Criminal Profiling

Fourth Edition

Visit the *Criminal Profiling, Fourth Edition* companion Web site at:

http://www.elsevierdirect.com/companions/9780123852434

The *Criminal Profiling* Web site hosts color figures from the book, appendices from the previous three editions, and brand new appendices to accompany this edition. Topics covered include Criminal Profiling Guidelines from the Academy of Behavioral Profiling, the Whitechapel murders, the JonBenet Ramsey case, California v. Charles B. Davis, and the homicides of Maria and Gaetano Russo.

Criminal Profiling
An Introduction to Behavioral Evidence Analysis

Fourth Edition

Brent E. Turvey
Forensic Solutions, LLC
Sitka, Alaska, USA

ELSEVIER

AMSTERDAM · BOSTON · HEIDELBERG · LONDON
NEW YORK · OXFORD · PARIS · SAN DIEGO
SAN FRANCISCO · SINGAPORE · SYDNEY · TOKYO
Academic Press is an imprint of Elsevier

Academic Press is an imprint of Elsevier
The Boulevard, Langford Lane, Kidlington, Oxford, OX5 1GB, UK
30 Corporate Drive, Suite 400, Burlington, MA 01803, USA
525 B Street, Suite 1800, San Diego, California 92101-4495, USA

1.1.1 Library of Congress Cataloging-in-Publication Data
Criminal profiling : an introduction to behavioral evidence analysis / muticontributed
book.—4th ed.
    p. cm.
Includes index.
ISBN 978-0-12-385243-4
1.   Criminal behavior, Prediction of. 2.   Criminal investigation—Psychological aspects.
HV8073.5.T87 2011
363.25'8—dc22

2010053946

1.1.2 British Library Cataloguing-in-Publication Data
A catalogue record for this book is available from the British Library.

For information on all Academic Press publications,
visit our Web site: www.elsevierdirect.com

Printed in China
14 15 16 9 8 7 6 5

Then I look about me at my fellow-men; and I go in fear. I see faces, keen and bright; others dull or dangerous; others, unsteady, insincere—none that have the calm authority of a reasonable soul.

—H. G. Wells, The Island of Dr. Moreau

Contents

Section 1   An Introduction to Criminal Profiling

Foreword to the Third Edition

Men of genius do not excel in any profession because they labor in it, but they labor in it because they excel.

—William Hazlitt (1778–1830)

In the 1970s, I was introduced to profiling at the FBI Academy when several classes were taught to the American Society of Crime Lab Directors. I saw this field as an adjunct to crime scene investigation and I had a great deal of enthusiasm for its merits. Later in my career, I worked with the FBI-trained profiler for the California Department of Justice (CA DOJ) and even considered transferring out of the crime lab business to follow a similar path. The successor to the original DOJ profiler caused me to rethink my position.

In the early years of profiling's development at the FBI, the public knew little about the actual methods used by profilers, or that there were such things as profilers at all. They perhaps knew, for example, that a profiler had helped with the Atlanta Child Murders, but little else. It was the later films based on the works of author Thomas Harris that caught the public eye and caused profiling to become a profession of interest; in particular, *Mindhunter* (1986) and *Silence of the Lambs* (1991). As a direct result of these and other similar films, and of the TV shows that came after, ike *UNSUB (Unknown Subject)*, *Millennium*, *Profiler*, and more recently *Criminal Minds*, more than a few criminal justice students have been inspired to become profilers.

However, many of the television programs became more supernatural in their orientation, with the profiler having "flashes" of the crime as it had occurred. This did not provide a real sense of what profilers actually can and cannot do. Profiles do not come in a flash or vision; they take long hard work examining physical and behavioral evidence. This was something that I wanted my own students to understand.

During the 1990s, when I worked for CA DOJ, I often invited our DOJ profilers to lecture in my crime reconstruction class. They had been trained by the FBI and could explain some of the methods and services that were available. On one such occasion, one of my students asked, "What happens if there are different opinions or interpretations about a profile?" The profiler responded, in essence, "That could never happen. We get together before a report is finalized and all come to an agreement." The "we" referred to the DOJ profiler and the FBI profiling unit back in Quantico. Bear in mind, this statement was made to a class of forensic scientists; all of them were criminalists with at least 10 years in crime labs, and who actively responded to crime scenes. We were shocked that there could not be different opinions about the same evidence. That everyone must reach a consensus before an FBI-style profile could be drawn up was unbelievable.

Criminalists frequently disagree about the interpretation of physical evidence and do not always reach consensus. You can't compromise a physical fact, just the interpretation. And interpretations can vary.

For someone interpreting the characteristics of a person committing a crime to say that all profilers (in the field and back at Quantico) must reach agreement before a report could be written just blew our minds. While this tradition builds consensus and squashes dissent (and lets it appear as though the final report has passed a form of peer review), it's fairly bad practice. At that moment, my class realized that FBI-style profiling was not an infallible discipline, despite what we were previously led to believe. Good science dictates that we cannot always agree; there must be room for differing opinions and interpretations. As Samuel Butler wrote,[1]

> Then he saw also that it matters little what profession, whether of religion or irreligion, a man may make, provided only he follows it out with charitable inconsistency, and without insisting on it to the bitter end. It is in the uncompromisingness with which dogma is held and not in the dogma or want of dogma that the danger lies.

The pioneering work done by the FBI in forming their profiling group was certainly groundbreaking and commendable. However, as is too often believed within closed law enforcement circles, they considered themselves somehow unique, considerable, and exceptional. FBI profilers continue to believe that criminal profiling can only be performed by those trained in a very specific program by the FBI or by those who have "apprenticed" under an FBI-trained profiler. The exclusivity of the group has rendered it just that—a closed society of narrow-thinking law-enforcement investigators. Ironically, they were and are actually treading in the realms and research of other established professionals: forensic scientists, forensic psychologists, forensic psychiatrists, and criminologists. And being a closed circle working outside of their actual profession (the formal education and actual experience of FBI profilers varies greatly), they don't always know what they are doing or when they are wrong. With a propensity for quashing dissent and everyone having to agree all the time, I guess it's not a surprise that their methods haven't changed substantially in three decades.

Film, television, and good public relations by the FBI have continued to inspire students toward criminal profiling as a career choice. However, even in the mid 1990s, there were no organized programs of study, no specific practice standards or principles, and the only publicized route was through law enforcement—specifically the FBI. For those students unfamiliar with the players and the field, there was no visible profession to enter. This remains a problem for students interested in FBI profiling, because the FBI has fewer than 20 "profilers" working for them at any given time—and they often don't even call themselves profilers anymore.

What does it take for a vocation to become a profession? Is forensic science a profession? This basic question has caused many heated discussions at forensic science meetings. According to one definition, which is as good as anything I've seen,[2]

> A profession is an occupation that requires extensive training and the study and mastery of specialized knowledge, and usually has a professional association, ethical code and process of certification or licensing.

> In many legal regimes that have "regulated professions" the issues of "public safety" or "client welfare", harm, ethics, accreditation or credentialing, licensing, peer discipline, special knowledge, judgment, training, practical experience and oaths of conduct are common to the regulated

---

[1] Butler, S. (1903) *The Way of All Flesh*, United Kingdom: Grant Richards Pub.
[2] *Profession* at Wikipedia.com; www.en.wikipedia.org/wiki/Profession.

professions. One or more of these factors may suffice to distinguish the profession from a related trade. The professional is obligated and sworn to exercise expert judgment on behalf of the client's interest. The client is not usually assumed to understand the complexities of the professional's special knowledge domain.

In the Preface to the First Edition of this textbook (1999), Brent Turvey wrote that criminal profiling "has not yet achieved the status of a profession." He then gave several reasons why. However, in the past few years there have been developments that may have overcome his reasoning, not the least of which is that Dr. Saferstein correctly refers to the field as the "profiling profession" at the end of the first paragraph of the Foreword to the First Edition.

When Brent Turvey first moved to California, criminalist Keith Inman told him "his first onus was to his profession."[3] That made an impression on him. The public face of criminal profiling was at that time almost exclusively law enforcement. The only entry, it was often stated, was through law enforcement, and within that construct only a few were allowed to become profilers. Brent did his homework and realized that there was a community of professionals already practicing criminal profiling beyond this narrow scope, and he saw the need to bring them together.

In 1998, after he finished the manuscript for the first edition of this book, Brent reached out to a group of forensic scientists, mental health professionals, and investigators. He wanted them to meet with him under one roof. The group included NYPD Detective John Baeza, ex-FBI profiler Mike Chamberlin, Dr. Michael McGrath, and myself. The subject of discussion was the formation of a professional association for profilers. The result of that meeting was the formation of the Academy of Behavioral Profiling (ABP). The ABP was the first independent professional organization for criminal profilers, with firm educational requirements and a published code of ethics. Brent took the additional measure of inviting several people from various parts of the world to participate in the formation of the association. The first step was taken to establish profiling as a profession: an *association*.

The ABP has various levels of membership, from students to affiliates, to full members in the investigative, forensic, behavioral, criminological, or general sections. The membership, currently almost 200 strong, is able to participate in an on-line forum for discussion of events in the field, to attend the ABP's annual meeting, and to publish their work in the *Journal of Behavioral Profiling*.

Full membership requires, among other things, an examination—the Profiling General Knowledge Exam (PGKE). The exam was designed by an international committee of investigators, forensic scientists, and behavioral scientists at the request of the ABP's PGKE Committee. The PGKE was completed and first administered in 2001. This testing process is a second step toward the establishment of criminal profiling as a profession: *certification*.

The ABP also undertook the task of developing practice standards. After many long discussions and extensive rewrites, the Board of Directors published these guidelines in 2000.[4] The guidelines have been refined over the years, and they have reached a pinnacle in the current edition of this text. At this point, the field of profiling meets the major criteria for being a profession. The only remaining question is whether there is extensive specialized knowledge in the field.

---

[3] Personal communication with the author.
[4] Baeza, J., Chisum, W.J., Chamberlin, T.M., McGrath, M., Turvey, B., Academy of Behavioral Profiling: Criminal Profiling Guidelines, *Journal of Behavioral Profiling* 1(1) (January, 2000).

This text, now in its third edition, certainly shows a wealth of specialized knowledge. It provides clear principles and practice standards, a strong code of ethics, and an undeniable map of the connection between criminal investigation, forensic science, criminology, mental health, and criminal profiling. These are the last threshold steps in demonstrating professionalism.

Henry Ward Beecher stated, "To become an able and successful man in any profession, three things are necessary, nature, study and practice."[5] One must have the nature to want to understand the field, the ability to study and learn about the field, and the desire to practice in the field to be a professional. The novella *Profession* by Isaac Asimov reiterates this theme. Asimov shows it is the ability to think, to learn, to be innovative, and to strive to improve the profession that makes a professional, not the title.[6]

Brent's body of work, ably supported by that of many others, fits the criteria necessary for criminal profiling to be considered a profession. Not only has Brent helped to build the profession, but also he has worked within the community to create courses of training and written material that have assisted others to learn the methods. The third edition of *Criminal Profiling* is a worthy furtherance of that effort and represents another tremendous step forward in the advancement of criminal profiling methods and research.

—**W. Jerry Chisum**

---

[5] Henry Ward Beecher (1813–1887); www.brainyquote.com/quotes/authors/h/henry_ward_beecher.html.

[6] Asimov, I. *Profession, Astounding Science Fiction* (July 1957).

Preface to the Fourth Edition
Criminal Profiling: The Imperatives of Scientific Methodology and a Behavioral Science Education

Criminal profiling is a subdiscipline of forensic criminology (Turvey, Petherick, and Ferguson, 2010). It is, therefore, a discipline within criminology, rooted in the behavioral sciences and forensic sciences alike. Thus it is imperative that students seeking to develop the skill of profiling educate themselves properly, and thoroughly, in scientific methodology and the behavioral sciences.

Generally speaking, criminal profiling involves making inferences about the physical, habitual, emotional, psychological, and even vocational characteristics of criminals. However, there are many different methods of criminal profiling, and all vary with respect to the soundness of underlying theory, logic, and insight. Some methods are abstract, general, and trait predictive; others are concrete, specific, and state descriptive. Some rely on offender group statistics; some rely solely on experience; and some rely on examining case-specific behavioral evidence.

The variety of profiling methods used around the world, across agencies and analysts, has resulted in a state of professional confusion. Profilers are often poorly educated in the forensic and behavioral sciences and consequently are confused about who they are and where they fit within the criminal justice system; other criminal justice professionals recognize and are confused about the same things, resulting in more than a little skepticism and even animosity; the media adds to myth by portraying profilers as ball-gazing supercops; and the general public views profilers as a more specialized form of psychic. And too many inept and uneducated profilers are benefiting from this lack of professional cohesion and the ignorant misperceptions it allows to persist.

If criminal profilers are to be taken seriously in the twenty-first century, as professional operatives with a substantive contribution to offer the criminal justice system, then there are areas in which reforms must be made. Education is the first.

METHODOLOGY

The method of criminal profiling that one claims to use will dictate the education necessary to use it. This methodology must be clearly and unequivocally defined. If a profiler does not know or cannot explain the method he is using to perform his examinations and reach his conclusions, then those conclusions can hardly be considered professional, reliable, or even acceptable.

The professional criminal profiler deals with facts and evidence, not assumptions and emotional hyperbole. He or she seeks to educate, not advocate. A profiler's method of choice will therefore be objective and necessarily rooted in the tenets of the scientific method. Learning what this is and what it means is vital to staying on a professional path, as opposed to remaining a profiling ingénue.

A criminal profiling method with a solid scientific foundation will be associated with one or more textbooks covering all aspects in detail—from definitions of key terms to related theory, to the nature of behavioral examinations involved, to the limitations of conclusions that may be offered. While this seems a minor hurdle, it is rare for any criminal profiling method to achieve. Most methods are associated with thinly prepared and poorly researched texts, or memoirs, without clear definitions or practice standards. Many are written by those who lack scholarship or the ability to explain how they arrived at a particular conclusion beyond summoning their "years of experience." Others wrap themselves in nearly unintelligible jargon, to confuse readers into believing that science has been employed when it actually hasn't.

The best criminal profiling texts are those that provide insight into criminal investigation and behavioral evidence by fusing real-world case experience, relevant behavioral and forensic science scholarship, and the scientific method. They provide tools, set limits, and don't leave the reader with the impression that criminal profiling is the domain of a select few. Exclusivity, whether from a law-enforcement profiler or an academic, is intended to dampen scrutiny from "outsiders." A true professional not only invites professional scrutiny, but also provides the means for it in the methods used.

If a criminal profiler is using a heuristic method of his or her own, without clear and consistent terms, definitions, and practice standards, it signals a lack of professionalism and accountability. It also demonstrates the absence of scientific education and training. This is not desirable, as the mandates of good science (e.g., objectivity, the scientific method, and transparency) are also crucial to professionalization.

SKILL IDENTIFICATION AND DEVELOPMENT

Given a clear and identifiable profiling methodology, the knowledge, skills, and abilities necessary for competent performance should become evident. This information can then be used to identify the necessary course of education, training, and experiences required to develop those skills and abilities. It will also allow for the development of professional competency tests, to assess whether basic thresholds of knowledge have been achieved and are being maintained.

Regardless of the method being used, the following knowledge, skills, and abilities are generally of benefit to every criminal profiler:

1. Knowledge of the criminal justice system in general
2. Knowledge of the various methods of criminal investigation
3. Knowledge of the scientific method
4. Knowledge of the science of logic
5. Knowledge of forensic science and the various methods of physical evidence collection and examination
6. Knowledge of victims, crime, and criminals
7. Knowledge of human sociology in relation to the study and examination of victims, crime, and criminals
8. Knowledge of human psychology in relation to the study and examination of victims, crime, and criminals
9. Knowledge of mental illness in relation to the study and examination of victims, crime, and criminals
10. Knowledge of drugs and alcohol in relation to the study and examination of victims, crime, and criminals
11. Knowledge of human anatomy and physiology

12. Knowledge of human sexuality in all of its contexts and incarnations
13. The skill and ability to perform competent research
14. The skill and ability to write competently and professionally
15. The skill and ability to make valid arguments based on sound logic and reasoning
16. The skill and ability to write reports that meet judicial standards
17. The skill and ability to give effective courtroom testimony
18. The ability to travel
19. The ability to examine evidence relating to the violent, the sexually graphic, the bizarre, and the grotesque without becoming overwhelmed by personal feelings
20. The ability to meet deadlines
21. The ability to recognize bias and work toward maintaining objectivity
22. The ability to keep a confidence and to maintain confidential information
23. The ability to remain honest and ethical despite the short-term rewards for professional dishonesty and unethical practice

EDUCATION

The development of a firm base of theoretical knowledge, and its practical application, can often be found in a formal college or university education. Successful completion of a degree program demonstrates the ability to commit to a long-term course of study and to see it through to completion. It is evidence to others regarding one's professional dedication and personal stamina. Therefore, less formal education is not better. However, too much college or university education of low quality can be worse, especially when it is not honed by actual experience with crime, criminals, and victims.

It should go without saying that criminal profiling involves the application of the behavioral sciences to criminology. Given this fundamental intersection of applied knowledge, it is hard to argue that one can be a qualified behavioral analyst if one does not possess a formal education in at least one of the behavioral sciences (e.g., psychology, sociology, criminology, social work). Too many criminal profilers still fail this basic litmus test, yet offer their services as though such a foundation is irrelevant.

Again, if you do not have a formal behavioral science education, you really have no business performing behavioral evidence examinations of any kind.

A criminal profiler's final educational path should be dictated by the method that she or he intends to use. If the profiler intends to use a method that involves statistical analysis, she or he must have a formal education that involves mathematics and statistics. If she or he intends to engage in scientific practice, he or she must have a formal education that features understanding and applying the scientific method. If the profiler wishes to examine and reconstruct crime scene behavior, he or she must study forensic science. Formal education provides the theoretical foundation required to give their eventual internships and work experience meaning.

EXPERIENCE

Experience is important to the development of knowledge, skills, and abilities. Criminal profilers must gain experience being correct, being incorrect, and being corrected. In this way they learn how to recognize when they are wrong, how to self-correct, and how to express scientific humility. Experience is accumulated from formal internships, mentoring, on-the-job training, and, of course, from life in general.

However, the experiences accumulated must be relevant, and, for them to have any value, they must be informed by outside knowledge and sound theory. This is why formal education must come first. For example, police officers often stand watch over crime scene security. This does not mean that they have knowledge and experience related to investigating crime, unless they are performing the duties of a detective. More experience standing watch over scene security will not teach them to be a good investigators. Detectives, on the other hand, often attend and witness the autopsy in cases of homicide. However, this does not mean that they are qualified to perform the autopsy, as they do not have the same education, training, and background as a forensic pathologist. Their job as witnesses to the autopsy is not the same as the forensic pathologist's job in performing it, and each is educated and trained to take different things away from the experience.

In addition, there is the issue of quantity vs. quality. Dr. Paul L. Kirk (1902–1970), the father of modern forensic science, offered the following thought (1974, p. 16): "The amount of experience is unimportant beside the question of what has been learned from it." If one does not learn from experience, and repeats the same errors time and time again, then experience has little meaning. Someone may have been doing their job for 20 years, but it may also be the same year of errors repeated 20 times.

Another concern regarding experience is that it is used as a shield, to argue the soundness and veracity of conclusions. This is actually a logical fallacy referred to as an *appeal to authority*. When a purported professional offers a conclusion based solely on the authority or expertise of themselves or others, their logic and reasoning is without solid foundation. Dr. John Thornton, a practicing criminalist and a former professor of forensic science at the University of California (UC) at Berkeley warns that (1997, pp. 17):

> Experience is neither a liability nor an enemy of the truth; it is a valuable commodity, but it should not be used as a mask to deflect legitimate scientific scrutiny, the sort of scrutiny that customarily is leveled at scientific evidence of all sorts. To do so is professionally bankrupt and devoid of scientific legitimacy, and courts would do well to disallow testimony of this sort. Experience ought to be used to enable the expert to remember the when and the how, why, who, and what. Experience should not make the expert less responsible, but rather more responsible for justifying an opinion with defensible scientific facts.

Consequently, appeals to authority have no place in professional or scientific practice.

BEA

In order to competently and effectively execute the methods of examination and classification provided in this text, in relation to *behavioral evidence analysis*, the following education and training are required:

1. *An undergraduate degree in a behavioral science* (psychology, sociology, criminology, social work): This will provide an understanding of human behavior and related behavioral theory and will also provide exposure to the scientific method. A criminal justice degree is not the same as a criminology degree, and most CJ programs will only prepare you for a career in law enforcement or corrections.
2. *Undergraduate term papers*: Many undergraduate courses allow students to choose term paper research subjects. As much as possible, research and write on subjects related to criminal profiling and related specialized areas of interest.
3. *A graduate degree in forensic science or a behavioral science*: As just about anyone can get an undergraduate degree, graduate work signals a professional-level commitment to your career. Students should choose a graduate program by seeking to study under someone who both published in their area of interest and also still has a hand in casework. Professional scholars without real-world experience make for poor teachers. They also lack the ability to help students get good internships.

4. *Graduate term papers*: Many graduate courses allow students to choose term paper research subjects. As much as possible, research and write on subjects related to criminal profiling and related specialized areas of interest.

5. *Graduate thesis*: It should go without saying that any graduate-level thesis should be written on a subject related to criminal profiling in some fashion—specifically oriented toward the student's specialized areas of interest. This presupposes that the student, by this time, has developed specialized areas of interest.

6. *Graduate internships*: Seek an internship that exposes you directly to the criminal justice system and its inhabitants. This can include a group home, the public defender's office, an ME or coroner's office, or a law-enforcement agency. Multiple internships are recommended for the broadest exposure. Even when college credit is not available, internships are still recommended. If your college or university program cannot offer you good internship possibilities, you are in the wrong program.

With this formal educational background, the student will be well suited to begin learning and eventually to apply BEA methodology in any career they decide to take up within or related to the criminal justice system. Bear in mind that it is a skill, not a job. The skill may be used in a career as an investigator, paralegal, lawyer, social worker, forensic examiner, or a mental health expert.

REFERENCES

Kirk, P., 1974. Crime Investigation, second edition. John Wiley & Sons, New York, NY.

Thornton, J.I., 1997. The General Assumptions and Rationale of Forensic Identification. In: Faigman, D., Kaye, D., Saks, M., et al. (Eds.), Modern Scientific Evidence: The Law and Science of Expert Testimony, vol. 2. West, St. Paul, MN.

Turvey, B., Petherick, W., Ferguson, C., 2010. Forensic Criminology. Elsevier Science, San Diego, CA.

Preface to the Third Edition
The Persistence of Faith-Based Profiling

The first step is admitting we have a problem.

Faith is often enough to make decisions in personal matters. Faith can give much needed hope and strength in times of personal crisis or difficulty. Faith can build relationships, give inspiration, and provide personal guidance. But personal faith is not to be confused with an actual proof, or actual evidence.[7] As such, personal faith and belief should not be imposed in a professional context where the burdens and consequences to others are grave—as in the criminal justice system.

Many people have transcendent or phenomenological belief systems that give their lives both meaning and bearing. Personal belief systems can take root at a very early age, sometimes as a part of our cultural or ethnic identity. As a result, they are almost impossible to remove without eroding the soil of substance that gives one both a sense of identity and purpose. As a consequence, most will not surrender a deeply held personal belief for fear it could lead to their spiritual loss or death. Therein lies the problem.

There is nothing inherently wrong with personal beliefs. Each person finds meaning and purpose in their own way and that is as it should be. We all have our own journey to take in life and it is deeply personal. However, there is a difference between faith and reason. As the reader will learn in the pages that follow, it is not the position of this work that personal faiths and beliefs are a problem unless they get in the way of objective forensic investigation and examination.

Let us speak clearly: faith and the phenomenological must have no influence over the objective investigation of fact. This includes religious faiths, spiritual beliefs, the metaphysical, the paranormal and the supernatural. These are personal matters and should remain personal.

In faith-based reasoning, the premise of an argument and the conclusion are a matter of personal belief and subsequently considered above criticism. Those who question the premises of such beliefs, religious and otherwise dogmatic, are labeled heretics, or worse. In faith and personal belief, there is little room for critical thinking, and no place for doubt. As a consequence, the nature of faith runs contrary to knowledge building.[8]

Criminal investigation and forensic examination are professional endeavors in the service of the criminal justice system. Any conclusion that is not based on actual proofs susceptible to testing does not belong in

---

[7] An apt analogy would be that *faith* is akin to believing what an apple will taste like based on what others have said; *proof* is akin to actually having eaten an apple oneself.

[8] It cannot be overemphasized that organized religions are but one form of faith or belief. There are also "religions" or belief systems organized around charismatic people, popular methodology, and popular agencies and institutions. When students or professionals cannot or do not question, and give uncritical loyalty to a person, method, or institution without seeking proofs, they are treading on the same grounds—faith and belief over reason.

the structural supports of a criminal investigation, or a forensic examination. The reason for this should be obvious. When we rely on faith-based reasoning to support a conclusion, we are more susceptible to bias, and there is no way of knowing whether or not we are wrong. For a conclusion to be reliable and valid our methods must be susceptible to independent review, and the conclusion itself must be falsifiable. That is to say, there must be actual proofs that everyone can experience, and there must be identifiable mechanisms for disproving our conclusions should our reasoning be biased or faulty.

As we will learn, criminal profilers will often serve as both criminal investigator and forensic examiner. Criminal investigators are tasked with serving the criminal justice system by establishing the objective facts and evidence of a given case. Forensic examiners are subsequently tasked with interpreting the facts and evidence objectively. These are enormous responsibilities that must not be taken lightly. When we act in service of our personal needs and beliefs, our objectivity can be tainted, our methods distorted, and our conclusions biased. Emotions can rush the soundest judgment; dogma can bury the clearest evidence. As explained in James and Nordby (2003, p. 4),

> When emotions overcome reason, a zealous forensic scientist may intentionally or inadvertently deny real justice. Results are misinterpreted, or worse, falsified. Such flawed science may not be easy to spot, since it can only appear through the results of the scientific investigation.

If we can agree to this—that we must maintain our objectivity—we can agree that personal faith and belief should have no part in the performance of what should be the cold and dispassionate rendering of a criminal investigation or forensic examination.

Is faith-based reasoning actually a problem in the criminal justice system, and specifically in the field of criminal profiling? Sadly, more than a century after the 1894 publication of the first textbook advocating for more objective and scientific methods of criminal investigation,[9] the answer is Yes. Despite repeated attempts to educate practitioners, there persists throughout the geography of criminal investigation and forensic examination no shortage of faith-based motivations, faith-based methodology, and faith in examiner charisma or affiliation over actual knowledge and efficacy. As is often the case, ignorance and ego are the culprits.

Three general issues, all related, require some discussion before we tackle their influence on criminal profiling in specific: religion, the popular media, and psychics.

WORKING FOR GOD

Thank God for narcissism.

—FBI Profiler Roy Hazelwood (Ret.) (Ramsland, 2005)

Those who do not recognize a separation between church and state, who perceive a personal duty to protect or act on religious or moral truth, and who are overly zealous in doing so, may deem it acceptable to supersede a professional duty to protect or act upon actual facts. Referred to as the *appeal to consequences of a belief*, this may be a rationalization involving the fallacious argument that the consequences of accepting whether a certain proposition is true or false have a bearing in determining the claim's truth—or there will negative consequences now or in the hereafter. When they are self-serving or just plain wrong, the consequences can be dire.

---

[9] Handbuch fur Untersuchungsrichter als System der Kriminalistik (Criminal Investigation: A Practical Textbook for Magistrates, Police Officers and Lawyers) by the legendary Austrian jurist Dr. Johann (Hans) Baptist Gustav Gross (1924).

Investigators and forensic examiner's alike are handmaidens to the various justice systems of mankind. Consequently, they must serve the various laws of mankind. They must serve objectivity, not passion; they must serve facts and proofs, not beliefs or superstitions. If they cannot serve in this manner, then they are unfit to serve at all.

It must be admitted that not everyone agrees with this position. Some view this work as a moral or religious calling. According to the self-proclaimed *Homicide Investigator's Bible*, homicide investigation is part of a Christian mandate to serve the "FIFTH COMMANDMENT Book of Exodus, 20 of the Holy Bible" in which "The Lord God said… Thou Shalt Not Kill." The text also concludes its preface with: "We work for God."[10] This is an admirable declaration in the service of personal faith and belief.

However, this declaration is more than just misplaced in the realm of homicide investigation, or any work performed in the service of the justice systems in the Western world. Why? Because pretending that the Bible and the Ten Commandments are somehow served by modern law oversimplifies a very complex reality. Further explanation is necessary.

In order to rationally discuss the Ten Commandments in an investigative and forensic context, we should probably start by getting them right. The fifth commandment is "Honor your father and your mother, so that you may live long in the land the Lord your God is giving you," (NIV Study Bible, Exodus 20:12; p.116). It is not "Thou shalt not kill," as described in Geberth (2006). This numbering remains true regardless of which version of the Bible one invokes.

The most accurate translation of the sixth commandment is "You shall not commit murder"(NIV Study Bible, Exodus 20:13). The translation referenced by the *Homicide Investigator's Bible* is chosen from the King James Bible, a text known by theological scholars to be rife with translation errors, intentional and otherwise (see generally Ehrman, 2005, and Norton, 2005). This is particularly true with respect to the sixth commandment. In the King James Bible, it reads: "Thou shalt not kill" (King James Bible, Exodus 20:13). The problem is that the verb appearing in the original Hebrew is not actually translated as "kill." The verb used in the Torah forbiddance is *ratsah*, which is most accurately translated as "murder"—used in the rest of the Bible to describe killing out of anger, killing the weak, or killing in the commission of a crime like robbery. Faulty translations of the original Hebrew and subsequent Greek texts, however motivated, have led to a great deal of confusion on this matter.

Murder is a crime. There can be no disputing this, whether one is an investigator, a profiler, a judge, or a theologian. However, while the Bible is general in its prohibitions and punishments, the law of man is rich with detail. In most Western countries there are degrees of murder, there are mitigating factors, and there are aggravating factors. The variations are such that the same facts will yield very different punishments from court to court, state to state, or country to country, depending on how those facts are interpreted. This can range from a few years in prison for manslaughter or negligent homicide, to the death penalty for premeditated murder. In the Bible, however, there is but one ultimate punishment for murder or any other intentional non-homicidal offense against God (i.e., idolatry, adultery, improper sexual behavior, cursing or attacking your father or mother, failure to put down a bull that tends to gore people, being a sorceress, taking advantage of widows or orphans, etc.): those found guilty are to be stoned to death, impaled on a stick, killed by the sword, or burned alive.[11]

---

[10] Taken from "The Oath of Practical Homicide Investigation," and the preface of Geberth (1996).

[11] There is actually a distinction between accidental and premeditated murder in the Bible, but none of the rich variation that we see in Western penal systems. Moreover, the determination of what is intentional and what is not seems to be left for reasonable men to decide (see generally NIV Study Bible: Exodus 21-23).

This is probably as good a place as any to acknowledge that the origins of our legal system, in fact of the legal systems in most countries, is tribunals in which the church was the arbiter of justice. This is because most crimes, especially of an interpersonal nature, were deemed to have been committed against God—so the church took the responsibility for bringing the offender to justice.[12]

No longer is this the case in most Western legal jurisdictions, especially where it is recognized that there is, or should be, a separation of church from state because of potential abuses and emotional influences (though there are marked exceptions that linger, in terms of both laws and those who judge them). In the United States, for example, this sentiment is a permanent part of our Constitution. The First Amendment begins: "Congress shall make no law respecting an establishment of religion, or prohibiting the free exercise thereof. ..." This was tested in 1801, when The Danbury Baptists Association (representing a relgious minority in Connecticut) wrote then president Thomas Jefferson to complain that their religious liberties were seen only as privileges by the Connecticut state legislature that could be revoked at will, not as immutable rights. Jefferson responded with a now well-known letter confirming that religious belief is personal and separate from the will and authority of the state. Consequently, those working in service of the state could not influence law making (and by extension law enforcement) with the preferences of their particular faith. Jefferson wrote (1802):

> Believing with you that religion is a matter which lies solely between man & his god, that he owes account to none other for his faith or his worship, that the legitimate powers of government reach actions only, and not opinions, I contemplate with sovereign reverence that act of the whole American people which declared that their legislature should make no law respecting an establishment of religion, or prohibiting the free exercise thereof, thus building a wall of separation between church and state.

This doctrine, with language lifted directly from Jefferson's letter, was first cited in the U.S. Supreme Court, Reynolds v. United States, 98 U.S. 145 (1878). George Reynolds, a member of the Church of Jesus Christ of Latter Day Saints, argued that he had a religious duty to marry multiple times and was therefore improperly indicted of the crime of bigamy. The Supreme Court disagreed, and the Supreme Court of the Utah Territory upheld his eventual conviction.

So in reality, far from the creed of the *Homicide Investigator's Bible*, investigators and forensic examiners in the United States and similar legal systems do not work for God. They do not investigate on behalf of the fifth, sixth, or any other commandment, or seek to enforce Biblical or other religious punishments. They do not work not to protect religious belief systems based on personal or popular interpretations of writings in religious texts. They do not investigate offenses against God. And they do not seek to impale suspects, stone them, or burn them at the stake.[13]

Or at least they shouldn't.

---

[12] What's more, the current jury system also has its basis in religion, whereby a defendant who could find 12 people of good character willing to testify to the defendant's innocence must surely be innocent because these witnesses surely would not lie before God.

[13] We are speaking mostly of Western countries. This is primarily because in the Muslim world there is no such thing as the *secular* (not pertaining to or connected with religion). All parts of Muslim life are governed by religious faith. Shari'a, for example, is the Islamic belief system inspired by the Koran, the Sunna, Arabic legal systems, and work of Muslim scholars over the first two centuries of Islam. Shari'a, often referred to inappropriately as Islamic Law, acts a strict guide for all aspects of Muslim life—public, private, religious, civil, and criminal. Consequently, the separation of church and state is considered by many in the Muslim world as a violation of their faith, and an intolerable insult to God.

Consider the case of 50-year-old polygamist Warren S. Jeffs, the President of the Fundamentalist Church of Jesus Christ of Latter Day Saints. As of this writing, he is in the Purgatory Correctional Facility in Hurricane, Utah. He faces trial for charges of rape as an accomplice—for arranging and performing "child bride" marriages. According to the Utah Attorney General's Office (Murphy, 2005):

> Jeffs is accused of arranging a marriage in 2002 between a 28-year-old man and a 16-year-old girl. An unnamed defendant has also been indicted on three felony counts of sexual assault and sexual conduct with a minor. The Mohave County Attorney's Office has also recently obtained indictments against two other men accused of taking part in arranged marriages with minors.

> "State, local and federal authorities will continue to jointly investigate allegations of child abuse, domestic violence and fraud in closed communities," says Shurtleff. "These efforts should serve notice that no one is above the law and we will vigorously prosecute crimes that victimize anyone under the guise of religion."

According to court records, this type of "child bride" marriage would be a common practice in Jeffs' church, with Jeff's presiding over the ceremonies. The situation is explained in Winslow (2006):

Polygamist Warren Steed Jeffs in court. As of this writing, he is awaiting trial for charges of rape as an accomplice – for arranging and performing "child bride" marriages.

Hildale/Colorado City Town Marshal Fred Barlow has pledged his allegiance to Fundamentalist LDS Church leader Warren Jeffs.

"I fill (sic) that without priesthood I am nothing," he wrote in a letter obtained by investigators for the Arizona Peace Officer Standards and Training board. The letter was given to the *Deseret Morning News* after a request under the Government Records Access Management Act (GRAMA.)

The letter was written in October 2005 when Jeffs was still a fugitive and begins, "Dear Uncle Warren." In it, Barlow says all of the police officers in the polygamous border towns of Hildale, Utah, and Colorado City, Ariz., are loyal to Jeffs and are working under his directions.

He updated Jeffs, who has since been captured, on a series of investigations by the Arizona Attorney General's Office and Arizona POST.

"I do not know exactly what we have ahead of us, but I do know that I and all of the other officers have expressed our desire to stand with you and the priesthood," Barlow wrote.

Arizona POST officials are investigating Barlow and two other members of the police force over their loyalties to Jeffs and refusal to answer investigators' questions about the FLDS leader.

Fred Barlow is facing several misconduct charges, along with officers Preston Barlow and Mica Barlow.

"In October 2005, Marshal Fred Barlow sought directions from and acknowledged previous direction on the operation of the Colorado City Marshal's Office from a federal fugitive," said Bob Forry, the manager of Arizona POST's Standards and Compliance Unit.

He added that the officers have refused to answer investigators' questions. Administrative hearings on their police certification have been scheduled for February in Phoenix. All law enforcement officers take an oath to uphold the laws of their respective states.

"These officers are truly conflicted between their religion and their duties as police officers," Forry said.

The Utah POST Council voted on Wednesday to begin an investigation into the actions of the entire Hildale/Colorado City Town Marshal's Office. Utah Attorney General Mark Shurtleff said Friday the letter makes him want to move quickly on suspending the police authority in the border towns.

Barlow's letter says he was praying Jeffs would be protected while he was on the lam.

"I love you and acknowledge you as my priesthood head," he wrote. "And I know that you have the right to rule in all aspects of my live (sic). I yearn to hear from you."

The letter is signed, "Your servant Fred J. Barlow Jeffs."

Arizona POST officials obtained the letter after Warren Jeffs' brother, Seth, was arrested in October 2005 outside Pueblo, Colo.

Search warrant returns from the Pueblo County Sheriff's Office that were obtained by the Deseret Morning News show a number of documents were being taken to Warren Jeffs, who was a fugitive at the time.

Among the items seized: a large box containing numerous envelopes addressed to "Warren Jeffs," "The Prophet," "Uncle Warren Jeffs," and other names; a banker box with miscellaneous documents titled, "Saturday Work Project January 2005–June 2005"; credit cards; 14 gift cards, valued at $500 each; VHS tapes, media cards, CDs, a Sony digital recorder, audio cassettes, computer floppy disks, a laptop, a Palm Pilot, seven cell phones, a donation jar with a picture of Jeffs marked "Pennies for the Prophet; and more than $135,000 in cash.

Seth Jeffs later pleaded guilty to a federal charge of harboring a fugitive and was sentenced to probation.

It is hard to imagine a situation where the conflict of interest between church doctrine and state law could be clearer. Yet an entire police agency has not only failed in their oath to protect and serve, they have admitting to working to aid a fugitive from justice because of their faith. The result has been a pattern of forced "child bride" marriages, statutory rape, and institutional control of females from a very young age going back generations—all sanctioned by local law enforcement. Not to mention further unlawful acts committed to protect their leader and conceal their crimes from the outside world.

This is but one recent example of religious or cultural beliefs inappropriately influencing the law and its enforcement, taken from many throughout history.

Investigators must work to establish the verifiable facts of a case, and thereby help protect the rights and property of citizens. All citizens. Not just those who share their religious beliefs; and not just those who subscribe to their subjective interpretations of religious texts. And those of similar faith cannot be immune to the rule of law. The intermixing of investigation, criminal profiling, politics, and religion has had a tragic history that will be explored further in the first chapter of this text.

In the context of personal faith and belief, things are made worse by the persistence of magical thinking.

A WORLD OF MAGICAL THINKING

I've never heard of or received information [from a psychic] that has even helped solve a case.
— *Sgt. Gary L. Plank, Criminal Profiler, Nebraska State Patrol* (Hammel, 2003)

It is of great concern that those who are guided in their investigations and examinations by faith and faith-based reasoning are more prone to believe in and waste finite resources on the phenomenological. Not in the modern age of science and reason? Think again. As explained in Sunstein (2005), people are not always that critical, that deliberate, or that bright. In fact, many are intellectually lazy, reaching only for the explanations and reasons within their immediate cognitive vicinity:

> It is well known that individuals do not always process information well. They use heuristics that lead them to predictable errors; they are also subject to identifiable biases, which produce errors. A growing literature explores the role of these heuristics and biases and their relationship to law and policy. For example, most people follow the representativeness heuristic, in accordance with which judgments of probability are influenced by assessments of resemblance (the extent to which A "looks like" B). The representative heuristic helps explain what Paul Rozin and Carol Nemeroff call "sympathetic magical thinking" including the beliefs that some objects have contagious properties and that causes resemble their effects. The representativeness heuristic often works well, but it can also lead to severe blunders.

> People also err because they use the availability heuristic to answer difficult questions about probability. When people use this heuristic, they answer a question of probability by asking whether examples come readily to mind.

So there are two big problems with the way people tend to reason: *magical thinking* and the *availability heuristic*. Magical thinking is often described in the cognitive psychology literature as a child-like belief that by wishing or believing something it becomes true, or that seeing two things together is proof that they are causally related despite the absence of any direct evidence. The availability heuristic is in play when judgments are made based on what one can remember, rather than complete or actual information. We tend to use the availability heuristic for judging the frequency or likelihood of events.

When magical thinking and the availability heuristic come together, resulting beliefs can be almost impenetrable. There is no better example of this than the influence of film and television. The popular media feeds an ever-increasing condition of *metacognitive dissonance* by providing false or distorted examples to populate our memory, which the public tends to believe because they want to, or because they don't know any better.[14]

---

[14] *Metacognitive dissonance*: Believing oneself capable of recognizing ones own errors in thinking, reasoning, and learning, despite either a lack of evidence or overwhelming evidence to the contrary. Examples: Believing oneself to be knowledgeable despite a demonstrable lack of knowledge; believing oneself to be incapable of error despite the human condition; believing oneself to be logical in one's reasoning despite regular entrapment by logical fallacies; believing oneself to be completely objective despite the persistence of observer effects.

THE POWER OF MEDIA

Fictional programs like Fox's *Millennium* (1996–1999), NBC's *Profiler* (1996–2000), and NBC's *Medium* (2005– today, based on a fictionalized version of the life of Allison DuBois, a self-described medium and psychic profiler), in combination with purported documentary programs like Court TV's current hits *Psychic Detectives* and *Haunting Evidence* (with "psychic" profiler Carla Baron) have made psychic phenomena not only seem mainstream, but valid as an investigative resource.[15]

For a variety of reasons, there are those who continue to argue that modern TV and film audiences are largely able to discriminate between fact and fiction, and that people do not uncritically accept and believe what they see on the screen just because it's in front of them, with good lighting, compelling images, and an emotive soundtrack. Surely, they argue, public faith and a belief in the supernatural are not simply a reaction to popular culture.

However, evidence to the contrary is overwhelming. Not just a mechanism for dispensing facts and properly vetted information, the popular media in any era have been an effective tool for propaganda, press relations, and "spin." In the past, conquerors would destroy libraries to erase the defeated cultures—and rewrite history as they saw it, unchallenged. The Bible, for example, has been edited, redacted, re-edited, re-translated, and infused with contrived stories and imagery to serve various agendas over the centuries (see Ehrman, 2005). Editorial cartoons in the print media have been used to spread true and false messages related to the character of political figures and their policies. Private individuals and governments have long used radio, newspapers, films, and television to spread propaganda and control information alike. Methods range from the creation of blatant propaganda material, to influences on filmmaking, to opinion-editorial pieces on various subjects of varying factual content, to biased reporting, all the way to news blackouts. Why? The availability heuristic and magical thinking. People believe what they read, what they see, and what they hear when it is put in front of them – and they very much want to believe what they feel. Put this all together in a compelling package and it can change the world for a second, a minute, an hour, or a lifetime.

Some modern examples should be given.

In 1973, when William Peter Blatty's book, *The Exorcist*, appeared as a feature film, the Catholic Church experienced a surge in numbers owing to the fear audiences developed in relation to evil spirits and demonic possession. To this day, and even as a result of being influenced by this film, there are educated people who believe whole-heartedly in demonic possession. The Catholic Church has supported the film since its release. In fact, the Catholic Church's position on this and similar films, like *The Exorcism of Emily Rose* (2005), is expressed plainly by Fr. James Lebar, exorcist for the archdiocese of New York:

> One of the reasons I'm willing to do interviews like this is so that this phenomenon comes to the attention of people, Catholic and non-Catholic, and they will be informed that a: The devil exists, b: He tries to trouble people, and c: If he troubles people so much that he possesses them, they can be helped through exorcism.

In other words, films can be very effective press relations when they are on message and of sufficient quality.

In 1977, *Jesus of Nazareth* was shown on television as a mini-series and prompted yet another surge in conversions. It is essentially a teleplay based on the life of Jesus Christ as told in the *Book of Matthew*. It broadcast on the NBC network in two three-hour installments—on Palm Sunday and Easter Sunday. The film

---

[15] The situation is not made better by syndicated talk show hosts, such as CNN's Larry King, who further legitimize psychics by regularly inviting them to speak on their respective programs simply to garner ratings.

has since been taken to all corners of the world and is still shown to people by missionaries in Third World countries. It was aired again the year of this writing on several cable television networks as part of what has become a Christmas tradition. The number of conversions owed to inspiration by this film are said to be in the tens of millions.

One might be inclined to argue that Western audiences of several decades ago were perhaps more open to media influence, and perhaps even less discriminating than audiences today. However this argument simply does not hold.

In 1988, the film version of Nikos Kazantzakis' *The Last Temptation of Christ* was released. It portrays Jesus Christ on the cross, in his last moments, tempted by a normal life with Mary Magdalene as opposed to dying without sin for the sins of mankind. Director Martin Scorsese billed it as a work of fiction; an exploration of what Jesus Christ might have been like as a normal human being. The idea of Jesus Christ as a mere human was so intolerable to some Christians that the film opened to violent denouncements from religious groups all over the world, as well as bomb threats to theaters that agreed to show it.[16] Those in opposition to the film's premise apparently believed that the film had the power would tarnish the image of Jesus Christ that the church had worked so hard to cultivate over the centuries.

In 2005, the film version of Dan Brown's *The DaVinci Code* was released. Worse to some Christians than *The Last Temptation of Christ*, this fictional work portrays Jesus Christ as a mortal who was in fact wed to Mary Magdalene, and argues that there exists a bloodline from that union which can be traced from their child to this day. Based on a variety of intriguing and even compelling evidence (some real and some highly dramatized), the questions raised by the book and film struck so much fear into organized religion that the film found itself banned by cities all over the world, and even some countries.

As with *The Last Temptation of Christ,* many in the church worried if people read the book, or saw the film, that they would believe it was true (BBC, 2005):

> Cardinal Tarcisio Bertone, Archbishop of Genoa, broke the church's official silence on the controversial book.
>
> Its story about the Church suppressing the "truth" that Jesus had a child with Mary Magdalene has convinced many fans.
>
> But the cardinal's spokesman denied reports that the clergyman was asked by the Vatican to hit back at the book.
>
> Carlo Arcolao told the BBC's News website that it had been the cardinal's own decision to make a public statement about the book.
>
> Mr Arcolao confirmed that the cardinal told an Italian newspaper: "It astonishes and worries me that so many people believe these lies."
>
> The archbishop told Il Giornale: "The book is everywhere. There is a very real risk that many people who read it will believe that the fables it contains are true."
>
> The book's publishers Random House were unavailable for comment.
>
> The book *The Da Vinci Code*, by Dan Brown, has been a publishing sensation around the world and is still in best-seller lists.

---

[16] The author vividly recalls going to see the film in Portland, Oregon, with armed guards screening all moviegoers.

Its conspiracy theories and thriller style, in which two code-breakers try to track down the truth behind the Holy Grail, have caught the imaginations of millions.

Its central claim is that the Holy Grail is really the bloodline descended from Jesus and Mary Magdalene—which the Church is supposed to have covered up, along with the female role in Christianity.

Brown has previously said: "All of the art, architecture, secret rituals, secret societies, all of that is historical fact."

Of great interest here is the lack of faith that the purported faithful elite continually display. If conversions are of substance, and the converted truly faithful, then film and television should be no threat. There should be no need to ban books, films, or ideas. But this is not how public perception works—faith is not typically a function of critical thinking, or of thoughtful reflection and careful study. Dogmatic advocates understand this, and understand the need to craft not only the message, but also how it is perceived. It is a direct understanding and manipulation of the availability heuristic.

The magical thinking by the public in effect here is this: If it's on the screen, it must be real; and perhaps conversely it's not real until it's on the screen.

But surely, as powerful as they are, film and television do not influence investigative professionals the same as an ignorant public. Surely professionals can distinguish between the fantasy world created on TV and the realities of a criminal investigation involving real people. Surely professionals are trained to know better than to believe what they see on TV.

Enter the wildly popular television show 24, aired on the Fox Network (currently in its sixth season, having been launched in the months following 9/11). Being the owner of every available boxed DVD set for each season, this author is a conversant and unrepentant fan of the show. It chronicles the life and career of the fictional Jack Bauer, a field operative in the fictional U.S. Counter Terrorism Unit (CTU). Each season is 24 episodes long, as story arcs take place in real time over the course of a single day. This creates drama and tension as Jack Bauer fights to unravel and thwart various cascading terrorist plots against the United States, both foreign and domestic, under crushing time constraints. To be blunt, the fictional Jack Bauer is both extreme and brutal. He tortures suspects, innocent and guilty alike, and executes whoever is necessary to protect the interests and security of the United States, or the lives of its citizens. It is great television, but it is only television. Or at least, that's how it is supposed to be.

Two circumstances prove beyond any doubt that military students and professionals alike are watching the fictional TV drama 24, and that they are taking the torture methods it depicts directly to the front line.

First, there are the admissions of former U.S. Army specialist Tony Lagouranis, who left the military with an honorable discharge in 2005. He and other members of his unit attempted to copy the interrogation methods and interrogator demeanor advocated by characters in the fictional program when interrogating prisoners during his 2004–2005 tour of duty in Iraq. His interview is quoted in Bennett (2007):

NEWSWEEK: How common were shows like 24 while you were in Iraq?

TONY LAGOURANIS: There were TVs everywhere in Iraq, so people were watching movies and television all the time. I don't know if it was specifically 24, because I hadn't watched it back then, but I do remember remarking all the time that it was just so common to see interrogation scenes. And they all seemed to have a common theme, that the interrogator would establish power over the detainee and then establish a threat that would make the detainee break—maybe the threat of torture, maybe actual torture.

NEWSWEEK: And soldiers would mimic that?

TONY LAGOURANIS: They were. Interrogators didn't have guidance from the military on what to do because we were told that the Geneva Conventions didn't apply any more. So our training was obsolete, and we were encouraged to be creative. We turned to television and movies to look for ways of interrogating. I can say that I saw that with myself, also. I would adopt the posture of the television or movie interrogator, thinking that establishing that simple power arrangement, establishing absolute power over the detainee, would force him to break.

NEWSWEEK: What kinds of television-type torture were soldiers actually imitating?

TONY LAGOURANIS: Mock executions and mock electrocution, stress positions, isolation, hypothermia. Threatening to execute family members or rape detainees' wives and things like that.

NEWSWEEK: What sort of training did you go through when learning how to interrogate?

TONY LAGOURANIS: We had some classroom training, we'd get Power Point presentations on what interrogation should be, but then we'd spend maybe a minute in the interrogation booth with a role player who was an instructor and we'd interrogate. And mostly we were judged on the form of our questions, whether or not we moved from question to question logically. It really didn't have to do with breaking the prisoner. It didn't have to do with coercion or reproaches, which in Iraq is pretty much all you did. So we really weren't trained at all for the mission we had in Iraq.

NEWSWEEK: And that's where television came into play?

TONY LAGOURANIS: The approaches that we were taught we could use, but we were encouraged to use more extreme tactics. We didn't have training in the more extreme tactics so people turned to television to learn what those might be.

NEWSWEEK: It must be easy to watch those shows and think everything will go smoothly—Jack Bauer always seems to get what he wants. How realistic is that?

TONY LAGOURANIS: [24] portrays Jack Bauer as this loose cannon who's operating outside the law but is doing what's necessary to save Los Angeles from a nuclear bomb. The message really is that everyone will break, at some point. But it's not as easy as they make it look. The point is that what he's doing is not an effective technique for gaining intelligence, and his success rate isn't lifelike at all. [Plus] the tactics he uses are completely illegal, under U.S. and international law.

This farce is an admission that in the absence of sufficient education and training, relatively inexperienced interrogators relied on a fictional television program to guide them in their real life interview interrogation tactics.

Second, the *24-effect* has now trickled down to the cadet level at West Point Academy in New York. It's so bad that in early 2007, Brigadier General Patrick Finnegan, Dean of the Academic Board, United States Military Academy, West Point, visited the set of *24* to urge its producers to cut down on torture scenes. He also invited Kiefer Sutherland, a producer as well as the actor who plays Jack Bauer, to visit West Point Academy and lecture on the evils of using torture to extract information from suspects. According to published reports, Mr. Sutherland has accepted that invitation. As explained in Wenn (2007),

Brigadier General Patrick Finnegan visited the set of *24* to urge its makers to cut down on torture scenes. He told the show's producers, "I'd like them to stop. They should do a show where torture backfires. The [cadets] see it and say, 'If torture is wrong, what about *24*?' "The disturbing thing is that although torture may cause Jack Bauer some angst, it is always the patriotic thing to do."

To be clear, the general asked the real-life actor to give a lecture at West Point Academy, to explain that he is only playing a fictional character in a television fantasy; to explain that Jack Bauer is not real; to explain that getting reliable intelligence from torture is not the norm; and to explain that torture itself is not only wrong but illegal. General Finnegan understands the influence of television on his cadets, and he is trying to stem the tide of ignorance that it creates. This is nothing short of an admission that his cadets are not able to tell the difference between television and reality.

Controlling and even manipulating the media has become a vital part of religion, politics, celebrity, and everything in between. As we will learn throughout this text, this includes the criminal justice system, and the field of criminal profiling.

BELIEF IN PSYCHIC PHENOMENA

The question of psychics and their utility was actually answered four decades ago. Back in 1979, the Los Angeles Police Department's Behavioral Science Services (BSS) (currently responsible for planning, developing, implementing, and administering the department's psychological services program) published a study of the efficacy of using psychics in a police investigation. The results of this study found that psychics often gave unverifiable insights and did no better than chance (or worse) when they offered specific details. The BSS ultimately concluded that psychics were not useful in aiding investigations (Reiser et al., 1979).

Contrary to the scientific evidence, the popular media, now firmly entrenched in a 24-hour news cycle, has saturated the globe with fictional and non-fictional accounts and images of psychics working to help solve crime. In the words of *Time* columnist Leon Jaroff (2004),

> They are ubiquitous, operating in shabby storefronts, appearing on national TV shows, keeping tabloids in business, working with naïve police departments and even participating in ludicrous studies by DARPA, the Defense Department's Agency for Advanced Research Projects. They are the psychics, a motley collection of mystics, charlatans, hoaxers and smooth con artists who have successfully buffaloed a good portion of the public into believing that they have supernatural powers.

Dampening belief in psychic ability as it intersects criminal investigation is made far worse for advocates of the scientific method and critical thinking by the *Homicide Investigator's Bible*. This widely used text dedicates five pages to the subject of purported psychics, ultimately advocating for their use by police. It first defines psychic ability in a way that is impossible to prove, support, or even defend with scientific fact—in other words, based entirely on belief (Geberth, 1996, p. 666; 2006, p. 718):

> [A] psychic is a person who learns to control a portion of the brain which is not generally used in order to see and feel things which the average person cannot experience.

This bold assertion presupposes that psychic phenomenon involves special areas of the brain, and that purported psychics actually do sense things that others do not—none of which has ever been proven. Next, the text suggests using psychics as an "investigative aid", even though they will often be wrong and of little investigative use (1996, p. 666; 2006, p. 718):

> It should be noted that information may not always be accurate and in some instances may be of no value to the investigation. However, this should not discourage authorities from using a psychic, especially in homicide cases where there is limited information. The use of a psychic can be considered as an additional investigative aid.

> There is no tenable reason for relying upon any purported "investigative aid" that provides inaccurate information, or information of no value. However this is precisely what is being suggested.

Unfortunately, the continued media attention on psychic phenomenon, and the support it has with a minority of police practitioners who provide training, bestow an unearned perception of reliability and validity on those who claim to be psychic. This is largely accomplished through unverified or unverifiable testimonials.[17]

Testimonials are interesting, but they are more associated with press relations and advertising than with analytical logic and the scientific method. Put another way, testimonials are irrelevant to the issues of reliability and validity—but they are necessary to sell a product, idea, or service when actual proofs are unavailable. And, when evocative, they influence the availability heuristic.

This wishful and magical thinking (that psychics are real; that some people, specifically psychics and profilers, have supernatural abilities) is alluring to the inexperienced and ignorant investigator, who is often desperate to try anything on a big case because they don't have enough training to know better. Accepting this and any other form of magical thinking has the additional benefit of not requiring the possession of actual investigative skill. It takes less ability, and less effort, to follow up on leads provided by a psychic and to believe in the supernatural, than it does to actually buckle down and work a case.

Consider the following examples of recent cases where police have used psychics. These demonstrate that not only are many investigators ignorant on the subject, but that they are necessarily ignorant of criminal investigation techniques as well. Given that the existence of psychic ability has NEVER been proven when proof should be relatively easy to find, this is a testament to the persistence of faith and belief over critical thinking and analytical logic.[18]

Example: The Case of Elizabeth Smart

Two faces of Brian David Mitchell, the polygamous kidnapper of Elizabeth Smart. In a Salt Lake City courtroom, he sings for the judge one day, and screams at her the next.

Elizabeth A. Smart, a 14-year-old girl from Salt Lake City, Utah, was kidnapped from her bedroom on June 5, 2002. Police found her alive 9 months later on March 12, 2003, a few miles from her home, in Sandy, Utah. Brian David Mitchell, 49, a drifter and self-described prophet calling himself "Emmanuel," had abducted her. Mitchell had done some work in the Smart family's home in November of 2001. Rather than focus on those obvious suspects with access to the home, and locating them and interviewing them, police spent a

---

[17] A testimonial is when someone personally vouches for a product, idea, or person: this product works; this idea is sound; or this person is of high caliber and wouldn't lie. The problem is that testimonials tend to be motivated by political or financial gain. As a consequence, many consumers are duped into buying or buying into the false and substandard.

[18] Consider also that hundreds of purported psychics are arrested each year for fraud and theft, usually after taking money from victims in fortune telling and money cleansing scams. And remember the study debunking psychic utility on major cases by Reiser et al. (1979).

lot of time during those nine months responding to psychic tips and their "visions." As reported in "Police, Archaeologists..." (2002),

> The months-old search for Elizabeth Smart took a strange twist last week when two Salt Lake City detectives—at the behest of a group of psychics—ventured into a crypt that holds the skeletal remains of ancient American Indians.
>
> Officials from PSI Tech, a Seattle-based company, claimed that more than a dozen of its members had determined the location of Elizabeth's body by using a special psychic process they call "Technical Remote Viewing."
>
> Independently, the company claims, 14 visionaries all pointed to a concrete burial vault built by the state of Utah about 10 years ago. The vault, located in Salt Lake City's This Is the Place State Heritage Park in the mouth of Emigration Canyon, contains the remains of 75 American Indians, many unearthed by construction projects around Utah.
>
> But the crypt was searched and no trace of the 14-year-old girl, snatched June 5 from her bedroom, could be found, said state archaeologist Kevin Jones.
>
> The investigators' fruitless Aug. 28 search through cobwebs and stale air was one example of how thousands of tips from self-proclaimed psychics have occupied overworked detectives desperately trying to crack the baffling case.
>
> "Many of these [psychic tipsters] are well-meaning, but these tips certainly take manpower away from the investigation," said Salt Lake City Police Chief Rick Dinse.
>
> Still, he said that investigators will check out every "psychic vision" if the tip is specific.
>
> "I don't encourage it or discourage it," Dinse said, speaking of psychics sharing their beliefs. In fact, Dinse said officers still may recruit a psychic to assist with the case.

Note that, as encouraged by the *Homicide Investigator's Bible*, the chief of police refused to cease the use of psychics in the Smart case, despite the fact that they were wrong each and every time.

Example: The Case of Australian Prime Minister John Howard

In April of 2006, a senior Australian Federal Police officer was suspended for consulting a psychic—Elizabeth Walker, a Scottish born medium based in New South Wales—over a threat to assassinate Prime Minister John Howard. As reported in Duff, Koutsoukis, and Shanahan (2006),

Elizabeth Walker is a Scottish born "medium" based in New South Wales, Australia.

> The ALP's spokesman for homeland security, Arch Bevis, said he would be greatly concerned if the AFP was using clairvoyants.

"I think, perhaps, this fellow has watched a few too many of the US detective shows," he said.

The AFP had doubled security staff between 2002 and 2005, Mr Bevis said, but that, apart from the comical aspect, the incident raised the serious issue of adequate training. "This does make you wonder … if the vetting of recruits is as thorough as it should be, and whether officers are receiving adequate training," he said.

Barry Williams, of Australian Skeptics, said he "would be very worried" if he were John Howard. "I know security and intelligence gathering can be a very hard job at times," he said.

"But if your critical faculties are intact and you are going to a psychic to ask for help on something like this, then I think you should be looking for another job."

What this helps demonstrate is that the law-enforcement community is divided on this issue of psychics. Some believe in psychics and want to use them; others recognize the use of psychics as a sign of investigative inability and ignorance. Yet there is pressure to use them because of a public saturated by media accounts of psychics helping the police. It takes a strong police agency with even stronger leadership to take a hard line against the use of psychics in the face of what can be overwhelming pressure, especially when it comes from a victim's family.

Example: The Case of Shawn Hornbeck

11-year-old Shan Hornbeck, reunited with his mother. He had been previously declared dead by "psychic" Sylvia Brown.

According to an FBI Missing Person's report, 11-year-old Shawn D. Hornbeck left his home riding a bicycle in Richwoods, Missouri, on Sunday, October 6, 2002, at approximately 1:00 p.m. He was headed to a friend's house, but never arrived. Shawn's family eventually reported him missing, and local law enforcement initiated an investigation.

In February 2003, *The Montel Williams Show* aired a segment with psychic Sylvia Browne. According to Boyle (2007),

Sylvia Browne told the family of missing Shawn Hornbeck he was dead shortly after the Missouri boy vanished—and later allegedly offered to help locate his body for $700 per half hour.

The popular TV clairvoyant appeared on the *Montel Williams Show* in February 2003, four months after Shawn disappeared, and told Pam and Craig Akers she believed their son was "no longer with us."

She also advised that his body could be found in a wooded area 20 miles from their Richwoods, Mo., home, near two large jagged boulders.

Browne's "vision" of his death caused search teams to redirect their efforts and drew dozens of calls from the public who believed they lived near the woods matching Browne's descriptions.

The family also claims the psychic then tried to cash in, which Browne vigorously denies.

Shawn Hornbeck was found alive and well in January of 2007. The 15-year-old Hornbeck was discovered living just a few miles away from his home with 41-year-old Michael Devlin, a 300-pound pizza parlor manager, and 13-year-old Ben Ownby. Hornbeck was found because police were actively searching for Ownby, who had been abducted from his family four days prior. A tip from a witness led authorities to Devlin, who was charged with both abductions.

These are cautionary tales meant to educate serious investigative and forensic professionals that the reality of psychic phenomena is this:
1. Anyone who claims to be a psychic is either mentally ill, an intentional fraud, or has become proficient at "cold reading" without knowing it.
2. Anyone who claims to be a psychic that has actual information about the case that only the offender could know is something else—a suspect or a witness.
3. Any professional who supports the use of psychics in criminal investigations suffers from a serious training deficiency, and their investigative abilities should be viewed with the utmost skepticism.

PROFILERS AND PSYCHICS: SPECIAL POWERS?

What do psychics and psychic abilities have to do with legitimate criminal profilers? Unfortunately, more than one might think. The confusion of psychic ability with criminal profiling has become an increasing problem, as too many profilers have repeatedly suggested over the years that the ability to profile is a special, near psychic intuition that not just everyone has. It is innate, they argue, and not something that can be taught except to those who belong to a particular group or organization. It should come as little surprise that such profilers also tend to support the use of psychics.

Many profilers have come to enjoy the suggestion that they are among an intellectual elite who have special knowledge and divining powers. This is an image that a number of profilers have actively cultivated in their reach for celebrity. It may even be argued that some are drawn to the profiling profession because of it. And it becomes more problematic as psychics pretend to be profilers, as profilers stump for psychics, and as profilers themselves claim to have near-psychic abilities.

The reach for celebrity through special powers has the effect of defining some areas of profiling as more priesthood than profession—something that less than informed or capable profilers need in order to maintain an aura of credibility and perceived infallibility. The belief that profiling is akin to special or psychic ability helps shield the fraudulent from legitimate scrutiny. By invoking a psychic aura, they avoid having to answer tough questions about how they arrive at their often general and inaccurate conclusions. In actuality, it should be a red flag suggesting a lack of training or worse, outright ignorance.

Consider the following prominent examples:

Robert Ressler, FBI Profiler (ret.)

In 1992, retired FBI Profiler Robert Ressler published his memoir *Whoever Fights Monsters* (Ressler and Schachtman, 1992).[19] There he discussed openly his belief in psychic ability, and admitted to consulting with purported psychic Noreen Renier in both his personal and professional life (pp. 238–239). According to Provence (2005),

> Former FBI agent Robert Ressler invited [psychic Noreen Renier] to lecture at the FBI Academy in Quantico in the early '80s.
>
> "I worked on several cases with her," says Ressler, now a consultant in Fredericksburg. "She worked with me—not the FBI, because the FBI never condoned working with a psychic."
>
> He mentions that Renier helped find a downed aircraft carrying FBI personnel and says that she predicted in 1981 that President Ronald Reagan would be shot.
>
> Ressler estimates he's referred "dozens" of law enforcement officers to Renier. He says that while he doesn't endorse psychic detective work, he doesn't refute it, either. "It can be useful. It can produce additional leads. It can solve cases," he says.
>
> He compares Renier's work to his own as a criminal profiler: "Sometimes it gets results, sometimes not."
>
> As for Renier's psychic abilities, "I don't think there's any question," he says. "She's been tested at Duke University."
>
> Court TV checks out people very carefully, notes Ressler. "The fact that Court TV is backing her is proof she's legitimate," he claims.

Note that as proof of the psychic's ability, Ressler states that she was tested at Duke University, and that Court TV backs her. Unfortunately, this line of reasoning does not hold up to scrutiny. The psychic contacted Duke University herself to be "tested" by undergoing "psychological evaluations and brain pattern monitoring." The result was not a confirmation of her psychic ability (Boyajian, 2001). Moreover, being on TV is not a professional credential or an endorsement of ability. Being on TV is at best recognition that one has a view or a personality that sells market share, nothing more.

John Douglas, FBI Profiler (ret.)

In 1995, FBI Profiler John Douglas wrote his memoir, *Mindhunter* (Douglas and Olshaker, 1995).[20] Like Ressler before him, he openly embraced the notions that not only are some psychics legitimate, but there may be a psychic component to criminal profiling. He further takes the position that criminal profiling is not entirely teachable. He describes his own method of rendering conclusions in the following passage (p.151):

> I try to think exactly as [the criminal] does. Exactly how this happens, I'm not sure, anymore than the novelists such as Tom Harris who've consulted me over the years can say exactly how their characters come to life. If there is a psychic component to this, I won't run away from it, though I regard it more in the realm of creative thinking.

---

[19] This title alone suggests that criminal offenders are "monsters" as opposed to just human beings, implying that those who fight them must have special monster fighting powers. It appeals to the market, as opposed to being based in reality.

[20] This title clearly suggests a special ability to get inside the mind of criminal offenders, and hints at the "psychic component" that Douglas flirts with.

Psychics can, on occasion, be helpful to a criminal investigation. I've seen it work. Some of them have the ability to focus subconsciously on particular subtle details at a scene and draw logical conclusions from them, just and I try and train my people to do.

Bear in mind that Douglas admits to not knowing how he comes up with his conclusions, and name-drops Thomas Harris to legitimize it. Essentially, he has compared what he does to psychic intuition and fiction writing. These are not the hallmarks of informed methodology, let alone objectivity and reliability.

Dr. Micki Pistorious, Investigative Psychologist

When FBI profilers advocated the use of psychics, and "embraced the possibility that [profiling] involves psychic powers" (Risinger, 2002), the door opened for psychics to start referring to themselves as profilers, and vice versa. The media embraced it, and FBI profilers raised no notable objections. In fact there is continuing evidence to suggest that they openly endorse this association.

One of the most notable examples is that of Dr. Micki Pistorius from South Africa. She studied under Dr. David Canter at the University of Liverpool, graduating with a Ph.D. in investigative psychology.[21] She is a former journalist, and worked for the South African Police Service as an "Investigative Psychologist" for six years before abruptly retiring in 2000. According to Johnson (1997),

[1994] was when Pistorius joined the [police] service, straight from completing her masters in psychology at Pretoria university. Until recently this former SABC journalist was the only person to whom the country's police could turn to for help whenever a serial killer was suspected.

The University or Pretoria, it should be noted, is a deeply religious learning institution. The Department of Psychology, where Dr. Pistorius studied, defines psychology in way that would be unacceptable in any scientific community:

Psychology is the scientific study of all the aspects of human behavior within the context of the person with him or herself, with his or her fellow man, with his or her environment and with the Creator.

More disturbing, Dr. Pistorius has repeatedly made claims that she has what can only be referred to as psychic experiences in which she reads the crime scene on a "quantum level," and then searches in her mind for the killer. Her own words explain her methods best (Phirippides, 2002):

[T]here's usually a wind, a peaceful wind, and I'd just absorb the energy flowing, of the crime scene, because that is the place the person acted out their fantasy. Sometimes after a while, the same day, sometimes a night, sometimes a week, the feeling would be translated.

The abyss is a very dark place in my mind where I managed to, on a mental plane, find these killers. It got so bad at one stage that on a Sunday afternoon I would get a feeling of sticky blood on my hands and I would feel the killer digging his hands into intestines, and then afterwards we'd find a crime scene which compares with that feeling I had.

'Psychic' is a difficult word for me. I can't predict the future, I can't hold the clothing of a missing person and tell you where they are. It goes a little beyond. In the beginning I was lured into it

---

[21] This program is not a psychology program, and it is not an investigative program. Investigative psychology is defined by the University of Liverpool as: "The application of psychological principles to all aspects of the analysis, investigation and prosecution of crime" (www.liv.ac.uk/study/postgraduate/taught_courses/investigative_psychology_msc.htm). This is explored in a later chapter.

without realising how it happened and it bothered me a lot so I started reading about it and I found the answer in quantum physics, in energy vibrations.

When I sit on a crime scene, if the body's been removed or not, I pick up the vibrations of energy and then it takes a while when this is translated into a pattern … and then I get this feeling. It's not like a visual picture, I can't tell you what the killer looks like, but I get the feeling and fantasy.

The manner in which a serial killer carries out his crime is a symbol of his personal agony. It is the job of the investigative psychologist to decipher the particular killer's fantasy.

Clearly, Dr. Pistorius believes she is having certain metaphysical experiences. Some might call these hallucinations. Some might call them wishful thinking or playing to an audience or market. In any event, none of her "experiences" are verifiable, nor have her profiles and methods been subjected to outside validation or review.

While the word "psychic" may be difficult for Dr. Pistorius, legitimizing psychics is apparently not. In 1995, she wrote a testimonial letter for Cape Town psychic Gypsy Niyan, as a credential authenticating her work with the police. Niyan produced the letter to journalists in 2003, after she was denied an audience with local police to give assistance on an unsolved series of poisonings. The media published her grievance, and her psychically derived profile of the suspect (Williams, 2003):

Gypsy Niyan said: "My initial feeling is that he is medium-dark in colouring, so he is not fair or blonde. He is swarthy-looking, stocky and foreign-looking. He might be a South African citizen, but is of foreign extraction. He is someone with a way out to a foreign country if he needs to run."

Niyan believes his motives were not only money—the extortionist has demanded R500 000 from Pick 'n Pay—but "some kind of a revenge thing."

Niyan produced a testimonial signed by top profiler Micki Pistorius. The letter, dated 1995, read in part that Niyan "has assisted the South African police in an unofficial capacity in the investigation of the station strangler serial killer case in Cape Town, as well as the River Strangler serial killer case in Durban." Pistorius also wrote that "in all these cases (Niyan) was particularly accurate in describing crime scenes."

The case remains unsolved.

Despite retiring in 2000 owing to "post-traumatic stress" (Phirippides, 2002), Dr. Pistorius apparently continues to consult with South African police, and they also continue to consult with psychics:

During the investigation into the murder of [Juanita] Mabula and the deaths of the other two women, [Deputy Police Commissioner Marius] Visser has been in contact with a South African psychologist who is regarded as an expert on serial killings in South Africa, Dr Micki Pistorius, to get some guidance on possible ways to approach the investigation of the three young women's deaths.

He has in the meantime also met a supposed South African psychic, Sue du Randt, who had offered to use her alleged supernatural abilities to help with the investigation, Visser said yesterday.

Her participation has however not yet borne fruit for the investigations either.

According to retired FBI Profiler Robert Ressler, it was his involvement with Micki Pistorius in 1994, when she was still a Ph.D. student of Dr. David Canter's at Liverpool and only a volunteer with the South African Police Service, that led to her being allowed to form the Investigative Psychology Unit in 1995 (Ressler and Schachtman, 1998; p.213). Ressler often touts her as "one of the world's best criminal profilers" in books and interviews (Phirippides, 2002). This is significant given the absolute faith Dr. Pistorius has in her psychic abilities, and the fact that she does not hide it.

Clint Van Zandt, FBI Profiler (ret.)

In 2001, Clint VanZandt, a retired FBI Profiler and Hostage Negotiator went on CNN's *Larry King Live* to participate in a program called "Are Psychics for Real?" His answer to the question was in step with that of other FBI profilers that have openly discussed the subject (King, 2001):

> [A]s an FBI agent, you know, you have to keep your mind open, and I'm not going say I'm a skeptic. I would listen if somebody could help solve a crime, Larry.

> When I was in Waco, dealing with David Koresh, and a psychic sent a letter in and said: If you say the word—I think it was Beelzebub—to David Koresh, he will come out. I read the letter, I got a three-by-five card and I wrote that word on 3-by-5 card, and I shoved it in front of the face of the negotiator talking to David Koresh on the phone.

> The negotiator says: "What am I supposed to do with this?" I said, "Use the word in the sentence." He said, "I don't know how to." I said: "Make up a sentence." So we did, and we used it.

> I would have loved David Koresh to come marching out with those little kids behind him, Larry, but it didn't happen. And there were situations where we have tried, and it didn't happen.

> But if you exhaust law enforcement investigation, if you exhaust psychological profiling, if the victim's family or the police say, "I would like to try a psychic," I would say, anything that can help, and anything that would help a victim's family, I would not stand in the way.

Like Geberth, Douglas, Ressler, and Pistorius, retired FBI profiler Clint Van Zandt believes that psychics may be real, and believes that investigative resources should be wasted indulging them. This belief persists despite that fact that his experience has shown just how little value they actually have.[22]

THE PROBLEM

The media affect the hearts and minds of the public—perpetuating magical thinking by influencing the availability heuristic. A segment of the public is fascinated with and/or believes in the supernatural—often as an adjunct to personal religious faith. The media have embraced this market by courting psychics, profilers, psychic profilers, and profilers who suggest that they have special powers, or may be a bit psychic. Because the media have an effect on what people believe, it is now in a continuous feedback loop with respect to psychics and near psychic profilers: the public believes—the media provide—the public believes more—the media provide more.

Clearly there are also more than a few professional criminal profilers, and criminal investigators, who are in the dark with respect to understanding how criminal profiling interpretations are actually made—theirs

---

[22] This also begs a very important question: what is an FBI hostage negotiator doing reading letters from psychics while involved in on-scene hostage negotiations with a heavily armed and entrenched religious sect? That such a letter was even taken seriously speaks to how seriously under-trained the on-scene negotiators were, trying anything because, in Van Zandt's own words, they simply did not know what else to do.

or others.[23] Too many are supplementing this ignorance with claims of special abilities because it intersects with personal belief systems, makes for light work, and most importantly it sells. And they are training others to think the same way —through their publicized interviews, their memoirs and their example.

Criminal profiling is not akin to being psychic, and it is not the result of having special, innate abilities. Continually playing to the popular market (the public) by suggesting it is has hurt the credibility of the field tremendously. It has also resulted in the waste of untold investigative time and resources.

When investigators and forensic examiners believe that findings are inspired by special abilities, or by divine providence, we will not question them, nor will we be receptive to the questions of others. This is anathema to critical thinking, analytical logic, and the scientific method, which are so vital to reality based criminal profiling, let alone actually working cases to a meaningful result.

THE SOLUTION

The first step is admitting we have a problem. Faith-based reasoning of any kind, while often important in one's personal life, has no place in the objective investigation of facts, or in their subsequent forensic examination. It promotes bias, and is not susceptible to falsification. To that extent, there is a problem of magical thinking that is endorsed by some profilers, embraced by a particular segment of the public, and perpetuated for profit by the media.

In the short term, the legitimate profiling community must openly separate itself from faith-based reasoning of any kind. This means an end to playing up religious and psychic influences with respect to profiling interpretations. It means refusal to endorse magical thinking in any way, shape, or form as it coincides with the popular media. It also means a move toward methods that embrace the scientific method, analytical logic, and critical thinking. In other words, it means we need to be showing our work and embrace methods that are verifiable. There is no tenable reason for doing otherwise.

Education is the only long-term solution to the problem of faith-based profiling, as misplaced faith is rooted in the worship of particular profiling personalities and methods, in combination with ignorance and an unwillingness to question anything for fear of being labeled harmful to the "faith."

The purpose of this third edition is to move evidence-based criminal profiling closer to a full embrace of the scientific method and all that it can bring to bear on the interpretation of behavioral evidence. We will discuss the role that intuition plays in logic and reason; we will learn how interpret the behavioral evidence rationally and deductively. We will learn principles and practice standards. We will identify what actually works and how, what actually doesn't and why, and we will not bow to any particular profiling faith or celebrity. Criminal profiling is not a priesthood—it is a skill that can be taught and learned. Only through serious, critically oriented students does it have the potential to become more reliable, and more useful as a forensic discipline.

---

[23] Former NYPD Policeman Richard "Bo" Dietl, who often refers to himself as criminal profiler during media appearances, stated during a January 17, 2007 interview on Fox News' *The Real World with Nick Cavuto*: "Don't you watch *24*? They're out there. Terrorist cells are out there." Mr. Dietl was citing the fictional television program *24* as evidence that terrorist cells from the Middle East are working inside the United States, and that the racial profiling of all Muslims (i.e., anyone who wears a turban) is reasonable, useful, and necessary in the wake of 9/11. This would be an example of the availability heuristic revealing a lack of actual knowledge about a subject by a purported expert in criminal profiling. It would also be an example of the problem that some profilers have with believing what they see on TV, and the pervasive nature of the *24 effect*.

REFERENCES

BBC, 2005. Church Fights DaVinci Code Novel. Tuesday, March 15. Available from: www.news.bbc.co.uk/2/hi/entertainment/4350625. stm (accessed 19.12.06.).

Bennett, J., 2007. TV's Guide to Torture. Newsweek (February 27).

Boyajian, R., 2001. ESP Made Easy. Independent Florida Alligator (April 21).

Boyle, C., 2007. She Told Them Boy Was Dead. New York Daily News (January 18).

Braser, K., 2006. Courts Battling CSI Effect. Evansville Courier and Press (December 4).

Douglas, J., Olshaker, M., 1995. Mindhunter: Inside the FBI's Elite Serial Crime Unit. Scribner, New York, NY.

Duff, E., Koutsoukis, J., Shanahan, L., 2006. The Police, the PM and the Psychic. The Age (April 9).

Ehrman, B., 2005. Misquoting Jesus. HarperCollins, New York, NY.

Geberth, V., 1996. Practical Homicide Investigation, third edition. CRC Press, Boca Raton, FL.

Geberth, V., 2006. Practical Homicide Investigation, fourth edition. CRC Press, Boca Raton, FL.

Gross, H., 1906. Criminal Investigation. Ramaswmy Chetty, Madras, India.

Hammel, P., 2003. Police Are Reluctant to Rely on Psychics. Omaha World-Herald (February 23).

James, S., Nordby, J., 2003. Forensic Science: An Introduction to Scientific and Investigative Techniques. CRC Press, Boca Raton, FL.

Jaroff, L., 2004. So Far, Psychics Are Batting .000. Time.com December 27.

Jefferson, T., 1802. Personal Letter to Nehemiah Dodge, Ephraim Robbins, & Stephen S. Nelson, a committee of the Danbury Baptist Association in the state of Connecticut. January 1.

Johnson, A., 1997. The Woman Who Stalks the Killers Electronic Mail and Guardian. Johannesburg, South Africa (October 8).

King, L., 2001. Are Psychics for Real? CNN, Interview with FBI Profiler Clint Van Zandt, Aired March 6.

Matera, A., 2005. Interview with an Exorcist: Fr. James Lebar Talks about "The Exorcism of Emily Rose". Godspy Magazine (October 3).

Murphy, P., 2005. Warren Jeffs Indicted: Shurtleff Applauds Mohave County's Investigation, News release. Utah Attorney General's Office June 10.

Norton, D., 2005. A Textual History of the King James Bible. Cambridge University Press, New York, NY.

Phirippides, S., 2000. Transcript of Interview with Micki Pistorius. Carte Blanche Interactive (www.carteblanche.co.za), (July 2).

Police, 2002. Archaeologists Wary of Psychics' Theory of Smart Mystery. The Salt Lake Tribune (September 7).

Provence, L., 2005. NEWS—Medium Rare: Psychic Offers Help in Rapist Hunt. The Hook (February 3).

Ramsland, K., 2005. Interview with Roy Hazelwood. Court TV Crime Library; www.crimelibrary.com/criminal_mind/profiling/ hazelwood/4.html, (accessed on December 19, 200).

Reiser, M., Ludwig, L., Saxe, S., Wagner, C., 1979. An Evaluation of the Use of Psychics in the Investigation of Major Crimes. Journal of Police Science and Administration 7 (1), 18–25.

Ressler, R., Schachtman, T., 1992. Whoever Fights Monsters. St. Martin's Press, New York, NY.

Ressler, R., Schachtman, T., 1998. I Have Lived the Monster. St. Martin's Press, New York, NY.

Risinger, M., 2002. Three Card Monte, Monty Hall, Modus Operandi and "Offender Profiling": Some Lessons of Modern Cognitive Science for the Law of Evidence. Cardozo Law Review (November).

Sunstein, C., 2005. Group Judgments: Statistical Means, Deliberation, and Information Markets. New York University Law Review (June).

Wenn, U.S., 2007. Army Invites Sutherland to Give Anti-Torture Speech. Hollywood.com (February 26).

Williams, M., 2003. Psychic's Vision of the Pick 'n Pay Poisoner. The Cape Argus (July 12).

Winslow, B., 2006. Town Marshal Pledges His Allegiance to Jeffs. Deseret Morning News (December 9).

Acknowledgments

This fourth edition of *Criminal Profiling* represents a great evolution of thought, theory, and methodology in the discipline. The core principles remain, while the mechanisms for examination and classification have been refined, and hopefully more clearly expressed. The more cases we work, the more professionals we work with, the more possibilities we encounter, the more theory and methods are shaped by practice.

However, the thanks for the refinements in this edition must go to my students. This includes those I have taught at Oklahoma City University and Bond University; through the Academy of Behavioral Profiling and Forensic Solutions; and in every workshop and lecture that I've been invited to give at colleges and police agencies since 2008. These students, some new to the subject and some already case-working professionals in the criminal justice system (law enforcement and otherwise), have provided an endless stream of questions, commentary, and criticisms. Every case a new theory; every theory a new doubt; and every doubt a new revelation. They have provided me with the crucible that is Socratic teaching—with inquiry and debate and doubt and energy. For this I am deeply grateful.

As much as I have learned working cases, testifying in court, and working with police officers and attorneys from different parts of the United States and around the rest of the world—learning how to teach that to others effectively is only possible when students are honest about the mistakes you've made trying to teach them. I am ever the student of my students, and often feel as though I've gotten more from them than they actually understand. This edition is dedicated to them in the hopes that they will realize their contribution to its evolution and continued success.

—Brent E. Turvey

About the Authors

JANSEN ANG

Jansen Ang is part of the Behavioral Sciences Program, Home Team Academy, Ministry of Home Affairs, Singapore.

EOGHAN CASEY, M.A.

Eoghan Casey is Director of Training at Stroz Friedberg, LLC, a nationally recognized leader in digital forensics, electronic discovery, and cyber-crime response (www.strozllc.com). He conducts industry-leading courses on best practices and technical tools derived from his active docket of case and experience managing complex investigations and preserving, harvesting, and analyzing relevant digital evidence. He is the author of widely used textbooks, including *Digital Evidence and Computer Crime* (second edition), *Handbook of Computer Crime Investigation*, and *Child Exploitation and Pornography*, and Editor-in-Chief of the journal *Digital Investigation*. Eoghan can be contacted at mailto:ecasey@strozllc.com.

JEFFERY CHIN

Jeffery Chin is part of the Behavioral Sciences Program, Home Team Academy, Ministry of Home Affairs, Singapore.

W. JERRY CHISUM, B.S.

William Jerry Chisum has been a criminalist since 1960. He studied under Paul Kirk at UC Berkeley, where he received a bachelor's degree in chemistry. He worked in San Bernardino, then set up the Kern County Laboratory in Bakersfield. He has been involved in laboratory management and administration for most of his career. He has been President of the California Association of Criminalists three times. He has also served as President of the American Society of Crime Lab Directors. In October of 1998, he retired from 30 years of service with the California Department of Justice and continues working through a private consultancy. He is a founding member of the Academy of Behavioral Profiling, where he currently serves as Vice-President. He is also a co-author of *Crime Reconstruction* (2006), also with Elsevier Science. He can be contacted at www.profiling.org.

CRAIG M. COOLEY, J.D.

Criag M. Cooley is a Staff Attorney with the Innocence Project in New York, New York. Mr. Cooley received his J.D. from Northwestern University School of Law (2004). He completed his M.S. in forensic science at the University of New Haven (2000). During graduate school he worked as an Investigative Intern with the Sacramento County Public Defenders Office and as a Graduate Research Assistant for the California Department of Justice's Bureau of Forensic Services. Prior to his work with the Innocence Project, Mr. Cooley worked as an Assistant Federal Defender in Las Vegas, Nevada (2005–2007), where he (and his unit—Capital Habeas Unit) represented Nevada death row inmates in federal and state post-conviction proceedings. Mr. Cooley's research and writings have been published in the *George Mason University Civil Rights Law Journal, New England Law Review, Indiana University Law Journal, Stanford Law and Policy Review, Oklahoma City University Law Review*, and *Southern Illinois University Law Journal*.

JODI FREEMAN, M.Crim.

Jodi Freeman holds an honors bachelor's degree in health sciences from the University of Western Ontario, Canada, with a double major in health sciences and criminology. She recently graduated from Bond University, Australia with a master's degree in criminology. During her master's program, Jodi completed an independent study under Brent Turvey, in the area of behavioral evidence analysis. In 2010, Jodi undertook a crime scene analysis internship with Forensic Solutions. Working in this role, she continues to assist with research, casework, and workshop facilitation. Jodi can be contacted at: mailto:jodi.freeman@rogers.com.

MAJEED KHADER

Majeed Khader is part of the Behavioral Sciences Program, Home Team Academy, Ministry of Home Affairs, Singapore.

MICHAEL MCGRATH, M.D.

Michael McGrath, M.D., is a Board Certified Forensic Psychiatrist, licensed in the State of New York. He is a Clinical Associate Professor in the Department of Psychiatry, University of Rochester School of Medicine and Dentistry, Rochester, NY, and Medical Director and Chair, Department of Behavioral Health, Unity Health System, Rochester, NY.

Dr. McGrath divides his time among administrative, clinical, research and teaching activities. His areas of expertise include forensic psychiatry and criminal profiling. He has lectured on three continents and is a founding member of the Academy of Behavioral Profiling. He can be contacted at: mailto:mmcgrath@profiling.org.

EUNICE TAN

Eunice Tan is part of the Behavioral Sciences Program, Home Team Academy, Ministry of Home Affairs, Singapore.

ANGELA N. TORRES, Ph.D.

Angela Torres majored in psychology at the University of California, Berkeley. She then went on to complete her doctorate in clinical psychology with a forensic focus at Sam Houston State University in Huntsville, Texas. After course work, she was a pre-doctoral Intern at the Federal Medical Center in Rochester, Minnesota. She is currently a post-doctoral Fellow in Forensic Psychology at Central State Hospital in Petersburg, Virginia. Her interests include: sex offender risk assessment, gender/sexuality/cultural issues, malingering, and general forensic assessment.

BRENT E. TURVEY, M.S.

Brent E. Turvey spent his first years in college on a pre-med track, only to change his course of study once his true interest took hold. He received a bachelor of science degree from Portland State University in psychology, with an emphasis on forensic psychology, and an additional bachelor of science degree in history. He went on to receive his master of science in Forensic Science after studying at the University of New Haven, in West Haven, Connecticut.

Since graduating in 1996, Brent has consulted with many agencies, attorneys, and police departments in the United States, Australia, China, Canada, Barbados, and Korea on a range of rapes, homicides, and serial/multiple rape/death cases, as a forensic scientist and criminal profiler. He has also been court qualified as an expert in the areas of criminal profiling, forensic science, victimology, and crime reconstruction.

In August of 2002, he was invited by the Chinese People's Police Security University (CPPSU) in Beijing to lecture before groups of detectives at the Beijing, Wuhan, Hanzou, and Shanghai police bureaus. In 2005, he was invited back to China again, to lecture at the CPPSU, and to the police in Beijing and Xian—after the translation of the second edition of this text into Chinese for the university. In 2007, he was invited to lecture at the First Behavioral Sciences Conference at the Home Team (Police) Academy in Singapore, where he also provided training to their Behavioral Science Unit.

He is the author of *Criminal Profiling: An Introduction to Behavioral Evidence Analysis* (1999, 2002, 2008), and co-author of the *Rape Investigation Handbook* (2004) and *Crime Reconstruction* (2006)—all with Elsevier Science. He is currently a full partner, Forensic Scientist, Criminal Profiler, and Instructor with Forensic Solutions, LLC, and an Adjunct Professor in Criminology at Oklahoma City University. He can be contacted at mailto:bturvey@forensic-science.com.

An Introduction to Criminal Profiling

CHAPTER 1

A History of Criminal Profiling

Brent E. Turvey

We must gather wisdom while we are not required to use it; when the time for use arrives, the time for harvest is over.

—Hans Gross, *Criminal Psychology*

CONTENTS

Criminal Profiling: An Introduction to Behavioral Evidence Analysis, Fourth Edition
© 2012 Elsevier Ltd. All rights reserved.

KEY TERMS

Academy of Behavioral
Profiling

Blood libel

Criminal profiling

Criminology

Handbuch für
Untersuchungsrichter, als

System der Kriminalistik (1893)
[a.k.a. Criminal Investigation,
A Practical Textbook for
Magistrates, Police Officers,
and Lawyers (Gross, 1906)]

Malleus Maleficarum

Pseudo-rational attribution

Pseudo-rational attribution
effects

Salem Witch Trials

Spanish Inquisition

Before we begin our study of current evidence-based criminal profiling methods and fundamentals, we must first understand what has come before. This is done in the hope that we may uncover how we have come to this place and time. That is the province of history—to provide a look back, to gauge progress and wandering, to mark the growth and depth of our placements and philosophies, to let us know what we have been and what we are becoming.

History, the chronicling and study of past events, is a quiet but feared discipline. History reminds us where our knowledge and wisdom came from when we lose sight of those who cut the path. History teaches us what has been lost to fire and fancy, despite conquering or dominant ideologies that would leave us ignorant of all that came before. History collects, history records, and history remembers. And it patiently waits for unsatisfied minds to discover it.

From this it may be rightly inferred that the purpose of studying history is not to learn dry facts for later academic recitation in order to appear intellectual. The study of history is about going back to see what has come before in order to honestly gauge where we are right now and, it is hoped, why. The study of history is about digging beneath and beyond cultural and institutional indoctrination because what you know, and what you've been told, are not always so.

The study of history is for critical thinkers—those who will not blindly and politely accept what they have been handed by someone claiming to be an authority. It is for those who would rather come to understand things and their relationships for themselves. It is for those who understand the value of hunting down information and sourcing it, and who would prefer not to be led by the hand into intellectual servitude. It is a bold and dangerous journey that can educate, inspire, and inflame a lifetime of study.

It has been argued that a competent, accurate history of any subject can only be written generations after an event or series of events. This supposedly helps provide the requisite clarity and objectivity on the part of historians and presumably keeps them from feeling the pressure to paint facts in a light more favorable to their confederates. This can be true. It is also true that objectivity can never be attained in even the most detached recounting of history because, despite valiant efforts, one cannot hope to separate the message from the messenger. The historian Edward Cheney offers a warning that is well worth our consideration (Cheney, 1988):

> Everything comes to the reader as interpreted by the historian. Everything is seen through the medium of personality ... the reader is at the historian's mercy. ... The conflicts of the past are perpetuated by the very chroniclers who recount their history. Thus history sells its birthright of truth for a mess of the pottage partisanship.

This is something to keep in mind when reading this or any of the available histories of criminal profiling[1] or histories of anything else for that matter. The historical view here will, despite all attempts at objectivity, be presented through the eyes of the author, in the author's language. It is intended to examine the nature of the roles and contributions of multiple organizations and disciplines to the field as it has developed. While admittedly incomplete, it should lay the groundwork for a basic understanding of those contributing perspectives. Readers are encouraged to use this historical rendering as a first blush only and to look beyond for a more complete understanding of the history and origins of criminal profiling.

Inferring the traits of individuals responsible for committing criminal acts has commonly been referred to as *criminal profiling*. Professionals engaged in the practice of criminal profiling have historically included a broad spectrum of investigators, behavioral scientists, social scientists, and forensic scientists. Their involvement in unsolved casework has most commonly been concerned with criminal investigative efforts and suspect identification. In that capacity, a wide variety of faith-based, inductive (statistical/experiential), and deductive (logical/rational) criminal profiling techniques have been sought out to help identify criminals, narrow suspect pools, assist with case linkage, and develop investigatively relevant leads and strategies with respect to unsolved cases.[2] As we will learn, various incarnations of profiling methodology also have a long-standing forensic tradition.[3]

Criminal profiling has also been referred to, among less common terms, as *behavioral profiling, crime scene profiling, criminal personality profiling, offender profiling, psychological profiling, criminal investigative analysis,* and, more recently, *investigative psychology*. Because of the variety of profilers, their respective methods, and their various levels of actual education on the subject, there remains a general lack of uniformity or agreement in the applications and definitions of these terms across and even within some profiling communities. Consequently, these terms are used inconsistently and interchangeably. For our purposes, we will be using the general term *criminal profiling*.

As students will learn, there has been a considerable and uneasy relationship between criminal profiling, politics, religion, and prejudice—such that each has too often been an expression for the other. Historically, investigators working for various religions or governments have used profiles and profiling to demonize a particular group, often in the most literal sense. The result has been much ignorance, and much blood.

We cannot ignore this part of criminal profiling history. It must be studied. We must learn its lessons to better avoid becoming its victims.

---

[1] Even with the first publication of a more complete historical rendering (Turvey, 2002), histories of criminal profiling are still noticeably few, and they infrequently begin with anything other than the FBI's involvement in the practice or some mention of profiling Hitler (which was actually a psychological assessment, not a profile). Brief mass media histories of criminal profiling remain the most common, written as a paragraph or two at the beginning of a piece about a particular criminal profiler, personality, or profiling technique.
[2] See general discussions of criminal profiling use and efficacy in Gross (1924), Depue et al. (1995), Kirk (1974), Cooley and Turvey (2002), Petherick (2002), and Turvey (1999). It will become evident throughout this text that specifically identifying criminals is one of the more hazardous uses of criminal profiling—because it is more susceptible to bias and abuse.
[3] As explained in Thornton (1997): "Forensic" comes to us from the Latin *forensus*, meaning "of the forum." In Ancient Rome, the forum was where governmental debates were held, but it was also where trials were held. It was the courthouse. So forensic science has come to mean the application of the natural and physical sciences to the resolution of conflicts within a legal setting.

BLOOD LIBEL

It's not just an act of murder and of a ritual murder. Removing the blood from the body and then using it for a ritual or religious purpose—there is something horrific, but yet as fascinating as it is repulsive in this notion.

—Professor Robert Wistrich, University of Jerusalem (Levinson, 2004)

One of the first documented uses of criminal profiling involves the demonization of Jews with a fairly crude form of profiling (Figure 1.1). Its origins are found in a report made by the anti-Semite scholar Apion to the Roman Emperor Caligula in 38 CE. Apion felt the Jews of Alexandria, where he had studied, had too many rights and privileges. Apion, documented in the writings of Flavius Josephus (*Contra Apionem*, circa 90s CE), falsely reported to Caligula that the Jews were often responsible for the ritual killing and eating of Greeks as part of Passover.

This idea of ritual abduction and murder by depraved Jews took particular hold in the 1100s because of widespread European anti-Semitism, and because of one monk's desire to martyr a slain child. As discussed in Levinson (2004):

> The origins of this anti-Semitic myth, known as the blood libel, lie in medieval England. In 1144, a skinner's apprentice called William went missing in Norwich. When his body was found, the monks who examined the corpse claimed that the boy's head had been pierced by a crown of thorns.
>
> Some years later, a monk called Thomas began to gather evidence about William's death. His main aim was to establish the boy as a holy martyr and draw pilgrims to the cathedral. Almost as an incidental matter, he accused the Jews of Norwich of killing the boy.

FIGURE 1.1
A fifteenth-century woodcut of Jews murdering the child Simon of Trent. This alleged "murder" is one of the sources of the medieval blood libel. Jews can be recognized by the circular patches sewn on their clothing and by the moneybags they carry. Found in facsimile of Hartmann Schedel's *Nuremburg Chronicle* or *Buch der Chroniken*, printed by Anton Koberger in 1493.

"The unforeseen outcome of what Thomas did was to create the blood libel, which then itself takes on a life of its own," says Dr Victor Morgan, of the University of East Anglia.

The *blood libel*, or false accusation of ritual killing, is an early and persistent form of criminal profiling because it involves a predetermined set of crime-related characteristics used to infer and consequently accuse a particular suspect pool—namely the Jews. From the available literature cited in this work, the general profile used included one or more or the following elements:

- A young Christian male goes missing.
- A Jewish community is nearby.
- The child goes missing on or just prior to Passover.
- The body may have injuries that appear to be the result of a ritual.
- The body may have lost a great deal of blood or may simply appear so.

The inference is then drawn that the Jewish community has effected a ritual abduction, torture, and murder, and this fear is fanned by some preexisting anti-Semitic sentiment. As the term implies, the accusations are libelous—intentionally false and inflammatory. The blood libel is therefore not just one of the first uses of profiling, it is one of the earliest documented forms of false reporting.

Unfortunately, blood libel cases have followed us to the twentieth century and threaten to remain with us for as long as there is value in anti-Semitic rhetoric. Levinson (2004) describes the path blood libel has taken across the centuries and why:

> The accusation that Jews would drain the blood of children and then use it for ritual purposes is bizarre, as Judaism has a powerful taboo against blood. Indeed, kosher butchering is meant to remove all blood from meat. But the idea seems to have had a powerful hold on the mediaeval imagination....
>
> The blood libel spread across England and Continental Europe over the centuries, with hundreds of accusations, all based on hysteria rather than evidence. There were notorious blood libel cases in Lincoln in 1255 and Trento, Italy, in 1475. Many Jews were executed. Others were killed by mobs seeking revenge.
>
> There was another rash of accusations in the late 19th and early 20th centuries in Eastern Europe—societies gripped by economic transformation and political uncertainty, climaxing with the Beilis case of 1913.

In 1911, Mendel Beilis (Figure 1.2) was arrested by the Kiev Secret Police and put on trial for the ritual murder of a Christian boy. He was jailed for two years while prosecutors tried to build their case, all the while concealing exculpatory evidence. Beilis was ultimately acquitted in 1913—sort of. As Murav (2000) explains:

FIGURE 1.2
Mendel Beilis, who worked at a brick factory outside of Kiev.

> In March 1911 in Kiev, the body of a thirteen-year-old boy, Andrei Iushchinskii, was found in a cave. Soviet scholar Alexandr Tager, who used archives closed until 1917, showed that Iushchinskii was murdered by a gang of thieves headed by Vera Cheberiak because the gang believed Iushchinskii was going to inform the police about them. Iushchinskii and Cheberiak's son were friends. Vera Cheberiak was arrested and released in July of the same year, at which time Mendel Beilis was arrested. Beilis had been identified as the "man with the black beard," whom witnesses claimed they saw with Iushchinskii.

He was a clerk at a brick factory on the territory of which Iushchinskii's body was found. Beilis was tried in 1913. The indictment charged that he had committed the murder "out of religious fanaticism, for ritual purposes." Two questions were put to the jury. The first suggested that the murder had been committed in such a way as to allow the perpetrator to harvest the maximum amount of blood from the victim's body. The language of the question implied that the purpose was to consume the blood. The question asked whether it had been shown that Iushchinskii had been subjected to wounds which produced "five glasses of blood" and then subjected to a second series of wounds which killed him and left his body in a state of "almost complete bloodlessness." The second question was whether Beilis was guilty of the crime. The jury, consisting mostly of peasants, answered "yes" to the first question, but acquitted Beilis. The jury's finding left open the possibility that ritual murder had been committed.

According to Murav (2000), the state used the expert testimony of a Catholic priest to cement their case regarding the ritualistic behaviors and motives of Jews, including their "dogma of blood."

Sadly, in the new millennium, blood libel accusations continue to be made against the Jewish community in the context of religious extremism and ongoing conflict in the Middle East.[4]

WITCHES AND THE MEDIEVAL INQUISITIONS

Thou shalt not suffer a witch to live.[5]

—King James Bible, Exodus 22:18

Whether the belief that there are such beings as witches is so essential a part of the Catholic faith that obstinately to maintain the opposite opinion manifestly savours of heresy.

—*Malleus Maleficarum*

One of the first published texts that offered explicit instruction on the subject and practice of profiling criminal behavior is the *Malleus Maleficarum* (*The Witches' Hammer*). Two Dominican monks, Henry Kramer and James Sprenger, professors of theology of the Order of Friars Preachers, originally published this work around 1486. Written in Latin, it was intended as a rationale and guide for those involved with the Inquisition (namely the authors), to assist in the identification, prosecution, and punishment of witches.

Upon publication, *Malleus Maleficarum* was fully sanctioned by the Catholic Church in fear of being made impotent by the existence of heretics, nonbelievers, and the failed Crusades against the Muslims, which had been waged in vain to occupy and control the Holy Land. Included in the *Malleus Maleficarum* was the bull of Pope Innocent VIII (Figure 1.3), written two years previously on December 9, 1484.[6]

The papal bull was an official church mandate from Innocent VIII explaining the powers and jurisdictions of the Inquisitors. It effectively deputized Kramer and Sprenger as unimpeachable enforcers working directly at the request of Innocent VIII, the Catholic Church, and, more specifically, God. Anyone who got in their way was in defiance of divine will and consequently a heretic.

---

[4] Only recently has the United Nations Commission on Human Rights acknowledged the blood libel as one form of anti-Semitism.

[5] In the NIV Study Bible (Exodus 22:18; p. 119), the same verse reads, "Do not allow a sorceress to live."

[6] A *bull* is formal papal document with papal seal, or *bulla*.

FIGURE 1.3

Innocent VIII (1432–1492) was born Giovanni Battista Cibo. He became pope in 1484. After several failed attempts (starting in 1488), Innocent VIII successfully launched the Fourth Crusade to invade the Holy Land with the intent of recapturing the Kingdom of Jerusalem. The Islamic general Saladin, a Sunni Muslim and sultan of Egypt, had claimed Jerusalem in a military victory in 1187. This Fourth Crusade failed miserably: the army ran out of money in Venice and never made it to the Holy Land. These bankrupt crusaders ultimately wound up working for the Venetians as a mercenary force. They attacked Christian and Muslim cities alike, including Constantinople. Innocent VIII was infuriated by this and excommunicated the entire Crusade as well as the city of Venice. He is remembered for his miserably failed crusade, for being bad with money, and for his undying zeal against witches and other heretics. It is likely that these symptoms were all related.

When the *Malleus Maleficarum* was written (Figure 1.4), and in years since, the Catholic Church held that witches and other heretics were in league with the Devil and, moreover, that they were fanatically bent on the destruction of God and the Catholic Church, and on the domination of Western civilization.

According to the *Malleus Maleficarum*, witches and other criminals may be identified by specific circumstances, abilities, and characteristics—as defined by the experiences of both authors in concert with their interpretation of the Bible (Kramer and Sprenger, 1971). Witches were described primarily as women who

- have a spot, scar, or birthmark, sometimes on the genitals and sometimes invisible to the Inquisitor's eye[7] (Figure 1.7)
- live alone
- keep pets (a demon in animal form known as a *familiar*)
- suffer the symptoms of mental illness (auditory or visual hallucinations, etc.)
- cultivate medicinal herbs
- have no children

FIGURE 1.4

Alphonsus Joseph-Mary Augustus Montague Summers (1880–1948), a Catholic priest, a devout believer in witches, and a "vampirologist," was the first to translate the *Malleus Maleficarum* into English, circa 1928. His published works include *Demonology and Witchcraft* (1926), *The Vampire: His Kith and Kin* (1928), and *The Vampire in Europe* (1929).

The authors provide case examples throughout, although upon close inspection they seem to be misogynistic fables more than anything else. One, for example, could be interpreted to suggest that women may suffer consequences for being "quarrelsome" with the honest men they meet (pp. 136–137):

> [I]n the diocese of Basel, in the district of Alsace and Lorraine, a certain honest labourer spoke roughly to a certain quarrelsome woman, and she angrily threatened him that she would soon avenge herself on him. He took little notice of her; but on the same night he felt a pustule grow upon his neck, and he rubbed it a little, and found his whole face and neck puffed up and swollen, and a horrible form of leprosy appeared all over his body. He immediately went to his friends for advice, and told them of the woman's threat, and said that he would stake his life on the suspicion that this had been done to him by the magic art of that same witch. In short, the woman was taken, questioned, and confessed her crimes. But when the judge asked her particularly about the reason for it, and how she had done it, she answered: "When that man used abusive words to me,

---

[7] This was referred to as the witch's mark, or the Devil's mark.

I was angry and went home; and my familiar began to ask the reason for my ill humour. I told him, and begged him to avenge me on the man. And he asked what I wanted him to do to him; and I answered that I wished he would always have a swollen face. And the devil went away and afflicted the man even beyond my asking; for I had not hoped that he would infect him with such sore leprosy." And so the woman was burned.

Specific descriptions of witches, devils, and murderers found in the *Malleus Maleficarum* are telling of the Inquisitors' profiling methods and reasoning, which are entirely faith based. Some examples include the following:

- Witches have the power make men impotent and unable to copulate (p. 4):

    [T]here are those writers who speak of men impotent and bewitched, and therefore by this impediment brought about by witchcraft they are unable to copulate, and so the contract of marriage is rendered void and matrimony in their cases has become impossible.

- Witches use spells, images, and charms (p. 13):

    [W]itches use certain images and other strange periapts, which they are wont to place under the lintels of the doors of houses, or in those meadows where flocks are herding, or even where men congregate, and thus they cast spells over their victims, who have oft-times been known to die.

- And witches cannot bear children (p. 23):

    [T]o beget a child is the act of a living body, but devils cannot bestow life upon the bodies which they assume; because life formally only proceeds from the soul, and the act of generation is the act of the physical organs which have bodily life. Therefore bodies which are assumed in this way cannot either beget or bear.

    Yet it may be said that these devils assume a body not in order that they may bestow life upon it, but that they may by the means of this body preserve human semen, and pass the semen on to another body.

With respect to murder, the *Malleus Maleficarum* explains that dead bodies will flow blood from their wounds when their murderer is near.[8] Moreover, the living will be seized with fear when a dead body is present—even when they don't know it's there (p. 13):

In the presence of a murderer blood flows from the wounds in the corpse of the person he has slain. Therefore without any mental powers bodies can produce wonderful effects, and so a living man if he pass by near the corpse of a murdered man, although he may not be aware of the dead body, is often seized with fear.

Burr (1896) explains the typical rationale for identifying a witch at trial using the *Malleus Maleficarum* as a guide, which presents the innocent with inescapable dilemmas (p. 31):

Either Gaia[9] has led a bad and improper life, or she has led a good proper one. If a bad one, then, say they, the proof is cogent against her; for from malice to malice the presumption is strong. If, however, she has led a good one, this also is none the less a proof; for thus, they say, are witches wont to cloak themselves and try to seem especially proper. …

---

[8] There is some reason to think that this passage may be one origin for the beliefs about the dead held by Dr. Micki Pistorius of South Africa, as discussed in the preface of this text. She is a graduate of the University of Liverpool's investigative psychology program and was mentored by Dr. David Canter. She practices the belief that violent crime scenes, and murderers, can be perceived on a psychic level.

[9] *Gaia* was the name used for a female culprit by the Roman law—like using John or Jane Doe for unidentified males and females in various forensic contexts.

Therefore it is ordered that Gaia be haled away to prison. And lo now a new proof is gained against her by this other dilemma: Either she then shows fear or she does not show it. If she does show it (hearing forsooth of the grievous tortures wont to be used in this matter), this is of itself a proof; for conscience, they say, accuses her. If she does not show it (trusting forsooth in her innocence), this too is a proof; for it is most characteristic of witches, they say, to pretend themselves peculiarly innocent and wear a bold front.

Moreover, none was allowed to defend the witch, neither through witness testimony nor legal counsel. Guilt was assumed, and the result of the legal proceeding preordained (p. 32):

[I]n these trials there is granted to nobody an advocate or any means of fair defense, for the cry is that the crime is an excepted one, and whoever ventures to defend the prisoner is brought into suspicion of the crime—as are all those who dare to utter a protest in these cases and to urge the judges to caution; for they are forthwith dubbed patrons of the witches. Thus all mouths are closed and all pens blunted, lest they speak or write.

The penalties for heresy and witchcraft prescribed by Kramer and Sprenger (1971) were specific and brutal— providing a strong deterrent against any outward appearance of disbelief in God or the Catholic Church. The accused were often tortured and typically were executed whether they confessed or not (pp. 5–6).

As for doubts raised against some of the more fantastical claims regarding the existence of witches and their powers, a brief excerpt gives some insight into the authors' ability to make a rational defense of their methods and means (Kramer and Sprenger, 1971, p. 89):

We pray God that the reader will not look for proofs in every case, since it is enough to adduce examples that have been personally seen or heard, or are accepted at the word of credible witnesses.

The instruction given is explicit that readers of the *Malleus Maleficarum* should take what they are being told on the basis of the expertise and credibility of the authors alone, without applying any scrutiny.[10] Their methods were faith based, their conclusions were final, and their authority was divine. Unfortunately, many readers heeded their plea to avoid seeking proofs—they failed to question the logic of Inquisitors out of fear or ignorance, or both. Consequently, during the time of the Medieval Inquisitions, one could be branded a witch or heretic by mere accusation, tried by an Inquisitors' court, tortured, and ultimately burned at the stake.

The faith-based profiling methods used by Medieval Inquisitors to prove the identity of witches and other heretics played on irrational fears and were logically unsound, personally and politically motivated, and divinely sanctioned. They were also consequently ripe for abuse. Abuse, however, was the point. When the *Malleus Maleficarum* was written, the Catholic Church was fighting on all fronts against what it perceived as direct threats to its authority and legitimacy—and had been for centuries. Heathens, heretics, Jews, and Muslims appeared to challenge the Catholic Church from without and within, and anyone who questioned its supreme authority was labeled as such.

The *Malleus Maleficarum* gave Inquisitors a divine mandate to dispose of a particular group of heretics and heathens. The fight for hearts, minds, and wealth was everywhere. Inspiring fear and obedience to the Catholic Church through abuse of power and manipulation with faith was their intention—fear God and

---

[10] This kind of reasoning has survived even in today's modern profiling and forensic community. Assertions and opinions are often levied as fact on the basis of expertise alone, with no substantive foundation or explanation. Thornton (1997, pp. 15–17) warns us against this practice, where he states: "Experience should not make the expert less responsible, but rather more responsible for justifying an opinion with defensible scientific facts." We explore this seriously in future chapters.

give total subservience to the Catholic Church, or else. The irony was that, by fomenting the Inquisitions, the Catholic Church became exactly what it purported to despise. As a result, it is believed that some 30,000 suspected witches in England and 100,000 suspected witches in Germany were put to death.

This is probably a good time to remind ourselves that the abuse of faith-based profiling methods did not stop, or even start, with witches. The Catholic Church initiated the first of the Medieval Inquisitions in 1184 (called the Episcopal Inquisition), centuries before the publication of the *Malleus Maleficarum*, in response to the heretics' gaining traction in the south of France.[11] The Medieval Inquisitions focused on any group or religion posing threat to the divine authority of the Catholic Church, and they spanned the centuries. The Medieval Inquisitions, ordained and administered by the Catholic Church, were separate from the Spanish Inquisition, which was administered by the Spanish government.

The Spanish Inquisition (1478–1834)

Nobody expects the Spanish Inquisition!

—Cardinal Ximinez of Spain in *Monty Python's Flying Circus*[12]

The Spanish Inquisition was originally ordained by the Catholic Church to assist the Spanish government with the identification of *conversos*, mainly Muslims (Moors) and Jews (*marranos*), who had pretended to convert to Christianity but secretly continued the practice of their former religion. To help Catholics better inform on their heretical neighbors, religious behavioral profiling was one of the tools of choice.

Some history and geography are required for context. Bear with the dates, as they are necessary to establish who were allies and who were slaves, until when—and why.[13]

In 711, Muslim forces invaded Spain from Africa to conquer the Visigoths, who were primarily Roman Catholic. Jews of the Iberian Peninsula, enslaved by the Visigoths for almost a century, were subsequently freed and allowed to form their own communities. For the next 750 years, Spain was largely under Muslim control, with some minor Christian kingdoms remaining in the north. During this time, the kingdom of Cordoba became perhaps the greatest cultural center in the world. It established a library with hundreds of thousands of texts; mosques were built, along with public baths, orchards, courtyards, and aqueducts; and the population swelled to more than half a million people. Other kingdoms in Spain experienced similar cultural and intellectual growth. Many Jews ultimately immigrated to Spain from the east to enjoy religious freedom, resulting in a historical exchange of culture and knowledge.

In 1031, however, the kingdom of Cordoba dissolved into smaller Muslim kingdoms; the noble Arabian families began to disagree; and the Christian kingdoms in the north of Spain began the *Reconquista*—the centuries-long process of reconquering Spain. This would prove to have a fairly horrible outcome for the Jews—especially since so many had emigrated there from the east or from England and France.[14]

---

[11] The heretics of the Episcopal Inquisition were the Cathars, also known as the *Albigensians*. Theirs was a Christian religion based on apocryphal scriptures and the writings of the Persian (Iranian) Prophet Mani. Mani presented himself as a savior and as an apostle of Jesus Christ. The Catholic Church disagreed—violently.

[12] *Monty Python's Flying Circus*, Season 2, Episode 2; originally aired September 22, 1970, on the BBC.

[13] Attentive students will realize that these events are important not only for contextualizing the history and use of faith-based profiling but also for contextualizing modern conflicts in the Middle East.

[14] In 1290, all Jews were expelled from England, with most moving to Spain. In 1306, all Jews were expelled from France, with most moving to the Spanish cities of Barcelona and Toledo.

FIGURE 1.5
The Iberian Peninsula, today consisting primarily of Spain and Portugal— as well as the small but significant British territory of Gibraltar—just 16 miles off the coast of Africa.

In this context, Spain was unified by the 1469 marriage between Isabel of Castilia and Ferdinand of Aragon (uniting the two largest Christian families in the north of Spain)—whose rule saw the Muslims lose their remaining Spanish territories. King Ferdinand and Queen Isabella set themselves to the task of re-Christianizing Spain or, in their view, purifying it. Fearing that there were traitors in their midst who might open the gates for Muslim armies seeking to take back the Iberian Peninsula, armies looming a mere 16 miles away, they went to work (Figure 1.5). In their minds, the Jews were a threat to Spanish purity and to Catholic supremacy, and were not to be trusted.

In 1478, Pope Sixtus IV (predecessor to Pope Innocent VIII) reluctantly authorized the Spanish Inquisition, giving total authority of its administration to the secular government under King Ferdinand and Queen Isabella. It began in earnest not two years later. By 1487, Innocent VIII appointed Tomas de Torquemada, a Dominican priest and Queen Isabella's confessor, to be the first Grand Inquisitor of Spain. His administration of the Spanish Inquisition was characterized by meticulous brutality and vigorous expeditions of torture against any and all accused (Longhurst, 1962, pp. 91–92).

In 1492, all Spanish Jews were ordered expelled from Spain.[15] Torquemada's office established a profile of Jewish behavior to help Catholics inform on their neighbors based on a book written specifically for

---

[15] The same year that Christopher Columbus discovered the "New World," claiming it for God and Queen Isabella.

his office, titled *Censure and Confutation of the Talmud*. Adoption of this text by Torquemada rendered the practices of Judaism itself (accurately described or not) an ad hoc criminal profile to be used as behavioral evidence against the accused of "secret Judaizing" (Longhurst, 1962, p. 101).

The appointment of Torquemada was the beginning of the Spanish Inquisition, but by no means its end. Worldwide death estimates over its full course range from the tens of thousands to a million or more. The true numbers are not known.

WITCHES AND PURITANS (1688–1692): GOODWIFE ANN GLOVER AND THE SALEM WITCH TRIALS

The Medieval and Spanish Inquisitions involved Catholics who felt strongly that Jews and others outside their faith were blasphemous and needed to be eradicated. Ironically, the *Salem Witch Trials* involved religious reformers commonly referred to now as *Puritans*. The Puritans believed that the Church of England was beyond reform and held strongly that Catholics were the blasphemers. Beginning in the 1600s, many Puritans fled England for North America, so that they could practice their particular form of religious extremism beyond the reach of the church and the King of England. But there was more than that, as Moriarty (2001) explains:

> "Magical thinking" and an unquestioned belief in the invisible world were part of the belief system of early New Englanders, faithful Puritans and non-believers alike. While "folk persons" may have believed in "spells" and the use of poppets and potions, likewise intellectuals held a universal belief in the "unseen hand" that animated natural events.

FIGURE 1.6
On November 16, 1688, Goodwife Ann Glover was hanged in Boston, Massachusetts, for being a witch. This placard currently hangs outside on the brick wall of the tavern bearing her name in Boston's North End District, Goody Glover's.

To be clearer, the Puritans believed strongly that only a select few were going to heaven, that God had already decided who they were, and that the Devil, capable of the supernatural, was behind every evil deed.

Goodwife Ann Glover (Figure 1.6)

In 1689, the Reverend Cotton Mather, Puritan minister of the Old North Church in Boston, authored his now infamous text, *Memorable Providences, Relating to Witchcrafts and Possessions* (Mather, 1689).[16] In much the same sensational style and fashion as a modern-day true crime novel or memoir, it presents the case of a mason named John Goodwin. In 1688, it was alleged that Mr. Goodwin's children had become possessed by demons because of a witch in their midst—their widowed Irish housekeeper, Ann Glover (a.k.a. Goodwife[17] Ann Glover, a.k.a. Goody Glover). It was written in the first person, with Mather presenting himself as a reluctant, humble, but expert fighter of witches, demons, and the Devil.

---

[16] According to Moriarty (2001): "Some scholars opine that the genesis of the Salem witchcraft trials may have been the publication in 1689 of Cotton Mather's widely disseminated treatise, *Memorable Providences*."

[17] *Goodwife* was a courtesy title for a married woman, not unlike the modern use of the title *Mrs*.

FIGURE 1.7
Examination of a Witch by T. H. Matteson, 1853. Depicts a forensic examination conducted in search of "The Devil's Mark."

According to Mather (1689, Sect. III), John Goodwin's eldest daughter, 13-year-old Martha, confronted Ann Glover about stealing the linens (clothes and other items from the laundry). Martha and several of her siblings subsequently fell violently ill, suffering "The Diseases of Astonishment." Over the course of a few weeks, as the children's symptoms worsened, various doctors were consulted, including a family friend named Dr. Thomas Oakes. After examining the children, Dr. Oakes bravely ruled out all natural causes, declaring that (Mather, 1689, Sect. IV) "nothing but an hellish Witchcraft could be the Original of these Maladies."

Their symptoms, the purported effects of witchcraft, and what one author has recently come to refer to as "witchcraft syndrome evidence" (Moriarty, 2001), included the following (Mather, 1689, Sect. V):

> Sometimes they would be Deaf, sometimes Dumb, and sometimes Blind, and often, all this at once. One while their Tongues would be drawn down their Throats; another while they would be pull'd out upon their Chins, to a prodigious length. They would have their Mouths opened unto such a Wideness, that their Jaws went out of joint; and anon they would clap together again with a Force like that of a strong Spring-Lock. The same would happen to their Shoulder-Blades, and their Elbows, and Hand-wrists, and several of their joints. They would at times ly in a benummed condition and be drawn together as those that are ty'd Neck and Heels; and presently be stretched out, yea, drawn Backwards, to such a degree that it was fear'd the very skin of their Bellies would have crack'd. They would make most pitteous out-cries, that they were cut with Knives, and struck with Blows that they could not bear. Their Necks would be broken, so that their Neck-bone would seem dissolved unto them that felt after it; and yet on the sudden, it would become, again so stiff that there was no

stirring of their Heads; yea, their Heads would be twisted almost round; and if main Force at any time obstructed a dangerous motion which they seem'd to be upon, they would roar exceedingly.[18] … and this while as a further Demonstration of Witchcraft in these horrid Effects, when I went to Prayer by one of them, that was very desirous to hear what I said, the Child utterly lost her Hearing till our Prayer was over.

The logic used by Dr. Oakes and Mather was equal parts swift and flawed, with strong notes of circular and *post hoc, ergo propter hoc* reasoning.[19] It went something like this: The symptoms were caused by the housekeeper because they came after the eldest daughter's confrontation with her; the housekeeper was obviously a witch because these were classic symptoms of witchcraft; these were obvious symptoms of witchcraft because the woman was so obviously a witch.

According to Mather, the "washerwoman" Ann Glover evidenced at least the following characteristics consistent with being witch—a profile he developed once she had been arrested and he was able to examine her: she was a "hag"; she was afflicted with the same symptoms as the children; she gave a blasphemous response when asked if she believed in God (she was Irish-Catholic, so any answer consistent with that faith would have been blasphemous to a Puritan reverend); she could not accurately recite the Lord's Prayer; and the children, whose symptoms had subsided with her incarceration, became ill again when in the presence of one of Goody Glover's female relatives. Mather also made certain that her body was examined for the witch's mark (Mather, 1689, Sect. VII).

Mather further advised that incriminating evidence consistent with the rituals of witchcraft was found in Ann Glover's home when it was searched by the authorities (Mather, 1689, Sect. VIII):

> Order was given to search the old womans house, from whence there were brought into the Court, several small Images, or Puppets, or Babies, made of Raggs, and stuff't with Goat's hair, and other such Ingredients. When these were produced, the vile Woman acknowledged, that her way to torment the Objects of her malice, was by wetting of her Finger with her Spittle, and streaking of those little Images.

Mather's examinations and inferences echoed earlier writings on the subject, notably those of William Perkins, minister of Finchingfield, Essex, in his book from 1613, *A Discourse of the Damned Art of Witchcraft; So Farre*. Minister Perkins offered the following profile of a witch, arguing these characteristics to be infinitely more reliable than lesser proofs accepted in some jurisdictions. But then he also explained that being accused of witchcraft was fairly reliable proof of the fact. Taken from Perkins (1613, pp. 44–47):

- They have the Devil's mark.
- They lie or give inconsistent statements.
- They have a *familiar*—a demon in animal form.

At her trial, Ann Glover refused to speak in anything but her native Irish language. This caused a great deal of confusion about the precise content of her testimony. Subsequently, Mather conveniently interpreted her refusal to renounce the Catholic faith as a confession to witchcraft. She was shortly thereafter convicted and sentenced to death. On November 16, 1688, in the city of Boston, Ann Glover was hanged for being a witch.

---

[18] This particular set of symptoms would be mimicked almost precisely in 1692 by the witch accusers in Salem, as is discussed in the next section. They were also featured prominently in a famous scene in the film *The Exorcist* (1973). The endurance of the demonic possession myth has been greatly assisted by this now iconic image of twisting heads and satanic roars.

[19] Circular reasoning occurs when the premise of an argument assumes the conclusion to be true; *post hoc ergo propter hoc* is Latin for "after this, therefore because of this." These fallacies of logic are discussed in future chapters.

Three hundred years later, on November 16, 1988, the Boston city council formally recognized that Ann Glover had suffered an injustice. They proclaimed that day "Goody Glover Day," condemning her arrest, trial, and execution.

Mather's true-crime memoir, *Memorable Providences, Relating to Witchcrafts and Possessions* (Mather, 1689), was a best seller and widely read throughout New England. This "case study" of children possessed at the hand of a witch would become the prototype for investigating and establishing the characteristics of witches and the evidence of witchcraft in Salem.

The Salem Witch Trials

The events in Salem, from June through September of 1692, followed naturally as a result of Ann Glover's witch trial in Boston and the publication of Mather's sensational memoir detailing his involvement.

It began locally, in 1689, when Salem Village negotiated with and hired its new minister, Rev. Samuel Parris from Boston. Parris moved to Salem Village with his wife, a son, two daughters, and a slave, Tituba, brought with him from Boston by way of his earlier days in Barbados. The community eventually became unhappy with his ministerial abilities and stopped paying him on a regular basis. In October of 1691, the community failed to support a tax increase to pay for his salary and the firewood he would need to last through the winter. Worse, some vowed to drive him out of the community. As a consequence, Parris began preaching about a conspiracy in the Village—a conspiracy against the church and himself alike. He naturally attributed this to Satan's taking hold of the community.

On January 20, 1692, 9-year-old Elizabeth Parris and 11-year-old Abigail Williams, her cousin and from the same home, began acting in a fashion quite similar to the Goodwin children in Boston only four years previously. Eventually, other young girls in Salem Village began acting similarly. With talk of witchcraft already in the air, Dr. William Griggs arrived in mid-February to examine all of the afflicted girls. Finding nothing physically wrong with them, he concluded that the cause was supernatural. Then began the accusations.

Before the Salem Witch Trials came to an end, 20 people had been executed (14 women and 6 men), at least 5 people had died in prison, and more than 150 had been jailed. Most of those executed were hanged, but one man was actually crushed beneath rocks. The evidence against the accused in each case included the conclusion that they fit a particular profile—that of a witch. As explained in Moriarty (2001),

> Prosecutorial profile evidence is defined as a proffered conclusion about the existence of criminal activity that is based upon observable behaviors or physical features of an alleged perpetrator. Profile evidence does not seem to possess the clear causal relationship that syndrome evidence does when associated with criminal activity. However, relevant profile evidence rests on an assumption that the accused's behavior is affiliated with the criminal behavior in a meaningful fashion. Thus, profile behaviors or features were indicative of witchcraft, if not actually caused by it.

> Of primary significance for profile evidence was the belief that witches acted in abnormal ways and displayed identifying features. There was testimony about inexplicable acts committed by the defendants—such as remarkable feats of strength—that supported convictions for witchcraft. Witchcraft experts also permitted the use of certain behavioral tests, such as the "touching test" and the "recitation of the Lord's Prayer test." The judges also decreed significant the display of curious physical features, commonly referred to as "witches' marks." The experts indicated that these behaviors and physical phenomena, along with physical symptoms, were consistent with witchcraft. This type of evidence is collected here under the heading of "witchcraft profile testimony."

It is worth mentioning that the Puritans prided themselves in being fair and rational in their methods. They employed the best judges, experts, and texts available. Unfortunately, "Despite [the Puritans'] claimed concern for fairness and certainty, defendants were convicted on flimsy and insubstantial evidence premised strongly upon the belief in the invisible world" (Moriarty, 2001).

The Salem Witch Trials are a dark and painful bruise on the history of criminal profiling. Not just because of what was done under the guise of informed justice but because forensic experts of that time were making particular errors in logic and reasoning that are repeated by profilers today. This becomes evident in the later chapters of this text. Serious students are encouraged to seek out the references provided in this section regarding the Salem Witch Trials in order to learn these lessons more completely.

Additionally, as with other early examples of criminal profiling, the Salem Witch Trials were facilitated by prejudice and ignorance, and the publication of pseudo-authoritative books used to legitimize both. The result was a localized form of mass *pseudo-rational attribution*.[20]

Mass pseudo-rational attribution in criminal profiling tends to work this way: A societal ill is perceived, be it heresy, immorality, impurity, or economic loss; an explanation is conceived, falsely blaming a particular group, be they real or imagined; and profiles and punishments follow—studiously described and prescribed—carried out under the aegis of written law, religious doctrine, or both. The aptly named "witch hunt" is a consequence of mass pseudo-rational attribution, but it is only one of many possible *pseudo-rational attribution effects*.[21] The hope is that in the modern era we can learn these lessons and, at the very least, avoid similar pitfalls.

MODERN PROFILERS: A MULTIDISCIPLINARY HISTORICAL PERSPECTIVE

Modern criminal profiling is, owing to a diverse history, grounded in the study of crime and criminal behavior (criminology), the study of mental health and illness (psychology and psychiatry), and the examination of physical evidence (the forensic sciences). In its many forms, it has always involved the inference of criminal characteristics for investigative and judicial purposes. The reasoning behind those inferences, however, has not always been consistent. It ranges from a basis in statistical argumentation, to examining specific criminal behaviors, to subjective intuitive opinions based on personal belief and experience. We break our historical study of the subject apart in just that fashion.

The Search for Origins: Criminologists

Integral to criminal profiling has been both understanding origins of crime and classifying criminal behavior. This pursuit falls under the banner of *criminology*, which is the study of crime, criminals, and criminal behavior. Criminology involves the documentation of factual information about criminality and the development of theories to help explain those facts. A review of the literature suggests that two

---

[20] In criminal profiling, this refers to a form of false deduction defined as the practice of falsely suggesting that traits, conditions, phenomena, or causal relationships exist because they can be traced to a divine or authoritative source—usually written—which was actually penned in response to a prejudice or belief, rather than providing evidence and reason. It is pseudo-rational because its mimics reason by the citation of an unquestioned authority—evading the delivery of verifiable proofs.

[21] In criminal profiling, pseudo-rational attribution effects refer to any of the various consequences of pseudo-rational attribution, including false accusations, witch hunts, and miscarriages of justice, such as wrongful arrests, convictions, and executions.

types of criminologists have intersected criminal profiling theory more than the rest: those who study the physical characteristics of criminals in order to make inferences about criminal character, and those who are concerned with applied criminal investigation.

Physical Characteristics of Criminals

The renowned Italian physician Cesare Lombroso (1835–1909) is generally thought to have been one of the first criminologists to attempt to formally classify criminals for statistical comparison.[22] In 1876, Lombroso published his book *The Criminal Man*. By comparing information about similar offenders, such as race, age, sex, physical characteristics, education, and geographic region, Lombroso reasoned, the origins and motivations of criminal behavior could be better understood and subsequently predicted.

Lombroso studied 383 Italian prisoners. His evolutionary and anthropological theories about the origins of criminal behavior suggested that, based on his research, there were three major types of criminals (Bernard and Vold, 1986, pp. 37–38):

> *Born criminals*. These were degenerate, primitive offenders who were lower evolutionary reversions in terms of their physical characteristics.

> *Insane criminals*. These were offenders who suffered from mental or physical illnesses and deficiencies.

Criminaloids. These were a large general class of offenders without specific characteristics. They were not afflicted by recognizable mental defects, but their mental and emotional makeup predisposed them to criminal behavior under certain circumstances. This classification has been compared to the diagnosis of psychopathic personality disorder that came later from the psychiatric community.

According to Lombroso's theory of criminal anthropology, there are 18 physical characteristics indicative of a born criminal, providing at least 5 or more are present. The physical characteristics Lombroso thought indicated a born criminal included (Bernard and Vold, 1986, pp. 50–51)

1. Deviation in head size and shape from the type common to the race and region from which the criminal came
2. Asymmetry of the face
3. Excessive dimensions of the jaw and cheekbones
4. Eye defects and peculiarities
5. Ears of unusual size, or occasionally very small, or standing out from the head as do those of the chimpanzee
6. Nose twisted, upturned, or flattened in thieves, or aquiline or beaklike in murderers, or with a tip rising like peak from swollen nostrils
7. Lips fleshy, swollen, and protruding
8. Pouches in the cheek like those of some animals
9. Peculiarities of the palate, such as a large, central ridge, a series of cavities and protuberances such as are found in some reptiles, and cleft palate
10. Abnormal dentition

---

[22] Jean Morris Ellis wrote an altogether gushing book called *Character Analysis* (Ellis, 1929), in which she unabashedly argued that the research of the European anatomist Dr. Francis Joseph Gall (1758–1828) was the basis for most current thinking in both character analysis (a.k.a. phrenology) and criminology. Others have argued that Gall was the first criminologist (Dickman et al., 1977).

11. Chin receding, or excessively long, or short and flat, as in apes
12. Abundance, variety, and precocity of wrinkles
13. Anomalies of the hair, marked by characteristics of the hair of the opposite sex
14. Defects of the thorax, such as too many or too few ribs, or supernumerary nipples
15. Inversion of sex characters in the pelvic organs
16. Excessive length of arms
17. Supernumerary fingers and toes
18. Imbalance of the hemispheres of the brain (asymmetry of the cranium)

Lombroso's theory of criminal origins was evolutionary in nature, suggesting that criminals represented a reversion to a more atavistic (apelike) human state. Noncriminals, of course, were thought to be more evolved and therefore less apelike. Lombroso felt that, based on his research, he could recognize those physical features that he had correlated with criminality. This notion was something akin to a "mark of Cain," by which all evil could be biblically identified and classified, to be subsequently cast from Eden.

Many criminologists since Lombroso have made similar attempts to classify and label criminals and potential criminals based on intelligence, race, heredity, poverty, and other biological or environmental factors. They include body-type theorists.

In 1914, the American character analyst Gerald Fosbroke published the first edition of his work *Character Reading through Analysis of the Features*. In it, he argued the following (Fosbroke, 1938, p. xx):

> As our bodies and minds grow so do our character traits mature. As our characters form, our faces evolve, upon them is written largely the story of what we are, whether strong or weak, for those who will to read.
>
> Our faces are literally made by ourselves. Nature does not contradict or lie. What we are we reflect in our structures.

Fosbroke's work was based, by his own account, on "thirty years of observation and study" (Fosbroke, 1938, p. xx). Examining the physical features of an individual's face, Fosbroke reasoned, would reveal his or her character .

This era also gave us the widely referenced work of the German criminologist Dr. Erich Wulffen, the ministerial director and head of the Department of Crime—Pardon and Parole—and of the Administration of Prisons of the Ministry of Justice of Saxony, *Woman as a Sexual Criminal* (Wulffen, 1935). Dedicated entirely to female criminal behavior, and not just sex crime as the title implies, Dr. Wulffen's book explored social, psychological, biological, and moral causes. Wulffen also argued for various female criminal profiles and motives, adducing the necessary examples along the way. For example, of the *murderous wife,* he states (pp. 232–233):

> The cases resemble one another very closely, and the methods of carrying them out are almost stereotyped. ... The husband may be brutal; he mistreats his wife and drinks excessively; or he spends his life in other dissipations, neglecting her, etc. ... [S]he is disappointed in marriage; feels forsaken, suppressed; her sexual needs can find gratification only outside of the marriage bonds; a lover comes along, who later becomes the accomplice in the murder. Only rarely does the woman venture to commit the crime herself. ... In the details of the crime she shows a certain inventiveness. An originally slight inclination or indifference for the husband are easily turned into disinclination or hate. ... The murder is regarded as a freeing from the subjugation by the male and is therefore supported by strong impulses. ... When a man is her abettor or accomplice in the crime the female murderess is sure, courageous and reckless.

Throughout the text, Dr. Wulffen continually argues (in keeping with the title) that most female crime is related to peculiar female sexuality, female sexual disturbances, or female sexual abnormalities.

The German criminologist Ernst Kretschmer moved deep into the predictive arena with his research. He proposed that there is a high degree of correlation between body type, personality type, and criminal potential. In 1955, Kretschmer proposed that there were four main body types, based on an unconfirmed study of 4,414 cases. The types were as follows (Bernard and Vold, 1986, pp. 57–58):

- *Leptosome or asthenic.* Those who are tall and thin. Associated with petty thievery and fraud.

- *Athletic.* Those with well-developed muscles. Associated with crimes of violence.

- *Pyknic.* Those who are short and fat. Associated most commonly with crimes of deception and fraud, but sometimes correlated with crimes of violence.

- *Dysplastic or mixed.* Those who fit into more than one body type. Associated with crimes against decency and morality, as well as crimes of violence.

Kretschmer's theories, however, were viewed as extremely dubious because he never disclosed his research, his inferences and descriptions were always incredibly vague, and no specific comparisons were performed with noncriminal populations. In short, he would not submit his findings for any form of peer review, and his approach was clearly unscientific. As a result, many argued that the theories born of his findings were nothing more than unfounded inference and correlation masquerading as science. The assumption beneath many of the criminological studies into biological and environmental criminal origins has been, and continues to be, that if the right combination of shared characteristics can be decoded, then criminal behavior can be predicted, and criminal potential can be inferred and manipulated. Of course, sharing arbitrary characteristics with any one criminal type does not make one a criminal, and the term *criminal* should be applied only to reflect a legal reality, rather than being the basis for an inductive probability.[23]

Furthermore, while Lombroso's and Kretschmer's specific theories may seem absurd to some in light of modern wisdom, the scientific community has yet to abandon the spirit of Lombroso's three essential criminal classifications. Both modern criminologists and the modern scientific community of forensic neurologists, psychiatrists, and psychologists continue to look for the "mark of Cain." Today's tools include CAT scans, cutter enzymes, and heuristic personality inventories. Modern methods of correlating brain abnormalities, genes, or personality types with criminal potential could be criticized in the same fashion as the theories of Lombroso: an unconscious intention of the scientific community to stamp preconceived ideas about the origins of criminal behavior with the approval of science.

Investigative Criminologists

Sir Arthur Conan Doyle (1859–1930)[24]

Crime is common. Logic is rare.

—Sherlock Holmes in *The Adventure of the Copper Beeches*

---

[23] Retired FBI profiler Robert K. Ressler is one of the modern-day proponents of utilizing the inductive findings of Dr. Kretschmer in criminal profiling and references their use in his own casework (Ressler and Shatchman, 1992, p. 4).

[24] Parts of this section have been adapted from Chisum and Turvey (2007).

FIGURE 1.8

Sir Arthur Conan Doyle.

Arthur Conan Doyle (Figure 1.8) was born in Edinburgh on May 22, 1859. He received a Jesuit education and went on to study medicine at the University of Edinburgh Medical School under Dr. Joseph Bell in 1877.

In 1886, Conan Doyle split his time between his medical practice and his writing of the first story that was to launch the fictional career of Sherlock Holmes, "A Study in Scarlet," published in 1887 (Figure 1.9). It has been widely theorized that he composed the name Sherlock Holmes based on the American jurist and fellow doctor of medicine, Oliver Wendell Holmes, and Alfred Sherlock, a prominent violinist.

In "A Study in Scarlet," through the character of Dr. John Watson, Conan Doyle outlined the evidence-based method of inference and deduction that would become the defining element of Sherlock Holmes's fictional reconstruction and criminal profiling casework (Conan Doyle, 1887):

Like all other arts, the Science of Deduction and Analysis is one which can only be acquired by long and patient study, nor is life long enough to allow any mortal to attain the highest possible perfection in it. Before turning to those moral and mental aspects of the matter which present the greatest difficulties, let the inquirer begin by mastering more elementary problems.

Let him, on meeting a fellow mortal, learn at a glance to distinguish the history of the man, and the trade or profession to which he belongs. Puerile as such an exercise may seem, it sharpens the faculties of observation, and teaches one where to look and what to look for. By a man's finger-nails, by his coat-sleeve, by his boots, by his trouser-knees, by the callosities of his forefinger and thumb, by his expression, by his shirt-cuffs—by each of these things a man's calling is plainly revealed. That all united should fail to enlighten the competent inquirer in any case is almost inconceivable.

Conan Doyle's protagonist also held fast to the principle of eliminating unnecessary bias and reducing preconceived theories in any interpretation of the facts. Through Holmes, Conan Doyle chastised those impatient for results in the absence of evidence: "It is a capital mistake to theorize before you have all the evidence. It biases the judgment" (Conan Doyle, 1887).

The second Sherlock Holmes story, "The Sign of the Four," was written for *Lippincott's Magazine*, and other subsequent stories were written for *The Strand Magazine*. In carefully woven plots, Conan Doyle continually referenced observation, logic, and dispassion as invaluable to the detection of scientific facts, the reconstruction of crime, the profiling of criminals, and the establishment of legal truth.

Sir Arthur Conan Doyle's work with fictional crime fighting did not just entertain and inspire others, although that would have been enough to heavily influence the forensic sciences, specifically crime reconstruction and criminal profiling, forever; it also had practical applications in his own work outside of writing and medicine. Conan Doyle, it is often forgotten, was a chief architect of the concept of postconviction case review in the early twentieth century and a firm believer in overturning miscarriages of justice.

An example is the case of George Edalji (Figure 1.10), an Indian who had been wrongly convicted of mutilating and killing sheep, cows, and horses. In 1903, someone was inflicting long, shallow cuts to animals in the Great Wyrley area of the United Kingdom, under cover of night, causing them to bleed to death. Anonymous, taunting letters were written to the police and the letters identified the offender as George Edalji, a local Indian solicitor. Edalji was arrested and a trial was held. Edalji was found guilty and was sentenced to seven years in prison. However, there was a public outcry that an injustice had been done and that Edalji had been framed for reasons of race.

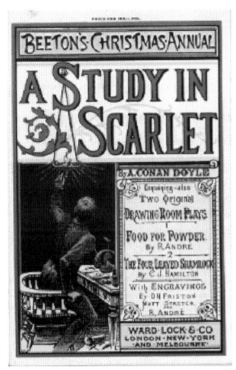

FIGURE 1.9
"A Study in Scarlet," published in November 1887 as the main part of Beeton's Christmas Annual.

FIGURE 1.10
George Edalji at his trial in 1903.

FIGURE 1.11
Sir Arthur Conan Doyle at work in his home office.

In 1906, Sir Arthur Conan Doyle learned of the Edalji case and became deeply concerned about the circumstances of the conviction; he set about examining the facts for himself (Figure 1.11). When the forensic evidence and the context of the crimes pointed away from Edalji's involvement, Conan Doyle became determined to educate the public. The British government took notice in more ways than one ("The George Edalji Case," 2005):

> As he reviewed the facts it seemed to Conan Doyle that the evidence was overwhelming.

> Edalji was innocent. The bloody razors found in the Edalji home were later discovered to be merely rusty razors. The handwriting expert who testified that Edalji's handwriting matched the writing on the taunting letters was discovered to have made a serious mistake on another case causing an innocent man to be convicted. The mud on George's boots was of a different soil type than that of the field where the last mutilation took place. The killings and letters continued after Edalji was prosecuted.

> And then there was the final piece of evidence that Conan Doyle gathered. The evidence that he saw in an instant the first time he set eyes on George Edalji. Conan Doyle stated, "He had come to my hotel by appointment, but I had been delayed, and he was passing the time by reading the paper. I recognized my man by his dark face, so I stood and observed him. He held the paper close to his eyes and rather sideways, proving not only a high degree of myopia, but marked astigmatism. The idea of such a man scouring fields at night and assaulting cattle while avoiding the watching police was ludicrous. … There, in a single physical defect, lay the moral certainty of his innocence."

Conan Doyle wrote a series of articles for the *Daily Telegraph* about the Edalji case. He outlined everything in great detail. These articles caught the public's attention and that caught the attention of the British government. At that time there was no procedure for a retrial so a there was a private committee meeting to consider the matter. In the spring of 1907 the committee decided that Edalji was innocent of the mutilations, but still found him guilty of writing the anonymous letters.

Conan Doyle found anything less than a finding of innocent on all charges a miscarriage of justice, however the decision made a huge difference for Edalji. The Law Society readmitted him. Edalji was once again able to practice as a solicitor. It is important to note that partially as a result of this case the Court of Criminal Appeal was established in 1907. So not only did Conan Doyle help George Edalji, his work helped to establish a way to correct other miscarriages of justice.

It should be remembered that when he discovered the likely culprit in the crimes (a school student and butcher's apprentice) and made it known, Conan Doyle began to receive anonymous threatening letters.

FIGURE 1.12

A middle-aged Oscar Slater pictured in his home.

Also, the panel that was eventually appointed to investigate Conan Doyle's new evidence in the Edalji case was made up of three commissioners, one of whom was a cousin of the original lead investigator. Conan Doyle was disgusted by their slander of Edalji and their collusion to protect each other's reputations even while being forced to pardon him for crimes he clearly had not committed. Conan Doyle's involvement with the Edalji case left him more than a little jaded, to say the least.

In 1909, a German named Oscar Slater (Figure 1.12) was tried and convicted in Edinburgh for murdering an elderly woman named Marion Gilchrist with a hammer the year before. Gilchrist had been bludgeoned to death, her personal papers had been rifled through, and a diamond brooch had been stolen. That case came to Conan Doyle's attention as well, and once again he was compelled to investigate. What he learned did not require much deduction, only observation and the force of indefatigable publicity ("The Oscar Slater Case," 2005):

While it was true that Slater did posses a small hammer it wasn't large enough to inflict the type of wounds that Miss Gilchrist had sustained. Conan Doyle stated that a medical examiner at the crime scene declared that a large chair, dripping with blood, seemed to be the murder weapon.

Conan Doyle also concluded that Miss Gilchrist had opened the door to her murderer herself. He surmised that she knew the murderer. Despite the fact that Miss Gilchrist and Oscar Slater lived near one another, they had never met.

The Case of Oscar Slater caused some demand for a new trial. However the authorities said the evidence didn't justify that the case be reopened. In 1914 there were more calls for a retrial. New evidence had come to light. Another witness was found that could verify Slater's whereabouts during the time of the crime. Also, it was learned that before Helen Lambie [Gilchrist's only servant] named Slater as the man she'd seen in the hallway the day of the murder she had given the police another name. Unbelievably, the officials decided to let the matter rest.

Conan Doyle was outraged. "How the verdict could be that there was no fresh cause for reversing the conviction is incomprehensible. The whole case will, in my opinion, remain immortal in the classics of crime as the supreme example of official incompetence and obstinacy."

The matter probably would have ended there in 1914, but in 1925 a message from Oscar Slater was smuggled out of Peterhead Prison, addressed directly to Conan Doyle. In it, he begged Conan Doyle not to forget his case and also to make one last effort to free him. Reinvigorated, Conan Doyle began lobbying once more, writing everyone he knew in the media and government.

As a result of the renewed interest, an investigative journalist in Glasgow named William Park published a book about the case that brought public interest in the Slater case to a fever pitch. The story was in every newspaper.

Helen Lambie was subsequently sought out and found living in the United States; she then confessed during an interview that she had actually known the real murderer, just as Conan Doyle had suggested years before. She further confessed that the police had talked her out of this initial identification and persuaded her she was mistaken. In short, she confessed to falsely accusing Oscar Slater of a crime she knew he did not commit to protect someone of her acquaintance whom she refused to name.

Mary Barrowman, a 14-year-old girl at the time of the murder who claimed she bumped into a man under a lamppost running from Gilchrist's apartment on the day of the murder, also came forward. She confessed that she had, under some pressure by police, tailored her eyewitness identification to match the accused.

In 1927, having been contacted by Conan Doyle, the secretary of state for Scotland ordered the release of Oscar Slater. Eventually, an appeal was granted. However, officials still refused to admit to any wrongdoing and would not suggest corruption or blame other officials for any breakdowns or wrongdoing. Slater's conviction was ultimately overturned on a technicality, allowing the authorities to save face. According to Gildart and Howell (2004, p. 3):

> Arthur Conan Doyle had always been convinced of Slater's innocence. An inquiry into the verdict in 1914 had upheld the original decision, but in 1927 Conan Doyle sent to [Prime Minister J. Ramsay] MacDonald a copy of a newly published book by William Park, *The Truth about Oscar Slater*. This suggested both the weakness of the prosecution's case and that the police had suppressed inconvenient evidence.

> Discussions between MacDonald and the secretary of state for Scotland, Sir John Gilmour, preceded Slater's release on 15 November 1927. The Court of Criminal Appeal for Scotland had only been inaugurated the preceding year and had no power to deal with cases that predated its foundation. However a single-clause bill was passed that permitted Slater to appeal [championed by Arthur Conan Doyle].

> [Lord Craig Mason] Aitchison appeared for Slater before the High Court of Justiciary in July 1928. He spoke for 13 hours, claiming that "the Crown's conduct of the case was calculated to prevent and did prevent a fair trial" [*The Times*, July 10, 1928]. The verdict was given on 20 July. The court ruled against the defense claim that on the basis of the evidence offered at the original trial the jury had acted unreasonably. Similarly new evidence did not justify the overturning of the original verdict. However the appeal was allowed on the ground that the judge in 1909, Lord Guthrie, had misdirected the jury; he had underlined the prosecution's emphasis on Slater's unattractive character. The defendant had allegedly lived off prostitution. This was held to have weakened the presumption of innocence [*The Times*, July 21, 1928, pp. 10–13; Marquand (1977), pp. 412–413; for a location of the trial in the context of anti-Jewish prejudice, see Barber (2003)].

Though it was not the absolute exoneration Conan Doyle's efforts sought, an innocent man was set free, the level of public debate on the justice system was raised, and the creation of the court of criminal appeal was successfully leveraged.

Sir Arthur Conan Doyle was far more than the creator of a popular fictional character. He was a medical doctor and a scientist. He was a forensic practitioner and a forensic reformer. He believed in logic and he believed in the scientific examination of evidence, and he taught these philosophies through his stories, which remain inspirational to modern forensic scientists and criminal profilers. When Conan Doyle died in 1930 of heart disease, he had helped to create much of the philosophical forensic landscape that we currently find ourselves navigating.

Dr. Johann (Hans) Baptist Gustav Gross (1847–1925)[25]

A thousand mistakes of every description would be avoided if people did not base their conclusions upon premises furnished by others, take as established fact what is only possibility, or as a constantly recurring incident what has only been observed once.

—Dr. Hans Gross (1906)

Hans Gross (Figure 1.13) was born on December 26, 1847, in Graz, Austria. He studied criminology and the law, and he eventually came to serve as an examining magistrate of the Criminal Court at Czernovitz. During this time, Gross observed firsthand the failings of apathetic and incompetent criminal investigators, as well as criminal identifications made by flawed and biased eyewitness accounts. He also became painfully familiar with the continuous stream of false suspect, eyewitness, and alleged victim accounts that poured into his office as a regular matter of course. These experiences led him to the conclusion that because people were essentially unreliable, and investigators were often their own worst enemy, a methodical, systematic way of determining the facts of a case was needed.

FIGURE 1.13
Dr. Hans Gross.

It is not known whether the works of Conan Doyle directly inspired Gross, but both men were moving in precisely the same direction at precisely the same time. In 1893, the same year that Conan Doyle killed the Sherlock Holmes character, Gross finished writing his seminal work, *Handbuch für Untersuchungsrichter, als System der Kriminalistik* [*Criminal Investigation, A Practical Textbook for Magistrates, Police Officers, and Lawyers* (Gross, 1906)]. This was a landmark publication, in which Gross proclaimed the virtues of science against intuition and of a systematic approach to holistic crime reconstruction and criminal profiling against uninformed experience and overspecialization.

The success of his groundbreaking book was, without exaggeration, unparalleled in the history of forensic science, crime reconstruction, and criminal profiling. The forensic community, as it existed, perhaps made fertile and hungry by the works of Conan Doyle, enthusiastically devoured *System der Kriminalistik*. The book achieved a fifth edition and by 1907 had been translated into eight languages, including French, Spanish, Danish, Russian, Hungarian, Serbian, English, and Japanese, each version with an overwhelmingly supportive foreword written by a forensic contemporary impatient to see it printed and adopted in his respective country. As described in Thorwald (1966, pp. 234–235),

> You had only to open Gross's book to see the dawning of a new age. … Each of his chapters was an appeal to examining magistrates (his word for criminologists) to avail themselves of the potentialities of science and technology far more than they had done so far.

---

[25] This section has been adapted from Chisum and Turvey (2007).

Gross became a professor of criminal law at the University of Czernovitz, a professor of criminology at the University of Prague, and later a professor of criminal law at the University of Graz. With the success of *System der Kriminalistik* as a platform, he launched other professional ventures that continue to contribute significantly to the development of forensic science. In 1898, Gross began serving as the editor for the *Archiv fur Kriminalanthropologie und Kriminalistik*, a journal to which he was a frequent contributor. He also introduced the forensic journal *Kriminologie*, which still serves as a respected medium for reporting improved methods of scientific crime detection. In 1912, he established the Museum of Criminology, the *Kriminalmuseum*, at the University of Graz.

Arguably a founding father of modern criminal profiling, Gross wrote authoritatively on the importance of carefully studying offender behavior. In *Criminal Investigation*, for example, he offers various methods for profiling the behavior of murderers, arsonists, thieves, counterfeiters, and females falsely reporting rape, to mention just a few (Gross, 1924). Strong examples of his philosophy that criminals can be best understood through their crimes are found throughout *Criminal Investigation*, including this passage on the investigative utility of *modus operandi* (Gross, 1924, p. 478):

> In nearly every case the thief has left the most important trace of his passage, namely, the manner in which he has committed the theft. Every thief has in fact a characteristic style or modus operandi which he rarely departs from, and which he is incapable of completely getting rid of; at times this distinctive feature is so visible and so striking that even the novice can spot it without difficulty; but on the one hand the novice does not know how to group, differentiate or utilise what he has observed, and on the other hand the particular character of the procedure is not always so easy to recognise.

In his other well-known work, *Criminal Psychology*, he shows the same underlying propensity toward the necessity of criminal profiling (Gross, 1968, pp. 54–55):

> Is it not known that every deed is an outcome of the total character of the doer? Is it not considered that deed and character are correlative concepts, and that the character by means of which the deed is to be established cannot be inferred from the deed alone? ...Each particular deed is thinkable only when a determinate character of the doer is brought in relation with it—a certain character predisposes to determinate deeds, another character makes them unthinkable and unrelatable with this or that person.

Gross also offers a variety of insights. The following discussion is a good example. It argues for the inclusion of females, mothers of victims in particular, as suspects in child-murder cases regardless of their character or circumstance (Gross, 1968, pp. 358–359):

> With regard to child-murder the consideration of psychopathic conditions need not absolutely be undertaken. Whether they are present must, of course, be determined, and therefore it is first of all necessary to learn the character of the suspect's conduct. The opportunity for this is given in any text-book on legal medicine, forensic psychopathology, and criminal psychology. There are a good many older authors. Most of the cases cited by authorities show that women in the best of circumstances have behaved innumerable times in such a way that if they had been poor girls child-murder would immediately have been assumed. Again, they have shown that the sweetest and most harmless creatures become real beasts at the time of accouchement, or shortly after it develop an unbelievable hatred toward child and husband. Many a child-murder may possibly be explained by the habit of some animals of consuming their young immediately after giving birth to them. Such cases bind us in every trial for child-murder to have the mental state of the mother thoroughly examined by a psychiatrist, and to interpret everything connected with the matter as psychologist and humanitarian.

The significance of *System der Kriminalistik* cannot be understated. It was the first comprehensive textbook to systematically cover the integrated philosophy and practice of scientific criminal investigation, forensic analysis, crime reconstruction, and criminal profiling. Its philosophies have not been diminished by the passage of time and should be required study for any student of these subjects.

O'Connell and Soderman (1935)

In 1935, the first edition of *Modern Criminal Investigation* was published by coauthors John J. O'Connell, deputy chief inspector of the New York City Police Department (and dean of the police academy), and Harry Soderman, D.Sc., head of the Institute of Police Science in the School of Law at the University of Stockholm, Sweden. The second edition opens with the following directive to investigators (O'Connell and Soderman, 1936, p. 1):

> Knowledge of the *modus operandi* of criminals and methods, their apprehension, skill, patience, tact, industry, and thoroughness, together with a flair peculiar to the successful detective, will be everlasting primary assets in detective work.

O'Connell and Soderman (1936) provide quite detailed profiles of different types of criminals. In regard to the crime of burglary, they describe the various personality characteristics of *loft burglars, window smashers, store burglars, residence burglars, flat and apartment-house burglars, house mobs, supper burglars, night burglars,* and the different types of *private-dwelling burglars* (pp. 302–313). In regard to the crime of larceny, they describe the various personality characteristics of *sneak thieves, pickpockets, swindlers,* and *confidence men* (pp. 330–355). They give the same attention to the different types of robberies (pp. 362–376) and arson, including the pyromaniac (p. 382).

It is interesting to note that while O'Connell and Soderman (1936) provide the above coverage with an emphasis on what we would refer to as criminal profiling, their coverage of homicide investigation in general (pp. 251–296) is more systematic. They do not talk about typical offenders; rather they discuss how the examination of physical evidence and offender actions can lead to good suspects. Their emphasis remains consistently on the recognition and reconstruction of physical evidence. In their investigative guidelines (pp. 254–260), they are explicit about determining the characteristics of the perpetrator through what may be referred to as *crime analysis*: the examination of behavioral evidence, such as motive, weapons used, routes taken, vehicle use, and items taken.

In terms of criminal profiling, the works of investigative criminologists have been folded into the works of forensic scientists. This was perhaps the next logical course of disciplinary evolution. Criminal investigation has become more about fact gathering (through interview and interrogation), forensic investigation has been placed under the banner of physical evidence and the forensic sciences, and the psychosocial aspects of crime remain more the province of the behavioral sciences.

The Search for Origins: Forensic Scientists

Forensic pathology is the branch of medicine that applies the principles and knowledge of the medical sciences to problems in the field of law (DiMaio and DiMaio, 1993, p. 1). It is the charge of the forensic pathologist to document and understand the nature of the interaction between victims and their environment in relation to their death. In medicolegal death investigations, the forensic pathologist is in charge of the body of the deceased and all of the forensic evidence that is related to that body (wound patterns, diseases, environmental conditions, victim history, etc.).

Whitechapel (1888)

During the Whitechapel (a.k.a. Jack the Ripper) murders in Great Britain in 1888, Dr. George B. Phillips, the divisional police surgeon (the equivalent of a forensic pathologist), engaged in a more direct method of inferring criminal characteristics. Rather than comparing the characteristics of statistically averaged offenders, he relied on a careful examination of the wounds of a particular offender's victims. That is to say, he inferred a criminal's personality by examining the behavior of that particular criminal with his victim. In this paradigm, offender behavior is manifested in the physical evidence as interpreted by an expert in the field of wound-pattern analysis.

For example, Dr. Phillips noted that injuries to one of the Whitechapel victims, Annie Chapman, indicated what he felt was evidence of professional skill and knowledge in their execution (Figure 1.14). In particular, he was referring to the postmortem removal of some of Annie Chapman's organs and what he felt was the cleanliness and preciseness of the incisions involved. As discussed in Appendix I of the first edition of this work (Turvey, 1999), the premises of this and other conclusions about the unknown offender's characteristics deserve a more critical eye.

Whatever the basis of inferences regarding the unknown offender's level of skill, the implication of this type of interpretation is very straightforward. As Dr. Wynne E. Baxter, coroner for the South Eastern District of Middlesex, stated to Dr. Phillips during a coroner's inquest into the death of Annie Chapman, "The object of the inquiry is not only to ascertain the cause of death, but the means by which it occurred. Any mutilation which took place afterwards may suggest the character of the man who did it." Behavior, they understood, was evidence suggestive of personality characteristics (Sugden, 1995, p. 131).

FIGURE 1.14
Front page of the *Police News*, September 22, 1888, depicting illustrations of the fate of Annie Chapman.

At the time of the Whitechapel murders, coroners were required to inquire into the nature, character, and size of all wounds and to document them thoroughly (though not necessarily by photograph). This practice speaks to the value placed, even then, on what today may be referred to as wound-pattern analysis.[26] It is extremely unlikely that the Whitechapel murders were the first crimes in which investigators and forensic personnel engaged in wound-pattern analysis. However, the investigation does offer some of the earliest written documentation of the types of inferences drawn from violent, aberrant, predatory criminal behavior by those involved in criminal investigations.

Dr. Paul L. Kirk (1902–1970)[27]

This is evidence that does not forget. It is not confused by the excitement of the moment. It is not absent because human witnesses are. It is factual evidence. Physical evidence cannot be wrong; it cannot perjure itself; it cannot be wholly absent. Only its interpretation can err.

—Dr. Paul Kirk (1953, p. 4)

FIGURE 1.15
Dr. Paul Kirk. Source: John E. Murdock, ATF Forensic Lab, Walnut Creek, California.

Paul Leland Kirk was born in Colorado Springs, Colorado, in 1902. He was first and foremost a scientist, but he was also a man of practical application as opposed to pure theory. He was educated at Ohio State University, where he received a B.A. in chemistry; the University of Pittsburgh, where he received an M.S. in chemistry; and the University of California, where he received a Ph.D. in biochemistry (Figure 1.15).

From 1929 to 1945, Kirk served as a professor of biochemistry at UC Berkeley. Later in his career, he would tell students that he was initially drawn to forensic science in his early teaching days when a biochemistry student approached him with a question about a deceased dog and whether it could be determined if the dog had been poisoned. Investigating this issue piqued Kirk's forensic curiosity. Soon after, authorities contacted him to examine the clothing of a rape victim—they wanted to know whether anything on the clothing could be found, at the microscopic level, to associate the victim with her attacker. Kirk's discovery of fibers from the attacker's shirt, and the subsequent conviction of the rapist, sealed his interest and secured his reputation for solid results based on careful examinations. Subsequently, in 1937, Kirk assumed leadership of the criminology program at UC Berkeley. Under his leadership, the program gained momentum and its reputation grew.

In 1953, subsequent to his work on the Manhattan Project during World War II, Kirk published the first edition of his seminal forensic textbook, *Crime Investigation*, a treatise on criminal investigation, crime reconstruction, and forensic examination that endures to this day as a foundational industry standard with few equals (Kirk, 1953).

Kirk took a much bolder position on the importance of crime reconstruction and behavioral evidence analysis than most are aware. He repeatedly discussed what could only be referred to as criminal profiling in

---

[26] Understanding the nature and extent of victim and offender injuries is considered an important aspect in criminal profiling to this day. Knowing what happened to a victim, through the specific injuries (or lack thereof) and other forensic evidence, is crucial to the goal of understanding the characteristics of the offender responsible. Modern criminal profilers have come to a deep appreciation of how forensic pathology, as well as the many other forensic sciences, can provide this type of information.

[27] Parts of this section have been adapted from Chisum and Turvey (2007).

both editions of *Crime Investigation* (Kirk, 1953, 1974). He viewed criminal profiling as the natural outcome of physical evidence examination (Kirk, 1974, pp. 4–5):

> The study of physical evidence can be a material aid in locating the perpetrator of a crime. …

> Physical evidence is often very useful to the police investigator before he has a suspect in custody or, in fact, before he even has suspicion of a possible perpetrator. If, for instance, the laboratory can describe the clothes worn by the criminal, give an idea of his stature, age, hair color, or similar information, the officer's search is correspondingly narrowed.

> Frequently it is possible to indicate a probable occupation, or to describe a habitat with remarkable accuracy from careful examination of some apparently trifling object found at the scene of the crime. Such facts do not necessarily constitute proof of guilt of any particular person, but they may give a background that is of the greatest value. …

> As an illustration of the possibilities and the pitfalls attendant upon deductions from laboratory findings, the following example is illuminating. From the examination of a glove left at the scene of a burglary, the following inferences were drawn:

> 1. The culprit was a laborer associated with building construction.
> 2. His main occupation was pushing a wheelbarrow.
> 3. He lived outside the town proper, on a small farm or garden plot.
> 4. He was a southern European.
> 5. He raised chickens, and kept a cow or a horse.

As suggested by this passage, Kirk was an advocate of the investigative use of criminal profiling well before its potential was recognized by even the criminal investigators of his time.

This advocacy continued in the first edition of *Fire Investigation* (1969), where Kirk provided a basic guideline for crime reconstruction and criminal profiling that has not been significantly eroded by developments in either field. First, he defined three types of arsonists (pp. 159–160): arson for profit, arson for spite, and arson for "kicks."

Kirk explains how his arson typology may not be important to lab analysts, but that the overall investigation can benefit (p. 160):

> It is evident that the investigator of the physical evidence of the fire is concerned very little with the type of arsonist who may have set it. However, there are differences in the *modus operandi* which he may note in the investigation, and these can be of great help in both tracing the arsonist and in producing information useful for trial purposes.

Kirk also argues that fire investigators should have sufficient knowledge of fire to get inside the mind of the arsonist (Kirk, 1969, p. 161):

> It has been noted for a long time that the investigator of crime is most effective when he can place himself in the role of the criminal; the best investigators are those who can do this most effectively. They can learn to think as the criminal thinks, react as he reacts, and from this they can estimate how he operates.

Subsequent to the works of Dr. Paul Kirk, other forensic science texts have given a nod (or a chapter) to the important role that physical evidence examination and crime reconstruction can play in both criminal profiling and suspect development (Bevel and Gardner, 2002; Lee et al., 1983; DeHaan, 1997; DiMaio and DiMaio, 1993; Geberth, 1996, 2006; James and Nordby, 2003; Lee, 1994).

The Search for Origins: Behavioral Scientists

Psychiatry is the branch of medicine that deals with the diagnosis and treatment of mental disorders. A forensic psychiatrist, or alienist, is a psychiatrist who specializes in the legal aspects of mental illness. The psychiatrist is trained to elicit information specific to mental disorders through face-to-face clinical interviews, a thorough examination of individual history, and the use of tested and validated personality measures. Historically, psychiatrists don't commonly apply their expertise to investigative matters, but they do apply it to forensic ones.

Previously in this chapter we discussed the case of Mendel Beilis, who was arrested in 1911 by the Kiev Secret Police and put on trial for the ritual murder of a Christian boy. Criminal profiling was used in this case as well, in the form of expert testimony from a forensic psychiatrist. By virtue of comparison to similar cases, Dr. Ivan Sikorsky opined on the issue of motive, and the characteristics of blood libel cases specifically. According to Murav (2000; p.246):

> [T]he act of indictment relied on psychological and anthropological findings of Dr. Ivan Sikorskii, a psychiatrist and a professor at Kiev University. The indictment paraphrased Sikorskii, who alleged that based on historical and anthropological considerations, and judging from the way the murder was committed, that is, the gradual extraction of the victim's blood from his body, that the crime showed a similarity to other murders in Russia and elsewhere. Its psychological basis was, according to Professor Sikorskii (here the indictment directly quotes him), "the racial revenge and vendetta of the sons of Jacob" against subjects of another race.

FIGURE 1.16

George Metesky, New York's "Mad Bomber," 1957.

In the United States, the work of the American psychiatrist Dr. James A. Brussel of Greenwich Village, New York, is considered by many to have advanced the investigative thinking behind the criminal profiling process significantly. As a clinician, his approach to profiling was diagnostic. Dr. Brussel's method included the diagnosis of an unknown offender's mental disorders from behaviors evident from the crime scene. He would infer the characteristics of an unknown offender, in part, by comparing the criminal behavior to his own experiences with the behavior of patients who shared similar disorders. Dr. Brussel also subscribed to the opinion that certain mental illnesses were associated with certain physical builds, not unlike the theories of criminologists a century before (specifically Ernst Kretschmer in the case of the "Mad Bomber"). As a result, an unknown offender's likely physical characteristics were included in Dr. Brussel's profiles of unsolved cases (Brussel, 1968, pp. 32–33).

During the 1940s and 1950s, the "Mad Bomber" terrorized the city of New York (Figure 1.16). He set off at least 37 bombs in train stations and theaters all over the city. Dr. Brussel was asked to analyze the case, and he determined that the person responsible for the crimes had the following characteristics (Brussel, 1968, pp. 29–46):

Male

Knowledge of metalworking, pipefitting, and electricity

Had suffered some grave injustice by Con Ed, which had rendered him chronically ill

Suffered from paranoia

Suffered from insidious development of his disorder

Had a chronic disorder

Suffered from persistent delusions

Had unalterable, systematized, logically constructed delusions

Was pathologically self-centered

Had a symmetric "athletic" body type due to his paranoia

Middle-aged, due to onset of mental illness and duration of bombings

Good education, not college but most if not all of high school

Unmarried

Possibly a virgin

Lived alone or with a female, mother-like relative

Slavic

Roman Catholic

Lived in Connecticut

Wore a buttoned, double-breasted suit

On December 25, 1956, the *New York Times* carried a story containing some of Dr. Brussel's predictions about the bomber. It did not contain the prediction about the double-breasted suit (Brussel, 1968, p. 47). When the police finally identified and arrested George Metesky for the bombings in 1957, Dr. Brussel's profile was determined to be generally accurate. Contrary to popular belief, Matesky was arrested wearing faded pajamas, not a double-breasted suit (Brussel, 1968, p. 69). He was allowed to change before being taken into custody, and that is when he put on a double-breasted suit—a common style at the time.

Between June 1962 and January 1964, 13 sexual strangulation homicides were committed in the city of Boston, Massachusetts, that law enforcement believed were related. Traditional investigative efforts by law enforcement to develop viable suspects and identify the "Boston Strangler" were unsuccessful. A profiling committee composed of a psychiatrist, a gynecologist, an anthropologist, and other professionals was brought together to create what was referred to as a "psychiatric profile" of the person responsible for the killings.

The profiling committee came to the conclusion that the homicides were the work of two separate offenders. They based their opinion on the fact that one group of victims was older women and one group of victims was younger women. The profiling committee also felt that the psychosexual behavior differed between the victim groups. They decided that the older victims were being strangled and murdered by a man who was raised by a domineering and seductive mother, and that he was unable to express hatred toward his mother and as a result directed it toward older women. They concluded that he lived alone and that, if he were able to conquer his domineering mother, he could express love like a normal person. Furthermore, they were of the opinion that a homosexual male, likely an acquaintance, had killed the younger group of victims.

FIGURE 1.17

Albert DeSalvo, arrested for the "Green Man" crimes in November 1964. He was never tried for the crimes committed by the "Boston Strangler."

Not everyone agreed with the profiling committee. Law enforcement invited Dr. Brussel into the investigation in April of 1964, in the hope that he would provide them with the same types of insights that helped solve the Mad Bomber case in New York. Dr. Brussel disagreed with the profiling committee, being of the opinion that the homicides were the work of a single offender. But by then the killings had stopped, and the profiling committee was disbanded.

In November 1964, Albert DeSalvo was arrested for the "Green Man" sex crimes (Figure 1.17). He subsequently confessed to his psychiatrist that he was the Boston Strangler. Since he so closely "fit" the profile that Dr. Brussel had provided law enforcement, DeSalvo was identified as the offender and the case was closed without charges being filed. In 1973, while he was serving his sentence for the Green Man crimes, DeSalvo was stabbed to death in his cell by a fellow inmate. DeSalvo was never tried for, or convicted of, the crimes committed by the Boston Strangler, and therefore neither profile has ever been validated.[28]

In late 2001 (when the second edition of this text was already in press), the possibility was raised that DeSalvo's initial confession may have been false. As discussed in "DNA Doubts" (2001):

A forensic investigation has cast doubts over whether the man who confessed to being the Boston Strangler actually was the infamous 1960s serial killer, and raised the possibility that the real murderer could still be at large.

DNA evidence found on one of the 11 women killed by the Boston Strangler does not match that of Albert DeSalvo, who had confessed to murdering the women between 1962 and 1964.

James Starrs, professor of forensic science at George Washington University, told a news conference that DNA evidence could not associate DeSalvo with the murder of 19-year-old Mary Sullivan— believed to be the Boston Strangler's last victim.

DeSalvo said he was the killer while serving a life sentence on unrelated crimes. He later recanted, but was knifed to death in 1973 before any charges could be brought.

Sullivan's body was exhumed last year and DeSalvo's a few weeks ago as part of the efforts by both their families to find out who was responsible for the murders.

The women were all sexually assaulted before being strangled.

Professor Starrs said an examination of a semen-like substance on her body did not match DeSalvo's DNA.

"I'm not saying it exonerates Albert DeSalvo but it's strongly indicative of the fact that he was not the rape-murderer of Mary Sullivan," Professor Starrs said.

Professor Starrs also found that Mary Sullivan's hyoid bone had not been broken, which is inconsistent with a strangulation death. This evidence contradicts DeSalvo's confession, which he recanted while in prison.

---

[28] According Dr. Brussel's own memoir, the Mad Bomber case represented the first time that the police had ever consulted with him on a case (Brussel, 1968, p. 12). It is also interesting to note that he stated (Brussel, 1968, p. 15): "I felt that my profession was being judged as well as myself. And, curiously, I was one of my own accusers in this bizarre trial of wits. Did I really know enough about criminals to say anything sensible…?"

It should be noted that only one of Brussel's profiles was ever partially validated (though it was not formally written, so one can never be certain). The other is merely presumed to be valid without any sort of investigation or corroboration. The concern here is that reliance on a profile alone—any profile—for the ultimate closure of a case leaves open the possibility that justice may not be fully served. Today, Brussel's method of profiling would be generally referred to as a *diagnostic evaluation*, which is discussed in later chapters.

The Federal Bureau of Investigation (FBI)

During the 1960s, an American law enforcement officer, Howard Teten, began to develop his approach to criminal profiling while still at the San Leandro Police Department in California. Teten studied under and was inspired by Dr. Paul Kirk, the internationally renowned criminalist, Dr. Breyfocal, the San Francisco medical examiner, and Dr. Douglas Kelly, a psychiatrist noted for his work in the Nuremberg war trials. They were his instructors at the School of Criminology, at the University of California, Berkeley, during the late 1950s. His inspiration for the work also included the work of Dr. Hans Gross (who is cited extensively in this text). A multidisciplinary understanding of forensic science, medicolegal death investigation, and psychiatric knowledge became the cornerstone of Teten's investigative skills early on and shaped his approach to criminal profiling. He also sought out and spent hours discussing cases with Dr. James Brussels, to develop his appreciation of the mental heath perspective (Hazelwood and Michaud, 1998, p. 116).

As a special agent for the Federal Bureau of Investigation, Howard Teten initiated his criminal profiling program in 1970. He taught criminal profiling techniques as an investigative aid, to be used in conjunction with other investigative tools. Teten taught his first profiling course, called applied criminology, to the FBI National Academy in 1970. Later that same year, Teten rendered his first actual profile as a FBI agent in Amarillo, Texas. In 1970, Teten also teamed with Pat Mullany, then assigned to the New York Division of the FBI, to teach abnormal psychology as it applies to criminal profiling. Mullany and Teten team-taught at several other schools around the country during the next year while Mullany was stationed in New York. The pair would dissect a crime, Mullany would talk about a range of abnormal behavior, and Teten would discuss how that behavior could be determined from the evidence found at the scene.

In 1972, the new FBI academy opened and Teten requested that Mullany be transferred there. Shortly after coming to the FBI academy, Teten and Mullany applied their concepts to the first FBI hostage negotiation guidelines. In 1974 and 1975, Mullany negotiated several major hostage situations successfully with these new techniques. These adaptations, based on criminal profiling techniques, were the first to be taught to all FBI negotiators. They were later modified and expanded by FBI Special Agents Con Hassel and Tom Strenz.

Also in 1972, an FBI agent named Jack Kirsch started the FBI's Behavioral Science Unit (BSU). Kirsch was a former newspaper reporter for the *Erie Dispatch Herald*. He was a major contributor to criminal profiling in that he was farsighted enough to give both Mullany and Teten the freedom to do research and to construct profiles in addition to their regular duties. After they had helped solve a number of cases, the word spread. Soon, police departments were making daily requests for profiles. Special Agents Con Hassel and Tom Strenz were subsequently trained to handle half of the teaching of the applied criminology course.

Heading the BSU after Jack Kirsch were Special Agent John Phaff and then Special Agent Roger DePue in 1978. Special Agent John Douglas took over the BSU when DePue retired. Neither Pat Mullany nor Howard Teten, the formative minds behind the development of early criminal profiling techniques at the FBI, ever headed the unit (Teten, May 5, 1997, personal communication). Mullany went on to become Assistant Special Agent in Charge of the LA office, and Teten became chief of research and development.

According to McNamara and Morton (2007), the FBI's National Center for the Analysis of Violent Crime (NCAVC) was created subsequent to the profiling unit:

> NCAVC was created in 1985 during an expansion of the FBI's Behavioral Science Unit (BSU).
>
> The BSU was one of the instructional units of the FBI's Training and Development Division. In 1994, the FBI created the Critical Incident Response Group (CIRG), and the operational behavioral components of the NCAVC were transferred to CIRG, where they now reside.
>
> The NCAVC is comprised of four units: three Behavioral Analysis Units (BAUs) and the computer data–based Violent Criminal Apprehension Program (ViCAP) Unit. BAU-1 handles cases involving threat assessments or counter-terrorism; BAU-2 handles all cases involving adult victims, including serial murder, murder and serial sexual assaults; and BAU-3 handles crimes involving child victims.
>
> The units have a threefold mission. The primary purpose of each is to provide operational investigative case support. This is done by either working with case investigators on-site, having the investigators travel to the NCAVC in Quantico, Virginia, for a case consultation, or discussing the case with the investigators remotely.
>
> The BAUs offer a broad array of operational services for case investigators: crime-scene analysis, profiles of unknown offenders, investigative recommendations, interview strategies, search warrant affidavit assistance, prosecution strategies, case-linkage analysis and expert-witness testimony.
>
> Second, in collaboration with other law enforcement agencies and academic institutions, the units also conduct research into a number of violent crime areas. This includes statistically based research and interviews of convicted violent offenders. The research includes many factors, such as offender characteristics, victim characteristics and the interaction between victims and offenders. They apply the insight gained from this research to the practical operational investigative support they provide to investigators.
>
> The third mission of the BAUs is to share the knowledge gained through operational experience and research with law enforcement agencies through a variety of training venues.

At the turn of this past century, a significant shift occurred within the NCAVC, manifesting a factionalization of profiling cultures and agendas. During the early months of 2000, in their written profiles and court testimony,[29] FBI profilers stopped referring to themselves as being specifically affiliated with the NCAVC's "Behavioral Science Unit." Instead, they began referring to themselves as being affiliated only generally with the NCAVC. By mid-2000, they were referring to themselves as being affiliated specifically with the "Behavioral Analysis Unit." This was not a minor change—it signaled a complete restructuring of organization and alignment.

Until 2000, the BSU had maintained what was referred to within it as a "three-legged stool" model: conducting research; providing education and training within the law enforcement community; and providing case consultations to support the efforts of police investigations (DeNevi and Campbell, 2004). However, the model began to change when Stephen Band, a Ph.D. in counseling psychology, took over the unit in 1998. Under his administration, the pre-existing cultural rift in the BSU between those who worked cases and those who performed teaching and research worsened. The two groups, one aligned with law enforcement investigators and the other with educated behavioral scientists, did not respect each other or work well together.

---

[29] The author has one of the largest private collection of criminal profiles assembled, exceeding 150 at last count, partially acquired through the process of discovery in legal actions.

Apparently, the separate BAU was formed to alleviate the cultural tensions and to prevent an implosion of everything that had been built within the BSU thus far.

The BAU was officially created in 2000 as part of the BSU, subordinate to Dr. Band. However, the BAU physically removed itself from Quantico and began performing case consultations with law enforcement from an off-site office location. This made real supervision impossible and rendered the BAU essentially autonomous.

To shore itself up after the split, the NCAVC/BSU and its various branches subsequently reached out to the academic community in an unprecedented fashion. As explained in Winerman (2004; p.66):

> Among those in the profiling field, the tension between law enforcement and psychology still exists to some degree. …

> Stephen Band, PhD, is the chief of the Behavioral Science Unit, and clinical forensic psychologist Anthony Pinizzotto, PhD, is one of the FBI's chief scientists.

> The unit also conducts research with forensic psychologists at the John Jay College of Criminal Justice in New York.

Additionally, the BSU even authorized a congratulatory biography of itself, titled *Into the Minds of Madmen* (DeNevi and Campbell, 2004). The book relays some of the formative history and events related to the BSU up until 2004 (the date of publication), including insight on its more prominent past members. However, the book almost entirely ignores the existence of the BAU and by extension any modern case-working FBI profilers. Perhaps most telling is the last chapter in the BSU biography, which laments (DeNevi and Campbell, 2004; p.396):

> The current initiatives of the Behavioral Science Unit, the expertise and the quality of staff, foretell a significant and bright future for the Behavioral Science Unit. However, one cannot help but think that the "three-legged stool" described by Ken Lanning has parts that are missed by the Behavioral Science Unit and the National Center for the Analysis of Violent Crime. The need to work, play, learn, research, laugh, and even cry together was the basis for the success of the Behavioral Science Unit in the 1980s. Until that ability to conduct research, provide consultative services, educate, and train are brought back together under that "three-legged stool" concept, there will be something missing.

As bright as this future may have looked in 2004, Dr. Stephen Band resigned as director of the BSU in 2005. The state of FBI profiling is currently unclear, as many of its big names and major practitioners have retired. The cultural rift between law enforcement and psychologists, however, remains.

The Modern Profiling Community

Today's profiling community is made up of professionals and nonprofessionals from a variety of related and unrelated backgrounds. At the forefront is the *Academy of Behavioral Profiling (ABP)*,[30] founded March 1999 (the author is one of five founding members and a voting member of the board of directors). The

---

[30] The ABP is not affiliated with, or adjunct to, any university, organization, or agency, and as such is not as susceptible to the political influences that such institutions engender. This is a major issue in terms of building objective standards and guidelines within the professional community. Additionally, the majority of the ABP's ethical guidelines are unexceptionable within the forensic community: don't lie about your findings or your credentials, don't steal other people's ideas, be impartial, and so on. However, several of the ethical guidelines have somewhat more teeth, including the requirement that ABP members "maintain the quality and standards of the professional community by reporting unethical conduct to the appropriate authorities or professional organizations" and that ABP members "make efforts to inform the court of the nature and implications of pertinent evidence if reasonably assured that this information will not be disclosed in court." These, in concert with the other ethical guidelines, provide that ABP members must be essentially intolerant of unethical conduct from any forensic professional. The subject of ethics is discussed further in other chapters of this text.

ABP is the first international, independent, multidisciplinary professional organization for those who are profiling or who are studying profiling. It has a student section; an affiliate section for the interested, nonprofiling professional; and four full member sections (Behavioral, Criminology, Investigative, and Forensic). As stated in the "Letter from the Editor" in the first issue of the *Journal of Behavioral Profiling* (Turvey, 2000):

> The Academy of Behavioral Profiling (ABP; www.profiling.org) was formed, in part, to address the rapid de-professionalization of this field. Not content to watch the decline of the profession, those who participate in this organization are determined to build something meaningful and legitimate within the field. A multi-disciplinary effort comprised of forensic, behavioral, and investigative professionals, it has developed a professional code of ethics, the first written criminal profiling guidelines, and is currently developing a profiling general knowledge exam.

Rather than being merely a training organization or a social organization, the ABP has developed firm practice standards and ethical guidelines, which the membership agrees to follow under penalty of various levels of sanction. And more recently, it has developed and deployed the Profiling General Knowledge Exam for those seeking to become full members. The goal of the organization is to provide structure and support for those diverse professionals actively involved in profiling work, as well as to allow members to advance within that structure based solely on their knowledge and the quality of their work.

Regardless of who is involved and regardless of the professional outlook, criminal profiling still is not typically a career in itself—although there are individuals who have made it so. Rather, it is a multidisciplinary skill that is nurtured and developed once one has become proficient in other requisite disciplines. Hence, there are few full-time criminal profilers, but this is changing as awareness of what profiling involves increases, as more competent training becomes available, as the literature increases, and as those in the profiling community begin to communicate.

SUMMARY

Inferring the traits of individuals responsible for committing criminal acts has commonly been referred to as *criminal profiling*. Criminal profiling has a legal history that can be traced back to the blood libeling of Jews in Rome, 38 CE. Over the past 200 years, professionals engaged in the practice of criminal profiling have included a broad spectrum of investigators, behavioral scientists, social scientists, and forensic scientists. The practice has never been the province of a single discipline or agency.

The FBI's involvement in profiling began during the 1960s, with a few courses taught by self-trained FBI-employed profilers, based on their own education and experience. During the 1980s, the FBI formalized its profiling efforts and methods with the development of the Behavioral Science Unit, which was involved in profiling-related research, training, and case consultation. In 2000, the BAU was formed within, and then separated physically from, the BSU, owing to cultural disagreements between its law enforcement and psychologist factions. These tensions have continued throughout the subsequent decade, despite internal efforts to reform. The future of FBI profiling is, at present, unclear.

Modern criminal profiling is, owing to a diverse history, grounded in the study of crime and criminal behavior (criminology), the study of mental health and illness (psychology and psychiatry), and the examination of physical evidence (the forensic sciences). In its many forms, it has always involved the inference of criminal characteristics for investigative and judicial purposes. The reasoning behind those inferences, however, has not always been consistent. It ranges from a basis in statistical argumentation, to examining specific criminal behaviors, to subjective, intuitive opinions based on personal belief and experience.

Questions

1. True or False: The Federal Bureau of Investigation (FBI) was the first to develop and publish criminal profiling techniques.
2. The *Malleus Maleficarum* was developed by members of the clergy and endorsed by the Catholic Church, to facilitate the profiling and subsequent criminal prosecution of _____.
3. Name one of the first criminologists to attempt to formally classify criminals for statistical comparison.
4. The Spanish Inquisition was ordained by the Catholic Church to assist the Spanish government with the identification of _____.
5. Criminal profiling is a multidisciplinary community. Name three general or specific professions from which profilers tend to hail (e.g., criminal investigator).
6. One of the first published attempts to apply the scientific method to criminal investigation and criminal profiling techniques was_____ .

REFERENCES

Bernard, T., Vold, G., 1986. Theoretical Criminology, third ed. Oxford University Press, New York, NY.

Bevel, T., Gardner, R., 2002. Bloodstain Pattern Analysis, second ed. CRC Press, Boca Raton, FL.

Brussel, J., 1968. Casebook of a Crime Psychiatrist. Bernard Geis Associates, New York, NY.

Burr, G. (Ed.), 1896. The Witch Persecutions, in Translations and Reprints from the Original Sources of European History, vol. 3, no. 4. University of Pennsylvania History Department, Philadelphia, PA, pp. 1898–1912 .

Cheney, E. P., 1988. What Is History. University Archives, University of Pennsylvania, p. 76. Cited in.Novick, P, 1988. That Noble Dream. Cambridge University Press, New York, NY, p. 46.

Chisum, J., Turvey, B., 2007. Crime Reconstruction. Elsevier Science, Boston, MA.

Conan Doyle, A., 1887. A Study in Scarlet. Beeton's Christmas Annual November.

Cooley, C., Turvey, B., 2002. Reliability and Validity: Admissibility Standards Relative to Forensic Experts Illustrated by Criminal Profiling Evidence, Testimony, and Judicial Rulings. Journal of Behavioral Profiling 3 (1).

DeHaan, J., 1997. Kirk's Fire Investigation, fourth ed. Prentice Hall, Upper Saddle River, NJ.

DeNevi, D., Campbell, J., 2004. Into the Minds of Madmen: How the FBI's Behavioral Science Unit Revolutionized Crime Investigation. Prometheus Books, New York, NY.

Depue, R., Douglas, J., Hazelwood, R., Ressler, R., 1995. Criminal Investigative Analysis: An Overview. In: Burgess, A., Hazelwood, R. (Eds.), Practical Aspects of Rape Investigation, second ed. CRC Press, New York, NY.

Dickman, T., Savitz, L., Turner, S., 1977. The Origin of Scientific Criminology: Franz Joseph Gall as the First Criminologist. In: Meier, R.F. (Ed.), Theory in Criminology. Sage, Beverly Hills, CA, pp. 41–56.

DiMaio, D., DiMaio, V., 1993. Forensic Pathology. CRC Press, New York, NY.

DNA Doubts over Boston Strangler, 2001. BBC News December 6.

Ellis, J., 1929. Character Analysis, second ed. Jean Morris Ellis, Los Angeles, CA (self-published).

Fosbroke, G., 1938. Character Reading through Analysis of the Features. Doubleday, Garden City, NY.

Geberth, V., 1996. Practical Homicide Investigation, third ed. CRC Press, New York, NY.

Geberth, V., 2006. Practical Homicide Investigation, fourth ed. CRC Press, Boca Raton, FL.

The George Edalji Case, 2005. The Chronicles of Sir Arthur Conan Doyle. Retrieved June 21, 2005, from www.siracd.com/life_case1.shtml.

Gildart, K., Howell, D., 2004. Dictionary of Labour Biography, vol. 7. Palgrave Macmillan, Hampshire, UK.

Gross, H., 1906. Criminal Investigation. G. Ramasawmy Chetty, Madras, India.

Gross, H., 1924. Criminal Investigation. Sweet & Maxwell, London, England.

Gross, H., 1968. Criminal Psychology. Patterson Smith, Montclair, NJ.

Hazelwood, R., Michaud, S., 1998. The Evil That Men Do. St. Martin's Paperbacks, New York, NY.

James, S., Nordby, J., 2003. Forensic Science: An Introduction to Scientific and Investigative Techniques. CRC Press, Boca Raton, FL.

Kirk, P., 1953. Crime Investigation. Interscience, New York, NY.

Kirk, P., 1969. Fire Investigation. John Wiley & Sons, New York, NY.

Kirk, P., 1974. Crime Investigation, second ed. John Wiley & Sons, New York, NY.

Kramer, H., Sprenger, J., 1971. The Malleus Maleficarum, reprint, Dover, New York, NY.

Lee, H., 1994. Crime Scene Investigation. Central Police University Press, Taoyuan, Taiwan.

Lee, H., DeForest, P., Gaensslen, R., 1983. Forensic Science: An Introduction to Criminalistics. McGraw-Hill, New York, NY.

Levinson, H., 2004. A Dark Lie through the Ages. BBC News, January 23.

Longhurst, J., 1962. The Age of Torquemada. Coronado Press, Sandoval, NM.

Mather, C., 1689. Memorable Providences, Relating to Witchcrafts and Possessions Printed at Boston in N. England by R.P.

McNamara, J., Morton, 2007. Cracking the BTK Case. The RCMP Gazette 69 (1).

Moriarty, J., 2001. Wonders of the Invisible World: Prosecutorial Syndrome and Profile Evidence in the Salem Witchcraft Trials. Vermont Law Review 26, pp. 43-99.

Murav, H., 2000. The Beilis Ritual Murder Trial and the Culture of Apocalypse. Cardozo Studies in Law and Literature Fall/Winter.

O'Connell, J., Soderman, H., 1936. Modern Criminal Investigation. edited reprint, Funk & Wagnalls, New York, NY.

The Oscar Slater Case, 2005. The Chronicles of Sir Arthur Conan Doyle. Retrieved June 21, 2005, from www.siracd.com/life/life_case2.shtml.

Perkins, W., 1613. A Discourse of the Damned Art of Witchcraft; So Farre. Universitie of Cambridge, Cambridge, MA.

Petherick, W., 2002. The Fallacy of Accuracy in Criminal Profiling. Journal of Behavioral Profiling 3 (1).

Ressler, R., Shachtman, T., 1992. Whoever Fights Monsters. St. Martin's Press, New York, NY.

Sugden, P., 1995. The Complete History of Jack the Ripper. Caroll & Graff, New York, NY.

Thornton, J.I., 1997. The General Assumptions and Rationale of Forensic Identification. In: Faigman, D., Kaye, D., Saks, M., Sanders, J. (Eds.), Modern Scientific Evidence: The Law and Science of Expert Testimony, vol. 2. West, St. Paul, MN.

Thorwald, J., 1966. Crime and Science. Harcourt, Brace, & World, New York, NY.

Turvey, B., 1999. Criminal Profiling: An Introduction to Behavioral Evidence Analysis. Academic Press, London, England.

Turvey, B., 2000. Criminal Profiling and the Problem of Forensic Individuation. Journal of Behavioral Profiling 1 (2).

Turvey, B., 2002. Criminal Profiling: An Introduction to Behavioral Evidence Analysis, second ed. Elsevier Science, Boston, MA.

Winerman, L., 2004. Criminal Profiling—The Reality behind the Myth: Forensic Psychologists Are Working with Law Enforcement Officials to Integrate Psychological Science into Criminal Profiling. The APA Monitor 35 (7), July.

Wulffen, E., 1935. Woman as a Sexual Criminal. Falstaff Press, New York, NY.

CHAPTER 2

Criminal Profiling: Science, Logic, and Cognition

Wayne A. Petherick and Brent E. Turvey

A thousand mistakes of every description would be avoided if people did not base their conclusions upon premises furnished by others, take as established fact what is only possibility, or as a constantly recurring incident what has only been observed once.

—Hans Gross, *Criminal Investigation* (1968, p. 16)

CONTENTS

<table>
<tr><td colspan="3">KEY TERMS</td></tr>
</table>

Critical thinking	Logic	Observer effects
Deductive argument	Logical fallacies	Science
Falsification	Metacognition	Scientific knowledge
Inductive argument	Metacognitive dissonance	Scientific method
Inference	Non sequitur	Speculation

A criminal profile is a collection of inferences about the qualities of the person responsible for committing a crime or a series of crimes. This sounds basic and it is. However, definitions are required, as there has been a tendency to gloss over the basic yet complex issues this brings to our doorstep.

Let's break it down. An *inference* is a particular type of conclusion based on evidence and reasoning. This is different from a *speculation*, which is a conclusion based on theory or conjecture without firm evidence. The job of any competent forensic examiner is to make certain that speculations are guarded against, while inferences are evidence-based, logical, and rational.

With no shortage of inferences based on a variety of methods,[1] the criminal profiling community and the literature it spawns suffer greatly from an absence of accuracy and applied understanding with respect to precisely what an inference is and how to make one without becoming lost in fallacy.

This chapter explains how valid inferences are made against the framework of criminal profiling. It requires the use of the scientific method, an applied understanding of the science of logic, and knowing how to know when you are wrong. It also requires some understanding of bias.

BIAS

Paul L. Kirk (1974, p. 4) has written, "Physical evidence cannot be wrong; it cannot be perjured; it cannot be wholly absent. *Only in its interpretation can there be error*" (italics added). This passage is of particular interest to all forensic examiners, because they are defined by their interpretive role with regard to the evidence. The challenge is that much of what forensic examiners confront represents ambiguous stimuli—evidence that might be interpreted in more than one way depending on a variety of subjective influences.

When asked about bias, the majority of forensic examiners, including criminal profilers, claim that they are entirely objective when performing their analyses, or that they try very hard to be. They also hold firm that their employer/agency, their emotions, and their personal beliefs have no influence over their final conclusions. To admit otherwise would be professional suicide, as objectivity and emotional detachment are prized above all other traits in the course of a forensic examination—that is, one ultimately bound for court. One could even argue that objectivity is a necessary and defining trait.

Given the professed and necessary objectivity of forensic examiners and their presumed scientific training, it could be asked how bias may yet persist in their results or inferences. This is a perfectly reasonable question. Some forensic examiners claim that it does not, and that an objective aspect combined with scientific

---

[1] Specific methods of criminal profiling not related to those taught in this text are described in Chapter 3, "Alternative Methods of Criminal Profiling," with a discussion of strengths and weaknesses.

training is sufficient to cure most, if not all, ills that may infect their examinations and subsequent results. However, this is untrue because it ignores a fundamental principle of cognitive psychology—the pervasive nature of *observer effects*.

As cognitive psychologists have repeatedly documented, tested, and illustrated, "[T]he scientific observer [is] an imperfectly calibrated instrument" (Rosenthal, 1966, p. 3). Their imperfections stem from the fact that subtle forms of bias, whether conscious or unconscious, can easily contaminate their seemingly objective undertakings. Observer effects are present when the results of a forensic examination are distorted by the context and mental state of the forensic examiner to include the examiner's subconscious expectations and desires.

Identifying and curtailing this kind of bias is a considerable task when one takes into account the forensic community's affiliation with both law enforcement and the prosecution. Specifically, this association has fashioned an atmosphere in which an unsettling number of forensic professionals have all but abandoned objectivity and have become completely partial to the prosecution's objectives, goals, and philosophies. They may even go so far as to regard this association as virtuous and heroic, and they may believe any alternative philosophy to be a manifestation of something that is morally bankrupt. So strong is the influence of this association between forensic evidence examination and law enforcement that some forensic examiners have even deliberately fabricated evidence or testified falsely so that the prosecution might prove its case; however, they are the extreme end of the spectrum.

It is fair to say that the majority of practitioners in the forensic community routinely acknowledge the existence of overt forms of conscious bias. That is, they generally recognize and condemn forensic ignorance, forensic fraud, and evidence fabricators when they are dragged into the light and exposed for all to see. Moreover, the forensic community seems to realize that, to effectively serve the criminal justice system, they must immediately eliminate individuals, procedures, or circumstances that call into question examiner objectivity and neutrality (although this may be called into question in some specific cases, when forensic science organizations essentially fail in their duty to regulate membership, thereby protecting inept and unethical examiners).

Although the forensic community is somewhat alert to the potential for extreme forms of outright fraud and overt bias, it tends to be less able to understand and accept that well-documented forms of covert bias can taint even the most impartial scientific examinations. This is disheartening for the simple reason that covert and subconscious biases represent a far greater threat to the forensic community than do the small percentage of overtly biased, dishonest, or fraudulent forensic examiners.

To grasp the elusive yet powerful nature of subconscious bias requires a brief lesson in cognitive psychology. Cognitive psychology is the psychological science that studies cognition, the mental processes that are believed to underlie behavior. The following is a well-established principle of cognitive psychology: An individual's desires and expectations can influence his or her perceptions, observations, and interpretations of events. In other words, the results of observations are dependent on at least two things: (1) the object or circumstance being observed and (2) the observer's state of mind. Cognitive psychologists have coined several terms to described this phenomenon, including *observer effects*, *context effects*, and *expectancy effects* (Neisser, 1976; Risinger et al., 2002; Rosenthal, 1966; Saks, 2003). Readers may consider them essentially interchangeable.

There can be no doubt that observer effects exist and subconsciously influence forensic examiners. The pervasive failure of the forensic community to confront this and to design safeguards speaks volumes about what James Starrs (1991), professor of forensic science, refers to as "institutional bias" (p. 24):

> Institutional bias in the forensic sciences is manifested by the policies, programs, or practices of an agency, an organization or a group, whether public or private, or any of its personnel which benefit or promote the interests of one side in a courtroom dispute, while either denying or minimizing the interests of the other side.

Currently, criminal profiling tends to be so strongly associated with law enforcement's investigative efforts that there is no reasonable hope of disentanglement in the near future. What can be accomplished in the short term is the recognition of this form of bias and the open embrace of methods and mechanisms to blunt its effects.

SCIENCE AND THE SCIENTIFIC METHOD[2]

Strict adherence to the scientific method is the first in a series of steps that can blunt the effects of even the most pervasive forms of bias. Unfortunately, the forensic community as a whole, including criminal profilers, remains uninformed about defining it, let alone applying it. Faigman et al. (1997, p. 47) are rather unforgiving, but honest, when observing:

> The subject of the scientific method … has been described innumerable times, in a multitude of works on manifold subjects, from elementary school textbooks to post-graduate treatises. And yet it remains a subject that is foreign to most lawyers and judges.

Thornton (1997b, p. 14) goes further and includes most forensic practitioners in the mix of those who do not understand what the scientific method is or how to apply it correctly:

> Those individuals engaged in "scientific" work rarely study the scientific method. To be sure, those engaged in research are expected to pick up the scientific method somewhere along the way; for the most part scientists don't study the implementation of the scientific method.

On the same subject, he also writes (Thornton, 1997a, p. 485):

> Many, perhaps even most, forensic scientists are not just inattentive to the scientific method, but ignorant. … I don't believe that forensic scientists lack the wit to be able to defend their use of the scientific method, but rather that the necessity to do so has not generally been thrust upon them.

Even as this fourth edition goes to press, these insights are as accurate and useful as ever. If nothing else, they remind us that basic explanations of these subjects are essential.

The relationship between scientists, the scientific method, and science is thus: Scientists employing the scientific method can work within a particular discipline to help create and build a body of scientific knowledge to the point where its theories become principles and the discipline as a whole eventually becomes a science. The discipline remains a science through the continued building of scientific knowledge, which is regarded as a process rather than a result.

Scientific knowledge is any knowledge, enlightenment, or awareness that comes from examining events or problems through the lens of the scientific method. The accumulation of scientific knowledge in a particular subject or discipline leads to its development as a science. The classic definition of a *science*, as provided by Thornton (1997b, p. 12), is "an orderly body of knowledge with principles that are clearly enunciated," as well as being reality oriented with conclusions susceptible to testing.

A strong caution is needed here. The use of statistics does not make something scientific. The use of a computer does not make something scientific. The use of chemicals does not make something scientific. The use of technology does not make something scientific. Wearing a lab coat does not make one's conclusions scientific. Science is found in the interpretations, or inferences, made by the scientific examiner. The question is this: Was the scientific method used to synthesize the knowledge at hand, and has that

---

[2] Portions of this section have been adapted from Chisum and Turvey (2007).

knowledge been applied correctly to render subsequent interpretations, with the necessary humility? If forensic examiners are not scientific in their methods of examination, then it does not matter how many books, research studies, or agreeable colleagues they are able to cite in defense of their positions.

The scientific method is a way to investigate how or why something works, or how something happened, through the development of hypotheses and subsequent attempts at falsification through testing and other accepted means. It is a structured process designed to build scientific knowledge by way of answering specific questions about observations through careful analysis and critical thinking. Observations are used to form testable hypotheses, and, with sufficient testing, hypotheses can become scientific theories. Eventually, over much time, with precise testing marked by a failure to falsify, scientific theories can become scientific principles. The scientific method is the particular approach to knowledge building and problem solving employed by scientists of every kind.[3]

The first step in the scientific method is observation. An observation is made regarding some event, fact, or object. This observation then leads to a specific question regarding the event, fact, or object, such as where or when an object originated or how an object came to possess certain traits.

The second step in the scientific method is attempting to answer the question that has been asked by forming a hypothesis, or an educated estimate, regarding the possible answer. Often, there is more than one possible answer, and a hypothesis for each one must be developed and investigated.

The third step in the scientific method is experimentation. Of all the steps in the scientific method, this is the one that separates scientific inquiry from others. Scientific analysts design experiments intended to disprove their hypotheses. Once again, scientific analysts design experiments intended to disprove their hypotheses, not to prove them. At least one major forensic science text that provides readers with chapters on crime reconstruction and criminal profiling has failed to emphasize this crucial aspect of the experimentation or "testing" phase in theory development. Rather, crime reconstruction and criminal profiling are incorrectly presented in an overly simplified fashion for use by investigators looking to prove their theories (Baker and Napier, 2003, p. 538; Miller, 2003, pp. 128–129). These works collectively leave the door open for confirmatory bias. Inferences regarding crime-related actions or events are not intended to verify, confirm, or prove investigative theories. Rather, they are meant to support or refute investigative theories. The words *support* and *confirm* are worlds apart. The former suggests assistance, and the latter suggests finality. This difference may sound semantic to some, but it is not.

If the job of the criminal profiler were merely to work toward confirming law enforcement theories, then there would be no point in performing an in-depth analysis of any offense or related behavior. Confirmation is easy to find if that is what one looks for—all one needs to do is ignore everything that works against a prevailing theory and embrace anything that even remotely supports it. But that is not what the scientific method is about. The absolute cornerstone of the scientific method is falsification.[4]

---

[3] It is important to explain that scientists use the scientific method to build knowledge and solve problems; its use defines them. If one is doing something else, then one is not actually a scientist. Faigman et al. (1997, p. 48) warn: "Not all knowledge asserted by people who are commonly thought of as scientists is the product of the scientific method."

[4] The authors have found that this has often been the best way to proceed when working with others to solve a problem, make a decision, or interpret the known facts. It is essentially brainstorming: coming up with all kinds of ideas regardless of their merit, getting them all down for everyone to see, and then killing off the weak with logic and reason, one at a time, as a group. The strongest solutions and theories will necessarily withstand this process. As Lee et al. (1983, p. 2) explain: "Forensic scientists engaged in reconstruction of events follow the essential principles of the scientific method. … In attempting to reconstruct the events that took place at the crime scene, for example, the first step is careful observation and assembly of all the known facts. Different hypotheses can then be entertained to see how well one or another corresponds to all the facts. As additional facts are disclosed by further observation or by experimental testing, it may be possible to arrive at a theory of what took place."

Science as Falsification

These considerations led me in the winter of 1919–20 to conclusions which I may now reformulate as follows.

1. It is easy to obtain confirmations, or verifications, for nearly every theory—if we look for confirmations.
2. Confirmations should count only if they are the result of risky predictions; that is to say, if, unenlightened by the theory in question, we should have expected an event which was incompatible with the theory—an event which would have refuted the theory.
3. Every "good" scientific theory is a prohibition: It forbids certain things to happen. The more a theory forbids, the better it is.
4. A theory which is not refutable by any conceivable event is nonscientific. Irrefutability is not a virtue of a theory (as people often think) but a vice.
5. Every genuine test of a theory is an attempt to falsify it, or to refute it. Testability is falsifiability; but there are degrees of testability: Some theories are more testable, more exposed to refutation, than others; they take, as it were, greater risks.
6. Confirming evidence should not count except when it is the result of a genuine test of the theory; and this means that it can be presented as a serious but unsuccessful attempt to falsify the theory. (I now speak in such cases of "corroborating evidence.")
7. Some genuinely testable theories, when found to be false, are still upheld by their admirers—for example by introducing ad hoc some auxiliary assumption, or by reinterpreting the theory ad hoc in such a way that it escapes refutation. Such a procedure is always possible, but it rescues the theory from refutation only at the price of destroying, or at least lowering, its scientific status. (I later described such a rescuing operation as a "conventionalist twist" or a "conventionalist stratagem.")

One can sum up all this by saying that the criterion of the scientific status of a theory is its falsifiability, or refutability, or testability.

—Sir Karl R. Popper (1963, pp. 33–39)

If a hypothesis remains standing after a succession of tests or experiments fail to disprove it, then it may become a scientific theory, which may be stated or presented with a reasonable degree of scientific certainty.

Scientific theories that withstand the test of time and study eventually become scientific principles. Although there is no universal agreement as to whether and when a scientific theory crosses the line to become a scientific principle, it is accepted that a scientific theory, developed with the assistance of the scientific method, has a greater degree of reliability and acceptance than mere observation, intuition, or speculation. With regard to criminal profiling, this may be explained in terms of establishing what traits are evidenced by established crime-scene behavior or not, as opposed to predicting or confirming that traits may or may not exist based on research or subjective experience. To argue for the presence of certain profile characteristics, one must establish the presence or absence of certain and relevant behaviors—not simply guess them or assume them, and then arbitrarily apply research findings that may or may not apply within the context of a particular case.

The correct use of the scientific method is impossible, however, without critical thinking and the science of logic to accurately synthesize, interpret, and apply the results.

Critical Thinking

The problem is not teaching the inferrer to think: the problem is the examination of how inferences have been made by another and what value his inferences may have for our own conclusions.

—Dr. Hans Gross (1924, p. 16)

There are many definitions of the term *critical thinking*. Their unifying concept is that critical thinking involves indiscriminately questioning assumptions in any arguments encountered in any context. This means rigorously questioning the assumptions beneath the reasoning and opinions of others as well as our own.[5] Paul and Scriven (2004) offer the following description:

> Critical thinking is the intellectually disciplined process of actively and skillfully conceptualizing, applying, analyzing, synthesizing, and/or evaluating information gathered from, or generated by, observation, experience, reflection, reasoning, or communication, as a guide to belief and action.

Sadly, most of the students and many of the professionals encountered by the authors have no idea what critical thinking is, what it involves, or why it is necessary. In fact, it is likely that most students reading this text will have never formally encountered the concept of critical thinking.

This may have something to do with the death of Socratic teaching methods in many universities or an increase in the number of unqualified instructors teaching pedantically from a script rather than using knowledge they have earned or built themselves. No matter the subject or reason, students have been, and continue to be, conditioned not to question, not to think critically, and to accept information as fact by virtue of the alleged expertise of their instructors. This reality is a dangerous, ego-driven farce. As Popper (1960, pp. 70–71) cogently explains, "no man's authority can establish truth by decree." This explicitly provides that questioning assumptions is a basic tenet of any forensic discipline. The danger of not questioning becomes apparent as we continue through this text. That students have been conditioned away from the virtues of critical thinking in any university setting is also ironic—the greatest gift given to a student by a liberal arts education used to be strong reasoning and critical thinking skills. That was the theory, at any rate.

For our purposes, the tragedy is compounded further because good critical thinking skills are at the heart of what makes a competent criminal profiler. Therefore, before we continue with this chapter, or with the rest of this text for that matter, we need to give ourselves permission to think outside of the confines that our colleagues, friends, parents, instructors, and experiences have placed around our minds. We need to give ourselves permission to question any and all assumptions, premises, and arguments and demand corroboration, no matter what the source. We need to free ourselves from the old habits of simply listening, taking notes, and accepting, and get into the habit of asking those who would purport to know things—why?

A brief overview of critical thinking is necessary. As described in Paul and Scriven (2004):

> Critical thinking can be seen as having two components:
>
> 1. a set of skills to process and generate information and beliefs; and
> 2. the habit, based on intellectual commitment, of using those skills to guide behavior.
>
> It is thus to be contrasted with:
>
> 1. the mere acquisition and retention of information alone (because it involves a particular way in which information is sought and treated);
> 2. the mere possession of a set of skills (because it involves the continual use of them); and
> 3. the mere use of those skills ("as an exercise") without acceptance of their results.

---

[5] Thornton (1997b, p. 20) provides a useful standard against which to measure the reasoning of others: "Forensic science cannot be viewed solely in terms of its products; it is also judged by the legitimacy of the processes by which evidence is examined and interpreted. Any opinion rendered by a forensic scientist in a written report or in court testimony must have a basis in fact and theory. Without such a basis, conclusions reached are bereft of validity and should be treated with derision."

Critical thinking varies according to the motivation underlying it. When grounded in selfish motives, it is often manifested in the skillful manipulation of ideas in service to one's own, or one's group's, vested interest. As such, it is typically intellectually flawed, however pragmatically successful it might be. When grounded in fair-mindedness and intellectual integrity, it is typically of a higher order intellectually, although subject to the charge of "idealism" by those habituated to its selfish use.

For the purposes of forensic examination (which, again, includes criminal profiling) the application of critical thinking to casework means a staunch refusal to accept any evidence or conclusions without sufficient proof. It involves the careful and deliberate determination of whether to accept, reject, or suspend judgment about any information or related findings. It means skeptical gathering of evidence, skeptical examinations, and the skeptical interpretation of results.

This includes the following tasks:

1. Evaluating the nature and quality of any information and its source
2. Recognizing bias in all of its forms, including all of the sources of bias
3. Separating facts from opinions
4. Distinguishing between primary sources of information (unaltered—direct from the source) and secondary sources of information (altered—interpreted or summarized through someone else)
5. Synthesizing information.

The problem with critical thinking is that in some circumstances it is easier, and even alluring, to accept what others have told us or shown us rather than to investigate matters for ourselves. There may even be harsh consequences for questioning information or findings when they come from those who perceive themselves as our betters (or our supervisors). Some people simply don't like to have their "facts" questioned, and in such cases profilers may have a standing policy to avoid criticism. They don't want to appear rude or upset their clients. In reality, failing to be critical at all levels of examination protects inadequate information and subsequent conclusions; it is the best way to guarantee unreliable results.[6]

Although this can be useful as a practical matter, making things easier and keeping everyone happy, it does not make inferences based on uncritically accepted information or conclusions more reliable. Forensic examiners are warned to embrace the limitations and accept the consequences of any information taken uncritically when conducting their analysis.[7]

---

[6] Consider the following sworn testimony of then FBI profiler Robert Hazelwood. It was made before the Senate Armed Services Committee in a response to a succession of questions and answers regarding investigative assumptions that were left unchecked in the FBI's analysis of the death of Clayton Hartwig aboard the USS *Iowa* (USS Iowa, 1990, pp. 25–26): "Whenever we [the FBI's profiling unit] are requested to do a case for an investigative agency, we make the assumption that we are dealing with professionals. They provide us with the materials for review, and that's what we review." This helpful assumption circumvents the entire concept of critical thinking and makes profiling conclusions far less informed and reliable. Additionally, it may serve the purpose of absolving blame should the profiler be found to be wrong: It wasn't my fault because the information I had was bad.

[7] One of the authors (Turvey) was asked to examine a series of sexual homicides as well as a single case of arson for the purpose of case linkage (see Chapter 14, "Case Linkage"). In the course of examination, it was learned that the initial determination of arson had been made using shoddy practices and with disregard for NFPA guidelines (discussed in Chapter 16, "Fire and Explosives: Behavioral Aspects"). Subsequently, the theory of arson was disconfirmed by a more informed independent fire investigator's analysis. The author's final report reads, "Since the criminal behavior of arson may not be assumed, this case is necessarily eliminated from any linkage analysis prepared in a forensic context for comparison to other crimes." It further explains why to do otherwise would be unethical: "According the Ethical Guidelines of the Academy of Behavioral Profiling, Members must 'render opinions and conclusions strictly in accordance with the evidence in the case.' Available online at http://profiling.org/abp_conduct.html."

The Science of Logic

In the broadest sense, *logic* can be defined as the process of argumentation, or, as Farber (1942, p. 41) describes it, "a unified discipline which investigates the structure and validity of ordered knowledge." According to Bhattacharyya (1958, p. 326):

> Logic is usually defined as the science of valid thought. But as thought may mean either the act of thinking or the object of thought, we get two definitions of logic: logic as the science (1) of the act of valid thinking, or (2) of the objects of valid thinking.

Burch (2003, p. 1) provides us with an applied definition and identifies the role that logic plays:

> Logic is the organized body of knowledge, or science, that evaluates arguments. An argument is a group of statements, the purport of which is that some of them (the premises) should support, imply, provide evidence for, or make reasonable to believe another particular one of them (the conclusion).

All of these descriptions are useful, because it is the ultimate purpose of logic to analyze the methods by which valid judgments are obtained in any science or discourse. This is achieved by the formulation of general laws that dictate the validity of judgments (Farber, 1942). But more than providing a theoretical framework for structuring arguments, the basic principles of logic allow for a rigorous formulation and testing of any argument, such as the characteristics inferred in a criminal profile.

McInerney (2004) outlined the following basic principles of logic:

The principle of identity. A thing is what it is. Existing reality is not a homogeneous mass, but it is composed of a variety of individuals. In criminal profiling, this principle may be used to argue for individually profiling particular crimes—that is, treating each case as an individual event, rather than as an extension of "similar" crimes.[8]

The principle of the excluded middle. Between being and nonbeing, there is no middle state. Perhaps the best way to view this in the context of criminal profiling is "either a crime (or an action) has occurred, or it has not." The key to establishing the validity of this premise is in carrying out a detailed and complete crime reconstruction to establish exactly what has occurred and what has not. Only through a full and complete forensic evaluation can the true nature and quality of the thing be known and then gauged.

The principle of sufficient reason. There is sufficient reason for everything. This may also be called the principle of causality. This principle states that everything in the known universe has an explanation for its existence. Implied here is that nothing in the physical universe is self-explanatory or the cause of itself, and, perhaps most important, that all instances of a thing must have an explanation that is realistic within accepted bodies of knowledge. Farber (1942) suggests that knowledge in its primary sense means true knowledge, in that it conforms to established facts of reality. In short, any argument put forth must not be sensational or rely on phenomenological explanations for its cause or existence. With respect to criminal profiling, this bars the examiner from assuming facts for the purpose of analysis or from using Martians, UFOs, or Bigfoot to explain events. And it requires that criminal profilers carefully establish the behavior that they intend to profile.

Induction

As already explained, the construction of a criminal profile is about making inferences; it is about the construction of rational arguments. There are essentially two general categories of reasoning behind the criminal profiling process, as with most forms of logic and argumentation. One can be described

---

[8] That is, of course, unless the point of the exercise is to determine if a crime is part of a series or if a crime is proven to be part of a series.

as *inductive reasoning*, referring to a comparative, correlational, or statistical process, often reliant on subjective expertise that is most associated with the development of psychological syndromes. The other has been described by the author as *deductive reasoning* and refers to a forensic-evidence-based, process-oriented method of investigative reasoning about the behavior patterns of a particular offender. This was formally explored in the first edition of this text (Turvey, 1999) and was inspired in part by sex offender research models published in Knight and Prentky (1990, p. 26).

Thornton (1997b, p. 13) offers the clearest explanation of the relationship between inductive and deductive reasoning:

> Induction is a type of inference that proceeds from a set of specific observations to a generalization, called a premise. This premise is a working assumption, but it may not always be valid. A deduction, on the other hand, proceeds from a generalization to a specific case, and that is generally what happens in forensic practice. Providing that the premise is valid, the deduction will be valid. But knowing whether the premise is valid is the name of the game here; it is not difficult to be fooled into thinking that one's premises are valid when they are not.

> Forensic scientists have, for the most part, treated induction and deduction rather casually. They have failed to recognize that induction, not deduction, is the counterpart of hypothesis testing and theory revision. They have tended to equate a hypothesis with a deduction, which it is not. As a consequence, too often a hypothesis is declared as a deductive conclusion, when in fact it is a statement awaiting verification through testing.

An inductive argument, then, is where the conclusion is made likely, a matter of some probability, by offering supporting conclusions. It is at best a prediction about what might be true. As Burch (2003, p. 7) explains,[9]

> There are several common types of inductive arguments, including predictions about the future, arguments from analogy, inductive generalizations, (many) arguments from authority, arguments based on signs, and causal inference.

A good inductive argument provides strong support for the conclusion offered, but this still does not make the argument infallible. A criminal profile is a set of offender characteristics (conclusions) based on premises that should be articulated in the body of the profile itself. As already suggested, deductive reasoning involves conclusions that flow logically from the premises stated. It is such that if the premises are true, then the subsequent conclusion must also be true. Inductive reasoning involves broad generalizations or statistical reasoning, where it is possible for the premises to be true while the subsequent conclusion is false.

Inductive arguments lead to the development of hypotheses and come in a variety of forms (Lee et al., 1983, p. 2). Two types of inductive arguments, however, seem to be more prevalent in criminal profiles than others. The first is the inductive generalization, which argues from the specific to the general (many of those the author has encountered believe that this is the only defining characteristic of inductive reasoning, having gone as far as their dictionary to research the matter). In this instance, conclusions are formed about characteristics from observations of a single event or individual or a small number of events or individuals (Walton, 1989, p. 198). Then a hasty generalization is made suggesting that similar events or individuals encountered in the future will share these initially observed, or sampled, characteristics. In *The Logic of Scientific Discovery*, Karl Popper argues against the use of generalizations by noting (Popper, 2003, p. 4):

---

[9] On the same page, Burch (2003) provides a stern warning to those looking to oversimplify this issue for lack of actually understanding the difference between induction and deduction. He states, "One should not use as a criterion for distinguishing deductive from inductive arguments the claim that deductive arguments go from general to particular, while inductive arguments go from particular to general." The use of this single criterion, or a variant, indicates a simplistic and incomplete understanding of these subjects.

It is far from obvious from a logical point of view, that we are justified in inferring universal statements from singular ones, no matter how numerous; for any conclusion drawn in this way may always turn out to be false: no matter how many instances of white swans we may have observed, this does not justify the conclusion that all swans are white.

The second type of inductive argument common to criminal profiling is the statistical argument. The truthfulness of statistical arguments is a matter of probability, a matter of likelihood (Walton, 1989, p. 199). They may sound good, even convincing, and tend to play to our "common sense" stereotypes. This is one of the reasons they are so seductive. But they are inherently unreliable and problematic.

It is also important to keep in mind that an inductive argument can contain both inductive generalizations and statistical arguments; they are not mutually exclusive.

For clarity and accuracy, inductive arguments should contain the requisite qualifiers, such as *normally, likely, often, many, rarely, most, some, probably, usually, always, never,* and so on. The trouble is that many criminal profilers have stopped using such qualifiers in their reports because they know that inductive reasoning is far weaker and far less accurate than deductive reasoning. Other major reasons for the failure to qualify conclusions and premises alike include ego and ignorance; many profilers do not really wish to share the weakness of their arguments with end users, or they open themselves to the questions and criticisms that would follow. And, perhaps most dangerous of all, many more are ignorant of the difference.

One common example of inductive argumentation in criminal profiling may be found in the issue of inferring offender sex.[10] Crime figures from the United States in 2002 (Federal Bureau of Investigation, 2002) suggest that 90% of people who committed murder in that year were male. Federal Bureau of Investigation (FBI) profilers (who currently refer to themselves as Criminal Investigative Analysts) use these and similar data to make inductive inferences in their profiles to this day. This language is taken directly from an FBI profile (a.k.a. criminal investigative analysis) written by SSA James McNamara (2000):

> The behavior at this crime scene indicates that the offender is a more mature male. We would expect him to be in his late 20s or early 30s at least. It should be noted that we mean the offender's emotional age, not necessarily his chronological age. Statistically speaking, absent any forensic or eyewitness evidence to the contrary, we believe the offender to be a white male. Most interpersonal violence is intra racial. No suspect should be eliminated based on age or race alone. The FBI's Uniform Crime Report for 1998 (the most recent edition) indicates for white female victims of homicide, white males were the offenders in 86% of the cases.

The inductive qualifiers in this example include "statistically speaking," "most," and "86%." Even though this specific statistic is relatively compelling, and many arguments are nowhere near this certain, it does not mean that every homicide committed in a given year will be committed by a male. Therefore, the final inductive argument above provides a degree of certainty largely dependent on a single variable plucked from the data out of context. The percentage will differ, for example, depending on the type of homicide, the weapon used, and a whole host of complicating variables. We also know without having to look at formal studies that women do in fact commit the crime of homicide. Inferring that most homicides are committed by a male, and therefore assuming and subsequently inferring that the offender in the present case must be male, is borderline unethical—without explicit qualification, it leaves a false impression in the mind of those reading the profile.

---

[10] Sex refers to the division of a species into male or female. Gender refers to sexual identity as it relates to society or culture. For example, someone who is born with male reproductive organs may choose later in life to transition outwardly toward female dress, habits, and expression. That person's sex would remain male, although the person would be considered female with respect to gender. The authors have encountered much ignorance on this subject.

The lack of certainty the profiler has about his or her conclusions should be reflected in the end product by the language used to convey the characteristic. Unfortunately, this does not always happen, and occasionally a profiler may stray into offering uncertain characteristics as though they had been unequivocally established. This may be referred to as offering an inductive conclusion deductively or, depending on the structure and the formation of the argument, a false deduction.

As already suggested, inductive profiles may also involve arguments where the premises themselves have been assumed. That is to say, too many inductive profilers do not bother to check the validity of their premises or simply assume a premise for the sake of arguing a conclusion. This happens far more than most profilers care to admit, often because they do not possess the knowledge or ability to check the veracity of their premises. We revisit this theme more than once throughout this text.

Although this section may appear to advocate the abandonment of inductive methods or argumentation, the authors agree that induction has many appropriate uses when applied in the context of the scientific method. Most importantly, induction provides a useful starting point in generating theories that may later be subjected to testing before developing a deductive conclusion.

Deduction

Deductive reasoning, strictly speaking, involves arguments whereby, if the premises are true, then the conclusions must also be true. In a deductive argument, the conclusions flow directly from the premises given (Walton, 1989, p. 110). Or, as Lee et al. (1983, p. 2) describe it,

> In deductive logic, a conclusion follows inescapably from one or more of the premises. If the premises are true, then the conclusion drawn is valid.

Burch (2003, p. 6) reminds us:

> When the arguer claims that it is impossible for the conclusion to be false given that the premises are true, then the argument is best considered a deductive argument. When the arguer merely claims that it is best considered improbable that the conclusion be false given that the premises are true, then the argument is best considered an inductive argument.

A deductive argument is structured so that the conclusion is implicitly contained within the premise; unless the reasoning is invalid (as in a false deduction or a non sequitur), the conclusion follows as a matter of course. It is designed so that it takes us from truth to truth. That is, a deductive argument is valid if (Alexandra, Matthews, and Miller, 2002, p. 65)

> - It is not logically possible for its conclusion to be false if its premises are true.
> - Its conclusions must be true, if its premises are true.
> - It would be contradictory to assert its premises yet deny its conclusions.

For these reasons, it is incumbent on the criminal profiler to establish the veracity and validity of every premise before attempting to draw conclusions from them. Inferences without this level of care are not deductive.

A criminal profile that results from a deductive argument is by no means static. Like any forensic report, its conclusions should be re-examined when new facts and information become available. However, a criminal profile that results from this process is by no means static and may be updated in light of new information. Further evidentiary considerations, such as new physical evidence, may be incorporated into the decision process to update the conclusion. Also, new advances in science and understanding may challenge long-held assumptions and question the current hypothesis. This is not a problem with the process, because a deduction can only operate within the realm of established laws and principles. Farber (1942, p. 48) makes clear this tenet of argumentation:

> Every "logical system" is governed by principles of structure and meaning. A system that claims to be a "logic," i.e., which operates formally with one of the various definitions of implication, possibility, etc., is subject to the laws of construction of ordered thought, namely, to the fundamental principles of logic. This requirement imposed on all systems cannot amount to a law that there shall be law. The specific application is provided by the rules in each system.

When the laws or principles of a logical system, such as a crime scene, change because of new knowledge from further testing or observation, so too must the nature of the deductions made.[11]

Fallacies of Logic[12]

Perhaps the most revealing indicator of the absence of analytical logic and the scientific method in a criminal profile is the presence of logical fallacy. Logical fallacies are errors in reasoning that essentially deceive those whom they are intended to convince. This does not mean that the fallacious criminal profiler is being intentionally deceptive. What it does mean is that some criminal profilers lack the intellectual dexterity to know whether and when their reasoning is flawed. This is discussed further in the next section, Metacognition.

Forensic examiners of all disciplines would do well to learn more about fallacies in logic and reasoning in order to avoid them in their own work as well as identify them in the work of others. Common logical fallacies in criminal profiling and the forensic disciplines in general include, but are certainly not limited to, the following:

Suppressed Evidence or Card Stacking

This is a one-sided argument that presents only evidence favoring a particular conclusion and ignores or downplays the evidence against it. It may involve distortions, exaggerations, misstatements of facts, or outright lies. This is not an acceptable practice for any forensic practitioner.

Example

One of the authors (Turvey) was asked to examine two separate instances of sexual homicide for the purpose of case linkage in postconviction (*Illinois v. Anthony Mertz*, 2003). This included reviewing the trial testimony of the prosecution's expert in criminal profiling, retired FBI profiler James Wright of Park Dietz and Associates. As described in the author's report,

> According to Mr. Wright's own testimony regarding the homicides of Amy Warner (1999) and Shannon McNamara (2001) (pp. 1964–1965): "The—the scenes were—were different in a lot of respects but there were some similarities. Certainly one was the—the attack of the throat and also that the arms were extended over the head, which is also something that's fairly consistent with what some of the witnesses have said about when they were attacked by Mr. Mertz, is that the arms were extended over the head and down. Those are the two biggest things, is the attack of the throat and the arms." The many differences conceded are not discussed or explained in the testimony of Mr. Wright. …

---

[11] The explicit mechanics of deductive profiling are detailed in Chapter 5, "An Introduction to Behavioral Evidence Analysis."
[12] This section has been adapted from Chisum and Turvey (2007).

When comparing the behavioral evidence in these two cases, of greatest significance are the distinctive differences between them. This includes the following:

1. The lack of blood evidence elsewhere in her residence suggests that Amy Warner (AW) was attacked and died in the same location—in her living room on her couch.
2. According to crime scene investigator Richard Caudell, Shannon McNamara (SM) was apparently attacked as she slept. The evidence suggests that a struggle began in her bedroom and continued in the bathroom, where she was eventually overcome. Then, dead or dying, she was moved to the living room of her apartment where she was posed or "put on display."
3. AW suffered a "massive incise wound" to her neck; SM suffered some lesser incise wounds to the neck, and manual strangulation, including a fractured hyoid bone.
4. SM had a washrag stuffed tightly into her mouth.
5. AW was discovered hanging headfirst off of the couch in her living room, her head resting on a pillow on the floor; SM was found lying on her back in her living room, on the floor, in a position to be discovered by the first person to open the front door.
6. AW was discovered wearing "a pink short sleeved blouse with no brassiere," nude from the waist down; SM was nude, however her arms were above her head, with her shirt pulled over her head onto her arms.
7. AW was discovered with her face in full view; SM was discovered with her face covered by her arms and shirt, evidencing depersonalization (Burgess et al., 1992; p. 352).
8. SM suffered a "widely gaping" postmortem incised wound to the upper abdomen, exposing a portion of her bowel.
9. SM suffered an incise wound to her external genitalia.
10. SM suffered multiple stab and incise wounds to her buttocks and anus.
11. SM suffered three parallel incise wounds across her back.
12. SM suffered one incise wound along the length of her back.
13. The motive for AW's murder is consistent with anger or retaliation, as evidence by the brutality and overkill in her injuries, and the lack of other motivational evidence.
14. The motive for SM's murder is consistent with sexual assault in combination with a desire to engage in eroticized post-mortem mutilation, as evidence by the extensive post-mortem mutilation to sexualized areas of the body, and the post-mortem display.

It should be mentioned that Wright testified that he was asked to render an opinion in court as to whether or not Mertz, the defendant, was responsible for both cases described here. This is most certainly a form of criminal profiling; naming the individual responsible renders not just some, but all, offender characteristics. Moreover, testifying whether a specific individual is responsible for a specific crime directly invades the province of the jury. It is one matter to compare offense behavior and connect scenes or offenses in a behavioral or even evidentiary sense. Wright's testimony went beyond that; he named the person responsible. This is not only unethical expert conduct in many professional circles, it is usually inadmissible. Doing so while card stacking, or suppressing clear evidence unfavorable to the preferred position of one's client, removes logic and reason from the effort.

Appeal to Authority

Appeal to authority occurs when someone offers a conclusion based on the stated authority or expertise of themselves or others. Such reasoning can be fallacious when the authority lacks the expertise suggested; when the authority is an expert in one subject, but not the subject at hand; when the subject is contentious and involves multiple interpretations, with good arguments on both sides; when the authority is biased; when the area of expertise is fabricated; when the authority is unidentified; and when the authority is offered as evidence in place of defensible scientific fact.

Example

When FBI agents write criminal profile reports (a.k.a. criminal investigative analysis reports), it is not uncommon for them to offer collective opinions on behalf of the FBI's entire National Center for the Analysis of Violent Crime (NCAVC) or Behavioral Analysis Unit (BAU), as though every member has reviewed all of the evidence in the case and has independently concurred. Opinions tend to be expressed in this fashion when the individual profiler lacks sufficient education, training, or experience on a particular issue—or in profiling in general. A recent case report from a BAU profiler reads in the first paragraph, "It is the collective opinion of the BAU." Other reports read, "we believe" or "we feel" or "we conclude"—to summon support for opinions by virtue of a collective agency authority that can never truly be measured, tested, or cross-examined.

It is common for forensic experts of all kinds to offer their years of experience as evidence of reliability and accuracy. However, experience, reliability, and accuracy are not necessarily related. Though skill and ability are potential benefits of age and experience, it does not follow that those with experience will necessarily gain skill or ability, let alone be reliable and accurate in their examinations. As Thornton (1997b, p. 17) explains, summoning experience instead of logic and reasoning to support a conclusion is an admission to lacking both:

> Experience is neither a liability nor an enemy of the truth; it is a valuable commodity, but it should not be used as a mask to deflect legitimate scientific scrutiny, the sort of scrutiny that customarily is leveled at scientific evidence of all sorts. To do so is professionally bankrupt and devoid of scientific legitimacy, and courts would do well to disallow testimony of this sort. Experience ought to be used to enable the expert to remember the when and the how, why, who, and what. Experience should not make the expert less responsible, but rather more responsible for justifying an opinion with defensible scientific facts.

In other words, the more experience of quality and substance one has, the less one will need to tell people about it in order to gain their trust and confidence—the quality of one's experience is demonstrated through the inherent quality of one's methods and results.

Furthermore, experience in finding, collecting, or packaging evidence (a.k.a. crime scene processing or crime scene investigation) is not related to experience interpreting the meaning of evidence in its context (e.g., crime reconstruction and criminal profiling). This would be an appeal to false authority. As O'Hara (1970, p. 667) explains, the role of crime scene investigator and the role of evidence interpretation should not intersect:

> It is not to be expected that the investigator also play the role of the laboratory expert in relation to the physical evidence found at the scene of the crime. ... It suffices that the investigator investigate; it is supererogatory that he should perform refined scientific examinations. Any serious effort to accomplish such a conversion would militate against the investigator's efficiency.

> ...In general the investigator should know the methods of discovering, "field-testing," preserving, collecting, and transporting evidence. Questions of analysis and comparison should be referred to the laboratory expert.

Appeal to Tradition

The appeal to tradition reasons that a conclusion is correct simply because it is older, traditional, or "has always been so." It supports a conclusion by appealing to long-standing, institutional, or cultural opinions, as if the past itself were a form of authority. This argument may be stated in a way that suggests the tradition of using a method is equivalent to establishing the reliability and validity of a method. In other words: If it didn't work, nobody would use it. This is far from true.

Example

In *Tennessee v. William R. Stevens* (McCrary, 2001), when queried as to the reliability of "crime-scene analysis" and "motivational analysis," retired FBI profiling expert Gregg O. McCrary stated, "[T]he proof ... [that] there is validation and reliability in the process is that it's being accepted. Uh—it's being used and the demand is just outstripping our resources to provide it." Furthermore, "[H]e explained that this type of analysis is 'not a hard science where you can do controlled experiments and come up with ratios in all this,' but the increased demand for such services exemplifies its effectiveness."

This line of reasoning is a direct appeal to both the past tradition of, and current demand for, FBI profiler assistance as evidence of its efficacy. The trial court recognized this fallacy and concluded that the expert's testimony regarding the motivation of the suspect did not comply with Tennessee Rule of Evidence 702 "in terms of substantially assisting the tr[ier] of fact because there is no trustworthiness or reliability." In the end, the trial court opined, "Although this type of sophisticated speculation is undoubtedly very helpful to criminal investigators, it is not sufficiently reliable to provide the basis for an expert opinion in a criminal trial." The Tennessee appellate court affirmed the trial court's decision by noting, "the Court is not convinced that this type of analysis has been subjected to adequate objective testing, or that it is based upon longstanding, reliable, scientific principles." Consequently, a tradition of use and a high demand for services do not equal reliability or accuracy.

Argumentum ad Hominem, or "Argument to the Man"

Ad hominem argument attacks an opponent's character rather than an opponent's reasoning. Because of its effectiveness, it is perhaps the most common logical fallacy. It is important to note that, even if they are true, arguments against character are not always relevant to the presentation of scientific conclusions, logic, and reasoning.

Example

In *United States v. O. C. Smith* (McCrary, 2005), retired FBI profiler Gregg O. McCrary provided a criminal investigative analysis (CIA) to the prosecution regarding the alleged abduction and assault of O. C. Smith that ended in a bomb's being strapped to his chest and his being suspended from a fence. McCrary's report details the accounts of a number of people known to O. C. Smith, including their beliefs that Smith's claims were false. For example, McCrary cites Dr. Steven Symes, a colleague of Smith, and notes, "Dr. Symes believes that the June 2002 attack on Dr. Smith is just too unusual, too detailed and too complicated and far fetched for him to believe" (p. 28). Further, McCrary cites Richard Walter, a prison therapist, who has known Smith for a period of years. Walter did not believe that the attack on Smith was real

> because the defendant is physically fit, machismo, rough and ready, smart and doesn't like to be touched. He advised that Dr. Smith likes to pretend he is on covert operations and Walter doesn't believe Dr. Smith would allow someone to tie him up easily with wire and a bomb. ... Mr. Walter believes that the June 2002 incident was dramatic, could be considered "overkill" and involved too much planning to be legitimate. Mr. Walters believes that Dr. Smith manufactured the incident for theater.

A good deal of Mr. McCrary's report could be distilled to ad hominem commentary about O. C. Smith's character rather than substantive forensic analysis of the crime or related behavior. That is to say, large sections of the report read like "Person X does not like O. C. Smith and believes his report is false, therefore his report is likely to be false." It is illogical to suggest that, because someone has qualities that others may or may not like, the person must also lack credibility.[13]

Emotional Appeal

Emotional appeal attempts to gain favor based on arousing emotions or sympathy to subvert rational thought.

Example

In 2001, one of the authors (Turvey) was retained as an expert in a civil action involving accusations of rape against a supervisor made by multiple subordinates. Opposing counsel had hired retired FBI profiler Greg M. Cooper to examine the complainant's statements. Cooper prepared what he referred to as a "behavioral investigative analysis" report, which was premised, inappropriately, on the assumption that the rapes did in fact occur. The report concludes that the victims shared similar characteristics and heightened risk, and that the offender groomed them in a similar fashion while committing the crimes in a similar manner.

However, the report itself was not written as an objective forensic document. It was written almost like an excerpt from a true-crime novel, using sensational and emotional language (such as "conviction," "cloak of deception," and "menacing sexual predator") and using inappropriately rendered analogies (such as "for the kill," "the hunt," and "wolf in sheep's clothing") to subtly play to the emotions of the reader, as opposed to maintaining an objective forensic stance. At times the report lapsed into what can be described as a stream of consciousness, with specific ruminations about the beliefs and fantasies of the offender. One such passage reads as though the author is purporting to channel the offender's post-offense mental state (Cooper, 2001, p. 4): "Having conquered his prey and satiated his fantasies, the 'charm' recedes." While this style of writing may be acceptable in a true-crime novel, or in a memoir, it has no place in an objective forensic report.

Post Hoc, Ergo Propter Hoc, *or "After This, Therefore Because of This"*

This fallacy occurs when one jumps to a conclusion about causation based on a correlation between two events, or types of events, that occur simultaneously.

Example

One of the authors (Turvey) examined a case involving the murder of a factory worker (Figure 2.1). The evidence demonstrated that, as he lay sleeping, the victim was stabbed twice in the heart through the chest, in the same wound path. The bloody steak knife used to kill him had been taken from a knife block in his kitchen and was found by investigators on the floor next to his bed. Subsequently, the bed was either set on fire or caught fire accidentally from cigarettes burning at the scene. It was not possible to determine which with the available evidence. The arson investigator reasoned, without direct facts or evidence of arson, that evidence of homicide was proof enough that the fire must have been set to conceal it. The author wrote in his report, "The opinions expressed in the arson investigator's report seem to assume that arson must have

---

[13] If someone possesses the specific characteristic of dishonesty, then certainly this must be taken into account when considering the truth of his or her statements. However, not liking someone, thinking that he or she dresses funny or looks strange, or similar irrelevant personal attacks do not have a logical bearing on the individual's truthfulness.

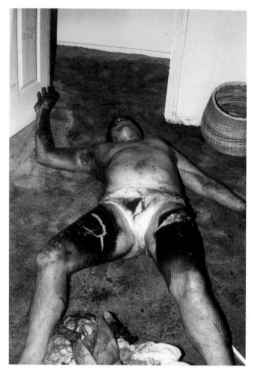

FIGURE 2.1
A 47-year-old male homicide victim who was stabbed to death while sleeping in his home. After working their way through the house, firefighters encountered his corpse, which was face down on his bed. He was removed from the bed to this position.

occurred because there was a homicide, and work backwards from that assumption without interest in proving it to any reliable degree. This is a basic fallacy of logic that incorrectly presumes 'with this, therefore because of this.' "

Hasty Generalizations

Hasty generalization occurs when one forms a conclusion based on woefully incomplete information or by examining only a few specific cases that are not representative of all possible cases.

Sweeping Generalization

Sweeping generalization occurs when one forms a conclusion by examining what occurs in many cases and assumes that it must or will be so in a particular case. This is the opposite of a hasty generalization.

Example

In *California v. Jennifer and Matt Fletcher* (2004), the prosecution asked FBI profiler SSA Mark Safarik to perform an analysis of a crime scene involving the police officer Joel Shanbrom, who was shot to death in his home (Figure 2.2). In that case, Shanbrom's wife, Jennifer, told police that intruders entered their home while she was bathing their child. She stated that she heard them shoot her husband while she hid with their son. SSA Safarik determined that the scene was actually a domestic homicide that had been staged to appear like a burglary gone wrong. SSA Safarik's criminal investigative analysis, dated June 17, 2002, provides the following lines reasoning to support this finding, among others (Safarik, 2002):

FIGURE 2.2
Joel Shanbrom, 32, was a five-year veteran police officer for the Los Angeles Unified School district. He patrolled schools in Verdugo Hills. His wife of seven years, Jennifer, worked at a dental office. Both were moonlighting, selling life insurance for Primerica, partnered with Matt Fletcher. On March 18, 1998, Joel Shanbrom was shot and killed in his home by a .410 shotgun, with three shots using mixed loads (birdshot and a slug). Jennifer told police that armed men entered their home and killed her husband while she and their son, Jacob, 3, hid in a concealed upstairs bathroom. A few years later, Jennifer Shanbrom married Matt Fletcher. Police saw this as evidence of an affair and arrested them both four years after Joel's murder. FBI profiler Mark Safarik testified that the scene was staged and that Jennifer's story did not add up. With no physical evidence whatsoever linking either to the crime, both were convicted based on this testimony.

- "Burglaries generally occur in unoccupied dwellings." (p. 11)
- "Experientially, if the offender was a stranger and had departed the residence from this door [the sliding glass door in the family room], he would not [have] bothered closing the door behind him." (p. 19)

These are sweeping and hasty generalizations, respectively. It is true that burglars enter both occupied and unoccupied dwellings with the intent to steal property— not just unoccupied dwellings. However, what is generally true based on SSA Safarik's understanding of the statistics is of no concern regarding the analysis of a particular case. Just because something is common in his experience does not prove that it actually occurred. Arguing in this fashion is a sweeping generalization. His argument is an inductive theory awaiting verification through forensic analysis and testing—not a deductive conclusion. It may also be true that SSA Safarik's experience has been that strangers do not close the door behind them when leaving the scene of a crime, but there is no way to verify it in this case. However, there are also no published studies of this issue, and his experience with residential burglary is unquantified, leaving us to understand that it is characterized by the four years he spent as police investigator in a small police department in Northern California. Arguing from such a narrow experience base, and without the support of the published literature, is a form of hasty generalization. Either way, again, his statement is an inductive theory awaiting verification through forensic analysis and testing—not a deductive conclusion.

False Precision

False precision occurs when an argument treats information as being more precise than it really is. It is characterized by conclusions that are based on imprecise information that must be taken as precise in order to adequately support the conclusion.

Example

Robert Lee Yates, Jr., was a serial murderer who picked up women in the area of Spokane, Washington—many while they were working as prostitutes to pay for their drug addictions (Figure 2.3). Some he frequented regularly and was quite friendly with, giving them rides, advice, and gifts. Others he shot in the head, and then he dumped their bodies in remote outdoor locations. (Except for Melody Murfin, whom he buried beside his house under concrete.)

In *Washington v. Robert Yates* (2003), the Tacoma Police Department contacted profiler Robert D. Keppel, Ph.D., and his longtime friend at the Pierce County district attorney's office, assistant prosecutor Barbara

FIGURE 2.3

Robert Yates, 50, a decorated military pilot, has admitting killing 13 people, 10 of whom were prostitutes. He is one of the worst serial murderers ever identified in the history of Washington State. Excerpt of statement read by Robert Yates to his jury: "I lived a double life. I stayed in denial; denial of my needs, denial that someone, somewhere could help me. Through my denial, because I couldn't face the truth, I thought I could be self-correcting, that if I kept it all to myself, someday it would all go away. That's denial. By my denial, I blinded myself to the truth—the truth that no one is so alone in this world as a denier of God. But that was me, alone and in denial." Robert Yates received the death penalty in October of 2002.

Corey-Boulet.[14] The police wanted Keppel to review 12 homicide cases to determine whether there was a behavioral linkage. Keppel provided his clients with a "modus operandi and signature analysis" report dated March 26, 2002 (Keppel, 2002). That report offers the opinion that the cases are linked in the context of behavioral evidence and in light of the rarity of some of the offense behavior as determined by the computerized Homicide Investigation and Tracking System (HITS) database in Washington State. At the time, Keppel performed a key word search of the 1,541 cases in the database involving women killed between 1981 and 2002.

According to Keppel and Weis (1993, p. 1),

> HITS is a computerized murder and sexual assault investigation program that collects and analyzes information pertaining to specific serious criminal offenses. The system relies on law enforcement agencies in Washington State to voluntarily submit information to HITS investigators.

One of the authors (Turvey) was retained as an expert in criminal profiling and linkage analysis to examine the Yates case, including the results of Keppel's modus operandi and signature analysis report. After requesting and examining a great deal of discovery material related to the HITS program, the author learned that most agencies in Washington State do not actually submit their cases to HITS—which is why the database has so few cases in it. The HITS budget includes subscriptions to major newspapers around Washington State, and HITS analysts cull these publications for cases, which are subsequently entered into HITS in order to fill the database. These and other concerns were expressed in the authors' report, which reads in part (Turvey, 2002):

6. Unreliable HITS Data

   The data in the HITS case database is unreliable (and subsequent conclusions drawn from the data are equally unreliable) for the following reasons:

   A. HITS data uncritically relies on information and opinions provided by the requesting agency as reliable (according to the Memo from John Turner, Chief Criminal Investigator of HITS to Mary Kay High dated April 30th, 2002, p. 2, Q11);
   B. Many of the HITS form fields involve providing crime reconstruction opinions that may be beyond the ken of a given criminal investigator.
   C. Many of the HITS form fields involve subjectively derived profiling-oriented, legal, and psychiatric opinions rather than objective facts (motive, psychopathy, victim risk, face covering, symbolic artifacts, offender anger, offender lifestyle). It should also be noted that the HITS Coding manual uses the term "Crazy People" to define the mental/insane category and inaccurately defines psychopathic as someone that commits psychotic offenses;
   D. The HITS database is apparently populated by case information at various levels of verification and reliability;
   E. The HITS database is populated by an unknown number of unverified cases drawn from media/newspaper accounts (according to HITS SOP, Newspaper Descriptions dated 9/5/95 as well as the Memo from John Turner, Chief Criminal Investigator of HITS to Mary Kay High dated April 30th, 2002, p. 2, Q6);

---

[14] The unfortunate case of assistant prosecutor Barbara Corey-Boulet is discussed in Chapter 12, "Victimology."

7. Unknown Case Linkage Error Rate

   The case linkage error rate for HITS or those using HITS results is unknown.

   A. According to job description information provided in relation to HITS, Tamara Matheny (a HITS Crime Analyst) maintains a monthly log of all positive investigative analysis. I have not seen this log in the discovery material provided.
   B. According to the Memo from John Turner, Chief Criminal Investigator of HITS, to Mary Kay High dated April 30th, 2002 (p. 3, Q17), asking for a showing of the error rate of HITS is too vague. This answer seems evasive. It is apparently not known how often probabilistic HITS linkages are right and how often they are wrong.

   Without this information, the reliability of HITS query results must remain in question.

8. False Negatives

   The false negative case linkage rate for the HITS database is unknown. That is to say, it is not known how often HITS results, or the interpretation of HITS results, have unlinked a known offender and their known offense. This is stated in the Memo from John Turner, Chief Criminal Investigator of HITS, to Mary Kay High dated April 30th, 2002 (p. 3, Q19). Without this information, the reliability of HITS query results must remain question.

9. False Positives

   The false positive case linkage rate for the HITS database is unknown. That is to say, it is not known how often HITS results, or the interpretation of HITS results, have linked a known offender and an offense known to have been committed by another offender. This is stated in the Memo from John Turner, Chief Criminal Investigator of HITS, to Mary Kay High dated April 30th, 2002 (p. 3, Q20). Without this information, the reliability of HITS query results must remain question.

Subsequent to the filing of this report, the court agreed with the author that the HITS database is too unreliable for forensic conclusions, and it barred Keppel's testimony and the related findings.

It bears mentioning that presenting precise statistics or numbers in support of an argument gives the appearance of scientific accuracy when it may not actually be the case. Many find math and statistics overly impressive and become intimidated by those who wield numbers, charts, and graphs with ease. This is especially true with DNA evidence, whose astronomic statistical probabilities are often presented by those without any background in statistics and without a full understanding of the databases that such probabilities are being derived from.

In light of varying DNA databases and subsequent impressive statistics being read in court to bedazzled jurors, and the outright fabrication of statistics related to hair comparisons, the caution offered in Kirk and Kingston (1964, p. 434) is more appropriate now than ever: "Without a firm grasp of the principles involved, the unwary witness can be led into making statements that he cannot properly uphold, especially in the matter of claiming inordinately high probability figures." A more specific criticism of forensic practices was provided in Moenssens (1993):

> Experts use statistics compiled by other experts without any appreciation of whether the database upon which the statistics were formulated fits their own local experience, or how the statistics were compiled. Sometimes these experts, trained in one forensic discipline, have little or no knowledge of the study of probabilities, and never even had a college-level course in statistics.

Those using statistics to support their findings have a responsibility to find out where the statistics come from, how they were derived, and what they mean to the case at hand. This must happen before the user forms conclusions and certainly before he or she testifies in court. The user also has a responsibility to refrain from presenting statistics without understanding or explaining their limitations.

METACOGNITION

Ignorance more frequently begets confidence than does knowledge.

—Charles Darwin (1871, p. 3)

As is discussed throughout this text, the field of criminal profiling is replete with examples of incompetent assessment and illogical inference. Examples include instances where the conclusion drawn about the offender doesn't match the available evidence, where that same evidence is misinterpreted by the profiler, or where profilers have gone beyond their knowledge and skills to provide an inference outside their area of expertise. Some instances are obvious and may be even be characterized as deliberate attempts to misinform or mislead. Others may be the result of bias: A law enforcement profiler may subconsciously tailor an assessment so that its features match a suspect already in custody.

However, not all falsehood and incompetence is deliberate or subconsciously influenced. Many practitioners in the forensic community use inappropriate methods and weak or flawed logic simply because they do not know any better. At the most basic level, these profilers are not aware that what they are doing is inept because they lack the cognitive ability to recognize competency and incompetency alike. This relates to an area of cognitive psychology known as metacognition.

Metacognition (a.k.a. metamemory, metacomprehension, and self-monitoring) refers to "the ability to know how well one is performing, when one is likely to be accurate in judgment, and when one is likely to be in error" (Kruger and Dunning, 1999, p. 1121). At a fundamental level, metacognition can be conceived of as thinking about thinking. For metacognitive ability to engage, there must first be a level of self-awareness: This entails explicit knowledge that one exists separately from other people and full recognition of one's capabilities, strengths, weaknesses, likes, and dislikes. Then practitioners must possess the requisite knowledge relating to their particular field in order to perform competently; they must know the basic principles and practice standards that they should employ and be able to explain why. Finally, they must have the cognitive capacity to stop or pause during the performance of a task or examination, reflect on their work and results, apply critical thinking skills, and critique their own performance to that point.

It has been demonstrated that, with respect to the nature of expertise, novice practitioners tend to possess poorer metacognitive skills than do expert practitioners, for lack of experience confronting their own errors or with problem solving particular to the geography of their domain. Moreover, Kruger and Dunning (1999, p. 1122) suggest that, based on these findings, "unaccomplished individuals do not possess the degree of metacognitive skills necessary for accurate self-assessment that their more accomplished counterparts possess." As Kruger and Dunning (1999, p. 1121) explain,

> [W]hen people are incompetent in the strategies they adopt to achieve success and satisfaction, they suffer a dual burden: Not only do they reach erroneous conclusions and make unfortunate choices, but their incompetence robs them of the ability to realize it. Instead … they are left with the mistaken impression that they are doing just fine.

As discussed in the Preface, we refer to this particular phenomenon as metacognitive dissonance—believing oneself capable of recognizing one's own errors in thinking, reasoning, and learning, despite either a lack of evidence or overwhelming evidence to the contrary. General examples include believing oneself to be knowledgeable despite a demonstrable lack of knowledge; believing oneself to be incapable of error despite the human condition; believing oneself to be logical in one's reasoning despite regular entrapment by logical fallacies; and believing oneself to be completely objective despite the persistence of observer effects. Miller (1993, p. 4) explains: "It is one of the essential features of such incompetence that the person so afflicted is incapable of knowing that he is incompetent. To have such knowledge would already be to remedy a good portion of the offense."

It is a chief purpose of this text to arm criminal profilers with the knowledge that they need to rid themselves of any burdens they suffer related to metacognitive dissonance. Awareness of the problem is a threshold step. The next steps involve taking to heart the tools and cautions that have been and will be further described in application. This includes the full embrace of all that critical thinking, the scientific method, and the science of logic have to offer. It is our hope that in the process, readers learn to recognize and call out the non sequiturs in their own work, as well as that of others. This can and will make the criminal profiling community more competent as a whole and more deserving of the trust that it is regularly afforded.

SUMMARY

Criminal profilers need to understand how valid inferences are made. This requires the use of the scientific method, an applied understanding of the science of logic, and knowing how to know when you are wrong. It also requires some understanding of bias.

The forensic community's affiliation with both law enforcement and the prosecution has fashioned an atmosphere in which an unsettling number of forensic professionals have all but abandoned objectivity and have become completely partial to the prosecution's objectives, goals, and philosophies.

The scientific observer is also inherently imperfect. This stems from the fact that subtle forms of bias, whether conscious or unconscious, can easily contaminate their seemingly objective undertakings. Observer effects are present when the results of a forensic examination are distorted by the context and mental state of the forensic examiner, to include the examiner's subconscious expectations and desires. A strict adherence to, and a full embrace of, the scientific method is the first in a series of steps that can blunt the effects of even the most pervasive forms of bias.

Questions

1. Explain the difference between an *inference* and a *speculation*.
2. Metacognition is the ability to know oneself when one is _____.
3. _____ is the cornerstone of the scientific method.
4. True or False: The goal of the scientific method, in application, is to prove the validity of a hypothesis or theory.
5. If an examiner's methods or results are influenced by the real or perceived expectations of his or her employer, this would be an example of _____.
6. When examiners question the reliability of information or inferences they are expected to rely on in their findings, this is an example of _____.

REFERENCES

Alexandra, A., Matthews, S., Miller, M., 2002. Reasons, Values and Institutions. Tertiary Press, Croyden, Victoria, Australia.

Baker, K., Napier, M., 2003. Criminal Personality Profiling. In: James, S., Nordby, J. (Eds.), Forensic Science: An Introduction to Scientific and Investigative Techniques. CRC Press, Boca Raton, FL.

Bhattacharyya, S., 1958. The Concept of Logic. Philosophy and Phenomenological Research 18 (3), 326–340.

Burch, R., 2003. Study Guide for Hurley's a Concise Introduction to Logic, eighth ed. Thompson-Wadsworth, Ontario, Canada.

Burgess, A.N., Burgess, A.W., Douglas, J., Ressler, R. (Eds.), 1992. Crime Classification Manual. Lexington Books, New York, NY.

California v. Jennifer and Matt Fletcher, 2004. Superior Court, Case No. PA 040748-01, Los Angeles County, CA.

Chisum, W.J., Turvey, B., 2007. Crime Reconstruction. Elsevier Science, Boston, MA.

Cooper, G., 2001. Behavioral Investigative Analysis Report, undated, Borthick v. Benjamin et al. received August 10; on file with the authors.

Darwin, C., 1871. The Descent of Man. John Murray, London, England.

Faigman, D., Kaye, D., Saks, M., et al. (Eds.), 1997. Modern Scientific Evidence: The Law and Science of Expert Testimony, vol. 1. West, St. Paul, MN.

Farber, M., 1942. Logical Systems and the Principles of Logic. Philosophy of Science 9 (1), 40–54.

Federal Bureau of Investigation (FBI), 2002. Uniform Crime Report. Available from www.fbi.gov/ucr/cius_02/html/web/index.html (accessed 23. 09. 04.).

Gross, H., 1924. Criminal Investigation. Sweet & Maxwell, London, England.

Gross, H., 1968. Criminal Psychology. Patterson Smith, Montclair, NJ.

Keppel, R., 2002. Modus Operandi and Signature Analysis, report regarding Washington v. Robert Yates, dated March 26; on file with authors.

Keppel, R.D., Weis, J., 1993. Time and Distance as Solvability Factors in Murder Cases. Journal of Forensic Science 39 (2), 286-401.

Kirk, P., Thornton, J.I., 1974. Crime Investigation. John Wiley & Sons, Inc, New York, NY.

Kirk, P., Kingston, C., 1964. Evidence Evaluation and Problems in General Criminalistics. Journal Forensic Science 9, 434–437.

Knight, R., Prentky, R., 1990. Classifying Sexual Offenders: The Development and Corroboration of Taxonomic Models. In: Marshal, W., Laws, D., Barbaree, H. (Eds.), Handbook of Sexual Assault. Plenum Press, New York, NY.

Krueger, J., Dunning, D., 1999. Unskilled and Unaware of It: How Difficulties in Recognizing One's Own Incompetence Lead to Inflated Self-Assessments. Journal of Personality and Social Psychology 77 (6), 121–134.

Lee, H., DeForest, P., Gaensslen, R., 1983. Forensic Science: An Introduction to Criminalistics. McGraw-Hill, New York, NY.

McInerney, D.Q., 2004. Being Logical: A Guide to Good Thinking. Random House, New York, NY.

McNamara, J., 2000. Criminal Investigative Analysis report, Amy J. Blumberg—Victim, USDOJ: FBI, February 9.

Miller, M., 2003. Crime Scene Investigation. In: James, S., Nordby, J. (Eds.), Forensic Science: An Introduction to Scientific and Investigative Techniques. CRC Press, Boca Raton, FL.

Miller, W.I., 1993. Humiliation. Cornell University Press, Ithaca, NY.

Moenssens, A., 1993. Novel Scientific Evidence in Criminal Cases: Some Words of Caution. Journal of Criminal Law and Criminology 84 (1), 1–21.

Neisser, U., 1976. Cognition and Reality: Principles and Implications of Cognitive Psychology. W. H. Freeman & Co, New York, NY.

O'Hara, C., 1970. Fundamentals of Criminal Investigation, second ed. Charles C Thomas, Springfield, IL.

Paul, R., Scriven, M., 2004. Defining Critical Thinking, Foundation for Critical Thinking. www.criticalthinking.org/aboutCT/definingCT.shtml.

Popper, K., 1960. On the Sources of Knowledge and of Ignorance. In: Proceedings of the British Academy of Sciences. pp. 39–71.

Popper, K., 1963. Conjectures and Refutations. Routledge & Keagan Paul, London, England.

Popper, K., 2003. The Logic of Scientific Discovery. Routledge classics, London, England.

Risinger, D.M., Saks, M.J., Thompson, W.C., Rosenthal, R., 2002. The Daubert/Kumho Implications of Observer Effects in Forensic Science: Hidden Problems of Expectation and Suggestion. California Law Review 90 (1), 1–56.

Rosenthal, R., 1966. Experimenter Effects in Behavioral Research. Appleton-Century-Crofts, New York, NY.

Safarik, M., 2002. Criminal Investigative Analysis Report, California v. Jennifer and Matt Fletcher, June 17; on file with the authors.

Saks, M.J., 2003. Ethics in Forensic Science: Professional Standards for the Practice of Criminalistics. Jurimetrics: Journal of Law, Science and Technology 43, 359–363.

Starrs, J.E., 1991. The Forensic Scientist and the Open Mind. Science and Justice 31, 111–134.

Tennessee v. William R. Stevens, 2001. No.M1999-02067-CCA-R3-DD, May 30.

Thornton, J.I., 1997a. Courts of Law v. Courts of Science: A Forensic Scientist's Reaction to Daubert. Shepard's Expert Sci. Evid. Q. 1 (3), 475 484–485.

Thornton, J.I., 1997b. The General Assumptions and Rationale of Forensic Identification. In: Faigman, D., Kaye, D., Saks, M., et al. (Eds.), Modern Scientific Evidence: The Law and Science of Expert Testimony, vol. 2. West, St. Paul, MN.

Turvey, B., 1999. Criminal Profiling: An Introduction to Behavioral Evidence Analysis. Academic Press, London, England.

Turvey, B., 2002. Report regarding Washington v. Robert Yates, May 28, 2002; on file with the author.

Turvey, B., 2007. Forensic examination report, Illinois v. Anthony Mertz, June 17.

The USS *Iowa*, 1990. The USS *Iowa*: Guilt by Gestalt, Congressional Testimony. Harper's Magazine 25–28 March.

Walton, D., 1989. Informal Logic: A Handbook for Critical Argumentation. Cambridge University Press, New York, NY.

CHAPTER 3

Alternative Methods of Criminal Profiling

Wayne A. Petherick and Brent E. Turvey

CONTENTS

Criminal Profiling: An Introduction to Behavioral Evidence Analysis, Fourth Edition

KEY TERMS

Availability heuristic	Distance decay	Least effort principle
Criminal investigative	Geographical profiling	Nomothetic
analysis (CIA)	Idiographic	Nomothetic offender profiles
Diagnostic evaluation (DE)	Investigative psychology (IP)	Organized/disorganized typology

There are two ways of viewing the application of logic to the development of scientific knowledge (Novick, 1988, p. 34). The first takes a position that facts, appropriately shaped and organized, will divulge their intrinsic connections to each other. In this system of reasoning, such facts are assumed to be evidence of inherent truths separate from the desires of those examining them. Further, in this system of reasoning, observations are considered the purest, most honest form of study. It is consequently believed that one should observe the facts and not poison their meaning with the construction of inductive hypotheses that go beyond the observable.

The second view takes the position that science requires the imposition of our hypotheses and theories on the facts to give them meaning—that our speculations bring order to chaos. In fact, it was Charles Darwin who wrote in 1861 (p. 34):

> About thirty years ago, there was much talk that geologists ought only to observe and not theorize; and I well remember someone saying that at this rate a man might as well go into a gravel-pit and count the pebbles and describe the colors. How odd it is that anyone should not see that all observation must be for or against some view if it is to be of any service!

In this text, we take a view that is closely aligned to Darwin's. That is to say, the study of criminal behavior, and the search for related patterns, is a directed study. It is governed by an understanding of how and why people think and act. When confronted with a particular crime, it is the job of the criminal profiler to draw from this knowledge to speculate and theorize using the factual and testable elements established in a particular case. However, knowledge about crime and criminal behavior is useful only inasmuch as it might help us render informed theories about what may have occurred in a particular case. In keeping with the scientific method, the formation of these theories is not the end of a profiler's analysis but the beginning. Only through testing and attempts to falsify do theories become meaningful when applied to interpretations of patterns in a specific case. Each time we succeed at failing to disprove something, we come closer to understanding the meaning beneath the specific patterns that we find. Unfortunately, this basic construct of scientific thought and reason evades many in the criminal profiling community.

In the previous chapter, we discussed how valid inferences are made and how scientific knowledge is built. In this chapter, we discuss the two different types of knowledge that this creates: idiographic and nomothetic. We also discuss the major styles of nomothetic profiling, with an exploration of their strengths and weaknesses.

IDIOGRAPHIC VERSUS NOMOTHETIC STUDY

In terms of the study of crime and criminals, or any subject for that matter, there are two major approaches to research and subsequent knowledge building. The first is *nomothetic* knowledge, referring to the study of the abstract: examining groups and universal laws.[1] The second is *idiographic* knowledge, referring to the study of the concrete: examining individuals and their actual qualities. Idiographic study concentrates on specific cases and the unique traits or functioning of individuals.

According to Hurlburt and Knapp (2006, p. 287), "Psychologists use the term 'idiographic' to refer to the characteristics of unique individuals and 'nomothetic' to refer to universal characteristics." Moreover, they explain that these terms have been a part of the American psychological landscape since as early as 1898. Consequently, these concepts have a history of application that we can learn from.

Again, nomothetic studies are those conducted on groups, and idiographic studies are those conducted on individuals. In terms of criminal profiling, it is fair to say that there are nomothetic methods and idiographic methods. A primary goal of idiographic (e.g., deductive) criminal profiling, as is discussed in subsequent chapters, is to study and determine the unique characteristics of the particular offender(s) responsible for a specific crime. The primary goal of nomothetic criminal profiling studies is to accumulate general, typical, common, or averaged characteristics of offender groups. These characteristics are abstract in the sense that they do not necessarily exist in each individual case—they represent the theoretically possible and, at best, probable. Problems arise when nomothetic methods are used inappropriately to make overly confident inferences or conclusive interpretations about individual offenders—in other words, when broad nomothetic knowledge is applied to answer narrow idiographic questions.

There are several ways to conceptualize the differences between idiographic and nomothetic profiling techniques. In general, the authors like to use the example of 20 mobile phones in 20 unmarked boxes. To learn the contents of a specific box (i.e., box #20), you may approach the problem using either nomothetic or idiographic study.

Nomothetically speaking, you can use your experience with previous mobile phones and conclude that box #20 will likely contain a unit consistent with phones you've owned or seen in the past. But in reality, these characteristics rely heavily on you, your preferences, and your available memory.[2] Ultimately, they will have nothing to do with what is more or less likely to be in box #20. If you like black phones and have perhaps always gravitated toward darker colors when they are available, for example, your experience will not lead you to the correct inference if the phone is pink.

Also nomothetically, you can approach the problem in a more organized and pedantic fashion. You can open boxes #1 through #19, examine the features of every phone you find, and then create a list of common or recurring characteristics. Using this list, you can inductively theorize about the likely characteristics of mobile phone #20. You can present this inference using computer models with tables, charts, and graphs. You can even use math to generate probabilities based on the sample you studied. Unfortunately, despite all the attention to detail, the results will be no more useful than using your experience, because any interpretation about what might be in one box based on examining the contents of the other boxes is a prediction, not a conclusion. It is an informed prediction, but it is a prediction nonetheless. Approaching the same problem from an idiographic viewpoint, you can open box #20 and examine the contents directly, interpreting the characteristics irrespective of all other phones.

---

[1] This should go without saying, but not all knowledge derived nomothetically results in universal laws or even useful generalizations. Occasionally, the best we may hope for is to develop a theory or theories about the group under study, and the theory may not apply outside of the study group. Knowing the difference, and saying it out loud, is an indication of scientific honesty.

[2] This is referred to as the *availability heuristic*, which is discussed in the preface to the third edition of this book. It involves answering a question of probability by asking whether examples come readily to mind. What we recall becomes what we believe is likely. This is a common yet grave metacognitive breakdown.

In the end, nomothetic study will yield general knowledge about mobile phones that may or may not be applicable to solving the particular problem of identifying the contents of an unopened box. It will certainly assist researchers who need to discuss and describe group trends that may be found. However, in answering questions about a specific problem or situation separate from the group, nomothetic knowledge fails. It may be used appropriately to help generate theories, but nomothetic study is not fit for rendering conclusions that are phone specific: a phone may or may not have a physical keypad; it may or may not have a camera; it may or may not have a clamshell design; battery talk time varies; power supply varies; service range varies; everything varies. There are just too many types of mobile phones with too many combinations of variable features to make an accurate let alone useful inference about the contents of the last box using nomothetic knowledge (Figure 3.1).

Even the notion that the unopened box contains a mobile phone is in fact an inductive theory based on nomothetic study and knowledge. You've been told the box has a phone in it, but until the box has been opened, the box's content is an assumption. The unopened box may contain a cell phone, a rock, or nothing at all. Until the box is opened and examined, theories about its contents are only that.

Now consider that we are dealing not with boxes and phones but with crime scenes and offenders. Inside each scene is contained the behavioral patterns of a particular offense. If we study 20 crime scenes as a group (nomothetically), looking for common or recurrent patterns, we will learn little about the uniquely integrated expressions of the individual offenders responsible for each crime. The result will be averaged

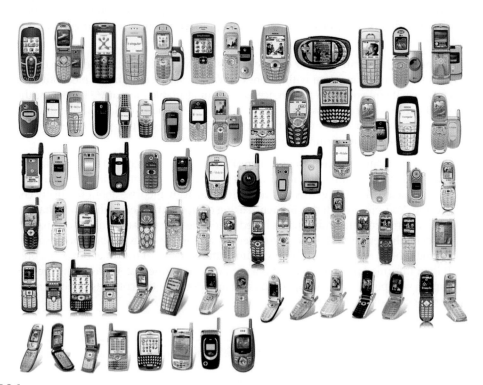

FIGURE 3.1
Modern cell phones come in a wide variety of shapes, styles, models, colors, sizes, and configurations with a seemingly endless combination of features.

But is criminal investigative analysis actually a form criminal profiling? The literature is in fact unanimous that, yes, it is. Depue et al. (1995, p. 115) states explicitly that the term criminal investigative analysis is merely an FBI replacement term for criminal profile:[8]

> A criminal investigative analysis (CIA) of an illegal and violent act may give the client agency a variety of useful information depending on the service requested. Previously termed "psychological profiling" and "criminal personality profiling," the term "criminal investigative analysis" was coined to differentiate the procedure from that used by mental health professionals.

This is also discussed in TaFoya (2002, para. 1), which states "Criminal Investigative Analysis is the terminology used by the FBI to describe what is more popularly known as Profiling—psychological or criminal."[9] Geberth (1996) offers a similar definition in his glossary of investigative terms (p. 841):

> Criminal Investigative Analysis—The current term utilized by the FBI Behavioral Sciences Unit at Quantico to define their Psychological Profile and Criminal Personality Profiles of Offenders.

It is also helpful to consider that the Royal Canadian Mounted Police (RCMP), which is currently in charge of the International Criminal Investigative Analysis Fellowship (ICIAF) and related training efforts, offers the following definition:[10]

> Criminal Investigative Analysis (CIA), also known as criminal profiling, is an investigative tool used within the law enforcement community to help solve violent crimes. The analysis is based on a review of evidence from the crime scene and from witnesses and victims. The analysis is done from both an investigative and a behavioural perspective. The analysis can provide insight into the unknown offender (characteristics and traits) as well as investigative suggestions and strategies for interviews and trial.

While this may seem a minor point, it can be significant to the admissibility of a given profiler's expert testimony—as is discussed in later chapters. For our purposes here, it is enough to understand that criminal investigative analysis is a method of criminal profiling. Any practitioner suggesting otherwise is either ignorant of the literature or being intellectually dishonest.

But how is criminal investigative analysis a nomothetic method of criminal profiling? This has to do with the fact that it is based primarily on knowledge built from studying groups rather than individuals—one group of offenders, to be more precise. The CIA method arose primarily from the FBI's Criminal Profiling Project, a study of 36 incarcerated offenders and their 118 respective victims conducted between 1979 and 1983.[11] The project's research focused on the development of offender classifications from an examination of various features of their crimes (see Burgess and Ressler, 1985). The goal was to determine whether there were any consistent features across offenses that might be useful in classifying future offenders (Petherick, 2005). A number of FBI-backed publications have resulted from this research, including Burgess, Hartman, Ressler, Douglas, and McCormack (1986); Ressler and Burgess (1985); Ressler, Burgess, and Douglas (1988); Ressler, Burgess, Douglas, Hartman, and D'Agostino (1986); and Ressler, Burgess, Hartman, Douglas, and McCormack (1986).

---

[8] The authors of this work (Roger Depue, John Douglas, Roy Hazelwood, and Robert Ressler) are all retired FBI agents who worked in its respective profiling units, and they are among the collective fathers of FBI criminal profiling methodology. If nothing else, they would at least be considered experts at explaining the origins of the terms used by the FBI.

[9] William L. TaFoya, Ph.D., is a retired FBI agent and was assigned to the FBI Academy from 1980 to 1990, where he worked for the then Behavioral Sciences Unit.

[10] Provided on the RCMP website at www.rcmp-grc.gc.ca/techops/crim_prof_e.htm. Page updated on April 20, 2005.

[11] This project was funded by the National Institute of Justice from 1982 to 1985 (Burgess and Ressler, 1985).

On a methodological level, the original 36-offender study was heavily criticized by the peer reviewers involved in the project (Fox, 2004). The sample size was small (N = 36), and not all of the offenders were serial in nature. Of the 36 offenders in the sample, 25 were serial murderers and 11 were sexual murderers who had committed either a single homicide, double homicide, or spree murder (Ressler and Burgess, 1985). Putting them in one group seems counterintuitive. Even the authors commented (p. 7):

> Several limitations of the study are to be noted. First, the study population of 36 offenders and 118 victims yielded a relatively small database. This data was further reduced by incomplete or missing data for some variables. Incomplete records, conflicting responses, and offender unwillingness to respond to certain questions all contributed to the missing data situation.
>
> As a result, some variables did not have sufficient responses for analysis, with the multivariate analysis most severely impacted. We performed a multivariate analysis to compare a set of crime scene variables with a set of profile variables. As a profiling objective is to proceed from crime scene data to a likely criminal profile, it would be useful to find the minimal number of variables that, when considered jointly, predict the profile characteristics. However, because of the limited database, results of the multivariate analysis appeared to have little utility and, as a result, are not presented.

The interviewers relied heavily on the self-report of the participants, potentially biasing the information on which the study was based, although perhaps most importantly, no inter-rater reliability was used to determine the degree to which discrete characteristics were judged. FBI agents who could not decide which category an offender fit into were told to force them into one category or another (Ressler and Burgess, 1985). Homant and Kennedy (1998) provide another aspect to the critique, in that the classification was seemingly made on the basis of information about the offender and the crime scene involved. As Burgess and Ressler (1985) noted, the study was exploratory and the concepts had been in use for some time (see Hazelwood and Douglas, 1980). Therefore, the results may actually be a self-fulfilling prophecy rather than reflecting any empirically valid classification system useful in identifying the personality and behavioral characteristics that are the cornerstone of the offender profile. If the agents had something in mind when conducting an interview, it may have introduced a level of cognitive bias that would make it easier to find the characteristics expected. Therefore, subsequent discovery that the classifications led to significant differences on a number of crime scene variables would be circular. Additionally, the study has never been replicated on an international level, so its application outside of the United States is questionable (Petherick, 2003; Woodworth and Porter, 1999).

Although widespread validation has not been undertaken, some attempts have been made to apply the CIA methodology to cases of serial sexual homicide of elderly females (Safarik et al., 2000). The data for this study were 33 cases of sexual assault for which an offender had been caught where the victim was over 60 years of age. The offenders had all committed at least two assaults. Using statistically averaged offender characteristics, the authors claim an 80% to 85% accuracy rate (which is in line with Pinizzotto's [1984] claim of accuracy for the BSU profilers). However, while the authors discuss the relatively limited frequency of elderly sexual assault (only about 2% to 3% of assaults in the United States per year are on elderly females), the small sample size may represent a problem in determining the degree to which these results apply to a broader sample. This may be particularly true since the research sample was less than 10% of the annual number of assaults involving elderly female victims. What's more, there is no discussion or rationale for the inclusion of cases in the study—it is not clear how they were selected. This, too, may affect the results.

However, it appears that small sample size, an issue also noted in Beasley (2004), is only one of a number of criticisms leveled at the research used to develop CIA. Consider, for example, the main critique presented by Canter et al. (2004). This latter study, applying the method to another population of serial offenders, provides the most damning indictment of criminal investigative analysis to date (p. 296):

> From the start, then, they were illustrating how certain offense behavior and certain offender characteristics combined in their sample. They never set out to test the discriminatory power of their dichotomy on a sample that was not specifically drawn up to illustrate this dichotomy.

While the results from Canter and colleagues were quite extensive and detailed, some of the major findings are summarized as follows:

- Almost twice as many disorganized crime scene actions as organized can be readily identified, suggesting the disorganized category is more detailed.
- The frequency varies in the sample from the 91 cases in which the victim was kept alive during the sexual acts through to the 3 cases in which there was dismemberment. This suggests that, at least in some situations, few criteria will be present.
- There are some indications that certain features of the organized category may be more indicative of base rate features in serial murder rather than discrete variables useful for distinguishing between organized and disorganized features.
- Disorganized aspects co-occur even less frequently than organized ones.

ORGANIZED VERSUS DISORGANIZED

One result of the Criminal Profiling Project and the subsequent publications cited earlier was the further development of the FBI's organized/disorganized dichotomy. This system instructs profilers to classify offenders by virtue of the level of sophistication, planning, and competence evident in the crime scene. It is easy to teach and easy to use.

Despite past suggestions that the organized/disorganized terminology was an outgrowth of the FBI's 36-offender study published in 1985, the terminology was actually in use before then. The terms first appeared in their original forms, *organized nonsocial* and *disorganized asocial,* in *The Lust Murderer* (see Hazelwood and Douglas, 1980). Therefore, the 36-offender study is best thought of as further developing an existing concept rather than generating a new one.

The organized/disorganized crime scene classification theory represents a conceptual division, most commonly referred to as a *dichotomy*, a term that means a division into two polarized or contradictory parts or opinions. The FBI's then Behavioral Science Unit (BSU) developed the organized/disorganized dichotomy in the 1980s as an attempt to more effectively communicate and teach profiling tools.[12] The organized/disorganized dichotomy, arrived at through "years of experience" (Ressler et al., 1988, p. 121), was intended to simplify the language of crime scene profiling for unsophisticated law enforcement agencies requesting profiles. It also lent itself effectively as a teaching tool for FBI students of criminal profiling techniques—students who have been almost exclusively law enforcement.

As Ressler and Shachtman (1992, pp. 113–114) explain,

> Amassing this knowledge was one thing. Communicating it to our audience—those police officers who sought our help in tracking down violent criminals—was another. To characterize the types of

---

[12] This eight-man unit is currently referred to as the Behavioral Analysis Unit. Before that it was referred to as the Profiling and Behavioral Analysis Unit and the Behavioral Sciences Unit.

offenders for police and other law enforcement people, we needed to have a terminology that was not based on psychiatric jargon. It wouldn't do much good to say to a police officer that he was looking for a psychotic personality if that police officer had no training in psychology; we needed to speak to the police in terms that they could understand and that would assist them in their searches for killers, rapists, and other violent criminals. Instead of saying that a crime scene showed evidence of a psychopathic personality, we began to tell the police officer that such a particular crime scene was "organized," and so was the likely offender, while another and its perpetrator might be "disorganized," when mental disorder was present.

It is a simple concept. An organized crime scene (characteristics shown in Table 3.1) is one with evidence of planning, where the victim is a targeted stranger, the crime scene reflects overall control, there are restraints used, and aggressive acts occur before death. This suggests that the offender is organized (characteristics shown in Table 3.2), with the crime scene being a reflection of the personality of an offender, meaning the offender will have average to above average intelligence, will be socially competent, will prefer skilled work, will have a high birth order, will have a controlled mood during the crime, and may also use alcohol with the crime.

A disorganized crime scene shows spontaneity, where the victim or location is known, the crime scene is random and sloppy, there is sudden violence, minimal restraints are used, and there are sexual acts after death. This is again suggestive of the personality of the offender, with a disorganized offender having below average intelligence, being socially inadequate, having a low birth order, having an anxious mood during the crime, and using minimal amounts of alcohol. Despite having these discrete classifications, it is generally held that no offender will fit neatly into either category, with most offenders being somewhere between the two: these offenders are called "mixed."[13]

This classification system is easy to use and can be applied almost without any deep case analysis or thinking, making it especially seductive to those without formal education in, or knowledge of, human psychology

| Table 3.1 Crime Scene Characteristics of the Organized and Disorganized Offender ||
Psychopathic (Organized) Crime Scene Characteristics	Psychotic (Disorganized) Crime Scene Characteristics
Offense planned	Offense spontaneous
Victim is a targeted stranger	Victim or location known
Personalizes victim	Depersonalizes victim
Controlled conversation	Minimal conversation
Crime scene reflects overall control	Crime scene random and sloppy
Demands submissive victim	Sudden violence to victim
Restraints used	Minimal restraints used
Aggressive acts before death	Sexual acts after death
Body hidden	Body left in plain view
Weapon/evidence absent	Evidence/weapon often present
Transports victim	Body left at death scene
From Ressler and Burgess, 1985.	

[13] As explained in Burgess et al. (1992, p. 9): "It should be emphasized that the crime scene rarely will be completely organized or disorganized. It is more likely to be somewhere on a continuum between the two extremes of the orderly, neat crime scene and the disarrayed, sloppy one."

Table 3.2 Offender Characteristics of the Organized and Disorganized Offender	
Psychopathic (Organized) Offender Characteristics	**Psychotic (Disorganized) Offender Characteristics**
Average to above average intelligence	Below average intelligence
Socially competent	Socially inadequate
Skilled work preferred	Unskilled work
Sexually competent	Sexually incompetent
High birth order	Low birth order
Father's work stable	Father's work unstable
Inconsistent childhood discipline	Harsh discipline as a child
Controlled mood during the crime	Anxious mood during crime
Use of alcohol with crime	Minimal use of alcohol
Precipitating situational stress	Minimal situational stress
Living with partner	Living alone
Mobility, with car in good condition	Lives/works near the crime scene
Follows crime in news media	Minimal interest in the news media
May change jobs or leave town	Significant behavior change
From Ressler and Burgess, 1985.	

(i.e., the majority of law enforcement). In fact, that is the type of analyst it was designed for. The organized/disorganized dichotomy gives undereducated law enforcement personnel ready access to unsophisticated, simple labels with important forensic mental health and diagnostic implications. This is not necessarily a good thing.

The dichotomy is the epitome of an inductive/nomothetic profiling approach. If a crime scene has organized characteristics (determined by a group study examining shared scene traits), it is reasoned that the offender must also be organized and share the characteristics of other organized offenders (determined by group study examining shared offender traits). If a crime scene has disorganized characteristics, it is conversely assumed that the offender must also be disorganized.

The profiling implications of this classification system are that disorganized offenders are inferred to be psychotic. That is to say, by virtue of a messy crime scene, offenders are determined to be suffering from a mental illness that afflicts them with a psychosis. Because they leave behind lots of evidence, there is thought to be a deterioration of normal intellectual and therefore social functioning, and a partial or complete withdrawal from reality.

Conversely, organized offenders are determined to be psychopathic. That is to say, by virtue of a relatively clean crime scene they are thought not to be suffering from a mental illness that afflicts them with a psychosis. They are determined to be aware of, and to understand, the nature and quality of their behavior.

This author does not agree with or advocate the use of the organized/disorganized dichotomy, because it is a false dichotomy, arising from mistaken ideas about the developmental nature of criminal behavior and the role of crime reconstruction. There are some straightforward arguments supporting this position.

First, the majority of crime scenes present somewhere on a continuum between the two extreme classifications of organized and disorganized, not as simply one or the other. The FBI's Crime Classification Manual (CCM)

(Burgess et al., 1992, p. 9) states this plainly. This fact has not kept the ignorant, as well as the unqualified, from attempting to cram crime scenes, and subsequent offenders, into these extreme classifications. Clearly, this has been one of the most overlooked passages in the CCM.

Second, only a competent forensic analysis, performed by qualified forensic scientists, can give insight into how and why a crime scene presents the way that it does in a given case (the process of determining what happened in a crime scene is generally referred to as *crime reconstruction*). The amount of evidence left behind or not left behind must be viewed in the context of a dynamic series of events. It cannot be interpreted at a glance through an isolating construct by the untrained.

Third, it is not generally possible to discriminate between the origins of behavior that can result in "disorganization" at a crime scene. Consequently, crime scenes involving the following can be difficult to distinguish with respect to their shared "disorganized" characteristics: domestic/intimate homicide involving rage, drug/alcohol-related homicide, and homicide committed by the mentally ill. Given the alternate possibilities, inferring that mental illness must be a cause or a factor is not appropriate. This issue is discussed in more detail in Chapter 10, "Criminal Motivation."

Fourth, a crime scene evidencing organized characteristics does not automatically suggest a psychopathic offender. As already mentioned, psychopathy is a specific personality disorder. It is not evidenced merely by a lack of psychotic behavior.

Fifth, labeling an offender using the dichotomy may cause a failure to account for an offender's development over time. Some offenders become more competent and skilled over time, leaving less evidence and engaging in more precautionary acts. Other offenders may become less competent and skillful over time, decompensating by virtue of a deteriorating mental state or increased use of controlled substances.

Sixth, and related to the second and fifth arguments, the organized/disorganized dichotomy inappropriately hinges offender classification on modus operandi (MO) considerations. It takes into account what appears to have occurred physically, but does not take into account why it occurred. This bears pointing out because those who constructed the dichotomy at the NCAVC know the difference between offender MO and signature behaviors, and they understand the investigative dangers of ignoring signature considerations. However, paradoxically, they have constructed and still advocate a crime scene classification tool that appears to completely ignore those concerns.

Seventh, an ethical danger of the organized/disorganized dichotomy is that it essentially and undeservedly empowers those who use it to speak from a clinical perspective on issues that have courtroom relevance. This is evidenced by the following passage from Ressler and Shachtman (1992, pp. 3–4):

> Looking at the crime-scene photographs and the police reports, it was apparent to me that this was not a crime committed by an "organized" killer who stalked his victims, was methodical in how he went about his crimes, and took care to avoid leaving clues to his own identity. No, from the appearance of the crime scene, it was obvious to me that we were dealing with a "disorganized" killer, a person who had a full-blown and serious mental illness.

The author of this statement presumes the ability to essentially diagnose a mental illness without the benefit of clinical interviews, years of clinical training, or a competent forensic reconstruction of what is actually in the photos, to say nothing of actually meeting the offender in person before rendering such an important clinical opinion. This is not a legitimate forensic practice.

And eighth, the classification of a scene and offender as organized or disorganized is rarely presented as merely a theory, as all nomothetic knowledge should be.

The current prevalence of use of the FBI method may be due to the mythology surrounding the bureau itself (see Jenkins, 1994). As Canter et al. (2004, pp. 294–295) observe,

> It is important to draw attention to the source and status of the reports typically used to inform criminal investigative analysis. … This information is most often disseminated in the form of popular books, clearly intended for a non-technical and inexpert audience, rather than in peer-reviewed journals. As a consequence it is less likely to be subjected to informed examination and the form of critical consideration usual within a professional or scholarly framework. However, if anything, this enhances rather than detracts from the wide uptake of these ideas by law enforcement practitioners who have no scientific training. Furthermore the mechanism, that Canter and Young (2003) has called the "Hollywood effect," whereby loosely formulated and often unsubstantiated theories and models are featured in widely disseminated movies and given extra credibility by such broadcast, means that these ideas can become part of apparently accepted expertise that juries and other lay groups will be prepared to accept. This also can lead to the possibility that the ideas may be incorporated into practice casually and applied in a less systematic manner than their original authors had intended. The organized/disorganized dichotomy has probably suffered this fate, being cited in a number of Hollywood films and drawn upon as a valid model by police investigators around the world.

The popularity of the FBI method may also be a function of its simplicity; as we've discussed, it requires little training or knowledge to apply and provides prefabricated templates of offender characteristics.

Despite having being entirely debunked at this point as a false dichotomy, the organized/disorganized classification remains in wide use today by nomothetic profilers who may in fact be ignorant of the current state of the literature.[14]

The Stages of Criminal Investigative Analysis (CIA)

CIA is ideally comprised of a number of steps or stages in which information about the crime is gathered and determinations are made about its relevance and meaning. Despite the fact that an articulated methodology is available, there is some anecdotal evidence to suggest that practitioners of the FBI method do not adhere strictly to all steps or stages, and that they may not be qualified to perform certain analyses proposed as part of the method (e.g., crime scene reconstruction; see Chisum, 2000; Superior Court of California, 1999).

Ressler et al. (1988) suggest that CIA is a six-step method, although in reality it has five steps, with the sixth step being the arrest of an offender, if identified. The first five steps are profiling inputs, decision process models, crime assessment, criminal profile, and investigation. The final phase (ostensibly the sixth) is apprehension.

In another article preceding *Sexual Homicides: Patterns and Motives* (Ressler et al. 1988), Douglas and Burgess (1986, p. 9) suggest a seven-step process, which is "quite similar to that used by clinicians to make a diagnosis and treatment plan." The seven steps are as follows:

1. Evaluation of the criminal act itself
2. Comprehensive evaluation of the specifics of the crime scene(s)
3. Comprehensive analysis of the victim
4. Evaluation of preliminary police reports

---

[14] For a study that debunks this dichotomy beyond the discussion provided here, see Canter et al. (2004).

5. Evaluation of the medical examiner's autopsy protocol
6. Development of profile with critical offender characteristics
7. Investigative suggestions predicated on the construction of the profile

Criminal Investigative Analysis: Efficacy in Casework

The profiling community has roundly criticized criminal investigative analysis as both methodologically deficient and outdated—yet it is still in wide use. As explained in the second edition of this text (Turvey, 2002, p. 349):

> FBI profiling has failed detailed peer reviews of both casework and publications. This includes a peer review of the FBI's Criminal Profiling Project involving the study of 36 incarcerated offenders and their 118 respective victims (Darkes et al., 1993; Turvey, 1999). According to Nobile (1989), "the Justice Department rejected the study for government publication after outside reviewers flayed its statistics and methodology." Despite the utter failure of their methodology in this study, FBI agents sought publication elsewhere, in Ressler et al. (1988). This study is foundational for many current FBI profiling concepts, methods, and research models.

Specifically, FBI-trained profilers have been criticized by the court and independent peer reviewers for the following practices (Darkes et al., 1993; Homant and Kennedy, 1998; *New Jersey v. Fortin*, 2000; *Pennsylvania v. Christopher Distefano*, 1999; *Tennessee v. William R. Stevens*, 2001; Turvey, 1999):

Lack of reliability
Unsystematic gathering of offender biographical material for research/study
Uncritical reliance upon offender interviews as the source of data worthy of research/study
Failure to use appropriate control groups
Uncritical reliance upon law enforcement theories and opinions as fact
Treatment of investigative hypotheses and theory as fact
Failure to be forthcoming about the weaknesses of opinions and conclusions
Failure to compare profiles with actual offenders when outcomes are known
Failure to base opinions on data susceptible to testing
Cronyism (evident in both the community and the published research)

Moreover, according to Howard Teten (the first FBI profiler), in an FBI study of 192 cases in which profiling was performed, 88 cases were solved. Of those 88 cases, the profile helped with the identification of the suspect only 17% of the time (15 cases). So the known efficacy rate for FBI profiling (criminal investigative analysis) is 15 out of 192 (Teten, 1995, p. 45).

Of course, the FBI is not unaware of the limitations of their profiling methodology. According to Hazelwood (1995, pp. 176–177), a criminal profile, also known as criminal investigative analysis (Depue et al., 1995, p. 115), is an investigative tool only. Therefore, the following disclaimer should precede each such report prepared by members of the FBI's Behavioral Analysis Unit:

> It should be noted that the attached analysis is not a substitute for a thorough and well-planned investigation and should not be considered all-inclusive. The information provided is based upon reviewing, analyzing, and researching criminal cases similar to the case submitted by the requesting agency. The final analysis is based upon probabilities. Note, however, that no two criminal acts or criminal personalities are exactly alike and, therefore, the offender may not always fit the profile in every category.

The caution demonstrated in the disclaimer is explained in Depue et al. (1995, p. 125), where it is stated that:

> CIA [criminal investigative analysis] and profiling should be used to augment proven investigative techniques and must not be allowed to replace those methods; to do so would be counterproductive to the goal of identifying the unknown offender.

The authors have read the disclaimer on FBI profiles when reviewing criminal investigative analysis reports for court purposes. However, they have made note that the disclaimer is regularly absent when FBI profilers submit CIA reports intended for trial, when expert testimony may be needed. It could be argued that the inclusion of the disclaimer at trial might hamper admissibility, because it addresses the issue of limited reliability. The exclusion of the disclaimer seems significant, however, as the conclusions are based on the same methodology as reports prepared by FBI profilers during an investigation.

DIAGNOSTIC EVALUATIONS (DE)

The term *diagnostic evaluations* does not refer to or represent a single profiling method or unified approach. It is instead a generic description of the services offered by medical and mental health professionals who rely on clinical experience when giving profiling opinions about offenders, crimes scenes, or victims. Diagnostic evaluations are done on an as-needed basis, usually as one part of a broad range of services being offered. As discussed in Chapter 1, some of the earliest examples of profiling available are diagnostic evaluations conducted by forensic psychiatrists.[15]

In a study of the range of services offered by police psychologists, for example, Bartol (1996) found that on average, 2% of the total monthly workload of in-house psychologists was profiling, and that 3.4% of the monthly workload of part-time consultants was criminal profiling. These results are not particularly interesting, other than they demonstrate that a percentage of profiling is being done by psychologists. However, the fact that 70% of the police psychologists surveyed did not feel comfortable with profiling and felt that the practice was extremely questionable is very interesting. Furthermore (Bartol, 1996, p. 79),

> One well-known police psychologist, with more than 20 years of experience in the field, considered criminal profiling "virtually useless and potentially dangerous." Many of the respondents wrote that much more research needs to be done before the process becomes a useful tool.

The authors of this work have also noted that more than a few forensic pathologists have shown a willingness to engage in profiling-related interpretation of victim and offender behavior, either in a didactic written form as part of the medicolegal death investigation or as part of courtroom testimony when asked to support expert opinions (Figure 3.2).

Without a clear and identifiable process, profiles based on diagnostic evaluations are heavily idiosyncratic, relying to a large degree on the specific background of the clinical profiler. One's education, training, and experience dictate the approach taken at a given point in time, with the profile being an outgrowth of the clinician's understanding of criminals and criminal behavior, flavored with his or her own take on personality and mental illness (Gudjonsson and Copson, 1997).

---

[15] Copson (1995) suggests that over half of the profiling in the United Kingdom is being conducted by psychologists and psychiatrists using a clinical approach.

FIGURE 3.2

During the 2007 trial of record producer Phil Spector for the murder of actress Lana Clarkson (pictured), forensic pathologist Dr. Vincent Dimaio (also pictured) testified for the defense. As support for his opinion that the shooting death was actually a suicide, he discussed certain aspects of the physical evidence and buttressed them with references to victimology and victim profile statistics. With respect to victimology: "Dimaio supported the suicide argument by characterizing Clarkson as a depressed, aging, out-of-work actress with health and financial problems who was 'at the end of her rope' " (Ryan, 2007a) and "said his reading of e-mails and other evidence from Clarkson's personal computer painted her as a depressed, destitute woman with drug and alcohol problems, 'no skills,' and flagging prospects in Hollywood. … She was an actress who was 40 years of age. I'm sorry. It's sex discrimination but that's the way it is," Dimaio said with a shrug. With respect to profiling: "Dimaio also ticked off a list of statistics which supported suicide. He said 87 percent of women who kill themselves do so by shooting themselves and 76 percent of those fire into their heads. He said that in his experience, 99 percent of intra-oral gunshots, those discharged within the mouth, are suicide" (Ryan, 2007b).[16]

Turco (1990) provides an adaptation of the diagnostic approach through psychodynamic theory. Like Liebert (1985, p. 151), Turco is critical of anyone without clinical experience:

> The experienced clinician has an underlying inherent understanding of psychopathology, experience with predictability, a capacity to get into the mind of the perpetrator and a scientific approach without moral judgement or prejudice. … The most productive circumstance likely to arise is when the profiler has both clinical (as opposed to academic) training and law enforcement experience. One cannot expect to obtain a graduate degree and make accurate predictions in the absence of a sound theoretical basis or clinical experience.

While it is possible that personality and learning theories have a role to play in assessing the likely characteristics of an offender, an overreliance on them may be counterproductive, as may be the case with the application of any general types—that is, they will apply in some cases but not others, and there is no way to determine their suitability with any certainty before an offender is apprehended and the case is unequivocally resolved.

In examining the role of forensic psychiatrists, McGrath (2000, p. 321) provides the following reasons why they may be particularly suited to providing profiles:

---

[16] Under cross-examination, the prosecutor presented Dr. DiMaio with a chart of Centers for Disease Control (CDC) statistics which showed that in 2003, the year of the shooting, women in the victim's age and ethnic group were more likely to kill themselves by overdosing on drugs—not shooting themselves. Dr. DiMaio explained that the CDC's death certificate information was often incorrect, so the statistics are flawed. The lesson here is that if you are going to cite statistics, make sure that you get them right and apply them correctly.

- Their background in the behavioral sciences and their training in psychopathology place them in an enviable position to deduce personality characteristics from crime scene information.
- Forensic psychiatrists are in a good position to infer the meaning behind signature behaviors.
- Given their training, education, and focus on critical and analytical thinking, forensic psychiatrists are in a good position to "channel their training into a new field."

Although these may seem obvious areas in which forensic mental health specialists can apply their skills, McGrath also notes that any involvement in the profiling process should not revolve around, or focus on, treatment issues.[17] That is, psychiatrists should not confuse their role as investigative advisors with their role as mental health diagnosticians: "It is critical that the psychiatrist or psychologist not fall prey to role confusion and descend into treatment advice and options when acting as a profiler" (Petherick, 2006a, p. 45). In addition to the potential problems that role division poses to their involvement, it is also true that those conducting diagnostic evaluations seldom have extensive experience in law enforcement or related areas (Wilson et al. 1997). West (2000, p. 220) provides similar commentary:

> However, it has to be conceded that many clinicians, whatever their professional background, do not routinely review crime scene data or witness depositions during the course of their involvement with offenders/patients. Instead, the clinical approach, with its often exclusive focus on the person of the offender, tends to preclude consideration of more exact details of the offense. All too often it is easier to believe the offender than to read the witness depositions or observe the crime scene. It seems inevitable that such omissions might lead to serious errors in any assessment.

Moreover, because their involvement in profiling tends to be sporadic, mental health specialists may lose touch with the requirements of a police investigation and therefore offer vague or irrelevant suggestions. Ainsworth (2001) claims that a profile produced by a mental health professional may contain statements about the inner workings of the offender's mental processes that will not be directly observable, and that the explanations provided may not be as useful to investigators as those from other approaches. The problem may go further than the type of advice offered in DE profiles and extend into the political difficulties of getting invited to assist with a police investigation. According to Canter (1989, p. 13), the difficulty is that

> Police officers are unlikely to admit psychologists to their investigations unless some mutual trust and reciprocal benefit is expected. This is a tricky cycle to break into, because it is difficult to make a contribution until some experience has been gained, yet difficult to gain experience until some contribution can be offered.

With regard to their role, Tamlyn (1999) claims that forensic clinicians in the United Kingdom rely on the goodwill of their employer to allow them to undertake profiling duties at potential expense to their employers. This means that many will work on their own time and be largely unpaid. It is unlikely that this situation will differ in other countries where mental health experts act in the advisory capacity of profilers. In fact, there are few "full-time" profilers from any discipline, and most offer the services as an adjunct to their usual duties.

---

[17] Dr. Michael McGrath is a forensic psychiatrist and president of the Academy of Behavioral Profiling. He is also a contributor to this text and co-author of Chapter 4, titled "Forensic Psychology, Forensic Psychiatry, and Criminal Profiling: The Mental Health Professional's Contribution to Criminal Profiling."

Although diagnostic evaluations do not comprise a unified approach with a clear theoretical framework, Copson et al. (1997, p. 16) outline the principles of clinical profiling. According to these authors, each piece of advice should be

- Custom made: the advice should not rely on the recycling of some kind of generic violent antisocial criminal stereotype;
- Interactive: at a range of levels of sophistication, depending on the officers' understanding of the psychological concepts at issue; and
- Reflexive: the advice should be dynamic, insofar as every element has a knock-on effect on every other element, and evolving, in that new information must lead to reconsideration not only of the element(s) of advice affected but of the construct as a whole.

They also identify a number of dangers (Copson et al., 1997, p. 16):

- There is an imperative to please that must be recognized and overcome; otherwise, objectivity will be undermined by tendencies to over-interpretation and unequivocality.
- Close interaction with the officers leaves the profiler open to allegations of improper collusion, such as tailoring a profile to fit a known suspect, or devising an interviewing strategy that is unethical or even unlawful.
- The mass of data that is produced by an interactive and reflexive process means that recording is an extremely difficult and time-consuming business, even to the extent that sometimes a written report never emerges.
- The reduction of a mass of data into a summary document—and more especially the failure to produce a summary document—leaves the profiler open to being misrepresented.

These issues are not peculiar to clinical profiling though, and some, if not all, of these problems will plague most profiling methods to varying degrees.

INVESTIGATIVE PSYCHOLOGY (IP)

The main advocate of investigative psychology (IP) is Dr. David Canter, a British psychologist who promotes a research-based approach to the analysis of individual offender behavior. IP is nomothetic, inductive, and dependent on the amount and accuracy of data collected. Although many inductive methods are criticized on the basis of sample size, Canter has performed research aimed at improving the samples on which his ruminations are based. The results are inductive but based on more empirically robust evaluations. However, enhanced empirical robustness does not make the results conclusive when applied in idiographic contexts (e.g., to the interpretation of offense behavior in a particular case). In other words, IP results remain entirely abstract and theoretical.

Like the FBI approach, IP identifies profiling as only one part of an overall methodology. This is explained in Canter (2000, p. 1091):

> The domain of investigative psychology covers all aspects of psychology that are relevant to the conduct of criminal and civil investigations. Its focus is on the ways in which criminal activities may be examined and understood in order for the detection of crime to be effective and legal proceedings to be appropriate. As such, investigative psychology is concerned with psychological input to the full range of issues that relate to the management, investigation and prosecution of crime.

As Canter (2004, p. 7) further explains:

> The broadening and deepening of the contributions that psychology can make to police investigations, beyond serial killers and personality profiles, to include the effective utilization

of police information, through interviews and from police records, as well as the study of police investigations and decision support systems, has led to the identification of a previously unnamed domain of applied psychology … called … Investigative Psychology.

According to the program's description on the University of Liverpool website, investigative psychology provides:

[A] scientific and systematic basis to previously subjective approaches to all aspects of the detection, investigation and prosecution of crimes. This behavioral science contribution can be thought of as operating at different stages of any investigation, from that of the crime itself, through the gathering of information and on to the actions of police officers working to identify the criminal then on to the preparation of a case for court.

Further, to distinguish between IP and those idiosyncratic profiling approaches, Canter (1998, p. 11) notes the following:

Investigative psychology is a much more prosaic activity. It consists of the painstaking examination of patterns of criminal behavior and the testing out of those patterns of trends that may be of value to police investigators. … Investigative psychologists also accept that there are areas of criminal behavior that may be fundamentally enigmatic.

The Five-Factor Model

The IP method has five main components, commonly referred to as the *five-factor model*, that reflect an offender's past and present. They are interpersonal coherence, significance of time and place, criminal characteristics, criminal career, and forensic awareness. We now address these in turn.

Interpersonal coherence refers to a person's style of interaction when dealing with others, where crime is an interpersonal transaction involving characteristic ways of dealing with other people (Canter, 1995). Canter believes that offenders treat their victims similarly to the way that they treat people in their daily lives—that is, criminals carry out actions that are a direct extension of the transactions they have with other people (Wilson and Soothill, 1996). For example, a rapist who exhibits selfishness with friends, family, and colleagues in his daily life will also exhibit selfishness with his victims. Similarly, offenders may select victims who possess characteristics of people important to them (Muller, 2000). This belief is not unique to IP, and most profiling approaches rely on the notion of interpersonal coherence in developing offender characteristics (Petherick, 2003).

As Canter (1989, p. 14) explains, "interpersonal processes gain much of their psychological nuance from the time and place in which they occur." The second component of the five-factor model holds that *time and place* are signifiers of some aspects of the offender. That is, the time and place are often specifically chosen by the offender and so provide further insight into the offender's actions in the form of mental maps. The implication is that "an offender will feel more comfortable and in control in areas which he knows well" (Ainsworth, 2001, p. 199). Two considerations are important: first, the specific location and, second, the general spatial behavior that is a function of specific crime sites (Canter, 1989). Canter (2003) dedicated a whole work to these aspects, which are largely based on the foundational theory of environmental criminology.

The offender's locational choices have been the subject of extensive examination in how offenders decide on place (see Snook et al., 2005), in the accuracy of various groups in determining an offender's residential location (Snook et al., 2002; Snook et al. 2004), and in the utility of geographic profiling models (Canter and Larkin, 1993; Canter et al., 2000; Godwin and Canter, 1997; Kocsis, 1997; Kocsis and Irwin, 1997;

Kocsis et al., 2002; Santilla et al., 2003). Snook et al. (2005) discuss a variety of factors that influence crime-site decisions (pp. 149–152):

Series chronology. Serial murderers often increase their spatial knowledge by learning from past experiences, which alters their spatial decision making.

Age. Until recently, research has shown that younger criminals tended to commit crimes closer to home, while older offenders were more likely to travel.

Intellectual capability. While the literature on the intelligence levels of serial murder is limited, some research suggests that there is a link between cognitive capacity and journey to crime, with "smarter" criminals traveling farther from home. It may be, then, that more intelligent serial murders will travel farther, with their IQ having a direct impact on the distances covered.

Marital status. Depending on the strength of the marital relationship, married offenders may travel shorter distances because of their accountability to a significant other, which affects the time they have available and therefore distance they can travel in furtherance of criminal enterprise.

Employment status. Like marriage, employment may restrict an offender's ability to travel, although the authors note that employment can also increase the offender's capacity for travel (by allowing access to vehicles, etc.).

Motive. Citing research by Holmes and DeBurger (1988), Snook et al. (2005) suggest that motive plays a role in a serial murderer's spatial decision making.

Mode of transportation. Obviously, transportation affects the offender's ability to acquire and deal with victims, especially if the victim must be moved.

Then, Snook and colleagues used a sample of 50 German serial murderers and examined the location of their crimes in relation to their homes. Considering the factors just listed, the first crime was closest to the offender's home 47% of the time, the second closest 34% of the time, and the third closest 36% of the time. If averaged across all offenders, however, none of the first crimes was closer to the offender's home than the other two. When age was analyzed, it was shown that older (German) serial murderers dumped the victims' bodies closer to home than did younger murderers, with intellectual capacity increasing the home-to-crime distance. The distances traveled by married offenders were not significantly greater than those of unmarried offenders, nor did employment status affect locations. Offenders who committed crimes for sexual motives traveled a median of 10 km, while those motivated by burglary traveled a median of 8.8 km (although the differences were not significant). As would be expected, the distance traveled was greatest with a car (median = 15.5 km), followed by public transport (median = 5.9 km) and walking (median = 2.2 km).

Criminal characteristics provide investigators with an idea of the type of crime they are dealing with. The goal is to determine "whether the nature of the crime and the way it is committed can lead to some classifications of what is characteristic…based upon interviews with criminals and empirical studies" (Canter, 1989, p. 14). This is an inductive component of the approach, and it is similar to attempts made by the FBI in applying the organized versus disorganized typology.

Studying the offender's *criminal career* provides an understanding of how offenders may modify behavior in light of experience (Nowikowski, 1995). The criminal career may exhibit adaptation and change, with learning and experience leading to responses to victim, police, or location dynamics. For example, a criminal may bind and gag a current victim, based on the screams and resistance of a past victim (Canter, 1989). Learning and experience may account for the evolution of modus operandi displayed by many offenders, who learn through subsequent offenses and continuously refine their behavior. Furthermore, the nature and types of precautionary behaviors may provide insight into whether the offender has experience with, or exposure to, investigative practices.

Finally, *forensic awareness* applies to learning based on past experience with the criminal justice system. Perpetrators may be sophisticated enough to use techniques that hinder police investigations, such as wearing a mask or gloves, or to make attempts to destroy other evidence (Ainsworth, 2000). A rapist may use condoms to prevent the transfer of biological fluids used for DNA analysis.

The criticisms of investigative psychology parallel those of other inductive approaches. McGrath (2000) is concerned that these approaches use predictions about offender characteristics or behaviors that may not be applicable to a specific case (that is, the average does not apply to every single case). Therefore, generalizations may erroneously guide the conclusion, as opposed to the conclusion's being offense specific.

GEOGRAPHIC PROFILING

Geographic profiling focuses on determining the "probable spatial behavior of the offender within the context of the locations of, and the spatial relationships between, the various crime sites" (Rossmo, 1997, p. 161). It assumes that an offender's home or other locations he or she is familiar with can be determined from their crime locations. As with other branches of profiling, geographic profiling is not intended to be an investigative panacea; rather, it is a tool to assist law enforcement in prioritizing search areas (Laverty and McLaren, 2002; Ratcliffe, 2004; Rossmo, 1997). Ideally, a geographic profile should only follow from, and augment, a completed full criminal profile (Rossmo, 1997), although this appears not to be the case, with Rossmo (2005) identifying geoprofiling as a form of offender profiling.

Its practitioners characterize geographic profiling as a decision support system used to identify the likely geographic region of an offender's home location (Rossmo, 2000), although it may also identify where he or she works (Ratcliffe, 2004) or other locations that are familiar (referred to as *activity nodes*). Essentially, geographic profiling makes use of the nonrandom nature of criminal behavior, presupposing that most crimes have patterns (Wilson, 2003):

> Crimes are not just random—there's a pattern. It has been said criminals are not so different from shoppers or even from lions hunting prey. When an offender has committed a number of crimes, they leave behind a fingerprint of their mental map, and you can decode certain things from that. We put every crime location into a computer program and it produces a map showing the most probable areas the police should target.

Despite the relatively recent advances in the use of computers in geographic profiling, its theoretical basis has been around for some time. The next section considers some of its theoretical underpinnings (Figure 3.3).

Lazy Criminals: The Least Effort Principle

The *least effort principle* at its most fundamental level suggests that, given two alternative courses of action, people will choose the one that requires least effort—that is, people will adopt the easiest course of action. According to Rossmo (2000, pp. 87–88),

> When multiple destinations of equal desirability are available, the least effort principle suggests the closest one will be chosen. The determination of "closest," however, can be a problematic assessment. Isotropic surfaces, spaces exhibiting equal physical properties in all directions, are rarely found within the human geographic experience.

FIGURE 3.3
After being terminated from the Vancouver police department, geoprofiler Darby Kim Rossmo, Ph.D., took a job with the police foundation in Washington, D.C. As of this writing, he is a research professor in the department of criminal justice at Texas State University. The least effort principle, distance, decay, and circle theory feature prominently in his geoprofiling theories.

As this statement suggests, the ability to impose arbitrary concepts of nearness onto crime is made difficult by the fact that our geographic environment is largely nonuniform. This means that not only does the layout of the environment affect an offender's decisions, but our physical location in a three-dimensional space comes into play as well. This may be particularly critical in major cities, such as New York and Sydney, Australia, where high-density housing is the norm. In rural areas, where travel routes are typically straighter and naturally larger, the application of the least effort principle may also be problematic. The caution is not necessarily against the application of the least effort principle generally, but against applying the same principle in an open environment that one applies in city spaces.

Distance Decay

Distance decay refers to the idea that the frequency of his or her crimes decreases as the offender travels farther from home (Rengert et al. 1999; Van Koppen and de Keijser, 1997). Distance decay is a geographical expression of the principle of least effort (Harries, 1999) and results when an offender shows a preference for closer-to-home crime sites.

Distance decay does not mean that crime sites are closely clustered around the offender's home, because this would obviously constitute a risk of the offender's discovery. Therefore, Rossmo (2000) posits the existence of a comfort or "buffer zone" directly around the offender's home. Within the comfort zone, targets are viewed as less desirable because of the perceived risk associated with offending too close to home (Rossmo, 2000). This is confirmed by Van Koppen and de Keijser (1997, p. 1), who note that "offenders rarely commit offenses on their own doorstep, presumably because the chances of recognition by people who know them are higher."

Distance decay is also affected by opportunity in the same way that the least effort principle is. According to Rengert et al. (1999), regardless of how much criminals would like to choose the locations of their offenses, they are unable to, given the lack of opportunities and the random and unpredictable behavior of others, which may foil even the best laid plans (pp. 428–429).

The Circle Theory

Another basis for geoprofiling is the *circle theory*, first discussed by Canter and Larkin (1993) and developed directly from environmental psychology research.[18] Two models of offender behavior, known as the "marauder" and "commuter" models, were developed from the circle theory. The marauder model assumes that offenders will "strike out" from their base in the commission of their crimes, whereas the commuter model assumes that offenders will travel a distance from their base before engaging in criminal activity. The base is not necessarily the home location of the offender; it may be some other place to which the offender has a psychological or physical affinity (Canter et al., 2000, p. 458):

---

[18] The utility of circle theory has been examined or tested in Kocsis and Irwin (1997), Meaney (2004), and Snook et al. (2002), with mixed results.

The "base" in question that provides the anchor for the criminal activity may take many forms. For some forms of base, delimiting the area where this base may be will be of more assistance to an investigation than for others. It will be of particular value when the base is in fact the home or some other location with which the offender will be known to have some affinity, such as a workplace or frequently visited recreation facility. It will be of less value when the base is an anonymous stopover point on a lengthy route that the offender is following, or any other location from which it is difficult to identify the offenders.

These two models are shown graphically in Figure 3.4.

In Canter and Larkin's study, they found no support for a commuter model in a sample of 45 sexual assaulters, but, in 41 of the 45 cases, the offender's home was within the circle, which, they suggest, is a "strong support for the general marauder hypothesis as being the most applicable to these sets of offenders" (Canter and Larkin, 1993, p. 67).

While circle theory seems plausible and attractive, it poses some problems. First, Canter and Larkin (1993) identified 91% of offenders as marauders, but classifying an offender as a marauder or commuter when the offender's home base is not known may be a matter of luck or educated guess.[19] If the profiler relies on a statistical probability that the offender is a commuter, then the same general cautions apply as with any inductive method (e.g., whether the degree of probability is statistically anomalous; in this particular study this would imply an error rate of 9%). In addition, the following cautions apply (Petherick, 2006b):

- The "base" may not be at the center of the circle of crimes, which would affect search areas, and the population of densely populated areas will also be important.
- The eccentricity of the model is important because it may reflect the developmental processes of the offender whereby he or she travels farther from home during different parts of the offense.
- As a result, the differences between marauding and commuting offenders could be explained by increases in criminal skill or confidence.
- The representation of ranges using circles is overly simplistic; research has shown that in North America, city expansion from downtown areas may be better indicated by elliptical or sectoral patterns.
- The number of offenses per offender was relatively small.
- It is possible that the information used in the modeling was not an accurate representation of all of the offenses committed by the offenders.

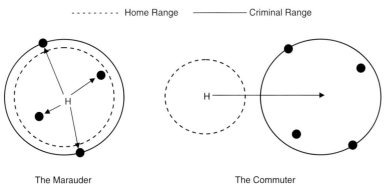

FIGURE 3.4
The marauder and commuter hypotheses.

The Marauder   The Commuter

---

[19] The same theory applied to a different sample may well produce results that are far less convincing than a result of 91%. Remember, this is one set of results with one sample.

Limitations of Geographic Profiling

In all nomothetic and inductive profiling methods, problems arise when broad theories are applied to actual cases in too certain a fashion. In the Washington, D.C., sniper case, there was legitimate concern about the application of geographic profiling. The concerns ranged from the estimation of "anchor points" (when none existed) through to low probabilities. Grierson (2003) cites Keith Harries, a pioneer of geographic profiling, as saying "in the sniper case [Rossmo's algorithm] was just not able to handle the level of variation in the data" (the D.C. sniper case is discussed at the end of this section).

In the first edition of this text (Turvey, 1999, pp. 262–263), we identified a number of concerns with geographic profiling that remain unresolved. They include the following:

- This method breaks the same tenet of behavioral-evidence analysis as the others: it takes a single manifestation of offender behavior (offense location selection) and attempts to infer its meaning out of the overall behavioral and emotional context that it was produced in.
- This method is actually employed without the benefit of a psychological profile. Though Rossmo states that he requires a full psychological profile for a competent geographical analysis, he has been known to proceed without one or to construct his own.
- Since it ignores overall behavioral evidence and case context and does not utilize full criminal profiles, geographic profiling cannot, and does not, distinguish between two or more offenders operating in the same area.
- This method assumes that all cases that are submitted have been positively linked by law enforcement. It does not check the veracity of this or any other information provided by law enforcement.
- This method assumes that offenders most often live near or within easy reach of their offense area.
- Rossmo's dissertation very competently outlines the weaknesses and the shortcomings of the published research on serial murder. Then, his dissertation goes on to base theories regarding geographic profiling, and the CGT (Criminal Geographic Targeting) software, on those admittedly flawed studies.
- The technology used in CGT is impressive, but amounts to only so much scientification. Inferences regarding offender anchor points and spatial behavior must still be drawn by the analyst.

McGrath (2000) has similar reservations, believing that geographic profiling may not be effective with a small number of cases and that it is further hamstrung when cases have not been linked (the same may apply if the case linkage is questionable). Also, the theory of geographic profiling is largely derived from the analysis of burglaries and other property crimes, so its larger-scale application to interpersonal crimes may not be sustainable. Similarly, a change of crime site resulting from interruption or change of opportunity may not provide significant insight into the offender, because the choice of where to offend is not made entirely by the offender and so is not reflective of his or her "mental map." That the crime site may be incorrectly identified or that crimes may not be reported are also possibilities (Ainsworth, 2001).

Geoprofiling Unit Closed

It should not need mentioning that any method of criminal profiling must be abandoned if it does not work. Certainly this was part of the decision-making process revealed in *Rossmo v. Vancouver (City) Police Board* (2001, at ¶21 and ¶38, respectively), where the following claims were made by the Vancouver Police Department (VPD) about Dr. Darby Kim Rossmo and his geoprofiling techniques:

> A cursory analysis seems to suggest that a choice to extend the contract would not be a good business decision. In short, there is little apparent evidence of enhanced policing outcomes. And establishing the extent and durability of prestige is problematic.

The question for the Vancouver Police Department and the Police Board is to what degree do we wish to continue what is essentially an international police program. There have been no definitive applications of geographic profiling in the [VPD] and the department is facing significant budget issues that require decisions on funding priorities.

This underscores that, while Rossmo enjoyed being flown around to give training, his unvalidated techniques had not helped with any casework at home. Consequently, there was no cost-benefit argument to be made that might keep the Geoprofiling Unit alive. In "Profiling Section Wasn't Good Value," the Vancouver *Sun* reported (June 28, 2001):[20]

> The contract of a detective-inspector in charge of the city police's geographic profiling section was terminated because the department felt it wasn't getting good value for its money, deputy chief Gary Greer testified Wednesday.
>
> The termination had nothing to do with jealousy or the existence of a so-called boy's club on the force, he said in B.C. Supreme Court.
>
> "It wasn't cost effective," he said.
>
> Kim Rossmo, a 22-year member of the force, is suing for wrongful dismissal after his five-year contract wasn't renewed last Dec. 31.

Greer was an inspector when he recommended that Rossmo's job be one of three positions the police department cut to meet city budget requirements .

Rossmo's lawsuit against the city of Vancouver and the Vancouver Police Department for wrongful termination was ultimately dismissed.

Geoprofiling the D.C. Sniper(s)

In October of 2002, because of his associations with the FBI, authorities tapped Rossmo to assist in the D.C. area sniper case (Figure 3.5). At the time, Rossmo was working in D.C. as director of research for the Police Foundation, a private nonprofit agency that trains police departments in law enforcement strategies. All of the assumptions of his software were put to a very public test in a case that had not been solved, and the result was a dismal failure.[21] Grierson (2003, pp. 63–68) provides a two-sided discussion of the outcome:

> "Geographic profiling isn't about prediction," Rossmo says. "Efforts to predict the location of crimes don't show a lot of focus." Instead of pushing forward into an unknown future, Rossmo's method pulls back to an origin, to the time and place the crimes were hatched. A center.
>
> "You know those sprinklers where the little metal thing hits the water stream and it sprays around in a circle?" Rossmo asks. "You could look at that and say, 'There's a good probability that the next drop of water will land within this ring,' but it'd be hard to know precisely where. If you took the sprinkler away, though, and I looked at the pattern of water, I could tell you where the sprinkler was."

---

[20] It was acknowledged that Rossmo's international celebrity was good for the Vancouver Police Department (VPD). However, this comment shows that it is hard to quantify celebrity and prestige. In reality, the actual return to the VPD was difficult to gauge because geoprofiling was not solving cases.

[21] Previously, Rossmo had great public success applying his model to already solved cases where the offender was known, although this could have biased the results, given the "artful" nature of Rossmo's geoprofiling technique.

FIGURE 3.5
John Allen Muhammad, a 42-year-old desert storm veteran, and his 17-year-old stepson, John Lee Malvo, were arrested, tried, and convicted for the shooting deaths of 10 people and for wounding 3 others critically in and around Washington, D.C., throughout the Baltimore-Washington metropolitan area, and along interstate 95 in Virginia. Before they were arrested, FBI profilers assumed that the shootings were the work of a single white male, likely a loner, who lived in the area. Instead, it turned out to be precisely the opposite.

What Rossmo hoped to do with his algorithm was to add rigor to the traditionally somewhat "soft" science of profiling, to create something that, once the crime sites were established, leaned more on deduction than induction. (Here's the difference: When Sherlock Holmes notices that the tips of your fingers are yellow and concludes you are a smoker, he's being inductive; when he concludes that if you are a smoker you cannot be the killer, because the killer is known to be fatally allergic to cigarette smoke, he is being deductive.)

"Induction is what most science is: You record observations and make generalizations about them," Rossmo says. "The only true deductive system is mathematics."[22] You might think of Rossmo out

---

[22] This is actually false, as we have demonstrated here. Mathematics can be deductive, but so can logic and reasoning. And induction is not by itself science. It is among the first steps of the scientific method.

walking his faithful hound, Rigel. Rossmo himself is "soft science"—a sleuth out gathering data from crime sites—while Rigel represents "hard science." The dog is off like a shot, programmatically, when the evidence is placed under his nose.

On the surface, the Beltway sniper case seemed a perfect candidate for geographic profiling, if only by default. Here was a serial killer against whom the arsenal of high-tech forensic tools—the mass spectrometers and gas chromatographs and scanning electron microscopes that can practically pull a DNA sample from an errant thought—appeared useless; whoever it was seemed to glide across the landscape without leaving a trace. What the sniper was leaving, in every pool of blood in every suburban gas station or parking lot, were data points. And Rossmo knew what to do with those.

And yet: Early on in the rampage, Rigel guessed the sniper's anchor point to be somewhere in the northern suburbs of D.C. (It turned out, in fact, that the killers may have had no anchor point at all.) It's tough to say whether it hurts or helps Rossmo's cred to point out that every pseudo-profiler who went on a TV news show with a half-cocked opinion was spectacularly wrong. In any case, though, when an anonymous tip attributed to the snipers gave police the clue they needed, the solution still seemed to be a long way away, buried deep in those 15,000 daily tips and an armada of irrelevant white vans.

"There are instances where profiling will probably be quite helpful, and there are a lot where it doesn't work at all," says Keith Harries, a professor of geography at the University of Maryland Baltimore County and a pioneer in "geography of crime" research. "In the sniper case, [Rossmo's algorithm] was just not able to handle the level of variation in the data."

As Ned Levine, a Houston-based urban planner who himself developed a geographic profiling model called Crimestat for the National Institute of Justice, points out, the two men arrested in the sniper case, John Allen Muhammad and John Lee Malvo, never kept a home base for long. (They had lived most recently in Washington State.) The distances they traveled were so large as to make the models imprecise. They killed not in areas they knew, but in areas like areas they knew. Which, in increasingly homogeneous America, can encompass quite a lot of real estate. Itinerant assassins like Andrew Cunanan and Aileen Wuornos have resisted accurate geoprofiling. (Evidence shows that U.S. serial killers are almost twice as nomadic as serial killers from elsewhere.) The increasing mobility of offenders and the increasing complexity of travel patterns could, Levine suggests, create ever-larger problems for geoprofilers. …

Rossmo's competitors assert Rigel hasn't yet proven itself. In the long run, they believe, Rossmo's model will reveal itself as no more accurate than their own—indeed no more accurate than straight centrography, the old pushpin method. "The business of the training is a way of making it seem terribly special and exotic, and imply that there are all sorts of skills that they can charge a lot of money for," says David Canter, director of the Center for Investigative Psychology at the University of Liverpool, who sometimes makes his own program, Dragnet, available free to researchers as open-source software. No one has ever done a head-to-head comparison of all the competing models, but, says Levine, "it's certainly overdue."

Rossmo says he can't discuss the Beltway Sniper case in any detail, in part because he doesn't have all the details about the suspects' movements throughout the killing spree. But he is pretty sure that Rigel wasn't as wrong-footed as it appeared. "Based on everything I know, the patterns of their behavior seemed, geographically, to be what we expected. That's all I'll say. I didn't find anything very surprising." In any case, he says, with any methodology there are assumptions and limitations. "I'd say of the requests I've received, 85 percent of the time we could provide some help," he says.

Dr. Rossmo is currently a research professor in the Department of Criminal Justice at Texas State University and the director of the Center for Geospatial Intelligence and Investigation. His recent publications have focused on applying geoprofiling techniques to animal foraging and the hunting behavior of sharks.[23]

CONCLUSION

As evident by the inclusion of this chapter, the authors are concerned about the reliability of many currently available methods of criminal profiling. This has to do with the fact that nomothetic profilers habitually isolate individual behavior and then interpret it out of context. Further, they tend not to explain, let alone understand, the differences between theories and conclusions. This may be a reflection of the close association between law enforcement and criminal profiling. Law enforcement investigators applying profiling techniques either do not have a strong scientific background or come to it late and with a law enforcement bias. In any case, nomothetic profilers too often apply their unique heuristic knowledge of crime and criminals to interpretations of individual cases as though they are somehow conclusive and relevant when often they are neither.

Criminal investigative analysis (CIA) is an unfinished, untested, nomo-inductive, law enforcement–oriented profiling method based on a small study of inappropriately grouped offenders from the 1970s. This study, which focused on unvalidated offender interviews, was used to further the FBI's organized/disorganized dichotomy, along with the current incarnation of criminal investigative analysis. The dichotomy has been debunked as false and lacking real-world application; and CIA, despite an overall lack of reliability, is being used in a forensic context to achieve criminal convictions, despite its original investigative purpose, by analysts who don't seem to understand the difference.[24] CIA-profile conclusions are too often rooted in general crime statistics, unqualified reconstructions of the evidence, and heuristic "experiential" interpretations of the evidence buttressed by fallacious appeals to the presumed authority of FBI-trained profilers.

Diagnostic evaluations (DE) represent the profiling work of clinicians (medical doctors and mental health professionals) operating in a forensic context with varying degrees of education, training, and experience. Individual clinicians approach the task of profiling from within the confines of their own treatment models and experience in a highly subjective fashion. The result is a lack of uniform methods and application and an overall detachment from the real-world case concerns of detectives who are trying to solve cases. DE profile conclusions are diagnostically oriented, ranging from exhaustively complex psychodynamic interpretations of obscure offense behavior to one-page diagnoses that have been cut and pasted directly from a clinical guide.

Investigative psychology (IP) is an attempt to bring science to profiling, but it fails because math and statistics are not by themselves scientific. They become scientific only in their interpretation and application. Certainly some interesting and even useful research has been published in the area. However, when applied to an actual criminal case, an IP profile deems it sufficient to blast statistics across its pages, citing study after study, but often without connecting the research or the percentages to the case at hand. An IP profile is more often than not a dissertation-style data dump, which is of no value to police investigators, who often work

---

[23] See Le Comber et al. (2006).
[24] This issue is explored throughout the text via case example.

without a strong background in research methods and statistics. The IP model is purely academic and often entirely irrelevant.

Geographic profiling is essentially the same as investigative psychology, from an end user standpoint, with the exception that geoprofilers have no trouble providing criminal profiles with their work as well. It is profiling through numbers; it presents inductive probabilities as the ceiling of scientific inquiry. This is despite the fact that geoprofilers are not typically educated or trained in the areas related to criminal profiling (or the scientific method in some cases). Moreover, unlike IP, geoprofiling has the added benefit of a map with a circle or a wedge drawn on it, which can have as good as a 50–50 chance of derailing the investigation if detectives actually use it to narrow their search.

If this review sounds harsh, that's because it's meant to be. Investigatively and forensically speaking, nomothetic methods should be used to examine individual cases only with the greatest of caution and with utter humility about their limitations. This means theory development only. In their current application, this is not what happens. Instead, it is more often the case that nomothetic profilers present inductive-nomothetic methods and findings as conclusive, and without regard for their actual limitations. This practice is scientifically dishonest at best. As is discussed throughout this text, there have been some disastrous consequences.

SUMMARY

The application of the scientific method creates the two different types of knowledge: idiographic and nomothetic. Nomothetic (group) study results in knowledge about the characteristics of groups, which is not only useful but necessary when trying to define groups, solve group-related problems, or generate initial theories about issues in specific cases. Nomothetic offender profiles, therefore, are characteristics developed by studying groups of offenders. Furthermore, nomothetic profiles represent an average, or abstract.

There are four main types of nomothetic profiling: criminal investigative analysis (CIA), diagnostic evaluations (DE), investigative psychology (IP), and geographic profiling.

The FBI's profiling method, criminal investigative analysis, is the most commonly known nomothetic method of criminal profiling. At its core is the widely used organized/disorganized dichotomy, based on the FBI's Criminal Profiling Project—a study of 36 incarcerated offenders and their 118 respective victims conducted between 1979 and 1983. Despite its notoriety and use by law enforcement, CIA and its methods have been widely debunked in the published literature as lacking accuracy, efficacy, and utility.

Diagnostic evaluations are not a single profiling method or representative of a unified approach. They are services offered by medical and mental health professionals who rely on clinical experience when giving profiling opinions about offenders, crime scenes, or victims. DE profiles are commonly offered as a footnote to primary reports, such as mental health evaluations, personality inventories, or autopsy findings.

Investigative psychology purports to cover all aspects of psychology that are relevant to the conduct of criminal and civil investigations. It involves research on various offender groups. Commonly, the result is a profile that is more or less a literature review of published studies examining ostensibly similar cases.

Geographic profiling focuses on determining the likely location of the offender's home, place of work, or some other anchor point. It assumes that an offender's home, or other locations the offender is familiar with, can be determined from the crime locations. It is based on theories and assumptions built from group studies of offenders that do not necessarily hold true in individual cases.

Questions

1. Knowledge developed based on the study of groups may be referred to as_____.
2. Knowledge developed based on the study of individual cases may be referred to as_____.
3. True or False: Nomothetic offender profiles represent an abstract that does not exist in the real world.
4. The FBI's current method of criminal profiling is_____.
5. True or False: Nomothetic profiles represent a prediction regarding potential offender characteristics, not an actual analysis.
6. According to a study by the FBI's first profiler, Howard Teten, the bureau's method of profiling helped with the identification of the suspect only _____% of the time.
7. _____involves the examination of spatial relationships between an offender's home and the locations of the offender's crimes.

REFERENCES

Ainsworth, P.B., 2000. Psychology and Crime: Myths and Reality. Longman, Harlow, Essex, UK.

Ainsworth, P.B., 2001. Offender Profiling and Crime Analysis. Willan, Cullompton, Devon, UK.

Baeza, J., Chisum, W.J., Chamberlin, T.M., McGrath, M., Turvey, B., 2000. Academy of Behavioral Profiling: Criminal Profiling Guidelines. Journal of Behavioral Profiling 1 (1).

Bartol, C.R., 1996. Police Psychology: Then, Now and Beyond. Criminal Justice and Behavior 23 (1), 70–89.

Beasley, J.O., 2004. Serial Murder in America: Case Studies of Seven Offenders. Behavioral Science Law 22, 395–414.

Burgess, A.N., Burgess, A.W., Douglas, J., et al. (Eds.), 1992. Crime Classification Manual. Lexington Books, New York, NY.

Burgess, A.W., Ressler, R.K., 1985. Sexual Homicides: Crime Scene and Pattern of Criminal Behavior. National Institute of Justice Grant 82-IJ-CX-0065.

Burgess, A.W., Hartman, C.R., Ressler, R.K., Douglas, J.E., McCormack, A., 1986. Sexual Homicide: A Motivational Model. Journal of Interpersonal Violence 1 (3), 251–272.

Canter, D., 1989. Offender Profiles. Psychologist 2 (1), 12–16.

Canter, D., 1995. Psychology of Offender Profiling. In: Bull, R., Carson, D. (Eds.), Handbook of Psychology in Legal Contexts. John Wiley & Sons, New York, NY.

Canter, D., 1998. Profiling as Poison. Interalia 2 (1), 10–11.

Canter, D., 2000. Investigative Psychology. In: Siegel, J., Knupfer, G., Saukko, P. (Eds.), Encyclopedia of Forensic Science. Academic Press, Boston, MA.

Canter, D., 2003. Mapping Murder: The Secrets of Geographical Profiling. Virgin Books, London, England.

Canter, D., 2004. Offender Profiling and Investigative Psychology. Journal of Investigative Psychology and Offender Profiling 1, 1–15.

Canter, D., Larkin, P., 1993. The Environmental Range of Serial Rapists. Journal of Environmental Psychology 13, 93–99.

Canter, D., Young, D., 2003. Beyond "Offender Profiling": The Need for an Investigative Psychology. In: Carson, D., Bull, R. (Eds.), Handbook of Psychology in Legal Contexts, second ed. Wiley, New York, NY.

Canter, D., Coffey, T., Huntley, M., Missen, C., 2000. Predicting Serial Killer's Home Base Using Decision Support System. Journal of Quantitative Criminology 16 (4), 457–478.

Canter, D., Alison, L.J., Alison, E., Wentink, N., 2004. The Organized/Disorganized Typology of Serial Murder: Myth or Model? Psychology, Public Policy and Law 10, 293–320.

Chisum, W.J., 2000. A Commentary on Bloodstain Analyses in the Sam Sheppard Case, Journal of Behavioral Profiling 1 (3).

Copson, G., 1995. Coals to Newcastle? Part 1: A Study of Offender Profiling, Police Research Group Special Interest Series Paper 7. Home Office, London, England.

Copson, G., Badcock, R., Boon, J., Britton, P., 1997. Articulating a Systematic Approach to Clinical Crime Profiling. Criminal Behavior and Mental Health 7, 13–17.

Darkes, J., Otto, R.K., Poythress, N., Starr, L., 1993. APA's Expert Panel in the Congressional Review of the USS *Iowa* Incident. American Psychologist 8–15 January.

Darwin, C., 1994. Observation, 18 September 1861. In: Burckhart, F., Browne, J., Porter, D., Richmond, M. (Eds.), The Correspondence of Charles Darwin. Cambridge University Press, Cambridge, MA.

Depue, R., Douglas, J., Hazelwood, R., Ressler, R., 1995. Criminal Investigative Analysis: An Overview. In: Burgess, A., Hazelwood, R. (Eds.), Practical Aspects of Rape Investigation, second ed. CRC Press, Boca Raton, FL.

Douglas, J.E., Burgess, A.E., 1986. Criminal Profiling: A Viable Investigative Tool against Violent Crime. FBI Law Enforcement Bulletin 55 (12), 9–13.

Fox, J., 2004. Personal communication with Wayne Petherick, 16 March.

Geberth, V.J., 1996. Practical Homicide Investigation: Tactics, Procedures and Forensic Techniques, third ed. CRC Press, Boca Raton, FL, pp. 89–91.

Godwin, G.M., Canter, D., 1997. Encounter and Death: The Spatial Behavior of US Serial Killers. Policing 20 (1), 24–38.

Grierson, B., 2003. The Hound of the Data Points: Geographic Profiling Pioneer Kim Rossmo Has Been Likened to Sherlock Holmes; His Watson in the Hunt for Serial Killers Is a Digital Sidekick—An Algorithm He Calls Rigel. Popular Science 262 (4), 62–68.

Gudjonsson, G., Copson, G., 1997. The Role of the Expert in Criminal Investigation, In Jackson, J., Bekerian, D. (Eds.), Offender Profiling: Theory, Research and Practice. John Wiley & Sons, Chichester, Sussex, UK.

Harries, K., 1999. Mapping Crime: Principles and Practice, Crime Mapping and Research Centre. U.S. Department of Justice, Washington, DC.

Hazelwood, R., 1995. Analyzing the Rape and Profiling the Offender. In: Burgess, A., Hazelwood, R. (Eds.), Practical Aspects of Rape Investigation, second ed. CRC Press, Boca Raton, FL.

Hazelwood, R.R., Douglas, J.E., 1980. The Lust Murderer. FBI Law Enforcement Bulletin 49 (4), 1–5.

Holmes, R., DeBurger, J., 1988. Serial Murder. Sage Publications, Newbury Park, CA.

Homant, R., Kennedy, D., 1998. Psychological Aspects of Crime Scene Profiling: Validity Research. Criminal Justice and Behavior 25 (3), 319–344.

Hurlburt, R.T., Knapp, T.J., 2006. Münsterberg in 1898, Not Allport in 1937, Introduced the Terms "Idiographic" and "Nomothetic" to American Psychology. Theory and Psychology 16 (2), 287–293.

Jenkins, P., 1994. Using Murder: The Social Construction of Serial Homicide. Aldine de Gruyter, New York, NY.

Kocsis, R.N., 1997. Criminal Profiling the Residence Location of Serial Rape and Arson Offenders. Australian Police Journal 51 (4), 250–253.

Kocsis, R.N., Irwin, H., 1997. An Analysis of Spatial Patterns in Serial Rape, Arson and Burglary: The Utility of the Circle Theory of Environmental Range to Psychological Profiling. Psychiatry, Psychology and Law 4 (2), 195–206.

Kocsis, R.N., Cooksey, R.W., Irwin, H.J., 2002. Psychological Profiling of Sexual Murders: An Empirical Model. International Journal of Offender Therapy Comp. Criminology 46 (5), 532–554.

Laverty, I., MacLaren, P., 2002. Geographic Profiling: A New Tool for Crime Analysis. Crime Mapping News, Summer, pp. 5–8.

Le Comber, S.C., Nicholls, B., Rossmo, D.K., Racey, P.A., 2006. Geographic Profiling and Animal Foraging. Journal of Theoretical Biology 240 (2), 233–240.

Liebert, J.A., 1985. Contributions of Psychiatric Consultation in the Investigation of Serial Murder. Inernational Journal of Offender Therapy Comp. Criminology 29 (3), 187–199.

McGrath, M.G., 2000. Criminal Profiling: Is There a Role for the Forensic Psychiatrist? Journal of the American Academy of Forensic Psychiatry and the Law 28 (3), 315–324.

Meaney, R., 2004. Commuters and Marauders: An Examination of the Spatial Behavior of Serial Criminals. Journal of Investigative Psychology 1, 121–237.

Meloy, J.R., 1998. The Psychology of Stalking. In: Meloy, J.R. (Ed.), The Psychology of Stalking: Clinical and Forensic Perspectives. Academic Press, London, England.

Muller, D., 2000. Criminal Profiling: Real Science or Just Wishful Thinking? Homicide Studies 4 (3), 234–264.

New Jersey v. Fortin, 2000. No.A-95/96-98, Supreme Court of New Jersey, 2000 (745 A.2d 509).

Nobile, P., 1989. The Making of a Monster. Playboy, July.

Novick, P., 1988. That Noble Dream. Cambridge University Press, New York, NY.

Nowikowski, F., 1995. Psychological Offender Profiling: An Overview. Criminologist 19 (4), 225–251.

Pennsylvania v. Distefano, 2001. August 16, 2000 (2001 WL 923333).

Petherick, W.A., 2003. What's in a Name? Comparing Applied Profiling Methodologies. Journal of Law and Social Challenges June, 173–188.

Petherick, W.A., 2005. Criminal Profile: Into the Mind of the Killer. Hardie Grant Books, Sydney, Australia.

Petherick, W.A., 2006a. Criminal Profiling Methods. In: Petherick, W.A. (Ed.), Serial Crime: Theoretical and Practical Issues in Behavioral Profiling. Academic Press, Boston, MA.

Petherick, W.A., 2006b. Geographic Profiling: The Devil Is in the Distance, Journal of Behavioral Profiling 6(1), June.

Pinizzotto, A.J., 1984. Forensic Psychology: Criminal Personality Profiling. Journal of Police Science and Administration 12 (1), 32–40.

Ratcliffe, J.H., 2004. Crime Mapping and the Training Needs of Law Enforcement. European Journal on Criminal Policy and Research 10, 65–83.

Rengert, G.F., Piquero, A.R., Jones, P.R., 1999. Distance Decay Reexamined. Criminology 37 (2), 427–445.

Ressler, R.K., Burgess, A.W., 1985. Crime Scene and Profile Characteristics of Organized and Disorganized Serial Murderers. FBI Law Enforcement Bulletin 54 (8), 18–25.

Ressler, R.K., Shachtman, T., 1992. Whoever Fights Monsters. Pocket Books, New York, NY.

Ressler, R.K., Burgess, A.W., Douglas, J.E., Hartman, C.R., D'Agostino, R.B., 1986. Sexual Killers and Their Victims: Identifying Patterns through Crime Scene Analysis. Journal of Interpersonal Violence 1 (3), 288–308.

Ressler, R.K., Burgess, A.W., Hartman, C.R., Douglas, J.E., McCormack, A., 1986. Murderers Who Rape and Mutilate. Journal of Interpersonal Violence 1, 273–287.

Ressler, R.K., Burgess, A.W., Douglas, J.E., 1988. Sexual Homicides: Patterns and Motives. Lexington Books, New York, NY.

Rossmo v. Vancouver (City) Police Board, 2001. Available at www.hamiltonhowell.ca/cases/rossmo.htm (accessed 8, 06.06.).

Rossmo, D.K., 1997. Geographic Profiling. In: Jackson, J., Bekerian, D. (Eds.), Offender Profiling: Theory, Research and Practice. Wiley, Chichester, Sussex, UK.

Rossmo, D.K., 2000. Geographic Profiling. CRC Press, Boca Raton, FL.

Rossmo, D.K., 2005. Geographic Profiling Update. In: Campbell, J.H., DeNevi, D. (Eds.), Profilers: Leading Investigators Take You Inside the Criminal Mind. Prometheus Books, Amherst, NY.

Ryan, H., 2007a. First Defense Witness at Spector Trial Says Actress's Death Was Suicide. CourtTV.com, June 28.

Ryan, H., 2007b. Prosecutor Accuses Expert of Misleading Jurors to Help Phil Spector. CourtTV.com, June 28.

Safarik, M.E., Jarvis, J., Nussbaum, K., 2000. Elderly Female Serial Sexual Homicide: A Limited Empirical Test of Criminal Investigative Analysis. Homicide Studies 4 (3), 294–307.

Santilla, P., Zappala, A., Laukannen, M., Picozzi, M., 2003. Testing the Utility of a Geographical Profiling Approach in Three Rape Series of a Single Offender: A Case Study. Forensic Science International 131, 42–52.

Snook, B., Canter, D., Bennell, C., 2002. Predicting the Home Location of Serial Offenders: A Preliminary Comparison of the Accuracy of Human Judges with a Geographic Profiling System. Behavioral Science and Law 20, 109–118.

Snook, B., Taylor, P.J., Bennell, C., 2004. Geographic Profiling: The Fast, Frugal, and Accurate Way. Applied Cognitive Psychology 18, 105–121.

Snook, B., Cullen, R.M., Mokros, A., Harbort, S., 2005. Serial Murderers' Spatial Decisions: Factors That Influence Crime Location Choice. Journal of Investigative Psychology and Offender Profiling 2, 147–164.

Superior Court of California, 1999. The People of the State of California v. Douglas Scott Mouser, Available from www.corpus-delicti. com/mouser_101999_prodan_direct.html (accessed 11. 11. 05.).

TaFoya, W.L., 2002. Profiling: A Measure of Last Resort, Police Futurists International. Available from www.policefuturists.org/ newsletter/webarticles/profiling.htm (accessed 4. 07. 07.).

Tamlyn, D., 1999. Deductive Profiling: A Clinical Perspective from the UK. In: Turvey, B.E. (Ed.), Criminal Profiling: An Introduction to Behavioral Evidence Analysis. Academic Press, London, England.

Tennessee v. Stevens, 2001. No. M1999-02067-CCA-R3-DD, May 30, 2001 (Tenn.Crim.App.2001).

Teten, H., 1995. Offender profiling. In: Bailey, W. (Ed.), The Encyclopedia of Police Science. Garland Publishing, New York, NY.

The Vancouver Sun, 2001. Profiling Section Wasn't Good Value, Vancouver Police Deputy Chief Says, June 28.

Turco, R.N., 1990. Psychological Profiling. International Journal of Offender Therapy Comp. Criminology 34, 147–154.

Turvey, B., 1999. Criminal Profiling: An Introduction to Behavioral Evidence Analysis, Academic Press, London, England.

Turvey, B., 2002. Criminal Profiling: An Introduction to Behavioral Evidence Analysis, second ed. Elsevier Science, London, England.

van Koppen, P.J., de Keijser, J.W., 1997. Desisting Distance Decay: On the Aggregation of Individual Crime Trips. Criminology 35 (3), 505–515.

West, A., 2000. Clinical Assessment of Homicide Offenders: The Significance of Crime Scene in Offense and Offender Analysis. Homicide Studies 4 (3), 219–233.

Wilson, C., 2003. Mapping the Criminal Mind. New Science 178 (2392), 46–49.

Wilson, P., Soothill, K., 1996. Psychological Profiling: Red, Green or Amber? Police Journal, July, 349–357.

Wilson, P., Lincoln, R., Kocsis, R.N., 1997. Validity, Utility and Ethics of Profiling for Serial Violent and Sexual Offenders. Psychiatry, Psychology and Law 4 (1), 1–12.

Woodworth, M., Porter, S., 1999. Historical Foundations and Current Applications of Criminal Profiling in Violent Crime Investigations. Expert Evidence 7, 241–264.

CHAPTER 4

Forensic Psychology, Forensic Psychiatry, and Criminal Profiling

The Mental Health Professional's Contribution to Criminal Profiling

Michael McGrath and Angela Torres

CONTENTS

Criminal Profiling: An Introduction to Behavioral Evidence Analysis, Fourth Edition

KEY TERMS

Competency to stand trial	Forensic psychologist	Projection
Countertransference	Forensic psychology	Transference
Forensic psychiatrist	Insanity (a.k.a. criminal	
Forensic psychiatry	responsibility)	

Forensic psychology and *forensic psychiatry* refer to the application of the behavioral sciences to legal questions (Hess, 1999). Common psycholegal questions that forensic mental health professionals answer involve (1) risk for future sexual offense recidivism, (2) competency to stand trial, and (3) criminal responsibility/ sanity at the time of the offense. In addition, forensic psychologists and psychiatrists, with their knowledge of human behavior, can add a unique perspective to ongoing investigations in the form of offender profiling. Profiling is often poorly understood, even by practitioners. Popular lore, driven by films and books, leads many to believe profiling is part of forensic psychology. In fact, few profilers have any background in the psychological sciences.

PSYCHOLOGY AND PSYCHIATRY

Psychology and psychiatry are two closely related fields but have some important differences. Both fields rely on the behavioral sciences. Psychiatrists are physicians who specialize in psychiatry after completing medical school. They can evaluate patients, diagnose illnesses (both psychological and medical), and prescribe medication. Psychologists are doctoral-level clinicians. They have studied psychology and have various levels of training in conducting research. They also are qualified to perform and interpret psychological measures, such as personality assessments, intelligence tests, and neuropsychological testing. There are practitioners in both forensic psychiatry and psychology who gained their expertise through experience, but currently there is an expectation that one has taken some advanced education and training to qualify as an expert in these fields (Bersoff et al., 1997).

In forensic work, the client can be the court (for a court-ordered assessment), or it can be one of the attorneys (retaining an expert to perform an assessment of an individual). The person (i.e., a defendant) evaluated in the forensic context may refuse to cooperate, and the forensic psychologist or forensic psychiatrist may have to complete the evaluation based solely on collateral information, although this is not common. Reliable collateral information is important in clinical and forensic evaluations and is essential in forensic assessments.

A pitfall for the clinician is performing both a therapeutic and a forensic role with the same person. Ethical guidelines generally recommend avoiding such a scenario (Committee on Ethical Guidelines for Forensic Psychologists, 1991). It is difficult if not impossible to maintain an objective mindset when you have had, or have, an ongoing relationship with a person who has a vested interest in what expert opinion you form. For example, how can a psychiatrist maintain objective neutrality when evaluating his own patient for psychological damages when he knows the patient is in dire financial straits? How can a clinician provide ongoing therapy to someone who may hold onto symptoms (consciously or unconsciously) that may lead to financial gain in a pending lawsuit where he or she is an expert witness for the patient? Such ethical conflicts must be both acknowledged and resolved.

Forensic mental health professionals may conduct evaluations in both civil and criminal cases. Civil cases involve matters related to property or torts (i.e., injury or some other loss that can be addressed through a lawsuit). Some evaluations involve risk assessments and child custody evaluations, for example. Criminal cases are those that involve a criminal act. Some common criminal evaluations are criminal responsibility at the time of offense (sanity) and competency to stand trial.

INSANITY AND COMPETENCY TO STAND TRIAL

Inability to stand trial is often equated with insanity, when that is not the case. *Competency to stand trial* relates to a defendant's current ability to understand his or her legal predicament (e.g., charges, possible outcomes) and to assist an attorney with his or her defense (Roesch et al., 1999). Insanity (or criminal responsibility) relates to the defendant's mental state at the time of the offense (Golding et al., 1999). There are different standards in different jurisdictions, but generally a person needs to be able (at the time of the crime) to understand that what he or she was doing was wrong or against the law. Many assume that a severe mental illness makes one incompetent or insane, but that also is not the case. While a severe mental illness (such as schizophrenia or bipolar disorder) or mental defect (such as mental retardation or brain trauma) is a prerequisite, such a disorder must then lead to an inability to meet the legal criteria for either competence to stand trial or criminal responsibility.

It is commonly believed that someone who has been acquitted by reason of insanity has "gotten away with it" (Hans and Slater, 1983). In reality, the insanity defense is rarely used and even more rarely succeeds. When it does result in an acquittal, the individual is usually committed to a secure mental health facility. It is a well-known fact in legal circles that individuals who successfully plead insanity are usually hospitalized (kept in a mental health facility) for much longer than they would have been incarcerated if they had pleaded or been convicted at trial (Callahan et al., 1992; Sloat and Frierson, 2005).

Case Example: Andrea Yates

The case of Andrea Yates (Figure 4.1) is well known, both because of the psychiatric aspects of the case and because of the accompanying issues regarding psychiatric testimony. It is illustrative of typical and atypical features related to forensic mental health assessment. Yates was a mother of five children, ranging in age from 6 months to 7 years old. She had suffered from depression (believed to be postpartum depression) and psychosis for some time and had been treated with antipsychotic medication and antidepressants (Parnham et al., 2004).[1] In 1999, she had attempted suicide by overdose, taking her father's medication. In March of 2001, her father passed away and it appears she began to deteriorate from then on. She was hospitalized and released to outpatient care shortly before the homicides. Two days before the killings, she was seen by her psychiatrist, who lowered her antidepressant medication but kept her off antipsychotic medication. On June 20, 2001, after her husband had gone to work, Yates methodically drowned her five children. She then called 911 to report what she had done and called her husband at work. Yates was taken into custody, and the judge issued a gag order around the case.

Yates told examiners that she believed she was not a good mother, that the mark of the devil was hidden under her hair, and that her children would suffer in Hell. At the time of her arrest and incarceration, the jail psychiatrist reported that Yates had no insight into her mental illness, was "profoundly" depressed, and

---

[1] Unless otherwise indicated, information related to the Yates case was drawn from the appellant brief filed with the Texas First District Court of Appeals. Quotation marks indicate text quoted from the brief, not necessarily actual quotes of speech.

FIGURE 4.1
Former nurse Andrea Yates was arrested on June 20, 2001, after calling Houston police to report that she had drowned her four boys and infant daughter in the bathtub. Yates is pictured here with her sons and husband, Rusty Yates.

was psychotic (not in touch with reality). For example, she thought that the cartoons her children watched "were sending them messages" (p. 29).

Andrea Yates reported to the psychiatrist that she began hearing voices after the birth of her first child. She also said she heard growling noises and reported "feeling" she was in the presence of Satan. Further, the children were not doing well (spiritually) and it was her fault. "She was convinced they were doomed to suffer in the fires of Hell." It was the psychiatrist's impression that Yates was "actively hallucinating [hearing voices] during the interview." Yates advised it was her belief that "her children would be tormented and they would perish in the fires of Hell if they were not killed" (p. 30). Yates was diagnosed with major depression, with psychotic features, with onset postpartum (i.e., postpartum psychosis). The jail psychiatrist advised during trial that Andrea Yates was the sickest patient she had ever treated. A psychologist performed neuropsychological testing on Yates while she was incarcerated. It was the psychologist's opinion that she suffered from schizophrenia and a comorbid depressive disorder.

In a high-profile case like this, questions related to competency to stand trial quickly surface and the defense moved to have Yates found incompetent. In September 2001, a jury deliberated over two days after hearing expert testimony from both defense and prosecution experts, to determine if Yates had "a rational as well as factual understanding of the proceedings against her" and the ability to work with her attorneys. The jury found Yates competent to proceed with her legal case. A different jury would later hear the criminal case.

There seemed to be no question that Yates was psychiatrically very ill. The question for the court was whether she met the criteria under Texas law for an insanity defense. The Texas statute requires that the person (as a result of a severe mental disease) did not know that what he or she was doing was wrong at the time the person did it.

Several defense experts testified that, in their opinion, Yates was unable to know right from wrong at the time she killed her children. One defense expert, Dr. Phillip Resnick, saw Yates several weeks after the homicides and again several months later. He noted that over time, Yates had memory alterations related to the events. This is important, as the new or altered memories are "often more rational" because of clinical improvement in the individual, in this case because of appropriately prescribed medication. Dr. Resnick testified that it was "possible for an individual to believe that an act was illegal, but yet not perceive it as wrong" (p. 40). The case, to a great extent, centered on whether Yates understood that killing her children was considered a criminal act. She did. She understood that society would see her behavior as bad. But, as Dr. Resnick testified, she believed the homicides were the right thing to do as Satan was inside her and her children would suffer eternal damnation if she did not kill them. She did, however, know the difference between right and wrong. So even though she believed what she was doing was right in a moral sense, she knew what she was doing was wrong in a legal sense.

Dr. Park Dietz (Figure 4.2), a forensic psychiatrist, was the only expert in behavioral science who testified for the prosecution. He examined Yates on November 6 and 7, 2001. By then she had been treated with antidepressant and antipsychotic medications. Dr. Dietz agreed that Yates suffered from a major mental disorder, schizophrenia, but disagreed that she met the criteria in Texas for an insanity defense. In assessing Yates's ability to appreciate the wrongfulness of her actions, he divided the crime into three phases: prehomicides, homicides, and posthomicides. In the prehomicide phase, he noted that Yates hid her plan from others and attributed the impetus for the killings to Satan. This negates the fact that she hid what she was planning, because carrying out the plan was necessary to save the children's souls. If she had told someone and was stopped, (in her mind) the children would suffer eternal damnation. He testified (p. 53) that if she believed her children were in danger or that Satan was inside her, she would have sought counseling or help in dealing with the situation. This line of reasoning imposes a rational standard on an irrational psychotic process. Regarding the homicides phase, he noted that Yates admitted that she knew her actions were illegal, that she would be arrested, and that society would see her behavior as "bad." Dr. Dietz opined if Yates actually believed she was saving her children, "she would have attempted to comfort them before the drownings." That may or may not be accurate. Once again, a rational standard was applied to a psychotic act.

In the posthomicide phase, Dr. Dietz opined that covering the children's bodies was evidence of "guilt or shame over her actions." This is an opinion, not a fact. It may be accurate, and it may not. Regardless, the emotion of shame or guilt after killing one's children does not rule out having acted for their ultimate benefit.[2] Also, she had told the 911 operator that she had done "something wrong," needed to be punished, and was ready to go to Hell. Yates had voiced a belief that her execution would kill Satan, but Dr. Dietz said she did not mention that at the time of the homicides. He gave his expert opinion that "at the time of the drownings, Ms. Yates knew her actions were wrong in the eyes of the law, wrong in the eyes of society and wrong in the eyes of God" (p. 55).

FIGURE 4.2
Forensic psychiatrist Park E. Dietz, M.D.

Dr. Dietz testified at the trial that weeks before the homicides, Yates had watched an episode of *Law & Order* on television in which a woman drowned her children and was found not guilty by reason of insanity. The fact that Yates watched *Law & Order* was included in information from an expert who had evaluated her for competency to stand trial. It was later noted that no such episode aired.

---

[2] If God had allowed Abraham to complete the sacrifice of his son, Isaac, would Abraham not have felt some guilt and shame at what he had done? Would he have covered the body?

Additionally, the prosecution used the nonexistent episode in cross-examining a defense expert (p. 62). Finally, the prosecutor used the issue of the nonexistent episode during summation (p. 63): "She gets very depressed and goes to Devereux and at times she says these thoughts came to her during that month. These thoughts came to her, and she watches 'Law and Order'; regularly she sees this program. There is a way out. She tells Dr. Dietz, that there is a way out."

A producer of *Law & Order* contacted the defense to advise that no such episode had ever been made. When it was brought to Dr. Dietz's attention that his testimony was false in regard to the *Law & Order* episode, Dr. Dietz wrote a letter, dated March 14, 2002, to the district attorney's office advising of the situation. "I also wish to clarify that Mrs. Yates said nothing to me about either episode or about the *Law & Order* series." The court rectified this by giving a stipulation to the jury that, if Dr. Dietz would testify, his testimony would be that he was in error regarding the *Law & Order* episode. This was after the verdict, but before sentencing.

Yates was convicted of capital murder in the deaths of three of her children and sentenced to life in prison. An appeal was filed on January 6, 2005, and the Texas First Court of Appeals overturned her conviction. After a retrial, on July 26, 2006, Yates was found not guilty by reason of insanity for the deaths of three of her children, Noah, John, and Mary.

Case Example: Jeffrey Dahmer

In some cases, FBI-trained profilers have waded into the water of forensic mental health assessment. One of the first cases on record, and certainly one of the most notorious, was that of Jeffrey Dahmer. This case involved mental health professionals and FBI profilers alike.

On July 22, 1991, police officers arrested Jeffrey Dahmer. A handcuffed man had escaped from Dahmer's apartment and was spotted by two Milwaukee police officers. Upon questioning, the man reported an encounter with a man that left him very uncomfortable and gave police the address of an apartment. Jeffrey Dahmer opened the door. Pictures of bodies and body parts, as well as body parts (including heads), were found in the apartment. Subsequent investigation revealed a 13-year killing spree.

Dahmer killed 17 victims between 1978 and 1991. His modus operandi was to invite homosexual men or boys to his apartment and drug them. When they were incapacitated, he would strangle them. He reported having sex with some bodies and occasionally eating body parts. Dahmer decided to plead guilty but insane (available in Wisconsin law) and went to trial. He was found guilty in 1992 and sentenced to 15 consecutive life terms. In November 1994, while Dahmer was in prison, another inmate killed him.

At Dahmer's trial, defense and prosecution experts offered opinions as to his sanity. Insanity was a hard sell, as Dahmer did not have a major diagnosable mental illness (to the level of a psychosis), in spite of the bizarre nature of his crimes. Although Dahmer had initially entered a plea of not guilty by reason of insanity, he changed this to a plea of guilty but insane. A not guilty by reason of insanity adjudication is an acquittal; a guilty but insane adjudication is a guilty verdict. Consequently, this would result in Dahmer's serving his sentence in a psychiatric facility under the jurisdiction of the corrections department in Wisconsin. Once "cured" (i.e., not requiring psychiatric hospitalization), he would be sent to a regular prison.

As previously mentioned, a former FBI profiler evaluated Dahmer for the defense. This was a scenario that was essentially unheard of before the Dahmer trial. Robert Ressler, one of the more notable members of the FBI's Behavioral Science Unit, had retired from the FBI in 1990. In one of his co-authored memoirs, *I Have Lived in the Monster* (Ressler and Shachtman, 1997, pp. 107–160), he describes his interview/evaluation of Dahmer. Ressler makes it clear (p. 109) that he believed he was evaluating Dahmer's "mental condition." The result of an evaluation of Dahmer's mental condition was relevant to Dahmer's plea of guilty but insane, and

FIGURE 4.3
The court rejected Jeffrey Dahmer's insanity plea. On February 17, 1992, he was sentenced to 15 consecutive life sentences. On November 28, 1994, another inmate at the Columbia Correctional Institute in Wisconsin murdered Dahmer.

should have been conducted by a qualified psychiatrist or a psychologist. Even Ressler admitted (p. 108): "It was unlikely that I would ever get to testify in this case, because of the presence of expert psychiatrists on both sides." He noted: "My friend Park Dietz was going to appear for the prosecution, but in this instance my opinion differed from his and I agreed to consult for the defense" (p. 107). Since Park Dietz, a forensic psychiatrist, had the opinion that Jeffrey Dahmer was sane at the time he committed his crimes, if Ressler had a different opinion, it would seem reasonable to infer that his opinion was that Dahmer was insane. In another paperback memoir (Ressler and Shachtman, 1992, p. 280), the former FBI profiler stated: "There was no way to view this tormented man as having been sane at the time of his crimes." It could be argued that Ressler appeared willing to offer an expert opinion that Dahmer was insane. He did not, however, appear in court. The salient point is that Ressler, who is neither a psychologist nor a psychiatrist, appeared willing to offer what he believed was an expert opinion as to Dahmer's responsibility in the commission of his crimes (Figure 4.3).

Ressler's involvement in the Dahmer case highlights the danger when those with investigative experience confuse or conflate their presumed area of expertise with other professions. Note the following section from *I Have Lived in the Monster* (Ressler and Shachtman, 1997, pp. 107–108):

> In my view, Dahmer was neither a classic "organized" nor a classic "disorganized" offender: while an organized killer would be legally sane, and a disorganized one would be clearly insane under law, Dahmer was both and neither—a "mixed" offender—which made it possible that a court could find him to have been insane during some of the later murders.

Aside from the fact that Ressler relied on a dichotomy that has never been validated and is essentially worthless from any perspective, investigative or scientific, he attached psycholegal meaning with apparent implied certitude to an investigative tool.[3] This is not an acceptable practice.

Case Example: O. C. Smith

Dr. O. C. Smith was a locally well-known physician and was at one time the medical examiner for Shelby County, Tennessee. Dr. Smith left work on June 1, 2002, a Saturday night, and was found several hours later by a security guard. The doctor was tied with barbed wire to a window grate in an outside stairwell and had an explosive device around his neck. He also had chemical burns to parts of his face from a caustic material allegedly thrown in his face by the assailant. He stated he had been attacked by a man and tied with the wire, as if crucified. The man only spoke briefly to him and left: "Push it, pull it, twist it, and you die. Welcome to death row."

---

[3] The organized/disorganized dichotomy is discussed in Chapter 3, "Criminal Profiling: Science, Logic, and Cognition."

A bomb squad removed the device. They determined that the device was real and could have exploded. The local police, the Bureau of Alcohol, Tobacco and Firearms (ATF), and the FBI each performed their own investigation of the case. This level of interest came in part because, three months earlier, another explosive device had been left in a hallway in the building where Dr. Smith worked. Additionally, a year earlier, a letter had been sent to the district attorney's office threatening Dr. Smith. However, early in the investigation into the attack on Dr. Smith, federal investigators were forming the opinion that he was not telling the truth.

The case of Dr. O'Brien C. Smith (Figure 4.4) is interesting on several levels. First, it presents an investigative dilemma: Was the doctor a victim or a liar? Second, without actually having interviewed Dr. Smith, a forensic psychiatrist attempted to present trial testimony that the doctor suffered from a mental illness, the diagnosis of which relied on wanting to be a victim of a crime. Third, an ex-FBI profiler submitted a report for the prosecution wherein he appears to come close to offering a psychological opinion.

As noted, federal investigators doubted Dr. Smith's story, for several reasons. For one thing, although a caustic chemical was thrown into his face, none got into his eyes. Also, while barbed wire had been wrapped several times around Dr. Smith's face and head, there was limited injury. Further still, investigators were leery of his claim of being overpowered, especially when he was known to carry a firearm on occasion. On the other hand, there was no doubt that the device attached to his chest was a live explosive and could have gone off. Dr. Smith was arrested for lying to federal authorities and illegally possessing an explosive device. They pressed forward with charges in federal court. Ultimately, local authorities made no such charges.

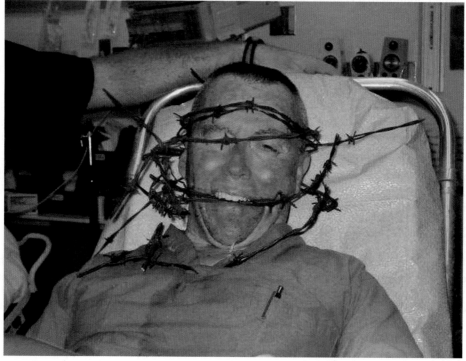

FIGURE 4.4
Dr. O. C. Smith as photographed while receiving medical attention on the night he was found in 2002.

Dr. Park Dietz submitted a report to the attorney general's office (Dietz and Ankrom, 2004) and was prepared to testify for the prosecution that, in his opinion, Dr. Smith suffered from a mental illness recognized by Dr. Dietz, specifically factitious victimization disorder.[4] While others have used the term factitious victimization, it has had limited use in the context of being a diagnosable mental illness. The concept has been used more broadly in the context of describing a behavior (i.e., falsely claiming oneself or another to have been a victim of a crime or situation when that claim is false). Dr. Dietz was proposing that such behavior is diagnosable as a discrete mental illness. The first known public reference to factitious victimization by Dr. Dietz is in a *Time* magazine article in April of 2004 (Fonda, 2004). In this article (on the false report of Audrey Seiler that she had been abducted), Dr. Dietz is cited as stating that false reports of being a victim that are not motivated by money or revenge are rare. The infamous Tawana Brawley case was mentioned, noting that Dr. Dietz testified to the grand jury in 1988. The grand jury did not believe the black teenager's claim of gang rape by several white men. "Dietz coined the term factitious victimization disorder to describe what occurs when someone claims to be a victim to win sympathy and support. The motives for individuals who stage their own victimization range from trying to get out of exams to stirring a boyfriend to pay more attention, Dietz says." There is no mention in the article that Dr. Dietz was claiming that factitious victimization was a mental disorder.

In the "Analysis, Discussion and Conclusions" section of the Smith report, Dietz notes (p. 43):

> Behavioral analysis of the facts of this case suggests that the events in question are the product of a mental disorder suffered by the defendant. The phenomenon that would account for this behavior is well-known in certain mental health and law enforcement circles, but is not familiar to most laymen.

This is an interesting statement, as familiarity with the case would not lead to this assertion. There is nothing in the facts of the case, even if one assumes Dr. Smith was lying about the assault, requiring the introduction of a mental illness to explain either the "facts" or the motivation. Also, the purported mental illness is not as "well known" as described. There is very little published literature that discusses the concept of false victimization and even less that claims it is a diagnosable mental disorder. Describing the psychodynamics of a behavior does not make the behavior a diagnosis.

Dr. Dietz presents his argument by noting that psychiatry has a category of mental illnesses that falls under the category of factitious disorder (FD) in the *Diagnostic and Statistical Manual of Mental Disorders,* Fourth Edition, Text Revision (DSM-IV-TR) (American Psychiatric Association, 2000). This category covers a mental illness wherein a person presents physical or psychological symptoms to obtain whatever psychological benefit that would accrue from the role of being ill. Munchausen's syndrome may be the most familiar form of a factitious disorder. In this illness, a person is motivated to appear physically ill, often undergoing diagnostic tests and even operations in an effort to assume the sick role. The DSM-IV-TR specifically preempts having external incentives for the behavior(s). In other words, the goal of the illness is to assume the sick role, not to make money (as in a lawsuit), or to get out of work, or to evade some other responsibility. These behaviors (e.g., feigning or exaggerating symptoms for secondary gain) are better described as malingering. There are two main types of FD: FD in which psychological symptoms dominate the picture and FD in which physical symptoms predominate. There is also an FD Not Otherwise Specified (NOS), which allows for the diagnosis of FD when the clinical picture consists of factitious symptoms not meeting the criteria of the first two mentioned. The most famous example of FD NOS is Munchausen's syndrome by proxy, whereby a

---

[4] Dr. Dietz had not examined Dr. Smith, as the defense declined the opportunity. Therefore, Dr. Dietz worded his opinion: "I conclude with reasonable medical certainty that a clinician examining the defendant who had access to all of the above-referenced data would conclude that at the time of the events in question, the defendant suffered from Factitious Disorder Not Otherwise Specified, specifically Factitious Victimization" (p. 48).

caretaker reports or induces signs or symptoms of illness in another, often a child. Please note well that the motivation remains one of assuming the "sick role." In Munchausen's by proxy, the role of caretaker of an ill child is usually expected to garner sympathy for the caretaker. Although it is not required for diagnosis, there is an expectation that one who suffers from factitious disorder has an inner compulsion to act out the behaviors that lead to the diagnosis and therefore that the sufferer would have a history of numerous episodes/events over the course of years. The case of Dr. O. C. Smith does not fit the diagnostic category of factitious disorder.

Dr. Dietz (2004, pp. 43–45) presents a literature review (Burgess and Hazelwood, 2001; Dohn, 1986; Eisendrath, 1996; Eke and Elenwo, 1999; Feldman et al., 1994; Feldman-Schorrig, 1996; Fliege et al., 2002; Ford et al., 1988; Gibbon, 1998a, 1998b; Goldstein 1998; Gutheil, 1989, 1992; Kanin, 1994; Matas and Marriott, 1987; McDowell and Hibler, 1987; Pathe et al., 1999; Sederer and Libby, 1995) related to factitious disorders and false allegations of sexual assault, highlighting that for something to be factitious the reporter (by definition) has to be lying. He then relies on the fact he has assumed Dr. Smith to be lying[5] to form the opinion (p. 44): "If Dr. Smith self-inflicted the chemical burns and abrasions that he suffered during the events in question, a diagnosis of factitious disorder would be technically correct." The authors would argue that this is circular reasoning. Dr. Dietz then goes on (p. 44) to opine that (assuming he is correct in making a diagnosis of factitious disorder): "it would be more accurate and insightful to regard the event as factitious victimization, since the role he sought to acquire was that of a crime victim rather than a patient."

In Dr. Dietz's report, he offers 18 articles or chapters (noted earlier) as he makes his case for a diagnostic entity of factitious victimization. The sources cover the topics of factitious disorder in general, false reports of sexual assaults, and the concept of false reporting of a crime as a type of factitious disorder. Sources that (in the authors' opinion) discuss the diagnosis of factitious victimization, factitious sexual assault, factitious sexual harassment, or factitious report of a crime number only 6 (Dohn, 1986;[6] Eisendrath, 1996;[7] Pathe et al., 1999;[8] Feldman et al., 1994;[9] Feldman-Schorrig, 1996;[10] Gibbon, 1998b[11]), encompassing a total of 12 cases.

Dr. Dietz, assuming he has proven that the scenario surrounding Dr. Smith falls into the category of a diagnosable factitious disorder (which the authors do not accept), then goes on to claim Smith meets criteria for the new diagnostic subcategory of factitious victimization. On page 44 of the report, Dr. Dietz specifically notes he has described scenarios wherein someone falsely reports being a victim of a crime as "factitious victimization" and states that in DSM-IV it would fall under Factitious Disorder Not Otherwise Specified. As (apparent) criteria for this diagnosis, he lists (p. 45): (1) "Childhood trauma or loss, such as abuse or emotional deprivation during childhood, as this is a risk factor." (2) "A prior history of false allegations, as such behavior is often repetitive. If the defendant were the author of the JMJ[12] communications, this factor

---

[5] Apparently without knowing this to be the case, as he states (p. 45), when assuming the doctor is a pathological liar, a fact that was not established: "If any of the following unlikely stories were to prove untrue, as I expect they will [emphasis added], this factor [pathological lying] would be present." Note well that Dr. Dietz indicated only one "unlikely story" would be enough for him to make a diagnosis of *pseudologia fantastica*. This would seem to be a ridiculously low threshold.

[6] One case report of a false "diagnosis" of rape.

[7] One report of a woman who falsely reported a physical assault.

[8] One case of factitious stalking.

[9] Four cases of false reports of rape.

[10] Four cases of factitious reports of sexual harassment.

[11] One case report of a false report of rape.

[12] Three threatening letters sent in 2001 to a defense attorney, a district attorney general, and a newspaper reporter. The letters contained religious references and appeared to reference Dr. Smith's involvement in the Workman death penalty case.

would be present." (3) "A prior history of intentionally self- inflicted wounds. If any of the defendant's scars were the result of intentionally self-inflicted injury, this factor would be present." (4) *Pseudologia fantastica*, a form of pathological lying." There is no known validity or reliability to these four criteria being used to make a diagnosis for a disorder that is not an agreed-upon diagnostic category. Criterion 1, if interpreted broadly enough, includes half or more of the human race. Criterion 2 (in the O. C. Smith case) presumes guilt, a fact that has not been established.

If taken at face value, the diagnosis of factitious victimization can be made if one has had a childhood trauma or loss, a prior history of a false allegation, a prior history of a self-inflicted injury, and one is a liar. What appears lost in all this is that Dr. Dietz gives as a motivation for the behavior (p. 46):

> The available record suggests that Dr. Smith was losing control at the Medical Examiner's Office, had a history of repeated marital infidelity, became excessively involved with the Workman case, and was exposed to a high-profile case in which a man had a bomb affixed to his body.[13] These factors are likely to be involved in his decision to use this particular form of bomb-related pseudo-crucifixion to expiate his guilt, achieve a form of martyrdom, gain the sympathy of his coworkers and family, and elicit the support of the wider law enforcement community whom he betrayed.

Note well that Dr. Smith's guilt had not been established, and it was not clear how well founded some of the assumptions (e.g., that Dr. Smith was a pathological liar and inflicted wounds on himself in the past) were on which Dr. Dietz appears to rest his opinion. Regardless, there is nothing in the motivation requiring the diagnosis of a mental illness called factitious victimization. If one has lied about being the victim of a crime to be seen sympathetically by others and to take pressure off oneself, this does not require diagnosis of a specific mental disorder related to lying about being a victim of a crime to make sense. Dietz further notes (p. 46) that "His motivation for staging the events was psychological and not intended to produce monetary or other obvious external gain," yet the authors would argue that the very things listed by Dietz are external gains. Simply because some gains are "psychological" does not make it a mental illness. Even if one assumes that Dr. Smith arranged events to garner sympathy, one does not need to diagnose a mental illness to explain the behaviors. Diagnosing (as opposed to understanding) behaviors can be brought to absurd levels, as offered by Feldman and Hamilton (2006) when they seem to suggest that the "role of unemployed person" is a potential and treatable illness. Apparently one can diagnose it by identifying a "job-hopper" who appears to be looking for employment but sabotages his or her success in various ways. The authors would suggest that any diagnosis of such a malady, as well as many so-called factitious disorders, can be adequately described or diagnosed under a different rubric, such as a personality disorder or antisocial behavior.

Gregg O. McCrary, a retired FBI profiler, also submitted a 56-page report in the Smith case (McCrary, 2005). It was his opinion after reviewing the evidence that the June 1–2 (the event crossed midnight), 2002, crime scene was staged. He went further, stating (p. 45):

> Presenting a false crime is analogous to "Munchausen's syndrome" wherein an individual presents with a feigned or self induced illness. ... This syndrome is based on a pre-occupation with manipulation. ... Rather than feign or produce an ostensibly legitimate illness, some individuals feign or create an ostensibly legitimate crime. The goal is to manipulate the criminal justice system in the service of underlying pathological needs. Because the condition is chronic, most individuals who do have this have a history of other attempts that tend to be less dramatic in content. This lesser efforts

---

[13] The only high-profile case found by the authors where a bomb was strapped to a person occurred on August 28, 2003, when a pizza delivery man robbed a bank and was killed when the device exploded. This was about a year after Dr. Smith was found wrapped in barbed wire with a bomb around his neck.

[sic] may include self-inflicted and pathological lying usually involving stories of dramatic events in which the individual is central. … Based upon the totality of the circumstances, it is my opinion that the April 2001 letters, the March 13, 2002 discovery of incendiary and explosive devices … and the alleged assault on Dr. O. C. Smith on June 1–2, 2002 are related incidents, staged by Dr. Smith for unknown psychological reasons.

One might be tempted to believe that McCrary is offering a psychological opinion here. Although not explicitly offering a diagnosis, he has equated Dr. Smith's report of assault and harassment with a chronic (mental) disorder due to a psychological motivation. The point must be made again: simply being able to offer a psychological explanation for a behavior does not make it a mental illness.

As with Ressler in the Dahmer case, the question of whether McCrary is qualified to make such inferences is appropriate. On his website (www.criminalprofiler.com), McCrary's biography notes he is an adjunct professor of forensic psychology at both Marymount University in Arlington, Virginia, and Nova Southeastern University in Ft. Lauderdale, Florida. He was awarded a B.A. degree in fine arts from Ithaca College in New York and did graduate work in criminal justice at Long Island University. Additional graduate work at the University of Virginia is cited, but a specific area of study is not mentioned. McCrary was awarded a master's degree in psychological services from Marymount University of Arlington, Virginia, in 1992. However, this is not a degree one would be expected to pursue to practice as a psychologist. It appears better suited to prepare one for further study or to practice as a school guidance counselor.

There is a further discrepancy, however. When he was retained in the Sam Sheppard civil case in 2000 (*The Estate of Sam Sheppard v. State of Ohio*, Case No. 312322), McCrary's curriculum vitae (CV) listed his 1992 degree as a master's of arts in psychological services. When retained for the O. C. Smith case, McCrary's CV listed his degree as a master's of arts in psychology, a degree Marymount University did not offer in 1992.[14]

McCrary did not appear as a witness in the Smith trial. After a pretrial evidentiary hearing, Dr. Dietz was allowed to testify to the existence of factitious disorders, including factitious victimization. He was not allowed to specifically opine that Dr. Smith suffered from one, as he had not examined him.[15] The jury could not reach a verdict, and a mistrial was declared. Eventually, all charges were dropped in lieu of a new trial, all but exonerating Dr. Smith.

Psychics

The issue of psychics must be addressed because many law enforcement agencies will "use" a psychic "when all else fails." Unfortunately, this lends credence to the belief that psychics are real. Robert Ressler brought a psychic to the FBI academy to lecture (Ressler and Shachtman, 1992). John Douglas (Douglas and Olshaker, 1995, p. 148) suggests that psychics "should be a last resort." While waiting until other means have failed is helpful, this mentality still endorses the use of psychics in criminal investigations. That law enforcement ever uses a psychic is sad commentary on our society, but occasionally law enforcement officers lament that if they don't use a psychic on a cold case they will be pressured to do so by family or some other quarter.[16]

The authors were not sure whether to list Micki Pistorius, a South African criminal profiler, as a psychologist or a psychic.[17] Ultimately, we do so as a commentary, and cautionary tale, regarding psychics who cloak their advice with psychological garb to imply legitimacy.

---

[14] All documents are on file with the author and editor of this text.

[15] As previously mentioned, the defense had declined to allow Dr. Dietz to examine Dr. Smith.

[16] For those who cling to the belief that using psychics in an investigation is helpful, the authors would recommend Nickel (1994).

[17] Dr. Pistorius is discussed in more length and context in the Preface to the Third Edition.

Dr. Pistorius is an "investigative psychologist" who, having studied IP under Dr. David Canter, worked for the South African Police Service for six years (Pistorius, 2005). In discussing whether profiling is an art or a science, she makes the following claims (p. 10):

- A "vibe" is a vibration of energy. Quantum physics teaches us that all matter vibrates, even thoughts vibrate, creating an energy field.
- Everyone has the ability to respond to energy fields in this way, but some people have a greater sensitivity than others.
- Crime scenes are laden with the residual energy fields of the killers and the victims and the acts that were committed there.
- Over time a profiler can develop a sixth sense to tune into this vibration of energy.
- Delta brainwaves are responsible for our instincts.

Keep in mind that Dr. Pistorius is arguably the preeminent profiler (at least by reputation) in South Africa. She continues (p. 11):

- My delta brainwaves were highly activated when I was working on a crime scene and this allowed me to tune into the "vibes" of the killer.
- We all have these brainwaves, but my delta brainwaves are apparently more active than average
- [M]y ability to "pick up the vibes of the killer" is not mumbo-jumbo (which is something I have been accused of); there is a scientific explanation for it.
- I could "feel" when they were killing and describe the crime scene to the detectives as if I were looking through the killers' eyes, even though I might have been hundreds of kilometers away at the time of the killing.

It is difficult to read her work and wonder how anyone in her right mind would let Dr. Pistorius near a crime scene or be part of an investigation. Yet it happens. These quotes are no different from the commentary one might expect from a professed psychic.

FORENSIC PSYCHOLOGISTS AND PSYCHIATRISTS AS PROFILERS[18]

Criminal profiling, as practiced by many, is more art than science. It is clearly a collection of proficiencies, with few practitioners engaged in criminal profiling full time. It is best considered one aspect of the practice of a well-rounded individual.

A significant aspect of criminal profiling is knowledge of human behavior and skill in interpreting its meaning, yet most profilers have no formal background or education in the behavioral sciences. In fact, law enforcement often looks askance at including a psychologist or a psychiatrist in an investigation, delegating their involvement as the second-to-last resort, with psychics generally occupying the last-resort niche.

Forensic psychologists and psychiatrists have a unique understanding and training in mental processes, physiology, thinking, human behavior, and psychopathology. Because of this, forensic mental health professionals can be well positioned to acquire further education related to investigations and the forensic sciences, which would allow them to review available evidence and offer an informed assessment (i.e., criminal profile) of the kind of individual who may have committed a particular criminal

---

[18] The remainder of this chapter is adapted, in part, from McGrath (2000).

act. It is incumbent upon them, as well as on all professionals, not to overreach or to go further than the evidence allows.

The behaviorally trained profiler may offer investigative advice, including proactive strategies and sometimes interviewing strategies in the event the offender is caught, although unless the strategies are carefully formulated, in some circumstances this last role may contravene professional ethics. The behaviorally trained profiler may also be utilized at the trial level to inform legal strategy. To competently profile, a forensic psychiatrist or psychologist needs to ensure that he or she has had adequate experience evaluating criminal offenders, so as to gain applied knowledge of antisocial individuals, especially those who fall into the category of sexual deviancy and sex offenders. Psychologists and psychiatrists may have much to offer when they are careful to limit investigative input to supportable opinions and to avoid mere speculation, with investigatively relevant insights being the goal of consultation, not the compilation of psychodynamically interesting, but ultimately useless, conjecture. Forensic psychiatry and forensic psychology share several characteristics with offender profiling, as discussed next.

Practice Is an Art

Forensic psychiatry and forensic psychology and profiling can be thought of as being based on scientific principles, but the actual application of one's skill, education, training, and experience to a specific case is an art. When evaluating a person in a forensic setting, the psychologist or psychiatrist relies on the science of the field (diagnostic criteria, theories of behavior, etc.). The application of that scientific base is dependent on the skill of the practitioner; in turn, the skill of the practitioner is dependent on the person's education, training, and experience. It should be no different with a criminal profiler. While accepting that the practice of a field may be an art, reliance on one's experiential knowledge in the absence of a scientific mindset or approach opens the door to error. For example, it was not that long ago that we were taught that the Sun revolved around the Earth or that there was an "organized/disorganized" dichotomy that was helpful in determining the characteristics of serial killers.

Need for Critical Thinking

Critical thinking skills are extremely important for the three fields. One must be willing to question every aspect of a case. The profiler must not simply review reports or information for inclusion in his or her profile but should critically review the data, ensuring that results or inferences are reasonable and supported by the evidence. One cannot assume the facts of a case.[19] One should be willing to question the supplied "facts" and evidence as necessary. If the profiler asks an investigator if the victim had a significant other (SO) and the response is that the SO was already considered and has been "cleared," the profiler should ask on what basis and assess to his or her own satisfaction if the SO is in the clear. If the investigator is troubled by this approach, the authors would suggest they do not want the services of a qualified profiler. Incredibly, FBI profilers doing an equivocal death analysis[20] in the USS *Iowa* explosion stated to a congressional committee looking into the botched investigation that it was not their practice to critically examine information supplied to them by others.

---

[19] The reader is referred to Thompson (1999). This book shows how institutional bias and a lack of critical thinking, as well as an unwillingness to question the validity of evidence, led to erroneous conclusions.

[20] This is what others would call a *psychological autopsy*. Since those performing the "autopsy" did not have a psychological background, it would be necessary to change the name ascribed to what they were doing.

"Whenever we are requested to do a case for an investigative agency, we make the assumption that we are dealing with professionals. They provide us with materials for review, and that's what we review" (The USS *Iowa*, 1990, pp. 25–28).

Independent Analysis

The profiler/psychiatrist/psychologist should (ideally) work in concert with, but independent of, the agency that engaged him or her. Subtle pressure to find what the client wants needs to be scrupulously resisted. The results of not adhering to this should be obvious. A tragic example of in-house pressure was the Branch Davidian standoff in Waco, Texas. In that scenario, an FBI profiler was pressured to change his assessment of how David Koresh would respond to various siege tactics. The profiler recommended negotiating with Koresh, while supervisors favored "tactical pressure" on the compound (U.S. Department of Justice, 1993). After being advised that his memos cautioning against an aggressive approach were "tying their hands," he wrote another memo supporting a more aggressive strategy. This memo was part of the argument to utilize a gas attack on the compound, an attack that resulted in significant loss of life (Freedman, 1995).

Review of All Available Data

Clearly, having access to all available data will make for a more informed opinion. Just as the forensic psychiatrist or psychologist will want to review all available records and interview the defendant in a criminal case before forming an opinion, the profiler will want to visit the crime scene (if possible) and review all available data related to victimology and forensic evidence.

If this is not possible for any reason, the omission and the reasons for it should be clearly elucidated in the report. All parties involved should be clearly informed about what was done, what was not done, and why.

Reliance on the Facts of a Particular Case or Cases

Just as a forensic psychologist/psychiatrist should not form an opinion based solely on his or her experience, the profiler needs to be careful to make inferences from the data in the case at hand. A forensic psychiatrist or psychologist would not make a diagnosis based on one symptom, no matter how often he or she may have seen the symptom in a certain diagnosis. In an analogous fashion, the fact that most homicides are intraracial tells a profiler little in a specific case, unless there are other indicators relevant to race.

Need to Avoid Advocacy

Forensic psychiatrists, psychologists, or profilers can be advocates for their opinions but should not advocate for either side in an adversarial (legal) arena or even on the investigative level. It is not the profiler's role to help a particular side prevail or to help a particular entity prove something. The profiler's only duty is to render opinions consistent with the facts of a case. Subtle pressures to assume an advocacy position abound and the best defense is awareness.

Contextual Differences

A psychiatrist or psychologist practicing from his or her office may diagnosis a mental illness and prescribe a course of treatment. At some later date, the practitioner could be asked in court, during a lawsuit or criminal action unrelated to the treatment, what the diagnosis was. The practitioner should consider the context. If testifying as a fact witness, he or she would give the diagnosis in the medical record. If testifying as an expert, the practitioner should reply that he or she has no forensic opinion, because the patient was never examined for the purpose of testifying in court. The evaluation of the patient would (and should) be markedly different in the two contexts, treatment versus forensic. With profiling, the profiler needs to understand the difference between rendering an investigatively helpful profile and a profile meeting a court-level threshold that imparts probative value. It is inappropriate to offer a criminal profile developed for investigative purposes in a court of law and to imply that it meets the standard of a court proceeding, unless the profile was developed to that standard initially.

Ethical Practice

Both profiling and forensic psychiatric or psychological practice need to be performed in an ethical manner. Practitioners in these fields need to take reasonable care that others do not misuse their work product and do not materially misrepresent their expertise. In addition, the profiler needs to understand that his or her profile cannot and should not be used to indicate the guilt of a particular individual. If asked if a specific person "fits" a profile, it is reasonable to indicate if it is so. But one should offer that "fitting" a profile is not the same as an identification. The standard is no different from the standard for a criminalist who offers an opinion that two hairs are a "match." Not attempting to add what a "match" means from a scientific perspective[21] is to mislead the jury.

What Would a Forensic Psychiatrist or Psychologist Need to Competently Profile?

A forensic psychiatrist or psychologist who would like to pursue profiling as part of his or her professional repertoire would need to have adequate experience evaluating criminal offenders to gain applied knowledge of antisocial individuals, especially those who fall into the category of sexual deviancy and sex offenders. He or she would need to gain extra knowledge in the forensic sciences and in investigative issues to be able to understand what will and what will not be helpful to the investigator in the field. The avenues one may pursue to gain such knowledge are varied, and there is no agreed-upon curriculum. A significant amount of work can be done through reading of applied texts and taking available courses online, at colleges and universities, and through professional organizations. One caveat is that the practitioner will need to use his or her critical thinking skills to weed out dubious courses or programs. Taking a one-day profiling course from someone who claims you will learn what you need to know to competently profile is likely to be unhelpful.

Role of the Forensic Psychologist or Psychiatrist as Profiler

A forensic psychologist or psychiatrist acting as a profiler can consult with law enforcement, prosecutors, or defense attorneys on a specific issue related to profiling or on a "cold case," or act as part of a multidisciplinary team (profiler + investigators + forensic scientists) engaged in a current investigation. The psychiatrist/psychologist-profiler can provide investigatively relevant interpretations related to crime scene behaviors and victimology, with the key word being "relevant." Opining that vaginal mutilation is an unconscious attempt on the part of a murderer to get back to the womb may meet the needs of the profiler, but it is not likely to be of much help to the investigator attempting to solve the crime. In contrast, inferring (if warranted) that emasculation of a young boy in a sexual assault was an attempt to undo a homosexual act by turning the boy into a girl may save the investigators time by avoiding their concentrating on overt homosexuals as suspects.

---

[21] That is, that the hairs share similar characteristics, but one cannot state with certainty that they came from the same source.

The forensic psychiatrist/psychologist-profiler can serve as a consultant to other profilers, laying claim to added expertise in the behavioral sciences, just as a profiler more proficient in the forensic sciences might entertain a question in his or her area of expertise from the psychiatrist. A forensic psychiatrist/psychologist can also educate other nonpsychiatric profilers about the psychiatric pitfalls of profiling (discussed next). Lastly, the forensic psychiatrist/psychologist can act as a researcher, using his or her knowledge of the behavioral sciences as a nexus for research in applied offender profiling, an area so far neglected by all disciplines.

Psychological Pitfalls and the Profiler

Whatever the educational and training background of the profiler, there are certain issues or problems that he or she must be aware of and make efforts to avoid or to minimize their effect on the work product.

Bias

Profilers, like all other human beings, are subject to bias, both conscious and unconscious. Whether the issue is dislike of pedophiles or men who physically abuse women, one must be on guard not to let personal biases influence a profile. The issue is not that one needs to get rid of all negative feelings but rather that one needs a mature outlook and to minimize the number of preconceived (ill-conceived?) notions one brings to a case. One can view autopsy photos of a mutilated corpse and exclaim that the perpetrator of the crime is sick, but this is not helpful to the investigation and does little to put the profiler in the mindset of the offender.

Transference

Transference is a psychoanalytical term for the phenomenon that occurs when a patient relates to a therapist in a manner that mimics other relationships from the patient's past. An example is when a male patient interacts with a male therapist as if he were the patient's father. Countertransference is the term for a similar phenomenon in reverse (i.e., the feelings that the patient evokes in the therapist). In a less formal sense, one could talk about transference in other situations, although psychiatrists and psychologists would argue the specifics. The authors suggest that it is possible for a profiler to experience transference in a case (as could anyone on the investigative or legal team). In other words, the profiler could react unconsciously to a case based on some facet that strikes him or her. This unwarranted emphasis could affect the profiler's judgment and the direction of a resulting profile. The issue could be related to prior case material or to aspects of the profiler's personal life. For example, a profiler could have had a bad relationship with his or her father and unconsciously assume that the offender in a case is a male when in fact no evidence exists to indicate the sex of the offender. The unconscious need is to punish the father, but this gets played out in the profiler's work product.

Projection

Projection is a psychoanalytical term for ascribing to others the thoughts, feelings, or motives of oneself. For example, a man may be sexually attracted to his friend's wife. The man then tells his friend that he had better watch his wife, as she appears to be attracted to him. It is possible (in the authors' opinion) for a profiler to project part of his or her unconscious issues into/onto a crime scene or victimology assessment. For example: A female profiler has ambivalent feelings about motherhood. She has a teenage child who is difficult to control and she resents the child and wishes she were not responsible for her. In assessing victimology in a case where a 12-year-old girl was abducted, the profiler focuses on some signals that the mother and the victim did not get along and pursues an avenue of case analysis unconsciously designed to prove that the mother wanted to get rid of the child victim.

All the issues mentioned (bias, transference, and projection) can only be minimized, not realistically eliminated entirely. Potential profilers are cautioned to know themselves, to keep themselves healthy both mentally and physically, and to have a life with gratification outside of profiling. Case conferencing with colleagues is often helpful in limiting bias, transference, and other issues. For the sake of clarity, these issues can never be entirely negated, but through awareness of them and their impact we can minimize their harmful effects.

The forensic psychiatrist or psychologist has much to offer the developing field of behavioral profiling. He or she can bring a technically proficient aspect of the behavioral sciences to the professional table. Some, but not all, forensic psychiatrists and psychologists will make good behavioral profilers, just as some investigators and forensic scientists, but not all, will make good profilers. If one is willing to invest the necessary extra effort to educate oneself to the basic forensic sciences and investigative issues, the field of offender profiling has much to offer the forensic psychiatrist or psychologist and much to gain from his or her expertise.

SUMMARY

Forensic psychology and psychiatry involve the application of the behavioral sciences to legal questions. Common psycholegal questions that forensic mental health professionals answer involve (1) risk for future sexual offense recidivism, (2) competency to stand trial, and (3) criminal responsibility/sanity at the time of the offense. In addition, forensic psychologists and psychiatrists, with their knowledge of human behavior, can add a unique perspective to ongoing investigations in the form of offender profiling.

Forensic psychologists and psychiatrists are specifically trained mental health professionals with set levels of education, patient contact, licensure, and certification. Not everyone who calls himself or herself a psychologist, or a forensic psychologist, in the profiling community can meet these standards. Those employing profilers should be particularly wary of those who cloak their advice with psychological garb to imply legitimacy, including so-called investigative psychologists and psychics.

Forensic psychologists and psychiatrists have a unique understanding of, and training in, mental processes, physiology, thinking, human behavior, and psychopathology. Because of this, forensic mental health professionals can be well positioned to acquire further education related to investigations and the forensic sciences, allowing them to review available evidence and to offer an informed assessment (i.e., criminal profile) of the kind of individual who may have committed a particular criminal act. However, they are also bound to operate within set ethical limits and guidelines.

Questions

1. What are the differences between a forensic psychologist and a forensic psychiatrist?
2. True or False: The role of the mental health professional is to get the patient to confess to involvement in a crime.
3. Give an example of projection.
4. Explain the difference between sanity and competency to stand trial, if any.
5. What is *collateral information*, and how is it used?

REFERENCES

American Psychiatric Association, 2000. Diagnostic and Statistical Manual of Mental Disorders, fourth ed–Text Revision, American Psychiatric Association, Washington, DC.

Bersoff, D., Goodman-Delahunty, J., Grisso, T., Hans, V., Poythrees, N., Roesch, R., 1997. Training in Law and Psychology: Models from the Villanova Conference. American Psychologist 52 (12), 1301–1310.

Burgess, A.W., Hazelwood, R.R., 2001. False Rape Allegations. In: Hazelwood, R.R., Burgess, A.W. (Eds.), Practical Aspects of Rape Investigation: A Multidisciplinary Approach, third ed. CRC Press, New York, NY, pp. 177–197.

Callahan, L.A., McGreery, M.A., Cirincione, C., Steadman, H.J., 1992. Measuring the Effects of the Guilty but Mentally Ill (GBMI) Verdict: Georgia's 1982 GBMI Reform. Law and Human Behavior 16, 447–462.

Committee on Ethical Guidelines for Forensic Psychologists, 1991. Specialty Guidelines for Forensic Psychologists. Law and Human Behavior 15 (6), 655–665.

Dietz, P., Ankrom, L., 2004. Report to Patrick Harris, Esq, Assistant U.S. Attorney General, December 7.

Dohn, H.H., 1986. Factitious Rape: A Case Report. Hillside Journal of Clinical Psychiatry 8 (2), 224–231.

Douglas, J., Olshaker, M., 1995. Mindhunter: Inside the FBI's Elite Serial Crime Unit. Pocket Books, New York, NY.

Eisendrath, S.J., 1996. When Munchausen Becomes Malingering: Factitious Disorders That Penetrate the Legal System. Bulletin of the American Academy of Psychiatry Law 24 (4), 471–481.

Eke, N., Elenwo, S.N., 1999. Male Genital Mutilation: "Whodunnit?" Journal of Clinical and Forensic Medicine 6, 246–248.

Feldman, M.D., Hamilton, J.C., 2006. Job-Hopping and Factitious Victimization (letter to the editor). Southern Medical Journal 99 (10), 1142–1143.

Feldman, M.D., Ford, C.V., Stone, T., 1994. Deceiving Others/Deceiving Oneself: Four Cases of Factitious Rape. Southern Medical Journal 87 (7), 736–738.

Feldman-Schorrig, S., 1996. Factitious Sexual Harassment. Bulletin of the American Academy of Psychiatry Law 24 (3), 387–392.

Fliege, H., Scholler, G., Rose, M., Willenberg, H., Klapp, B.F., 2002. Fictitious Disorders and Pathological Self-Harm in a Hospital Population: An Interdisciplinary Challenge. General Hospital Psychiatry 24, 164–171.

Fonda, D., 2004. Abduction Overruled. Time April 4. Available at www.time.com/time/magazine/article/0,9171,607807,00.html.

Ford, C.V., King, B.H., Hollender, M.H., 1988. Lies and Liars: Psychiatric Aspects of Prevarication. American Journal of Psychiatry 145 (5), 554–562.

Freedman, D., 1995. FBI Analyst Says He Was Ignored on Waco. Washington Times May 1, A1, A20.

Gibbon, K.L., 1998a. False Allegations of Rape in Adults. Journal of Clinical and Forensic Medicine 5, 195–198.

Gibbon, K.L., 1998b. Munchausen's Syndrome Presenting as an Acute Sexual Assault. Medical Science and Law 38 (3), 202–205.

Golding, S.L., Skeem, J.L., Roesch, R., Zapf, P.A., 1999. The Assessment of Criminal Responsibility. In: Hess, A.K., Weiner, I.B. (Eds.), The Handbook of Forensic Psychology. second ed. John Wiley & Sons, New York, NY, pp. 379–408.

Goldstein, A.B., 1998. Identification and Classification of Factitious Disorders: An Analysis of Cases Reported during a Ten Year Period. International Journal of Psychiatry and Medicine 28 (2), 221–241.

Gutheil, T.G., 1989. Borderline Personality Disorder, Boundary Violations, and Patient-Therapist Sex: Medicolegal Pitfalls. American Journal of Psychiatry 146 (5), 597–602.

Gutheil, T.G., 1992. Approaches to Forensic Assessment of False Claims of Sexual Misconduct by Therapists. Bulletin of the American Academy of Psychiatry and Law 20 (3), 289–296.

Hans, V.P., Slater, D., 1983. John Hinckley, Jr., and the Insanity Defense: The Public's Verdict. Public Opinion Quarterly 47 (2), 202–212.

Hess, A.K., 1999. Defining Forensic Psychology. In: Hess, A.K., Weiner, I.B. (Eds.), The Handbook of Forensic Psychology, second ed. John Wiley & Sons, New York, NY, pp. 324–347.

Kanin, E.J., 1994. False Rape Allegations. Archives of Sexual Behavior 23 (1), 81–89.

Matas, M., Marriott, A., 1987. The Girl Who Cried Wolf: Pseudologia Phantastica and Sexual Abuse. Canadian Journal of Psychiatry 32 (4), 305–309.

McCrary, G.O., 2005. Report to Patrick Harris, Esq, Assistant U.S. Attorney General, January 21.

McDowell, C.P., Hibler, N.S., 1987. False Allegations. In: Hazelwood, R.R., Burgess, A.W. (Eds.), Practical Aspects of Rape Investigation: A Multidisciplinary Approach. Elsevier, New York, NY, pp. 275–299.

McGrath, M., 2000. Forensic Psychiatry and Criminal Profiling: Forensic Match or Freudian Slipup? Journal of Behavioral Profiling 1 (1).

Nickel, J., 1994. Psychic Sleuths: ESP and Sensational Cases. Prometheus Press, Buffalo, NY.

Parnham, G., Odom, W., Shefman, D., 2004. Appellant brief in *Andrea Yates v. State of Texas*. 01-02-00462-CR and 01-02-00463-CR, filed in the Texas Court of Appeals, 1st District of Texas, Houston, Texas, April 30.

Pathe, M., Mullen, P.E., Purcell, R., 1999. Stalking: False Claims of Victimization. British Journal of Psychiatry 174, 170–172.

Pistorius, M., 2005. Profiling Serial Killers and Other Crimes in South Africa. Penguin Books, London, England.

Ressler, R.K., Shachtman, T., 1992. Whoever Fights Monsters. St. Martin's Press, New York, NY.

Ressler, R.K., Shachtman, T., 1997. I Have Lived in the Monster. St. Martin's Press, New York, NY.

Roesch, R., Zapf, P.A., Golding, S.L., Skeem, J.L., 1999. Defining and Assessing Competency to Stand Trial. In: Hess, A.K., Weiner, I.B. (Eds.), The Handbook of Forensic Psychology, second ed. John Wiley & Sons, New York, NY, pp. 327–349.

Sederer, L.I., Libby, M., 1995. False Allegations of Sexual Misconduct: Clinical and Institutional Considerations. Psychiatric Service 46 (2), 160–163.

Sloat, S.M., Frierson, R.L., 2005. Juror Knowledge and Attitudes Regarding Mental Illness Verdicts. Journal of the American Academy of Psychiatry Law 33 (2), 208–213.

The USS *Iowa*: Guilt by Gestalt, 1990. Congressional Testimony. Harper's Magazine March, 25–28.

Thompson II, C., 1999. A Glimpse of Hell: The Explosion on the USS *Iowa* and Its Cover Up. W.W. Norton & Company, New York, NY.

U.S. Department of Justice, 1993. Report to the Deputy Attorney General on the Events at Waco, Texas. Available online at www.usdoj.gov/05publications/waco/wacofour.html.

An Introduction to Behavioral Evidence Analysis

Brent E. Turvey[1]

CONTENTS

---

[1] This chapter is adapted from, and builds heavily on, Petherick and Turvey (2008).

KEY TERMS

Behavioral evidence	Crime scene analysis	Individuation
Behavioral evidence	Forensic analysis	Intuition
analysis (BEA)	Forensic victimology	Nomothetic offender profile
Common sense	Identification (or	Observer bias
Confirmation bias	Classification)	Practice standards
Criminal profiling	Idiographic offender profiles	Principles

To bring facts in relation to each other, to connect them in such a way that their functional significance becomes visible, to separate the essential from the accidental, to draw conclusions from certain premises—all these are logical operations.

—Theodore Reik (*The Unknown Murderer*, 1945, p. 26)

Idiographic (individual case) study builds knowledge about the characteristics of a particular case. It is necessary when trying to understand the peculiar characteristics, dynamics, and relationships between a particular crime scene, victim, and offender. *Idiographic offender profiles*, therefore, are characteristics developed from an examination of a single case, or a series of cases linked by a single offender. An idiographic profile is therefore concrete—it describes an actual offender who exists in the real world.

A *nomothetic* profile is an average, or a prediction; it does not describe a real offender walking around and breathing in the real world. However, profilers use both nomothetic and ideographic information to render the conclusions in their profiles. The trick is using nomothetic information in theory generation, and not presenting it as a firm or deductive conclusion.

The purpose of this chapter is to discuss the general method, principles, and practice standards of *behavioral evidence analysis (BEA)*. Given the discussions of alternative profiling methodology offered in this text so far, one might anticipate that this chapter will undertake to explain how vastly superior BEA is to current inductive/nomothetic methods. One might further anticipate that this chapter will exalt the infallibility of BEA. But even ego must give way to reason. Not only will this chapter refrain from presenting BEA as purely scientific or infallible, it will also refrain from presenting it as purely deductive.

THE INFERENCE OF TRAITS

In the most basic terms, *criminal profiling* is the inference of distinctive offender traits from physical and/or behavioral evidence. From the physical evidence left behind in relation to criminal activity, such as an offender's hair and semen, the criminal profiler may deduce that the offender is a male with a particular color of hair, perhaps even of a particular race.[2] Similarly, from behavioral evidence, inferences about the offender's background, habits, and personality (a.k.a. offender traits) may also be possible. As explained in Kidder (2005, p. 390):

---

[2] This type of deduction may of course be made by anyone capable of reading and understanding the results of physical evidence analysis in a given case and is certainly not limited to the profiler. Such deductions, given their heightened reliability, should form the initial core of any criminal profile.

Traits represent individual characteristics, which are either inherited or acquired, and refer to tendencies to act or react in certain ways (Drever, 1964). Key to this definition is the fact that having a particular trait does not guarantee predictable performance, but an individual possessing a certain trait will be more disposed to react to a given situation in a certain way (McKenna, 1994). Trait theorists view traits as broad, general guides that lend consistency to behavior.

BEA methodology suggests that examination of crime-related behavioral evidence over time, along with subsequent offender physical, personal, and psychological traits, can reveal individual offender trait correlations, patterns, and propensities. Some personal and psychological traits may be stable across a criminal career, some are situationally determined, and some will evolve (or even devolve).

BEA is generally consistent with Allport's dynamic *Trait Theory of Personality* (Allport and Odbert, 1936), which emphasizes the consideration of an individual's uniquely patterned personality traits as they change over time. BEA is built around the notion that individuals are unique, and that the examination of those differences is highly revealing. It therefore emphasizes ideographic examination over nomothetic.

Allport's *trait theory* also divides personality traits and dispositions into three general categories: *cardinal*, *central*, and *secondary*. *Cardinal traits* are the small number of dominant, pervasive and stable traits that define an individual to others and guide the majority of their decisions (e.g., extremely religious, extremely frugal, narcissistic, and altruistic); *central traits* are core characteristics and behavioral tendencies that accurately describe an individual, while not consistently dominating their decision-making processes and subsequent behavior (e.g., educated, intelligent, shy, and honest); and *secondary traits* are transitory preferences and moods, which are often situational and therefore less enduring (e.g., hungry, angry, impatient, or nervous).

While this theory provides a sound theoretical platform for BEA interpretations, its considerations also become important when attempting to understand and to explain the durability of inferred offender characteristics, or when comparing the characteristics evident across multiple cases in linkage analysis efforts.

BEHAVIORAL EVIDENCE ANALYSIS (BEA) DEFINED

Behavioral evidence is any physical, documentary, or testimonial evidence that helps to establish whether, when, or how an action has taken place. Any form of physical evidence may also be behavioral evidence under the right circumstances. Footprints and footwear impressions can indicate presence; standing, walking, or running; and direction. Bloodstain patterns can indicate presence, injury, contact, or movement and direction. Fingerprints can indicate presence, contact, and use of an object. Semen and sperm can indicate presence, contact, sexual behavior, and ejaculation. Injuries can indicate weapon type, presence, contact, the amount of force, and even intent. Ligature patterns can indicate strangulation, binding, and resistance. Toxicological testing can indicate the presence of drugs, alcohol, or toxins in a victim or offender's system, and these also have an impact on cognition, judgment, state of mind, and health—all of which influence behavior. Photo images and video footage from the media, security cameras, cell phones, digital cameras, and camcorders operating at the time of an event can provide limited but specific documentation of behavioral evidence. To be useful, behavioral evidence must be examined and considered as a whole, in a directed and purposeful fashion, in order to achieve meaningful results. It cannot be surmised inconsistently, without focus, or based solely on the subjective insights of experience. That's where BEA comes in.

BEA is an ideo-deductive method of crime scene analysis and criminal profiling. It involves the examination and interpretation of physical evidence, forensic victimology, and crime scene characteristics. For the purposes of criminal profiling, the results of these individual examinations can be analyzed for behavioral patterns and clusters that suggest offender characteristics of investigative or forensic relevance. BEA is ideographic in that it is concerned with studying the aspects of individual cases and offenders through the lens of forensic analysis—not groups of similar cases and presumably similar offenders. It is deductive in that inferences and conclusions are not inductive theories or nomothetic predictions in disguise. They are based on critical thinking, the scientific method, and analytical logic.

BEA conclusions are meant to be the result of the most complete understanding of the events surrounding the commission of the crime. A BEA-style crime scene analysis or criminal profile will not render a conclusion unless the evidence exists to support it. Instead of relying on averaged (nonexistent/abstract) offender statistics, BEA profilers conduct a detailed examination of a scene and related behaviors to determine which characteristics are evidenced. This approach requires more work, more study, and more humility than the alternative methods of profiling discussed in previous chapters.

In general, the information used to develop a BEA profile is drawn from at least the following individual examinations: forensic analysis, forensic victimology, and crime scene analysis.

FORENSIC ANALYSIS (A.K.A. EQUIVOCAL FORENSIC ANALYSIS)

Forensic analysis, in general, is the first step in BEA, and refers to the examination, testing, and interpretation of any and all available physical evidence. A thorough forensic analysis must be performed on the physical evidence to establish the corresponding behavioral evidence in a case before a BEA profile can be attempted. One cannot offer a BEA profile based on unproven conjecture or guesswork masquerading as fact—and until the results of the forensic analysis are known, that is the only kind of information available to the profiler. A thorough forensic analysis is required to establish the strengths and limits of the existing physical evidence. This threshold demand ensures the integrity of the behavior and subsequent crime scene characteristics that are going to be analyzed by the criminal profiler.

Consequently, the victim and offender behavior used to create a profile must be established from reliable sources. Behavioral evidence cannot simply be assumed or inferred by those without sufficient forensic education, training, and experience— or by those with an agenda. This means understanding and applying the scientific method with respect to evidence interpretation (as discussed in Chapter 2). This also means settling for nothing less than established reconstruction techniques applied by qualified forensic scientists.[3] A competent forensic analysis requires an informed crime reconstruction (see Chapter 11). There are more than a few practicing criminal profilers who suffer from a metacognitive block in this area; they believe that by virtue of being criminal profilers they are also somehow qualified to perform crime reconstruction. Even with the best intentions, the resulting behavioral evidence interpretations tend to range from the intellectually incomplete to the utterly incompetent. If a criminal profiler is not also a forensic scientist and not properly educated and trained in crime reconstruction methods and their limits, then he or she should not keep their own counsel when seeking to understand and integrate a picture of crime-related behavior from the physical evidence.[4]

---

[3] Many criminal profilers accept the theories of the detectives or attorneys who contact them as factual reconstructions of events that are fit for analysis. While the theories are a fast way for the profiler to get information, neither investigators nor attorneys are forensic scientists. All forensic examiners, profilers included, should know this, and are admonished to treat theories with the appropriate level of distrust.

[4] For a complete reference, see Chisum and Turvey (2011).

We discuss this further in the "Behavior Evidence Analysis Standards of Practice" section of this chapter. Suffice it to say that the scientific method demands that criminal profilers be skeptical; they must work to disprove theories, not prove them; they must abandon disproved theories; and they must embrace theories that have yet to be disproved as the most valid. They must also know enough to recognize when they are wrong.

FORENSIC VICTIMOLOGY

As explained in Ferguson and Turvey (2009, p.1), *forensic victimology* is the scientific "study of violent crime victims for the purposes of addressing investigative and forensic questions." It involves the accurate, critical, and objective outlining of a victim's lifestyle and circumstances, the events leading up to an injury, and the precise nature of any harm or loss suffered. Establishing the characteristics of a particular offender's victim choices can lead to inferences about fantasy, motive, modus operandi, knowledge, and skill.

Forensic victimology includes an assessment of victim risk and exposure. The profiler is interested in not only the amount of exposure to harm that a victim's lifestyle routinely incurs, but also the amount of exposure the victim suffered at the actual time of the attack. From this information, the profiler may determine the amount of exposure that the offender was willing to allow in order to acquire the victim. This is inherently useful in contextualizing other offender behavior and choices related to the crime.

CRIME SCENE ANALYSIS

Crime scene analysis (a.k.a. crime analysis) is the analytical process of interpreting the specific features of a crime and related crime scenes. Potential crime scene characteristics that must be established or at least considered include, among many others, method of approach, method of attack, method of control, location type, nature and sequence of sexual acts, materials used, evidence of skill or planning, any verbal activity, precautionary acts, contradictory acts, modus operandi, signature behavior, and the amount of time spent in the commission of the crime. Crime scene characteristics are interpreted from an integrated examination of the established behavioral evidence and victimology. Because they depend on evidence, and complete evidence is not always be available, not all crime scene characteristics may be established in every case. This can limit any subsequent findings, and in some cases may even prevent meaningful profiling efforts.

The results of crime scene analysis may be used to compare cases for linkage analysis purposes (see Chapter 14), or they may be used to render a criminal profile.

BEHAVIORAL EVIDENCE ANALYSIS: GOALS AND PURPOSE

Perhaps the most common misconception about criminal profiling is that its main purpose is to achieve a static, inflexible result, not unlike a clinical diagnosis. The result is then presumably applied to a crime or series of crimes and can then be used to suggest precisely *whodunit*. This is evidenced by the persistent yet inaccurate belief that there is an average psychological or behavioral pattern or profile that describes a typical serial murderer, a typical rapist, or even a typical crime scene.

This clinical view of profiling regards clusters of offender behavior, and subsequent penal classifications, as potential mental health disorders that can be diagnosed for the purposes of recommending treatment or delineating cause. It is a highly desirable position to take if one is a mental health practitioner. However, the goals of offender assessment and treatment are unrelated to the goals of criminal profiling. Clinicians have treatment goals—profilers have explicit investigative and forensic goals.

Humans learn, change, and grow. Humans are also affected by time, place, and each other. Therefore a deductively rendered criminal profile cannot be regarded as a static, fixed result that will hold true for all time. It must evolve and must become more refined as it is checked against new evidence and related cases over time. That is to say, when a new offense is committed, when a new attack occurs or a new body is located, and when new evidence is collected and analyzed, the integrity of the criminal profile must be reassessed. A deductively rendered profile learns. New information is not used to support the old profile, or to pigeonhole the offender, or to rationalize investigative assumptions. It is used to make a more complete and more accurate profile of the offender responsible for the crime(s) at hand.

Behavioral evidence analysis, therefore, should be viewed not as a process aimed at a fixed result, but as an ongoing, dynamic, critical, analytical process that examines offender behavior as it changes over time. It is a criminological effort, not a clinical one.

The first responsibility of the criminal profiler, as opposed to the treatment-oriented clinician, is fact finding in a criminal investigation for the purpose of serving justice.[5] The profiler serves the justice system. The clinician serves the client/patient. This is an important difference in terms of ethical obligations when considering the potential goals and purposes of behavioral evidence analysis.

With that onus in mind, a criminal investigation of any kind should start with the assumption that every human on the planet is a suspect. That is to say, the suspect set is universal. One of the purposes of BEA is to assist an investigation, at any phase, in moving from that universal set of suspect characteristics to a more discrete set of suspect characteristics. It cannot typically point to a specific person, or individuate one suspect from all others. It can, however, give insight into the *general* characteristics of the offender(s) responsible. This type of insight can be used to educate an investigative effort, as well as attorneys, judges, and juries in a forensic context (e.g., criminal proceedings, civil proceedings, and public hearings).

BEHAVIORAL EVIDENCE ANALYSIS: CONTEXTS

Behavioral evidence analysis has two separate but equal contexts, divided not by the method that is employed to arrive at conclusions, but rather by their divergent goals and priorities. Goals and priorities are dictated by a necessity that is dependent upon when, in a given case, a profiler's skills are requested. The two time frames typically include the *investigative phase*, before a suspect has been arrested (or before a defendant is taken to court with a lawsuit), and and the *trial phase*, while a suspect is being tried for a crime (or put on trial for damages).

The investigative phase of a criminal case gets a lot of the media attention and is the primary focus of popular fiction on the subject of criminal profiling. When we think of a criminal profiler, we have been conditioned to think of unsolved serial murder cases, and of remote locations where teams of forensic scientists work to recover decaying human remains. Profilers are often characterized as being socially alienated individuals,

---

[5] It is worth noting that the process of criminal investigation starts from the moment that law enforcement responds to a crime scene, and does not end until that case is completely out of the criminal justice system. For some cases, especially those involving homicide, this may never happen. It must also be noted that there are criminal investigators working hard for both sides of the courtroom in any legal proceedings, civil or criminal.

deeply troubled by their own selfless insights into the minds of the unknown offenders that they are hunting. This view presented by fiction and the media not only is completely skewed but also is only the first half of the equation.

The trial phase is the second half of the equation, and has received much less explicit attention not only in the media but in the published literature. Although it is equally important, it often lacks the romance and drama associated with high-profile serial cases, making it less marketable.

Investigative Phase

The investigative phase involves behavioral evidence analysis of the patterns of unknown perpetrators of known crimes. Criminal profilers tend to be called in to extremely violent, sexual and/or predatory cases when witness testimony, confessions, and/or physical evidence have not been enough to move the investigation forward. The decision to call a profiler into an investigation is typically reactive, with agencies waiting months or even years (if at all) due to a lack of access to a profiler, or to a lack of understanding of what criminal profiling is and how it can aid an investigation.

Primary Goals

- Evaluating the nature and value of forensic and behavioral evidence in a particular crime or series of related crimes
- Reducing the viable suspect pool in a criminal investigation
- Prioritizing the investigation into remaining suspects
- Linkage of potentially related crimes by identifying crime scene indicators and behavior patterns (i.e., modus operandi and signature)
- Assessment of the potential for escalation of nuisance criminal behavior to more serious or more violent crimes (i.e., harassment, stalking, voyeurism)
- Providing investigators with investigatively relevant leads and strategies
- Helping keep the overall investigation on track and undistracted by offering fresh and unbiased insights
- Developing communication, interview, or interrogation strategies when dealing with suspects

Trial Phase

The trial phase of criminal profiling involves behavioral evidence analysis of known crimes for which there is a suspect or a defendant (sometimes a convicted defendant). It takes place in the preparation for hearings, trials, and post-conviction proceedings. Guilt, penalty, and appeal phases of trial are all appropriate times to use profiling techniques, depending on the evidence at issue.

Primary Goals

- Evaluating the nature and value of forensic and behavioral evidence to a particular crime or series of related crimes
- Helping to develop insight into offender fantasy and motivations
- Developing insight into offender motive and intent before, during, and after the commission of a crime (i.e., levels of planning, evidence of remorse, precautionary acts, etc.)
- Linkage of potentially related crimes by identifying crime scene indicators and behavior patterns (i.e., modus operandi and signature)

BEHAVIORAL EVIDENCE ANALYSIS THINKING STRATEGIES

To best achieve any of the goals of behavioral evidence analysis, a criminal profiler must first and foremost be a critical, analytical thinker. As already discussed, profilers must have strong, well-honed critical thinking skills and approach cases both objectively and methodically. They must have enthusiasm for detail, be willing to question all assumptions, and be familiar enough with forensic science and criminal investigation to ask all of the right questions.

In addition to this, and evidenced by the principles and practice standards discussed, criminal profilers must also know themselves. They must know who they are and have a firm grasp of their own personality. They must be able to distinguish their own needs, tastes, desires, and morality so that they may more clearly perceive the needs, tastes, desires, and morality of a given offender. That means profilers must know who they are with an extremely irregular level of personal comfort: All of the questions that they have put to the life of the victim, they must put to themselves. They must know their strengths, fears, fantasies, and weaknesses. This is not a simple or by any means trivial point.

In the absence of self-knowledge and critical thinking skills, profilers risk transference of their own issues, needs, and morality into a profile. It bears repeating that it is not uncommon for untrained and undisciplined profilers to create profiles that tell more about their own needs than about the patterns of behavior being profiled. To avoid this pitfall, and to keep the BEA process a critical, analytical, and objective endeavor, profilers are admonished to follow these general guidelines regarding thinking strategies (some topics inspired by Depue et al., 1995, pp. 119–123).

Life Experience

It is often suggested that age will beget experience, which will beget wisdom. This is not the case at all. There are quite a number of people in the world who fail to learn from their mistakes, or their successes, and who are ultimately denied wisdom, or applied knowledge, of any kind. Life experience does not necessarily equal special knowledge or insight. Furthermore, not all investigative or law enforcement experience is equal. Note the differences below, just as a comparative example:

- 15 years in law enforcement
- 15 years as a homicide detective
- 15 years as a homicide detective in a rural county
- 15 years as a sex crimes detective
- 15 years as a sex crimes detective in a major metropolitan police department
- 7 years in vice; 8 years on patrol
- 3 years on patrol; 12 years as a guard at the jail

While each example represents 15 years in what can be generally referred to as law-enforcement experience, the specific nature and quality of that experience are quite varied. Kirk and Thornton (1974, p. 16) provide an excellent crystallization of this thought: "The amount of experience is unimportant beside the question of what has been learned from it."

The point is that, before we go around applying investigative or law-enforcement experience, or accepting the experiences of another, as the basis for our reasoning, we must have an understanding of the precise nature of that experience. Subsequently, the applied knowledge gained from that experience must be measured, weighed, and applied appropriately rather than indiscriminately. Not all experience is of equal quality or measure, despite how similar it may first appear.

Intuition

Invariably, an accumulation of any amount of life experience leads to intuition. That is, knowing or believing without the use of reason, or rational, articulable processes. If we have a belief, or something that we "just know," and are unable to articulate the reasoning behind it, it is likely that intuition is the culprit.

Seductive as they are, intuitions and gut instincts can be extensions of bias, prejudice, stereotyping, and accumulated ignorance. They can be extremely damaging to investigative efforts and should be left out of investigative strategy, suggestions, or final profiles unless reasonable, articulable arguments for their inclusion exist. Thornton (1997, p. 17) is very clear about the substitution of intuition or experience for scientific fact based on deductive logic:

> Experience is neither a liability nor an enemy of the truth; it is a valuable commodity, but it should not be used as a mask to deflect legitimate scientific scrutiny, the sort of scrutiny that customarily is leveled at scientific evidence of all sorts. To do so is professionally bankrupt and devoid of scientific legitimacy. ... Experience ought to be used to enable the expert to remember the when and the how, why, who, and what. Experience should not make the expert less responsible, but rather more responsible for justifying an opinion with defensible scientific facts.

Avoid Moral Judgments

Never use terminology in a profile that describes an offender as sick, crazy, nuts, a scumbag, worthless, immoral, etc. This terminology represents a moral judgment based on a profiler's personal feelings. Personal feelings have no place in a criminal profile. A good way to achieve objectivity is by not using adjectives, or using as few as possible, when describing an offender's personality characteristics.

Common Sense

Common sense is best defined as native good judgment. Put another way, it refers to knowledge accumulated by an individual that is useful for, but specific to, making decisions in the locations that he or she frequents. Common sense, then, is not common. What is socially acceptable, reasonable, and expected does not always transfer from country to country, state to state, city to city, neighborhood to neighborhood, or even person to person. Therefore, using our own common sense, our own eyes and beliefs, to gain insight into the behavior of another can be an expedition into the absurd. It assumes, incorrectly, that the offender and the profiler share a perception of what is common sense, as though they are creatures that inhabit the same culture.

As an example, in one's own home it is usual to remove garbage and food scraps to an area external to the living space. This makes perfect sense for reasons of health and comfort. However, if one is to go camping, this same action makes less sense, because, depending on the location, one runs the very real risk of attracting predators, some of which pose a threat to health or life.

THE PRINCIPLES OF BEHAVIORAL EVIDENCE ANALYSIS

Principles are the fundamental truths and propositions that provide the foundation for any given field of study. The basic principles of BEA identified by the authors, and drawn from the behavioral and biological sciences, include, but are certainly not limited to, the following:

1. *The principle of uniqueness:* Individuals develop uniquely over time, in response to biological, environmental, and subsequent psychological factors. However similar their past and present, no two

people will develop in precisely the same fashion. This is because each person is born with a unique genetic profile and temperament, is raised into their own culture surrounded by other uniquely formed individuals, and develops a unique constellation of associations with respect to pleasure, pain, taste, and distaste.

2. *The principle of separation:* Individuals have their own unique constellation of associations with respect to pleasure, pain, taste, and distaste—independent of the profiler. Consequently, no victim or offender should be treated as a mirror. This principle is meant to remind profilers that there are certain psychological pitfalls they should strive to avoid. This includes *vanity profiling;* the attribution of our own thoughts and motives (e.g., sexual fantasies, responses to danger, and belief systems) to others. Profilers must be aware of the fact that victims and offenders will act differently and choose differently than they might because they are different. Profilers also must be aware of and guard against potential *projection* and *displacement* (these concepts are well established in the behavioral science literature as psychological defense mechanisms). Both can occur subconsciously, and therefore without the profiler's knowing it at the time.[6] *Projection* occurs when we attribute our own unacceptable or unwanted thoughts and/or emotions to others. The classic example is infidelity: those with thoughts of infidelity may accuse their partners of cheating on them. In a profiling context, a profiler may imbue the offender and crime scene behavior that he or she is examining with all of the unwanted feelings that he or she has—resulting in a profile that is more about the profiler than the offender. Such profiles are more common than is generally known. This may be a conscious or subconscious process. *Displacement,* however, occurs when our mind redirects emotion from a "dangerous" object to a "safe" object. Examples include getting angry with a victim or offender because of an argument at home, or shifting anger related to feelings of sexual frustration from a lover to a victim or an offender. This, too, can result in a profile that is more about the conflicts and frustrations in the profiler's life than in the offender's. This is a subconscious process, and may account for many of the richly detailed profiles that purport to get deep inside the mind of "killers."

3. *The principle of behavioral dynamics:* Offense-related behavior, including modus operandi, is not static. It can evolve, or devolve, over time and over the commission of multiple offenses. It is also subordinate to contextual factors, such as victim and offender experience, mental dexterity, psychological influences (mental illness, mood, etc.), personal toxicology (drugs, alcohol, etc.), and offense location. Consequently, not every crime committed by the same criminal must be similar, and not every criminal always reflects the characteristics evident in the crime scene that they leave behind.

4. *The principle of behavioral motivation:* As explained in Petri (1981, p. 3), motive is the concept we use to describe the forces acting on or within a person to initiate and direct behavior. No one acts without motivation. All behavior has underlying causes and origins. The origins may be conscious or subconscious, however. They can also be the result of either brilliant or incompetent reasoning. Motive-related decisions, whether planned or reactionary, are strongly influenced by emotions, mental defect and mental illness, and the use of drugs and alcohol.

5. *The principle of multidetermination:* As explained in Groth (1979, p. 13), offense-related behavior, such as rape and aggression, is "complex and multidetermined," serving multiple aims and purposes.

---

[6] *Conscious* thought occurs when one is aware; it is deliberate and purposeful. *Subconscious* thought occurs when one is not aware; it is suppressed, unplanned, and not deliberate. The notion of the very existence of subconscious thought is difficult for some to accept because it tends to mitigate responsibility—hence those looking to assign blame or punish may ignore this possibility in their casework, and fail to admit or recognize their own subconscious tendencies.

A single behavior/choice/action can result from a combination of motives. Consider a rapist who chooses to bring a heavy Mag-Lite flashlight along during the commission of an offense. It may serve multiple functions: as a source of light, a weapon to help control the victim, a weapon to punish the victim, and for insertion into the victim's mouth, vagina, or rectum in an act of substitution. One behavior, the act of bringing a flashlight, serves multiple functions to a single offender.

6. *The principle of motivational dynamics:* An individual offender is capable of multiple motives over the commission of multiple offenses, or even during the commission of a single offense. During a single offense, one serial rapist may evidence a range of behaviors from sadistic to angry to remorseful—and then rob the victim for profit. Across multiple offenses, a serial murder may rape one victim and then stab her to death to eliminate a potential witness, and then one month later might go out of his way to shoot a parked male couple to death, then rob them, because of a hatred for homosexuals. This principle should preclude the pigeonholing of specific offenders because of their known offenses. From an investigative and forensic standpoint, having one part of the picture (known offenses) is not the same as having the whole picture.

7. *The principle of behavioral variance:* Different offenders can invoke the same or similar behavior/choice/action for completely different motives. For example, some rapists use guns, but not all for the same reason. One offender brings a gun for protection and does not show it during the offense; another offender brings a gun to achieve and maintain control over the victim; and yet another needs the gun as part of a fantasy, pointing the gun at the victim's head during the act of rape. One behavior, the act of bringing a gun, serves multiple functions to different offenders. This principle should preclude the profiler from assuming that a behavior will always mean the same thing. A gun is not always an instrument of death; a kiss is not always an act of intimacy.

8. *The principle of unintended consequences:* Not all of the results of behavior are intended. Consequences are not always foreseen. Judgment may be impaired. Perception may be altered. And accidents do happen. For example, bombs go off prematurely or not at all; guns jam; aim is poor; and fire can burn out of control or die off quickly for lack of fuel. This should preclude the profiler from assuming that the scene, as it was found, is also as it was intended.

9. *The principle of memory corruption:* This refers to the fact that witness statements are inherently unreliable for a variety of reasons. First, memory is not a fixed record of events. It changes as new memories are formed. It can also be corrupted by the "forgetting curve,"[7] weapon focus,[8] cross-racial identification, bias, suggestion, expectation, and the human tendency to "fill in the blanks" (Gambell, 2006). Memory can also be affected by the use of perception-altering substances, such as drugs and alcohol. And finally, witnesses may tell partial truths, half-truths, and outright lies for a number of reasons, including embarrassment, an attempt to conceal their involvement in a crime, or an attempt to conceal their involvement in the crime at hand. All of these forces can contribute to conscious and subconscious corruptions of memory that should prevent any forensic examiner from relying on a single witness without corroboration.

---

[7] As explained in Gambell (2006), "That memory becomes less accurate with time has been established since 1885, when Hermann Ebbinghaus created the 'forgetting curve.' Through research, Ebbinghaus found that memory fades up to fifty percent within an hour, sixty percent in the first twenty-four hours, and gradually declines thereafter. Since then, research has shown that recognition is extremely high immediately following an event, but then fades quickly."

[8] As explained in Gambell (2006), "Stress and anxiety can result in a person narrowing her attention. Although this may be a natural reaction to allow the person to confront what is threatening her, it also results in a decrease in 'perceptual scope and acuity.' When a crime involves a weapon, witnesses often focus their attention on that weapon. This distracts the witness from other important details of the event and often results in an incorrect eyewitness identification. Research has shown that up to fifty percent of identifications made when a weapon was present during the crime are incorrect."

10. *The principle of reliability:* The results of forensic examinations, including criminal profiling, are only as reliable as the underlying evidence and reasoning. Behavior must be reliably established. Logic and reasoning must be without fallacies. If the behavior has been assumed and not established, if the logic has fallacies, then the profile is invalid. This principle should preclude the profiler from assuming facts for the purposes of analysis, and from failing to winnow flawed logic and reasoning from the analysis.

Behavioral Evidence Analysis Standards of Practice

In behavioral evidence analysis, practice standards are the fundamental rules that set the limits of evidentiary interpretation.[9] They offer a standard for evaluating acceptable work habits and application of methods. Consistent with practice standards explained in Thornton (1997, p. 18), for all forensic examiners, they are specifically designed to help reduce bias, employ analytical logic and the scientific method, and form hypotheses and conclusions only in accordance with the known evidence.

It should go without saying that all forensic practitioners have a duty to strive for objectivity, competence, and professionalism in their work. Forensic examiners should want their findings to be accurate and their methods to be reliable. There are few forensic practitioners who would disagree with Lee (1993), who provides that "Perhaps the most important issue in forensic science is the establishment of professional standards. An assessment is needed of standards of practice in the collection, examination, and analysis of physical evidence."

Practice standards define a minimum threshold of competency. They also help define a practitioner's role and outline a mechanism for demonstrating their facility. They are a compass for diligent practitioners to follow and a screen against which those who have lost their way can be delayed and educated.

As this suggests, the purpose of defining practice standards is not only to help professionals achieve a level of competency but also to provide independent reviewers with a basis for checking work that purports to be competent. Practice standards set the bar and are a safeguard against ignorance, incapacity, and incomprehension masquerading as science and reason. In a field in which the most common argument tends to be that conclusions are accurate simply because of how many years a practitioner has been on the job, the need for providing practice standards should be self-evident.

The major published works that cover forensic examination may be aggregated to assist in defining basic yet essential practice standards that apply to forensic practitioners of almost every kind (Bevel and Gardner, 1997, 2001; Chisum and Rynearson, 1997; DeForest et al., 1983; DeHaan, 2002; Gross, 1924; Inman and Rudin, 2000; Kirk, 1953; Kirk and Thornton, 1974; Lee, 1994; Locard, 1934; O'Connell and Soderman, 1936; O'Hara, 1956, 1970; Saferstein, 1998; Thornton, 1997; Turvey, 2002). In these collected texts, authored by practitioner-educators, the scientific method, analytical reasoning, and objectivity are prized above all else, whereas emotion, intuition, and other forms of bias posing as knowledge are shunned. With the assistance of these works, the following generally accepted practice standards can be offered:

1. Criminal profilers must strive diligently to avoid bias.

Dr. Paul Kirk wrote of forensic examination, "Physical evidence cannot be wrong; it cannot be perjured; it cannot be wholly absent. *Only in its interpretation can there be error*" (Kirk and Thornton, 1974, p. 4). With this simple observation, Kirk was referring to the influences of examiner ignorance, imprecision, and bias on the reconstruction of physical evidence and its meaning. The evidence is always there, waiting to be understood. The forensic examiner is the imprecise lens through which a form of understanding comes.

---

[9] This section has been adapted from Chisum and Turvey (2007, pp. 116–124).

Specifically, there are at least two kinds of bias that objective forensic examiners need to be aware of and to mitigate in their casework in order to maintain their professional lens—observer bias and confirmation bias.

Observer bias may be described as the conscious or unconscious tendency to see or to find what one expects to see or to find. In a practical sense, this means that the forensic examiner might develop an expectation of findings based on information and opinions he or she learned from the popular media, witnesses, and the opinions and findings of others. These influences are particularly insidious because, unlike overt fraud, they can be subconscious. Unless intentionally screened or recognized by the examiner in some fashion, influences can nudge, push, or drag examiner findings in a particular direction.

Confirmation bias may be described as the conscious or unconscious tendency to affirm previous theories, opinions, or findings. It is a specific kind of observer bias in which information and evidence are screened to include those things that confirm a position and to actively ignore, not to look for, or to undervalue the relevance of anything that contradicts that position. It commonly manifests itself in the form of looking only for particular kinds of evidence that support a given case theory (i.e., suspect guilt or innocence) and actively explaining away evidence or findings that are undesirable. As stated previously, this can be the selection of the evidence to examine by persons advocating a particular theory or by persons interested in "watching the budget" so that potentially exculpatory evidence is not selected for analysis because that would cost more money or require too much time.

Wrestling with confirmation bias is extremely difficult, often because it is institutional. Many forensic examiners work in systems in which they are rewarded with praise and promotion for successfully advocating their side when true science is about anything other than successfully advocating any one side. Consequently, the majority of forensic examiners suffering from confirmation bias have no idea what it is or that it is even a problem. This is related to the reality that having information about possible suspects can consciously or subconsciously influence the final profile, causing it to be tailored, as discussed in Burgess et al. (1988, p. 137):

> Information the profiler does not want included in the case material is that dealing with possible suspects. Such information may subconsciously prejudice the profiler and cause him or her to prepare a profile matching the suspect.

While this guideline is useful with respect to blocking didactic suspect material, suspects may emerge naturally from the pool of witnesses to the crime or the crime scene. This is information that the profiler must have. In such instances, strict adherence to practice standards, as well as to the tenets of critical thinking, analytical logic, and the scientific method, will be the profiler's best safeguard.

What must be understood by all forensic examiners is that the primary value of forensic science to the justice system (the forensic part) is their adherence to the scientific method (the science part), and that this demands as much objectivity and soundness of method as can be brought to bear. Success in the forensic community must be measured by the diligent elimination of possibilities through the scientific method and peer review, not through securing convictions.

2. **Criminal profilers are responsible for requesting all relevant evidence and information in order to perform an adequate victimology, crime scene analysis, or criminal profile.**

Criminal profilers must define the scope of evidence and information they need to perform an adequate reconstruction, partial or otherwise, and make a formal request from their client, employer, or the requesting agency. Upon receiving that evidence, they must determine what has been made available and what is missing. This basic task is incumbent upon every forensic examiner.

When a criminal profiler is not able to base his findings on complete information as he defines or understands it, this must be made clear as part of his conclusions. Basic requests for information must include

- A list of all agencies that responded to the crime scene and/or have assisted in the investigation to date
- All available crime scene documentation, including collection and security logs, notes, sketches, and photos
- All available investigative reports and notes from all responding/assisting agencies
- All available forensic reports, notes, and laboratory findings from all responding/assisting agencies
- All available medical reports and notes, including trauma-grams and injury photos
- All available medical examiner reports and notes, including trauma-grams and autopsy photos
- All relevant investigative and forensic testimony from any court proceedings to date
- A list of all witnesses to the crime or crime scene
- Any documentation of witness statements, including recordings, transcripts, and investigative summaries
- All available victim information and history

3. **Criminal profilers are responsible for determining whether the evidence they are examining is of sufficient quality to provide the basis for an adequate victimology, crime scene analysis, or criminal profile.**

The harsh reality is that crime scene processing and documentation efforts in the United States are often abysmal if not completely absent, and they are in need of major reform (see DeForest, 2005). Crime scenes throughout the United States are commonly processed by police-employed technicians or sworn personnel with little or no formal education, to say nothing of training in the forensic sciences and crime scene processing techniques. The in-service forensic training available to law enforcement typically exists in the form of half-day seminars or short courses taught by nonscientists who, on their own, in no way impart the discipline and expertise necessary to process crime scenes adequately for the purposes of victimology, crime scene analysis, or criminal profiling.

In order to determine whether evidence is of sufficient quality to provide the basis for these efforts, the most important considerations are the following:

1. The ability to identify the item of evidence (evidence number, collected by, at the following location, with a description)
2. The ability to conceptually if not literally place the item back in the crime scene where it was found in relation to the other items of evidence. This is accomplished through competent sketches and related written and photographic documentation. Memory is not a reliable substitute for hard documentation
3. The ability to identify every person who handled the item subsequent to its collection. Is the chain of evidence secure and complete?
4. The ability to identify every test that was performed on the item, who performed the tests, and the results

If crime scene documentation and processing efforts are not sufficient to the task of allowing the criminal profiler to establish the previously mentioned considerations, then those efforts were at best inadequate. Profilers must make note of such deficiencies in their analysis and factor them into their conclusions, and they may even need to explain that they cannot derive certain conclusions because of them.

It is important to note that the profiler cannot know absolutely everything about any item of evidence. Nobody can. The challenge is to consider all that is known when performing a reconstruction and be prepared to incorporate new information as it may come to light. This means appreciating that new information about any item of evidence, or its history, may affect any conclusions about what it means.

4. Criminal profilers must, whenever possible, visit the crime scene.

It is highly preferable that the criminal profiler visit the crime scene. The following are examples of the kind of information that may be learned:

1. The sights, smells, and sounds of the crime scene, as the victim and the offender may have experienced them
2. The spatial relationships within the scene
3. Observation of potential transfer evidence firsthand. Vegetation, soil, glass, fibers, and any other material that may have transferred onto the victim or suspects may become evident or may transfer onto the profiler, providing examples of what to look for on a suspect's clothing or in a suspect's vehicle
4. The attentive profiler may discover items of evidence at the scene previously missed and subsequently uncollected by crime scene technician efforts. This is far more common than many care to admit, and it is one of the most important reasons for visiting the crime scene

In many cases, it will not be possible for the criminal profiler to visit the crime scene. This occurs for a variety of practical reasons, including time limitations, budgetary limitations, legal restrictions, the alteration of the scene by forces of nature, or the obliteration of the scene by land or property development. If the profiler is unable to visit the crime scene for whatever reason, this must be clearly reflected in his or her findings.

It is not disputed that the primary reason for documenting a crime scene is to provide for later reconstruction and behavioral analysis efforts. Therefore, the inability of the criminal profiler to visit the scene does not preclude crime scene analysis and criminal profiling efforts across the board. Competent scene documentation by forensic technicians may be sufficient to address the issues in question, or it may not. Each case is different and must be considered separately and carefully with regard to this issue.

5. Criminal profiling, crime scene analysis, and victimology conclusions, and their basis, must be provided in a written format.

Hans Gross referred to the critical role that exact, deliberate, and patient efforts at crime reconstruction can play in the investigation and resolution of crime. Specifically, he stated that just looking at a crime scene is not enough. He argued that there is utility in reducing one's opinions regarding the reconstruction to the form of a report in order to identify problems in the logic of one's theories (Gross, 1924, p. 439):

> So long as one only looks on the scene, it is impossible, whatever the care, time, and attention bestowed, to detect all the details, and especially note the incongruities: but these strike us at once when we set ourselves to describe the picture on paper as exactly and clearly as possible. ...

> The "defects of the situation" are just those contradictions, those improbabilities, which occur when one desires to represent the situation as something quite different from what it really is, and this with the very best intentions and the purest belief that one has worked with all of the forethought, craft, and consideration imaginable.

Moreover, the criminal profiler, not the recipient of the report (i.e., investigators, attorneys, and the court), bears the burden of ensuring that conclusions are effectively communicated. This means writing them down. This means that the profiler must be competent at intelligible writing, and reports must be comprehensive with regard to examinations performed, findings, and conclusions.

Orally communicated conclusions should be viewed as a form of substandard work product. They are susceptible to conversions, alterations, and misrepresentations. They may also become lost to time. Written conclusions are fixed in time, are easy to reproduce, and are less susceptible to accidental or intentional conversion, alteration, and misrepresentation. An analyst who prefers orally communicated conclusions to written conclusions reveals a preference for conclusive mobility.

Apart from their relative permanence, written conclusions also provide the criminal profiler with the best chance to document methods, conclusions, arguments, and the underlying facts of the case. This includes a list of the evidence examined, when it was examined, and under what circumstances. Generally, a written report should include, but need not be limited to, the following information:

- A preliminary background section, describing the profiler's involvement in the case
- A chain of custody section, describing and detailing the evidence that was examined or included in the profile
- A descriptive section, in which the profiler thoroughly describes the examinations performed (e.g., forensic analysis, victimology, crime scene analysis), with consideration of the facts and evidence
- A results section, in which the profiler lists any results and conclusions, including their significance and limitations
- The intended users of the end result include detectives, judges, and jurors: The report should be worded so that there is no question in the reader's mind about what is being said

If a crime scene analysis or criminal profile cannot be written down in a logical form and easily understood by its intended user, then, apart from having no value, it is also probably wrong.

6. **Criminal profilers must demonstrate an understanding of behavioral science, forensic science, and the scientific method.**

Crime scene analysis, victimology, and criminal profiling are multidisciplinary examinations of the behavioral evidence based on the principles of the forensic and behavioral sciences. Given the advanced level of knowledge required, it is unclear how a criminal profiler could perform any of these examinations competently without receiving a baseline of formal education and ongoing training in these areas from non-law-enforcement forensic and behavioral scientists.

In stark contrast to the pro-law-enforcement, FBI-oriented criterion bizarrely mandated in Napier and Baker (2003, p. 532),[10] the authors strongly recommend that a purported expert in the area of criminal profiling satisfy at least the following minimal criteria:

1. At least an undergraduate education in a behavioral science (psychology, sociology, social work, criminology, etc.). Graduate-level education in these areas is preferable. This criterion disqualifies those with undergraduate degrees in unrelated areas, such as music, police administration, public administration, and education. It should be noted that there are some online university programs

---

[10] The criterion mandated by Napier and Baker (2003), both former FBI profilers, is that a CIA analyst be a former police detective, a former crime scene technician, a near forensic scientist, and have "studied" under FBI "certified" analysts while solving violent crimes. Unfortunately, while such persons exist in the fictional television world of *CSI*, they do not exist in the real world. These requirements actually exclude most of the FBI profilers that the authors have encountered, as their background in these areas tends to come from short courses taught by law enforcement rather than training by forensic or behavioral scientists (CVs on file with authors). It should be noted that Michael R. Napier's highest educational achievement is a Bachelor of Science in Education, which is a program of undergraduate study designed to prepare individuals for teaching careers; Kenneth P. Baker's highest educational achievement is an Ed.S.—a graduate degree designed especially for directors of education, educational superintendents, school principals, curriculum specialists, and religious educators. It is an intermediate professional degree, between a master's and a doctorate. Relevance to criminal profiling: zero.

that offer graduate degrees in behavioral science related areas, without an undergraduate degree requirement, without a thesis requirement, and without actual class time. These programs should be considered essentially worthless, as they are designed for professional advancement and résumé enhancement as opposed to the discovery of knowledge and actual learning.

2. Advanced study of, and a working knowledge of, the published criminal profiling literature in the areas of behavioral evidence analysis, criminal investigative analysis, and investigative psychology—including the limitations and weaknesses of each.

3. Advanced study of, and a working knowledge of, the published literature in the forensic sciences, specifically that related to evidence analysis and crime reconstruction.

4. Advanced study of, and a working knowledge of, the methods, procedures, and requirements of a criminal investigation.

5. An approach to casework in accordance with objective forensic examination, as opposed to a law-enforcement one.

7. Reconstruction conclusions must be based on established facts. Facts may not be assumed for the purpose of analysis.

Many criminal profilers are willing to provide a certain interpretation of offense behavior based on experiential comparisons to unnamed cases, factual guesses and assumptions, or nonexistent physical evidence. If the underlying facts have not been established through investigative documentation, crime scene documentation, the examination of physical evidence, or corroborating eyewitness testimony, then any reconstruction of those facts is not a reliable or valid inference of events. This includes hypothetical scenarios.

8. Crime scene analysis and criminal profiling conclusions must be valid inferences based on logical arguments and analytical reasoning.

In the process of establishing the facts that are fit for analysis, facts must be sifted and distinguished from opinions, conjectures, and theories. Inductive hypotheses must further be delineated from deductive conclusions, and conclusions must flow naturally from the facts provided. Furthermore, the reconstruction must be reasonably free from logical fallacies and incorrect statements of fact.

9. Crime scene analysis and criminal profiling conclusions must be reached with the assistance of the scientific method.

The scientific method demands that careful observations of the evidence be made and then hypotheses generated and ultimately tested against all of the known evidence and accepted facts. Subsequently, the criminal profiler must provide not just conclusions but all other postulated theories that have been falsified through examinations, tests, and experiments. Falsification, not validation, is the cornerstone of the scientific method. Theories that have not been put to any test, or that appear in a report or in courtroom testimony based on rumination and imagination alone (i.e., experience and intuition), should not be considered inherently valid or reliable.

10. Crime scene analysis and criminal profiling conclusions must demonstrate an understanding of, and clearly distinguish between, individuating findings and all others.

The concept of identification and individuation is often misunderstood. *Identification* or *classification* is the placement of any item into a specific category of items with similar characteristics. Identification does not require or imply uniqueness. *Individuation* is the assignment of uniqueness to an item. To individuate an item, it must be described in such a manner as to separate it from all other items in the universe (Thornton, 1997, p. 7).

In the presentation of findings, profilers will find themselves using statements that suggest varying degrees of confidence. Vague terms or terms of art, such as "probably," "likely," "identify," "match," "consistent with," and "reasonable degree of scientific certainty," are among those used to qualify the certainty of findings. Unchecked, this language can be misleading to those it is intended to assist. Confidence statements must be qualified and discussed to the point of absolute clarity. Without clarification, findings may be misunderstood, misrepresented, and misapplied.

If the criminal profiler provides individuating findings of any sort, the nature of the uniqueness and how it was established must be clearly presented. When the profiler has given findings, there must remain no question whether the findings are individuating and no question about how this was determined. The purpose of presenting findings is to clarify the evidence, not muddle it.

11. **Criminal profilers must demonstrate an understanding of the conditions of transfer (Locard's exchange principle and evidence dynamics).**

Identifying and individuating physical evidence is only one part of crime scene analysis. Equally important is the need to establish the source of evidence and the conditions under which it was transferred to where it was ultimately found. Profilers must not be quick to oversimplify complex issues, such as the examination and interpretation of physical evidence, or to disregard those circumstances that can move, alter, or obliterate that evidence.

12. **Any evidence, data, or findings on which crime scene analysis or criminal profiling conclusions are based must be made available through presentation or citation.**

It is not acceptable for the criminal profiler to provide conclusions based on phantom databases, phantom data, phantom research, phantom evidence, or unseen comparisons. Data, research, and evidence must be detailed to the point where others reviewing their work may easily locate or identify it, in the same way we cite the endeavors of others in written work. Data, research, and evidence that cannot be duplicated or identified by the court in some fashion should not find its way into forensic conclusions.

These minimum practice standards should be applied to the evaluation of any method of crime scene analysis and criminal profiling, both the general and the specialized, in order to show due diligence. If a criminal profiler is able to meet these standards, then a minimum threshold level of professional competency has indeed been achieved. Subsequently, the recipients of their conclusions may be assured that, whatever the findings, they may be independently investigated and reviewed for reliability, accuracy, and validity. It bears pointing out that a profiler who fails to climb even one of the rungs prescribed will not have reached this threshold. In failing, they should have their findings questioned, as well as subsequent reports and testimony viewed with disfavor. This is echoed in the chapters that follow.

It is important to clarify that these practice standards do not leave anyone behind, but they do require everyone to show their work. Crime scene analysis and criminal profiling are not easy or rote. Conclusions must be earned and that means competency must be demonstrated and peer review embraced. A profiler has a duty to formulate conclusions with the full reach of everything that forensic science, the scientific method, and analytical logic have to offer. Without these tools, profilers are at risk of not being able to recognize forensic and scientific illiteracy in themselves or others.

These practice standards may also raise the ire of some criminal profilers who have been doing the work based on intuition and experience, perhaps for years, and who are unaccustomed to explaining themselves or their methods apart from stating their alleged vast experience. If peer review and criticism are not welcome at a conclusion's doorstep, if instead such visitors are met with hostility and derision, then something other than ineptitude dwells within. To be clearer, the absence of the scientific method and logical inference in any behavioral analysis should not be a point of pride because it is ultimately evidence of ignorance. A crime scene analysis or criminal profile in the absence of the scientific method, analytical logic, and critical thinking is called a guess. The justice system is no place for ignorance or guessing. Consequently, it is not unreasonable to expect that anyone interpreting behavioral evidence in such a manner be prepared to explain why.

SUMMARY

Behavioral evidence analysis (BEA) is an ideo-deductive method of crime scene analysis and criminal profiling. It involves the examination and interpretation of physical evidence, forensic victimology, and crime scene characteristics. For the purposes of criminal profiling, the results of these individual examinations can be analyzed for behavioral patterns and clusters that evidence offender characteristics of investigative or forensic relevance. BEA is idiographic in that it is concerned with studying the aspects of individual cases and offenders through the lens of forensic analysis, not groups of similar cases and offenders. It is deductive in that inferences and conclusions are not inductive theories or nomothetic predictions in disguise. They are based on critical thinking, the scientific method, and deductive logic. BEA is consequently guided by strict adherence to set principles and practice standards that embrace these concepts.

Questions

1. What are three of the primary goals of BEA in the investigative phase?
2. Allport divides personality traits into three categories. What are they and how are the different?
3. True or False: Life experience results in wisdom and therefore is a reasonable basis for interpretations and conclusions.
4. BEA involves three different kinds of examinations as part of crime scene analysis. What are they?
5. All behavior has underlying causes and origins. The origins may be conscious or subconscious, however. This is related to the principle of _____?
6. The forgetting curve is associated with which principle of BEA?
7. Explain why profilers should be responsible for requesting case materials in writing.

REFERENCES

Allport, G.W., Odbert, H., 1936. Trait-Names: A Psycho-lexical Study. Psychology Monographs 47 (211).

Bevel, T., Gardner, R.M., 1997. Bloodstain Pattern analysis: With an Introduction to Crime Scene Reconstruction. CRC Press, Boca Raton, FL.

Bevel, T., Gardner, R.M., 2001. Bloodstain Pattern analysis: With an Introduction to Crime Scene Reconstruction, second edition. CRC Press, Boca Raton, FL.

Burgess, A., Douglas, J., Ressler, R., 1988. Sexual Homicide: Patterns and Motives. Lexington Books, New York, NY.

Chisum, J., Turvey, B., 2011. Crime Reconstruction, second edition. Elsevier Science, San Diego, CA.

Chisum, W.J., Rynearson, J.M., 1997. Evidence and Crime Scene Reconstruction, fifth edition. Shingleton Press, Shingleton, CA.

DeForest, P., Gaenssien, R., Lee, B., 1983. Forensic Science: An Introduction to Criminalistics. CRC Press, Boca Raton, FL.

DeForest, P.R., 2005. Crime Scene Investigation. In: Sullivan, L.E., Rosen, M.S. (Eds.), Encyclopedia of Law Enforcement. Sage Publications, New York, NY, pp. 111–116.

DeHaan, J., 2002. Kirk's Fire Investigation. Prentice Hall, Upper Saddle River, NJ.

Depue, R., Douglas, J., Hazelwood, R., Ressler, R., 1995. Criminal Investigative Analysis: An Overview. In: Burgess, A., Hazelwood, R. (Eds.), Practical Aspects of Rape Investigation, second edition. CRC Press, New York, NY.

Ferguson, C., Turvey, B., 2009. Victimology: A Brief History with an Introduction to Forensic Victimology. In: Petherick, W., Turvey, B. (Eds.), Forensic Victimology. Elsevier Science, San Diego, CA.

Gambell, S., 2006. The Need to Revisit the Neil v. Biggers Factors: Suppressing Unreliable Eyewitness Identifications. Wyoming Law Review.

Gross, H., 1924. Criminal Investigation. Sweet & Maxwell, London, England.

Groth, A.N., 1979. Men Who Rape: The Psychology of the Offender. Plenum Press, New York, NY.

Inman, K., Rudin, N., 2000. Principles and Practices of Criminalistics: The Profession of Forensic Science. CRC Press, Boca Raton, FL.

Kidder, D., 2005. Is It "Who I Am," "What I Can Get away with," or "What You've Done to Me"? A Multi-Theory Examination of Employee Misconduct. Journal of Business Ethics 57, 389–398.

Kirk, P., 1953. Crime Investigation. Interscience Publishers, New York, NY.

Kirk, P., Thornton, J., 1974. Crime Investigation, second edition. John Wiley & Sons, New York, NY.

Lee, H., 1993. Forensic Science and the Law. Connecticut Law Review, 1117–1124.

Lee, H., 1994. Crime Scene Investigation. Central Police University, Taoyuam, Taiwan.

Locard, E., 1934. Manuel de Technique Policiere: Les Constats, les Empreintes Digitsles, second edition. Payot, Paris.

Napier, M., Baker, K., 2003. Criminal Personality Profiling. In: James, S., Nordby, J. (Eds.), Forensic Science: An Introduction to Scientific and Investigative Techniques. CRC Press, Baco Raton, FL.

O'Connell. J., Soderman, H., 1936. Modern Criminal Investigation. Funk and Wagnalls, New York, NY.

O'Hara, C., 1956. Fundamentals of Criminal Investigation. Charles C. Thomas, Springfield, IL.

O'Hara, C., 1970. Fundamentals of Criminal Investigation, second edition. Charles C. Thomas, Springfield, IL.

Petherick, W., Turvey, B., 2008. Behavioral Evidence Analysis: An Ideo-Deductive Method of Criminal Profiling. In: Turvey, B. (Ed.), Criminal Profiling: An Introduction to Behavioral Evidence Analysis, third ed. Elsevier Science, San Diego, CA.

Petri, H., 1981. Motivation: Theory and Research. second edition. Wadsworth Publishing Inc, Belmont, CA.

Reik, T., 1945. The Unknown Murderer. Prentice Hall, New York, NY.

Saferstein, R., 1998. Criminalistics: An Introduction to Forensic Science, sixth ed. Prentice Hall, Upper Saddle River, NJ.

Thornton, J.I., 1997. The General Assumptions and Rationale of Forensic Identification. In: Faigman, D., Kaye, D., Saks, M., Sanders, J. (Eds.), Modern Scientific Evidence: The Law and Science of Expert Testimony, vol. 2. West Publishing Co, St. Paul, MN.

Turvey, B., 2002. Criminal Profiling: An Introduction to Behavioral Evidence Analysis, second edition. Elsevier Science, Boston, MA.

CHAPTER 6

An Introduction to Crime Scene Analysis

Brent E. Turvey

Erroneous statement of facts based on false premises is in reality a much greater danger than deficiencies of deductive powers.

—Theodore Reik (*The Unknown Murderer*, 1945, p. 35)

CONTENTS

Criminal Profiling: An Introduction to Behavioral Evidence Analysis, Fourth Edition

KEY TERMS

A priori investigative bias   Crime scene investigation   Forensic assessment
Corpus delicti   Crime scene processing   Threshold assessment
Crime scene analysis   Equivocal forensic analysis

Crime scene analysis (crime analysis) is the analytical process of interpreting the specific features of a crime and related crime scenes. It involves an integrated assessment of the forensic evidence, forensic victimology, and crime scene characteristics.[1] The results of crime scene analysis (CSA) may be used to determine the limits of the available evidence and the need for additional investigative and forensic efforts, as in a threshold assessment (discussed shortly). When sufficient behavioral evidence is available, these same results may also be used to infer offender modus operandi (MO) and signature behaviors, evidence of crime scene staging, crime scene motive, and offender characteristics, or to assist with linkage analysis efforts.

Crime scene analysis is not to be confused with the task of *crime scene processing*, which involves recognizing, documenting, collecting, preserving, and transporting physical evidence at and from a crime scene. Non-scientist police officers and crime scene technicians generally perform this duty on behalf of a police agency.

However, CSA does depend heavily on the overall results *crime scene investigation*, which includes crime scene examination and documentation, laboratory analysis, of physical evidence, scientific interpretation of results, and scientific crime reconstruction. As explained in DeForest (2005, pp. 111–113),

> It would not be an exaggeration to assert that crime scene investigation ranks with the most intellectually challenging and difficult of human activities. It is also one of the most misunderstood. In practice, crime scene investigation is rarely carried out efficiently or effectively. Successful outcomes, when and where they occur, are often fortuitous rather than following from intelligently adaptive plans or designs. ...

> In most law-enforcement jurisdictions in the United States, scientific expertise is absent from the initial crime scene investigation. This is true for many other parts of the world as well, and it is a situation that needs to be rectified. An argument can be made that crime scene investigation should be carried out exclusively by forensic scientists, but at the very least, experienced forensic scientists should form part of the crime scene investigation team. ...

> The term crime scene processing is commonly used as a synonym for crime scene investigation. This is unfortunate and betrays an ignorance about the nature of crime scenes and what is necessary to extract the relevant information from them. Crime scene investigation should not be perceived as a mechanical process, carried out in a rote fashion. Too commonly, this is the way it is viewed by law enforcement policy makers; administrators; supervisors; and perhaps, surprisingly, those who actually "process" the crime scene. Change is necessary. ...

---

[1] Schlesinger (2009) provides a generous outline of issues related to crime scene analysis as they are intended to serve FBI profiling methods. FBI methods are quite different with respect to how conclusions are reached, and certain concepts (such as signature) are presented with too much confidence qirh the certainty of findings. However, the contrast between FBI Crime Scene Analysis methods and those provided here may be helpful to some. See also Chapter 13 for detailed exploration of offender MO and signature.

The stages of the crime scene investigation extend beyond the work at the scene. Once the evidence has been analyzed in the laboratory, the scientific interpretation of the laboratory results may lead to a reconstruction of the event.

CSA is intended to provide a language for categorizing, explaining and comparing victim and offender behavior that has been established by available reconstruction interpretations. Ultimately, it is an interpretive stage of crime scene investigation as it is defined by DeForest (2005), subsequent to crime scene processing and later reconstruction efforts.[2] The relationship between physical evidence and crime scene analysis may be expressed in the following manner: crime scene processing efforts provide a foundation of physical evidence; physical evidence is examined and interpreted through laboratory analysis and crime reconstruction efforts to provide behavioral evidence; behavioral evidence is examined and classified by the crime scene analyst or criminal profiler to establish evidence of motive, staging, offender MO and signature behaviors, and compare cases for linkage purposes.

CSA involves examining, assessing, and integrating the findings of least the following investigative and forensic protocols, if not more when available:[3]

1. Crime scene protocols (law enforcement and/or crime lab)
   a. Crime scene investigation reports
   b. Laboratory analysis reports
   c. Chain of custody documents
   d. Crime reconstruction reports
2. Investigative protocols (law enforcement)
   a. Incident reports
   b. Investigative action reports
   c. Evidence submission reports
   d. Witness statements and interviews
   e. Victim statements and interviews
   f. Suspect confessions and denials
   g. Suspect elimination protocols
3. Medicolegal investigation protocols (hospital and/or ME/coroner)
   a. Medical/toxicological reports
   b. Wound pattern analysis reports
   c. Sexual assault protocols/reports
   d. Autopsy protocols/reports
4. Forensic victimology[4]
   a. Death investigations: shared duty of police and ME/coroner
   b. Sex crimes: shared duty of police and SANE[5]

---

[2] *Crime reconstruction* is the determination of the actions and events related to a crime. See Chapter 11.

[3] Every agency that is responsible for the above areas of examination should have written protocols (of varying clarity, quality, and soundness) that dictate their actions and responsibilities. Moreover, these protocols are not private or confidential—as they must be made available for court. If an agency that is responsible for one of these areas of examination does not have written protocols, this is evidence of an overall lack of competence and professionalism. It also signals the absence of good scientific practice.

[4] See Chapter 7.

[5] Sexual assault nurse examiner.

In cases of *post-conviction review*,[6] the following documentation should also be available:

1. Probable cause statements
2. Suspect arrest warrants
3. Search warrants and documentation
4. Hearing and trial transcripts
5. Court decisions

As already mentioned, the results of CSA may be used to determine both the limits of the available evidence and the need for additional investigative and forensic efforts. When sufficient behavioral evidence is available, these same results may also be used to infer evidence of staging, crime scene motive, MO and signature behaviors, offender characteristics, or to assist with linkage analysis efforts.

In cases where a profile is the desired outcome, information about suspects should be avoided whenever feasible. As explained in Schlesinger (2009, p. 76), "The profiler needs to review all of the information in the investigation except for the suspect list, which could unwittingly influence his opinion." This also means avoiding interviews of suspects and premature theories about who may be responsible. In reality, this is not entirely possible, as theories will be continuously thrust upon the profiler from all directions. It is also true that strong suspects may be a witness of some kind with information about the crime scene or case facts that must be considered by the profiler. Avoiding suspects and premature theories will not just be difficult, in many cases it will be impossible. Profilers must bear this burden with conscious deliberation and must learn to recognize the preconceived and the premature so as to cautiously set them aside in their examinations.

FORENSIC ASSESSMENT/EQUIVOCAL FORENSIC ANALYSIS

Forensic assessment is a general term that refers to any examination, evaluation, or appraisal of the evidence record and related to the findings in a given case. This includes physical evidence (e.g., DNA, bloodstain patterns, and wound patterns); statement and testimonial evidence (e.g., written or typed communications, statements to authorities, formal interviews with authorities, and sworn testimony); documentary evidence (e.g., financial records, phone records, still photos, audio recordings, video recordings, cell phone logs, Internet browser history/cache, GPS history); and behavioral evidence.

Any scientific assessment of evidence requires examiner objectivity and skepticism (see Chapter 2). Therefore any scientific assessment will also consider alternate theories regarding the evidence and what it means. It will take on what may be referred to as an equivocal aspect. The word *equivocal* refers to anything that can be interpreted in more than one way or any interpretation that is questionable. An *equivocal forensic analysis* refers to a review of the entire body of physical evidence in a given case, questioning all related assumptions and conclusions. If the physical evidence, and any subsequent reconstruction, lacks veracity or merit, then so does any report upon which it is based.

Purpose

A forensic assessment, or equivocal forensic analysis, helps to preserve the criminal profiler's objectivity by protecting him or her from investigative and forensic assumptions or premature theories. Many examiners assume that the cases they are asked to review have been thoroughly and competently investigated. They assume that law-enforcement and crime lab personnel have worked together to form cohesive, informed theories about victim–offender behavior and basic crime scene characteristics (e.g., whether a scene is

---

[6] CSA conducted subsequent to a conviction, as part of the appeals process.

primary, secondary, or a disposal site; whether victims in a particular series knew each other; whether there is evidence of sexual assault). As a consequence, many forensic examiners do not see the need to question the assumptions of law enforcement or the conclusions of forensic personnel. They view it as bad form, or perhaps even as impolite. Such attitudes are an anathema to the mandates of good science.

The objectivity and skepticism required by a scientific approach assist the profiler with avoiding the trap of *a priori investigative bias*. A priori investigative bias is a phenomenon that occurs when investigators, detectives, crime scene personnel, or others somehow involved with an investigation come up with theories uninformed by the facts. These theories, which are most often based on subjective life experience, cultural bias, and prejudice, can influence whether investigators recognize and collect certain kinds of physical evidence at the scene. A priori investigative bias can also influence whether certain theories about a case are ever considered.

Similarly, in *Criminal Investigation*, Dr. Hans Gross has explained the concept of *preconceived theories*. The discussion is so valuable, and the volume so difficult to obtain, that it is best presented here in nearly its entirety. Despite the original text's being over a century old, his writings are still terribly relevant (Gross, 1924, pp. 10–12):

Section iv— Preconceived Theories

The method of proceeding just described, that namely, in which parallel investigations are instituted, which to a certain extent mutually control each other, is the best, and one is tempted to say the only, way of avoiding the great dangers of a "preconceived theory"—the most deadly enemy of all inquiries. Preconceived theories are so much the more dangerous as it is precisely the most zealous Investigating Officer, the officer most interested in his work, who is the most exposed to them. The indifferent investigator who makes a routine of his work has as a rule no opinion at all and leaves the case to develop itself. When one delves into the case with enthusiasm one can easily find a point to rely on; but one may interpret it badly or attach an exaggerated importance to it. An opinion is formed which cannot be got rid of. In carefully examining our own minds (we can scarcely observe phenomena or a purely psychical character in others), we shall have many opportunities of studying how preconceived theories take root: we shall often be astonished to see how accidental statements of almost no significance and often purely hypothetical have been able to give birth to a theory of which we can no longer rid ourselves without difficulty, although we have for a long time recognized the rottenness of its foundation.

Nothing can be known if nothing has happened; and yet, while still awaiting the discovery of the criminal, while yet only on the way to the locality of the crime, one comes unconsciously to formulate a theory doubtless not quite void of foundation but having only a superficial connection with the reality; you have already heard a similar story, perhaps you have formerly seen an analogous case; you have had an idea for a long time that things would turn out in such and such a way. This is enough: the details of the case are no longer studied with entire freedom of mind. Or a chance suggestion thrown out by another, a countenance which strikes one, a thousand other fortuitous incidents, above all losing sight of the association of ideas end in a preconceived theory, which neither rests upon juridical reasoning nor is justified by actual facts.

Nor is this all: often a definite line is taken up, as for instance by postulating, "If circumstances M. and N. are verified then the affair must certainly be understood in such and such a way." This reasoning may be all very well, but meanwhile, for some cause or other, the proof of M. and N. is long in coming; still the same idea remains in the head and is fixed there so forcefully that it sticks even after the verification of M. and N. has failed, and although the conditions laid down as necessary to its adoption as true have not been realized.

It also often happens that a preconceived theory is formed because the matter is examined from a false point of view. Optically, objects may appear quite different from what they really are, according to the point of view from which they are looked at. Morally, the same phenomenon happens, the matter is seen from a false point of view which the observer refuses at all costs to change; and so he clings to his preconceived theory. In this situation the most insignificant ideas, if inexact, can prove very dangerous. Suppose a case of arson had been reported from a distant locality, immediately in spite of oneself the scene is imagined; for example, one pictures the house, which one has never seen, as being on the left-hand side of the road. As the information is received at headquarters the idea formed about the scene becomes precise and fixed. In imagination the whole scene and its secondary details are presented, but everything is always placed on the left of the road; this idea ends by taking such a hold on the mind that one is convinced that the house is on the left, and all questions are asked as if one had seen the house in that position. But suppose the house to be really on the right of the road and that by chance the error is never rectified; suppose further that the situation of the house has some importance for the bringing out of the facts or in forming a theory of the crime, then this false idea may, in spite of its apparent insignificance, considerably confuse the investigation.

All this really proceeds from psychical imperfection to which every man is subject. Much more fatal are delusions resulting from efforts to draw from a case more than it can yield. Granted that no Investigating Officer would wish by the aid of the smallest fraud to attach to a case a character different from or more important than that which it really possesses, yet it is only in conformity with human nature to stop the more willingly at what is more interesting than at what belongs to everyday life. We like to discover romantic features where they do not exist and we even prefer the recital of monstrosities and horrors to that of common every day facts. This is implanted in the nature of everyone, and though in some to a greater, in some to a lesser, extent, still there it is. A hundred proofs, exemplified by what we read most, by what we listen to most willingly, by what sort of news spreads the fastest, show that the majority of men have received at birth a tendency to exaggeration. In itself this is no great evil; the penchant for exaggeration is often the penchant for beautifying our surroundings; and if there were no exaggeration we should lack the notions of beauty and poetry. But in the profession of the criminal expert everything bearing the least trace of exaggeration must be removed in the most energetic and conscientious manner; otherwise, the Investigating Officer will become an expert unworthy of his service and even dangerous to humanity. We cannot but insist that he should not let himself slip into exaggerations, that he should constantly with this object criticize his own work and that of others; and that he should examine it with extra care if he fail to find traces of exaggeration. These creep in in spite of us, and when they exist no one knows where they will stop. The only remedy is to watch oneself most carefully, always work with reflection, and prune out everything having the least suspicion of exaggeration. It is precisely because a certain hardihood and prompt initiative are demanded of Investigating Officers that one finds in the best of them a slight leaning towards the fictitious: one will perceive it in careful observation of oneself and get rid of it by submission to severe discipline.

Because of the prevalence of preconceived theories, we must admit that the recognition, documentation, collection, and examination of physical evidence prior to the criminal profiler's involvement is potentially incomplete, uninformed, biased, incompetent, and even criminally affected. Though it may seem otherwise, this is not an anti-law-enforcement view. Investigators must appreciate that competent criminal profilers will want to establish the veracity of investigative assumptions and not take anything on faith. The reason for this is simple: A profile is only as good as the information used to render it. Given the investigative and potential courtroom consequences of an incorrect forensic examination, it is not asking too much that criminal profilers should be expected to question the sources of the information on which they are basing their interpretations and opinions.

The overall level of forensic science knowledge and training within the judicial and law-enforcement communities remains very low (National Institute of Justice, 1997). In many cases it is even nonexistent.[7] Horvath and Meesig (1996) report, and this author agrees, that physical evidence is rarely used in criminal investigations at all.[8] This is not because of a lack of evidence availability, according to the study. Rather, physical evidence and forensic analysis are often ignored, even when available, due to the attitudes and mindsets of individual investigators and prosecutors who only see the value of physical evidence in light of their own limited knowledge and experiences.

Cases where physical evidence is exploited to its fullest value are the exception rather than the rule. In many cases a great deal of physical evidence is not recognized or collected. Even when physical evidence is collected, it is rarely analyzed, but sits on an evidence shelf for undetermined periods of time. Furthermore, the reputation of the forensic sciences for reliably delivering credible and objective findings has taken a severe hit in recent years with the publication of the National Academy of Sciences Report, and a seemingly never-ending succession of crime lab scandals that has plagued the United States since at least 1997. As explained in O'Brien (2010),

> [D]oes forensic evidence really matter as much as we believe? New research suggests no, arguing that we have overrated the role that it plays in the arrest and prosecution of American criminals.
>
> A study, reviewing 400 murder cases in five jurisdictions, found that the presence of forensic evidence had very little impact on whether an arrest would be made, charges would be filed, or a conviction would be handed down in court.
>
> A mere 13.5 percent of the murder cases reviewed actually had physical evidence that linked the suspect to the crime scene or victim. The conviction rate in those cases was only slightly higher than the rate among all other cases in the sample. And for the most part, the hard, scientific evidence celebrated by crime dramas simply did not surface. According to the research, investigators found some kind of biological evidence 38 percent of the time, latent fingerprints 28 percent of the time, and DNA in just 4.5 percent of homicides.
>
> "Forensics had no bearing on the outcome at all," said Ira Sommers, professor of criminal justice at California State University, Los Angeles, who coauthored the research with colleague and fellow professor Deborah Baskin. "It was not a significant predictor of the district attorney charging the case and had no relation to actually getting a conviction. That's a pretty stunning finding considering all the hype around forensic evidence."
>
> And according to Baskin and Sommers, there's reason to believe that the findings aren't limited to murder cases alone. In research yet to be published, the California professors say they have made similar conclusions regarding the small role that forensic evidence plays in solving other

---

[7] An irony of law-enforcement training has been observed by this author repeatedly: larger investigative agencies in higher crime jurisdictions are forced to spend their budget fighting crime, while smaller investigative agencies with less crime to investigate are able to spend a greater portion of their budget on training. The result is often that large agencies have very experienced investigators with very little formal training, and smaller agencies have well-trained investigators with no experience applying what they have learned. For this reason, it is also common for investigators in the smaller agencies not to know when or how to apply what they have spent time and money learning.

[8] The only exception is perhaps DNA, which has become a forensic mainstay that is, rightly or wrongly, anticipated by juries.

crimes as well. In assault, robbery, and burglary cases, investigators collect forensic evidence less than a third of the time, the researchers have found, and only a small fraction of that evidence ever gets submitted to a lab for study, making it essentially "a nonfactor," Sommers said, "a rare phenomenon."

The new research, to be published in the *Journal of Criminal Justice*, comes at a time when forensic science is already under siege, with some questioning whether certain forensic practices are even that scientific. The National Academy of Sciences authored a report last year questioning the reliability of many forensic methods, deploring the lack of standardization and certification within the trade, and calling for sweeping reforms. The report, which gave voice to concerns that many forensic scientists had been whispering for years, reached the White House, where President Obama directed a subcommittee on forensic science to study the suddenly prickly matter.

That committee is expected to report its findings and make policy suggestions in the coming weeks. Meanwhile, twice in the last 18 months, the Senate Judiciary Committee has held hearings generally bemoaning the state of American forensic science—and perhaps with good reason.

Hundreds of crime labs across the country are unaccredited; laws in most states don't require them to be. And even those with accreditation have had problems. In 2008, the city of Detroit shuttered its crime lab after an audit found a 10 percent error rate in ballistic evidence. Last year, New York's inspector general chastised the state police there for overlooking evidence that a crime lab analyst was fabricating data. Just last spring, San Francisco was forced to shutter its drug analysis unit after allegations that an analyst was skimming seized drugs for personal use. And Massachusetts hasn't been immune to problems. In 2007, the state Executive Office of Public Safety commissioned a report that documented a backlog of untested DNA from 16,000 cases, including homicides and sexual assaults—a discovery that the report labeled "a crisis."

Meanwhile, across the country, a backlog of DNA evidence continues to fester and grow despite the $330 million dedicated since 2004 to attack the mountain of untested evidence. The problem, according to a special report published in June by the National Institute of Justice, is that crime labs' capacity for the work has not kept pace with increased demand for testing.

In other words, even when physical evidence is understood and valued by investigators and prosecutors, it may lack credibility or even availability. This forensic fatigue results in a diminished role for forensic evidence and a lack of emphasis on it in criminal investigations and subsequent prosecutions.

In cases where physical evidence has been collected and analyzed properly, the results of that analysis are infrequently used for anything in court other than to promote prosecutorial theory (Horvath and Meesig, 1996). It is also the experience of this author that, when it is believed the physical evidence might not match up with case theories, it may remain on the shelf, untested and unanalyzed. To say nothing of evidence that is uncollected for the same reason.

All of these possibilities being the case, potentially influencing the nature and quality of the information and interpretations that a criminal profiler gets up front, the need for an equivocal mindset is apparent. With so much room for omission and error, all forensic examiners must be capable of competently determining the meaning and limits of physical evidence and must not be afraid to question any investigative assumptions or conclusions. This is not to suggest that profilers assume the information they are getting is incorrect, but rather that they have a responsibility to establish what is known and knowable about victim and offender behavior for themselves before they undertake to profile.

Inputs

Nobody creates a criminal profile alone. Behind each criminal profile should be a mountain of information and evidence collected by a hundred people. Their subsequent role in the creation of a criminal profile is at least as important as the role of the profile itself. Those who do not admit the role of others in their own profiling process are either being dishonest or are creating uninformed profiles.

It is a very basic concept: good crime scene investigation begets more competent physical evidence begets a more competent reconstruction begets a more competent criminal profile. That means everyone needs to cooperate, and nobody should render a criminal profile in a vacuum. Everyone works together, and everyone does the best job that they can, or the result will reflect it.

While every case is different and has its own unique peculiarities in terms of what occurred and how it was documented, there are basic items of forensic information, or *inputs*, that should be reviewed and considered before a competent criminal profile can be rendered.

A brief summary of common reconstruction/behavioral inputs is given below, but students are urged to avail themselves of the following references for a better understanding of the forensic sciences, their role in establishing behavioral evidence, and the nature of the documentation that can and should be available to them when performing a forensic assessment:

- Chisum and Turvey (2011) *Crime Reconstruction*
- DeHaan (2006) *Kirk's Fire Investigation*
- DeForest, Gaensslen, and Lee (1983) *Forensic Science: An Introduction to Criminalistics*
- Dolinak, Matshes, and Lew (2005) *Forensic Pathology: Principles and Practice*
- Faigman, Kaye, Saks, and Sanders (Eds.) (2005) *Modern Scientific Evidence: The Law and Science of Expert Testimony*
- Gross (1924) *Criminal Investigation*
- Kirk and Thornton (1974) *Crime Investigation*
- Inman and Rudin (2000) *Principles and Practice of Criminalistics*
- Petherick and Turvey (2009) *Forensic Victimology*
- Saferstein (2010) *Criminalistics: An Introduction to Forensic Science*
- Savino and Turvey (2010) *Rape Investigation Handbook*

Full details on each of these references are available in the "References" section at the end of this chapter.

The exact nature of any documentation and reports generated in relation to a particular case will vary based on the type of crime, the availability of evidence at the scene, the skill of forensic personnel involved, and the skill of investigators involved. The criminal profiler will want all of it, avoiding biasing influences as he can, and will want to examine it with enthusiasm.

Crime Scene Video

The first documentation of any crime scene in its pristine, undisturbed state should be in the form of photos and video. Video is low-cost and relatively easy to render, and it can provide an uninterrupted, context-rich record of the crime scene. In the absence of being able to visit the scene, video, in combination with thorough still photos, is the best way to appreciate the nature and extent of the crime scene as it relates to the events that took place in it.

In reality, however, scene video is only sporadically available. And even when it is, all that may get documented is a few minutes of some technician's shoes. The truth is, very often the video camera is handed to the least trained, least important person at the crime scene—and they tend to document the conversations and mistakes of others inside the tape. Consequently, the result is not always all that good with respect to quality, let alone thoroughness.

In some jurisdictions, police agencies have stopped documenting crime scenes using video. This is often because video has been used against the prosecution in the past to show uncollected evidence of importance, to document crime scene errors in collection or contamination, or generally to disrupt prosecution theories of the case. In any case, when video is not a part of law-enforcement crime scene processing efforts, the forensic examiner should be aware that this is not necessarily an accident. Rather, it may be deliberate attempt to narrow the record of evidence.

Crime Scene Photos

Ideally, crime scene photos provide, in concert with video, the best chance to see physical evidence from the crime scene in context and up close. Depending upon the nature of the scene, they also provide the opportunity to look for environmental items that have psychological value (literature, sexual paraphernalia, etc.) and the potential sources of unexplained wound patterns on the body of the victim, either of which may have been otherwise undocumented. They also provide the opportunity to find new items of evidence that may have been uncollected or simply missed.

In reality, however, the quality of crime scene photos tends to be low to extremely low. Context of evidence is not provided, pictures are out of focus, and generally not enough photos are taken. This is an area where law enforcement needs time and training. When few or limited crime scene photos have been provided or taken, it is an indication of one or more the following: the crime scene photos show something that the police agency involved does not want others to see; the crime scene photos have been lost or temporarily misplaced for lack of organization; or crime scene photos were not taken because of a lack of leadership or clear assignments made at the crime scene by the lead investigator. In cases of extreme disorganization, when cases move quickly from investigation to prosecution, the lead investigator may not be aware that he is, and was, in charge of the case until much later in the process.

Investigators' Reports

Any personnel that enter a crime scene, or whose names appear on a security log (when there is a security log—which is not often enough), may be required to write a report of their activities and observations. This is by no means universal, as standard operating procedure for report writing varies from agency to agency. The importance of these reports is that they can be used to help establish who saw what, who collected what, and whether that record is consistent with other reports and any reconstructed physical evidence. Criminal profilers should pay close attention to these reports because they often offer important insights into crime scene detail that may not otherwise get mentioned.

In this author's experience, new officers tend to write the most detailed and consequently most useful reports. They do not have the training or experience to know what is trivial, so they are more likely to include everything that occurred. Seasoned officers with more experience tend to leave out a great deal and recount only what they believe is important. In any case, the reports reflect the personality and experience of the person writing them, so no two are precisely alike. Criminal profilers should therefore read all that are available to get the most complete picture of crime scene activity and observations.

Crime Scene Sketches

Before any crime scene is released, a *rough* crime scene sketch should be made (hand-drawn and not to scale, but with notes of evidence collected and measurements). A smooth crime scene sketch can be rendered later: to scale, with carefully drawn measurements, and the location of all evidence collected marked in a clear fashion. The purpose of any sketch is to show the relationship of the physical evidence that was collected to the physical environment where it was found. The crime scene sketch is also useful for its evidentiary value in determining what might not have been collected.

Crime Scene Evidence Logs and Evidence Submission Forms

Every item of evidence that has been recognized, documented, and collected at the crime scene (including things like rolls of film and videotape) should be on the evidence logs. This provides a record of what was found and where and by whom. This record can be compared with items in the documentation (scene photos and videos) that may not have been collected, that may have been lost, or that may still require analysis by the crime lab. Not everything that gets collected makes it to the lab for analysis.

The evidence submission forms should be compared to the crime scene evidence logs to determine what was sent where, when, and for what tests. Not everything that is submitted to a crime lab for analysis gets the appropriate attention, because it is the investigators in charge who decide what tests get done, as opposed to the forensic scientists who receive the evidence. Following up on these items, and knowing what type of information they can give to the investigation, in terms of potential behavior, is very important.

Results of Forensic Analysis

Typically, the criminalists from a crime lab prepare the reports detailing the results of any forensic analysis. They have performed these tests on physical evidence submitted to them by investigators. It is the investigator who decides what evidence, if any, to submit to the crime lab, and which tests will be run on that evidence.

There are many different types of physical evidence and subsequent analysis that can be performed on them. As stated at the beginning of this section, readers are encouraged to avail themselves of the references that are provided and familiarize themselves with the great breadth of possibilities. This is by no means a small task, and even the most learned professionals require regular updates and training.

Medical Examiner's and Coroner's Reports

The medical examiner (ME) or coroner, depending on jurisdiction, has the responsibility for establishing cause, manner, and time of death. They may also comment on the nature and origin of wounds. Theirs is a forensic report, and not a medical one. Depending upon the laws regulating the area where the crime was committed, and the nature of the death, an autopsy may have been performed and an autopsy report may have been generated. Or not. The person performing the autopsy may be a coroner or a medical examiner, and they may simply be referred to as a forensic pathologist.

The Centers for Disease Control (CDC) estimate that medical examiners and coroners investigate 20% of the roughly 2 million deaths that occur in the United States each year. Investigative practices and requirements vary widely between and within jurisdictions. Currently, 22 states in the United States use a medical examiner system, 11 use a coroner system, and 17 use a combination.

Medical examiners may have state, district, or county jurisdiction and are appointed. They must be licensed physicians and may even be Board Certified Forensic Pathologists (there are less than 1000 BCFPs in the United Sates). *Coroners*, however, are most often elected or appointed officials, and they are generally not required to be licensed physicians. In some cases, they need only meet an age requirement and reside in the district. This can have an enormous influence on the nature and quality of the medicolegal death investigation performed in a given case, and it can make the necessity of an equivocal forensic analysis even more crucial to a competent criminal profile.

Autopsy Photos

Autopsy photos can form some of the most important documentation in a death investigation. They should provide close-up and contextual shots of all internal and external injuries, both before and after the victim has been cleaned up for autopsy. They also provide an excellent opportunity for finding overlooked or misinterpreted wound patterns. These should be reviewed in the context of the autopsy report, and should be compared to statements made by representatives of the ME or coroner's office who were at the scene (and likely filed their own, separate investigative reports).

Sexual Assault Protocol

In some cases, the sexual assault protocol may be handled by a forensic nurse or sexual assault nurse examiner (SANE), either through a medical facility, such as a hospital or clinic emergency room, or through the local ME/coroner's office in cases involving the death of the victim. In other cases, the sexual assault protocol may be handled by someone with absolutely no training or experience in the recognition or documentation of forensic evidence. In any case, the professionals who perform these protocols write their own reports and opinions, document injuries on diagrams and with photos, and collect evidence for submission to the crime lab. Or at least they should. Not all sexual assault protocols are complete or even adequate.

The criminal profiler, investigators, and criminalists should review all of this documentation. This evidence, including any wound patterns, should be compared with the victim's statements, when available, for consistency. Any inconsistencies need to be understood and explained.

Often, investigators will suggest that a sexual assault crime scene cannot be barricaded off, perhaps because the victim was attacked on a busy street, or in an unknown location, or in an assailant's vehicle. Subsequently, it will be argued that no physical evidence could be collected because there was no crime scene. This is not the case.

Even when a physical, protected location is denied the investigators, either by a fluke of circumstances or by the design of a precautionary offender, there is still potential transfer evidence that can be collected on the victim. In any case where a sexual assault is suspected or alleged, a sexual assault protocol may be performed on the victim. Physical evidence transfers (from the offender and from the locations involved in an attack) onto the victim's clothing and the victim's person occur in a variety of recognizable and collectable forms. The victim, when available, is an extension of the crime scene.

Written and Taped Statements from Witnesses and Victims

When possible, get any audiotape associated with transcribed interviews from witnesses and victims. The flavor of what was said, as much as the content, is important in the review of this documentation for facts and inconsistencies. It is almost impossible to get a clear understanding of the nature of a conversation from a written transcript alone.

In many cases, the law-enforcement agency will have their personnel avoid taping interviews and rely instead on the investigator's memory to provide an interview summary. This is much less reliable than a recorded and transcribed statement, as memory is selective, and the focus tends to be on what is important to support or refute case theories of the moment. Such documentation should be regarded as substandard and unreliable for forensic purposes.

Results

An equivocal forensic analysis provides information regarding the strengths and weaknesses of the physical evidence that may or may not establish the evidence relationships to a criminal investigation. Criminal profilers must therefore be trained in the same manner as forensic scientists. They must also learn to work closely with reconstruction criminalists, forensic pathologists, and other forensic scientists. One person cannot possibly interpret all of the evidence in a case for himself or herself.

The following list is adapted liberally from *Forensic Science: An Introduction to Criminalistics* by Lee et al. (1983, pp. 29–30). These authors agree that the aim of forensic science in every investigation is to provide useful information that helps make the facts of the case clear. In general, these are the types of evidence of behavior relationships that can be established with competently recognized, documented, collected, analyzed, and reconstructed physical evidence.

Corpus Delicti

The *corpus delicti*, literally translated as the "body of the crime," refers to the essential facts that show a crime has taken place. To establish the crime of burglary, for instance, a forensic analysis of the crime scene for physical evidence could include searching for items of evidence such as, but not limited to,

- Tool marks and fingerprints at the point of entry
- Broken doors or windows
- Glass in the burglar's shoes and pants from broken glass at the scene
- Ransacked rooms
- Missing valuables
- Footwear impressions on the ground outside of the residence at the point of entry

To establish a rape or sexual assault, however, a forensic analysis of the crime scene for physical evidence could include searching for items of evidence such as, but not limited to,

- The victim's blood at the crime scene
- The rapist's semen/sperm in the victim's orifices
- A weapon with transfer evidence of some kind
- Wound patterns on the victim
- Torn pieces of victim clothing
- Fibers from ligatures used by the rapist to bind the victim
- Hair/fibers from the victim in the rapist's vehicle
- The rapist's pubic hair on the victim

Modus Operandi

All criminals have a *modus operandi* (or MO, method of operation) that consists of their habits, techniques, and peculiarities of behavior. Sometimes this MO is somewhat consistent, but often it grows and changes over time as the offender becomes more skillful, including what has been successful, excluding what has been unsuccessful (O'Hara, 1970, p. 597). Physical evidence can help establish the MO.

To establish the MO in the crime of burglary, for instance, a forensic analysis of the crime scene for physical evidence could include searching for items of evidence such as, but not limited to,

- Tools used to gain entry (screwdriver, hacksaw, keys to the front door, etc.)
- Types of items taken (valuables vs. impulse items, cash, jewelry, credit cards, sport memorabilia, clothing, etc.)
- Lack of fingerprints at the point of entry, suggesting a gloved offender

To establish the MO in the crime of rape, a forensic analysis of the crime scene for physical evidence could include searching for items of evidence such as, but not limited to,

- The type of restraints used on the victim, from fiber and wound pattern evidence, if any
- Tire marks nearby suggesting the type of vehicle used, if any
- Wound patterns on the victim indicating a type of weapon used (i.e., incision marks from a knife or bite marks on the victim's back)
- Tape found on the victim's person used to cover the eyes or the mouth

Signature Behavior

Some criminals commit actions in the crime scene that may be referred to as *signature behaviors*. As described in *California v. Odell Clarence Haston* (1968),[9]

> Professor McCormick states: 'Here [i.e. in the matter of proving identity by means of other-offenses modus operandi evidence] much more is demanded than the mere repeated commission of crimes of the same class, such as repeated burglaries or thefts. The device used must be so unusual and distinctive as to be like a signature.' (McCormick, Evidence (1954) 157, p. 328.)

McCormick is cited again on the subject of signature behaviors in *California v. Rhonda Denise Erving* (1998), stating that they must be:

> . . . sufficiently distinctive so as to support the inference that the same person committed both acts.

> The pattern and characteristics of the crimes must be so unusual and distinctive as to be like a signature. (1 McCormick [on Evidence (4th ed.1992)], § 190, pp. 801–803.)

Signature behaviors establish the theme of the crime; they are committed to satisfy psychological and emotional needs. Physical evidence can be used to help establish signature behaviors and their context.

To establish signature behaviors in the crime of burglary, for instance, a forensic analysis of the crime scene for physical evidence could include searching for items of evidence such as, but not limited to,

- Slashing the clothing in the closets
- Ejaculation, urination, and/or defecation in specific locations
- Stealing female undergarments

---

[9] The term "signature" was used in legal parlance to describe unique patterns of MO well before the FBI got involved in the practice of criminal profiling. John Douglas, as many of us are aware, has claimed to be, and is commonly referred to as, the originator of this term. This reference suggests otherwise.

- Furniture destruction
- Vandalization of vehicles in the garage

To establish the signature behaviors in the crime of rape, a forensic analysis of the crime scene for physical evidence could include searching for items of evidence such as, but not limited to,

- Type of ligature used
- Specific sequences of sexual acts
- Level of injury to the victim (from minimal to brutal)
- Specific type of weapon used
- Personal items taken from the victim not related to theft, such as identification, clothing, or inexpensive jewelry

Linking the Suspect to the Victim

Blood, tissue, hair, fibers, and cosmetics may be transferred from a victim to an offender. Furthermore, items found in the possession of the suspect can be linked back to the victim. Examples include

- The victim's vaginal epithelial cells dried onto an offender's penis or clothing
- The victim's skin cells and hairs on a piece of rope in an offender's vehicle
- The victim's blood on an offender's knife
- The victim's artificial nails broken off during a struggle and left in an offender's vehicle

It is also possible that trace evidence can be transferred from a perpetrator onto a victim. Suspect's belongings and clothing should be examined thoroughly for this type of trace evidence. Victims and their belongings, of course, should be similarly examined.

Linking a Person to a Crime Scene

Linkage of a person to a crime scene is a common and significant linkage provided by physical evidence analysis. Fingerprints and glove prints, blood, semen, hairs, fibers, soil, bullets, cartridge cases, tool marks, footprints or shoe prints, tire tracks, and objects that belonged to the criminal are examples of deposited evidence (Lee, 1994, p. 5). Depending on the type of crime, various kinds of evidence from the scene may be carried away. Stolen property is the most obvious example, but two-way transfers of trace evidence can be used to link a suspect, a victim, or even a witness, to a crime scene.

Disproving or Supporting a Witness's Testimony

Physical evidence analysis can indicate conclusively whether a person's version of a set of events is credible or whether the person is being deceptive. A simple example would be a driver whose car matches the description of a hit-and-run vehicle. An examination of the car may reveal blood and other tissue on the underside of the bumper. The driver may explain the findings by claiming to have hit a dog. A simple species test on the blood could reveal whether the blood was from a dog or from a human.

Identification of a Suspect

The most conclusive evidence for individuating and identifying a suspect includes fingerprints, bite-mark evidence, and some kinds of DNA. A fingerprint found at a scene, or on a victim's skin or possessions, and later identified as belonging to a particular person, results in an unequivocal identification and individualization of that person.

In rape/sexual assault cases, DNA can be used to make identifications from the following sources (not by any means an exclusive list):

- Sperm left behind at the scene or on the victim
- Blood left behind at the scene from injuries inflicted by the victim
- Tissue collected beneath the victim's fingernails during defensive activity
- Pubic hair left behind at the scene or on the victim

In rape/sexual assault cases, bite-mark evidence can be used to make identifications from the following sources (not by any means an exclusive list):

- Bite marks inflicted on the victim's back during the victim's struggle, intended to make the victim compliant
- Bite marks made to victim's genital areas as part of the sexual attack
- Bite marks made to the victim's face and extremities as a part of a punishment (child abuse)

Providing Investigative Leads

Physical evidence analysis can be helpful in directing an investigation along a productive path. In a hit-and-run case, for example, a chip of paint from the vehicle can be used to narrow down the number and kinds of different cars that may have been involved. In a rape/sexual assault case, DNA evidence can be used to quickly rule out suspects. And bite-mark evidence can be used to generate suspects if submitted to local area dental organizations (when feasible).

This author has developed the *threshold assessment* as a tool for the delivery of these and other types of investigative leads.

THE THRESHOLD ASSESSMENT

A *threshold assessment* (TA) is an investigative document that reviews the initial physical evidence of behavior, forensic victimology, and crime scene characteristics for a particular case, or a series of related cases, in order to provide immediate direction. It is not informed by complete access to all crime scene documentation, victim information, or the full analysis and interpretation of physical evidence by the necessary forensic scientists. It makes assessments of what is *currently understood* to be fact. It can include suggestions regarding potential evidentiary connections and analysis, insight into interview strategy, and any investigatively relevant first impressions that the profiler has regarding investigative priority and direction.

As presented in Baeza et al. (2000),

4.0 THRESHOLD ASSESSMENT

A *Threshold Assessment* is an investigative report that reviews the initial physical evidence of crime related behavior, victimology, and crime scene characteristics for a particular unsolved crime, or a series of potentially related unsolved crimes, in order to provide immediate investigative direction. It should include what is generally known of events, what is not, and suggestions regarding any means by which the former may be established. It is not to be confused with, or presented as, a *Criminal Profile*.

4.1 Guidelines

A *Threshold Assessment* should include the following elements:

4.11 Overview of the established facts of the case relevant to crime related behavior as appropriate.

4.12 Overview of the established facts of the case relevant to victimology as appropriate.

4.13 Overview of the established facts of the case relevant to crime scene characteristics as appropriate, with supporting argumentation.

4.14 Initial hypothesis regarding potential motivational behaviors and aspects, as appropriate, with supporting argumentation.

4.15 Initial hypothesis regarding potential offender characteristics, as appropriate, with supporting argumentation.

4.16 Suggestions regarding further facts that need to be determined or established in order to address logical breaks in the sequence of events surrounding the crime, including suggestions regarding additional forensic analyses that may be performed on available physical evidence.

4.17 Suggestions regarding further victimological information gathering.

4.18 Investigatively relevant suggestions regarding potential strategies or avenues for suspect development.

A TA should not include firm conclusions or opinions. That is the place of a full criminal profile. A TA is meant to be an investigative compass, or "to do" list, compiled in any phase of a case, that outlines what is known and what needs to be investigated further. It provides initial observations, concerns, and priorities. It should be made up of investigatively relevant questions, investigatively relevant suggestions, and first impressions where appropriate.

Although it can have the same written structure as a criminal profile, a TA is rendered under different circumstances for different purposes. It should therefore not be presented as, or used for the same purpose as, a full criminal profile. It is important to keep the different circumstances and purposes of criminal profiles and TAs in mind when writing reports, or when reading any reports generated by another criminal profiler who may not know the difference.

Why a Threshold Assessment?

There are two main reasons for making a threshold assessment of a case, as opposed to simply waiting for more information and rendering only a full criminal profile.

First, as already discussed, it provides investigative direction. A TA compiles and presents information and suggestions in a way that is concise and effective. It serves the general profiling goal of keeping an investigation on track. It also directs investigators to gather the type of information that will assist in creating the full criminal profile, and that will provide additional grist for leads, theories, and opinions apart from the profiling effort. This is because the type of suggestions for information gathering in the TA (designed to inform a criminal profile) will help everyone involved in an investigation, not just the criminal profiler.

Second, and most often in the investigative phase, is the issue of public safety. In cases where danger is imminent, we may not be able to wait for a criminal profile. We may decide that it is in the best interest of the affected community to draw up some insights based on initial and consequently incomplete information. Investigators may only have time to get a profiler's first-blush response from available case materials in order to organize investigative efforts within a given time constraint.

The decision to construct a threshold assessment should be made only after a basic cost–benefit analysis of doing so has been made. The cost of writing down seductive, and potentially misleading, ideas and insights that may be extremely difficult to dislodge later on should be weighed against the benefits of being able to organize effective investigative strategy in a timely manner. In the experience of this author, the trouble with using a TA comes about when it is presented as, or used as a replacement for, a criminal profile. If the members of a case effort are aware, up front, of the nature and purposes of a given TA, then the miscommunications and overstatements of opinions that are the hallmark of investigative disaster can be more easily avoided. This requires not only truth in advertising on the part of the criminal profiler (not overstating or misrepresenting information in the TA), but also a responsibility on the part of other members of the case effort to use the information in the TA appropriately.

This outlook and designation also has implications for courtroom use, because the TA cannot be confused with a criminal profiler's firm opinions about the characteristics of a given offender. First, it has fewer conclusions and only seeks to provide preliminary investigative direction. Second, it is based on necessarily incomplete (and potentially inaccurate) information. Consequently, it is a working report.

SUMMARY

Crime scene analysis (crime analysis, CSA) is the analytical process of interpreting the specific features of a crime and related crime scenes. It involves an integrated assessment of the crime scene protocols, investigative protocols, medicolegal protocols, and forensic victimology to determine crime scene characteristics. The results of CSA may be used to determine the limits of the available evidence and the need for additional investigative and forensic efforts, as in a threshold assessment. When sufficient behavioral evidence is available, as determined by a forensic assessment, these same results may also be used to infer offender MO and signature behaviors, evidence of crime scene staging, crime scene motive, offender characteristics, or to assist with linkage analysis.

CSA is not synonymous with criminal profiling; it describes the state of the crime scene and does not go further to describe the characteristics of the offender responsible. Because it is based on the physical and behavioral evidence left behind at the scene, it has natural limits. These limits require that practitioners be sufficiently educated and trained in behavioral and forensic sciences. Without a background studying and applying the scientific method and the limits of evidence, practitioners risk assuming too much, treating theories as facts, and over-interpreting the scene.

Questions
1. Define the term *crime scene analysis* (CSA).
2. What are the four investigative and forensic protocols that should be relied upon in performing a CSA?
3. A CSA may be used to determine crime scene motives. What else may it be used for?
4. What is the purpose of maintaining an equivocal mindset when performing a CSA?
5. What is a threshold assessment?

REFERENCES

Baeza, J., Chisum, W.J., Chamberlin, T.M., McGrath, M., Turvey, B., 2000. Academy of Behavioral Profiling: Criminal Profiling Guidelines. Journal of Behavioral Profiling 1 (1).

Claifornia v. Odell Clarence Haston, 1968. No. 11710, Supreme Court of California, En Bank, August 19.

California v. Rhonda Denise Erving, 1998. No. B111324, April 29, 1998 (73 Cal. Rptr. 2d 815).

Chisum, W.J., Turvey, B., 2011. Crime Reconstruction, second edition. Elsevier Science, San Diego, CA.

DeForest, P., 2005. Crime Scene Investigation. In: Rosen, M., Sullivan, L. (Eds.), Encyclopedia of Law Enforcement, vol. 1. State and Local, Sage Publications, Thousand Oaks, CA, pp. 112–116.

DeForest, P., Gaensslen, R., Lee, H., 1983. Forensic Science: An Introduction to Criminalistics. McGraw-Hill, New York.

DeHaan, J., 2006. Kirk's Fire Investigation, sixth edition. Prentice Hall, Upper Saddle River, NJ.

Dolinak, D., Matshes, E., Lew, E., 2005. Forensic Pathology: Principles and Practice. Elsevier Science, Boston, MA.

Faigman, D., Kaye, D., Saks, M., Sanders, J. (Eds.), 2005. Modern Scientific Evidence: The Law and Science of Expert Testimony, vol. 2. West Publishing Co, St. Paul, MN.

Gross, H., 1924. Criminal Investigation. Sweet & Maxwell, London, England.

Horvath, F., Meesig, R., 1996. The Criminal Investigation Process and the Role of Forensic Evidence: A Review of Empirical Findings. Journal of Forensic Science 41 (6), 963–969.

Inman, K., Rudin, N., 2000. Principles and Practice of Criminalistics. CRC Press, Boca Raton, FL.

Kirk, P., Thornton, J.I., 1974. Crime Investigation, second edition. John Wiley & Sons, New York, NY.

Lee, H. (Ed.), 1994. Crime Scene Investigation. Central Police University Press, Taoyuan, Taiwan.

Lee, H., DeForest, P., Gaensslen, R., 1983. Forensic Science: An Introduction to Criminalistics. McGraw-Hill, New York, NY.

National Institute of Justice, 1997. National Guidelines for Death Investigation. Research Report 167568, National Institute of Justice, Washington, DC.

O'Brien, K., 2010. The Case against Evidence: From Fingerprints to High-Tech CSI, Forensic Science Plays a Much Smaller Role than You Would Think. The Boston Globe November 7. www.boston.com/news/science/articles/2010/11/07/the_case_against_evidence/.

O'Hara, C., 1970. Fundamentals of Criminal Investigation. Charles C Thomas, Springfield, IL.

Petherick, W., Turvey, B., 2009. Forensic Victimology, second edition. Elsevier Science, San Diego, CA.

Reik, T., 1945. The Unknown Murderer. Prentice-Hall, New York, NY.

Saferstein, R., 2010. Criminalistics: An Introduction to Forensic Science, tenth edition. Prentice Hall, Upper Saddle River, NJ.

Savino, J., Turvey, B., 2010. Rape Investigation Handbook, second edition. Elsevier Science, San Diego, CA.

Schlesinger, 2009. Psychological Profiling: Investigative Implications from Crime Scene Analysis. Journal of Psychiatry and Law 37, 73–84.

SECTION

2

Forensic Victimology

CHAPTER 7

Forensic Victimology[1]

Brent E. Turvey and Jodi Freeman

CONTENTS

---

[1] This chapter has been adapted from and builds heavily on the concepts originally published in *Criminal Profiling: An Introduction to Behavioral Evidence Analysis*, third edition (Turvey, 2008) and *Forensic Victimology: Examining Violent Crime Victims in Investigative and Legal Contexts* (Turvey and Petherick, 2009).

KEY TERMS

Deification	Offender exposure	Victim exposure
Forensic victimology	Situational or incident	Vilification
Lifestyle exposure	exposure	

CHALLENGES

While this chapter asserts the importance of studying the victim, forensic victimology has largely been over-looked as an important component of crime scene analysis. There can be no doubt that part of the reason for this absence of attention is because it is not easy to study victims. In fact, there are many circumstances under which profilers and investigators will be actively discouraged from doing so.

First, there are emotional challenges. The coping mechanisms of overtaxed, underpaid, and undervalued detectives, investigators, and forensic personnel involve continuous doses of personal detachment and dissociation from the victim and the horrible things that they have suffered. The victim is compartmentalized and seen as an object. The victim's body, living or dead, and all of the terrible things that it has endured, is regarded as evidence to be analyzed and catalogued. The advantage of this coping mechanism is that there is no emotional investment, no opening up to be affected by the pain and suffering of a fellow human. The disadvantage is that we risk surrendering our humanity when we regard victims and their suffering as objects.

We risk losing our humanity because compartmentalization and distancing demand that we continually reinforce our view of the victim as an object. If we humanize victims, we know that there is the risk of recognizing that they are not unlike our own daughter, son, mother, father, sister, brother, wife, husband, or friend. To maintain the necessary detachment, we may actively avoid or suppress information about the victim as a person. We do not get to know victim; we do not familiarize ourselves with the victim's personal life outside of the crimes committed against them. We avoid the victim's family. We do not wish to make time to see them as people—all because it might affect us emotionally; it might make us feel bad. However, these reasons are not sufficient.

Conversely, some investigators cross the line and identify too closely with victims. They see themselves as protectors and the victims as objects of their own rescue fantasy. When this happens, the line between investigator of fact and advocate is violated. Otherwise thorough professionals avoid investigating clear inconsistencies; obvious falsehoods are explained away or swept under the rug; and false reporters are given cover and, in some cases, encouragement.

When profilers or investigators take on a case, they must take on the whole case—good and bad—and they have a responsibility to do the best job possible, not just the best job with those parts that are comfortable and safe. Anything less than this is a disservice to real victims and, in a broader sense, the criminal justice system. Those who cannot overcome their emotional disabilities are not going to fully meet their professional responsibilities and may even contribute to miscarriages of justice.

Second, there are political challenges. In some cases, the culture within which an investigator or forensic examiner operates openly encourages the marginalization, vilification, or deification of certain victim populations. When the profiler takes a stance that is at odds with the accepted view within their culture, chances are that he or she will feel pressure to move their findings back into step. They may even be advised to stop generating findings at all. In other cases, there may be direct political pressure to cast a victim in a certain light or gloss over a victim's actual history in favor of a popular theory or stereotype. A dead child is better portrayed as an angel without blemish; a homosexual found dead in a motel room is better portrayed as a worthless deviant; prostitutes are regarded as drug-addicted liars on the make (especially if they are minorities); and attractive white females never lie and always need at least double the normal amount of detectives working their case, if not all available male personnel. Such circumstances are all too common.

These realities explain why the performance of a thorough victimology is not routine practice for many detectives, investigators, and forensic personnel. When gathered without regard to a predetermined outcome, victimology forces us to get to know the victim better than we know most of the people in our own lives. It opens us up to potential internalizations, where we make a victim's personal feelings our own. It opens us up to potential transference, where we shift our thoughts and feelings about other people onto the victim. It can even raise doubts about the victim's story or complicity, as may be the case when things are not as they were first reported. Getting to know the intimate details of a victim's history and personality is not professionally or emotionally safe. Moreover, getting to know the victim prevents the easy stereotypes from maintaining a hold over the investigation. Getting to know the victim is rough on all levels, but it is necessary for the objective investigator and examiner.

FORENSIC VICTIMOLOGY AND THE SCIENTIFIC METHOD

Forensic victimology is an applied discipline as opposed to a theoretical one. The forensic victimologist seeks to examine, consider, and interpret particular victim evidence in a scientific fashion in order to answer investigative and forensic (i.e., legal) questions. The unimpeachable philosophy of forensic victimology is that victim facts are preferable to victim fictions; that victim evidence must be gathered and examined in a consistent, thorough, and objective fashion as with any other form of evidence; and that interpretations of any victim evidence must comport with the tenets of the scientific method.

The guiding principle for studying victims in investigative and forensic contexts is this: a comprehensive understanding of victims and their circumstances will allow for an accurate interpretation of the facts of a case, which will allow for an accurate interpretation of the nature of their harm or loss, and subsequently tell us about the offender. The less we know about the victim, the less we know about the crime and the criminal. Consequently, the way we collect and develop victim evidence is just as important as our eventual interpretations: they must not be weak, narrow, or based on unproved assumptions.

Victim Background/History

Developing a clear and factually complete victim history as part of a thorough case examination is universally understood as best practice for just about any of the helping professions, as it provides a baseline against which to compare current circumstances, behavior, illness, or injury. For example, medical and mental health specialists of every kind accept that what presents in a given case is a reflection of, and can be affected by, past events. Moreover, they are mindful that any diagnosis or treatment must take into account the changes brought about by past treatment efforts. In addition, both medical and mental health professionals are trained to recognize behavioral indicators of those presenting false symptoms (e.g., drug-seeking behavior and malingering). Consequently, the failure of medical and mental health practitioners to take an adequate history prior to diagnosis and treatment is generally considered an unacceptable practice.

The importance of gathering victim background information is understood within the forensic professions as well. For example, medical examiners, coroners, and their respective death investigators understand this, as reflected in the National Institute of Justice (NIJ) manual, *Death Investigation: A Guide for the Scene Investigator* (1999, p. 39):

> Establishing a decedent profile includes documenting a discovery history and circumstances surrounding the discovery. The basic profile will dictate subsequent levels of investigation, jurisdiction, and authority. The focus (breadth/depth) of further investigation is dependent on this information.

Sex crime investigators understand this as well, as reflected in the importance of gathering information related to the complainant's criminal, medical, and mental health background prior to conducting formal interviews, as provided in Savino and Turvey (2011). This is because sex crimes investigators are solely responsible for investigating and determining the veracity of the complaints they receive. Without victim history, they have no context for investigating allegations of sex crimes and the forensic evidence (or lack thereof) that presents.

Victim history is also a required component of sexual assault examinations, performed by medical specialists as part of their dual treatment and evidence-gathering mission. As explained in Jamerson (2009, p. 114),

> [I]ntake and history information is necessary to competently inform and prioritize the physical examination. … Each patient is unique; any treatment and forensic efforts should be individually crafted to his or her particular condition and history.
>
> *Medical history*[2] is a significant component of the evaluation in the context of any suspected sexual assault, child molestation, or domestic assault. It provides a baseline of information for the examiner so that recent trauma and injury can be discriminated from past conditions and events. Therefore, it must cover all body systems. In this way, the examiner can identify any acute or chronic problems, as well as any history of past injury or surgeries. It also informs the nature, extent, and sequence of the forensic medical exam. A failure to document and report medical background information prevents informed medical treatment and leaves the forensic examiner without the proper context for accurate interpretations. Ultimately, conducting an accurate forensic medical examination in the absence of a patient medical history is not possible.

This also specifically includes (pp.117–120) "recent consensual sexual activity," "post-assault activities," "history of drug abuse," history of mental health and behavioral problems, and history of STDs—all of which can be instrumental in determining whether sexual activity occurred, the type of sexual activity, the parties involved, and the reliability of the account provided.

The forensic necessity for this extensive history-gathering effort is affirmed in the National Institute of Justice (NIJ) guidelines, *A National Protocol for Sexual Assault Medical Forensic Examinations* (2004), which provides that informed sexual assault examinations require a complete victim history (p. 81):

---

[2] *Medical history* is the information about a patient gathered by a health care professional for the purposes of making examinations, providing treatment, and rendering a diagnosis. It commonly involves asking patients questions regarding the current and former state of their physical and mental health. Without this background information, examinations, treatments, and diagnoses are at best uninformed and at worst potentially lethal.

Coordinate medical forensic history taking and investigative interviewing. Examiners typically ask patients to provide a medical forensic history after initial medical care for acute problems and before the examination and evidence collection. This history, obtained by asking patients detailed forensic and medical questions related to the assault, is intended to guide the exam, evidence collection, and crime lab analysis of findings.

Inherent in the scientific method and the professional guidelines mentioned is the understanding that evidence observed in relation to an alleged victim or crime scene may not be the result of the criminal activity being reported. Such evidence may in fact be the result of some previous and unrelated activity or event. In fact, sex crime investigators and forensic examiners will not necessarily know what features of complainant or victim history are relevant to a forensic assessment until well after they have begun their work.

Because it not always possible to know which factors of victim history are going to be relevant, professional guidelines, as well as the scientific method, require that a broad net be cast at the outset of every case. In one case the primary issue may become a question of toxicology (e.g., how many drinks and how intoxicated was the reporting party). In another it may be a question of where an alleged murder occurred (e.g., which room did the victim normally occupy, where is it in relation to location where the body was found, and could they physically occupy that space). In yet another there may be a question of sexual habits or preferences (e.g., were they virgin, did they engage in sadomasochistic activity resulting in frequent bodily injury of a sexual nature, did they often have more than one sexual partner on they day of the alleged sexual assault). All of these issues and related details have been a deciding factor in criminal cases. Each victim is different, each case is different, and therefore less victim history is not better.

Avoiding Logical Fallacy

The propensity to assume that everything found in a crime scene or in relation to a crime must somehow be related is a common logical fallacy, referred to as *Post hoc, ergo propter hoc*, or *"after this, therefore because of this."* For example, a victim or complainant may present with extensive bruising of the shins and may not clearly recall its origins. Such injuries might be related to a sexual assault, depending on the events described. Or, after conducting a history, the forensic examiner may learn that the complainant played a soccer game in the days preceding the alleged attack, in which her shins were repeatedly kicked. This is true for injuries related to sexual activity as well.

The forensic examiner interpreting any victim injury without the proper history could improperly proceed with the assumption that the injury must be related to a sexual assault. Therefore, collecting history from the complainant, as well as collateral sources (e.g., friends, family members, other witnesses), is necessary to ensure that the most complete and accurate information is relied upon before examinations and scientific interpretations of the evidence are finalized.

With these as our standards, it is not possible to avoid the fact that the best way to objectively build case knowledge and render valid interpretations is through the scientific method.[3] This means developing a clear and honest picture of victim history, rendering victim theories in accordance with the established facts, and working to disprove those theories to avoid confirmation bias.

---

[3] The scientific method is discussed in Chapter 2.

Goals of Forensic Victimology

Forensic victimology is an essential component of crime scene analysis, and therefore an unavoidable feature of any criminal profile. The information gathered from a thorough victimology has the potential to affect each stage of a criminal profile, from crime reconstruction to establishing offender motivation. The goals of forensic victimology include, but are not limited to, the following:

- **Assist in understanding elements of the crime.** By studying the victim, the examiner is better able to understand the relationship between a victim and his or her lifestyle and environment, and subsequently of a given offender to that victim. Victimology provides the context for the victim-crime scene interaction, the offender-crime scene interaction, and the victim-offender interaction.
- **Assist in developing a timeline.** Retracing a victim's last known actions and creating a timeline are critical to understanding the victim as a person, understanding the victim's relationship to the environment, understanding the victim's relationship to other events, and understanding how the victim came to be acquired by an offender. (The timeline is discussed later in the chapter.)
- **Define the suspect pool.** In an unsolved case, where the offender is unknown, a thorough victimology defines the suspect pool. The victim's lifestyle in general and his or her activities in particular must be scrutinized to determine who had access to them, what they had access to, how and when they gained and maintained access, and where the access occurred. If we can understand how and why an offender has selected known victims, then we may also be able to establish a relational link of some kind between the victim and that offender. These links may be geographic, work related, schedule oriented, school related, hobby related, or they may be otherwise connected. The connections provide a suspect pool that includes those with knowledge of, or access to, the related area.
- **Provide investigative suggestions.** A thorough victimology compiled in the investigative stage will offer suggestions and provide direction to the investigation. Such suggestions may include interviewing those in the defined suspect pool, interviewing witnesses about discrepancies in their statements or contradictions with timeline information, and examining any physical evidence that may have been overlooked during the initial investigation.
- **Assist with crime reconstruction.** By understanding the victim's behavior patterns, the examiner is better equipped to complete a thorough crime reconstruction. Knowing why a victim was in the location where he or she was acquired or what the victim was doing in that location will provide the examiner with information that may be necessary when inferring the most reasonable behavior of that victim.
- **Assist with contextualizing allegations of victimization.** Developing a clear and factually complete victim history will provide context to the allegations of victimization. Victimological information may also support or refute the allegations of victimization.
- **Assist with the development of offender modus operandi.** Knowledge of the victim's pattern of behavior in relation to the location where the victim was acquired may assist with the development of the offender's modus operandi (MO), specifically in victim selection. For example, an offender who is trolling for victims may choose to acquire an opportunistic victim at a location with increased victim availability and vulnerability, such as a busy pub with intoxicated patrons. This information tells us about the offender's MO or the choices made during the commission of the crime.
- **Assist with the development of offender motive.** Without a thorough examination of victim history, the examiner may overlook important victimological information that may reflect the offender's motivation. For example, an examiner can only appropriately establish a list of items missing from a crime scene if it is known what the victim had in his or her possession at the time of victimization. Without this information, a profit-oriented motivation may be disregarded.

- **Assist with establishing the offender's exposure level.** *Offender exposure* is the general amount of exposure to discovery, identification, or apprehension experienced by the offender. The context surrounding the point at which the offender acquired the victim may assist with establishing the offender's level of exposure. For example, an offender who acquires a victim in broad daylight is at an increased risk of detection and apprehension, which may suggest an increased level of confidence or skill.
- **Assist with case linkage.** When determining whether a series of crimes can be behaviorally linked, victim selection is an important behavioral factor that cannot be ignored during a linkage analysis. A study of the victims across a series of cases may reveal a unique connection between the victims, or the exposure levels of the victims may allow the examiner to support or refute a linkage.
- **Assist with public safety response.** If we can understand how and why offenders have selected their previous victims, then we have a better chance of predicting the type of victim they may select in the future. This will allow the appropriate public safety messages to be delivered to the public with the aim of reducing the exposure levels of those affected individuals. For example, an offender who enters multiple residences through unlocked windows may prompt a public safety message to be delivered to affected communities warning them to lock their windows and doors.
- **Reduce victim deification and vilification.** The objective, scientific, and thorough examination of victims assists in reducing victim deification and vilification.

Deification involves idealizing victims based on who or what they are, without consideration of the facts (e.g., young schoolchildren, missing adolescents, and others who are favored in the press or by public opinion). Because of the political or public culture of a certain area or region, certain victim populations tend to be more politically or publicly sympathetic. This view facilitates rationalizations about time expended on the deified case while other investigations suffer, and it does not allow for an unbiased victimology by virtue of depriving the crime and the investigation of true victim context. Deification has the capacity to accomplish the following:

- Remove good suspects from the suspect pool
- Provide coverage for the false reporter
- Provide coverage for suspects who are family or household members

Vilification involves viewing a victim as worthless or disposable by virtue of who or what they are, without consideration of the facts (e.g., the homeless, the poor, minority groups, and prostitutes). This view presumes that it is okay, or not as bad, to commit crimes against people of certain lifestyle, races, religions, or creeds. Ultimately, this tends to be guided by an investigator's subjective sense of personal morality—or that of a like-minded community. Ultimately, it facilitates investigative apathy. Examples of vilified groups, or groups toward which there is no lack of apathy, commonly include the following:[4]

- The homeless/mentally ill
- Homosexuals
- Minority populations within particular regions, such a immigrants and Native Americans
- Prostitutes
- Drug dealers
- Drug addicts
- Teen runaways who becomes prostitutes or drug addicts
- Individuals of particular religious beliefs

---

[4] It is not insignificant that this list is similar to the victim typology developed by von Hentig (1948). Von Hentig classified victims in terms of their propensity for victimization, and there can be no question that such "propensity" lends itself to vilification.

If we idealize victims or vilify them, we will not learn who they were. Forensic victimology reduces victim bias by examining the victim through an objective and scientific lens.

■ **Help establish the nature of victim exposure to harm or loss.** An examination of the harmful elements experienced by a victim, throughout his or her life and at the time of crime commission, will allow the examiner to determine the victim's level of exposure to suffering harm or loss. Victim exposures are discussed in the following section.

VICTIM EXPOSURE ANALYSIS

Victim exposure is the amount of contact or vulnerability to harmful elements experienced by the victim. It is not necessarily from the victim's perspective, but what we as criminal profilers perceive for a given victim.

In previous editions of this text, victim risk has been defined as victim exposure. However, the concept of *victim risk* refers to the possibility of suffering harm or loss and is associated with predictions about potential harm—what might happen. By utilizing the concept of victim risk, one may infer a conclusion based upon a statistical analysis of the potential to be harmed as being part of a demographic group. However, these conclusions often do not account for the victim's particular characteristics and context or how the victim interacts with the offender. Making conclusions about the victim's level of harm based on statistical analyses or probability estimates of risk does not accurately reflect how a specific victim's lifestyle contributed to his or her harm, nor does it necessarily provide investigative relevance. Exposure analysis, on the other hand, is concerned with examining harmful elements that are actually present. This concept examines how an environmental factor or personal trait of the victim specifically increased his or her contact with harm.

It is important to remember that the victims are not responsible for the predatory acts of offenders. This may seem like an obvious concept, but, unfortunately, many people do blame the victim as being partially or wholly responsible for certain crimes committed against them. Detectives might blame a prostitute, in whole or in part, for being the victim of a violent crime. The same detective might view a student in a similar situation as being an unfortunate victim of circumstance. However, establishing victim "blame" does not add anything to the investigative effort. All citizens have moments of vulnerability, no matter what level of harm their lifestyle and circumstances expose them to. Criminals are not entitled to commit crimes just because citizens have these moments of vulnerability. As we discuss, profilers must understand the difference between *lifestyle exposure* and *situational exposure*.

Categorizing Victim Exposure

Criminologist Hans von Hentig had a progressive view of victims, openly suggesting that some indeed contributed to their own victimization by virtue of elements that may or may not have been beyond their control. He published *The Criminal and His Victim: Studies in the Sociobiology of Crime* (1948), which contained a chapter devoted solely to discussing these theories. Von Hentig argued for acknowledging the responsibility some victims had in becoming victimized. He even developed a system of categorizing victims along a continuum that depended on their contribution to the criminal act, although currently his terminology may be considered politically incorrect (offensive).

Von Hentig originally classified victims into one of 13 categories, which could easily be described as a list of characteristics that increase victim exposure to harmful elements (adapted from pp. 404–438; discussion by the authors):

1. *The young.* Von Hentig was referring to children and infants. From a contemporary view, children are physically weaker, have less mental prowess, have fewer legal rights, and are economically dependent on their caretakers (parents, guardians, teachers, and so forth); therefore, children have the potential to be exposed to a wider range of harm than do adults. Moreover, they are less able to defend themselves and sometimes are less likely to be believed should they seek assistance. Children suffer emotional, physical, and sexual abuse by parents or guardians (who are often under the influence of drugs and alcohol), children are bullied at school because of some aspect of their appearance or personality, and children are forced into acts of prostitution or sold into slavery by impoverished parents. Each child suffers different levels and frequencies of exposure to different kinds of harm.

2. *The female.* Von Hentig was referring to all women. From a contemporary view, many women are physically weaker than men. Many women have been culturally conditioned, to varying degrees, to accept male authority and many women are financially dependent on males in their lives (fathers, husbands, and so forth). To make matters worse, many Western women are conditioned to believe that their value is associated with their bodies, or specifically, their sexuality. In its extreme form, this can lead to promiscuity and prostitution, each with its varying exposures to harm.

3. *The old.* Von Hentig was referring to the elderly. In a contemporary sense, the elderly have many of the same vulnerabilities as children: they are often physically weaker and mentally less facile, and they may be under someone else's care. These vulnerabilities can expose them to a range of harms, from the theft of personal property to physical abuse.

4. *The mentally defective and deranged.* Von Hentig was referring to the feeble-minded, the "insane," drug addicts, and alcoholics. Many who suffer from any of these conditions have an altered perception of reality. As a consequence, depending on the level of their affliction, their personality, and the environment, these potential victims can be at risk of harming themselves and others to varying degrees. They also suffer many of the same exposures as children and the elderly.

5. *Immigrants.* Von Hentig was referring to foreigners unfamiliar with a given culture. Anyone traveling to a different culture is exposed to varying gaps in communication and comprehension. These gaps can, depending where the foreigners go and whom they encounter, expose them to all manner of confidence schemes, theft, and abuse, to say nothing of prejudices.

6. *Minorities.* Von Hentig was referring to the "racially disadvantaged," as he put it. The correct name for their vulnerability is *prejudice.* Groups against which there is bias or prejudice by another may be exposed to varying levels of abuse and violence.

7. *Dull normals.* Von Hentig was referring to "simple-minded persons," as he put it. Contemporarily, we might consider these people as having the same type of exposure to harm as those who are mentally defective and deranged.

8. *The depressed.* Von Hentig was referring to those with various psychological maladies. Today, we know that individuals with mental disorders may expose themselves to all manners of danger, intentional and otherwise. Furthermore, they may take (nontherapeutic) psychotropic medication that alters perception, affects judgment, and impairs reasoning.

9. *The acquisitive.* Von Hentig was referring to those who are greedy and are looking for quick gain. Such individuals may suspend their judgments or intentionally put themselves in dangerous situations in order to achieve their goals.

10. *The wanton.* Von Hentig was referring to promiscuous persons. People who engage in indiscriminate sexual activity with many different partners expose themselves to disease and varying personalities. Some of these personalities may be healthy and supportive; some may be narcissistic, jealous, and destructive.

11. *The lonesome or heartbroken.* Von Hentig was referring to widows, widowers, and those in mourning. Currently, loneliness is at epidemic proportions—due to more than half of marriages ending in divorce, the rise of the culture of narcissism since the late 1970s (see, generally, Lasch, 1979),

and diminishing intimacy skills across all cultures. Thus, loneliness doesn't apply just to those in mourning. Those who are lonely or heartbroken are prone to substance abuse and can be easy prey for con artists, the abusive, and the manipulative.

12. *The tormentor.* Von Hentig was referring to abusive parents. Today, we identify abusive caretakers and abusive intimates and family members of all kinds. All abusers expose themselves to the harm they inflict, the resulting angst (with the exception of the psychopath, who feels no remorse), and the degree to which their victims fight back. For example, the abusive mother who gets drunk and punches a child exposes herself to the risk of injuring her hand, the risk of misjudging her strike and even her balance, and the possibility that the child might punch back.

13. *The blocked, exempted, or fighting.* Von Hentig was referring to victims of blackmail, extortion, and confidence scams. Contemporarily, such victims are still exposed to continual financial loss or physical harm, or they must suffer the consequences that come from bringing the police in to assist, such as the attention of law enforcement and the resulting publicity.

From a nomothetic view, these are interesting and even useful classifications with important theoretical implications. However, the idiographic victimologist must study each victim to determine the extent to which a classification has a bearing on the harm actually suffered. Some children are smart and fast; some women are strong and self-assured; some of the elderly are resourceful; immigrants can learn languages and customs; and the "blocked" may decide to go to the police, despite the potentially painful consequences.

Ultimately, the aim is to arrive at an understanding of victims in the context of their lifestyle and conditions, in order for exposure to be fully understood and described to others. The question to be investigated and answered is: *What is this particular victim exposed to?* Ask when and how a particular victim's lifestyle places the individual in harm's way, if at all. For example, an adolescent male may have a high exposure to domestic violence by virtue of living with a parent who is an abusive alcoholic. At the same time, the teen may have a low exposure to being abducted, raped, and killed by a stranger, by virtue of a fixed schedule with a great deal of group activity and adult supervision.

Victim exposure can, and should, be categorized further in terms of *lifestyle exposure* and *situational exposure*.

Lifestyle Exposure

A victim's *lifestyle exposure* is related to the *frequency* of potentially harmful elements experienced by the victim and resulting from the victim's usual environment and personal traits, as well as past choices. Assessing lifestyle exposure requires an investigation and assessment of the victim's personality, and his or her personal, professional, and social environment.

Generally, lifestyle factors can influence harm to the victim in three ways:

1. By creating a perceived conflict with an offender
2. By increasing the victim's presence around offenders or those predisposed toward criminality
3. By enhancing an offender's perception of victim vulnerability.

There are many lifestyle factors that are commonly known to increase victim exposure and vulnerability to harm. However, we find even the most experienced investigators and examiners can fail to consider them in their individual assessments—especially when it suits their purposes. It should also be noted that, generally speaking, not all lifestyle factors can be said to have the potential to increase harm to a victim. Thus, to argue that a lifestyle factor influences victim-offender dynamics, the factor needs to be both potentially harmful, in the sense that its presence could be argued to influence opportunity for harm to occur, and also relevant, within the context of who the particular victim was and the criminal behavior that occurred.

Notable lifestyle factors include, but are not limited to, the following examples:

Careers

- **Attorneys.** It is true that attorneys do have regular contact with criminals, which provides an increased lifestyle exposure to violence and the possibility of retaliation. However, these crimes tend to be underreported by attorneys and the media, leading to a lack of general awareness outside of the legal community.
- **Law enforcement.** Law-enforcement officers have regular contact with a variety of criminals and controlled substances. This results in an increased lifestyle exposure to violence and the possibility of retaliation for simply showing up at work on any given day. These officers also suffer higher rates of divorce, depression, alcoholism, domestic violence, and suicide than regular citizens. Law-enforcement officers are therefore exposed to dangers on the job, at home, and at every place in between, from themselves, their cases, and those they love.
- **Prostitutes.** A *prostitute* is any person who engages in sexual activity for payment. Because prostitution is often illegal and therefore unregulated, prostitutes are often defined by their willingness to get into vehicles or go into hotel rooms with men they don't know, to perform sex acts without being seen by others. This increases their exposure to potential assault, rape, robbery, kidnapping, and even homicide, to say nothing about the risks related to drug abuse and venereal disease, both of which form a crime and criminal nexus with prostitution.
- **Drug dealers.** Drug dealing is among the most violent and dangerous criminal occupations that exist, no matter the community or the culture. It commonly involves the presence of drugs, cash, and firearms—each of which attracts crime and may be used in the perpetuation of violence of just about every kind. Like prostitution, it creates a nexus of crime and criminals.

Afflictions

- **Drug addiction.** Drug addiction involves a steady progression of drug use, increased dosages, and decreased dosage intervals. Each drug affects the addict differently, depending upon the amount taken, personal chemistry, and the other drugs in the system. The one universal consequence of drug use is impairment of the ability to think rationally.
  Drug addiction can also be associated with progressively violent and criminal drug-seeking behavior. This behavior is characterized by an intense focus on supporting a drug habit regardless of the cost or consequences. Drug addicts who engage in drug-seeking behavior exist on a continuum that includes falsifying the symptoms of illness to get prescription medications, stealing medication from neighbors under a false pretext, stealing items of value for conversion to cash to buy drugs, engaging in prostitution to support a drug habit, and robbing a pharmacy. Drugs addicts do whatever they believe will get them their drug. Period. This essentially completes the nexus of crime and criminals associated with drugs and prostitution.
- **Alcoholism.** *Alcoholism* is a particular kind of drug addiction that is not necessarily illegal—though it can result in illegal activity because of the lack of inhibition and impairment of rational thought that necessarily results. Furthermore, alcoholics may be very difficult to identify if they develop high functioning, coping, rationalization, and concealment skills. Alcoholics' persistent lack of judgment, memory, and dexterity combine to increase their vulnerability to harm from themselves and others.

- **Mental disorders/defects.** An organic mental defect or a mental disorder is a health problem that significantly affects how a person feels, thinks, behaves, and interacts with other people.

Personal Traits

- **Aggressiveness.** People who are more aggressive and confrontational in their behavior are more likely to evoke aggressive behavior in others (see Singer, 1981).
- **Impulsivity.** Impulsive behavior is executed without planning or forethought. As a consequence, impulsive individuals are generally unprepared to meet the challenges that they face, and they fail to consider the actual consequences of their actions.
- **Self-destructive behavior.** Some individuals engage in behavior that routinely puts them in harm's way. Such behaviors exist on a continuum from reckless to overtly self-destructive. The actions can include driving too fast, binge drinking or eating, overmedicating, and spending beyond one's means.
- **Passivity.** Passive individuals are those who allow or accept the actions and choices of others without question or defiance. This passivity can persist even when they are put in situations that expose them to harm or loss, and it is especially problematic if they are known to be passive, as others might see them as excellent targets.
- **Low self-esteem.** Those with low self-esteem are more apt to be depressed, to engage in self-destructive behaviors, and to be taken advantage of or otherwise victimized. Low self-esteem can create a strong desire to gain and maintain the approval of others—a tendency that is ripe for abuse by those with bad intentions. Low self-esteem can also foster the belief that one deserves to be victimized.
- **Aberrant sexual behavior.** Sexual promiscuity can lead to increased exposure to sexually transmitted disease and jealous or possessive lovers. Extreme sexual behavior can actually be physically dangerous, depending upon the types of behaviors involved.

It should be noted that any combination of these elements could have a synergistic effect. In other words, two or more of these factors or similar circumstances, when combined, are likely to enhance the frequency and effects of the others. For example, chronic drug abuse can contribute to and enhance aggressiveness and impulsivity, and a mental disorder can lead to and exacerbate abusive relationships. These circumstances do not typically occur in a vacuum, and those afflicted are rarely able to self-correct.

Assessing Lifestyle Exposure

The authors have developed an objective method of classifying the lifestyle exposure level of victims. The categories of exposure used in the method have been adapted from Turvey and Petherick (2009) and have been influenced by similar classifications from Hazelwood (1995).

With respect to lifestyle exposure,

> *Extreme-exposure victims* are those who are exposed to the possibility of suffering harm or loss every day (7 days a week). The following examples illustrate extreme-exposure victims:

- A prostitute who engages in sexual activity for money on a daily basis
- An alcoholic who is constantly intoxicated
- A prisoner who lives in a confined environment with constant exposure to criminals

> *High-exposure victims* are those who are exposed to the possibility of suffering harm or loss more often than not (4–6 days a week). These victims are frequently exposed to harmful elements; however, the exposure is not constant. For example, a child who lives in an abusive and neglectful environment during the week with his mother but lives in a healthy environment with his father on weekends. This child is exposed to harm or loss during the week but is removed from the harmful environment on the weekend.

Medium-exposure victims are those who are exposed to the possibility of suffering harm or loss less often than not (1–3 days a week). An example is a college student who engages in excessive drinking to the point of intoxication every weekend.

Low-exposure victims are those who are rarely exposed to the possibility of suffering harm or loss (less than once a week). These victims rarely engage in behaviors, or put themselves in positions, that increase their exposure or vulnerability to experiencing harm or loss.

Because lifestyle exposure refers to the *frequency* of exposure, the above categories of victim exposure are defined by timeframes. The examiner must acknowledge that not every victim trait or characteristic can be perfectly slotted into one of the above categories. For example, a child who accesses the Internet unsupervised on a daily basis is at an increased risk of communicating with online predators, but daily, unsupervised use of the Internet or chat rooms will not necessarily elevate the child's lifestyle exposure to extreme. These categories are merely a guideline to establishing the victim's lifestyle exposure and must be evaluated in the context of the specific victim's lifestyle, personal traits, and choices.

Situational/Incident Exposure

A victim's *situational* or *incident exposure* refers to the amount of actual exposure or vulnerability to harm resulting from the environment and the victim's personal traits *at the time of victimization*. This is distinct from lifestyle exposure, which again refers to harmful elements that exist, generally, in a victim's everyday life. A few useful analogies are in order.

Consider the issue of alcohol. Being a person who routinely becomes intoxicated increases one's lifestyle exposure to the many harmful effects of alcohol. However, unless a victim is actually intoxicated at the time of victimization, it does not necessarily raise situational exposure. It is possible to have a high lifestyle exposure related to alcohol abuse, but a low situational exposure from lack of alcohol use or abuse at the time of victimization. The opposite is also true.

Consider also the use of firearms. A person who does not own a firearm, does not use a firearm, does not have one in the home, or does not live with or interact with individuals who do, has a decreased lifestyle exposure to the harmful effects of firearms. However, if a victim is at a shooting range for the first time with a new friend or romantic interest and is accidentally shot, it must be recognized that the situational exposure to harm from firearms was quite high at the time of victimization. This is true even if the victim was not participating or holding a gun, because the victim had a situational proximity to multiple loaded firearms being discharged by multiple persons of varying skill.

However, not all immediately harmful exposures are as transparent and easy to recognize from the victim's perspective as these basic examples might suggest. Harmful exposure may not even be apparent to investigators, owing to investigative apathy, or the reliance on false investigative assumptions about who and what was present during the crime. The situational harm coming from persons, environments, and circumstances related to a particular crime must be thoroughly investigated, carefully established, and never assumed.

Notable situational factors include, but are not limited to, the following:

- **Time of occurrence.** Certain times of day can result in more exposure to various kinds of harm than others. However, any interpretation of the effect of this factor is highly dependent on the location of occurrence as well as other converging circumstances. Time of day cannot be considered in a vacuum. Time of day is a factor heavily influenced by the regular activities of the victim, the victim's proximity to abusers, and subsequent supervision—all of which is very often a function of age.

- **Location of occurrence.** Location is one of the most important factors to consider in terms of situational exposure. Certain environments contain a great deal of criminal activity, others may place a victim outside the immediate reach of assistance, and still others may physically isolate or confine the victim.
- **Proximity to criminal activity.** Nearness in space, time, or relationship to criminal activity increases one's incident exposure. This can include victim nearness to crime and criminals, or direct victim participation and involvement in criminal activity. The more violence associated with a proximal crime, the greater subsequent victim exposure to harm.
- **Number of potential victims.** It is generally true that there is safety in numbers; in other words, the buddy system can remove one from the path of harm, or speed one away from harmful circumstances. This is true as long as the people one is with are not at an increased lifestyle or situational exposure. If your buddy is intoxicated, he's not an asset, he's a liability. The same is true if your buddy has a temper, he just got in a fight with his significant other and is distressed, or he has a mental disorder and is not taking medication.

  Also, some more competent and confident offenders prefer to select victims in pairs in order to use one to control the other, such as a mother and a child. This situation is one of the exceptions that proves the rule. Examples include abusive parents who threaten the life of other family members should anyone tell the police, or the rapist who selects a mother with small children to gain her total compliance by threatening to harm the children.
- **Availability of weapons.** The availability of any weapon or material in a given environment increases the likelihood that it will be used in a physical altercation, should one ensue, or that someone will accidentally injure himself or herself or others while handling it for any number of legitimate or illegitimate purposes. The availability of a shotgun in an environment increases victim exposure to shotgun injury or fatality; the availability of knives in an environment increases victim exposure to sharp force injury or fatality; the availability of coat hangers in an environment increases victim exposure to related ligature injury or fatality. However, a weapon's availability does not cause its use.
- **Care and supervision.** Individuals become more willing to engage in criminal activity when they are not being watched. That is to say, criminal propensity can increase as supervision and accountability decrease.
- **Victim state of mind or perception.** This factor refers to the victim's emotional state before, during, and following an attack, as evidenced by convergent patterns of behavior and any reliable witness accounts. An agitated or distressed emotional state, for example, may increase victim incident exposure. Additionally, a victim who feels safe in a particular environment or situation will act differently from a victim who does not. Many variables, including the presence of drugs, alcohol, mental disorder, or a heightened emotional state, such as anger or sadness, affect this directly.
- **Drug and alcohol use.** The use of mind-altering substances may decrease physical reaction time, impair judgment, and alter one's perception of reality. Either drug or alcohol use increases victim situational exposure dramatically, even for otherwise low-exposure victims. One thing that one cannot do under the influence of drugs or alcohol is think rationally.

The existence of any one circumstance is not necessarily enough to be a tipping point for victim harm, unless direct harm is inherent (such as with drug and alcohol use). Having a gun in the home will not cause someone to use it for violence, having drugs in the home will not make someone use them, leaving a child unsupervised at school will not cause the child to be raped. It is the synergy of corresponding factors and circumstances that exposes victims to ever-increasing levels of harm.

Assessing Situational Exposure

The authors have developed a more transparent method of classifying situational exposure. These categories of exposure have been adapted from Petherick and Turvey (2009) and have been influenced by similar classifications from Hazelwood (1995).

With respect to situational exposure,

> *High-exposure victims* are those who are exposed to harm or loss immediately prior to victimization. These victims are already suffering actual harm or loss prior to the point of victimization. For example, a young child who is abducted while home alone in an unsafe environment was already suffering harm and neglect by their primary caregiver prior to the point of victimization.
>
> *Medium-exposure victims* are those who are vulnerable to harm or loss immediately prior to victimization. These victims are not suffering actual harm or loss prior to victimization, but the environment or personal traits of the victim increase their vulnerability or susceptibility to experiencing harm. For example, a female who is walking alone late at night has increased vulnerability due to the time of day and the environment, because the offender is provided with an available and vulnerable victim and darkness/isolation reduce the offender's exposure level.
>
> *Low-exposure victims* are those who are exposed to little contact or vulnerability to harm or loss immediately prior to victimization. The environment and personal traits of these victims do not expose them to harmful elements or increase their vulnerability to harmful elements prior to victimization. It is important to note here that most of us are generally exposed to at least some level of vulnerability to harm or loss at any point in time, whether it is within our immediate environment or it reflects our personal traits.

Case Example: Paige Birgfeld

Consider the unsolved case of Paige Birgfeld, a single 34-year-old mother of three from the upper-class suburbs of Grand Junction, Colorado (Figure 7.1). She went missing on Thursday, June 28, 2007. Several days later, her car was found burning in an empty parking lot less than three miles from her home (Figure 7.2). A cursory

FIGURE 7.1

As of this writing, Paige Birgfeld remains missing from her home in Grand Junction, Colorado. Foul play is suspected, but her body has not been found.

FIGURE 7.2

Paige Birgfeld's car, a red 2005 Ford Focus, was found burning in a parking lot in an industrial area near her Grand Junction home on July 1, 2007. Police believe this may have been an attempt to conceal physical evidence of a crime.

glance at her life painted a picture to investigators that did not suggest an association with anything that might expose her to danger; quite the opposite, in fact. She was involved with her family and community, had several business ventures going, and was well regarded by those who knew her.

A careful examination of her life, however, revealed something else—a history of exposure to bad people, bad choices, and bad things and a not-so-hidden career that would change the face of the investigation completely. As Martin (2007a) describes,

> Investigators have used bloodhounds and interviewed family and friends to try to unravel the mysterious disappearance of Paige Birgfeld, a Grand Junction mother of three missing for nearly a week. "She was here in Grand Junction, and there was nothing out of the ordinary," said her father, Frank Birgfeld. "And then she simply vanished."
>
> The search for the 34-year-old began Saturday, when she was reported missing by family members. Birgfeld was last seen Thursday night, said Mesa County sheriff's spokeswoman Heather Gierhart. Sunday night, her red Ford Focus was found burning in an empty parking lot about 3 miles from her house. Frank Birgfeld, who lives in Centennial, said the fire appeared to have been started inside the car, as if to destroy evidence.
>
> "I can tell you that (police) never considered this a missing persons matter," Birgfeld said. "They were actively investigating this as much more."
>
> But the Sheriff's Office is saying anything is possible. "Whether she walked away or staged her disappearance or was the victim of something, we're open to all possibilities," Gierhart said.
>
> Friends said Paige Birgfeld had told them she was afraid of one of her ex-husbands, Rob Dixon. …
>
> "My children would ask me if Dad was going to kill me," she wrote under the name Paige Dixon in a posting in March on chefsuccess.com, a forum for people like herself who sold Pampered Chef products. "I can't imagine what they were thinking life would be like after he killed me. … I would gladly sacrifice every penny of child support if he would stay away!"
>
> Rob Dixon was arrested on charges of domestic violence after allegedly shoving Birgfeld during an argument, according to a police report and court records. He later pleaded guilty to a lesser charge of harassment. Sheriff's investigators have not named Dixon as a suspect in the disappearance.
>
> Dixon's lawyer, Scott Robinson, said his client was in Philadelphia last week. Dixon moved there to work as a paramedic after the couple's divorce. He had planned, however, to move back to Colorado to be closer to his three children, ages 3, 6 and 8, Robinson said. Dixon returned to Colorado on Sunday after he learned about Birgfeld's disappearance, Robinson said. Gierhart said Dixon has answered questions and cooperated fully with police investigators.

Further investigation revealed Birgfeld had been living a double life, a holdover from her days working as a stripper years before. Separate from her other business ventures, some of which may have actually been covers, she was also a female escort who advertised her services on the Internet. *Escort* is a term that is commonly used by prostitutes in their written ads. It allows them to advertise their services legally in adult magazines, on the Internet, and even in the Yellow Pages. As Martin (2007b) describes,

> For most of last week, friends and family of a missing Grand Junction mother were surprised on an almost-daily basis as they learned the secrets she had been keeping.

Over the weekend, they found out one more: She went by another name. Paige Birgfeld, 34, occasionally told people her name was "Carrie," police said, also announcing for the first time that they suspect she is the victim of foul play. Birgfeld used the pseudonym with customers of an escort agency before she disappeared June 28, Mesa County sheriff's spokeswoman Heather Gierhart said. The investigation is focusing on people who were in contact with "Carrie" and the agency, "Models Inc.," around the time she went missing, Gierhart said.

Birgfeld's involvement with the escort service was a surprise to friends and family last week. "We didn't know any of this," her mother, Suzanne Birgfeld, said Sunday. But, she said, the new information helps the search for her daughter, whose three children, ages 8, 6 and 3, are beginning to really miss her. "We added the name 'Carrie' to some of the fliers we're handing out," she said, adding that she did not know where the name came from. …

The picture that friends have painted of Birgfeld is of a beautiful, committed mother who sold Pampered Chef products and taught dance to preschoolers to get by. Investigators previously said any explanation was possible, including the theory Birgfeld staged the whole thing. They kept an open mind even after her car was found July 1 engulfed in flames in an empty parking lot about 3 miles from her home.

Shockley (2007) details Birgfeld's complete ad for "escort" services (Figure 7.3):

A news release distributed Saturday by the Mesa County Sheriff's Office said the missing mother of three children was known to some escort-service customers of Models Inc., as Carrie. …

FIGURE 7.3

One of the Web sites where Paige Birgfeld advertised—www. naughtynightlife.com.

The Web page at www.naughtynightlife.com, linked to "Carrie" offers a physical description nearly identical to Birgfeld. The Web page describes Carrie as a 29-year-old white female, 5 feet, 4 inches tall, 112 pounds with hazel eyes and dark blonde hair. The sheriff's office has described Birgfeld as 34, a white female, 5 feet, 4 inches tall, 110 pounds with hazel eyes and sandy hair.

"Carrie" of Grand Junction, with Models Inc., according to the Web site, offers services such as escort, erotic massage, private dancer, groups and parties—available all hours of the day on an "incall & outcall" basis. She travels "within Colorado and neighboring states by chartered jet only," according to the Web page, and she lists Parachute, Rifle, Silt, Delta and Montrose, among "cities I travel to."

A complete background detailing where the danger was coming from in Birgfeld's life has yet to be fully divulged as of this writing. With each new victimological revelation, the suspect pool expands and the sources of harm unfold. An informed thumbnail sketch is provided in Montero (2007):

[Paige] was 18. It was a big moment for her. She was already dating Ron Biegler in Colorado, and he decided to move to Gainesville, Fla., to be near her. They lived across the street from the University of Florida football stadium, and Biegler said after several months there, Paige considered herself married to him.

There was only one problem. "She wanted to be a stripper in Florida and I just didn't want her to do it," Biegler said. "And she never did while we lived there."

Biegler was an odd match for Paige Birgfeld. With [his] long, blond hair, tattoos and [his] being the lead guitarist in a rock band, the Birgfelds weren't sure what to make of her boyfriend. Even Biegler acknowledged the mismatch. "I married over my head," he said.

They had met without really knowing it years before their eventual marriage. But it was when Biegler saw her in a parking lot and offered to jump-start her car that he decided he wanted to go out with her. He was 19 and she was 16. Within days, they went out to dinner and a movie. After the date, Biegler was too shy to make the first move. So Birgfeld leaned in to kiss him, and Biegler moved away. "She took it as a rejection," Biegler said. "That wasn't the case at all. I was just nervous." She never let him live it down.

After they moved back to Colorado, they got married in 1995 and lived in a small house in Aurora. Paige worked hard at decorating the house. She really loved the home, even if it was small. Biegler had his instruments in the basement and continued to work on his music while doing odd jobs. And then the issue of stripping came up again. Biegler was still opposed but didn't want to tell her what to do. So a few nights a week, she'd go to the now-defunct Mile High Saloon strip club and dance under the stage name Madison. For about three years, she did it. Biegler didn't see her perform very often and said she didn't like him going there.

But she had her reasons for stripping. "She wanted to pay for her breast augmentation," Biegler said. "I also don't think she felt very pretty or attractive, and I think stripping made her feel better about herself and made her feel more powerful."

When they divorced in 1997, it wasn't because of the stripping. She said she was ready to have kids. He wasn't. She was 24. A year later, she met Rob Dixon at the Mile High Saloon. Dixon lavished Paige with gifts—jewelry, cars and plenty of money. Dixon was wealthy and said he wanted to have children. …

But the couple's relationship was tempestuous. Court records indicate that in October 2005, Dixon allegedly slapped his wife on the shoulder and punched her in the throat as she held their baby after accusing her of giving topless massages. He was arrested on suspicion of third-degree assault and misdemeanor child abuse. He pleaded guilty to a lesser charge of harassment. The case against him was dismissed last month after he completed terms of a yearlong deferred sentence, his attorney said.

Frank Birgfeld said the couples' finances were shaky. And Dixon often found his name in the *Daily Sentinel* newspaper because of a questionable investment he recommended as an official of the Grand Junction Rural Fire District. Paige's father said Dixon filed for bankruptcy and his daughter began trying to make money to keep a house that had been valued at $900,000. The mortgage payments were overwhelming, as were the expenses of maintaining the home. The couple divorced in 2006. …

Jamie Silvernail, a 28-year-old mom, met Paige four years ago but really got to know her in late 2006, when they lived together in the big house. Silvernail said she would see how busy Paige was—sometimes doing housecleaning in the middle of the night just to keep up.

She also noticed Paige leaving the house late at night after the kids were in bed. Those were the escort calls. "I didn't ask about it, but you kind of knew," Silvernail said. "She was someone who just did what they had to do to survive. She was intent on keeping the house and family together and would do whatever it takes."

Silvernail also said Paige seemed to extend herself for everyone. She took on a leadership role in the Grand River Playgroup and was one of the most willing donors of time to the Grand Junction MOMS club. In addition, Paige was juggling Pampered Chef parties, teaching kids dance through a business she ran called Brain Dance and doing small jobs such as selling baby slings.

Motherhood seemed to be her primary focus. Throughout her house, the only magazines are about mother-child-related issues. Her bedroom, where the three kids slept with her—the 8-year-old in a small bed nearby—is littered with children's toys, including a small Elmo chair. …

Paige Birgfeld met a problem the night of June 28. Earlier that Thursday, she drove to Eagle to meet Biegler—a rendezvous the two had been planning for a couple of months. Biegler said it was going well, but he didn't want to push it. Still, he said the spark between them had been rekindled.

He said she joked with him again that if she tried to kiss him, he'd probably reject her. He didn't. As she left Eagle, she told him she'd call him in a couple of hours to make sure he got back to Denver safely. When she called around 9 p.m., she wasn't home yet—deterred by roadwork in Grand Junction. He said the conversation was run of the mill because he knew they were supposed to talk again later that night. They didn't.

Biegler called Paige's cell phone Friday and waited in anticipation of her voice. Click. Straight to her voice mail. He called her other phone. Click. Straight to her voice mail. He didn't leave any messages, figuring he would talk to her later. Never thinking he wouldn't. And now, weeks later, knowing he won't.

As of this writing, authorities have all but cleared her ex-husbands of any wrongdoing and continue to search through her client list for what are commonly referred to these days as "persons of interest." The case remains open and active.

VICTIMOLOGY GUIDELINES

Weston and Wells (1974, p. 97) provide a quick checklist of preliminary victimological queries that have been proven to be most useful in eliciting investigative information. This is the kind of information that should be gathered immediately, ideally before the investigator arrives at a given crime scene.

1. Did the victim know the perpetrator?
2. Does the victim suspect any person? Why?
3. Had the victim a history of crime? A history of reporting crimes?
4. Did the victim have a weapon?
5. Had the victim an aggressive personality?
6. Has the victim been the subject of any field [police] reports?

The problem with this checklist is that it may require some misleading assumptions and interpretations prior to the start of the investigation. For example, unless it there is no doubt about the identity of the offender, this is a question to be answered by virtue of an investigation. Also, it presumes that there was actually a crime committed. Not all complaints are founded; not all deaths are homicides. Again, this is something that can only be established by a thorough investigation. The lesson here is that victim information, and victim history, has long been considered essential to professional investigators of fact, to the point of developing these kinds of conceptual checklists.

Turvey and Petherick (2009) also provide basic victimological inquires that have been useful when applied to actual casework. Gathering this information, along with the careful examination of physical evidence, provides the starting point for investigative activity. Again, no one checklist can suffice; the victimologist must be willing to sift through each victim's history carefully, with no preconceived theories. When compiling a forensic victimology, it is important to reference the case material that each piece of information was taken from, ensuring the reader can locate the original document.

The following adapts those victim guidelines into a more cohesive set of objective packages that must be gathered and assessed by the criminal investigator and profiler alike, as with any intelligence. There can be no mistake as to the importance of this effort, and the investigative clarity it will provide. Conversely, the failure to collect these data packages leaves gaping holes in the investigation through which unexamined theories of the crime will most certainly escape.

Again, the gathering and assessment of these packages provides context, and should lead to additional information and evidence. They are not the end of the inquiry but rather the beginning.

Personal Package

1. Sex
2. Race
3. Height
4. Weight
5. Hair color/length/dyed
6. Eyes: color/glasses/contacts
7. Clothing/jewelry
8. Personal items: contents of wallet, purse, handbag, backpack, briefcase, suitcase, or medicine bag
9. Grooming/manner of dress
10. Smoker or non-smoker
11. Hobbies/skills

12. Routine daily activities and commitments
13. Recently scheduled events
14. Upcoming scheduled events

Digital Package

1. Cell phone: calls, chats, address book, GPS, photos, video
2. Laptop/desktop: email, calls, chats, documents, address books, browser history, photos, video
3. Personal Web sites: recent browser history, social network activity (e.g., Facebook, Twitter), blogs, dating Web sites, and other personal subscription Web sites
4. Financial Web sites/payment history: stocks, mutual funds/401k, credit cards, and online banking
5. Personal GPS device: recent trips, destinations, bookmarked points of interest

Residence Package

1. Physical home address
2. Location/condition of bedroom
3. Evidence of music/literature/personal interests
4. Personal correspondence
5. Personal sexual items/explicit material
6. Missing items
7. Signs of violence
8. Location/condition of personal vehicle
9. Hard line phone calls (incoming and outgoing)
10. 911 calls and criminal history of residence

The investigator or profiler should spend time, when possible, with the victim's personal items, in the personal environments (hangouts, work, school, home/bedroom, etc.). Examine any available photo albums, diaries, or journals. Make note of music and literature preferences. Do this to find out who the victims seemed to believe they were, what they wanted everyone to perceive, and how they seemed to feel about their life in general.

Relationship Package

1. Current and previous intimate or marital partner(s)
2. Current and previous family members
3. Current and previous household members
4. Current and previous friends
5. Current and previous co-workers/classmates
6. History of relationship counseling

Employment Package

1. Educational background and history
2. Current occupations/job titles (many people have multiple employers)
3. Place of employment/work schedule/supervisor
4. Employment history

5. Work phone: calls, chats, address book, GPS, photos, video
6. Laptop/desktop: email, calls, chats, documents, address books, browser history, photos, video
7. Business GPS device: recent trips, destinations, bookmarked points of interest
8. Business vehicle: logs, travel (times/ destinations), GPS device
9. Business insurance policies

This list can be adapted for students, with the school as the employer, class schedule as work schedule, and teachers as supervisor, and so forth.

Financial Package

1. Wallet/purse: contents, cards, personal items
2. Credit cards/history
3. Bank accounts/history
4. Property ownership (residences and vehicles)
5. Stocks/mutual funds/401k/retirement benefits
6. Insurance policies

Medical Package

1. Current state of intoxication (alcohol and drug levels)
2. Current medical conditions (physical and mental)
3. History of serious medical conditions
4. Current medications (see purse, desk drawers, and medicine cabinets)
5. Current treatment regimes
6. Current treatment professionals
7. Recent medical appointments
8. Addictions (drugs, alcohol, or obsessive behavior)

Court Package

1. Criminal history (active investigations, protection orders, arrests, warrants, convictions)
2. Civil court history (lawsuits, judgments, and role)
3. Witness history (previous depositions or testimony given in legal proceedings)
4. In-state and out-of-state records
5. Evidence of victim criminal activity during the crime
6. Evidence of ongoing victim criminal activity unrelated to the crime

These packages should be used to

1. Compile a list of the victim's daily routines, habits, and activities
2. Compile a complete list of victim family members with contact information
3. Compile a complete list of victim friends with contact information
4. Compile a complete list of victim coworkers/schoolmates with contact information
5. Create a timeline of events using witness statements, digital evidence, and physical evidence

Everyone should be interviewed, as people with important information often do not come forward. Many well-meaning witnesses wait for someone to approach them out of ignorance with respect to how the investigative process works. Investigators must be pro-active in this regard.

Creating a Timeline: The Last 24 Hours

The general purpose here is to familiarize the forensic victimologist with the last known activities of the victim and subsequently determine, if possible, how a given victim got to a place and time where an offender was able to access him or her. The picture needs to be built from the ground up. It is a rewarding and illuminating process that should not be overlooked.

A good approach to creating this timeline of locations and events includes at least the following steps:

■ Compile all witness data
■ Compile all available forensic evidence
■ Compile all of the police/media crime scene photographs and video
■ Compile all security stills and video covering the crime scene and any paths taken by the victim or offender to or from it
■ Create a linear timeline of events and locations
■ Create a map of the victim's route for the 24 hours before the attack, as detailed as possible
■ Physically walk through the victim's last 24 hours using the map and forensic evidence as a guide
■ Document expected background elements of the route in terms of vehicles, people, activities, professionals, and so on for the time leading up to, during, and after the victim was acquired. It is possible that the offender is, or was masquerading as, one of those expected elements

Attempt to determine the following:

■ The point at which the offender acquired the victim
■ The place where the offender attacked the victim
■ How well the attack location can be seen from any surrounding locations
■ Whether the offender would need to be familiar with the area to know of this specific location or get to it
■ Whether knowledge of the route would require or indicate prior surveillance
■ Whether this route placed the victim at higher or lower exposure to an attack
■ Whether the acquisition of the victim on that route placed the offender at higher or lower exposure to identification or apprehension

SUMMARY

Forensic victimology is concerned with the investigation and examination of particular victims alleged to have suffered specific crimes, which is an idiographic form of knowledge building. It is intended to serve both investigative and forensic goals, which are very different in scope and reliability with respect to findings. In order to reduce bias and achieve a minimum threshold of reliability, the forensic victimologist must request a sufficient amount of victim information, determine its reliability, and perform examinations in accordance with the practice standards provided. A key feature of this is an applied understanding of the scientific method and an emphasis on theory falsification.

Forensic victimology assists in establishing the nature of victim exposure to harm or loss. Victim exposure can be categorized in terms of *lifestyle exposure* and *situational exposure*. Victim *lifestyle exposure* is concerned with studying the *frequency* of potentially harmful elements experienced by the victim and resulting from the victim's usual environment and personal traits, as well as past choices. Victim *situational* or *incident exposure* refers to the amount of actual exposure or vulnerability experienced by the victim to harm, resulting from the environment and personal traits *at the time of victimization.*

In order to use victimology effectively in the course of an investigation, a complete picture of the victim history is required. Ignoring victim history, in part or whole, creates gaps in the investigative and factual record that will make victim related interpretation incomplete, if not inaccurate.

Questions

1. List three goals of forensic victimology.
2. _____ is the amount of contact or vulnerability to harmful elements experienced by the victim.
3. True or False: *Situational/incident exposure* is concerned with studying the frequency of potentially harmful elements experienced by the victim.
4. List the three ways that lifestyle factors can influence harm to the victim.
5. Provide an example of an *extreme lifestyle exposure* victim.

REFERENCES

Hazelwood, R., 1995. Analyzing Rape and Profiling the Offender. In: Hazelwood, R.R., Burgess, A.W. (Eds.), Practical Aspects of Rape Investigation: A Multidisciplinary Approach, second edition. CRC Press, Boca Raton, FL.

Jamerson, C., 2009. Forensic Nursing: Approaching the Victim as a Crime Scene. In: Turvey, B., Petherick, W., (Eds.), Forensic Victimology. Elsevier Science, San Diego, CA.

Lasch, C., 1979. The Culture of Narcissism. W.W. Norton & Co, New York, NY.

Martin, N., 2007a. Woman's Disappearance Baffles Family, Police. Denver Post July 3.

Martin, N., 2007b. Secret Life Surprises Kin, Pals of Missing Woman. Denver Post July 9.

Montero, D., 2007. Paige's Secret Life. Rocky Mountain News July 14.

National Institute of Justice, 1999. Death Investigation: A Guide For The Scene Investigator. NIJ, Research Report NCJ 167568. Washington, DC.

National Institute of Justice, 2004. A National Protocol for Sexual Assault Medical Forensic Examinations. U.S. Department of Justice, Office on Violence Against Women, Washington, DC, NCJ 206554, September.

Savino, J., Turvey, B., 2011. Rape Investigation Handbook. Elsevier Science, Boston, MA.

Shockley, P., 2007. Escort Web Link Missing Woman's? Free Press July 9.

Singer, S., 1981. Homogenous Victim-Offender Population: A Review and Some Research Implications. Journal of Criminal Law and Criminology 72, 779–788.

Turvey, B., 2008. Criminal Profiling: An Introduction to Behavioral Evidence Analysis, third edition. Elsevier Science, San Diego, CA.

Turvey, B., Petherick, W., 2009. Forensic Victimology: Examining Violent Crime Victims in Investigative and Legal Contexts. Elsevier Science, San Diego, CA.

von Hentig, H., 1948. The Criminal and His Victim: Studies in the Sociology of Crime. Yale University Press, New Haven, CT.

Weston, P., Wells, K., 1974. Criminal Investigation: Basic Perspectives, second edition. Prentice-Hall, Englewood Cliffs, NJ.

CHAPTER 8

Sexual Deviance

Brent E. Turvey

Prosecutors confuse the presence of traditional symbols of violence (whips, chains, handcuffs), utilized in a theatrical and self-conscious simulation of power relationships, as the presence of real dominance and exploitation. I wish to dispel this confusion and advocate for a more culturally informed legal treatment of this behavior.

—Pa (2001, p. 53)

CONTENTS

KEY TERMS

Exhibitionism

Fetishism

Infidelity

Sadomasochism

Sexual arousal

Sexual asphyxia

Sexual coercion

Sexual deviance

Sexual fantasy

"Open" relationship

Pornography

Criminal profilers and investigators have a duty to be thoroughly knowledgeable about the prevalence, nature, and variety of human sexual behavior. This means not confusing one's limited personal sexual experience for "normal." It also means avoiding the tendency to judge and to demonize those who engage in what may be considered deviant sexual activities. This is an area where many profilers and investigators not only are lost, but also are without resources.

Criminal profilers must become comfortable with human sexuality in order to conduct a thorough and informed victimology, and to ably examine related behaviors in their proper context, without bias. They must also develop an understanding of how sexual preference and desire may manifest themselves in the course of non-criminal activities. This will help prevent the confusion of non-criminal sexual activity with sex crimes, and inform the criminal profiling process as it relates to the need for sexual honesty.

EVERYBODY LIES

Sexual behaviors and their diverse underlying motivations are among the most difficult to study for a variety of reasons. However, the greatest barrier to sexual truth is undoubtedly the fact that most people lie about their sexual habits, or at the very least are actively working to conceal their true sexual self from public scrutiny. They most often lie about the age at which they lost their virginity; the number of sexual partners they've had; sexual prowess, virility, and experience; the nature of the sex acts that they have performed or would be willing to perform; and, in extreme cases, they lie about their sexual orientation.

The reasons for these lies, fabrications, and concealments are many, but the more outstanding motivations deserve our attention.

First is the desire for privacy. The sexual self is perhaps the most closely guarded aspect of one's personal life. It is also among the most intimate faces that one person can show another. In the majority of cultures it is not regarded as something to be shared casually or openly. In fact, its privacy is often regarded as part of its inherent value. Given this reality, it is no surprise that most people are unwilling to be completely honest about their actual sexual fantasies, preferences, or history.

Second, there is embarrassment. Many people are embarrassed by their sexuality, and by the need to satisfy sexual impulses, because of either their upbringing or some early trauma. For whatever reason, they fear public scrutiny and humiliation related to some or all of their sexual practices or feelings. These individuals will not admit to desiring, let alone enjoying, any number of sexual activities.

Third, there are social, cultural, religious, and even legal taboos against certain sexual activities. These prohibitions, and the consequences that can follow, provide enough motive to lie or to remain silent about any sexual habits or propensities that are prohibited. Failure to do so may expose one to being judged, labeled, and sanctioned by colleagues, friends, family, and even the justice system.

Finally, many people are sexually reactive, lacking reflection or insight into the nature and extent of their own sexuality. They often haven't thought about who they are as a sexual person, or how that might be relevant to their relationships with sexually intimate partners. When asked about their sexual habits and history, their awareness of what they have done and with whom, or even why, is minimal, if it exists at all.

All of these motivating factors combine to create an abundance of ignorance regarding human sexuality. When research is conducted or official inquiries are made based on self-reporting, the answers are often a function of the respondents' rising to meet social, cultural, or religious expectations in their answers: they deny fantasizing, they deny masturbating, they deny engaging in oral or anal sex, and they deny indulging in their sexual impulses and sharing infidelities.

Obviously, then, it is difficult to define and to discuss the nature and extent of deviant sexual behavior. The discussion requires thoughtful consideration of primary influences on sexual development, arousal, and fantasy, leading up to the contextualization of major forms of sexual deviation. It also requires honesty about the sexual habits and propensities that are evident in the world around us.

DEFINING DEVIANT SEXUAL BEHAVIOR

For the purposes of this chapter, *sexual deviance,* or *sexual aberration,* is defined as any eroticized activity that differs from accepted or typical sexual norms. This definition is similar to the definition provided by Francoeur (1995, p. 592), which refers to sexual deviance as: "Any sexual behavior that deviates from what a society considers normal (qv) or typical, usually with the connotation that the aberrant behavior is criminal or at least antisocial." Criminal sexual behavior is discussed in a subsequent chapter, which leaves us with the rare and the antisocial (that which is self-serving and misanthropic).

The concept of sexual deviance is not fixed or universal. Rather, it is defined inconsistently by the needs and beliefs of those classifying, discussing, or studying it. Each religion has its own sexual prohibitions, subject to wide interpretation and changing with time and place. Each culture has its own sexual mores, depending on the dominant groups in a region. Even professionals approach the subject with their own ends in mind: the clinician seeks to treat, the criminologist seeks to understand, the courts seek justice, and the lawyer seeks to defend. Every group has its own purported set of norms and their subsequent deviations.

This chapter takes the criminological view of sexual deviance—our goal is understanding, as opposed to punishment or treatment. The topic is approached scientifically and without consideration of moral constructs like "right" and "wrong," or religious constructs like "good" and "evil." These are subjective measures and often are selectively applied, leading to little if any insight. The aim of the criminal profiler is to objectively understand the nature of major forms of sexual deviance, as well as their origins and motives.

MODERN SEXUAL DEVELOPMENT

Sexual development begins at infancy as children investigate their bodies through self-touch, which includes their genitals. As they grow and explore their bodies, they learn what is appropriate from the reactions of others. As described in Allen et al. (2008b, pp. 517–518), the influences on sexual development are a complex blend from the beginning:

> Families are the primary context in which messages about sexuality are first communicated. Children's earliest learning occurs as they observe and make meaning from their parents' actions. Parents who provide a stable and secure home environment facilitate their children's ability to form stronger sexual and emotional relationships as they develop (DeLamater and Friedrich,

2002). A positive socialization context for children allows them to experience more connection and emotional bonds with significant others, learn to regulate their behavior through the imposition of consistent limits, and develop a stable sense of self and personal autonomy (Barber and Olsen, 1997).

Socialization is complex, and multiple contexts, such as peers, schools, and social institutions, interact, particularly as children transition to early then later adolescence (Peterson and Hann, 1999). Although families provide the foundation for children's socialization, not all parents are interested in or are adept at providing for children's positive sexual socialization.

When parents are less interested and less able to provide positive sexual socialization for their children, other sources of information take on a greater role in the early formation of sexual identity. In the modern age, these sources are the mass media and the Internet. As explained in Allen et al. (2008b, pp. 518–519),

Competing with the idea that families, parents, and peers are the main socializers of adolescent sexuality, Brown, Halpern, and L'Engle (2005) claimed that in the 21st century, private electronic media has become the primary sexuality educator of youth. Summarizing data from the Kaiser Family Foundation Report of 1997, DeLamater and Friedrich (2002) stated that young teens (ages 10–15) consider the mass media (e.g., movies, TV, magazines, music), as more important sources of information about sex and intimacy than parents, peers, and sexuality education programs. Mass media helps construct, reflect, challenge, and exploit human sexuality and gender relations. Sex is used to sell everything from household products to luxury vehicles and fast food; explicit sex acts are shown on prime-time television; and pornography is easily available on the Internet. Children and adolescents are increasingly exposed, often unintentionally, to pornographic or violent images, or both, at younger ages through aggressive advertising, personal Internet use, and various entertainment outlets (Greenfield, 2004; Valkenburg and Soeters, 2001). …

Although sex saturates both private and public discourse and is used to persuade and sell, Americans, both historically and today, are queasy about acknowledging the sexual desire of children and youth (Irvine, 2004). If adults are reticent to proactively and fairly address sexuality issues, such as the tension between sexual exploitation and repression, then, young people will remain vulnerable to misinformation from the very institutions (e.g., families, school, faith communities, and the media) that are charged with providing sex education. Young people will be left to generate their own ideas about what constitutes healthy sexual development and positive sexual decisions (Baber, 2000; Russell, 2005).

If young people begin their sexual careers with an inadequate knowledge about what constitutes sex, they are unprepared for the risks and responsibilities, including unwanted pregnancy, sexually transmitted infections, and participation in sexually coercive behavior. They are also unprepared to act with agency on behalf of their own sense of sexual desire. Lacking the knowledge to be empowered, their threshold for error—and the possibility of making mistakes—is lowered.

As children grow into and through adolescence with these competing influences on their sexual perceptions, their own physical development (e.g., pubic hair, breasts, body odor, acne) also has an enormous impact on their self-esteem and the subsequent development of social skills. The impact of physical development is measured not only by how they perceive themselves, but also by how they believe others perceive them.

Sexually related trauma can also have a significant impact on sexual development, either by muting it, stopping it, increasing it, or distorting it. Trauma includes being the victim of sexual rumors, name-calling or bullying by peers, sexual coercion, and, of course, sexual abuse. There is no one single way that sexually related trauma manifests in a child's actions or development, but it is generally believed that pre-pubescent boys and girls who engage in age-inappropriate sexual behavior do so because of exposure to, or experience with, explicit sexual material or activities. Such exposure may come from the actions and activities of adults, intentionally or otherwise, but it may also come from peers.

This raises the question of what precisely are age-inappropriate behaviors. In other words, *what is normal sexual behavior for teenagers these days?* It is fair to say that most adults, and parents, believe they know what is going on in the lives of their children. Many authority figures purport to have special insight as well. However, most do not have the first clue—as many are willfully ignorant of how the world has changed since their own adolescence, or they are too self-centered to take notice.

Let's alleviate some misconceptions. One of the better descriptive studies was conducted on Australian teenagers by Sauers (2007), who found the following:

- Teenage (ages 13–19) boys and girls generally remember starting to masturbate between ages 9 and 11; 61% of girls reported masturbating twice a week or more, as opposed to 89% of boys
- By the time they turned 16, 51% of girls and 65% of boys reported having either given or received oral sex; notably, 24% of girls and 19% of boys age 13–14 and reported participation in the same activity
- By the time they turned 15, 34% of girls and 34% of boys reported engaging in sexual intercourse; by age 16, the numbers increased to 43% of girls and 52% of boys
- Anal sex was by far the least common sexual activity, with only 12% of teenage girls and 25% of teenage boys reporting that they had engaged in anal sex. However, this is not nearly rare enough to make anal sex a deviant behavior

These findings agree with those published in the United States by the Centers for Disease Control in 2005 (Jayson, 2009):

> The generational divide between baby-boomer parents and their teenage offspring is sharpening over sex.
>
> Oral sex, that is.
>
> More than half of 15- to 19-year-olds are doing it, according to a groundbreaking study by the Centers for Disease Control and Prevention.
>
> The researchers did not ask about the circumstances in which oral sex occurred, but the report does provide the first federal data that offer a peek into the sex lives of American teenagers.
>
> To adults, "oral sex is extremely intimate, and to some of these young people, apparently it isn't as much," says Sarah Brown, director of the National Campaign to Prevent Teen Pregnancy.
>
> "What we're learning here is that adolescents are redefining what is intimate." Among teens, oral sex is often viewed so casually that it needn't even occur within the confines of a relationship. Some teens say it can take place at parties, possibly with multiple partners. But they say the more likely scenario is oral sex within an existing relationship.
>
> Still, some experts are increasingly worrying that a generation that approaches intimate behavior so casually might have difficulty forming healthy intimate relationships later on.
>
> "My parents' generation sort of viewed oral sex as something almost greater than sex. Like once you've had sex, something more intimate is oral sex," says Carly Donnelly, 17, a high school senior from Cockeysville, MD. "Now that some kids are using oral sex as something that's more casual, it's shocking to (parents)."…

A study published in the journal *Pediatrics* in April supports the view that adolescents believe oral sex is safer than intercourse, with less risk to their physical and emotional health.

The study of ethnically diverse high school freshmen from California found that almost 20% had tried oral sex, compared with 13.5% who said they had intercourse.

More of these teens believed oral sex was more acceptable for their age group than intercourse, even if the partners are not dating.

"The problem with surveys is they don't tell you the intimacy sequence," Brown says. "The vast majority who had intercourse also had oral sex. We don't know which came first."

The federal study, based on data collected in 2002 and released last month, found that 55% of 15- to 19-year-old boys and 54% of girls reported getting or giving oral sex, compared with 49% of boys and 53% of girls the same ages who reported having had intercourse.

Though the study provides data, researchers say, it doesn't help them understand the role oral sex plays in the overall relationship; nor does it explain the fact that today's teens are changing the sequence of sexual behaviors so that oral sex has skipped ahead of intercourse.

"All of us in the field are still trying to get a handle on how much of this is going on and trying to understand it from a young person's point of view," says Stephanie Sanders, associate director of The Kinsey Institute for Research in Sex, Gender and Reproduction at Indiana University, which investigates sexual behavior and sexual health.

"Clearly, we need more information about what young people think is appropriate behavior, under what circumstances and with whom," Sanders says. "Now we know a little more about what they're doing but not what they're thinking."

Consider also the anecdotal evidence offered in the Canadian documentary film *Oral Sex Is the New Goodnight Kiss,* detailed in Shipman and Kazdin (2009):

They don't give their names, but viewers can see their faces plainly and what these teens are saying is shocking parents.

"I ended up having sex with more than one person that night and then in the morning I was trying to get morning-after pills," one of the girls said. "I was, like, 14 at the time."

It's just one of dozens of stories from teenage girls in a new documentary by Canadian filmmaker Sharlene Azam that aims to shed light on the secret, extremely sexual lives of today's teens.

After four years researching for the documentary, Azam told *Good Morning America* that oral sex is as common as kissing for teens and that casual prostitution—being paid at parties to strip, give sexual favors or have sex—is far more commonplace than once believed.

"If you talk to teens [about oral sex] they'll tell you it's not a big deal," Azam said. "In fact, they don't consider it sex. They don't consider a lot of things sex."

Evidence of this casual attitude may be seen in the fact that more than half of all teens 15 to 19 years old have engaged in oral sex, according to a comprehensive 2005 study by the Centers for Disease Control's National Center for Health Statistics.

Oral Sex Is the New Goodnight Kiss

In the documentary *Oral Sex Is the New Goodnight Kiss*, girls as young as 11 years old talk about having sex, going to sex parties and—in some extreme situations—crossing into prostitution by exchanging sexual favors for money, clothes or even homework and then still arriving home in time for dinner with the family.

"Five minutes and I got $100," one girl said. "If I'm going to sleep with them, anyway, because they're good-looking, might as well get paid for it, right?"

Another girl talked about being offered $20 to take off her shirt or $100 to do a striptease on a table at a party.

The girls are almost always from good homes, but their parents are completely unaware, Azam said.

"The prettiest girls from the most successful families [are the most at risk]. We're not talking about marginalized girls," she said. "[Parents] don't want to know because they really don't know what to do. I mean, you might be prepared to learn that, at age 12, your daughter has had sex, but what are you supposed to do when your daughter has traded her virginity for $1,000 or a new bag?"

Sex Favors Traded for Relationship Stability

For some of the girls, the sexual favors are not about clothes or money, but used to keep a relationship together in a chillingly objective way.

"I think there's very much trading for relationship favors, almost like 'you need to do this [to] stay in this relationship,'" one girl told *Good Morning America*.

"There's a lot of social pressure," said another. "Especially because of our age, a lot of girls want to be in a relationship and they're willing to do anything."

The girls laughingly admitted they never talk to their parents about their sexual activity.

"I mean, we're not looking for our future husbands," one girl said. "We're just looking for, maybe like … at our age, especially, I think all of us, both sexes, we have a lot of urges, I guess, that need to be taken care of. So if we resort to a casual thing, no strings attached, it's perfectly fine."

We started this chapter by explaining that everyone lies about their sexual activity, or seeks to conceal it from particular groups. Teenagers are no different, admitting readily that authority figures, including their parents, are the very last people they will admit their sexual habits to. What this means is that the real numbers regarding who is doing what with whom, and when, are actually higher than the studies cited above would indicate.

In any case, it is clear that modern teenagers have developed sexually in a manner that is distinct from the perceptions afforded generations past. Both boys and girls masturbate with frequency and are having more sex at younger ages; they also are having a great deal more oral sex, and often it is in exchange for something other than emotional intimacy—including money. Moreover, anal sex is not at all uncommon from a statistical perspective. These realities must be embraced as we move forward with any discussion regarding what is sexually deviant and what is not. While the current generation of teens represents a departure from traditionally held sexual values and ideology, they are established as a group unto themselves with their own uniquely developed sexual norms and frequencies.

SEXUAL AROUSAL

Sexual arousal is "an emotional and motivational state arising from an interaction between genital response, central arousal, information processing of sexual stimuli, and behavior" (de Jong, 2009, p. 237). There are two kinds of sexual arousal, generally speaking: subjective and genital. Subjective arousal is the emotional aspect, which includes "an awareness of autonomic arousal, expectation of reward, and motivated desire" (de Jong, 2009, p. 237). It relates to what one feels regarding anticipated or imminent sexual activity. In contrast, genital arousal refers to "vasodilation of genital tissues: In females, this response leads to vasocongestion of the genital tissues and lubrication, and in males, erection" (de Jong, 2009, p. 237). Genital arousal may be associated with subjective arousal, but not necessarily. Both can occur separately, and for very different reasons. Specifically, genital arousal is not necessarily evidence of subjective arousal, as it can be an uncontrollable bodily response to any number of internal and external circumstances.

Sexual arousal is a multidetermined function of individual biology, chemistry, and psychology. Variation in arousal occurs because everyone's brain chemistry is different. Moreover, individual pleasure and pain associations are differently experienced and constructed (which can alter and be altered by brain chemistry). So while we all look similar with similar parts distinguished by sex, we really aren't. Each of us is a unique and changing blend of our biology, our history, our current chemistry and toxicology, and our environment.

Visual, auditory, and tactile stimuli play a major role in human sexual activity. Put more simply, seeing things, hearing things, and touching things can cause sexual arousal. However, a male's erection, a primary indicator of sexual arousal, also occurs as a result of harmony achieved among nerves, hormones, blood vessels, and psychological factors. Again, each of these elements is stimulated and dampened differently in different individuals (Savino & Turvey, 2004).

Because of the hyper-variable nature of sexual arousal, human beings have experimented with all manner of sexual stimulation, ranging from the mundane to the bizarre, and human sexual desires and activities can encompass elements that the average person has never heard of (McGrath and Turvey, 2008). Anything, it seems, can be eroticized.

SEXUAL FANTASY

Sexual fantasy refers to the deliberate act of imagining a behavior, event, or series of events that one finds personally arousing. According to Strassberg and Lockerd (1998, pp. 403–404),

> Research has demonstrated that sexual fantasizing can be a normal, adaptive, and healthy aspect of sexuality for both men and women. … Apparently, almost everyone at least occasionally engages in sexual fantasizing, either to enhance the pleasure of other sexual activities (e.g., intercourse or masturbation) or as a pleasurable act in and of itself.

Specific fantasies are meaningful in themselves as didactic narratives of desire, but they can also reveal hidden or subconscious desires that have yet to be fully realized. As described in Freidman and Downey (2000, p. 567), "Underneath one narrative is another, and under that yet another, arranged in layers as is the mind itself." It is further important to note that some fantasies are meant as templates for future sexual activities, while many others are intended to remain unfulfilled.

Sexual fantasy is also useful as a window to evolutionary development, as explained in Wilson (1997, p. 27):

> Sexual fantasies provide an interesting window to the evolutionary instincts underlying sexual behaviour because they are less subject to constraints of civilization, morality and social convention

than sexual behaviour itself. In fantasy, people are relatively free to indulge their primitive lusts and brutish impulses in ways that might be unacceptable in reality. Fantasies can also be employed selfishly, without regard for the preferences and sensitivities of one's partner, hence they are better placed to reveal the differing biological natures of men and women than either sexual behaviour or public statements of opinion.

Sexual fantasies commonly involve themes of power, romance, and an exploration of the unusual or even forbidden. For example, a less commonly acknowledged reality is that fantasies involving force and coercion are very common among women (Strassberg and Lockerd, 1998, p. 404):

> Researchers examining sexual fantasies have found remarkable similarity across different samples of both men and women in terms of the general content of the most frequently occurring of such fantasies. Themes such as sex with an imaginary lover, reliving a previous sexual experience, sex with a stranger or famous person, or sex in a different or exotic place, are frequently reported among those occurring most often by both men and women (e.g., Hariton and Singer, 1974; Knafo and Jaffe, 1984; Pelletier and Herold, 1988). Another theme reported by men involves their using some type of force or coercion in their sexual interaction. A surprising related finding has been the large percentage of women who report themes of force or coercion, *against them,* in their sexual fantasies (e.g., Price and Miller, 1984; Sue, 1979). For example, Hariton and Singer (1974) found that the fantasy of being "overpowered or forced to surrender" was the second most frequently reported sexual fantasy among the women they surveyed; 48% of their subjects reported having this fantasy at least some of the time during intercourse. Similarly, Knafo and Jaffe (1984) found that the fantasy of being overpowered ranked first among women's sexual fantasies during intercourse, while Pelletier and Herold (1988) reported that more than half of their female subjects engaged in fantasies of forced sex. Others have also reported this theme among women's fantasies, but at lower levels of frequency/popularity (Davidson, 1985; Davidson and Hoffman, 1986; Gold and Clegg, 1990).

> It has often been noted that women's fantasizing about being forced into having sex should not suggest that they actually wish to be raped (e.g., Davidson and Hoffman, 1986). These "force" or "coercion" fantasies "tend to be overlaid by romantic images—in many cases, more like seduction than actual force" (Lance, 1985, p. 66). The men in these fantasies tend to be described by the women as attractive and otherwise desirable; men the women would (in other circumstances) *choose* for a sexual partner. The scenario reported often describes this desirable partner as being overwhelmed by his attraction to the woman to the extent that he is willing to use force or coercion to get her to submit. These fantasies do not usually involve (i) the women being hurt in any way, nor (ii) the man being seen as otherwise undesirable as a lover.

In their own study of women's sexual fantasies, Strassberg and Lockerd (1998) found that (pp. 408-409): "It can be seen that virtually all subjects reported having sexual fantasies and that a wide range of fantasy themes were common among the women. Of particular note are the two themes involving force; "being overpowered and forced to surrender," and "forced to expose my body to a seducer," reported by 55% and 35% of subjects, respectively, with 64% reporting at least one of these fantasies."

It becomes clear that many consider the sexual fantasy a safe venue for the private expression of otherwise deviant desires. They may even act on them so long as there is a level of safety and control. This is normal and healthy for both sexes. However, problems will arise when intimate partners are coerced or forced to participate in fantasy-related activities that they find less than enjoyable, as is discussed shortly. Problems will increase and compound when fantasy-related activity involves painful and even illegal activity, as is discussed in the chapter on *sex offenders*.

PORNOGRAPHY

Pornography has been defined inconsistently over the centuries, but it has always been around in one form or another. Generally speaking, there are many different kinds of pornography—and not all of it may be taken equally. However, what precisely constitutes pornography is generally found in the eye of the beholder.

As described in Langevin et al.(1988, p. 337),

> Pornography literally means "the writing of harlots" but usually implies any materials used primarily to create sexual excitement and pleasure. It appears in all media: photographs, writing, music, and, in the twentieth century, movies, videos, and television. It is not always clear what forms of erotica are included under the definition, e.g., nudity per se, bondage or sexual aggression etc., and even nonsexual aggressive material may be labeled "pornography."

> The terms "soft core" and "hard core" have been used in attempts to differentiate more and less socially, morally, or legally acceptable depictions or descriptions of nudity and sexual acts but reliable differentiation of these categories is far from established.

> Some writers differentiate pornography based on its intent or its effect. If the material is intended to be sexually arousing, regardless of the viewer's perception, it can be called pornography. Similarly, one can argue that, regardless of the author's intentions, if some material is primarily viewed as sexually arousing, then it is pornographic. Neither definition elucidates the nature of pornography and, technically, almost any material could be considered pornographic.

More recently, Kingston et al. (2009, p. 218) offered a thoughtful discussion of definitions:

> [T]he Attorney General's Commission on Pornography (1986) noted that "the range of materials to which people are likely to affix the designation 'pornographic' seems to mean in practice any discussion or depiction of sex to which the person using the word objects" (U.S. Department of Justice, 1986, p. 227).

> In general, the terms pornography and sexually explicit material have been utilized as overarching conceptualizations describing various media materials (e.g., films, Internet) displaying sexual content (sexual acts or body parts) that are primarily designed to stimulate sexual arousal. ... In one study, Senn and Radtke (1990) differentiated between erotica, nonviolent pornography, and violent pornography:

> 1. Erotica, which was defined as sexual "images that have as their focus the depiction of mutually pleasurable sexual expression between people who have enough power to be there by positive choice. ... They have no sexist or violent connotations and are hinged on equal power dynamics between individuals as well as between the model(s) and the camera/photographer" (p. 144).
> 2. Nonviolent pornography, which was defined as sexual "images that have no explicitly violent content but may imply acts of submission or violence by the positioning of the models or the use of props. They may also imply unequal power relationships by differential dress, costuming, positioning ... or by setting up the viewer as voyeur (the model is engaged in some solitary activity and seems totally unaware or very surprised to find someone looking at her)" (p. 144).
> 3. Violent pornography, which was defined as sexual "images that portray explicit violence of varying degrees perpetrated against one individual by another" (p. 144).

The author generally accepts these distinctions, with the addition of (4) criminal pornography, involving the depiction of actual sex crimes or underage children, and (5) bestial pornography, depicting sex acts with animals (which may or may not be criminal, depending upon jurisdiction). By including these last two categories, almost all pornography may be classified. It should be noted that the first three definitions have nothing to do with nudity, while the last two tend to imply it.

People use pornography during intercourse or masturbation to stimulate or facilitate specific sexual desires or contexts. They may also use it for voyeuristic purposes—out of a sexual desire to witness others engaged private or in sexual activity, as is discussed later.

Historical Access to Porn

It should be explained that, in generations past (even 20 years ago), access to explicit sexual material was fairly limited. Before the advent of lithographs and still photographs, carnal knowledge could only be gained by reading written accounts, looking at drawings, or through direct experience. This made the solicitation of exotic dancers, strippers, and prostitutes a right of passage for many young men. Still photos of sexual acts and illegally made 8-millimeter and 16-millimeter porn films ("stag films") circulated in the Americas and Europe during the first half of the twentieth century. However, access was very limited and viewing films was a particularly onerous process. They required privacy and technology, neither of which was necessarily available.

Later (Shimizu, 2006, pp. 243–244): "during the Golden Age of pornography in the 1960s to the 1980s, many films like *Deep Throat*, *Behind the Green Door*, and *The Devil in Miss Jones* made huge profits, as couples began to attend screenings in movie theaters together." During this same time period, magazines featuring explicit pictures of various sexual acts made their way into the mainstream—they were sold over the counter at adult bookstores and then through aptly named convenience stores across the United States. Eventually, film gave way to video, and video to DVD, and DVD to archived and even live Internet streaming. As explained in Kingston et al. (2009, p. 218):

> The sale of pornography in various media, including magazines, video, cable television, and the Internet is an extremely large multibillion-dollar industry. In recent years, there has been a great increase in the use of the Internet to access pornography, which has, in part, been influenced by the easy accessibility, affordability, and anonymity provided to its users (Cooper, 1998). Indeed, recent reports have suggested that easily available sexually explicit materials are one of the most widely used materials or searched topics on the Internet (D. Brown, 2003; Lam and Chan, 2007).

All this is to say that only recently, in perhaps the last 10 years, has porn of all kinds been so easily available in such an accessible and affordable format. Those raised in generations where access to porn was far more restricted will have a different view of it, as well as perhaps less insight into the ready availability of its many forms. They may also have diminished insight into what precisely constitutes statistical deviance from accepted sexual norms based on porn—as the current generation is not just watching porn but many are actually creating it for their intimate partners with digital video, digital cameras, and cell phone technology. And they are using public and private Web sites on the Internet to distribute it, as is discussed shortly.

Porn as Harmful

Despite repeated studies, there is no reliable evidence to suggest that the use of pornography is associated with violent or criminal behavior, although it can bear on attitudes toward sex and interpersonal relationships. Moreover, it can cause severe feelings of inadequacy when intimate partners believe they are in sexual competition with idealized pornographic images.

Langevin et al. (1988, pp. 358–359) found in their sex offender study that: "The impression gained from the offenders in this study was that erotica use was not a pertinent factor in their sex offenses nor to their legal situation. … Present results did not support the conclusion of the Meese Commission that there was a causal association of sexual violence and use of violent pornography. The violent sex offenders in the Ontario sample did not differ remarkably from nonviolent sex offenders. There were few differences in Alberta and Ontario sex offenders in overall use of erotica." Further, they explain that:

> It has been suggested that exposure to erotica can entrench sexual habits such as preferentially seeking out children for sex (Marshall, 1988). Presumably, masturbating to pictures of children will establish pedophilic tendencies and lead to sexual contact with young children and to crime. If this is indeed so, it can be true only for a small minority of sex offenders. In this study, the majority of sex offenders were similar to controls and were exposed predominately to nude adult females. This creates some difficulty for the masturbatory conditioning theory of sexual anomalies …
> because it has to explain why masturbating with pictures of adult females leads to pedophiles' acting out with children rather than establishing conventional sexual behavior. Pedophilic offenders embellish their fantasies of children, not those of the adult female.

> Similarly, the number of regular users of erotica is too small to support the masturbatory conditioning model of sexual deviance. Only 10.3% to 26.9% of sex offenders were regular users of any erotica media, *at some time in their lives.*

Kingston et al. (2009, pp. 227–228) rendered similar findings, arguing:

> Although the extant literature we have reviewed does not currently enable us to determine a direct causal link between pornography use and aggressive behavior, in several individual studies (e.g., Kingston et al., 2008; Vega and Malamuth, 2007) and meta-analytic reviews … researchers have supported the notion that pornography may influence negative attitudes or beliefs and aggressive behavior among sexual and nonsexual offenders (Malamuth et al., 2000; Seto et al., 2001). However, with the goal of developing improved scientific causal models, the relation between pornography and aggressive behavior may be better framed in terms of the confluence of several risk and protective factors.

> The suggestion that media has a uniform effect on all individuals is considerably simplistic and, as such, increasing attention has focused on a variety of individual and cultural differences that moderate the way in which pornography influences arousal, attitudes, and behavior. As indicated earlier, several background factors, such as cultural and home environments, as well as peer environments, have been implicated as important moderating variables. In addition to background factors, several stable personality characteristics (e.g., IS orientation, psychopathy) are likely factors to consider in developing a causal model. Rather than viewing these factors as "casual-link variables" (i.e., if this third factor was not present, pornography consumption is otherwise harmless), individual difference variables should be viewed within the cumulative—conditional—probability conceptualization described earlier, such that it is the confluence of relevant factors that affects the probability of a particular outcome.

Also, while consistent exposure to overtly pornographic material may reinforce negative stereotypes of male–female relationships, as well as cause unrealistic ideals, it should be pointed out that the same may be said of "embedded sexual content" in the mass media, including soap operas, music videos, glamour magazines, and romance novels. Kingston et al. (2009, p. 217) explain that:

> It has also been found that greater exposure to soap operas and music videos is associated with more stereotypical sexual attitudes, greater endorsement of dysfunctional relationship models, and greater acceptance of sexual harassment. Similarly, greater exposure to sexually oriented media genres is

associated with adolescent perceptions that "everybody is doing it," referring not only to perceptions about sex, but also affairs, abortions, divorce, and having children out of wedlock. Correlational findings appear to be somewhat stronger and more consistent among women than men, and it should be emphasized that results have been inconsistent with regard to other media types (e.g., exposure to prime-time television programming; Ward, 2003).

As with any vice, porn becomes particularly harmful to the self and personal relationships should it become an addiction. Consider the following extreme cases of porn addiction described in Ranney (2005):

> "I suspect if there was a forensic examination of all the personal computers in Lawrence, some similar-size collections would show up in some very shocking places," said [Rev. Darrell] Brazell, pastor at New Hope Fellowship, 1449 Kasold Drive.

> Brazell, who said he's been "clean" for five years, counsels and coordinates faith-based support groups for men addicted to pornography. … Brazell … was addicted to pornography for 15 years.

> Convicted killer Martin K. Miller says Brazell helped him overcome his own addiction.

> During his trial, Miller credited Brazell with helping him overcome his addiction, noting that he had given up porn Sept. 15, which was almost two months after his wife was killed.

> Miller also testified he first had a "problem" with pornography when he was 10 or 11 years old.

> His ever-escalating addiction, Miller said, caused him to participate in an online adult dating service, which led to his having an extramarital affair with a Eudora woman that included role-playing, bondage, spanking and explicit photographs.

> Prosecutors argued that Miller, a carpenter, wanted his wife out of the way so he'd be free to pursue sexual relationships with other women and so he could collect more than $300,000 in life-insurance money.

> Clearly, Brazell said, Miller's addiction to pornography caused him to act irrationally.

> "That's the bottom-line evidence of addiction: You do something you don't want to do," he said.

> Christian men, Brazell said, are especially susceptible to becoming addicted to pornography and, consequently, masturbation.

> "As a Christian, you believe that pornography and masturbation are morally wrong," he said. "And yet, because of so many issues that we grow up with, you're attracted to it, which causes all kinds of shame and guilt—you're in pain."

> As this pain intensifies, Brazell said, so too does the attraction to pornography. "You wind up in this downward spiral that after a while, you can't get out of," he said. "The addict within you does things the rational self would never do."

> Non-Christians, Brazell said, may be less vulnerable to pornography addiction because they experience less shame.

> Miller testified that his addiction was so out of control that after he was charged in his wife's murder and released on bond, he used money from his children's bank account to buy a new computer to replace the machine seized by police.

> He said he intended to use the computer for business, but soon began logging onto pornographic Web sites and accessing adult dating sites. Miller attributed his actions to habit and curiosity. "Some of it (was) fantasy," he said.

Brazell called pornographic Web sites the "crack cocaine of sex addiction."

The sites are especially addictive, he said, because they're easy to find, relatively cheap and, as long as they don't involve children, perfectly legal. ...

Martin Miller, who testified that he had a pornography addiction, was sentenced to life in prison Wednesday afternoon for the murder of his wife, Mary E. Miller. ...

[Cynthia] Akagi [an assistant health education professor at Kansas University] said male students tell her it's common for them to log on to a "favorite porn site when their partner's not around."

"Keep in mind, this is a generation that's grown up on the Internet," she said. Akagi said she's surprised that for much of society, pornography addiction remains under the radar.

She added, "Many things break up marriages these days, and this is certainly one of them."

At Bert Nash Community Mental Health Center, Marciana Crothers, an addiction specialist, said few people have sought counseling for pornography addiction.

"Typically, we see people who are more disturbed by someone else's use of pornography," Crothers said. "I've only had one couple come in (seeking help) for themselves."

Crothers attributed the low numbers to the inherent differences between pornography and alcohol, drugs and gambling. Porn addiction is easier to maintain and hide.

"First of all, as long as it's not child pornography, it's legal and readily accessible—unlike drugs," she said. "Second, when you're drinking, your friends and family get tired of you and start to leave you alone. It's an abandonment that may cause you to seek treatment."

"But with the Internet, you can take part in these adult chat rooms and have unlimited access to people," she said. "It's a lot easier to hide than, say, a drinking problem."

Those addicted to gambling, she said, often seek treatment because they've bankrupted their families. But the Internet, she said, is loaded with free or low-cost pornography.

It's also true, Brazell said, that being addicted to pornography carries a stigma that gambling, alcohol and drugs do not.

"It's much more shameful and difficult to admit to having a sexual addiction," Brazell said. "You can talk about being addicted to alcohol or drugs and it's, 'OK, sure, yeah, here's who can help.' But as soon as you say the word 'sex,' you're a pervert or some kind of child molester."

Brazell said most of the men who take part in his support groups drive in from out of town.

"There aren't a lot resources out there," he said. "Most churches are too terrified to deal with this."

McDonough-Taub (2009) discusses the indicators of sexual or porn addiction:

Indicators of Sexual Addiction

So how do you know if someone you work with suffers from a sex or porn addiction? While a conclusive diagnosis for sexual addiction should only be carried out by a mental health professional, the following behavior patterns compiled by Dr. Patrick Carnes, a pioneer in the field, can indicate its presence in any environment.

1. Acting out: a pattern of out-of-control sexual behavior
2. Experiencing severe consequences due to sexual behavior, and an inability to stop despite these adverse consequences

3. Persistent pursuit of self-destructive behavior
4. Ongoing desire, or effort, to limit sexual behavior
5. Sexual obsession and fantasy as a primary coping strategy
6. Regularly increasing the amount of sexual experience because the current level of activity is no longer sufficiently satisfying
7. Severe mood changes related to sexual activity
8. Inordinate amounts of time spent obtaining sex, being sexual, and recovering from sexual experiences
9. Neglect of important social, occupational, or recreational activities because of sexual behavior.

But what are the telltale signs of what this looks like in the workplace?

Here are just a few of the most likely behavioral clues:

- Hiding Internet use or secretive behaviors
- Declining work performance
- Withdrawing from others
- Increased irritability
- Losing sleep and declining health
- Declining interpersonal skills
- Inappropriate sharing of sexual beliefs with others

Porn as Mainstream

The question arises whether porn is mainstream (culturally accepted and common). Clearly there are those who wish it weren't. This is not the reality, however. In the United States, for example, most porn is not illegal unless it depicts real sex crime or children. So, from a legal perspective, it is not generally deviant.

More recently, the pornography industry determined the dominant format for DVD players. This is because, from a purely commercial standpoint, the mainstream film industry knows that people will buy the DVD player that supports their porn, as is described in Mearian (2006):

> Just as in the 1980s, when the Betamax and VHS video formats were battling it out for supremacy, the pornography industry will likely play a major role in determining which of the two blue-laser DVD formats—Blu-ray Disc and HD-DVD—will be the winner in the battle to replace DVDs for high-definition content. …
>
> The pornography industry, which generates an estimated $57 billion in annual revenue worldwide, has always been a fast leader when it comes to the use of new technology, according to analysts. …
>
> Paul O'Donovan, an analyst at Gartner Inc., said pornography's support of either DVD format will be a "strong factor" to the uptake of the technology by the general marketplace, but even more critical is Sony's adoption of the technology. …
>
> Steve Hirsch, head of the adult film studio Vivid Entertainment Group, said he's currently using the HD-DVD format because it was the first to be available, but his studio will begin burning to the Blu-ray format as soon as it's available.

"The adult industry has always been ahead of the curve when it comes to technology. We don't have any theatrical distribution issues, nor do we have 'big box' retailers, like Wal-Mart and Blockbuster, to cater to. We're forced to find distribution wherever we can," Hirsch said.

Hirsch, who founded Vivid Entertainment in 1984, said the porn industry—just as in the 1980s—will have a big influence on the outcome of the latest high-definition video-format wars. In the 1980s, Hirsch said VHS tapes started selling for $50 a piece, and Betamax sold for $55. "Therefore, we pushed VHS harder, and in that sense, we did have something to do with VHS winning out," said Hirsch, whose studio pulls in an estimated $100 million in revenue a year.

"It was the adult industry who jumped right in and were putting movies on both VHS and Beta. We pushed the actual technology more than anyone else," he said. "The adult industry has always been ahead when comes to technology."

In 2008, Blue-ray Disc became the dominant format following the decision of many in the porn industry to produce their titles in that medium.

Consider also the porn-related statistics from the Internet, which indicate that (Ropelato, 2009):

1. 42.7% of Internet users are doing so to view porn (72% male; 28% female)
2. There are 4.2 million pornographic Web sites (12% of total Web sites)
3. There are 68 million searches performed for pornography per day (25% of total search engine requests)
4. There are 1.5 billion pornographic peer-to-peer downloads per month (35% of all downloads)
5. 20% of surveyed men admit to accessing porn while at work, in contrast to 13% of women
6. 17% of surveyed women admitted to addiction to Internet porn
7. 47% of Christians surveyed admitted to Internet related sexual addiction
8. Porn generates 100 billion dollars a year in revenue worldwide; the U.S. porn revenue alone exceeds the combined revenues of ABC, CBS, and NBC

Porn, in all its incarnations, is undeniably an accepted part of our culture, is commonly viewed by men and women alike (though with different frequencies), and is a highly traded commodity. Moreover, with revenues reaching 100 billion dollars, it is a major employer. Arguing that porn is not mainstream, or rather that it is deviant, may be ideologically accurate from some perspectives, but not by virtue of economy, statistical volume, and prevalence.

DEVIANT SEXUAL BEHAVIOR

Deviant sexual behaviors, in the non-criminal sense, are those that are uncommon, antisocial, or in violation of an interpersonal covenant of some kind (e.g., monogamy or marriage). The following examples are offered as those most often encountered in the casework of the author, and they are not meant to be wholly representative. They are given in no particular order of importance.

Exhibitionism

Exhibitionism refers to sexual arousal achieved from showing others one's own genitals, or from sex acts (e.g., masturbation, oral sex, vaginal sex, and anal sex) committed in front of an audience, often in public. Despite the research on female sexual fantasies, which revealed exhibitionism rates high among females' fantasies, definitions have tended to associate exhibitionism with males exposing themselves to females for the purposes of eliciting shock or embarrassment. Money (1988, pp. 78–79) explains that females often engage in exhibitionism:

> As an act of paraphilic exhibitionism, a woman may display her genitals in public if she wears no panties and, with a short skirt, sit so as to expose the pudenda. Another possibility is to arrange to copulate in a park or other public place to attract onlookers, and to assume a position that allows display of the genitalia.
>
> Men to whom a female exhibits usually do not take offense and do not call the police, whereas the reverse is far more likely to be true in the case of the male exhibitionist.

Money goes on to explain that exhibitionism is a highly individual and idiosyncratic ritual behavior, and not a precursor to rape.

The motives for exhibitionism range from sexual attention seeking, to a desire to shock, to satisfying masochistic desires for self-humiliation, and even to demonstrating sexual ownership and submission. In such cases, sexual arousal is strongly associated with achieving the exposure of one's body, and, in fewer cases, with performing public sex acts. However, acts of "public" exhibitionism have become more common; the Internet is rife with Web sites dedicated to those who wish to post images and video of themselves engaged in various stages of undress and explicit sex acts. Special categories include things like public flashing, public sex in bathrooms and changing rooms, and reflections from the bathroom mirror.

Exhibitionism is deviant in that it plays against established social conventions relating to sexual privacy and discretion. However, it only becomes a full-blown paraphilia when it begins to interfere with quality of life, normal and routine functioning, or the ability to achieve and maintain intimate relationships.

Fetishism

Fetishism refers to the attribution of erotic or sexual significance to a nonsexual inanimate object or nonsexual body part (Francoeur, 1995). It is a generally rare sexual proclivity. Examples of the objects of a fetish include feet, high-heeled shoes, knee-high boots, stockings, underwear, piercings, guns, material (e.g., silk, satin, leather, or latex), hair, hands, and uniforms (e.g., nurse, police officer). Fetishists tend to be highly specific in their associations between objects and sexual arousal, so that they are meticulous collectors. They will prefer particular kinds of shoes, particular kinds of hair, and particular types of feet, and they will collect and catalog as much as they can, using the objects during masturbation or sexual intercourse. If the object is not a body part, the fetishist's partner will likely be asked to wear it or otherwise involve it in their erotic play.

Although fetishism is not a crime itself, fetishists are often identified publicly by association with other illegal sexual activity related to the fetishism or satisfying their fetish, such as theft, trespassing, and sexual assault.

Consider the case of 27-year-old Joshua Gonzalez of Bridgeport, Connecticut, a local barber with a history of drug convictions (Tepfer, 2009):

> A convicted felon has been charged with kidnapping two Fairfield women at gunpoint and, in a re-enactment of a scene from a fetish movie, forcing them to wear prom dresses and stockings before sexually assaulting them.
>
> Joshua Gonzalez, 27, of East Main Street, was charged Monday with two counts each of first-degree kidnapping, unlawful restraint, fourth-degree sexual assault, reckless endangerment, threatening and one count of criminal possession of a firearm.

The incident took place about 8:45 p.m. Sunday, police said, as the two 22-year-old Fairfield women were leaving an East Main Street apartment building after visiting a friend. Police said Gonzalez confronted them with a handgun and forced them into his apartment in the same building.

Inside, Gonzalez told the women to give up their cell phones and then handed them two formal prom dresses and nylon stockings, which he ordered them to put on, police said.

When the women protested, police said, Gonzalez handed them a black book and told them to write their complaints in it. He then handed one of the women several bullets and told her to hold them, police said.

Gonzalez told the women the scenario was his re-creation of a scene from a fetish movie called *The Stocking Secret*, according to police.

While the women pleaded with Gonzalez to let them go, police said, he forced them to lie on a bed on either side of him and to fondle him while he touched them.

After about 45 minutes, police said, Gonzalez held a gun on the women while forcing them to watch him take a shower.

Gonzalez eventually allowed the women to leave, and they immediately called police, according to the report.

It should be noted, again, that most fetishists are not criminals nor are they necessarily engaged in criminal behavior. Nor is fetishism a precursor to criminal sexual behavior. Rather, the fetishist who engages in criminal acts gets noticed, creating a false perception in many people's minds.

Sexual Coercion

Sexual coercion refers to the psychological, emotional, and even physical manipulation of one intimate partner by the other to achieve domination and control. This includes (Goetz and Shackleford, 2009): "withholding benefits, threatening relationship defection, and manipulating their partners by reminding them of their 'obligation' to have sex (e.g., "If you love me, you'll have sex with me")." Sexual coercion falls just short of physical threats and force, making it difficult for many to perceive as rape, though it often is, because the victim perceives very real physical, economic, or social consequences if she or he fails to acquiesce.

Sexual coercion occurs in intimate relationships, but it can also be committed by employers, guardians, police officers, and teachers. Anyone in a position to impose sanctions or take away benefits may use the threat of doing so to engage in sexual coercion.

On one end of the spectrum, sexual coercion is deviant in that it exploits the covenant of an intimate relationship for explicit personal sexual gain; on the other, it is rape and therefore a violation of law.

"Open" Relationships

An *"open" relationship* is one where intimate partners are free to pursue sexual relationships with other partners. If the intimate partners are married, then it is referred to as an "open" marriage. There are different kinds of open relationships, to meet the various emotional and sexual needs of those involved. Some permit sex outside the relationship but not love (e.g., swinging and partner "swapping"). Others allow both sex and love outside the relationship, which is called *polyamory*.

Open relationships are deviant in that they are rare and even more rarely work out. That is to say, sexual jealousy almost invariably overtakes one of the partners involved, leading to a breakdown of the relationship and an eventual break-up. This often happens because one of the partners develops a more intimate attachment to someone outside the primary relationship and initiates a break-up. Or it happens because one of the partners becomes jealous of, and hurt by, the pleasurable sexual activities being continually experienced by the other.

On the rare occasion that an "open" relationship succeeds, it is because both partners are comfortable with their own sexuality and happy with their core relationship and no one was leveraged into the deal through any sexual coercion or belief that they had to do it to satisfy their partner.

While Internet Web sites dedicated to swinging, or "the lifestyle," abound, run by a few to fuel the sexual fantasies of the many, an actual census of participants has been difficult owing to the negative social stigma associated with the practice. However, as with many sexual taboos of the past, and clearly facilitated by the attention that "swinging" has received on the Internet, that stigma may be showing signs of retreat.

Consider the following feature regarding what organizers have dubbed "Swingfest" (Layne, 2009):

> It's the biggest convention of its type, and its founders live in South Central Pennsylvania. The event's called Swingfest. It's a convention for couples who "swap."
>
> It was created by Jason Jean. He and his wife, Russy, are swingers. They have been swinging for 13 of their 15 years of marriage, but they don't like the label.
>
> "The word swinger just seems old and dirty," Jason says.
>
> "It has kind of a negative connotation to it," Russy adds.
>
> Instead the Jeans call it "The Lifestyle," and the Hershey-area couple is using that lifestyle for swinging business success.
>
> "The lifestyle is in little pockets all over the country," Jason explains. "There was nothing national or international that encompassed the entire lifestyle."
>
> To fill that void, Jean started Swingfest, the biggest swingers party ever. Almost 12,000 people showed up to the inaugural event in Miami last year. They're hoping for a similar turnout this October when the swingers convention returns to South Florida. ...
>
> Jason and Russy say they've heard all kinds of criticism regarding everything from safe sex to promiscuity.
>
> "This is emotional monogamy," Russy explains. "It doesn't have to be physical monogamy."
>
> "We always practice safe sex," Jason adds. "That's a must."
>
> The two say swinging has improved their marriage and made them more honest and open with one another.
>
> "It's all about honesty. It's about trust, communication," Jason says.

For the most part, those involved in open relationships and "swingers" in particular view sexual intimacy and emotional intimacy as strictly separate considerations. Furthermore, they view sex as a recreational activity, not just as an expression of romantic love. Rather, it is treated as both, and practitioners rave about always looking for and experiencing something new, refreshing, and exciting with respect to their sexual partners.

The honesty referred to by those in "the lifestyle" is a nod to the underlying belief that sex with one person, the same person, for an entire lifetime, runs contrary to human desire—and as such creates sexual dissatisfaction and even fosters the urge to commit infidelity. Monogamy naturally leads to cheating, they argue, and destroys relationships rather than nurturing them. As explained in an in-depth feature on the subject (ABC News, 2006):

> About 4 million people are "swingers," according to estimates by the Kinsey Institute and other researchers.
>
> Swingers have become a multimillion-dollar travel industry, so be careful when you pick a family vacation spot. (Watch out for code words like "clothing optional," "adult fun" and "couples only.") Hundreds of resorts now cater to the lifestyle. There are also swingers' conventions that take over entire resorts. Inside, thousands of couples play out sexual fantasies.
>
> "It's a worldwide phenomenon," according to award-winning journalist Terry Gould.
>
> When Gould was assigned to write a news story about swinging, he assumed it would be all sleaze. He was surprised when he went to an elegant club. "I met bankers and lawyers, and I started talking to these people," he said.
>
> Gould then spent three years researching the lifestyle and the people who swing. "Most of them don't drink and most of them don't use drugs. They believe in raising children in clean-cut, stable environments. They match our paradigm of the sunny suburbanite," he said. In his book *The Lifestyle: A Look at the Erotic Rites of Swingers*, Gould concluded couples swing in order to *not* cheat on their partners.
>
> "They see it as consensual, co-marital sex and something that they're doing in order to spice up their own relationships. They are not going to a swing club to have sex with other people. They're going there to get hot for each other," Gould said.
>
> Chris and Lavonne are new to the lifestyle. They've been married five years, and about a year ago decided they wanted to experiment. They checked out Web sites where thousands of people seeking strangers to have sex with can find one another.
>
> Brian and his wife run such a site, and it's very popular. "We have a half million members. We have 70,000 per day that visit," he said.

Even with 4 million participants, which is a liberal estimate of those in open relationships across the United States, swinging is yet to be considered mainstream. However, all indications are, with Web sites, public events, and travel accommodations proliferating widely, that societal values are more than willing to stretch in that direction.

Infidelity

Infidelity refers to any violation or betrayal of the mutually agreed rules and boundaries of an intimate relationship. Typically, it refers to a sexual infidelity, although this is not always true, as rules vary from couple to couple. As explained in Allen et al. (2008a, pp. 243–244),

> In the United States, the vast majority of marrying individuals expect to be monogamous (Wiederman and Allgeier, 1996) and disapproval rates of extramarital sex are high (Johnson et al., 2002), yet up to 34% of men and 19% of women in older cohorts report engaging in extramarital sex

at some point in their lives (Wiederman, 1997). When infidelity occurs, it is typically viewed as a marital betrayal and is in fact one of the most commonly cited reasons for marital dissolution (Amato and Previti, 2003).

This is echoed in Andrews et al. (2008, p. 348):

> While expectations of sexual exclusivity are a pervasive feature of human romantic relationships (Buss, 1994), evidence suggests that selection has favored a certain amount of sex outside those relationships (extrapair copulation, or EPC). For instance, men across cultures tend to express more interest than women in sex with multiple partners (McBurney et al., 2005; Schmitt, 2003), especially when there are no constraints or costs to consider (Fenigstein and Preston, 2007).

This expectation of sexual exclusivity, or fidelity to a given set of rules and boundaries, makes infidelity a deviant behavior by its very nature. Those who are engaging in infidelity are breaking the rules they have set down for themselves, making their actions deviant because they break social or religious conventions.

The primary predictor of infidelity is poor communication, particularly if is premarital. As described in Allen et al. (2008a, p. 253),

> Overall, the strongest and most consistent effects were found on relationship (stress) variables, particularly observed communication. Generally, our findings suggest that couples who go on to experience infidelity show more problematic communication premaritally, such as lower levels of positive interaction and higher levels of negative and invalidating interaction. …[F]emale invalidation continued to be a risk factor for later male infidelity even after controlling for male invalidation. Because of the high overlap between partners' communication behaviors, it may be best to conceptualize risk at a couple level for communication behaviors. For example, rather than conclude that men who communicate less positively premaritally are more likely to go on to engage in infidelity, it may be better to focus on the notion that couples who have lower levels of positive communication are more at risk for later infidelity. Similarly, rather than one partner "driving" another to be unfaithful, a context of problematic couple communication may leave an individual more receptive to extramarital relationships.

Other predictors include low self-esteem, neuroticism (with impulsivity and low dependability), religion acting as a dampener, and pregnancy, as explained in Whisman et al. (2007, p. 323): "Compared with husbands whose wives were not pregnant, husbands whose wives were pregnant were more likely to have engaged in sexual infidelity during the past 12 months." During pregnancy, marital dissatisfaction is often at an all-time high—until children arrive.

Infidelity is among the most devastating events that any intimate relationship can suffer, and it is one the hardest to overcome. In fact, as previously mentioned, it is the foremost cause of relationship dissolution. Consider the facts and emotional context provided in O'Gorman (2007):

> When a spouse cheats, the devastation is felt by the entire family. Trust is broken and no one looks at the cheater in the same way again. People who cheat on a partner lose the respect of family, friends, and even co-workers (if they are aware). Yet, infidelity is at an all time high in our country. Can a marriage survive infidelity? If so, will it ever be the same again?

> I was in a marriage where my husband was unfaithful. I've had many years to gain some insight and understanding of the issues caused by infidelity, and have received personal counseling to deal with these issues. These statistics by the Associated Press are very concerning:

- 22 percent of married men have strayed at least once during their married lives.
- 14 percent of married women have had affairs at least once during their married lives.
- Younger people are more likely candidates; in fact, younger women are as likely as younger men to be unfaithful.
- 70 percent of married women and 54 percent of married men did not know of their spouses' extramarital activity. ...

> In my own marriage, having been married for nineteen years, I trusted him completely. He was a Sunday school teacher, an excellent father, and had been a very good husband to me. No one could have convinced me he was cheating if he hadn't told me himself. After that, my world as I knew it was over.

Even couples who initially strive to overcome infidelity often fail in the long run because insurmountable resentments build on both sides, as one partner is unable to let go of the pain, and the other resents the broken promise of forgiveness.

Sadomasochism

A certain percentage of the population engages various forms of sexually oriented bondage and domination/sadomasochism (BD/SM). Sadomasochistic relationships are about the eroticization of pain, power, and emotional humiliation. *Sadomasochism* is defined as a consensual activity involving polarized role-playing, intense sensations, and feelings, actions, and fantasies that focus on playing out or fantasizing dominant and submissive roles as part of the sexual scenario (Francoeur, 1995, p. 556). Sadists derive sexual pleasure from inflicting pain, and masochists derive sexual gratification from receiving it.

As explained in Pa (2001, pp. 53–54):

> Media depictions of S/M as a violent sexual pathology at best represent dismal ignorance of sociological and psychological information, and at worst, portray hateful smear tactics against a legally vulnerable community. The legal discourses surrounding S/M often reflect stereotypes propagated in the media. ...

> S/M sex includes a wide range of sexual activities "between two consenting adults that may include, but is not limited to, the use of physical and/or psychological stimulation to produce sexual arousal and satisfaction." S/M sex is difficult to define precisely because of the wide range of activities involved and the paucity of research on this subject. There are four major categories of sadomasochistic behavior, although variations are numerous. They include: (1) infliction of physical pain, usually by means of whipping, spanking, slapping or the application of heat and cold; (2) verbal or psychological stimulation such as threats and insults; (3) dominance and submission, for example, where one individual orders the other to do his or her bidding; (4) bondage and discipline, involving restraints such as rope and chains and/or punishment for real or fabricated transgressions. Other variations include fetishistic, exhibitionistic and voyeuristic components, intense and/or frustrated genital stimulation, age-play (infantilism, diapering), body mutilation (piercing, scarring, corsetting, tattooing), role reversal (cross-dressing) and defecation (urination, enemas, fecal play).

> Given this wide range, analysts have observed five features generally present in an S/M encounter:

> 1. Dominance and submission—the appearance of control of one partner over the other;
> 2. Role-playing—the participants assume roles that they recognize are not reality;
> 3. Consensuality—a voluntary agreement to enter into SM "play" and to honor certain "limits";

4. Sexual context—the presumption that the activities have a sexual or erotic meaning;
5. Mutual definition—participants must agree on the parameters of what they are doing, whether they call it SM or not.

Sadomasochistic relationships are inherently deviant because they are generally rare, and because they eroticize pain and humiliation while directly encouraging antisocial behavior—despite the consensual context.

Sexual Asphyxia and Autoerotic Asphyxia

Sexual asphyxia is the consensual or forced reduction of oxygen to the brain to enhance physical or psychological pleasure in association with sexual arousal. It can be practiced both as an autoerotic activity and as a consensual sadomasochistic act between two or more people. *Autoerotic asphyxia* is the deliberate induction of hypoxia with the intent of causing heightened sexual arousal. These are discussed in a subsequent chapter.

SUMMARY

People routinely lie about or conceal their sexual habits and histories. This makes it difficult to define sexual deviance from a statistical perspective, because common sexual practices are not well established. It also makes it difficult to define it from an ideological perspective because of the disparity between self-reporting and actual sexual behavior.

In the absence of consistent parenting, children and adolescents are being educated about sex and sexuality by their peers and by the Internet. The result is a level of exposure to explicit sexual material, and pornography, that has not been experienced by generations past. This in turn may be partially responsible for an overall shift and even loosening of sexual norms away from traditionally professed values of sexual restraint and discretion.

Sexual arousal is a multidetermined function of individual biology, chemistry, and psychology. Variation in arousal occurs because everyone's brain chemistry is different. Moreover, individual pleasure and pain associations are differently experienced and constructed. Because of the hyper-variable nature of sexual arousal, human beings have experimented with all manner of sexual stimulation; anything can be eroticized.

The associations that drive individual sexual arousal are reflected in sexual fantasy. These are didactic narratives of desire, but they can also reveal hidden or subconscious desires that have yet to be fully realized. Sexual fantasies commonly involve themes of power, romance, and an exploration of the unusual or even forbidden.

Sexual fantasies are reflected in personal choices with respect to pornography, which is widespread and has become mainstream. While consistent exposure to overtly pornographic material may reinforce negative stereotypes of male–female relationships, as well as cause unrealistic ideals, it should be pointed out that the same may be said of "embedded sexual content" in the mass media, including soap operas, music videos, glamour magazines, and romance novels. However, pornography is not associated causally with violent or criminal behavior. It does become a problem when its use as a fantasy aid turns into an addiction.

Deviant sexual behavior, in a noncriminal sense, is defined as any sexual behavior that is uncommon, antisocial, or a violation of an interpersonal covenant of some kind (e.g., monogamy or marriage). It includes such things as exhibitionism, fetishism, sexual coercion, open relationships, infidelity, sadomasochism, sexual asphyxia, and autoerotic asphyxia.

Questions

1. True or False: The concept of sexual deviance is not universal.
2. What are the two kinds of sexual arousal?
3. After reviewing the chapter, how would you define pornography?
4. Select and define one form of sexually deviant behavior.
5. Why might an open relationship be problematic?

REFERENCES

ABC News, 2006. The "Lifestyle"—Real-Life Wife Swaps. ABCNews.com. September 6; www.abcnews.go.com/print?id=2395727.

Allen, E., Rhoades, G., Stanley, S., Markman, H., Williams, T., Melton, J., Clements, M., 2008. Premarital Precursors of Marital Infidelity. Family Process 47 (2), 243–259.

Allen, K., Husser, E., Stone, D., Jordal, C., 2008. Agency and Error in Young Adults' Stories of Sexual Decision Making. Family Relations 57 (4), 517–529.

Allen, M., Emmers, T., Gebhardt, L., Giery, M.A., 1995. Exposure to Pornography and Acceptance of Rape Myths. Journal of Communications 45, 5–26.

Amato, P.R., Previti, D., 2003. People's Reasons for Divorcing: Gender, Social Class, the Life Course, and Adjustment. Journal of Family Issues 24, 602–626.

Andrews, P., Gangestad, S., Miller, G., Haselton, M., Thornhill, R., Neale, M., 2008. Sex Differences in Detecting Sexual Infidelity: Results of a Maximum Likelihood Method for Analyzing the Sensitivity of Sex Differences to Underreporting. Human Nature 19, 347–373.

Baber, K.M., 2000. Women's Sexualities. In: Biaggio, M., Hersen, M. (Eds.), Issues in the Psychology of Women. Kluwer, New York, NY.

Barber, B.K., Olsen, J.A., 1997. Socialization in Context: Connection, Regulation, and Autonomy in the Family, School, and Neighborhood, and with Peers. Journal of Adolescent Research 12, 287–315.

Brown, D., 2003. Pornography and Erotica. In: Bryant, J., Roskos-Ewoldsen, D. (Eds.), Communication and Emotion: Essays in Honor of Dolf Zillmann. Lawrence Erlbaum Associates, Mahwah, NJ.

Brown, J.D., Halpern, C.T., L'Engle, K.L., 2005. Mass Media as a Sexual Super Peer for Early Maturing Girls. Journal of Adolescent Health 36, 420–427.

Buss, D.M., 1994. The Evolution of Desire: Strategies of Human Mating. Basic Books, New York, NY.

Cooper, A., 1998. Sexuality and the Internet: Surfing into the New Millennium. Cyberpsychological Behavior 1, 181–187.

Davidson, J.K., 1985. The Utilization of Sexual Fantasies by Sexually Experienced University Students. Journal of American College Health 34, 24–32.

Davidson, J.K., Hoffman, L.E., 1986. Sexual Fantasies and Sexual Satisfaction: An Empirical Analysis of Erotic Thought. Journal of Sex Research 22, 184–205.

de Jong, D., 2009. The Role of Attention in Sexual Arousal: Implications for Treatment of Sexual Dysfunction. Journal of Sex Research 46 (2–3), 237–248.

DeLamater, J.D., Friedrich, W.N., 2002. Human Sexual Development. Journal of Sex Research 39, 10–14.

Fenigstein, A., Preston, M., 2007. The Desired Number of Sexual Partners as a Function of Gender, Sexual Risks, and the Meaning of "Ideal". Journal of Sex Research 44, 89–95.

Francoeur, R., 1995. The Complete Dictionary of Sexology. Continuum Publishing Co, New York, NY.

Freidman, R., Downey, J., 2000. Psychoanalysis and Sexual Fantasies. Archives of Sexual Behavior 29 (6), 567–586.

Goetz, A., Shackleford, T., 2009. Sexual Coercion in Intimate Relationships: A Comparative Analysis of the Effects of Women's Infidelity and Men's Dominance and Control. Archives of Sexual Behavior 38, 226–234.

Gold, S.R., Clegg, C.L., 1990. Sexual Fantasies of College Students with Coercive Experiences and Coercive Attitudes. Journal of Interpersonal Violence 5, 464–473.

Greenfield, P.M., 2004. Inadvertent Exposure to Pornography on the Internet: Implications of Peer-to-Peer File-Sharing Networks for Child Development and Families. Applied Developmental Psychology 25, 741–750.

Hariton, E.B., Singer, J.L., 1974. Women's Fantasies during Sexual Intercourse: Normative and Theoretical Implications. Journal of Consulting and Clinical Psychology 42, 313–322.

Irvine, J.M., 2004. Talk About Sex: Battles over Sex Education in the United States. University of California Press, Berkeley, CA.

Jayson, S., 2009. Teens Define Sex in New Ways. USA Today October 19; www.usatoday.com/news/health/2005-10-18-teens-sex_x.htm.

Kingston, D.A., Fedoroff, P., Firestone, P., Curry, S., Bradford, J.M., 2008. Pornography Use and Sexual Aggression: The Impact of Frequency and Type of Pornography Use on Recidivism among Sexual Offenders. Aggressive Behavior 34, 341–351.

Kingston, D., Fedoroff, P., Marshall, W., 2009. The Importance of Individual Differences in Pornography Use: Theoretical Perspectives and Implications for Treating Sexual Offenders. Journal of Sex Research 46 (2–3), 216–232.

Knafo, D., Jaffe, D., 1984. Sexual Fantasizing in Males and Females. Journal of Research on Personality 18, 451–462.

Lam, C.B., Chan, D.K.-S., 2007. The Use of Cyberpornography by Young Men in Hong Kong: Some Psychosocial Correlates. Archives of Sexual Behavior 36, 588–598.

Lance, K., 1985. Your Secret Sex Life. Ladies Home Journal 102, 64–68, 140–141.

Langevin, R., Lang, R., Wright, P., Handy, L., Frenzel, R.R., Black, E.L., 1988. Pornography and Sexual Offences. Sex Abuse l (3), 335–362.

Layne, C., 2009. Dauphin County Couple Starts World's Biggest Swingers Party—Swingfest. WPMT-TV, July 26; www.fox43.com/news/newsatten/wpmt-pmnews-swingfest09-07-26-2009,0,6812315.story.

Malamuth, N.M., Addison, T., Koss, M., 2000. Pornography and Sexual Aggression: Are There Reliable Effects and Can We Understand Them? Annual Review of Sexual Research 11, 26–91.

Marshall, W.L., 1988. The Use of Sexually Explicit Stimuli by Rapists, Child Molesters, and Nonoffenders. Journal of Sex Research 25, 267–288.

McBurney, D.H., Zapp, D.J., Streeter, S.A., 2005. Preferred Number of Sexual Partners: Tales of Distributions and Tales of Mating Systems. Evolution of Human Behavior 26, 271–278.

McDonough-Taub, G., 2009. Porn at Work: Recognizing a Sex Addict. MSNBC, July 16; www.cnbc.com/id/31922685/.

McGrath, M., Turvey, B., 2008. Sexual Asphyxia. In: Turvey, B. (Ed.), Criminal Profiling: An Introduction to Behavioral Evidence Analysis. third edition. Elsevier Science, London, England.

Mearian, L., 2006. Porn Industry May Decide Battle between Blu-Ray, HD-DVD. Computerworld.com, May 2; www.computerworld.com/s/article/print/111087/Porn_industry_may_decide_battle_between_Blu_ray_HD_DVD_.

Money, J., 1988. Lovemaps: Clinical Concepts of Sexual/Erotic Health and Pathology, Paraphilia, and Gender Transposition In Childhood. Adolescence, and Maturity. Prometheus Books, New York, NY

O'Gorman, K., 2007. Infidelity: How One Woman Survived Spouse's Cheating. Associated Content, June 8; www.associatedcontent.com/article/267617/infidelity_how_one_woman_survived_spouses.html?cat=41.

Pa, M., 2001. Beyond the Pleasure Principle: The Criminalization of Consensual Sadomasochistic Sex. Texas Journal of Women and the Law 11, 51–92.

Pelletier, L.A., Herold,, E.S., 1988. The Relationship of Age, Sex Guilt, and Sexual Experience with Female Sexual Fantasies. Journal of Sex Research 24, 250–256.

Peterson, G.W., Hann, D., 1999. Socializing Children and Parents in Families. In: Sussman, M., Steinmetz, S.K., Peterson, G.W. (Eds.), Handbook of Marriage and the Family. second edition. Plenum Press, New York, NY.

Price, J.H., Miller, P.A., 1984. Sexual Fantasies of Black and White College Students. Psychology Reports 54, 1007–1014.

Ranney, D., 2005. Minister Who Was Addicted to Porn Says Case Not Rare. LJWorld.com, July 21; www2.ljworld.com/news/2005/jul/21/minister_Who_Was_Addicted_Porn_Says_Case_Not_Rare/?martin_miller_trial.

Ropelato, J., 2009. Internet Pornography Statistics—2006. Top Ten Reviews. www.internet-filter-review.toptenreviews.com/internet-pornography-statistics.html.

Russell, S.T., 2005. Conceptualizing Positive Adolescent Sexuality Development. Sexuality Research and Social Policy: Journal of NSRC 2 (3), 4–12.

Sauers, J., 2007. Sex Lives of Australian Teenagers. Random House Australia, Sydney, Australia.

Savino, J., Turvey, B., 2004. Rape Investigation Handbook. Elsevier Science, Boston, MA.

Schmitt, D.P., 2003. Universal Sex Differences in the Desire for Sexual Variety: Tests from 52 Nations, 6 Continents, and 13 Islands. Journal of Personal and Social Psychology 85, 85–104.

Senn, C.Y., Radtke, H.L., 1990. Women's Evaluations of and Affective Reactions to Mainstream Violent Pornography, Nonviolent Erotica, and Erotica. Violence Victimology 5, 143–155.

Seto, M.C., Maric, A., Barbaree, H.E., 2001. The Role of Pornography in the Etiology of Sexual Aggression. Aggression and Violent Behavior 6, 35–53.

Shimizu, C., 2006. Queens of Anal, Double, Triple, and the Gang Bang: Producing Asian/American Feminism in Pornography. Yale Journal of Law and Feminism 18, 235–276.

Shipman, C., Kazdin, C.T., 2009. Oral Sex and Casual Prostitution No Biggie. ABCNews.com, May 28; www.abcnews.go.com/GMA/Parenting/Story?id=7693121&page=1.

Strassberg, D., Lockerd, M.D., 1998. Force in Women's Sexual Fantasies. Archives of Sexual Behavior 27 (4), 403–414.

Sue, D., 1979. Erotic Fantasies of College Students during Coitus. Journal of Sex Research 15, 299–305.

Tepfer, D., 2009. Bridgeport Man Reenacts Fetish Movie in Sexual Assault of Two Fairfield Women. The Stamford Advocate, July 29; www.stamfordadvocate.com/ci_12933875.

U.S. Department of Justice, 1986. Attorney General's Commission on Pornography: Final report. U.S. Government Printing Office, Washington, DC.

Valkenburg, P.M., Soeters, K.E., 2001. Children's Positive and Negative Experiences with the Internet. Communication Research 28, 652–675.

Vega, V., Malamuth, N.M., 2007. Predicting Sexual Aggression: The Role of Pornography in the Context of General and Specific Risk Factors. Aggressive Behavior 33, 104–117.

Ward, L.M., 2003. Understanding the Role of Entertainment in the Sexual Socialization of American Youth: A Review of Empirical Research. Development Review 23, 347–388.

Whisman, M., Gordon, K., Chatav, Y., 2007. Predicting Sexual Infidelity in a Population-Based Sample of Married Individuals. Journal of Family Psychology 21 (2), 320–324.

Wiederman, M.W., 1997. Extramarital Sex: Prevalence and Correlates in a National Survey. Journal of Sex Research 34, 167–174.

Wiederman, M.W., Allgeier, E.R., 1996. Expectations and Attributions Regarding Extramarital Sex among Young Married Individuals. Journal of Psychology and Human Sexuality 8, 21–35.

Wilson, G., 1997. Gender Differences In Sexual Fantasy: An Evolutionary Analysis. Personality and Individual Differences 22 (1), 27–31.

CHAPTER 9

Sexual Asphyxia

Michael McGrath and Brent E. Turvey

CONTENTS

KEY TERMS

Asphyxia	Masochism	Sexual asphyxia
Autoerotic asphyxia	Sadomasochism	Sexual fantasy

Criminal Profiling: An Introduction to Behavioral Evidence Analysis, Fourth Edition

Human beings have experimented with all manner of sexual stimulation, ranging from the mundane to the bizarre. Human sexual desires and activities can encompass things the average person has never heard of, for example, ampotemnophilia, an erotic fixation on having a limb amputated (Money et al. 1977). The general public is, for the most part, unaware of such practices. Unfortunately, many criminal investigators also are equally ignorant and are subsequently unprepared when confronted by uncommon sexual practices in casework.

While some sexual practices can be considered physically dangerous in a general way (e.g., sadomasochistic behaviors or engaging in sexual activity with a horse[1]), sexual asphyxia stands out as having the clear potential to result in a lethal end. Various autoerotic practices can be seen to pose some inherent danger, such as the use of electricity (Brokenshire et al., 1984; Tan and Chao, 1983), vacuum cleaners (Imami and Kemal, 1988), and the insertion of objects into the rectum (Byard et al. 2000). Autoerotic asphyxia, though, appears to present the most obvious risk of death to the practitioner. Although asphyxia can be accomplished through a variety of mechanisms (Ikeda et al., 1988; Leadbetter, 1988; McLennan et al., 1998; Minyard, 1985; O'Halloran and Dietz, 1993) that result in decreasing the flow of oxygen to the brain, this chapter concentrates on asphyxia induced via a constriction of the neck. Nonasphyxial autoerotic deaths and asphyxial deaths not induced by ligature or constriction around the throat are often self-evident (by virtue of the bizarre and complex apparatus involved) and generally do not present as a significant investigative mystery.

PROBLEM WITH SEXUAL ASPHYXIA

Sexual asphyxia can be practiced both as an autoerotic activity and as a consensual sadomasochistic act between two or more people.[2] Conversely, nonconsensual sexual asphyxia would be for the needs (sexual or otherwise) of the person restricting the other person's oxygen source and is best described as an intentional criminal act. As Pa (2001, pp. 53–54) notes,

> Media depictions of S/M as a violent sexual pathology at best represent dismal ignorance of sociological and psychological information, and at worst, portray hateful smear tactics against a legally vulnerable community. The legal discourses surrounding S/M often reflect stereotypes propagated in the media. …
>
> S/M sex includes a wide range of sexual activities "between two consenting adults that may include, but is not limited to, the use of physical and/or psychological stimulation to produce sexual arousal and satisfaction." S/M sex is difficult to define precisely because of the wide range of activities

---

[1] In 2005, a "friend" dropped off a 45-year-old man from Enumclaw, Washington, to an area hospital. By the time doctors determined that the man was dead, his friend was gone. According to the King County medical examiner's office, the man had died of "acute peritonitis due to perforation of the colon" that caused fatal internal bleeding. The dead man's driver's license led police to family, friends, and eventually a rural farm in Enumclaw where they seized videotapes of various men engaged in sexual acts with the horses boarded there. The videotapes, featuring hundreds of hours of sexual acts filmed at the farm, were found hidden in a field. It was eventually determined that the dead man, Boeing worker Kenneth Pinyon, had suffered the fatal trauma while being sodomized by an Arabian stallion named Bullseye maintained at the farm for stud purposes. Because Washington State had no bestiality laws in place at the time, James Tait, 54, who lived at the farm, could only be charged with trespassing in relation to the other man's death (Sullivan, 2005). The incident is the subject of the documentary film *Zoo*, released in 2007.

[2] Sadomasochism is defined as a consensual activity involving polarized role playing, intense sensations, and feelings, actions, and fantasies that focus on playing out or fantasizing dominant and submissive roles as part of the sexual scenario (Francoeur, 1995, p. 556).

involved and the paucity of research on this subject. There are four major categories of sadomasochistic behavior, although variations are numerous. They include: (1) infliction of physical pain, usually by means of whipping, spanking, slapping or the application of heat and cold; (2) verbal or psychological stimulation such as threats and insults; (3) dominance and submission, for example, where one individual orders the other to do his or her bidding; (4) bondage and discipline, involving restraints such as rope and chains and/or punishment for real or fabricated transgressions. Other variations include fetishistic, exhibitionistic and voyeuristic components, intense and/or frustrated genital stimulation, age-play (infantilism, diapering), body mutilation (piercing, scarring, corsetting, tattooing), role reversal (cross-dressing) and defecation (urination, enemas, fecal play).

Given this wide range, analysts have observed five features generally present in an S/M encounter:

1. Dominance and submission—the appearance of control of one partner over the other;
2. Role-playing—the participants assume roles that they recognize are not reality;
3. Consensuality—a voluntary agreement to enter into SM "play" and to honor certain "limits";
4. Sexual context—the presumption that the activities have a sexual or erotic meaning;
5. Mutual definition—participants must agree on the parameters of what they are doing, whether they call it SM or not.

As this statement indicates, when consensual sexual asphyxia results in death, the death is unintended. It is not an intentional act of homicide. This can be difficult to ascertain in some circumstances, as the surviving participant may not be eager to trust the police with understanding the difference between a consensual/accidental sexual asphyxia and an intentional homicide. Moreover, drug or alcohol use/abuse may also add another layer of confusion. The result can be a situation that some investigators may find distasteful to the point of a failure to investigate and some prosecutors may be eager to exploit to the point of ignoring historical and contextual evidence that can establish asphyxia as a regular part of a particular individual's sexual activities.

As Pa (2001, p. 52) explains, the elements of a consensual sadomasochistic (S/M) sexual encounter can be confounding:

Criminal prosecution for S/M sex should occur only where the victim claims he or she was sexually assaulted because there was no clear consent to the S/M encounter, consent was revoked, or the perpetrator exceeded the scope of consent. Criminal prosecution of S/M sex in any other circumstance is a misapplication of criminal assault law. This is because such prosecutions mistake S/M sex as only violence. Prosecutors confuse the presence of traditional symbols of violence (whips, chains, handcuffs), utilized in a theatrical and self-conscious simulation of power relationships, as the presence of real dominance and exploitation.

In cases of autoerotic asphyxia, the investigation may be complicated by well-meaning relatives or significant others who alter the scene—for example, by removing pornography or female clothing from a male victim—out of personal embarrassment or the wish to preserve the dignity of the deceased.

Autoerotic asphyxia is the deliberate induction of hypoxia with the intent of causing heightened sexual arousal. It can be mistaken for either a homicide or a suicide. It is incumbent upon investigators and criminal profilers to understand the nature of sexual asphyxia, the signs of such behavior present at a death scene, and how to delineate it from a suicide or a homicide. Unfortunately, some of the literature carries a subjective moral tone, although it may be subtle. For example, Holmes (1991) includes sexual asphyxia in his book *Sex Crimes*.

Errors in judgment can have psychological, civil, and criminal repercussions. While not relieved of grief about the death of a loved one, a family may take some solace in knowing the death was accidental, not suicide. Also, insurance companies may refuse to pay if the death is a suicide (depending on the specific clauses or time frame of the policy), unnecessarily adding to the burden of a family dealing with the death of a loved one. Furthermore, some insurance policies pay more for an accidental death claim (Miller and Milbrath, 1983) than for a death from other causes. Finally, law-enforcement resources may be wasted on a homicide investigation into what is actually an accident. Worse still, an innocent person could be charged with a crime that has not been committed.

Discussions of sexual asphyxia have been problematic, and widespread dissemination of information on the practice via the media has resulted in at least one death (O'Halloran and Lovell, 1988). However, there are exceptions. For example, the acclaimed HBO (2002) series *Six Feet Under* started one episode with a portrayal of an accidental autoerotic asphyxial death.[3] In any case, because of the propensity for certain individuals to mimic what they see reported in the media, many news agencies and media groups are understandably hesitant to give the subject any but the vaguest coverage. This has had the effect of leaving much of the general public underinformed regarding the various incarnations of sexual asphyxia—both with respect to the dangers involved and the fact that it exists at all.[4]

NATURE OF SEXUAL ASPHYXIA

Sexual asphyxia goes by several names, including *le petit mort*, asphyxiophilia, and Koczwarism, among others. It is called "hypoxyphilia" in the DSM-IV-TR (American Psychiatric Association, 2000) and is mentioned under sexual masochism in the section on paraphilias.[5]

It is not known when or how the practice of sexual asphyxia arose. Penile erection (with or without ejaculation) as a consequence of hanging has likely been well known for millennia. Aside from what tales a hangman might tell, public hangings offered the general populace a view of the phenomenon. The first historical mention of sexual asphyxia was in the seventeenth century, when it was suggested as a treatment for impotence (no doubt because of its ability to cause an erection even in the dying), with reference to death by autoerotic asphyxia dating at least back to 1791 (Dietz, 1979).

DeBoisemont (1856) first reported the practice in the medical literature in 1856. A reference to erection during hanging appears in Herman Melville's *Billy Budd* (1900) and Samuel Beckett's (1954) *Waiting for Godot*. A description of assisted sexual asphyxia appears in *Justine* by the Marquis de Sade (De Sade, 1965). Resnik (1972) reports that purposeful asphyxia can be found in Eskimo children ("probably sexual"), the Celts, Shoshone-Bannock Indian children, and some South American tribes. Theories put forth as to the psychodynamic or developmental genesis of the behavior (Friedrich and Gerber, 1994; Resnik, 1972; Rosenblum and Faber, 1979) offer no investigative assistance. Hazelwood and Dietz (1983) are probably correct in noting that most practitioners learn of the behavior accidentally or from others.

---

[3] HBO (2002): *Six Feet Under*, "Back to the Garden," season 2, episode 20.

[4] It bears mentioning that sexual arousal from sadomasochistic stimuli is not exactly rare in the general population. As cited in Pa (2001): "Research indicates that approximately 5–10% of the U.S. population have experimented with S/M sex." The 1990 Kinsey Institute New Report on Sex estimates that the U.S. population "engages in S/M for sexual pleasure on at least an occasional basis, with most incidents being either mild or stage activities involving no real pain or violence."

[5] *Le petit mort*, the little death; asphyxiophilia, from the Greek *philia* for "love of," *a* for "not" or "lack of," and *sphyzein* for "to throb." Taken literally, it means the love of not having a pulse. Koczwarism: in eighteenth-century Europe, Frantisek Koczwara was well known as a double-bass player and as a dabbler in sadomasochism. In 1791, he met his end after a session with a prostitute that included sexual asphyxia.

The practice must provide some positive reinforcement; otherwise it would not likely be repeated. It is assumed that the decreased availability of oxygen leads to lightheadedness, which when coinciding with orgasm is subjectively felt to result in an enhancement of the sexual feelings (Resnik, 1972). While there are clearly fantasy factors operating in the behavior, actually dying as a result of the practice is usually not part of the fantasy scenario, although that has occurred (Litman and Swearington, 1972).

Furthermore, a significant number of Internet websites are dedicated to a variety of consensual sexual asphyxia–related activities, from social clubs to the dissemination of pornography. Masochism appears to be a persistent, integral part of the fantasy throughout. Those who enjoy these practices achieve sexual arousal and gratification from the physical act of being choked, the psychological component of degradation and humiliation that is associated being used in such a fashion, as well as the element of actual danger that is involved.

One such Web site is www.necrobabes.com, a fantasy-oriented Web site dedicated, in part, to "Tastefully erotic death scenes through asphyxia, shooting, knives" and "Sexy strangled, suffocated, hanged & drowned babes. It takes your breath away!"[6] While this Web site is dedicated to archiving and disseminating pornographic material related to consensual fantasies involving the aforementioned, it has been used at least once by someone who crossed the line from consensual fantasy to criminal reality.[7] In 2001, one of its subscribing members killed someone.

Patrick Russo, a church worship leader, had a membership in necrobabes.com. Along with other digital evidence, his membership was used as evidence against him in court when he was put on trial for the murder of IBM employee Diane Holik. The following account is taken entirely from the court record (Texas v. Patrick Anthony Russo, 2007):

> A violent thunder and rainstorm descended upon Austin in the afternoon of November 15, 2001. In the same general time frame, Diane Holik was murdered by ligature strangulation in her own home at 6313 Pathfinder in the Great Hills subdivision in Austin, where she lived alone. Holik's last known telephone conversation occurred at 3:30 p.m. on November 15, 2001, and her computer had been shut down at 3:59 p.m. the same day.

> Holik was a supervisory employee of IBM and worked out of her home. She was in daily and weekly contact with certain IBM coworkers across the country in the same supervisory field. They worked as a team in managing new college "hires" for IBM. Holik was engaged to be married and planned to move to Houston where her fiancé lived. She was eager to sell her Austin home. The house was listed with a realtor for $435,000, and there was a "For Sale" sign in the front yard.

> Teena Fountain, an IBM coworker from Oak Park, Illinois, testified that on the morning of November 16, 2001, she was contacted by co-workers, Diane Kapcar of Dallas and Cynthia Barajas of Los Angeles, California, who reported that Holik had missed a scheduled "meeting," and that they had been unable to contact her by any available means.

> Knowing that the Austin storm had spawned some tornadoes, Fountain called the Austin Police Department that afternoon asking for a check on Holik. Austin police officers checked Holik's house

---

[6] Taken from descriptions of subject areas at www.necrobabes.com/index1.html. This Web site claims to archive more the 35,000 images and videos of commercial and amateur depictions related to sexual asphyxia; last accessed July 2007.

[7] In the great debate about such Web sites, it must be remembered that the majority of sexual fantasy between consenting adults is a healthy form of sexual expression and even sexual development. Like all things sexual, it can be turned into something destructive, just as reproductive acts and acts of intimacy are made acts of violence in crimes involving rape. Bearing that in mind, fantasy play that involves asphyxia is extremely dangerous to act out or act upon, even when merely simulated.

about 5:30 p.m. on November 16, 2001. All the doors and windows were locked. Dogs inside the house appeared to have left fecal matter on the carpet, indicating that they had been confined for some time. Holik's realtor and neighbor, Lakki Brown, saw the police officers. She opened the front door for them.

Holik's body was found face down on the floor in an upstairs guest bedroom. The body was fully clothed and there was no evidence of a sexual assault. Holik's neck bore the marks of a ligature, which was never found. Holik's wrist bore indentations showing discernible redness, indicating that her heart was still beating when the wrists were bound. The indentations appeared to have been made by plastic zip ties or flex-cuffs once used by police to bind prisoners' wrists together. No zip ties were found on the body or in the house. When the police officers rolled the body over, a charm fell out of Holik's hair. It was shown at trial that she wore the charm on a necklace. No such necklace was found. No rings were found on the body. Her $17,500 engagement ring was missing. A jewelry box, which contained a substantial amount of jewelry, including some very expensive pieces, was missing from the master bedroom. A spare front door key with a ribbon was missing from the doorknob of a ground floor door.

Dr. Elizabeth Peacock, deputy medical examiner, performed the autopsy and determined the cause of death to be homicide by ligature strangulation. Dr. Peacock estimated that Holik died between 3:00 p.m. on November 15 and 3:00 a.m. on November 16, 2001. …

During the course of their investigation, the police learned that, on November 15, 2001, some Great Hills residents, who had "For Sale" signs in front of their houses, had been approached by a man who claimed to be interested in buying their homes. The man told some that he would return with his wife on the weekend to see the house, that he had recently sold a ranch or some property, and that he would be paying cash. The man gave different names to some of the homeowners. At least two homeowners testified that the man came to their houses twice on November 15, 2001, in the Great Hills subdivision. A composite drawing of the man was prepared by an artist [who was guided by a description] from one of the homeowners. A homeowner from another subdivision saw the drawing in the newspaper and called the police. When trying to sell her home, a man, generally fitting the description, came to her home in May 2001 just after her husband left for work. He returned on November 5, 2001, at the same time. On this latter date, she took note of the license plate number on his van. Using this number, the police were able to identify appellant as the man they were seeking.

Appellant [Patrick Russo] worked at the New Life In Christ Church in Bastrop. He was a worship leader and music director. On November 17, 2001, there was a church staff meeting. According to the pastor, Jim Fox, appellant stated that God had gotten his attention during the November 15 storm, and that it was a determining time in his life. Appellant was ready to submit to the authority of the pastor. There had been a power struggle between the two at the church. Appellant appeared broken and downcast when making his statements.

In the early morning hours of November 21, 2001, police officers executed a search warrant at appellant's Bastrop home. Appellant agreed to go with the officers to the Austin police station, telling his wife that the inquiry possibly had something to do with his parole status. He was interviewed during the transport and at the station. Appellant told the detectives that he became lost during the storm in a residential area of Austin. He said that he did not enter any houses. Appellant also said that he stopped at only one house to ask for directions, which he received from an older gray-haired man. …

Later the same day, appellant went to the home of his pastor and discussed his conversation with the police. Pastor Fox stated that appellant felt that he was going to be arrested for killing a lady.

Appellant said that some jewelry had been taken from the victim. It was later shown that the police did not inform appellant that any jewelry was missing from the Holik home. ...

Approximately twelve realtors testified that in 2001, a man, whom most of these witnesses identified as appellant, had contacted them about a home or homes he needed to see immediately, and who indicated that he was a cash buyer and could afford houses from $200,000 to $700,000. He insisted that he be shown only vacant houses. In many situations, he wanted to meet the woman realtor alone at the site of the vacant house. Many of realtors were "uncomfortable" while showing homes to the man. Appellant's telephone number was given and identified. The realtors' telephone numbers appeared on appellant's phone bill.

Appellant's wife, Janet, was a schoolteacher for the Smithville Independent School District. Appellant received approximately $50.00 a week for his work at the church. He was a full-time unskilled employee at a custom-cabinet-making company. Appellant only worked there about thirty hours a week, but appellant voluntarily quit that job.

The prosecution offered evidence of appellant's financial condition during the time period in question. Cathy Vance, a forensic analyst with the white-collar crime unit in the district attorney's office, analyzed appellant's financial records. Her testimony demonstrated that appellant and his wife had more than $40,000 in available monies in 1999, but that at the time of the offense, they had approximately $1,796.19. The evidence shows that appellant and his wife had a $199,000 mortgage on their trailer home in Bastrop.

There was an extensive crime scene investigation at the victim's home. During the autopsy, police officers collected biological evidence from the victim's left hand. The police officers also recovered a green towel found on a couch downstairs. Brady Mills, the supervising criminalist at the Department of Public Safety (DPS) laboratory in Austin, extracted DNA from a swab of the victim's left hand. He compared the samples with known DNA samples from the victim, the appellant, the victim's fiancé, and a male co-worker. The fiancé and co-worker were excluded, but Mills could not exclude DNA samples from the victim or appellant on the swab. Appellant's DNA could not be excluded from four of nine loci considered by Mills.

Kimberlyn Nelson of Mitotyping Technologies at State College, Pennsylvania, testified that she specialized in mitochondrial DNA testing. All persons inherit mitochondrial DNA from their mothers—so maternal relatives have the same "M-DNA." Nelson examined seven hairs recovered from the victim's home. Appellant could not be excluded from two hairs retrieved from a green towel found in the living room.

Dr. Ranazit Chakraborty, Director of the Center for Genome Information of the University of Cincinnati College of Medicine, reviewed the findings by Mills and Nelson. He testified that he hypothesized the coincidental chances of obtaining the same nuclear DNA results in this case would be one in 16,817. When Dr. Chakraborty considered the mitochondrial DNA, he decided that the coincidental chance of obtaining the same profile in this case is one in 12.9 million people.

On June 18, 2003, a search warrant was issued authorizing the search of appellant's home and the seizure of his personal computer "and its content." The computer was seized pursuant to the warrant. Detective Roy Rector, a computer forensic examiner with the Austin Police Department, was initially requested to look for references in the computer to the victim, her address, or her realtor. No such references were found. His search was broadened to consider the Internet history, searching for documents relating to real estate, including Web pages. More than 136 such documents in the temporary Internet files folder or unallocated clusters (deleted files) were located. Several of the Internet pages related to the realtors who testified at trial.

Rector presented the information extracted from the computer to the prosecutor, who noticed that the computer's Internet history (which contained no Web pages or images) made reference to a Web site named "necrobabes.com," which was later determined to be an asphyxiation-type pornographic Web site. On November 18, 2003, a second search warrant was issued, that authorized the search of the hard drive of appellant's computer for "[i]nformation pertaining to death by asphyxiation" as well as other information and photos and text from the Web site named "necrobabes.com."

Joseph Schwaleberg, the record custodian of Generic Systems, a billing company that controlled access to the "necrobabes.com" Web site, testified that a "Tony Russo" with the same home and email address as appellant purchased a six-month membership on July 21, 2001. An earlier membership had been issued on February 28, 2001, to a "Janet Russo" at the same address. Passwords were issued allowing entry to the said Web site as a result of the memberships. Rector recovered two hours, thirty-six minutes, and fifty-five seconds of Internet history of the "necrobabes.com" Web site. The Web site was accessed or visited by appellant's computer in the month prior to the victim's murder, including on November 13, 2001, two days before the offense occurred. The Web pages viewed by appellant included manual and ligature strangulation. Some 1,200 "necrobabes.com" related images were recovered.

Dr. Richard Coons, a psychiatrist and an attorney, testified concerning his training in human sexuality. He qualified as an expert witness for the State. Dr. Coons viewed the images shown to have been accessed by appellant on his computer from the "necrobabes.com" Web site as well as photographs of the victim's body. Dr. Coons was presented with a hypothetical scenario based on the evidence admitted at trial (except evidence of robbery). He indicated that the material from the erotic asphyxiation Web site tended to reveal the motive for the killing of the victim, which was sexual sadism. Dr. Coons explained that a sexual sadist is sexually stimulated with a fantasy life and becomes obsessive. The person will "play out" the fantasies, searching out potential victims. The person is aroused by watching and controlling another with knives or guns or injuring them by other methods, including ligature strangulation. In many such encounters, Dr. Coons explained, there is no completed sexual act. The underlying purpose can be killing, dominating, or humiliating another.

The doctor testified that in his opinion, the hypothetical scenario strongly suggests that the defendant in the scenario sought sexual gratification through ligature strangulation.

In 2004, Patrick Russo was convicted for the murder of Diane Holik and sentenced to life in prison. In 2007, the court of appeals in Austin, Texas, upheld that conviction.

DEMOGRAPHICS

Despite the vast number of amateur Web sites dedicated to the subject, the true extent of sexual asphyxia is unknown. The majority of cases come to light due to the death of the practitioner, although there is some literature related to living practitioners (Money et al., 1991; Rosenblum and Faber, 1979; Wesselius, 1983). Consequently, little is available in the professional literature describing those who practice this behavior and do not die.

The DSM-IV-TR (American Psychiatric Association, 2000, p. 573), summarizing data from the United States, England, Australia, and Canada, offers a range of "one to two hypoxophilia-caused deaths per million population are reported each year." Various authors report autoerotic asphyxial death mortality figures from an apparent low of 250 deaths per year (Wesselius, 1983) to a higher, yet "conservative," estimate of 500 to 1,000 such deaths annually (Burgess and Hazelwood, 1983). As discussed in Erman (2005, p. 2173):

> To date, hard numbers on the death rate of autoerotic asphyxiation have been difficult to produce. The number of deaths per year resulting from autoerotic asphyxiation has been variously calculated to lie between forty and two thousand. But because of underreporting, the number of annual incidents or practitioners is largely unknown. Thus the only firm statement one can make about autoerotic asphyxiation is that throughout the general population "death by autoerotic asphyxiation is statistically rare." Nonetheless, experts and courts have tended to concur that most incidents of autoerotic asphyxiation end in survival and do not produce serious or permanent injury. As a result of this information and its obscure and inconclusive nature, one cannot say that practitioners of autoerotic asphyxiation ought to expect to die.

Until fairly recently, the literature reflected the belief that autoerotic asphyxia was an adolescent male activity (Adelson, 1974; Resnik, 1972) and that female devotees of the practice were either extremely rare or nonexistent. Several papers have alerted the forensic community to the fact that female autoerotic asphyxia is not as rare as believed (Byard and Bramwell, 1988; Byard et al., 1990; Danto, 1980) and may be more problematic than male autoerotic asphyxia in sorting out the behavior from a sexual homicide or a suicide.

Hazelwood and Dietz's (1983) study of 157 cases of suspected autoerotic fatalities gave the following breakdown: 132 (84.1%) asphyxial (i.e., typical); 18 (11.5%) atypical; 5 (3.2%) asphyxial with a partner; and 2 (1.3%) autoerotic suicide. Uva (1995), in a review of autoerotic asphyxial deaths in the United States, reports that the incidence of such deaths is increasing, when, in fact, it may be only that the reporting or identification of such deaths may be increasing. Most cases involve young males, but the age range is large.

Blanchard and Hucker's (1991) study of 117 male autoerotic deaths in Canada gave a range of 10 to 56 years, with a mean of 26 years. A third of the men were under 19 years of age. Behrendt and Modvig (1995), reporting on 46 male autoerotic deaths in Denmark, gave an age range of 10 to 71 years, with a mean of 31; 64% of the men were younger than age 29. One study (Sheehan and Garfinkel, 1987) reported that 31% of the adolescent hangings in a section of Minnesota from 1975 to 1985 were autoerotic asphyxial deaths.

Balassone and Hightower (2007, p. A1) provide a contemporary discussion regarding adolescent practice:

> Nothing about P.K.'s behavior, his bare bedroom walls or unkempt closet hinted at how he would die.

> "I had no clue," the 18-year-old's mother said, thinking back on the hours she spent with her son March 31 before he tied a pair of sweat pants around his neck and choked himself to death.

> Coroners call P.K.'s hanging death an accident. The Modesto man had been "experimenting with autoeroticism," starving his brain of air to achieve a rush that heightens sexual fantasy and stimulation. ...

> P.K.'s case is at least the third accidental hanging from autoerotic choking among adolescent or teenage boys from the Northern San Joaquin and Sacramento valleys in the past two years.

> In October 2005, a 12-year-old Manteca boy was found dead by his grandmother, a karate belt wrapped around his neck. A final report by the San Joaquin County coroner determined the cause of death was an accidental hanging "due to autoerotic activity."

> In March, a 16-year-old boy from Folsom was found to have died from autoerotic asphyxiation. He was found hanging from a tree in a neighborhood park just a few doors from his family's house.

Cutting off oxygen to the brain can cause someone to lose consciousness in just seconds, said Kristi Herr, chief deputy coroner in Stanislaus County. If the pressure is not relieved quickly, the brain begins to swell. The practice can be fatal in as few as three or four minutes. …

P.K. spent the day shopping and having lunch with his mother, visiting his grandmother and helping carry groceries into the house. He had plans for spring break and was looking forward to a winter cruise with the family, D.K. said.

When P.K. disappeared, his parents assumed he was at a friend's house. His father, searching for clues to his son's whereabouts, found P.K. two days later in his bedroom closet. …

Dr. Mark Super, Sacramento County's chief forensic pathologist, helped investigate the death of the Folsom teenager in March. Super said the best estimates of deaths from autoerotic asphyxiation in the United States are 500 to 1,000 each year.

Super said these cases can be missed by coroners who rule the deaths to be suicides rather than accidental hangings. "In more rural areas, where people are not very experienced, they might not know these things exist," said Super, who's worked in the field for 25 years.

Sometimes, the scene where victims are found can be altered, accidentally or on purpose, by parents, police or paramedics who respond, Super said. The more ritualistic scenes can be cleaned up and bodies may be clothed to prevent embarrassment to the family, he said.

Super said the same feeling of light-headedness that attracts young children to play "the choking game" is the driving force behind autoerotic asphyxiation, although the purposes are different.

When playing the choking game, children may cut off their air supply alone or in groups of friends by using their hands, clothing or rope.

"It's done kind of to get a high, to get vivid dreams," Super said. "That is kind of addicting."

Super said the phenomenon of choking for sexual pleasure is "predominantly male" and the practice is often done privately. Some victims will pad the ligature they use to constrict their neck to prevent visible bruises or marks. …

Although it's young men who die of autoerotic asphyxiation most frequently, it's unknown if they experiment with it more than other groups because there is so little information about it, said sexologist Kathryn Ando of San Francisco.

Carol Queen of the Center for Sex and Culture, based in San Francisco, said constricting the air flow to the brain adds to the sensation of arousal for those who practice autoerotic asphyxiation. "It is seen to involve erotic feelings or an erotic thrill," she said. …

"There were no clues he'd done this before. No marks. I don't know why anyone does it. It only takes one time," D.K. said tearfully as she stood in the small, now-empty closet where her husband found their son's body. "I can't be angry, though. I think he was curious and made the wrong choice."

Stanislaus County Deputy Coroner Misty Leach said P.K. was on the family's computer so often that his parents transferred it from the living room to his bedroom.

The Sacramento Valley Hi-Tech Crimes Task Force analyzed the computer after his death and found multiple "images, sketches, cartoons, photos, video files and Web pages" depicting autoeroticism, Leach said. There were no e-mails or writings found on the subject, said Detective Lydell Wall with the task force.

Leach said most of the images had been viewed by P.K. in the week before his death. She spoke to P.K.'s friends but none of them knew he was involved in autoeroticism.

"The weird thing is (he) never brought the topic up," a friend said in an e-mail message. "He was mostly the quiet guy."

Mostly quiet, his friends say, until "game time." P.K. loved playing computer games such as "Dungeons & Dragons" and card games like Magic: The Gathering, which is based on a fantasy world of wizards, elves and demons. ...

Super, the Sacramento pathologist, said it's important for parents to know what their children may be looking at on the Internet.

Child safety experts urge parents to keep computers in common areas of the home and to know what their children have posted on social networking sites such as Facebook and MySpace.

"Some parents don't realize that it's natural to be interested in these things, but they don't know they may be trying this stuff," Super said.

"Parents need to be savvy that this kind of stuff can happen even though they think their teenager is quote-unquote normal."

Super said he would like to see information about autoerotic asphyxiation included in sexual education classes, at least in general terms.

"It's like drugs, alcohol or anything else," he said. "If they tell kids how to put on condoms, why don't they talk about autoerotic ... if it's going to save somebody's life?"

That's easier said than done, said Vicki Bauman, director of prevention programs for the Stanislaus County Office of Education. Bauman said area school districts are required to teach basic sexual education curriculum, including abstinence, safe sex practices, sexually transmitted diseases, alcohol and drug abuse. But they are hesitant to add more controversial topics for fear of upsetting parents. "We're always hitting a brick wall, so we're really sensitive when we do these types of classes," Bauman said.

She has no plans to address autoerotic behavior but does hope to have experts talk about the dangers of the choking game with superintendents, principals and teachers this fall.

"We have concerns about bringing something to light that's so deadly," Herr said. "I don't want the coroner's office to be responsible for giving any instructions or ideas."

FINDINGS AT THE DEATH SCENE

Death scenes will vary, but certain findings can be expected. At a minimum, to form an opinion that a death is the result of autoerotic asphyxia, the investigator would need to find evidence that the activity was repetitive and likely pursued for sexual stimulation.[8] There should be evidence that death was not an expected outcome. Pornography, mirrors, and other fantasy aids help such a determination, as does finding padding between the ligature and the neck. Evidence of an escape mechanism (even if only consisting of

---

[8] The exceptions would be that it is the practitioner's first time, or the practitioner is at a different place from his usual location, such as a hotel room or staying at a friend's house.

the ability to stand, thereby releasing tension on the ligature) must be present. The presence of semen at the death scene is not by itself proof that the deceased was masturbating or had an orgasm. Semen on the ground or on the victim's underwear or leg is possibly due to sexual activity, but it is also possibly due to postmortem rigor mortis (Spitz and Fisher, 1993). And most suicides are not discovered nude or partially nude, as many autoerotic death victims are. On the other hand, lack of nudity or partial nudity in no way rules out an autoerotic death.

Various authors list criteria to determine whether a death is an autoerotic fatality. Hazelwood and Dietz (1983) give 12 autoerotic death scene characteristics, not all of which are necessary. As expanded on and discussed in Turvey (2000),

1. Location. In autoerotic deaths, the location is likely to be a secluded area with a reasonable expectation of privacy (e.g., a locked bedroom, bathroom, basement, attic, garage, workshop, motel room, or wooded area).
2. Body position. In asphyxial hanging deaths, the victim's body may be partially supported by the ground, or the victim may even appear to have simply been able to stand up to avoid strangulation.
3. High-risk elements. These are items that are brought into the autoerotic activity to enhance physical or psychological pleasure. They include anything that is potentially harmful or reduces judgment, such as drugs, alcohol, or weapons. These elements increase the risk of autoerotic death.
4. Self-rescue mechanism. This is any provision that allows the victim to voluntarily stop the high-risk element's effect (e.g., literature dealing with escape mechanisms, a slipknot in a ligature around the victim's neck, the freedom to punch a hole in a plastic bag sealed over the victim's face, a remote safety button on a power hydraulic within or near the victim's reach, keys for locks, or the ability to simply stand up and avoid asphyxiation altogether).
5. Bondage. This refers to the use of special materials or devices that physically restrain the victim (e.g., handcuffs, leather harnesses, wrist manacles, elaborate ligature configuration). These items have psychological/fantasy significance to the victim. The presence of this characteristic can lead investigators to believe that a death was homicidal when it was not. In cases of autoerotic death, it is important to establish that the victim could have placed the restraints on himself or herself, without assistance. (Literature dealing with bondage may be found at the scene or investigation may reveal that such literature was available to the deceased.)
6. Masochistic behavior. This refers to inflicting psychological (humiliation) or physical pain upon sexual areas of the body, or other body parts. It is important to look not only for indicators of current use but also for healed injuries suggesting a history of such behavior, when appropriate (e.g., literature dealing with sadomasochism, spreader bar between the ankles, genital restraints, ball-gag, nipple clips, cross-dressing, suspension).
7. Clothing. The victim may be dressed in fetishistic attire or in one or more article of female clothing. However, cross-dressing or fetishistic attire may be absent. Clothing is not always a useful indicator in cases of autoerotic death. It is possible for victims of autoerotic fatalities to be fully dressed, nude, or in a state of partial undress.
8. Protective measures. The victim often will not want injuries sustained during regularly occurring autoerotic behaviors to be visible to others. Injuries may be inflicted only to areas that are covered by clothing, or the victims may place soft, protective material between their skin and restraining devices or ligatures to prevent abrasions and bruising (e.g., a towel may be placed around the victim's neck beneath a hanging ligature, or wrist restraints may be placed over the victim's clothing, etc.).
9. Sexual paraphernalia and props. These are items found on or near the victim that assist in sexual fantasy (vibrators, dildos, mirrors, erotica, diaries, photos, films, female undergarments, method for recording the event [an audiotape recorder, video camera, etc.]).

10. Masturbatory activity. The absence of sperm or semen at the scene does not rule out autoerotic death. The victim may or may not have been manually masturbating at the time of death. Evidence of masturbation strongly supports a determination of autoerotic death, however, and may be suggested by the presence of sperm or semen, tissues, towels, and lubricant on hands and sexual areas. In cases involving females, sexual devices may be present.

11. Evidence of prior autoerotic activity. This includes evidence of behavior similar to that found at the scene that predates the fatality (permanently affixed protective padding, plastic bags with repaired "escape" holes, pornography from many different dates, a large collection of erotica, complex high-risk elements [very complex ligature configurations], complex escape mechanisms, healed injuries, grooves worn in a beam from repeated ligature placement, homemade videotape of prior autoerotic activity, witness accounts of prior autoerotic behavior, etc.).

12. No apparent suicidal intent. The victim had plans for future events (e.g., the victim made plans to see close friends or to go on a trip in the near future). Absence of a suicide note is not necessarily an indication of an autoerotic event. If one is present, it must be determined that it was written around the time of death and is not a prop (part of a victim's masochistic fantasy). Other indicators that the victim did not commit suicide are that the victim had no history of depression, had recently paid monthly bills, and had spoken to friends of looking forward to a specific event.

The authors suggest the following death scene findings are necessary to determine that a death is due to autoerotic asphyxia:

1. There is an expectation of privacy
2. There is no convincing evidence of suicidal intent
3. There is no evidence of another actor at the scene
4. There is an apparatus to induce hypoxia
5. The apparatus includes an escape mechanism, even if it is as simple as standing up
6. The victim could have placed any bindings found

There could be a seventh criterion: evidence of repetitive activity. While this is certainly valuable evidence, its absence cannot rule out an autoerotic death. For one thing, the event could be the first (and fatal) time the individual attempted the behavior. Additionally, the practitioner may not be where he or she usually practices the behavior, so, while the asphyxia was a repeated practice, the location would not indicate that. For example, the victim could be found hanging in a hotel he or she happened to be staying at.

Other influences on death scene findings include the friends and family of the victim. When friends or family members discover a loved one who has died from autoerotic asphyxia, their first impulse may be to sanitize the scene. They may remove and dispose of embarrassing items (pornography, articles of female clothing, sexual devices) and generally may act to preserve their loved one's dignity before notifying authorities. This is not criminal behavior done with criminal intent, and it should not be treated as such. However, investigators must be aware that this type of intervention can and does happen, and they must anticipate dealing with it. If an autoerotic death is suspected but the expected findings are absent, those who discovered the body should be questioned about altering the scene.

FINDINGS AT AUTOPSY

Specific autopsy findings will vary, depending on the actual manner and mode of death. While the cause of death may be autoerotic asphyxia, the manner of death may vary because of the use of a ligature or some other hypoxia-inducing apparatus. Even within the context of a ligature-related sexual asphyxia, the actual mode of ligature will affect autopsy findings. Some of the findings associated with hanging oneself from a ceiling beam will differ from those related to hypoxia induced with a ligature while lying down or in some other position. Of note, conjunctival and facial petechiae, often assumed to be related to hypoxia, are likely a result of hydrostatic pressure and not anoxia per se (Ely and Hirsch, 2000). A constriction around the neck impedes venous return from the head but is often not tight enough to completely cut off arterial flow to the brain. This results in increased pressure in the blood vessels, and the capillaries (the smallest vessels) begin to "leak."

Complete suspension of a victim by ligature will cause a pale face, while incomplete suspension will lead to a dusky, purple, and often swollen appearance (Spitz and Fisher, 1993). It is worth noting that the amount of pressure to the neck required to cause unconsciousness is quite low (Spitz and Fisher, 1993). An excellent description of the findings related to asphyxial deaths is presented in Spitz and Fisher's (1993) third edition of *Medicolegal Investigation of Death*.

FINDINGS OF PSYCHOLOGICAL AUTOPSY

The victim of accidental autoerotic asphyxial fatality should lack a history consistent with suicidal behavior. Such a history would consist of recent or chronic depression, a belief by associates that the deceased was at risk of killing himself or herself, and so on. While to some degree one of the underlying dynamics of sexual asphyxia clearly must be a death wish, this is also true of many activities (e.g., skydiving) that are not equated with conscious suicidal behavior. To relegate sexual asphyxia to a niche of suicidal behavior misses the point. It is a multidetermined activity that is more likely overtly related to sexual satisfaction than to any other cause.

As in any suspected homicide or suicide, assessment of victimology is a necessity. Taking the time to get to know and understand the victim can help guide opinions in equivocal cases. Psychological information can be helpful in equivocal death investigations (Jobes, Berman, and Josselson, 1986), yet true psychological autopsies are often neglected. A useful discussion is offered in Chapter 14 of this work.

It is an error to rely on one source of information when investigating an equivocal death. A close relative (such as a mother) will need to see the deceased in one way, while a lover may offer another view. Still more information may be gleaned from co-workers and others. The more information gathered from different sources, the more likely it is the investigator will get a clear picture of the deceased. It is not unheard of for individuals who practice sexual asphyxia to decide to end their lives (Byard and Botterill, 1998). Also, an apparent sexual asphyxial death can be reviewed, taking into account death scene variables and mental health history, to determine whether suicide was the victim's intent (Frazer and Rosenberg, 1983).

FEMALE SEXUAL ASPHYXIA

Although it is mostly a male activity, women do engage in sexual asphyxia. Gosink and Jumbelic (2000) offer a male-to-female ratio of greater than 50:1 (which may well be accurate) without citation. Byard et al. (1990) give the same figure.

Female victims of autoerotic asphyxia tend to be found naked, often without excessive or elaborate apparatus/props. The mere presence of a nude female in a death scene may account for a high level of underreporting or mislabeling of female autoerotic deaths. This is especially true when female victims of autoerotic fatalities are deeply involved with self-binding and other sadomasochistic behavior. This scenario can readily appear to investigators as a sexual homicide, perhaps the work of a sexual predator.

Female autoerotic death scenes do not present the same as male autoerotic death scenes. Danto (1980) reported on the case of a 21-year-old black female who was found nude in her bathroom by her boyfriend and another male. She was leaning over the bathtub with her head submerged. There was an abrasion on the side of her head. Her wrists appeared to have been bound with cord and a similar cord was wrapped around her neck. Additionally, a heavy iron bolt was found under the victim's buttocks. The case was open for over a year until it was determined to be an autoerotic death. While using the bolt as a dildo, the woman had passed out from the constriction around her neck, struck her head on the tub, and subsequently drowned. Byard and Bramwell (1988) reported on a 19-year-old white female found dead in her bedroom by family. She was lying on the bed with rope wrapped around her neck and tied to her ankles. She was wearing panties, and a hairbrush handle was inserted into her vagina.

Byard et al. (1990) presented a comparison of male and female autoerotic death scenes. They gave an age range in males of 9 to 80 years, and in females of 19 to 68 years. Male death scenes were characterized by the presence of pornography, unusual attire, devices to cause real or simulated pain, bizarre props, and evidence of fetishism, but these characteristics were absent from female death scenes. These differences are not definitive, though. Gosink and Jumbelic (2000) presented an atypical female autoerotic death scene that included pornographic and bondage magazines, videotapes, pornographic photographs, ligatures around the breasts, and a mirror situated to allow the victim to view herself, as well as a ligature around the neck. In general, however, most female autoerotic death scenes lack many of the attributes of the male death scene. One review of nine episodes of female autoerotic activity (Byard et al., 1993), including eight deaths, revealed that the majority of the women did not use props or unusual clothing (five women were completely naked). The authors of the study point out that investigators initially misinterpreted four of the nine episodes.

DIFFERENTIATING BETWEEN ACCIDENTAL DEATH FROM SEXUAL ASPHYXIA AND OTHER CAUSES

The investigator or criminal profiler is best prepared to correctly assess an equivocal death if aware of the potential choices. Autoerotic deaths are uncommon, but they do occur. The very idea of autoerotic behaviors (let alone asphyxia) is morally repugnant to some and discomfort with such subjects only interferes with the ability to assess such death scenes. When confronted with a possible autoerotic death scene, one can use the criteria noted earlier to form a preliminary assessment.

This should be followed by a psychological assessment of the victim (the depth of which will vary according to need). The autopsy findings should be consistent with the type of autoerotic death suspected. Although it is uncommon, homicide or suicide masquerading as an autoerotic death needs to be considered. The following factors may be helpful in making a determination of autoerotic asphyxial death:

1. Was there a reasonable expectation of privacy?
2. Were doors/windows locked from the inside?
3. Was it possible for the victim to place whatever ligatures are present on himself or herself?
4. If a nonligature method of asphyxiation was utilized, was it possible for the victim to engage it by himself or herself?
5. Was there padding on ligatures to prevent visible marks?
6. Was there evidence of fantasy or fetishistic activity?
7. Was there evidence the behavior had occurred before?
8. Is there lack of evidence that the victim committed suicide?
9. Are any injuries consistent with what is found at the death scene and attributable to behavior of the victim or inadvertent motion of the victim after losing consciousness?

This issue commonly arises when survivors attempt to claim life insurance and death benefits. For example, there may be an accidental death clause, waivers, and other associated benefits. According to Achampong (1987, p. 191),

> The accidental death benefit may be added to the basic death benefit in a life insurance policy, if the insured meets the particular insurer's underwriting requirements for the coverage. The accidental death benefit is provided in an amount equal to the policy face, hence the reference to "double indemnity" in the context of the accidental death benefit.

Therefore, the families of those who have died accidentally from autoerotic asphyxia may have a strong financial motivation to have the court or their insurer educated on the matter if the death benefits have been denied. Conversely, insurers may be confronted with lawsuits by those demanding death benefits that have been denied, so they too may wish to educate themselves independently. Consequently, criminal profilers are regularly called to consult on such cases and to examine the issue of accidental versus intentional death for the client and perhaps even the court, and they should be prepared with knowledge of the subject.

SEXUAL HOMICIDE WITH ASPHYXIA: A LETHAL HOOKUP

One of the authors (Turvey) was asked to consult on a case involving a sexual homicide with ligature strangulation. The circumstances are described in Chiem and Wilson (1998, p. 3):

> Cook County prosecutors said in court that [34-year-old Patrick] Bailey met [William Rosenbaum, 33] late Friday night at a "leather" club frequented by mostly gay men in the 5000 block of North Clark Street.
>
> Around 2 a.m. Saturday, police said, Bailey and a man in his 20s checked into a room at the Edens Motel, 6020 N. Cicero Ave., where Bailey registered using his own name.
>
> While the men engaged in sex, "Bailey put a belt around the victim's neck and pulled to the point where the victim passed out," said Cook County Assistant State's Atty. Kristen Piper.
>
> Bailey then pulled out a hunting knife, which he had brought to the motel, and stabbed the victim in the back, stomach and chest, Piper said. Authorities also alleged that Bailey mutilated the victim's body.
>
> Piper said Bailey then tried to drag the victim's body into the trunk of his car, but the man was too heavy. Bailey allegedly dragged the body back to the room, left the motel and went home, authorities said. A motel employee found the body around 12:30 p.m. Saturday.
>
> The Cook County medical examiner's office said the victim, who has not been identified, died of strangulation and multiple stab and incision wounds. Police collected several knives and a coat hanger at the scene. …
>
> A graduate of Maine East High School and Oakton Community College, Patrick Bailey seemed quiet and unassuming, his brother said. He had worked as a salesclerk at a Park Ridge discount store. …
>
> About a year ago, Bailey moved back in with his older brother and elderly mother, who shared a modest townhouse. He lived in Ohio for several years before that, said the older brother, Mike Bailey.
>
> According to Mike Bailey, his brother wanted to be closer to his mother as he sought treatment for Hodgkin's disease. Before his arrest, Patrick Bailey was undergoing chemotherapy, Mike Bailey said. … "He's a very non-violent person," said Mike Bailey. "He grew up around here, and he never once ran into trouble. He never raised his temper."

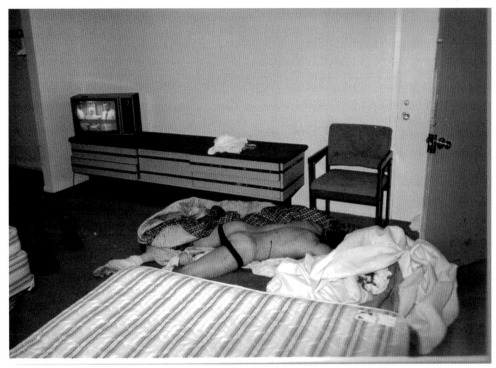

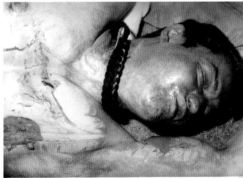

FIGURE 9.1 AND 9.2
Patrick Bailey and William Rosenbaum engaged in consensual sex at a hotel after hooking up at a gay bar in Chicago. Subsequent to their consensual encounter, Bailey asphyxiated Rosenbaum, stabbed him, and cut off one of his nipples.

In this case, an accidental death resulting from a consensual sexual encounter could not be argued because the victim was sexually mutilated (his nipple was cut off postmortem) (Figures 9.1 and 9.2). However, the author prepared a report of findings detailing a lack of planning and a lack of precaution. The following was excerpted from Turvey (1999):

Offense Planning

It is my opinion that there is an overall absence of criminal planning evident in this case. The basis for my opinion on this issue resides in the consideration of the following facts:

1. The defendant brought a shoulder bag with him to Chicago. This bag contained music CDs, medicine, cigarettes, folding pocketknives, and some "personal items." This is consistent with items packed in a bag for short duration or "overnight" travel purposes.
2. Available materials were primarily associated with the commission of the offense, including a belt and a coat hanger. The pocketknives used by the defendant came from his "overnight" bag.
3. The defendant has a known history of "cruising" bars, and having consensual sexual encounters with other males in that context.
4. There is no physical evidence of fantasy materials related to the defendant that could be considered evidence of prior sexual fantasies involving sexual bondage or sexual asphyxia.
5. There is an overall absence of precautionary acts evident in this case.

Precautionary Acts

Precautionary acts are those acts that are meant to hamper or defeat investigative or forensic efforts. It is my opinion that there is an overall absence of precautionary acts evident in this case, which is related conceptually to an overall lack of planning. The basis for my opinion on this issue resides in the consideration of the following facts:

1. The defendant made no attempt to conceal his identity when he registered for the motel room. He allowed himself to be seen by Eden Motel clerk Don Brewer, and provided Mr. Brewer with a photocopy of his driver's license (DL). This provided for the identification and location of the defendant.
2. The body of the victim was left in the scene, where it was certain to be found by housekeeping at the next cleaning. This provided for the discovery of the crime.
3. The belt ligature was left in place on the victim at the scene. This provided for linkage of the belt to the commission of the crime.
4. There is no evidence that attempts were made to obscure the identity of the victim by obscuring or removing identifying body parts. This facilitated the identification of the victim.
5. There is no evidence that attempts were made to clean up the blood and pattern evidence at the primary crime scene, the motel room. This includes the blood pools, splatters, and drag marks. This also includes bloody footwear patterns in the bathroom, on the carpet in the bed area, and on the concrete outside the door. This provided for the discovery of the crime.
6. There is no evidence that attempts were made to clean up or clean out the vehicle used by the defendant in association with the crime. This provided for further association of the defendant with the crime.
7. The defendant went to his home. He did not flee his residence or go "on the run" subsequent to the crime. Given the fact that he had provided his DL information to the motel, this further provided for law enforcement's ability to locate the defendant in association with the crime.
8. The defendant removed items from the scene that he took home with him, which were located without any difficulty by law enforcement. This included a broken piece from the belt found around the victim's neck, a motel key for room #19, and a bloody rag. This provided for further association of the defendant with the crime.
9. There is no evidence that attempts were made to clean, permanently discard or destroy items of evidence that could be associated with the crime, including the knives, a pair of

bloodstained boots, and other items of clothing belonging to the defendant. This provided for further association of the defendant with the crime.

Initially, police considered Patrick Bailey a potential serial killer because of the aberrant nature of the crime scene behavior, but this was ruled out by a thorough investigation. The context of the death scene allowed attorneys to argue that the murder was not premeditated and may have, in fact, resulted from some form of mental derangement. Patrick Bailey was convicted of murder, spared the death penalty, and sentenced to 60 years in prison.

SUMMARY

Sexual asphyxia can be practiced both as an autoerotic activity and as a consensual sadomasochistic act between two or more people. When consensual sexual asphyxia results in death, the death is unintended. Conversely, acts of nonconsensual sexual asphyxia would be for the needs of the person restricting the other person's oxygen source and are best described as an intentional criminal act. These can be difficult to discriminate in some circumstances, as the surviving participant may not be eager to trust the police with understanding the difference between a consensual/accidental sexual asphyxia and an intentional homicide. Moreover, drug or alcohol use/abuse may add another layer of confusion.

Until fairly recently, the literature reflected the belief that autoerotic asphyxia in particular was an adolescent male activity and that female devotees of the practice were either extremely rare or nonexistent. However, these misconceptions have been slowly eroded. Currently, there is no typical or predominant profile of someone who engages in any kind of sexual asphyxia. It is known to be practiced by both sexes and to have been practiced in many cultures for hundreds of years.

Interpretation of autoerotic asphyxia in death scenes has been particularly problematic in the absence of information and training available to law enforcement and other death scene investigators. Scenes and autopsy findings vary, but certain findings can be expected. At a minimum, to form an opinion that a death is due to autoerotic asphyxia, the investigator would need to find evidence of asphyxia and that the activity was repetitive and likely pursued for sexual stimulation. Correct interpretations regarding sexual asphyxia–related deaths rely heavily on thorough crime scene investigation, deliberate crime reconstruction, and thorough victimology.

Questions

1. True or False: Evidence of sexual asphyxia is in itself evidence of a crime.
2. List three things to look for at a death scene where autoerotic asphyxia is suspected.
3. Explain how participation in sexual asphyxia might be arousing to a masochist.
4. What is the relationship between sexual asphyxia and masturbation?
5. Why are some people unable or unwilling to be honest about the nature and extent of their sexual behavior, even when participating in anonymous scientific studies?

REFERENCES

Achampong, F., 1987. Death from Autoerotic Asphyxiation and the Double Indemnity Clause in Life Insurance Policies: The Latest Round in Accidental Death Litigation. Akron Law Review 21, 191–199.

Adelson, L., 1974. The Pathology of Homicide. Charles C Thomas, Springfield, IL.

American Psychiatric Association (APA), 2000. Diagnostic and Statistical Manual of Mental Disorders, fourth ed, American Psychiatric Association, Washington, DC.

Balasonne, M., Hightower, E., 2007. A Deadly Game. The Modesto Bee May 26, p. A1.

Beckett, S., 1954. Waiting for Godot. Grove Press, New York, NY.

Behrendt, N., Modvig, J., 1995. The Legal Paraphiliac Syndrome. Accidental Autoerotic Deaths in Denmark 1933–1990. American Journal of Forensic Medical Pathology 16 (3), 232–237.

Blanchard, R., Hucker, S., 1991. Age, Transvestism, Bondage and Concurrent Paraphilic Activities in 117 Fatal Cases of Autoerotic Asphyxia. British Journal of Psychiatry 159, 371 357.

Brokenshire, B., Cairns, F., Koelmyer, T., Smeeton, W., 1984. Deaths from Electricity. New Zealand Medical Journal 97, 139–142.

Burgess, A., Hazelwood, R., 1983. Autoerotic Asphyxial Deaths and Social Network Response. American Journal of Orthopsychiatry 53 (1), 166–170.

Byard, R., Botterill, P., 1998. Autoerotic Asphyxial Death—Accident or Suicide? American Journal of Forensic Medical Pathology 19 (4), 377–380.

Byard, R., Bramwell, N., 1988. Autoerotic Death in Females: An Underdiagnosed Syndrome? American Journal of Forensic Medical Pathology 9 (3), 252–254.

Byard, R., Eitzen, D., James, R., 2000. Unusual Fatal Mechanisms in Nonasphyxial Autoerotic Death. American Journal of Forensic Medical Pathology 21 (1), 65–68.

Byard, R., Hucker, S., Hazelwood, R., 1990. A Comparison of Typical Death Scene Features in Cases of Fatal Male and Female Autoerotic Asphyxia with a Review of the Literature. Forensic Science International 48, 113–121.

Byard, R.W., Hucker, S.J., Hazelwood, R.R., 1993. Fatal and Near-Fatal Autoerotic Asphyxia Episodes in Women. American Journal of Forensic Pathology 14 (1), 70–73.

Chiem, P., Wilson, T., 1998. City Slaying Suspect under New Scrutiny: Police Seek Possible Links to Other Deaths. Chicago Tribune April 28, 3.

Danto, B., 1980. A Case of Female Autoerotic Death. American Journal of Forensic Medical Pathology 1 (2), 117–121.

DeBoisemont, A., 1856. Du Suicide et de la Folie Suicide. Germer Baillere, Paris as cited in Uva (1995).

De Sade, M., 1965. Justine, Philosophy in the Bedroom, and Other Writings. Grove Press, New York, NY.

Dietz, P., 1979. Kotzwarraism: Sexual Induction of Cerebral Hypoxia, paper presented at the American Academy of Psychiatry and the Law, annual meeting, Baltimore Maryland, November, as cited in Hazelwood, R., Burgess, A., Groth, A., 1981. Death during Dangerous Autoerotic Practice. Social Science and Medicine 15, 129–133.

Ely, S., Hirsch, C., 2000. Asphyxial Deaths and Petechiae: A Review. Journal of Forensic Science 45 (6), 1274–1277.

Erman, S., 2005. Word Games: Raising and Resolving the Shortcomings in Accident Insurance Doctrine That Autoerotic-Asphyxiation Cases Reveal. Michigan Law Review 103 (8), 2172–2208.

Francoeur, R., 1995. The Complete Dictionary of Sexology. Continuum Publishing Co. New York, NY.

Frazer, M., Rosenberg, S., 1983. A Case of Suicidal Ligature Strangulation. American Journal of Forensic Medical Pathology 4 (4), 351–354.

Friedrich, W., Gerber, P., 1994. Autoerotic Asphyxia: The Development of a Paraphilia. American Academy of Child and Adolescent Psychiatry 33 (7), 970–974.

Gosink, P.D., Jumbelic, M.I., 2000. Autoerotic Asphyxiation in a Female. American Journal of Forensic Medical Pathology 21 (2), 114–118.

Hazelwood, R., Dietz, P., 1983. Autoerotic Fatalities. DC Heath (Lexington Books), Lexington, MA.

Holmes, R., 1991. Sex Crimes. Sage Publications, London, England.

Ikeda, N., Harada, A., Umetsu, K., Suzuki, T., 1988. A Case of Fatal Suffocation during Autoerotic Practice. Medicine, Science and Law 28, 131–134.

Imami, R., Kemal, M., 1988. Vacuum Cleaner Use in Autoerotic Death. American Journal of Forensic Medical Pathology 9 (3), 246–248.

Jobes, D., Berman, A., Josselson, A., 1986. The Impact of Psychological Autopsies on Medical Examiner's Determination of Manner of Death. Journal of Forensic Science 31 (1), 177–189.

Leadbetter, S., 1988. Dental Anesthetic Death. American Journal of Forensic Medical Pathology 9 (1), 60–63.

Litman, R., Swearington, C., 1972. Bondage and Suicide. Archives of General Psychiatry 27, 80–85.

McLennan, B., Sekula-Perlman, A., Lippstone, M., Callery, R., 1998. Propane Associated Autoerotic Fatalities. American Journal of Forensic Medical Pathology 19 (4), 381–386.

Melville, H., 1900. Billy Budd. Northwestern University Press, Evanston, IL.

Miller, E., Milbrath, S., 1983. Medical-Legal Ramifications of Autoerotic Asphyxial Death. Bulletin of the American Academy of Psychiatry and Law 11 (1), 57–68.

Minyard, F., 1985. Wrapped to Death. American Journal of Forensic Medical Pathology 6 (2), 151–152.

Money, J., Jobaris, R., Furth, G., 1977. Amepotemnophilia: Two Cases of Self-Demand Amputation as a Paraphilia. Journal of Sex Research 13 (2), 115–125.

Money, J., Wainwright, G., Hingsburger, D., 1991. The Breathless Orgasm: A Lovemap Biography of Asphyxiophilia. Prometheus Books, Buffalo, NY.

O'Halloran, R., Dietz, P., 1993. Autoerotic Fatalities with Power Hydraulics. Journal of Forensic Science 38 (2), 359–364.

O'Halloran, R., Lovell, F., 1988. Autoerotic Asphyxial Death following Television Broadcast. Journal of Forensic Science 33 (6), 1491–1492.

Pa, M., 2001. Beyond the Pleasure Principle: The Criminalization of Consensual Sadomasochistic Sex. Texas Journal of Women and the Law 11, 51–92.

Resnik, H., 1972. Eroticized Repetitive Hangings: A Form of Self-Destructive Behavior. American Journal of Psychotherapy 26, 4–21.

Rosenblum, S., Faber, M.M., 1979. The Adolescent Sexual Asphyxia Syndrome. Journal of American Academy of Child Psychiatry 17, 546–558.

Sheehan, W., Garfinkel, B., 1987. Case Study: Adolescent Auroerotic Deaths. Journal of the Academy of Child and Adolescent Psychiatry 27 (3), 367–370.

Spitz, W., Fisher B., 1993. Medicolegal Investigation of Death, third edition. Charles C Thomas, Springfield, IL.

Sullivan, J., 2005. Videotapes Show Bestiality, Enumclaw Police Say. Seattle Times July 16.

Tan, C., Chao, T., 1983. A Case of Fatal Electrocution during an Unusual Autoerotic Practice. Medicine, Science and Law 23 (2), 92–95.

Texas v. Patrick Anthony Russo, 2007. Court of Appeals of Texas, Austin No. 03-04-00344-CR, June 7.

Turvey, B., 1999. Crime Scene Analysis. Illinois v. Patrick G. Bailey, File No. 98-1017, December 5.

Turvey, B., 2000. Autoerotic Death. In: Knupfer, G., Saukko, P., Seigal, J. (Eds.), Encyclopedia of Forensic Science. Academic Press, London, England, pp. 290–295.

Uva, J., 1995. Review: Autoerotic Asphyxiation in the United States. Journal of Forensic Science 40 (4), 574–581.

Wesselius, C., 1983. A Male with Autoerotic Asphyxia Syndrome. American Journal of Forensic Medical Pathology 4 (4), 341–345.

CHAPTER 10

False Reports

Brent E. Turvey and Michael McGrath

Not only must the self-made victim be exposed, but innocent people who may be suspected must be protected.

—Hans Gross, *Criminal Investigation* (1924, p.14)

CONTENTS

KEY TERMS

False report (or false
allegation)

False reporter

False reporting

False swearing

Mandated reporter

Obstruction of justice

Perjury

Everyone lies at some point in life, either to protect himself or to protect others. In some instances, these untruths may be referred to as "white lies"—when they are harmless, perhaps beneficial to those around us, and contribute to the greater good. Under other circumstances, a lie may be an utter betrayal of personal or professional commitments, intended to conceal an abuse of power, an inappropriate consideration or relationship, or a sexual infidelity. Lying is not, by itself, a crime, unless it occurs under a certain set of circumstances prohibited by law.

Almost without exception, it is a crime to lie to a police officer or any other *mandated reporter*[1] with respect to involvement in, or the occurrence of, criminal activity. Many criminal statutes address this kind of lies, and they may be counted as misdemeanors or felony violations. They include

- *Obstruction of justice:* Obstructing, delaying, or preventing the communication of information relating to a violation of any criminal statute by any person to a criminal investigator by any means (e.g., bribery, intimidation, and false statements).
- *False swearing:* A false statement, oral or written, made under oath or penalty of perjury.
- *Perjury:* A lie communicated under oath or penalty of perjury about a material fact in a criminal matter. A particular kind of false swearing.
- *False reporting:* The false report, conveyance, or circulation of an alleged or impending criminal offense.

As is evident from the legal terminology, in some jurisdictions, false reports are a crime even when they are reported indirectly to authorities by a third party—such as a friend, spouse, employer, counselor, or medical professional.

For the purposes of this work, a *false report,* or *false allegation,* refers to any untruthful statement, accusation or complaint to authorities asserting that a crime did or will occur. A *false reporter* is one who makes false allegations or reports (Turvey and McGrath, 2009). Criminal profilers have a professional responsibility to understand the phenomenon of false reporting because those requesting their services may not, and because it is a possibility that must be considered in every case where there is a complaining witness. People lie, and not all pertinent lies are revealed in time to prevent a criminal investigation or even an arrest.

Police agencies without sufficient experience, professional training, or good leadership may be unaware that false reporting, or making false allegations, is itself a crime. This is true even if the false reporter is in law enforcement; law-enforcement personnel do not have special immunity from the law. Even if police agencies are aware that false reports are a crime, pressure from colleagues, supervisors, community leaders, or even victim's advocates may serve as a political disincentive to pursue false reporters. Consequently, many

---

[1] A mandated reporter is *any* professional who is bound by law to report evidence of crime, abuse, or neglect. This includes police officers, doctors, nurses, teachers, social workers, mental health professionals, and many others (Turvey, 2009).

false reporters are not investigated, let alone charged and arrested. The criminal profiler may at some time be confronted with such a case, and with an investigator or agency that lacks the expertise to recognize it—or the leadership and integrity to be honest about it.

The police have a legal obligation to identify false allegations, to arrest those responsible for initiating them, and to assist with their conviction. False reports drain valuable departmental resources, to say nothing of potentially leading to wrongful arrests and convictions. Given that many false reporters are repeat offenders, a firm zero tolerance policy and judicious enforcement of the law can save time and money by preventing future false reports from the emboldened. Proper enforcement of the law may also act as a powerful deterrent to others considering false reporting when the consequences for making false allegations are publicized. A convicted false reporter may be fined, may be required to perform community service, and may even serve jail time. When it is warranted, they may also be remanded for mental health evaluation and treatment.

HISTORICAL CONTEXT

False reports of crime to authorities are nothing new. They have been a part of documented history for thousands of years (Figure 10.1).

Consider the biblical example of Joseph and Potiphar's wife, memorialized in Guido Reni's oil on canvas rendering from about 1631 C.E. According to Genesis 39:7–20, Joseph, a Hebrew slave, had repeatedly rebuffed the sexual advances of his master's wife. She was, however, persistent and not to be denied. On one occasion, she was able to get hold of Joseph's garment as he tried to leave the house, and he ran out without it. Angered by Joseph's refusals, she placed his clothing in her bedroom, to make it appear as though he had raped her. She then reported Joseph's "crime" to the men of her household, who in turn informed her husband, Potiphar (also a captain of Pharaoh's guard). Needless to say, Joseph went to prison for a crime that he did not commit, because Potiphar did not doubt his wife.

This example, although ancient and unsubstantiated, is representative of a particular source of false allegations still encountered in the modern age: the spurned lover. It is significant that a text written thousands of years ago includes such an example, probably as a cautionary tale.

From the Middle Ages to modern times, false accusations have been used to serve personal, social, political, and religious agendas. They have been key in the historical persecutions of Jews that came to be referred to as "blood libel" (Dundes, 1991; see Chapter 1). Medieval Inquisitions were also fueled by false accusations of heresy and witchcraft (again, see Chapter 1). In the nineteenth century, the Austrian jurist Dr. Hans Gross provided one of the earliest and arguably most informed professional discussions of false allegations (1924, pp. 13–14). Written for the investigator, his coverage includes such topics as the various motivations for filing false reports, the occurrence of self-injury, and the related responsibilities of the investigating officer. This indicates that the problem of false reporting was by no means foreign to his century, or to his courtroom. Twentieth-century "witch hunts" continue to involve false reports of crime, including repressed memory fiascos and sex abuse trials like the Wenatchee sex ring trials (Barber and Lange, 2001) and the McMartin preschool debacle (McHugh, 2008).

FIGURE 10.1
Guido Reni's "Joseph and Potiphar's Wife," 1631.

HIGH-PROFILE CASES

There have been many high-profile cases involving false reports of crime, ranging from simple deceptions to staged evidence and self-injury. This is due to the willingness of false reporters to lie and to refuse to back down even when the facts are against them. Such cases are fanned by the eagerness of both the media and the public to get behind a story with the right kind of "victim," involving a crime that hits all of the right racial or emotional notes. Consider the following representative list, taken from many cases over the years.

- In 1994, Susan Smith reported that a black male had abducted her two young sons during a carjacking (Terry, 1994). She later admitted to driving her car into a lake, with the two boys seat-belted in, drowning them. Her apparent motive was to rid herself of child-rearing responsibility in order to pursue a romantic interest. She was charged with multiple counts of murder.

- In March 2004, Audrey Seiler, a 20-year-old sophomore at the University of Wisconsin, disappeared from her apartment. She was found four days later lying in a marsh. She claimed a man had abducted her at knifepoint. Later she was forced to admit staging the whole thing, blaming it on depression brought on by poor grades and a recent break-up with her boyfriend (Parmar, 2004). She was charged with obstructing an investigation.

- Jennifer Wilbanks, a 32-year-old medical assistant (later nicknamed the "runaway bride") disappeared while out jogging on April 26, 2005, four days before her 600-guest wedding. She was declared missing and a nationwide media frenzy ensued, during which some in the psychic community declared her dead or in danger. A police investigation revealed that she was overwhelmed by her upcoming wedding and got "cold feet." She bought a bus ticket, traveled to Las Vegas and then to Albuquerque, and then called the police—falsely reporting that she had been abducted. Later, after questioning, she admitted she had run away on her own. She was charged with making a false report, was fined, and was given community service.

- Crystal Gail Mangum accused members of the Duke University lacrosse team of dragging her into a bathroom, raping her, and shouting racial slurs during an off-campus party in March of 2006. However, none of this came to light until after she was arrested the same night as her alleged rape for public intoxication. Duke University lacrosse team players Reade Seligmann, David Evans, and Collin Finnerty were charged with first-degree kidnapping and first-degree sexual offense. The case was ultimately dismissed as false, with the overzealous prosecutor in charge, Mike NiFong, disbarred and convicted of criminal contempt of court. The false allegations made national news and increased racial tensions. The accuser was mentally unstable and her motives included avoiding criminal charges, profit, and revenge.

- In 2008, Ashley Todd, a 20-year-old college student from College Station, Texas, was a supporter of, and volunteer for, presidential candidate John McCain. In a story that made national headlines, she reported that a tall black man who was politically motivated had attacked her with a knife at an ATM. Ms. Todd claimed her assailant robbed her, then pinned her to the ground and carved the latter "B" onto her face—an alleged reference to presidential candidate Barack Obama. Later, she confessed to making the whole thing up and to carving the letter on her own face—backward—but she did not know her motives. She was charged with filing a false report and remanded for a mental health evaluation.

- In late 2010, Bethany Storro, 28, a deli clerk in Vancouver, Washington, reported to police that she had been the victim of an unprovoked acid attack by a young black woman (Figure 10.2). The story gained national media attention and was widely believed by the public despite many inconsistencies—such as Storro's statement that wearing sunglasses saved her eyes. As reported in Potter and Friedman (2010),

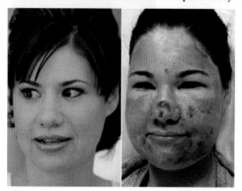

FIGURE 10.2

Bethany Storro, before and after the "acid attack" which she eventually confessed to staging.

Storro had claimed she was attacked outside a coffee shop on Aug. 30. "A woman approached her and said, 'Hey pretty girl,' and she turned around and she asked if she wanted something to drink, and my daughter said, 'No,'" Storro's mother, Nancy Neuwelt, told reporters at the time. She said the woman then threw a cup of liquid in Storro's face.

Storro appeared on "Good Morning America," her head covered in gauze. "It was like it almost didn't hurt right away because of the panic, you know, like, what just happened, and you're so focused on that, and then once I let it soak in I could start to feel it burning through my flesh," she said from her hospital bed. She said that by sheer luck, she had bought a pair of sunglasses just minutes before, which protected her eyes.

Attention grew. Storro was invited to be a guest on Oprah Winfrey's show, but then news outlets began to report suggestions that police suspected the attack was faked. On Tuesday the Oprah appearance was canceled.

- Storro subsequently confessed to the hoax, stating to police that she had smeared drain cleaner on her face in a suicide attempt. She was charged with theft related to the almost $30,000.00 in donations that she procured from the public under false pretenses after appearing on television. She is, as of this writing, under psychiatric care and awaiting trial.

- During 2010, it was revealed that at least three individuals in Canada have faked cancer in order to hold fundraisers and defraud the public by soliciting donations.[2] The cases were widely covered by the Canadian media. *Christopher Gordon*, 39, of Toronto, falsely claimed to friends and family that he had a brain tumor, held a fundraiser, and received more than $3000.00. *Jessica Ann Leeder*, 21, of Timmins, pretended to have stomach and lung cancer and received more than $5000.00 in donations from the community. *Ashley Anne Kirilow*, 23, of Burlington, confessed to faking cancer, running a phony charity, and collecting thousands of dollars in donations from hundreds of people (Figure 10.3). According to Kennedy (2010): "She shaved her head and eyebrows, plucked her eyelashes and starved herself to look like a chemotherapy patient. She told anyone she met she had been disowned by drug-addicted parents, or that they were dead." Her parents are alive but divorced.

FIGURE 10.3

Ashley Anne Kirilow, a Canadian woman who faked cancer and defrauded hundreds out of charitable donations in the thousands of dollars, shaved her head, plucked her eyebrows, and starved herself to mimic the effects of chemotherapy. She also had the words "Won't Quit" tattooed across both of her knuckles.

FREQUENCY OF CASES

The precise number of falsely reported crimes is unknown, because statistics are not regularly collected nor are they broadcast outside of law enforcement. Moreover, because investigating agencies may not correctly identify cases as false reports (for the reasons previously stated), any reported figures are going to be unreliably low.

---

[2] Such cases are quite common in the United States and perhaps this is why they are not as widely reported in the media.

There has been some research specific to the area of falsely reported rapes, resulting in published figures ranging from 8% to 41%:[3]

1. MacDonald (1973) provided false report rates for 1968: they were 18% nationwide and 25% in Denver, Colorado.
2. Greenfeld (1997), quoting United States Bureau of Justice Statistics, provided a nationwide false report rate of 8% in 1995 and 15% in 1997.
3. Brown et al. (1997) conducted research to address the issue of genital injury in female sexual assault victims presenting to the San Louis Obispo General Hospital emergency room in California between 1985 and 1993. Their study revealed a false report rate of just over 13%, involving women who ultimately removed themselves from the research being conducted.
4. Kanin (1994), in his study of an unnamed Midwestern city in the United States revealed a 41% false report rate
5. Kennedy and Witkowski (2000), in their attempt to replicate the Kanin study in a suburb of Detroit, found a false report rate of 32% between 1988 and 1997.
6. In April of 2002, Her Majesty's Crown Prosecution Service Inspectorate and Her Majesty's Inspectorate of Constabulary published "A Report on the Joint Inspection into the Investigation and Prosecution of Cases involving Allegations of Rape." The report revealed that, out of 1,379 cases studied, 11.8% were false reports.
7. Lea et al. (2003) gathered data in a constabulary in the southwest of England from 1996 to 2000. They revealed an 11% false report rate.
8. Jordan (2004) studied police rape and sexual assault files in New Zealand. The study revealed a false report rate of 41%.

These numbers, while varying by location and year, combine to suggest that false reports of rape are not rare, but common. (Certainly it may be stated that false reports are not uncommon for every other type of crime.)

The regular occurrence of false reports and their drain of resources away from legitimate victims of crime are not news to professional law-enforcement agencies. Many no longer tolerate false reporters of any kind and have started to respond. The University of Southern California Department of Public Safety (campus police) has recently warned students that it will call upon the LAPD to prosecute false reporters (Martinez, 2010). A campus police spokesman stated that one pattern that has emerged is students falsely reporting a crime, such as a robbery, to elicit sympathy from parents when grades are poor. Police in Clarke County, Georgia, are also fed up with the phenomenon: "This is becoming an epidemic and we're taking a stance" (Johnson, 2010). Examples of false reports from Clarke County include a female UGA law student reported a robbery and beating to garner sympathy during her divorce; a male UGA student reported a beating and robbery to obtain free medical care after injuring himself while intoxicated; a soldier on leave reported a robbery at knifepoint because he had spent too much money and did not want his wife to know. An Athens-Clarke police spokesman noted accurately that false reports of crime not only waste taxpayer money and police time, but also harm the community by inflating crime rates and perceptions of safety.

---

[3] Dunleavy (1999), in an editorial in the New York *Post* on the now infamous Oliver Jovanovic false report case, quoted then district attorney Linda Fairstein, the sex crimes DA, from an interview in *Penthouse* magazine, where she stated, "There are about 4,000 reports of rape each year in Manhattan, of these half of them didn't happen." In a 2000 article, it was stated that out of 2,000 uninvestigated cases in Philadelphia, from 1995 to 1997, investigators determined that "600 were false reports or allegations that did not amount to crimes" (Fazlollah and McCoy, 2000).

While precise statistics are not available regarding the many different kinds of false reports that can occur, and the frequency of false claims may vary by agency and region, it reasonable to agree that false reports are common enough to have become a very real problem in many jurisdictions. Serious study of the phenomenon is required, as are corresponding educational and training efforts within law enforcement.

With respect to behavioral evidence analysis, precise statistics regarding the frequency of false reporting have no value when examining the facts of a particular case. The criminal profiler must simply acknowledge that false reports can occur and that they should be considered as a possibility in every case. The question for the criminal profiler is whether the case at hand is a false report, and whether and how that possibility can be eliminated.

MOTIVATIONS

The specific motives often attributable to false reporters discussed below may be further illuminated with the typology presented in Chapter 13. As with any list of potential motives for human behavior, there is no bright yellow line between them. Human behavior is multi-determined, and therefore multiple motives may apply to the actions of a single false reporter, and this is true for false reporters of all different types of crimes. The following discussion of motives is not intended to be exhaustive.

Profit

A profit motive involves financial or material gain (see Chapter 13). In some cases, the false reporting of crimes is used to leverage a lawsuit against an apartment building or a hotel and its owner for negligent security. False allegations of a sexual assault or burglary may also be filed to get better accommodations within an apartment building or a housing complex. Under some rental/lease agreements, such a move is automatic if victimization of a certain type is suffered. Along the same lines, many false reporters present to hospitals and clinics with claims of rape, injury, or assault in order to obtain drugs (often called pill-seeking behavior) or treatment related to unwanted pregnancy, AIDS, or sexually transmitted infections. This motive also applies in insurance fraud cases where property is alleged to have been stolen, damaged, or destroyed in a crime that the property owner staged or intentionally initiated.

Wherever there is a financial or material gain for being victimized, a percentage of reports will be frauds.

Anger and Revenge

Anger and revenge involve instrumental or expressive retaliation for real or perceived wrongs. These motives may reflect a prior relationship with the accused. Similarly, anger and revenge can motivate accusations of spousal abuse in acrimonious divorces cases and accusations of child physical or sexual abuse and neglect in child-custody battles. The same motives are manifest in accusations of inappropriate conduct or sexual assault in schools and other employment settings, where students or employees retaliate against instructors, supervisors, or co-workers in response to poor evaluations, social rejection, or spurned sexual advances.

Crime Concealment

Some false allegations are meant to hide evidence of actual criminal activity, or at least to misdirect law enforcement investigators in their efforts. For instance, it is not uncommon for victims of domestic violence to seek hospital care for their injuries but to report being the victim of a stranger crime in order to protect an intimate partner or household member. In extreme cases, the false reporter may stage an intimate or domestic homicide to look like a stranger burglary gone wrong or a kidnapping.

Another form of crime concealment involves a preemptive allegation or counter-allegation when a criminal investigation or criminal charges seem imminent. In such cases, the false reporter hopes that pending criminal investigations, accusations, or arrests will be delayed or forgotten when they have become the victim. In other cases, crimes are reported by an offender in order to physically move agency resources to something more serious.

Concealment of Illicit Activities

Some individuals report being the victim of a crime in order to conceal forbidden activities, such as improper sexual activity or an extramarital affair that involved unexplainable absences, sexually transmitted disease, or a pregnancy. This motive can also apply to those who have abstained from the use of drugs or alcohol for some period of time and then suddenly relapse. In an attempt to invent an excuse for their behavior, they will make a false report of a crime. They may claim that someone else forced them to ingest drugs or alcohol against their will. They may also claim that they returned to using drugs or alcohol to deal with the pain of being victimized.

Mitigation of Responsibility

This motive involves a desire to explain or to deflect scrutiny from personal failings and obvious irresponsibility. Perhaps the most common form of false reporting, it is made to avoid what many would regard as minor consequences. In extreme or pathological cases, this type of false report may also indicate a mental defect of some kind. This motive applies to individuals who stay out past family or legally imposed curfews, as well as to students with late homework assignments, bad grades, or chronic tardiness or absenteeism. In adults, it applies to employees who are late to or absent from work or who have failed to complete major projects, to meet deadlines, or to meet other obligations and subsequently may face sanctions. Such false reports are not routinely made directly to the police, but through a third party (e.g., parent, counselor, friend, or intimate partner), and can be the beginning of a snowball effect that results in a wrongful arrest or even conviction.

Mental Defect—A Contributing Motivational Factor

Some false reporters suffer from personal and emotional problems, or chemical imbalances, that manifest as mental health issues. Included are those who are said to be "crying out for help" as well as those with a specific personality disorder or mental illness. As described in Rumney (2006, p. 130), "there may be non-malicious allegations from people with particular medical conditions who genuinely believe they are victims of rape or other sexual offenses, but who are mistaken, as opposed to being malicious." This is true of non-sexual false reports as well.

False reports related to mental defect can also include those who want attention from friends, family, intimate partners, or the media. When attention-seeking behavior manifests as a false report of a crime, it suggests deep personal and emotional turmoil and may be the result a full-blown mental disorder.

TYPES OF FALSE REPORTS

The authors have found that many professionals and students are unaware of the breadth and scope of false reporting. They simply do not know how common it is, and they are unable to conceive its magnitude. Suffice it to say that any crime can be falsely reported when sufficient motivation is present. The following is a list of examples culled from hundreds of false allegations reported in the United States during November 2010.

False Report of Murder

In Richmond, Indiana, 38-year-old Angela Boyd falsely reported that her 15-year-old daughter had been raped and murdered by her biological father in Iowa. She arranged a funeral service at the New Life Church of Nazarene, bringing an urn that allegedly contained her daughter's ashes and a box labeled "Donations to the Autistic Society in Memory of Kaitlin" for attendees to fill. She also gave an emotional statement about her daughter's life during the service that was so compelling it brought many in attendees to tears. When Boyd's brother took the podium at the end of the service to reveal that "Kaitlin" was alive and living elsewhere in a home for disabled children, Boyd fled the church, crying (Mijares, 2010).

False Report of Kidnapping

Cailey L. Summers, 18, of Cedar Rapids, Iowa, faked her own kidnapping to get the attention of her boyfriend. As reported in Gravelle (2010),

> Summers sent several text messages to her boyfriend that she'd been kidnapped from the Casey's General Store, 380 33rd Ave. SW, about 11:30 p.m. The boyfriend called police, and when officers went to the store, she pulled through the lot riding in a car. The car's driver returned to the store, where officers stopped the vehicle and questioned Summers.

Summers admitted sending to the texts and also calling police to report the fake kidnapping. She was charged with making a false report.

Amada Gonzalez-Herrera, 27, of Beaverton, Oregon, reported to police that she had been kidnapped and raped. As reported in Staff (2010),

> She previously claimed that a man got in her car while she was at a stop sign and subsequently raped and robbed her.

> Detectives have been diligently working on the case since Mrs. Gonzalez-Herrera reported the alleged crime.

> Over the last two days they have been gathering evidence that was slowly pointing to a false claim by Mrs. Gonzalez-Herrera. The victim's car was seized and taken to the Sheriff's Office for processing. Members of the Forensics Sciences Section searched that car and found evidence that the rape had not occurred in the car as the victim had claimed. She also claimed that the suspect forced her to take out $300 from an ATM, [but] they found the stolen money in the glove box.

Once confronted with the contradicting evidence, Mrs. Gonzalez-Herrera admitted that she may have imagined the events and it was all in her head. Mrs. Gonzalez-Herrera has voluntarily agreed to a mental evaluation and is currently at an area hospital.

As is common in Oregon, she was not arrested for making a false report despite unequivocal legal statutes criminalizing such behavior, and no charges have been filed as of this writing.

False Report of Rape and Sexual Assault

Desiree Freeman, a 22-year-old Bethlehem, Pennsylvania, woman, has been accused of lying to police about being raped when she was actually engaging in prostitution. According to the police report, she (Buck, 2010)

> ...initially told police that she was raped on Oct. 17 by two men behind Lopes Seafood and Mini Market in the 800 block of East Fourth Street, according to the complaint. During a second interview with police on Oct. 29, Freeman admitted to making up the story, the complaint says. The complaint says Freeman was upset that she did not get paid for the encounter and decided to tell police the men raped her, records say. Freeman will be charged by summons with making a false report to police.

Police report that she had been a prostitute for about one year and was using the money to buy food.

False Report of Child Abuse and Neglect

Amanda Irene Morgan, 22, of Clinton Township, Michigan, falsely reported that her husband had abandoned their 1-year-old daughter in their family minivan outside a mobile home park. She reported that her husband had dropped her off at work, and that she had been notified by a friend of the van's location. She further claimed that she had contacted relatives to investigate and to retrieve the child from the minivan on her behalf. Initially, charges had been filed against the husband for child abuse. However, an actual investigation revealed that she had fabricated the elaborate story because of marital problems. The child was with a babysitter and had at no point been left alone. Mrs. Morgan was charged with false report of a felony, and faces up to four years in prison if convicted (Ferretti, 2010).

False Report of Hate Crimes

Alray Nelson, an openly homosexual Native American, was serving as student body president of Fort Lewis College in Durango, Colorado. In November of 2010, he was arrested for falsely reporting anti-gay hate crimes. As reported in Meloy (2010),

> Alray Nelson stepped down from his post as student body president just prior to being placed under arrest on suspicion of filing false reports, local newspaper the Durango *Herald* reported on Nov. 17.

> Alray had made several claims, including that he had received threatening e-mails and notes, and that he had been drugged. "During the course of our investigation, we determined that these incidents did not occur, and there is evidence to believe that Alray filed false reports with multiple law-enforcement agencies," said Durango PD Det. Alex Hutchison.

This type of false report is not uncommon on college and university campuses, or among minority groups seeking personal, social, or political attention for their issues. This is not to say that all such complaints are false, because hate crimes are a very real problem. However, the possibility of false reporting must not be ignored simply because a minority group is involved.

False Report of Robbery

In Memphis, Tennessee, three female co-workers planned and staged a robbery of their own pizza restaurant. As reported in McKenzie (2010),

> For a manager and two employees of a Domino's Pizza outlet, things fell apart after the manager was robbed of store receipts she took to deposit about 2 a.m. Saturday at a First Tennessee Bank at 2015 East Brooks in Whitehaven, according to police and a court affidavit.
>
> Another Domino's employee called police after seeing two women, one armed with a .22-caliber handgun, rob the manager. The robbers fled, but officers caught them after a brief foot chase. The manager, Daibrei Nunley, 24, of Memphis, admitted to planning the robbery and falsely claiming that she was held up, according to the affidavit.
>
> Her two co-workers, Marcia Milam, 21, and Desiree Hines, 21, both of Memphis, also confessed.
>
> Police charged Nunley with theft and filing a false report, Hines with theft and unlawful possession of a weapon, and Milam with theft.

"Inside" employee theft/fraud cases are common to many businesses, although generally they are not violent; this is the reason that many security cameras point at employees as well as customers.

False Reports for Insurance Fraud

False reports of crimes to insurance companies are common and costly. In the United Kingdom, one survey found that over half of all stolen goods crimes were false reports. As reported in Coombs (2010),

> Stories include a man who claimed he was robbed in Windsor Street, Uxbridge, and his passport taken. He went as far as issuing a detailed description of the suspect.
>
> But when his lies began to unravel he confessed that he had lost his passport and did not want to pay for a new one, and was just after a crime reference number.
>
> Another tall tale involved a girl in Elm Avenue, Ruislip, who told police she was attacked in an alley by a man who stole her Apple iPhone.
>
> Probing by police led her to admit she had just dropped her phone down the toilet, and had made up the story because her expensive gadget was not insured.
>
> Detective Chief Inspector Tariq Sarwar said: "False reporting is totally unacceptable and wastes a considerable amount of police time and resources that could be better spent helping genuine victims and catching criminals."
>
> "They also artificially increase the levels of reported crime and affect the public confidence in the police."
>
> "A dishonest minority of people are intent on making false reports, usually to make a fraudulent insurance claim of some kind to gain a replacement upgraded mobile phone."
>
> "False reporting of offences is taken extremely seriously and those making such claims are committing a criminal offence. A warning goes out to anyone who is thinking of making a false report that every effort is made to establish whether a crime has genuinely occurred."

In the United States, it is not uncommon to find cases where people have ditched their own vehicles, or set them on fire, to collect the insurance subsequent to a false automobile theft report. Consider the case described in Queally (2010):

> A former East Orange police officer admitted today to torching his car on an Essex County street last year so he could collect on the insurance, authorities said.
>
> Kareem Spence, 35, of South Plainfield, faces up to five years in prison after pleading guilty to insurance fraud for setting fire to his 2002 Cadillac Coupe DeVille on Rich Street in Irvington in May 2009, said Acting Essex County Prosecutor Robert Laurino. Spence claims he set the blaze because the vehicle, on which he owed $8,000, had 122,000 miles on it and repeatedly overheated.
>
> Investigators from the Irvington Fire Department and the prosecutor's arson unit suspected the car fire was set intentionally after they found towels soaked in gasoline in the vehicle's trunk.

Similar false claims are also not uncommon among homeowners and business owners in financial difficulty.

False 911 Calls

Intentionally making a false report of a crime to 911 is a crime in most jurisdictions, but penalties are not always steep, even when they are enforced. Many states have recognized the waste of time and resources that such calls cause, as well as the harm they represent to real victims of crime who suffer associated delays in response. As a deterrent, states have increased the fines for such calls and in some instances have made such false reports a felony.

False 911 calls involve prank calls, calls from emotionally disturbed or attention-seeking individuals, and calls from those who want the chance to be seen as heroic. Consider the following representative examples, each causing a significant drain on responder time and agency resources:

- In Doylestown, Wisconsin, Jean Vick, 47, confessed to making multiple false 911 calls. As reported in Ebert (2010),

  > Vick had faced 19 charges of "obstructing an officer" after the Columbia County Sheriff's Office spent, according to the criminal complaint, more than 100 hours of response time and investigation for the bogus calls. The charges carried a possible total of 14 years in jail and $190,000 in fines.
  >
  > According to the criminal complaint, Vick placed 19 prank calls to 911 in 2009 and 2010. On at least one call, Vick told dispatchers that her daughter was being held with a gun to her head. On others, Vick said someone was hurting her.

- Vick claimed she suffered from depression, and began making the fake calls after her son died of cancer. She was given probation and a small fine and was remanded to counseling.
- Dustin R. Bentivegna, 24, a former Footville volunteer firefighter from Janesville, Wisconsin, confessed to two misdemeanor charges of reporting a false emergency. As reported in Sullivan (2010), quoting the original criminal complaint,

  > Four reports of a natural gas odor were made to 911 between Aug. 30 and Sept. 3. The Footville Fire Department responded to three calls, and the Janesville Fire Department responded to one call.
  >
  > All four calls were unfounded, and they came from the same phone number. The number belonged to Bentivegna, who initially denied making the calls. He later admitted making the calls knowing that no emergency existed.

Bentivegna told investigators he wanted to wear his firefighter uniform, drive or ride in the fire truck and investigate calls.

Bentivegna was a probationary volunteer firefighter training to become a regular volunteer firefighter. He had been with the department for about six weeks when he was arrested. He was then fired.

- He was also convicted and fined for impersonating a police officer in an unrelated case.
- Lewis Bunnell, 43, of Indianapolis, Indiana, was arrested for making 13 fake calls to 911 in a 24 hour period. In one instance, he called to report a dead body. When confronted by police investigators, he told them that he was depressed and had issues with alcohol abuse (Nichols, 2010).

CONCLUSION

In the absence of a thorough victimology and a thoughtful reconstruction, false reports can be easy to miss. Consequently, every criminal complaint must be given the same level of investigative and forensic attention. False reports are a problem for all of the professional communities that encounter them, and they are more frequent than those with pro-victim or political agendas would have us believe.

SUMMARY

False allegations of crime have a long documented history. They also occur much more commonly than is generally understood or accepted. Empirical studies of false allegation frequencies have often failed, not just because of law enforcement ignorance in recognizing false reporters, but also because of the political agendas of those involved with victims of crime. False reporters span all crimes, ages, and walks of life, and they are capable of staging both injuries and evidence to support their claims. Ultimately, false reporting is a possibility in every case; the possibility of a false report must be eliminated and its absence cannot be assumed.

Questions

1. Give three common motives for false reporting.
2. True or False: False reporting is a crime.
3. Why is the statistical frequency of false reporting unimportant to a BEA profile?
4. Give two examples of how false reporters can use their claims to make money.
5. True or False: False reporting is a possibility in every case with a complaining witness.

REFERENCES

Barber, M., Lange, L., 2001. Jury Finds City, County Negligent in Child Sex Ring Case—Couple Awarded $3 Million. Seattle Post-Intelligencer, Wednesday, August 1.

Brown, C., Crowley, S., Peck, R., Slaughter, L., 1997. Patterns of Genital Injury in Female Sexual Assault Victims. American Journal of Obstetrics and Gynecology 176(3), 609–616.

Buck, M., 2010. Bethlehem Woman Charged with Making a False Report after Claiming Rape. Leighvalleylive.com, November 2; www.lehighvalleylive.com/bethlehem/index.ssf/2010/11/bethlehem_woman_charged_with_m_1.html.

Coombs, D., 2010. Half of Stolen Goods "Crimes" Are Falsified. Uxbridge Gazette, November 17; www.uxbridgegazette.co.uk/west-london-news/local-uxbridge-news/2010/11/17/half-of-stolen-goods-crimes-are-falsified-113046-27669309/.

Dundes, A., 1991. The Blood Libel Legend: A Casebook in Anti-Semitic Folklore. University of Wisconsin Press, Madison, WI.

Dunleavy, S., 1999. Cybersex Victim's Kin: She's a Liar. New York Post, July 26; www.cybercase.org/shesliar.html.

Ebert, A., 2010. Doylestown Woman Gets Probation for Faking 911 Calls. Portage Daily Register, November 19; www.wiscnews.com/portagedailyregister/news/article_a6ecf18a-f456-11df-8b3a-001cc4c03286.html.

Fazlollah, M., McCoy, C., 2000. Timoney Commends Rape-Squad Reforms. Philadelphia Inquirer, December 13; www.inquirer.philly.com/packages/crime/cofax/00dec13inq.asp.

Ferretti, C., 2010 Mom Charged with False Report of Abandoned Baby. The Detroit News, November 16; www.detnews.com/article/20101116/METRO03/11160394/1412/METRO03/Mom-charged-with-false-report-of-abandoned-baby.

Gravelle, S., 2010. Cedar Rapids Woman Charged with Faking Her Own Kidnapping. The Gazette.com, November 1; www.thegazette.com/2010/11/01/cedar-rapids-woman-charged-with-faking-her-own-kidnapping/.

Greenfeld, L.A., 1997. Sex offense and Offenders: An Analysis of Data on Rape and Sexual Assault. NO. NCJ-163392, U.S. Department of Justice, Office of Justice Programs, Bureau of Justice Statistics, Washington, DC.

Gross, H., 1924. Criminal Investigation, third edition. Sweet and Maxwell, London, England.

Her Majesty's Crown Prosecution Service Inspectorate/Her Majesty's Inspectorate of Constabulary, 2002. A Report on the Joint Inspection into the Investigation and Prosecution of Cases Involving Allegations of Rape. Home Office, London. April; www.inspectorates.homeoffice.gov.uk/hmic/inspections/thematic/aor/them02-aor.pdf.

Johnson, J., 2010. Fake Crime Reports Becoming a Real Pain. Athens Banner-Herald: Online Athens, February 28; www.onlineathens.com/stories/022810/new_568808185.shtml.

Jordan, J., 2004. Beyond Belief? Police, Rape and Women's Credibility. Criminal Justice: International Journal of Policy and Practice 4 (1), 29–59.

Kanin, E., 1994. False Rape Allegations. Archives of Sexual Behavior 23 (1), 81–92.

Kennedy, B., 2010. Woman Faked Cancer to Raise Money. The Toronto Star, August 6; www.thestar.com/news/gta/article/844614.

Kennedy, D.B., Witkowski, M., 2000. False Allegations of Rape Revisited: A Replication of the Kanin Study. Journal of Security Administration 23, 41–46.

Lea, S.J., Lanvers, U., Shaw, S., 2003. Attrition in Rape Cases. British Journal of Criminology 43, 583–599.

MacDonald, J., 1973. False Accusations of Rape. Medical Aspects of Human Sexuality May;170–194.

Martinez, N., 2010. DPS Hopes to Crack down on False Crime Reports. Daily Trojan, March 23; www.dailytrojan.com/2010/03/23/dps-hopes-to-crack-down-on-false-crime-reports/.

McHugh, P.R., 2008. Try to Remember: Psychiatry's Clash over Meaning, Memory, and Mind. Dana Press, Washington, DC.

McKenzie, K., 2010. Guns Used to Threaten Store Clerk, Customer at Two Stores. The Memphis Commercial Appeal, November 23; url: http://www.commercialappeal.com/news/2010/nov/23/crime-report-plan-rob-their-own-pizza-place-goes-a/.

Meloy, K., 2010. Police: Gay Colorado College Student Body President Faked Hate Crimes. Edgeboston.com, November 18.

Mijares, L., 2010. Police Stumped on Charges for Mom Who Faked Daughter's Funeral. Gant Daily, November 17; www.gantdaily.com/2010/11/17/police-stumped-on-charges-for-mom-who-faked-daughters-funeral/.

Nichols, L., 2010. Man Arrested for Fake 911 Calls. WXIN-FOX59, November 10; www.fox59.com/news/wxin-man-arrested-for-fake-911-call-111010,0,973768.story.

Parmar, N., 2004. Crying Wolf: Fabricated Crimes. Psychology Today, July 01; www.psychologytoday.com/articles/200408/crying-wolf-fabricated-crimes.

Potter, N., Friedman, E., 2010. Acid Attack Was Faked: Bethany Storro Admits to Police She Maimed Herself. ABCNews.com, September 16; www.abcnews.go.com/US/acid-attack-victim-bethany-storro-tells-police-faked/.

Queally, J., 2010. East Orange Police Officer Admits to Lighting Car on Fire for Insurance Money. The Star-Ledger,. November 19; www.nj.com/news/index.ssf/2010/11/east_orange_police:officer_adm.html.

Rumney, P.N.S., 2006. False Allegations of Rape. Cambridge Law Journal 65 (1), 128–158.

Staff, 2010. Woman Who Claimed to Be Raped and Kidnapped Recants Story. Salem-news.com, November 11; www.salem-news.com/articles/november112010/report-recanted.php.

Sullivan, S., 2010. Former Firefighter Gets Probation for 911 Calls. GazzetteXtra.com, November 26; www.gazettextra.com/news/2010/nov/24/former-firefighter-gets-probation-911-calls/.

Terry, D., 1994. A Woman's False Accusation Pains Many Blacks. New York Times, November 6; www.nytimes.com/1994/11/06/us/a-woman-s-false-accusation-pains-many-blacks.html.

Turvey, B., 2009. Victimity: Entering the Criminal Justice System. In: Turvey, B., Petherick, W. (Eds.), Forensic Victimology: Examining Violent Crime Victims in Investigative and Legal Contexts. Elsevier Science, San Diego, CA.

Turvey, B., McGrath, M., 2009. False Allegations of Crime. In: Turvey, B., Petherick, W. (Eds.), Forensic Victimology: Examining Violent Crime Victims in Investigative and Legal Contexts. Elsevier Science, San Diego, CA.

SECTION 3

Crime Scene Analysis

CHAPTER 11

An Introduction to Crime Reconstruction

W. Jerry Chisum and Brent E. Turvey

The prosecutor seeks to convict the defendant by making the crime more heinous in nature. The defense seeks to exonerate the defendant. Both theorize about how the crime occurred, with different objectives. Both cannot be correct and, lacking a reconstruction, both are probably wrong. The theories are alternatives and [must] be examined against the evidence.

—W. Jerry Chisum (in Turvey, 2002, p.93)

CONTENTS

Criminal Profiling: An Introduction to Behavioral Evidence Analysis, Fourth Edition

KEY TERMS

Action evidence	Directional evidence	Ownership evidence
Associative evidence	Evidence dynamics	Psychological evidence
Assumption of integrity	Inferred evidence	Secondary transfer
Chain of custody	Limiting evidence	Sequential evidence
Contact evidence	Locard's exchange principle	Staging
Crime reconstruction	Locational/positional evidence	Temporal evidence

Crime reconstruction is the determination of the actions and events surrounding the commission of a crime (Chisum and Turvey, 2007). A reconstruction may be accomplished by using the statements of witnesses, the confession of a suspect, the statement of a living victim, or by the examination and interpretation of physical evidence.

Some refer to this process as crime scene reconstruction. A crime scene is any location where criminal activity is known to have taken place. In most reconstruction efforts, the crime scenes are not actually being put back together as they were; only some of the actions and sequences of events are being established (or disproved). At the evidentiary level, this is in no small part due to the natural limits and capabilities of science. Consequently, the term *crime scene reconstruction* is at best an inaccurate description of what forensic science is actually able to contribute to the cause of justice.

As mentioned in previous chapters, some examiners confuse crime reconstruction with the specific task of *crime scene processing* and the overall field of *crime scene investigation*. These are not the same thing (see Chapter 6). Suffice it to say that forensic scientists perform crime reconstruction: it is based on the evidence processing done at crime scenes, the results of the scene investigation, and the subsequent analysis of physical evidence.

While unnecessary in nomothetic (e.g., statistical or experiential) profiling methods, crime reconstruction is vital to ideo-deductive methods like behavioral evidence analysis (BEA). In order to analyze the behavior that has occurred in a particular crime scene, it must first be established by means of a competently rendered *reconstruction* of events. This sounds like an obvious step, but it is too often skipped by inexpert examiners who believe they can simply read the scene with a glance. Crime scene behavior may not be assumed for the purpose of analysis, it is not done with a glance, and being a profiler does not automatically qualify one as a reconstructionist. This means that profilers must rely heavily on the work of a variety of forensic scientists and have a strong background in the subject themselves.[1]

Crime reconstruction requires the ability to put together a puzzle using pieces of unknown dimensions without a guiding picture. *Like profiling, it is a forensic discipline based on the forensic sciences, the scientific method, analytical logic, and critical thinking.* The next logical question is this: How?

APPROACHING THE RECONSTRUCTION

There are several different approaches to the problem of reconstruction. However, the specific approach used by the reconstructionist is not all that must be considered. Ethics, bias, practice standards, the crime scene investigation, chain of custody, evidence dynamics, and many other related issues must be considered. Each shapes and influences the analytical methods used and the behavioral inferences made. The purpose of this chapter is to introduce the criminal profiler to the problem of crime reconstruction and related considerations, to enable an informed behavioral evidence analysis. Without this foundation, the profiler is guessing, assuming, or otherwise ineptly fabricating the crime-related events that are supposed to be analyzed.

Crime reconstruction is based at least in part on a firm understanding of Locard's exchange principle. As stated by Dr. John Thornton, a practicing criminalist and a former professor of forensic science at the University of California (UC) at Berkeley (Thornton, 1997, p. 29):

> Forensic scientists have almost universally accepted the Locard Exchange Principle. This doctrine was enunciated early in the 20th century by Edmund Locard, the director of the first crime laboratory, in Lyon, France. Locard's Exchange Principle states that with contact between two items, there will be an exchange of microscopic material. This certainly includes fibers, but extends to other microscopic materials such as hair, pollen, paint, and soil.

By recognizing, documenting, and examining the nature and extent of evidentiary traces and exchanges in a crime scene, Dr. Locard postulated that criminals could be traced and later associated with particular locations, items of evidence, and persons (i.e., victims). He regarded this postulation as both obvious and ancient, and

---

[1] A chapter in a forensic science text by two retired FBI profilers states that "Crime scene reconstruction is a process within CIA [criminal investigative analysis] that provides the investigator an understanding of how the victim was approached and controlled, as well as the likely interactions between the offender and the victim"; then, later, "A special part of crime analysis is the ability to reconstruct and sequence criminal acts as they occurred in the interaction between the victim and the offender" (Baker and Napier, 2003, p. 538). The reader is left with the impression that crime reconstruction is a special province of FBI profilers, that they are qualified to perform crime reconstruction, and that it is the function of investigators. This is not just misleading, it is false. The majority of FBI-trained profilers do not have college-level forensic science or behavioral science qualifications. *Criminal investigative analysis* is the FBI's method of criminal profiling and is discussed in Chapter 3 of this text.

he likened the recognition and examination of trace evidence to hunting behavior as old as mankind (Locard, 1934, p. 7). The prey, for example, in the normal course of drinking at a watering hole, leaves tracks and spoor and other signs that betray its presence and direction; the hunter deliberately seeks out this evidence, picks up the trail, and follows. Every contact leaves a trace that may be discovered and understood. The detection and identification of exchanged materials is interpreted to mean that two objects have been in contact. This is the cause-and-effect principle reversed; the effect is observed and the cause is concluded. Understanding and accepting this principle of evidentiary exchange make possible the reconstruction of contacts between objects and persons. Consequently, the incorporation of this principle into evidentiary interpretations is perhaps one of the most important considerations in the reconstruction of crime.

CRIME RECONSTRUCTION AND EXPERIENCE

The most common method of crime reconstruction is to base interpretations on experience. Dr. Hans Gross (1924) emphasized the importance of learning from experience in the late nineteenth-century. He wrote that the scientific investigator must take pains to learn from everything he observes, not only in his work but also in his daily life. And question everything; question why something has happened, or what has caused it to happen—then investigate.

The reconstructionist, Gross posited, must learn to see effects from causes and then reverse the process and establish causes from the effects. When similar events occur at a later time, the reconstructionist should then be able to extrapolate what he has learned about effects and infer the potential causes responsible. The learning and the discipline urged by Gross should make it clear that he was not advocating the value of raw and uneducated experience but, rather, experience tempered with extensive learning and what he referred to as an "encyclopaedic knowledge."

As this suggests, experience is not unimportant, but it can lead the naïve, ignorant, or inept reconstructionist astray when applied in isolation. Regardless of the quality of our experiences, and our capacity to learn from them, the experiences we have in everyday life prepare us to make inferences about the possible causes of the effects we see only when we seek to learn from them. Consequently, the use of one's experience as a knowledge base for developing reconstruction hypotheses and theories, or for inferring the cause from an examination of the effects, is commonplace. It is important to bear in mind that not all experience is equal, not all experience is sufficiently instructive, and not everyone actually learns from his or her experiences.

For these same reasons, it also unacceptable to argue "in my experience" as a sole premise to explain how and why an event must have occurred. Any inference regarding an event must be supported by factual details submitted to thoughtful analysis and rigorous logic. The thoughtful reconstructionist will also prepare citations from the published literature in support of the interpretations when necessary, as he or she may be asked to provide the basis for their knowledge in court. The purely "experience-based reconstructionist" may give examples of his conclusions to demonstrate how he reconstructs but often will not be able to show the logic and science behind his methods. He will also be unable to cite the literature in support of his findings. The absence of such "long division" in his work is in effect an absence of science.[2]

---

[2] The ability to cite the published literature when necessary is a not a pedantic or high-minded exercise in bookish propensity. It is actually a demonstration that one's knowledge extends beyond one's experience—that effort has been made to research and learn from the theories and experiences of others. Without this support, along with analytical logic, the inept or biased reconstructionist may get away with claiming any interpretation of events that suits him. However, literature citation can backfire. One must be careful when selecting references. Once you have established the "expertise" of a reference (which you do by citing it), opposing counsel can cross-examine you on anything in the entire article or text. Be certain that you have informed responses prepared.

A valuable discussion of this issue is found in the writings of Dr. John Thornton (1997, p. 17):

> Virtually everyone agrees that an expert's bare opinion, unsupported by factual evidence, should be inadmissible in a court of law. And yet, precisely that sort of testimony is allowed every day in courts throughout the country by judges who believe that every statement uttered by a person with a scientific degree or employed by an agent called "scientific" is therefore a scientific opinion. Courts permit expert testimony from those with specialized knowledge. But how is a court to gauge such knowledge? The answer generally lies in the education and experience of the prospective witness. A convenient means is to look for a measure of scientific education, and a university degree in a scientific discipline will ordinarily meet that test.
>
> With an educational requirement satisfied, a court will then look at experience. But experience is very difficult to evaluate. The more experience the better, but rarely is there any effort exerted to distinguish between 10 years of experience and 1 month of experience repeated 120 times, or 1 month of experience spread out over 10 years. Furthermore, some experts exploit situations where intuition or mere suspicions can be voiced under the guise of experience. When an expert testifies to an opinion, and bases that opinion on "years of experience," the practical result is that the witness is immunized against effective cross-examination. When the witness testifies that "I have never seen another similar instance in my 26 years of experience ...," no real scrutiny of the opinion is possible. No practical means exists for the questioner to delve into the extent and quality of that experience. Many witnesses have learned to invoke experience as a means of circumventing the responsibility of supporting an opinion with hard facts. For the witness, it eases cross-examination. But it also removes the scientific basis for the opinion. ...
>
> Testimony of this sort distances the witness from science and the scientific method. And if the science is removed from the witness['s testimony], then that witness has no legitimate role to play in the courtroom, and no business being there. *If there is no science, there can be no forensic science.*
>
> Experience is neither a liability nor an enemy of the truth; it is a valuable commodity, but it should not be used as a mask to deflect legitimate scientific scrutiny, the sort of scrutiny that customarily is leveled at scientific evidence of all sorts. To do so is professionally bankrupt and devoid of scientific legitimacy, and courts would do well to disallow testimony of this sort. Experience ought to be used to enable the expert to remember the when and the how, why, who, and what. Experience should not make the expert less responsible, but rather more responsible for justifying an opinion with defensible scientific facts.

Failure to appreciate the limitations of bare experience untempered by analytical logic, critical thinking, and the scientific method can lead some analysts to wrongly believe that they should learn and be able to conclusively "read" the events that have transpired in a crime scene simply by standing in it and looking around. It may further confuse some analysts into believing that scientific examinations and scientific inquiry are an impractical investigative burden, as opposed to a necessary form of theory validation or exclusion. This kind of vanity reconstruction, based on presumed expertise from years of experience performing various tasks, is simply that—vanity substituting for scientific inquiry. Courts that allow any form of reconstruction testimony to proceed along these lines contribute mightily to stalling the development of crime reconstruction as a scientific discipline.

REASON, METHODS, AND CONFIDENCE

The reconstructionist must be capable of critical thinking.[3] That is, the reconstructionist must have the ability to discern fact from speculation, must be able to postulate or theorize alternative solutions for events, must be able to connect facts together, and must further make informed judgments about what questions are important to ask of the evidence in the case at hand.

The process may be regarded as something like this:

- Observe the evidence of events and related clues
- Determine what might be learned of events from each observation
- Postulate what the clue or observation means in light of the crime
- Propose alternative explanations for events
- Eliminate alternatives with analytical logic, critical thinking, and experimentation
- Sequence events until the picture is completed

Put this way, it seems deceptively simple.

Sir Arthur Conan Doyle, through his fictional characters Sherlock Holmes and Dr. John Watson, showed how one could derive information regarding events from close observation and attention to detail. He claimed it was a form of deductive logic. Although no offense is meant to Conan Doyle, it is relatively easy to use deductive logic when you can contrive the facts to fit a single theory of "whodunit" in a fictional story. The use of deduction in actual casework, in which multiple theories may explain known events, is much more difficult.

In 1983, Joe Rynearson and W. Jerry Chisum published the first edition of their text, *Evidence and Crime Scene Reconstruction*, for the course they had been teaching on the subject since 1976. Rynearson has continued to update the text periodically. One of the primary changes in each edition has been the treatment of how reconstruction is actually performed. Early efforts were primarily case oriented, showing examples and hoping the students could understand the process. The text discussed the "Sherlockian" philosophy of finding and eliminating alternatives. Then it explained the logic used by putting it into flowcharts. It further discussed the roles that evidence plays in reconstruction as a classification scheme. This scheme is discussed later because it is the basis for understanding reconstruction. It was introduced at several forensic science professional meetings and conferences throughout the late 1970s and early 1980s.

Subsequent to the Chisum and Rynearson text, other practitioners began to write about what they thought the process of crime reconstruction should involve. For example, Jerry Findley and Craig Hopkins wrote an overview of reconstruction in 1984. They describe it as (pp. 3–4)

> the process of applying logic, training, experience, and scientific principles to:
>
> (1) The crime scene itself (i.e., location, environment, condition, etc.)
> (2) Physical evidence found at a crime scene.
> (3) The results of examinations of physical evidence by qualified experts.
> (4) Information obtained from all other sources in order to form opinions relative to the sequence of events occurring before, during, and after the criminal act.
>
> In essence, reconstruction is the sum total of the investigation demonstrated in its tangible form.

---

[3] Critical thinking is a purposeful, reflective, and goal-directed activity that aims to make judgments based on evidence rather than conjecture. It is based on the principles of science and the scientific method.

These authors discuss the degrees of certainty on a scale of 1 to 10, with 1 being mere speculation and 10 an absolute certainty. They suggest that, the larger the information base and the better the information, the closer the reconstructionist can be to a 10; however, reconstructions will usually fall short of this ideal goal.

They also enumerate the concepts that they explain (Findley and Hopkins, 1984, p. 12): "There are 5 sources of information, 5 tests of a witness' story, 2 types of reconstruction, 7 requirements and 3 goals of a reconstruction." They further stress caution in reconstructions, stating, "The investigator must not try to reconstruct with insufficient or unreliable information or jump to a conclusion before all the data is available" (p. 15).

We have a great deal of enthusiasm for this specific sentiment, which is in accordance with our previously rendered practice standards. However, we reserve a measure of respect for the practice of assigning a specific numeric value to the confidence of what is ultimately an opinion. Numeric values look a lot like math, and many consider math among the hardest of the hard sciences. This and similar practices may have the unintended (or perhaps intended) consequence of making opinions look more certain or reliable than they actually are, without the burden of showing any underlying work. There is no established means of consistently assigning numeric value to reconstruction certainty—such an assignment is a function of the reconstructionist's subjective judgment and experience, not a function of any particular mathematics. Assigning a numeric value, or even a statistical probability, to reconstruction certainty is ultimately misleading.

In reality, the known evidence in a case either

- Supports a reconstruction theory,
- Does not support a reconstruction theory,
- Refutes a reconstruction theory, or
- Is inconclusive.

Consequently, a reconstructionist may characterize a theory only by saying that the theory is:

- *Supported by/consistent with the physical evidence and known circumstances.* This is used for describing results that favor a particular theory or explanation of events.
- *Inconsistent with/eliminated by/disproved by the physical evidence and known circumstances.* This is used for describing results that show the particular theory or explanation of events is out of alignment with the facts.
- *Inconclusive, or not disproved/not eliminated, by the physical evidence and known circumstances.* This is used for addressing alternatives that remain untested or examinations that result in inconclusive results.

EVENT ANALYSIS

Tom Bevel and Ross M. Gardner initially wrote separate articles regarding the technique they use to perform crime reconstruction. They advocate the methods espoused by the military, based on naval research. They have since published these methods in *Bloodstain Pattern Analysis, with an Introduction to Crime Scene Reconstruction* (1997). In this text, they describe what is referred to as *event analysis*. They state (p. 20), "Reconstruction is the end purpose of analysis; it requires not only the consideration of the events identified, but whenever possible the sequence of those events." Bevel and Gardner delineate event analysis as follows:

- Collect data and, using all evidence, establish likely events
- Establish from the data specific snapshots or event segments of the crime

- Consider these event segments in relationship to one another in order to establish related event segments
- Order or sequence the event segments for each identified event
- Consider all possible sequences and, where contradictory sequences exist, audit the evidence to determine which is the more probable
- Establish the final order or sequence of the events themselves
- Flowchart the overall incident based on the event and event-segment sequencing

One caution offered by Bevel and Gardner is that there is no way to be certain of one's conclusions regarding a reconstruction. The analysis may be logical and based on scientific facts, but, just as is true for the conclusions of an archeologist, there is no one standard by which the results can be assessed (pp. 20–21).

This is perhaps one of the greatest limits of crime reconstruction. There are always unknowns with regard to the evidence—holes in the sequence or gaps in timing that cannot be filled. The physical evidence provides a record, but it is ultimately limited to itself. For instance, we may be able to say a certain person was in a certain location at one time, then in a different location at another time. However, it may be impossible to determine the precise route taken from one place to another, the time elapsed, or the manner of travel. Also, there is often no true record of the total event that we can consult to ascertain whether our conclusions are valid. We have only our science, or logic, and our reasoning to guide us through the evidence so that we may explain its strengths and limits to others. Ultimately, what the evidence *cannot* show is as important as what it *can*.

Apart from the incomplete record in the evidence, another barrier to full reconstruction is the complexity combined with the volume of evidence: the amount of evidence and the sequence of events may simply be too overwhelming.

In this text, we take a different approach. We look to the physical evidence based on its role in the crime. This approach allows each item to be evaluated for what it can contribute to the reconstruction of the overall incident or crime. We also break down the crime into segments, as is explained later.

THE ROLE OF EVIDENCE: RECONSTRUCTION CLASSIFICATIONS

The essence of analysis is the breaking down of complex problems or information into its component parts. In crime reconstruction, the information is in the form of physical evidence, and the complex problem to resolve is what happened during the commission of the crime.

Crime reconstruction requires that evidence be broken down and examined using a different mode, and with a different goal, than may be familiar to many forensic specialists. Most classification schemes that describe forensic evidence are based on the type of analysis being performed, the section of the laboratory involved (trace evidence, biological evidence, serological evidence, drugs, firearms, toxicology, etc.), or even the type of crime that produced it. These classifications may assist with the process of triaging evidence as it comes into the crime lab, and perhaps even shed a small amount of light on its context. In crime reconstruction, however, these classifications are not very informative. The reconstructionist needs to consider evidence with regard to the role it plays in the crime and what it can establish regarding the events that have taken place.

The following evidence classification employs the fundamental Who, What, When, Where, How, and (sometimes) Why questions that are the focus of crime reconstruction. The basic types of evidence are:

- Sequential
- Directional
- Locational

- Action
- Contact
- Ownership
- Associative
- Limiting
- Inferential
- Temporal
- Psychological

It should be noted that, in any given case, one piece of evidence may, and probably will, fit into more than one of these categories.

Sequential evidence (Figure 11.1) is anything that establishes or helps to establish when an event occurred or the order in which two or more events occurred. Examples:

- A footprint over a tire track shows that an individual was present subsequent to the vehicle's passing.
- Blood found under the glass from a broken window at a burglary/murder establishes that the window was broken after the blood was deposited. This may call witness statements into question and begin to suggest the possibility of *staging*.
- Radial fracture patterns in plate glass from multiple gunshots can be used to establish the firing sequence.

Directional evidence (Figure 11.2) is anything that shows where something was going or where it came from. Examples:

- Footprints may be used to help indicate potential direction of travel.
- Projectile trajectory analysis can help establish the origin and direction of bullets, spears, arrows, and other missile weapons.

FIGURE 11.1
This elderly victim of a sexual homicide was manually strangled in her home, next to her bed. Note that contents of the open dresser drawers and ransacked personal items are dumped on the body, indicating that a debilitating attack took place prior to the search for valuables. This evidence indicates a particular sequence of events in that particular room.

FIGURE 11.2
The above photo shows bloody drag marks in the back hallway of a store. They lead from the front area, to the woman's bathroom, back out again, down the hallway, and finally into the men's bathroom. The victim was a college student who died as the result of a single gunshot wound to the head; she was found mostly nude in the men's bathroom. The bloody drag marks indicate both a sequence of events (the victim was dragged down the hall and into both bathrooms after she was shot), and the direction that the body came from.

- Bloodstain pattern analysis can be used to determine the direction of blood that is dripped, cast, smeared, spattered, wiped, or swiped.
- Wound pattern analysis can be used to determine the direction of abrasions and other injuries to the skin via an examination of piled epithelium; the epithelium piles in the direction of travel of the object that created the abrasion.

Locational/positional evidence shows where something happened, or where something was, and its orientation with respect to other objects at the location. Examples:

- A single fingerprint inside the passenger window could indicate that a particular person was inside a vehicle at some point. However, if the fingerprint is pointed down and at the top of a window that rolls down, it may only mean that a person standing outside the vehicle placed a finger inside the glass.
- The orientation of a tool mark on a door or window may indicate a potential point of offender entry into a scene and subsequently suggest the need to look for other transfer evidence from the offender at that location.
- Bloodstains or spatters can indicate where a victim was injured or where the victim, offender, or even bystanders may have been standing, sitting, or lying. They can also be used to help determine where intermediate objects may have been located, by virtue of void patterns.
- Livor mortis is the settling of the blood in the lower (dependent) portion of the body, causing a purplish-red discoloration of the skin. When the heart is no longer beating, gravity causes the red blood cells to sink into the tissue. This discoloration does not occur in the areas of the body that are in contact with the ground or another object because the capillaries are compressed. Livor mortis becomes fixed after roughly 10 hours and may be used to determine whether a body has been moved after this time if the pattern is inconsistent with the victim's final resting position.
- Indentations in a carpet show where something (e.g., a chair) had been placed and can indicate that it was moved.
- A pile of cigarette butts in one location may indicate the location where someone lay in wait.

Action evidence (Figure 11.3) defines anything that happened during the commission of the crime. This may seem a basic issue, but it is crucial when establishing the elements of a crime as required by law. Misinterpretation of action evidence at any point during the reconstruction can cause criminal charges to be brought against an innocent person and failure to charge a guilty party with the totality of the crimes that have been committed. Examples:

- Bloodstains and patterns indicate an injury to the offender or a victim or that a blood source was moved rapidly, resulting in cast-off patterns.
- Gunshot wounds, bullet holes, and cartridge casings indicate that a firearm was discharged.

FIGURE 11.3
This man was found to have died from multiple sharp force injuries in a bathroom. Additionally, his jeans were unzipped, there was unflushed urine in the toilet, and there was blood spatter on the toilet. The context of this evidence combines to support the conclusion that the victim was attacked while urinating. This would be action evidence and locational evidence, at the very least.

- Sharp force injury indicates that a sharp force weapon was used (knife, sword, razor, box-cutter, etc.).
- A broken window with glass on the floor next to the door lock indicates that the window was broken to gain entry (of course, this can be staged as well).

Contact evidence is something that demonstrates whether and how two persons, objects, or locations were at one point associated with each other. Examples:

- Trace evidence, such as hairs, fibers, soil, and glass, may be used to suggest an association between persons, objects, and locations.
- A fingerprint on a glass can be used to indicate that a particular person was holding it at one point.
- The victim's blood on the soles of the suspect's shoes indicates contact with a location where the victim was bleeding.
- Two toothbrushes and two wet towels would indicate that two persons were residents (conversely, only one toothbrush could indicate a single occupant).

Ownership evidence is something that helps answer the Who question with a high degree of certainty. It includes any evidence that may be connected to, or associated with, a particular person or source. It also includes individuating forms of physical evidence. Examples:

- Written signatures
- Driver's licenses
- Credit cards
- Computer IP addresses
- PIN numbers
- Mail
- E-mail
- Serial numbers
- Vehicle identification numbers
- DNA
- Fingerprints

Associative evidence is usually a form of trace evidence that can be identification or ownership evidence. The finding of common materials on the suspect and victim, the suspect and the scene, or the scene and the victim is used to suggest contact, in accordance with Locard's exchange principle. Although associative evidence indicates certain or potential contact between persons or environments, it cannot by itself indicate when that contact occurred. This requires the presence of other circumstantial evidence. Examples:

- A bloody footprint on linoleum places a person at the scene.
- Fibers found on a body that match the fibers in the trunk of a vehicle.
- Double-base gunpowder found on both the suspect and the victim.
- Vegetation found in the trunk of a vehicle possibly used for hauling a body that is consistent with the vegetation found at the crime scene and on the body.

Associative evidence takes on a higher degree of importance when there is more than one type involved. For example, if all the previous examples were discovered in one case, the reconstructionist would first be inclined to postulate that the vehicle (associated with the crime via fibers and vegetation) was used to transport the body. If the owner of the vehicle were also the person whose bloody footprint was discovered on the floor, and the blood belonged to the victim, the tightening circle of associations would increase the importance of this evidence.

FIGURE 11.4

This door in rear of a residence associated with a child sexual homicide was nailed shut and blocked with numerous undisturbed boxes. The condition of this door excludes it as a point of entry or exit for the offender.

Limiting evidence defines the nature and boundaries of the crime scene (Figure 11.4). Determining the nature and limits of the crime scene is perhaps one of the most difficult tasks in crime reconstruction. It is made difficult by the fact that reconstruction is most often performed after the scene is released, and that first responders, without any forensic training, often determine scene limits by arbitrarily throwing up barrier tape wherever it seems appropriate. This may or may not reflect the actual limits of the scene and the evidence. By the time crime scene investigators (CSIs) realize that there is evidence outside of the tape, it is often already trampled upon by a variety of well-meaning crime scene personnel. Examples of limiting evidence are:

- Points of entry and exit to and from a scene
- Walls inside a building
- Doors inside a building
- Geography and landscape of an outdoor scene
- Fences on a piece of property
- Location of the known scene (indoor, outdoor, vehicle, etc.)
- The confines of a vehicle (car, truck, boat, cruise ship, etc.)
- The beginning and end of blood trails
- The beginning and end of drag marks
- The location of items dropped by the offender when fleeing the scene

The absence of any evidence that should be there given the known action evidence that specifically suggests a secondary scene. This includes the absence of blood at a scene where the victim has exsanguinated, the absence of teeth on the ground from a victim whose teeth were knocked out during a fight, and so forth.

Limiting evidence is important because it helps establish whether there are secondary crime scenes and whether the evidence search area must be expanded to include other nearby locations.

Inferred evidence is anything that the reconstructionist thinks may have been at the scene when the crime occurred but was not actually found. Examples:

- A contact gunshot to the face of a victim produces a quantity of blood on the table where she was sitting. A void pattern is formed on the table with a specific outline. It is inferred that the package of cocaine described by a witness was consistent with this outline and may have been removed after the victim was shot.
- A deceased victim is found without his wallet.
- A deceased married victim is found without his wedding ring.
- A deceased female is found outdoors without her underwear.
- A victim is found stabbed to death in her residence, but the knife is not found.
- A victim is found shot to death in his residence, but the gun is not found.

It is important when dealing with inferred evidence to refrain from assuming that the offender must have removed it from the scene, even when the reconstructionist knows precisely what it is. For example, a witness or even crime scene responders may have stolen cash or a wallet from the victim's body, and a female victim found without underwear may simply not be in the habit of wearing underwear. Questions must be asked, and their answers known, before informed inferences regarding what the offender may or may not have removed from the scene can be made.

Temporal evidence is anything that specifically denotes or expresses the passage of time at the crime scene relative to the commission of the crime. Examples:

- It is known that the electricity was turned off at a main switch to a home. The victim was shot during this time. The electricity was turned back on. The clock in the bedroom was one that reset itself to midnight. Therefore, to establish the time of death, the time that the crime lab looked at the clock was subtracted from the present time to give the time when the clock was turned back on.
- A clock that is knocked off a nightstand during a struggle then stops when it hits the floor, affixing the time.
- A new stick candle is lit during the commission of a crime. It is discovered still burning, with only half of the wax remaining. The length of time it takes to burn this candle halfway may be established via experimentation with a candle of precisely the same type.
- A bowl of ice cream is placed on a kitchen counter just prior to the commission of a murder. It is barely melted when police arrive. The more expensive the ice cream, the less air is injected into it during its manufacture and the longer it takes to melt. The length of time it takes to melt may be established via experimentation with ice cream of precisely the same brand and flavor.
- A forensic pathologist uses the decrease in body temperature, rigor and livor mortis, analysis of the vitreous humor, and examination of the gastric contents to determine a victim's approximate time of death.
- A forensic entomologist uses the life cycle of insects found on a dead body to approximate how many days the victim's body has been susceptible to those insects.

Psychological evidence (i.e., motivational evidence) is any act committed by the perpetrator to satisfy a personal need or motivation (Figure 11.5). This type of evidence is more commonly the province of the criminal profiler and the behavioral scientist. Examples:

- A man murders his wife in their bedroom and stages the scene to look like a burglary gone wrong. This is done to conceal his otherwise obvious connection to the crime and the crime scene.
- An offender tortures his victim, sexually, to satisfy a sadistic motivation.
- An offender records his attack of a victim to both humiliate the victim and to relive the event later for fantasy purposes.

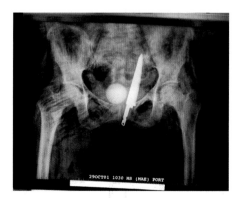

FIGURE 11.5

This image is an x-ray of the abdomen of an adult female victim of a sexual homicide. A knife has been inserted into her vagina, along with a golfball, postmortem. Penetrating the vagina, or rectum, with a knife or other object is strong psychological evidence. It is an act that, in the proper context, may suggest sexually related anger, jealousy, and/or punishment.

- An offender beats his victim repeatedly with the butt of a pistol out of rage.
- An offender binds and gags a victim during an attack at a private location where no one would hear the screams to prevent the victim from disrupting the offender's fantasy of victim compliance.

Ultimately, there are no bright yellow lines between these evidence classifications. In fact, it may be more useful for reconstructionists to consider them questions to ask of each item of evidence. What can this tell us about sequence? What can this tell us about contact? What does this tell us about action? What does this tell us about ownership? In this way, evidence relationships are less likely to be lost, and the fullest picture of events may be allowed to emerge.

EVIDENCE DYNAMICS

Crime reconstruction is an exacting process that often yields imprecise results containing evidentiary holes, sequential gaps, and alternate possibilities. This is not necessarily evidence of poor science and examiner inability. Establishing and revealing evidentiary frailty, however, can be an indication of scientific honesty. Forensic scientists are responsible for remembering, and reminding others, that what the evidence does not support is often just as important as what it does support.

The more we learn about physical evidence—how it can be affected by external forces and distortions—the more we come to appreciate that it is not necessarily an abiding and precise record of actions and events. Even under the best circumstances, physical evidence must be interpreted through a successive layer of necessary and uncontrollable influences. As a consequence, though it is often the most objective record of events, physical evidence and reconstructive interpretations can infrequently be expressed in terms of absolute certainty.

The purpose of this section is to discuss those necessary and uncontrollable influences, which we refer to as *evidence dynamics*,[4] and how reconstructionists must endeavor to account for them in their interpretations.

Crime reconstruction efforts are concerned with interpreting the physical evidence of the effects of actions and events related to the commission of a crime. However, frequently missing from this analysis is the recognition and consideration of the influences that can change physical evidence prior to, or as a result of, its collection and examination. The general term *evidence dynamics* has been developed by the authors to refer to any influence that adds, changes, relocates, obscures, contaminates, or obliterates physical evidence, regardless of intent. This term was deemed appropriate because all forms of physical evidence are at the mercy of environmental change, activity, and time.

Evidence dynamics are at work even before the crime happens, as well as during the interval that begins as physical evidence is being transferred or created. The influences continue and do not stop affecting the evidence throughout its life, until it has been completely destroyed. For those who are familiar with such influences, and account for them in their analyses, this terminology provides a necessary and useful descriptor. As we discuss, an appreciation of evidence dynamics is requisite, and often pivotal, to any examinations done by the laboratory and to the subsequent reconstruction of the events of the crime.

---

[4] *Evidence dynamics* as a formal concept was first described by the authors in Chisum and Turvey (2000). Portions of that article have been used to develop the current chapter.

DYNAMIC INFLUENCES: PRE-DISCOVERY

Crime reconstructions are too often built on an *assumption of integrity*—that evidence left behind at a scene has been guarded and left undisturbed prior to the arrival of police investigators and other responders. This assumption involves the mistaken belief that taping off an area, limiting access, and setting about the task of taking pictures and making measurements somehow ensures the integrity of the evidence found within. Subsequently, any conclusions reached through forensic examinations of that evidence are wrongly assumed to be a wholly reliable lens through which to view the crime. Though reconstruction is made easier with this assumption, it is not made more accurate.

Reconstructionists must accept that each item of evidence at a crime scene will go through some or all of the following before it is actually recognized:

1. Transference or creation at the scene
2. Changes due to time (blood and semen dry; dead bodies decompose, stiffen, and equalize with room temperature)
3. Changes due to the environment (rain, heat, cold, and wind)
4. Alteration/destruction/creation by individuals performing their duties, including first officer(s) at the scene, paramedics, crime scene investigators, crime lab personnel, and lost or confused supervisors
5. Recognition or discovery that it is evidence (sometimes only after stepping on it or in it)

Each of these processes, legitimate and uncontrollable alike, has the potential to leave its mark on the evidence—to alter it in some irremediable way.

Consider the following forms of evidence dynamics:

The Other Side of the Tape

The placement of crime scene security tape by first responders sets into motion a series of expectations and events that defines the scope of all evidence-processing efforts. Under the best circumstances, first responders may fully grasp the complexity of the crime scene and the involvement of surrounding areas; or they may be limited by natural barriers in the environment, such as active freeways, cliffs, or bodies of water; or they may have inaccurate preconceived ideas about where the crime occurred; or they may simply be misinformed about the nature of events; and, under the worst circumstances, they may simply lack proper training or concern about the importance of the physical evidence (Figure 11.6).

FIGURE 11.6

Then crime scene investigator Eddie-Joe Delery, of the NOPD crime lab, is shown photographing a spent .40 caliber shell casing at the scene of a shooting in June, 2007. A man was riding his bike along a stretch of road when someone fired at least three shots at him. The cyclist was hit three times and fled the scene. When officers arrived, he kicked off his shoes in a fit of anger for having been shot. Quite by coincidence, the shell casings landed next to a dead pigeon on the side of the road. Supervisors insisted that the pigeon's cause of death be determined, to eliminate its involvement in the crime. CSI Delery opened the pigeon up to find no bullet wounds, and its bones crushed. It was determined that bird had been hit by a car.

The dynamics of "the other side of the tape" are explained in plain but effective language by Eddie-Joe Delery, a retired forensic examiner for the New Orleans Police Department's crime lab (personal communication with Turvey, July 23, 2005):

> Every time I roll up on a scene and see the tape coming off the back of a patrol car, tied to a telephone pole or something like that, I just shake my head. Everybody's so worried about searching inside that tape, by the time they realize the crime took place on the other side of it they've walked all over the evidence. And that's if they didn't park their vehicle on it.

The limiting effect of crime scene tape is tremendous. First responders have a duty to understand and implement competent barrier efforts; scene technicians have a responsibility to understand and implement competent search and collection efforts. Each must grasp the dangers of setting up the tape and working only on one side of it.

When it is relevant, the reconstructionist is advised to consider whether the tape accurately defined the scene and whether subsequent evidence search and collection efforts reflect the most informed picture of the evidence, given the nature of the crime. If, for example, evidence was found outside the tape and search efforts were not expanded accordingly, it suggests an incomplete investigative and processing effort.

The Crime Scene

Before the crime occurs, the area where it eventually takes place may already contain items that are "evidence" of everyday activities, such as cigarette butts, beer or soft drink cans, fibers, evidence of recent sexual activity, old bloodstains—the potential list is endless. The reconstructionist has a responsibility to differentiate between preexistent items and actual evidence of the crime. That is, each item of evidence must somehow be associated with the crime; its association may not be assumed merely by establishing its presence in the scene.

The person who "recognizes" the evidence at a crime scene must also have the ability to make this distinction or there will be useless items collected as though they are relevant and relevant items ignored as though they are useless. Mistakes in this effort can result in a reconstruction that is not only erroneous but also may point to the wrong actions and even the wrong suspect.

Example

> One of the authors (Turvey) recently examined a post-conviction case out of Oklahoma where a very highly regarded bloodstain analyst examined what he thought was high-velocity blood spatter on a car believed to be associated with a shooting death. In a bit of profiling, the bloodstain analyst testified at trial, in the pre-DNA era, that the bloodstains on the car door almost certainly came from a shooting incident and were most likely associated with a homicidal death. The defendant, Richard Tandy Smith, was convicted. Eighteen years later, DNA proved that the substance was indeed blood, but that it did not match the homicide victim in the case. The bloodstain was unrelated to the homicide, and its origins have been lost to time.

Offender Actions

The actions of an offender during the commission of the crime, and in the post-offense interval, directly influence the nature and quality of evidence that is left behind. The actions can include precautionary acts, ritual or fantasy, and staging (Figure 11.7).

FIGURE 11.7
According to Brown (2006, A1), Rebeccah Huston, a 32-year-old veterinary technician from Kennewick, Washington, was carjacked at gunpoint and forced into a garbage dumpster, where she spent an entire night. She was found early the next day at Solid Waste Management of Ukiah. She was not unconscious, bound, or restrained in any way. As a result of her night in the cold, she suffered from hypothermia. She also suffered a laceration to her head from when the dumpster was picked up, emptied into a garbage truck and the garbage was compacted. She was treated at a local hospital and later released.

- *Precautionary acts* involving physical evidence are behaviors committed by an offender before, during, or after an offense that are consciously intended to confuse, hamper, or defeat investigative or forensic efforts for the purposes of concealing the identity of the perpetrator and/or his connection to the crime, or even the crime itself. They include disposal of the body, clipping victim's fingernails or removing their teeth or fingers to prevent identification, cleaning up the blood at the scene, picking up shell casings—essentially anything that changes the visibility, location, or nature of the evidence.
- *Staging* of the crime scene is a specific type of precautionary act that is intended to deflect suspicion away from the offender. Staging often involves the addition, removal, and manipulation of items in the crime scene to change the apparent "motive."
- *Ritual* or *fantasy* may also influence the offender's actions during a crime and can include postmortem mutilation, necrophilia, and purposeful arrangement of a body or items in a scene. Fantasy may also be involved with items found in the suspect's home environment that show planning or pre-/post-incident fantasies.

Staging

A *simulated* or *staged crime scene* is one in which the physical evidence has been purposefully altered by the offender to mislead authorities or misdirect the investigation.

The formal recognition of crime scene staging as a discrete subject in the literature began with the work of Dr. Hans Gross in the late 1800s (Gross, 1924). His insights, provided more than a century ago, resonate through the literature with conspicuous agreement: In each case, examine the forensic evidence carefully, reconstruct the crime meticulously, corroborate/compare victim and witness statements with the evidentiary findings, and assume nothing. Since that time, the only published study of the subject, beyond the various case reports that appear in the journals each year, is Turvey (2000).

Each investigator, profiler, and forensic examiner has his or her own subjective sense of the elements that, when discovered at a crime scene, indicate staging. Or at least, that is what they say in court. The elements can include :

- There is no sign of forced entry
- Forced entry is evident
- The drawers in a room have been removed and carelessly dumped out to give a "ransacked" appearance
- The drawers in a room have been removed and carefully stacked to protect or preserve the content

- No search for valuables is apparent
- Only particular items have been stolen
- No items have been stolen
- The victim had life insurance
- The victim's death benefited a family member, household member, or intimates in some way other than life insurance (anger, revenge, trust fund, unfettered access to a large bank account, etc.)

Any or all of these circumstances may raise the suspicion of the alert investigator, and there is nothing inherently wrong with suspicion. However, these circumstances also occur in cases in which there is no staging. Careful readers will note that they are not even useful as red flags because they cover almost all possibilities with respect to each particular circumstance (i.e., the point of entry will either be forced or not, items of value will either have been stolen or not, and the scene will either be ransacked or not). Suspicion justifies further investigation; it tells the investigator where to look for more evidence. Suspicious circumstances are not themselves evidence, however. They are hypotheses that must be tested with the evidence; they do not signal the end of inquiry, but its beginning. If forensic examiners do their long division and work to disprove these theories, they may discover that what appears to be evidence of staging may ultimately be something else.

Let us consider the issue of "ransacking." If the crime scene "appears ransacked," and this appearance used to support the inference of staging, at least the following must be established:

- That the ransacked appearance is a departure from the normal appearance of the scene
- That the ransacked appearance is the direct result of offender activity, and not crime scene personnel
- That the ransacked appearance was unrelated to a search by the offender for items of value (cash, checkbooks, jewelry, firearms, etc.)
- That the ransacked appearance was unrelated to a search by the offender for a specific item of interest (vehicle keys, illicit drugs, prescription medications, personal items of a fetishistic value, etc.)

If the forensic examiner can eliminate these possibilities, then it can be argued that ransacking may support the inference that the scene was staged. We emphasize *may* because it is only one indication and must be considered in the context of the other evidence.

Let us also consider "valuables." The issue of whether valuables have been taken from the crime scene is often a major consideration with respect to establishing the elements and motive of a crime. Some examiners are comfortable assuming that the offender took valuables, despite having no evidence that any such items even existed, because it is helpful in promoting their theory of a case. For those examiners and all others, a certain threshold line of inquiry for each item of value is required:

- What was the item? What is its value?
- Where was the item located in the scene?
- Who knew of the item's existence?
- Who knew where the item was located?
- What barriers did the offender overcome to locate and remove the item? (Was it hidden or in a safe? Was it in plain sight on the kitchen table?)
- What evidence demonstrates that it was actually removed from the scene?
- What evidence demonstrates that it was the offender who removed it from the scene? Has forensic testing established a clear association of any kind?
- Has the item been located? If so, where?

Those who are staging a crime scene to look like a burglary gone awry often forget to remove valuables. Or they may simply remove a few items of value to create a superficial illusion. Or the scene may not have been staged at all. For example, the following are all possibilities when considering why there are items of obvious value remaining in the scene:

- The offender was interested in items of a personal or fetishistic nature, which may have been removed from the scene undetected
- The offender was under the influence of controlled substances during the crime and was fixated on locating something specific
- The offender was not there to steal anything but had entered to satisfy other desires, such as rape or fetish burglary, for which there may or may not be clear evidence, depending on the level and quality of scene documentation

As with any circumstance at the crime scene, the removal of valuables must be considered in context with all of the other evidence. Cash is particularly difficult because proving its existence is not always easy, although it is certainly not impossible. Seeking to answer the questions in the threshold line of enquiry will set the reconstructionist on the right path and help to establish the relevance of the items of value that have been stolen from the scene or that may have been left behind.

Staging is a possibility in every case. Therefore, in every case, it must be considered and excluded before it is abandoned as an explanation. It cannot be proven, however, through mere observation, intuition, and surmise. The evidence must be reliably established, the conclusions must be empirically tested and logically rendered, and alternative explanations must be eliminated. Only then may staging be considered as the most viable explanation for events.

Victim Actions

The victim's activities prior to a crime may result in artifacts that are mistaken for evidence that is related to the crime. The actions of a victim during an attack and in the post-offense interval can also influence the nature and quality of evidence that is left behind. This includes defensive actions, such as struggling, fighting, and running, which can relocate transfer evidence, causing secondary transfer. The victim's actions may also include cleaning up a location or their person after an attack.

Secondary Transfer

Transfer evidence is produced by contact between persons and objects (Cwiklik, 1999; Lee, 1995). Secondary transfer refers to an exchange of evidence between objects or persons that occurs subsequent to an original exchange, unassociated with the circumstances that produced the original exchange. In a discussion regarding fiber evidence that can be generalized to any form of transfer evidence, Deedrick (2000) explains:

> Fibers can also transfer from a fabric source such as a carpet, bed, or furniture at a crime scene. These transfers can either be direct (primary) or indirect (secondary). A primary transfer occurs when a fiber is transferred from a fabric directly onto a victim's clothing, whereas a secondary transfer occurs when already transferred fibers on the clothing of a suspect transfer to the clothing of a victim. An understanding of the mechanics of primary and secondary transfer is important when reconstructing the events of a crime.

Witnesses

The actions of witnesses in the post-offense/pre-discovery interval can influence the nature and quality of evidence that is left behind. This includes actions taken to preserve victim dignity, as well as the deliberate theft of items from the scene upon discovery of an incapacitated or deceased victim. It also includes any other well-intentioned yet destructive efforts.

Weather/Climate

The meteorological conditions (e.g., temperature, precipitation, and wind) at a crime scene can influence the nature and quality of all manner of evidence that is left behind. This includes the destruction or obliteration of evidence, as well as the effects of climate on body temperature and decomposition.

Inclement or extreme weather in particular can destroy evidence, destroy crime scenes, and in some cases prevent responders from getting to the scene altogether. If too much time elapses under such conditions, the chance to locate, secure, and retrieve evidence may be lost. A corpse in the water may bloat and eventually disintegrate. A hard rain may wash away footprints in the soil.

There are rare exceptions to the destructive properties of weather, however. For example, extreme cold may preserve the body of a murder victim that becomes frozen in an outdoor disposal scene. This may keep areas of injury from decomposing and preserve DNA evidence for testing. Extreme heat and dryness, on the other hand, may mummify a corpse and cause it to shrivel.

Hurricane Katrina

At 7:10 a.m. EDT on August 29, 2005, Hurricane Katrina (Figure 11.8) made landfall in Louisiana as a Category 3 storm. Maximum winds were near 125 mph. It was the most destructive hurricane in U.S. history, obliterating, rending, and flooding buildings and homes and destroying lives all along the Gulf Coast. As explained in Cruz (2007):

> Nearly two years after Hurricane Katrina cut its destructive path through the Gulf Coast, the NOPD has found little relief. Six FEMA trailers make up its headquarters. The traffic department and SWAT team also call several double-wide units home. Seventy-two officers have left the force this year. Of the 1,200 that remain (down from 1741 before the storm), there is only a single fingerprint examiner and only one expert firearm examiner. This year, the deadliest city in America has seen over 90 killings, eight of them in the past week and a half alone. In 2006, the city saw 161 murders (only one of which has resulted in a conviction).

> The list of woes went on and on. Because of a lack of storage space, criminal evidence is still kept in the back of an 18-wheel truck. The city's crime lab just reopened after finally finding a home on the University of New Orleans campus. The resources that most major cities take for granted just haven't existed for the past 22 months. And according to [New Orleans Police Department Deputy Superintendent Anthony] Cannatella, it's not just the infrastructure—it's the manpower. Several hundred of his officers still live in temporary housing. "They live in FEMA trailers, they come to work in a FEMA trailer, and they patrol FEMA trailers," said Cannatella. "It's demoralizing. We say FEMA trailer like it's something specially built. It's not."

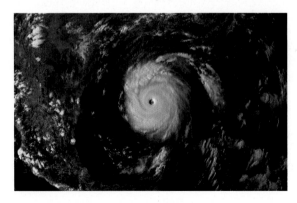

FIGURE 11.8
Hurricane Katrina, pictured here the day before it landed, was the most destructive hurricane in U.S. history.

Decomposition

Naturally occurring rates of decomposition can obscure, obliterate, or mimic evidence of injury to a body. Because of this, in combination with the odor and the associated revulsion experienced by examiners, there is a perception that everything else has decomposed as well. Consequently, the clothing from a decomposed body will normally receive less attention for trace or transfer evidence. This is a mistake, because hair, fiber, and other synthetic transfer evidence can endure well beyond biological material.

As previously mentioned, the rate of decomposition is affected by climate. Body temperature, in particular, changes to meet room or environmental temperature after death. In a freezer, this means a decrease in temperature; in a heated indoor or outdoor environment, it means an increase. The temperature change affects the rate of decomposition as well as the onset and duration of both rigor mortis and livor mortis (Knight, 1996).

Insect Activity

The actions of flies, ants, beetles, and other insects can obliterate or mimic the wounds on a body (Figure 11.9, left and right). They may also move, remove, or destroy the transfer evidence. The evidence of their activities may also appear to the inexperienced to be evidence of torture.

Animal Activity/Predation

The feeding activities of all manner of indigenous wildlife, from ants to mice, coyotes, and bears, can relocate body parts, obliterate patterns, and further obscure, obliterate, or mimic injury to a body. At each scene, the forensic examiner should establish what kinds of animals may be found there, what their habits are, and how they may affect the evidence. Their effects may be minor, as when a housecat walks through a bloodstain pattern leaving obvious paw-prints across a kitchen floor, or they may be significant, as when a coyote chews a body left outside and carries away extremities.

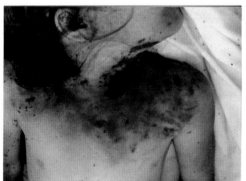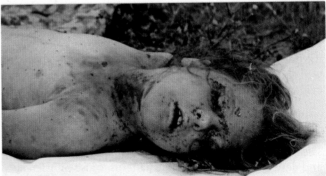

FIGURE 11.9
This child victim of sexual homicide was discovered nude, beneath a blanket from her bedroom, in her backyard. She died from manual strangulation. Examiners initially believed that the injuries evident on her neck were consistent with abrasions and bruising from manual strangulation. Upon close inspection of the photograph, it becomes clear that the pronounced "abrasions" are actually post-mortem ant bites. The ants are actually visible in the photo, and have characteristically focused their attention on the tissue damaged during the attack—including her neck. The dark areas of "bruising" are actually fingerprint powder left behind from an attempt to realize latent prints.

Fire

When fire is involved, either intentional fire or accidental, its result can be the burning, obscuring, and even destruction of all manner of physical evidence related to criminal activities.

In cases involving arson, evidence of the actions of the offender may be obscured if not eliminated (concealing homicide, concealing theft), but evidence of the arson may remain. For a more complete discussion, see Chapter 16 "Fire and Explosives: Behavioral Aspects."

Fire Suppression Efforts

Fire suppression efforts typically involve the use of high-pressure water, heavy hoses, and perhaps chemicals. The job of fire suppression personnel is to put out the fire; evidence preservation is secondary to this goal. Any fire suppression activities, alone or in concert, can relocate or destroy the evidence, obliterate patterns, cause potentially misleading transfers, and/or add artifact evidence to the scene.

The First Responder/Police Personnel

The duty of the first responder on the scene is to protect life, not to preserve evidence. First responders must first protect their own lives and then the lives of others by giving first aid and determining that potential suspects are no longer a threat to personal or public safety. That is, the first-responder officer cannot protect public safety if he is incapacitated; therefore, the officer must first ensure his own safety by searching the premises for suspects, bombs, or other hazards. The officer cannot worry about footprints or fingerprints during this search. After that, the officer must render aid to victims and establish that the scene is secure from further danger. The first responders should be interviewed, if not at the scene, then before the reconstruction is finalized.

Furthermore, detectives and other law enforcement personnel should know to refrain from touching evidence at the scene before it is properly documented. When possible, a strict "hands in the pockets" policy must be enforced among those not saving lives or documenting or collecting evidence. Otherwise, their actions may relocate evidence, obliterate patterns, cause transfers, and add artifacts to the scene.

When it is relevant, the reconstructionist must avail herself of all reports and notes detailing such activities to prevent misinterpretation. If no such documentation exists, the reconstructionist should realize that there is a serious gap in the reliability of the evidence and must so qualify her report. Moreover, it is arguably the duty of the reconstructionist to document and report the absence of such vital scene documentation, as well as any other failings or shortcomings in scene processing efforts. In this way, misrepresentations of the evidence by overly certain examiners or legal professionals may be prevented.

The Emergency Medical Team

The actions of emergency medical personnel engaged in life-saving activities at the crime scene may relocate and destroy evidence, obliterate patterns, cause transfers, tear clothing, and add artifacts. Additionally, they may intentionally inflict therapeutic injuries to the victim, such as cuts or punctures. This is expected and necessary.

Should a victim be transported to a medical facility, treatment rendered there can also change the nature of injuries. This will cause problems for subsequent examination and interpretation of the injuries (e.g., at autopsy). Again, this is expected and should not be misinterpreted.

When it is relevant, the reconstructionist must avail himself of all reports and notes detailing the activities of the emergency medical team, to prevent misinterpretation. If no such documentation exists, the reconstructionist should request that it be sought and created.

Security

Proper scene security must be maintained at all times. This means limiting access to only necessary personnel and controlling it by means of a security officer who logs the entry times, exit times, reason for entry, and duties performed of each person who passes through the tape. This is a basic concern that is part of every scene-processing training course and program that the authors have encountered. However, it is still regularly ignored. Sometimes, a reminder is needed.

However, gentle reminders may not be enough. In one case, a Minneapolis police sergeant became so disturbed by the lack of security at a double homicide scene that he wrote e-mail to his supervisors to make an official record of his concern (Chanen and Collins, 2005, p. 1B):

> A Minneapolis police sergeant sent an e-mail to his supervisors questioning why nonpolice personnel were walking around a taped-off crime scene where two men were shot to death in a north Minneapolis restaurant nearly two weeks ago. Members of the Police Community Relations Council (PCRC) were given copies of the e-mail that Sgt. Robert Berry sent to police administration and Fourth Precinct supervisors relating his concerns about the crime scene following the March 4 fatal shootings of Frank Haynes, 21, and Raliegh Robinson, 68, both of Minneapolis.
>
> PCRC member Ron Edwards said the e-mail suggested that the crime scene may have been contaminated by unauthorized people.
>
> In his e-mail, Berry said "people moved freely" and could have destroyed evidence. He said one woman was "confidently walking beyond the crime scene tape, as a number of others had, then passed by an officer and into a door leading into the restaurant from the south side."
>
> Berry said officers were hesitant to question those entering the site because they were concerned about creating controversy.
>
> "The officers do not know who should or should not be allowed inside these scenes. Some of them were flat out ignored when they inquired about a person's presence inside the perimeter," Berry said in the e-mail. "This should never be the case."
>
> Several community leaders were seen walking around the crime scene that stretched for blocks more than an hour after the shooting occurred at 3010 Penn Av. N. Some of them stood beside Police Chief Bill McManus behind the crime scene tape as he answered questions from reporters.
>
> Lt. Lee Edwards, head of the homicide unit, said at Wednesday's meeting that the scene was not contaminated, but he did cite other sites that hadn't been properly secured. He told attendees that police officials have already addressed internally the issues Berry raised. Capt. Rich Stanek said there still may be times when people will be allowed behind crime tape.

Although administrators may think that there are legitimate reasons for passing unchecked into or through the tape when one is not directly involved in the processing effort, this is entirely mistaken and can add to the evidence or even obliterate it.

Another example taken from one of the author's case files (Chisum) includes the following: A major West Coast city department had three employees (supervisors) shot by an employee who had "gone postal." The shooter was arrested at the scene, so there was no question about the identity of the perpetrator. The crime lab shared the same building and was at the crime scene with the homicide investigators within 10 minutes of the shooting.

The lab personnel started into the scene and took only a few photos before they were then removed from the scene so that police captains could "evaluate the scene." An hour later, they re-entered the scene, but again only for a few photos. This time, the chief (no longer) ordered them to stay out while the local TV station made a "documentary recording" (publicity) of the scene. When the lab personnel were finally allowed to enter the crime scene, they found it was a "shambles"—cam wheel tracks ran through blood, and cartridge casings recorded in the first few photos had been moved and some had been stepped on. Footprints were found in blood, but they were not the defendant's.

The proper way to handle this scene would have been to establish a command center. The captains could have "evaluated the scene" from this command center with a direct feed to the video cameras the techs carried. The only persons who should have been allowed into the scene should have been the trained lab personnel. (The chief originally came from an East Coast city where image was important, so he had wanted all the publicity he could get, to show how "good" he was at his job. The TV video was never shown.)

Once aid has been rendered and danger has been eliminated, the crime scene may be secured. Subsequently, the search for evidence may begin. The dynamic influences on physical evidence do not end with its recognition, however.

DYNAMIC INFLUENCES: POST-DISCOVERY

Crime reconstruction is at the end of, and dependent on, a long line of necessary investigative and forensic processes. Each item of evidence collected from a crime scene will go through some or all of the following processes:

1. Protection (from the environment and those in it)
2. Documentation (notes, sketches, photos, video, etc.)
3. Collection/packaging/marking
4. Preservation before delivery to the lab and in the lab
5. Transportation (to the forensic lab)
6. Identification (as a general kind of evidence based on its properties)
7. Comparison (to knowns, unknowns, and controls)
8. Individualization (as a unique piece of evidence)
9. Interpretation (consideration with other evidence from the case)
10. Disposition (storage/destruction/loss/deterioration)

As with pre-discovery influences, each of these processes has the potential to leave its mark on the evidence. A crime scene in high-traffic public areas like sidewalks and subways can wreak havoc on evidence collection efforts, even to the extent that law enforcement may refuse to process it if too much time has passed. Packaging items of clothing in plastic may result in static electricity, which can pull away valuable fiber evidence, or bacterial growth, which causes degradation of biological or botanical evidence. Transportation may shake and jar a dead body, causing fluids to purge from the injuries or the mouth and nose. Examination may result in the intentional sectioning and destruction of evidence portions. Reconstructionists must consider these and related influences and attempt to account for them in their interpretations.

Consider the following incarnations of post-discovery evidence dynamics.

Failure to Search or Recover

Even when the pre-discovery evidentiary influences have been accounted for or even avoided, it is still possible that crime scene personnel may fail to adequately recognize the true scope of the scene and to perform an adequate search for evidence. As a result, areas at or related to the scene may be insufficiently searched and documented to support reconstruction interpretations, and evidence may be missed entirely.

Consequently, the police investigation and the forensic investigation are deprived of the most complete picture possible. The failure to recognize evidence, the failure to conduct a complete and thorough search the first time through, and the failure to document the entirety of the scene each represent a missed opportunity to learn more about the crime. Recovering from these missed opportunities can be time-consuming, expensive, and, to some extent, impossible.

Evidence Technicians

Evidence technicians [crime scene investigators (CSIs)] are charged with evidence recognition, preservation, documentation, collection, and transportation. They are expected to locate and protect physical evidence without damaging it, without causing potentially misleading transfers, and without adding artifact evidence to the scene. They are expected to document and preserve, as much as possible, any pattern evidence. They are also expected to collect and package the evidence in a manner that preserves it for subsequent analysis and interpretation.

An important step in this process is documenting the scene prior to entering so that any changes that do occur as a result of their efforts are evident to those interpreting the documentation at a later time.

Coroner/Medical Examiner

The actions of the coroner or medical examiner while removing the body from the scene can alter evidence, obliterate patterns, cause potentially misleading transfer, and add artifact evidence. Influential events include the physical removal of the body from the location where it was discovered, the placement of the body into a "body bag," transporting the body from the scene, storing it, and reopening it for examination at a later time. These actions may change pattern evidence on the body and clothing of the victim, and they may relocate or destroy potentially valuable transfer evidence.

Premature Scene Cleanup

When a crime occurs in a public place, especially one that is highly visible or well traveled, there is sometimes an irresistible urge to clean up any signs of extreme violence left in the wake, including bloodshed, body parts, and brain matter. If it is done prematurely, cleanup will hamper crime scene investigation efforts.

Packaging/Transportation

How evidence is packaged and transported is also important. Clothing evidence with wet stains, for example, should not be folded in manner that transfers the stains to other parts of the garment. They must be removed and dried or preferably wrapped in butcher paper so the stains cannot transfer. Also, whenever possible, avoid placing multiple items of evidence in a single package, under a single number. This provides for potential cross-contamination and confusion in evidence tracking.

Svensson and Wendel (1974, p. 35) offer further suggestions:

> Evidence that is to be sent to a laboratory for further examination should be packaged in such a way that it does not run the risk of breaking, spoiling, or contamination, which might destroy its value as evidence.
>
> Containers should be tight and, depending on the nature of the material, strong enough that they will not break in transit.
>
> If the evidence consists of several objects, they should be packaged in separate containers or wrapped individually in paper. Each item should be clearly marked as to contents and then packaged in a shipping container. Loose evidence is thereby kept from contaminating other evidence. In some cases, it may be necessary to fix articles to the container separately so as not to come in contact with each other. Bottles and other glass vessels that contain liquids should not be packaged with other evidence, since they may break and contaminate other material.

Whatever specific evidence collection guidelines are adopted, they must preserve the evidence in transport, prevent cross-contamination, prevent spoilage, and provide for later identification. If evidence collection guidelines fail in any of these respects, then they are insufficient to the purposes of forensic science in general and crime reconstruction specifically.

Storage

Evidence storage is a subject that is infrequently discussed because it is often the source of extreme angst for police departments and their respective crime labs. Commonly, they do not have enough space to store the evidence they collect or sufficient and qualified personnel available to keep it properly inventoried. Deficiencies in this area can be disastrous, resulting in evidence being lost or destroyed, and cases dismissed.

Those with questions about evidence packaging and storage are encouraged to contact the American Society of Crime Lab Directors (www.ascld.org) because it has developed related standards and protocols for labs seeking accreditation.

Examination by Forensic Personnel

The purposeful actions of forensic scientists will remove evidence, obliterate patterns, may cause potentially misleading transfers, and can add artifact evidence. Forensic examination involves opening the packaged evidence, exposing it to the "lab" environment, exposing it to the forensic examiner, and submitting it to procedures that may require its physical separation or even destruction.[5] Although the last is often unavoidable and even expected, the first two can introduce unknown, unexpected, and questionable results when proper procedures are absent or ignored.

---

[5] The "lab" environment is really any place that the evidence is opened and examined. This may be a secure forensic lab with forensic examiners in protective clothing, or it may be a back office in a police department shared by a CSI unit, with a folding table in the middle on which they examine evidence as well as eat their lunch. The reconstructionist is better off knowing which is the case.

Premature Disposal/Destruction

At some point, an item of evidence may be slated for lawful disposal or destruction. Cases may be adjudicated, statutes of limitation may run out, and biological or chemical hazards may exist that make such measures necessary. However, physical evidence must not be destroyed before proper documentation and forensic examination have taken place. Unfortunately, those charged with the custody of evidence are commonly prone to neglect, mistakes, and ignorance with respect to the performance of these duties.

The inappropriate "house-cleaning" that takes place in some crime labs has been attributed largely to miscommunication and ignorance. However, the practice of specifically targeting some types of evidence, like untested rape kits, for destruction has been criticized as an intentional effort to prevent post-conviction testing that could result in an overturned conviction or even an exoneration.

To account for these post-discovery influences, a record must be kept of the people, places, and processes that the evidence has endured since the time of its recognition at the scene. This record is usually referred to as the *chain of custody*. Even though a reliable chain may be established, physical evidence may have been altered prior to or during its collection and examination. Unless the integrity of the evidence can be reliably established, and legitimate evidentiary influences accounted for, the creation of a chain of evidence does not by itself provide acceptable ground on which to build reliable forensic conclusions. It is, however, a good start, and without it evidence should not be considered sufficiently reliable for courtroom opinions.

Chain of Custody/Chain of Evidence

The chain of custody is the record of everyone who has controlled, taken custody of, or had contact with a particular item of evidence from its discovery to the present day. It has tremendous importance with respect to providing context for, and a record of, any scientific examinations. It also has considerable value with respect to establishing the origins of, and influences on, evidence presented in court.

For some items of evidence, a chain of custody may not be known or established prior to its recognition. Investigators may have to work hard in order to establish how it got where it was found. For other items, the chain of custody prior to recognition may be readily evident and undisputed. Accepting these limitations of the evidence, and working within them when interpreting the elements of the crime, is part of the normal investigative and forensic process.

The official chain of custody typically begins with the person who first found the item of evidence. In this way, potential evidence transfer, evidence contamination, and evidence loss are tracked. Because of the increase in potential influences on the evidence, the fewer people handling the evidence, the better. As described in O'Hara (1970, p. 69),

> The number of persons who handle evidence between the time of commission of the alleged offense and the ultimate disposition of the case should be kept at a minimum. Each transfer of the evidence should be receipted. It is the responsibility of each transferee to insure that the evidence is accounted for during the time that it is in his possession, that it is properly protected, and that there is a record of the names of the persons from whom he received it and to whom he delivered it, together with the time and date of such receipt and delivery.

O'Hara gives more specific instructions regarding the creation of the chain (p. 78):

> Evidence should be properly marked or labeled for identification as it is collected or as soon as practicable thereafter. The importance of this procedure becomes apparent when consideration is

given to the fact that the investigator may be called to the witness stand many months after the commission of the offense to identify an object in evidence which he collected at the time of offense. Indeed, defense counsel may require that the complete chain of custody be established, in which case each person who handled the evidence may be called to identify the object.

Photographs and measurements of the evidence that document its condition and location in the crime scene are also an important and commonly overlooked part of the chain of custody. Those looking for doubt can, in some cases, legitimately suggest weakness in a chain of custody that does not have this level of documentation.

As already shown, not everyone enthusiastically participates in the process of rendering a solid chain of evidence. Moreover, even when it is considered to be of importance, there is no guarantee that those responsible will know what they are doing. It is therefore not uncommon for the various chains of custody in a given case to be inconsistent, weak, and, for some items, nonexistent.

Consider the following case example of a chain of custody in utter confusion, from evidence to interviews, and the consequences.

The Case of Jamie Penich

In 2001, Jamie Lynn Penich, a 21-year-old junior majoring in anthropology at the University of Pittsburgh, was in Korea studying at Kiem Yung University for a semester (Figure 11.10). Penich and seven other students had traveled to Seoul for a weekend of sightseeing. Some of them, including Penich, went dancing and drinking at Nickleby's, an expatriate bar frequented by U.S. military in Seoul's party district, to celebrate St. Patrick's Day.

Penich was found dead in her hotel room at approximately 8 a.m. on March 18, 2001. Though initial police reports indicated she was strangled, her autopsy report determined that she had been stomped to death (Figure 11.11). There were imprints of jogging shoes on her chest, and she had sustained extensive head, neck, and facial injuries. U.S. Army CID became involved because they suspected a U.S. soldier had committed the crime. They investigated the scene, the suspects, and the evidence.

As reported in *Stars & Stripes* (Kirk, 2001):

> [Forensic scientist Brent] Turvey criticized the evidence collection and investigation methods in the Penich case, citing gathering up garments from the crime scene and placing them all in the same container as irregular.

FIGURE 11.10
Jamie Lynn Penich, 21-year-old anthropology major.

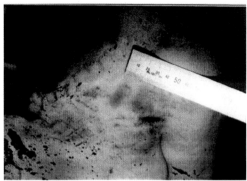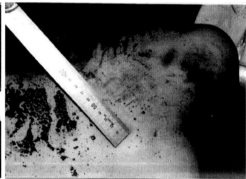

FIGURE 11.11
Autopsy photos of Jamie Lynn Penich's left shoulder reveal distinctive blunt force patterns left behind by footwear. This is action evidence consistent with stomping.

Korean police brought two pieces of evidence collected at the crime scene—a black jacket and a brown pullover—to a lab in the same bag, Korean forensic officials said. Turvey said that evidence should not have been clumped together.

"Every item of clothing—every shoe, every sock—should have its own bag," Turvey said. "You should never ever put two items in the same bag."

Penich's roommate in the hotel said the jacket completely covered Penich's face when she found the body. Two other witnesses said they remember Penich's face was covered with what they believed to be her black jacket.

The jacket is not seen over Penich's head in numerous crime scene photos shared with *Stars and Stripes*, or in the autopsy report. In some photos, the jacket is seen near Penich's body.

Another area of contention is whether Penich was sexually assaulted or had intimate relations with her attacker.

Lee Won-tae, chief medical examiner and director of the Department of Forensic Medicine in Seoul, said he's worked more than 800 murder cases. He said that evidence collection hinges on the quality of the detective. "Sometimes, they [investigators] are very highly qualified," Lee said. He said he considers the Yongsan Police Department officials good at collecting evidence. Lee said his lab was unable to get a DNA fingerprint from semen samples on two pairs of underwear belonging to The Netherlands woman and Penich, respectively.

During the autopsy, investigators also took a sample from Penich's body that tested positive for semen.

Lee said it was not unusual to not recover DNA. Turvey agreed, but said it could be a case of inexperience. "I would say that's very possible [to not get DNA results] if the lab doesn't have experience doing that kind of test," Turvey said. "Another lab with more experience may be able to find something."

Turvey also questioned the role of U.S. investigators.

One soldier originally suspected in the murder told *Stars and Stripes* that U.S. Army Criminal Investigation Command, known as CID, agents came to his barracks room to check his clothing. They donned goggles, turned off the room lights, and scanned the clothes with a special light, he said.

"They told me it was to see if [my clothes] had any body fluids, traces of blood," he said.

The agents found nothing, the soldier said, and allowed him to keep his clothes.

"This is ridiculous and speaks to the horrible level of training in forensic science on the part of CID investigators," Turvey said. "The clothes should simply have been taken and submitted to a lab for analysis. Investigators should not be doing that kind of thing themselves."

Marc A. Raimondi, chief of public affairs for CID in Virginia, said CID agents are well trained.

"We are better trained than any federal law enforcement agency in the country," he said.

According to Raimondi, agents routinely use a Polilight4 to find biological fluids and stains. The light uses selected wavelengths across the visible spectrum to fluoresce or identify stains or latent fingerprints for analysis.

Turvey said that method might not show all traces of fluids that could be present. Investigators can use other methods to detect blood, and clothes can be analyzed for fibers, he said. "There are so many things they can do with evidence," Turvey said. The soldier said CID agents returned a few weeks later to confiscate his clothing.

It is flawed when evidence is not collected immediately and retained, Turvey said. Delaying evidence collection makes analysis more problematic, he said.

Eventually, the FBI re-interviewed 20-year-old Kenzi Snider, a fellow student and traveling companion who had befriended Jamie Penich during their time together at Kiem Yung University. She was back in the United States at the time. FBI agents claim that Snider ultimately confessed to the crime during their interview; however, that interview was not recorded (Arnold, 2002).

[FBI Special Agent Mark] Divittis and [U.S. Army Criminal Investigations Division Agent Mark] Mansfield conducted the two-day interview [of Snider] along with another federal investigator.

In her confession, Snider told investigators she and Penich had been in a bar on the night of March 17. The two went to the motel and into Penich's motel room, said Linwood Smith, special agent with the FBI.

The two went into the bathroom, where they began kissing and groping, Smith said. The touching led to Snider performing oral sex on Penich, he said.

When Penich attempted to unbutton Snider's pants, Snider hit her in the face and knocked her into the bathtub, Smith said.

Snider dragged her into another room and stomped on her head, he said. …

One sticking point for Snider's defense team is that the confession was not recorded or videotaped. The only records are signed statements by Snider and a series of notes taken by investigators.

"The FBI does not tape interviews or interrogations," Divittis said. "It is not necessary, and it would be hard on the victim's family to have to hear it. People would not even understand the interrogation."

The defense disagreed.

"Don't you think that it is important for the courts to see how a person is persuaded?" Weis asked.

The U.S. Army CID also does not tape interviews, Mansfield said.

Snider was arrested, extradited back to Korea, and put on trial for the murder of Jamie Penich. However, she was acquitted. According to published reports (Jae-Suk, 2003):

> South Korean court has acquitted an American woman accused of beating to death another U.S. student for allegedly making unwanted sexual advances.

> Seoul District Court Justice Kim Nam-tae said today there wasn't enough evidence to convict 21-year-old Kenzi Snider of killing Jamie Lynn Penich at a Seoul motel in 2001.

> Kim said the court decided not to consider the confession Snider made to FBI and U.S. military investigators because Snider claimed she had been coerced into making it.

> "There is no other evidence to find her guilty of the accused crimes. She is not guilty," Kim said.

In reviewing this case, it should become clear that the initial investigation focused on chasing after a single theory to the detriment of gathering evidence and establishing a solid chain. Furthermore, when evidence collection efforts did take precedence, they were often late, inadequate, and uninformed. This deprived the case of the forensic evidence it most certainly could have used at trial, forcing prosecutors to rely on a confession for which there was also no reliable chain.

QUESTIONING THE EVIDENCE DYNAMICS

As suggested previously, one way to assess the evidence dynamics that may be present in a given case involves a scrupulous study of the scene and of the chain of evidence. The reconstructionist must begin by establishing the known individuals, circumstances, and events that may have handled or affected the evidence in question. Then, for each item of evidence involved in the reconstruction, the reconstructionist must inquire about the history of that item by asking the following:

- What comprises its chain of custody (notes, sketches, photos, logs, signatures, etc.)?
- Is it consistent or are there gaps?
- What were the conditions at the scene at the time of the incident and then later at the time of discovery (indoor/outdoor, raining/sunshine, humid/dry, windy/ stuffy, etc.)?
- Was any effort made to record the environmental factors that might have affected the evidence?
- What did the item look like at the scene?
- When was the item collected?
- Was the exact location of the item documented? (Where appropriate, in three dimensions)
- Was the item of evidence collected properly?
- When and how was the item packaged?
- Was the collection documented? How?
- What effects did transportation have had on the item?
- Is the name of every individual and agency that has handled the item known? How?
- Is every test or examination that has been performed on the item of evidence known? How?
- Was the item stored properly after collection and prior to testing?
- What effects have forensic testing had on the item of evidence?
- What does the item of evidence look like now and why? How much change has been effected?
- Has the initial officer at the scene been interviewed to determine what was done to secure the scene?
- Have the EMTs been interviewed to determine what they observed upon entering the scene and what they did that might affect the evidence?

The inability to answer even one of these questions represents a broken link in the chain of evidence and may call into question subsequent interpretations. The answers to these questions begin to address the issue of evidence dynamics, and subsequently a clearer picture of influences is established. As a result, the reconstructionist may learn whether and when uncertainty, equivocation, or reexamination are warranted.

EVIDENCE DYNAMICS: THE INFLUENCE OF FUTURE TECHNOLOGIES

As time goes forward, physical evidence may suffer its ravages. But while we have focused largely on the destructive aspect of evidence dynamics, they are not always destructive. As time goes forward, so does technology. Our ability to recognize, collect, preserve, and extract information from evidence grows with each technological breakthrough.

Consider the crime scene in general. The problem of documenting a crime scene as it appears upon arrival is one that troubles anyone who's had the experience—there is simply too much. Crime scenes involve complex systems of interrelated evidence that can easily be missed by imperfect human investigators. This may soon be a problem no longer. Several companies market various tools for documenting crime scenes, recording millions of points within a few minutes. Eventually, crime scenes will not require individual measurements, because as computers record the positions of each of those points it will be a simple matter to determine the distance between two points or objects. The recording is also three-dimensional, so there is a complete picture of the scene. Even the size and angle of blood droplets is recorded so the point of origin can be determined.

Consider the evolution of fingerprint evidence. From powders, to chemicals, to lasers, to metals—the search for latent prints has been met with a variety of technological solutions. But now, the fingerprint itself has become evidence. Under the right conditions, scientists are able to extract DNA from cellular material left behind, and recently there has been a further development. As explained in Choi (2007):

> Standard methods for collecting fingerprints at crime scenes, which involve powders, liquids or vapors, can alter the prints and erase valuable forensic clues, including traces of chemicals that might be in the prints.

> Now researchers find tape made from gelatin could enable forensics teams to chemically analyze prints gathered at crime scenes, yielding more specific information about miscreants' diets and even possibly their gender and race.

Consider the evolution of blood and DNA evidence. First they were analyzed for blood type, then RFLP DNA, then PCR DNA, now STR DNA—with the evidence sample size needed growing smaller with each method. Now we don't even need blood. You can get DNA from any live cell, including saliva on a cell phone or sweat left on the nose guard of eyeglasses. If there is hair evidence, you can get DNA from the root, mitochondrial DNA from the cells in the shaft, or a toxicological history. There are currently companies engaged in forensic DNA testing for the purposes of predicting race and even eye color. It may not be too long before we can discover any number of characteristics from the smallest amount of DNA.

This aspect of evidence dynamics demonstrates the need for ongoing training of evidence collection and cold case personnel—to consider not just what the evidence reveals with today's methods and techniques, but what it could reveal with the technology of tomorrow.

CONCLUSION

Crime reconstruction is a scientific endeavor that is best performed by qualified forensic scientists. Criminal profilers must either have such a background or work closely with those who do. When the criminal profiler is not a practicing forensic scientist, additional education and training in the forensic sciences is necessary to effectively perform BEA-style profiles.

The failure to consider *evidence dynamics* as a part of any crime reconstruction process has the potential to provide for misinterpretations of physical evidence and inaccurate or incomplete interpretations. Any subsequent use of the reconstruction would have a diminished foundation and relevance, compounding the harm in legal, investigative, and research venues. It is the responsibility of forensic scientists to perform reconstructions of the circumstances and behaviors involved in a crime with diligence, and to be aware of the possibility of *evidence dynamics*, in order that their interpretations reflect the most informed and accurate rendering of the evidence. Evidence dynamics do not always preclude a meaningful reconstruction, but reconstruction interpretations are questionable when evidence dynamics have been ignored.

Because they are commonly present and are commonly ignored by undertrained forensic personnel, the criminal profiler must be fully aware of the effects of evidence dynamics when examining behavioral evidence.

SUMMARY

Crime reconstruction is the determination of the actions and events surrounding the commission of a crime. A reconstruction may be accomplished by using the statements of witnesses, the confession of a suspect, the statement of a living victim, or the examination and interpretation of physical evidence. It requires the ability to put together a puzzle using pieces of unknown dimensions without a guiding picture.

Like criminal profiling, crime reconstruction is a forensic discipline based on the forensic sciences, the scientific method, analytical logic, and critical thinking. It requires an understanding of Locard's exchange principle, the ability to recognize and mitigate bias, and the willingness to abandon theories once they have been disproved. This remains true regardless of which reconstruction method is used.

Crime reconstruction is a scientific endeavor that is best performed by qualified forensic scientists. Criminal profilers must either have such a background or work closely with those who do. When the criminal profiler is not a practicing forensic scientist, additional education and training in the forensic sciences is necessary to effectively perform BEA-style profiles.

The failure to consider offender actions, victim actions, and *evidence dynamics* as a part of any crime reconstruction process has the potential to provide for misinterpretations of physical evidence and inaccurate or incomplete interpretations. Any subsequent use of the reconstruction would have a diminished foundation and relevance, compounding the harm in legal, investigative, and research venues. It is the responsibility of forensic scientists to perform reconstructions of the circumstances and behaviors involved in a crime with diligence and to be aware these influences so that their interpretations reflect the most informed and accurate rendering of the evidence.

Questions
1. Give two examples of evidence dynamics.
2. Explain Locard's exchange principle.
3. What purpose does the chain of custody serve?

4. Give two examples of secondary transfer.

5. Define the term *crime reconstruction.*

6. What are some of the problems inherent with relying on experience alone when reconstructing crime?

REFERENCES

Arnold, L., 2002. Snider Discusses Confession to Killing: Hearing to Decide if Former MU Student Will Be Tried for Murder. The Herald-Dispatch October 3.

Baker, K., Napier, M., 2003. Criminal Personality Profiling. In: James, S., Nordby, J. (Eds.), Forensic Science: An Introduction to Scientific and Investigative Techniques. CRC Press, Boca Raton, FL.

Brown, B., 2006. Woman Picked up with Trash. Ukiah Daily Journal April 19.

Chanen, D., Collins, T., 2005. Sergeant Raises Questions about Site of Slayings. Minneapolis Star Tribune, March 17.

Chisum, W.J., Turvey, B., 2000. Evidence Dynamics: Locard's Exchange Principle and Crime Reconstruction. Journal of Behavioral Profiling 1 (1).

Chisum, W.J., Turvey, B., 2007. Crime Reconstruction. Elsevier Science, Boston, MA.

Choi, C., 2007. Fingerprint Technique Could Reveal Sex, Race: Gel Tape Could Enable Forensics Teams to Chemically Analyze Prints. www.msnbc.msn.com/id/19876020/ (accessed 20.07.07.).

Cruz, G., 2007. New Orleans: Police Still Underfunded. Time June 20.

Cwiklik, C., 1999. An Evaluation of the Significance of Transfers of Debris: Criteria for Association and Exclusion. Journal of Forensic Science 44 (6), 1136–1150.

Deedrick, D., 2000. Hairs, Fibers, Crime, and Evidence. Forensic Science Communications 2 (3).

Findley, J., Hopkins, C., 1984. Reconstruction: An Overview. Identification News, October, 3–15.

Gross, H., 1924. Criminal Investigation. Sweet & Maxwell, London (English translation of earlier work).

Jae-Suk, Y., 2003. Kenzi Snider Acquitted in Murder of Jamie Lynn Penich. Associated Press June 19.

Kirk, J., 2001. U.S. Forensic Scientist Says Investigation of Student's Murder Was Flawed. Stars and Stripes May 24.

Knight, B., 1996. Forensic Pathology, second edition. Oxford University Press, Oxford, England.

Lee, H. (Ed.), 1995. Physical Evidence. Magnani & McCormick, Enfield, CT.

Locard, E., 1934. Manuel de Technique Policière: Les Constats, les Empreintes Digitales, second edition. Payot, Paris, France.

O'Hara, C., 1970. Fundamentals of Criminal Investigation, second edition. Charles C Thomas, Springfield, IL.

Svensson, A., Wendel, O., 1974. Techniques of Crime Scene Investigation, second edition. Elsevier, London, England.

Thornton, J.I., 1997. The General Assumptions and Rationale of Forensic Identification, In: Faigman, D., Kaye, D., Saks, M., Sanders, J. (Eds.), Modern Scientific Evidence: The Law and Science of Expert Testimony, vol. 2. West, St. Paul, MN.

Turvey, B., 2000. Staged Crime Scenes: A Preliminary Study of 25 Cases, Journal of Behavioral Profiling 1 (3).

Turvey, B., 2002. Criminal Profiling: An Introduction to Behavioral Evidence Analysis, second edition. Elsevier Science, London, England.

CHAPTER 12

Crime Scene Characteristics

Brent E. Turvey and Jodi Freeman

CONTENTS

Criminal Profiling: An Introduction to Behavioral Evidence Analysis, Fourth Edition

KEY TERMS

Crime scene characteristics	Method of attack	Sexual act
Crime scene type	Methods of control	Staged crime scene
Location type	Missing items	Victim location
Location of the scene	Opportunistic element	Victim selection
Method of approach	Point of contact	Victim response
	Precautionary acts	Weapon

Crime scene analysis and criminal profiling methods are dependent upon a host of different variables that must be gathered, weighed, and interpreted. Chief among these are the characteristics evident in the crime scene. Hardly a text or a research paper on either subject can avoid them, and most rely heavily upon related factors as a basis for their utility or findings. It is the essence of criminological analysis: examination, interpretation, classification, and comparison of offenders, victims, and their characteristics.

Crime scene characteristics are the features of a scene as evidenced by offender behavior related to decisions about the victim and the offense, in accordance with their contextual meaning. Crime scene characteristics may be established by a thorough crime reconstruction, the use of forensic victimology, and a timeline of known offense-related behaviors. As always, behavioral analysts are cautioned to avoid relying upon a single source of information when rendering crime scene characteristics or any other form of behavioral evidence analysis, and to seek corroboration when possible. When a single source is used, such as a victim or witness statement, that must be made clear in the analysis and its limitations must be discussed.

LIMITATIONS

The crime scene characteristics discussed in this chapter are characteristics that the authors have found most useful in their casework and research. However, each crime scene is distinct from all others by virtue of its unique environmental influences, victim–offender disposition, victim–offender interaction, the physical evidence left behind, and whether that evidence is ultimately discovered and recovered. The concepts in this chapter are therefore intended as a flexible starting point and are not to be used as a pedantic checklist.

Dynamic influences on a crime scene also mean that not all crime scene characteristics will be known in every case; some will not be discernible from the available evidence. It is the examiner's responsibility to determine and to acknowledge the limits of the behavioral evidence in every case. The examiner must also be prepared to classify characteristics as *unknown* when evidence is lacking. Only an inept examiner forces offense-related behavior into a specific category or classification when behavioral evidence is insufficient or absent.

UTILITY

As already suggested, the purpose of establishing crime scene characteristics is a primary criminological concern. It provides descriptive behavior that classifies offender actions and choices during crime-related activity, which gives insight that can distinguish one offender from others. These features may then be compiled for criminology research purposes as part of an idiographic/case study, or it can be used to help answer investigative and forensic questions in a given case. Crime scene characteristics may also be used to compare multiple offenders with each other, for nomothetic/group study or for the purposes of investigative and forensic linkage analysis (see Chapter 14 "Case Linkage").

LOCATION TYPE

Location type refers to the physical environment of a crime scene. There are four general types, and the qualities of each dictate the nature and extent of evidence that can be discovered and recovered there, as well as the methods that may be used to do so. The four location types are not mutually exclusive:

- **Indoor crime scenes** exist inside a structure with walls and some form of ceiling/roof cover that protects the scene from elements of nature. Examples include houses, apartments, buildings, sheds, garages, warehouses, cabins, tents, and caves.
- **Vehicle crime scenes** are drivable and therefore mobile. They may also constitute a form of indoor crime scene, or the only relevant surface may be exterior. Examples include cars, trucks, boats, ships, trains, airplanes, motorcycles, bicycles, blimps, RVs, and ATVs.
- **Outdoor crime scenes** are exposed to natural elements. Examples include fields, forests, ravines, canyons, ditches, roadsides, deserts, beaches, and hillsides.
- **Underwater crime scenes** are at or beneath the surface of any body of water. Examples include lakes, ponds, creeks, rivers, oceans, reservoirs, and harbors.

Location of the Scene

Location of the scene refers to the descriptive qualities of the crime scene, which include its physical location and its relationship to the surrounding environment. For urban and suburban crime scene locations, the street address and cross-streets are included. For rural, outdoor, or underwater scenes, the precise physical location may be determined using a global positioning system (GPS) device. Key questions to address include:

- Who frequents the location and the surrounding area?
- What is located at the scene? What belongs there?
- What activities normally occur at that location and in the surrounding area?
- What kind of criminal activity occurs at that location and in the surrounding area, if any?
- How can the location and the surrounding area be reached (by vehicle, walking, hiking, airplane, etc.)? If the scene is outdoors, what is the terrain?
- What are the access points to the scene (e.g., doors, roads, or paths), and what security exists, if any?

CRIME SCENE TYPE

A *crime scene* is defined as an area where a criminal act has taken place (Lee, 1994, p.1). One of the most important considerations in crime scene investigation, reconstruction, and analysis is determining what type of crime scene we are presented with. By this we mean the investigator must establish the relationship of the crime scene to the offense behavior, in the context of the offense. When determining the *crime scene type* in a particular case, the examiner is warned not to use intuition or experience as a guide. Let the physical evidence tell the story. Work from the physical evidence out to a sound reconstruction, not from biased theories into a corner.

A criminal offense can take place in not just one but multiple locations. This means that many crime scenes can be related across a single offense by virtue of the role they play in the crime. Consider the following types of crime scenes. They are not mutually exclusive categories.

All crime scenes may be described as *primary crime scenes*, *secondary crime scenes*, or *tertiary crime scenes*.

Primary Crime Scene

The *primary crime scene* is the location where the offender engaged in the majority of his or her principal offense behavior. (Principal offense behavior is determined by motive and/or criminal statute, and includes homicide, sexual assault, or theft.) In many instances, the primary crime scene is the location where the offender spent the most time—for either criminal behavior or cleanup. It is also likely to be the place where the most physical evidence was deposited during the offense.

In more complex, involved, or prolonged criminal offenses, the concept of a primary scene may still be applied, but not without care. If attacks on multiple victims occur within a single offense at separate locations, it is most useful to separate the offenses and assign one primary scene for each victim. Similarly, if a single victim suffers multiple types of harm within a single offense, it is most useful to separate the offenses and assign one primary scene for each.

For example, in a sexual homicide there may be a primary sexual assault scene and a primary homicide scene. If multiple victims are involved, each victim may have his or her own primary sexual assault scene and a primary homicide scene. Or victims may be sexually assaulted and killed at the same location. This must be determined by a careful reconstruction of each crime, after which the appropriate classification can be applied.

Classifying the location where the offense began in a particular case as the primary crime scene misses the point of this effort and prevents meaningful criminological comparison to other offenses. It also ignores the complexity of criminal behavior. Not all offenders do just one thing with one victim at one place; some crimes are much more complicated and we must acknowledge this in our classifications.

Secondary Crime Scene

The *secondary crime scene* is the location where some of the victim-offender interaction occurred, but not the majority of it. Also, the secondary scene does not involve principal offense behavior, but rather supporting behavior. There can be several *secondary crime scenes* associated with a single crime.

For example, if the victim is abducted from one location and taken to another to be raped or killed, the location where the victim was abducted is a secondary scene.

If the secondary scene is the location where the body is found, the secondary scene is also the *disposal site.*

Intermediate Crime Scene

An *intermediate crime scene* is any crime scene between the primary crime scene and a *disposal site,* where there may be transfer evidence. This includes vehicles used to transport a body to a disposal site after a homicide and locations where a body has been stored before final disposal. It also includes ground that has sustained drag marks of any kind. *Intermediate crime scenes* are a type of *secondary crime scene.*

Dumpsite/Disposal Site

Dumpsite, or *disposal site,* is a rough term used to describe a crime scene where a body is found. It may be the primary scene, or it may be a secondary scene.

More often than not, the term *disposal site* is interpreted to imply that the victim was assaulted somewhere else and transported to this location after or just before death. This is an unfortunate and very dangerous investigative assumption to make. A disposal site may also be the primary crime scene; this possibility must not be excluded. It must be investigated and confirmed by the physical evidence.

Many criminal profilers and behavioral analysts encountered by the authors seem uninterested in interpreting the relationship of outdoor locations to the bodies of victims found within them. Often, it is assumed that an outdoor crime scene is both a primary scene and a disposal site, and other nearby potential underwater, indoor, or vehicle locations are ignored. Investigators will also fail to consider that the victim's home might be related to the crime and will miss the opportunity to include related evidence in their investigation.

This kind of error can occur for four reasons:

- The investigator or examiner has not visited the crime scene and therefore does not know the spatial relationships within the scene and related areas.
- The investigator or examiner has not questioned the assumptions of law-enforcement personnel and is taking their word for the relationship of the crime scenes(s) to the crime.
- The investigator or examiner has little or no knowledge, training, and experience in crime scene investigation and the forensic sciences.
- The investigator or examiner has not attempted to reconstruct the crime scene based on the available evidence.

The remedy for this problem is avoiding preconceived theories. This means not concluding anything without physical evidence, questioning all investigative assumptions no matter how strongly they are believed by others, and getting adequate education and training in forensic sciences.

Once it has been established that the crime scene at hand is a secondary disposal site, certain questions must be answered:

- How was the body transported there—were dragging, carrying, containers, wraps, or vehicles involved?
- What route was taken during transportation—direct, indirect, public, private?
- Why was the disposal site chosen—convenience, crime concealment, evidence destruction, or emotion/fantasy?
- Why was transportation away from the primary scene necessary?

Transporting a body under any circumstance is a cumbersome and risky proposition. The body can be heavy and unwieldy, and in some cases may even need to be dismembered. Just getting it out of, or away from, the primary scene exposes the offender to innumerable risks. However, there is often a reason for moving the body—namely, that the offender is somehow associated with the primary scene and would be a logical suspect if the body is found there. This reason must be considered when formulating investigative or offender trait theories.

Tertiary Crime Scene

A *tertiary crime scene* is any location where physical evidence is present but there is no evidence of victim–offender interaction. This includes a location where *evidentiary items* (e.g., a used weapon, bloody clothing) are stored after a crime has been committed. It can also include transfer evidence resulting from victim movement after the offense, such as vaginal purge subsequent to a sexual assault or bloody-hand transfer to areas and objects (outside the primary or secondary scenes) that are touched while escaping or seeking help.

Example

The following example illustrates the differences between crime scene types:

> An altercation occurs between a victim and offender in a high-rise apartment building. The altercation results in the victim's being pushed off the balcony of an apartment. The victim's body hits numerous balconies during the fall, leaving material and biological transfer evidence (e.g., fibers, blood, hair, and skin) in the process. The offender subsequently recovers the victim's body and transports it by vehicle to a rural location that dissociates the offender from the crime scene.

In this case, the *dumpsite/disposal site* is the rural location where the body is found. The apartment building where the initial altercation occurred is the *primary crime scene*. The *intermediate crime scene* is the vehicle that transported the victim's body. The vehicle is also a *secondary crime scene*. Each balcony that contains transfer evidence from the victim's fall is a *tertiary crime scene*.

By accurately determining the crime scene type in a given case and evaluating the nature of any evidence that has been found there, the potential for other related crime scenes will be revealed. Failure to accurately determine the crime scene type or to consider this determination at all will result in the loss of physical and behavioral evidence. It will also prevent the examiner, and anyone relying on his or her analysis, from understanding what actually happened.

VICTIM LOCATION

Victim location refers to description of the victim's physical location immediately prior to his or her encountering the offender. Establishing this information is essential to the timeline of events and can provide invaluable information regarding potential suspects and witnesses. It will assist with determining who could have committed the crime, what they needed to know, what they had to be capable of, and who could have seen it.

Key questions to address include the following:

- Who frequents the location?
- What activities normally occur at the location?
- What is the criminal activity like in the area surrounding the location?
- What is the victim's connection to the location (e.g., work, friend, family)?
- How often did the victim frequent this location? Why?
- Why was the victim there that day, and was the visit scheduled?

It is possible that the victim location shares the same descriptive qualities as the crime scene location, previously discussed.

VICTIM SELECTION

Victim selection refers to the process by which an offender chooses or targets a victim. Victim selection can be classified as *targeted* (selected in advance) or *opportunistic*.

Targeted Victim

A *targeted victim* is the primary object of the offense, resulting directly from the offender's motive for committing the crime. A targeted victim is selected in advance specifically because of who they are, what they are, what they know, or what they possess. A targeted victim may be in a relationship with the offender (spouse, parents, family member, co-worker, friend, roommate, therapist, teacher, etc.) or may have been in a past relationship with the offender. The offender may also intentionally target a victim because the victim has information, items, or valuables sought by the offender. Examples of targeted victim selection include: administrative homicides that eliminate a witness to a crime; abduction and physical torture of a victim for the purposes of eliciting information; stalking, abducting, and raping a victim as revenge or punishment for a real or perceived wrong; and killing an intimate partner.

Opportunistic Victim

An *opportunistic victim* is ancillary to the offense. In such cases, the offender is motivated by a desire to commit the offense and the victim is irrelevant. The victim is selected because of:

- *Availability*: This refers to a particular victim's accessibility to the offender. It is related to the concept of *offender exposure.*
- *Vulnerability*: This refers to the offender's perception of how susceptible a particular victim is to the method of approach and attack. It is also related to the concept of *offender exposure.*
- *Location*: This refers to the victim's particular locality in relation to the offender's. It is often a function of both offender and victim activities and schedules and is also related to the concept of *offender exposure.*

Opportunistic victims may also be chosen because they fit specific criteria preferred by the offender. These criteria may include:

- *Fantasy criteria:* Fantasy criteria mean that victims are selected by virtue of having traits that a particular offender views as desirable or necessary for the satisfaction of a particular fantasy. The nature of these desirable or necessary traits is revealed in the victimology and the offender signature behavior.
- *Symbolic criteria:* Symbolic criteria mean that victims are selected by virtue of sharing the characteristics of others in a relationship with the offender (spouse, parent, family member, co-worker, friend, roommate, therapist, teacher, etc.).

It is important to note that the criminal profiler will be unable to determine whether an opportunistic victim fits specific offender criteria unless there is a series of crimes with a repeated pattern of particular victim characteristics or the identity of the offender (along with his or her past behavior) is known.

POINT OF CONTACT

Point of contact is the precise location where the offender first approached and acquired the victim. This is a neutral term because it includes locations where the victim was encountered under some ruse devised by the offender, as well as locations where the offender may have attacked the victim and dragged him or her to some other primary or secondary scene. Examples include a jogging path where a victim was grabbed before being taken somewhere else and raped, a vehicle in a case of a carjacking, and the victim's bedroom in the case of a home invasion.

Establishing the point of contact provides a reference marker, forward and backward, for activity on the timeline of both victim and offender behavior. At the point of contact, the offense has reached the point of no return. It establishes the beginning of victim–offender interaction and sets the emotional tone for rest of the offense.

METHOD OF APPROACH

Method of approach refers to the offender's strategy for getting close to a victim. (This discussion is adapted from Burgess and Hazelwood, 1995, pp. 142–143.) It may be described as a *surprise*, a *con*, or *pre-existing trust*. These methods of approach are mutually exclusive.

Surprise

The *surprise* approach is characterized by an offender who gets close to a victim by lying in wait for a moment of vulnerability. This can mean waiting for a victim at a particular location commonly included in the victim's scheduled activities, which suggests selection in advance (Burgess and Hazelwood, 1995, p.143). It can also mean selecting a victim and waiting until he or she is distracted, preoccupied, or asleep before approaching. The term *surprise* describes the approach only and does not suggest a particular method of attack.

A surprise approach requires timing, at least some cover or distraction, and opportunity. However it does not require planning or criminal skill to be effective.

The surprise approach may be important in criminal cases where *lying in wait* indicates premeditation and is an aggravating factor. An *aggravating factor* is a circumstance that turns murder into first-degree murder. In some states this can mean the death penalty.

Con

The *con* approach is characterized by an offender who gets close to a victim by use of deception or subterfuge. (This discussion adapted from Burgess and Hazelwood, 1995, p.142.) A con can involve a simple ploy to momentarily divert attention, such as a casual question or request for assistance that allows the offender to get physically close enough to overpower the victim. It can also involve a more complex scheme whereby the offender obtains the victim's immediate and prolonged trust, in order to move the victim to a secondary location, to gain access to a particular location or area, or to obtain the victim's compliance. The term con approach describes the approach only and does not suggest a particular method of attack.

Depending on the complexity of the con, this method of approach requires criminal confidence, planning, and experience in order to be implemented without raising the victim's suspicion. It is not a method of approach used by a criminal novice.

For example, impersonating a police officer, or some other form of authority figure, is a common ruse that tends to work with the ignorant, the inattentive, and the unsuspecting. It incurs a minimal need for physical force and achieves victim compliance and/or limited victim resistance.

Pre-Existing Trust

The *trust* approach means the offender gets close to the victim by means of a current or past relationship with the victim. The approach is exploitative and may be utilized as part of a long-term plan or simply out of opportunity, depending on the motives of the offender.

The trust approach requires the offender's willingness to betray the trust of someone they know and does not necessarily require particular criminal confidence or skill unless the exploitation is planned well in advance. Therefore, when assessing this approach it is necessary to consider whether the victim was targeted or opportunistic.

Pre-existing *trust* differs from a *con* in that a con uses deception to gain the trust of a stranger prior to the attack—there is no relationship to exploit.

METHOD OF ATTACK

Method of attack refers to the offender's mechanism for initially overpowering a victim after making the approach. The method of attack is separate from the method of approach and must be examined independently. The method of attack may be described in terms of the weapon and the nature of the force involved. Examples include:

- Verbal threat of lethal force. "Do what I say or I'll kill you."
- Verbal command and threat of lethal force—controlling force with a gun. "Do what I say or I will shoot you."
- Verbal command—controlling force with a knife. "I have a knife in your ribs. Do exactly as I tell you."
- Blitz attack (outlined below).

Blitz

According to Burgess and Hazelwood (1995, pp. 142–143), in a *blitz* attack, the offender gets close to the victim and delivers an immediate, overpowering force (in other words, an attack). The blitz attack is intended to deprive the victim of any reaction time and to give the offender immediate control of the situation.

The authors consider that the concept of a blitz attack describes the method of attack only and not the offender's method of approach. The authors advocate its use as a descriptor for an offender's method of attack when there is an immediate, brutal application of controlling, sexual, punishing, or lethal physical force aimed at incapacitating or killing the victim. A blitz attack may follow any method of approach.

A blitz attack suggests offender anger and a lack of overall criminal skill, combined with a willingness to inflict heavy damage to the victim and to create the physical evidence that necessarily results from such an unpredictable exchange.

For example, in a *surprise* approach with a blitz attack, an offender may lie in wait for hours before jumping out of the bushes in a park and immediately applying brutal levels of force to a victim, with a knife or a rock.

In another example, an offender may approach a different victim in the same park with a ruse. They may spend a few minutes together before the offender decides to make a move. The ruse itself is not the attack; it is a con approach. The blitz comes when the offender applies brutal levels of force to overpower the victim.

USE OF FORCE

The nature and amount of force that offenders are willing to use in their offenses tell us a great deal about their skills, dispositions, and motives. Analyzing the use of force includes an assessment not only of the force used in the *method of attack*, but also of how it relates to the rest of the offense behavior. It should include a breakdown of when the offender used force and the related intent. It can also include an assessment of force not used. This is referred to as negative documentation— a record of areas where no evidence of injuries exists and of associated environments and scenes that contain no evidence or objects associated with injuries (Jamerson, 2009). Without such negative contrast, the context of force and any resulting injury is incomplete.

The types of intentional force most commonly found in criminal cases (discussed below) are not necessarily exclusive.

Lethal Force

Lethal force is a term that describes physically aggressive behavior that is sufficient to kill. It includes the intentional infliction of injuries to vital areas, such as the heart, head, or neck. It may involve a weapon, a chemical, or bare hands. The defining element is that the force used is sufficient to cause the victim's death. Lethal force can be *administrative* or *brutal,* or it can involve *overkill.*

Lethal force need not cause the victim's death immediately or at all, but, once it causes the victim's death, then it is lethal by definition, regardless of intent.

Administrative Force

Administrative force is a term used to describe behavior that is focused on the delivery of a specific, purposeful amount of injury in order to accomplish a particular goal. In such instances, the offender is focused on a narrow outcome and is operating without personal interest. The offender's delivery of the force lacks evidence of emotion, passion, or other personal motivations. It is characterized by a short time interval, a single method of injury or killing focused on a specific or vital area or organ (head, neck, chest, etc.), and an absence of time spent on extraneous activity (looking for valuables, looking for personal items, cleaning up the scene, etc.). Examples of administrative force include:

- A sniper killing a victim with a single shot
- Killing a victim with a single lethal dose of poison
- Breaking someone's hands or legs for failure to pay a debt

Administrative force is often associated with the work of paid or trained professionals, acting on behalf of others. However, it may also be evident in the crimes committed by non-impulsive sociopaths against individuals they know and profess to have personal feelings for.

Brutal Force

Brutal force is a term for physically aggressive behavior involving one or more injuries that result in tremendous damage, often to the point of death. However, brutal force does not always result in death, nor is it necessarily intended to kill. It is generally employed in the service of anger. Examples of brutal force include:

- Multiple blows to the face with a blunt object like a hammer
- A shotgun blast to the face
- Detonation of an explosive device that removes a limb

Overkill

Overkill is injury beyond that needed to cause death. It involves the repeated infliction of injury subsequent to the application of lethal force. Overkill is generally in the service of cumulative rage—anger and frustration that have built up over time. Common examples of overkill include:

- Multiple close-range gunshots requiring reloading
- A dozen or more stab wounds in the same general area of the victim's body

It is important to discriminate between injuries evidencing overkill and injuries inflicted on a victim who has a high endurance and keeps coming back despite repeated attempts to put him down.

Control-Oriented Force

Control-oriented force is physically aggressive behavior that is intended to restrict victim movements. Examples of control-oriented force include:

- Holding a victim manually to prevent movement or escape
- Gagging a victim to prevent screaming
- The use of restraints, such as handcuffs and ligatures, to prevent movement or escape
- Locking a victim in a room to prevent escape

Corrective Force

Corrective force is a term for physically aggressive behavior that is delivered in response to, or to prevent, undesirable or harmful victim behavior. Examples of corrective force include:

- Slapping a victim for screaming
- Punching a victim for refusing to take off their clothes
- Kicking a victim for refusing to get up

Defensive Force

Defensive force is physically aggressive behavior that is intended to protect the individual administering it from attack, danger, or injury. This term does not imply that the behavior was legally or morally justified. Rather, it is meant to describe behavioral intent. Examples of defensive force include:

- A victim's kicking a mugger in the groin in order to facilitate a flight to safety
- A victim's biting an offender during a sexual assault
- An offender with a gun fighting off the violent response of a would-be victim with blunt force

Defensive force may also be used to describe injuries that are self-inflicted in an attempt to escape or to resist the application of force. An example is bruising and fingernail marks sustained by a victim in his attempts to remove a ligature from around his neck.

Precautionary Force

Precautionary force is a term for physically aggressive offender behavior that results in wound patterns that are intended to hamper or to prevent the recognition and collection of physical evidence. Examples of precautionary acts that leave behind wound patterns include:

- Chopping off a victim's hands and head to hamper investigative efforts at identification
- Burning a victim's pubic area with fire to destroy evidence of sexual assault
- Placing a body in acid to obscure identifiable features or to dissolve it entirely

Experimental Force

Experimental force describes behaviors involving force that fulfill nonaggressive, psychological, and often fantasy-oriented needs. It does not require a conscious or living victim. Examples of experimental behaviors that leave behind wound patterns include:

- Postmortem biting or removal of the victim's flesh
- Postmortem or perimortem insertion of foreign objects into a victim's mouth
- Postmortem disembowelment

This behavior may also be associated with temporary chemically induced delusions or a full-blown mental disorder.

Physical Torture

Physical torture is the intentional and repeated infliction of nonlethal injury to a victim. For the requirements of torture, the victim must remain alive and conscious during the initial infliction of the injury so that he or she can experience the pain that follows. In most cases, there is a specific aim involved, such as getting information, obtaining a confession or a denouncement, sexual gratification (sadistic intent), or revenge.

Sexual Force

Sexual force is aggression or coercion that relates directly to the satisfaction of erotic or libidinous desires. Examples of sexual force include:

- Postmortem biting or removal of the victim's breasts
- Forcing a victim to engage in oral sex
- Vaginal or anal penetration

Sexual force may also be associated with sexual fetishes and paraphilias.

METHODS OF CONTROL

An offender's *methods of control* are used to manipulate, regulate, restrain, and subdue victim behavior during the offense. Methods of control can include the use of the following forms of force.

Control-Oriented Force

- Striking a noncompliant victim
- Choking a combative victim
- Biting a combative victim
- Using ligatures to bind or secure the victim's body
- Using handcuffs
- Using a gag to quell the victim's verbal activity

Verbal Threat of Controlling, Punishing, Sexual, or Lethal Force

- "Quit moving around, or I'll tie your hands behind your back."
- "Do that again, and I'll kill you."
- "Do what I say, or I'll put this in your ass."
- "Keep walking, or you'll really be taught a lesson."

Unarticulated Presence of the Physical Threat of Controlling, Punishing, Sexual, or Lethal Force

- Presence of a gun
- Presence of a knife
- Presence of a bat (or other blunt force weapon)
- Clenched and raised fists
- Physical intimidation by virtue of size
- Presence of handcuffs (or other obvious restraints)

When describing an offender's methods of control, the criminal profiler is admonished to be specific about the physical mechanisms of control and precisely how the control manipulated, regulated, restrained, or subdued victim behavior.

WEAPON AND WOUNDS

A *weapon* is any item found at, or brought to, the crime scene by the victim or the offender and used for the purposes of inflicting injury.

Not all offenders use a weapon, some because they do not have it within them to use a weapon, some because they do not have access to a weapon, some because they do not feel that they need a weapon, and some because the nature of their perception does not allow them to use a weapon (such as having a reassurance-oriented fantasy that the attack involves the consent of the victim and is therefore not actually a criminal act).

For the criminal profiler, key questions to address regarding any weapon include:

- What type of weapon is it (knife, gun, rope, rock, shovel)?
- Who does the weapon belong to (victim, offender, third party)?
- How did the weapon get to the crime scene?
- Where was the weapon found (on/near victim, discarded nearby, at another related crime scene)? Or was it not found?
- When during the crime was the weapon used (e.g., during the offender's approach, during the physical attack, during sexual attack)?
- How was the weapon used (defensive, precautionary, experimental, corrective, controlling, punishing, sexual, or lethal force)?

It is important to look at both the type of weapon used and the physical injuries or wounds sustained by the victim. An analysis of each weapon involved in the crime should include the type of wound it created. The use of a weapon in the crime may not be assumed; the evidence must demonstrate it.

The following list of general wound types is adapted from DiMaio and DiMaio (1993).

Blunt-Force Trauma

Blunt-force trauma is caused by forceful (e.g., crushing or shearing) contact with non-penetrating weapons or objects. Adelson (1974, p. 378) described the mechanisms of injury in blunt trauma as impacts delivered by a weapon's forceful contact with part or all of the victim's body and combinations of impact and forceful contact with an unyielding surface. Blunt-force injuries are divided into the following categories:

- **Abrasions.** An excoriation or circumscribed removal of the superficial layers of skin indicates an abraded wound. Examples include ligature furrows where movement caused the skin to break and redden, as well as the long marks left behind on a body dragged across a rough surface like concrete.
- **Contusions** are injuries (usually caused by a blow of some kind) in which blood vessels are broken but the skin is not. They can be both patterned (imprinted, not directional) and non-patterned. They include bruises and subcutaneous hemorrhages, the age of which can often determined by their color. Differentiating postmortem and antemortem contusions is also an important consideration in reconstruction (Adelson, 1974, p. 382).
- **Lacerations** are torn or jagged wounds that tend to have abraded and contused edges. They can be differentiated from sharp-force (penetrating) injuries by the recognition of tissues bridging from one side of the laceration to the other (indicating shearing or crushing force).

Burns

A *burn* is damage caused by heat, fire, or chemical. Burn injuries occur due to:

- Direct exposure to open flame
- Contact with hot objects
- Radiated heat waves
- Scalding hot liquids/steam
- Chemicals
- Microwaves

Sharp-Force Injury

Pointed, bladed, or sharp-edged objects and weapons cause sharp-force (penetrating) wounds. They may be divided into the following categories:

- **Stab wounds.** Stab injuries are the result of being pierced with a pointed instrument. The depth of the injury is usually greater than its width.
- **Incise wounds (cuts).** Incisions and cuts are the result of sharp instruments' being drawn across the surface of the skin, even into the tissue, and are longer than they are deep.
- **Chop wounds.** Chop injuries are the result of heavy instruments with a sharp edge. They go deep into the tissue, can be associated with bone fractures, and can have a combination of incised and lacerated characteristics. Examples include injuries inflicted by axes, hatchets, machetes, swords, and meat cleavers.

Gunshot Wounds

A firearm (rifle, handgun, or shotgun) delivers force from a distance with a single projectile or multiple pellets, which arrive at a target with enough force to cause either penetrating (entrance wound only) or perforating (entrance wound and exit wound) injuries. *Entrance wounds* are divided into the categories of contact, near contact, intermediate, and distant. Gunshot wounds also include *exit wounds* and *atypical entrance* and *exit wounds* (DiMaio and DiMaio, 1993).

Therapeutic and Diagnostic Wounds

Therapeutic and *diagnostic wounds* are injuries inflicted by emergency medical services (EMS) personnel during treatment. They include needle sticks and marks, various incisions and puncture marks, and even bruising caused by rough handling or transport. It is important, when interpreting wounds, to get a complete record of the activities of EMS personnel so that injury patterns unrelated to interactions between the victim and the offender can be distinguished.

Postmortem versus Antemortem Wounds

An important, but often overlooked, consideration in wound pattern analysis is whether wounds were inflicted before, during, or after death. This assessment is an involved and often imprecise process that may require more than just examining the wound. For some injuries, it may not be completely possible to determine if the injury was inflicted just before or just after death—hence, the use of the imprecise term *perimortem* injury.

Antemortem wounds are those that occur before death. They tend to be associated with injuries that result in a lot of bleeding, either internally or externally.

Postmortem wounds are inflicted after the victim's death. They commonly exhibit very little or almost no bleeding from broken arteries and veins. This is not a hard and fast rule, however, as every injury has its own peculiarities.

VICTIM RESPONSE

Victim response refers to the victim's reaction to the offender's behavior. There are two categories of victim response: *victim compliance* and *victim resistance*.

Victim Compliance

Victim compliance refers to the victim's acquiescence to an offender's demands readily and without hesitation. Some victims may even proactively ask what they can do to please the offender so that he will be on his way. This does not mean that the offender–victim interaction was consensual or that no crime took place. Victim compliance can be the result of fear of harm or a resignation to the horrible events that are about to take place.

Victim Resistance

Victim resistance refers to the victim's behavior that defies an offender.

Burgess and Hazelwood (1995, p. 143) provide three useful categories of victim resistance and give a well-placed warning not to confine the definition of resistance to *physical* or *verbal* but to include *passive resistance* as well. The categories are not mutually exclusive and each type of victim resistance may occur within a single crime.

The authors offer the caution that the descriptors that follow are not about victim blame or victim responsibility. A victim's response to an offender is influenced by his or her life history, experiences, and understanding of the world as expressed through their individual personality. What is extreme behavior for one victim may not be for another. This emphasizes the importance of developing a full victimology before assessing victim resistance. Find out who the victim is first, and that knowledge will provide insight into why the victim reacted the way he or she did.

- **Passive resistance.** In passive resistance, a victim defies an offender by nonaggressive means, such as the refusal to comply with the offender's commands or the refusal to eat or drink if in captivity for prolonged periods of time. In *Practical Aspects of Rape Investigation* (1995), Burgess and Hazelwood admonish us to remember that victim noncompliance is a form of resistance and may be all that certain victims are capable of (physically or psychologically).
- **Verbal resistance.** The term *verbal resistance* refers to the victim's defiance of an offender with words or vocalizations. It applies to a victim who shouts for help, who screams when attacked, who pleads for mercy, who verbally refuses to follow commands, or who tries to negotiate or bargain. Examples of verbal resistance include:
  - "Don't touch me."
  - "I'm not going anywhere with you."
  - "You'll have to kill me to rape me."
  - "I don't want to die."
  - "Please, I just don't want you to hurt me."
  - "Let me go and I won't tell anyone."
- **Physical resistance.** Physical resistance occurs when a victim defies an offender with physical force, which can include punching, slapping, scratching, biting, struggling, kicking, and running away. Physical resistance may also include the victim's unintentional self-inflicted injuries, including fingernail marks on the victim's neck resulting from an attempt to physically resist the use of a strangling ligature.

If a victim claims that physical force was used, attempts to confirm this statement should include examination of the victim's body and the areas of the offender's body that would have been affected or injured. Absence of injury does not always indicate that physical force was not used or that the victim is being untruthful.

NATURE AND SEQUENCE OF SEXUAL ACTS

A *sexual act* is any offender behavior involving sexual organs, sexual apparatus, or sexualized objects. Establishing the nature and sequence of sexual acts within an offense gives insight into offender *modus operandi* and offender *signature*. The physical evidence can allow limited determination (e.g., the nature is established but not the definite sequence), but often the determination relies heavily on witness accounts or victim interviews.

Sexual acts are an extension of offender force and should be evaluated similarly, as being defensive, precautionary, experimental, corrective, controlling, punishing, sexual/fantasy, or lethal.

Students are encouraged to seek out as many sources as they can that discuss human sexual behavior, fantasy, fetishes, and ritual. A comprehensive knowledge of human sexual behavior must be acquired before an investigator can examine or comment on it meaningfully. Any examiner who avoids such material (e.g., because it is personally distasteful) not only should refrain from examining any case involving actual or potential sexual behavior but also should seek out a new profession.

TIME

The evidence in a case may allow the criminal profiler to determine the amount of time (or approximate amount of time/time range) spent by the offender in performing various crime-related tasks. The timeline may provide insight into the offender's motivation as well as modus operandi and signature behavior. Some crimes are completed in minutes, while others may take days, and the reasons for the time elapsed can speak volumes about a case.

Examples of evidence that may be used to determine the amount of time involved in the offense include:

- Testimonial evidence (e.g., victim and witness statements)
- Forensic reports (e.g., medical examiner's report, entomology report, toxicology report)
- Documentary evidence (e.g., computers, cell phones or security devices that identify victim/offender movement and communication timelines prior to, during, and after the offense)

MULTIPLE OFFENDERS

The evidence in a case may allow the criminal profiler to provide an opinion about whether multiple offenders were involved in the commission of the crime. If more than one offender is involved, this fact will provide insight into the modus operandi and signature behavior of the offenders as well as the level of planning required. Examples of evidence that may support this opinion include:

- Physical evidence (e.g., DNA, fingerprints, footprints, wound patterns, number of weapons used)
- Testimonial evidence (e.g., witness statements and victim statements)
- Documentary evidence (e.g., images from cell phone cameras and security cameras)

PLANNING/PREPARATION

The extent of offender *planning* may be determined by assessing whether the offender possessed the means for the commission of the crime. For the criminal profiler, key questions to address regarding planning/preparation include the following:

- What did the offender bring?
- What did the offender use from the scene?
- What did the offender take?
- How did the offender take it?
- How many offenders were involved in the commission of the crime?
- Was the victim targeted?

As suggested by these questions, a determination of the extent of offender planning hinges on an assessment of both *precautionary acts* and *opportunistic elements*.

PRECAUTIONARY ACTS

Precautionary acts are actions that an offender takes before, during, or after an offense that are consciously intended to confuse, hamper, or defeat investigative or forensic efforts for the purposes of concealing the offender's identity, connection to the crime, and the crime itself. Examples of precautionary acts include, but are certainly not limited to, the following:

- **Clothing/disguise.** Offenders may change their appearance using disguises, masks, or bulky clothing. By disguising their physical features they make later identification by a victim or witness difficult or impossible.
- **Alteration of voice.** The offender may deepen his or her voice, increase its pitch, or affect an accent. This stratagem may serve precautionary or psychological/fantasy-oriented motives. The contact and language used may suggest the correct reason.
- **Use of a blindfold.** Use of a blindfold prevents the victim from seeing the offender's physical features. This may serve precautionary or psychological/fantasy-oriented motives. The role that a blindfold plays (function or fantasy) may not be clear without other contextual evidence.
- **Time of day.** Offenders may choose to act at a time of day when the scene is very dark so as to obscure their own physical features and to increase victim vulnerability
- **Location selection.** A location that is secluded, less traveled, and out of the visual range of any local residences may be preferred by certain offenders.
- **Victim selection.** Offenders may select complete strangers as victims (opportunistic victims), decreasing the likelihood that they may be connected to the crime at a later date.
- **Use of gloves.** When used during the commission of a crime, gloves prevent the transfer of fingerprints and biological fluids (e.g., sweat) from the offender's hands to objects and surfaces that he or she touches.
- **Use of a condom.** A condom inhibits the transfer of sperm (and therefore DNA evidence) to the victim or the crime scene. The offender can take the condom from the scene and dispose of it elsewhere.
- **Use of fire.** Fire can be used to damage or destroy the victim, the crime scene, and/or evidence of the offense. It may also be an expression of anger.
- **Disposing of the victim's clothing.** The offender may throw some (e.g., shirts, shoes, and socks) or all of the victim's clothing away. This serves the purpose of increasing the victim's shame, leaving the victim without protective footwear, and hampering the victim's ability to get help or to contact authorities. It also disposes of potential physical evidence.
- **Looking at or collecting victim identification.** The offender may examine, record, or take the victim's personal identification to learn the victim's name and address. This knowledge can be used in a threat of future violence to intimidate the victim, with the aim of preventing the victim from reporting the incident or at least of delaying reporting. In a homicide, removing the victim's identification may delay investigative efforts to identify the body.
- **Use of control-oriented force:** Offenders may use control-oriented force to prevent the victim from verbally or physically resisting and/or attracting attention to the crime and offender. For example, a gag prevents verbal resistance.
- **Use of a disposal site.** The offender may dispose of the victim's body at a location separate from the primary crime scene. This is a precautionary act that may prevent the discovery of evidence at the primary crime scene or may dissociate the offender from the primary crime scene.

MISSING ITEMS

Missing items refer to any items that originally belonged at a crime scene and were not found during crime scene investigation efforts. Establishing missing items may provide insight into offender *motivation, modus operandi,* and *signature behavior.*

When possible, compare a crime scene as it exists to how it existed before the crime occurred there. To make this comparison, the criminal profiler and forensic personnel will need solid documentation of the scene before the crime occurred. Use photos from recent events held at the location, ATM cameras, security cameras, and so on. Then develop a list of witnesses who know the area well and interview them extensively—the rule here is to be resourceful and to be thorough. Look for things that are

- New
- Missing
- Unchanged

A thorough victimology is also useful in determining what items may be missing from a crime scene. It is important to look at what the victim was wearing and what the victim had in his or her possession to accurately establish what items may be missing from the scene.

Why things are new, missing, or unchanged must be accounted for. Burgess and Hazelwood (1995, p. 153) place items taken by the offender in three categories:

Evidentiary Items

Evidentiary items are items that the offender believes may link him or her to the victim or to the crime. Examples include, but are not limited to,

- Items of the victim's clothing with bloodstain patterns, fibers, or semen on them
- Gifts, valuable items, or jewelry given to the victim by the offender
- Photographs of the victim and the offender together
- Letters written by the offender in the victim's possession

Taking this type of items from a crime scene is considered a *precautionary act.*

Valuables

Valuables are items taken from the crime scene that the offender believes may have financial value. The type of item taken by an offender for profit suggests not only the skill level and transportation capabilities of the offender but also the level of the offender's financial need. Examples include, but are not limited to,

- Credit cards
- Jewelry
- Cash
- Checkbooks
- TVs
- Laptops
- DVD players
- Cell phones
- Drugs

Personal Items

Personal items taken from the victim or the crime scene may have sentimental value to the offender. These items often have no financial value, but, if they do, that value is ancillary or incidental. Personal items are divided into two subjective categories, trophy and souvenir. The precise nature of each item must be determined on an item-by-item basis, and it cannot be done without knowing how the offender acquired it (context) and the offender or victim behavior that it is associated with. Note that items given as examples from either category could fit into both; they are not mutually exclusive categories.

- **Trophy.** A *trophy* is a symbol of victory, achievement, or conquest. It is associated with force, victim resistance, or victim subjugation and humiliation. The following are examples of trophies:
  - A torn garment worn by the victim
  - A lock of the victim's hair
  - Victim personal identification
  - Pictures taken of the victim during the attack
  - A weapon used on the victim, taken from the scene
  - A victim body part
- **Souvenir.** A *souvenir* is a reminder or token of remembrance that represents a pleasant experience. It is commonly associated with reassurance-oriented needs, but this may not be the case. The following are examples of souvenirs:
  - Victim undergarments taken from clothes hamper
  - Victim school identification
  - Pictures taken from the walls of the victim's home or taken out of the victim's personal photo album
  - A ring, necklace, or other inexpensive jewelry worn by the victim
  - Pictures taken of the victim during victim selection activity, before the offense

Taking these items from a crime scene is *signature behavior* and suggests offender motivation.

OPPORTUNISTIC ELEMENTS

Opportunistic elements are any unplanned elements that the offender seizes on for inclusion in an offense. They can be an opportunistic victim, an opportunistic offense, an opportunistic weapon, or an opportunistic location—anything that was not planned for but was utilized during the offense. Evidence of opportunistic elements or behavior in an offense does not necessarily imply an unplanned or previously unimagined offense.

In assessing whether a behavior or element (victim, location, etc.) is opportunistic, remember to look for any associated behaviors or elements that indicate planning. These include, but are not limited to,

- Evidence of victim surveillance
- Items brought to the crime scene specific to the crime committed
- Calls to the victim before the attack
- Intimate knowledge of victim's residence and personal schedule

It is not uncommon for investigators to mistakenly theorize that an offender's behavior was generally opportunistic when the victim appears to be an opportunistic victim (a mistake often made when an inadequate victimology has been done). They may therefore underestimate the offender's dangerousness or the likelihood that he or she will offend in the future. This can result in *a priori investigative bias*, which causes the failure to recognize the offender's planning behavior or the pattern of a serial offender. Indications that an offense is opportunistic include, but are not limited to,

- The offense occurs during the commission of another offense
- The offense occurs during offender non-criminal activity
- The offense lasts a very short period of time
- The offense is committed hastily—an abundance of easily discoverable evidence is left at the scene
- The offender uses available materials to disable the victim

THE BODY

In all cases, whether a victim survives or is dead, the victim's body is an extension of the crime scene. For an excellent reference on this subject, see DiMaio and DiMaio (1993). For the criminal profiler, key questions to address regarding the victim's body include the following:

- At what point during the offense was the body put in the scene?
- How did the victim or body physically get into the crime scene?
- How did the victim or body physically get into its final position at the crime scene?
- Why was the body left in the particular scene?
- What condition is the body in?
- Is the positioning of the body in keeping with the established facts of the offense?
- Is there evidence to suggest that the offender placed the body in a particular position?
- If the body was placed in a particular position, how is that posing meaningful?
- To whom is the posing meant to be meaningful (i.e., the offender, whoever finds the body, the victim, etc.)?

STAGING

As discussed in Chapter 11, a *staged crime scene* is one in which the physical evidence has been purposefully altered by the offender to mislead authorities or to misdirect the investigation (Turvey, 2000). Staging is a precautionary act committed after an offense that is consciously intended to confuse, hamper, or defeat investigative or forensic efforts for the purpose of concealing the offender's connection to the crime.

"Appears Staged"

Each investigator, profiler, and forensic examiner has his or her own subjective sense of the elements that, when discovered at a crime scene, indicate staging. Or, at least, that is what they say in court. These elements can include circumstances like:

- There is no sign of forced entry
- Forced entry is evident
- The drawers in a room have been removed and carelessly dumped out to give a "ransacked" appearance
- The drawers in a room have been removed and carefully stacked to protect or preserve the content
- There is no indication of a search for valuables
- Only particular items have been stolen
- The victim had no life insurance
- The victim's death profited a family member, household member, or intimates in some way other than life insurance (anger, revenge, trust fund, etc.)

Any or all of these circumstances may raise suspicion in the alert investigator, and there is nothing inherently wrong with suspicion. However, these circumstances also occur in cases where there is no staging. Careful examiners will note that they are not even useful red flags, because they cover almost all possibilities with respect to each particular circumstance (i.e., the point of entry will either be forced or not, items of value will have either been stolen or not). Suspicion justifies further investigation; it tells the investigator where to look for more evidence. Suspicious circumstances are not themselves evidence, however. They are hypotheses that must be tested with the evidence; they do not signal the end of the inquiry, but its beginnings.

Staging is a possibility in any crime and therefore must be considered and excluded during the crime analysis. The criminal profiler must test theories of staging against the physical evidence. None of the physical evidence can be excluded or ignored. The clearest determination of whether a crime scene has been staged depends on reconstruction of the physical evidence. In each case, examine the forensic evidence carefully, corroborate/ compare victim and witness statements with evidentiary findings, reconstruct the crime meticulously, and assume nothing.

VERBAL BEHAVIOR/SCRIPTING

Scripting refers to the language used by an offender during an offense, as well as the language he or she commands the victim to use. Scripting is used to direct the victim verbally and behaviorally. It indicates the offender's ideal fantasy regarding the offense—what will happen, what the offender will say, and what the victim will say in return (if anything at all). Language, then, is an extension of both psychological needs and force (or an extension of a lack of psychological/emotional need and a lack of force).

According to Burgess and Holmstrom (1979), there are 11 major themes in rapist/offender verbal behavior, which must be evaluated not only for content, but also for tone, attitude, and timing in the context of the attack. Because the 11 themes cover only certain kinds of selfish rapist motivations, ignoring others, the author has made additions to these themes indicated by boldface type (while they were developed to describe rapist language, there is no reason that these script categories are exclusive to rapists). They include:

- **MO-oriented orders and commands.** "Don't look at my face."
- **Signature-oriented orders and commands**. "Shake your ass for me. I want to see it move."
- Threats. "Don't look at my face, or I'll kill you."
- Confidence lines. "I'm going to show you how a real man feels."
- Personal inquiries of the victim. "What is your name? How old are you?"
- Personal revelations by the offender. "I love the way this feels."
- Obscene names and racial epithets. "Bitch." "Nigger."
- Soft-sell departures. "I'm not going to hurt you."
- Sexual insults. "You're barely worth raping."
- Possessiveness. "I own you."
- Taking property away from others. "You think that you can't be had by someone else?"
- **Intentional deceptions**. "My name is Paul. I live very close by, so don't watch me while I'm leaving."
- **Reassurance-oriented statements**. "My name is Paul. I won't hurt you."
- **Apologies**. "I'm sorry. This wasn't me."
- **Bargaining**. "If you do this, I'll let you go."
- **Personal compliments**. "You look so pretty."
- **Sexual compliments**. "You have really nice tits."
- **Self-deprecation**. "I am such a loser"
- **Rationalizations**. "This isn't me. I'm not going to rape you. I wouldn't do that."

SUMMARY

Crime scene analysis and criminal profiling methods depend upon a host of different variables that must be gathered, weighed, and interpreted. Chief among these are the characteristics evident in the crime scene. *Crime scene characteristics* are the features of a scene as evidenced by offender behavior related to decisions about the victim and the offense, in accordance with their contextual meaning. They may be established by a thorough crime reconstruction, the use of forensic victimology, and a timeline of known offense-related behaviors. It is an interpretive classification stage of crime scene investigation subsequent to crime reconstruction efforts. It is intended to provide a language for categorizing, explaining, and comparing victim and offender behavior that has been established by the reconstruction interpretations that are available.

Each crime scene is distinct from all others by virtue of environmental influences, victim–offender disposition, victim–offender interaction, the physical evidence left behind, and whether that evidence is ultimately discovered and recovered. Furthermore, not all crime scene characteristics will be known in every case; some will not be discoverable from the available evidence. Crime scene characteristics may be compiled for criminology research purposes as part of idiographic and nomothetic study, or they can be used to help answer investigative and forensic questions, including those related to case linkage efforts.

Questions

1. Explain the difference between a *primary crime scene* and a *dumpsite/disposal site*.
2. The *method of approach* characterized by an offender who gets close to a victim by lying in wait for a moment of vulnerability is referred to as a _____ approach.
3. List three types of *force* that offenders may use.
4. A determination of the extent of offender *planning* hinges on an assessment of both _____ and _____.
5. List three examples of *precautionary acts*.

REFERENCES

Adelson, L., 1974. The Pathology of Homicide. Charles C Thomas, Springfield, IL.

Burgess, A., Hazelwood, R. (Eds.), 1995. Practical Aspects of Rape Investigation: A Multidisciplinary Approach, second edition. CRC Press, New York, NY.

Burgess, A., Holmstrom, L., 1979. Rapist's Talk: Linguistic Strategies to Control the Victim. In: Deviant Behavior, vol. 1. Hemisphere, Washington, DC, pp. 101–125.

DiMaio, D., DiMaio, V., 1993. Forensic Pathology. CRC Press, Boca Raton, FL.

Jamerson, C., 2009. Forensic Nursing: Approaching the Victim as a Crime Scene. In: Turvey, B., Petherick, W. (Eds.), Forensic Victimology: Examining Violent Crime Victims in Investigative and Legal Contexts. Elsevier Science, San Diego, CA.

Lee, H. (Ed.), 1994. Crime Scene Investigation. Central Police University Press, Taoyuan, Taiwan.

Turvey, B., 2000. Staged Crime Scenes: A Preliminary Study of 25 Cases. Journal of Behavioral Profiling 1 (3).

CHAPTER 13

Interpreting Motive

Jodi Freeman and Brent E. Turvey[1]

The crime remains obscure as long as the motive remains unclear.
—Theodore Reik, *The Unknown Murderer* (1945, p. 40)

CONTENTS

---

[1] This chapter adapts and builds on the construct of motive as presented in Turvey (1996), Turvey (1999), Turvey (2002), and Turvey and Petherick (2008).

Criminal Profiling: An Introduction to Behavioral Evidence Analysis, Fourth Edition

KEY TERMS

Administrative crime scene behaviors	Expressive offenders	Power reassurance crime scene behaviors
Anger retaliatory crime scene behaviors	Goal-directed crime scene behaviors	Profit-oriented crime scene behaviors
Behavioral-motivational typology	Instrumental offenders	Sadistic crime scene behaviors
Contributing motivational factors	Intent	
	Motive	
	Power assertive crime scene behaviors	

Motive can be defined as the emotional, psychological, and material needs that impel and are satisfied by behavior. In a criminal prosecution, the determination of motive is not necessary. Yet, while this is a legal reality, the failure to make the determination of motive is a significant investigative shortcoming, and any investigation that has failed to yield the motive behind the crime is subsequently incomplete.

Determinations of motive are not made directly, as it is not possible to read the mind of any criminal. Nor are confessions regarding motivation reliable without corroboration. This is because motives are not always the product of deliberate thought; they can subconscious and therefore not directly perceived or understood by those experiencing them.

Criminal motives are most reliably inferred by reasoning from the facts developed during an investigation. As explained in O'Hara (1970, p. 14),

> [Motive] may be inferred from circumstances. ... Evidence relating to motive or state of mind is usually obtained by interviewing witnesses. A study of the crime scene and a reconstruction of the occurrence, including the suspect's prior and subsequent acts, may often be helpful.

This is consistent with Leonard (2001, p. 447), which goes further:

> Because motive cannot be proven directly, it is necessary to resort to circumstantial evidence of its existence. … [O]ne must infer the existence of a motive from matters that can be evidenced more or less directly, including other crimes, wrongs, or acts committed by the person. From the existence of motive, to the behavior of a person on the occasion in question requires, of course, a second inferential step. That step can lead to one of three facts: (1) that the person is the one who committed the act in question (identity); (2) that the act in question occurred [*actus reus*]; and (3) that the actor behaved with the required state of mind (in criminal cases, [*mens rea*]).

In some cases, motive is readily apparent from the evidence of offender behavior and choices; in others, this evidence is obscured. Only a thorough investigation of the victim, the crime scene, and known offender behavior will make criminal motivations clear.

Deliberate use of the scientific method is also necessary. An objective motivational analysis of any crime attempts to falsify potential theories about motive, not prove them. It also documents the absence of evidence in support of unproven or disproved motivations. If the behavioral analyst applies the scientific method, he or she will have a clearer picture of what impelled a person to act in a given situation, and what did not.

RATIONALE

Determining the motivation behind a crime provides several advantages to its investigation and subsequent defense, prosecution, or related sentencing efforts. These advantages include, but are not limited to,

- It reduces the suspect pool to those individuals with the requisite motives
- It can assist with investigative and forensic case linkage efforts in crimes with a similar motive
- Along with other class evidence (i.e., means, opportunity, associative evidence), motive can provide circumstantial bearing on offender identity
- Along with other contextual evidence, motive can provide circumstantial bearing on offender state of mind
- Along with circumstantial evidence, motive can provide circumstantial bearing on whether a crime has actually occurred

The act or behavior that is proof, or an element of, a crime is referred to as *actus reus*. On this subject, Leonard (2001, p. 489) offers some insight:

> In the typical criminal prosecution, there is ample evidence that the underlying criminal act occurred. … But sometimes there is a legitimate dispute about the occurrence of the act. Perhaps the alleged murder victim's body was never found, leaving doubt as to whether any killing took place. Or perhaps the condition of the body did not attest to the cause of death, whether natural, self-inflicted, or by the act of another. Moreover, there are some types of cases in which the lack of physical evidence or disinterested witnesses makes the commission of the criminal act a matter of dispute. This is obviously the case with charges of incest or other types of sexual crimes, though it can be true of other crimes as well. In any case in which the commission of the criminal act by any party is disputed, evidence that the person charged with the act had a motive to commit it can, in theory, be admissible to prove that the act occurred.

This reality has some disturbing implications. Consider the fact that some cases do not have an abundance of physical evidence connecting a suspect to a crime. Evidence can be lacking: because of the inadequate efforts of law enforcement to find, collect, or process existing evidence; when there is distance in time between the crime and its discovery, resulting in evidence's being forever lost, decomposed, or obliterated (see Chapter 11, the section titled "Evidence Dynamics"); or because the suspect is innocent. In a case where there is only motive, where that is the primary focus of the investigation, and forensic efforts are not applied to the crime scene, the result can be a miscarriage of justice.

MOTIVE: CRIME SCENE STATE OR OFFENDER TRAIT?

It is necessary at all times to be clear about what we mean when discussing general motivations with use of the typologies described. If the profiler is arguing that the crime suggests an anger motivation, does he or she mean that anger is suggested in the crime scene or that the offender will be of a generally angry personality when finally identified and apprehended? The reader will recall from earlier chapters that offender characteristics can take one of two forms: a *state*, a snapshot of a person evidenced by a cluster of behavior at one point in time, or a *trait*, a relatively stable and static portrait of a person that endures over time.

Perhaps one of the most fundamental differences between inductive (nomothetic) and deductive (idiographic) approaches is that induction represents an attempt to guess what a criminal *will be like when found*. Deductive approaches are meant to provide an understanding of the crime and criminal *at the time of the crime*. Induction offers a nomothetically derived prediction, while deduction offers an idiographic analysis.

Crime Scene Motives

When offering an inference of motive, profilers should clearly explain their purpose and reasoning. The idio-deductive profiler is interested in analyzing and understanding behavior in its context. Behavioral evidence is examined to interpret the motive, or motives, evident in a crime scene. It is used to perform an indirect assessment of one moment or a series of related moments. *Crime scene motives* are fixed in time, in relation to a particular event—that is to say that they already exist and will not change. Crime scene motives are also general and thematic. They should not be used to infer specific insights about the offender except when extraordinary and explicit behavioral evidence regarding the offender is gathered at the scene or in relation to the crime (e.g., a videotape of the offender with the victim, a cache of pornography gathered by the offender, messages written by the offender, a confession, or documentation of the offender's verbal behavior).

Any determination of motive based on behavioral evidence is affixed to the moment of that behavior. In other words, a confession to a motive directly after the fact has a half-life. A confession to a motive well after the fact has another motive altogether. The behavior at the scene is going to be the most reliable indicator or what was really going on.

Offender Motivation

Offender motivation is a separate construct that exists in the abstract. Because offender motivation is attached to an individual and their perceptions, it can change over time. In fact, this is likely. Like all people, offenders can change their minds about what it is they mean or meant with respect to their behavior. They can misremember, they can confabulate, and they can rationalize. Moreover, the dynamic nature of an offender's mental state and overall mood can account for motivational drift within an offense and motivational variation across offenses committed by the same offender.

Establishing offender motivations separate from crime scene behavior is typically outside of the interest of the criminal profiler seeking to examine a particular crime or a series of related crimes. It is more of a clinical construct and is best left to mental health professionals performing specific assessments of personality traits and characteristics—unless, again, offender-specific behavioral evidence is certain and overwhelming.

THEORIES OF MOTIVE

One can study motivation nomothetically, by looking for similarities that form groups; or one can study it idiographically, to determine the motivations evident relevant to a particular person or crime. One nomothetic lens considers whether offenders are instrumental or expressive in the commission of their crimes. *Instrumental offenders* are defined by their desire to achieve a specific end, usually financial or materially oriented. They are deliberate, calculating, and engage in acts of precaution to limit their exposure to being discovered, identified, and apprehended. *Expressive offenders* are defined by their heightened emotional state; their motive is personal, associated with jealousy, anger, power, or even sexual desire. As discussed in Kennedy (2006, p. 135),

> As a practical matter, criminologists have generally found the criminal who acts instrumentally to be more deterrable (or displaceable) than one whose crimes tend to be expressive in nature (cf. Nettler, 1989). Thus, a professional criminal who tends to choose a lucrative target carefully might be more sensitive to security measures than a morbidly jealous man who charges into his girlfriend's place of work and shoots her in front of many witnesses because he had recently heard rumors of her infidelity.

With respect to idiographic analysis, Petri (1986, p. 15) explains that:

> The study of motivation at the level of individuals involves research aimed at understanding motivational changes that occur to a person as a result of internal or external conditions.

Internal conditions are those that come from the individuals; *external conditions* are those that come from the environment. This construct for understanding motivation is useful, but it only gets us part of the way there. A closely associated consideration is whether internal and external conditions influencing behavior are *proximate* (immediate) or *pathological* (long term).[2]

Yarvis (1991, p. 5) provides a useful table of "proximate cause factors relevant to the study of homicidal behavior," all of which are internal, that apply to all types of violent crimes. Some of the factors are self-explanatory, and not all of them will be explicitly discernable from crime scene behavior alone:

1. The status of interpersonal relations (the ability to place value on others)
2. The status of impulsive control (the ability to check dangerous and self-destructive behavior)
3. The status of reality testing (ability to tell what is imaginary and what is real)
4. The status of rational thinking (the ability to think and reflect without disruption)
5. The status of cognition (the ability to accumulate information and recall it later when making decisions)
6. The status of self-image (the ability to maintain self-worth, avoiding depression and anger)

---

[2] Pathological factors include negative parental and/or sibling role models, instability in childhood, lack of safety in childhood, and disruption during childhood (Yarvis, 1991, p. 9). As these considerations are not proximate to the crime scene, they are best left to forensic mental health professionals to gauge and interpret.

7. The status of internalized values (the ability to refrain from antisocial beliefs and actions)
8. The status of integration/alienation and enfranchisement/disenfranchisement (the degree to which people feel connected to and invested in their respective homes and communities—how much they have to lose in terms of friends, family, and reputation)
9. The presence of mental disorders
10. The presence of substance abuse problems
11. The presence of specific rationalizing or justifying motives
12. The presence of intoxication
13. The presence of significant stresses

Even the most careless read of these proximal circumstances establishes the relevance of understanding the offender's emotional disturbance and perceptions of reality. When emotional disturbance is at a low, and the perception of reality is unaffected, it is reasonable to employ the *expectancy value theory*. This is a rational motivational approach, as Petri (1986, pp. 217–218) explains:

> The basic idea underlying expectancy-value theory is that motivated behavior results from the combination of individual needs and the value of goals available in the environment. Expectancy-value theories also stress the idea that the probability of behavior depends not only upon the *value* of the goal for the individual, but also upon the person's *expectancy* of obtaining the goal.

However, *expectancy value theory* does not always apply in violent crimes. An all too frequent mistake in motivational analysis occurs when rational models like this one are applied to irrational acts. This is exemplified by profilers who attempt to explain the actions, choices, and motives of those involved in violent crime using their own subjective sense of value and expectancy. We must also bear in mind that violent crime is inherently charged with emotion and frequently occurs within the context of drugs, alcohol, and mental illness.

If any of these influences are at work in the victim or the offender, they can direct whether and how a violent crime occurs. They also make absolutely clear the importance of gathering a complete history from the victim and offender alike.[3] Offense-related behavior must be placed in its proper context before motives can be understood or disproved.

MOTIVE VS. INTENT

Motive is distinct from *intent,* which may be defined as the end aim that guides behavior. Intent refers to a specific desired outcome, as made evident by a set of actions, while motive provides the reasoning behind action and desire. As explained in Leonard (2001, p. 446),

> [W]hen one has a reason to act in a certain way, it is just as easy, and accurate, to state that the person had a "motive" to act in a certain way as it is to state that the person developed the "intent" to behave that way, or developed a "plan" to do so. In all three cases, the inference flows from the initial reason. Thus, a person charged with arson in burning a building to collect insurance proceeds

---

[3] Suspect history is important for determining the specific motives of a crime in a clinical or forensic context, while crime scene behavior is used to establish the general motivational themes that are evident in a particular crime involving an unknown suspect. However, in a forensic context, the profiler is barred from examining suspect history to determine the motive of a particular crime unless guilt is not an issue. If guilt is not yet established, then the assumption of guilt is not appropriate when undertaking a motivational analysis.

could be said to have had a motive to burn the building for that reason, and also to have had a plan to do so. Obviously, the evidence also demonstrates that the person acted with intent, rather than by accident, in causing the fire. Evidence of other insured properties burned by defendant potentially would be admissible on any of the three theories if, for example, defendant denies committing the charged offense, or claims the fire began accidentally.

The following example illustrates the difference between motive and intent: A woman becomes angry with her husband for cheating on her with another woman. She takes out a large insurance policy on him. Then she waits until he falls asleep one night and shoots him. She proceeds to stage the crime scene to make it look like a stranger burglary gone wrong. It may be argued that she was *motivated* by revenge, crime concealment, and profit. It may further be argued that she *intended* to kill him, to conceal her crime, and to collect the insurance money. Motive (revenge) is the general need, and intent (to kill the husband and claim the insurance money) is the specific plan, or, aim. Crime concealment and profit become contributing motives in this case. These specific motivational constructs are discussed in the next section.

THE BEHAVIORAL-MOTIVATIONAL TYPOLOGY

To understand the general motivational themes of violent, predatory offenders, Dr. A. Nicholas Groth, an American clinical psychologist working with both victims and offenders conducted and published a study of more than 500 rapists (Groth, 1979). His work was treatment oriented: he wanted to classify the motivations of rapists to assist with the development of effective treatment plans. In his study, Groth found that rape, like any other crime that satisfies emotional needs, is complex and multi-determined. That is to say, the act of rape and its associated behaviors can serve a number of psychological needs (motives) for an offender (Groth, 1979). Groth's work formed the basis of the behavioral-motivational typology presented here.

Most of those engaged in criminal profiling have adopted the Groth typology and use it investigatively, in some form. First, the Groth typology was modified and used as a part of the basis for the *Crime Classification Manual*, a project designed to create a DSM-type reference specifically for criminals (Burgess et al., 1997). Then, from Groth's research and the work of those associated with the FBI's National Center for the Analysis of Violent Crime (NCAVC), Hazelwood (1995, pp. 160–170) developed the rapist motivational typology further, placing offender behavior into one of six classifications:

1. Power reassurance
2. Power assertive
3. Anger retaliatory
4. Sadistic
5. Opportunistic
6. Gang rape[4]

This motivational classification system, with some modifications, is useful for classifying most criminal behavior. The needs, or motives, that impel criminal behaviors remain essentially the same for all offenders, despite the variety of behavioral expressions that may involve burglary, kidnapping, child molestation, terrorism, sexual assault, homicide, or arson.

---

[4] "Opportunistic" and "gang rape" are not actually motives; they are subtypes of rapist modus operandi or signature behaviors. As such, they need not be incorporated here.

The following working typology shifts the emphasis from classifying *offenders* to classifying *crime scene behavior*. This changes the typology from a nomothetic offender labeling system to an idiographic tool from crime scene analysis. This typology is constructed as a guide to help investigators and criminal profilers classify behavior, in context, in relationship to the crime scene behavior evidenced and the offender need it serves. It is not intended for use as a diagnostic tool, where offenders are crammed into one classification or another and conclusively labeled. Therefore, it is not investigatively helpful to think of this as an offender typology, but rather as a crime scene–oriented *behavioral-motivational typology*.

Power Reassurance Behavior (Compensatory)

Power reassurance crime scene behaviors include those that are intended to restore the offender's self-confidence or self-worth through the use of low-aggression means. These behaviors suggest a lack of confidence and a sense of personal inadequacy on the part of the offender. This may also manifest itself in a belief/rationalization that the offense is consensual or that the victim is somehow a willing or culpable participant.

The following are examples of power reassurance behavior.

Verbal Behavior

- Reassures victim that the offender does not wish to harm the victim: "Don't worry, it will be over soon. I'm not going to hurt/rape you. I'm not that kind of guy."
- Compliments victim: "You're beautiful, I bet you have a lot of boyfriends/girlfriends. You have nice breasts. You have a pretty face."
- Asks for emotional feedback: "Do you like me? Tell me that you won't leave me. Tell me that you love me."
- Self-deprecation: "You wouldn't love me; nobody could. I'm so ugly, you're so beautiful. I don't have anything to offer anyone."
- Voices concern for victim welfare: "Am I hurting you? Do you need me to move this? Am I on your hair?"
- Apologetic: "I didn't mean it. Please forgive me. I know I wasn't supposed to do this. I hope you will be okay."
- Asks about the victim's sexual interests: "Are you a virgin? Do you do this with your boyfriend/girlfriend?"
- Asks victim to evaluate his sexual skills—sexual reassurance: "Do you like this? Does this feel good? Are you getting aroused?"

Sexual Behavior

- Foreplay attempt with victim (kissing, licking breasts, cunnilingus, anilingus, etc.)
- Involvement of the victim in sexual activity
- Allowing the victim to negotiate sexual activity
- Not forcing the victim to physically comply with sexual demands

Physical Behavior

- Does not harm the victim physically
- Minimal force used to intimidate the victim
- Relies on threats or the presence of a weapon to get victim compliance

MO Behavior

- Selects victims who live in the same general area, often near offender's home, work, or other places where the offender feels comfortable
- Targets victims in advance
- Engages in surveillance of victims
- Victim is alone or with small children when attacked
- Terminates the rape if the victim resists
- Attacks last a short period of time: duration increases with victim passivity
- Distribution of the attacks remains within same general area

Signature Behavior

- Engages in voyeuristic behavior with the victim before or after the attack
- Takes personal items from the victim, such as an undergarment, ring, or photograph
- Keeps a record of attack
- Makes obscene phone calls to the victim
- Contacts the victim after the attack (phone calls asking the victim out on a date, flowers sent to the victim's home, messages on the victim's answering machine telling him or her what a good time he or she had)

Offenders evidencing these behaviors or characteristics may attempt to recontact their victim after an attack. They might have expected the victim to respond erotically to their advances. In the offender's mind, the victim might even be in love with the offender and have enjoyed the attack. From the offender's point of view, at least in his or her own interpretation, it was more of a date.

The core fantasy motivating this rapist is that the victim will enjoy and eroticize the rape and subsequently fall in love with the rapist. This fantasy stems from the rapist's own fears of personal inadequacy, hence the term commonly applied to this rape is *an inadequate personality*. The rape is restorative of the offender's doubt about himself and therefore sexually and emotionally reassuring. It will re-occur as his need for that kind of reassurance arises.

Power Assertive Behavior (Entitlement)

Power assertive crime scene behaviors are intended to restore the offender's self-confidence or self-worth through the use of moderately to highly aggressive means. The behaviors suggest an underlying lack of confidence and a sense of personal inadequacy, which are expressed through control, mastery, and humiliation of the victim, while demonstrating the offender's sense of authority.

The following are examples of power assertive behavior.

Verbal Behavior

- Does not want the victim to be verbally or otherwise involved in the attack
- Gives sexual instructions/commands: "Suck this. Bend over. Hold still. Don't move. Shut up."
- Offender's pleasure is primary
- Acts "macho"
- Uses a great deal of profanity; language is offensive and abusive
- Demeans and humiliates the victim: "You are a whore. You are a slut. I own you. You're not so pretty now."

- Verbally explicit about sex: "I'm going to put my cock in your cunt. I'm going to cum in your ass. You are going to suck my dick."
- Verbal threats: "Do what I say and you won't get hurt. Shut up or I'll kill you. I don't want to have to teach you a lesson."

Sexual Behavior

- Offender does whatever he wants to the victim, sexually or otherwise
- There is a lack of fondling foreplay behavior
- Repeated attacks with a single victim
- Offender sexually punishes or abuses victims
- Offender engages in pulling, pinching, or biting behaviors
- Offender's goal is capture, conquer, and control
- Victim is a prop only, an object for his sexual fantasy

Physical Behavior

- Offender rips or tears the victim's clothing
- Offender forcefully gags victim to control verbal behavior
- Offender engages in the use of corrective force
- Offender engages in moderate, excessive, or brutal levels of force that increase with victim resistance or his level of sexual dysfunction during the offense
- Offender chooses locations for the attack that are convenient and safe

MO Behavior

- Victim is selected in advance or opportunistic (too good to pass up)
- Victim is chosen by availability, accessibility, and vulnerability
- Location of the offense is victim dependent
- Weapon is involved, or higher levels of force take its place
- Physical aggression is used to initially overpower the victim
- Victim is held captive in some fashion while being raped

Signature Behavior

- Attacks may involve brutal levels of force
- Sexual acts may include degrading sexual acts, such as anal penetration
- The offender may bring sexualized objects to the crime scene to utilize during the offense

Offenders evidencing this type of behavior wish to appear to have absolutely no doubt about their own adequacy and masculinity. In fact, they may be using their attacks as an expression of their own virility. In their perception, they are entitled to the fruits of their attack by virtue of being stronger.

These offenders may grow more confident over time, as their egocentricity tends to be high. They may begin to do things that might lead to their identification. Law enforcement may interpret this as a sign that the offender desires to be caught. What is actually true is that these offenders have no respect for law enforcement, have learned that they can commit their offenses without the need to fear identification or capture, and subsequently may not take precautions, which they have learned are unnecessary.

These offenders do not necessarily desire to harm their victims, but rather to possess them sexually. Demonstrating power over their victims is their means of expressing mastery, strength, control authority, and identity to themselves. The attacks are therefore intended to reinforce the offender's inflated sense of self-confidence or self-worth.

Anger Retaliatory Behavior (Anger or Displaced Anger)

Anger retaliatory motive is evidenced by crime scene behaviors that indicate a great deal of rage, either toward a specific person, group, or institution, or a symbol of them. These behaviors are commonly evidenced in stranger-to-stranger sexual assaults, domestic homicides, work-related homicides, and cases involving political or religious terrorists.

The following are examples of anger retaliatory behavior:

Verbal Behavior

- Verbally selfish—is not interested in hearing the victim
- Does not negotiate
- May blame victim for events and perceived events: "If you wouldn't have struggled I wouldn't have had to beat you like that. You think you are so hot. You think you're better than I am. It's people like you that are the problem. You don't understand; you have to be made to understand."
- Other angry, hostile language

Sexual Behavior

- Sexually selfish
- Sex is violent, an extension of the physical attack
- No foreplay
- Attempts to force victim to perform acts that the offender perceives as degrading or humiliating (fellatio or sodomy)

Physical Behavior

- Ripping of victim's clothing
- Dresses for the event (full military dress uniform, face paint, battle dress uniform [khakis or camouflage materials] etc.)
- Excessive or brutal levels of force with high amount of injury to the victim

MO Behavior

- Attack is unplanned, a result of an emotional reaction on the part of an offender
- Attack is skillfully planned and focused on a particular victim or victim population
- Offenses appear sporadic over time, occurring at any location, at any time of day or night (whenever the offender gets angry or whenever a particular victim type is accessible)
- Uses weapons of opportunity; if the attack is planned, offender will prepare for the event with excessive weaponry and ammunition
- Offender knows the victim, or the victim symbolizes something specific to the offender

Signature Behavior

- There is an immediate application of direct physical force to the victim; the offender attacks first, and then continues into any other behavior as an extension of that attack
- Duration of attack is very short—ends when the offender is emotionally spent
- Results in the offender's intentionally surrendering his life as part of a social, political, or personal message to others
- There is a lot of anger evident in the crime scene
- Collateral victims may result from the offender's anger and lack of planning; other victims surprise the offender in the heat of the moment or just get caught in the crossfire (this is often unintentional, but if it is intentional, it will be evidenced by offender's planning behavior)

Anger retaliatory behavior is just what the name suggests. The offender is acting on the basis of cumulative real or imagined wrongs from those who are in the offender's world. The victim of the attack may be one of these people, such as a relative, a girlfriend, or a co-worker. Or the victim may symbolize that person to the offender in dress, occupation, or physical characteristics.

The main goal of this offender behavior is to service the offender's cumulative aggression. The offender is retaliating against the victims for wrongs or perceived wrongs, and the offender's aggression can manifest itself across a wide range, from verbally abusive epithets to hyperaggressive homicide with multiple collateral victims.

Cumulative rage is evidenced by *overkill:* multiple injuries (e.g., gunshots, stabs, blunt-force trauma) beyond that necessary to cause death. In such cases, the violence employed involves direct physical contact (e.g., manual strangulation, sharp-force stabs penetrating to the weapon's hilt, cutting) and weapons of opportunity taken from the environment. It also may involve the use of multiple weapons. When dismemberment or disfigurement is featured, it is intended to humiliate, mutilate, or otherwise attack a specific location associated with a grievance (mouth, hands, genitals). It is not a precautionary act intended to conceal the identity of the victim.

It is important not to confuse anger retaliatory behavior with sadistic behavior. Although they can share some characteristics, the motivations are wholly separate. Also, non-terrorist anger retaliatory behavior shows a distinct lack of planning and overall offender preparedness.

Sadistic Behavior (Anger Excitation)

Sadistic crime scene behaviors are those that evidence the offender's sexual gratification from the victim's pain and suffering. The primary motivation for the behavior is sexual; however, the sexual expression for the offender is manifested in physical aggression, or torture behavior, toward the victim.

The following are examples of sadistic behavior.

Verbal Behavior

- Offender says things meant to gain the victim's trust and confidence—things that will lower the victim's guard: "Can you help me with this? I'm lost. Do I know you? You remind me of a friend I had back in school."
- Offender says things to entice the victim away from safe areas: "I have something I want to show you. Let me offer you a ride. Can I give you help with that heavy load up to your apartment?"

- During the attack, the offender may demand to be called a certain name that indicates the victim's subservience (Sir, Master, Lord, etc.)
- Offender asks, "Does it hurt? Did that hurt you? Can you feel that?" when engaged in rough sex acts or inflicting victim injury
- Calls the victim demeaning, humiliating names attesting to his view of the victim's worthlessness (e.g., bitch, slut, whore, cunt)

Sexual Behavior

- Offender is sexually stimulated by the victim's response to the infliction of physical or emotional pain
- Offender involves the use of sexual bondage apparatus and behaviors during the attack
- Offender performs sexual torture on the victim, including repeated biting, insertion of foreign objects into the vagina or anus, and the use of sexual torture devices on a conscious victim
- Offender prefers rough anal sex followed in frequency by forced fellatio
- Offender prefers ejaculating on specific parts of the victim's body
- Offender is sexually selfish; the victim's primary function is to suffer, sexually
- Offender records the attack for later fantasy activity (video, photos, journal, audio, maps, calendars, diaries, media clippings, etc.)
- Souvenirs and trophies are kept and hidden in secret but accessible places (home, office, vehicle, storage space, etc.)

Physical Behavior

- Brutal or high levels of force are used to inflict victim injury over a prolonged period of time
- Injuries are inflicted against specific areas of the victim's body of sexual significance to the offender (feet, nipples, anus, vagina, mouth, etc.)
- The intensity of specified sexual injuries increases with the rapist's anger (i.e., in response to a noncompliant victim or a victim who is too compliant), which increases with the level of sexual arousal

MO Behavior

- Offenders choose or impersonate an occupation that allows them to act as an authority figure, placing them in a position to identify and acquire victims (i.e., law enforcement, security guard, youth counselor, coach, etc.)
- Offenses are planned in exacting detail: victim type, location for selecting victim, location for attack, signature behavior, and disposal site are all determined in advance
- Offenses are executed methodically
- Offender assesses and selects victims by emotional vulnerability and gains the victim's confidence through seduction
- Victims are vilified by law enforcement (prostitutes, drug addicts, runaways, etc.)
- Victims are nonaggressive and have low self-esteem
- Victim is lured to a concealed area where the offender has a great deal of control (vehicle, basement, garage, hotel room, etc.)
- Offender increases aggression with each successive attack
- Offender kills the victim as a precautionary act

Signature Behavior

■ Special material brought with offender to the scene, containing weapons, bindings, and any sexual apparatus
■ The sexual attack lasts for an extended period of time
■ Offender is good at presenting the image of a loving and sincere individual
■ Victims are strangers to the offender (facilitates both MO and signature—it is easier to torture and humiliate and to inflict suffering on those whom one has no personal connection to, and it is also less likely that law enforcement will link the offender to the victim)

Sadistic behavior is perhaps the most individually complex. It is motivated by intense, individually varying fantasies that involve inflicting brutal levels of pain on the victim solely for the offender's sexual pleasure. The goal of this behavior is total victim fear and submission. Physically aggression has been eroticized. The result is that the victim must be physically and psychologically abused and degraded in order for the offender to become sexually excited and subsequently gratified.

A sadistic offense requires a conscious victim who is able to respond to the injuries inflicted by the offender. The pain and suffering experienced by the victim sexually arouses the offender. Therefore, postmortem injuries to sexual areas of the victim are not sadistic in nature. Sadism is also distinct from non-sexual torture, which is inflicted on victims for material or financial gain.

Administrative Behavior (Instrumental)

Administrative behaviors include those that service financial, material, or personal gain. Administrative behaviors can be found in all types of homicides, robberies, burglaries, muggings, arsons, bombings, kidnappings, and most forms of white-collar crime, to name just a few. Administrative behaviors are the exceptions that prove the rule of signature aspects, as they do not necessarily satisfy psychological or emotional needs. Administrative behaviors can further be broken down into *profit-oriented* behavior and *goal-directed* behavior.

Profit-Oriented Behavior

Profit-oriented behaviors result in material or financial gain. Examples of these behaviors include torture for money or information, theft of valuables, and addiction-directed drug-seeking behaviors, such as theft or prostitution of children.

The following are examples of profit-oriented behaviors.

Verbal Behavior

■ Offender gives simple commands to achieve victim compliance regarding the release of valuables: "Give me the money. Open the safe. Give me all of your jewelry. Where is the cash?"
■ Offender shows an interest in the value of items: "Is this real gold? Are these fake diamonds? This is cheap shit."

Sexual Behavior

■ Offender creates fantasy pornographic material using victim, which is sold for material or financial gain
■ Offender sells victim's sexual services for personal or material gain
■ Offender sells victim to another party as a "sexual slave" for personal or material gain

Physical Behavior

- Engages in behavior that is necessary to control the victim during the offense
- Moderate, commensurate force

MO Behavior

- Short offense duration
- Searches vehicles or residences in a targeted fashion for specific types of valuables
- Shows interest in completing an offense as quickly as possible and no interest in activities that may prolong the offense

Signature Behaviors

- Special materials with personal meaning brought with offender to the scene to complete the crime, including weapons, bindings, and any other distinctive apparatus
- Any behavior that was committed during the offense that prolongs the offender's exposure to apprehension without gaining the offender some sort of financial reward (which would have to be reviewed and assessed in the lens of the other motivational typologies)

Goal-Directed Behavior

Goal-directed behaviors fulfill personal gain specific to the offender. These behaviors are engaged in for a specific functional purpose, such as eliminating a living witness or eliminating a threat.

The following are examples of goal-directed behaviors.

Verbal Behavior

- The verbal behavior of the offender is limited

Sexual Behavior

- There is a lack of sexual behavior, because the offender's behaviors are functional. The presence of a sexual act indicates the behavior is not goal-directed for personal gain

Physical Behavior

- Offender engages in behavior necessary to complete a specific, purposeful goal
- The offender is focused and without distraction

MO Behavior

- Short offense duration with a single method of injury
- Victim is targeted specifically because of who they are
- Offender shows interest in completing an offense as quickly as possible and no interest in activities that may prolong the offense
- Offender's delivery lacks evidence of emotion or passion, or other motivations

Signature Behaviors

■ Any behavior that was committed during the offense that prolongs the offender's exposure to apprehension without gaining the offender the personal gain anticipated from the offense

Administrative crime scene behaviors are perhaps the most straightforward, because the successful completion of the offense satisfies the offender's needs. Purely administrative behavior does not involve emotional or psychological needs. Any behavior that is not purely administratively motivated, which satisfies an emotional or psychological need, must be examined with the lens of other motives.

For example, if a thief attacks a victim on a public street, stealing her purse and making a quick getaway, this is evidence of administrative behavior, specifically profit-oriented behavior. If the same thief brutally beats the victim, in the absence of any victim resistance, before stealing the purse, it is evidence of anger retaliatory behavior (i.e., it is behavioral evidence that more is going on with the offender than just the need to make a quick profit—although the specifics may be unclear from the crime scene behavior alone).

PSYCHOLOGICAL CRIME SCENE TAPE

The behavioral-motivational typology does not provide a dynamic, developmental scale that measures an offender over time. It is a tool for the assessment of offender behaviors at a particular moment, in a particular setting, with a particular victim. The behavioral-motivational typologies are not to be confused with a full criminal profile, nor by any means should they be considered an exclusive list of characteristics and potential signature aspects (motivational themes for behavior patterns). They can be used to provide a psychological snapshot of an offender during a single instance from which some reliable inferences about motives can be made.

All too often, investigators and criminal profilers use motivational typologies and other sorts of offender classifications to label a rapist's behavior with a single investigative "diagnosis." Investigators and inexperienced criminal profilers will often issue a report stating the offender characteristics that are associated with whatever typology appears to "match" the offender. They inappropriately use a typology as a boilerplate replacement for a thoroughly rendered criminal profile.

This practice results in misleading investigative generalizations and inappropriately pigeonholes an unknown offender into an inductive, inflexible classification. The typology becomes the equivalent of psychological crime scene tape—a barrier that investigators all too often fail to look beyond in the search for evidence.

There is also no bright yellow line between the classifications in the behavioral-motivational typology, meaning that a single offender can evidence behaviors suggestive of more than one motivation. It is also possible that an offender may evidence behaviors that reflect a change in motivation during a single offense. For example, a power reassurance rapist may evidence power assertive behavior if the victim resists the attack.

Human behavior and human needs are developmental in nature, not fixed and static. Offender signature behavior is expressive of multi-determined needs. Using the motivational typologies to "diagnose" an offender can have limiting effects on an investigation, not unlike improperly placed crime scene tape.[5] It can result in ignoring other offender motivational patterns, incorrect investigative assumptions, and

---

[5] The placement of crime scene tape determines, for some, where evidence will be looked for and where it will not. It is a common problem for investigators and forensic personnel alike; looking outside of the crime scene tape for evidence is simply not done because—well, the crime scene is viewed as everything inside the tape. The area outside the tape isn't the crime scene. Or so they may erroneously think.

ultimately overlooked physical and behavioral evidence. All of this working together facilitates the inability of investigators to link and investigate related cases. To avoid this pitfall, the motivational typologies should be used investigatively to suggest the motivations of an offender that are apparent in the given patterns of crime scene behavior, not as rigid diagnostic classifications.

CONTRIBUTING MOTIVATIONAL FACTORS

Contributing motivational factors are any circumstances that support or lead to the development of motive. These factors are not primary to the offense but have the potential to influence or to contribute to offender choices and behavior.

The existence and nature of contributing motivational factors will only become evident after a thorough crime scene analysis. Knowledge of these factors will provide examiners with a more complete understanding of an offender's rationale and how it was shaped. Examples of contributing motivational factors include, but are not limited to,[6]

- Mental illness
- Physical disabilities
- Drug and alcohol use
- Significant stress
- Sexual gratification
- Fear
- Financial problems
- Submissive tendencies
- Low self-esteem
- Self-preservation
- Zeal/bias

The above list is not exhaustive and the presence of any of these factors in a crime does not necessarily mean they are contributing factors. The following examples are intended to illustrate the difference between motives and contributing motivational factors:

An abused woman kills her husband with a single gunshot to protect herself and her children. This evidences an administrative, or goal-directed, motivation, intended to eliminate a threat. It is the removal of the threat that is satisfied by the woman's behavior. In this case, fear would be considered a contributing motivational factor.

In another example, a male offender sexually assaults a female victim through the use of low-aggression means. He is motivated by power reassurance or compensatory behavior that intends to restore his self-confidence or self-worth. It is his sense of self-worth that is satisfied by his behavior. The sexual act, or sexual gratification, is a component servicing the offender's underlying needs, and should be considered a contributing motivational factor.

It is important to note that a contributing motivational factor in one crime may be a primary motivation in another, stressing the importance of ideographic case analysis over broad generalizations. Consider the following example: a man loans a co-worker a small amount of money. The co-worker does not pay

---

[6] It is not a coincidence that numerous subordinate motivational factors have been borrowed from the Yarvis (1991) table of "Proximate Cause Factors Relevant to the Study of Homicidal Behavior." Internal proximate factors presented by Yarvis that are discernable from crime scene behavior or from knowledge of the offender have been included in our list of subordinate motivational factors.

it back and is even indifferent to the debt. Over time, the man becomes angry at his co-worker's attitude. They go out drinking one night, and an argument ensues over the unpaid debt. The man physically assaults the co-worker, who is subsequently hospitalized with severe injuries. The motivation in this case would be anger, with a financial motive as a contributing motivational factor. Profit is not the need that is satisfied by the argument and physical altercation, it is the anger toward the specific individual that is primary.

In a completely different scenario, an offender pickpockets a victim in a busy location. This offender demonstrates a purely administrative motivation that is profit oriented. Profit is the only need that is satisfied by the offense, and it is not merely a contributing motivational factor.

While the general motivation of a crime is discernable from crime scene behavior, a complete understanding of contributing motivational factors may require knowledge of the offender. Some factors cannot be established from the crime scene behavior alone and require specific background information about the offender. Profilers must acknowledge and accept this limitation. If the identity of the offender is not in question, only then may it be appropriate to discuss offender-specific motivational factors.

SUMMARY

Motive can be defined as the emotional, psychological, and material needs that impel and are satisfied by behavior. Determinations of motive are not made directly, as it is not possible to read the mind of any criminal. Nor are confessions regarding motivation reliable without corroboration. Motives are most reliably inferred by reasoning from the facts developed during an investigation.

Behavioral evidence is examined to interpret the motive, or motives, evident in a crime scene. It is used to perform an indirect assessment of one moment or a series of related moments. *Crime scene motives* are fixed in time, in relation to a particular event—i.e., they have already been acted on and will not change. Crime scene motives are also general and thematic.

Motive is distinct from *intent,* which may be defined as the end aim that guides behavior. Intent refers to a specific desired outcome as made evident by a set of actions, while motive provides the reasoning behind the action and desire.

Criminal profilers interpret the motives evident in a crime based on patterns evident in crime scene behavior. They do not interpret the motives of specific individuals, as this is best left to mental health professionals evaluating offenders in a forensic setting. Profilers must be careful, however, not to impose their own subjective values and expectations on the choices made by the victim or the offender during the crime, as this can mask or distort their findings. They must also embrace the limits of crime scene evidence and refrain from assuming or over-interpreting behavior in their interpretations.

The behavioral-motivational typology provided in this chapter does not provide a dynamic, developmental scale that measures an offender over time. It is a tool for the assessment of offender behaviors at a particular moment, in a particular setting, with a particular victim. There is also no bright yellow line between the classifications in the behavioral-motivational typology, meaning that a single offender can evidence behaviors suggestive of more than one motivation. It is also possible that an offender may evidence behaviors that reflect a change in motivation during a single offense.

Contributing motivational factors are any circumstances that support or lead to the development of motive. These factors are not primary to the offense, but have the potential to influence or to contribute to the offender's choices and behavior. The existence and nature of contributing motivational factors will only become evident after a thorough crime scene analysis.

Questions

1. List three goals of interpreting motive.
2. Explain the difference between power reassurance and power assertive behavior.
3. True or False: All postmortem injuries to the sexual areas of a victim are sadistic in nature. Explain.
4. Explain the two types of administrative behaviors. Provide an example of each.
5. Explain the difference between motivations and contributing motivational factors.

REFERENCES

Burgess, A., Burgess, A., Douglas, J., Ressler, R., 1997. Crime Classification Manual. Jossey-Bass, San Francisco, CA.

Groth, A.N., 1979. Men Who Rape: The Psychology of the Offender. Plenum Press, New York, NY.

Hazelwood, R., 1995. Analyzing the Rape and Profiling the Offender. In: Burgess, A., Hazelwood, R. (Eds.), Practical Aspects of Rape Investigation: A Multidisciplinary Approach, second edition. CRC Press, New York, NY.

Kennedy, D., 2006. Forensic Security and the Law. In: Gill, M. (Ed.), The Handbook of Security. Palgrave Macmillan, New York, NY.

Leonard, D., 2001. Character and Motive in Evidence Law. Loyola of Los Angeles Law Review 34, 439–536.

O'Hara, C., 1970. Fundamentals of Criminal Investigation, second edition. Charles C Thomas, Springfield, IL.

Petri, H., 1986. Motivation: Theory and Research, second edition. Wadsworth, Belmont, CA.

Reik, T., 1945. The Unknown Murderer. Prentice-Hall, New York, NY.

Turvey, B., 1996. Behavior Evidence: Understanding Motives and Developing Suspects in Unsolved Serial Rapes through Behavioral Profiling Techniques. Master's Thesis , University of New Haven, www.corpus-delicti.com/rape.html.

Turvey, B., 1999. Motivational Typologies. In: Turvey, B. (Ed.), Criminal Profiling: An Introduction to Behavioral Evidence Analysis. Academic Press, London, England.

Turvey, B., 2002. Criminal Motivations. In: Turvey, B. (Ed.), Criminal Profiling: An Introduction to Behavioral Evidence Analysis, second edition. Academic Press, Boston, MA.

Turvey, B., Petherick, W., 2008. Criminal Motivation. In: Turvey, B. (Ed.), Criminal Profiling: An Introduction to Behavioral Evidence Analysis, third edition. Elsevier Science, San Diego, CA.

Yarvis, R., 1991. Homicide: Causative Factors and Roots. Lexington Books, Lexington, MA.

CHAPTER 14

Case Linkage
Offender Modus Operandi and Signature

Brent E. Turvey and Jodi Freeman

You never know what is enough unless you know what is more than enough.
—William Blake, "The Marriage of Heaven and Hell"

CONTENTS

KEY TERMS

Behavioral commonality	Investigative link	Probative link
Behavioral dissimilarity	Modus operandi (MO)	Signature behaviors
Case linkage	Offender signature	X-factor
Interrupted/incomplete offense	Offense gone wrong	

Case linkage, also referred to as *linkage analysis,* is the process of determining whether there are discrete con-nections, or distinctive behavioral factors, between two or more previously unrelated cases by means of crime scene analysis. It involves establishing and comparing the physical evidence, victimology, crime scene characteristics, motivation, *modus operandi* (MO), and *signature behaviors* of each of the cases under review.[1] It also requires consideration of both behavioral similarities and dissimilarities.

Case linkage is seen in two different contexts: *investigative* and *forensic.* In investigative contexts, it is used to assist law enforcement by helping to establish where to apply investigative efforts and resources (e.g., identifying serial or pattern cases or closing cases by exceptional means).[2] In forensic (a.k.a. legal) contexts, it is employed to assist the court with determining whether or not there is sufficiently distinctive behavioral evidence to connect crimes together in their commission. This will be used to help decide specific forensic issues, such as whether similar crimes may be tried together or whether similar past crimes may be brought in as evidence.

EVIDENTIARY THRESHOLDS

While case linkage methods are used to assist both investigative and forensic efforts, it is important for exam-iners to understand the profound differences between investigative and forensic thresholds of evidence.

An *investigative analysis* is one that is conducted during an ongoing investigation while facts are still being established. It is meant to move the case forward and to lead investigators toward additional evidence. It exists with a level of uncertainty and is subject to rapid change as new evidence and information are con-tinuously gathered and integrated into the case.

---

[1] Woodhams and Toye (2007, p. 59) state: "Case linkage is typically conducted by crime analysts and involves the analyst engaging in a detailed behavioral analysis of criminals' crime scene actions (modus operandi [MO]) to determine whether there is a sufficient degree of similarity in behavior for the crimes to be attributed to a common offender." However, this definition does not deal with the issue of signature, or require a consideration of behavioral dissimilarity.

[2] As explained in Bennell et al. (2009, p. 293): "Of paramount importance in police investigations is the ability to accurately link crimes committed by the same offender. The correct identification of an offense series allows investigators to pool information from all relevant crime scenes, thus resulting in a more efficient use of investigative resources."

The investigative realm is more concerned with results than methods, as methods become irrelevant when they have revealed new facts and evidence—so long as there is no violation of due process or law. Investigative tools and their results are not necessarily designed or even intended for courtroom use. Therefore, they must be recalled, offered, and regarded with the requisite humility and uncertainty. Examiners who try to offer the results of their own investigative analyses in court without consideration of new facts and evidence uncovered during subsequent investigative efforts have a duty to be clear about this limitation with the court and with any other authority seeking to exploit what are essentially preliminary findings.

A *forensic analysis* is conducted in accordance with established professional and legal guidelines in order to allow for admissibility as evidence in court. It is based on the facts and evidence that are commonly brought forth to make a legal action or finding, and therefore it is less subordinate to rapid changes of facts and evidence (although it is not immune to them). A forensic analysis of behavioral evidence can take place only after the investigative phase of a case is completed, and all available physical evidence has been examined and interpreted. A scientific forensic analysis will also take into account the evidence that was not available and any natural limits of the findings. As this suggests, a higher standard of competency and professional methodology must be evident in the education, training, and techniques of forensic examiners, as well as in the rendering of their findings.

Unfortunately, many of those practicing in the forensic realm have a limited appreciation of its rules, as explained in Turvey and Petherick (2010, p. xxxviii):

> Achieving basic forensic knowledge is not a simple matter, as the mandates of the forensic realm place students at crossed purposes with scientific, public safety, and legal mandates. They must learn to distinguish scientific fact from legal truth; to appreciate how investigative thresholds for evidence are a great deal less than scientific standards, and a great deal different from legal ones; and to understand the role that they seek to uphold in the criminal justice system—be that of factual witness, impartial examiner, or zealous advocate—as well as the importance of each to the others.

> The varying issues, practices, and standards peculiar to the forensic realm are nothing short of vital to student survival and prosperity once employment has been secured. However, the authors have routinely observed that these same issues are too often all but foreign to those teaching coursework within criminology and criminal justice programs. Not all of the time, but more often than not.

It is the purpose of this chapter to educate readers regarding the investigative and forensic utility of linkage analysis, as well as its limits in each context.

With respect to behavioral evidence, case linkage efforts have most typically hinged on two concepts: *modus operandi (MO)* and *signature.*

MODUS OPERANDI

Knowledge of the modus operandi of criminals and methods of their apprehension skill, patience, tact, industry, and thoroughness … will be everlasting primary assets in detective work.

—O'Connell and Soderman (1936, p. 1)

Many criminals have a particular modus operandi … which consists of their characteristic way of committing a crime. Physical evidence can help in establishing MO. … [F]or example, the means used to gain entry, tools that were used, types of items taken, and other telltale signs … are all important.

— DeForest et al. (1983, p. 29)

FIGURE 14.1
Eugene François Vidocq
(1775–1857).

Modus operandi (MO) is a Latin term that means *method of operating*. It refers to the manner in which a crime has been committed (Gross, 1924, p. 478). Law enforcement has long held to the belief that understanding the methods and techniques criminals use to commit crime is the best way to investigate, identify, and ultimately apprehend them. This has traditionally required that the best detectives become living encyclopedias of criminal cases and behaviors. It has also demanded that they learn to utilize the knowledge and experience of known criminals to inform their investigative strategy.

In 1809, the French demonstrated a strong belief in this approach to criminal investigation through their faith in a former convict named Eugene Vidocq (Figure 14.1). He had been working as a police spy and was assigned by the government to form a *Brigade de Sûreté*. He organized and led this group of detectives, mostly former criminals themselves.

Vidocq and his detectives were paid based on the number of criminals that they apprehended. Within their first year, they had made more than 750 arrests. This led some to believe that Vidocq and his detectives were a perfect solution to the local criminal problem; they understood how criminals operated, had insights into their habits and methods of operation, and were putting that knowledge to work for the good of the state. However, this led others to suspect that Vidocq and his detectives committed many of the crimes themselves and then framed known criminals or detractors in order to close out the cases. In 1832, Vidocq was removed from office on the charge of instigating a crime for the purpose of uncovering it. Despite this, Vidocq appears to enjoy a favorable historical place as the first and very successful chief of the French *Sûreté Nationale*.

Whether Vidocq was a master detective or merely continued his criminal career through the *Sûreté*, a philosophy of criminal investigation emerged. To understand criminals, to develop competent investigative strategies, to link their crimes, and to successfully apprehend them, detectives needed to understand very intimately the particular methods criminals used to commit their crimes. This is an investigative philosophy that survives on an international level, in one form or another, to the present day.[3]

A criminal's modus operandi is made up of choices and behaviors that are intended to assist the criminal in the completion of the crime. An offender's modus operandi reflects *how* the offender commits the crime.[4] It is separate from the offender's motives or *signature* aspects, as these have to do with *why* an offender commits the crime.

The collection, storage, and examination of a criminal's modus operandi, whether on arrest cards or in computer databases, has traditionally been investigatively relevant for the following reasons. (This list was compiled with help from Weston and Wells [1974, p. 110] and DeForest et al. [1983, p. 29].)

---

[3]When the United States Secret Service began in 1865 in Washington, DC, to suppress counterfeit currency, its staff consisted partly of former counterfeiters. The agency also used the services of paid criminal informants. Moreover, law enforcement agencies still use criminal informants as a necessary means to gain access to, and knowledge of, the criminal world and "the street."

[4]According to Gross (1924, p. 478), repeat offenders like thieves have a characteristic style, or MO, that they rarely depart from. Weston and Wells (1974, p. 110) state more accurately that not all criminals have a particular MO, but some of them have distinctive enough methods to justify making investigative note of it. They go on to say that the modus operandi of criminals is their signature, which contradicts what they said immediately prior about not all offenders having a particular MO. *Black's Law Dictionary* (Black, 1990, p.1004) translates the phrase modus operandi as "method of operation of doing things," and states that it is "used by police and criminal investigators to describe the particular method of a criminal's activity." It goes on to discuss the term's use as reflected by the testimony of law-enforcement experts on the subject who have either confused modus operandi for offender signature or been less than enthusiastic in the pursuit of their investigative work: "It refers to a pattern of criminal behavior so distinct that separate crimes or wrongful conduct are recognized as work of the same person."

- Investigative linkage of unsolved cases by modus operandi
- Suspect identification by comparing known criminal modus operandi with the modus operandi evidence in unsolved cases
- Routine comparison of arrestee modus operandi with the modus operandi evidence in unsolved cases
- Development of investigative leads or suspect identity in unsolved cases by virtue of accumulating modus operandi information
- Suspect prioritization or elimination
- Clearance of unsolved cases[5]

To the criminal profiler, MO is also relevant because it can provide an array of information about the offender. This includes the involvement of choices, procedures, or techniques that can be characteristic of, or reflective of, the following:

- A particular discipline, trade, skill, profession, or area of knowledge, criminal and non-criminal
- Knowledge particular to the victim, suggesting surveillance, contact, or a prior relationship
- Knowledge particular to a crime scene, suggesting surveillance, contact, or intimate familiarity

Elements of Modus Operandi

An offender's MO behavior is functional in nature. It is comprised of learned behaviors that can evolve and develop over time. It can be refined as an offender becomes more experienced, sophisticated, and confident. It can also become less competent and skilled over time, decompensating by virtue of a deteriorating mental state or increased used of controlled substances (Turvey, 2000).

MO behaviors most often serve (or fail to serve) one or more of three general purposes:[6]

Protection of offender identity: e.g., wearing a mask during a daytime bank robbery, covering a victim's eyes during a rape, wearing gloves during a burglary, killing a witness to any of the above, and staging the crime scene

Successful completion of the crime: e.g., targeting and acquiring the victim, using a gag to silence a victim, using a weapon to control a victim, making a list of potential victims with pertinent information, and using a gun to kill the victim

---

[5] After making a burglary, robbery, or sex crime arrest, law-enforcement officers will often attempt to connect the suspect to other cases in their file for which there is tangible evidence. Similarities in other crimes may be uncovered and then thoroughly investigated. This is a legitimate investigative practice. However, historically, the procedures followed by the Washington, DC, Metropolitan Police Department, as well as many others throughout the United States, allow the following (Feeney, 2000):
[I]ndividual officers clear offenses without any assurance that the identity of the offender is reliably known. Officers are able to use the modus operandi method of clearance even where charges based on the cleared offenses are not filed, where the offender denies his involvement, and where no other evidence exists to connect him with the crimes. In one instance three thefts were cleared by a police officer because he "felt sure" a suspect arrested for a different theft was responsible, even though the suspect had not confessed to the thefts, there was no other evidence linking him to the thefts, and the modus operandi was different from the crime for which he was arrested.
In the author's view, this is not a legitimate or forensic practice, for what should be obvious reasons. Even when the MO in otherwise unconnected cases is precisely the same, a reasonable level of certainty has not been reached with respect to the absolute identity of the offender. Only physical evidence can provide that level of certainty.
[6] There are by far more foolish and ignorant criminals than there are criminal masterminds. As Gross (1924) argues, investigators throughout history owe a great deal of their case resolution to the sheer stupidity of criminals. He goes on to say (Gross, 1968): "The cleverest people do the most idiotic things. He makes the most progress who keeps in mind the great series of his own stupidities, and tries to learn from them."

Facilitation of offender escape: e.g., use of a stolen vehicle during the commission of a crime, disposal of a vehicle after the commission of a crime, and tying up/knocking out victims to prevent their escape and hamper their attempts to get help

General types of MO can include crime scene characteristics such as, but not limited to, the following. (This list was compiled with help from O'Connell and Soderman [1936, pp. 254–260].)

- Number of offenders
- Amount of planning before a crime
- Offense location selected
- Route taken to offense location
- Pre-offense surveillance of a crime scene(s) or victim
- Involvement of a victim during a crime (non-fantasy-related)
- Use of a weapon during a crime
- Use of restraints to control the victim during a crime
- Nature and extent of injuries to the victim
- Method of killing the victim
- Nature and extent of precautionary acts
- Location and position of the victim's clothing
- Location and position of the victim's body
- Items taken from victim or crime scene(s) for profit or to prevent identification[7]
- Method of transportation to and from the crime scene(s)
- Direction of escape/route taken from offense location

It is important to note that an offender's modus operandi can be an act or a *failure* to act. Common examples include *not* using a condom during a sexual assault, not using a firearm during the commission of a robbery, and not killing witnesses during the commission of a home invasion burglary. These are all choices that an offender makes.

In addition, readers are cautioned not to confuse MO, motive, and signature: these are very separate concepts, although related and even interdependent in the context of a linkage analysis.

Influences on Modus Operandi

An offender's MO behaviors are learned, and by extension they are dynamic and malleable. This is because MO is affected by time and can change as the offender learns or deteriorates. An offender's MO is therefore a function of both *fortifying* and *destabilizing* factors.

Fortifying Factors

Offenders may realize that some of the choices they make during a crime are more proficient and effective than others. They may subsequently repeat them in future offenses, becoming more skillful as well as strengthening or fortifying their MO. Over the course of a criminal career, offenders may also incorporate

---

[7] It is common for rapists to take driver's licenses or other forms of photo ID off their victims as an overt threat to their safety should they report the crime. By doing so, the rapists hope to achieve a level of intimidation. Such offenders are trying to send the message: "I know what you look like, I know where you live, and if you go to the police I will be back and they will not be able to protect you. I will remember you." Still others stalk or contact the victim after the offense.

MO choices that unintentionally reveal something about their identity, character, or experience. Common ways that offenders may learn how to commit crimes more skillfully, evade capture, and conceal their identity (i.e., fortifying factors) include, but are certainly not limited to, those listed here.

Educational and technical materials. Until they are captured and convicted, criminals have equal access to the same learning opportunities as any other citizen. Professional journals, college courses, textbooks, and other educationally oriented material available at a public library or via that Internet can provide offenders with knowledge that is useful toward refining their particular MO. The important lesson for the criminal profiler is that the offender's MO may reflect familiarity or proficiency with specialized knowledge or techniques, and this can be incorporated into the final criminal profile as well as provide investigatively relevant direction. For example, arsonists may read *Kirk's Fire Investigation* (DeHaan, 1997), rapists may read *Men Who Rape* (Groth, 1979) or *Practical Aspects of Rape Investigation* (Burgess and Hazelwood, 1995), murderers may read *Practical Homicide Investigation* (Gerbeth, 1996), and bank robbers may subscribe to security magazines.[8]

Trade or professional experience. Offenders may have been, or may currently be, employed in trades or professions that utilize special knowledge or that require proficiency with specialized techniques (electrician, plumber, telephone company, computers, military, law enforcement, pilot, and so on). Such specialized knowledge may find its way into an offender's MO and be reflected in the offense. The offense may also reflect an opportunity created by the offender's profession, by virtue of time, place, and victim availability.

Criminal experience and confidence. As offenders commit more of the same type of crime, they become more proficient at it. They may act more confidently, be able to handle the unexpected more smoothly (or even be prepared for it), or they may have tailored their precautionary acts to the type of criminal activity they expect to engage in. It is important to establish, in any crime, what the offender had planned for, as evidenced by what the offender brought to the crime scene and the behaviors the offender engaged in. The question that criminal profilers need to ask is whether the materials brought and the behaviors committed were appropriate to the crime. The next question is whether the materials brought and the behaviors committed suggest proficiency with another type of crime (suggesting a criminal history apart from the crime at hand).

Contact with the criminal justice system. Being arrested just once may teach an offender an invaluable lesson about how to avoid detection by law enforcement in the future. Furthermore, and ironically, a prison term in the United States is referred to by some in both law enforcement and the criminal population as "going to college." This is because in prison, younger and less experienced offenders have the opportunity to network with older and more experienced offenders who have already accumulated a great deal of criminal knowledge. Consequently, a prison term of only a few years has the potential to advance an offender's skill level far beyond that person's original MO. Once released, that offender may take this "education" and embark on criminal enterprises that previously would have been beyond his or her ability.

The media. Some offenders monitor investigations into crimes by paying close attention to media accounts in the newspapers and on television. It is important that investigators and profilers alike pay attention to the release of any such information to the media, when it was released, and how that may

---

[8] The author of this text is often asked about the practice of providing training and information to the public that might help a criminal become more proficient. However, the public availability of such material is not the problem. It's not so much a concern that criminals have access to books and materials like this, but that those responsible for investigating crimes don't. In any case, the law-enforcement community enjoys its share of current and future criminals (as does any profession). To argue in favor of providing such material only to law enforcement or only to a specially designated group is to ignore this reality.

affect the future crimes of a given offender in a serial case. Not only may information relating to a case provide an offender with insight into future precautionary acts, but also it may provide other offenders with adequate information to "copycat" a particular series and deflect investigative suspicion from themselves.

For example, a rapist may commit five different attacks in a single region. The serial nature of his crimes may have been undetected until DNA results demonstrated that the rapes were more than likely committed by the same offender. If the media publishes a headline that reads "Serial Rapist Linked to Five Attacks by DNA!" the rapist may alter his MO to prevent law enforcement from linking future cases. For example, he may use a condom during any future rapes. Or he may decide to make a more permanent change and get a vasectomy. In summary, the rapist may make a conscious attempt to prevent detection based on what he has learned from the media coverage of his crimes or similar cases.

Destabilizing Factors

MO may also deteriorate over time and become less skillful, less competent, more careless, and even more irrational than when the criminal behavior began. Common ways that an offender's MO can de-evolve or destabilize over time include, but are certainly not limited to,

- Deteriorating mental state
- Use of controlled substances
- Overconfidence, which can lead to carelessness
- Offender mood (e.g., agitated, excited, or otherwise distracted)
- Untested or unreliable tools or vehicles (e.g., weapons prone to jamming or misfire, and old and malfunctioning vehicles)

The American serial murderer Ted Bundy (Figure 14.2), who killed at least 30 victims across five states between 1973 and 1978, began his criminal career with a competent, well-thought-out MO. He was polite and friendly, was extremely mobile, and often approached his victims in a manner that made him appear helpless or weak and essentially non-threatening. He sometimes accomplished this by presenting himself as a motorist who needed assistance with a disabled vehicle, and he would often wear his arm in a sling. He also tended to select victims who were teenage females, stalking them and selecting disposal sites for their bodies well in advance of committing an actual crime. But his MO deteriorated remarkably over time.

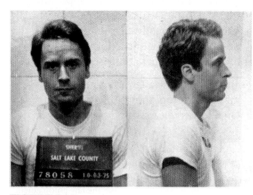

FIGURE 14.2
Theodore (Ted) Robert Bundy (1946–1989).

After being incarcerated and then escaping on two separate occasions in Colorado, he made his way to Florida. He began to drink heavily and he also began to interact with the bodies of his victims, keeping them for days after death. There was also evidence that, with some victims' bodies, Bundy shampooed their hair and applied makeup to their faces, rather than disposing of them immediately. In short, he began to leave more and more evidence behind, engaged in fewer precautionary acts, and became involved in more ritual behavior.

His victim selection also changed; he chose his last victim, a 12-year-old female student from Florida, totally because of her availability. This was a marked departure from his previous MO of carefully stalking victims in advance and selecting victims who were in their late teens and early twenties (Hickey, 1991, pp. 157–162).

X-Factors

An *X-factor* is any unknown or unplanned influence that can affect crime scene behavior during an offense. The successful completion of a crime, from an offender's perspective, depends on events conforming to expectations. Under real-life conditions, crime scenes, victims, and other extrinsic influences do not always conform to an offender's plans. This includes, among many possibilities,

- Weapon malfunction
- Unexpected witnesses
- Victim preparedness/response (e.g., Mace, a victim trained in self-defense)
- Ineffective method of killing or control, resulting in unplanned victim survival or death
- Vehicle malfunctions (e.g., faulty engine, out of gas, or flat tire)
- Increased security measures at pre-selected scene

The presence of any number of X-factors may force the offender to improvise or to make a hasty retreat, resulting in an *interrupted/incomplete offense* or even an *offense gone wrong.*

An *interrupted/incomplete offense* is one that does not contain enough MO behaviors to complete the offense. An incomplete crime might include the following: A victim, instead of being easy prey, turns around and kicks the offender in the groin. The offender may be stunned and limp away, or the victim may create an opportunity to flee the scene. Or, during the attack, a passerby might unwittingly witness the offender, who may then flee the scene. The offender may also choose to walk away from the offense for any reason. Either way, the event would not have included the full potential range of offender MO behaviors and would therefore be incomplete.

An *offense gone wrong* is one that contains unintentional, unplanned MO behavior, which increases the offender's risk or criminal status. An event gone wrong might include the following: The offender might accidentally use too much force, or the victim's response might be too violent for the offender and the offender's control-oriented choking could result in the victim's death. This turn of events can transform a serial rape investigation into a homicide investigation, increasing the offender's criminal status.

MO in Court: Case Example

California v. Kenneth Hernandez (1997) involved the prosecution of Kenneth Hernandez for sex crimes committed against two victims. According to the California Court of Appeals, the trial court committed a reversible error when it admitted into evidence a crime analyst's testimony about data contained in a sex crimes database from which the prosecutor argued circumstantial evidence of the defendant's identity and guilt.[9]

---

[9] The job title "crime analyst" does not automatically imply someone that also has the skills, knowledge, and expertise of a criminal profiler (as evidenced by the case at hand). A crime analyst is often a civilian working for law enforcement (or even in the private sector) who engages in mapping and sometimes interpreting crime trends within a given jurisdiction. As Douglass (1998) states, regarding modern computer-based crime-mapping tools: "Instead of the tedious process of poking color-coded pins into wall maps, crime analysts using the software can click a few computer buttons and create a custom map in seconds." This is an important job, but it does not necessarily involve education, training, or skills related to behavioral analysis and criminal profiling.

The following narrative is adapted entirely from the record provided by California v. Kenneth Hernandez (1997). On December 7, 1994, at around 5:20 p.m., the victim identified as "Monika" was attacked as she jogged on the sidewalk up Gilman Drive toward the University of California at San Diego (UCSD) in La Jolla. Her attacker, whom she identified at trial as Hernandez, came "out of nowhere" from the bushes between two condominiums, butting his head into her stomach and knocking her off balance. They both fell to the ground and the attacker laughed "a real sick laugh." He then reportedly put his hand up her sweatshirt and touched her breasts over her bra. He also reportedly put his other hand down her pants, touching her vagina. Monika then broke free from her attacker, who was unarmed, and ran to the nearby Marriott Residence Inn where she had the front desk receptionist call 911.

On January 2, 1995, shortly after noontime, the victim identified as "Jane" was attacked while she took a break from her jog to meditate in Rose Canyon. She reportedly stopped to help a woman and her small daughter calm their dog. While she was petting the dog, a man with long hair in a ponytail and wearing a black ski hat with green, yellow, and orange stripes; a black ski coat; and black shoes walked by. Jane thought that something was not right with the man and that he might be a "criminal, robber, not balanced," because he was "dressed for the dead of Wisconsin winter." The man followed her for a bit and then approached her when she had found a quiet place to sit. She put up her fists and said, "Don't hurt me, don't hurt me." According to the record (California v. Kenneth Hernandez, 1997), the attacker then did the following:

> [He] delivered a very sharp blow to the left side of her face, causing her to fall sideways. When he came around and started dragging her by her shirt collar across a clearing and into some bushes, Jane screamed and thought, "Oh, my God, my ticket's up. This is what rape is about. And when it's over I'm gonna be dead. Isn't that what rapists do?" After dragging her about eighty-seven feet, Hernandez threw her hard on the ground, told her to shut up and that he did not want to hurt her, giving her two to three more blows to the left side of her face. Jane started blacking out, was terror ridden, and was in shock, thinking she had to befriend this man and talk him out of what he was doing. She told Hernandez he reminded her of her ex-boyfriend, that they had just broken up and she was missing him so much that she was happy when Hernandez ran up to her. When Hernandez got on top of her, with his butt resting on her stomach and his hands on her shoulder area, Jane screamed she could not breathe because her sweatshirt was over her head and she wanted to kiss him so she could see his face. Hernandez just "chuckled," and said "Okay, lady, I'm gonna turn you over now."

> Hernandez rolled her to her stomach, ripped down her sweatpants to her ankles, pulled off one of her pant legs and pulled down her underpants. Jane said, "He spread the crease of my buttocks and started licking me from top of the crease down to the vagina and I thought I was gonna throw up."

> Hernandez, fully clothed, then lay full body on top of Jane, with his head over her right shoulder and rubbed his lower self up and down on her. He suddenly stopped, said, "Okay, lady, I'm gonna go now. Don't shout and don't scream," and ran south.

> Jane got up and started screaming. She told the man who came to her rescue she had been raped. Jane suffered severe headaches, neck trouble, a swollen face, scratches, scrapes and bruises as a result of the attack.

At the trial, the state sought to introduce the testimony of a sheriff's department crime analyst, Karen Goodman, to help prove the offender's identity in this case. The following narrative is provided in as much detail as necessary to show the nature of the database used and the reasoning behind the testimony of the crime analyst involved. It is excerpted entirely from the record of the California Court of Appeals provided by California v. Kenneth Hernandez (1997):

The court held an evidentiary hearing at which crime analyst Goodman testified she had worked for the SDPD [San Diego Police Department] for five years, accessing "various computer systems with law enforcement information to identify suspects, victim profiles, trends analysis on crimes." She had a bachelor of science degree and had received on-the-job training in her unit from people who had developed the various computer systems, from other crime analysts and from miscellaneous investigative units. She explained the computer systems contained law enforcement information "that's captured on crime cases, arrests, field interviews, citations" and that the actual computer system on which she ran the search for this case was named Sherlock. Goodman described the Sherlock system as: "[A]n in-house database that was developed by crime analysis. It was defined by the sex crimes unit, variables that we capture in there. Information that is put into the sex crimes file is from a sex crimes log, which each case that is assigned to a sex crimes detective has very specific information that's put down on a sex crimes log. In turn, that log is given to us and we enter it, give it to a clerical support person in the crime analysis unit who then enters each item into the Sherlock system, into the Sherlock sex crimes files." The entries to Sherlock were generally done within three to four days after a reported sex crimes incident. Sherlock was used daily in the normal course of business for the SDPD and its sex crimes database included every reported sex crime that went to a sex crimes detective. Goodman did not know whether there were any sex crimes not assigned to detectives which might not be entered into Sherlock or whether some sex crimes reported to the San Diego Sheriff's Department which occurred in the SDPD jurisdiction would necessarily be included. Sherlock's programs were limited to crimes occurring within the SDPD's jurisdiction. The SDPD frequently relied upon Sherlock, it was regularly used by the sex crimes unit, and it included separate database files on homicides and one that "captures unique descriptors of suspects." Goodman assumed a murder case in which a rape had occurred would be cross-referenced in both the homicide and sex crimes files.

Goodman explained that a crime analyst accessed information from the sex crimes file of Sherlock by picking certain variables and defining the criteria needed in a particular search and then selecting those from the system. Examples of the variables contained in Sherlock were physical descriptions of victims and suspects, such as height, race, sex; variables concerning the crimes, such as date, time, location, weapon; and various MO's like "binding or taping or things that would be key searchable items." For this case, she did a search on the sex crimes file contained in Sherlock; she did not search in any other database files.

Regarding the search, Goodman prepared a diagram showing the two police beats, beats 125 and 114, where the crimes in this case had occurred. She searched Sherlock for these two areas for sex crimes involving the specific criteria that the crimes have "suspects that were not Black," a "stranger," i.e., no relationship between victim and suspect, and were committed between January 1994 and June 1995. Her initial search produced eight separate incidents. After reviewing each, she narrowed her inquiry down to two cases which matched the MO she was given, based on place of attack and suspect description and "the 'MO' as well." The two cases were the ones with which Hernandez is charged here. Goodman explained that the other six cases were eliminated because they did not match the specific search criteria and did not involve a victim who had been attacked while jogging. For example, she eliminated those crimes where the attack took place other than in a canyon, i.e., in a vehicle or residence, where there were multiple suspects, where the victim was a male, and where the reported victim did not pursue the case. Goodman first worked on this case sometime after February 6, 1995, when she was asked to do so by Detective Gregg. At that point Gregg had one crime that had occurred within a canyon and that is how she came up with the other incident in this case for Gregg. Goodman opined the information from Sherlock was relied upon for the conclusion there was another connected case.

On cross-examination, Goodman testified the original information for the data in the sex crimes log comes from initial police officer reports by the investigating officer who responded to the crime scene, who would turn that report over to the sex crimes unit for entry into the sex crimes log. She explained the original information "is transferred from the crime case to the log by the clerical support or the sex crime detective and it's identified with the specific incident, location, time, and also a key synopsis of the case summary. That would be key words such as suspect actions or victim actions or statements." Assailant descriptions and any modifications would also be put in the log. After the log is prepared, a copy is given to Goodman's unit for crime analysis and inputting into Sherlock. After Goodman opined a person was not obligated by law to report a sex crime, the court stipulated there are "probably some people who don't report."

Goodman agreed the information actually put into Sherlock is not "exactly what's told to the original reporting officer. It's either … what's in the 911 tape, or … what's told to the reporting officer, or … it's an edited version of what is told to the sex crimes detective[.]"

Goodman stated the sex crimes file contained in Sherlock is not connected to any other law enforcement agency computer systems. She was not aware of anyone who periodically checked to ensure that all sex crimes occurring in certain beats within the SDPD jurisdiction were included in Sherlock. She knew of times where a person reported a sex crime that had occurred in the past, for instance over three years ago, that would be input in the sex crimes log only after it had been written up in a police report. Goodman was unsure of when the information on the December 7 incident against Monika in this case had been entered into the log.

Going to the reliability of the system, Goodman said her supervisor made "sure that the operations within the office are going as procedure permits." Any editing authority as to the sex crimes log would be with the detective assigned to a particular case. Goodman further stated: "The only reliability that I can attest to here is that of all the items that come from the sex crimes log they're put in a chronological order … and if something falls out of sequence or is not there, our clerical support would contact the sex crimes [unit] and identify a potential problem … that would mean that every case that was assigned to the sex crime detective … would be reported on there."

Goodman also acknowledged that a crime occurring outside the boundaries of the two beat areas for which she was asked to limit her search, even one block outside, would not be included in the data retrieved from Sherlock. She further admitted she did not rely solely on the computer data to arrive at her conclusion there was a similarity between the two incidents in this case; she looked into the sex crimes files and handwritten police reports to check on other variables that she had not used in retrieving data from Sherlock.

On redirect, Goodman testified the data entered into Sherlock daily from the sex crimes logs was not entered for the purposes of this litigation, but rather to assist her and other SDPD crime analysts and detectives with their jobs. On re-cross, Goodman conceded no other police agency used Sherlock. The court denied the defense motion to preclude Goodman's testimony.

Hernandez was subsequently convicted of six violent sex offenses involving these two victims, by virtue of victim identification and the expert testimony of the crime analyst. The court of appeals reviewed this case and reversed the conviction. It held that such methods of analysis, although a valuable investigative tool, do not meet the test of admissibility in the guilt phase of a criminal trial (California v. Kenneth Hernandez, 1997).

It is important to note that modern law-enforcement case databases suffer from the same limitations as those revealed in the given case. They are only as accurate as the information that is entered into the system. When this is done based on incomplete, unchecked, or outright inaccurate data (as is common in the investigative phase of a law-enforcement investigation), by non-scientists, the possibility of error is increased if not ever-present.

OFFENDER SIGNATURE

Those ideas which, in others, are casual or obscure, which are entertained in moments of abstraction and solitude and easily escape when the scene is changed, have obtained an immovable hold upon his mind.

—Charles Brockden Brown, 1962

The term *signature* has long been used in legal parlance to refer to an unusual, distinctive criminal modus operandi.[10] An early court decision, where MO evidence was inappropriately allowed to show offender identity (and dismissed by the court as a harmless error), cites *McCormick on Evidence* from 1954 (California v. Haston, 1968):

> Professor McCormick states: "Here [i.e., in the matter of proving identity by means of other-offenses' modus operandi evidence] much more is demanded than the mere repeated commission of crimes of the same class, such as repeated burglaries or thefts. The device used must be so unusual and distinctive as to be like a signature." (McCormick, *Evidence* (1954) 157, p. 328.)

However, MO behaviors frequently change and are not always that distinctive. Something more stable and enduring must also be considered to meet the burden of unusualness and distinctiveness mandated by the court. This requires an understanding and consideration of offender psychodynamics.

Offender Psychodynamics

Psychodynamics is a term that refers to how conscious and subconscious drives, emotions, and desires combine to determine personality and motivation. To understand offender psychodynamics, the criminal profiler must start with accepting that not all offenders are the same. They have different histories, different tastes, and different needs. Therefore, similar behaviors committed under similar circumstances by different offenders will not necessarily be for identical or even similar motivations.

According to the American psychologist Dr. John Money, the explanation for this behavioral-motivational distinctiveness is found in the mind's eye of the offender: each maintains a pattern of specific behaviors and subsequent associated feelings that he refers to as a *lovemap* (Money, 1988). *Lovemap* is a term that

---

[10] According to Douglas and Olshaker (1995, p. 69), the American criminal profiler John Douglas, a special agent with the Federal Bureau of Investigation and head of its Behavioral Sciences Unit in the 1980s, first coined the term "signature." He wrote: "Eventually, I would come up with the term *signature* to describe this unique element and personal compulsion, which remained static. And I would use it as distinguishable from the traditional concept of modus operandi, which is fluid and can change." Here, Douglas clearly states that he developed the term to help those investigators involved in criminal profiling distinguish offender behaviors that suggest psychological needs and themes. The research of this author makes clear that the term was in use in criminal courts long before Douglas began his career with the FBI.

Dr. Money developed to describe an idealized scene, person, or program of activities that satisfy the particular emotional and psychological needs of an offender.[11]

Lovemaps, needs, or fantasies develop in all people (not just criminals) as a part of the natural process of human development and can subsequently be affected by both biological and environmental factors. The development of offender's signature behavior necessarily follows a parallel path with sexual and emotional development. As a lovemap develops and related personality is shaped, the behaviors necessary to achieve individual needs are identified, incorporated, and developed. For some, the result may be a healthy expression manifested in nurturing and intimacy-seeking relationships. For others, at the more distant end of the continuum, the result may be the incorporation and development of antisocial and even criminal behaviors.

Dr. Money theorized that criminal behaviors result when the human developmental process is derailed and a person is able to make pleasurable associations with violent or otherwise criminal activity. These associations, varied and evolving over time, amount to a behavioral distinctiveness in the way that an individual offender seeks to satisfy emotional or psychological needs during the commission of a crime such as rape, homicide, arson, and other similar or serial offenses.

As an offender's fantasy develops over time, so does the need to live out those fantasies. When a violent or predatory fantasy is subsequently acted out, the act itself fuels the fantasy in the mind of the offender and causes it to evolve. The process is complementary and can facilitate the evolution of fantasy, signature behaviors, and overall offender signature over time.

SIGNATURE BEHAVIOR

Signature behaviors are those acts committed by an offender that are not necessary to commit the crime, but rather suggest psychological or emotional needs. An offender's signature behaviors are not functional in nature. As discussed in the previous section, they reflect psychodynamic relationships and predispositions that are generally more stable and enduring over time than those evident in their MO.

Repetition

Because of ongoing confusion amongst some analysts and attorneys, it is necessary to explain that the mere repetition of a given behavior across multiple offenses is not enough to make it a signature. It may simply be part of the offender's MO. Generally the following will be true of a signature behavior:

1. Takes extra time to complete, beyond more functional MO behavior
2. Unnecessary for the completion of the crime
3. Involves an expression of a need or emotion
4. May involve an expression of fantasy

---

[11] Money (1988, p. 290) defines the term *lovemap* as a "developmental representation or template in the mind and in the brain depicting the idealized lover and the idealized program of sexuoerotic activity projected in imagery or actually engaged in with that lover." In describing the development of lovemaps, Money explains (pp. 17–18):
Lifelong lovebonding that begins at age eight and continues through marriage into adulthood demonstrates that the imagery or erotic attraction and genital arousal can, like native language, be well established at an early age. Since there is a need for a name for this counterpart of native language, I have called it a lovemap…
Just as they absorb their society's native language, children absorb also its sexual percepts, negative as well as positive. Even as precepts of anti-sexualism are in the process of vandalizing a child's lovemap, they continue to be absorbed.

If a behavior satisfies these criteria, then it is a signature—that is to say, it is related to the offender's psychological and emotional needs (fantasy and motive) rather than functional crime-related needs.

Active and Passive Signature Behaviors

There are two types of signature behaviors: *active* and *passive*.

Active signature behaviors are conscious or deliberate acts committed by the offender. They result from an offender who is in control and intends to leave a specific psychological impression or to satisfy a particular emotional need. Examples can include, but are not limited to,

- Specific and repeated victim type
- Specific and repeated constellation of injuries to body
- Notes left at the scene
- Specific and repeated weapons that go beyond mere function
- Specific and repeated ligature/binding type or configuration

Active signature behavior represents a clear message from the offender; the offender is aware it is being sent and it is meant to be recognized and understood.

Passive signature behaviors are incidental in nature. They result from an offender who is not in control and unintentionally leaves a particular psychological impression. Examples can include, but are not limited to,

- Overkill or brutal levels of force
- Obsessive/compulsive behavior (e.g., stalking, harassment)
- Jealous or self-deprecating language or scripting

Passive signature behavior is the result of offenders who are not in control of their emotions and are unaware that their psychological needs may be revealed by what they are doing.

Limitations

It is important to accept that it may not always be possible to link or unlink cases using signature behaviors for the following reasons:

- An offender may not always leave behind evidence of signature behaviors
- An offender may engage in precautionary acts that conceal the evidence of signature behaviors (burning evidence, removing unknown fantasy items from the crime scene, staging the crime scene, etc.)
- Evidence of offender behavior may be lost, overlooked, or destroyed by forensic personnel and criminal investigators

SIGNATURE PATTERNS

While *signature behaviors* refer to specific acts committed by an offender, overall *offender signature* refers to the pattern or cluster of MO behaviors, signature behaviors, and motivations that are found within an offense. This pattern of behaviors may be unique to a particular offender and may be used to distinguish between crime scenes and potentially between offenders, it may be rare within a particular type of offense, or it may even be common.

Recognizing Offender Signature

An offender's signature is sometimes referred to inappropriately as a "calling card" or a "trademark" (Keppel, 1995). These terms evoke the vision of a static, inflexible, indelible psychological imprint of offender behavior on the crime scene. As should be clear to readers by now, this is a highly misleading description.

There are important limitations to the concept of offender signature that must be understood. Many serial or predatory offenders do not have a need to engage in personal expressions of emotion that are distinct to their individually formed personality. Furthermore, despite an offender signature's distinctiveness, which is a result of the many variables affecting the human developmental process, it is not truly appropriate to state that two crime scenes related by signature alone are psychologically "identical." The terms *identical* and *match* can be misleading to those who do not fully understand the concept and psychology of offender signature.

The term *match* may be used to suggest *identical*, shared characteristics between two things. But by their very nature, crime scenes and crime scene behaviors cannot be precisely the same across offenses, even when the same offender is responsible for them. Not only are the locations likely to be different, but the victims are most certainly different people with their own responses to offender behaviors that will in turn influence the offender's behavioral expressions, both MO-oriented and signature-oriented. One of the other primary reasons for the lack of absolute certainty in interpreting signature behaviors as unique to a specific offender is the subjectivity of the interpretation itself. While offenders may be psychologically distinct, profilers cannot see through the eyes of an offender with perfect, objective clarity. They can show the most likely perspectives and needs of the offender by demonstrating a strong convergence of the physical and behavioral evidence, but they cannot go so far as to call it a "psychological fingerprint."

When asked to make inferences about offender signature, criminal profilers may not have all the facts in the case, or they may be operating with flawed investigative assumptions. Consequently, a thorough criminal profiler will consider the following factors:

- Whether the amount of behavioral evidence is sufficient to make an interpretation of offender signature (e.g., Was there a competent crime scene reconstruction performed? Were the forensic protocols that the reconstruction is based on adequate? Was evidence of wound patterns lost due to bodily decay?)
- Whether the amount of behavioral evidence is fully representative of the offender's needs (e.g., Is there evidence of interruption during the crime? Did the offender have the time to do all of the things that he or she felt was important?)
- Whether the behavioral evidence suggests a signature that is part of an escalation or evolution in an offender's fantasy continuum or whether the offender signature appears to be relatively fixed over time

Case Linkage: Offender Signature in Court

Some researchers (Alison et al., 2002; Canter, 1995; Woodhams and Toye, 2007) have hypothesized that there is both "offender behavioral consistency" and "offender behavioral distinctiveness," which may be used in linkage analysis efforts to identify "crimes suspected of being committed by the same perpetrator on the basis of behavioral similarity." These researchers even go so far as to confuse courtroom acceptance of linkage analysis testimony as scientific evidence of its efficacy and accuracy—and therefore of its utility for court purposes. This is circular reasoning at best. Courtroom acceptance means that on a particular day, in a particular court, a particular judge allowed or disallowed particular evidence—and the reasons for admissibility can vary. Failure to understand the dynamics and unpredictability of this aspect of the forensic realm is a cardinal sin for any scientific forensic examiner.

Moreover, the assumptions of these researchers ignore two of the more important axioms of criminal profiling and behavioral evidence analysis.

1. Different offenders do similar things for different reasons (this is known as the *principle of behavioral variance*)
2. Individual offender behaviors are multidetermined; they can be the result of multiple offender motivations and multiple external influences (this is known as the *principle of multidetermination*)

The authors are not suggesting that case linkage efforts are futile because of the complex and dynamic nature of human behavior. Rather, case linkage is not always possible, and it is rarely certain. Oversimplifying the problem of interpretation with assumptions that ignore the principles of behavioral evidence analysis does not move us closer to accurate case linkage efforts—it moves us further away.

This position directly contradicts the *offender (behavioral) consistency hypothesis* originally proposed by Canter (1995) as an underlying assumption of profiling methods employed by investigative psychologists in their research. Canter's hypothesis predicts that offenders will show consistency (or similarity) in their criminal behavior across their series of crimes. Unfortunately, not only can behavioral manifestations of MO and signature vary across a series, but the series under examination may be only one type of crime, among more than one, being committed by an offender. An offender responsible for a series of rapes may also be responsible for a series of burglaries. An offender responsible for a series of homicides may also be responsible for a series of robberies or thefts. Offenders with such multiple criminal pathways are by no means rare, yet scholars lump and study offenders into fixed groups as though criminal diversification does not happen at all.

The offender consistency hypothesis is, ultimately, a form of limited nomothetic thinking uniformed by actual casework. It inappropriately pigeonholes offenders into categories that are useful for research purposes but artificially isolate them as a particular type (rapist, murderer, arsonist, burglar, stalker, etc.). This has the effect of causing offenders to be viewed as one-dimensional abstracts, as opposed to the multidimensional criminals who exist in reality. Again, this makes offender research easier, but not more accurate.

DISTINGUISHING MO AND SIGNATURE BEHAVIOR

An offender's MO, which is the method employed to commit the crime, is not the same thing as an offender's *motive*, which is the reason for committing the crime, or an offender's *signature behaviors*, which satisfy an offender's emotional and psychological needs and are typically not necessary for the completion of the crime.

The problem for criminal profilers is distinguishing between MO behaviors and signature behaviors. A related problem is that signature needs and MO needs may be satisfied by the same behavior. This is illustrated by the following example:

- In the case of one offender, for example, the act of covering a victim's face with her own shirt during a rape may be a part of a psychological desire, facilitating a fantasy that the victim is another person. This would be a *signature* behavior. In the case of another offender, the act of covering a victim's face with her own shirt during a rape may be part of a functional need to keep the victim from seeing his face and identifying him at a later time. This behavior would then be considered a part of the offender's MO.

Furthermore, the same act may also be intended to satisfy both MO and signature needs and therefore may be part of both the offender's MO and signature behaviors. This is illustrated by the following examples:

- Take the example of a male offender who anally rapes a female victim. Sexual assault is a modus operandi behavior that reflects how the offender committed the crime. The type of sexual assault in this case, anal rape, reflects the offender's *signature behavior*. Sexual assault can be committed in any number of ways; the specific behavior of anal rape is unnecessary for the completion of the crime and reflects the offender's psychological or emotional needs.
- The method of killing may be intended to satisfy both MO and signature needs. Take, for example, an offender who manually strangles a victim. Strangulation or asphyxiation is a modus operandi behavior intended to successfully complete the crime. However, the use of the offender's bare hands, opposed to any other method of killing, satisfies one of the offender's emotional or psychological needs. Furthermore, the process of manual strangulation requires an extended period of time and increased physical contact with the victim, another circumstance reflecting emotional or psychological needs of the offender.
- The number of offenders involved in a sexual homicide may also demonstrate how offender behavior can satisfy both MO and signature needs. The number of offenders involved in the commission of crime is a modus operandi behavior that assists in the successful completion of the crime. However, in the case of a sexual homicide, multiple offenders represent a shared sexual fantasy that reflects their emotional or psychological needs. In this case, the presence of multiple offenders is also a *signature behavior*.

To address the issue of whether a behavior is part of the MO, part of the signature, or both, criminal profilers must look for behavioral patterns and convergences. They must not fall into the inductive trap of interpreting behavioral meaning based on averaged meaning from unrelated offenses. Furthermore, they must not fall into the trap of interpreting a single behavior outside of the context of the facts of a given case and apart from the other behaviors in the offense. The meaning of a behavior to an offender can only be interpreted in context.

INTERPRETING BEHAVIORAL LINKAGE

Behavioral evidence is complex and multidetermined, and testimonial evidence is known to be unreliable. Therefore, it is accepted that physical evidence is the most reliable means of linking two or more cases together. When the physical evidence in a given case is insufficient, or when the law allows it, behavioral evidence may be employed as a secondary means of addressing the question of case linkage. However, there is no evidence or research to suggest that behavioral evidence alone may be used like fingerprints or DNA with respect to determining with any certainty that the same person must be responsible for two or more crimes. Furthermore, while there may be general or thematic similarities between some cases, the dissimilarities between them are of greater weight and importance to rendering final linkage conclusions. Linkage analysis efforts that fail to account for dissimilarity, focusing only on similarities, should be considered inadequate at best, if not biased.

To enable expression of linkage analysis findings in a manner that is useful to investigators and the court but does not mislead with respect to certainty, the author of this text has developed a series of confidence statements. The results of case linkage efforts, or linkage analysis, may be expressed with the following language:

- Behavioral dissimilarity
- An investigative linkage
- Behavioral commonality
- A probative link

Behavioral Dissimilarity

Behavioral dissimilarity means just that: behavioral factors have been compared and they are dissimilar. For example, two homicide cases are presented. One involves the use of a handgun with a single shot to the victim's head. The other involves manual strangulation. The two cases have evidence of a behavioral dissimilarity in the use of a weapon.

It is important to note that behavioral dissimilarities must be analyzed in the context of the entire crime and in relation to all offender behavior. The existence of dissimilar behavioral factors between crimes does not necessarily refute a linkage. Take for example, an offender who engages in unique signature behaviors with multiple victims of different exposure levels. Victim exposure in this case is a behavioral dissimilarity, but the different levels may reflect changes in the offender's modus operandi behavior over time and across offenses. Therefore, behavioral dissimilarities may exist within crimes that evidence a *probative link.*

An Investigative Linkage

An *investigative linkage* is a general class connection between one or more cases that serves to inform the allocation of investigative resources (i.e., in terms of behavior, general, or opportunistic circumstances of the offense; general similarities in modus operandi; and similar signature aspects evidenced by signature behaviors that are perhaps dissimilar). Such a link, as the name suggests, requires further investigation. It is not conclusive. An example of an investigative link would be finding two women murdered in their homes, in generally the same fashion, in the same community, over the course of a year. The general description is of interest, and resources should be applied to investigate further possible connections, as may be found in victimology, MO, signature behavior, and the physical evidence. During any one of these examinations, a more certain linkage may be established or refuted. If more information is not available, it must be remembered that an investigative linkage is not sufficient to suggest a *behavioral commonality* let alone a *probative link.*

Behavioral Commonality

A *behavioral commonality* is present when behavioral factors have been compared and they are similar but not *unique.*[12] For example, two convenience robberies occur in broad daylight. Both involve a .357-magnum handgun. Both involve an offender wearing a mask. These robberies evidence behavioral commonalities with respect to time of day, precautionary acts, location type, use of weapon, and even motive. However, this robbery pattern is not unique, especially in large urban areas.

Probative Link

A *probative link* is evidenced by either a unique offender *behavior* or a unique *offender signature* that is shared across two or more cases, with limited behavioral dissimilarity. It is a connection that is sufficiently distinctive

---

[12] *Unique* refers to a behavioral factor that is so rare as to behaviorally individuate one offense from all others; *unique* means that it is not repeated anywhere else. The use of this term implies the highest level of undisputed confidence.

to support the inference that the same person is responsible. Physical evidence, such as certain kinds of DNA, may also provide a probative link —and must therefore not be ignored unless intentionally set aside for court purposes.

When determining whether a unique offender signature exists between two or more crimes, the behavioral dissimilarities are also of importance. If significant behavioral dissimilarity exists between crimes that cannot be explained by evolving or devolving MO behavior, a probative link cannot be cited in the final case linkage analysis.

New Jersey v. Steven Fortin

One of the most comprehensive rulings related to the admissibility of linkage analysis evidence and testimony occurred in New Jersey v. Steven Fortin (1999–2007).

On April 3, 1995, 34-year-old Vicki Gardner, a Maine state trooper, was sexually assaulted, severely beaten about the face, and strangled by Steven Fortin (Figure 14.3), who pled guilty to this attack and was sentenced to a 20-year term of imprisonment.

In August of 1994, 25-year-old Melissa Padilla was sexually assaulted, severely beaten, robbed, and strangled to death in Avenel, New Jersey, while walking home after making purchases at a Quick Chek convenience store. Retired FBI profiler Roy Hazelwood was retained by the state to analyze case materials pertaining to

FIGURE 14.3
Steven Fortin, seated and surrounded by law enforcement officers, in the courtroom during his sentencing for the murder of Melissa Padilla, August 11, 1994. A photograph of Melissa Padilla and her four children is projected on a screen in the background.

the Padilla murder and the attack on Gardner for the purpose of determining whether the two crimes were committed by the same offender, based on a "linkage analysis" of both incidents. Such an analysis involves an evaluation of MO and signature behaviors from both crimes (New Jersey v. Steven Fortin, 1999).

According to Hazelwood (New Jersey v. Steven Fortin, 1999), there were 15 points of similar MO behavior in the crimes. They included the facts that they were both high-risk crimes, the crimes were committed impulsively, the victims were female, the age of the victims was generally the same, both victims crossed the path of the offender, the victims were alone, the assaults occurred at a confrontation point adjacent to or on a well-traveled highway, the assaults occurred during darkness, no weapons were involved in the assaults, both assaults involved blunt-force injuries inflicted with fists (and each victim's nose was broken), there was facial trauma (primarily to each victim's upper face, and no teeth were damaged), the lower garments were totally removed, with panties found inside the shorts or pants of the victims, their shirts were left on the victims and their breasts were free, and no seminal fluid was found in or on the victims.

Furthermore, according to Hazelwood, the offender demonstrated anger through five points of similar signature behavior in the crimes. They included bites to the lower chin, bites to the lateral left breast, injurious anal penetration, brutal facial beating, and manual frontal strangulation. The conclusion of Hazelwood's report stated:

> In my 35 years of experience with a variety of violent crimes committed in the U.S., Europe, Canada, and the Caribbean, I have never observed this combination of behaviors in a single crime of violence. The likelihood of different offenders committing two such extremely unique crimes is highly improbable.

> Based upon a comparison of the MO and the ritualistic behaviors of the two crimes, it is my opinion that the same person was responsible for the murder of Ms. Melissa Padilla and the subsequent attempted murder of Ms. Vicki Gardner.

Hazelwood proffered his true-crime memoir *The Evil That Men Do* (Hazelwood and Michaud, 1998) as a learned treatise on the subject, in which he argues that offender signature is as unique as fingerprints or DNA evidence. In this case, the court applied the New Jersey v. Gladys Kelly (1984) standard for admissibility, which includes "general acceptance" and "sufficiently outside the general knowledge of average fact-finder" language. The trial court judge denied the defense motion to exclude Hazelwood's testimony. Fortin was subsequently convicted of the capital murder of Melissa Padilla.

In 1999, the appellate division reversed the lower court's ruling on the admissibility of Hazelwood's testimony. It found that linkage analysis (consideration and comparison of offender MO and signature behavioral patterns) was not such that the testimony would be sufficiently reliable. It also held that linkage analysis involved an application of behavioral science and, as such, should be evaluated under the test for admission of scientific evidence. It further held that given the conclusive nature of Hazelwood's testimony, there could be no adequate limiting instruction given to the jury that could undo the damage of an expert's expressing an opinion that he believed the defendant was guilty of the crime charged (New Jersey v. Steven Fortin, 1999).

In 2000, the New Jersey State Supreme Court ruled to uphold the decision of the 1999 appellate court. Two issues were involved: first, whether the prosecution can introduce evidence of a similar crime on the issue of identity and, second, whether the state's proposed witness can be qualified as an expert on the ritualistic and signature aspects of crime and testify through the use of linkage analysis that the same person who committed the Maine crime committed the murder in New Jersey. The New Jersey State Supreme Court ruled that the proposed expert testimony concerning linkage analysis lacked sufficient scientific reliability and was therefore inadmissible but that evidence of the Maine crime is admissible on the issue of identity with an appropriate limiting instruction (New Jersey v. Steven Fortin, 2000).

The court took note of the fact that Hazelwood was substituting alleged case experience for defensible scientific fact and research, which Thornton (1997, pp. 15–17) explicitly warns against as an illegitimate forensic practice (New Jersey v. Steven Fortin, 2000):

> … Hazelwood had not seen in reviewing 4000 cases this combination of bite marks, anal tears, and brutal facial beatings to a victim. If there is such a database of cases, the witness' premise can be fairly tested and the use of the testimony invokes none of the concerns that we have expressed about the improper use of expert testimony.

The court also took note of the cronyism involved in the issue of linkage analysis and its impact on the scientific reliability of the discipline. According to Booth (2000),

> In order to be accepted as valid analysis, [Justice] O'Hern wrote, the analysis must be backed up by scientific and legal writings and judicial opinions. Hazelwood's report, he said, fails that test, especially since linkage analysis is a field in which only Hazelwood and a few of his close associates are involved.

> "Concerning consensus on acceptance of 'linkage analysis' in the scientific community, the other experts mentioned by Hazelwood in his testimony were either current or former co-workers," O'Hern noted. "In this respect, there are no peers to test his theories and no way in which to duplicate his results."

Of note is the partially dissenting view of Justice Long. She agreed with the other justices that Hazelwood was not qualified as an expert in the area of linkage analysis and that his testimony was unreliable. However, she felt that evidence of the Maine crime should not be admissible even with a limiting instruction. She wrote (New Jersey v. Steven Fortin, 2000):

> [I]t is my view that the reliability defects that, according to the Appellate Division and the majority, preclude Hazelwood from testifying as a scientific expert on linkage, are equally applicable to his proffer of uniqueness testimony. Linkage analysis is the procedure used by criminal investigators when the concentration of modus operandi and ritualistic characteristics in crimes is high, such that the investigator can conclude that the perpetrator is the same person. Uniqueness testimony is linkage analysis under another name. It is no more reliable when Hazelwood testifies as a crime investigator than when he does so as an "expert" in ritualistic behavior. In sum, while I would not allow the evidence of the Maine crime to be admitted without an expert, I agree with the Appellate Division that Hazelwood does not qualify.

The author of this text disagrees strongly with the opinions expressed by the expert in New Jersey v. Steven Fortin (2000) and is confused by the comparison of signature analysis with the hard science of forensic DNA analysis. They are not the same thing. One involves dynamic behavior, and one involves inflexible molecular chemistry. A comparison of the two is at best inappropriate and even misleading. The author agrees most strongly with Justice Long in this case for the reasons given in her opinion.

But the Fortin case did not end there. There was a retrial, and it dealt with the same issues all over again. Rather than use an FBI-trained expert already viewed askance by the court, the prosecution sought to enter into evidence the results of the FBI's Violent Criminal Apprehension Program (ViCAP) database search regarding the two cases (the search having been done by a new FBI profiler)—to demonstrate the unique signature nature of the crimes. However, the new FBI profiler completed the ViCAP form at the request of the Middlesex County prosecutor's office with the defendant's trial in mind years after the crimes. The information was not compiled and entered as part of the original investigation. Given this circumstance, the court was aware of the potential for bias. As explained in New Jersey v. Steven Fortin (2007),

Defendant [Fortin] was then convicted in the Superior Court, Law Division, Middlesex County, of capital murder, aggravated sexual assault, first-degree robbery, and felony murder and was sentenced to death. Defendant appealed. The Supreme Court, 178 N.J. 540, 843 A.2d 974, reversed and remanded. On retrial, the Superior Court, in ruling on several pretrial evidentiary motions, conditioned introduction of Maine assault and nonfatal strangulation on expert testimony, ruled that evidence of injuries suffered by victim in Maine assault and non-fatal strangulation other than the bite marks were admissible, and ruled that search results of FBI's Violent Criminal Apprehension Program were inadmissible.

Holdings: On grant of state's motion for leave to appeal, the Supreme Court, Albin, J., held that: (1) motion judge did not abuse her discretion by conditioning the admission of the Maine assault on the presentation of expert testimony; (2) motion judge did not abuse her discretion by requiring state to provide defendant with a database of cases supporting experts' testimony that bite marks inflicted during defendant's alleged sexual assault of victim and Maine police officer were unusual [and] that they constituted signature crimes; (3) state was permitted to show that the bite marks suffered by female police officer in Maine were inflicted in the course of a violent sexual assault; and (4) Violent Criminal Apprehension Program (ViCAP) database could not be used by state to show that a crime comparison search revealed similarities between victim's murder and Maine assault that were allegedly so unusual as to constitute a signature. …

In the retrial of defendant Steven Fortin for the capital murder of Melissa Padilla, the State intends to prove defendant's guilt by showing that he committed the crime in such a distinctive way that it may be said to bear his "signature." The State seeks to introduce as "other crimes" evidence pursuant to *N.J.R.E.* 404(b) defendant's sexual assault of Maine State Trooper Vicki Gardner, whom he vaginally and anally penetrated, strangled, and bit on both the left breast and chin. The State argues that the peculiar bite marks to the left breast and chin found on Padilla's battered body, combined with injuries inflicted from anal penetration and manual strangulation, were akin to a signature that identified defendant as Padilla's killer. The State submits that jurors, relying on their common experience and general knowledge, need no expert testimony to conclude that the trademark bite injuries in both the Gardner and Padilla cases had a singular author defendant.

To bolster that conclusion, the State offers the results of a computer search of the FBI's Violent Criminal Apprehension Program (ViCAP), a national database of reported violent crimes that yielded three crimes with strikingly similar features—the Gardner and Padilla sexual assaults, and a sexual crime committed in Washington State.

In ruling on pretrial motions, the motion judge held that determining whether the Gardner and Padilla sexual assaults are signature crimes is beyond the general experience and knowledge of an ordinary juror and therefore requires expert testimony to explain those features that uniquely tie the two crimes together. The judge determined that the State could present the expert testimony of a medical examiner and forensic odontologist to establish the uniqueness of the bite marks suffered by both victims, provided those experts produce a reliable database to support their opinions. With regard to the attack on Trooper Gardner, the motion judge limited the State to the signature-crime evidence—the bite marks—finding that other details of the assault would be irrelevant and unnecessarily inflammatory. Last, the judge concluded that because law enforcement authorities inserted the details of the Maine crime into the ViCAP database solely for the purpose of making an inexorable link between the Gardner and Padilla crimes, the ViCAP search results would not be admissible. The motion judge did allow the use of the ViCAP database, absent the Maine crime, as a means for supporting or attacking the reliability of the expert testimony.

We granted the State's motion for leave to appeal and now affirm the motion judge's ruling with the following modifications. The State must be permitted to present the bite-mark evidence in context and therefore *material* details of the Gardner sexual assault cannot be censored. Testimony describing that assault, however, is subject to specific jury instructions explaining the limited use of "other crimes" evidence under *N.J.R.E.* 404(b). Finally, because the State's experts have not relied on the ViCAP database to form their opinions, the ViCAP database should not be admissible to bolster those opinions. …

In his testimony, FBI Supervisory Special Agent Mark Safarik described the Violent Criminal Apprehension Program, more commonly known as ViCAP. Created in 1984, ViCAP is a national database of approximately 167,000 reported violent crimes (homicides, attempted homicides, and kidnappings) maintained by the FBI in Quantico, Virginia. The database represents about three to seven percent of the violent crimes committed since ViCAP's inception. Participation in ViCAP nationwide is voluntary. Law enforcement agencies that complete the ViCAP form answer numerous questions about the crime for inclusion in the national database.

The general purpose of ViCAP "is to identify similarities in crimes" through a computer search isolating particular characteristics in the commission of the offense. Through such a computer search focusing on specific crime criteria, one law enforcement agency can contact and cooperate with another agency working on a "similar case with similar characteristics." According to Agent Safarik, the "ViCAP system is looking for … solved or unsolved homicides, or attempted homicides, missing persons cases, kidnappings, where there is a strong possibility of foul play, or unidentified dead bodies, where the manner of death is suspected to be homicide." In the relevant time period, it does not appear that sexual assaults unrelated to kidnappings or homicides and attempted homicides were a targeted group for input into the ViCAP system.

Law enforcement authorities completed the ViCAP form for the Padilla murder in a timely manner for inclusion in the national database. The Maine State Police, however, did not complete a ViCAP form for the 1995 Gardner sexual assault. In 2004, in preparation for defendant's trial, the State requested that Agent Safarik submit a ViCAP form for the Gardner case. He did so with the assistance of a ViCAP analyst and the Maine State Police. Agent Safarik then ran a series of searches on the ViCAP system for specific criteria common to both the Padilla and Gardner crimes, such as manual strangulation, sexual assault, and bite marks on the face and chest. The searches yielded only three cases—the Padilla murder, the Gardner sexual assault, and a 1988 case from Washington State. The State argued that the searches showed that the similarities between the Padilla and Gardner crimes were so unusual as to constitute a signature. Significantly, Agent Safarik indicated both that the ViCAP database could not be released to defense counsel because of privacy concerns and that it was exempt from the Freedom of Information Act. …

The motion judge ruled that any comparative analysis of the two sexual assaults for the purpose of identifying them as signature crimes was beyond the ken of an ordinary juror and that the ViCAP database did not "provide independent support of a theory of uniqueness" between the two crimes. She therefore conditioned the admissibility of the Maine crime on expert testimony making the link between the two crimes. …

The motion judge rejected the State's position that the ViCAP matches could be used to support a theory that the Gardner and Padilla crimes were unique. She reasoned that the ViCAP database, at present, was not sufficiently crafted to isolate unique criteria. For example, she noted that the ViCAP data form had no boxes to check for bite marks to the chin. For that reason, she concluded that the overly broad factors listed in the ViCAP database did not permit a reliable uniqueness analysis. She also found that because the Gardner ViCAP form "was created for litigation purposes and was not within the regular course of police work," the match between the two crimes was not from "an unbiased generation of data" and thus was inadmissible. Last, she determined that the ViCAP database, without the Gardner information, "would be a reliable database upon which the [S]tate may rely to test the expert opinions."

As mentioned earlier, ViCAP is a national database containing approximately 167,000 cases of homicide, attempted homicide, and kidnapping. Completion of a ViCAP form by a law enforcement agency is on a voluntary basis. Lawrence Nagle, the supervising investigator on the Padilla case in 1994, testified that at the time of the Padilla investigation, it was the practice of the Middlesex County Prosecutor's Office to fill out ViCAP forms only for unsolved crimes.

Agent Safarik testified that various agencies follow different practices in determining when to complete a ViCAP form. The 167,000 cases in the database represent about three to seven percent of the homicides, attempted homicides, and kidnappings committed since 1984. The record does not reveal how many of those three to seven percent of cases were sexual assaults. Moreover, at least according to the ViCAP form's general instructions, ViCAP did not invite entries for violent sexual assaults falling outside of the categories of homicide, attempted homicide, or kidnapping. Accordingly, violent sexual assaults that did not end in a homicide, attempted homicide, or kidnapping may not be reflected in the ViCAP database. Viewed through that prism, the ViCAP database may only contain a very small fraction of the number of violent sexual assaults since 1984.

Significantly, although the State presented Agent Safarik to explain the functions of ViCAP, neither he nor any other expert witness vouched that a ViCAP crime match, such as the one in this case, constituted reliable signature-crime evidence. Only one case has been brought to our attention in which a signature-crime match from the ViCAP database was found to be admissible, and there the ViCAP searches were offered to support an expert's conclusion that the criminal behavior—posing bodies of murder victims in staged positions—was highly unusual. ...

It is noteworthy that only through the importuning of the Middlesex County Prosecutor's Office, which was preparing for defendant's murder trial, did Agent Safarik input a ViCAP form for the nine-year-old Gardner sexual assault. Thus, the Gardner ViCAP form was not submitted in the course of an ordinary investigative routine by the Maine State Police, but rather for litigation purposes—to find a match with the Padilla murder. Although the State maintains that the description of the Gardner crime on the ViCAP form is unassailable, it cannot be known in hindsight how the information would have been entered into the system for normal recordkeeping and investigative purposes. That is why the motion judge concluded that the State could not show that Agent Safarik's searches were based on "an unbiased generation of data."

Ultimately, the court found that ViCAP is a useful investigative tool, but in the case at hand it was used outside of investigative efforts. Moreover, ViCAP's scientific and subsequent forensic reliability could not be established, or even vouched for, sufficiently for court purposes. The inability to know the reliability of the database, let alone produce it for review by the defense, precluded its use as a forensic tool.

CASE EXAMPLE: COMMONWEALTH OF MASSACHUSETTS v. TIMOTHY IMBRIGLIO

The following is excerpted from Turvey (2009), a linkage analysis report prepared for defense attorney Matthew A. Kamholtz of Boston, in Commonwealth of Massachusetts v. Timothy Imbriglio (Case No. 9773CR0017). It was introduced into evidence with sworn expert testimony by one of the authors (Turvey):

This case involves the examination of two separate homicides for linkage analysis purposes:

- Gerald Rose, a 39-year-old white male found nude and strangled in his bedroom at his Taunton, MA home on February 18, 1992 (police reports indicate that he actually died on February 14, 1992).
- Henry Cohen, an 82-year-old white male found clothed and strangled up in the woods off the North side of Long Pond Road in Freetown, MA on November 15, 1996 (he had been left there on November 5th, 1996).

Henry Cohen

It should be noted that on March 3, 1999, Mr. Imbriglio pled guilty to larceny of more than $250 and manslaughter in relation to the death of Mr. Cohen.

In the Cohen case, Mr. Imbriglio specifically pled guilty to meeting Mr. Cohen at the southbound rest area on Route 140; agreeing to drive separately to another location (the Dunkin Donuts parking lot) to engage in oral sex performed on Mr. Imbriglio for money as a ruse; to walking Mr. Cohen into the woods, struggling with him, and robbing him; to leaving Mr. Cohen bound in such a manner as to eventually cause his death.

It should also be noted that the facts of plea agreement specifically provide that there was no assertion or evidence of sexual activity, and that the victim was in fact alive when Mr. Imbriglio left the scene.

The notable characteristics of this crime include the following:

1. Victim appears to have a history of frequenting rest areas to solicit male partners for oral sex, based on age, skill (e.g., writing down vehicle plate numbers), and comfort with participation.
2. The body was found at an outdoor crime scene.
3. Use of a ruse to gain victim confidence and compliance.
4. The victim was bound by his feet with his own shoelaces; this is use of available material for functional restraint in non-sexual context.
5. The victim was found with his own shoelace around his neck, and the cause of death was asphyxiation.
6. Absence of sexual activity.
7. Victim was found clothed.
8. According to police reports, the victim's wallet was found in his vehicle but without money in it.
9. The victim's vehicle appears to have been searched, at least from the photos of the passenger seat.
10. Stranger-on-stranger crime with profit motivation.

Gerald Rose

The notable characteristics of this crime include the following:

1. Victim has a history of frequenting rest areas to solicit male partners for sex, based on witness statements.
2. The body was found at an indoor scene.
3. There is an absence of forced entry at the scene.

4. The timeline strongly suggests that the victim died on Valentine's Day.
5. The victim died at his home, in his own bedroom.
6. The victim was found nude.
7. Recent sexual activity is evident from apparent semen on victim's leg and fecal matter found at scene.
8. The victim died as the result of ligature strangulation from multiple neckties (offender use of available material).
9. There is an absence of injury to victim other than ligature strangulation, which in concert with the victim's nudity, lifestyle, and the location of the offense suggest that the victim may have allowed himself to be tied up.
10. Neckties found around the victim's neck are multiple; that the victim appears to have submitted to binding, in this context, suggests a fetishistic/masochistic element to the behavior. Death may therefore have been the result of accidental sexual asphyxia. This possibility has not been eliminated.
11. The TV, VCR, and answering machine are missing from the victim's home; however, his wallet was not taken nor is there evidence of jewelry missing.
12. According to investigators, the scene appeared staged to look like a robbery. This examiner concurs that staging is a strong possibility. Crime scene staging is done to move investigation away from friends, family, and known suspects, not by strangers (Turvey, 2000).
13. The motive in this case appears to be sexually oriented along with crime concealment.

Conclusions

These cases evidence some *investigative links* with numerous and significant *behavioral dissimilarities*. As a consequence, it is highly inappropriate and even misleading to suggest that these two cases share …distinctive characteristics [sufficient] to [imply] a common offender.

It should be noted that the rest area in particular is not a distinctive feature of these two cases. Rather it is an investigative link. The nature of the rest area as a nexus for criminal/sexual activity demonstrates how large the suspect pool in the Rose homicide is. Homosexuals from the surrounding areas have frequented that rest area for many years to engage in sexual activity, in order to find and solicit sexual partners. Given this history, is it not a surprise that the defendant can be connected to both victims in some fashion. In particular, Mr. Rose's history of soliciting males for sexual activity at that rest area is extensive.

Investigative Links

As already mentioned, an investigative link is a superficial connection between one or more cases that serves to inform the allocation of investigative resources (e.g., similar victim type, crime type, geographic area, and motive).

The investigative links in this case include the following:
1. Both victims are homosexual males.
2. Both victims live within the same geographic region.
3. Both victims appear to have a history of frequenting rest areas to solicit male partners for sex.
4. Both victims were killed with a ligature, dying of asphyxia.

While these similarities are of interest, they are by no means unique. They also require further investigation to contextualize.

Certainly there are a percentage of homosexual men in the geographic region, and they exist in significant enough numbers to have developed a mechanism for meeting up at local rest areas. Moreover, of those homosexual men in that geographic region, only a certain percentage were murdered using ligatures. This creates an investigative link that must be examined.

However, once these superficial similarities are considered, the differences become stark: The [victims] are both men, but one is 39 and one is 82. Both lived in the same geographic region, but one was a locally high-profile political figure and the other was a retiree. Moreover, while both solicited men for sex, and at the same rest area, this actually increases the suspect pool rather than decreasing it, as it connects them both to a very specific covert homosexual sub-culture. And finally, while both were killed with a ligature, one involved multiple neckties in a fetishistic fashion during sexual activity, while the other involved a shoelace used to secure the victim during a robbery. These "similarities" do not bear out as distinctive connections.

Behavioral Dissimilarities

As already mentioned, behavioral dissimilarities refer to behavioral evidence components (e.g., MO, victimology, and offense signature) that have been compared and are dissimilar.

The behavioral dissimilarities in this case include the following:

1. *Victimology*: Cohen was an 82-year-old male retiree; Rose was a 39-year-old city planner with a boyfriend.
2. *Scene type*: Cohen was found at an outdoor crime scene in the woods; Rose was found in his own home, in his bedroom.
3. *Day/Season*: Cohen was killed in early November; Rose was killed on a holiday weekend in February (Valentine's Day).
4. *Victim clothing*: Cohen was clothed; Rose was nude.
5. *Sexual activity*: There was no evidence of sexual activity or contact in the Cohen case; in the Rose case, recent sexual activity is evident from apparent semen and fecal matter.
6. *Use of ligatures*: The use of ligatures in the Cohen case was functional and basic; the use of ligatures in the Rose case was complex and fetishistic in a sexual context.
7. *Evidence of injury*: Cohen's body evidenced contusions to the eyes, lips, and chin suggestive of control-oriented force related to a struggle; Rose's body evidenced no injury other than the ligature, suggesting the victim may have been compliant. Combined with the fetishism, this suggests a masochistic component to the Rose homicide.
8. *Evidence of theft*: Cohen's wallet and watch were found in his vehicle, but with no money in [the wallet], and his vehicle appears to have been searched—suggesting theft. Items of obvious value were left behind at the Rose scene, such as his wallet and jewelry, while the TV, VCR, and answering machine were taken.
9. *Evidence of staging*: Investigators in the Rose homicide believed that the scene was staged to look like a burglary; no staging is evident in the Cohen homicide.
10. *Type of crime*: [The] Cohen [homicide] is a confessed stranger crime with a profit motivation and no sexual activity; [the] Rose [case] presents as a staged sexual homicide in the context of sexual activity, to conceal the relationship between the victim and the offender.

These dissimilarities combine to suggest two entirely different motives, circumstances, and victim–offender relationships between the Cohen and Rose cases. This precludes the possibility of using offense behavior to suggest that the same person must be responsible for both crimes.

SUMMARY

Case linkage or *linkage analysis* refers to the process of determining whether there are discrete connections between two or more previously unrelated cases through crime scene analysis. It involves establishing and comparing the physical evidence, victimology, crime scene characteristics, motivation, modus operandi, and signature behaviors of each of the cases under review. It is seen in two different contexts: *investigative* and *forensic*. In investigative contexts, it is used to assist law enforcement by helping to establish where to apply investigative efforts and resources. In forensic contexts, it is employed to assist the court with determining whether there is sufficiently distinctive behavioral evidence to connect crimes together in their commission.

A criminal's modus operandi (MO) refers to the manner in which a crime has been committed. It is comprised of learned behaviors that can evolve and develop over time. It can be refined, as an offender becomes more experienced, sophisticated, and confident. It can also become less competent and skilled over time, decompensating by virtue of a deteriorating mental state or increased use of controlled substances.

Signature behaviors are those acts committed by an offender that are not necessary to commit the crime, but rather suggest psychological or emotional needs. While signature behaviors refer to specific acts committed by an offender, overall offender signature refers to the pattern or cluster of MO behaviors, signature behaviors, and motivations that are found within an offense. This pattern of behaviors may be unique to a particular offender and may be used to distinguish between crime scenes and potentially between offenders, it may be rare within a particular type of offense, or it may even be common.

When the physical evidence in a given case is insufficient, or when the law allows it, behavioral evidence may be employed as a secondary means of addressing the question of case linkage. However, there is no evidence or research to suggest that behavioral evidence alone may be used like fingerprints or DNA with respect to determining with any certainty that the same person must be responsible for two or more crimes. Furthermore, while there may be general or thematic similarities between some cases, the dissimilarities between cases are of greater weight and importance to rendering final linkage conclusions. Linkage analysis efforts that fail to account for dissimilarities, focusing only on similarities, should be considered inadequate at best, if not biased.

Questions

1. An _____ analysis is done during the investigation, while facts are still being established and for the purpose of moving the case forward and leading investigators towards additional evidence.
2. An offender's MO behavior often serves (or fails to serve) one or more of three general purposes. List these purposes.
3. Explain the difference between *active signature behaviors* and *passive signature behaviors*.
4. True or False: Signature needs and MO needs may be satisfied by the same behavior.
5. A _____ is a connection that is sufficiently distinctive to support the inference that the same person is responsible for a series of crimes.

REFERENCES

Alison, L., Bennell, C., Mokros, A., Ormerod, D., 2002. The Personality Paradox in Offender Profiling: A Theoretical Review of the Processes Involved in Deriving Background Characteristics from Crime Scene Actions. Psychology, Public Policy, and Law 8, 115–135.

Bennell, C., Jones, N., lnyk, T., 2009. Addressing Problems with Traditional Crime Linking Methods Using Receiver Operating Characteristic Analysis. Legal and Criminological Psychology, 293–310.

Black, H.C. (Ed.), 1990. Black's Law Dictionary. West, St. Paul, MN.

Booth, M., 2000. "Linkage Analysis" of Crime Profile Called Junk Science by N.J. Court. New Jersey Law Journal February 29.

Burgess, A.W., Hazelwood, R.R., 1995. Practical Aspects of Rape Investigation: A Multidisciplinary Approach, second edition. CRC Press, Boca Raton, FL.

California v. Haston, 1968. Crim. No. 11710, August 19 (70 Cal. Rptr. 419).

California v. Kenneth Hernandez, 1997. No. D024403, May 23 (63 Cal.Rptr.2d 769).

Canter, D., 1995. Psychology of Offender Profiling. In: Bull, R., Carson, D. (Eds.), Handbook of Psychology in Legal Contexts. Wiley, Chichester, England, pp. 343–355.

DeForest, P., Gaensslen, R.E., Lee, H., 1983. Forensic Science: An Introduction to Criminalistics. McGraw-Hill, New York, NY.

DeHaan, J., 1997. Kirk's Fire Investigation, fourth edition. Prentice Hall, Upper Saddle River, NJ.

Douglas, J., Olshaker, M., 1995. Mindhunter: Inside the FBI's Elite Serial Crime Unit. Scribner's, New York, NY.

Douglass, E., 1998. A Byte out of Crime: Mapping Software Helps Officers Put Pieces Together. Los Angeles Times February 16.

Feeney, F., 2000. Police Clearances: A Poor Way to Measure the Impact of Miranda on the Police. Rutgers Law Journal (Fall), 1–14.

Gerbeth, V., 1996. Practical Homicide Investigation, third edition. CRC Press, Boca Raton, FL.

Gross, H., 1924. Criminal Investigation. Sweet & Maxwell, London, England.

Gross, H., 1968. Criminal Psychology. Patterson Smith, Montclair, NJ.

Groth, A.N., 1979. Men Who Rape. Plenum Press, New York, NY.

Hazelwood, R., Michaud, S., 1998. The Evil That Men Do. St. Martin's Press, New York, NY.

Keppel, R., 1995. Signature Murders: A Report of Several Related Cases. Journal of Forensic Science. 40, 70–674.

McCormick, C., 1954. Handbook of the Law of Evidence. West Publishing Company, St. Paul, MN.

Money, J., 1988. Lovemaps: Clinical Concepts of Sexual/Erotic Health and Pathology, Paraphilia, and Gender Transposition in Childhood, Adolescence, and Maturity. Prometheus Books, New York, NY.

New Jersey v. Steven Fortin, 1999. 318 N.J. Super. 557.

New Jersey v. Steven Fortin, 2000. No.A-95/96–98, Supreme Court of New Jersey, 2000 (745 A.2d 509).

New Jersey v. Steven Fortin, 2007. 189 N.J. 579, 917 A.2d 746, decided March 28.

New Jersey v. Gladys Kelly, 1984. A.2d 364, July 24.

O'Connell, J., Soderman, H., 1936. Modern Criminal Investigation. Funk & Wagnalls, New York, NY.

Thornton, J.I., 1997. The General Assumptions and Rationale of Forensic Identification. In: Faigman, D., Kaye, D., Saks, M., Sanders, J. (Eds.), Modern Scientific Evidence: The Law and Science of Expert Testimony, vol. 2. West, St. Paul, MN.

Turvey, B., 2000. Modus Operandi, Encyclopedia of Forensic Science. Academic Press, London, England.

Turvey, B., 2009. Linkage analysis report, in re Commonwealth of Massachusetts v. Timothy Imbriglio, Case No. 9773CR0017; presented via expert testimony given March 9, 2010.

Turvey, B., Petherick, W., 2010. Forensic Criminology. Elsevier Science, San Diego, CA.

Weston, P., Wells, K., 1974. Criminal Investigation: Basic Perspectives, second edition. Prentice-Hall , Englewood Cliffs, NJ.

Woodhams, J., Toye, K., 2007. An Empirical Test of the Assumptions of Case Linkage and Offender Profiling with Serial Commercial Robberies. Psychology, Public Policy, and Law February, 44–46.

CHAPTER 15

Cyberpatterns: Criminal Behavior on the Internet

Eoghan Casey

The rather mundane reality is that every new technology can serve as a vehicle for criminal behavior, and the Internet is no exception. The extraordinary dimensions of this new technology, however, are its rapid growth and infinite capacity to make communication both universal and instantaneous. The planet, in a sense, becomes a replicant of the human cortex: billions of neurons synaptically firing at random or in concert, multitasking without interference—prefrontal websites, hemispheric chat rooms, temporal lobe flaming, occipital e-mail.

—Meloy, *The Psychology of Stalking: Clinical and Forensic Perspectives* (1998, p. 10)

CONTENTS

Criminal Profiling: An Introduction to Behavioral Evidence Analysis, Fourth Edition

KEY TERMS

Automated modus operandi	Dynamic modus operandi	Remote assessment
Cyberpatterns	Grooming	Spoofing
Cybertrails		

As organizations like IBM focus more energy on projects like the Second Life Virtual World and remotely controlled homes, the interdigitation between the physical and virtual worlds will continue to increase, creating new opportunities for criminal activity. Although it may be some time before we have virtual murders, offenders are currently using the Internet to acquire victims, gather information, fabricate alibis, protect or alter their identities, and communicate with other offenders. Terrorists are making extensive use of computers and the Internet to plan attacks, avoid apprehension, and communicate with the public. For instance, computers played a role in the planning and subsequent investigations of both World Trade Center bombings. Ramsey Yousef's laptop contained plans for the first bombing and, during the investigation into Zacarias Moussaoui's role in the second attack, more than 100 hard drives were examined (*United* States *v. Moussaoui*; *United* States *v. Salameh et al.*; *United* States *v. Ramsey Yousef*). Even traditional violent crimes in which the key forensic evidence is usually physical, such as homicide and sexual assault, can involve digital evidence either directly or incidentally (Reust, 2006a).

CASE EXAMPLE: PREMEDITATED FIRST-DEGREE MURDER

Prosecutors upgraded the charge against Robert Durall, 40, to first-degree murder based on what they described as evidence of premeditation found on his office computer. Durall had been charged with second-degree murder, but a coworker told police he had discovered a number of temporary files on Durall's office computer that showed Durall had conducted Internet searches using key words like kill + spouse, accidental + deaths, smothering, poison, homicides, and murder, according to court documents. A plus sign tells the search engine to pull up only sites that use both terms as key words (*Washington v. Robert A. Durall*, 2003).

Fortunately for investigators, computers record the actions and words of offenders and victims, creating a behavioral archive that can give insight into their thoughts, choices, motivations, interests, and desires. Given its ubiquity and investigative usefulness, investigators must learn to recognize digital evidence and to interpret it from a behavioral standpoint. It might not be obvious, particularly at the outset of an investigation, that a computer or the Internet holds key evidence, so it is advisable to search for potential digital evidence in all cases. This chapter discusses the usefulness of digital evidence in any type of criminal investigation and provides practical guidance for including digital evidence in the deductive criminal profiling process. The predominant focus is on using digital evidence in investigations of violent crime, but a portion of this chapter discusses how criminal profiling may be applied in investigations of computer intrusions and fraud.

CRIME AND COMPUTERS

Not surprisingly, as computers and networks become more prevalent, investigators are encountering an increasing amount of digital evidence of witness, victim, and criminal activity (Casey, 2004). Forensic examination of a floppy diskette that was sent to a television station by the Bind Torture Kill (BTK) serial killer led investigators to the church where Dennis Rader was council president. In another serial homicide case, investigators tracked down Maury Travis using a map that he had printed from the Expedia Web site and had sent to a reporter in St. Louis to show where another body was located.

A criminal can use the Internet proactively to enhance a modus operandi (MO) or he can use it reactively to avoid detection and capture (Turvey, 2000). For example, John E. Robinson, who referred to himself as "Slavemaster," used the Internet to con some of his victims into meeting him, at which time he sexually assaulted some and killed others (Rizzo, 2001). Robinson first used newspaper personal ads to attract victims and then used the Internet to extend his reach (McClintock, 2001). Robinson also used the Internet reactively to conceal his identity online, often hiding behind the alias "Slavemaster." When Robinson's home was searched, five computers were seized.

The Internet gives offenders greater access to victims, extending their reach from a limited geographical area to victims all around the world. Additionally, the Internet contains a significant amount of personal information about individuals, enabling a predator to search for particular types of potential victims. "One offender might search the Web for potential victims who are involved with church groups or online Bible discussions. Another offender might search for potential victims of a specific age by sifting through personal Web pages or AOL [America Online] user self-descriptions. Sexual predators can lurk in a Usenet newsgroup dedicated to victims of abuse (e.g., alt.abuse.recovery), or they may choose a particular online venue because it attracts potential victims who are located geographically near them" (McGrath and Casey, 2001). Furthermore, by giving offenders access to victims over an extended period of time (rather than just a brief encounter), the Internet enables offenders to gain control of their victims or to gain their victims' trust and possibly to arrange a meeting in the physical world.

In 2000, Lawrence Stackhouse found 15-year-old Diana Strickland's online profile, contacted her using the Internet, and then groomed[1] her until she and a girlfriend agreed to travel to his home in Pennsylvania, where he exploited them sexually for four days until the girlfriend called the police ("Protect Children from Predators on Internet, Parents Tell Congress," 2000). Also in 2000, e-mail and AOL instant messages provided the compelling evidence to convict Sharee Miller of conspiring to kill her husband and abetting the suicide of the admitted killer she had seduced with the assistance of the Internet. Miller carefully controlled the killer's perception of her husband, going so far as to masquerade as her husband to send the killer offensive messages ("Sex, Lies and Murder: *Michigan v. Miller*," 2001). In December 2004, Lisa Montgomery used an Internet chat room to contact 23-year-old Bobbie Jo Stinnett about looking at rat terriers the Stinnetts sold over the Internet. Montgomery later admitted to strangling Stinnett and cutting her open to kidnap her baby.

In late December 2005, 27-year-old Josie Phyllis Brown was reported missing in Baltimore. Digital evidence led investigators to a 22-year-old college student, John Gaumer. Brown and Gaumer met on the Internet site MySpace.com and arranged to meet for a date (Associated Press, 2006). On the night of her disappearance, Brown's mobile telephone records showed that she had talked to Gaumer before meeting with him, and police traced her telephone to a location many miles from where Gaumer claimed to have left her that night. After the web of evidence converged on Gaumer in February 2006, he led police to her body and admitted to beating Brown to death after their date. Gaumer used the Internet extensively to communicate with and to meet potential dates. Part of the evidence against him was a digital recording of "thumping noises, shouting and brief bursts of a woman's muffled screams" apparently created when

---

[1] Grooming is a general term used to describe the process by which a sexual predator gains control over his victim. According to Johnson (1997), "Perpetrators attempt to build both a trusting and fear-based relationship with their victim, with an end goal of being able to get sexual contact without significant resistance."

Gaumer's mobile phone inadvertently dialed Brown's phone number (McMenamin, 2007). In his confession to police, Gaumer stated that he removed her nose, jaw, teeth, and most of her fingertips in an attempt to thwart identification of her body and that he later sent an e-mail to her account to make it appear that he did not know she was dead.

CYBERTRAILS

Everyday activities leave a significant amount of digital data lying around. Third parties, such as mobile telephone providers, banks, credit card companies, and electronic toll collection systems, can reveal significant information about an individual's whereabouts and activities and are a staple source of evidence for criminal investigators.

Even when they are not consciously using networks, offenders and victims leave digital footprints as they move through the world, creating cybertrails that an investigator may be able to retrace to reconstruct where they were and what they were doing at particular times. For example, records from a missing person's mobile telephone provider or car navigation system may indicate where the person went and when.

Similarly, the computers and other digital devices, including cell phones and PDAs, that people use at home and work contain remnants of documents, photographs, Internet communications, and other details that generally reveal a great deal about their daily life, inner thoughts, and motivations. For example, Web browsers on a computer often maintain a list of all pages that have been viewed and can temporarily store recently viewed content in a cache to improve performance. This cached data can include Web-based e-mail and other activities that may be useful to investigators. Data that have been "deleted" often remain on a computer indefinitely and may be recoverable using digital forensic techniques and tools. Information posted on the Internet that an individual later altered or removed may also be recoverable through archives like the Way Back Machine (www.archive.org).

Handheld devices may contain entries or photographs that capture ongoing criminal activity or indicate where the victim was or whom she met with at a particular time. In an alleged rape case, a forensic examiner recovered cell-phone video that showed Dominic Jones having sex with a woman who had apparently passed out after drinking (Chanen and Xiong, 2007).

Various log files on servers may provide useful evidence in a case involving the Internet. For instance, sending an e-mail usually generates a record of the sender's location at a particular time, leaving traces on the device used by the sender, intermediate e-mail servers, and the recipient's computer. Therefore, in addition to looking for the contents of e-mail, an investigator can determine what messages passed through the system. If a message has been deleted to conceal a crime and cannot be recovered, there may still be evidence of its existence in the server's log files. Additionally, many e-mail server logs contain information about when individuals checked their e-mail, potentially recording their whereabouts at a particular moment.[2]

The detailed and personal nature of information that may be available on the Internet is demonstrated by the online statements and interactions between Taylor Behl and Ben Fawley (Bardsley and Huff, 2007). Behl went missing on September 5, 2007, and her body was found a month later in an isolated rural area that Fawley was familiar with. Fawley subsequently admitted to killing Behl and was convicted in August 2006. Behl's postings on Livejournal.com using the nickname "tiabliaj" were akin to online diary entries describing

---

[2] An e-mail program can be configured to periodically download e-mail automatically without requiring the user to be present at the keyboard. This emphasizes that care must be taken when interpreting digital evidence and attributing online activities to an individual.

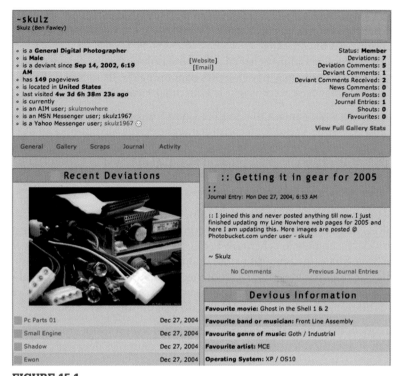

FIGURE 15.1
Ben Fawley's Web page on deviantart.com showing interests and computer-related information.

her thoughts and personal life, including interactions with Fawley. Fawley maintained a number of Web pages that contained a variety of information about him (Figure 15.1). The information in Figure 15.1, from one of Fawley's Web pages, includes various Internet accounts with the name "Skulz," a photograph of computer parts, and an indication that Fawley used both Windows and Macintosh operating systems. Another Web page that Fawley maintained under the nickname "line-nowhere" indicated that he had a number of computers: "I use MSIE on five of my PC's. I have Safari on the crapMac, but I have just added Firefox to three of my PC's as I find MSIE is a royal pain in the ass." When police searched Fawley's home, they seized significant amounts of computer equipment and storage media, as well as digital cameras and mobile telephones.

As the following examples demonstrate, while sexual predators exploit the Internet to identify and attract victims and facilitate their crimes, criminal investigators can exploit their associated cybertrails to track the whereabouts of the perpetrators and document their activity:

- A sexual predator might frequent AOL chat rooms because AOL has a high percentage of new Internet users who are not yet familiar with the risks of this new medium. Locating and examining the offender's AOL account could lead to valuable digital evidence. Recording all of the offender's chat sessions could result in a wealth of behavioral evidence.
- A sexual predator might frequent a local chat room to gain access to local victims. Determining that the offender is located in a certain area significantly limits the suspect pool. Monitoring chat rooms that attract individuals from that geographic area may lead to the offender or other victims.

- A sexual predator might frequent Usenet (alt.abuse-recovery, alt.teen-advise, alt.torture) looking for a specific kind of victim expressing particular vulnerabilities. A search of Usenet archives may lead to useful information about the offender.
- A sexual predator might post online personal ads or use online dating services to acquire a certain kind of victim. The ad/dating service may have log files containing the IP address(es) that the suspect used to post information or may have records that lead to other victims.

Even if digital evidence does not contain the "smoking gun," it can reveal actions, positions, origins, associations, activities, and sequences useful for reconstructing the events surrounding an offense (Casey, 2006). Therefore, whether computers and networks are involved directly or indirectly, it is productive for investigators to view cybertrails as an extension of the physical world, as opposed to a completely irrelevant and separate space. Taking this viewpoint enables investigators to incorporate cybertrails and the associated digital evidence into the investigative reconstruction process detailed in this text.

The primary assumption in deductive criminal profiling is that the choice of victims, the choice of crime scenes, and the actions of an offender in executing a crime provide telling information about the perpetrator. This assumption can be applied to cybertrails because (1) computers and networks are an extension of, and another means to mediate, the physical world; and (2) computer technology does not fundamentally change human behavior, but instead is simply a tool that facilitates, and captures virtual instances of, activity. An individual may do things on the Internet that he or she would not do in the physical world, but those online activities are still recognizable as, and reflective of, that person's behavior.

Just as following an offender's cybertrails can improve a profile, the profiling process can direct investigators to additional sources of digital evidence, as the following case examples demonstrate.

CASE EXAMPLE: DEATH THREAT

An individual was receiving anonymous threatening e-mail messages that made her fear for her life. The messages were sent through an anonymous e-mail service, making it difficult for investigators to identify the sender or origin of the messages. However, information contained in the messages suggested that the sender was in the same organization as the victim. Investigators believed that the sender would have initially sent himself a test message to ensure that no identifying information was disclosed in the e-mail header. The log files of the organization's e-mail server showed that one other individual in the organization had received a message from the same anonymous e-mail service. When this individual's computer was examined, an abundance of digital evidence was found indicating that he was responsible for the threatening e-mail.

CASE EXAMPLE: BLACKMAIL

In an extortion case, the offender sent a message to the victim from a Web-based e-mail account. The Internet protocol (IP) address contained in the e-mail header showed that the message was sent from a computer located in an Internet café, but investigators were unable to determine who was using the computer at the time. Believing that the offender may have checked the Web-based e-mail account for responses to his message, investigators obtained all records relating to that account from the Internet service provider. These records indicated that the offender had indeed connected to the e-mail account from his home computer.

CASE EXAMPLE: CHILD EXPLOITATION

Behavioral analysis of a sexual predator directed undercover investigators to particular online chat rooms that the offender trawled for victims and enabled investigators to pose as the type of victim that attracted the offender.

Digital evidence may be scattered across different media sources and in multiple online sites, and a profile of the perpetrator may help investigators identify other investigative steps to find additional sources of evidence. For example, if a profile indicates that the current victim probably was not the first to be targeted by the offender, investigators will be motivated to seek evidence relating to other victims. A profile may also suggest to investigators what types of victims to look for and where the offender might have come into contact with them.

As offenders become more aware of digital forensic techniques, they are employing concealment tools and techniques, such as encryption, misleading file names, or disk wiping. Therefore, it is important for a profiler to consider when digital evidence should be present but is absent. Given such direction, a trained forensic examiner may be able to recover and use these data to reveal evidence that a criminal sought to hide, and the examiner may thereby glean a great deal about an individual's activities.

PROFILING COMPUTER CRIMINALS

To date, the majority of efforts to apply profiling to crimes involving computers has focused on criminals who target computers. In one study, computer criminals were split into the following categories (Icove, Seger, and VonStorch, 1995):

- Computer crackers: groups and individuals
- Computer criminals: espionage and fraud/abuse
- Vandals: strangers and users.

In another study, hackers were stereotyped as white, middle-class, obsessive antisocial males between 12 and 28 years old, with an inferiority complex and a possible history of physical and sexual abuse (Rogers, 1999). Several other attempts have been made to create general profiles of computer criminals using information from media reports, offender interviews, and anecdotal observations.

Although these efforts to create inductive profiles give a general overview of past offenders and may be useful for diagnosing and treating associated psychological disorders, they are of limited use in an investigation. In fact, such generalizations about criminals may be misleading, prompting investigators to make incorrect assumptions about an offender. Since investigators usually require particulars rather than generalizations, criminal profiles should contain specific conclusions, substantiated by evidence. If a generalization is deemed necessary, it should be made with great care and extensive research or it is likely to be unhelpful in an investigation.

Studying past crimes can help investigators assess offenders and their motives and make strategic decisions in an investigation. Researchers concerned with computer-related crime have focused on dangerous critical information technology insiders (CITI)—individuals who threaten critical infrastructures from within an organization (Shaw, Ruby, and Post, 1998). This research focuses on threat assessment, attempting to predict the future behavior of high-risk individuals to mitigate the damage they might cause. According to this research, all CITIs have one common trait—introversion, which makes them "less likely to deal with stress in an overt, constructive manner, and less likely to seek direct assistance" (Shaw, Post, and Ruby, 1999). CITIs are also more likely to express their problems via e-mail than in person. Studies have identified six high-risk characteristics: a history of personal and social frustrations, computer dependency, ethical flexibility, reduced loyalty, a sense of entitlement, and a lack of empathy. These studies also provide several motivational categories in an effort to help identify and evaluate the risks associated with problem individuals (Table 15.1). These motivational categories overlap with those mentioned in Chapter 13: power reassurance (compensatory), power assertive (entitlement), anger retaliation, and profit oriented.

More recent empirical studies provide additional insight into computer crimes committed by individuals within an organization. In studies by the Secret Service/Carnegie Mellon University Software Engineering Institute (Keeney et al., 2005; Randazzo et al., 2004) and the Defense Personnel Security Research Center (Shaw and Fischer, 2005), the majority of the crimes surveyed had a profit motive, with some level of anger retaliation. Although the criminal activity was committed using computers, the method of attack was often nontechnical, generally taking advantage of the business to embezzle funds. The importance of digital evidence in these investigations was perhaps lower than one might expect, emphasizing the need to combine digital forensics with traditional investigative techniques like criminal profiling. In 74% of the cases surveyed, system logs helped identify the insider, while in 30% of the cases forensic examination of the targeted network, system, or data helped identify the subject.

Table 15.1 Motivational Categories of Critical Information Technology Insiders

Category	Motivational Descriptive Summary and Demonstrative Example
Explorers	Motivated by curiosity, rarely cause purposeful damage. Example: Idle employees access poorly protected network resources that they are not officially authorized to access.
Good samaritans	Motivated by a desire to "save the day" or to show off their abilities. Example: A system administrator on one system identifies a vulnerability on another system that is not the administrator's responsibility and breaks into the vulnerable system to fix it rather than informing the responsible system administrator.
Hackers	Motivated by a need to bolster self-esteem by violating access boundaries. Example: An individual connects his employer's secure network to the Internet in violation of policy, providing his friends on the Internet with access to the secure system and sensitive information it contains.
Machiavellians	Motivated by personal gain, damaging people and systems to achieve their goals. Example: An individual who enjoys traveling introduces malfunctions in her employer's equipment abroad so that she will be sent to other countries to repair the systems.
Exceptions	Believe that they are special and entitled to special treatment. Example: A system administrator has unique knowledge of an organization's computer systems and feels that he deserves better pay, benefits, and treatment than other employees.
Avengers	Motivated by specific perceived wrongs. Example: A system administrator hears that she is going to be laid off, so she encrypts patient files and holds them ransom in the hope of getting a better severance package.
Career thieves	Motivated by profit. Example: An individual embezzles money using an organization's computer system.
Moles	Motivated by profit but indirectly through espionage. Example: An individual who joins an organization with the express purpose of obtaining proprietary information that he can sell to competitors.

Psycholinguistic Analysis of Digital Communications

Shaw's more recent work has expanded from managing insider threats to using deductive profiling techniques in active investigations involving unknown offenders (Shaw, 2006, p. 26). Shaw uses a methodology called remote assessment and performs content analysis to extract information from written and spoken communications:

> Remote assessment refers to a portfolio of methods used to evaluate individuals and groups when direct contact methods (interviews, questionnaires, etc.) are not feasible or desirable. Sometimes referred to as Unobtrusive Methods, these techniques have been used by researchers concerned about disturbing the natural environment of their subjects.

Shaw's approach is useful when investigators have e-mail messages, Internet chat logs, or recorded audio that captures the offender's words. E-mail messages, newsgroup posts, and other online statements may contain unusual or repeated verbal behaviors or show a level of planning and forethought related to a criminal act. Software that implements psycholinguistic analysis has been developed to process electronic communications and to highlight noteworthy characteristics for a human analyst to evaluate (Shaw and Stroz, 2004).

In addition to psycholinguistic analysis of content, Shaw's remote assessment methodology takes into account the context of communications. The target, delivery method, time, related organizational events, and other context can give the profiler a better understanding of the offender and may reveal useful patterns of behavior. For example, an offender who attacks just before a company goes public may be attempting to harm the company financially. As another example, an offender's use of concealment technology when communicating shows technical sophistication and may suggest that the offender is known to the victim. This type of assessment can give insight into the offender's motives, state of mind, psychological disorders, and distinctive verbal behavior, such as unusual word usage or errors in spelling, that may help narrow the suspect pool. When dealing with an insider, such as an ex employee, it may be possible to compare writing samples of potential suspects.

CASE EXAMPLE: ANGRY INSIDER

Each board member of a company received an anonymous letter viciously disparaging the CEO and aspects of the company's operations, citing details that could only be known to an insider. Because of fears that the information in the letter might be made public and circulated to suppliers and customers, an investigation was launched to identify the sender.

After analyzing the profile of the author, a suspect pool of insiders was identified, and e-mail and other writings were compared to the anonymous letter writer, resulting in not only the sender's identification but also a method for managing his relationship with the company to mitigate the risk of further harm.

DIGITAL BEHAVIOR OF UNKNOWN OFFENDERS

Criminal profiling can be most useful when little is known about the offender(s), which is particularly important when offenders use the Internet to conceal their identities and activities. Criminal profiling assists investigators by:

- Distinguishing whether a single offender committed multiple crimes or multiple offenders are involved

- Providing likely offender characteristics to aid the technical investigation
- Identifying likely suspects from a given pool based on offender skill level, access to victim/target, and other technical characteristics
- Revealing modus operandi and signatures to help investigators search for related behaviors and to assess offender motivations
- Giving insight into offender motivations and general psychological state
- Assessing the dangerousness of offenders
- Revealing additional sources of evidence

In one case, a company and its customers were harassed by embarrassing e-mails containing derogatory information about the company and disturbing sexually explicit attachments that were spoofed to appear that company executives were the senders. After two years of repeated spoofed e-mail attacks, it remained unclear whether the perpetrator was an individual or a group, an insider or outsider, or even what the offender(s) wanted in order to stop their harassment.

Behavioral analysis of the harassing communications showed that one individual with a high technical skill level was responsible for all of the activities, and it indicated that the subject was a highly intelligent male over 30 who was extremely angry with the target company. This information led to further investigation of other anonymous contacts that had not previously been associated with the perpetrator of the harassing e-mail attacks. E-mail communications were established with the perpetrator and, with the assistance of a behavioral psychologist, additional information about the perpetrator was elicited from him about his motivation, culminating in a cyber-extortion demand. In the negotiations over the extortion demand, the perpetrator's state of mind was regularly assessed to evaluate the level of danger he posed to others.[3]

In this investigation, digital forensic analysis of the company's computer systems uncovered no evidence that the perpetrator was a malicious insider, but it did identify suspicious connections from computers at a nearby university, providing investigators with a solid lead and confirmation of an outside hacker. As suggested by the profile, the offender was technically skilled enough to conceal his identity by using publicly accessible computers at university computer laboratories and wireless access points. Subsequent surveillance of the locations used by the offender to send spoofed e-mails led investigators to a prime suspect who matched many of the characteristics detailed in the profile. Because the profile indicated that the offender might be dangerous and mentally unstable, investigators were cautious when they ultimately apprehended him. This case demonstrates how behavioral analysis of the digital evidence can provide investigators with information about the numbers of individuals involved in the criminal activity, the skill level of the individuals involved, other evidence that is actually related though may not superficially appear to be, and the physical security risk that the perpetrator poses.

An offender's online activities may also indicate that the offender is taking precautionary measures to avoid identification and apprehension. For instance, some offenders protect themselves by using computer-smart nicknames, such as "En0ch|an" instead of "Enochian." Because a search engine does not realize that the zero represents an "o" and the pipe (|) represents an "i," a search for "En0ch|an" will not find information labeled with "Enochian."[4] Additionally, offenders may use anonymous or forged e-mail messages to conceal their identities. Investigators should determine how much technical knowledge was required to perform such a task and whether every modification was necessary to conceal the person's identity or whether the

---

[3] For further description of this case, see Howell (2006) and Shaw (2006).
[4] To make matters worse, some search engines treat a pipe (|) as a separator and may therefore search for terms other than those specified.

modifications were instead created to fulfill a psychological need of the offender. Explaining how and why the offender conceals his or her identity may lead investigators to identifying information that the offender failed to hide or may help investigators narrow the suspect pool (e.g., to people who were intimately familiar with the victim and concealed their identify to avoid recognition by the victim).

CASE EXAMPLE: INTERNAL OFFENSE

A large company received an anonymous letter containing documents from an executive's computer. In addition to the concerns raised by the documents, the fact that someone was able to obtain access to these sensitive materials without the executive's knowledge raised security concerns. If the anonymous whistle-blower had gained unauthorized access to the executive's computer system or e-mail, this would have to be considered. A behavioral assessment helped focus the investigation on a person morally offended by the executive's activity, which was the subject of the documents and was a violation of corporate policy. The behavioral analysis of the anonymous whistle-blower's activities on the company's computer systems also supported the assessment that the security breach was specifically targeted at the executive and his activities and was not more far-reaching.

Feeling protected by some level of anonymity, individuals often do things on the Internet that they would only imagine doing in the physical world and express thoughts that they would otherwise keep to themselves. Digital evidence may also contain information that can be used to determine the offender's sex, age, occupation, interests, relationship status, and other potentially useful information. An offender's Web site and online presence can give the viewer an impression of the offender's self-image, state of mind, interests, and more. The choice of online nicknames can be revealing (e.g., Slavemaster, Zest, Dr. Evil), and an offender's Web pages may contain stories that give insight into his or her motives and fantasies and may have links to favorite areas online that can lead to other victims and additional evidence. This last point also applies to the physical world—an offender's Web page may contain references to, or photographs of, favorite locations that can be useful when looking for other potential victims or sources of physical evidence.

CASE EXAMPLE: CHILD EXPLOITATION

An offender's admissions about state of mind, sexual fantasy, or personal/sexual conflict can provide insight into his or her behavior and motivations. For instance, in one traveler[5] case, a profiler examined the offender's online activities and concluded that the offender believed he was genuinely in consensual relationships with his young victims. "He sees nothing about his behavior as criminal or exploitative. He believes that he is merely seizing the day, and that what he is doing benefits the children he exploits. His motive is not to physically harm his victims but to be loved and admired by them. He confuses his own identity with theirs, to an extent, projecting a childlike affect to them. An interview strategy that exploits these factors by being sympathetic to them will be successful in getting the most information from this suspect."

---

[5] A sexual predator who obtains victims online and then travels to meet them is commonly called a traveler.

MANAGING OFFENDER BEHAVIOR

An effective profile can help investigators decide whether attempts to contact and to communicate with the offender would be useful or harmful, and how to best approach the offender. It can also be helpful to know that certain sex offenders will confess to their crimes when treated in a certain manner, but the same approach may drive others into deeper denial.

In the same case involving the spoofed e-mails noted earlier, investigators decided to send an e-mail with a Web bug in an effort to learn more about an unknown offender. However, a profiler working on the case determined that the offender was highly skilled and would most likely notice and circumvent the tracking mechanism embedded in the e-mail. The profile also noted that the suspect was exhibiting signs of mental instability and was potentially dangerous. When law enforcement officers served a warrant at the suspect's home, they found not only digital evidence connecting him with the offense but also firearms and the recipe and ingredients for a poisonous toxin called ricin.[6]

VICTIMOLOGY

Given the growing number of people encountering and communicating with each other on the Internet, it is necessary to consider the possibility that the offender had contact with the victim using the Internet. For instance, during the investigation of Robinson, cooperation between law enforcement agencies overcame potential physical linkage blindness, and victims' bodies were located in two neighboring states (McClintock, 2001). Additional investigation of the offender's activities, combined with interviews of online witnesses, may reveal that an offender communicated with other victims on the Internet who have not yet been identified. Conversely, in the case of missing victims, a thorough analysis of their computers might lead to a common offender. Therefore, as a rule, victimology should include a thorough search of the Internet, pertinent computers, and handheld devices.

For example, suppose the victim in a homicide accesses the Internet through Verizon and uses her Verizon e-mail account to communicate with friends and family, but uses Google Mail to communicate with strangers. Her computer would contain e-mail from friends and family but might contain nothing to or from the strangers she encountered on the Internet. Of course, the diligent investigator would examine the victim's Web browser history, see the many connections to gmail.com, and obtain the victim's messages from Google.

In addition to exploring the possibility of an Internet link between the victim and offender, try to gain some understanding of the victim as an individual from his or her Internet activities. Every detail about the victim's life and behavior contributes to one's understanding of why that particular individual became a victim of a crime. Try to determine the what, why, where, how, and when of the victim's Internet activities by asking questions like the following:

- Did the victim have Web pages, post to Usenet regularly, use chat networks, or send/receive e-mail or text messages on a mobile phone? The contents and context of any such online activities help a profiler understand the victim.
- Did the victim use a parent's account, a personal account, or an anonymous account? If the victim was using an anonymous account, was he or she hiding from someone (e.g., abusive ex-boyfriend)?
- What did the victim get from the Internet that was not accessible otherwise (e.g., friendship, drugs, fantasy fulfillment)?
- Where did the victim access the Internet (e.g., at home, work, a café or bar)? Why did the victim pick that location to access the Internet (e.g., privacy, business, or to meet people face-to-face)?

---

[6] For further description of this case, see Howell (2006) and (Shaw 2006).

- Did the victim exhibit any behavior that sheds light on his or her mental state, sexuality, lifestyle, intelligence, or self-image? For example, was the victim involved with bondage and sadomasochism (BDSM) online groups?
- Are there discernible patterns in the victim's Internet activities that suggest habits or schedules? Were there any breaks in these patterns around the time of the crime?

When looking for information on the Internet, investigators should not limit themselves to computer queries. Interviewing individuals with whom the victim interacted on the Internet can uncover online nicknames and areas of the Internet that the victim used. A person's private online hangouts can be the most revealing from a victimology standpoint and may be the way the offender crossed cybertrails with the victim.

CASE EXAMPLE: HARASSMENT

A woman was being harassed and threatened over the Internet, primarily via a Hotmail account. The victim put a significant amount of personal information on the Internet, such as her age, home phone and address, background, photographs, and personal interests. The offender used a pseudo-anonymous e-mail account to hide his identity but did not have enough knowledge of the Internet to realize that the e-mail account did not provide complete anonymity (Hotmail headers contain the IP address of the sender's computer). Although the offender claimed to have located the victim through her Web page, he exhibited a high degree of familiarity with the victim's surroundings (e.g., town, residence), suggesting that he spent a significant amount of time in the area. Additionally, the offender did not suggest a face-to-face meeting and did not use the victim's phone number although it was provided on her Web page, perhaps because he was concerned that the victim would recognize or be repelled by him if they met or spoke. Perhaps the offender knew the victim or felt less confident/comfortable communicating in person. The e-mail messages contained some descriptions of the offender's fantasies and suggested a degree of mental instability.

It is also important to include digital evidence when assessing victim risk. Risk assessment on the Internet works in the same way as in the physical world, as the comparisons in Table 15.2 demonstrate.

Table 15.2 Analogous Risks in the Real and Virtual Worlds

Risk	Physical World	Internet
High-risk victim	Unattended child who talks with strangers while walking home from school	Unattended child in an Internet chat room who talks with strangers
High offender risk	Offender who acquires victims in an area that is surveyed by security cameras	Offender who acquires victims in an area of the Internet that is monitored or recorded
Low-risk victim	Individual who avoids going into certain areas unaccompanied and does not give personal information to strangers	Individual who avoids certain areas of the Internet and does not give personal information to strangers
Low offender risk	Offender who wears a mask and performs covering behavior to avoid detection	Offender who uses anonymity provided by the Internet and performs covering behavior to avoid detection

The Internet can influence victim risk, putting an otherwise low-risk victim at high risk of certain crimes. For example, if a woman makes a large amount of personal information available on the Internet and participates in online activities that expose her vulnerabilities, this can increase her risk of being stalked. If a woman who is reserved and cautious in the physical world uses the Internet to explore bondage and torture fantasies and arranges to meet an online acquaintance to act out these fantasies, this online activity can increase her risk of being raped or killed.

CASE EXAMPLE: TYPE "M" FOR MURDER

Sharon Lopatka traveled from Maryland to North Carolina to meet her killer. Friends described Lopatka as a normal woman who loved children and animals. Lopatka's activities on the Internet give a very different impression, however. Lopatka was evidently interested in sex involving pain and torture. Victimology that did not include her Internet activities would have been incomplete, lacking the most relevant aspects of her character and would probably describe her as a low-risk victim when, in fact, she was quite a high-risk victim. For instance, in the murder of Sharon Lopatka, the victim's home computer contained hundreds of e-mail messages that provided the crucial link between the victim and the murderer, Robert Glass. Before these e-mails were found, investigators believed that they were dealing with a low-risk victim, and without these e-mails, it is unlikely that the investigators would have found the offender.

Individual pieces of digital data may not be useful on their own, but patterns of behavior can emerge when the pieces of digital evidence are combined. A victim might always check e-mail at a specific time or might always frequent a particular area on the Internet. A disruption in this pattern could be an indication of an unusual event—determining what that event was could generate a key lead. If there was no break in the victim's routine, this consistency may help investigators hypothesize that the offender was aware of the victim's routine and planned the crime accordingly or that the offender happened upon the victim and took advantage of an opportunity. Discerning such patterns can be challenging when digital data are involved because there is often a massive quantity of information. Therefore, a thorough forensic analysis should always be performed to provide familiarity with the complete body of evidence and the opportunity to consider all possibilities before getting caught up with one detail or theory.

DEDUCTIVE PROFILING OF COMPUTER INTRUDERS

The same techniques discussed in this chapter can be useful for crimes committed on, not just using, computers, such as data breach cases and network intrusions. When an offender uses the Internet to commit crimes, it can be difficult to pinpoint all of the relevant evidence in the digital vastness. Knowledge of a criminal's MO and signature is very useful when scouring the Internet for information regarding a case because it gives investigators a clearer sense of what to look for and where to look. The Internet, however, has many areas that are private and may never show up in a routine search. Sometimes an offender's MO or signature will indicate that he uses one or another of these out-of-the-way places. Developing an understanding of the offender's MO can direct investigators to look for particular traces of digital behavior or to monitor particular virtual areas where the intruder is likely to appear.

CASE EXAMPLE: COMPUTER INTRUDER CAUGHT IN THE ACT

In a computer intrusion/information theft case, investigators determined how the offender operated and what he was looking for by carefully examining the compromised computers. Investigators used this knowledge to identify and monitor other machines on the network that would attract the intruder. After several hours, the intruder was detected on one of the systems being monitored, giving investigators one of the most vivid forms of evidence, a live recording of a crime in progress. While monitoring the intruder, investigators were able to determine that he was a recently fired employee who was dialing into the network from his home. They quickly obtained a search warrant for his personal computer and found copies of the stolen information on the hard disk.

For an in-depth example of MO and signature in the context of computer crime, consider the well-known case of Kevin Mitnick. Mitnick had an advanced MO that made it difficult to track him down. He would break into telephone networks, create a clever dial loop to hide his whereabouts, and use a cellular phone to dial into a large Internet service provider. He would then use advanced techniques to break into computers and steal software, credit cards, and data. A team that consisted of computer expert Tsutomu Shimomura and the FBI finally tracked Mitnick down using cellular-frequency direction-finding antennae. Although Mitnick's main motivation seemed to be profit, he exhibited some other behaviors that were clearly not necessary to commit crimes (i.e., signature behaviors). For example, in addition to breaking into Shimomura's computer and stealing advanced computer software, Mitnick allegedly left taunting voice messages on Shimomura's voicemail, possibly as a form of power reassurance (www.takedown.com/evidence/voicemail).

An interesting aspect of MO in the context of computers arises when criminals take advantage of computer automation during the commission of a crime—automated actions and offender behavior can be difficult to differentiate. Automation can be particularly problematic when several criminals use the same automated tools. For example, programs exist that automate certain methods of breaking into computer systems and hiding incriminating evidence, providing an automated modus operandi that makes multiple offenders almost indistinguishable. When every crime scene looks almost identical, it becomes more difficult to link cases committed by a single offender and to understand the unique motivations of different offenders.

To make case linkage even more difficult, offenders who use the Internet can change their modus operandi with relative ease. As offenders become more familiar with the Internet, they usually find new ways to make use of it to achieve their goals more effectively. An offender who uses the Internet creatively can change his or her modus operandi so frequently and completely that it is best described as dynamic. For instance, individuals who break into well-secured computer systems may have to develop a novel intrusion plan for each unique target. A dynamic modus operandi has also been seen when an offender is consciously trying to foil investigators. For instance, when a stalker becomes aware that investigators are preventing one method of terrorizing the victim (e.g., e-mail), he or she uses another method (e.g., ICQ).

Investigators who are able to extract key behavioral information from available digital evidence and who can make sound deductions based on that behavioral evidence are invaluable in an investigation involving the Internet. Determination of motivation and intent can be critical when available evidence does not provide a complete picture of the offender's actions. For instance, in data breach cases, one of the main questions that arises is whether the intruders gained access to confidential data stored on the compromised computer. When it is not possible to prove that the intruders did not access the data of concern, an assessment of their activities can reveal that their intent was not focused on the confidential data but rather to use the computer system for some other purpose, such as storage of contraband or to launch attacks against other systems on the Internet (Casey, 2003). In one case, forensic examination of the target systems found that the motivation for computer breach was not to steal sensitive data but to find storage space for pirated movies (Reust, 2006b). Additionally, investigators who can recognize signature behaviors in a digital setting are in a solid position to overcome the challenges of automated or dynamic modus operandi—they can use signature behaviors to link cases and make deductions about offenders.

Like an autopsy, the forensic analysis of the target computer systems will reveal a significant amount about an attack (Casey, 2004). However, it is important for investigators to realize that there may be other computers that contain significant amounts of relevant digital evidence. Just as a crime in the physical world can have multiple crime scenes, computer intrusions can have primary and secondary scenes, each containing potentially useful information. Computer intruders often perform surveillance of a target computer from one location, move (virtually) to another location on the network to break into the target system (potentially passing through several intermediate systems), gain unauthorized access to the target system and steal money or information, destroy the target system and all of the evidence it contains, and delete evidence on other systems that were used during the commission of the crime. A staging area used by a computer intruder may contain evidence related to the crime, tools left by the offender, and communications with cohorts, and could provide a link between an individual and the primary crime scene.

It can also be productive to perform a kind of victimology relating to the target computer(s) in an intrusion case. In crimes where computers are the targets, the underlying question is the same: Why did the offender choose the target computer, and what was the risk the offender was willing to take? Consider a well-protected computer, for example. If an offender overcomes many obstacles and exposes himself or herself to many risks to break into the computer, this ability may indicate that the offender was familiar with the target system, had a strong desire for something on the target system, and was skilled enough to overcome the obstacles and risks.

To assess victim risk when the target is a computer, gather information about the computer, including the make and model, the operating system, where it was located, what it contained, who had access to it, what other computers it regularly connected to, and how difficult it was to break into. Determine whether there were any previous unsuccessful attempts to access the computer. If an offender required a significant amount of knowledge about the target computer system to commit the crime, investigators should try to determine how this knowledge was obtained. Was it available only to employees of an organization? Could the offender have obtained the information through surveillance, and if so, what skill level and equipment were required to perform the surveillance?

In investigations of computer intrusions or violent crime, computers and the Internet may contain crucial information about the people involved. Profiling can utilize this rich repository of digitized human behavior to aid an investigation and can direct investigators to other potential sources of digital evidence that might otherwise be overlooked.

SUMMARY

As computers and networks become more prevalent, investigators are encountering an increasing amount of digital evidence of witness, victim, and criminal activity. A criminal can use the Internet proactively to enhance his current modus operandi or he can use it reactively to avoid detection and capture. Additionally, the Internet gives offenders greater access to victims, extending their reach from a limited geographical area to victims all around the world.

Everyday activities leave a significant amount of digital data lying around, especially from third parties, such as mobile telephone providers, banks, credit card companies, and electronic toll collection systems. Consequently, even when they are not consciously using networks, offenders and victims leave digital footprints as they move through the world, creating "cybertrails" that an investigator may be able to retrace to reconstruct where these computer users were and what they were doing at particular times.

To date, the majority of efforts to apply profiling to crimes involving computers have focused on criminals who target computers. Although these efforts to create inductive profiles give a general overview of past offenders and may be useful for diagnosing and treating associated psychological disorders, they are of limited use in an investigation. They can even be misleading.

Criminal profiling can be most useful when little is known about the offender(s), which is particularly important when offenders use the Internet to conceal their identities and activities. Feeling protected by some level of anonymity, individuals often do things on the Internet that they would only imagine doing in the physical world, and they express thoughts that they would otherwise keep to themselves. Digital evidence may also contain information that can be used to determine the offender's sex, age, occupation, interests, relationship status, and other potentially useful information.

When an offender uses the Internet to commit crimes, it can be difficult to pinpoint all of the relevant evidence in the digital vastness. The Internet, however, has many areas that are private and may never show up in a routine search. Sometimes an offender's MO or signature will indicate that he or she uses one or another of these out-of-the-way places. Developing an understanding of the offender's MO can direct investigators to look for particular traces of digital behavior or to monitor particular virtual areas where the intruder is likely to appear.

Questions

1. True or False: Hackers are mostly teenagers who play video games and have too much time on their hands.
2. Explain how an automated modus operandi is made possible.
3. Cybertrails are often created passively. Give three examples of how this might occur.
4. What is the purpose of a dynamic modus operandi?
5. Why might a predatory sex offender troll America Online (AOL) for victims, as opposed to somewhere else?

ACKNOWLEDGMENTS

The author thanks Brent Turvey for his efforts to enhance the body of knowledge in forensic science and crime reconstruction. The author also thanks his colleagues at Stroz Friedberg, LLC, in particular Beryl Howell and Eric Shaw, for their ongoing support.

REFERENCES

Associated Press, 2006. Police Charge Md. Student in Murder: UMBC Student Met Woman on MySpace.com, February 9.

Bardsley, M., Huff, S., 2007. Disappeared: Taylor Behl, Crime Library. Court TV. Available at www.crimelibrary.com/criminal_mind/forensics/taylor_behl.

Casey, E., 2003. Determining Intent: Opportunistic vs. Targeted Attacks. Computer Fraud & Security (4), 8–11.

Casey, E., 2004. Digital Evidence and Computer Crime: Forensic Science and the Internet, second edition. Academic Press, London, England.

Casey, E., 2006. Reconstructing Digital Evidence. In: Chisum, J., Turvey, B. (Eds.), Crime Reconstruction. Academic Press, London, England.

Chanen, D., Xiong, C., 2007. To a New Kind of Sleuth, Phones Leave a Rich Trail. Minneapolis *Star Tribune* (July 22).

Gudaitis, T., 1998. The Missing Link in Information Security: Three Dimensional Profiling. Cyberpsychological Behavior 1 (4), 321–340.

Howell, B., 2006. Real World Problems of Virtual Crime. In: Balkin, J. (Ed.), Cybercrime: Digital Cops in a Networked Environment. New York University Press, New York, NY, pp. 95–98.

Icove, D., Seger, K., VonStorch, W., 1995. Computer Crime: A Crimefighter's Handbook. O'Reilly & Associates, Sabastapol, CA.

Johnson, S., 1997. Psychological Force in Sexual Abuse: Implications for Recovery. In: Schwartz, B.K., Cellini, H.R., Kingston, N.J. (Eds.), The Sex Offender: New Insights, Innovations and Legal Developments, vol. 2. Civic Research Institute, Kingston, NJ, pp. 17-1–17-11.

Keeney, J., Kowalski, E., Cappelli, D., Moore, A., Shimeall, T., Rogers, S., 2005. Insider Threat Study: Computer System Sabotage in Critical Infrastructure Sectors. National Threat Center, U.S. Secret Service, CERT Coordination Center, Software Engineering Institute, Carnegie Mellon University, Washington, DC; Pittsburgh, PA.

McClintock, D., 2001. Fatal Bondage. Vanity Fair June.

McGrath, M., Casey, E., 2002. Forensic Psychiatry and the Internet: Practical Perspectives on Sexual Predators and Obsessional Harassers in Cyberspace, Journal of the American Academy of Psychiatry and Law 30 (1), 81–94.

McMenamin, J., 2007. Gaumer Convicted of Rape, Murder: Prosecutors Seeking Death Penalty for UMBC Student, Who Met Victim Online, Baltimore *Sun* (May 11).

Meloy, J.R. (Ed.), 1998. The Psychology of Stalking: Clinical and Forensic Perspectives. Academic Press, London, England.

Protect Children from Predators on Internet, Parents Tell Congress. 2000. Psychiatr. News May 5. Available at www.psych.org/pnews/00-05-05/protect.html.

Randazzo, M., Keeney, M., Kowalski, E., Cappelli, D., Moore, A., 2004. Insider Threat Study: Illicit Cyber Activity in the Banking and Finance Sector. National Threat Center, U.S. Secret Service, CERT Coordination Center, Software Engineering Institute, Carnegie Mellon University, Washington, DC; Pittsburgh, PA.

Reust, J., 2006a. Case Study: AOL Instant Messenger Trace Evidence. Digital Investigation 3 (4), 238–243.

Reust, J., 2006b. Network Intrusion Investigation: Preparation and Challenges. Digital Investigation 3 (3), 118–126.

Rizzo, T., 2001. Judge Says Robinson Must Stand Trial in Three Deaths. Kansas City Star, March 2. Available at www.kcstar.com/standing/robinson/case.html.

Rogers, M., 1999. The Psychology of Hackers: A New Taxonomy, paper presented at the RSA World Security Conference < San Jose, CA.

Sex, Lies and Murder: *Michigan v. Miller*, 2001. Court TV February 26. Available at www.courttv.com/trials/taped/miller.html.

Shaw, E.D., 2006. The Role of Behavioral Research and Profiling in Malicious Insider Investigations. Digital Investigation 3 (1), 20–31.

Shaw, E.D., Fischer, L., 2005. Ten Tales of Betrayal: An Analysis of Attacks on Corporate Infrastructure by Information Technology Insiders, vol. 1. Defense Personnel Security Research and Education Center, Monterrey, CA.

Shaw, E.D., Post, J.M., Ruby, K.G., 1999. Inside the Mind of the Insider, Business Continuity. Available at www.securitymanagement.com/library/000762.htm.

Shaw, E.D., Ruby, K.G., Post, J.M., 1998. Insider Threats to Critical Information Systems. Technical Report #2; Characteristics of the Vulnerable Critical Information Technology Insider (CITI) Political Psychology Associates. www.pol-psych.com.

Shaw, E.D., Stroz, E., 2004. Warmtouch Software: The IDS of Psychology. In: Parker, T. (Ed.), Adversary Characterization: Auditing the Hacker Mind. Syngress, Rockland, MA, pp. 145–170.

Turvey, B., 2000. Modus Operandi, Motive and Technology. In: Casey, E. (Ed.), Digital Evidence and Computer Crime: Forensic Science Computers and the Internet, second edition. Academic Press, London, England, pp. 147–167.

Washington v. Robert A. Durall, 2003. State of Washington Appellant File Date: 05/05/2003 47928-8-1.

CHAPTER 16

Fire and Explosives: Behavioral Aspects

Brent E. Turvey

Cruelty has a Human Heart
And Jealousy a Human Face:
Terror, the Human Form Divine
And Secrecy, the Human Dress …

—William Blake (ca. 1790), *A Divine Image*

CONTENTS

Criminal Profiling: An Introduction to Behavioral Evidence Analysis, Fourth Edition
© 2012 Elsevier Ltd. All rights reserved.

KEY TERMS

Accelerant	Explosions	Property
Arson	Group	Symbol
Bomb	Intended victim	Target
Broad targeting	Narrow targeting	
Collateral victims	Point of origin	

One of the most important behavioral evidence concepts to understand is the nature of the relationship between a person's behavior and their motives or needs. Human behaviors are a manifestation of human need. They are the expression of want, and can be windows to *intent*.

Consider the behaviors of fire setting and explosives use. They must be examined and considered just like any other criminal behavior. They can occur in a variety of contexts, and they can satisfy or be motivated by multiple offender needs. They are not limited to use in a particular kind of criminal offense or against any particular type of victim. Their use in a particular offense is constrained only by offender motive, offender intent, offender skill level, and the availability of materials.[1]

DEFINITIONS

The term *arson* is a penal classification. Like the terms rape and homicide, arson is used to refer to a certain constellation of criminal behaviors. The type of behavior generally described by the term *arson* is the intentional setting of a fire with the additional intent to damage or defraud (DeHaan, 1997, p. 482). Without these intents, the crime of arson has not been committed. There are of course noncriminal motives

---

[1] The author is often asked whether he is an expert arson profiler. The answer is that, while not specializing in arson investigation, the author routinely encounters fire setting and explosives use in casework and research. So while the author does not seek to work cases involving a serial arsonist, the behaviors involved are comparable to any other violent behavior in any other type of violent crime. Some violent criminals use guns, others use knives, and some use fire and explosives.

for starting fires. To foster the habit of staying away from subjective penal classifications that imply guilt, the author uses the neutral behavioral descriptor *fire setting* throughout the chapter.

The term *bomb* refers to an explosive that is detonated by impact, proximity, timing, or other predetermined means. An *explosive* is any material that can undergo a sudden conversion of a physical form to a gas with a release of energy. Explosives are used to create *explosions*, which are defined generally as the sudden conversion of potential energy (chemical or mechanical) into kinetic energy with the production of heat, gases, and mechanical pressure (DeHaan, 1997, p. 482). The manufacture of explosives into a bomb for use in a criminal offense is also offender behavior.

When fire setting and explosives are involved in criminal enterprise, the reconstruction and interpretation of related behaviors may appear difficult or impossible to those unaccustomed with it. This is because fire, explosions, and/or related suppression and rescue efforts will likely destroy some or most of the immediately recognizable physical evidence. What the behavioral examiner should understand is that this does not mean that there is no evidence, or that cases involving arson or explosives are difficult to solve. Consider the following advisory from Corry and Vottero (1997):

> Whenever a rash of arson fires makes the local news, a uniformed official under the glare of news cameras will often trot out the usual list of excuses about why arson fires are so difficult . ...

> The real problem occurs when present or prospective fire/arson investigators accept this bleak outlook as though it were fact. ... It has been our experience that most arson fires are not only possible to solve, in many cases, average arson fires are very easy to solve.

This is true when the investigation involves the deliberate and non-political pooling of skills and resources. Teamwork between the arson investigator, the laboratory criminalist, and the criminal profiler is mandatory for the successful reconstruction of fire scenes and the subsequent interpretation crime-related behaviors and motives.

The focus of this chapter is the use of fire and/or explosives in the furtherance of criminal activity. For specific texts devoted in part or in whole to the concepts and procedures involved in the investigation of fire setting and explosives use, the author strongly recommends the following:

- Chisum, W. J., and Turvey, B. (2011) *Crime Reconstruction*, 2nd Edition
- DeHaan, J. (1997) *Kirk's Fire Investigation*, 4th Edition
- Kirk, P. (1969) *Fire Investigation*
- National Fire Protection Association (1998) NFPA 921: Guide for Fire and Explosion Investigations, 1998 Edition

Full citations of these publications are given in the "References" section at the end of the chapter.

LIMITATIONS

Every fire scene presents its own natural limits on what a scientific investigation can reveal. Understanding and expressing those limits in each case, without bias, is a necessary part of the work. Competent interpretation of fire patterns is therefore the domain of a properly educated and trained fire investigator, who must have a scientific background. As explained in Kirk (1969, p. 2),

> To be a successful fire investigator, numerous facets of fires, fuels, people, and investigation procedures must be mastered and understood. The investigator must truly understand *how* a fire burns and that not all fires necessarily burn in the same way. These differences must be correlated with their causes, generally the nature of the fuels involved or the physical circumstances and environment of the fire.

This knowledge and skill are not afforded to all who seek or proclaim them and cannot be adequately conferred in a series of short courses or workshops. Moreover, the fire investigator community is full of long-standing myths propagated by the "experienced" that have passed for scientific evidence when nothing could be further from the truth. As explained in Russell (2006, pp. 42–43),

It is a long-standing problem. There are approximately 500,000 structural fires in the U.S. each year, with 10 to 15 percent deemed suspicious. "That's 70,000 chances to screw up," says John Lentini, a former crime lab analyst who manages fire *investigations* for Applied Technical Services in Marietta, Georgia. More than 5000 people are currently in prison in the U.S. for *arson*, and only recently have defendants had any hope of seeing their stories tested by rigorous experiments. ...

Fire *investigation* has always been more art than science. In the U.S., especially, it has been based largely on observations handed down through generations of firefighters and investigators. The hallmarks of *arson* have been thought to include extreme heat, complex patterns of cracks in windows and irregular burn marks on walls and floors, the latter suggesting the use of accelerants like gasoline or multiple points of origin. Yet until a couple of decades ago, there had been no studies of accidental fires, so there was nothing with which to compare suspected *arson* fires. Instead, proving *arson* fell to the experience of long-serving fire investigators. They routinely told juries that fires were too hot, too big or too fast-moving to be accidental.

"*Arson* murder is the only crime that can land you on death row based on the testimony of an expert witness who may not have attended college," says Lentini. For years, no one seemed to question the assumptions. Everyone accepted that fires that had been started intentionally with accelerants burned hotter than accidental fires, and that the depth of charring in wood revealed how fast a fire had burned, among other things. Never mind that there was no scientific research to support any of these beliefs.

All this began to change in the mid-1970s when a handful of fire experts started to look at the science. "We quickly realized that some of the things that were said in the books, and were being taught and used by investigators, didn't hold up," says John DeHaan, author of *Kirk's Fire Investigation*, a widely used text. "Fire scientists knew a lot about fires, fire engineers knew a lot about preventing them, fire investigators knew a lot about the aftermath, but the three groups never really talked to each other."

By the early 1990s, experts like Lentini and DeHaan were regularly debunking old myths through experiment. In October 1991 a massive brush fire in Oakland, California, killed 25 people and destroyed more than 3000 homes. The burnt-out buildings presented Lentini and his colleagues with numerous accidental fire scenes. They studied the remains of 50 houses and could find no scientific basis for several traditional indicators of *arson*.

Take a phenomenon called crazed glass—windows marked with a distinctive web of tiny, tightly spaced, random cracks. The effect was thought to result from the intense, rapid heating of an accelerated fire. However, Lentini's team discovered it in 12 of the 50 Oakland homes. It appeared most often on the fire's periphery, suggesting that it resulted from contact with water from firefighters' hoses rather than rapid heating.

Lentini then performed lab tests, subjecting glass to slow and rapid heating sources, including an 800 °C propane flame. He found that spraying cool water on glass that had been heated to over 500 °C reliably produced crazing, while rapid heating never did. It turns out the effect results from thermal shock: as the glass cools it contracts too rapidly to adjust smoothly. Lentini published his results in 1992, but even today some diehard investigators remain reluctant to accept it. "I still run into cases where they used crazed glass as an *arson* indicator," says chemist and fire consultant Gerald Hurst of Austin, Texas.

Meanwhile, understanding a phenomenon called "flashover" has also shed light on the true behavior of fires. ... Flashover occurs when a fire becomes so intense—approximately 600°C—that all the flammable materials that are present ignite simultaneously. Hot, deadly smoke billows, windows are blown out and flames gush from windows and doors, Flashover requires sufficient ventilation, but it can happen terrifyingly fast. A single burning armchair can bring a room to flashover point in less than five minutes. It also irrevocably alters the evidence a fire leaves in its wake, making it hard to tell *arson* from accident.

Given these limitations and concerns, criminal profilers should seek out and/or incorporate only the findings of adequately educated, trained, and experienced fire scene investigators into their analyses. That is to say, no forensic examiner is required to assume the competency of any other and should be hesitant to use their results when there is a legitimate doubt. This is especially true in fire scene investigation, where many of those rendering findings are insufficiently educated and trained to interpret what they are seeing within the mandates of good science, to say nothing of holding on to myths that have been debunked in the literature that many do not read.

FIRE AND EXPLOSIVES USE AS FORCE

The intentional use of fire and explosives is an extension of an offender's will to use force. Fire and explosives are meant to kill, injure, obliterate, or obscure their intended targets. However, they also leave behind visible, recognizable patterns that can be interpreted by the nature and the extent of the resulting human, structural, and environmental damage.

As extensions of an offender's will to use force, fire and explosives can be weapons that are used for the same motives as other types of force, from defensive to lethal. In order to interpret their motivational origins, like any other behavior, close attention needs to be paid to their context in terms of victimology and crime scene characteristics. As explained in DeHaan (1997, pp. 395–396), "Motives, devices, intents, and targets for arson fires are all interrelated to some degree ... the discovery of one can be used to suggest or deduce the others."

VICTIMOLOGY

With respect to intentional fires and explosions, one of the first things to establish is who or what the intended target was: who or what was meant to receive the force that was unleashed by the offender, and who or what was meant to suffer as a result. By extension, examiners may also determine who or what was not the target.

The targets of fire setting and explosives use can include individual people, but also groups, items, property, or symbols. In this context, a *target* is defined as the object of an attack from the offender's point of view. This is separate from the concept of the victim. The *intended victim* is the term for the person, group, or institution that was meant to suffer loss, harm, injury, or death. The intended victim and the target may be one and the same. There may also be more than one intended victim.

Because of the unpredictable, uncontrollable, and often imprecise nature of fire and explosives use, there may also be *collateral victims*. This term refers to victims that an offender causes to suffer loss, harm, injury, or death (usually by virtue of proximity), in the pursuit of another victim. "Once set, the fire is no longer responsive to the desires or dictates of the firesetter" (Geller, 1992).

Individuals

An *individual* is a victim who has been targeted for emotional, psychological, or precautionary reasons, as well as those who are collateral victims. Victims who have been targeted may also be symbolic. In this context, a *symbol* is any person who represents something, such as an idea, a belief, a group, or even another person.

Groups

A *group* can mean any collection of people unified by shared characteristics, such as sex, race, color, religion, beliefs, activities, or achievement. It also includes groups that are symbolic. In this context, a *symbol* can be any group that represents something, such as an idea or a belief.

Property: Objects and Symbols

The term *property* refers to structures, vehicles, or other objects. It includes things that have material or evidentiary value. For example, it could include one vehicle burned for insurance purposes by its owner, or another vehicle burned in precisely the same fashion to hide evidence related to vehicle theft by a stranger.

It also includes physical symbols and collateral objects (things that are unintentionally damaged or destroyed by virtue of proximity). In this context, a *symbol* can be any object or property that represents something more, such as an idea, a belief, an organization, or a person. Examples range from hate crimes involving bombs set off in churches and abortion clinics, to burning an ex-boyfriend's clothing (Figures 16.1 and 16.2).

FIGURES 16.1 AND 16.2
On March 9, 2009, Kim Eccott (see Figure 16.1), 23, used a cigarette lighter to set fire to clothing belonging to Mark Naylor, 47, while he was helping her move out of his apartment in Stowmarket, Suffolk, UK (see Figure 16.2). She was angry about their recent break-up and wanted a second chance, which he was unwilling to give. She therefore set fire to his expensive collection of designer suits in retaliation. The fire eventually destroyed two bedrooms and a bathroom, causing £25,000 worth of damage. She was arrested that day, pled guilty to arson, and received a 52-week jail sentence, suspended for two years with a two-year supervision order. It was felt by the court that she needed help more than punishment (Daily Mail Reporter, 2009).

CRIME SCENE CHARACTERISTICS

The extent and nature of preparations ... are all indications of the organization characteristics of the fire setter. Such characteristics ... can be used to focus on a possible motive and even develop a personality profile of the arsonist for use in the investigation.

—DeHaan (1997, p. 405)

The same crime scene characteristics detailed in Chapter 12 are appropriate, with minor adjustments, for the analysis of cases involving fire setting and the use of explosives. To that end, it must be determined what type of involvement caused the damage at the scene: fire, explosion, or both. The following additional characteristics should also be determined as they relate to the manufacture and/or deployment of incendiary or explosive materials and devices.

Accelerants and/or Explosive Material

An *accelerant* is any fuel (solid, liquid, or gas) that is used to initiate or increase the intensity or speed of the spread of fire. Once it has been established that an accelerant was used, it must further be determined whether the accelerant is native or foreign to the environment. The type of accelerant that the offender utilizes is dictated by experience, availability, motive, and intent (DeHaan, 1997, p. 415).

Some common accelerants include:

- Gasoline
- Kerosene
- Lighter fluid
- Potable liquors
- Newspaper
- Accumulated trash
- Rags
- Clothing

For example, DeHaan (1997, p. 407) points out that offenders often follow two guidelines in terms of materials use:

> (1) the simpler the better, and (2) use fuels available at the scene. Both guidelines minimize the materials that must be brought to the scene by the arsonist, and the fewer the number of times the individual is seen in the area (especially carrying containers or odd packages) the less the chances of being spotted by a witness. Simpler sets minimize the chances of elaborate devices failing to ignite, while they maximize the chances that the entire set will be destroyed by the fire or even normal suppression activities.

The explosive materials involved in an offense can range from crude, homemade, or improvised concoctions to commercially available explosive material and noncommercial explosives. Like accelerants, the type of explosive materials that an offender utilizes is also dictated by experience, availability, motive, and intent.

Point of Origin

The *point of origin* is the specific location at which a fire is ignited (DeHaan, 1997, p. 486), or the specific location where a device is placed and subsequently detonated. Do not discount the possibility of multiple points of origin until all of the facts of the case are in.

The point of origin is highly suggestive of the offender's intended target and the intended victim.

Method of Initiation

The way that an offender chooses to start, or delay, the burning of accelerant or the detonation of a device is dependent upon the types of fuels or explosives used, the amount of delay time that is desired, and the mobility of the target. Methods of initiation for fires, adapted from DeHaan (1997), include but are not limited to:

- Open flames (matches, lighters, and so on)
- Fuses (any length of readily combustible material)
- Smoldering materials
- Cigarettes
- Electrical arcs
- Glowing wires
- Chemical reaction (commercial or improvised)
- Black powder and flash powder

Methods of initiation for explosive devices, adapted from the National Fire Protection Association (NFPA) publication 921 (NFPA, 1998), include but are not limited to:

- Blasting caps
- Hot surfaces
- Electrical arcs
- Static electricity
- Open flame
- Sparks
- Chemical reaction (commercial or improvised)

Nature and Intent

Offender behavior may be used to infer intent. According to O'Hara (1970, p. 214),

> The actions of the suspect can frequently offer evidence of criminal intent. For example, anticipation of fire may be shown by such circumstances as the removal of valuable articles or the substitution of inferior articles. Ill feelings or unfriendly relations between the accused and occupants of the burned building may be shown. The absence of any effort to extinguish the fire or to turn on the alarm in the presence of opportunity is significant. The flight of the suspect may also be incriminating.

When considering the nature and intent of any fire or explosive used by an offender, it will be helpful to determine intentional versus actual damage. This means learning as much about the environmental structure and fuels in the point of origin as possible. This should be compared with the amount of accelerant or explosive used and the amount of damage incurred by the target. The more fuels or explosives used by offenders, the more damage they intended to inflict upon their target.

Another important element to bear in mind when considering the nature and intent of any fire or explosive used by an offender is the targeting. By that we mean to examine the devices, initiation, and origin for evidence of just what the fire or explosive was intended to inflict damage upon. Was it intended to harm, damage, kill, or destroy a narrow target selection, or a broad target selection? *Narrow targeting* refers to any fire or explosive that is designed to inflict specific, focused, calculated amounts of damage to a specific target. *Broad targeting* refers to any fire or an explosive that is designed to inflict damage in a wide-reaching fashion. In cases involving broad targeting, there may be an intended target near the point of origin, but it may also be designed to reach beyond that primary target for other victims in the environment.

Offender Skill

Manufacture, point of origin, method of initiation, and nature of the fire or explosion should all be taken into account when assessing the offender's skill level. The key questions include:

- How effective was the intended design and/or manufacture of the burn or the blast in achieving the offender's objective?
- How competently was the burn or blast delivered to the point of origin and initiated?
- Did the burn or blast achieve the offender's objective?

Motivation

The motives for fire setting and explosives use are not generally complex or difficult to understand, as explained by Corry and Vottero (1997):

> Most adults set fires for revenge, spite, to hide another crime, or for fraud. Many juveniles set fires during vandalism, for revenge, or to achieve some other "logical" criminal purpose. In many cases there is some type of direct connection between the arsonist and the structure [or object, or victim] that he sets on fire.

Consequently, there is a tendency on the part of those who study arsonists and bombers to develop tidy inductive offender typologies from which to predict offender characteristics once an offender has been classified. For example, the FBI's National Center for the Analysis of Violent Crime has suggested that there are six major motivations for arsonists, which they use to predict likely offender characteristics. They are (Burgess et al., 1997, pp. 165–166):

1. Revenge
2. Excitement
3. Vandalism
4. Profit
5. Crime concealment
6. Extremism

In point of fact, this is an adaptation of the Groth rapist typology (Groth, 1979) with some nonsexual motivations (points 4 and 5) and a non-motive (point 3) thrown in. The NCAVC "revenge" motivation and the "extremist" motivation listed above both correspond with Groth's *anger*-motivated offender (the extremist motivation, as defined, could also correspond with *reassurance* or *assertive* motivations). The NCAVC "excitement" motivation corresponds with Groth's *power*-motivated offender (or with *reassurance*, *assertive* or *sadistic* motivations—as defined this is not a very exclusive category because there are so many different kinds of offender "excitement").

Furthermore, "vandalism" is not an offender motive. It is a penal classification, or, as we have discussed, a constellation of behaviors. While reflective of motive, such as assertive-oriented needs, reassurance-oriented needs, the need for excitement, or revenge-oriented needs, it is not a motive in its own right. It would require further behavioral analysis before we could start understanding why the offender was doing it.

In any case, as already discussed in this work, prediction is not the intent of behavioral evidence analysis.

APPLYING THE BEHAVIOR-MOTIVATIONAL TYPOLOGY

By now students should understand that the author does not support the inductive use of motivational typologies, but he does support their deductive use. The motivational typology detailed in Chapter 13 is more than adequate to the task of classifying the actual behaviors associated with specific instances of fire setting and explosives use. It is a valuable tool for use in criminological assessments and should be applied to understand the motivations behind offender motives in context and without pigeonholing.

It is worth mentioning that, in addition to criminal motives, the use of fire and explosives may also involve non-criminal desires. Such is the case with what may be referred to as the *hero* or *vanity* arsonist. As explained in White (1996),

> The hero or "vanity" arsonist category is one of the most disturbing in the sense that a fair number of firefighters have been assigned to this group over the years. These firefighters who set fires "are believed to be … driven to fire-setting by boredom, vanity … or a nagging desire to be accepted as one of the guys." They "are most frequently motivated by ego" and "typically crave the celebrity status" that comes with "extinguishing the blaze, often arriving first at the scene. …" The "hero" arsonist may also be a security guard, a police officer, or a recently rejected applicant to one of these departments who is attempting to prove himself. These arsonists have no desire to hurt anyone; they seek public acclaim.

Firefighters and arson investigators who intentionally set fires may also do so for excitement, crime concealment, and profit-related motives. They are people, too, and it's not all about being the hero. Consider the case of two firefighters discussed in Zapotosky and Morse (2009):

> Two recent volunteer fire fighters in Prince George's County were charged with arson Thursday amid accusations that while on duty, they slipped into a vacant house, set fire to a sofa using a signal flare and returned minutes later to help extinguish the blaze.

> The allegations, which officials said could lead to more charges against more fire fighters, highlight a phenomenon that investigators and psychologists worldwide have studied for years: fire fighters setting fires for the thrill of putting them out.

> "The excitement is to respond to the fire—the action, the results from speeding to the fire with sirens blaring and suppressing the fire with bystanders figuratively applauding, that sort of thing," said Timothy G. Huff, a former FBI criminal profiler who has consulted on and written studies on the topic. "The hero thing is part of the excitement."

> He and others are quick to say that such people represent only a tiny fraction of all fire fighters. The scope of the problem is unclear because no one keeps data nationwide on the profession or volunteer affiliation of those who set fires. And it's difficult to generalize about what motivates arsonists.

> Jerome Engle, 46, a long-time volunteer fire fighter who spent time at several stations in Prince George's, and James R. Martinez, 24, a Prince George's volunteer who also is a paid fire fighter in Montgomery County, were charged in the case. They were indicted on charges including second-degree arson, burglary and malicious burning. …

> Engle left for another volunteer department a year and a half ago, and Martinez resigned for personal reasons in March, a Riverdale department official said.

Fire fighters who commit arson generally strike in their jurisdictions, Huff said. "It's common sense when you think about it," he said. "Otherwise, they wouldn't be responding to them."

Huff cited three common motives of fire fighter–arsonists, ranking excitement above profit and revenge. …

Pamela Kulbarsh, a psychiatric nurse and former member of the San Diego County Psychiatric Emergency Response Team, said fire fighter–arsonists often are volunteers who grow bored at their stations.

"A lot of people really crave that excitement and that attention," she said. Kulbarsh said some firefighter-arsonists have mental health issues such as antisocial behavior or histrionic personality disorder.

Both Engle and Martinez pled guilty to arson related charges in late 2010.

Precautionary-Oriented Fire Setting and/or Explosives Use

This motivational aspect is a more inclusive category than the FBI's crime concealment motivation given previously. Recall that a *precautionary act* is any behavior committed by an offender before, during, or after an offense that is consciously intended to confuse, hamper, or defeat investigative or forensic efforts for the purposes of concealing their identity, their connection to the crime, or the crime itself. Precautionary-oriented fire setting and/or explosives use refers to the use of fire or explosives as a precautionary act. That is, when they are used to conceal, damage, or destroy any items of evidentiary value. That includes the partial or complete immolation of a crime scene and/or the victim.

It should be noted that these types of precautionary acts are not always very thorough. Items intended for destruction should always be thoroughly examined by forensic scientists to exploit them for their full evidentiary potential, no matter how little may be left in terms of debris.

Examples include, but are not limited to,

Conceal, damage, or destroy the crime scene
- Setting a fire in an apartment after robbing it
- Burning a shed to destroy blood evidence left behind from an abduction-homicide
- Blowing up a residence with the victim inside, using the gas main, to conceal homicide

Conceal, damage, or destroy the victim
- Burning a victim's body in the woods after a rape-homicide
- Blowing a victim's body up with explosives and hiding the pieces in different locations to conceal a homicide
- Placing a victim's body in the trunk of a vehicle and burning the vehicle to conceal a homicide

Conceal, damage, or destroy evidentiary material linking the offender to the victim
- Setting a victim's pubic area on fire to conceal evidence of sexual assault or rape
- Burning bloody victim clothing
- Burning bloody offender clothing
- Burning records, deeds, titles, and policies

Conceal, damage, or destroy personal items linking the offender to the victim
- Burning pictures, videotape, computer hard drives, or other types or locations containing physical documentation of the victim and the offender together
- Burning gifts given to the victim by the offender
- Burning gifts given to the offender by the victim

The Profile of a Serial Arsonist? The Case of Allen Wayne Penson

Allen Wayne Penson was an unemployed resident of Walker County, Georgia. He was convicted of burglary and arson, for allegedly entering and setting fire to the Walker County Rescue Building and one of their vehicles. At his trial, prosecutors attempted to prove that Mr. Penson was a serial arsonist, not because of any physical evidence, but because he fit the FBI's profile of a serial arsonist.

Background

According to Georgia v. Allen Penson (1996),

> A person fitting the description of Penson was seen with a sandy-colored dog near the rescue building prior to the outbreak of the fire. Penson lived just 500 feet from the building and owned a sandy-colored dog. Investigators discovered blood at the scene indicating that someone may have broken a window to obtain entry. Penson had cuts or scratches on his arm which he claimed were from briars. Pursuant to a consent search of Penson's home, police found a sheet of ordinary notebook paper which had bloodstains on it. A volunteer member of the rescue squad identified the notebook sheet as a "doodle sheet" which he had scribbled on and had either thrown in the garbage or left on the desk in the break room.

Behavioral Issue

At trial, over the objections of the defense, the prosecution had an arson expert testify regarding the FBI's serial arsonist profile from a document titled, "Record on Essential Findings of the Study of Serial Arsons." The trial court permitted the expert to outline the serial arsonist profile, but instructed the prosecution not to apply the profile to Mr. Penson. They also prohibited the expert from giving the opinion that Mr. Penson was a serial arsonist. The FBI profile of a serial arsonist, according to the state's expert, is as follows (Georgia v. Allen Penson, 1996):

- White males between 18 and 27
- Loners
- Educational failures
- Homosexuals or bisexuals
- History of criminal activity
- Medical or mental problems
- Poor employment record
- Alcohol and drug abuse
- Dysfunctional family background
- Walkers who set fires within two miles of their home
- Act on the spur of the moment, usually for revenge

Prior to this testimony, through other witnesses, the state showed the following (Georgia v. Allen Penson, 1996):

> Penson was age 26, lived alone, had a tenth grade education, was unemployed, did not own a vehicle, and walked to the scene of the Walker County Rescue Building fire which was 500 feet from his home. The jury could observe for itself that Penson is a white male.

The prosecution was also allowed to introduce into evidence the circumstances of an unsolved fire in a vacant house in the same general area. This house had burned after Mr. Penson had been charged for the crime at hand and released on bond. No charges had been filed against Mr. Penson, but it was implied at trial that he was a suspect.

The defense appealed the conviction, arguing that the admission of the FBI serial arsonist profile into evidence at trial, as well as the uncharged fire, were reversible errors for the following reasons (Georgia v. Allen Penson, 1996):

- The profile did not rebut defendant's alibi
- The trial court's directive that its witness not apply the profile to the defendant was meaningless given state's extensive exploration of defendant's personal history and personality traits and transparent efforts to correlate this information to profile
- Evidence of Mr. Penson's guilt in relating to the Walker County Rescue Building fire, apart from the FBI profile, was not overwhelming
- No direct evidence of Mr. Penson's guilt relating to the vacant house fire was presented

Court Ruling

The Court of Appeals of Georgia determined that the admission of the FBI's serial arsonist profile through expert testimony was, by itself, a reversible error, given the lack of substantial evidence in the case and the amount of time that the prosecution spent establishing Mr. Penson's character. According to Georgia v. Allen Penson (1996),

> We are unable to accept the State's contention that even absent the serial profile evidence it had a "strong" circumstantial evidence case. Having reviewed the transcript and considered the totality of the State's evidence, we do not find the evidence was otherwise overwhelming, and we are unable to conclude that it is highly probable that the profile evidence did not contribute to the verdict.

The Court of Appeals of Georgia further determined that introducing the unsolved fire into evidence was an error, stating (Georgia v. Allen Penson, 1996):

> In view of the inflammatory serial arsonist insinuations implicitly directed at Penson, the failure of the State to make the requisite satisfactory showing of all three prongs of Williams, supra, was particularly egregious.

Mr. Penson's guilty verdict was subsequently reversed and remanded.

Discussion

The author has a great deal of enthusiasm for the findings of the Court of Appeals of Georgia in this case. Even at their very best, inductive statistical profiles regarding average offender types should be used for investigative purposes only. When they are used to substitute for any other real evidence of guilt, a miscarriage of justice becomes more than possible. It becomes likely.

The Murder of Melanie Richey: Pipe Bomb

Joseph Kelsey, 16, and two of his friends were convicted of charges relating to the sexual homicide of 15-year-old Melanie Richey on July 12, 1994.

Background

Melanie Richey was a student at Lakeside High School in McCormick County, Georgia. She knew her attackers from school. At the end of August, after she had been missing for six weeks, a dairy farmer discovered her body. According to South Carolina v. Joseph Kelsey (1998):

In early July 1994, sixteen-year-old Kelsey was staying with his friend, seventeen-year-old Mike Kirchner in Martinez, Georgia. On Monday, July 11, 1994, Kirchner left to go to work, leaving Kelsey, seventeen-year-old Geoffrey Payne, and seventeen-year-old Jamie Lynn Lee ("Defendants") alone in the house. Defendants decided to manufacture homemade pipe bombs. They initially constructed a bomb using copper tubing and gunpowder extracted from firecrackers. They detonated the bomb near a tree in Kirchner's backyard.

Defendants then decided to construct more sophisticated pipe bombs. To accomplish this, they shoplifted pipe material and shotgun shells from a nearby hardware store and Wal-Mart. Under the direction of Kelsey, they built three galvanized steel pipe bombs, one of which they detonated in Kirchner's backyard. The explosion produced a crater approximately four inches deep and one foot wide. It left bomb fragments in the side of Kirchner's house and in a nearby privacy fence. Kelsey placed the other two unexploded bombs in his travel bag inside Kirchner's house.

Later that evening, Defendants gathered at Kirchner's house for a party. In addition to Defendants, the following individuals showed up for the party: Tom Wurtzinger, April Reese, Tommy Speigel, and Joey Ingram. Everyone was drinking beer. At around midnight, Lee and Payne left the party to go to a nearby Texaco station, a popular "hang-out" area among local teens. When Lee and Payne arrived at the station, they spotted Melanie Richey standing near a telephone booth. They noticed something was wrong with her foot. In the process of sneaking out of her house to meet with a friend, Richey had severely cut her foot. Lee and Payne offered to take Richey to Kirchner's house in order to clean and bandage her injuries. Richey accepted.

Lee, Payne, and Richey returned to Kirchner's house at around 1:30 a.m. Lee and Payne helped Richey bandage her foot and then all three rejoined the party. Soon thereafter, Payne and Richey went outside on Kirchner's back porch where Payne repeatedly tried to coax Richey into having sexual intercourse with him. Richey refused Payne's advances. At several points during the night, Payne expressed to Lee his frustration over Richey's intransigence. Kelsey testified that at one point he overheard Payne tell Lee that he was so mad he could kill Richey.

Payne instructed Lee to crush up a tablet of Ecstacy, a mild hallucinogen. Payne poured the powder into a mixture of tea and water in order to hide the taste of the drug. Payne gave the drink to Richey and told her it would help calm a stomachache she had been complaining about earlier in the evening. Payne did not tell her that the drink was laced with Ecstacy. Kelsey testified that while this was going on, he was resting on the floor by the stereo and occasionally changing the music selection.

At around 3:30 a.m., Defendants decided to take Richey home. While Richey was waiting for Defendants outside of Kirchner's house, Payne asked Lee to get something to knock Richey out with. Lee retrieved a wrench from Kirchner's garage. Payne then suggested that Kelsey bring the unexploded pipe bombs. Kelsey complied by retrieving the bombs from his travel bag. Kelsey testified that he was unaware, at the time, of what Payne actually intended to do with the wrench and bombs.

Defendants and Richey then got into Lee's car, ostensibly to take Richey home. Lee was driving, Kelsey was in the passenger seat, and Payne and Richey were in the backseat. Although Richey had given them directions to her house, Lee detoured in the opposite direction. Richey asked where they were going; Payne replied that they were going to drive around for a while. Lee eventually drove across the Georgia border and into South Carolina. Lee testified that the music was "obscenely" loud in the car, and he was going about 90 m.p.h.

Soon after entering South Carolina, Lee noticed his tachometer go from 4200 to 6000 r.p.m. Lee looked down at the gear shift and discovered Richey's foot had knocked the gear into neutral. Lee turned around and saw that Payne had Richey in a "strangle hold type position." Lee continued to drive. A few minutes later, Lee "heard two quick, empty thud type sounds." He again turned around and saw that Payne still had Richey in a strangle hold. Lee further testified that Payne had the wrench in his hand. Kelsey testified that he had also turned around and saw that Richey's body was limp, her face was pale, and her lips were blue.

A few moments later, Payne leaned forward to tell Lee to turn the music down. According to Lee's testimony, Payne stated, "I'm pretty sure she's knocked out, guys." Payne then instructed Lee to go to "Scary Bridge" which crossed over Stevens Creek, the boundary line between Edgefield and McCormick counties. Lee drove to the bridge, where he parked the car.

Defendants got out of the car, leaving Richey in the backseat. Payne informed Lee and Kelsey that he was going to have sex with Richey. Payne took off his clothes and Richey's shorts. A few moments later, Lee warned Payne that a car was coming. Defendants quickly got back into Lee's car and began driving. After the approaching vehicle passed, Lee turned the car around and went back to the bridge. Lee testified that Richey was unconscious the entire time, and "she was definitely alive." Kelsey, on the other hand, testified that he had checked Richey's pulse, and he believed she was dead. Lee once again drove away from the bridge. He got approximately 100 feet down the road when Payne told him to stop the car. Defendants pulled Richey out of the car and carried her into the woods and up an embankment where they placed her on the ground. Lee returned to the car. Payne and Kelsey remained by Richey's body.

Kelsey testified that while he was standing over Richey's body, Payne instructed him to place a pipe bomb into Richey's mouth. Kelsey complied. Payne then lit the fuse, and the two ran. A few seconds later, the bomb exploded. Defendants returned to Kirchner's house where they fell asleep.

Mr. Lee pled guilty to accessory to murder after the fact, and agreed to testify against Geoffrey Payne and Joe Kelsey. He was sentenced to 10 years in prison. In February of 2000, he was granted parole with four years off for good behavior. Mr. Kelsey and Mr. Payne were sentenced to life in prison and will not be eligible for parole until September 2015.

Use of Explosives

In this case, the evidence suggests that the pipe bomb was used after the victim was dead. The offenders in this case constructed several pipe bombs specifically for detonation under what could be described as vandalism circumstances. There is no evidence to suggest that the pipe bombs were specifically intended for use on a human target in the above-described manner.

Having said that, there is evidence that the victim was alive when the pipe bomb was placed in her mouth and then detonated. The pipe bombs were essentially available materials, as was the wrench used to knock the victim out. The victim was also opportunistic, as the encounter with her could not have been planned for.

Arguably, the motive for the abduction and assault was sexual, as described. However, failing that and failing in their attempts to rape the victim, a twofold motive of retaliation and the need to kill a living witness emerged. The still living victim was taken to a secluded, remote secondary scene (over state lines), carried up into the woods, placed on the ground, and executed with a pipe bomb. The pipe bomb was chosen because it would kill (modus operandi behavior), and because it would carry the message of rage and indignation to the victim, as well as to those who found her body (signature/motivational behavior). So while the abduction and sexual assault were not very well planned, a great deal of thought and planning went into the disposal of the victim as a living witness and into the dissociation of the offenders from the crime.

Rape-Homicide: Arson for Crime Concealment

In late April of 2010, Robert Drown, Jr., pled guilty to charges relating to the 2007 murders of Jennifer Ison, 31, and her two daughters in Hitchins, Kentucky (Figures 16.3 and 16.4). This avoided a trial and a conviction that could have meant the death penalty. As detailed in Wood (2010),

> Ison and her daughters, Shannah, 10, and Marissa, 3, were found dead inside their burned out home in May 2007.

> Jennifer was strangled, Marissa died from smoke inhalation and Shannah's death was caused by blunt force trauma to the head

> He also pled guilty to rape, arson and burglary.

> Drown, a convicted sex offender, says he also raped Shannah before beating her and setting the home on fire.

A year prior, Drown had denied any involvement in the crimes during a jailhouse interview, described in Yohe (2008),

> [Drown] said he's currently married, with two step-daughters, ages 12 and 16. He said he's struggled with bipolar disorder since he was 20 years old.

> He had plenty to say about his treatment behind bars and denied the public perception that he's a ruthless evil monster.

> The convicted sex offender is charged with killing Jennifer Ison and her two young daughters last May, then torching their home to cover up the crime.

FIGURES 16.3 AND 16.4
In late April of 2010, Robert Drown, Jr. (Figure 16.4), pled guilty to charges relating to the 2007 deaths of Jennifer Ison, 31 (Figure 16.3), and her two daughters in Hitchins, Kentucky.

Drown said police have the wrong man, but he did explain how he met the delivery nurse a few days before her death.

"I met her at a bar, the Raging Bull, and about 10 minutes later, I was staying the night with her at her friend's house down in Kenova," Drown said.

Robert Drown said he wants a speedy trial, as soon as possible.

Drown was registered as a sex offender in Ohio and West Virginia and had been in a relationship with Ison prior to his crimes against her. She worked a registered nurse in the labor and delivery department at Cabell Huntington Hospital, West Virginia.

Insurance Fraud: Arson for Profit

Not only is it common for arson-related insurance fraud to increase during hard economic times in the United States, it is anticipated by the nation's insurance industry (Jay, 2009). This is true of American homes, and it is also true of American vehicles. As explained in Jay (2009, p. 24),

> Helen Marier, a Yuba County, Calif, resident, torched her Jeep Liberty to escape the $600 monthly payments, while her husband plunked his Nissan Titan into a river to collect a $29,000 insurance policy, prosecutors say. As America's economy sinks deeper into a trough, growing numbers of anxious drivers are illegally dumping unwanted vehicles in the hope that insurance payouts will help relieve the financial misery. …
>
> So-called vehicle give-ups have long been a common insurance crime. When a vehicle becomes too expensive or burdensome, a driver may torch it, drown it in a lake or a river, or simply abandon it in a remote location. The driver then tells the insurer that someone stole the doomed vehicle, demanding an insurance payout.

Jay (2009) also provided a checklist of red flags that may suggest "give-up" vehicles. However, in this author's experience, the checklist may be adapted and applied (in part) to the investigative considerations of any fire scene. For vehicles, the checklist includes:

1. An absence of damage to the ignition or steering lock
2. A lease agreement and the designated mileage has been exceeded
3. An absence of evidence suggesting break-in or other signs of forced entry
4. The owner is behind on payments
5. The owner is unemployed or otherwise financially distressed

As should be made clear by these red flags, which are by no means evidence of fraud on their own, the investigation of any fire scene must go beyond simply a rote cause and origin determination. It must involve a complete forensic victimology in order to provide context and investigative direction where needed.

Crack, Domestic Violence, and Arson

A jury found Pamela Newman guilty of first-degree arson. She was sentenced to a term of imprisonment not to exceed 25 years. During the trial, under cross-examination, the local fire marshal was asked his opinion regarding the profile of an arsonist. The court ruled that this was both outside of his area of expertise and inadmissible because it was in fact profiling testimony.

Background

On January 12, 2002, the Waterloo (Iowa) Fire Rescue and Police Departments responded to a fire at the home of Pamela Newman. The smell of gasoline and the pattern of the fire led them to conclude that the fire had been intentionally set. As described in Iowa v. Pamela Newman (2005), her stories did not add up:

> Over the course of the investigation into the cause of the fire, Newman gave several different accounts of what happened. At the scene of the fire, Newman told authorities she had been sewing in her living room and got up to go to the bathroom. She stated that when she got out of the bathroom the kitchen was on fire, and she did not know how the fire started.

> She explained that the snowmobile suit she was wearing at the time caught on fire as she ran through the kitchen to get out of the house and she rolled on the ground after escaping the house to put out the fire. She said she might have kicked a gas can left in the kitchen by a mechanic the previous day on her way out of the house. Newman also stated she had been cooking and could not remember whether she left the burners on. She told one officer on the scene that she was cooking and a gas can either near on or the stove had caught fire. She stated she was the only one in the home.

> At the police station Newman stated that during an argument with Darryl Speller he pinned her against a wall in the kitchen and poured gasoline over her. Newman stated that she escaped into the bathroom, but when she came out the kitchen was on fire.

> Darryl Speller, who had been living with Newman since June 2001, told officers on the scene he had been in the house when the fire started. Clothing worn by Newman and Darryl Speller the day of the fire tested positive for the presence of gasoline. After the fire, Newman made a claim on her homeowner's insurance for damage caused by the fire. Her claim was denied. …

> At trial, Newman testified that in August 2001 she caught Speller smoking crack cocaine. He was not working at the time and had become verbally and physically abusive. Therefore, in September 2001, Newman asked Speller to pack his things and move out. Between September 2001 and January 2002, Newman asked Speller twice to move his property out of her house and move his trucks, tires, and trailers off of her property.

> Newman and Ronald Speller, Darryl's brother, offered differing testimony about what transpired the day of the fire. Newman testified that Darryl lost his temper and pinned her in a corner of the kitchen in front of the bathroom door, where he kept her for approximately two hours. He banged her head up against the wall. At some point, he picked up a gas can and started pouring gas on Newman.

> While Darryl and Newman argued, Ronald Speller knocked at the front and back doors, telling Darryl to let Newman go. Newman testified that Ronald never came into the house. Newman begged Darryl to let her use the bathroom.

> When she came out, the kitchen was a wall of fire. Newman ran through the fire in the kitchen and fell in the dining room. The legs of her snowsuit caught fire; she ran across the street and rolled on the ground to put out the fire. Newman testified she lied to the authorities at the scene of the fire because she was scared of Darryl, who was still in the area.

> Ronald Speller testified that he went to Newman's house after receiving a phone call informing him that Darryl and Newman were arguing. According to Ronald, Newman invited him into the house. The two were in the garage area of the house, arguing about their relationship. At some point during the argument, Darryl told Newman the relationship was over. Newman dropped her lighted

cigarette onto the kitchen floor, picked up a gas can, went into the bathroom and started shaking it. She slipped and fell in the gas, got back up, and continued shaking the gas container in the kitchen, spilling gasoline on the floor. The gas on the kitchen floor ignited, and Ronald and Darryl ran out the back door.

Because she gave multiple versions of events and would have been burned to death if she had actually been in the bathroom when the first started, as explained by the experts, Newman was not believed by the jury and was subsequently convicted of first-degree arson.

Admissibility Issues

Newman's appeal stems in part from the fact that the court denied the testimony of the fire marshal, which would have been helpful to the defense. As described in Iowa v. Pamela Newman (2005),

> Dave Boesen, the Waterloo fire marshal, testified at trial that based on the evidence of the fire in the bathroom, if Newman had been in the bathroom during the fire, as she claimed, she would have been severely burned or would not have escaped at all.

> On cross-examination, Newman's attorney asked Boesen if aggressive fires, such as the one in this case, were generally set by men, which Boesen denied. The prosecutor then questioned Boesen about whether it was possible to profile arsonists, as it was with some other crimes. Boesen responded that there was no reliable body of evidence to support the profiling of people who set fires. Newman sought to introduce the expert testimony of John Woodland, a fire investigator, to show that the fire was more likely started by a man than a woman. In a report Woodland stated:

> I believe the "profile of the fire scene" is indicative of an act committed by a man, and not typically the act of a woman. The violence of the act, and the volume and type of fuel required to cause the level of damage observed, implies a confidence in and understanding of the fuel, not typically portrayed by women.

> Woodland's report served as an offer of proof as to his testimony. The district court ruled that Woodland could testify to the cause of the fire, the spread of the fire, and the types of burns that are on clothing.

The trial court determined that profiling testimony was outside the area of Woodland's expertise and would also invade the province of the jury. A discussion is provided in Iowa v. Pamela Newman (2005):

> Newman contends the district court abused its discretion by excluding Woodland's proposed testimony about psychological profiles and gender statistics in arson cases. She points out that Boesen was permitted to testify that aggressive fires could be set by a man or a woman. She believes Woodland should have been permitted to contradict that statement by testifying that aggressive fires are more likely to be set by a man. …

> The admission of expert opinion testimony is governed by Iowa Rule of Evidence 5.702, which provides: If scientific, technical, or other specialized knowledge will assist the trier of fact to understand the evidence or to determine a fact in issue, a witness qualified as an expert by knowledge, skill, experience, training or education may testify thereto in the form of an opinion or otherwise.

> Iowa has a liberal tradition in the admission of opinion evidence under rule 5.702. State v. Buller, 517 N.W.2d 711, 713 (Iowa 1994). In State v. Hulbert, 481 N.W.2d 329, 331 (Iowa 1992), the defendant claimed the district court abused its discretion by refusing to permit expert opinion testimony about

whether he fit the profile of a child molester. The supreme court concluded the district court had not abused its discretion. *Hulbert*, 481 N.W.2d at 333. The court noted, "expert psychological evidence may not be used to merely bolster a witness's credibility" because "veracity is not a 'fact in issue' subject to expert opinion." ... (citing *State v. Myers*, 382 N.W.2d 91, 97 (Iowa 1986)).

The court also determined expert testimony that a defendant does or does not fit a certain profile "clearly goes beyond ordinary character evidence. It comes cloaked with an aura of scientific reliability about the predisposition of certain individuals to commit the type of crime at issue." ... Therefore, this type of evidence improperly comments on the guilt or innocence of the defendant. ...

For the same reasons the supreme court found no abuse of discretion in the exclusion of expert opinion testimony on the issue of profile evidence in *Hulbert*, we determine the district court in this case did not abuse its discretion in excluding Woodland's proposed testimony on the issue of whether Newman met the profile of an arsonist. The evidence would have been presented merely to bolster Newman's credibility. ... Also, the evidence would have been an improper comment on Newman's guilt or innocence. ...

Furthermore, Woodland's proposed profiling testimony did not present any evidence concerning whether a specific female defendant, such as Newman, was guilty or innocent. By stating that most aggressive fires are set by men, this does not eliminate the fact that some aggressive fires are set by women. The underlying premise of Woodland's testimony was unreliable, and " 'unreliable evidence cannot assist a trier of fact.'" *Buller*, 517 N.W.2d at 713 (quoting *State v. Murphy*, 451 N.W.2d 154, 156 (Iowa 1990)).

Based on these considerations, the appeals court upheld the trial court's decision to exclude this type of testimony.

Use of Fire

In this case, the evidence suggests that the use of fire could have been intended to satisfy first an intense anger motivation related to a domestic altercation, and then profit.

SUMMARY

When present in a crime scene, fire setting and explosives use must be examined and considered along with every other criminal behavior. They can occur in a variety of contexts and they can satisfy or be motivated by multiple offender needs. They are not limited to use in a particular kind of criminal offense or against any particular type of victim. Their use in a particular offense is constrained only by offender motive, offender intent, offender skill level, and the availability of materials.

Every fire scene presents its own natural limits on what a scientific investigation can reveal. Understanding and expressing those limits in each case, without bias, is a necessary part of the work. Competent interpretation of fire patterns is therefore the domain of a properly educated and trained fire investigator.

The intentional use of fire and explosives is an extension of an offender's will to use force. The first concern of the criminal profiler is to establish the intended target or targets of that force, whether it is a person, group, object, property, or a symbol. Then the profiler must assess the crime scene characteristics, including the type of accelerant/explosives used, point of origin, method of initiation, and motive/intent. From these, and the effectiveness of their use, offender knowledge, skill, and ability may be inferred.

Questions

1. True or False: Fire destroys all physical evidence of criminal behavior.
2. List three motives for the use of fire in a crime scene.
3. List three methods of initiation commonly used by arsonists.
4. Give an example of fire used as a precautionary act.
5. True or False: According to the FBI-trained arsonist expert in Georgia v. Allen Penson, serial arsonists tend to be homosexuals or bisexuals.

REFERENCES

Burgess, A., Burgess, A., Douglas, J., Ressler, R., 1997. Crime Classification Manual. Jossey-Bass, San Francisco, CA.

Chisum, W.J., Turvey, B., 2011. Crime Reconstruction, second edition. Elsevier Science, San Diego, CA.

Corry, R., Vottero, B., 1997. A New Approach to Fire and Arson Investigation. In: Fire Investigation Guideline. Massachusetts State Fire Marshal, Boston, MA.

Daily Mail Reporter, 2009. Jilted Girlfriend Sets Fire to Ex-Partner's Designer Suits After He Dumped Her. The Daily Mail Reporter, London, UK. August 28. www.dailymail.co.uk/news/article-1209634/Jilted-girl-burns-boyfriends-flat-setting-designer-suits.html.

DeHaan, J., 1997. Kirk's Fire Investigation, fourth edition. Prentice Hall, Upper Saddle River, NJ.

Geller, J., 1992. Arson in Review: From Profit to Pathology. Psychiatric Clin. North America 15 (3, September), 623–645.

Georgia v. Allen Penson, 1996. No. A96A1248, July 11, 1996 (222 Ga. App. 253).

Groth, A.N., 1979. Men Who Rape: The Psychology of the Offender. Plenum Press, New York, NY.

Iowa v. Pamela Newman, 2005. No. 04-0690, Oct. 12 (Iowa App., 2005).

Jay, D., 2009. Driven to Desparation–Auto Dumping Surges as Economy Sours. Claims Magazine (February), 24, 26, 28, and 37.

Kirk, P., 1969. Fire Investigation. John Wiley and Sons, New York, NY.

National Fire Protection Association, 1998. NFPA 921: Guide for Fire and Explosion Investigations, 1998 Edition. In: Technical Committee on Fire Investigations. National Fire Protection Association, Quincy, MA.

O'Hara, C., 1970. Fundamentals of Criminal Investigation. Charles C Thomas, Springfield, IL.

Russell, S., 2006. Down in Flames. New Science (November 4), 192 (2576), 42–45.

South Carolina v. Joseph Kelsey, 1998. No. 24801, July 20 (502 S.E.2d 63).

White, E., 1996. Profiling Arsonists and Their Motives: An Update. Fire Engineering March, 149 (3), 80–85.

Wood, M., 2010. Robert Drown Pleads Guilty to Killing Mother and Daughters. WCHS-TV, April 28. www.wchstv.com/newsroom/eyewitness/100427_1591.shtml.

Yohe, R., 2008. Robert Drown Jailhouse Interview. WSAZ-TV, January 24. www.wsaz.com/news/headlines/14298477.html.

Zapotosky, M., Morse, D., 2009. Two Firefighters in Pr. George's Charged with Arson. Washington Post Friday, November 6. www.washingtonpost.com/wp-dyn/content/article/2009/11/05/AR2009110504793_pf.html.

4 SECTION

Offender Characteristics

CHAPTER 17

Inferring Offender Characteristics

Brent E. Turvey

It is still not sufficiently realized that the criminal at the moment of the act is a different man from what he is after it—so much so that one would sometimes think them two different beings.

—Theodore Reik, *The Unknown Murderer* (p. 42)

CONTENTS

Criminal Profiling: An Introduction to Behavioral Evidence Analysis, Fourth Edition

KEY TERMS

Behavioral consistency theory	Forensic identification	Peer review
Error rate	Forensic individualization	Personal identification
Falsification	Homology assumption	

Criminal profiling refers to the inference of offender characteristics. As we have discussed, there are more than a few ways to make these inferences—none of them equal. The analyst can predict offender characteristics based on statistical models, prior research, or experience (i.e., nomo-inductive reasoning); the analyst can use hard physical evidence to make deductions about physical characteristics (DNA to give sex and race, hairs to give hair color, footwear impression to give shoe size, etc); or the analyst can use analytical logic, critical thinking, and the scientific method to make deductions about offender relational and psychological characteristics based on an analysis of crime scene behavior (e.g., behavioral evidence analysis).

In this textbook, we have explained how the different methods of inferring offender characteristics achieve results of varying quality. Inferences based on statistics and experience can represent an unqualified or even inappropriate guess about an offender's possible characteristics because statistics and experience rely on the typical or abstract. Behavioral evidence analysis (BEA), on the other hand, seeks to examine the behaviors and patterns in a particular offense, then to make specific inferences about offender characteristics that are evident directly from crime-related behavior. Nomo-inductive methods of profiling predict based on aggregated past similar cases; ideo-deductive methods examine and interpret based on the case at hand.

This chapter describes the general purpose, mechanism, and limitations of BEA-oriented profiling inferences in the context of investigative and forensic issues. Other chapters deal with the interpretation of specific sets of offender characteristics, such as those related to psychopathy, sadism, sexual asphyxia, homicide, serial crime, and cybercrime.

THE HOMOLOGY DEBACLE[1]

Two theories accepted by those using predictive methods of criminal profiling are, as referred to by investigative psychologists, *behavioral consistency* and the *homology assumption*. Criminal investigative analysis (CIA) and investigative psychology (IP; see Chapter 3, "Alternative Methods of Criminal Profiling") fully embrace and to a large extent depend upon the reliability these methods. BEA does not. As explained in Woodhams and Toye (2007),[2]

> Offender profiling rests on several assumptions or hypotheses (for a comprehensive discussion of these, see Alison et al., 2002). The first is the homology assumption (Mokros and Alison, 2002), the hypothesis that there will be a relationship between offenders' characteristics and their crime scene behavior. An implication of this hypothesis is that offenders with similar characteristics will therefore display similar crime scene behaviors (Mokros and Alison, 2002). It follows that offenders with different crime scene behavior should possess different characteristics.

In essence, the behavioral consistency theory suggests that the same criminal will behave in relatively the same way across offenses, while the homology assumption provides that different criminals who commit similar acts will have similar traits or characteristics. These two theories posit that those characteristics are reflective of the offender's overall traits and disposition.

The problem with these theories is that the generalizations they allow don't work in real cases. Just because someone is angry while committing one crime does not guarantee that he or she will be generally angry in everyday life, nor that they will be angry in their other criminal behavior. The same is true for any other characteristic or personality trait—especially given the nature of compartmentalization (discussed in Chapter 22, "Serial Cases"). Time advances forward, and, with time, experience increases, mood changes, personal chemistry and toxicology change, and skills evolve. Time is a variable ignored by these theories.

It is possible for some characteristics to be *consistent* or *homologous*, and indeed this can be demonstrated in some cases. However, it is not a reasonable assumption in all cases, or even most cases. As already cited in this text, the research on consistency and homology has either refuted or failed to lend support for either theory.

BEA does not assume that crime-related behavior must reflect an offender's enduring core or cardinal traits. Rather, it seeks to establish what characteristics are evident in each crime. As a result, BEA profiles cannot indicate who a person is, who they might be, or even who they want to be—only what they are capable of showing the world through their actions.

PURPOSE

The purpose of a criminal profile is to assist in the process of establishing the core and cardinal characteristics of an offender that separate and ultimately distinguish him or her from the general population. The profile is rendered to define or refine the suspect pool in a criminal investigation. It is, by its nature, a tool

---

[1] A *debacle* is a sudden and ignominious failure. This section is adapted in part from Petherick (2007).
[2] Here, Woodhams and Toye (2007) refer specifically to the assumptions of investigative psychologists using predictive, nomo-inductive profiling methods. They do not speak for the ideo-deductive (BEA) community. Moreover, the regular omission of citation of ideo-deductive texts and treatises in their research is telling. It leaves readers with the false impression that no methodology other than CIA and IP exists.

intended for use in assisting the process of criminal identification. However, like many forensic methods, it is not suited for the task of *individuating* offenders on its own.

The common wisdom is that those in law enforcement know how to investigate all crime and are capable of developing suspects from the evidence. This is not always so. As explained in a review of law-enforcement clearance rates (Turvey, 2006),[3]

> In 2004, the United States experienced 13,662 murders and non-negligent homicides. The overall clearance rate for homicide was 62.6 percent. This means that 37.4 percent of all homicides were not cleared. The clearance rate drops further still when one examines only data from reporting cities with populations of 500,000 and over—to between 55 and 60 percent. Put another way, almost two out of every homicides committed remained unsolved—and more than two in the largest cities. It's the non-metropolitan areas and the smaller cities that raise the average—where stranger crimes are less frequent.

> In terms of the victim–offender relationship—42.9 percent of victims knew their offenders; 12.9 percent of victims died at the hands of strangers. However, in 44.1 percent of the cases, the victim–offender relationship was unknown.

> All cleared homicide cases involved a known victim–offender relationship. That relationship was 3.5 times more likely to be a known as opposed to unknown assailant. Back in 1993, the FBI's Uniform Crime Report stated that the primary reason for the drop in the national clearance rates "may be the victim/offender relationships composing today's murders are more likely to be unknown." Based on the empirical evidence provided, and the other factors previously discussed, this examiner is forced to concur. In other words, murder cases requiring investigative skills related to stranger crimes (developing and working the physical evidence, following all leads to their conclusion, long hours, complex problem solving, etc.) are solved with far less frequency.

> The data and issues are entirely similar with respect to rape investigation. In 2004, the United States experienced 80,939 forcible rapes. The overall clearance rate for forcible rape was 41.8 percent, down from 44.5 percent in 2003. This represents the lowest point of a steady decline that started back in 1996, when the clearance rate for rapes was 52 percent. …

> This preliminary review of rape and murder clearance rates, in combination with investigative realities and solvability factors, strongly suggests that investigative and forensic skill, ability and attentiveness are not being brought to bear in the majority of these cases. As a result, the vast majority of cases are being cleared because the victim–offender relationship is already known, and the investigation may focus on developing that presumed connection. In other words, criminal investigation is at this point reactive.

Therefore, criminal profiling has a role in cases where law-enforcement efforts have met a dead end, for whatever reason, and an objective external perspective may be useful. Those providing such assistance should not be afraid to cover the investigative and forensic basics. If these basics were widely known and regularly practiced, it is likely that profilers and others would be less necessary.[4]

---

[3] Data taken from the U.S.Department of Justice's Crime in the United States—2004.

[4] The plain truth is that not all law-enforcement agencies use basic suspect-development techniques or the forensic sciences to solve their cases. For example, Feeney (2000) cites a study of police case clearances that showed:
The most significant factor affecting clearance of the crimes was whether a suspect was named in the crime report. Sixty three percent of the 482 'cleared' cases involved named suspects—about half being persons known to the victim or a witness and about half being

CRIMINAL PROFILING AND CRIMINAL IDENTITY

Forensic identification is a general term that refers to the methods used to classify or individuate items of evidence for court (a.k.a. forensic) purposes. According to Inman and Rudin (1997), an item is identified when it can be placed into a class of items with similar (a.k.a. class) characteristics. However, an item can only be individualized if it has some unique feature or property that distinguishes it from all other items in the universe (Kirk and Thornton, 1974, p. 10).

Personal identification is a term that refers to establishing the precise identity of individuals, typically witnesses, victims, and offenders. There are relatively few reliable forensic methods that can be used to individualize a particular person. These include fingerprint analysis, RFLP (restriction fragment length polymorphism) and STR (short tandem repeat) DNA analyses, certain kinds of odontological evidence, and the far less reliable yet generally accepted identifications made by eyewitnesses.

What is referred to as "The Problem of Identity" is discussed thoroughly by the late criminalist Dr. Paul L. Kirk in both editions of his seminal work *Crime Investigation* (Kirk, 1953; Kirk and Thornton,1974). He raised valid concerns about expert testimony on the issue, including those related to bias, incompetence, and ignorance, all of which remain relevant today. According to Kirk and Thornton (1974, p. 15),

In the examination and interpretation of physical evidence, the distinction between identification and individuation must always be clearly made, to facilitate the real purpose of the criminalist: to determine the identity of source. That is, two items of evidence, one known and the other unknown, must be identified as having a common origin. On the witness stand, the criminalist must be willing to admit that absolute identity is impossible to establish. Identity of source, on the other hand, often may be established unequivocally, and no witness who has established it need ever back down in the face of cross-examination.

---

identified through on-the-scene arrests by the police or by store security officer. . . . "If a suspect is neither known to the victim nor arrested at the scene of the crime, the chances of ever arresting him are very slim."

In their study, which focused specifically on homicide cases, Cronin and Wellford (2000, p. 1) noted the dearth of research on the determinants of clearance rates for any type of crime, including homicide. They opened their work with the following statement: "Law enforcement's ability to make arrests following crimes appears to have significantly diminished in recent years. This is especially true for homicide." Their study further showed that (Cronin and Wellford, 2000, p. 6):

The probability of clearance increases significantly when the first officer on the scene quickly notifies the homicide unit, the medical examiners, and the crime lab and attempts to locate witnesses, secure the area, and identify potential witnesses in the neighborhood. These authors (Cronin and Wellford, 2000, p. 4) also found that the probability of clearance increased when:

- More than one detective was assigned to a case
- The crime scene was measured
- Detectives took less than 30 minutes to arrive at the crime scene
- Detectives followed up on witness information
- Detectives attended the postmortem examination (autopsy)
- The weapon was found at the crime scene
- Friends and neighbors of the victim were interviewed
- Computer checks were conducted on victims, witnesses, suspects, and guns
- The medical examiner collected specimens, recovered a projectile, or prepared a body chart

Solve rates in many cities throughout the United States continue to remain incredibly low, no doubt for the same reasons. According to one study of FBI crime statistics by the Emergency Response and Research Institute in Chicago (Macko, 1996), the U.S. cities with the lowest clearance rates of crime in general (including rapes and homicides) were Las Vegas, NV (20.7%); Detroit, MI (21.4%); Buffalo, NY (21.9%); San Francisco, CA (24.5%); and Miami, FL (25.7%).

What this combines to suggest is that there are many cases where the basic investigative actions described by Cronin and Wellford (2000) are not being taken, even within experienced police agencies. Hence there is a need for criminal profiling and other investigative measures beyond existing law enforcement strategies for fighting crime.

It is precisely here that the greatest caution must be exercised. The inept or biased witness may readily testify to an identity, or to a type of identity, that does not actually exist. This can come about because of his confusion as to the nature of identity, his inability to evaluate the results of his observations, or because his general technical deficiencies preclude meaningful results.

> To sum up: accurate identification must rest on a proper basis of training, experience, technical knowledge, and skill, and an understanding of the fundamental nature of identity itself. It should not be attempted without this kind of background, either by the police officer or the amateur. Highly experienced professional identification men make errors and overlook many significant matters. How much worse the situation would be if every police officer or amateur were to attempt the same identifications, merely because they had an interest in the matter and an opportunity to indulge their desires!

Thornton (1997, p. 5) agrees, and goes further, saying:

> In the comparison of physical evidence, it is often helpful to make use of the concepts of class characteristics and individual characteristics. Class characteristics are general characteristics that separate a group of objects from a universe of diverse objects. In a comparison process, class characteristics serve the very useful purpose of screening a large number of items by eliminating from consideration those items that do not share the characteristics common to all of the members of that group. Class characteristics do not, and cannot, establish uniqueness. Individual characteristics, on the other band, are those exceptional characteristics that may establish the uniqueness of an object. It should be recognized that an individual characteristic, taken in isolation, may not in itself be unique. The uniqueness of an object may be established by an ensemble of individual characteristics. A scratch on the surface of a bullet, for example, is not a unique event; it is the arrangement of the scratches on the bullet that may mark it as unique.

Although *forensic individuation* is a fundamental forensic concept, this author routinely encounters forensic and legal practitioners who have not heard of it, do not understand it, and subsequently do not apply it in their casework by imposing the requisite limits on their findings.

Kirk, an advocate of the investigative use of criminal profiling well before its potential was widely recognized by others, understood its limitations when applied to the issue of identity (Kirk and Thornton, 1974, p. 4):

> The study of physical evidence can be a material aid in locating the perpetrator of a crime. … Frequently it is possible to indicate a probable occupation, or to describe a habitat with remarkable accuracy from careful examination of some apparently trifling object found at the scene of the crime. Such facts do not necessarily constitute proof of guilt of any particular person, but they may give a background that is of the greatest value.

Well before this, Gross (1924, pp. 478–482) was of similar thought, and argued that an offender's characteristic method of operation should lead us by reason to investigate particular suspects, stopping short of the suggestion that the observance of characteristic offender methods could be used to individuate that offender without corroborating evidence.

There is furthermore a consensus in the literature that behavioral evidence and criminal profiling alone should not be used to individualize a particular person in relation to a particular crime or series of crimes (Burgess et al., 1992; Burgess and Hazelwood, 1995; Holmes and Holmes, 1996; Ingram, 1998). Criminal profiling methods may be used to suggest the type of person most likely to have committed the offense, but not to accuse a specific person. The reason for this limitation is that human behavior is complex and multi-determined. The oversimplification of the meaning behind complex human behaviors must be guarded against.

Reik (1945, pp. 44–45) offers criminal profilers and criminal investigators a useful caution with which to close our discussion:

> Middle-class society likes to represent the gulf between itself and the law-breakers as unbridgeable, and is frightened to find that even mass-murderers are made of the same stuff and behave in walks of life like the rest of us—your very neighbor might be a murderer. The complacency of conscious psychology and the superficiality of psychological observation in criminal investigation are nowhere clearer than in the treatment of the question whether a person is capable of a crime or not.

This refers to the fact that many investigators are continually amazed or blindsided by the actual guilt of those who had been eliminated from suspicion based on preconceptions of what a criminal should look like—despite powerful evidence that people from all backgrounds and walks of life are capable of all manner of criminal acts.

DEDUCING OFFENDER CHARACTERISTICS[5]

Deducing offender characteristics is about asking the right questions of offense-related behavior. First operationalize, or define, the characteristic (e.g., a sadistic offender motive). Second, establish what type of offense behavior provides evidence of that characteristic, and under which circumstances (e.g., evidence of offender sexual gratification from victim suffering). If the crime reconstruction includes those behaviors and circumstances, then the criminal profiler has a good argument for that characteristic.

Operationalizing offender characteristics is more than a simple academic exercise. It avoids ambiguity and informs those without knowledge of specific technical terms and concepts of their meaning. It sets forth how offender characteristics are manifested in offense-related behavior. It provides a means for discriminating between logical conclusions and those that are vague, potentially irrelevant, and unable to stand up to scrutiny. As discussed by McInerney (2004, p. 37),

> The most effective way to avoid vagueness or ambiguity in logical discourse is to define one's terms. We speak of defining terms, but actually what we are defining is the objects to which terms (words) refer. The process of definition, the mechanics of it, is the way we relate a particular object (the object to be defined) to other objects and thereby give it a precise "location". In defining a term or word, we relate it as rigorously as possible to the object to which it refers. There are two immediate practical benefits of carefully defining terms. Our own ideas are clarified, and, as a result, we can more effectively communicate them to others.

Consider the following crime scene behavior: During an anal sexual assault, the offender wraps a belt around the victim's neck and pulls her shirt up over her head, revealing her breasts. The offender is unconcerned with the victim's welfare and abuses her for whimpering. The offender completes the sodomy and leaves the victim with her shirt covering her face before leaving the crime scene.

Some profilers believe that when an offender displays a preference for anal sex and uses a belt as a ligature, it may mean the offender spent time in a prison environment. Additionally, crime data indicate that most crimes occur intra-racially (within the offender's own racial/ethnic group) and that offenders are typically the same age as the victim. Furthermore, in cases where the offender pulls the victim's shirt up over his or

---

[5] Portions of this section have been adapted from Petherick (2006).

her head, the profiler's experience may indicate that this is done to prevent the victim from identifying the offender. Lastly, most crimes occur within half a mile of the offender's residence (often referred to as the "half mile rule").

Because of these nomothetic beliefs, the profiler may infer that the offender has spent time in prison and may inform detectives how this may define the likely suspect pool. Furthermore, the profiler may infer that the offender is white (because the victim is white) and that the offender is the same general age as the victim. They may also advise that police should look for someone who lives in the area.

This is in fact how many profilers approach their casework. Simple yet weak generalizations dictate inferences made and the advice offered. The obvious problem with this type of profiling is that these generalizations stand a good chance of being wrong.

Approaching the case from a deductive and more scientific standpoint presents a number of hypotheses that can be measured against the evidence. At this point, we are not necessarily interested in developing a profile, but in presenting and testing our theories.[6] Once this has been thoroughly carried out, the process of inferring personality and behavioral characteristics can be attempted. Some initial hypotheses are:

■ The offender is male
■ The belt was used because of its availability to the offender
■ The belt was used because of personal preference
■ The offender found the belt near the scene
■ The offender pulled the shirt up over the victim's head to increase fear
■ The offender pulled the shirt up over the victim's head to prevent his identification
■ The offender pulled the shirt up to provide access to the victim's breasts
■ The offender pulled the shirt up to help him pretend the victim was somebody else

At this point, none of the competing hypotheses is necessarily any more correct than any other. They are hypotheses awaiting testing and they may or may not be borne out by further examination. Now let us consider them in turn:

■ The offender is a male: This has been established because the victim reports hearing a male's voice throughout the assault. Furthermore, the victim reports seeing a penis and physical examination yielded sperm in and around the victim's anus.
■ The belt was used because of its availability to the offender: There is nothing to suggest the origin of the belt. (It is possible that the offender brought the belt to the scene because of his preference for it.) Further discussion with the victim reveals that the offender was wearing tracksuit pants. This indicates the belt was not part of the offender's clothing; so another explanation must be sought. Further examination may indicate one of the following two theories may be correct.
■ The belt was brought along by the offender and used because of personal preference.
■ The offender found the belt near the scene.
■ The offender pulled the shirt up over the victim's head to increase fear: Finding another, more plausible reason may assist in determining whether this is the case. For example, did the offender call the victim by another name (suggesting it was to aid in fantasy), or did he play with the victim's breasts during the assault (suggesting the next explanation is most likely)?

---

[6] It should be noted however, and this can be seen in the examples that follow, that some conclusions follow directly from the collection of premises. Although it is a legal term used to assume culpability, the concept of *res ipsa loquitur* may apply here ("the thing speaks for itself").

- The offender pulled the shirt up to provide access to the victim's breasts (such as may be the case in foreplay).
- The offender pulled the shirt up over the victim's head to prevent his identification: A determination of when during the assault the shirt was pulled up would help to elucidate whether this was the reason. If it was done early in the offense, this reason becomes more likely, if it was done at the offense's conclusion, after the victim had already seen her attacker, this explanation becomes less plausible.
- The offender pulled the shirt up to help him pretend the victim was somebody else. This may be indicated by the offender's engaging in certain types of discussion with the victim, or by, for example, the offender's calling the victim by a name other than her own.

Once a complete examination of the facts has been undertaken and competing theories have been ruled out scientifically, then we can assert our conclusions by defining the characteristics and providing evidence supporting them. Employing the common structure of a deductive argument, referred to as *modus ponens*, is often most useful.[7] A *modus ponens* argument for the above example would be as follows:

- If (P) the victim had already seen the offender a number of times
- If (P) the victim could identify the offender after having seen him
- If (P) no other attempts had been made to obscure identification
- Then (Q) the victim's shirt was not pulled over her head for the purpose of preventing the offender's identification

In this example, if the premises (P) are true, then the conclusion (Q) must be true.

In *The Logic of Scientific Discovery*, Karl Popper (2003, p. 9) gives further explanation of testing theories and developing deductive conclusions:

> According to the view that will be put forward here, the method of critically testing theories, and selecting them according to the results of tests, always proceeds on the following lines. From a new idea, put up tentatively, and not yet justified in any way—an anticipation, a hypothesis, a theoretical system, or what you will—conclusions are drawn by means of logical deduction. These conclusions are then compared with one another and with other relevant statements, so as to find what logical relations (such as equivalence, derivability, compatibility, or incompatibility) exist between them.
>
> We may if we like distinguish four different lines along which the testing of theories could be carried out. First there is the logical comparison of the conclusions among themselves, by which the internal consistency of the system is tested. Secondly, there is the investigation of the logical form of the theory, with the object of determining whether it has the character of an empirical or scientific theory, or whether it is, for example, tautological.
>
> Thirdly, there is the comparison with other theories, chiefly with the aim of determining whether the theory would constitute a scientific advance should it survive our various other tests. And, finally, there is the testing of the theory by way of empirical applications of the conclusions which can be derived from it.

It should be apparent that the deductive process is very powerful in developing knowledge about a case. Not only does it help to point out what is fact and what is not, but also it highlights voids in current knowledge (to disprove one theory, we may need to seek out further information). Being able to establish, rather than

---

[7] A *modus ponens* argument follows the format *If P, then Q; P, therefore Q*. That is, if the premise (P) is true, it speaks to Q (the conclusion).

assume, what happened is a cornerstone of the overall process because, as Gross (1924) notes, nothing can be known if nothing has happened.

However, it's not really enough to define arbitrary characteristics and to look for evidence that they exist. The inference of offender characteristics should answer investigative or forensic questions and move the case forward rather than set it back. With respect to criminal investigation, characteristics that have proven to be investigatively relevant in the work of this author include the following.

Evidence of Criminal Skill

Offenders who have committed a particular crime more than once may become more skillful at its commission—they may get better and more proficient with time. Their skill may be thought of as a function of their *planning* and their *precautionary acts*.

Example

An offender enters a second-story apartment wearing gloves, a mask, and carrying a bag. He finds a sleeping female in her bedroom, wakes her, ties her up, and rapes her (he removes his gloves during the sexual attack and places them back on when he is through). He uses a condom that he brought with him. He leaves the victim tied up and quickly searches through her home. He ends up taking her jewelry, a handgun that was stored in the closet, and all of the cash in her purse.

First, in cases where burglary and sexual assault both occur, detectives from both the robbery unit and the sex crimes unit should be involved in the investigation. If the offense had involved a homicide, then a homicide detective should have also been asked to participate. Evidence of offender skill in the crime of rape includes precautionary acts specific to the nature of evidence transfer that commonly occurs. Two things that link a rapist directly to the crime are their physical description as given by a witness and the DNA from their ejaculate. This offender has skillfully prevented either from being a factor by wearing both a mask and a condom.

Evidence of skill in the crime of burglary includes precautionary acts specific to the nature of evidence transfer that commonly occurs. Two things that link a burglar directly to the crime are their physical description as given by a witness (actual or recorded via surveillance cameras) and their fingerprints left at the scene. This offender has skillfully prevented either from being a factor by wearing both a mask and gloves during the entry, search, and exit of the scene. If the offender had evidenced skill in the crime of burglary, but not in the crime of rape, this would also have provided the criminal profiler with useful information.

It is not uncommon for investigators to look only at murderers when investigating a murder, or only at rapists when investigating a rape. Evidence of particular criminal skill can be used to expand the suspect pool to criminals with a history of committing crime dissimilar to the one at hand. This kind of information assists with determining how to prioritize database searches of known criminal descriptions and MOs. It can also be used to suggest other type of MO influences that the offender may have been exposed to, such as:

- Educational and technical materials
- Trade or professional experience
- Contact with the criminal justice system
- The media
- Offender mood
- Various X-factors

Knowledge of the Victim

In the commission of the crime, an offender's choices may give us insight into the offender's relationship with the victim. Victim–offender relationships may be generally characterized in a number of ways, including, but not limited to,

- Stranger
- Relative
- Significant other
- Ex-significant other
- Lover
- Ex-lover
- Friend
- Ex-friend
- Acquaintance
- Employee
- Former employee
- Co-worker
- Former co-worker

The first question should be whether the offender is a stranger. That is to say, did the crime require special knowledge of, or access to, the victim's residence, place of work, schedule, habits, hobbies, beliefs, etc., to commit? If the answer is no, then strangers must be included in the suspect pool. If the answer is yes, then the question is what particular kind of knowledge about the victim was required, and who would have it? This begins to suggest the possible relationship between the victim and the offender.

Examples of circumstances that can support the conclusion that a prior relationship of some kind exists between the victim and the offender include crimes involving or requiring (these circumstances may also suggest extensive pre-surveillance, planning, and/or fantasy—context, context, context!):

- Use of the victim's name during the crime
- Absence of forced entry into a locked victim residence or secured work area
- Evidence of overkill in the attack upon the victim (more force than is necessary to subdue or eliminate the victim as a witness)
- Willingness of a victim to get into an offender's vehicle without a struggle

The context of these circumstances, and others, is informed by, and dependent upon, information developed in the victimology, specifically the *lifestyle exposure* and *situational exposure* of the victim.

Evidence that an offender required knowledge of the victim to effectively commit the crime can be used to expand the suspect pool to those with a relationship to the victim prior to its commission. This kind of information assists directly with suspect prioritization and development of investigative strategy.

Knowledge of the Crime Scene

In the commission of the crime, an offender's choices may give us insight into the offender's relationship with the crime scenes involved. This can include knowledge peculiar to certain geographic areas, neighborhoods, residences, buildings, and places of work. It includes, but is certainly not limited to, knowledge of:

- Security schedules
- Security devices

- Employee shift changes
- Location of valuables/safes/objects/apparatus
- Availability of materials at the scene
- Complex and/or unlighted travel routes used at night

For examples of how this is accomplished in actual casework, see the various online Appendices of this text at http://www.elsevierdirect.com/companion.jsp?ISBN=9780123741004.

It should further be understood that knowledge of a crime scene suggests knowledge of a victim if the crime scene is *strongly* associated with the victim (like the victim's residence, place of work, or vehicle).

Evidence that an offender required knowledge of the crime scene to effectively commit the crime can be used to expand the suspect pool to those with access to that scene. This kind of information assists directly with suspect prioritization and development of investigative strategy.

Example: Intimate Fetish Burglary

In a recent case, the author was asked to reconstruct and examine a residential burglary at the home of a single mother and her teenage daughter: the intrusion occurred while the daughter was home alone and taking a shower. The physical evidence, victimology, and crime scene characteristics made it clear that the intruder had been inside the home before. The following is an extract from the author's report in that case:

> The victim selection in this case is non-random. The intruder deliberately targeted this specific house and this particular victim. In order to complete this offense, the intruder needed to know which bedroom belonged [to the mother], that she had personal sexual items, and the precise [hidden] location of her sexual items. These could not have been randomly discovered [by a stranger] under the circumstances.
>
> The intruder also had to know that activity inside of the victim's bedroom could be suggested by the crack at the bottom her bedroom door. [Sealing the bottom of a bedroom door with clothing items] is a highly uncommon behavior for any intruder, and suggests the need to block smells, sights, or sounds. There was no evidence of foreign aromas in the home or room, and the walls are very thin. It is therefore reasonable to infer that the intruder was attempting to block the visibility of shadows moving about in the bedroom that would have been visible from the other side of the door, through the crack, once the black out curtain was opened. However, to know this was a necessary precaution to take, they would need foreknowledge of this vulnerability (experience being on the outside of that particular door while someone was inside moving around). In other words, this act demonstrates knowledge particular to the house.
>
> These elements combine to suggest planning and pre-surveillance inside of the home. However, it was not recent, as the child safety gate [immediately inside the point of entry] was unanticipated and subsequently knocked over.

Based on this and other behavioral evidence that demonstrated peculiar intimate knowledge of the victim and the scene, it was determined that the intruder in this case was likely a former intimate partner of the mother.

Knowledge of Methods and Materials

Criminals, like all people, use what is familiar to them. Consequently, their choice of methods and materials tends to reflect that familiarity, evidencing their skills and aptitudes, or lack thereof. This familiarity may be common to many, such as driving a stick-shift vehicle. Or it may be peculiar knowledge, such as the ability to fly a helicopter. Or it may be knowledge of investigative and forensic methods. Elicitation of these characteristics requires extensive examination of the offender's MO and signature behaviors. This kind of information also assists directly with suspect prioritization and development of investigative strategy.

This is not an exhaustive list of potential offender characteristics. They are merely the offender characteristics that have proven to be investigatively relevant in the work of this author. Keep in mind that many characteristics may not be apparent or inferable by virtue of the available evidence in a given offense. Also remember that one behavior is less meaningful outside of the context of other evident behaviors—less information about offender crime scene behavior, and choices, is not better. Individual offender behaviors can only be understood in the light of their relationship to others.

PROBLEM CHARACTERISTICS

There are three offender characteristics that routinely present a challenge to criminal profilers: offender age, sex, and intelligence. This author specifically recommends that the first two, age and sex, not be inferred without conclusive physical evidence. The third, intelligence, should be left out of an assessment altogether in favor of skill.

Age

If a profiler is going to be wrong, the offender's age is one of the most likely mistakes. Estimates regarding age have typically involved inferences based on witness accounts or behaviors that suggest mental illness. For example, if a criminal profiler had evidence of a behavior indicative of a psychotic state, the profiler might estimate the offender's age as being above 18 years (as it has been argued that this is the age after which psychosis tends to set in). Age estimates also tend to be based upon what a criminal profiler believes, from experience, is *likely* behavior for different age groups.

This author suggests, given the track record of inferring this particular offender characteristic, and given the increase of violent, aberrant crimes committed by increasingly younger offenders, that age should be left out of a criminal profile unless there is conclusive physical evidence.

Consider the following case, in which some American profilers voiced loud opinions that this particular offender was likely above the age of 30 and had visited the United States on at least one occasion. The offender turned out to be a 14-year-old boy.

Example (from Sugawara, 1997)

> [A] severed head was found in front of a junior high school in Kobe with a chilling note stuck in the 11-year-old male victim's mouth that declared "the beginning of the game . . . It's great fun for me to kill people. I desperately want to see people die." When police announced today that they had arrested a suspect in the murder, the horror that had gripped this relatively crime-free nation turned to relief—but then to horror again as it was revealed that the suspect is a 14-year-old boy. …

> Seishi Yamashita, chief investigator, said police questioned the boy and arrested him after he confessed to the crime. According to police, the boy said he beheaded the victim, Jun Hase, with a knife and a saw. Yamashita said police later searched the suspect's home and found the knife and other weapons. The boy told police he knew Hase.

Police declined to identify the suspect and said they were trying to determine the motive for the crime.

Hase's head was discovered May 27 by a school custodian in front of Tomogaoka Middle School in Kobe, a city of 1.5 million that is 300 miles west of Tokyo. His body was found later the same day in a forest near his elementary school. The beheading and the taunting note threatening more murders triggered a massive, four-week manhunt involving more than 500 investigators. …

A few days before Hase's head was found, two dead kittens turned up—one with severed limbs—near the same school. NHK television reported tonight that police tracked down the suspect after investigating the fate of the cats. Days after Hase's head was discovered, the killer sent a letter to the Kobe Shimbun newspaper. He blamed "the compulsory education system and the society that created that system that rendered me invisible, and I will exact revenge."

He said he might kill three people a week, and added, "If you assume I am a childish criminal able to kill only the young, you will be grossly mistaken."

Investigators originally thought the killer was between 20 and 40 years old, based on descriptions of suspicious persons in the area at the time of the slaying. Psychiatrists also concurred that it was probably someone in that age range, based on the writings. Hase's murder came two months after two schoolgirls were attacked in the area. Many residents feared the attacks were linked, although no proof has emerged. (Sugawara, 1997)

Sex

Like age estimates, opinions regarding the sex (male or female) of an offender also tend to be based upon what a criminal profiler believes, from experience, is *likely* behavior for different sexes. Females are often regarded, quite erroneously, as a weaker, less aggressive sex that is incapable of complex fantasy motivation. This is an outdated notion that can create investigative bias, resulting in the failure of authorities to investigate potential suspects because they have been eliminated on the basis of sex.

This author suggests, given the potential investigative misdirection such assumptions can cause, that opinions regarding offender sex also be left out of a criminal profile unless there is hard physical evidence (i.e., DNA evidence, evidence of a sexual penetration with a penis, or a competent witness/victim description).

Intelligence

Intelligence generally refers to a person's ability to acquire knowledge and to apply it effectively. However, it is a very vague and subjective term that has no actual investigative value. Most often, what the criminal profiler is concerned with is the offender's skill level. Very intelligent people may commit foolish or poorly planned offenses. Therefore, evidence of a low offender skill level suggests a lack of criminal experience and poor planning, not a lack of intelligence. Conversely, an offender of low intelligence may, by virtue of criminal experience, acquire a great deal of criminal skill. Therefore, evidence of a high criminal skill level is not a sure indication of a high level of offender intelligence.

This author strongly recommends that criminal profilers focus their efforts on the investigatively relevant offender characteristic of offender skill level and leave the subjective interpretation of offender intelligence to the forensic psychologists and psychiatrists (who are more qualified to make such estimations in the first place).

THE WRITTEN PROFILE

A criminal profile should be a written, court-worthy document. It should not be something that is done over drinks or on the telephone. There are several very important reasons for this.

First, a written criminal profile is less likely to be misrepresented. If the conclusions of an unwritten profile must go through several people before they reach those who can use the information, they may suffer brutal revisions. In any case, constructing a written profile is the only way that a criminal profiler can know that his or her conclusions are going to reach others, in context, without alteration or misrepresentation.

Second, those who need the information can more easily reference a written profile. It can be photocopied, faxed, scanned, e-mailed, and distributed with greater facility, which reduces the amount of time that it takes to convey the information. A written criminal profile provides for the investigative record of a case. In cases that are stalled for weeks, months, or years, for whatever reason, orally delivered profiles may be forgotten not only by those who requested the information, but by the criminal profilers themselves. Additionally, if an investigation changes hands or jurisdictions, a written profile can follow it.

Third, reducing one's reasoning to a written form is useful in establishing the logic involved in the process of forming particular conclusions. The clearer they are in the mind of the criminal profiler, the more easily they are written. During the process of clarifying arguments through writing, one's thinking may become more focused and more inclusive, or it may change entirely.

Fourth, a written criminal profile represents the methods and conclusions of a criminal profiler in a given case. This information can be used to validate the criminal profile at a later time. It can also assist the criminal profiler as a feedback mechanism for refining their technique in instances where the profile was in error, for whatever reason. A written criminal profile is subject to the scrutiny of peer review. Peer review is another mechanism for the criminal profiler to get feedback on the veracity of their profiling methods. In the absence of peer review, which independently seeks to validate or invalidate methods, techniques, and conclusions, a criminal profiler's particular method cannot be trusted by the community that it seeks to serve. Criminal profilers must be willing to submit their work to the scrutiny of their peers: written profiles may be independently peer reviewed as part of the adversarial process or full criminal profiles may be published, so that they receive criticism from the entire criminal profiling community. Peer review does not include written profiles that are submitted internally to private or law-enforcement groups only, or those that are submitted to groups with a vested interest in promoting their own competency. Peer review must be public, and it must be independent.

The unwillingness of a criminal profiler to write down his or her conclusions in a report suggests that the above issues are of no concern, or that they are of great concern.

CRIMINAL PROFILING AND *DAUBERT*

One way to assess the forensic value of criminal profiles in courts of law would be to apply the *Daubert* standard (Daubert v. Merrell Dow Pharmaceuticals, Inc., 1993). The first question is whether *Daubert* should even be applied to this particular forensic discipline. Since it is not a science in the traditional sense, it may legitimately be considered an area of specialized knowledge. Therefore, the opinions and testimony of criminal profilers, to be probative, may need only to be helpful when the subject matter would otherwise be incomprehensible to the trier of fact (Lilly, 1987; Thornton, 1994).

However, some legal commentators have made the argument that *Daubert* applies to all testimony, not just that which is labeled scientific (Jonakait, 1994; Saks, 1994). This argument has been upheld in the U.S. Supreme Court's ruling in Kumbo Tire Co. v. Carmichael (1999):

> The Daubert "gatekeeping" obligation applies not only to "scientific" testimony, but to all expert testimony. Rule 702 does not distinguish between "scientific" knowledge and "technical" or "other specialized" knowledge.

Consequently, even when it is accepted that criminal profiling testimony (opinions related to offender characteristics) will assist the trier of fact on a material issue, the following *Daubert* criteria may still need to be addressed: testability, peer review, error rates, and general acceptance. This author views the question of whether the application of *Daubert* criteria to criminal profiling is appropriate as solely the domain of the court. This is in no small part owing to the inconsistent case law and judicial rulings on the issue of admissibility standards for expert testimony across the United States and around the world.

In any case, *Daubert* (Daubert v. Merrell Dow Pharmaceuticals, Inc., 1993) does raise questions of sufficient interest that they require consideration.

TESTING AND FALSIFIABILITY

According to Thornton (1997), "The foundation of the scientific method, the most fundamental aspect, is the formulation and testing of hypotheses." He further stated (p. 13) that:

> Forensic scientists have, for the most part, treated induction and deduction rather casually. They have failed to recognize that induction, not deduction, is the counterpart of hypothesis testing and theory revision. They have tended to equate a hypothesis with a deduction, which it is not. As a consequence, too often a hypothesis is declared as a deductive conclusion, when in fact it is a statement awaiting verification through testing.

Practitioners of criminal profiling have behaved no differently. It is the experience of this author that many criminal profiles are built partially or wholly on surmises, hypotheses, or preconceived theories (see Gross, 1924, pp. 10–15 and Chapter 7 of this work) that are presumed to be infallible, with no attempts made to corroborate or falsify them. For example, FBI profilers have testified before the United States Senate Armed Service Committee that they do not make a habit of investigating the soundness of investigative assumptions, premises, or opinions in case materials provided by requesting agencies. According to FBI Special Agent Robert Hazelwood, "Whenever we are requested to do a case for an investigative agency, we make the assumption that we are dealing with professionals. They provide us with materials for review, and that's what we review" (The USS Iowa, 1990, pp. 25–26). FBI profilers have also been criticized by the court and independent peer reviewers for various unacceptable practices in casework and research (see Chapter 3).

What can be gathered from the criticism of nomo-inductive methodology is the following: unless there can be some qualification as to how inferences and theories regarding offender characteristics have been developed and tested against the case facts or alternate theories (through attempts to falsify), they should be treated with derision.

PEER REVIEW AND PUBLICATION

Given the untested nature and varying quality of much of the material published in the area of nomo-inductive criminal profiling, it cannot be said that peer review and publication have routinely played a significant role in determining whether the methodologies espoused in that material are valid and relevant.

The author has participated in the peer review process for the past decade, sometimes as an editor, sometimes as a reviewer, and sometimes as the one being reviewed. In that time, the author has uncovered numerous publications containing various errors, misrepresentations, and frauds. When directly confronted, the editorial staff at journals tend to ignore inquiries about what they've published, authors with phony credentials or fabricated data make indefensible denials, and professional organizations that support them simply bury their heads in the sand hoping it will all go away. Consequently, the author is of the view that peer review in the field of criminal profiling is not occurring to any great degree, nor can it in the current political environment.

This failure of peer review is not unique to the field of criminal profiling. Thornton (1994, p. 480) gives a well-keeled view when he states that, "it cannot be supposed that publication alone will suffice to prove the validity of a particular method." These concerns were expounded upon in McCook (2006), in response to the discrediting of stem cell research published by Woo-Suk Hwang at Seoul National University:

> Despite a lack of evidence that peer review works, most scientists (by nature a skeptical lot) appear to believe in peer review. It's something that's held "absolutely sacred" in a field where people rarely accept anything with "blind faith," says Richard Smith, former editor of the [*Annals of Internal Medicine, British Medical Journal*] and now CEO of United Health Europe and board member of the [*Public Library of Science*]. "It's very unscientific, really."
>
> Indeed, an abundance of data from a range of journals suggests peer review does little to improve papers. In one 1998 experiment designed to test what peer review uncovers, researchers intentionally introduced eight errors into a research paper. More than 200 reviewers identified an average of only two errors. That same year, a paper in the *Annals of Emergency Medicine* showed that reviewers couldn't spot two-thirds of the major errors in a fake manuscript. In July 2005, an article in *JAMA* showed that among recent clinical research articles published in major journals, 16% of the reports showing an intervention was effective were contradicted by later findings, suggesting reviewers may have missed major flaws.
>
> Some critics argue that peer review is inherently biased, because reviewers favor studies with statistically significant results. Research also suggests that statistical results published in many top journals aren't even correct, again highlighting what reviewers often miss. "There's a lot of evidence to (peer review's) downside," says Smith. "Even the very best journals have published rubbish they wish they'd never published at all. Peer review doesn't stop that." Moreover, peer review can also err in the other direction, passing on promising work: Some of the most highly cited papers were rejected by the first journals to see them.
>
> The literature is also full of reports highlighting reviewers' potential limitations and biases. An abstract presented at the 2005 Peer Review Congress, held in Chicago in September, suggested that reviewers were less likely to reject a paper if it cited their work, although the trend was not statistically significant. Another paper at the same meeting showed that many journals lack policies on reviewer conflicts of interest; less than half of 91 biomedical journals say they have a policy at all, and only three percent say they publish conflict disclosures from peer reviewers. Still another study demonstrated that only 37% of reviewers agreed on the manuscripts that should be published. Peer review is a "lottery to some extent," says Smith.

In other words, peer review is one of the areas where scientists behave unscientifically. Scientists sabotage each other, they make up data, misrepresent findings, and reviewers are not always competent to the task of ferreting any of this out. Peer review, far from being a silver bullet, is not a bullet at all. It can actually provide the bias and ineptitude that it is meant to correct.

There is only one true method to gauge the quality and competency of published work, and that is through an evaluation of the extent to which the scientific method has been employed. When ideographic or nomothetic studies are conducted and subsequently published, the scientific method must be readily apparent in both methods and interpretations. Moreover, any opinions, hypotheses, and theories should be sufficiently qualified as such. In this way, the inappropriate presentation of a theory or hypothesis as scientific fact may be avoided.

Ultimately, that something has been published is not by itself a guarantee of quality work.

ERROR RATES

To the uninitiated, it may sound like a straightforward and reasonable expectation that all methods of forensic identification should be tested and their error rates known to determine their reliability. However, according to Saks (1994, p. 429),

> Identification science consists largely of speculation, impression, and intuition. It is a field of assertedly scientific endeavor that, ironically, cannot offer sufficient research data in its own behalf simply because its basic theoretical notions have been subjected to virtually no empirical testing.

Saks (1994, p. 432) further explains:

> Forensic identification scientists, no doubt due in large part to their instructional role and function, tend to claim a most unscientific sort of infallibility, and have a history of exaggerating their wares. Within such a culture, ironically for one that calls itself a science, empirical research is viewed as a threat rather than a help or a defining part of its essence.

Thornton (1994, pp. 480–483) concurs:

> As a practicing forensic scientist, I consider this criterion to be the weakest of all those enunciated in *Daubert*.

> The problem is that we simply do not have good statistics on the rate of error of most tests conducted in operational crime laboratories, and it is doubtful that we can develop them. In most instances, we do not even have bad statistics. If anyone is skeptical, let them call up the FBI laboratory or any other major forensic laboratory and ask them how many times they have been right, and how many times they have been wrong.

In that the error rates of even hard forensic sciences are unknown, it seems inappropriate to hold an area of specialized knowledge such as criminal profiling to a higher standard than is currently being met by criminalists in crime labs.

Having said that, it must be admitted the error rates for criminal profiles are also unknown. As stated by Homant and Kennedy (1998, pp. 323–324),

> As far as we can determine, no one has attempted to assess the validity of crime scene profiling in real life situations. Such a study would present some unique problems. The main problem is the lack of objective criterion against which to test a sample of actual profiles. … Even when the identity of the offender is unambiguously determined, there is still a large subjective element in deciding how well the person fits the profile.

This author agrees with the concerns expressed in this passage. Though a uniform standard has been developed by which the internal consistency of profiles may be gauged in the form of recently published *Criminal Profiling Guidelines* (Baeza et al., 2000), these guidelines have only been adopted by the membership for which they were developed. Furthermore, there is the very real issue of subjectivity in the interpretation of whether or not an individual fits the soft characteristics that may be present in a criminal profile.

Further complicating issues are stated by Ingram (1998, p. 264):

> A profiler's determination, by nature, can be tested and proven accurate only if a person is caught and later confesses.

Just as a conviction is not factual evidence of guilt (confession or not), an acquittal is not factual evidence of innocence. Judges and juries acting on behalf of U.S. courts routinely convict the innocent and acquit the guilty. As such it is frequently impossible to make a reliable, unambiguous determination as to the precise identity of the offender in a given case. Without this information, reliability studies as to the accuracy of criminal profiling, and other methods of forensic identification, cannot be entirely meaningful.[8]

GENERAL ACCEPTANCE

It may be said without significant debate that criminal profiles are generally accepted as legitimate investigative tools by law enforcement and other investigative communities. This investigative acceptance, however, is not necessarily related to the validity of criminal profiles. This is not, after all, a professional community that necessarily rewards reliability and punishes incompetence. Consider that many criminal investigators also generally accept the investigative use of imprecise and unreliable investigative tools such as eyewitness identification, polygraphy, voice stress analysis and psychic intuition (see the Preface of the third edition of this book). Consider also that this acceptance may have something to do with the tendency of criminal profilers in major investigative agencies to overstate the confidence and certainty of their conclusions to less knowledgeable investigators who may be overwhelmed or seduced by an authoritative sounding federal acronym.

RECOMMENDATIONS

Criminal profiling and related techniques were developed as tools to be used in the investigative process to assist in the identification of *suspects*. There are also a number of useful forensic ends that they can serve which are not necessarily related to establishing offender identity, including focusing the suspect pool, explaining behavioral evidence, case linkage, and assistance in the development of investigative strategies.

There is something further to be said for the potential use of criminal profiles as an ingredient to assist in educating the trier of fact as to the general type of offender that may be responsible for a particular crime. Criminal profiles may be a reasonable aid to the trier of fact, given two very important caveats. First, the court must understand, and be explicit in its instructions to the jury about, the limits of behavioral evidence as described in this work. Second, criminal profilers must not disregard these limits and intrude on the issue of guilt by giving opinions about whether the accused fits a particular profile.[9] Criminal profilers should furthermore clearly articulate their opinions regarding the case, and lay out the characteristics that they have

---

[8] Thornton (1994) is refreshingly blunt on this issue, stating on p. 481, "Who is the final arbiter of correctness and error? The jury? No one that I know thinks that a conviction rate is a test for correctness for a prosecution witness, or an acquittal rate a test for correctness for a defense witness." In truth, this author has encountered many experts who hold these fallacies dear, except when their own testimony fails to find purchase with the judge or jury.

[9] The indulgence in such testimony by an expert, in this author's view, would need to be tempered with an explanation as to the limitations of criminal profiling, i.e., that it is not individuating and not suggestive of guilt or innocence. Ideally, this should come from the expert, as the court will not necessarily understand this to be so. Additionally, if the prosecution offers such testimony, the defense must be afforded the opportunity to retain similarly qualified experts.

inferred and the manner in which they inferred them. The jury should then be allowed the opportunity to consider the behavioral evidence in concert with the physical evidence, without a criminal profiler telling them how they should decide. Failure to fully engage these precautions invites jurors to "convict the accused based on character rather than convicting the accused because the force of the evidence convinces them that the accused is guilty of the conduct charged," as warned against by Imwinkelried and Mendez (1992).

This reasonable aid to the trier of fact would not be unlike a forensic scientist who testifies that a hair found in a suspect's vehicle is consistent with the head hair of a victim. Or that a black cotton fiber found on a victim's body is consistent with similar fibers from a suspect's shirt. These are items of class evidence that by their nature cannot provide the certainty of conclusive individuating tests or measures. Such testimony, it may be argued, has the same reliability and limitations as criminal profiling evidence. Similarly, it can take on greater meaning when combined with other circumstantial evidence. The difference being, of course, that a criminal profile may not always have the same exclusionary properties as hard physical evidence, depending upon the evidentiary basis for the offender characteristics.[10]

Though criminal profiling is not a science, it can be scientific with respect to its approach, and it may still be subject to *Daubert* criteria. Whether this is an appropriate standard by which to measure criminal profiling is a matter for individual courts to decide. A good argument may be made, however, that the overall utility of *Daubert* is lacking apart from the criteria that relates to hypothesis testing and falsification.

Criminal profiling is most certainly not reliable nor designed for individuating a specific offender who is or is not responsible for a specific crime. As already discussed, this position has the appearance of a consensus in the published literature and in some recent U.S. court decisions.[11] As a practicing forensic scientist and criminal profiler, the author must concur with this view. Until such time as more reliable research is published, and peer review and critical thinking are embraced by the practicing community as assets rather than shunned as liabilities, criminal profilers risk being treated with derision by the courts when they employ their craft in this manner.

CRIMINAL PROFILING IN COURT

When the liberty of an individual may depend in part on physical evidence, it is not unreasonable to ask that the expert witnesses who are called upon to testify, either against the defendant or in his behalf, know what they are doing.

—Dr. John Thornton in *Kirk's Crime Investigation* (1974)

---

[10] This author has prepared criminal profiles that include traits such as offender sex and offender race. However, this has been done only when supported by the physical evidence. In one case, race was given as Caucasian when a red pubic hair was found on the victim's body that could only be attributed to an offender. In other cases, sex was determined by virtue of the deposition of semen during an attack, or by virtue of a witness who provided a conclusive anatomical description of the attacker.

[11] There are experts who disagree with this and have testified as such. However, the certainty of their conclusions has been based on experience rather than published research or defensible scientific fact, as in New Jersey v. Steven Fortin (1999), and ultimately inadmissible. On that reliability issue, it is curious that in New Jersey v. Steven Fortin, the criminal profiler offered both his memoir and the fantasy/ritual chapter from Burgess and Hazelwood (1995) as proof that linkage analysis is as conclusive (individuating) as fingerprints or DNA. I find that position curious because another of the chapters from the same book (Depue et al., 1995) states, "It should be made clear that the profile is not intended to identify a particular person, but rather a personality type. Consequently, a profile may describe more than one person." In this author's view, this is the kind of inconsistency that is worth the court's time.

This section discusses the pros and cons of using criminal profiling (the inference of offender characteristics) as evidence in court. The discussion includes a review of cases involving criminal profiling testimony and subsequent court rulings. Nomo-inductive and ideo-deductive processes are identified, and the relevant issues in each case are discussed.

As the above implies, a secondary purpose of this section is to elucidate just how different deductive criminal profiling is from the inductive profiling techniques associated with psychological syndrome evidence.

Criminal Profilers in Court

Perhaps unsatisfied with the limited venue of criminal investigations, and perhaps also because of their involvement in it, criminal profilers have begun a new tradition in the new millennium—courtroom testimony. As discussed in Turvey (2000),

> Despite the investigative use intended for criminal profiling, it is becoming more common for criminal profilers to find themselves asked to give expert forensic opinions on criminal and civil matters in courts of law. Criminal profiling testimony has been sought relating to areas of specialized knowledge (i.e., victimology, offense planning, modus operandi, motive, foreseeability, etc.), as well as issues relating to offender identity. These identity issues encompass such things as likely offender characteristics and determinations relating to alleged *unique* behavioral patterns, common scheme or plan, and other behavioral characteristics of crimes that may be linked back to specific individuals. In some cases, under a variety of circumstances, the court has allowed criminal profiling testimony relating to offender identity into evidence.

This newer role for the criminal profiler is that of courtroom expert, and consequently that of forensic examiner.

A forensic examination differs from other forms of examination in that it is done, ultimately, for courtroom purposes. That is to say, opinions and conclusions formed during a forensic examination are distinguished by the possibility that they may become testimony or evidence in a court of law for use by the trier of fact. As such, the results of such examinations may deprive someone of their freedom (by sending them to prison), or their life (by assisting with the invocation of the death penalty).

Forensic examiners, therefore, have a great responsibility to the competency and thoroughness of their opinions and conclusions, and the standards for reaching them must be high.

The Problems

There are two related problems that complicate the use of criminal profiling during trial. The first is ignorance about the nature of criminal profiling and crime reconstruction. The second is the zeal (lack of restraint) with which many criminal profilers give opinions.[12] When these two problems intersect in a single case, it may be that a criminal profiler gives opinions with strong certainty regarding circumstances and behaviors that are assumed and not established.

---

[12] Though it comforts us to believe that no forensic scientist/examiner would engage in opining beyond the evidence, misrepresenting evidence, or outright lying to the court, recent examples of chronic misconduct by various forensic scientists around the world remind us that it is not beyond the realm of possibility. For original published research on the subject, see Turvey (2003).

Misperceptions

As detailed in this text, physical evidence and its interpretation are at the core of behavioral evidence analysis and criminal profiling. However, not every criminal profiler is qualified to reconstruct the physical evidence. Unfortunately, out of ignorance or arrogance, many incorrectly believe that they are.

Lack of Restraint

When criminal profilers examine materials in the trial phase of a case, they are forensic examiners whether they care to be or not. That is to say, their opinions may wind up in court, informing the judge or jury. However, forensic examiners often experience a degree of separation from the actual events in a crime scene. Crime reconstruction helps bridge that gap, but it can only provide as much information as was left behind and subsequently reconstructed. In an ideal forensic scenario, the following levels of separation still exist:

1. An offender leaves evidence of the crime behind at the crime scene (with or without attempts to conceal it)
2. A crime scene technician recognizes, documents, and collects some of that evidence (although either a great deal, or very little, may be missed)
3. A criminalist in a crime lab examines and tests some of that evidence collected by the technician and writes a report with opinions and conclusions (the criminalist may test only for specific things or for a great deal)

This rendering does not include evidence that is unrecognized at the scene, untestable, lost, accidentally thrown away, forgotten, or destroyed in testing. Thus, even in a perfect scenario, there are already at least three levels of separation between what actually occurred in the crime scene and what the evidence can reliably establish.

The point is that forensic reconstruction of events attempted by forensic examiners is only as informed as the evidence they have to work with. They cannot afford to assume facts that have not been established. Given the described levels of separation, there is a need for conservatism and qualification when forming opinions and conclusions about what happened.

Unfortunately, many forensic examiners proceed to reconstruct crimes in certain detail, almost as though they were there with a video camera recording the whole event. This is an irresponsible practice that can often be corrected by merely toning down the certainty of one's opinions. Forensic examiners are admonished to conclude and opine only on the evidence that they have before them, and not to overstate the certainty of their opinions regarding that evidence.

Consider the testimony and rulings in the following cases from the past 10 years.[13]

Virginia v. Shermaine Ali Johnson (1998)

Sixteen-year-old Shermaine Ali Johnson was tried as an adult, convicted, and sentenced to death for the murder of Hope Denise Hall on July 24, 1998.

---

[13] These are, or course, not the only cases on the record. They are, however, representative, and have been selected for their instructive value. Other cases covering similar but more specialized issues and testimony are discussed in other chapters.

Background

Hope Denise Hall was a 22-year-old mother and a part-time associate producer for WWBT-Channel 12. Her nude body was found on July 11, 1994, in her locked Halcun Manor apartment. She had suffered 15 stab wounds and a slit throat. She lived in the apartment with her 3-year-old son.

Police at Southampton Correctional Center, in January 1997, arrested Mr. Johnson for the rape and murder of Ms. Hall after a computer database search matched his DNA to blood and semen found in her apartment. His DNA matched blood found on a knife, broken glass, and semen found on a sheet in Ms. Hall's apartment. His semen was also found in her body (Blackwell, 1998).

At the time of his arrest, 16-year-old Mr. Johnson was already serving a 100-year sentence for the rape of two other women.

Expert and Opinion

The expert used by the prosecution in this case was FBI profiler Mark Safarik. Mr. Safarik holds a B.S. degree in human physiology, and had three years experience as a police detective prior to working for the FBI. According to his professional C.V., he had not testified in the area of criminal profiling prior to his involvement in this case.

The prosecution brought Mr. Safarik in to provide expert testimony that Mr. Johnson fit the profile of a serial rapist. Mr. Safarik stated in a hearing before the judge that (Blackwell, 1998):

> [H]e compared behavioral evidence in the Hall case to evidence from two rapes Johnson has been convicted of and found numerous similarities. He concluded there is a link between the sexual assaults and the murder.

According to the prosecutor's closing statement, there were many similarities between the two rapes and the rape-homicide, including (Blackwell, 1998):

> [T]he raping of the women and the consistent use of a steak knife in the attacks. The attacker, with whom the victims were acquainted, also asked for a glass of water, attacked the women from behind and demanded they remove their clothes before he raped them.

Issue

In the hearing regarding the admissibility of Mr. Safarik's testimony, the defense argued there was no evidence to support his opinion, and that it was an unfounded speculation (Blackwell, 1998).

Court Ruling

The trial court judge agreed with the defense. Mr. Safarik's expert testimony was not allowed on the grounds that the jury was capable of drawing its own conclusions about similarities in the cases. That is to say, the court decided that his opinions invaded the province of the jury.

Discussion

The author has mixed feelings regarding the findings of the trial court in this case. While the author has enthusiasm for keeping out the testimony of the expert in this case, and his opinion that Mr. Johnson fit the profile of a rapist, the ruling may have been too inclusive. It must be agreed that certain areas of expertise are beyond the ken of the general public. This should include modus operandi analyses, which appear to be at least in part at issue in this case. As such, this kind of testimony may be helpful in understanding the nature of the behavioral linkage between two or more crimes.

On a final note, the attempted use of a criminal profiler in this case seems odd, given that the physical evidence was so overwhelming. One gets the feeling that the prosecution may have been trying to get such testimony on the record in this case in order to establish a precedent for admission in future cases.

Tennessee v. William R. Stevens (2001)

William R. Stevens was convicted of two counts of first-degree premeditated murder and one count of especially aggravated robbery, in relation to the deaths of his wife, Sandi Stevens, and his mother-in-law, Myrtle Wilson.

Background

Mr. Stevens and his wife, Sandi, had been married approximately 3 years. Ms. Wilson had been living with them for approximately 6 months prior to the killings. Sandi Stevens and Myrtle Wilson were found dead in their home, each in her respective bedroom, on December 22, 1997. According to Tennessee v. William R. Stevens (2001):

> Sandi Stevens was found lying on her bed nude, with pornographic magazines around her head and a photo album containing nude photographs of her on the bed. Myrtle Wilson was also found lying on her bed; her nightgown had been pulled up and her underwear was on the floor. The medical examiner determined that Myrtle Wilson died from stab wounds and manual strangulation, and Sandi Stevens died from ligature strangulation. Several items of Sandi Stevens' were taken from the trailer, giving rise to the robbery charge. The Defendant's convictions for these crimes were based on the theory of criminal responsibility for the actions of another. The State's proof at trial established that the Defendant hired his eighteen-year-old neighbor and employee, Corey Milliken, to kill his wife and mother-in-law and to make it look like a robbery.

Mr. Stevens denied involvement in the crime. He suggested that Corey Milliken fabricated a "murder for hire fantasy" and that he killed Sandi Stevens and Myrtle Wilson in the perpetration of a sexual assault (Tennessee v. William R. Stevens, 2001).

Expert and Opinion

The expert used by the defense in this case was Gregg McCrary, formerly of the FBI's Behavioral Science Unit. This was only the second time that Mr. McCrary had testified for the defense. He holds an undergraduate degree in music, and a master's degree in professional psychology. In qualifying Mr. McCrary as an expert, he discussed his opinions about the disorganized nature of the crime (Tennessee v. William R. Stevens, 2001):

> During a jury-out offer of proof, Mr. McCrary testified that he was asked by the defense to conduct a crime scene analysis in which he would examine the evidence at the crime scene in order to determine the likely motive for the crime. He said that he specifically requested that he not be given any information regarding the suspect and that he was not engaging in criminal profiling, which is trying to determine the profile of an unknown suspect. Mr. McCrary described this crime scene as a "disorganized sexual homicide." He determined that Sandi Stevens was the primary target and was the focus of a sexual assault. He thought that Myrtle Wilson was simply a victim of opportunity who was in the wrong place at the wrong time. Mr. McCrary explained that in a disorganized homicide the victim and location are known to the offender, and there is minimal interpersonal contact between the victim and offender. He stated that usually a "blitz attack" or sudden violence is used. The crime scene is sloppy and in disarray. There is minimal use of restraints. Sexual acts

tend to occur after death, and there is post-mortem injury to the victim and indications of post-mortem sexual activity. He stated that the body is left at the scene, typically in view, and a great deal of physical evidence is left at the scene. The murder weapon is usually a weapon of opportunity obtained at the scene. There is generally a precipitating stressor that triggers the violent event in a disorganized homicide, and the crime usually involves transferred aggression from the person or persons who precipitate the stressing event to the victim.

Mr. McCrary contrasted a disorganized crime scene to an organized crime scene, such as the typical "contract killing," which usually involves a victim and offender who are strangers. There is some interpersonal contact prior to the crime, such as a con or ruse to lure a victim out. In an organized crime scene, the scene reflects an overall sense of control; restraints are often seen; there are aggressive acts prior to the death; the body is usually hidden, though sometimes it is left propped up or displayed for shock value; the murder weapon is a weapon of choice brought to the scene and taken away after the crime; offenders are more "evidence conscious," and there is usually transportation of the body.

In qualifying Mr. McCrary as an expert, he also discussed his opinions about the error rates of his analysis, and similar analysis by FBI profilers. He essentially testified that the true error rate is unknown, but that the proof of its accuracy is evident because of the widespread request for profiling services (Tennessee v. William R. Stevens, 2001):

> Mr. McCrary was asked whether a potential accuracy rate had been established, and he reported that the FBI had conducted one survey and determined that its agents were seventy-five to eighty percent accurate on crime scene analysis and profiling. He explained that this type of analysis is "not a hard science where you can do controlled experiments and come up with ratios in all this," but the increased demand for such services exemplifies its effectiveness. Mr. McCrary testified that there were seven agents in the FBI unit when he first entered the unit, there were twelve agents when he left the unit, and there are currently about forty agents in the unit. He said, "the proof ... [that] there is validation and reliability in the process is that it's being accepted. Uh—it's being used and the demand is just outstripping our resources to provide it."

After hearing Mr. McCrary's testimony in this area, the trial court disallowed it. It found that it dealt with the "behavior aspect of an offender and not the crime scene." That is to say, he was testifying about likely offender behaviors (crime reconstruction based on his experience rather than based on the physical evidence at the crime scene). The trial court further determined that his testimony in this area would not assist the trier of fact "because there is no trustworthiness or reliability" (Tennessee v. William R. Stevens, 2001). Ultimately, he was allowed only to testify generally about the crime scene, the staging, the possibility that there were two offenders, and the things that should have been done by the police. He was not permitted to testify as to what he believed to be the motive.

Mr. McCrary was qualified as an expert on the subject of criminal investigative analysis, a.k.a. criminal profiling (Tennessee v. William R. Stevens, 2001).[14] According to Tennessee v. William R. Stevens (2001),

---

[14] As previously discussed in this text, Depue et al. (1995, p. 115) state explicitly that the term *criminal investigative analysis* is merely an FBI replacement term for the term *criminal profile*:

> A criminal investigative analysis (CIA) of an illegal and violent act may give the client agency a variety of useful information depending on the service requested. Previously termed 'psychological profiling' and 'criminal personality profiling,' the term 'criminal investigative analysis' was coined to differentiate the procedure from that used by mental health professionals.

This would be an important distinction, as FBI profilers had found criminal profiling and psychological profiling generally inadmissible when they attempted to bring their testimony into court. The name change, then, was done to facilitate courtroom acceptance and get profiling in under another guise.

Mr. McCrary testified that he was asked by the defense to conduct a criminal investigative analysis of the crime scene in this case, which involves analyzing the crime scene, studying the victims to determine what might have elevated their risk for becoming victims, looking at underlying forensic reports, and looking at how the crime was committed. For this case, he was given photographs and a videotape of the crime scene, as well as the medical examiner's report. He testified that the crime scene was sloppy and in disarray. The crime scene showed a lack of control. There was a general trashing of the crime scene—clothes were thrown down, purses and pills were dumped, things were scattered, the Christmas tree was knocked over—all of which was unnecessary to commit the murders.

Mr. McCrary said that a "sex crime" is a crime of violence in which sex is used as a weapon or tool to punish, degrade, and humiliate the victim. He explained that "staging" is the purposeful alteration of a crime scene by the offender done to refocus the investigation away from the offender. During staging, an offender attempts to hide the true motive and reality of the crime by attempting to make the crime scene look like one type of crime when, in fact, it is another. He also said that "transfer blood" is a stain or impression of blood that occurs when an offender with blood on him or her touches another object. It can be important because patterns may be evident in the blood transfer, which can be linked to specific garments or items. Mr. McCrary testified that fingerprints, footprints, and hair samples can be important evidence at a crime scene. In addition, Mr. McCrary stated that it was important to corroborate a confession with evidence from the crime scene.

Mr. McCrary testified that based on the crime scene, it is possible that there could have been more than one offender. First, different weapons were used to kill the victims: Ms. Wilson was stabbed, and Ms. Stevens suffered ligature strangulation. Second, there was not a lot of transfer blood in Ms. Stevens' room where you would expect it to be, such as on the pill bottles or the pornographic magazines that were on the bed. The items had to have been touched and placed on the bed by an offender, but they were totally free of blood transfers. In addition, the "staging" of the crime scene seemed to have been accomplished without transferring any blood to the items that were thrown about the trailer. Mr. McCrary testified that there was a feeble attempt at "staging" to make the scene look like a burglary. He said that burglars do not necessarily throw clothes and other items around.

Mr. McCrary was asked by defense counsel whether pornographic magazines "play into a sex crime." He responded that keeping in mind the motive of a sex crime is to punish, degrade, and humiliate the victim, "the displaying of the pornographic literature around . . . this victim—uh—in my opinion, [may] best be interpreted as an attempt to further humiliate or degrade . . . this victim. And, it goes to the—goes to the motive of a sex crime."

Issue

The defense argued that the trial court erred in limiting Mr. McCrary's testimony. They assert that the trial court applied an incorrect legal standard and an unreasonable interpretation of Gregg McCrary's proffered testimony in finding the evidence inadmissible. They argued that Mr. McCrary was prepared to testify about characteristics of a crime scene and what those characteristics indicate, which is beyond the common understanding of the jury. They concluded that this ruling to limit Mr. McCrary's testimony had prevented them from putting on their defense (Tennessee v. William R. Stevens, 2001).

Court Ruling

The Tennessee Court of Appeals agreed that the trial court properly limited Mr. McCrary's testimony as unreliable. They also clearly identified the part of his testimony that they ultimately disallowed as criminal profiling (Tennessee v. William R. Stevens, 2001):

McCrary conceded that, to his knowledge, no court in the United States has ever admitted expert testimony which relied upon criminal profiling. Typically, a criminal profile is developed at the request of authorities who seek information regarding the race, sex, employment status, etc., of an unknown perpetrator. Although this type of sophisticated speculation is undoubtedly very helpful to criminal investigators, it is not sufficiently reliable to provide the basis for an expert opinion in a criminal trial. Likewise, although not technically considered "profiling," McCrary's attempt to analyze the "behavior of the offender based on all the forensic evidence" does not pass muster. Despite agreeing that human behavior is very complex and that there can be multiple motives for a homicide, McCrary intended to express an expert opinion that the killer in this case had not been hired to commit the murders but, instead, had committed a sexually motivated crime triggered by an upsetting event.

This Court does not doubt McCrary's assertion that his opinion is based upon years of research and experience. For that reason, the Court agrees that the opinion is not based entirely on speculation. However, the Court is not convinced that this type of analysis has been subjected to adequate objective testing, or that it is based upon longstanding, reliable, scientific principles.

The Tennessee Court of Appeals felt strongly that Mr. McCrary was attempting to do more than merely explain the characteristics of a crime scene. He was going to testify that he could determine the specific motive of the perpetrator by comparing the crime scene at issue to "typical" crime scenes in which the motivation is a sexual assault brought about by a precipitating stressor. He was trying to argue that a crime did or did not occur as described by the defense based on the manner in which a person behaved (Tennessee v. William R. Stevens, 2001).

To be admissible in Tennessee, expert testimony must *substantially* assist the trier of fact. The Tennessee Court of Appeals concluded that the trial court did not abuse its discretion by determining that the proposed expert testimony was not reliable enough to substantially assist the trier of fact, for the following reasons:

- Similar case precedent, limiting such testimony
- The 75% to 80% accuracy rate[15]
- The "special aura" of expert testimony[16]

Discussion

The author agrees with the decision in this case. The trial court rightly identified much of the opinion testimony proffered by Mr. McCrary as an unreliable form of inductive criminal profiling and kept it out. As already mentioned, if the Oklahoma Court of Appeals had been asked to address these same issues that were raised in Oklahoma v. Jimmy Ray Slaughter (1997), perhaps Mr. Hazelwood's testimony in that case would have been disallowed entirely. As with that case, there's nothing terribly wrong with discussing generalities when dealing with inductive profiles. But the science/research behind them should be examined thoroughly, and the expert should not try to match things up with absolute certainty for the jury.

---

[15] There is no forensic discipline that this author is aware of that would consider 70%, 80%, or even 95% an acceptable accuracy rate. Not in a court of law where expert testimony may cause the defendant to lose life or liberty. Bragging about such an error rate would seem problematic to say the least.

[16] The belief is that expert scientific testimony may be very prejudicial, or confuse the issues, or mislead the jury, because of its aura of special reliability and trustworthiness. The concern is that a jury may abandon its responsibility as fact finder and adopt the judgment of the expert. Hence, expert testimony needs to be admitted carefully.

United States v. Gordon E. Thomas III (2006)

Gordon E. Thomas was charged with sexual exploitation of children; possession of material shipped and transported in interstate and foreign commerce depicting minors engaged in sexually explicit conduct; and attempted receipt of images depicting minors engaged in sexually explicit conduct. The prosecution moved for pretrial detention for the safety of the community, and the defense objected. On April 28, 2003, the court ruled against pretrial detention in favor of conditional release, and the prosecution appealed. The original decision was upheld, but additional conditions were added to Mr. Thomas' release.

Ultimately, this 2006 opinion sets an important standard for evaluating expert testimony from FBI criminal profilers about future dangerousness.

Background

Taken entirely from United States v. Gordon E. Thomas III (2006):

> The charges against the defendant were the result of an investigation in which federal agents assumed the computer identity of a person overseas who had been advertising pornographic videos depicting children on the internet. Following the internet advertiser's arrest, agents continued to correspond with that person's customers, including Mr. Thomas. The government contends that the defendant, in response to one of these internet advertisements, paid $200 in exchange for child pornography videos. Following this transaction, the Postal Inspection Service executed a "controlled delivery" of child pornography to the defendant's home. A search warrant was executed at the defendant's home on January 3, 2003 during which a computer, video camera, CD-ROMs, floppy disks, and a number of videotapes were seized. Subsequent analysis of these items revealed that they contained approximately 16,000 images of child pornography. These images are the basis for the two charges that have been brought against the defendant regarding the receipt and possession of child pornography.
>
> In addition to the images just described, one of the videotapes seized from the defendant's home depicted an adult hand exposing the genitalia of a young girl who appeared to be asleep. The government states that this scene was created and produced by Mr. Thomas, while he was babysitting a friend's nine-year-old daughter. Mr. Thomas signed a written statement acknowledging that he had been advised of his rights, stating that he produced the scene and the video, but claiming that it was a onetime occurrence and that he never touched either the girl depicted in the video or any other child. This image, and the conduct associated with its creation, is the basis for the charge that has been brought against the defendant regarding the sexual exploitation of a child.
>
> Among the seized videotapes, there is also non-pornographic footage of young girls talking in a stairwell and otherwise present on the grounds of an apartment complex. The camera, however, zooms in on their crotch areas, and these portions of the video were allegedly taped surreptitiously through the peephole of an apartment door and from an apartment balcony. The government thus characterizes these portions of the videotapes as both "child erotica" and "surveillance" video, claiming that this is further evidence of the defendant's dangerousness to young girls in the community.

Expert and Opinion

The state relied in part on the testimony of SSA James Clemente from the Behavioral Analysis Unit (formerly the profiling unit). He testified as to how the defendant fit the characteristics of a preferential sex offender, specifically with regard to his future level of dangerousness for re-offending. As detailed in United States v. Gordon E. Thomas III (2006, with the original footnotes appended here in square brackets and italic type):

> The government presented the testimony of James Clemente. Mr. Clemente is a supervisory special agent ("SSA") with the Federal Bureau of Investigation's National Center for the Analysis of Violent Crimes ("NCAVC"), Behavioral Analysis Unit ("BAU"). *[SSA Clemente's curriculum vitae (CV) states that the mission of the NCAVC is to provide criminal investigative analysis of violent, sexual and serial crimes to law enforcement agencies worldwide. The NCAVC is comprised of three entities: the Behavioral Analysis Unit; the Child Abduction/Serial Murder Investigative Resource Center; and the Violent Criminal Apprehension Program. The three entities "represent the culmination of nearly 30 years of Criminal Investigative Analysis within the FBI."*
>
> *SSA Clemente's CV [also] states: "The Behavioral Analysis Unit is staffed by Supervisory Special Agents with an average of 18 years of law enforcement experience focused on violent and sexual criminal investigations. Many BAU members hold advanced degrees in areas including Law, Psychology, Entomology and Criminology.[17] Each member has completed the NCAVC's comprehensive 560-hour training regimen, as well as other advanced and specialized courses. All BAU members perform case analysis, conduct research, and provide training. Annually they analyze 1,500+ cases, conduct multiple ongoing research projects, and train 10,000+ law enforcement officers, prosecutors and health care professionals worldwide. BAU members also provide onsite Crime Scene Analysis and Expert Testimony.]* SSA Clemente has specialized training in the investigation of criminal sexual exploitation of children, as well as some graduate level education in clinical forensic psychology, criminology, and research methodologies. *[SSA Clemente also holds a J.D., a law degree, as well as a B.S. in Chemistry. He was previously assigned to the New York Field Division's Joint FBI/ NYPD Sexual Exploitation of Children Task Force. Prior to joining the FBI, he headed the Child Sex Crimes Prosecution Team for the New York City Law Department Clemnte CV).]* Additionally, SSA Clemente has analyzed and consulted on over 1000 child sexual exploitation and victimization cases, as well as conducting interviews of sex offenders and related research. SSA Clemente was offered, without objection, *[SSA Clemente also holds a J.D., a law degree, as well as a B.S. in Chemistry. He was previously assigned to the New York Field Division's Joint FBI/NYPD Sexual Exploitation of Children Task Force. Prior to joining the FBI, he headed the Child Sex Crimes Prosecution Team for the New York City Law Department Clemnte CV).]* and accepted by the Court, as an expert in "criminal investigative analysis" in light of his training and experience in investigating child sex offenders *[SSA Clemente explained that the term "child sex offender" is a law enforcement term that applies to those who commit crimes (of a sexual nature) against children under the age of eighteen. He further noted that, although the psychiatric term of pedophile applies to some child sex offenders, it does not apply to all, as the term pedophile is reserved for those individuals who are sexually attracted to prepubescent children. (Tr. 23, Apr. 28).]* and their characteristics and methods. In his written declaration, SSA Clemente defined the term "criminal investigative analysis" as "a law enforcement tool which utilizes investigative results, forensic findings and victim and offender behavior to assess cases. It is further used in child sexual victimization cases to dispel myths and misconceptions about individuals who sexually exploit or molest children." *[The FBI NCAVC website states, in part: The mission of the BAU is to provide behavioral based investigative and operational*

---

[17] While this may or may not be true, those members of the BAU who routinely perform casework and testify in court lack any such advanced qualification in areas related to behavioral science, crime or criminology—not unlike SSA Clemente whose education as a lawyer is unrelated to the area in which he is testifying as an expert.

support by applying case experience, research, and training to complex and time-sensitive crimes typically involving acts or threats of violence ... [including] Crimes Against Children ... BAU assistance to law enforcement agencies is provided through the process of "criminal investigative analysis." Criminal investigative analysis is a process of reviewing crimes from both a behavioral and investigative perspective. It involves reviewing and assessing the facts of a criminal act, interpreting offender behavior, and interaction with the victim, as exhibited during the commission of the crime, or as displayed in the crime scene. BAU staff conduct detailed analyses of crimes for the purpose of providing one or more of the following services: crime analysis, investigative suggestions, profiles of unknown offenders, threat analysis, critical incident analysis, interview strategies, major case management, search warrant assistance, prosecutive and trial strategies, and expert testimony. Federal Bureau of Investigation, Critical Incident Response Group, NCAVC, Mission Statement (2003), available at www.fbi.gov/hq/isd/cirg/ncavc.htm (last visited January 4, 2006).] (Declaration, ¶ 5).

SSA Clemente further explained that preferential child sex offenders exhibit: (1) long-term and persistent patterns of behavior; (2) children as preferred sexual objects; (3) well-developed techniques in obtaining child pornography and or child victims; and (4) fantasy-driven behavior. (Declaration, ¶¶ 7-11) (Tr. 23-24, Apr. 28). He characterized a collection of child pornography as the most telling sign of a preferential child sex offender. (Declaration, ¶ 14). SSA Clemente asserted that because such offenders are often sexually attracted to children of a particular age group, they must periodically search out and groom new children for victimization, because the children they are sexually interested in grow up and "age out" of their desired age range. SSA Clemente stated that such classification is significant, because preferential offenders are "much more likely" to re-offend than situational offenders, as preferential offenders' behavior is compulsive in nature, and therefore less easily controlled. (Tr. 34-35, Apr. 28) *[SSA Clemente's declaration explained that there are preferential and situational child sex offenders: Situational child sex offenders do not have a dominant sexual attraction to children. As a result, their sexual activities with children tend to result from accidental or circumstantial access to children rather than a methodical effort to pursue children. Their offenses can be described as opportunistic and impulsive in nature. Preferential child sex offenders, on the other hand, find themselves sexually attracted to children, usually of a particular age group or other specific characteristics ... These offenders must periodically search out new [child victims] because the children they are sexually interested in always grow up and "age out" of their desired age range. Their sexual behavior with children, therefore, is typically repetitive and predatory in nature ... [and they] tend to engage in highly predictable behavior patterns. Declaration, ¶¶ 6-7).]*

SSA Clemente formed his opinions regarding Mr. Thomas, the defendant in this case, after reviewing interview reports, evidence summaries, statements made by Mr. Thomas, and the images and the video seized during the search discussed previously. He also consulted with the principal investigator and Assistant United States Attorney involved in the prosecution of this case. He did not, however, interview the defendant.

SSA Clemente opined that Mr. Thomas has exhibited all four of the typical hallmarks, or behavioral characteristics, of a preferential child sex offender. First, he equated the defendant's collection of child pornography and erotica, amassed over a period of six years, with a long-term and persistent pattern of behavior. Second, SSA Clemente found that Mr. Thomas's collection, which focused almost exclusively on prepubescent girls between the ages of five and thirteen, demonstrated his interest in children as preferred sexual objects. Third, he characterized the defendant's friendship with the mother of the child he videotaped as an effort to gain access and control over that child and her sister. He further assessed Mr. Thomas's relationship with these two girls as typical "grooming" behavior exhibited by such offenders. SSA Clemente thus concluded that Mr. Thomas utilized two welldeveloped or sophisticated techniques, that is, his friendship with the girl's mother and grooming behavior, to gain access to child victims. Fourth, SSA Clemente found that both the child pornography collection and the videotaping of his friend's daughter demonstrated fantasy-driven behavior, noting that the collection was very directed and goal oriented, and the level of risk the defendant took to make the tape was high.

Additionally, SSA Clemente found it significant that the video created by Mr. Thomas spliced together the non-pornographic images of young girls characterized as surveillance video, adult pornography, and the images of the genitalia of his friend's daughter in such a way as to satisfy himself, thus providing additional insight into Mr. Thomas's predilections. Therefore, SSA Clemente concluded that the defendant's behavior, in combination with his child pornography collection that predominantly featured prepubescent girls, demonstrate that he is a preferential child sex offender.[18]

SSA Clemente testified that although it is impossible to predict future criminal behavior with absolute certainty, the best indicator of future behavior is a past pattern of behavior. He stated that the risk of this defendant reoffending is high because Mr. Thomas's conduct regarding his friend's daughter crossed the line separating fantasy from active molestation. (Declaration, ¶ 20) (Tr. 39-40, Apr. 28). He further assessed that Mr. Thomas's overall conduct, which had progressed from private fantasy, to collection of child pornography, to production of child pornography, to actual molestation of a child by exposing and touching her genital areas, demonstrated an escalation of behavior. (Tr. 40, Apr. 28).

SSA Clemente believed some of the assertions made by Mr. Thomas in his written statement did not indicate acknowledgment of his sexual attraction to young girls or acceptance of responsibility for his behavior, but rather represented an attempt to rationalize his conduct. (Tr. 38, Apr. 28). He also stated that because Mr. Thomas had victimized an unrelated child, that is, an extrafamilial child, he was much more likely to re-offend, and that the literature clearly supported this assertion. (Tr. 40-41, Apr. 28). Specifically, SSA Clemente testified that in his opinion there was a "high" risk, which he further defined as "more likely than not", that Mr. Thomas would reoffend if released, even under the proposed conditions, pending trial. (Tr. 75-77, Apr. 28). However, SSA Clemente also testified that he did not believe Mr. Thomas was at the "highest" possible risk for re-offense if released pending trial. (Tr. 75, Apr. 28).

When questioned by the Court regarding the basis for his opinions, SSA Clemente identified his experience as a criminal investigator, the institutional knowledge of the FBI,[19] and a study of inmates in a Sex Offender Treatment Program at the Federal Correctional Institution in Butner, North Carolina. See Andres E. Hernandez, Psy.D., *Self-Reported Contact Sexual Offenses by Participants in the Federal Bureau of Prisons' Sex Offender Treatment Program: Implications for Internet Sex Offenders* (2000)

---

[18] It is disturbing to note, as an objective forensic expert, that SSA Clemente was willing to both assume the guilt of the defendant for the purposes of his analysis, and also opine as to an ultimate issue. Such testimony would be a violation of ABP ethical guidelines, as well as the practice standards set forth in this text.

[19] This is basically testimony that SSA Clemente has some kind of special knowledge uniquely available to those who work for the FBI. Unfortunately, he is unable to quantify or even describe this knowledge. The inference we are left with is that it must be secret. However, given the rules of discovery in the United States, experts are not allowed to rely upon "secret" foundations for their opinions and testimony.

("Hernandez Study"). The primary objective of this study was to "examine the incidence of sexual offending involving contact crimes (e.g., child sexual abuse, rape) of program participants, including those inmates convicted of non-contact sexual offenses (e.g., possession of child pornography)." The results of this study were that 90 subjects convicted of crimes involving the production, distribution, receipt, and possession of child pornography, or the luring of a child and traveling across state lines to sexually abuse a child, had committed an additional 1,622 sexual crimes which had never been detected by the criminal justice system. However, when questioned by the Court regarding the basis for his risk assessment as to this defendant, SSA Clemente was unable to explain how his methods or techniques had been error-checked or peer reviewed for accuracy and reliability.

Court Ruling

The court ultimately found that FBI BAU agent's expert opinions must be reliable, and that Clemente's weren't. Moreover, it found that peer review of BAU methods was lacking, and that the research Clemente had cited was being applied incorrectly. When asked to defend his opinions, he routinely cited his law enforcement experience and status as an FBI agent while engaged in circular reasoning (United States v. Gordon E. Thomas III, 2006):

> In light of this expanding role, and the considerable authority and even mystique in which these experts are cloaked due to their status within the FBI, it is essential to establish the reliability of such expert testimony. *See Cochran* at 89 (noting that "[b]ecause of the *status* of the FBI's Profiling and Behavioral Assessment Unit as the only organization in the world that specializes in the investigation of bizarre and brutal crimes, *testimony by members of the unit will always be powerful evidence"*) (emphasis added). *See also* D. Michael Risinger & Jeffrey L. Loop, *Three Card Monte, Monty Hall, Modus Operandi & "Offender Profiling": Some Lessons of Modern Cognitive Science for the Law of Evidence*, 24 Cardozo L.Rev. 193, 251 (2002) (opining that questionable profiling data at issue in the article could have been easily validated or invalidated for the simple reason that the FBI had access to data that would settle the issue of raw accuracy and that the FBI should not benefit from "their own failure to aid the generation of defensible data"); Henry F. Fradella, Adam Fogarty & Lauren O'Neill, *The Impact of Daubert on the Admissibility of Behavioral Science Testimony*, 30 Pepp. L.Rev.. 403, 444 (2003) (noting that "[t]here appears to be only one area in which Daubert is not being rigorously applied to behavioral science testimony ... [which is] 'expert opinions' offered by law enforcement officers based on their years of experience in the field when they offer opinions with regard to modus operandi or other aspects of the ... criminal mind" and that "[e]xplorations into their theoretical knowledge base, as well as the validity and reliability of both their methodologies and their conclusions, appear to have escaped Daubert review"). ...

> The Court recognizes that SSA Clemente has certain expertise in criminal investigative analysis regarding the characteristics and behavioral patterns of child sex offenders, based on specialized knowledge, acquired primarily through experience and anecdotal information. *[However, expertise in criminal investigative analysis regarding sexual offenses against children does not, based on the evidence presented, equate necessarily to expertise in risk assessment. Shreve v. Sears, Roebuck & Co., 166 F.Supp.2d 378, 391 (D.Md.2001 (finding that "the fact that a proposed witness is an expert in one area, does not ipso facto qualify him to testify as an expert in all related areas"). See also Gross v. King David Bistro, 83 F.Supp.2d 597, 600-01 (D.Md.2000) (determining that because the proposed testimony was unreliable, the proposed expert's experience and training were "immaterial").]*

SSA Clemente's testimony patently demonstrated that the *Daubert* factors were not satisfied, with the arguably sole exception of general acceptance within the law enforcement community. The Supreme Court, however, expressly rejected the *Frye* "general acceptance" standard for scientific evidence, and replaced it with the two-pronged gatekeeping test set forth by *Daubert*. 509 U.S. at 597, 113 S.Ct. 2786, 125 L.Ed.2d 469. *Kumho Tire Co.*, of course, later extended *Daubert* to all expert evidence. 509 U.S. at 584-89, 113 S.Ct. 2786, 125 L.Ed.2d 469.

First, SSA Clemente was unable to demonstrate that his risk assessment methodology had been (or could be) tested. When asked by the Court whether his methodology had been tested or validated, SSA Clemente, in a series of answers largely unresponsive to the Court's inquiry, asserted that his methodology was "outside of scientific analysis" and failed to identify anything that could be even remotely construed as either testing or validation. (Tr. 75-78, Apr. 28). *[SSA Clemente characterized his opinion as a risk assessment, testifying that he "[did] not predict behavior" but rather "evaluate[d] the risk based on ... criminal investigative analysis ... [and] provide[d] an opinion as to the level of risk [of] reoffending as it relates to this person and a risk to the community." (Tr. 53, Apr. 28).]*

Moreover, the typology *[A typology is defined as "the study of types, as in a systematic classification." Webster's II New Riverside Dictionary, 1249 (Riverside Publishing Co., 1994).]* of a preferential sex offender, *[See Kenneth V. Lanning, Child Molesters: A Behavioral Analysis 26-30(National Center for Missing & Exploited Children, 2001) (describing the typology of a preferential sex offender). The typology developed and described by Mr. Lanning, characterized by four hallmarks, is substantively identical to that described in both SSA Clemente's declaration and his testimony, as discussed supra.]* to which SSA Clements repeatedly referred as the foundation of his analysis, apparently is based entirely on anecdotal case studies and interviews. *[SSA Clemente testified that his risk assessment methodology, which he described as "one aspect of criminal investigative analysis," is based "on largely anecdotal studies of cases [because] it's very difficult to conduct empirical research in this area." (Tr. 71-72, Apr. 28). He later reiterated that it was "based on years of interview[s]." (Tr. 77, Apr. 28). Finally, in answer to a series of questions regarding the basis for his risk assessment, SSA Clemente responded: "Now, have we published studies indicating [that people who meet the four hallmarks of a preferential sex offender do re-offend]?" No, we haven't. We're in the process of doing probably the first long-term empirical study on this area." (Tr. 82, Apr. 28). See also Kenneth V. Lanning, Child Molesters: A Behavioral Analysis 1 (National Center for Missing & Exploited Children, 2001) (acknowledging that the preferential sex offender typology is based on anecdotal information and "the totality of [the author's] acquired knowledge and expertise").]* SSA Clemente was unable to offer even any retrospective studies establishing the validity of this typology. *[THE COURT: But even a retrospective study, going back and looking at offenders and then looking back at their characteristics, have you published anything that looked at say 100 ... re-offenders, identified their characteristics and looked at it that way, retrospectively, and published it?*

THE WITNESS: Yeah. I have not. One of the things that I did when I joined the unit was make a push towards empirical studies ... I'm an attorney, and I know the relative weight that can be applied to anecdotal versus empirical. We had a huge amount of anecdotal information. We didn't have empirical. (Tr. 82-83, Apr. 28).] (Tr. 82-83, Apr. 28).

SSA Clemente admitted that the typology of a preferential sex offender, which is the essential predicate to his risk assessment methodology, as well as re-offense risk assessment regarding such offenders, requires additional research to achieve validation. *[SSA Clemente testified that* the Behavioral Analysis Unit is associated with a longitudinal study, with over 1,000 subjects, that is ongoing. (Tr. 80, Apr. 28). However, the results of that study are not yet available, and thus cannot assist the Court in this matter. Additionally, SSA Clemente testified that the results, analysis, and typology of a preferential sex offender, as promulgated by the BAU, had been published in the Journal of the American Medical Association ("JAMA"). (Tr. 83, Apr. 28). However, the Court's research revealed that a sole JAMA article stated merely that "[r]esearchers in a child sex offender program based in Seattle, Washing[ton], have provided a qualitative study of the attitudes and modus operandi of men who have sexually abused children." Peter J. Fagan, Ph.D., Tomas N. Wise, M.D., Chester W. Schmidt, Jr., M.D. & Fred S. Berlin, M.D., Ph.D., Pedophilia, 288 J. Am. Med. Assoc. 2458, 2460 (2002) (citing Conte JR, Wolf S., Smith T., What Sexual Offenders Tell Us about Prevention Strategies, 13 Child Abuse Negl. 293-301). The Court was unable to obtain the study cited by the JAMA article, neither of which was offered or even specifically identified by SSA Clemente. However, while the cited reference indicates that the study addressed the "attitudes and modus operandi" of certain abusers, it does not reveal whether it in fact validated the BAU's typology for preferential sex offenders.] (Tr. 80, Apr. 28). SSA Clemente therefore acknowledged that his opinions were based on anecdotal case studies and interviews, albeit "a huge amount," and lacked an empirical basis. (Tr. 83, Apr. 28).

While the Court recognizes, as SSA Clemente testified, that collecting empirical data is difficult in this context, this difficulty cannot, by itself, render a risk assessment methodology reliable or exempt it from any sort of testing or validation. Thus, the first *Daubert* factor was not met.

Second, no specific literature was offered demonstrating that his methodology has been subjected to meaningful peer review analysis. While SSA Clemente testified that the typology of a preferential sex offender has been *referenced* in a number of publications outside the field of criminal investigative analysis, no studies or publications were offered in which SSA Clemente's peers, that is, other criminal investigative analysts, *analyzed* or *validated* the typology. [SSA Clemente testified that the typology was "accepted" by the International Fellowship of Criminal Investigative Analysis as "a good model for analyzing for criminal purposes the behavior of child sex offenders." (Tr. 84, Apr. 28). However, with no other evidence beyond SSA Clemente's assertion, it does not constitute meaningful peer review. See United States v. Horn, 185 F.Supp.2d 530, 555 (D.Md.2002).] (Tr. 84, Apr. 28).

Additionally, while SSA Clemente described a process wherein some oversight is provided to BAU staff by an advisory and research board, it does not appear to comprise meaningful peer review in the present legal context. (Tr. 60, Apr. 28). *See United States v. Horn*, 185 F.Supp.2d 530, 555 (D.Md.2002) (explaining that "peer review as contemplated by *Daubert* and *Kumho Tire* must involve critical analysis that can expose any weaknesses in the methodology or principles underlying the conclusions being reviewed").

Third, SSA Clemente was likewise unable to explain what, if any, error rate applied to his risk assessment technique, which he repeatedly referred to as one aspect of criminal investigative analysis. On cross-examination, the following colloquy transpired:

Q: Does your office have any sort of program or procedure in place to assess cases over time to determine whether there is an error rate that applies to your analysis?

A: Absolutely. Our office is set up like a think tank. We do consultations with a board ... [a]nd basically, when you're going to testify as an expert, you have to present the testimony you're going to give to this committee and they will approve or disapprove it based on our track record over the years....

Q: What do you meant by your track record? Track record of what?

A: On consulting of cases, of giving expert testimony, the accuracy of it and so forth.

Q: Well, by track record are you saying that in 1990 you gave an opinion that a person was a preferential sex offender who had been actively molesting and you tracked that years later to see if that was true or not?

A: Well, for example-sure. You go through the whole case. The case is not close -

Q: And you have never been wrong?

A: That first-

Q: Other than that example you gave me?

A: That he was a preferential offender?

Q: Yes. That sort of thing. Is there any error control over those sorts of opinions, that a person is an offender who is an active molester, and it turns out years later that he is not? Is there any way to pick that up?

A: Well, the only way I would make that determination is if there were evidence that would amount to that determination. I have never-well, I will be able to tell one case. (Tr. 58-60, Apr. 28).

Obviously, there is no known error rate regarding the application of the required predicate of his risk assessment methodology, that is, the determination of whether a defendant is a preferential sex offender. Thus, the third *Daubert* factor was not met.

Finally, as the foregoing discussion demonstrates, there is minimal, if any, evidence that there are any standards controlling the operation of SSA Clemente's methodology. While there is apparently some oversight exercised by the board previously described, SSA Clemente failed to identify any measures that might properly be termed "standards" in this context. Thus, the fourth *Daubert* factor was also not met.

Certainly, the precise factors articulated by *Daubert* need not be applied to every expert in every case. *See Kumho Tire Co.,* 119 S.Ct. at 150. However, *Daubert* and *Kumho,* in conjunction with Fed.R.Evid. 702, mandate that the Court's gatekeeping function must be fulfilled by inquiring into factors that fairly assess reliability. SSA Clemente claimed that his area of expertise and methodology were not "scientific" and that while analogies could be made to the scientific method, it should not be strictly applied to his testimony. (Tr. 77, Apr. 28).

Many social scientists, as SSA Clemente has done, rely primarily on real-world experience to arrive at their conclusions. As one court found, prior to *Kumho Tire Co.,* while the *Daubert* factors "must be applied when an expert bases his testimony on scientific hypotheses which are capable of being refuted by controlled experimentation ... [they] may be applied in differing degrees when it comes to non-Newtonian science or other specialized knowledge." *United States v. Hall,* 974 F.Supp. 1198, 1202 (C.D.Ill.1997) (internal quotation marks omitted). Nonetheless, the court emphasized that "there must be *some* degree of reliability of the expert and the methods by which he has arrived at his conclusions." *Id.* The court explained that expert social science testimony based on "real-world experience rather than experimentation" must meet certain quantitative and qualitative requirements, including threshold number of experiences, sufficient similarity of those experiences "in nature to form a valid basis for comparison," publication in scholarly journals, and meaningful peer review. *Id.* at 1202-03.

However, as demonstrated previously, SSA Clemente's assessment, with the exception of number of experiences, did not even meet the less rigorous factors sometimes applied to 'soft' social sciences in determining reliability. ...

In his testimony, SSA Clemente referred to and relied on the Hernandez study for his view on Mr. Thomas' recidivism. SSA Clemente noted that this study found that 54 of 62 inmates who were convicted for the mere possession of child pornography admitted, during the course of the study, which was conducted while they were incarcerated for the child pornography charges, that each of them had actually committed approximately 30 instances of molestation which had been undetected. Thus, SSA Clemente used the Hernandez Study to argue that Mr. Thomas, merely on the basis that he possessed a collection of child pornography, was at a high risk of re-offending, and at a higher risk than the recidivism statistics would indicate, if he were released under the proposed conditions pending trial. The Hernandez Study is so dissimilar to the instant facts that it did not 'fit' the purpose for which it was used by SSA Clemente. *See United States v. Horn,* 185 F.Supp.2d 530, 553 (D.Md.2002) (explaining that factors establishing reliability and relevance must "fit" the case at issue and that careful examination can "expose evidentiary weaknesses that otherwise would be overlooked"). While SSA Clemente testified that sexual offender recidivism statistics are inaccurate because many such crimes remain undetected, it is speculative to conclude that Mr. Thomas is likely to molest a child, under the proposed strict conditions, during the approximately six week period *[The defendant was scheduled for trial approximately six weeks from the conclusion of the detention hearing when the Court issued its bench ruling in this matter.]* pending trial. *[See George B. Palermo, M.D., & Mary Ann Farkas, Ph.D., The Dilemma of the Sexual Offender 171-72 (2001). The authors state: "Sex offenders are portrayed as more likely to reoffend than other types of offenders. The offender is characterized as one who repeats his sexual conduct or is likely to repeat it ... [y]et research is inconclusive regarding the recidivism rates of sex offenders as compared to other offenders even though improvements have been made using actuarial methods. There is no clear evidence that sex offenders are any more likely to recidivate than any other type of offender and there is no empirical basis to assess which sex offenders present the most immediate risk for reoffending." Id. (internal citations omitted). ...]*

SSA Clemente raised the Hernandez Study in making the point that recidivism statistics are understated because many instances of molestation are never reported to, or detected by, the justice system. While that may indeed be so, the issue is the extent of that understatement in the available recidivism statistics, and how such understatement affects re-offense risk assessment in the context of the typical period of time pending trial, which is generally a few months and certainly less than a year.

SSA Clemente's approach in no way accounted for, or even acknowledged, how the proposed conditions of release in this case might mitigate such a risk.

Notably, the Hernandez Study subjects reported having committed molestation offenses when they were under no such strict supervision or conditions as those proposed in the instant case. Nonetheless, SSA Clemente maintained that, because in his opinion Mr. Thomas was at a "high" risk for reoffending pending trial, he should be detained, without explaining why the proposed conditions would or could not mitigate the alleged risk. Therefore, the Court finds that the Hernandez Study simply does not fit the facts of this case, and thus adversely affects the reliability of SSA Clemente's risk assessment. *See Gross v. King David Bistro,* 83 F.Supp.2d 597, 600-01

(D.Md.2000) (finding a proposed expert's testimony unreliable because the empirical data cited by the proposed expert was "simply too nascent and tepid to support his conclusion"). ...

SSA Clemente based his opinion on what he characterized as a "pattern" of past behavior. However, the Court is not convinced that collecting child pornography and the sole incident of molestation in evidence in this case equate to the pattern asserted. The Court, as stated earlier, in no way minimizes the seriousness of the conduct underlying the molestation charge. However, there was no evidence whatsoever of any other acts of molestation, and thus this conduct may, on Mr. Thomas's part, indeed have been an aberration, as he argued.

Notably, a recent publication's authors concluded, following an exhaustive review of the empirical issues relevant to various tests used to determine the dangerousness, antisociality and recidivism risk of sexual offenders, that "it remains an empirical question as to whether all individuals who access, view, and download child pornography, eventually escalate into contacting children and molesting them." George B. Palermo, M.D., & Mary Ann Farkas, Ph.D ., The Dilemma of the Sexual Offender 66-67 (2001) (citing a personal communication with Anthony J. Pinizzotto, Ph.D., of the FBI Academy, for this assertion).

Moreover, while the Court fully appreciates the significance of the sophisticated techniques and grooming behavior used by some serial child molesters to gain access to children, the government's argument that, because Mr. Thomas molested the girl in the video, his friendship with her mother and his occasional babysitting of the victim and her two siblings *ipso facto* constituted such techniques and grooming. Thus, the Court is not convinced, even applying the typology of a preferential sex offender as defined by SSA Clemente, that Mr. Thomas's behavior actually comprises such grooming and techniques, or that the totality of his conduct, given the evidence to date, can accurately be assessed as the typology of a preferential sex offender. ...

4. The Court's Conclusion as to SSA Clemente's Opinion

In *Daubert,* the Supreme Court held that Federal Rule 702 required that scientific evidence be "not only relevant, but reliable." 509 U.S. 579, 113 S.Ct. 2786, 2795, 125 L.Ed.2d 469, 481 (1993). In determining reliability, the Supreme Court provided four factors that could be used, while noting that the analysis should be flexible. *Daubert,* 509 U.S. at 594, 113 S.Ct. 2786, 125 L.Ed.2d 469. In *Kumho Tire Co. Ltd. v. Carmichael,* 526 U.S. 137, 119 S.Ct. 1167, 143 L.Ed.2d 238 (1999), the Court held that the principles enunciated in *Daubert* applied to all expert testimony, not merely scientific evidence. Although experts with specialized knowledge may extrapolate from existing data, "nothing in either *Daubert* or the Federal Rules of Evidence requires a district court to admit opinion evidence that is connected to existing data only by the *ipse dixit* of the expert." *Kumho Tire,* 526 U.S. at 157 (finding no abuse of discretion in rejecting opinion of expert) (internal citation and quotation marks omitted) (emphasis added). Clearly, *Daubert* and *Kumho Tire Co.,* as well as Rule 702, require that expert opinion evidence be connected to existing data by something more than a chain of dubious inferences that amount to an expert's assertion that "it is so because I say it is so." [Black's Law Dictionary 743 (5th ed.1979) (defining ipse dixit as "[h]e himself said it; a bare assertion resting on the authority of an individual").]

Failure to satisfy four out of the five *Daubert* factors, and most of the less rigorous criteria sometimes applied in the social science context, combined with a lack of any other persuasive indicia of reliability, forced the Court to conclude that the principles and methods underlying SSA Clemente's opinions were insufficiently reliable. Moreover, even assuming the reliability of SSA Clemente's methodology, that is, application of the preferential sex offender typology by a non-examining criminal investigative analyst combined with actuarial data, his methodology was not well supported in this case.

In summary, while SSA Clemente repeatedly stated that he could not predict what this defendant would do if released, he nevertheless insinuated that because there is admittedly very strong evidence that the defendant committed one act of molestation, that he most likely has committed others and will undoubtedly commit more. This is circular reasoning at best, and without more, cannot serve as clear and convincing evidence of a re-offense risk in a detention determination.

Although SSA Clemente has strong law enforcement and criminal investigation credentials, they cannot serve as a substitute for a proven, reliable method or technique that can be independently verified when it comes to such risk assessment. As *Daubert* and its progeny make clear, while experts are not required to be *right*, their testimony must be based on methods and techniques that constitute a reliable foundation.

Discussion

The court correctly identified, perhaps for the first time, a complete range of failings with respect to FBI profiler testimony—from the "aura" of FBI expertise, to unvalidated methodology, to misapplied research, to logical fallacies, to lack of peer review. In the end, these considerations rightly add up to a lack of expert reliability. This ruling also provides an excellent template for future courts, given that FBI profiling methodologies do not differ significantly across cases. It also signals the education of the court with respect to the particulars that should be of concern regarding this type of highly speculative testimony.

The only issue not sufficiently covered by this ruling was that of expert qualification. One is left to wonder why the FBI sent a lawyer to testify about behavioral science issues, as opposed to an actual behavioral scientist. Additionally, the claims of casework and training are not consistent with the testimony of FBI other profilers. If the defense had preserved this issue with an objection, the court's *Thomas* opinion could have been far more exhaustive in its condemnations.

THE FUTURE OF CRIMINAL PROFILING IN COURT

The following is an example of how criminal profiling testimony may be used responsibly in a court of law. It the first known case of a criminal profiler testifying as an expert in criminal profiling, where they have been allowed to give their explicit *expert profiling opinions in the guilt phase of a criminal trial*, without fear of reversal. Provided for the reader is background on the case, an overview of pertinent forensic issues, and the author's forensic conclusions. Note that while general offender characteristics are provided, the author did not seek to opine on the issue of guilt or innocence as it relates to a specific suspect (generally referred to in courts as *the ultimate issue*).

Wisconsin v. Peter Kupaza (2000)

At the end of July in 1999, 25-year-old Mwivano Kupaza's dismembered body parts were found in several plastic bags that had been placed inside of duffel bags, floating in the Wisconsin River near Spring Green. Her arms, legs, feet, and head had been disarticulated at the joints by a razor-sharp instrument, like a scalpel. A similar instrument had been used to remove the skin from the victim's face,

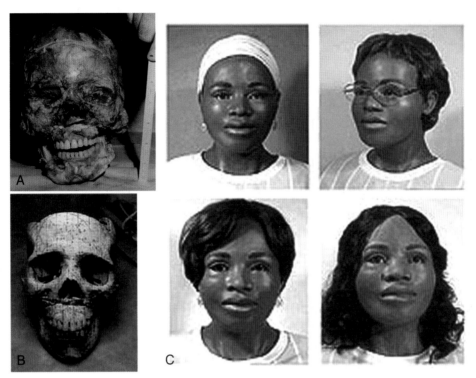

FIGURE 17.1
(a) Skull of Mwivano Kupaza. Skin has been removed from the head, face, and neck by the offender. This behavior goes beyond what would be needed to simply obscure the victim's features to hamper identification. (b) Skull of Mwivano Kupaza after being prepared for craniofacial reconstruction. (c) Skull of Mwivano Kupaza after craniofacial reconstruction has been completed. These various aspects were put on a flyer that was distributed in the area where the body was found as an aid to victim identification.

head and neck (Figure 17.1a, b, and c). This dismemberment severely hampered investigative efforts. An autopsy performed on the recovered body parts failed to reveal a cause of death.

Because of the extensive dismemberment and mutilation, the victim was not actually identified until early February of 2000. This occurred when Shari Goss, Peter Kupaza's ex-wife, recognized what she thought appeared to be Mwivano's face on a handbill posted in a Westby, Wisconsin, store. With this tip, law enforcement turned to a fingerprint examiner from the Wisconsin State Crime Laboratory, who was able to compare prints from the body that matched those Mwivano had left on a form for a Madison abortion clinic in October 1997.

That same month, another Tanzanian immigrant, 40-year-old Peter Kupaza, the victim's cousin, was charged with the murder. Kupaza was divorced, living alone in a single-bedroom apartment, and had formerly been employed by the state of Wisconsin in various capacities. He had worked for the state Department of Financial Institutions as a support services assistant, the state Department of Natural Resources providing customer service for state park displays at regional recreation shows, and at the state Department of Workforce Development as a temporary employee processing unemployment insurance claims. Mwivano Kupaza had previously been living with her cousin, Peter, near Madison.

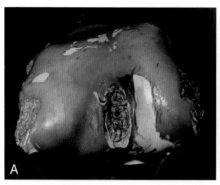
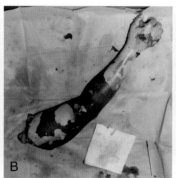
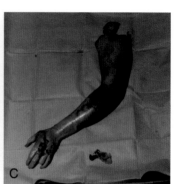

FIGURE 17.2
(a, b, and c) Torso and limbs of Mwivano Kupaza.

The trial began in June, 2000. The prosecution's case focused on conflicting statements made by Kupaza to the police about Mwivano's whereabouts, a fingerprint found on a letter from their common postal mail box belonging to Mwivano (left after she was supposed to have returned to Tanzania), and the fact that a dog gave a positive indication for human biological fluids in Peter Kupaza'a apartment (where Mwivano had lived with her cousin for a time) and vehicle.[20]

Shari Goss, Peter Kupaza's ex-wife, testified that he was familiar with knives and had knowledge relating to how to slaughter animals. According to her, this was a product of growing up in Tanzania where people raise and butcher their own livestock. She also testified that a duffel bag in which body parts were found was similar to one she had given her ex-husband.

The state's forensic pathologist, Robert Huntington III, testified that the victim's body parts had been meticulously detached from one another. Huntington referred to the act as "disarticulation," in that the body was taken apart joint by joint (Figure 17.2a, b, and c). He testified that it demonstrated a great knowledge of anatomy on the part of the offender.

In June, 2000, the state of Wisconsin allowed expert crime reconstruction and criminal profiling testimony from the author in the guilt phase of Wisconsin v. Peter Kupaza (2000) for the defense.[21] This testimony was allowed owing to the opinion published by the Court of Appeals in Wisconsin v. Richard A.P. (1998). In *Richard*, the Wisconsin Court of Appeals held (and the State Supreme Court denied review) that the exclusion of defense expert testimony in the guilt phase by psychologist Dr. Charles Lodl as to

---

[20] Of note is the fact that one would expect human biological fluids in any home. A great deal was made of the findings in the car as well. The car was subsequently sprayed with Luminol, an enzymatic blood enhancement reagent, with negative findings. The prosecution and the dog's trainer argued that the dog's sense of smell was more sensitive than the Luminol test. This is not the case, however, as a dog's sense of smell requires the scent to be airborne, while Luminol does not. The negative finding of the Luminol test is proof of the dog's inaccuracy. It should also be noted that the state did not call any of its own forensic scientists to testify, as their findings conflicted with the findings of the dog and subsequent theories relating to the defendant's guilt. The forensic scientists from the state lab were called as witnesses for the defense.

[21] As discussed in this work, and in Turvey (2000), criminal profilers already testify in U.S. courts on a regular basis in relation to a variety of issues, but not often during the guilt phase, and not overtly (i.e., openly called profilers offering profiling opinions). For example, the medical examiner in Wisconsin v. Peter Kupaza testified to some of the same opinions as the author, only under the umbrella of medical expertise.

Richard's profile, for comparison to the profile of a child molester, was a reversible error. It also agreed that profiling evidence was outside the general knowledge of the jury and must be supported by expert testimony, both with respect to the theory itself and whether the defendant exhibits character traits consistent with that profile.

The following are the conclusions provided by this author to the defense, dated May 30, 2000. These conclusions were the basis for expert testimony ultimately provided to the court and jury:

> It is this examiner's opinion that the residence of Peter Kupaza, at 1118 Pleasant View, Apt. 107, Madison, WI, is not the location where this victim was dismembered. The basis for my opinion on this issue resides in the consideration of the following items:
>
> 1. The absence of significant bloodstains and/or bloodstain patterns at the residence, which would be expected with the degree of manual disarticulation and skin removal evident in this case (i.e., under carpets, beneath tiles, behind baseboards, etc.). It is important to note that a single, small bloodstain was found in the bathroom on the edge of the baseboard only a few inches from the tile floor. This is highly consistent with incidental transfer from an accidental cut related to shaving of the foot/ankle area, as well as other incidental injury scenarios.
> 2. The lack of evidence related to human tissue or body fluids associated with the victim's disarticulated joints, such as fatty tissue, skin, and synovial fluids, discovered at the location. Any of these would be somewhat expected with the nature and degree of manual disarticulation and skin removal evident in this case (i.e., under carpets, beneath tiles, behind baseboards, etc.).
> 3. The lack of evidence such as detailed in items 1 and 2 associated with Peter Kupaza's vehicle, a 1997 Silver/Gray Nissan Altima.
> 4. Fiber evidence associated with a duffel bag used in the disposal of the victim's body is excluded as having come from either the residence or vehicle discussed above. This supports the association of the victim's nude, deceased body with another location.
>
> It is this examiner's opinion that this crime contains a number of components that, in concert, could be used to support the interpretation of a sexual motivation. It should be noted that by themselves any of these components would not be as compelling. However, when combined they suggest the strong possibility of a sexual aspect within this crime. The basis for my opinion on this issue resides in the consideration of the following items:
>
> 1. The victim's body was found nude, which is not entirely explained by the possibility that the removal of the victim's clothing may have been part of a precautionary act.
> 2. The victim's body shows no evidence of injury caused by premortem violence. Moreover, there is a significant lack of what is commonly referred to as "overkill" (i.e., multiple blows to the face, crush injuries to the skull, multiple stabs, etc.), which would be suggestive of offender anger and/or a violent confrontation.
> 3. The offender(s) spent an inordinate amount of time with the victim's body in the postmortem interval. Specifically, there is evidence of careful attention paid to the skillful separation of the victim's joints with a sharp instrument, the removal of the skin covering the victim's head with a sharp instrument and the removal of the skin on the victim's thighs with a sharp instrument. It is important to note that the careful dismemberment of the victim is not entirely explained by the possibility that it may have been part of a precautionary act to prevent victim identification. This is given the increased risk of offender discovery involved in such a time consuming effort, and the disinterest in the removal or obliteration of the victim's hands, fingers and teeth.

4. The victim's feet were not found. Feet are a commonly and readily fetishized body part. The majority of the victim's dismembered body was located subsequent to a directed search effort in the same general area. Given this, in concert with the nature of the postmortem activity in this case, the victim's feet are conspicuously absent, in my view.

It is important to note at this point that despite the typical persistence of sperm and hair evidence in the vaginal vault and anal cavity subsequent to sexual activity (including rape), and the death range estimated, a sexual assault exam was not performed in this case. It is also important to note that despite the extensive drug toxicology performed at the time of autopsy, and despite the level of alcohol in the victim's blood (the victim was not known to drink), no toxicological screens for poison appear to have been conducted. This examiner is at a loss as to why neither of these things was done at the time of autopsy, as they would seem to be important steps in reconstructing the victim's demise.

It is this examiner's opinion that this crime evidences an offender(s) with medical knowledge. The basis for my opinion on this issue resides in the consideration of the following items:

1. This victim was not dismembered with commonly associated chopping instruments such as a hatchet, cleaver or machete applied to areas of bone (such as a butcher might use).
2. There is no evidence that a sawing instrument such as a hacksaw, band saw, skill saw, or radial saw was used.
3. There is evidence that the offender(s) separated the victim's head, arms, legs, and feet at their respective joints with the utmost deliberation, precision and care, using a very sharp cutting instrument not unlike a scalpel.

Based on these facts, the time requirement, and the significant emotional requirement involved, it is further the opinion of this examiner that the offender(s) responsible for this crime has experience with performing precisely this kind of disarticulation, most likely with another human victim.

FIGURE 17.3

Peter Kupaza on the stand, responding to questions about the murder of his cousin, Mwivano Kupaza.

In June of 2000, despite the extraordinary lack of any direct physical evidence of guilt, a Sauk County jury took nine hours to decide that Peter Kupaza killed and then dismembered Mwivano Mwambashi Kupaza, sometime in late July 1999. Peter Kupaza (Figure 17.3) was subsequently sentenced to life in prison, having been convicted of first-degree murder.

The overt use of criminal profiling testimony in this case is significant as it sets a precedent in Wisconsin that will in all likelihood be mirrored in courtrooms around the United States. In any case, it is clear that all criminal profilers have a responsibility to learn what it means to have opinions heard in court and the potential consequences of those opinions. The desired result would be to help govern their *forensic* opinions in a mindful, conscientious, and responsible manner.[22] For better or worse, criminal profilers are unquestionably out of the investigative basement and in the courtroom.

---

[22] Forensic opinions (opinions given in, and subsequently worthy of, the courtroom) and investigative opinions are by no means the same thing. Investigative opinions and speculations are used to engine an investigation, and are under continual refinement as new facts become available. Forensic opinions are more or less final, based on a static sum of case information at a given time or point, and are not necessarily going to be susceptible to proof or testing through further investigative processes.

SUMMARY

Behavioral evidence analysis (BEA) is an ideo-deductive method of criminal profiling that seeks to examine the behaviors and patterns in a particular offense and then make specific inferences about offender characteristics that are evident directly from crime-related behavior. The purpose of BEA is to provide insight into criminal behavior and to define or refine the suspect pool in a criminal investigation. It is not, however, a tool suited for the task of *individuating* offenders in its own right.

Deducing offender characteristics is about asking the right question of offense-related behavior. The first part of the question is defining the characteristic. The second part is agreeing upon what type of behavior evidences that characteristic. If the behavior is evident in the scene, in the proper context, that characteristic is evident. Offender characteristics that tend to be investigatively and even forensically relevant include criminal skill, knowledge of the victim, knowledge of the crime scene, and knowledge of methods and materials. Problem characteristics, where profilers are often wrong, include age, sex, and intelligence. To best determine and document which characteristics are evident, the profile must be a written document and not a conceptual abstract.

Criminal profilers are often asked to give testimony in court to help address forensic issues. The *Daubert* standard of admissibility is one way to assist with determining whether or not the testimony of a particular method of profiling should be admissible. Though criminal profiling is not a science, it can be scientific with respect to its approach, and it may still be subject to *Daubert* criteria. Whether or not this is an appropriate standard by which to measure criminal profiling is a matter for individual courts to decide. A good argument may be made, however, that the overall utility of *Daubert* is lacking apart from the criteria that relate to hypothesis testing and falsification.

Questions
1. True or False: BEA employs the scientific method.
2. Explain the difference between identification and individuation, with examples of each.
3. What are two advantages to having a written as opposed to a verbal profile?
4. Offense skill is a function of what two elements?
5. If the offender demonstrates specific knowledge of the crime scene, suggesting that he or she has been there before, how does this affect the suspect pool?

REFERENCES

Baeza, J., Chisum, W.J., Chamberlin, T.M., McGrath, M., Turvey, B., 2000. Academy of Behavioral Profiling: Criminal Profiling Guidelines. Journal of Behavioral Profiling 1 (1).

Blackwell, L., 1998. Murder Trial Verdict May Come Soon. Richmond Times Dispatch (July 24).

Bureau of Justice Statistics, 2006a. Criminal Victimization in the United States, 2005. NCJ 215244, U.S. Department of Justice (December).

Bureau of Justice Statistics, 2006b. Drug Use and Dependence, State and Federal Prisoners, 2004. NCJ 213530, U.S. Department of Justice (October).

Burgess, A.G., Burgess, A.W., Douglas, J., Ressler, R., 1992. Crime Classification Manual. Lexington Books, New York, NY.

Burgess, A., Hazelwood, R. (Eds.), 1995. Practical Aspects of Rape Investigation. second edition. CRC Press, Boca Raton, FL.

Cronin, J., Wellford, C., 2000. Clearing up Homicide Clearance Rates. National Institute of Justice Journal (April).

Daubert v. Merrell Dow Pharmaceuticals, Inc, 1993. 113 S. Ct. 2786.

Depue, R., Douglas, J., Hazelwood, R., Ressler, R., 1995. Criminal Investigative Analysis: An Overview. In: Burgess, A., Hazelwood, R. (Eds.), Practical Aspects of Rape Investigation, second edition. CRC Press, Boca Raton, FL.

Feeny, F., 2000. Police Clearance: A Poor Way to Measure the Impact of Miranda on the Police. Rutgers Law Journal (Fall), 1–114.

Gross, H., 1924. Criminal Investigation. Sweet & Maxwell, London, England.

Holmes, R., Holmes, S., 1996. Profiling Violent Crimes: An Investigative Tool, second edition. Sage, Thousand Oaks, CA.

Homant, R.J., Kennedy, D.B., 1998. Psychological Aspects of Crime Scene Profiling: Validity Research. Criminal Justice and Behavior 25 (3), 319–343.

Ingram, S., 1998. If the Profile Fits: Criminal Psychological Profiles into Evidence in Criminal Trials. Journal of Urban and Contemporary Law 54, 239–266.

Inman, K., Rudin, N., 1997. An Introduction to Forensic DNA Analysis. CRC Press, Boca Raton, FL.

Inwinkelried, E.J., Mendez, M., 1992. Resurrecting California's Old Law on Character Evidence. Pacific Law Journal 23, 1005–1041.

Jonakait, R.N., 1994. Real Science and Forensic Science. Shepard's Expert and Scientific Evidence Quarterly 1 (3), 435–455.

Kirk, P., 1953. Crime Investigation. Interscience Publishers, New York, NY.

Kirk, P., Thornton, J.I., 1974. Crime Investigation, second edition. John Wiley & Sons, New York, NY.

Kumho Tire Co. v. Carmichael, 1999. 526 U.S. 137.

Lilly, G., 1987. An Introduction to the Law of Evidence, second edition. West, St. Paul, MN.

McCook, A., 2006. Is Peer Review Broken? The Scientist 20 (2), 26.

McInerney, D.Q., 2004. Being Logical: A Guide to Good Thinking. Random House, Westminster, UK.

Mokros, A., Alison, L.J., 2002. Is Offender Profiling Possible? Testing the Predicted Homology of Crime Scene Actions and Background Characteristics in a Sample of Rapists. Legal and Criminological Psychology 7, 25–43.

New Jersey v. Steven Fortin, 1999. 318 N.J. Super. 557.

Oklahoma v. Jimmy Ray Slaughter, 1997. 450 P.2d 839.

Petherick, W.A., 2006. Developing the Criminal Profile: On the Nature of Induction and Deduction. Journal of Behavioral Profiling 6 (1), 2–12.

Petherick, W.A., 2007. Criminal Profiling: A Qualitative and Quantitative Analysis of Methods and Content. Doctoral dissertation, Bond University.

Popper, K., 2003. The Logic of Scientific Discovery. Routledge Classics, London, England.

Reik, T., 1945. The Unknown Murderer. Prentice-Hall, New York, NY.

Saks, M.J., 1994. Implications of the Daubert Test for Forensic Identification Science. Shepard's Expert and Scientific Evidence Quarterly 1 (3), 427–434.

Sugawara, S., 1997. Japanese Arrest 14-Year-Old in Decapitation of 11-Year-Old. Washington Post Foreign Service June 29, A26

Thornton, J.I., 1994. Courts of Law v. Courts of Science: A Forensic Scientist's Reaction to Daubert. Shepard's Expert and Scientific Evidence Quarterly 1 (3), 475–485.

Thornton, J.I., 1997. The General Assumptions and Rationale of Forensic Identification. In: Faigman, D., Kaye, D., Saks, M., Sanders, J. (Eds.), Modern Scientific Evidence: The Law and Science of Expert Testimony, vol. 2. West, St. Paul, MN.

Turvey, B., 2000. Criminal Profiling and the Problem of Forensic Individuation. Journal of Behavioral Profiling 1 (2).

Turvey, B., 2003. Forensic Frauds: A Study of 42 Cases. Journal of Behavioral Profiling 4 (1).

Turvey, B., 2006. Beneath the Numbers: Rape and Homicide Clearance Rates in the United States. Journal of Behavioral Profiling 6 (1), 36–47.

United States v. Gordon E. Thomas III, 2006. No. CRIM. CCB-03-0150, WL 140558, January 13.

The USS Iowa: Guilt by Gestalt, 1990. Congressional testimony, Harper's Magazine (March), 25–26.

Wisconsin v. Peter Kupaza, 2000. Case No. 00-CF-26.

Wisconsin v. Richard A.P., 1998. No. 97-2737-CR.

Woodhams, J., Toye, K., 2007. An Empirical Test of the Assumptions of Case Linkage and Offender Profiling with Serial Commercial Robberies. Psychology, Public Policy, and Law 13, 59–85.

CHAPTER 18

Psychopathy and Sadism
Interpreting Psychopathic and Sadistic Behavior in the Crime Scene

Brent E. Turvey

I have no brother, I am like no brother;
And this word "love," which graybeards call divine,
Be resident in men like one another and not in me:
I am myself alone.

—Shakespeare, *King Henry VI*, Part 3, Act 5, Scene 6

He's not afraid of pain as most people are. He won't hold back. Once an impulse gets hold of him, a guy like this is capable of practically anything.

—Harrington, *Psychopaths* (1972, p. 171)

CONTENTS

KEY TERMS

Antisocial personality disorder	Lustmurder	Sadism
Lack of empathy	Psychopath	Sociopath
Lack of remorse	Psychopathy	

Many criminal profilers are not concerned with, and often not qualified to perform, the evaluation, diagnosis, and treatment of criminal offenders. Why, then, should they concern themselves with the diagnostic constructs of psychopathy and sadism? The answer is that these two particular offender classifications are behaviorally determined. That is to say, the diagnosis of psychopathy or sadism is largely dependent on behavioral evidence. The criminal profiler, in some cases, will address behavioral patterns and crime scene characteristics that may incidentally be a part of a particular clinical diagnosis. An analogy would be that while criminal profilers may not be allowed to bake the forensic psychologist's cake, they might show up in the kitchen with a few ingredients that the forensic psychologist can use (or at the very least should not ignore).

It is not the purpose of this chapter to argue the root causes of extreme offender behavior like psychopathy or sadism. These vary with the individual and are best left for the clinician to assess rather than for the profiler to infer from the scene alone. For the criminal profiler, it is enough that psychopaths and sadists exist and may commit violent crimes that require investigation.[1] The purpose of this chapter is to discuss psychopathy and sadism as behavioral constructs, breaking them down into components that may be evident in a crime scene.

---

[1] It remains the opinion of this author that most criminals are largely made, a product of circumstances and environments, and not born. However, this is not meant to imply that criminals must come from unhealthy homes. Even environments rich with love and opportunity can produce a psychopath, sadist, or other violent criminal. This is something that many researchers do not wish to accept, causing the continued search for genetic influences that never quite explain anything—at best they only correlate.

PSYCHOPATHY

More than 200 years ago, Philippe Pinel, a French physician, used the phrase *manie sans delire* to describe an unusual case of a man who did not fit into the categories of mental disturbance that were recognized at the time. Pinel characterized the patient as remorseless and lacking in restraint. The phrase he chose to describe this patient's condition, when translated to English, means simply "madness without confusion," or as Dr. Robert Hare interprets it, "insanity without delirium" (Hare, 1993, p. 25). This was one of the first attempts to describe what we may refer to in modern terms as a psychopath—an individual capable of enjoying what most would consider horrible, heinous acts, and recognizing the harmful consequences of those acts to others, but incapable of feeling remorse and unwilling to stop.

Pinel did not consider these individuals immoral (someone whose beliefs are contrary to accepted morality) but rather amoral (someone who does not care about conventional interpretations of right or wrong and gives those issues no weight in decisions). However, there were others who considered these patients not only immoral but also evil. The debate on this issue persists.[2]

In 1835, the English alienist J. C. Pritchard came up with the term moral insanity, which he applied in instances where abnormality or "insanity" expressed itself in a particular field of morality. Then, in 1888, Toch began substituting the term psychopathic inferiority for Pritchard's term. But Toch implied a biological predisposition for the disorder rather than a wholly environmental cause (Toch, 1979).

In a 1952 revision of the psychiatric nomenclature, according to Cleckley (1976, pp. 10–11), the term psychopathic personality was officially replaced by sociopathic personality, hence the word sociopath found its way into the literature. Then in 1968, that was replaced by personality disorder, antisocial type.

As it stands, there have been a lot of revision and a lot of confusion about the diagnosis of psychopathy, the meaning behind the behavioral manifestations, and the causes of the overall disorder. This is in the grand tradition of the mental health and criminological professions; each person who encounters these and related terms has interpreted them in his or her own unique way using subjective measures. Even today, qualified clinicians and the public alike confuse psychopathy with antisocial personality disorder (ASPD). As Hare (1996) explains,

> The distinction between psychopathy and ASPD is of considerable significance to the mental health and criminal justice systems. Unfortunately, it is a distinction that is often blurred, not only in the minds of many clinicians but also in the latest edition of DSM-IV.

> Most psychopaths (with the exception of those who somehow manage to plow their way through life without coming into formal or prolonged contact with the criminal justice system) meet the criteria for ASPD, but most individuals with ASPD are not psychopaths. Further, ASPD is very common in criminal populations, and those with the disorder are heterogeneous with respect to personality, attitudes and motivations for engaging in criminal behavior.

For the purposes of this work, to stem any confusion, the following definitions will apply:

- *Psychopathy.* A personality disorder evidenced by a distinctive cluster of behaviors and inferred personality traits defined by the *Hare Psychopathy Checklist–Revised* (PCL-R) (Hare, 1991).
- *Psychopath.* A social predator (diagnosed with psychopathy) who often charms and manipulates his or her way through life. Psychopaths are completely lacking in conscience and in feelings

---

[2] The author leans toward Pinel's opinion on this issue, finding the study of crime and criminality through the lens of morality to be uninformative, divisive, and futile.

for others; they take what they want and do as they please without the slightest sense of guilt or regret (Hare, 1993). This term is used when psychological, biological, and genetic factors have contributed to the development of the syndrome, as well as social forces and early life experiences.[3]

■ *Sociopath*. This term is used to describe the same behavior manifestations and inferred personality traits as are evident in a psychopath. The explicit exception is that sociopaths have a syndrome forged entirely by social forces and early experiences (Hare, 1993).

Psychopathic Characteristics

As Walsh and Kosson (2007, p. 31) explained,

Psychopathy is among the most important and widely researched individual differences related to violent criminality (Hare, 2003). The psychopathic personality is characterized by a constellation of traits including impulsivity, callousness, and irresponsibility.

The "distinctive cluster of behaviors and inferred personality traits" that Hare is referring to are found in the *Hare Psychopathy Checklist–Revised*. Adapted from Hare (1991), they are as follows:

Callous lack of empathy
Conning/manipulative
Criminal versatility
Failure to accept responsibility for actions
Glibness/superficial charm
Grandiose sense of self-worth
Impulsivity
Lack of remorse or guilt
Poor behavioral controls
Early behavioral problems
Irresponsibility
Juvenile delinquency
Lack of realistic long-term goals
Many short-term marital relationships
Need for stimulation/proneness to boredom
Pathological lying
Parasitic lifestyle
Promiscuous sexual behavior
Revocation of conditional release
Shallow affect

Hare (1991) gives the following instructions regarding the use of these criteria:

The 20 items of the PCL-R measure behaviors and inferred traits considered fundamental to the clinical construct of psychopathy. Most of the traits are treated as open concepts. That is, the rater is provided with a description of a trait and with some behavioral exemplars and is asked to make a judgment about the extent to which a person has the trait. ...

---

[3] The author is aware that this diagnostic construct has been updated and continues to be updated on a regular basis. However, our concern is with behavioral manifestations of individual traits and not with the diagnosis of particular disorders. Those who wish to keep up to date should reference Dr. Hare's website at www.hare.org.

Although clinical judgment and inference are required, the scoring criteria are quite explicit, and with some training, the items are not difficult to score.

This gives us an important piece of information: These traits exist in varying degrees of intensity, thus individual psychopaths will manifest them in varying degrees of intensity. All psychopaths are not equal, and by extension all psychopathic behavior is not equal. Psychopathic behavior exists on a continuum.

As previously stated, criminal profilers are interested in what offenders do in relation to an offense. They are not precisely interested in what offenders have to say about their offense behavior—other than in comparison to what they've actually done. Information regarding an offender's personality characteristics must be derived directly from the offense behavior as established by the physical evidence and not from insights requested from offenders days, months, and even years after an event. Information gathered from an offender in an interview may be nothing more than a rationalization or nothing less than a total lie.

Bear in mind that the presence of one characteristic is not by itself proof of psychopathy. It is only when the traits cluster together and in an enduring and intense fashion that psychopathy becomes a possibility. There are, however, traits that that tend to define psychopathy, such as lack of remorse and deceitfulness. As Porter and Woodworth (2007, p. 93) explained,

> Psychopaths long have been characterized as persistent liars to the extent that duplicity is regarded as a defining characteristic of psychopathy. For example, Cleckley (1976) viewed untruthfulness and insincerity as being important features of the disorder. The PCL-R (Hare, 1991, 2003) contains two items that consider deception: "pathological lying" and "conning/manipulative" (Hare, 2003). Further, one of the three main factors identified in Cooke and Michie's (2001) model of psychopathy is an arrogant and deceitful interpersonal style. Several theoretical frameworks have been proposed to explain psychopathic deception. Affective factors have been implicated; anxiety and guilt which may inhibit or interfere with deception in most people are largely missing in the psychopath (Ekman, 2002; Lykken, 1995). Lykken (1995) proposed that because psychopaths experience less anxiety than non-psychopaths, they are able to deceive more adeptly than others. In fact, it has been suggested that psychopaths may even experience "duping delight" from successfully deceiving others (Ekman, 1991; Porter, Birt, & Boer, 2001; Raskin & Hare, 1978). Evolutionary factors also have been implicated; psychopaths exhibit a reproductive strategy intended to maximize the number of reproductive partners but invest few resources into caring for the offspring (MacMillan & Kofoed, 1984; Mealey, 1995; Wiebe, 2004). In order for such a strategy to be effective, prodigious deception (i.e., infidelity, denial, false promises) may be required, referred to by Mealey (1995) as a "cheater strategy."

Next are some sample explanations regarding how characteristics associated with psychopathy may be inferred from physical evidence. They are not the only possibilities. As with all behavioral evidence, the meaning should only be inferred in the context of other offender behavior, and then only when there is adequate documentation.

Lack of Empathy

A lack of empathy is suggested by the inability to understand and to identify with the situations, feelings, or motives of others. Empathy is a complex emotion. It must be understood at the outset that people can do horrible things, identify closely with their victims, and learn to live with the angst that accumulates. Consequently, an absence of empathy may not simply be inferred just because the offender commits a crime that causes victim discomfort, pain, and suffering. It may also not be inferred when clear evidence of empathy is present. Examples of empathy include :

- A rapist lays down a coat or a blanket for the victim at an outdoor crime scene
- An abductor decides not to molest a victim after the victim cries and instead lets the victim go, perhaps even driving the victim back to where the abduction occurred
- An offender negotiates with a victim and compromises by using a condom, loosening restraints, or otherwise accommodating a victim's request

However, a lack of empathy may be inferred when an offender evidences a total lack of interest in a victim's response to discomfort, pain, and suffering during an offense or when an offender mocks a victim's response to discomfort, pain, and suffering.

Conning/Manipulative

This characteristic is suggested by behavior that is intentionally deceptive for personal gain. It can be inferred when an offender uses a deception or a "con" method of approach to get close to the victim. It may also be inferred when offenders get what they want by using their victims' emotions or beliefs against them.

Criminal Versatility

This characteristic can be inferred when an offender evidences MO behavior that suggests competency with criminal activity other than that typically necessary for a given type of offense. An example would be a rapist who evidences burglary skills, such as like wearing gloves, disabling alarms, and stealing easily sold, untraceable valuables. This characteristic may also be inferred when an offender has been linked to other criminal activity by physical evidence.

Failure to Accept Responsibility for Actions

This characteristic refers to offenders who blame everyone but themselves for their situations or who do not feel obligated to address the consequences of their behavior. This can be inferred when an offender blames the victim or the authorities during the attack. This may be found in the form of language used during the offense, notes left behind at the scene, or messages sent to others about the offense.

Glib and Superficial

Glib and *superficial* are terms that refer to behaviors that are done with little concern or thought, with intent to be evasive, deflect emotion, or conceal a lack of emotional depth. In some psychopaths, these behaviors appear contrived and lack substance. In others, they appear quite sincere. The effectiveness of these behaviors has to do with the skills of the psychopath, as well as the ability of the person perceiving the behavior to recognize deception or secondary gain. This characteristic can be inferred when a verbally facile offender exudes an insincere and superficial charm as part of a con that is used to acquire a victim's trust in the offender's method of approach. It may also be inferred when the offender makes jokes during the offense.

Grandiose Sense of Self-Worth

This characteristic can be inferred when offenders evidence an inflated view of themselves and their abilities. For example, they may speak in an unrealistically conceited manner and appear to be indifferent about law enforcement's present or future investigative efforts to apprehend them (lack of precautionary acts). They may also exaggerate past accomplishments or current reputations and prospects.

Impulsivity

Impulsivity is a propensity toward behavior that is not thought out, where consequences are not fully understood. It may be inferred when an offender consistently initiates offense behavior in a reactionary fashion, without planning. Impulsivity may be attributable to drug use, mental defect, or extremely low self-esteem (that is, when people are constantly trying to distract themselves from the pain of their emotions or trying prove their worth to others).

Lack of Remorse or Guilt

Remorse and guilt are characterized by moral anguish and regret for actions. As with empathy, remorse is a complex emotion. It must be understood at the outset that people can do horrible things, feel intense remorse, and learn to live with the angst that accumulates. Consequently, a lack of remorse may not be inferred just because an offender commits a crime that causes victim discomfort, pain, and suffering. It also may not be inferred when clear evidence of remorse is present. Examples of remorse include:

- The offender shows intense emotion during or immediately after the commission of an offense
- An offender apologizes or cries in front of the victim during or immediately after the commission of an offense
- Evidence of undoing: attempts at the scene to cancel or reverse the consequences of the crime, such as cleaning up evidence of a homicide victim's injuries and making it appear as though the victim is unharmed and simply asleep
- An offender uses drugs or alcohol during or immediately following the commission of an offense

A lack of remorse may be inferred when an offender shows no emotion or shows anger or delight in the face of victim suffering. This may also be inferred when an offender is able to engage in extremely violent crimes and then immediately participate in regular, nonviolent activities without apparent distress or emotional leakage. An example would be shooting a prostitute in the head and hiding the body just before going home to a family dinner.

Poor Behavioral Controls

This characteristic refers to violent, damaging, or reactionary behavior that is not controlled, even when the consequences may be harmful to the offender. It may be inferred when an offender is easily angered or frustrated and when the offender frequently responds with verbal or physical aggression.

Motivations

Perhaps the most important thing to understand about the motivations of the criminal psychopath is that they are no different from the motivations of other, non-psychopathic criminals. Criminal psychopaths are susceptible to the same needs and inducements as others.

Where psychopaths may differ from other offenders is in the means that they will use to satisfy their needs. The psychopath uses methods that can be particularly brutal, lack sympathy, and exploit vulnerabilities and that are carried out in the absence of any remorse whatsoever, as we have previously discussed. Psychopaths are not encumbered by distress or moral angst. They do not place any value on those outside of themselves, other than as a source of pleasure, and they view the socialized world of rules and negotiation as an onerous imposition.

It has been said by wise men that inside every human being there is a war between good and evil that can never be won. Psychopaths, however, having no remorse regarding the suffering of others to compass their behavior, are not encumbered by this internal conflict. It has been argued that most psychopaths in general lack the ability to take the perspective of others and therefore do not have access to that information in their decision-making process (Cleckley, 1976, p. 343).

The lack of remorse, the absence of negative emotional consequences, is argued to be a facilitating factor for the psychopath's violent, destructive behavior. This is what allows a psychopath on any range of the spectrum the psychological and emotional facility to do what the rest of us consider horrible, cruel, and morally wrong. They have no sympathy for the pain of others, no remorse for the harm they inflict, and often a high level of impulsivity. Therefore, normally socialized people are one or both of two things to the psychopath: either a source of amusement and gratification or in the way.

For all of our discussion so far about psychopathic criminality, we have largely ignored an important truth that is not pleasant for many to consider when understanding the motivations of criminal behavior. Not all psychopaths are criminals (just as not all criminals are psychopaths). Psychopaths exist in many cultures and are often encouraged. According to an article by William Krasner, written in the 1950s, cited by Harrington (1972, p. 23),

> This is no accident ... there are very definite aspects to our culture pattern which give them [psychopaths] encouragement. In America, we put great value on the acquisition of material gain, prestige, power, personal ascendance, and the competitive massing of goods.

Hare (1996) writes an equally stern indictment, arguing:

> We live in a "camouflage society," a society in which some psychopathic traits—egocentricity, lack of concern for others, superficiality, style over substance, being "cool," manipulativeness, and so forth—increasingly are tolerated and even valued. With respect to the topic of this article, it is easy to see how both psychopaths and those with ASPD could blend in readily with groups holding antisocial or criminal values. It is more difficult to envisage how those with ASPD could hide out among more prosocial segments of society. Yet psychopaths have little difficulty infiltrating the domains of business, politics, law enforcement, government, academia and other social structures.

Case Examples

The following case examples are provided to give readers an applied sense of the variety of criminal offenses involving psychopathy, as well as the motivational possibilities. Readers are once again reminded that these are behaviors, not motives, and are expressive of offender needs. Approaching psychopathic behavior from this perspective should provide for a more penetrating understanding of offenders in a given situation. Consider the following cases.

Profile of a Psychopath: United States v. Aquilia Barnette (2000)

Aquilia Barnette was convicted in federal court of numerous crimes relating to the murders of Donald Lee Allen and Robin Williams. They included use of a firearm in a carjacking that results in death, commission of a carjacking that results in death, and use of a firearm while violating the Interstate Domestic Violence Act that results in death. He was sentenced to death (United States v. Aquilia Barnette, 2000).

Background

Aquilia Barnette and Ms. Robin Williams began dating in 1994. In March of 1995, they moved into an apartment together in Roanoke, Virginia. In April 1996, Williams broke up with Barnette. He left their apartment and returned to Charlotte, North Carolina, where he lived with his mother (United States v. Aquilia Barnette, 2000).

Barnette was not happy about the break-up and continued to pursue Williams. According to United States v. Aquilia Barnette (2000):

> Miss Williams continued to live in the apartment she had shared with Barnette, but a friend, Benjamin Greene, was staying with her because she was afraid to remain there alone. On April 30, 1996, Miss Williams woke Greene up, telling him "he was here," referring to Barnette. Greene looked out of the window and saw Barnette smashing the windows of Greene's car with a baseball bat. Greene attempted to call the police, but the telephone wires had been cut. Barnette saw Miss Williams in the apartment and began to strike at the windows with the bat. He then threw a fire bomb through a gap he had kicked open in the front door, setting the apartment on fire. Barnette fled the scene after Greene fired shots at him, and Miss Williams and Greene escaped the flames by jumping out of a rear window. Miss Williams was hospitalized with second and third degree burns to her hands and arms. Miss Williams identified Barnette to the Roanoke police, who issued a warrant for his arrest and notified the Charlotte Police Department. The Charlotte police, however, did not arrest Barnette.

> On May 20, 1996, Barnette purchased a 12-gauge shotgun in Charlotte using his brother's, Mario Vonkeith Barnette's, Virginia driver's license. He returned the gun the next day and exchanged it for a semi-automatic shotgun. He sawed off the stock and barrel of the new gun and taped a flashlight to its barrel. On June 21, 1996, Barnette took the gun and walked from his mother's house to the nearby intersection of Billy Graham Parkway and Morris Field Road. Donald Allen stopped his blue Honda Prelude at that intersection shortly after midnight. Barnette approached Allen's car with the shotgun and ordered Allen to get out of the car. Allen complied and also threw down his wallet after Barnette demanded it. Barnette then forced Allen to walk at gunpoint to a drainage ditch across the road. After reaching the ditch, Barnette shot Allen three times in the back and left his body in the ditch. Barnette took Allen's wallet and car and drove to Bertha Williams', Robin Williams' mother's, house in Roanoke, Virginia. Miss Williams had been living with her mother since the firebombing incident.

> After arriving at Mrs. Williams' house, Barnette went into the backyard and cut the home's telephone wires. He then attempted to enter the home though the side kitchen door, but after finding that it was locked, he fired the shotgun into the door and kicked it in. Mrs. Williams was inside the house holding her eight-month-old granddaughter when Barnette entered the house. Mrs. Williams told Miss Williams to run, and Miss Williams ran out the front door. Barnette entered the house, confronted Mrs. Williams, and followed Miss Williams out the front door, chasing her across the street. A neighbor, Sonji Hill, was standing in her doorway, calling the police, when Barnette ran by. Barnette saw her making the call, and from 50 feet away, he pointed the shotgun at her and told her to hang the phone up or he would shoot her. Miss Hill hung up the phone and retreated into her apartment, where she called the police again.

> Miss Williams fell down as she was running away from Barnette, and he caught up with her, grabbed her by the hair, and dragged her back to her mother's house. He told Miss Williams that he planned on killing her and himself. Mrs. Williams came out of the house as they returned, and Miss Williams

broke free from Barnette and went with her mother toward the house. Barnette then shot Miss Williams twice. He fired the first shot from 10 to 12 feet away, hitting Miss Williams in the side. The second shot, fired from four to five feet away, hit her in the back. When Barnette fired both shots, Mrs. Williams was close enough to her daughter to touch her. Miss Williams died from these injuries.

Barnette left the scene of the murder in Allen's car, driving to Knoxville, Tennessee where he stole new license plates for the car. He then drove to Charlotte, North Carolina where he abandoned the car in a shopping center parking lot on June 24, 1996. Police officers discovered the car that night and found the shotgun Barnette used in the murders in a nearby dumpster.

On June 25, 1996, Barnette arranged to turn himself in to the authorities at his mother's house. He subsequently took the police to the scene of Allen's murder and showed them where to find the body. He ultimately confessed to the two murders and the carjacking (United States v. Aquilia Barnette, 2000).

Behavioral Determination

In the penalty phase of this case, the government called a number of witnesses, including Dr. Scott Duncan. Dr. Duncan gave the opinion that Barnette would be a future danger in prison based on three factors (United States v. Aquilia Barnette, 2000):

> ... the Psychopathy Checklist Revised, research on predicting future dangerousness, and an actuarial analysis comparing Barnette to groups of people with characteristics similar to him. Dr. Duncan found that Barnette was likely to be violent in the future. He testified that, in his opinion, Barnette was a psychopath.

Dr. Duncan further testified to the following (United States v. Aquilia Barnette, 2000):

> Q. Before you tell us how you came to that conclusion, will you describe for the jury what a psychopath is?
>
> A. Certainly. In general, a psychopath is an individual who lacks the ability to feel at the same level and have the intensity of what feelings are as compared to nonpsychopathic individuals. Typically they are very callous, manipulative, calculating, individuals that will often exploit other people. There is research to suggest that biologically, they do not respond to what nonpsychopaths view as fear and anxiety, which are two emotions that make up what we refer to as remorse or guilt. The psychopath is an individual that has little if any ability to feel remorse or guilt for behavior they engage in. ...
>
> Q. Why is it important to establish whether or not a defendant is a psychopath?
>
> A. Well, psychopaths are—criminal psychopaths are twice as likely to engage in future criminal behavior when compared to noncriminal psychopaths. Criminal psychopaths are three times as likely to engage in violent future criminal behavior when compared to nonpsychopathic criminals. Although in any prison population only about 20 percent of that population typically are psychopaths, they are responsible for over 50 percent of violent crimes that are committed. Also, identifying someone as a psychopath helps institutions to be able to place them either in a maximum or lower security penitentiary based on what they score out. ...
>
> Q. Now, do psychopaths look any different than other people?

A. No, sir. The psychopath, probably one of their best assets and probably one of the greatest fears of nonpsychopaths is their ability to look normal. We would all like to be able to think that we can pick out the psychopaths from the nonpsychopaths in the community, but none of us are immune to that. … The psychopath, as I say, has the ability to look very normal. However, if you know what you are looking for, it is kind of like seeing a bowel [sic] of fruit, and you say to yourself, gosh that bowl of fruit looks wonderful, it looks very good. But when you get close to the bowel [sic] of fruit and pick it up you realize that it's fake fruit. And the psychopath is a lot that way. And they look very, very normal, but when you know what to look for, you can see things in their behavior, not their appearance necessarily as much as things in their behavior, which identify them as psychopaths.

To rebut the testimony by Dr. Duncan that Barnette was a psychopath (and related testimony based on the *Hare Psychopathy Checklist—Revised*), the defense asked to recall its own risk assessment expert. The district court denied the motion. When Barnette was given the death penalty, the defense appealed the decision.

The Fourth Circuit U.S. Court of Appeals ruled that this denial was a reversible error. The trial court should have let the defense put its own expert back on the stand to address that issue. According to Mealey's *Daubert* Reports (2000),

"While Barnette essentially alleges that the district court made an improper initial determination that the Psychopathy Checklist Revised was reliable scientific evidence, he does not contest its relevancy," the panel said. When deciding whether to admit the testimony based on the Psychopathy Checklist Revised, the court considered Barnette's objections to the test, that the list had not been standardized as to the black population (Barnette is black) or as to the post middle-age population.

"Barnette offered two articles written by his own expert, Dr. Cunningham, to support his position, but no other evidence. On this record, the decision to admit the evidence was not a clear error of judgment. Taking into account the discretion afforded the district court's decision, we are of the opinion that its examination of the issue was sufficient and that the record does not support a determination that admitting the evidence was an abuse of discretion."

The Fourth Circuit U.S. Court of Appeals subsequently reversed the death sentence and remanded Barnette for a new sentencing hearing.

Discussion

This author agrees that, when psychopathy is given as a diagnosis offered by a qualified psychologist or psychiatrist, such testimony is appropriate during the penalty phase (after a defendant has already been found guilty, and guilt is not at issue). This author agrees that, when based on observable fact such as the behavior-oriented PCL-R, such testimony may be beneficial to the trier of fact in determining how long the offender needs to be put away. If the court did so more often, the court might avoid the problem of having to rely on civil commitments, as is discussed in the cases that follow.

As for adequate access to rebuttal witnesses, the author absolutely supports this. The failure of the trial court to allow the defense expert to get back on the stand and at least discuss the shortcomings of the PCL-R is almost belligerent. This would not have been a good decision to let stand.

Crawford Wilson: Psychopathic Rapist

Crawford Wilson is what may be colloquially referred to as a one-man crime wave. His juvenile record includes car theft, petty theft, and fighting. His adult criminal record includes felony convictions and imprisonment for auto theft, grand theft, two unauthorized uses of a weapon, two burglaries, armed robbery, and possession of burglary tools (Minnesota v. Crawford Wilson, 2000).

Wilson's known career as a sex offender began in 1962 with an attempted rape. As detailed in Minnesota v. Crawford Wilson (2000),

> Part of his history includes sexually molesting a stepsister when she was 8 years old and he was 17 or 18. Before moving to Minnesota in 1981, Wilson lived in Illinois. Wilson has acknowledged that he committed five or six rapes during the time he lived in Illinois. Wilson was paroled from an Illinois state prison on October 2, 1981. He began raping women in Minnesota in January 1982, while still on probation.

> Wilson's current incarceration is the result of a series of rapes of 11 women during a six-month period in 1982. He preyed on unknown women of widely varying ages. In each instance, Wilson used a knife to subdue and intimidate his victim, who was accosted either in her own apartment or apartment building. Generally, Wilson was intoxicated when he committed these crimes. He would blindfold, gag, and tie up the victim before raping her. Some assaults involved multiple acts of penetration. In some instances, Wilson cut off a victim's clothing with the knife while she was bound, and he physically struck at least two of his victims. He routinely remained in the victim's apartment for a period of hours after the rape, rummaging through the victim's belongings and then stealing cash and personal items.

> In 1982, Wilson pleaded guilty to five counts of criminal sexual conduct in the first degree and was sentenced to 25 years in prison. During his incarceration, Wilson received four discipline reports relating to sexual behavior. In December 1983, he exposed his penis to a female visitor. In October 1986, he was found to be involved in anal intercourse with a fellow inmate. In August 1991, Wilson attempted to hug and kiss a female corrections officer, telling her he fantasized about having sex with her. Finally, in June 1997, Wilson was seen standing naked in front of his window, masturbating in full view of a female officer.

According to the record, Wilson continued to engage in other misconduct during his incarceration as well, including verbal abuse; disobeying a direct order; disorderly conduct; possession of contraband, drug paraphernalia, and alcohol; use of intoxicants; unauthorized possession of property; conspiracy to smuggle; and smuggling (Minnesota v. Crawford Wilson, 2000).

In August of 1999, Crawford Wilson was committed to the Minnesota Sex Offender Program as a sexual psychopathic personality (SPP) and as a sexually dangerous person (SDP).[4]

---

[4] Minnesota enacted a "psychopathic personality" (PP) law in 1939 that provides for indefinite civil commitment of dangerous sex offenders to the Department of Human Services for treatment. County attorneys and the attorney general's office used the law to commit high-risk sex offenders to the Minnesota Security Hospital at St. Peter upon their release from prison (Minnesota, 1994). Commitment as an SPP in Minnesota requires evidence that a person has engaged in a habitual course of misconduct in sexual matters, has an utter lack of power to control his or her sexual impulses, and is therefore dangerous to others. Commitment as an SDP in Minnesota requires evidence that a person engaged in a course of harmful sexual conduct, manifests a sexual, personality, or other mental disorder, and is therefore likely to engage in acts of harmful sexual conduct (Minnesota v. Crawford Wilson, 2000).

Behavioral Determination

Crawford Wilson appealed the finding that he was an SPP and an SDP. However, according to the court-appointed examiner, Dr. Roger C. Sweet, Wilson is (Minnesota v. Crawford Wilson, 2000):

> a sexually dangerous person (SDP), meeting all three elements of Minn.Stat. § 253B.02, subd. 18c, based on the following: (1) Wilson is a career criminal with a history replete with violent sexual and nonsexual criminal behavior; (2) his PCL-R degree of psychopathy approaches the cutoff point for indication of psychopathy; (3) his MMPI-2 and MCMI-III results indicate a propensity for violent behavior; (4) he is chemically dependent and use of mood-altering substances contributes to his impulsive, unreflective behavior; (5) he has not yet successfully completed a chemical dependency or sexual offender treatment program; and (6) the combination of psychopathy and a deviant sexual arousal pattern is associated with a greater sexual offense recidivism rate.

Dr. Sweet explained that Wilson's score of 27 on the *Hare Psychopathy Checklist—Revised* (PCL-R) was above the cut-off score of 25 used by many researchers to classify an individual as a psychopath. He further gave the following opinion (Minnesota v. Crawford Wilson, 2000):

> [Mr. Wilson] exhibits a moderately deviant pattern, more characteristic of a "power assertive" rapist who regards rape as an expression of his virility and/or an "anger retaliatory" rapist, who rapes as an expression of hostility and rage.

The Court of Appeals of Minnesota agreed that Wilson was indeed an SPP and an SDP. In its decision, the court explained that the Sexually Dangerous Person Act allows civil commitment of sexually dangerous persons who have "engaged in a prior course of sexually harmful behavior and whose present disorder or dysfunction does not allow them to adequately control their sexual impulses, making it highly likely that they will engage in harmful sexual acts in the future" (Minnesota v. Crawford Wilson, 2000),

Discussion

This is one of those cases in which there can be little doubt of an offender's continued danger to society. Whether or not he suffers from a defect of the brain, his behavior clearly shows that despite incarceration or parole, he will engage in sex crimes. In this author's view, Crawford Wilson is one of the many poster children for the pro–civil commitment lobby.

Leon James Preston: Juvenile Sex Offender

Not entirely dissimilarly from the ruling in the case of Crawford Wilson, the Court of Appeals of Minnesota recently upheld the civil commitment of 25-year-old Leon James Preston. The largest difference is that Preston was a juvenile sex offender, convicted of charges relating to the sexual assaults of at least eight juvenile girls when he was between the ages of 14 and 17. The victims included, in the following order (Minnesota v. Leon James Preston, 2001),

- Preston's 8-year-old cousin. He attacked her at her home.
- A 9-year-old girl whom he rode with on a school bus. He assaulted her approximately 30 to 45 different times.
- A 4-year-old girl in a park. He attacked her twice during the same day.
- An 8-year-old girl at a park. He attacked her on at least 15 separate occasions.
- Preston's 5-year-old half-sister. He attacked her during his confirmation party.
- A 9-year-old neighborhood girl whom Preston babysat for. He attacked her in a park, on the school bus, and at her house.
- The 12-year-old daughter of a family friend. He molested her in her bedroom.

The last of these attacks occurred while Preston was in and out of inpatient treatment at the Hoffman Center. He was removed from that program for twice having sexual contact with a 14-year-old male resident; he persuaded the younger male to perform fellatio on him (Minnesota v. Leon James Preston, 2001).

Behavioral Determination

Court-appointed psychologists determined that Preston was impulsive, self-centered, and antisocial, all of which they felt indicated he was a psychopath. They also determined that he did not seem to recognize that he had a problem and did not believe that treatment would be necessary or beneficial. Preston actually told them that he thought he could design a program for dealing with his sexual addiction issues. The psychologists felt that this plan was vague, inadequate, insufficient, unrealistic, and "strikingly shallow" (Minnesota v. Leon James Preston, 2001).

Preston was subsequently committed to the Minnesota Sex Offender Program at St. Peter and at Moose Lake as both a sexually dangerous person and a sexual psychopathic personality. He appealed this decision on the basis that he was able to control his impulses (he was able to plan assaults, groom victims, and wait for opportune time to offend) and therefore did not meet the requirement of having "an utter lack of power to control the person's sexual impulses" (Minnesota v. Leon James Preston, 2001).

While this argument is an interesting one, the Court of Appeals of Minnesota provided an equally interesting response when they denied Preston's appeal. According to Minnesota v. Leon James Preston (2001),

> Though grooming victims and planning behavior can show the ability to control the sexual impulse, and thus negate the requirement for commitment under the sexual psychopathic personality statute that the offender have an utter lack of control over sexual impulses, where the grooming behavior itself is uncontrollable, the impulse is likewise not controllable.

Discussion

The issue is framed from a legal standpoint, and legally the statute involved requires that to be considered a sexually dangerous person and a sexual psychopathic personality, an offender must have an utter lack of power to control sexual impulses. That's fine. However, the author is of the opinion that the Court of Appeals of Minnesota's reasoning in this case is specious. That is to say, planning is not evidence of impulsivity. This is a case of an offender who not only groomed numerous victims in numerous contexts but also attacked several of his victims on multiple occasions over a period of months. Much thought and deliberation went into these crimes. Given that many sex offenders engage in complex grooming and planning behaviors, the author fails to understand how such an uninformed statute made it on the books and subsequently remains there in active use.

SADISTIC BEHAVIOR[5]

In general parlance, and in the mass media, the accepted use of the term *sadistic* describes a variety of criminal behaviors. Most often, it describes any perceived cruel act, without respect to specific motivation or context. Learned professionals have not advanced much beyond this vaguely defined usage. In the

---

[5] This section was originally published as Baeza, J., and Turvey B., Sadistic Behavior, in Turvey, B. (2002) *Criminal Profiling: An Introduction to Behavioral Evidence Analysis,* second edition, Elsevier Science, London, England.

investigative community, it may be used to describe the motive of a serial rapist. In the criminological community, it may be used to define an offender group that is being studied for shared characteristics. In the clinical community, it may be used to describe the fantasies of a patient. In some cases, the application of this term may be appropriate and accurately convey what is meant by its invocation. In other cases, however, the application may be inappropriate and arguably misinformed by the sensationalistic and inconsistent body of literature that has come into existence on the subject of sadism. Professional usage of the term is often broad, equating the enjoyment of any cruel act with sadism and it is often tainted by moral umbrage instead of scientific objectivity.

Background

The term *sadism* is derived from the name of a French author who lived from 1740 to 1814, Donatien-Alphonse-François de Sade, better known as the Marquis de Sade. Many regard his existing body of work as important erotic literature because it effectively, intelligently, and indelibly renders descriptive images of sexual arousal driven by physical suffering. This passage from "Justine" (de Sade, 1990, p. 569), for example, describes sadistic rape by a monk who achieves sexual gratification through his victim's pain and humiliation:

> He spreads, he presses, thrusts, tears, all of his efforts are in vain; in his fury the monster lashes out against the altar at which he cannot speak his prayers; he strikes it, he pinches it, he bites it; these brutalities are succeeded by renewed challenges; the chastened flesh yields, the gate cedes, the ram bursts through; terrible screams rise from my throat. … Never in my life have I suffered so much.

> … Inflamed by lust, the beast strikes with all his force … daring to mix love with these moments of cruelty, he fastens his mouth to mine and wishes to inhale the sighs agony wrests from me.

Subsequently, Krafft-Ebing in 1898 (Krafft-Ebing, 1997, p. 20) adopted the term sadism for professional use and classified it as one of the subdivisions of *paraphilia* (a perversion of the sexual instinct), evidenced by the following:

> It consists in this that the association of lust and cruelty, which is indicated in the physiological consciousness, becomes strongly marked on a physically degenerated basis, and that this lustful impulse coupled with presentations of cruelty rises to the height of powerful affects. …

> The quality of sadistic acts is defined by the relative potency of the tainted individual. If potent, the impulse of the sadist is directed to coitus, coupled with preparatory, concomitant or consecutive maltreatment, even murder, of the consort ("Lustmurder"), the latter occurring chiefly because sensual lust has not been satisfied with the consummated coitus.

Arguably this definition can be reduced to the idea that sadism was thought to involve sexual gratification achieved through the cruel treatment and subsequent suffering of a "consort" (i.e., a spouse, partner, or victim). In keeping with this definition, Krafft-Ebing (1997) adduces a total of 15 sadistic cases. Each case but one consistently involves an argument that the offender tortured a conscious creature for the purposes of achieving sexual gratification. The exception, case number 25, involves a patient who developed an adolescent association between seeing blood flow from the fingers of females and his own sexual arousal, an image that made its way into his sexual fantasies but never manifested itself with an actual victim.

Sadism was not necessarily associated with criminality or murder. According to Krafft-Ebing (1997), when sadistic acts did result in homicide, the homicide could be referred to as lustmurder. In this paradigm, the classification of a homicide as a lustmurder requires that the cruel treatment, which can include but is not limited to "strangling, stabbing, and flagellation" (Krafft-Ebing, 1997, p. 34), is indeed oriented toward the sexual gratification of the offender. In other words, the application of the term lustmurder assumes that offender behavior services primarily sexual desires.

Furthermore, while all sadistic murders may be classified as lustmurder, not all lustmurder involves sadism. Krafft-Ebing (1997) adduces a total of 13 cases of lustmurder, only one of which is also sadistic. In fact, the majority of the cases presented involve quick deaths for the victims and postmortem activity, such as sexual penetration, blood drinking, evisceration, organ removal, or mutilation. From this we can reasonably infer that the homicidal classification of "lustmurder" suggested by Krafft-Ebing was indeed intended to be used as a nonspecific and intentionally inclusive term to describe almost all sexually motivated crimes that involve homicide, not just sadistic ones. Arguably, this is no different in application than the broadly inclusive term given by Burgess et al. (1988, p. 1), referring to "the killing of a person in the context of power, sexuality, and brutality."

Sadism: An Applied Standard

For the purposes of this review, a behavioral requirement to establish evidence of sadism was inferred from the background provided earlier, as well as the DSM-IV (American Psychiatric Association, 1994):

> The paraphilic focus of Sexual Sadism involves acts (real, not simulated) in which the individual derives sexual excitement from the psychological or physical suffering (including humiliation) of the victim. Some individuals with this Paraphilia are bothered by their sadistic fantasies, which may be invoked during sexual activity but not otherwise acted on; in such cases the sadistic fantasies usually involve having complete control over the victim, who is terrified by anticipation of the impending sadistic act. Others act on the sadistic sexual urges with a consenting partner (who may have Sexual Masochism) who willingly suffers pain or humiliation.

Still others with sexual sadism act on their sadistic sexual urges with nonconsenting victims. In all of these cases, it is the suffering of the victim that is sexually arousing. Sadistic fantasies or acts may involve activities that indicate the dominance of the person over the victim (e.g., forcing the victim to crawl or keeping the victim in a cage). They may also involve restraint, blindfolding, paddling, spanking, whipping, pinching, beating, burning, electrical shocks, rape, cutting, stabbing, strangulation, torture, mutilation, or killing.

From the preceding definition, a basic behavioral standard can be inferred, which we propose should be required to warrant the use of the term sadistic when describing offender behavior:

1. The intentional infliction of psychological or physical suffering on a conscious victim who is able to experience pain and/or humiliation
2. The infliction of such suffering over a period of time, to support an inference that the suffering was inflicted intentionally and that the offender was sexually aroused by it
3. The association of the intentional infliction of suffering with the offender's sexual arousal or gratification

Some authors suggest that necrophilia and other postmortem behaviors are sadistic in nature. In agreement with Dietz et al. (1995, p. 362), the proposed standard reaffirms that no behavior taking place after a victim is unconscious or deceased meets the burden required for use of the descriptor sadistic:

> The critical issues are whether the victim suffered, whether the suffering was intentionally caused, and whether the suffering sexually aroused the offender. This is why neither sexual nor cruel acts committed on an unconscious or dead victim are necessarily evidence of sadism; such a victim cannot experience suffering.

Further still, some authors make a distinction between the terms sadism and sexual sadism, arguably to accommodate the expanded usage that has evolved in general parlance. The proposed standard reaffirms that sexual gratification is inherent to sadistic behavior, distinguishing it from other forms of cruelty. This is in keeping with the origins of the term, borne out in the behavior and lifestyle of the Marquis de Sade (Seaver and Wainhouse, 1990) and described in the *Psychopathia Sexualis* (Krafft-Ebing, 1997). As such, the term sexual sadism is considered redundant.

This standard is applied with the thought that while many offenders may or may not have sadistic fantasies, what is at issue for investigative or courtroom purposes is the nature and extent of actual behavior. Using this standard, which shares a professional and a historical basis, the authors will now evaluate offender behaviors that have been described as sadistic in the existing literature.

Confusion of Sadism and Lustmurder

Analysis arguably involves the systematic consideration of facts to form conclusions. Predictions are the guesses that one entertains based, presumably, on some form of analysis. Assumptions, on the other hand, are those items that have been accepted as truth or fact without proof.

As already discussed, lustmurder has been defined (Holmes, 1991; Krafft-Ebing, 1997) as any sexually motivated homicide, without respect for sadism. It is a broadly inclusive term that can arguably be used to describe almost any homicide with a sexual element and includes sadistic homicides. It can also include the many forms of non-sadistic homicide.

There are many examples in the literature of authors who either make the assumption that the term sadism and the term lustmurder (or some equivalent) are synonymous, or who use the occurrence of postmortem lustmurder behaviors to predict that the offender is a sadist (Bain et al., 1988; Birnes and Keppel, 1997; De Burger and Holmes, 1988; Geberth, 1996; Geberth and Turco, 1997; Holmes, 1991; Langevin, 1990; Simon, 1996).

One example of a prediction of sadism based on the assumption that postmortem lustmurder behaviors and sadism are synonymous includes Birnes and Keppel (1997). In this work, the authors argue that "if the crime scene looks as though the killer spent time sexually manipulating the victim after death, then he was probably an excitation [sadistic] killer."

Another example is Geberth and Turco (1997, p. 53). In this work, the authors assume that lustmurder involves sadism regardless of victim suffering, based on the assumption that such offenders may be fantasizing about victim suffering either in the crime scene or at a later time.

De River recognizes that even though the offender may not witness any prolonged degree of suffering on the part of the victim, he is likely to "[call] upon his imagination and fancy to supply him with the necessary engrams to satisfy his craving for his depravity." This is not unlike lustmurderers who torture victims before killing them, and then recall "an after-image (engram) of the sensation produced by the physical torture and mutilation, extending beyond time and space." The sadistic scenario is thus conjured in the imagination, be it a recreation of the actual crime scene or the product of fantasy. In each instance, lustmurders are viewed as the behaviors of sadistic sexual psychopaths.

Predictions and assumptions are not facts, and fantasy is not behavior. This distinction may not be important in a treatment setting. However, as will be discussed, it is crucial in the process of investigative and forensic work, where analysis and opinion cannot assume behaviors for which there is no evidence. Further examples of this confusion are elucidated throughout the rest of this chapter and the effects of this confusion are discussed in the conclusion.

Definitions in the Literature

Over the years, many learned researchers have attempted to describe or otherwise elucidate the condition of sadistic offenders. The result has been mixed. In this section, we review some of the more prominent and commonly referenced descriptions of sadism and discuss their veracity in terms of both clarity and adherence to the standard we have proposed.

Burgess et al. (1978, p. 15) described sadism as follows:

> The sadistic offender finds pleasure in hurting the child. … Sexuality becomes an expression of domination and anger. In some way the child symbolizes everything the offender hates about himself, and thereby becomes an object of punishment. The victim's fear, torment, distress, and suffering are important and exciting to the sadistic pedophile, since only in this context is sexual gratification experienced. … His intention is to hurt, degrade, defile, or destroy the child. Sexuality and power are in the service of anger.

This definition appears to be in conflict with itself. The issue of sexual gratification from victim suffering is appropriately raised; however, it is sandwiched within the concept that sexuality and power are servicing aggression and anger. When sexuality and power service anger and aggression, the associated behaviors are best described as anger-retaliatory (see the later section of this chapter called "Generalized Behavioral Assumptions") and not as sadistic. Sadistic behaviors actually involve the use of anger and aggression in the service of sexual gratification. Analysts applying this conflicted definition might confuse anger-retaliatory behavior for sadistic behavior in their casework.

In his work, Groth (1979, pp. 44–45) described sadism this way:

> There is a sexual transformation of anger and power so that aggression itself becomes eroticized. The offender finds the intentional maltreatment of his victim intensely gratifying and takes pleasure in her torment, anguish, distress, helplessness and suffering. … Usually his victims are strangers who share some common characteristic, such as age, appearance, or occupation. They are symbols of something he wants to punish or destroy. … Excitement is associated with the inflicting of pain upon his victim. … Hatred and control are eroticized, so that he finds satisfaction in abusing, degrading, humiliating, and in some cases, destroying his captive.

Again, this presentation appears internally conflicted. It appropriately argues the eroticization of aggression and the need for victim suffering but then goes on to emphasize what can only be described as nonsexual anger-retaliatory motivations involving hatred, punishment, and victim destruction. Again, analysts adhering to this definition might confuse anger-retaliatory behavior for sadistic in their casework.

Cleckley (1988, pp. 290–291), on the other hand, stretched his description of psychopaths to include an element of sadism:

> In a broader sense it might be said that the apparently willful persistence with which they bring humiliation and emotional suffering upon those who love them, as well as failure and unpleasant circumstances upon themselves, marks all psychopaths as both sadists and masochists. Only in this sense, however, are these impulses common or consistent, and the gratification is probably not the directly erotic sensation enjoyed by perverts who literally whip others or have themselves whipped.

This usage of the term sadism ignores two requirements. In an applied sense, it either assumes the intent of the offender to cause suffering or ignores the issue of offender intent altogether. Furthermore, it purposefully removes the requirement of achieving sexual gratification through victim suffering. It ultimately suggests that general cruelty and sadism are really the same thing, regardless of intent or context. While it is possible that Cleckley was being somewhat facetious in this discussion of sadism, in the overall context of his work a reader may not be certain. Therefore, analysts adhering to this generalized description might infer that all psychopaths are also sadists; sadistic behavior may be assumed, and not established, in their case analysis.

Langevin (1990, p. 106) gave a description of sadism that appears to associate it with features of the more inclusive lustmurder:

> Sadism is a sexual anomaly whereby an individual derives sexual gratification from the power and control over his victim, from their fear, terror, humiliation, and degradation, as well as from their injury and death …

> Usually sadists are men who are aroused as much by the force and power as by the sexual acts. They may also engage in bizarre ritualistic behavior and, in conjunction with the sexual entrapment of their victims, they may be sexually aroused by the unconscious or dead body.

This definition is somewhat appropriate and arguably meets the proposed standard for sadism. However, it is potentially confusing because it mentions the possibility of postmortem activity and arousal without qualification. While it is possible that an unconscious or dead body may arouse some sadists, this arousal is non-sadistic and requires separate discussion and description. In a discussion about the defining characteristics of sadistic behavior, the discussion of non-sadistic traits that may be associated with them should be properly qualified to avoid potential confusion.

De Burger and Holmes (1988), Holmes (1991), and Holmes and Holmes (1996) propose a serial killer typology that includes visionary, mission-oriented, hedonistic, and power/control types. In particular, the hedonistic type is broken further into two categories: the lust-oriented killer and the thrill-oriented killer. According to De Burger and Holmes (1988, p. 77),

> Both the lust and the thrill-oriented types of killers may be sadistic with their victims. Yet, unlike the lust killer, the thrill-oriented murderer is primarily impelled to kill not by sexual motives but by a craving for excitement or bizarre experiences. In short, the act or process of killing is enjoyable for this kind of serial murderer.

> This description inappropriately gives the impression that thrill-oriented killers who are not sexually motivated may be referred to as sadistic. If thrill-oriented killers are not sexually motivated, then by definition they cannot be referred to as sadistic; sadism requires a desire for sexual gratification.

Of the lust-oriented killer, Holmes (1991, p. 67) argued further:

> This type of serial killer is motivated by the hunger for sexual gratification. Unfortunately, many such killers are sadistic to the extent that their sexual pleasure depends on the amount of torture and mutilation they can administer, and ultimately on the killing of their victims.

This description directly associates sadism with victim mutilation and victim killing. Given that immediately after this description, Holmes (1991) presents an example where victim mutilation is inflicted postmortem, it is worth noting that victim mutilation is only sadistic when it is carried out with a living, conscious victim. This must be established by a forensic reconstruction and cannot be assumed. It is further worth noting that the act of homicide is not necessarily sadistic in nature (even when sexually motivated) and is often ancillary to an occurrence of sadistic behaviors.

Furthermore, Holmes (1991, p. 126) defines sadism as "sexual gratification received from the punishment of another person" and further states of sadistic rapists that they "seek revenge and punishment from another person by the use of violence and cruelty. The victim is typically only a symbol of the source of his anger."

As with other authors, these definitions are conflicted. They appropriately argue the eroticization of aggression but ignore victim suffering and emphasize what can only be described as nonsexual anger-retaliatory motivations involving punishment and displaced rage. As Dietz et al. (1995, pp. 364–367) warn, analysts adhering to such definitions might proceed to confuse anger-retaliatory behavior for sadistic in their casework.

Dietz et al. (1990, p. 165) say, "a sexual sadist is someone who has established an enduring pattern of sexual arousal in response to sadistic imagery." This description is ambiguous, as the term "sadistic imagery" is not defined. It could refer to imagined behavior, it could refer to actual behavior, or it could refer to both. In any case, it is not commonly regarded as a helpful practice to use the word being defined in its own definition. The ambiguity is carried over into other works (Burgess et al., 1992; Dietz et al. 1996).

Fortunately, Burgess et al. (1992, p. 136) provide helpful, accurate elucidation by adding, "the offender derives the greatest satisfaction from the victim's response to torture," and further still, "the offender's sexual arousal is a function of the victim's pain, fear, or discomfort" (p. 227).

Perhaps one of the most helpful and informed definitions of sadism, however, can be found in Dietz et al. (1995, pp. 361–362):

> Sexual Sadism is a persistent pattern of becoming sexually excited in response to another's suffering. … Inflicting pain is a means to create suffering and to elicit the desired responses of obedience, submission, humiliation, fear, and terror.

There is little room for misinterpretation in this definition, and it easily meets the proposed standard for sadism. These researchers also do their readers the important service of explaining that sadism and criminality are not necessarily the same thing and that many criminal behavior patterns are routinely confused for sadism, including anger- or revenge-motivated cruelty and postmortem mutilation.

Case Examples

Throughout the literature, reference is made to certain high-profile cases as exemplars of sadistic behavior. The cases often involve "serial murderers" whose crimes have been sensationalized not only through all-but-fictional "true crime" novels but also in the media. This section reviews the most prominent of these cases, discussing offenders whose behaviors have been inappropriately labeled sadistic and offenders who actually exhibit sadistic behavior.

Non-Sadistic Cases

Jerome Brudos

Jerry Brudos, a 30-year-old father of two who lost his job as an electrician just months before his arrest, was alleged by authorities to have been responsible for the strangulation deaths of the following women (Turvey, 1994):

- Linda K. Slawson, 19, who disappeared while selling encyclopedias in the Brudos family's neighborhood in Portland, Oregon
- Janet S. Whitney, 23, who disappeared on November 26, 1968, after her car broke down near the Santiam Rest Stop off Interstate-5 just north of Albany, Oregon
- Karen A. Sprinker, 19, who disappeared on March 27, 1969, from the Meier and Frank Co. store parking garage in Salem, Oregon

- Janet Shanahan, 23, who was found stuffed in the trunk of her own car on April 23, 1969, at the intersection of Cross and Maple in Eugene, Oregon
- Linda Dawn Salee, 22, who disappeared on April 23, 1969, from the Lloyd Center shopping mall in Portland, Oregon

Brudos was arrested, pled "innocent by reason of insanity" and made a confession, and mental exams were ordered. After the courts declared him "sane," he recanted his confession and was subsequently convicted on three counts of murder. He was not tried or convicted for the murders of Linda K. Slawson or Janet Shanahan.

According to information and opinions given in Holmes (1991, p. 67), Brudos was best described as a lust killer:

Elaborate stalking, carefully planned activities regarding the extermination of the victim, and sexual experimentation after death (necrophilia) are often elements in lust killings; mutilation of the victim is often perpetrated as well. Jerry Brudos, a serial killer from Oregon, was such a killer.

According to information and opinions given in Geberth and Turco (1997, p. 55), however, which are based on accounts of Brudos's crimes rendered by the imagination of a true-crime author:

Jerry Brudos, dubbed "The Lust Killer," murdered four young women during 1968 and 1969 in a series of lust murders that were predicated on a sadistic and bizarre plan to kidnap and kill women, whom he would force to dress and pose in various sexually provocative positions. …

The behaviors … are appropriately described as psychopathic sexual sadism.

More specific information upon which these conclusions are made can be found in Geberth (1996, pp. 437–438), where Geberth opines of Brudos's offense behavior with his victims, the majority of which are fetishistic and postmortem: "In each case the victim was taken to his garage workshop, which he had equipped for this purpose and where he acted out his sadistic sexual fantasies." Geberth relates only two case examples where premortem behavior (other than that related to victim acquisition) is significant. According to Geberth (1996, p. 437), regarding Brudos's behavior with Karen Sprinker,

[The victim] … was brought to his garage workshop alive. He had sexual intercourse with the victim and then took pictures of her dressed in various stolen undergarments which he had in his collection. He then strangled her. However, he wasn't finished with his outrages. He performed necrophilia with the corpse and then cut off both her breasts to make plastic molds.

Furthermore, according to Geberth (1996, p. 437), regarding Brudos's behavior with Linda Salee,

He brought her back to his garage, where he strangled her as he was raping her. He then hung her corpse from a hook in the ceiling and undressed the body, which he subjected to electrical charges to see if he could make the body dance.

As argued, however, none of the behaviors related by Holmes (1991), Geberth (1996), or Geberth and Turco (1997) satisfy the proposed standard for sadistic behavior. While easily fitting into the vague and inclusive category of lustmurder, Brudos's sexual desires were geared toward non-interactive or deceased victims. He did not intentionally torture his victims before killing them. Nor was victim suffering demonstrably to facilitate his sexual arousal. Rather, he had strong necrophilic (postmortem) desires associated with fetishism.

Nathaniel Code

According to information and opinions given in Burgess et al. (1992, pp. 265–267), Nathaniel Code was best described as an anger-retaliatory offender, evidencing rage and overkill in his offense behavior:

> Nathaniel Code ... killed eight times on three separate occasions. The first homicide [victim], a twenty-five-year-old black female, occurred 8 August 1984. Code stabbed her nine times in the chest and slashed her throat.

> Approximately one year later, on 19 July 1985, Code struck again, this time claiming four victims: a fifteen-year-old girl, her mother, and two male friends. Code nearly severed the girl's head from her body. Her mother died from asphyxiation and was draped over the side of the bathtub. Code shot one of the males in the head, leaving him in the middle of the bedroom. The other male was found in the front bedroom, shot twice in the chest with his throat slashed.

> The last case took place on 5 August 1987. The victims were Code's grandfather and his two young nephews, ages eight and twelve. The boys died of ligature strangulation. Code stabbed his grandfather five times in the chest and seven times in the back. ...

> Nathaniel Code had a very distinctive calling card. The injuries suffered by the victims demonstrated one aspect of his signature. Code employed a bloody method of attack and overkill. ... Code wounded nearly all of the victims far beyond what was necessary to cause death (overkill). ...

> Code forced the mother to witness her daughter's death as part of his ritual of control, formed from his rage. If the victim's response threatened his sense of domination, Code reacted with anger and the excessive violence that led to overkill. ...

> In all three cases, the victims were bound with electrical appliance or telephone cords acquired at the scene. ... He used a handcuff style configuration, with a loop around each wrist. He also bound the ankles handcuff style and connected them to the wrists by a lead going through the legs.

As argued in this description, Code's offenses contained a theme of domination and control, driven by rage and not sexual gratification.

As Birnes and Keppel (1997) argued,

> There was also a shift from an ultimately unsatisfying assault in the primary sexual continuum—the killer ejaculated at the first homicide—to the concentrated use of secondary sexual mechanisms to produce a pathological sense of power—the killer's anger was the focus of the assault, and not sexual satisfaction.

They also argued:

> Nathaniel Code's sexual satisfaction ... made its appearance indirectly and was defused. His major concentration was the substitution of sexual release through an expression of power exhibited through ritualistic binding and cutting of his victims. In other words, the process of carrying out his anger through torture and forced submission substituted for sexual gratification.

This seems to be somewhat in agreement with Burgess et al. (1992). However, Birnes and Keppel (1997) present the Code case as their primary example of sadistic behavior in a crime scene. Having repeatedly argued that anger and rage are being serviced by this offender's behavior, such a classification seems paradoxical. Analysts adhering to this conflicted description might proceed to confuse anger-retaliatory behavior for sadistic in their casework.

Ted Bundy

Perhaps the most commonly analyzed serial murderer in the literature is Theodore (Ted) Robert Bundy, who was 43 years old when put to death for his crimes in 1989. He is credited with having killed at least 20 victims from January 1974 to February 1978, although he confessed to many more. His known victims were females, ages 12 to 26, spanning the United States across Washington, Oregon, Utah, Colorado, and Florida. He is widely referred to as a psychopathic sexual sadist.

- "Ted Bundy, in addition to being a serial killer, must be viewed as a serial sadistic rapist" (Holmes, 1991, p. 81)
- "Far from being the Rudolph Valentino of the serial killer world, Ted Bundy was a brutal, sadistic, perverted man" (Ressler and Schactman, 1992, p. 63)
- "Clinically speaking, Ted Bundy was a sexual psychopath who enjoyed killing women in the context of expressing his sadistic sexual fantasies" (Geberth, 1996, p. 748)

Simon (1996) noted generally of Bundy's offense behavior:

> With his arm in a cast, he would get them into his car, or to some isolated spot, and then bludgeon them with a short crowbar concealed in the removable arm cast. While the women were unconscious or semiconscious, he would then commit gross sexual acts, including anal assault. Bundy bit various body parts, sometimes biting off a victim's nipple or leaving bitemarks on her buttocks. He killed the victims by strangulation. He mutilated and decapitated their bodies, and severed their hands with a hacksaw. He would leave the bodies in secluded spots and return to them after several days to commit necrophilic acts such as ejaculating into the mouth of a disembodied head.

Birnes and Keppel (1997), opining on Bundy's fantasies and motivations, argued:

> He wanted to attack only those who didn't know him and to make sure they were unconscious or dead as soon after he met them as was possible. He was a necrophile who carried his victims over the threshold of death where he could exercise complete control over their corpses. That was the only relationship his fantasy allowed him.

And, later,

> Ted's intention was to spend his time with dead victims, not put himself in jeopardy by dealing with live ones. That's why he knocked his victims out almost immediately, transported them to a dump site, and murdered them so that he could experience sexual gratification through necrophilia.

There are numerous accounts of Bundy's necrophilic and other postmortem fantasy-oriented behavior related in the literature. None of them relates behavior that could be described as sadistic. There are, however, behavioral instances worth discussing.

First, during an interview with Supervisory Special Agent (SSA) Bill Hagmaier of the FBI, Bundy stated that after he kidnapped Janice Ott and Denise Naslund from Lake Sammamish on July 14, 1974, one of them had to watch as the other was killed (Geberth, 1996, p. 751). Given the context of this offense and subsequent postmortem activity, sadistic intent cannot be reliably argued regarding this act. Bundy's preferred behavioral interaction was with an unconscious or deceased victim; therefore, the fact that one victim had to watch as the other was killed was ancillary to Bundy's primary motives. This, of course, assumes that Bundy was being truthful in his account.

Second, one of the two victims that Bundy killed at the Chi Omega sorority house in Tallahassee, Florida, on January 15, 1978, had been bitten (Geberth, 1996, p. 753). Some might argue that this constitutes a sadistic act. However, arguments relating to the bite mark in the literature do not discuss whether the victim was conscious, unconscious, or deceased when the bite mark was inflicted. This would need to be established before an informed behavioral analysis could be made. Further still, the context of the biting is during what could be described as violent rage. So, even if the bite was inflicted premortem, it arguably did not occur in the required context for sadistic intent.

Finally, as referenced by Geberth (1996, p. 752), Bundy is known to have given the following statement, which, at face value, might be interpreted by some as evidencing a sadistic fantasy:

> You feel the last bit of breath leaving their body. You're looking into their eyes. A person in that situation is God! You then possess them and they shall be a part of you, and the grounds where you kill them or leave them become sacred to you, and you will always be drawn back to them.

Upon closer analysis, there is no mention of sexual arousal and gratification, and there is no discussion of prolonged victim agony or suffering. This statement is arguably about power and control only. It does not refer to achieving sadistic needs.

Jack the Ripper

Perhaps the most infamous and sensationalized serial murderer of all time is the self-named "Jack the Ripper." He is credited with having killed at least five female victims between August 31 and November 9, 1888, in the Whitechapel section of the East End of London. According to Eckert (1981),

> Each victim was a woman of the streets who was a heavy drinker and apparently heavily intoxicated when she was killed. All except one were strangled, had their throats cut, and were mutilated after they were killed. The victim who was not mutilated was strangled and saved from desecration when the killer was startled and interrupted before carrying out postmortem mutilation. The last victim was killed indoors, and all deaths occurred late in the evening or in the early morning hours.

> This killer was never identified, and subsequently never apprehended.

At least one heavily referenced work has described these offenses as sadistic: "His two assaults were ritualized, compulsive, and highly sadistic, much along the lines of the classic case of Jack the Ripper" (Burgess et al., 1992, p. 230).

However, Eckert (1989) and Turvey (1999) both interpret this offender's behavior as demonstrably non-sadistic, they describe an offender who evidences both anger-retaliatory and reassurance-oriented behaviors. According to Turvey (1999, p. 330), "There is a lot of passive anger evidenced in these crimes, and other behaviors speak to a lot of inadequacy on the part of the offender." Key behaviors included the following:

- The lack of sexual assault to the victims.
- The fact that the victims were overpowered on the street, killed, and mutilated in a short space of time save the last victim, discovered indoors.
- The lack of any evidence of torture to a living, conscious victim.
- Power over the victim's sexuality by humiliating them with postmortem mutilation and displaying of their bodies. This behavior is also experimental in nature, as opposed to ritualistic (he does different things with the organs from each body—not the same thing every time).
- The need to instill fear, terror, or shock in the public and law enforcement, thereby demonstrating his power and superiority to law enforcement.

■ The need to have his actions seen or heard about by others; the need to have his victims found and his "work" on display.

Sadistic Cases

Neville G. C. Heath

As an example of a psychopathic sadist, Cleckley (1988, pp. 291–293) presents the case of Neville G. C. Heath. At the time of his arrest in 1946, Heath was a 29-year-old former Royal Air Force officer who had been court-martialed in 1941 for charges related to fraud and being absent without leave. His personality was described as charming, profoundly sincere, and irresistible to women; he was said to have the ability to impress others easily as a man of wealth and intelligence.

On Friday, June 21, 1946, the dead body of 32-year-old film extra Margery Gardner was found in room number 4 of Pembridge Court Hotel in Notting Hill, London. Her ankles were bound with a handkerchief. Additionally, her nipples had been bitten off, and there were many whip marks on her back, chest, stomach, and face. The forensic pathologist, Dr. Keith Simpson, determined that she had suffocated, either from a gag or from having her face pressed into a pillow. The room her body was found in was registered to Mr. and Mrs. N. G. C. Heath.

On July 6, 1946, the dead body of 21-year-old Doreen Marshall, formerly of the Women's Royal Naval Service, was found in Branksome Chine. She was discovered in some rhododendron bushes, naked with the exception of her left shoe. Her clothing had been placed on top of her. Before her death, her hands had been bound, and they bore defensive cut marks suggesting that she tried to resist a knife attack. She died of exsanguination, after having her throat cut.

Heath was charged only with the murder of Margery Gardner, but the details of the Doreen Marshall killing were allowed into evidence. Though his lawyers tried to plead Heath's insanity, the jury found him guilty on September 24, 1946. He was executed by hanging one month later. According to Cleckley (1988, p. 292),

> Each of the two young women tortured and killed by Heath within a period of three weeks was cruelly butchered. The sexually sadistic quality of Heath's behavior on these two occasions is made plain by the nature of the mutilations. A nipple was bitten entirely from one girl's breast. … With the other girl, this had almost been accomplished. At the autopsy both showed that some instrument, perhaps a poker, had been thrust with violence into the vagina, rupturing it and damaging the abdominal viscera. In one of the victims the poker had apparently been driven far up into the abdominal cavity and twisted about with great violence. One body had been lashed severely by a heavy, metal-tipped whip. … The abdomen of one woman had been ripped open so extensively that the intestines emerged and spread sickeningly over the area about her body. One deep gash started below the genital organs and extended up into the breast. …

> The victims were tightly bound and gagged. Points brought out at the autopsies indicate that Heath wanted the women to remain alive as long as possible to experience the agony resulting from his vicious torture and that he seemed to relish the butchery, particularly while the victims still remained conscious and capable of feeling it. Apparently, he also found perverse sexual satisfaction in continuing after death the gruesome and protracted mutilation of the bodies.

Many of the offense behaviors related in this account, in context, are arguably sadistic. They include whipping the victims, binding their limbs, gagging their mouths, premortem insertion of items into the vagina (with violent twisting), premortem mutilation with the knife, and premortem biting of the victims' breasts. However, not everything that a sadist does is sadistic. Any postmortem acts committed by the offender (e.g., cutting or mutilating), although perhaps sexually motivated, could not have induced the requisite victim suffering and should not be described as sadistic.

Paul

As an example of a sadistic offender, Burgess et al. (1978, p. 16) present the case of "Paul," a single white 19-year-old male who was convicted of four rapes but later admitted to more than 20. According to his account, he would typically select an innocent-looking girl, around the age of 12, and force her into the woods with a knife. He further related the following:

> Then I'd give her a choice: I would rape her or cut off her hair. I'd tie her hands behind her back with my belt, put the point of my knife between her eyes, and threaten to kill her. Then I'd get undressed and make her lick my body and blow me because I knew she wouldn't want to do it. I'd get all shaky and excited. I would keep her scared and frightened—her fear and suffering gave me pleasure. Sometimes while the girl was blowing me I'd burn her with a cigarette on her shoulder and ass and "come off" in her mouth, sometimes I would punch her and stomp on her hand with my workboots. … Even now when I think about a girl getting beat up, or see it on television, I get a "hard-on."

All of the offense behaviors related in this account, in context, are arguably sadistic. Aggression and violence are in the service of increasing sexual gratification. Note, however, the absence of homicide. As discussed, sadistic behavior does not necessarily result in a homicidal act.

Generalized Behavioral Assumptions

A review of the literature makes it evident that many authors advocate that certain behaviors are always sadistic, irrespective of their context. These authors cite their own experiences of behavioral associations in casework, or more often they reason that, for certain behaviors, one can assume extended victim suffering and assume that the offender's motive and intent were to inflict and enjoy that suffering to service sexual gratification.

These authors are introducing generalized and potentially inaccurate behavioral assumptions into the motivational analysis of individual offender behavioral patterns. As already discussed, unless a behavior is intentionally inflicted on a living, conscious victim for the purpose of achieving sexual gratification, it does not qualify as sadism. Broad generalizations regarding the motivations of a single behavior across multiple offenders, based on the motives of other offenders, deprives individual behaviors of their context and meaning (Turvey, 1999, p. 171).

The inference of motivation from physical evidence of behavior, and behavioral patterns, for investigative or courtroom purposes, is an expedition into the realm of forensic examination regardless of the professional involved. Forensic examination is about the exploration of possibility. Until proper forensic tests and analysis have been undertaken and the context of the offense behaviors narrowed by virtue of crime reconstruction efforts, those possibilities cannot be reliably inferred.

More to the point, a forensic examiner can form opinions regarding only the behavioral elements of an offense for which there is physical and behavioral evidence. Consider the following examples from the literature.

Rape

The generic term *rape* is not a specific behavior but rather a penal classification that represents the occurrence of a variety of potential offender behaviors. These can include, depending on the laws of the region, forcible penetration of a victim's vagina with a foreign object, forcible penetration of the victim's mouth with a penis, or forcible penetration of a victim's anus with a finger. Accordingly, when used as the only descriptor of an offender's behavior, this term has limited behavioral meaning.

Knight et al. (1988), Hazelwood et al. (1991), and Turvey (1999) agree, based on initial studies conducted by Groth (1979) and continued research efforts, that the psychological needs satisfied by rapist behavior can be described by four general categories:

- Power-reassurance (compensatory). Nonaggressive behavior that normalizes an attack for an offender, which restores an offender's doubts about his desirability
- Power-assertive (exploitative). Aggressive but nonlethal behavior that shows no outward doubt of masculinity, which restores an offender's inner doubts and fears
- Anger-retaliatory (displaced). Behavior in which high levels physical and sexual aggression service feelings of cumulative rage
- Anger-excitation (sadistic). Behavior, where offender aggression is put in the service of causing victim pain and suffering to service the offender's sexual gratification

As to the sadistic aspect of any rape behavior in general, however, Dietz et al. (1995, p. 362), argue:

> Rapists cause their victims to suffer, but only sexual sadists intentionally inflict that suffering, whether physical or psychological, to enhance their own arousal.

If the acts involved in a particular rape (e.g., some kind of forced penetration) are used as torture, over time, to humiliate the victim and cause suffering specifically to sexually arouse the offender, then a reasonable argument for their classification as sadistic can be made. In the absence of these types of acts, other psychological needs may be at work. Therefore, it is the duty of the forensic examiner to analyze the established patterns of behavior in a particular case and form opinions about the nature of individual behaviors within the context of those patterns.

Anal Assault

Anal assault is a term that may refer, generally, to any physical attack of the anus. Some examiners consider this behavior sadistic in any context because it involves the infliction of pain to a victim associated with a sexual act. Such an interpretation also assumes the intent of an offender to inflict suffering.

It is certainly true that some offenders, for the purposes of servicing their own sexual gratification, insert objects into a victim's rectum in order to witness their subsequent suffering. This could be described accurately as a sadistic behavior. However, some offenders force objects into a victim's orifices, including the anus, either premortem to service anger-retaliatory motivations, or postmortem to service fantasy-based reassurance-oriented motivations.

For example, Krafft-Ebing (1997, pp. 230–231) adduces case number 216, that of a lustmurder, involving a 19-year-old male laborer, referred to as "K," who killed a 10-year-old girl named Anna:

> [H]er body was found about fifty paces from the main road, in a copse. The face was turned to the ground; the mouth was gagged with moss; [there were] signs of a criminal assault about the anus. …
>
> K. was arrested. At first he denied the deed; but afterwards made a complete confession. He had strangled the child, and when she stopped kicking and resisting, committed sodomy upon her.

In this case the anal rape, referred to here by the general term sodomy, occurred after the child was unconscious, possibly even after the child was deceased. In either case, the burden for sadism is not met. The anal rape behavior described in this case arguably falls more within the parameters of reassurance-oriented.

Strangulation

Both manual and ligature strangulation involve the restriction of oxygenated blood to a victim's brain by compressing the arteries in the neck. It is true that some offenders engage in the practice in order to bring the victim in and out of consciousness, achieving sexual gratification from the victim's intermittent suffering responses. This could be described accurately as a sadistic behavior. However, some offenders employ strangulation in their offense behavior not for fantasy but for function. Manual and ligature strangulation may be used in the process of subduing, controlling, punishing, or killing a victim separately from sadistic motivations.

For example, Krafft-Ebing (1997) adduces case number 18, that of a lustmurder, involving a 26-year-old homeless man named Vacher who was found "guilty of eleven murders, which are acts of sadism, Lustmurder. They consisted of strangling, cutting of the throat and ripping open of the abdomen, mutilation of the corpse, especially the genitals, eventually gratification of the sexual lust on the corpse."

In this example, sadism is also attributed to the overall aspect of the crimes by the author. Paradoxically, the majority of the acts committed on the victim were postmortem. Strangulation was Vacher's method of killing, but there is no evidence, as argued, that killing the victims was anything other than functional. That is to say, the offender could not engage in his preferred behaviors (postmortem mutilation) with a living, conscious victim, and sexual gratification was not associated with any premortem activity. The behavior in this case, as argued by Krafft-Ebing (1997), does not meet the burden required for use of the term sadistic.

Biting

Brittain (1970), while widely referenced in the literature, does not give a specific operational definition of sadistic behavior in his opinion piece on the topic. He does remark of biting that:

> Bite marks may be found and are most commonly on the breasts or neck of the victim but they are not restricted to these sites. They can vary from being minor to being very severe. They can occur in homosexual as well as heterosexual sadistic murders.

It should be noted that this vague behavioral discussion is representative of Brittain's overall approach to the topic of sadism. He first adduces examples of behaviors that might be sadistic, but then he fails to define specific contexts in which sadism is a certainty.

Some offenders bite their victims, leaving visible and identifiable bite marks on the surface of the skin and in the tissue beneath. Geberth (1996, pp. 636–639) discusses three possibilities motivating the infliction of bite marks:

- Sadistic pleasure, commonly associated with ecchymotic or "suck mark" patterns
- Punishment or anger, commonly associated with cases involving child abuse
- Defensive action, which can arguably be associated with both victims and offenders who are fighting off physical attacks

Therefore, while biting can be a sadistic act, it is not necessarily so. Any sadistic motivation associated with biting behavior must be established and cannot be assumed.

Killing the Victim

Some offenders kill their victims. However, the act of killing is not evidence, by itself, of sadism. First, there must be victim suffering. Even then, victim suffering may be ancillary to an offender's purpose. There must, again, be evidence of offender sexual gratification from that suffering. Sadists, arguably, would want to keep their victims alive and conscious as long as possible in order to continue their gratification from that suffering. The earlier on in the offense a victim is killed, the less likely it is that there would have been an opportunity for sadistic behavior.

Killing a Victim in Front of Another Victim

As discussed in the previous example, some offenders kill their victims. However, the act of killing is not evidence, by itself, of sadism. Nor is the act of killing one victim in the presence of another inherently sadistic. As one possibility among many, homicide may be precautionary in nature, to rid the offender of a living witness. In such a case, any suffering or trauma experienced on the part of the second living, conscious victim is ancillary to the offender's motives. As another possibility, homicide may be retaliatory in nature, done in the presence of living victims who witness the act but are not the object of the offender's rage.

Postmortem Mutilation

Postmortem mutilation of a victim is perhaps the one behavior that is most consistently, and quite erroneously, described as sadistic. As already discussed, this is likely in no small part due to the confusion in the literature between lustmurder and sadism. For example, one clinician (Simon, 1996) describing sadistic behavior argued:

> Serial sexual killers are always sadistic, sometimes necrophilic, often both. They all obtain sexual thrills from the hurt and terror they produce in their victims, and from the total power they wield over their victims, alive or dead.

Aside from being a broad generalization that does not hold true when applied to known serial murder cases, this statement suggests that sadistic behavior can include power exercised over a dead, nonresponsive victim. As already discussed, by definition, unconscious or deceased victims cannot give a sadist the type of feedback required for sexual arousal (crying, screaming, begging, whimpering, struggling, etc.). Therefore, postmortem acts (such as necrophilia), or acts committed on an unconscious victim, cannot be accurately described as sadistic.

For example, Bain et al. (1988) adduce the case of an alleged sadist, Mr. A, who "murdered a woman and had intercourse with the corpse. He then removed the genitals and was contemplating eating them when he was interrupted by a third party and fled the scene of his crime." The behavior in this case, as argued by Bain et al. (1988), does not meet the burden required for use of the term sadistic.

As another example, Holmes (1991, p. 124) defines necrosadism as "interest in having sex with dead bodies; necrosadistic killers murder to have sex with the dead." This term is, for lack of a better word, an oxymoron. The dead cannot suffer. Sadism requires victim suffering. Therefore, this term is not only inappropriate, but misleading.

Expressing "Sadistic" Tendencies in a Post-Offense Interview

Many authors base their interpretations of sadistic offense behaviors on statements made by an offender during post-offense interviews. Clinical training and experience interviewing sex offenders aside, there are a number of practical reasons why the results of any post-offense offender interviews should not be taken at face value. According to Abel and Rouleau (1990, p. 10), in cases where parole is a possibility:

> To be forthright and honest about the number of his sex crimes, or the degree to which he used force and violence during his assaults, may severely jeopardize the offender's opportunity to leave prison and might extend his incarceration should he be found guilty of new sex crimes that were revealed during questioning.

However, in cases where parole is not a possibility, there are equally compelling reasons for offenders to deceive interviewers about the nature and extent of their criminal behavior. These include the following:

■ Offenders may perceive the possibility of a plea or deal and may fashion the details of their criminal activities to fit those particular needs
■ Offenders may be embarrassed by certain aspects of their activity with victims (e.g., they may not wish to admit that they prefer to engage in sexual activity with the dead and may subsequently relate that such activities were premortem)
■ Offenders may wish to be perceived as more intelligent and competent than their criminal activities suggest (e.g., an offender may agree to being a sadist or proffer what the offender perceives to be sadistic details in the crimes or fantasies after hearing that sadists are the most intelligent offenders)
■ Offenders may wish to be perceived as tougher, more dangerous, or more accomplished than their criminal activities suggest, to service their own egos or their criminal reputation (e.g., offenders may admit to offenses that they did not commit or proffer what they perceive to be sadistic fantasies or details regarding their crimes in order to be perceived as more dangerous by those in prison and in the general public)

CONCLUSION

After a thorough examination of the publications referenced in this literature review, the authors have formed several conclusions relevant to forensic casework.

First, and perhaps most important, the term sadistic is not consistently applied within the literature by investigators, criminologists, or those in the treatment community. Moreover, it is often vaguely defined and broadly employed.

Second, two common misinterpretations of sadism are evident in the literature:

1. Behaviors motivated by punishment and anger are misinterpreted as sadistic
2. Postmortem necrophilic or mutilation behaviors are misinterpreted as sadistic

The second type of misinterpretation may occur in some instances because of an examiner's assumptions that mutilation is always premortem. This assumption, which appeared to occur numerous times in the literature, may suggest a lack of reliance on competently, objectively reconstructed offender behavior when forensic opinions are being formed. That is to say, examiners may assume behaviors that are not being established by the physical evidence for the purposes of forming opinions regarding offender sadism. This practice is not justifiable.

Third, a number of authors (De Burger and Holmes, 1988; Geberth, 1996; Geberth and Turco, 1997; Holmes, 1991; Holmes and Holmes, 1996) consistently referenced fictionalized and sensationalized "true crime" novels as primary source material for their research regarding specific offender behaviors. This practice undermines the credibility of accounts given in legitimate research, raising issues of reliability and objectivity. Most disturbing is a practice in the professional community where some adopt as fact the sensationalized, fictionalized reconstructions of offenses by "true crime" authors as proper data for study.

Finally, in reference to those offenses described as sadistic or lustmurder, the author notes frequent and liberal use of relative moral descriptors. In fact, some authors have devoted sections of their professional work to discussing the moral disposition of particular offender types and, as evidenced by excerpts in this chapter, frequently use such subjective and relative terms as:

Bad
Cold blooded

Crazy
Evil
Monstrous
Perverse

These subjective terms and moral positions form the basis for emotional arguments, not logical ones. Their meaning is furthermore culturally subjective. Therefore, while they do give readers insight into the personal belief system of the authors who use them, they arguably act as a tangible barrier between researchers and their understanding of individual offender motivations. The use of such terms does not advance the cause of objective research.

SUMMARY

Psychopathy and sadism are offender classifications that are behaviorally determined. That is to say, the diagnosis of psychopathy or sadism is largely dependent on behavioral evidence. Because criminal profilers may encounter and address related behavioral patterns and crime scene characteristics, they must have an appreciation for the history and interpretation of both.

Psychopathy is characterized by a constellation of traits, including impulsivity, callousness, and irresponsibility, that are detailed in the *Hare Psychopathy Checklist—Revised*. All psychopaths are not equal, and by extension all psychopathic behavior is not equal. Psychopathic behavior exists on a continuum.

While motivated by the same things as other criminals, the psychopath can use brutal and exploitative methods that can be carried out in the absence of any remorse whatsoever. Psychopaths are not encumbered by distress, empathy, or remorse.

Sadism is a clinical term that has been adopted for non-clinical usage. Most often it is used to incorrectly describe any perceived cruel act without respect to specific motivation or context. A historical review of the origins of the term reveals that sadism refers to the intentional infliction of psychological or physical suffering on a conscious victim, able to experience pain or humiliation, for the purpose of the offender's sexual gratification.

Misunderstandings of the origins of the term have also led to its confusion as a synonym for the generic concept of lustmurder in the pseudo-professional literature. This has in turn led to the misclassification of many high-profile offenders as sadistic and the incorrect assumption that certain behaviors are inherently sadistic. While these practices are good for book sales and the enhancement of criminal prosecutions, they are nonetheless inaccurate. Given the forensic implications of interpreting sadistic behavior in a crime scene, the profiler has a duty to approach such interpretations with informed humility.

Questions

1. Give three examples of psychopathic behavior.
2. Explain the difference between psychopathy and antisocial personality disorder.
3. True or False: It is possible to commit a sadistic act on a corpse.
4. What is the primary motivation for sadistic behavior?
5. Give three examples of sadistic behavior.

REFERENCES

Abel, G., Rouleau, J., 1990. The Nature and Extent of Sexual Assault. In: Marshall, W.L., Laws, D., Barbaree, H. (Eds.), Handbook of Sexual Assault: Issues, Theories, and Treatment of the Offender. Plenum Press, New York, NY.

American Psychiatric Association, 1994. Diagnostic and Statistical Manual of Mental Disorders, fourth edition. American Psychiatric Association, Washington, DC.

Bain, J., Dickey, R., Hucker, S., Langevin, R., Wortzman, S., Wright, P., 1988. Sexual Sadism: Brain, Blood, and Behavior. Annals of the New York Academy of Science 528, 163–171.

Birnes, W., Keppel, R., 1997. Signature Killers: Interpreting the Calling Cards of the Serial Murderer. Pocket Books, New York, NY.

Brittain, R., 1970. The Sadistic Murderer. Medicine, Science and Law 10, 198–207.

Burgess, A.W., Burgess, A.G., Douglas, J., Ressler, R., 1992. Crime Classification Manual. Lexington Books, New York, NY.

Burgess, A., Douglas, J., Ressler, R., 1988. Sexual Homicide: Patterns and Motives. Lexington Books, New York, NY.

Burgess, A., Groth, A.N., Holmstrom, L., Sgroi, S., 1978. Sexual Assault of Children and Adolescents. Lexington Books, New York, NY.

Cleckley, H., 1976. Mask of Sanity, fifth edition. Mosby, St. Louis, MO.

Cleckley, H., 1988. The Mask of Sanity, fifth edition. Mosby, Augusta, GA.

De Burger, J., Holmes, R., 1988. Serial Murder. Sage, Newbury Park, CA.

De Sade, M., 1990. Justine. In: Seaver, R., Wainhouse, A. (Eds.), The Marquis de Sade: Justine, Philosophy in the Bedroom, and Other Writings. Grove Press, New York, NY, pp. 447–743.

Dietz, P., Hazelwood, R., Warren, J., 1990. The Sexually Sadistic Criminal and His Offenses. Bulletin of the American Academy of Psychiatry and the Law 18, 163–178.

Dietz, P., Hazelwood, R., Warren, J., 1995. The Criminal Sexual Sadist. In: Burgess, A.W., Hazelwood, R. (Eds.), Practical Aspects of Rape Investigation: A Multidisciplinary Approach. second edition. CRC Press, Boca Raton, FL.

Dietz, P., Hazelwood, R., Warren, J., 1996. The Sexually Sadistic Serial Killer. Journal of Forensic Science 41 (6), 970–974.

Eckert, W.G., 1981. The Whitechapel Murders: The Case of Jack the Ripper. American Journal of Forensic Medicine and Pathology 2 (1), 53–60.

Eckert, W.G., 1989. The Ripper Project: Modern Science Solving Mysteries of History. American Journal of Forensic Medicine and Pathology 10 (2), 164–171.

Geberth, V., 1996. Practical Homicide Investigation, third edition. CRC Press, Boca Raton, FL.

Geberth, V., Turco, R., 1997. Antisocial Personality Disorder, Sexual Sadism, Malignant Narcissism, and Serial Murder. Journal of Forensic Science 42 (1), 49–60.

Groth, A.N., 1979. Men Who Rape: The Psychology of the Offender. Plenum Press, New York, NY.

Hare, R., 1991. Psychopathy and the DSM-IV Criteria for Antisocial Personality Disorder. Journal of Abnormal Psychology 100 (3), 391–398.

Hare, R., 1993. Without Conscience. Pocket Books, New York, NY.

Hare, R., 1996. Psychopathy and Antisocial Personality Disorder: A Case of Diagnostic Confusion. Psychiatric Times 13 (2).

Harrington, A., 1972. Psychopaths. Simon & Schuster, New York, NY.

Hazelwood, R., Reboussin, R., Warren, J., Wright, J., 1991. Prediction of Rapist Type and Violence from Verbal, Physical, and Sexual Scales. Journal of Interpersonal Violence 6 (1), 55–67.

Holmes, R., 1991. Sex Crimes. Sage, Newbury Park, CA.

Holmes, R., Holmes, S., 1996. Profiling Violent Crimes: An Investigative Tool, second edition. Sage, Thousand Oaks, CA.

Knight, R.A., Lee, A., Prentky, R.A., Rosenburg, R., 1988. Validating the Components of a Taxonomic System for Rapists: A Path Analytic Approach. Bulletin of the American Academy of Psychiatry and Law 16 (2), 169–185.

Krafft-Ebing, R., 1997. Psychopathia Sexualis. Velvet, London, England.

Langevin, R., 1990. Sexual Anomalies and the Brain. In: Marshall, W.L., Laws, D., Barbaree, H. (Eds.), Handbook of Sexual Assault: Issues, Theories, and Treatment of the Offender. Plenum Press, New York, NY.

Mealey's *Daubert* Reports, 2000. 4th Circuit Finds No Error in Admission of Psychopathy Opinion, Mealey's *Daubert* Report (May 2000), Mealey. Cited in United States v. Aquilia Barnette (2000) Nos. 98–05, 98–11.

Minnesota, 1994. Psychopathic Personality Commitment Law. State of Minnesota, Office of the Legislative Auditor Executive Summary, February 25.

Minnesota v. Leon James Preston, 2001. No. C5-00-1715, June 12 (629 N.W.2d 104).

Minnesota v. Crawford Wilson, 2000. No. C3-00-434, August 22 (2000 WL 1182807).

Porter, S., Woodworth, M., 2007. I'm Sorry I Did It … But He Started It: A Comparison of the Official and Self-Reported Homicide Descriptions of Psychopaths and Non-Psychopaths. Law and Human Behavior 31, 91–107.

Ressler, R., Schactman, T., 1992. Whoever Fights Monsters. St. Martin's Press, New York, NY.

Seaver, R., Wainhouse, A. (Eds.), 1990. The Marquis de Sade: Justine, Philosophy in the Bedroom, and Other Writings. Grove Press, New York, NY.

Simon, R., 1996. Bad Men Do What Good Men Dream: A Forensic Psychiatrist Illuminates the Darker Side of Human Behavior American Psychiatric Press, Washington, DC.

Toch, H. (Ed.), 1979. Psychology of Crime and Criminal Justice. Holt, Rinehart, and Winston, New York, NY, Chapter 14.

Turvey, B., 1994. [Interview with Jerome H. Brudos] Author's notes, unpublished, Oregon State Penitentiary, June 7, 1994.

Turvey, B., 1999. Criminal Profiling: An Introduction to Behavioral Evidence Analysis. Academic Press, London, England.

United States v. Aquilia Barnette, 2000. Nos. 98-5, 98-11, May 2, 2000 (C.A.4) (N.C.).

Walsh, Z., Kosson, D., 2007. Psychopathy and Violent Crime: A Prospective Study of the Influence of Socioeconomic Status and Ethnicity. Law and Human Behavior 31, 209–229.

Sex Crimes

Brent E. Turvey

CONTENTS

KEY TERMS

Bestiality (or zooerasty)

Child molestation

Consent

Fetish burglary

Necrophilia

Physical or mental disability

Preferential bestiality (or zoophilia)

Rape

Sexual assault

Sex crime

Sexting

Sodomy

Voyeurism

Criminal profilers have a duty to be fully versed in the prevalence, nature, and variety of sex crimes that may be encountered in research and casework. Those who enter the profession ignorant of the subject do it a disservice, and those who avoid study of the subject would do best to leave it immediately. One cannot be a competent criminal investigator or criminal profiler without significant exposure to, and a healthy appreciation of, human sexuality and its criminal manifestations.

The term *sex crime* generally refers to any confluence of criminal and sexual acts. In some cases, sexual activity is inherently criminal, such as that involving a lack of consent. In other cases, sexual activity occurs between "consenting" parties but still involves a crime, as with prostitution in certain jurisdictions. As explained in Torres and van der Walt (2009, p. 450), "the law not only defines who can be a 'victim' of sexual assault, but also which specific sexual behaviors can be criminalized, even between consenting adults." Consider the description provided in Griffin and West (2006, pp. 143–144):

> "Sex crime" is a term that identifies a multitude of possible offenses toward an individual or community that either directly or indirectly relates to sex. A few of the most common sex crimes include child molestation, exhibitionism, incest, rape, and voyeurism. There are many manifestations of each of these crimes. For example, rape is often categorized in one of two ways: acquaintance rape and stranger rape. ... However, it should be noted that sex crimes are not the same as sexual disorders.

Those who commit sex crimes are accurately referred to as sex offenders. However, sex offenders are not all alike. They are varied, each with his or her own constellation of behaviors, motives, and capabilities existing on a broad continuum of intensity and severity.

Unfortunately, and owing to persistent ignorance, there is a public and professional tendency to regard all of those who commit sex crimes as essentially the same. A perspective that remains true to this day was offered in East (1946, p. 529):

> Sexual offenders are perhaps more liable to be misjudged by prejudice and ignorance than the majority of criminals. Bias is almost inevitable if their conduct is reviewed solely in the light of narrow personal experience and the tastes and distastes of the assessor. Many persons of both sexes are grossly ignorant on sexual matters in spite of the modern tendency to discuss the subject with a considerable amount of freedom. Some husbands, in effect, commit rape upon their wives because they do not understand the art of married life and do not realize that a woman is at a disadvantage unless a psychical approach precedes each physical contact. Such sexually unaesthetic men and women, manifestly incompetent to pass judgment upon the interrelationships of the sexes, may be called upon as members of a jury to assess the guilt of a sexual offender.

Currently, the primary cause of this same general lack of accurate knowledge is the uncritical acceptance of film, television, and media accounts of crime—fiction and non-fiction alike. In particular, the author is continually amazed at the extent to which film and television are viewed as reliable sources of information, even among those who absolutely know better. This has resulted in uninformed education, uninformed legislation, uninformed investigative and adjudication efforts, and even uninformed ideas about treatment.

THE HISTORICAL VIEW

Throughout history, each culture has sought to define unacceptable (e.g., criminal) sexual behavior in ways that best reflect prevailing attitudes and beliefs. These determinations and related penalties are by no means uniform or static, differing and evolving radically across cultures and generations. As explained in East (1946, p. 528),

> Ideas change with the times. The Mosaic Law imposed the penalty of death on both parties when a married woman committed adultery. The old Roman Law punished adultery on the part of the wife but not on the part of the husband. Although under Roman Law a father had the right to kill both his married daughter and the accomplice if she was taken in adultery either in his house or her husband's, a husband had no such right as to his wife in any case, and no such right as to her accomplice unless he was an infamous person or a slave taken in his own home. By a law of [King] Cnut [Canute], a woman was to forfeit both nose and ears for adultery, and in the seventeenth century the ecclesiastical law punished both adulterous accomplices with extreme severity.

Torres and van der Walt (2009) make a direct link between ownership and the concept of sexual violation, arguing that modern sex crimes statutes originated from laws related to property crime (p. 445):

> Interestingly, it is property law that has shaped and defined who can be a victim of a criminal sexual act. Historically, children, slaves, animals, and other similarly classed groups have been considered the property of white, land-owning men. Until fairly recently, women in particular were viewed as the property of their fathers and subsequently of their husbands after marriage. Such beliefs are the basis for modern marriage traditions, such as the father "giving away the bride" at her wedding. In a legal sense, this often exempted husbands from being charged with rape related to any sexual acts they committed with their wives, whether she agreed to them or not.

And marital rape did not become illegal in all 50 of the United States until 1993 (Woolley, 2007).

More recently, the United States Supreme Court decriminalized sodomy, also described in Torres and van der Walt (2009, p. 450):

> Sodomy may be defined as any sexual act that does not involve a penis penetrating a vagina. It can include behaviors such as manual stimulation of a partner (e.g., mutual masturbation), oral sex, anal sex, and the use of sexual toys (e.g., vibrators, dildos). Anti-sodomy laws originally served to punish people for engaging in sexual behavior for the sake of pleasure only, that is, sexual behavior that does not lead to the potential conception of a child. More recently, sodomy laws were used to criminalize acts between consenting gay and lesbian people.

In the deciding case, Lawrence v. Texas (2003), the U.S. Supreme Court held that (p. 585):

> A law branding one class of persons as criminal based solely on the State's moral disapproval of that class and the conduct associated with that class runs contrary to the values of the Constitution and the Equal Protection Clause, under any standard of review. I therefore concur

in the Court's judgment that Texas' sodomy law banning "deviate sexual intercourse" between consenting adults of the same sex, but not between consenting adults of different sexes, is unconstitutional.

Hough (2004) offered the following historical context for *Lawrence* (pp. 105–106):

> References to sodomy can be traced back to biblical times. Historically, the definition of sodomy has often been confusing, but the courts have almost always defined sodomy as an act done by men. In fact, in the late twentieth century, courts and theorists found sodomy between women to be a legal impossibility. …

> In colonial times, laws against sodomy were often not directed at homosexual conduct, but were focused on sexual acts between men and children, men raping women, or men engaging in bestiality.

> These laws were created on the grounds that sodomy was immoral and unchristian. It has only been in recent history that sodomy has been attached to a certain type of person, rather than just to a particular sexual activity. In today's society, sodomy laws have defined the place of gay people in American society. Even in cases where sodomy is referred to in a gender-neutral way, the assumption is that it refers to homosexual acts only, not to sodomy in other contexts. The existence of sodomy laws has limited homosexuals to a second-class position in society, whether or not the laws have actually been enforced. This second-class status is reflected in derogatory synonyms for sodomy such as: unnatural offense, abominable and detestable crime against nature, and buggery.

> Until the Supreme Court's landmark decision in *Lawrence v. Texas*, states were allowed to prohibit sodomy and prosecute homosexual couples who engaged in consensual sexual acts.

Obviously, then, the concept of sex crimes is dynamic, originating from time-specific cultural morality, as opposed to broadly held universal values. Historically, this is evident when the state legislates against sexual activity between consenting adults, is later forced to admit its prejudice, and then reverses itself. This becomes clearer as other offenses, and their cultural exceptions, are discussed.

CONSENT

A major factor in the consideration of whether or not a sex crime has been committed is the issue of consent. *Consent* refers to the act giving permission with full awareness of the consequences. In some instances the victim is able but unwilling to give consent for sexual contact, as is the case with almost all stranger crimes (barring those involving sex workers, where consenting to sexual contact with strangers is part of the job description). However, strangers do not commit the majority of sex crimes; most are committed by an acquaintance, friend, relative, or even an intimate. In other instances, the victim is willing but unable to give consent, as is the case when the victim is too young or impaired by drugs, alcohol, or some mental defect.

Age

Age is a factor in consent when the victim is legally viewed as too young to give consent. That is to say, many societies hold that its citizens must reach a minimum age before they are considered mature enough, knowledgeable enough, or simply aware enough to sign contracts, make medical decisions for themselves, and consent to sexual activity. These things, and many others, require informed consent to varying degrees. According to Torres and van der Walt (2009, p. 448), many men [become] entangled in "statutory rape" charges. These are crimes of "consensual" sex between a person (most often the female) who is below the legal age of consent with someone (most often the male) who is of legal age of consent to sex.

Given that the age of consent varies from one legal jurisdiction to the next, being charged with a sex offense and labeled culturally "deviant" may be only a matter of living in the wrong zip code and raising the ire of the local prosecutor. This is because one jurisdiction's sex offender is often another's legal intimate partner—and because, even when it is a crime, the prosecutor has broad discretion in what are referred to as "consent cases."

Drugs and Alcohol

Alcohol is a drug; it is a substance that causes a physiological change when it enters the body. We mention both drugs and alcohol in our discussion only because students, along with many professionals, would not include the alcohol drug if we used only the term *drugs*. This inappropriate separation exists because professional and colloquial understanding of the term "drug" is fairly uneven.

In some instances, drugs are intentionally yet surreptitiously given to a victim by an offender to facilitate rape. There are in fact many different kinds of "date rape" drugs, including sedatives, sleeping pills, and, more specifically, Rohypnol. They can all incapacitate victims, induce sleep, and cause memory loss, depending upon type and dosage.

However, the number one such drug is alcohol: along with other well-known side effects, it lowers inhibitions, impairs judgment, and ultimately prevents informed consent (Bates, 2007). It is also the case that alcohol does not generally require surreptitious delivery—victims regularly ingest alcohol to excess, and of their own free will. In fact, alcohol is often used recreationally precisely because of its narcotic effects, rather than in spite of them. However, this creates an environment of increased risk wherever such activity takes place, especially within large groups of strangers (e.g., bars and certain kinds of parties).

Alcohol is also the number one drug associated with rape, as reported in the *Journal of the American Medical Association* (Cole, 2006, p. 504):

> According to a 2003 US Department of Justice (DOJ) report (available at www.cops.usdoj.gov/mime/open.pdf?Item=269), rape is the most common violent crime at U.S. universities. The incidence of rape is estimated to be 35 per 1000 female college students per year in the United States, although less than 5% of these rapes are reported to police. Women may decline to report rape for a variety of reasons, including shame, fear of social isolation from the assailant's friends, and self-reproach for drinking with the assailant before the rape.

> Ninety percent of college women who are raped know their assailants, according to the DOJ report.

> Most rapes occur in social situations, such as at a party or studying together in a dormitory room, and about half of perpetrators and rape survivors are drinking alcohol at the time of the assault, according to a National Institute on Alcohol Abuse and Alcoholism (NIAAA) review of recent studies of alcohol and sexual assault (available at www.pubs.niaaa.nih.gov/publications/arh25-1/43-51.htm). Henry Wechsler, Ph.D., of the Harvard School of Public Health, in Boston, who has conducted studies of alcohol use by college students, says that most nonconsensual sex is fueled by alcohol. "Alcohol is the number 1 rape drug," says Wechsler.

This is further supported by findings reported in Cowan (2008, pp. 904–905):

> Research has shown that the level of alcohol use in sexual assault cases is alarmingly high. Andrea Finney's 2004 summary of various research studies in this area shows that around 60% of perpetrators have been drinking just prior to the offense of sexual assault. However, statistics on the proportion of victims who have been drinking prior to the offense vary widely and depend partially on the sample—for instance, in student populations, up to 81% of incidents can involve drinking on the part of the victim. There has been no substantive research on intoxication of victims in the U.K. to date and the data referred to by Finney is generated in the U.S. However, more recent research in the U.K. (aimed at analyzing the attrition rate in rape cases rather than the rate of alcohol consumption per se) found that in a sample of 676 cases over eight police force areas, 38% of victims aged 16 and above had been drinking, though not necessarily to the point of intoxication, prior to the assault.

As already suggested, drugs and alcohol in sufficient quantities can prevent the user from thinking rationally, and consequently from being able to form any kind of rational intent (victims and offenders alike). This bears directly on cases of rape involving drug and alcohol use, described in Cowan (2008, pp. 900–901):

> A complainant's intoxication can impact consent in a rape trial in two possible ways. First, the complainant and the defendant could disagree about the fact or level of intoxication—i.e., capacity, so that the defendant claims either that the complainant was not drunk at all, or that she was not drunk to the degree that she was incapable of consenting but merely was disinhibited, and therefore she was in fact capable of, and did, consent. Second, there could be disagreement about whether or not there was consent—i.e., the defendant claims that the complainant gave consent, albeit drunken, and that she was capable even though intoxicated, whereas the complainant states that she cannot remember what happened because she was extremely drunk but that she knows that she did not want to have sex with the defendant (and she may also claim that she was too drunk to resist). The claim then could be either that she was not intoxicated (enough) and capable, or, that despite a high level of intoxication, she did consent.

Though referring specifically to alcohol intoxication, the issues discussed in Cowan (2008) remain the same with other drugs that cause similar mental defects. This temporary state of being incapable of rationally appraising the nature of one's own conduct is referred to as mental incapacity.

Physical or Mental Disability

In many jurisdictions, it is a crime to have sexual contact with person who is incapable of consent by reason of being physically or mentally disabled. Physical or mental disability refers to any physical or mental disease or defect that causes a permanent state of being incapable of rationally appraising the nature of one's own conduct. An example of a physical disability that precludes the possibility of consent is being in a coma, and there are many cases involving healthcare workers accused of, and convicted of, raping patients in various coma wards. An example of a mental disability that precludes the possibility of consent is mental retardation (or developmental disability), which is accompanied by a lower-than-average IQ and low cognitive functioning.

TYPES OF SEX CRIMES

At the beginning of this chapter, we explained that sex offenders are varied, each with their own constellation of behaviors, motives, and capabilities existing on a broad continuum of intensity and severity. Some offenders are fixated or preferential, with a pathological, long-term attraction to deviant sexual behavior that goes back to adolescence. Others may be referred to as regressed, with deviance being a temporary or experimental interest in response to anxiety, conflict, stress, or crisis in their adult relationships (see, generally, Burgess et al., 1978). This is all necessarily reflected in their history, and in the nature of the crimes they commit.

Consider the following types of sex crimes (discussed in no particular order), with the understanding that this is by no means a complete list.

Rape/Sexual Assault

Depending upon the legal jurisdiction, the terms *rape* and *sexual assault* may be used almost interchangeably, but this is improper from a criminological standpoint. As explained in Savino and Turvey (2004), rape is nonconsensual sexual penetration. It is a form of sexual assault, a term that refers generally to any nonconsensual sexual contact. Therefore, it is possible for a victim to be sexually assaulted without being raped (penetrated). Neither requires force or evidence of force, only a criminal intent on the part of the offender and the absence of consent on the part of the victim.

Like the crime of homicide, there are generally different degrees of rape or sexual assault, with increasing levels severity and associated penalties, defined explicitly within criminal statutes. There are too many variations to relate here, so readers are encouraged to reference their local penal law.

As explained in McKibbin et al. (2008, p. 86):

> Rape is a fact of life across cultures (Rozee, 1993; Sanday, 1981). In American samples, estimates of the prevalence of rape vary with the population studied, but are as high as 13% for women (Kilpatrick, Edmunds and Seymour, 1992). Rape is likely more common, however, because rapes often go unreported (Greenfield, 1997; Kilpatrick et al. 1992). Researchers estimate that 67–84% of rapes are not reported.

In this context, data reported to and then by the U.S. Department of Justice, Bureau of Justice Statistics, provide the following (Rand, 2008): in the United States, there was a 25% increase in total reported rapes and sexual assaults between 2005 and 2007 (from 190,600 to 248,300 cases). Reported victims were most often female (236,980, or 95%, of all reported cases), and reported offenders were most often non-strangers, such as friends, acquaintances, and intimates (58%). Interestingly, 91% (226,410) of reported cases did not involve a weapon of any kind, with the clear weapon of choice being a knife in 3% (6,280) of reported cases. Firearms were the least reported weapons of choice, at less than 1% of total cases.

As explained in Turvey (2004) motive is the emotional, psychological, and material needs that impel and are satisfied by behavior. Intent is the aim that guides behavior. Motive is the general need, and intent is the specific plan. Many rapes are committed to satisfy a rapist's emotional or psychological need to express power, anger, or sadistic desire (for rapist typologies, see Groth, 1979; McKibbin et al., 2008; and Turvey, 2008). Profit may also be an adjunct, as creating an opportunity to rob the victim may play a role. In these cases, power, anger, sadism and profit are the possible motives (with no bright line between them), and rape is the intent.

Child Molestation

Child molestation is a particular subclass of sexual assault, referring to "any sexual contact with a child or adolescent below the age of consent," (Torres and van der Walt, 2009; p. 433). It includes a broad spectrum of criminal sex offenses from incest to pedophilia, and represents the largest percentage of convicted sex offenders (Lindsay et al., 2004).

Despite continued social concern regarding "stranger danger," the greatest threat to children still comes from the people they know and are meant to trust. This is discussed in Torres and van der Walt (2009, pp. 453–454):

> More often then not, the sexual abuse of children occurs in their own homes (Marshall, Serran, and Cortoni, 2000). These children are often abused by someone within their immediate or extended family. This can take the form of incest, a biological relative having sexual contact with a child, or a stepparent, stepsibling, or pseudo-parent. These children are often chosen because of the perpetrators' access and opportunity to be alone with them. These victims are extremely vulnerable and have limited resources to report the abuse. Due to these offenders' access to their victims, the abuse is often longstanding and increasingly more intrusive. These types of offenses have an enormous impact on their victims, as the confusion caused by being harmed by a person who is supposed to care for you is difficult to comprehend and overcome.

There have been numerous attempts to classify child molesters by type but most have failed because of the similarities between them, and the inability of researchers to key in on discrete differences between populations. This may be owing to the poor research that has been done on the subject thus far, and the lack of consistently understood definitions. Jensen et al. (2002, p.40) explain that:

> While much effort has been devoted to categorize child molesters into discrete subtypes, researchers continue to find more similarities than differences between groups. Predatory pedophiles frequently seek employment or volunteer placement in order to gain access to children while their counterparts are more likely to molest children that wander into their domain. However, opportunistic or "situational" offenders can have more victims than predatory pedophiles and can be just as aroused to children. Both groups abuse more children than initially detected and engage in a series of behaviors to ensure continued access to victims.

> Contrary to what offenders usually tell people when they are first confronted, child sexual abuse is never accidental, unplanned or harmless. Once in treatment, child molesters describe a series of specific cognitive and behavioral steps that precede and continue throughout the offending process.

> These steps include:

> . placing themselves in a situation or environment in which they can offend,

> . developing an attraction to and selecting a specific child to abuse,

> . engaging the child and/or family in a relationship,

> . desensitizing and disarming the child and his/her family,

> . sexualizing the relationship and abusing the child,

> . maintaining the child's cooperation and silence, and

> . avoiding discovery and/or prosecution.

> Child sexual abuse should not be regarded as an act but rather, as a process. …

This is useful to note because of the many rationalizations offered by child molesters when they are caught, and the believability with which they are rendered. In point of fact, the average grooming time put into a single child by a molester is nine months. That is to say, the offender engages in no sexual contact or intimations, spending on average about nine months gaining the child's trust, and the offender may have multiple child targets in various stages of grooming at any one time. While it is easy to classify child molestation and related criminal sexual behavior as statistically and even ideologically deviant, there are some apparent exceptions.

For example, in certain cultures, incest is considered a right of the father. It may also be encouraged in places where there is a high incidence of HIV, such as Barbados, as a safer alternative to an extramarital affair.

Additionally, there are parents, including many single women, who sell or allow sexual access to their children for money or drugs or to keep from losing an intimate partner who has a preference for, or a financial interest in, child sex.

Consider the following case, reported in Larkin (2008):

A woman who has lived in Burlington and East Montpelier [Vermont] is in jail on sordid charges—based in part from entries in her child's diary—that she allowed her young daughter to be raped and molested.

Vermont State Police investigators arrested 40-year-old Stacey Parnitzke, of East Montpelier, Friday at Vermont District Court in Barre, where Parnitzke had gone to appear for a court check-in for a September DUI case.

Shane E. Casey, 38, who is described as a transient in court documents, was also arrested on Friday in Barre.

The two are facing charges based on allegations by the woman's daughter that her mother sexually abused her and forced her to have sex with Casey on numerous occasions.

Casey and Parnitzke were taken to Vermont District Court in Burlington, where they were both charged with aggravated sexual assault on a child and jailed in lieu of $25,000 bail.

The charge carries a maximum penalty of life in prison or a fine of up to $50,000.

The case came about in October 2007 when Parnitzke's 11-year-old daughter, who has been living with her father in California for the past year and a half, disclosed to her father that while she and her mother were living in England her mother would bring men home from her AA meetings and force the girl, starting at the age of five, to let the men rape her.

California authorities contacted police in Burlington because Parnitzke and her daughter had moved there in 2004 and because the child said her mother's boyfriend, Casey, raped her in a Burlington North End apartment on numerous occasions, according to court documents.

Parnitzke met Casey in Vermont some time in 2006, according to court documents.

The girl was interviewed at a child advocacy center in San Jose, CA, in October and investigators in Burlington worked on the case in Vermont.

According to court documents, Parnitzke would force her daughter to watch a pornographic movie, telling her daughter it was a "Disney" movie, and then force her daughter to do what she saw in the movie.

The girl told investigators she remembers seeing her mother getting injected with a hypodermic needle by the men and sometimes the needle would be put into the child while she was getting raped.

The child kept a diary, in which she tallied every time she was forced to let Casey rape her. The child told investigators her last count of tallies was 15 and that she thought she was raped while living in England approximately 10 times. Investigators retrieved the diary from Parnitzke's storage and found evidence of the child's list; days she was allegedly raped were marked with an "S" for Shane.

The child also told investigators she thought someone might have taken photographs while she was getting raped both in England and in Vermont because she saw a flash on several occasions. According to court documents, the child told investigators her mother sexually abused her on numerous occasions, as well.

The child's father told police Parnitzke called him in March 2006 and asked him to take their daughter because she could not take care of her anymore.

On Sept. 2, 2007, police responded to a single-vehicle accident on Route 2 in East Montpelier near Country Campers. Police found Parnitzke, who had lost control of her 1995 Dodge Caravan, to have a blood alcohol content of .274 percent and a half-pint of Bacardi rum in her purse.

Parnitzke was subsequently charged with DUI and on Friday she was at the Barre court for a check-in on her case when investigators from the Chittenden Unit for Special Investigations arrested her for aggravated sexual assault on her daughter.

Parnitzke was also charged with domestic assault against her mother in Burlington in November 2006.

According to court documents, Parnitzke and Casey are separated but share a newborn son together.

It must be noted that this type of occurrence is often viewed as rare to non-existent. Certainly it occurs, and has always occurred, but to what extent is unknown.

Bestiality

Bestiality, also referred to as zooerasty, refers to any sexual act with an animal, while zoophilia, or preferential bestiality, refers to "a clear preference for engaging in sex with animals" (Earls and Lalumiere, 2009, p. 605). In some jurisdictions, bestiality, or animal molestation and cruelty, are crimes all on their own. In others, bestiality may be treated as a property crime, and the offender charged only with trespassing.

Consider the following case example in the United States, taken from Sullivan (2005):

Police began investigating James Tait, 54, and another man who lived at the rural Southeast King County farm after the Seattle man died of injuries suffered during intercourse with a horse at a neighboring farm, Enumclaw police said.

The criminal-trespassing charge stems from a July 2 bestiality session involving Tait, the 45-year-old Seattle man and a horse in a neighbor's barn, charging papers say. According to the King County Medical Examiner's Office, the Seattle man died of acute peritonitis due to perforation of the colon. ...

King County prosecutors say it's the most-severe charge they could file; Washington is one of more than a dozen states that does not outlaw bestiality.

"There is no evidence of injury to the animal to support animal-cruelty charges," said Dan Satterberg, the county prosecutor's chief of staff. "This is the only crime we can charge."

When interviewed by *The Seattle Times* July 15, the horse's owners said they had known their neighbors for years. The couple, who asked to have their names withheld to protect their privacy, said they were shocked when police showed them a home video of the July 2 incident that investigators seized from their neighbor's home. The couple identified their barn and their horse.

According to the King County Sheriff's Office, which also investigated, the farm was known in Internet chat rooms as a destination for people who want to have sex with livestock. Authorities didn't learn about the farm until July 2, when a man drove to Enumclaw Community Hospital seeking medical assistance for a companion. Medics wheeled the Seattle man into an examination room and realized he was dead. When hospital workers looked for the man who had dropped him off, he was gone, Enumclaw police said.

Using the dead man's driver's license to track down relatives and acquaintances, investigators were led to the Enumclaw farm.

Because the other man who lived at the farm wasn't there the night the Seattle man died, he wasn't charged with trespassing, Satterberg said. Tait will be arraigned Oct. 27; he faces up to a year in jail and a $5,000 fine if convicted. …

In the wake of the man's death, State Sen. Pam Roach, R-Auburn has said she plans to draft legislation making bestiality illegal in Washington.

It should be noted that, historically, bestiality has been treated as an extremely rare phenomenon without a great many preferential offenders. Case studies of curious and inexperienced rural adolescents abound. However, the Internet has given researchers a valuable tool for researching the subject with more accuracy and insight. As explained in Earls and Lalumiere (2009, p. 607),

More recently, investigations of zoophilia have moved beyond the case study method. There have been several quantitative group studies of community samples. The emergence of these studies is due in large part to the availability of Internet sites devoted to zoophilia or bestiality. Although one must be wary of reports from sometimes unverifiable sources, the internet provides an unparalleled source of potentially zoophilic individuals from the general community. … The group studies conducted to date suggest that some men and women who admit having had sex with animals have a clear preference for such activities. In addition, the data obtained from Internet surveys reveal that sex with animals is rarely a substitute for sex with humans, and that many respondents live happy and productive lives.

Because of the recent window offered into human sexual behavior and preferences by the Internet, bestiality is among the many types of sex crimes that are entering an era of more accurate research. At the very least, we have learned that it is more common, and more preferential, than has been previously suggested.

Voyeurism

Voyeurism is one of many non-contact sex offenses, such as public masturbation and sexual harassment. It refers to a sexual interest in, or the practice of spying on, people engaged in intimate or private behaviors, such as undressing, sexual acts, urinating, or defecating. This includes "perpetrators looking through windows with the hope of seeing people in various states of undress; taking pictures of others in bathrooms; and viewing others in dressing rooms without their knowledge" (Torres and van der Walt, 2009, p. 459).

Definitions of voyeurism in a clinical sense have failed to keep up with culture and technology, given the prevalence of sexually themed reality TV shows and the ease with which voyeur-oriented pornography can be viewed, even unintentionally, on the Internet. Metzle (2004, p. 127) explains that:

DSM-IV (1994) defines voyeurism as the practice of looking specifically at "unsuspecting individuals, usually strangers, who are naked, in the process of disrobing, or engaging in sexual activity." And psychiatric textbooks employ terms that further modify the diagnosis based on the content of voyeuristic acts—such as "pictophilic voyeurism" and its dependence on "viewing obscene or pornographic pictures or video tapes." Yet evidence also suggests that the notion of voyeurism has limited relevance in a world where it is at times difficult to distinguish hard-core paraphiliacs who require psychiatric interventions from the many amateurs who simply watch VTV programs.

On that note, the proliferation of Web sites dedicated explicitly to criminal and non-criminal voyeuristic pleasure reveals that viewing this sort of material is broadly appealing, making it less statistically and culturally uncommon (or deviant) than previously understood.

As with most of the sex offenses discussed in this chapter, there is a stunning lack of quality reference material and research—with legislation and treatment models developed based on thinly examined case vignettes. It is hoped that with the advent of the Internet and related communications technology, better research and insight are on the horizon.

Fetish Burglary

As mentioned previously, a sexual fetish is the attribution of erotic or sexual significance to a nonsexual inanimate object or nonsexual body part. As explained in Lowenstein (2002, p. 136), "among the objects frequently sought as fetishistic are shoes, bras, and panties, etc. Sometimes in a search for fetishist objects housebreaking occurs as the individual searches for women's used bras or panties." When burglary is committed in whole or in part to gather such items for sexual purposes, it may be properly referred to as a fetish burglary. Gebhard et al. (1965, p. 413) refer more generically to "fetish theft."

Consider the case of Tyrel Pitka, as reported in Morris (2006):

> A man accused of burglarizing at least 27 houses in the Valley and committing strange, solitary sex acts inside was sentenced Tuesday to seven years in prison.
>
> Tyrel Pitka, 20, was charged with two counts of first-degree burglary and one count of second-degree burglary. Superior Court Judge Larry Weeks sentenced Pitka to 12 years, then suspended five years of the sentence. He also placed Pitka on five years probation and ordered him to receive sex-offender treatment.
>
> According to court testimony and documents, Pitka admitted to burglarizing at least 27 homes. Investigators said they linked Pitka to several other burglaries, but he wasn't charged with those crimes. According to investigators, Pitka started hitting homes in Mendenhall Valley on Nov. 22, 2005, working from trails that crisscross the Loop Road area and scouting for houses where the occupants were gone. From December to January of the same year, Pitka went to Sitka.
>
> Officials said Pitka committed three burglaries in Sitka. In February when Pitka returned to Juneau, he started burglarizing houses again, until his arrest on April 7. According to court records Pitka committed one burglary in Angoon.
>
> Juneau District Attorney Doug Gardner said in court that Pitka used money from the robberies to buy drugs and alcohol. The crimes also had strong sexual overtones.
>
> In a sentencing memorandum, Gardner said Pitka "searched the residences in many of the cases for pornography, sex toys, or other personal and intimate photographs...In addition, the defendant made a video tape of himself masturbating, using a victim's video camera, and masturbated while in at least two of the locations...leaving semen in two stuffed toy animals."

In court, Gardner said that Pitka also used his victims' computers to look at pornography. In one of Pitka's filming sessions, he recorded over a video of a woman giving birth to her son. In another incident, Pitka returned a sex toy to the house of its owner with a vulgar, suggestive note attached to it.

It is noteworthy that fetish burglars prefer used objects and garments. That is to say, they cannot simply buy perfume, clothing, or other items at the store to satisfy their desires in private. The items must have been owned previously, touched, or otherwise possessed by someone (often a specific person) so that there is greater meaning in the acquisition. However, the items taken need not be soiled or freshly used, as many fetish thieves take clothes, for example, directly off clotheslines or out of public dryers (Gebhard et al., 1965).

Although the true prevalence of fetish burglary is unknown, as law-enforcement agencies do not keep such statistics, fetishism itself "tends to begin during adolescence or even before. It persists for most of the individual's life. Frequently such individuals are shy and socially withdrawn. They may well be ashamed of their dependence on their particular fetish, and hence attempt to keep their fetish secret" (Lowenstein, 2002, p. 136). As with bestiality, the recent window offered into human sexual behavior and preferences by the Internet moves fetishism in all its forms into an era of more accurate research.

Necrophilia

Necrophilia refers to a persistent sexual arousal associated with the dead, or sexual activity with the dead. A literature review for the term reveals a dearth of consistent terminology as well as an utter lack of any meaningful research. Rather, the subject of necrophilia seems to be infrequently covered by legitimate professionals, and even then the coverage is thin, uninformed, and deeply misleading. What can be said is that verifiable cases are quite rare.

Most often, necrophilia enters public awareness in one of two ways. First, it is often revealed as an adjunct to the activities of sexual murderers who sexually violate the corpses of their victims. Sometimes this is done for pure sexual gratification, and sometimes it is done for anger-motivated humiliation of the corpse of someone the offender knows. Also, in some jurisdictions necrophilia is considered an aggravating factor that increases the severity of criminal charges associated with murder. Second, necrophilia is often revealed as part of a funeral home scandal, where current or former employees are found to have been committing sex acts on bodies in their care. Certainly, there are other instances, but these are the most commonly reported.

Consider the following example, reported in Cornell (2009, p. 5):

> A former morgue worker already in prison for having sex with a body awaiting autopsy was indicted Thursday on two more charges of sexually abusing corpses.

> The latest charges against 55-year-old Kenneth Douglas of Cincinnati accuse him of assaulting two women's bodies at the Hamilton County morgue in 1991.

> Douglas, an attendant at the morgue from 1976 to '92, was convicted last year of having sex with the body of a 19-year-old murder victim in 1982. He is serving a three-year prison sentence, which includes 18 months for corpse abuse and 18 months for a parole violation on an unrelated drug conviction.

> Prosecutor Joe Deters said the case is "just beyond belief" and that the new charges are based on DNA testing. He said there is not enough evidence left to determine whether more corpses might have been abused because DNA evidence wasn't saved in many cases.

Deters said he suspects Douglas had more victims in the 16 years he worked at the county morgue. "I'm sure there are more," Deters said. "I'm certain of it, but we'll never be able to prove it."

The numbers Douglas gave investigators in interviews ranged from one victim to possibly more than 100, Deters said.

Douglas' attorney, Norman Aubin, said he hadn't seen the new evidence and would confer with Douglas after he studies the charges.

A grand jury indicted Douglas on two counts of gross abuse of a corpse for allegedly sexually assaulting the bodies of Charlene Edwards, 23, and Angel Hicks, 24, both of Cincinnati.

Edwards was strangled in October 1991. Mark Chambers, convicted of voluntary manslaughter in her death, was released on parole in 2000.

Hicks died of a blunt impact to the head. Her death was ruled a homicide, but the defendant in that case was found not guilty at trial.

The first corpse abuse case against Douglas involved 19-year-old Karen Range, who was murdered in her Cincinnati home. David Steffen, a door-to-door salesman, was convicted in 1983 of rape and aggravated murder.

Steffen acknowledged stabbing Range but always denied that he raped her, saying he attempted to but was physically unable. A DNA test—not available at the time he was tried—confirmed in 2007 that he had not raped her.

Meanwhile, Douglas was convicted of the drug trafficking offense last year and was ordered to provide a DNA sample, as required by Ohio law. That sample matched the 1982 sample from Range, prosecutors said.

The maximum sentence Douglas could receive if convicted of the new charges is 18 months on each one.

While currently necrophilia is deemed deviant from a legal perspective as part of "abuse of a corpse" statutes, some people are not satisfied with the leniency of resulting sentences. In Wisconsin, for example, there has been significant re-interpretation of the law by the state's supreme court, which now enables prosecutors to charge corpse molesters with rape. As discussed in the *Harvard Law Review* (Criminal Law, 2009, pp. 1780–1781):

On September 2, 2002, Nicholas Grunke, Alexander Grunke, and their friend Dustin Radke attempted to excavate a female corpse at a local cemetery so that Nicholas could engage in sexual intercourse with the corpse. The Grunkes and Radke brought excavation tools, a tarp, and condoms to the cemetery, and proceeded to dig a hole into the body's gravesite. The three men managed to expose the top of the corpse's vault, but fled after being unable to open the vault and hearing another car driving into the cemetery. A police officer subsequently arrived at the cemetery in response to a call reporting a suspicious vehicle on the grounds. The officer encountered Alexander Grunke, noticed his supplies, and placed him in custody.

The Grunkes and Radke were charged in a Wisconsin state court with damage to cemetery property, attempted criminal damage to property, and attempted third-degree sexual assault. The sexual assault statute prohibits "sexual intercourse with a person without the consent of that person." The statute provides, in relevant part, that "'[c]onsent' … means words or overt actions by a person who is competent to give informed consent indicating a freely given agreement to have sexual intercourse or sexual contact," and establishes a presumption that mentally ill persons or persons "unconscious or for any other reason … physically unable to communicate unwillingness to an act" are incapable of consent. Finally, section 940.225(7) states that the statute "applies whether a victim is dead or alive at the time of the sexual contact or sexual intercourse."

The Grunkes and Radke were convicted by the trial court of sexual assault. The court of appeals overruled the trial court, and the case was kicked up to the Wisconsin Supreme Court, which in turn reversed the appellate court. The Wisconsin Supreme Court held that the dead cannot give active consent—making necrophilia a form of rape, and death a physical condition that prohibits consent.

Prostitution/Soliciting/Sex Trafficking

In many jurisdictions, it is a crime to offer money for sex, to receive money for sex, to transport persons across borders for the purposes of prostitution (a.k.a. trafficking), or to live off the earnings of a prostitute. In other words, it is very often a crime to be a prostitute, to solicit the services of a prostitute, to traffic in prostitutes, or to "pimp" them out. This is by no means universal, as there are legalized forms of prostitution in many countries, usually restricted to a particular area.

A contemporary view of how girls and young women are "recruited" into prostitution is offered in Hotaling et al. (2006, pp. 185–186), who report that the average age of recruitment is 13:

> These pimps and traffickers systematically and methodically break down their "prey," socially isolating them away from family and friends. Their victims become embedded in a social system typified by living in transient hotels close to the "whore strolls," traveling from city to city, and socializing with other transient persons also involved in prostitution. These pimps use severe and immediate violence to force their victims to participate in the sex industry. A common theme reported by SAGE clients about guerilla pimping is that a woman or girl is physically picked up, thrown into a trunk, and transported to cities throughout the United States. SAGE has rescued individuals who did not know what city they were in or even what cities they had been trafficked through while forced to work in the sex trade, which includes prostitution, strip clubs, escort services, and websites such as Craigslist and sites created by the pimps themselves. They were sold on the back pages of alternative newspapers and sex trade magazines. They had been transported in trunks of cars and isolated in out-of-the-way motels and single-room occupancy hotels throughout the country while being brutalized, raped, tortured, and repeatedly sold to those who demand them. Harsher methods reported by SAGE clients involve beating, raping, sodomizing, drugging, and starving a woman or girl before "turning her out" on the streets or other sex industry arenas.
>
> Pimps will often create a sense of ownership by giving their victims new identities and supplying fake identification, such as identification cards, driver's licenses, social security cards, and birth certificates. With a young woman or girl's former identity gone, she then belongs to the pimp.

Brown (2008, pp. 489–490) summarizes the statistical prevalence and social consequences of prostitution, providing support for the notion of sex workers being enslaved in many cases:

> The trafficking of women and children for prostitution is a rapidly growing area of international criminal activity and cause for international alarm. More than 700,000 people are trafficked each year worldwide, some 50,000 to the United States. The overwhelming majority of those trafficked are women and children. At least 100,000 illegally-immigrated women prostitutes work in the United States. The trafficked women have backgrounds of poverty, illiteracy, civil strife, and low social and political status. Traffickers can exploit the conditions of trafficked women for their own

financial gain. Women are lured into traveling to unknown regions with the promise of high wages and civilized working conditions. Instead, the women encounter slave-like wages, inhumane working conditions, and indebtedness to their traffickers. Women who are trafficked for the sex industry may fare worse than other trafficking victims due to the violence they face. Prostitutes who immigrate from Asia often sell for $20,000 each in the United States. But the smuggling fees keep trafficked women ensnared to their trafficker, and fear of reprisals keep the women from seeking help. In addition, trafficked women may suffer retribution and deportation if they seek help from law enforcement, which makes them reluctant to do so. These women may also face ostracism, and even potential death upon returning home.

It should also be noted that the presence of the U.S. military has also had an impact on local prostitution in areas surrounding military bases, both at home and abroad, as explained in Chang (2001, pp. 627–628):

The sex industry developed to serve stationary forces, those on shore leave, and military men engaging in R&R. Rest & Recreation (sometimes called Intoxication and Intercourse by GIs) is an enlisted man's vacation of sorts. They are allowed a short period of time off, and there are frequent designated R&R "locations" that have been established and developed specifically for this purpose. Designation as an R&R location can be quite lucrative for local economies that develop the types of entertainment that appeal to U.S. military personnel. In 1967, Thailand completed a pact with the United States to provide R&R leave for American soldiers. This treaty secured economic developmental perks. The Industrial Finance Corporation, a consortium of international investors, loaned four million dollars to build the infrastructure needed to accommodate this military tourism, including hotels, restaurants, bars, and nightclubs.

This industrialization, however, was subject to a bust or boom cycle. When the military was present, the economy was stimulated. When they were not, absent a sufficient local or sex tourism business to sustain the thousands of prostituted women and their corresponding establishments (bars, hotels, etc.), the economy entered a depression.

Soto (2007, pp. 561–562) offered a similar argument, explaining that:

Demand is what drives severe forms of trafficking in persons, and the United States military's presence in overseas operations has fueled that demand for decades. Historically, the United States military has accepted, encouraged, and even aided severe forms of trafficking in persons. Currently, there are brothels in proximity to nearly every United States military base, and there is significant evidence to indicate that many of the prostitutes in the brothels are victims of severe forms of trafficking. Moreover, there is evidence indicating that American military personnel know that the prostitutes in the brothels are victims of severe forms of trafficking but continue to patronize the brothels anyway.

This is not to say that all military personnel agree with prostitution or use the services of prostitutes, but rather that it is clearly accepted and encourage by many within the military. It is even a feature of recruitment in some instances. There is no denying this, as the evidence exists and has existed for generations. The only question is what it means.

While it is more than fair to classify the constellation of sex crimes associated with prostitution as deviant from a legal perspective, it is difficult to classify them as deviant from an ideological perspective. There are a number of reasons for this. First, they are broadly prevalent—implying broad acceptance by large cross-sections of society. Second, the severe negative consequences to those involved, and society at large, are widely ignored, with almost no public outcry. Third, many of those in law enforcement selectively enforce prostitution statutes. Law enforcement is generally aware of where prostitution occurs and who is involved, but it is unwilling to make arrests, due to lack of resources and insufficient public motivation. Fourth, and finally, the constellation of sex crimes associated with prostitution is tacitly accepted by many in the government and the military who support, encourage, and ultimately rely on the services of prostitutes.

DEVELOPMENTAL ISSUES

According to the research and literature review conducted by Beauregard et al. (2004), three factors are found to be consistently associated with the sexual preferences of rapists. They are described as (p. 158) "a sexually inappropriate family environment, use of pornography during childhood and adolescence, and deviant sexual fantasies during childhood and adolescence." A sexually inappropriate family environment refers to one that involves (p. 155) "(1) witnessing incestuous behavior within the family; (2) being a victim of incestuous behavior; and (3) witnessing promiscuous sex within the family." The convergence of these circumstances creates a perfect foundation for the development and nurturing of deviant sexual preferences through modeling and vicarious learning. Such preferences are then reinforced by a cycle of fantasy, use of pornography or sexual "props," and the physical gratification and chemical release achieved during masturbation.

It should be noted that this cycle recapitulates how non-criminal behaviors are developed and nurtured as well.

FEMALE SEX OFFENDERS

There are by far more male than female sex offenders, and males are by far more aggressive. However, it must be admitted that cultural values have played a role here. Females are traditionally viewed as victims, and males are traditionally viewed as aggressors. This generalization colors and contextualizes everything about the study of sex crime. It is borne out in the following by Gebhard et al. (1965, p. 10):

> If a man walking past an apartment stops to watch a woman undressing before the window, the man is arrested as a peeper. If a woman walking past an apartment stops to watch a man undressing before window, the man is arrested as an exhibitionist. The essence of the matter is simply that women are less prone to behavior that offends society, and society refuses to take offense at acts committed by women which would, if committed by men, lead to arrest and conviction.

While these scenarios are certainly true under the right circumstances, it is also true that the female sex offender is not "as rare as proverbial hen's teeth" (p. 10). Strickland (2008, p. 474) provides insight into why this reality has remained hidden:

> Sexual abuse has historically been viewed as a male crime against adult women and children, with men committing approximately 95% of the sex crimes in the United States (Finkelhor, Hotalling, Lewis & Smith, 1990; Knopp & Lackey, 1987). Cultural resistance has hindered the identification of sexual crimes committed by women. Although cases of female sexual abuse of children have been documented since the 1930s (Bender & Blau, 1937; Chideckel, 1935). women sexual offenders have remained well hidden.

> In cases of female sexual abuse, either the abuse is not found out for many years, or if discovered, it is dismissed or disbelieved. It has been only since the mid-1980s that a small sample of female sex offenders have been described in the scientific literature and only since the 1990s that this group has been studied more systematically (Hislop, 2001). Historically, these crimes have been underreported

and unidentified by victims and easily dismissed by adults (Allen, 1991; Hislop, 1999). Sexual abuse by women tends to be minimized and justified as an extension of the women's nurturing role, rather than as harmful or [constituting assault] (Denov, 2001).

Rizzo (2007) offers additional context, based on the interviews of 12 female sex offenders for the Kansas City *Star* in the United States:

> One is a white-haired grandmother who sews and plays piano. Another attends college while raising two small children. A third operates a business but avoids intimate relationships.
>
> All are female sex offenders—perpetrators of perhaps the most underreported and least understood criminal behavior.
>
> Society has been slow to recognize that women are capable of committing such crimes and even slower in trying to figure out what to do with them when they do.
>
> And though they still represent a small percentage of convicted sex offenders, they are being arrested in greater numbers each year, possibly because more victims are willing to report their crimes, experts say.
>
> Unlike most male offenders, many were drawn to their victims by loneliness and the need for emotional attachment. Others got caught up in the crimes alongside husbands or boyfriends. ...
>
> "At present, the research and literature about this unique segment of the sex offender population remains in its infancy," the Center for Sex Offender Management recently reported. "And there is no evidence-based guidance or other consensus about the most effective approaches to working with them."
>
> The extent of female sex offending is unknown. Nationwide, females make up about 6 percent of those arrested for sex crimes other than forcible rape.
>
> But a variety of sources indicate that female offenders are more prevalent, experts say.
>
> The proportion of females in sex offender counseling programs has nearly doubled from two years ago, the Center for Sex Offender Management reports.
>
> And some victim surveys uncovered surprising news: As many as 63 percent of females and 27 percent of males said that women had victimized them.
>
> There are a variety of theories about why such crime is underreported.
>
> The stereotype of women as nurturing caregivers who don't engage in violent or harmful behavior may be one factor. The misperception that females cannot physically abuse unwilling males is another.
>
> A third factor is the mindset of law enforcement officers and treatment providers who, because of wider societal stereotypes, react with disbelief or minimize the seriousness of reports.
>
> One offender interviewed by the Kansas City *Star* said that although she acted alone, she had to convince investigators that her then-husband was not involved.
>
> In one study of women who said they were the victims of sex abuse by other females when they were children or adolescents, 70 percent reported that they never told anyone, according to Julia Hislop, author of a book on female sex offenders.
>
> Of those who did, 21 percent said they were not believed, she said.

"This is a very hidden experience," said Hislop. "People do not come forward."

Both male and female victims may be reluctant to report crimes involving women because of fear of how they will be perceived, the experts say.

Boys are socialized to not be victims, Hislop said. They may worry that their masculinity will be questioned, and they are often met with the reaction that they got "lucky." Girls may be afraid that it will call into question their own sexual identity.

"It often creates a great deal of confusion for them," she said.

The "lucky guy" reaction toward male victims often keeps them from recognizing they were harmed, experts say.

In her study of female sex offenders, Strickland (2008) found that prevalence is unknown, varying widely from source to source, with strong evidence of significant under-reporting. She reported that (p. 475):

In those cases of sexual abuse reported to the authorities, women perpetrators comprise about 4% of the cases (Finkel & Russell, 1984). The percentage of female sex offenders identified through Child Protection Agencies ranged from 1.5% to 12.5% (Kercher & McShane, 1985; Margolin & Craft, 1989; Rowan, Langelier & Rowan, 1988). Victims receiving treatment who have identified female perpetrators ranged from 2% to as much as 39% (Cupoli & Sewell, 1988; Kasl, 1990; Kendall-Tackett & Simon, 1987; Mendel, 1995). In Faller's (1989) study, female perpetrators molested 8% of the boy victims, whereas 29% were molested by both female and male offenders. … Studies using anonymous surveys have reported that 17% to 75% of respondents were abused by females (Crewdson, 1998; Etherington, 1997; Weber, Gearing, Davis & Conlon, 1992). In surveys of college students, 1% to 15% of the students surveyed reported sexual contact with women in childhood. (Condy, Templer, Brown & Veaco, 1987; Haugaard & Emery, 1989). Females appear to account for even higher percentages of childhood sexual contact than reported by male college students (43% to 60%; Burgess, Groth. Holmstrom & Sgroi, 1987; Risin & Koss, 1987).

Strickland closed her study by offering the following profile of the female sex offender (p. 486):

Female sexual offenders, due to overall severe childhood trauma and deprivation, including severe sexual abuse, have few skills to negotiate their social and sexual contacts. Distorted sexual values, beliefs, and knowledge, coupled with emotional neediness and dependency issues, increase their risk for engaging in dysfunctional relationships. They lack the necessary skills to get their emotional and sexual needs met with appropriate partners—namely healthy, consensual adults. This inability increases their risk of getting their sexual needs met by children.

This all combines to demonstrate that female sex offenders are historically misunderstood, vastly underreported as males and females play to gender roles (whether experiencing victimization, sitting on a jury, or conducting sex research), and are increasingly common in the criminal justice system as society gains awareness.

SEX CRIMES AND COMMUNICATIONS TECHNOLOGY

Technology does not cause sex crime, but it can facilitate it. That is to say, technology is morally neutral. A handgun, pepper spray, and a set of handcuffs fixed on the belt of a law-enforcement officer serve one purpose, while the same tools in the kit of a rapist can serve another. A searchable database of names, addresses, and e-mails is one thing to an old college friend, another to a salesman, and yet another to a sex offender. Computer technology, the Internet, and virtual worlds are much the same as any other tool or environment: ripe for abuse by those with criminal intentions. Any other view tends to remove personal responsibility in favor of blaming something external for criminal choices.

Virtual Worlds and Exploitation

As explained in Hughes (2002, p. 127), there is no shortage of those willing to use to Internet, and related communications technology, for the sexual exploitation of various victim populations:

> New communications and information technologies have created a global revolution in communications, access to information, and media delivery. These new communications and information technologies are facilitating the sexual exploitation of women and girls locally, nationally and transnationally. The sexual exploitation of women and children is a global human rights crisis that is being escalated by the use of new technologies.

> Using new technologies, sexual predators and pimps stalk women and children. New technical innovations facilitate the sexual exploitation of women and children because they enable people to easily buy, sell and exchange millions of images and videos of sexual exploitation of women and children. These technologies enable sexual predators to harm or exploit women and children efficiently and, anonymously.

> The affordability and access to global communications technologies allow users to carry out these activities in the privacy of their home.

> The increase of types of media, media formats, and applications diversifies the means by which sexual predators can reach their victims.

In years past, sex offenders of all types trolled for victims using e-mail discussion lists and variously themed chat groups hosted by service providers like CompuServe and America Online. Then they used Web-based chats through social networking sites like MySpace and Facebook. Facebook actually removed over 5,500 registered sex offenders from active membership between May 1, 2008, and January 31, 2009. This was done out of concern for the potential exploitation of its other members by a presumably predatory criminal population. From a pure liability standpoint, it is difficult to argue with this broad policy, but it by no means solves the problem.

In a related move to stamp out the facilitation of a particular type of sex crime, the popular online classified advertisement Web site Craigslist implemented a policy to remove ads involving solicitation for sexual services. Kopytoff (2009) reports that:

> Pressured by law enforcement, Craigslist launched a crackdown on prostitution in May by promising to review adult ads. While largely stamping out overt solicitations for paid sex, the new policy has prompted a proliferation of more vaguely worded offers of good times, sensual massages and overnight companionship.

> By many accounts, prostitution hasn't been eliminated on Craigslist. It's simply more discreet.

> "Offers of sex for sale are now disguised—though their intent is transparent," said Connecticut Attorney General Richard Blumenthal, who plans to ask Craigslist to take more aggressive action soon.

> Craigslist implemented its new guidelines amid criticism by various state attorneys general, led by Blumenthal, who accused the company of operating an online brothel. Clean up the ads or face a lawsuit, the attorneys general warned.

> Under its new policies, Craigslist staffers or contractors—it's not clear which—monitor adult ads and block those that solicit prostitution or include graphic images. New adult listings cost $10, or $5 to be reposted, payable by credit card only.

Jim Buckmaster, Craigslist's CEO, said the new adult category is for legal services only, including massages, exotic dancing and escorts—illegal services are unwelcome.

Moreover, he said the strict standards ensure that the ads are tamer than what's routinely published in weekly newspapers, telephone Yellow Pages and on other Web sites.

As for prostitutes masking their ads with vague language, Buckmaster said: "We are no more able to read the minds of people placing ads than are classifieds editors at newspapers and the Yellow Pages."

In mid-September of 2010, Craigslist removed the adult services section from its Web site entirely; however, personal ads offering similar services may still be found in other sections.

It is useful to note that, in general, online adult classified ads for services like those offered by escorts often mirror ads found in the print media (e.g., magazines and phone books). The message is the same, only the technology by which it is delivered has changed.

In a more recent trend, as other forms of online communication reach new levels of security awareness, sex offenders are exploiting the connectivity provided in other more nascent or less matured technologies. As reported in Cox (2009),

Cyber predators are now using game consoles and mobile phones with Internet access in their efforts to snare children for sex.

WA [Western Australia] Police yesterday issued the warning about the emerging phenomenon, revealing deviants were luring youngsters by building rapport and trust through their knowledge of interactive, online games.

WA Police have not yet arrested or charged anyone for directly grooming children through X-Box 360, PlayStation 3 and Wii consoles, but detectives said their intelligence showed it was a developing trend. "Adult child sex offenders are using these mediums to try to engage children, firstly by starting to chat to them about how to play games and talking generically about how the games are played," Det-Insp Darren Seivwright told The Sunday Times. "After they gain the trust and groom the child online, it then becomes more pointed towards sexual behavior. ... Because gaming consoles are played by young people, that creates another environment where adult online offenders can make contact and gain the trust of children...Mobile phones with Internet capabilities are also problematic. ... Texting is so popular among young people. If they have a mobile phone that also has Internet connection, they can chat and it is much harder for adults to supervise."

The surge in online crime and the shocking rape and murder of eight-year-old schoolgirl Sofia Rodriguez-Urrutia Shu in June 2006 prompted an expansion of the police Sex Crimes Division, including more resources to the Sex Assault Squad and to counter cyber predatory crimes.

The police warning comes as detectives from the Online Child Exploitation Squad this week apprehended a man from Perth's southern suburbs after he allegedly engaged in explicit online chat with a police officer posing as 14-year-old girl, sent her webcam images of his genitals, encouraged her to masturbate and arranged to meet her for sex.

The man, who cannot be named for legal reasons, faces 12 charges, including seven counts of using electronic communications with intent to procure a child for sexual activity and five counts of using electronic communications with intent to expose a child to indecent material.

He appeared in Perth Magistrates Court on Friday, when the case was adjourned. He was released on bail to next appear in court in September.

Det-Insp Seivwright said each month investigations were begun into about 25 new "targets"—or suspects—by police from the online squad, signaling an explosion in the number of predators preying on youth through the Internet.

He said parents needed to be increasingly vigilant and monitor their children's use of mobile phones and game consoles, including online opponents.

Last financial year, the squad investigated 214 online targets, arrested 57 people and laid 220 charges after spending 1038 hours online. Thirty-one inquiries were referred to interstate or overseas police for further investigation.

"Law enforcement agencies worldwide are trying hard and really grappling with trying to keep abreast of emerging technology," Det-Insp Seivwright said.

Det-Insp Seivwright said parents should ask regular questions of their children, including who they were communicating with as well as the nature of the conversations. Tell-tale indicators of danger included behavioral changes such as children becoming introverted, spending more time in their bedrooms or being obsessive about spending time online, he said.

With respect to sex crime, the virtual world is in many ways no different than the actual world it emulates: sexually explicit material is widely available, sexually explicit activity is facilitated by evolving communication technologies, and sex offenders have access to victim populations wherever people gather. The advantage of the Internet, and other proprietary virtual worlds with corresponding communication technologies, is that sex offenders can use them to search for, target, and even stalk, groom, or surveil their intended victims from a distance, and with varying levels of anonymity. Like opening any public park, grocery story, nightclub, or shopping mall, opening a virtual-world site without consideration for protections invites tragedy.

"Sexting" as a Crime

Consider the legal and social issues surrounding of the current practice of "sexting"—engaging in sexually explicit cell-phone conversations via text messaging, with equally explicit images and even video added to enhance the narration. Sometimes this is a welcome form of courtship and intimacy; sometimes it is an unwelcome intrusion on privacy; and sometimes it is a crime regardless of intent. As explained in Celiuzic (2009),

A 15-year-old Pennsylvania girl is facing child pornography charges for sending nude photos of herself to other kids. A 19-year-old Florida man got thrown out of college and has to register as a sex offender for 25 years because he sent nude pictures of his girlfriend to other teens.

The growing phenomenon of kids using their cell phones and computers to share racy photos and videos is known as "sexting." It is a problem that society is having trouble dealing with, and the punishments do not fit the perceived crimes, attorney Larry Walters told *Today*'s Matt Lauer Tuesday in New York. …

Walters was joined by Internet safety consultant Parry Aftab, who campaigns against the dangers presented to juveniles by modern communications technology. While Walters talked about how inappropriate it is to treat juveniles the same as adult pedophiles, Aftab talked about the very real dangers that sexting can lead to.

Aftab didn't argue with Walters' assertion that the law has not caught up with technology. But, she said, "We don't really have a choice. There's nothing else out there, and we are relying on prosecutorial discretion, meaning the prosecutors won't bring these cases. But when kids are out of hand, prosecutors are saying enough is enough."

Kids may not think there is any harm in sending revealing pictures to boyfriends and girlfriends, but Aftab brought up the case of Jesse Logan, an 18-year-old high school student from Cincinnati who killed herself after her ex-boyfriend sent nude pictures of her to other girls in her school. Jesse's mother, Cynthia Logan, and Aftab visited *Today* last week to talk about the tragic case.

They told of how some of the girls who received Jesse Logan's pictures harassed and bullied her for months. Cynthia Logan alleges that school officials did not take steps to stop the harassment. Jesse told her story to a local television station, and when that didn't stop the harassment, she hanged herself in her bedroom last July.

It should be noted that, immediately prior to sex-texting using cell phones, there was (and still is) live online chatting, which may include video streaming (e.g., webcams), e-mail, and typed and handwritten written notes and letters with Polaroid pictures—all of which have been used to the same end. So, rather than creating desire and creating pathology, it is fairer to say that technology reveals it by creating opportunity.

SUMMARY

Criminal profilers have a duty to be fully versed in the prevalence, nature, and variety of sex crimes that may be encountered in research and casework. Sex crimes are, by definition, deviant from a legal perspective. However the cultural and ideological deviance of a particular sex crime can vary widely. Confounding the issue is that the majority of sex crimes have not been studied or even defined with adequacy and consistency. This leaves inferences regarding the nature and frequency of many sex offenses without legitimate scientific foundation, subject to the bias of belief and narrowly perceived experience. It is also true that sex crimes are themselves not static or universal constructs; instead, they evolve with cultural expectations and the re-interpretation or abolition of criminal statutes.

Sex crime statutes teach us what was or remains ideologically deviant in a given society. However, the prevalence of individual sex offenses, and the extent to which they are tolerated or even encouraged, provides insight into changes that may be coming, or into the inability of a culture to acknowledge a problem for fear of needing to take responsibility for the consequences. Clearly, a great deal more study and research, from a scientific perspective, is needed across the spectrum of sexual offenders and their offenses.

Questions
1. Define the term *sex crime*.
2. What does *consent* refer to?
3. What is the difference between rape and sexual assault?
4. True or False: There are far more females than male sex offenders.
5. Facebook removed how many registered sex offenders from active membership:
    a. 1,750
    b. 2,250
    c. 2,500
    d. 5,500
    e. 7,000

REFERENCES

Bates, J., 2007. Alcohol is the True Date Rape Drug. Nursing Standards 21 (29), 26–27.

Beauregard, E., Lussier, P., Proulx, J., 2004. An Exploration of Developmental Factors Related to Deviant Sexual Preferences Among Adult Rapists. Sex Abuse 16 (2), 151–161.

Brown, G., 2008. Little Girl Lost: Las Vegas Metro Police Vice Division and the Use of Material Witness Holds against Teenaged Prostitutes. Catholic University Law Review 57 (Winter), 471–509.

Burgess, A., Groth, A.N., Holmstrom, L., Sgroi, S., 1978. Sexual Assault of Children and Adolescents. Lexington Books, New York, NY.

Celiuzic, M., 2009. Teen "Sexting": Youthful Prank or Sex Crime? TODAYShow.com Available from: www.commonsensemedia. org/about-us/press-room/daily-digest/sexting-porn-or-prank (accessed 10.03.09.).

Chang, E., 2001. Engagement Abroad: Enlisted Men, U.S. Military Policy and the Sex Industry. Notre Dame Journal of Law, Ethics and Public Policy 15, 621–652.

Cole, T., 2006. Rape at US Colleges Often Fueled by Alcohol. Journal of the American Medical Association 296 (5), 504–505.

Cornell, S., 2009. Corpse Abuser Faces New Counts. Fort Wayne *Journal-Gazette*, Indiana, February 27.

Cowan, S., 2008. The Trouble with Drink: Intoxication, (In)Capacity, and the Evaporation of Consent to Sex. Akron Law Review 899–922.

Cox, N., 2009. Police Warning to Parents about Online Sex Predators. Perth Now. Available from: www.news.com.au/perthnow/ story/0,27574,25933849-2761,00.html (accessed 15.08.09.).

Criminal Law, 2009. Statutory Interpretation—Wisconsin Supreme Court Applies Sexual Assault Statute to Attempted Sexual Intercourse With a Corpse.—*State v. Grunke*, 752 N.W.2D 769 (WIS. 2008). Harvard Law Review 122 (April), 1780–1787.

Earls, C., Lalumiere, M., 2009. A Case Study of Preferential Bestiality. Archives of Sexual Behavior 38, 605–609.

East, W.N., 1946. Sexual Offenders—A British View. Yale Law Journal 55 (April), 527–557.

Gebhard, P., Gagnon, J., Pomeroy, W., Christenson, C., 1965. Sex Offenders: An Analysis of Types. Harper & Row Publishers, New York, NY.

Griffin, M., West, D., 2006. The Lowest of the Low? Addressing the Disparity between Community View, Public Policy, and Treatment Effectiveness for Sex Offenders. Law and Psychology Review 30 (Spring), 143–169.

Groth, A.N., 1979. Men Who Rape: The Psychology of the Offender. Plenum Press, New York, NY.

Hotaling, N., Miller, K., Trudeau, E., 2006. The Commercial Sexual Exploitation of Women and Girls: A Survivor Service Provider's Perspective. Yale Journal of Law and Feminism 18, 181–190.

Hough, N., 2004. Sodomy and Prostitution: Laws Protecting the "Fabric of Society". Pierce Law Review 3 (December), 101–124.

Hughes, D., 2002. The Use of New Communications and Information Technologies for Sexual Exploitation of Women and Children. Hastings Women's Law Journal 13 (Winter), 127–146.

Jensen, C., Bailey, P., Jensen, S., 2002. Selection, Engagement and Seduction of Children and Adults by Child Molesters. Prosecutor (November/December)40–47.

Kopytoff, V., 2009. Mixed Views on Craigslist Crackdown on Hookers. San Francisco Chronicle (August 9).

Larkin, D., 2008. Vermont Couple Face Child Sexual Abuse Charges. Rutland *Times-Argus*, Vermont, January 8.

Lawrence v. Texas, 2003. 539 U.S. 558.

Lindsay, W.R., Murphy, L., Smith, G., Murphy, D., Edwards, Z., Chittock, C., et al., 2004. The Dynamic Risk Assessment and Management System: An Assessment of Immediate Risk of Violence for Individuals with Offending and Challenging Behavior. Journal of Applied Research in Intellect. Disabilities 17, 267–274.

Lowenstein, L.F., 2002. Fetishes and Their Associated Behavior. Sexual Disabilities 20 (2), Summer.

McKibbin, W., Shackelford, T., Goetz, A., Starratt, V., 2008. Why Do Men Rape? An Evolutionary Psychological Perspective. Review of General Psychology 12 (1), 86–97.

Metzle, J., 2004. Voyeur Nation? Changing Definitions of Voyeurism, 1950–2004. Harvard Review of Psychiatry 12 (March/April), 127–131.

Morris, W., 2006. Sex Burglar Gets Seven Years. Juneau *Empire* Available from: www.juneauempire.com/stories/110106/loc_20061101015.shtml (accessed 01.11.08.).

Rand, M., 2008. Criminal Victimization, 2007. In: Bureau of Justice Statistics Bulletin. December, NCJ 224390. U.S. Department of Justice, Washington DC.

Rizzo, T., 2007. Female Sex Offenders: Underreported and Little Understood. Kansas City *Star* Missouri, June 02.

Savino, J., Turvey, B., 2004. Rape Investigation Handbook. Elsevier Science, Boston, MA.

Soto, J., 2007. We're Here to Protect Democracy. We're Not Here to Practice It: The U.S. Military's Involvement in Trafficking in Persons and Suggestions for the Future. Cardozo Journal of Law and Gender 13 (Summer), 561–577.

Strickland, S., 2008. Female Sex Offenders: Exploring Issues of Personality, Trauma, and Cognitive Distortions. Journal of Interpersonal Violence 23 (4), 474–489.

Sullivan, J., 2005. Trespassing Charged in Horse-Sex case. Seattle *Time*s. Available from: www.seattletimes.nwsource.com/html/localnews/2002569751_horsesex19m.html (accessed 01.12.08.).

Torres, A., van der Walt, A., 2009. Sexual Offenders and Their Victims. In: Petherick, W., Turvey, B. (Eds.), Forensic Victimology: Examining Violent Crime Victims in Investigative and Legal Contexts. Elsevier Science, San Diego, CA.

Turvey, B., 2004. Rapist Modus Operandi and Motive. In: Savino, J., Turvey, B. (Eds.), Rape Investigation Handbook. Elsevier Science, Boston, MA.

Turvey, B., 2008. Criminal Profiling: An Introduction to Behavioral Evidence Analysis, third edition. Elsevier Science, London, England.

Woolley, M., 2007. Marital Rape: A Unique Blend of Domestic Violence and Non-Marital Rape Issues. Hastings Women's Law Journal 18 (Summer), 269–293.

CHAPTER 20

Domestic Homicide

Brent E. Turvey

I would look forward to the times when they faulted, so I could whip them … I would think with each blow of the switch: Now you are aware of me!

—William Faulkner, *As I Lay Dying*

CONTENTS

KEY TERMS

Domestic child homicide	Honor killing	Mutual violent control
Domestic elder homicide	Intimate terrorism	Situational couple violence
Domestic homicide:	Intimate homicide	Violent resistance

Domestic homicide occurs when one family member, household member, or intimate kills another. It is often the result of accumulated as opposed to situational rage, and therefore it is commonly associated with long-term fighting, abuse, or betrayal. It also frequently occurs in association with drug and alcohol use. Consequently, it involves some of the more violent and aberrant behaviors that criminal profilers will need to examine.

It is well known that domestic homicide is a regular occurrence in the United States, to say nothing of the rest of the world. In the United States alone, more than three women are murdered by an intimate partner every day (Bureau of Justice Statistics [BJS], 2003). According to FBI statistics, domestic homicide is more than twice as likely to involve the killing of a female victim (BJS, 1996) and regularly results in the death of more than one person at the hands of the offender, as well as the offender's own death.[1]

It is also well known that drugs and alcohol play a significant role in domestic violence. Some studies have shown that as many as 92% of batterers used alcohol or drugs before domestic assaults (Brookoff et al., 1997) and that the use of alcohol or drugs is one of the most significant risk factors for domestic violence (Bennett et al., 1994). Whatever the current or local statistics surrounding the reader, it is enough to know that the association between substance abuse and domestic violence will make itself clear in actual case-work to the point of frustration and exhaustion. It is, however, a mistake to assume that this association is necessarily causal. In some cases, substance abuse may be symptomatic of other issues (as a self-medicating/coping mechanism) as opposed to being the explicit reason for violence.

However, it is not well known that many domestic abuse and neglect deaths fail to be counted as domestic homicides. Often, such deaths occur within the context of ongoing domestic violence between parents that spills over into abusive behavior toward children or other domestic victims. In any case, law-enforcement agencies routinely fail to code these and other crimes correctly for a variety of reasons (Johnson et al. 2000). Consequently, the grim reality is that, as bad as the problem of intimate, child, and elder domestic homicide appears, it actually is much worse.[2]

RISK AND EXPOSURE

According to the research presented in Johnson et al. (2000), several circumstances increase one's risk of domestic homicide. The high-risk factors (written from the perspective of female victims) are (pp. 283–284):

1. Prior history of domestic violence
   - escalation of violence
   - past homicide attempts; choking
   - rape and sexual violence
   - violence toward pets
   - violence during pregnancy

---

[1] According to a Florida study conducted in 1994 (Task Force, 1997), 38% of domestic homicides involve multiple victims, usually combining a spouse homicide and suicide or child homicide. According to a San Francisco study, from 1995 to 1996, 43% of the male murderers in domestic homicides killed themselves after killing the woman (Hallinan, 1997).

[2] The study conducted by Johnson et al. (2000) revealed that the Florida Department of Law Enforcement (FDLE) itemized 230 domestic homicides for 1994. The researchers discovered that there were actually 319 domestic homicides, roughly a third more than had been officially counted. In 1995, the FDLE itemized 195 domestic homicides, and the final total revealed by the researchers was actually 295. One of the other reasons cited for this ongoing misclassification was the fact that the law-enforcement agencies did not code boyfriend/girlfriend homicides as domestic when the two people did not officially live together. Such coding methodologies conceal the real numbers.

2. Escaping violent relationships
   - marital estrangement
3. Obsessive possessiveness
   - extreme jealousy
   - stalking
   - obsessiveness about the relationship
   - suicide attempts or threats
4. Prior police involvement
5. Prior criminal history of the perpetrator
6. Threats to kill
7. Alcohol/drug problems
8. Protection orders
9. Acute perceptions of betrayal
10. Child custody disputes
    - past attempts to kill or abduct children
    - severe abuse of children
    - sexual abuse of children
11. Mental illness of perpetrator (paranoia, schizophrenia, depression)
    - severe abuse as child
12. Hostage taking
13. Children are hers not his
14. Change in circumstances
    - unemployment
15. Her fear!

As far as the courts are concerned, depending upon the facts and the victim's perceptions in the particular case, whether the research is deemed to suggest a greater degree of risk or a risk of death is far less important to the court than is the court's per se heightened vigilance when confronted with any number of these factors.

It should be noted that these risk factors are in fact sex and gender neutral and they apply to males and females.

Criminal profilers must recognize, investigate, examine, understand, and explain these factors in the preparation of *any* victimology. The existence of any one or a combination of more of them (aside from 13 and 14) is enough to raise the risk for being the victim of a domestic homicide to medium or high levels. Sources of information that can have a direct bearing on these factors include medical records, court records, mental health records, phone records, e-mail records, prescriptions on hand, personal toxicology and personal diaries. Failure to gather this kind of information leaves the analyst in the dark with respect to the risks and exposures of a particular victim. In domestic homicides, the factors are also necessary to establish the context of the crime.

Given that exposure to domestic violence and abuse increases the risk of becoming a victim of domestic homicide, risk factors for suffering domestic violence must be considered as well. As Wilson (2005) observed, they include the age of the woman (women in their child-bearing years are at greatest risk), being a mother of children not related to the male aggressor, and making threats to leave or actually leaving the male. Wilson noted (p. 306) with respect to domestic homicide: "there does seem to be a tendency for men who kill their female intimates to do so when the women are in their child-bearing years." She went on to discuss the issue of threats to leave or actual departure as a precipitating event, citing some fairly alarming research (Wilson, 2005, pp. 307–309):

Perhaps the largest single trigger for male violence is a woman's threat or attempt to leave her partner. Ironically, where domestic violence is already a problem, the very act that is undertaken in order to assure survival often ends up activating a dose of lethal violence.

The evidence that women are at a particularly high risk of violence or homicide when they are poised to leave or recently have left a relationship is overwhelming. Three quarters of homicide victims and eighty-five percent of victims of severe (but non-fatal) abuse had tried to leave the relationship within the past year. In situations where abuse is ongoing, leaving can end the violence, but when it does not, the abuse often becomes more extreme.

According to one report, an attempt to leave was the precipitating factor in forty-five percent of femicides. In another study by Brewer and Paulsen, while female-initiated separation was a motivating factor in fifty-six percent of the cases of wife killing, this trend was not found in situations where men initiated the separation. In a study of 293 women killed by intimates in North Carolina from 1991 to 1993, Beth Moracco and her colleagues at the University of North Carolina School for Public Health found that forty-two percent had been killed after they threatened to separate, tried to separate, or had recently separated from their partners.

Women are at particularly high risk in the two months after the separation. The proximity in time of the deadly attack to the separation is not a coincidence. In cases in which the husband's abuse does turn deadly, it is often clear that the event that precipitated the lethal attack was her departure. In the aftermath of uxoricide, it is often noted that husbands did precisely what they threatened to do, and husbands often admit that their spouse's desertion was the cause of the deadly violence. Hence, there is rarely any question as to what motivated the murder—in these cases, the women who died were attempting to leave their killers.

Just as lethal assaults increase when a wife threatens to leave, so do non-lethal assaults. As Wilson and Daly point out, "[a] credible threat of violent death can very effectively control people, and the … evidence on risks to estranged wives suggests that such threats by husbands are often sincere." This remark underscores the proprietary aspect of this type of violence. In fact, sexual jealousy and fear of desertion both elicit similar aggressive reactions. Clearly, killing a wife is not utilitarian if the goal is to assure access for future procreation. Ironically, what motivates this type of homicide is clearly not a desire to be free of the woman. Were that the case, presumably the man would allow her to leave. Instead, Wilson, Johnson, and Daily propose that uxoricide occurs when male proprietariness gets carried to an extreme. In many cases, the male may have used the threat of lethal violence in the past in a less counterproductive way to successfully prevent his wife from leaving. Proprietary uxoricide may occur in cases where men use more force than intended, attempting to intimidate their wives into staying. Equally likely, however, is the possibility that the man was simply carrying out a promise he made the woman before she left, adopting the attitude, "If I can't have her, then no one shall."

However, this does not answer the question of whether or not pregnancy is, by itself, a factor that increases risk of domestic violence or homicide.

PREGNANCY AS A RISK FACTOR

In recent years, there has been considerable media coverage of intimate homicides involving pregnant women. Headlines, copy, and pundits have repeatedly and incorrectly affirmed that homicide is *the* leading cause or *a* leading cause of death for pregnant women. Much of the related reporting has been biased, inflammatory, or just plain uninformed—often fuelled by victim's advocates and victims' groups that, while well intentioned, are prone to react emotionally rather than based on a careful reading of the facts. This circumstance has been made worse by reporters and some less-than-informed criminal profilers citing incorrect or nonexistent data and research to support their particular social or political view.

The actual study at the heart of these numbers, published in the *American Journal of Public Health* (Chang et al., 2005), reported that, between 1991 and 1999, 31% of all pregnancy-related deaths that were also injury-related deaths were the result of homicide. Specifically, they found that homicide was not the leading cause of death for pregnant women, as many in the media have been eagerly reporting:

> For the years 1991 through 1999, 7342 deaths were reported to the PMSS [Pregnancy Mortality Surveillance System]. A majority of the reported deaths (n=4200 [57.2%]) were pregnancy-related (e.g., they occurred during or within 1 year of pregnancy and were causally related to pregnancy)[see Chang et al. 2003]. A total of 1993 deaths (27.1%) were pregnancy associated and injury related. The remaining 1149 (15.7%) deaths included those that were pregnancy associated but not caused by injuries or pregnancy complications and those that were not pregnancy associated (e.g., the time interval between the end of pregnancy and maternal death exceeded 1 year).

> Of all pregnancy-associated injury deaths (n=1993), 617 (31.0%) women died as a result of homicide, ranking homicide as the second leading cause of total reported injury deaths among pregnant women and postpartum women, following deaths caused by motor vehicle accidents (44.1%). The rest of the pregnancy-associated injury deaths were attributed to unintentional injuries (12.7%), suicide (10.3%), and other (2.0%).

> When interpreting this report's finding that homicide is the second leading cause of injury-related death among pregnant and postpartum women, it is important to note that our findings regarding homicides involving pregnant and postpartum women are similar to national statistics on homicide among all women of reproductive age (regardless of whether they are pregnant or not).

According to the study, there were 4,200 pregnancy-related deaths between 1991 and 1999 (pregnancy-related death was defined as death that occurred during, or within 1 year of, pregnancy and were causally related to pregnancy). Note that 1,993 (47.5%) of these pregnancy-related deaths were also injury related; 613 (14.6%) of pregnancy-related deaths were the result of homicide. This makes clear that homicide is not in fact the leading cause of death among pregnant women, nor is it even the leading cause of death among all pregnancy-associated injury deaths. In fact, more recently, research by Taylor and Nabors (2009) has found that domestic violence may actually decrease during pregnancy.

This research matters because certain "experts" have no difficulty going on television and stating the opposite—and the media are quick to repeat it, and the public is very quick to believe.

Certainly, any victim's pregnancy is a potential motive for any violence that might be suffered. It must absolutely be considered when preparing a victimology. However, as with all factors, it must be considered in its particular context, and its value should not be overstated simply because it makes a good sound bite. This is an area where experts can do the most good by educating themselves so that they may in turn educate the public in an honest and informed fashion when asked to do so. When any expert crosses the line into unrestrained advocacy, providing opinion that is free of the facts, then his or her public service is political, not scientific, and is a professional violation of the public trust.

THE DYNAMICS OF ABUSIVE RELATIONSHIPS

It is important for criminal profilers to understand how to recognize, perceive, and communicate abusive relationship dynamics, to grasp what precisely motivates them, and to assess the risk and actual exposure involved.

The dynamics of intimate violence—the way it begins, expresses, and evolves—are complex. Yet they are driven by a sense of overall powerlessness experienced on the part of the aggressor. This powerlessness is expressed by the assertion of power and control over the victim. As explained in Burke (2007, p. 555): "Outside the realm of criminal law, social scientists almost universally describe domestic violence as an ongoing pattern of conduct motivated by the batterer's desire for power and control over the victim." Burke then explained more precisely why domestic violence is different from other forms of interpersonal violence, with respect to qualitative and quantitative features (pp. 567–569):

A. Quantitative Factors: Frequency and Duration

Compared to assaults between strangers or non-intimate acquaintances, violence between intimates is more likely to involve repeated assaults over a period of time, rather than a one-time incident of violence. One quantitative aspect of domestic violence is its frequency. One expert estimates that sixty-three percent of men who assault their wives repeat the behavior. That estimate is consistent with the results of the National Violence Against Women Survey, which found that more than sixty-five percent of the women who reported being physically assaulted by an intimate partner said they were victimized multiple times by that same person. Nearly twenty percent of the assaulted women recalled ten or more incidents, and the average number of assaults by the same partner was nearly seven. Domestic violence is quantitatively distinct from non-intimate violence not only in its frequency, but also in its duration. The same survey found that nearly seventy percent of women who had been assaulted by an intimate partner reported that their victimization lasted more than one year. For more than a quarter of the women, the victimization occurred over more than five years, and the average duration of the violence was four and a half years. Indeed, even the language used to describe the experience of domestic violence reflects its frequent and prolonged character. We say that a woman who has been assaulted by her husband is "battered" or "beaten," or has been subjected to "domestic violence," suggesting a general status or a continued phenomenon. In contrast, when a person has been assaulted by a stranger or casual acquaintance, we say he has been "attacked" or "assaulted," or has gotten into a "fight," suggesting a one-time act of violence, not violence more generally.

B. Qualitative Factors: Power and Control

The frequency and duration of domestic violence distinguish it quantitatively from other examples of criminal violence, but they also give rise to a qualitative distinction. Social scientists universally speak of domestic violence in terms that transcend the physical injuries from individual incidents of assault. Instead, they speak of domestic violence as a pattern of conduct that uses physical battering as just one method of inflicting emotional trauma.

Although social scientists caution that there is no singular profile of a domestic abuser's psychology, they commonly use a framework of power and control to explain the coercive nature of domestic violence, emphasizing that the intended harm goes beyond physical injury. Empirical evidence supports the theory that domestic violence is often driven by a desire to control. For example, men who are jealous, controlling, or verbally abusive are statistically more likely to assault, rape, or stalk their partners. Many domestic violence offenders suffer from low self-esteem and little self-control, and may physically retaliate against exercises of independence by their intimate partners.

In a discussion of the contradictions found in domestic violence research, specifically regarding the issue of male versus female victims, Ver Steegh (2005, pp. 1382–1384) referred to a domestic violence typology that may be useful:

> Disquieting inconsistencies [in domestic violence research], as well as major contradictions, are either ignored or become the subject of rancorous cross-professional debate. For example, for the past twenty-five years, researchers have engaged in an intense debate concerning how often assaults occur and whether men and women are equally violent. The controversy stems from the contradictory findings of various studies. Epidemiological "family conflict" studies show higher overall assault rates with nearly equal rates of assault by men and women. In contrast, so-called "crime" studies and police call data show lower overall annual assault rates and much higher rates of assault by men than by women.

> The "family conflict" studies have been criticized by service providers and some feminist scholars who challenge the methodology of the studies, particularly the use of reliance on the Conflict Tactics Scale. These critics believe that the studies focus too heavily on specific acts of aggression and too little on resulting injury and the context of the behavior. "However, both groups of researchers agree that women are ten times as likely as men to be injured as a result of domestic violence." Differences also stem from definitional issues. The family conflict researchers define domestic violence narrowly in terms of physical assault, while service providers and clinical researchers define it broadly to include all types of maltreatment.

> In the final analysis, despite the high level of acrimony, these studies may not actually contradict each other. As Murray Straus explains, researchers may in fact be observing and measuring different phenomena. He asserts that both groups of researchers are correct. They are merely studying different populations experiencing different types of violence. He speculates that, "these two types of violence probably have different etiologies and probably require different types of intervention."

> Researcher Michael P. Johnson has taken the process of integrating competing studies to its conclusion by developing a comprehensive typology that accounts for contradictory research and connects contrasting perspectives. Based on his analysis of the "family conflict" and the "feminist" studies discussed above, he concludes that women's advocates and service providers are primarily observing one type of domestic violence, Intimate Terrorism, while family conflict researchers are predominantly measuring another type of violence, Situational Couple Violence.

The Johnson typology of intimate personal violence (IPV) provides four discrete categories that are meant to take an offender's use of threats, economic control, privilege and punishment, children, isolation, emotional abuse, and sexual control into account. The categories are intimate terrorism (IT), violent resistance (VR), situational couple violence (SCV), and mutual violent control (MVC). They are determined based on offender motivation and the overall pattern of offense behavior. According to Johnson (2006, pp. 1009–1010),

> "[I]ntimate terrorism" refers to relationships in which only one of the spouses is violent and controlling. The other spouse is either nonviolent or has used violence but is not controlling. ... [Then there are] cases in which the focal spouse is violent but not controlling, and his or her partner is violent and controlling. I call it violent resistance, and it is almost entirely a woman's type of violence in this sample of heterosexual relationships. Of course, that is because in these marriages almost all of the intimate terrorism is perpetrated by men, and in some cases the wives do respond with violence, although rarely are they also controlling. ... "[S]ituational couple violence" [refers to] individual noncontrolling violence in a dyadic context in which neither of the spouses is violent and controlling. ... "[M]utual violent control" refers to controlling violence in a relationship in which both spouses are violent and controlling.

According to Mills (1999), a good way to describe the emotional abuse dynamics occurring in a relationship is via the typology presented below. A caution is added that, as with any behavioral motivational typology, the categories of abuse are not exclusive. The following has been adapted from Mills (1999), with the sex-specific term *woman* replaced by the generic term *victim*:[3]

1. *Rejection.* This includes criticizing, punishing, or judging the victim, refusing to help them, and routinely discounting their opinion.
2. *Degradation.* This includes verbally abusing the victim and physically humiliating them.
3. *Terrorization.* This involves threatening to harm the victim, threatening to harm their loved ones, and punishing the victim by playing on their fears. It can include things like setting unrealistic expectations, with threat of loss and harm if they are not met.
4. *Social isolation.* This involves preventing the victim from engaging in normal social activities and other interactions with people.
5. *Mis-socialization.* This involves corrupting the victim by encouraging them to engage in criminal or delinquent behavior.
6. *Exploitation.* This involves using the victim to support the abuser and their abusive lifestyle.
7. *Emotional unresponsiveness.* This includes showing detachment and lack of involvement with the victim, and interacting with them only if absolutely necessary. It also includes failure to express affection, caring, and love toward the victim.
8. *Close confinement.* This includes restricting the victim's movement, even to the point of imprisonment.

INTENT

In many cases, the courts have recognized that behavioral evidence may be sufficient to support the conclusion that a domestic homicide was committed in the heat of passion. For example, domestic homicide may follow a confession or admission of adultery made to the offender by the intimate partner, thus warranting a reduction of subsequent charges from murder to manslaughter (Smith, 2000). As a result, criminal profilers may find themselves asked to examine domestic homicides in regard to the issue of intent. Examining the crime scene and related offense behavior may yield an informed understanding of this issue. As Smith (2000) discussed,

> The degree of homicide in any particular case depends upon the intent, purpose, or design of the defendant, and it is the element of malice which distinguishes murder from manslaughter. Thus, while murder is regarded generally as the killing of one human being by another with malice aforethought, either express or implied, a homicide, even though intentional, is regarded as the lesser crime of voluntary manslaughter where the killing was committed under the influence of passion produced by an adequate or reasonable provocation and before a reasonable time has elapsed for the passion to cool and reason to assume control, the killing not being the result of wickedness of heart or cruelty or recklessness of disposition.

However, not all domestic homicides are the result of a sudden onset of uncontrollable rage. Many long-term spouse abusers, for example, plan and choose their actions very carefully.

---

[3] There is a great deal of literature about female victims of domestic abuse. The author agrees that women are far more often the victims of domestic abuse. According to Rennison (2003), 85% of intimate partner violence victims were in fact women. However, men may be victims as well. Bearing that in mind, the generic term *victim* is the appropriate term for use in objective behavioral evidence analysis.

- They can be selective about the time and place that they exhibit their physically violent behavior. They will more than likely become physically violent with their intimate partners and/or children in the privacy of their home, rather than in public.
- They can be selective about whom they beat. They will become physically violent with intimate partners and/or children, but not with bosses or co-workers.
- They can be particular about where they injure their victims. They often injure only those body areas that can or will be covered by clothing. Or, if they want to keep the victim from leaving the home, injuries may be delivered to a body area where all will see them. If the victim leaves the home, he or she is faced with the embarrassment of having to explain the injury.
- They can calculate how long and how badly they will injure their victims. They take care that injury will not interfere with daily chores or other expected duties.

This kind of calculated behavior pattern evidences an offender who does not suffer from a loss of control when he or she commits a crime. While still an expression of rage, actions are focused and managed. Even those crimes that contain, or are the result of, rage may be well planned or carefully thought out.

To distinguish such cases, criminal profilers must be thorough and determine whether an individual crime evidences cumulative rage, situational passion, planned retribution, or some combination of these factors.

INTIMATE HOMICIDE

An *intimate homicide* occurs when a current or former intimate relationship partner kills the other. It is a sub-type of domestic homicide. In such cases, the victim and offender do not always live together, but they must be, or have been, involved in a deep personal relationship of some kind. Often it is a sexual or romantic relationship, and the motive is almost exclusively anger/revenge, profit, or a combination of the two.

DOMESTIC CHILD HOMICIDE

A *domestic child homicide* occurs when a parent or caretaker kills a child. Too often, the author has observed or been asked to examine child homicides where police have focused on stranger suspects and failed to investigate suspects within the victim's home or family. The rule in all child homicides is simple: Investigate and eliminate the family and household members first, including caretakers. Then friends. Then neighbors. Essentially those with access to, and who spend time with, the child need to be eliminated first. If the resources exist, other detectives should be working a parallel investigation on the possibility of a stranger's having committed the offense (with the first attention paid to local area registered sex offenders, recently paroled child molesters, etc.). Failure to do this, for whatever reason, results in an imbalanced investigation and a lack of certainty regarding any suspect who is accused.

According to research conducted by the Correctional Service of Canada (1995), children who are killed before their first birthday (the crime of *infanticide*) are most often killed by a family member, usually by their parent (about three-quarters of such victims) and are equally at risk from their father and mother. A very small number of these children are killed by acquaintances (such as baby-sitters or friends) and an even smaller number are killed by strangers.

This information is useful to criminal profilers in that it indicates investigative priorities in a child homicide. It should not be used conclusively, however. Statistics are not evidence, they merely point the investigation in a certain direction that may or may not be fruitful. Statistics are not a substitute for a thorough investigation. The investigation must still be performed.

"HONOR KILLINGS"

One of the great oxymorons of our time, an *honor killing*, is the murder of an individual, almost always a girl or woman, by members of, at the direction of, or on behalf of, their family. Honor killings occur because of the belief that the woman's actions have brought dishonor to the family or community. As explained in Mayell (2002),

> Hundreds, if not thousands, of women are murdered by their families each year in the name of family "honor." It's difficult to get precise numbers on the phenomenon of honor killing; the murders frequently go unreported, the perpetrators unpunished, and the concept of family honor justifies the act in the eyes of some societies.

> Most honor killings occur in countries where the concept of women as a vessel of the family reputation predominates, said Marsha Freemen, director of International Women's Rights Action Watch at the Hubert Humphrey Institute of Public Affairs at the University of Minnesota.

> Reports submitted to the United Nations Commission on Human Rights show that honor killings have occurred in Bangladesh, Great Britain, Brazil, Ecuador, Egypt, India, Israel, Italy, Jordan, Pakistan, Morocco, Sweden, Turkey, and Uganda. … [T]he practice was condoned under the rule of the fundamentalist Taliban government in Afghanistan, and [it] has been reported in Iraq and Iran.

> But while honor killings have elicited considerable attention and outrage, human rights activists argue that they should be regarded as part of a much larger problem of violence against women.

> In India, for example, more than 5,000 brides die annually because their dowries are considered insufficient, according to the United Nations Children's Fund (UNICEF). Crimes of passion, which are treated extremely leniently in Latin America, are the same thing with a different name, some rights advocates say.

> "In countries where Islam is practiced, they're called honor killings, but dowry deaths and so-called crimes of passion have a similar dynamic in that the women are killed by male family members and the crimes are perceived as excusable or understandable," said Widney Brown, advocacy director for Human Rights Watch.

> The practice, she said, "goes across cultures and across religions."

> Complicity by other women in the family and the community strengthens the concept of women as property and the perception that violence against family members is a family and not a judicial issue.

A particularly distressing feature of honor killings is that it is commonly believed the more brutal and degrading the death—the more suffering endured by the victim—the more honor is restored to the family. In such cases, the community is often complicit, as are some in law enforcement. Those who commit honor killings are often open about their participation and are applauded as heroes, while the victims are vilified as deserving or somehow earning their fate.

DOMESTIC ELDER HOMICIDE

Domestic elder homicides involve a caretaker (often a family member, private nurse, etc.) who kills an elder in his or her charge. An elder person is one who is roughly 65 years old or older and who may have physical or mental limitations that restrict the person's ability to carry out normal activities. A caretaker is a person who has care, custody, and control, or is in a position of trust with an elder (adapted from Powers, 2001).

Criminal profilers are admonished to be particularly thorough in preparing the victimology of an elderly person, as they are unlikely to have reported past abuse. This may be because of feelings that the mistreatment was normal or that the law could do nothing to help, or it may be because they were so physically isolated that there were no opportunities to ask for help. The most common reason for a failure to report abuse, however, may be related to the fact that 90% of elder abusers are members of the victims' families (Korpus, 2001). As Moskowitz (1998, p. 100) noted,

> [V]ictims are often particularly reluctant to proceed against family members because of embarrassment, shame, lack of third party emotional support, and failure of the criminal justice system to accommodate victims' needs.

According to Powers (2001), five motives are commonly related to killing the elderly—none of which are specific to the elderly, and some of which are consistent with similar motives for killing children (burden, profit, sexual assault). They include:

- Killing to be rid of a burden
- Killing for profit
- Killing out of hatred of the elderly person
- Killing for revenge
- Killing in commission of sexual assault

Red flags for foul play in the death of an elder, according to Powers (2001), include, but are not limited to,

- Death is unexpected and the victim is being tended by a caregiver with unusually high emotional stress
- Unusual interest in the victim by a much younger or previously unknown person, especially when the interest developed in a relatively short time frame
- Isolation of victim from family, friends, social activities, religious activities
- Unusually high mortality rates in a caregiving setting
- Unexpected changes in health with previously unseen symptoms
- Changes in the victim's will, power of attorney, trust or other fiduciary instrument, particularly when contrary to the victim's previously expressed wishes
- Significant and unusual expenditures of the victim's assets

DISCUSSION

Domestic homicide occurs in every race, culture, creed, and religion. It happens in every city, state, and country. And anyone can be victim—no matter his or her age or station. Examiners must be prepared for the volume and variety of cases that will present. They must further guard against the belief that such crimes have typical features, or that certain suspects are immune from consideration by virtue of their station or disposition.

Certain individuals are at greater risk of becoming the victim of a domestic homicide by virtue of their lifestyle, habits, intimates, and history. The majority of at-risk individuals are women, but men are at risk as well. In any case, the prevalence and brutality of domestic violence makes the need for a thorough victimology crucial, and the demands of objectivity are sometimes difficult. Barring direct evidence and a confession (which can and does happen), only a thorough victimology offers hope that we can determine precisely how victims have met their demise, and whether domestic homicide is a possibility that cannot be discarded.

SUMMARY

Domestic violence is more than physical injuries from individual incidents of assault. It is a pattern of conduct that uses physical battering as just one method of inflicting emotional trauma. In this chapter, the Johnson typology of intimate personal violence is discussed. The typology provides four categories that take into account an offender's use of threats, economic control, privilege and punishment, children, isolation, emotional abuse, and sexual control. The chapter also considers the Mills behavior motivation typology of eight types of abuse dynamics, including rejection, degradation, terrorization, social isolation, mis-socialization, exploitation, emotional unresponsiveness, and close confinement, which often happen in intimate violence situations.

The risk factors for domestic homicide are discussed, including pregnancy, attempting to leave the relationship, and so on. Further, issues with the reporting and presentation of statistics of domestic homicide and violence are discussed in some detail, with a focus on the media's misrepresentation of research about the risk of pregnant women becoming victims.

It should now be clear that the ways that intimate violence begins, expresses, and evolves are quite complex. They are often driven by the aggressor's overall sense of powerlessness and may present in various ways depending on the context of the situation, the people involved, and the precipitating factors.

Questions

1. True or False: Violence between intimates is less likely to involve repeated assaults over a period of a time as opposed to a one-time incident of violence.
2. Name and describe three of the different types of abuse dynamics discussed in Mills (1999).
3. True or False: The primary cause of death for pregnant women in the United States is homicide.
4. What is one of the most significant risk factors for domestic violence?
5. What are some of the most significant risk factors for domestic homicide?
6. True or False: Men cannot be the victims of domestic violence.

REFERENCES

Bennett, L.W., Tolman, R.M., Rogalski, C.J., Srinivasaraghavan, J., 1994. Domestic Abuse by Male Alcohol and Drug Addicts. Violence Victimology 9, 59–368.

Brookoff, D., O'Brien, K., Cook, C.S., Thompson, T.D., Williams, C., 1997. Characteristics of Participants in Domestic Violence. Journal of the American Medical Association 277, 1369–1373.

Bureau of Justice Statistics, 1996. Female Victims of Violent Crime. No. NCJ-162602, U.S. Department of Justice, Washington, DC, December.

Bureau of Justice Statistics Crime Data Brief, 2003. Intimate Partner Violence, 1993–2001. U.S. Department of Justice, Washington, DC, February.

Burke, A., 2007. Domestic Violence as a Crime of Pattern and Intent: An Alternative Reconceptualization. George Washington Law Review 75 (April), 552–612.

Chang, J., Elam-Evans, L.D., Berg, C.J., et al., 2003. Pregnancy Related Mortality Surveillance: United States, 1991–1999. MMWR Surveillance 52 (Summer), 1–8.

Chang, J., Berg, C., Saltzman, L., Herndon, J., 2005. Homicide: A Leading Cause of Injury Deaths among Pregnant and Postpartum Women in the United States, 1991–1999. American Journal of Public Health 95 (3), 471–477.

Correctional Service of Canada, 1995. A Profile of Homicide Offenders in Canada, Number B-12, Research Division, Correctional Research and Development, Correctional Service of Canada.

Hallinan, T., 1997. Domestic Terror: Family and Domestic Violence Homicide Cases in San Francisco 1993–1994. San Francisco Family Violence Project, San Francisco District Attorney's Office, March 31.

Johnson, J., Lutz, V., Websdale, N. (panelists), 2000. Death by Intimacy: Risk Factors for Domestic Violence, Symposium Speech. Pace Law Review 20 (Spring), 263–296.

Johnson, M., 2006. Conflict and Control: Gender Symmetry and Asymmetry in Domestic Violence. Violence against Women 12 (11), 1003–1018.

Korpus, K., 2001. Extinguishing Inheritance Rights: California Breaks New Ground in the Fight against Elder Abuse but Fails to Build an Effective Foundation. Hastings Law Journal 52 (January), 537–554.

Mayell, H., 2002. Thousands of Women Killed for Family "Honor". National Geographic News February 12.

Mills, L., 1999. Killing Her Softly: Intimate Abuse and the Violence of State Intervention. Harvard Law Review 113 (December), 550–558.

Moskowitz, S., 1998. Saving Granny from the Wolf: Elder Abuse and Neglect—The Legal Framework. Connecticut Law Review 31, 77–204.

Powers, S., 2001. Elder and Dependent Adult Homicide: Prevention, Investigation and Prosecution. Los Angeles County District Attorney's Office, April.

Rennison, C., 2003. Intimate Partner Violence, 1993–2001. Bureau of Justice Statistics, U.S. Department of Justice, Washington, DC. Publication No. NCJ197838.

Smith, J., 2000. Spouse's Confession of Adultery as Affecting Degree of Homicide Involved in Killing Spouse or His or Her Paramour. American Law Reports June 2000 (93 A.L.R.3d 925).

Task Force, 1997. Florida Governor's Task Force on Domestic and Sexual Violence. Florida Mortality Review Project 45, table 12.

Taylor, R., Nabors, E., 2009, . Pink and Blue . . . or Black and Blue? Examining Pregnancy as a Predictor of Intimate Partner Violence and Femicide. Violence against Women 15 (11), 1273–1293.

Ver Steegh, N., 2005. Differentiating Types of Domestic Violence: Implications for Child Custody. Louisiana Law Review 65 (Summer), 1379–1429.

Wilson, M.J., 2005. An Evolutionary Perspective on Male Domestic Violence: Practical and Policy Implications. American Journal of Criminal Law (Summer), 291–323.

Mass Murder

Brent E. Turvey

CONTENTS

KEY TERMS

Genocide

Mass murder

This chapter covers *mass murder* (mass killing), an all too common focus of the author's casework. The phrase *mass murder* is commonly defined as the murder of multiple victims during a single event, at one or more associated locations. This construct is distinct from serial crime classifications, such as *killing sprees* and *serial murder,* which are discussed in Chapter 22.[1]

The definition of mass murder appears straightforward, and it should be. For any event to be described thus, there must be multiple victims and they must all be victims of criminal homicide. This also means that they must all be dead. It is not permissible to refer to a case as a mass murder, or any related subtype, should there be doubt whether the alleged victims are dead or should there be doubt that their deaths were the result of a homicide.

For example, if multiple family members go missing it is not a legitimate forensic practice to assume that they are dead and/or must have been killed. They may have been in an accident. They may have simply moved away without telling anyone. Until each of their deaths has been investigated and homicide has been established by a proper reconstruction of the forensic evidence, their demise is impossible to know and irresponsible to guess at. A determination of mass murder requires the existence and examination of multiple dead bodies. Deaths may not be assumed and the manner of death may certainly not be inferred without the proper physical evidence.

Furthermore, if multiple persons are discovered dead in a particular location it is not a legitimate forensic practice to assume that their deaths must have been the result of a homicide. They may have died from something in the environment. They may have committed mass suicide. Again, until homicide has been established as the manner of death by a proper reconstruction of the forensic evidence, it is impossible to know and irresponsible to guess. This is especially problematic in cases where there has been significant decomposition.

Practitioners who make assumptions for the purposes of their analysis are showing either ignorance or bias.

MASS MURDER VERSUS GENOCIDE

Genocide is the deliberate and organized killing of large groups of people who are distinguished by their personal, political, and religious beliefs; their nationality; and/or their ethnicity. Genocide is a subtype of mass murder. Most commonly, genocide is committed by a government against another state or minority, or by one group that is in competition or conflict with another. It is also important to note that genocidal campaigns do not involve just killing, but also may be characterized by mass rape, torture, and other abuses. There are, unfortunately, many examples of this both historically and presently.

The purpose of this textbook is to discuss the interpretation of behavioral evidence in order to investigate crimes committed by individuals, not those authorized by, or committed on behalf of, governments or nations. The latter effort would be tremendous and deserves its own fair and accurate textbook. Consequently, the subject of genocide is not covered further in this book.

---

[1] Levin and Madfis (2009) add the caveats that mass murder is antisocial and not sponsored by the state. This author considers the antisocial caveat redundant; murder, by its very nature, is antisocial. Moreover, the caveat regarding state sponsorship is problematic. Certainly governments can sponsor acts of intentional or negligent mass murder. In extreme cases, some of these incidents can fall into the category of genocide (discussed shortly). However, there are examples of illegal state-sponsored killings of small groups, such as dissidents, witnesses, or civilians executed without due process. Although they are not the subject of this text, there is no reason to pretend this kind of killing does not happen and that in some instances is determined to be criminal.

Students interested in the subject can begin their studies with the following general works, and then advance to specialized research of individual conflicts:

- Jones, A. (2010) *Genocide: A Comprehensive Introduction*, second edition
- Kiernan, B. (2009) *Blood and Soil: A World History of Genocide and Extermination from Sparta to Darfur*
- Weitz, E. (2005) *A Century of Genocide: Utopias of Race and Nation*

Full details on these titles may be found in the "References" at the end of the chapter.

MASS MURDER AND THE MEDIA

Because of available cell phone and Internet technology, and the competitive nature of the 24-hour news cycle, the relationship between violent crime and the media has approached a critical mass. Victims and offenders alike communicate directly with news outlets before, during, and after the commission of crimes. It's a matter of narcissism and supply and demand. Certain offenders want to be seen and remembered, and the media wants to increase veiwership and sell market-share. Fortunately for both, the public wants to see offenders commit crimes, victims suffer, and the authorities either rise or fall in their efforts to respond. Not surprisingly, this is of particular delight to the media in the United States, which has progressed from merely reporting these events to delivering dramatic, real-time coverage, which may be viewed by victims and their loved ones during a prolonged incident.[2] Hostage situations and those involving mass murder are regularly televised live, pieced together with video and still images from phone cams at the scene, audio of frightened 911 calls, and interviews with victims, family members, and first responders from outside the barrier tape.

In April of 2007, 23-year-old Virginia Tech student Cho Seung-Hui, a senior and English major, committed a mass murder with the highest body count in the history of U.S. school shootings. As described in Shapira and Jackman (2007),

> An outburst of gunfire at a Virginia Tech dormitory, followed two hours later by a ruthless string of attacks at a classroom building, killed 32 students, faculty and staff and left about 30 others injured yesterday in the deadliest shooting rampage in the nation's history.
>
> The shooter, [Cho Seung-Hui], wore bluejeans, a blue jacket and a vest holding ammunition, witnesses said. He carried a 9 mm semiautomatic and a .22-caliber handgun, both with the serial numbers obliterated, federal law enforcement officials said. Witnesses described the shooter as a young man of Asian descent—a silent killer who was calm and showed no expression as he pursued and shot his victims. He killed himself as police closed in.
>
> He had left two dead at the dormitory and 30 more at a science and engineering building, where he executed people taking and teaching classes after chaining some doors shut behind him. At one point, he shot at a custodian who was helping a victim. Witnesses described scenes of chaos and grief, with students jumping from second-story windows to escape gunfire and others blocking their classroom doors to keep the gunman away.

---

[2] One of the first examples of this new role of the media is the 1999 shooting at Columbine High School in Littleton, Colorado, in which two students killed 13 people before taking their own lives. During the attack, students hiding throughout the school could view live coverage of the event on classroom televisions equipped with cable connections. A more recent example is the April 2007 Virginia Tech shootings, which claimed 33 lives (including that of the shooter) and became the deadliest school shooting in U.S. history. Students on campus captured video of the attack using their cell phones and uploaded it to the Internet for media dissemination in near real time.

In keeping with the new relationship between the media and mass murder, and the narcissism at work behind this particular crime, Cho Seung-Hui mailed photographs, video, and writings to NBC News that detailed and documented his motives and state of mind. The network aired the material, and the public consumed it without hesitation. As per Cho's intent, international mass media coverage and infamy followed. This caused great distress among the victims, their families, and the Virginia Tech community in general.

MYTHS

There are a number of myths that must be dispelled regarding the phenomenon of mass murder.

First, it is not a uniquely American problem. It happens all over the world, in all nations and cultures.

Second, mass murderers are not always lone, unemployed, psychotic gunmen. Many adult mass murderers are employed and are either married or in relationships. Many also hold deeply felt personal beliefs, or perceive terrible grievances, as opposed to suffering from a detachment from reality. In other words, they tend to know what they are doing and to plan their crimes in detail, whether it be with respect to the amount of ammunition they pack or the placement of an explosive at a crowded location for maximum effect. Whether they also suffer from mental illness is another question entirely, and not all mental illness results in psychosis.

Third, mass murder doesn't happen in just one type of place. Mass murder can happen in any place where people gather—a school, a factory, a church, a business office, a police department, a military base, a hospital, a subway, or a home. Neither the existence of security checkpoints and personnel, nor holy ground, nor children has proven an effective deterrent to a committed mass murderer.

Finally, there is no one nomothetic "profile" that can be rendered from studying cases of mass murder. The murderers are diverse in their individual traits, methods, and motives. They come from all nations, cultures, and economic backgrounds; they use all manner of weapons with very different levels of skill; and they don't all want the same thing. Mass murder is a behavioral expression of a personal motive, and it is in no way represented by a typical offender type.

For example, consider the case of Charles Carl Roberts IV. On October 2, 2006, he defied all school shooter archetypes to date (Holusha, 2006):

> A lone gunman walked into a one-room schoolhouse in a largely Amish community in southeastern Pennsylvania today and shot as many as 10 girls, killing three immediately before turning the gun on himself and dying at the scene, according to the state police.
>
> The school is just outside Nickel Mines, a tiny village about 55 miles west of Philadelphia (Figure 21.1).
>
> The man, identified as Charles Carl Roberts IV, 32, who lived in the area, was evidently nursing a long-ago grievance expressed in notes left for his wife and children, said Jeffrey Miller, commissioner of the state police. He said the gunman lined the girls against the blackboard, bound their feet and shot them execution-style in the head.
>
> "He split them up, males and females," Commissioner Miller said. "He let the males go, some of the adults go. He bound the females at the blackboard, and apparently executed them."
>
> Three of the girls were dead at the scene in Nickel Mines, Pa., and seven others were rushed to nearby hospitals, some of them severely wounded. An earlier Associated Press report quoted a local coroner as saying there were six people dead, but the coroner later said he was unsure, The A.P. said. ...

FIGURE 21.1
Amish men standing outside of the barrier tape put up to secure the perimeter by the Pennsylvania State Police, pictured, on October 2, 2006, in Nickel Mines, PA.

"There was some issue in the past" that had left the gunman with a desire to harm female students, Commissioner Miller said. He said that the murders were premeditated and that the gunman had called his wife— without telling her he was holding hostages in a school—[and told her] that he would not be coming home.

Commissioner Miller said Mr. Roberts called his wife from a cell phone, saying he was "acting out in revenge for something that happened 20 years ago."

"It seems as though he wanted to attack young, female victims," he said, according to The Associated Press.

The gunman released about 16 boys in the class, a pregnant teacher's aide and three women with small children before the shooting began, Commissioner Miller said. The principal teacher escaped at that time and ran to a nearby property to call 911.

The gunman, who was not Amish, evidently chose the small, private Amish school in Lancaster County about 55 miles west of Philadelphia because the security would be lax, Commissioner Miller said. He said when police tried to talk to the gunman over loudspeakers to begin negotiations, Mr. Roberts made a cell-phone call from inside the building threatening to start shooting unless police pulled back.

He was armed with an automatic pistol and a shotgun and had barricaded the doors to the school with structural lumber to slow down the police, who tried to charge in once the shooting started.

Police said the gunman worked as a truck driver who collected milk from nearby farms for processing and sale. Police said he walked his own children at a nearby bus stop before borrowing a relative's pick-up truck and heading for the Amish school.

Commissioner Miller of the State Police said the gunman was not wanted for any crimes and apparently did not have a criminal record.

Far from being revenge oriented, as suggested by some, the schoolhouse takeover appears to have been a power-assertive sex crime followed by suicide. This is detailed in Knight (2006):

"He wasn't agitated, he wasn't screaming, he was just taking control," said Commissioner Jeffrey Miller, of the Pennsylvania Police, as he recounted the last moments of Charles Carl Roberts IV, a milk lorry driver, who shot ten Amish schoolgirls at close range yesterday morning.

In the first insight into the possible motives of Roberts, a respected and well-liked father of three, Mr. Miller said that the gunman had called his wife, Marie, on a mobile phone soon after taking the schoolgirls hostage and said he had attacked two young relatives as a 12-year-old.

"I'm not coming home, the police are here," he is reported to have said before directing her to suicide notes in which Roberts said he had [been] assailed by dreams of assaulting young people again.

Police said today that Roberts had panicked when ten state troopers surrounded the one-room Georgetown Amish School in the tiny village of Nickel Mines, Pennsylvania, and started "executing" the schoolgirls rather than following what appeared to be a plan "to victimise them in many ways."

Three girls died instantly when Roberts shot them in the back of the head and two more succumbed to their injuries overnight.

Five others remain in hospital after being shot in the head and back. All of the victims were students. The dead girls were named today as Naomi Rose Edersol, 7, Anna Mae Stolzfus, 12, Marian Fischer, 13, and sisters Lina and Mary Liz Miller, aged 7 and 8.

Roberts then killed himself as police broke through the windows of the school. Officers had to free the dead and wounded from wires that bound their ankles.

Roberts had nailed closed the side door of the school and blocked the main entrance with a piece of wood and desks. As well as equipping himself with 600 rounds of ammunition and a change of clothes, he also brought plastic handcuffs, planks of wood mounted with ten pairs of hooks, apparently to restrain his victims, and KY jelly, a sexual lubricant.

At a news conference this afternoon, Mr. Miller said that rambling suicide notes left for Roberts's wife, Marie, and his three children suggested that the gunman, a home-schooled Christian, acted out of grief for a daughter who died nine years ago and as a furious reaction to his alleged attack on two relatives as young as 3 when he was just 12 years old.

Mr. Miller said that Roberts's confession had come as a complete surprise to his wife and that interviews with his family, although ongoing, had yet to corroborate any wrongdoing. "They have no knowledge of any molestation of family members or anyone else," he said.

Although it is unclear what, if any, crime Robert committed as a young boy, his assault, America's third fatal school shooting incident in the last week, was meticulously planned. Mr. Miller said today that Roberts parked his milk lorry outside the Nickel Mines Auction House, just yards from the school, after every shift and that the unprotected building represented "a target of opportunity."

Based on his phone call and suicide letters, investigators believed he wanted to attack girls of a certain age rather than members of the Amish community.

Police discovered a checklist and receipts that showed Roberts was buying equipment for the attack up to six days ago. A handwritten list in a notebook read: "Tape. Eyebolts. Tools. Nails. Hoes. KY. Bullets. Guns. Binoculars. Earplugs. Batteries. Flashlight. Candle. Wood."

This case underscores how mass murder can vary in offender background, motive, modus operandi, and victimology—despite the stereotypes that nomothetic archetypes have created.

NOMOTHETIC PROFILES OF MASS MURDER

There is no one nomothetic offender profile that can be rendered from looking across all cases of mass murder. However, a literature review reveals four substantial studies of the phenomenon have been conducted (Fox and Levin, 1998; Hempel et al., 1999; Mooney and Orav, 2000;

Gray et al., 2001).[3] Fox and Levin (1998) studied 483 cases involving 697 mass murderers, examining offender, victim, and crime characteristics. They also compared their data to other types of murders. Hempel et al. (1999) provided a profile of mass murderers based on a study of 40 cases. Mooney and Orav (2000) studied 440 cases, but examined only temporal patterns and issues, with an eye toward developing protective programs to reduce stress and violence in public places.[4] Gray et al. (2001) studied 34 cases of adolescent mass murderers (19 years old or younger), providing both a profile and a motivational typology. However, all of this nomothetic offender research results in archetypes that fall apart when applied as predictions to actual cases.

NOMOTHETIC DATA: NUMBERS AND AVERAGES

The purpose of creating an average or inductive nomothetic profile seems to be twofold. First, researchers want to see if they can identify patterns in known cases, most often to identify the causes of crime. By extension, prevention initiatives may be imagined, designed, and implemented for a variety of circumstances. Second, researchers may want to use such profiles forensically, either to assist in criminal investigations or to provide the basis for expert courtroom testimony. Whether inductive/nomothetic profiles are useful to this second end is addressed below.

According to Hickey (1991, p.3), mass murderers are those who kill several victims within a few moments or hours. He suggests that mass murderers generally have the following characteristics:[5]

- Give little thought or concern to inevitable capture or death
- Commit crime in public places
- Motive is retaliatory: based in rejection, failure, and loss of autonomy
- Offense is an effort to regain a degree of control over their lives

Fox and Levin (1998) provide a somewhat similar definition:[6]

> Mass murder consists of the slaughter of four or more victims by one or a few assailants within a single event, lasting but a few minutes or as long as several hours.

---

[3] Lindquist and Lidberg (1998) published details of the 14 mass shootings that occurred in Sweden from 1960 to 1995. The most interesting part of their study is the depth of detail provided in the presentation and analysis of the 14 offenders. Despite its weaknesses, the anecdotal value of this work is fairly high. However, no conclusion is reached regarding the typical/nomothetic profile of a Swedish mass shooter.

[4] As their data, Mooney and Orav (2000) examined newspaper reports on 440 "mass slayings/rampages" from 1920 to 1996. News reports are not, in this author's opinion, a legitimate data source for scientific research. While useful for illustrating the type of crime that can and does occur, news reports are not reliable enough to meet the rigors that scientific research demands. Those of us who regularly perform casework in any area know how flawed and inaccurate the specific details in media reporting can be. That a researcher would use news reports in the place of actual case material for scientific data suggests an overall lack of access to, and contact with, real case material. Furthermore, the use of news reports as a data source creates a sample bias. As discussed in Fox and Levin (1998), what is most common is not the most publicized:

While the most publicized type of mass murder involves the indiscriminate shooting of strangers in a public place by a lone gunman, other kinds of mass killing are actually more common. Included within this definition are, for example, a disgruntled employee who kills his boss and coworkers after being fired, an estranged husband or father who massacres his entire family and then kills himself, a band of armed robbers who slaughter a roomful of witnesses to their crime, and a racist hatemonger who sprays a schoolyard of immigrant children with gunfire.

If a researcher lacks access to real case material, then the next question may be whether the researcher is sufficiently prepared and experienced to conduct meaningful research in that particular area.

[5] Using a method similar to the method employed by Mooney and Orav (2000), Hickey (1991, pp. 242–255) cites 70+ newspaper articles and true-crime novels as references for offender behavioral information. This includes true-crime novels on every major case presented in the work. Additionally, no offender interviews conducted by Hickey are cited.

[6] Note that this study is not based on their recently revised definition of "multiple victims," but instead requires "four or more."

According to their research, mass murderers most often have the following characteristics:

- Male (94.4%)
- 20–29 years old (43.3%)
- White (62.9%)
- Has a relationship with the victim of some kind (Family = 39.4%; Other = 38.2%)

Hempel et al. (1999) studied 30 mass murderers in the United States and Canada during the past 50 years. According to their research, mass murderers generally share the following characteristics:

- Male
- Single or divorced
- 40–50 years old
- Paranoid and/or depressive conditions
- Recently suffered a major loss related to employment or relationship
- Alcohol plays a very minor role
- Death occurs by suicide or at the hands of others

According to Gray et al. (2001), mass murderers are those who intentionally kill three or more victims in one event. They studied 34 adolescent offenders, acting alone or in pairs, from 1958 to 1999. According to their research, adolescent mass murderers generally share the following characteristics:

- Male
- 17 years old
- Described as "loners" by others
- Abused alcohol or drugs
- Had been bullied by others in the past
- Have depressive symptoms and historical antisocial behaviors
- Recently suffered a perceived failure in love or school

TYPES OF MASS KILLERS

The purpose of building a typology is to provide a common language for describing a systematic grouping of offenders. Offenders can be grouped into types by a vast number of variables relating to motivation, crime scene types, victim selection, and so forth. The construction of typologies, again, is a search for patterns to the same ends as described above for inductive profiles. The great problem with typologies, as previously discussed, is that they can, and often have, become unquestioned criminal stereotypes.

Fox and Levin (1998) argue that their research suggests that a unified typology of multiple murder can be constructed using five categories of motivation applicable to both serial and mass killing: power, revenge, loyalty, terror, and profit.

Of the power-oriented mass killer, Fox and Levin (1998) state:

> The thirst for power and control also inspired many mass murderers—particularly the so-called pseudocommando killers—who often dress in battle fatigues and have a passion for symbols of power, including assault weapons.

Of the revenge-oriented mass killer, Fox and Levin (1998) state:

> Many multiple murders, especially mass killings, are motivated by revenge, either against specific individuals, particular categories or groups of individuals, or society at large. Most commonly, the murderer seeks to get even with people he knows—with his estranged wife and all her children or the boss and all his employees.

Of the loyalty-oriented mass killer, Fox and Levin (1998) state:

> A few multiple murderers are inspired to kill by a warped sense of love and loyalty—a desire to save their loved ones from misery and hardship. ... Typically, a husband/father is despondent over the fate of the family unit and takes not only his own life but also those of his children and sometimes his wife, in order to protect them from the pain and suffering in their lives. ...
>
> Multiple murders committed by cults reflect, at least in part, the desire of loyal disciples to be seen as obedient to their charismatic leader.

Of the profit-oriented mass killer, Fox and Levin (1998) state:

> Some serial and mass murders are committed for profit. Specifically, they are designed to eliminate victims and witnesses to a crime, often a robbery.

Of the terror-oriented mass killer, Fox and Levin (1998) state:

> Some multiple homicides are in fact terrorist acts in which the perpetrators hope to "send a message" through murder. ...
>
> It is not always possible to identify unambiguously the motivation for a multiple murder, to determine with certainty whether it was inspired by profit, revenge, or some other objective.

This is by far the most comprehensive and least inflammatory typology, based on perhaps the most inclusive and reliable study of mass murder to date.[7]

However, preliminary research published in Turvey (2001) and continued follow-up suggest that the current literature is populated by nomothetic offender profiles that are investigatively useful only when applied to specific kinds of cases (by first making certain assumptions, such as offender age and offender motive), or not very useful to the investigative process by virtue of general inaccuracy. On the other hand, the motivational typology developed by Fox and Levin (1998) appears to have stood up generally well in the face of the cases examined in that study. More research on how these inductive profiles and typologies may apply to specific cases is clearly needed.

The author would argue that, before this research can begin, criminologists should move away from applying merely a body count requirement. Offender groups must be further broken down into more specific mass murder subgroups before meaningful research can be attempted. This requires separating offenders by age, location type, and motivation. Examples of mass murder subgroups would include:

- Adolescent mass murderers at grade schools
- Adult mass murderers at grade schools

---

[7] Inflammatory profiles that use emotionally charged terms like "rampage" and "annihilator" do not deepen our understanding of the mass homicide phenomenon. However, they do show a bias toward moral judgment, the sale of newspapers, and the subsequent prosecution of suspected mass homicide offenders. Such typologies are not the tools of the objective forensic examiner.

- Teen mass murderers at universities
- Military personnel who commit mass murder at their own or friendly military bases, at home and abroad
- Adult mass murderers at abortion clinics
- Domestic self-radicalized terrorists

Given the differing skills, motives, policies and preventative security issues suggested by each, it would also be useful to study mass murder subgroups by their preferred method of killing. Some use hunting rifles at a distance, some use automatic weapons, some use handguns, and some use explosives, fire, or biochemical agents. In fact, there are some that use a combination of these. All require different levels of offender knowledge, skill, access, and ability, and they are not equally deterrable by policy or proactive security measures.

An encouraging research trend in this area is seen in Levin and Madfis (2009). Their study explores the origins of mass murder committed by students at their respective schools. Levin and Madfis (2009) use existing criminological theory to explain how mass murder is the result of cumulative factors that eventually lead to a power-oriented fantasy that is eventually made real (p. 1227):

> To explain the genesis of mass murder committed by students at their schools, the authors propose a five-stage sequential model in which several criminological theories (strain theory, control theory, and routine activities theory) are brought to bear collectively to demonstrate their cumulative effect. These stages are as follows: chronic strain, uncontrolled strain, acute strain, the planning stage, and the massacre. Long-term frustrations (chronic strains) experienced early in life or in adolescence lead to social isolation, and the resultant lack of prosocial support systems (uncontrolled strain) in turn allows a short-term negative event (acute strain), be it real or imagined, to be particularly devastating. As such, the acute strain initiates a planning stage, wherein a mass killing is fantasized about as a masculine solution to regain lost feelings of control, and actions are taken to ensure the fantasy can become reality. The planning process concludes in a massacre facilitated by weapons that enable mass destruction in schoolrooms and campuses, where students are closely packed together.

While Levin and Madfis (2009) provide a mostly theoretical commentary on proposed stages, and do not offer any concrete findings, they make a good conceptual shift away from what hasn't been helpful. Until all criminologists stop making the mistake of lumping all mass murderers into the same pile in their research efforts, the differences between subgroups will remain hidden.

MASS MURDER PROTOCOLS

While every case is different, there are certain general questions that the behavioral analyst will need to answer for building a suspect profile. In cases involving known offenders, this same information may be useful for court proceedings as well.

1. Assess the type of weapons used by the mass murder during the crime, as well as their capacity for inflicting damage, the amount of ammunition involved, and weapon functionality.
2. Determine the knowledge, skill, ability, planning, and access required to acquire and effectively employ those specific weapons at the crime scene(s) involved in the case at hand.
3. Determine the actual target(s) and/or victim(s); discriminate between these and any collateral victims. Unless the offender experienced one or more barriers to their actions that required eliminating collateral targets, the primary and secondary targets will likely have been among the first to die.
4. Conduct a thorough victimology of the primary and secondary victims.

5. Conduct a damage assessment: Determine the actual vs. the intended damage inflicted, and the actual skill involved, given the victim and the method of killing employed.
6. Look for messages sent or left by the offender in the 24 hours prior to the crime—via phone, e-mail, social network, video diary, written letters, or any other means. These may be sent to friends, family, estranged and would-be intimates, enemies, co-workers, classmates, instructors, supervisors, or even media outlets. Such messages are left to provide an explanation or apology for the offender's actions and are more common when the offender does not expect or plan to survive.
7. Assess crime scene characteristics and possible motives for the offense.

Starting with this checklist, and incorporating the specific crime scene analysis protocols offered in this text, investigators and behavioral analysts should be able develop the most complete possible understanding of the case with the evidence available.

SUMMARY

There is no one nomothetic "profile" that can be rendered from studying cases of mass murder. Mass murderers are diverse in their individual traits, methods, and motives. They come from all nations, cultures, and economic backgrounds; they use all manner of weapons with very different levels of skill; and they don't all want the same thing. Mass murder is a behavioral expression of a personal motive, and it is in no way represented by a typical offender type.

The most complete understanding of a mass murder or any other case is best found in a behavioral assessment of the crime using the BEA crime scene analysis protocols offered in this text.

Questions

1. Define the term *mass murder*.
2. True or False: The newspaper is a reliable source of data that is fit for empirical research.
3. Give three potential motives for mass murder, with examples.
4. List three weapons commonly employed by mass murderers.
5. True or False: Mass murder is an international phenomenon that occurs across all nations and cultures.

REFERENCES

Fox, J.A., Levin, J., 1998. Multiple Homicide: Patterns of Serial and Mass Murder. Crime and Justice 23, 407–455.

Gray, B.T., Hempel, A.G., Meloy, J.R., Mohandie, K., Shiva, A.A., 2001. Offender and Offense Characteristics of a Nonrandom Sample of Adolescent Mass Murderers. Journal of the American Academy of Child and Adolescent Psychiatry 40 (6), 719–728.

Hempel, A.G., Meloy, J.R., Richards, T.C., 1999. Offender and Offense Characteristics of a Nonrandom Sample of Mass Murderers. Journal of the American Academy of Psychiatry and Law 27 (2), 213–225.

Hickey, E., 1991. Serial Murderers and Their Victims. Brooks/Cole, Pacific Grove, CA.

Holusha, J., 2006. Students Killed by Gunman at Amish Schoolhouse. New York Times October 2.

Jones, A., 2010. Genocide: A Comprehensive Introduction, second edition. Routledge Press, New York, NY.

Kiernan, B., 2009. Blood and Soil: A World History of Genocide and Extermination from Sparta to Darfur. Yale University Press, New Haven, CT.

Knight, S., 2006. Amish School Shooter's Sex Crime Secret. The Age October 4.

Levin, J., Madfis, E., 2009. Mass Murder at School and Cumulative Strain: A Sequential Model. American Behavioral Science 52 (9), 1227–1245.

Lindquist, O., Lidberg, L., 1998. Violent Mass Shootings in Sweden from 1960 to 1995. American Journal of Forensic Medicine and Pathology 19 (1), 34–45.

Mooney, J.J., Orav, E.J., 2000. Time Trends in a Study of 440 Mass Slayings/Rampages Occurring in Public Places. Journal of Forensic Science 4 (5), 1028–1030.

Shapira, I., Jackman, T., 2007. Gunman Kills 32 at Virginia Tech in Deadliest Shooting in U.S. History. Washington Post April 17, A01.

Turvey, B., 2001. Mass Killings: A Study of Five Cases. Journal of Behavioral Profiling 2 (1).

Weitz, E., 2005. A Century of Genocide: Utopias of Race and Nation. Princeton University Press, Princeton, NJ.

CHAPTER 22

Serial Cases: Investigating Pattern Crimes

Brent E. Turvey

CONTENTS

KEY TERMS

Arranged aspect	Preselected aspect	Serial homicide/murder
Convenience aspect	Remorse aspect	Serial rape
Cooling-off period (or cooling interval)	Serial arson	Staged aspect
Precautionary aspect	Serial bombing	
	Serial crime	

What is it, what nameless, inscrutable, unearthly thing is it; what cozening, hidden lord and master, and cruel, remorseless emperor commands me; that against all natural lovings and longings, I so keep pushing. …

Is it that by its indefiniteness it shadows forth the heartless voids and immensities of the universe, and thus stabs us from behind with the thought of annihilation. … Wonder ye then at the fiery hunt?

—Herman Melville, *Moby Dick*

Serial crime refers to any series of two or more related crimes (Petherick, 2005, pp. 143–149). Despite the limits set upon us by traditional nomothetic reasoning, this does not necessarily mean two or more related crimes of the same type (i.e., rape, homicide, burglary, stalking, etc.). Unfortunately, many investigators and researchers are stuck in a nomothetic mode—a function of how crime has been studied (chunked into similar groups), as opposed to how criminals actually behave and how crime must consequently be investigated. From a practical standpoint, it is not the type of crime that defines the existence of a series, but the inference that the same offender is committing them. Nomothetic research and study have worked very hard to blind us to the reality that many offenders are not just rapists, not just murderers, not just arsonists, not just stalkers, not just burglars, or not just bank robbers. In fact, many serial offenders (a.k.a. serialists) commit crimes of multiple types in the course of a criminal season or career. Keeping this criminal versatility in mind is one of the steps that can lead to offenders' identification and apprehension. And the opposite is also true.

CASE EXAMPLE: BRENT J. BRENTS

Brent J. Brents (Figure 22.1) was, as a teenager, convicted of multiple counts of child molestation. Once released as an adult after years in prison, he resumed old habits. By the time he was finally apprehended in 2005, the failure of investigators to sign his arrest warrant and the failure of supervisors to follow up and provide oversight had already allowed multiple tragedies. His arrest was also the result of the nation's most intense manhunt of the time. According to Pankratz and McPhee (2005),

> As an adult, the 35-year-old Brents, who is wanted by police on suspicion of sexually assaulting three women and two girls in Denver, has been in and out of jail for molesting children.
>
> "It was either boys or girls; it didn't matter to him. The guy is a scum bucket—to put it mildly," said retired Denver police Detective Carrolyn Priest.
>
> In 1988, when Brents was 18, Priest was hot on his trail because he was raping children in Denver, she said. "At that time, he was using a ploy to get kids to go with him to find a pet, like a dog or a cat," Priest said. "He [said he] just wanted them to help him find it, and then he tried to coax them down an alley."
>
> In February 1988, he raped a 6-year-old boy in a trash bin between the 2200 blocks of South Lincoln and South Sherman streets, according to court records. A few days later, he forced a 9-year-old girl into a garage at knifepoint before raping her. He threatened to kill her if she screamed, the records show.
>
> As a juvenile, Brents assaulted children in Adams County and was sentenced to the Lookout Mountain School for Boys, records show.
>
> Priest has been following the latest investigation. Her husband, Jon Priest, is commander of the Denver police homicide unit and works nights. His unit was actively involved in investigating Monday night's assault on two girls and their grandmother in the 800 block of Vine Street and the Friday assaults of a shop owner near East Sixth Avenue and Clarkson Street and a woman in a home in the 1100 block of Adams Street.

FIGURE 22.1A AND B
Brent J. Brents, a one-man crime wave who began serial offending as a teenager, is pictured at the time of his capture and arrest in February of 2005 and at the time of his sentencing in July of 2005. During his trial, he wrote of his crimes in letters to the press: "Sex has little to do with it. ... It's the control, the domination, the fear, the hurt, the power. It's shameful, disgusting, perverted, brutal, hateful and senseless but bottom line it is who I am. ... I am my father, my mother, sick, evil, twisted, confused, angry, sad, lonely."

A former girlfriend of Brents said he told her that he was sexually assaulted as a child and that his father was fatally shot when he was young. She requested anonymity because she said Brents sexually assaulted her child.

The 32-year-old woman, who has three boys, said she dated Brents in August and September [of 2004] until she learned he had been convicted of sexual abuse of a child. "He had told me that he went to prison for hitting a woman, but he had been convicted of sexual assault on a child," she said. "I broke off the relationship immediately."

Before [she learned] of the conviction, the couple attended church together, she said. Even though Brents worked odd jobs and had little cash, she said he was unselfish toward her family.

One of the great tragedies of this case was the system-wide failure that allowed Brents to remain free in late 2004 even after he had confessed to yet another molestation offense. This was detailed in Abbott and Langbein (2005, p. A5):

An arrest warrant issued in Aurora for Denver sex crime suspect Brent J. Brents languished for more than a month awaiting the investigative officer's signature, Aurora and Arapahoe County officials acknowledged Thursday. …

Brents—who is suspected of raping five people, including two grade-school-age girls and their grandmother in a four-day siege of fear and violence—could have been arrested months before, when a mother reported to Aurora police that he had sexually assaulted her 8-year-old son.

But Aurora police opted to gather more evidence, Chief Ricky Bennett said Thursday. When his officers questioned Brents about the mother's accusations on Nov. 23, Brents made "statements," Bennett said, but he stopped short of characterizing them as a confession. "These are difficult cases," Bennett said. "Your victim is a child. We're not talking about adults here, who can give specific and direct information. We treat them a little bit differently."

Brents is a registered sex offender in Aurora with a lengthy history of sex crimes. He was released from prison last summer. Detectives said they think he previously worked at fast-food businesses and has ties to drug dealing, Whitman said. "He is a career criminal, he's a parolee, he's a registered sex offender, he's a pedophile, he's about as evil as you can be," the chief said during an interview on Fox News.

The chief said that Brents was identified Wednesday as a suspect in the three Denver attacks through the FBI's National DNA database. …

Paperwork sat unsigned.

Meanwhile, that Brents was still walking free at the time of the latest attacks, which occurred in East Denver last Friday through Monday, drew words of shock and outrage.

"This is one of the most disturbing cases I have ever seen," said criminal profiler Brent E. Turvey, based in Alaska. "There is a huge negligence lawsuit building here. It's huge. If they even have the shade of a confession, you'd take him into custody. … I can't imagine that this wouldn't rise to that level."

Bennett and Arapahoe County District Attorney Carol Chambers said officers followed "the preferred method" by waiting for a judge to decide if they had enough evidence to arrest Brents. But even after the police presented their case against Brents to Arapahoe County prosecutors in early December, paperwork for Brents' arrest sat unsigned for more than a month while district attorney staffers left messages for officers, who didn't respond, Chambers said.

Bennett said the 8-year-old boy who allegedly was sexually assaulted was safe even though Brents wasn't arrested. "The mother was aware of the issue," Bennett said. "The mother brought this issue forward to us. The mother, I would hope and believe, would keep the child safe and away from this predator."

But Chambers blasted the chain of events as "not acceptable to me. We should be much more aggressive with getting those warrants issued and getting people in custody."

Boy's mom dated Brents

The boy's mother, who dated Brents before learning of his acts against her son, described her child as a prisoner in his own home while Brents came and went in the neighborhood, even as the unsigned arrest warrant awaited action. "We've seen him in and out," the mother said, anger edging her voice. "He was here. My son saw him all the time."

The woman, who began dating Brents in October, didn't know she had a relationship with a convicted child molester until her mother-in-law's gut reaction led to a mini-investigation. When the woman introduced her parents to Brents over dinner, her stepmother said she felt uncomfortable with Brents' interactions with her kids.

A family member who works at the Boulder County Justice Center would later run a background check on Brents, finding out the secrets of his past. And her 8-year-old son would tell her of inappropriate sexual contact. The boy endured repeated questions from police and a forensic interviewer. He was asked to point to an anatomical drawing of a little boy and explain in the best way he could what happened to him.

He told authorities of the inappropriate touching that he said occurred while his mother slept on the opposite side of the bed, according to the arrest affidavit. And he told the forensic interviewer that Brents didn't come over anymore "because he was touching my private parts," the affidavit says. His mother, looking back, also told police that her son had insisted on wearing his jeans to bed one night.

Police estimate that Brents molested the boy repeatedly between Sept. 1 and Nov. 11, court records show. "I feel guilty; I'm supposed to take care of my kids," the mother said, adding that a family therapist was trying to get Brents arrested. …

Bennett said the officer who was supposed to sign the arrest warrant affidavit had been transferred out of the crimes against children unit and was working a later shift. …

From release to manhunt: A chronicle of the delay after contact

- July 12, 2004: Brent Brents is released from prison.
- July 13: Brents registers with the Aurora police as a sex offender.
- Nov. 9: Aurora patrol officer takes offense report from a mother who says Brents sexually assaulted her 8-year-old son.
- Nov. 10: Three detectives begin work on the case.
- Nov. 23: Detectives interview Brents. He is not in custody. He claims the sexual contact with the boy was unintentional, occurring as he slept on a bed with the child and the child's mother. Brents is not arrested.
- Early December: Detectives present case against Brents to Arapahoe County district attorney seeking an arrest warrant.
- Dec. 14: DA's staff telephones detective, saying arrest warrant affidavit is ready to be signed.
- Dec. 21: DA's staff again telephones for detective to come sign arrest warrant affidavit.

- Jan. 11, 2005: Detective whose signature is required rotates from the crimes-against-children detail to another unit, where he works a later shift. Police Chief Ricky Bennett said Thursday he can't explain why the detective didn't sign the arrest warrant affidavit sooner.
- Jan. 19: Aurora police victims advocate asks DA's staff about the status of the case. DA's staff then takes arrest warrant to Aurora police headquarters and detective signs it.
- Jan. 26: Judge signs arrest warrant.
- Feb. 11: Aurora police let Denver police know they're looking for Brents for sexual assault on a child. Two women are raped in separate attacks that Denver police later link to Brents.
- Feb. 14: Two school-age girls and their grandmother are sexually assaulted in a Cheesman Park-area home. Denver police later link Brents to the attacks.

Source: Aurora Police and Arapahoe County District Attorney's Office.

Subsequent to his arrest on February 18, 2005, the specific details of Brents' crimes were published after detectives working the case were interviewed by the press (Lindsay, 2005, p. A5):

Six women and two girls were victimized in the knifepoint assaults in three Denver neighborhoods between October and February. Investigators say the cases were linked to Brents by DNA evidence, witness accounts and Brents' admissions to police.

Brents has claimed to have committed dozens of other sexual assaults. On Monday, the defendant, a convicted child molester who was released from prison last summer, was formally advised of charges in two additional cases involving sexual assaults that took place in January. ...

The day Brents was arrested, he said he hadn't slept in a week and referred to himself as a "sociopath" in an interview with Denver homicide Lt. Jon Priest. "I'm tired of what's going on in my head," he told Priest.

Brents described how he would "just flip out. There's this thing in my brain that just goes f------ stupid. It's just this weird thing in my head. It's not even sexual. It's more like this animalistic s---."

Denver detectives testified that in all the attacks, Brents threatened to kill the women with a knife if they screamed or resisted.

Brents was arrested Feb. 18 in Glenwood Springs after one of the most intensive manhunts in Denver history.

He fled in a stolen car with a 27-year-old woman he is accused of repeatedly raping in a vacant Denver apartment near East 10th Avenue and Marion Street where he was hiding out. That woman, Aida Bergfeld, later died of a drug overdose. She told police Brents raped her "more times than she can count" during a 12½ hour period ending Feb. 18, Detective Martin Vigil said.

Brents told police he shot Bergfeld up with heroin to make her more compliant, Priest said. He then tied her up and put her in the closet when he left the apartment to get cigarettes, according to Priest's testimony.

Apartment manager Tiffany Engle was choked and beaten with a board when she went to check on the apartment and surprised a naked Brents in the middle of a sexual assault, Priest said.

Brents said he began choking Engle and hit her over the head because she wouldn't stop screaming, Priest said. "He said she kicked him and he just lost it," Priest said. "He said he felt he strangled her enough that she was within seconds of dying," Priest said. "He said he had studied martial arts and knew how to shut off the blood flow for a quicker reaction. He said he had strangled a number of people until they turned blue and passed out. He said he used it as a control."

Engle, who had been tied up, was able to crawl out of the apartment for help after Brents fled in her car. She nearly died and had to undergo a lobotomy to relieve swelling in her brain, Vigil said.

Four days earlier, on Feb. 14, police allege, Brents sexually assaulted two girls and their 67-year-old grandmother in the 800 block of Vine Street. Brents allegedly forced the grandmother into the basement, where he raped her and left her tied up on a mattress.

One of the girls told police she hugged her stuffed hippopotamus while Brents raped her in her bed, said Detective Larry Black. "She said she had to stand there while he took her sister and sexually assaulted her," Black said. "She said she just closed her eyes during that assault."

The grandmother was able to escape and run for help while the girls were being attacked. Brents told police he simply planned to rob the 44-year-old owner of a pet store on East Sixth Avenue at knifepoint, but decided to rape her Feb. 11 after she cut her finger on his blade and bled all over the money she was removing from the cash register, Priest said.

The woman told police Brents took her to a back bathroom and bent her head over a toilet where she watched blood from her thumb dripping into the water while he raped her, said Detective Tamara Molyneaux.

In another attack Feb. 11, a 29-year-old woman said Brents attacked her in her apartment in the 1100 block of Adams Street when she came home from work. The woman said Brents held a knife to her throat during the rape and choked her almost to the point of unconsciousness, threatening to impregnate her, said Detective Gilbert Lucio.

Brents also is charged with raping a 25-year-old woman at knifepoint behind a dumpster near Colfax Avenue. At one point during the Oct. 20 attack, the woman said they heard police sirens, prompting Brents to remark, "Isn't it crazy that I'm raping you right next to Colfax?" said Detective Mylous Yearling.

During his trial, Brents fuelled the press further with letters detailing his crimes, motives, and various states of mind. As described in Herdy (2005, p. A4),

After picking up a 15 year-old prostitute on Colfax Avenue, Brent J. Brents pulled his car into an abandoned garage and attacked. "I open her door, pull her out by her hair and put a K-Bar military knife to her throat," he wrote. "She tells me I'm going to have to kill her. No problem I tell her. I start choking her and black out. Some time later when I come back there is a girl, purple, barely breathing tears flowing and trying to focus on me."

The account of that previously unreported assault is part of a 49-page journal Brents wrote over the course of several weeks and sent to a Denver Post reporter.

In his writing, Brents detailed how he kidnapped, raped and nearly killed the girl he held captive for 24 hours. He also described another near-fatal attack on a property manager.

Brents also recounted the horror of his childhood and how he became a man who felt compelled to inflict pain upon others.

Sickened by his own acts at times, Brents said, he realizes he should never be allowed to leave a prison cell. "I am a villain in every way," he wrote. "I'm not proud of it, I don't like it, I'm ashamed of it."

The details of the assault on the teenager, Denver district attorney spokeswoman Lynn Kimbrough said, fit with other acts police believe Brents committed. "We suspect there may be scores of victims like this who never reported," Kimbrough said.

It was early one January morning, Brents wrote, when he picked up the girl, whom he described as Hispanic, and offered her $40 for sex. After driving her to an abandoned house that was partially burned, he pulled into the garage and shut its doors. After choking the girl, Brents waited for her to recover, he wrote, before raping her repeatedly. He then choked her into unconsciousness, tied and gagged her and left her, going off to be with friends.

When he returned hours later, he continued to rape the girl, whom he injected with heroin before he let her go the next morning, he said.

"This is just one of the many but it shows how violent and (sadistic) I had become. A lot of the times I was doing these things I thought about what had happened between my Dad and my Mom and me."

Brents said he was raped by his father beginning at age 4, and said he was sexually abused by his mother beginning at age 6. He said he would often see his mother's face when attacking a victim. "Sex has little to do with it," he wrote. "It's the control, the domination, the fear, the hurt, the power. It's shameful, disgusting, perverted, brutal, hateful and senseless but bottom line it is who I am."…

The case that haunts him the most, Brents said, is that of Tiffany Engle, an apartment manager who found him hiding in a Capitol Hill apartment. "One minute she's alive and fierce," Brents wrote. "And I suddenly come to like I just woke up. She's dying I know it she knows it. Somehow she reaches up and touches my cheek and says please. No sound comes from her mouth, but I read her eyes. I stop choking her. There is a pool of blood under her head. I'm not sure when I hit her with the 2×4. But here I am straddling her. Her hair is messed up I try to straighten it, her panties are showing, I pull her skirt down to make her decent."

"Later in a bathroom in Evergreen I'm looking at Tiffany's blood on my hands I look at me in the mirror and I don't know me. I am everything I hate. I am my father, my mother, sick, evil, twisted, confused, angry, sad, lonely."

Ultimately, Brents agreed to plead guilty across the board. In July of 2005, he was sentenced to more than 1,500 years in prison (Langbein, 2005, p. A6):

Here's a breakdown of Brent J. Brents' sentence in Arapahoe County:

- 90 years to life: On aggravated charges in a Feb. 4 attack, attempted rape and robbery of a 49-year-old woman in her Aurora apartment.
- 100 years to life: On aggravated charges for sexually assaulting a child multiple times between Sept. 1 and Nov. 10, 2004. Brents molested an 8-year-old boy with whom he shared a home in Aurora while dating the boy's mother.

In January of 2006, four of the female victims of Brent J. Brents reached a $240,000 settlement with the city of Aurora. As explained in Langbein (2006, p. A7),

The four victims are:

- A 49-year-old Aurora woman who was followed home from a bus stop on Feb. 4. Brents forced his way into her apartment. He beat her, attempted to sexually assault her and then robbed her.
- A 29-year-old woman who was raped Feb. 11 in her apartment near the corner of 12th Avenue and Adams Street. Brents slipped in through an unlocked door and held her at knifepoint. She suffered cuts to her hand, forearms, shoulder and stomach. He threatened to kill her if she screamed.

- Hours later, on the same day, Brents threatened a 44-year-old pet shop owner with a knife. He changed the sign in the shop window, in the 800 block of East Sixth Avenue, from "Open" to "Closed." He raped her in a back room.
- A 33-year-old apartment manager checking on a property in the 1000 block of Marion Street stumbled upon Brents and a 27-year-old victim Feb. 18 in a supposedly vacant unit. She was savagely beaten and tied up. She has undergone several brain and head surgeries.

The four had filed intent-to-sue notices within the 180-day deadline last year that allowed them to pursue a lawsuit in state court.

These victims filed their intent-to-sue notices against the city and others for negligence with respect to the unsigned warrant previously mentioned, which allowed Brents to remain free and attack at least 10 more people.

The Brents case illustrates not just systemic failures related to serial crime investigation, but also the wide variety of crimes that a single offender can leave in his or her wake. Classifying Brents as a child molester is correct. Classifying him as a serial rapist is correct. Classifying him as a kidnapper is correct. Even after these classifications, we won't have begun to understand what created him, what drives him, or what he was moving toward on a given day. The Brents case is a testament to the principles of behavioral dynamics and motivational dynamics (see Chapter 5).

Looking at Brents through any one classification lens presents an accurate but completely uninformed view of his total criminal career—because each time we look, he's different. This is the legacy of nomothetic study. Researchers want to classify offenders—lump them into a particular group, compare them, and find similarities. Then profilers and others generalize those findings to similar offenders that they've also lumped in, using the same narrow lenses, to apply research on supposedly similar offenders predictively.

Nomothetic research leaves an inductive stain of false theories on the investigative community that seeks to educate itself about how to understand and investigate serial criminals. Serial rapists are labeled and treated as a serial rapist abstract. Child molesters are labeled and treated as a child molester abstract. The problem is, as discussed in previous chapters, the abstract offender does not exist in real life. Consequently, the only way to understand Brent J. Brents is through a careful ideographic analysis of the behavioral evidence in the crimes he committed. Pigeonholing Brents as a particular type of offender will make nomothetic predictions easier, it will make research easier, and it will make good headlines; however, it won't be accurate, and it won't teach us anything about what he's actually done.

The purpose of this chapter is to help do away with the stale nomothetic thinking strategies related to serial crime investigation and to do so in the context of discussion of serial rape and serial homicide behavior. For those interested in going beyond these narrow subjects, a good place to start is the textbook *Serial Crime* (Petherick, 2005).

TERMS AND DEFINITIONS

Because of the legal consequences of offender behavior, and perhaps because separate law-enforcement units each tend to have a separate investigative focus, serial rape and serial homicide have been rendered all but unrelated. Sex crimes detectives work sex crimes; homicide detectives work homicides; juvenile crimes detectives work juvenile crimes; major crimes detectives work major crimes.[1] Unless detectives in separate units communicate with each other (which is not common), it is unlikely that any one detective has access to the whole picture. As the author argued in the first edition of this text in 1999, this is a mistake.

---

[1] In smaller departments, of course, a group of two to five detectives may run the whole detective squad and work everything that comes through the door.

The motivations for homicide, rape, and sexual assault–related behaviors are the same. The only notable exception is rape behavior. Both fire setting/explosives use and the act of homicide can be motivated by precautionary needs. This author is unaware of any case where rape or sexual assault has been used as a precautionary act.

Investigators and profilers alike would do well to keep two very important things in mind, placing serial rape and serial homicide behavior on the same level of priority:

1. The act of homicide is not a motive. It is a behavior that expresses an offender need. A related series of homicides can easily contain sexual aspects and motives that are expressed by sexualized behavior for which homicide is ultimately a precautionary act. A series of homicides may also contain living victims who successfully evaded capture, escaped captivity, or were released by the offender.
2. The act of rape is not a motive. It is a behavior that can express other offender needs beyond those of pure sexual gratification. Any series of related rapes may also include victims who were killed, either accidentally or intentionally, by the offender. Rape or sexual assault cases that involve offenders using any amount of force can easily become homicides given the right set of circumstances.

Serial in Nature

What makes something serial in nature? According to Ressler (1992, p. 29), the term *serial killer* was first coined by the Federal Bureau of Investigation (FBI) profiler Robert K. Ressler to describe offenders who are obsessed with fantasies that go unfulfilled, pressing them onward to the next offense. It was used as a red flag. This is because the economy of law enforcement is such that decisions are made on a daily basis to determine how their scarce resources may be allocated against their current caseload. The term serial killer puts associated cases at the top of that resource-allocation pile. The media and general public love it, however, because of its sensational aspect. It looks scary, it sounds scary, and it sells.

This author prefers the terms *serial homicide* or *serial murder* because they most accurately relate the behavior of legal interest while being the least sensational. In that spirit, we will use the definitions provided here. These are intended to be investigatively useful for suggesting the allocation of resources, but they are so broad as to be useless for academic research purposes.

- Serial homicide/murder: Two or more related cases involving homicide behavior
- Serial arson: Two or more related cases involving fire-setting behavior
- Serial bombing: Two or more related cases involving the use of explosives
- Serial rape: Two or more related cases involving rape or sexual assault behavior

These are not exclusive descriptors and are meant to describe the types of cases presented as opposed to describing a particular type of offender. That is to say, just because a series of rapes or homicides have been identified, it does not mean that the offender should be pigeonholed as a serial rapist or a serial murderer. Certainly we can refer to an offender that way and be accurate, so long as we bear in mind that they can be other things as well. This is a lesson taken from the Brents case, among many others.

SERIAL HOMICIDE

Sense of power. I don't know. Vulnerable. I dreaded, just … I got a very … got a rush out of it, got a high out of it. Call it what you want. I had no real excuse why other than I like to do it. (Pause). I don't know how to describe it.

—Convicted serial murderer, Joe Roy Metheny, Maryland v. Metheny, 2000

For investigative purposes, serial homicide may be defined as two or more related cases involving homicide behavior with a *cooling-off period* in between (Egger, 1984; Petherick, 2005). What precisely constitutes a cooling-off period has been ill defined in the literature. That ends now. A cooling off period, or cooling interval, refers to the psychological component that makes serial murderers so horrible to the imagination; it refers to the interval during which the offenders psychologically disconnect, separate, or compartmentalize themselves from the behaviors and motives that led to, or culminated in, homicidal behavior and then reintegrate back into their non-criminal lives and activities. As discussed in Fox and Levin (1998),

> The compartmentalization that allows for killing without guilt is actually an extension of an ordinary phenomenon used by normal people who play multiple roles in their everyday lives. An executive might be heartless and demanding to all his employees at work but be a loving and devoted family man at home. Similarly, many serial killers have jobs and families, do volunteer work, and kill part-time with a great deal of selectivity. Even the cruelest sexual sadist who may be unmercifully brutal to a hitchhiker or a stranger he meets at a bar might not ever consider hurting family members, friends, or neighbors.

For some, the cooling interval is immediate—as instant as flipping a switch. For others, the cooling interval can span hours or even days. This is in stark contrast to mass murders and crime sprees, where offenders enter the psychological landscape of offense behavior, resign themselves to it, and do not come back until set tasks have been completed or they have been stopped.

It should also be noted that the cooling interval does not refer to the entire time between offenses, only the time it takes to psychologically extract and reintegrate. Once reintegrated, serial offenders may enter an extended period of dormancy, or they may go back out and engage in victim-seeking behavior the very next day—all depending on how they feel. There's no predicting which will be the case.

This is all particularly troubling because it means that those who are capable of serial murder are not completely defined by that fact—in an emotional sense. It means that they can have emotions and beliefs that are separate from, and even mask, their homicidal side. It means that we can be standing next to such people in a bank, be working with them, be dating them, be married to them, and not necessarily have the first clue. Or we can have all the clues and not know what they mean.

Media and the Serial Murderer Archetype

At this point, it would be absurd to suggest that world culture is not fascinated by the serial killer archetype—crafted, packaged, and sold to the public by the popular media. The archetype is a brilliant and manipulative psychopath who revels in all manner of pleasures produced by all manner of victim suffering and humiliation, moving deliberately, expertly, and undetected. It is an image of potency, control, and of freedom from law or consequence. It is essentially a romantic image of someone who is governed by pure id.[2]

---

[2] In Freudian theory, the human psyche is composed of three parts: the ego, the superego, and the id. The id is the division of the psyche that is totally unconscious and serves as the source of irrational, emotional, instinctual impulses and demands for the immediate satisfaction of primitive needs.

As Ebrite (2005, p. 691) discusses, the media archetype has an impact on how we view serial murderers in real life:

> Serial killers fascinate American society. Society evinces this fascination in music, films, and literature. ...
>
> The extent to which popular art and the media saturate society with fodder for its macabre fascination with serial killers results in dehumanizing the serial killer. This dehumanization can rise to the level of creating an absolute lack of empathy by society for either the abuses perpetrated on individuals who later become serial killers or any other circumstances that arguably contributed to serial killers' development.
>
> The absence of empathy and humanity creates a response in the collective mind of society, and by extension the minds of jurors, that the only adequate means of dealing with these creatures is to exterminate them because, as one prospective juror explained, the mention of the words "serial killer" conjures images of a "beyond hope situation."

Kennedy (2006) discusses the public fascination with serial murder in a survey of books about crime and law. Unlike Ebrite, Kennedy argues that, thanks to an undying public interest in their grotesque expressions of deviance, lawlessness, and personal freedom, serial murderers enjoy a form of celebrity as antiheroes (Kennedy, 2006, p. 1288):

> One might be tempted to dismiss interest in serial killers as simply a morbid obsession with the grotesque. This interest ranges in its forms from the concentrated obsession of some who bid for serial killer memorabilia on websites purveying hair and other artifacts of notorious serial murderers, to the more general interest in fictional and factual accounts of serial killers in movie and book form. ...
>
> There has long been a somewhat standard account of why we are fascinated with certain types of criminals generally. Our fascination with criminals reflects contradictory impulses. We are simultaneously repelled by the deviance of their crimes, but we also experience a vicarious thrill at the freedom from social constraint that they experience.

This attention and celebrity is not born out of admiration for the characteristics of real-life serial murderers, but out of the need to maintain specific yet varied illusions that many in the general public find comforting and entertaining. The sales receipts for media products about serial murderers indicate that there are those who want to believe that serial murderers are both evil and romantic, that serial murderers experience the ultimate power and the ultimate thrill in exercising that power by completely owning and completely disposing of the lives of their victims, and that serial murderers know things that can never be known by those of us who do not engage in the unchecked domination and destruction of others.

These images are, of course, manufactured by the industry that is in the business of profiting from serial killer fictions.[3] They are the myths we buy into. Anyone who doubts this should spend some time in the true-crime and mystery sections of the local bookseller to see what is being published, watch an episode of any crime series on television, or simply go to the movies. This "experience" directly impacts our availability heuristic with respect to knowledge of serial murderers—knowledge that is more contrived than anything else.

---

[3] The industry selling us the myth of the serial killer includes the popular media, in collusion with less than knowledgeable true-crime authors, certain caseworkers who play to the image of monster-fighter, and certain academics who just want to have a hand in any part of something that sounds dangerous. What it amounts to is trading on victim pain without any educational value, selling the myth for profit and celebrity.

Serial Killer Myths

Despite all the press and hype, the reality is that serial murderers are nothing like the pervasive archetypes being sold to us every time we pick up a newspaper, read a book, watch TV, or go to the movies. They are often arrogant without particular brilliance; they can be childish and quick to anger; they frequently lack control of their impulses and ego; many use drugs or alcohol and are consequently less than skillful and deliberate; and, because they have to do a lot of lying, they also tend to lack the necessary depth for self-reflection, let alone intimacy. In other words, they are commonly depressed, frustrated, angry, and powerless—unlike the romanticized characters of fiction that we crave or the real-life characters we fictionalize as evil and brilliant to make their takedown seem more of an accomplishment. As Kennedy (2006, p. 1293) observes,

> Perhaps serial killing comes not from a powerful person but a powerless one, a person who lacks basic capacities that most people enjoy: the capacity to empathize with others, to enjoy emotional and sexual connection with others. The dissatisfaction one might experience at the inability to experience such connections might be aggravated or given shape by a sense of entitlement that white male privilege creates, but it would not be an extension of that sense of privilege in [a] straightforward sort of way....

> Such a lack of power, whether it is the product of nature or nurture, plays little or no part in popular narratives about serial killers for a reason. ... [S]uch an alternate story about serial killers would not lend itself to the morally instructive purposes which these stories serve in contemporary society. We need powerful—not pathetic—monsters to keep the national morality play of punishment going.

Ebrite (2005, p. 691) is more specific in cataloguing the myths related to those who commit serial homicide, expertly blasting many long-held yet inaccurate assumptions:

> No universal formula exists to quantify serial killer status. ...

> Although the stereotypical image of the serial killer is one of an intelligent Caucasian male, twenty to thirty years of age, who targets predominantly young women or men in their late teens or early twenties, in reality, the profile is much more varied. Indeed, serial murderers are found throughout the globe, have representatives from various ethnicities and both genders, and are not universally as intelligent as popular films and novels portray them.

> Although male serial murderers predominantly commit the types of sexually sadistic murders involving ritual mutilation, necrophilia, or cannibalism, the serial killer phenomenon is not exclusive to the male gender. Society commonly misperceives that only males serially murder. Such a misperception results from the graphic and visceral nature of their crimes, usually evincing strong elements of sexual sadism, which attracts more attention from the media when compared to the generally less explosive facts surrounding the crimes of female serial killers.

> Another public misperception of serial killers concerns the killers' level of intelligence. Society's belief that serial murderers are exceptionally cunning and intelligent is not necessarily accurate. While the most notorious serial murderers—those who have the greatest number of victims—tend to possess higher than average intelligence, less intelligent serial murderers exist. The killers of below average intelligence, however, are probably not as notorious because they do not have the ability to sustain their activities over a long period of time without being captured by law enforcement.

Hinch and Hepburn (1998) go further; they assert that no typical profile of a serial murderer exists, and that none of the existing typologies is adequate to the task of classifying actual serial murderers as they exist in casework. It is useful to note that the serial murder typologies cited within have not changed substantially since the publication of Hinch and Hepburn (1998):[4]

> According to Hickey (1991), three assumptions about the core characteristics of serial killers influence the development of typologies: serial killing is psychogenic, the locus of motives is internal, and the reward for killing is psychological. As we noted about the definition of serial murder, these assumptions exclude those serialists who are externally motivated (e.g., hit men, terrorists, politically or religiously motivated killers, and black widows). Many cases do not fit easily into existing categories, or straddle several typologies (Gresswell and Hollin, 1994; O'Reilly-Fleming, 1996). Typologies overlap and conflict with one another. Some are based on motivation while others are based on psychiatric diagnosis. Still others use the criminal offense, or the crime scene, or the geographical mobility of the offender as the basis for classification (Gresswell and Hollin, 1994; Hickey, 1997; Holmes, 1989). The inevitable conclusion we draw from this is that there is no such thing as a typical serial killer. As a result, classification attempts are misleading and tend to reinforce the stereotypes.

The author agrees with this assessment but would also argue that the behavior-motivational typology developed and offered in Chapter 11, since the publication of Hinch and Hepburn (1998), is more than adequate for the investigative and forensic purposes of crime scene analysis: first, because it is based on evidence of crime scene behavior (it is more objective than offender post-offense interviews alone); second, because it does not purport to be an exclusive classification system—rather it states clearly that most offenders will evidence behaviors from multiple motivations (no pigeonholing); third, because it is designed to explore general motivations as opposed to specific ones. This is because the general motivations for criminal behavior have remained largely unchanged, from a historical perspective (for a general discussion, see Turvey, 2004).

The study of serial murder to date has been, in this author's opinion, both racist and ethnocentric, due to the fact that media sources rarely cover nonwhite serial murder and serial rape, and media sources are the primary material for the majority of serial and mass murder research (e.g., Fox and Levin, 1998; Hickey, 1991). Aside from the race factor, cases are also chosen for media publication by virtue of their sensational qualities. According to Fox and Levin (1998),

> Although the most publicized and prominent form of serial killing consists of a power-hungry sadist who preys on strangers to satisfy sexual fantasies, the motivations for and patterns of serial homicide are quite diverse. Included within our definition of serial homicide are, for example, a nurse who poisons her patients in order to "play God," a disturbed man who kills prostitutes to punish them for their sins, a team of armed robbers who execute store clerks after taking money from their cash registers, and a satanic cult whose members commit a string of human sacrifices as an initiation ritual.

The following case example (as well as the other case examples of serial homicide adduced in this text) is provided to give readers an applied sense of serial homicide offenses, as well as the motivational possibilities. Students are once again reminded that rape and homicide are behaviors, not motives, and express offender needs. Moreover, just because a serial offender can be labeled a serial murderer does not mean that

---

[4] For a recent and straightforward review of these typologies, which comes to no conclusion regarding their efficacy or utility, see Homant and Kennedy (2005).

this completes our understanding of the person's offenses. Approaching cases from this perspective should provide for a more penetrating understanding of what homicidal serialists are capable of.

Gary L. Ridgway: The Green River Killer

I think he's either in prison for something else, or dead, because I don't see how he could quit doing that cold turkey.

—Det. Dan Richmond (retired), head of detectives for the King County Sheriff's Office (Cabrera, 2001, p. 2)

In August of 2001, prompted by advances in DNA technology and cold case successes, detectives in Washington State decided to reexamine and essentially reopen the Green River Killings case—an unsolved serial murder case unparalleled to others in the region's history. This effort was publicized in Cabrera (2001, p. 2):

> The King County Sheriff's Office has been looking for the Green River Killer since 1982, when the first of his 49 victims in the Pacific Northwest was discovered.
>
> Now, encouraged by DNA advances that allow testing of even flakes of skin, investigators are bringing in lab technicians from the FBI and other agencies to help identify promising evidence. …
>
> The Green River Killer abducted most of his victims—young women who were prostitutes and runaways—in a red-light district south of Seattle. The victims' bodies were found in or next to the nearby Green River, and in densely wooded areas near Seattle and Portland, Ore. The bodies had all been reduced to skeletal remains by the time they were found, probably having decayed for several months.
>
> When [King County sheriff's detective Tom] Jensen started working on the case, a taskforce of dozens of investigators was following thousands of leads, interviewing victims' friends, witnesses and possible suspects. But in the end, virtually all the group could conclude was that the killer might be driving a primer paint-spotted pickup truck with a canopy, and might look like one of several composite drawings. An FBI profiler concluded only that the killer was probably a white man in his 30s or 40s who had issues with women and spent a lot of time in the woods.

A few months after beginning this new DNA initiative, police had Gary L. Ridgway (Figure 22.2) in custody—a man who had been considered a suspect in the mid-1980s and from whom DNA samples had been taken but never tested. As reported in Ith et al., (2001),

> Even as police and body-sniffing dogs yesterday pored through the home and former homes of Gary Leon Ridgway, the man they say is responsible for four slayings in the Green River serial-killer case, the King County sheriff remains firm: He's not ready to declare that he has captured the Green River killer.
>
> But with 45 other dead women attributed to the notorious killer, and the possibility that scores of other dead and missing women could be connected to the case, sheriff's detectives are trying hard to tie the 52-year-old truck painter to as many deaths as they can. …

FIGURE 22.2

Gary L. Ridgway, the Green River Killer, standing in court with one of his defense attorneys. Ridgway ultimately confessed to murdering at least 48 women over the course of a few years in the early 1980s—many of them prostitutes. Detectives believe that they did not get the full story from Ridgway and that the true number is much higher.

Police say they have DNA evidence tying him to the deaths of Opal Mills and Marcia Chapman. Mills was found on the bank of the Green River near Kent on Aug. 15, 1982, the same day the bodies of Chapman and Cynthia Hinds were found in the water, weighed down by rocks. …

Police say they also have DNA evidence tying Ridgway to Carol Christensen, found in woods outside Maple Valley in May 1983. Her death may be unique in the Green River saga because it was staged, with props apparently not seen in any other cases. Investigators never have said what they think the staging meant.

Christensen was found strangled with fishing line, with a paper sack over her head. A cleaned trout lay across her neck, another on her shoulder, records show. Sausage was scattered about. An odd-sized wine bottle was placed on her abdomen, and her hands were draped over the bottle.

Soon it became clear that Gary Ridgway had been a police suspect for a long time. Evidence of his involvement had been in their hands for decades, and the media probed investigators for answers about what took them so long to put it all together. McCarthy (2002) details how Ridgway initially became a suspect:

Ridgway came to police notice again in February 1984, when a prostitute, Dawn White, reported him after she became uneasy about the way he approached her for sex on the Pacific Highway. Ridgway was interviewed, given a polygraph and cleared. Later that year Rebecca Guay, another prostitute, came forward with a lurid tale of how Ridgway nearly strangled her back in 1982, after taking her into the woods and partly undressing her. Ridgway admitted being with Guay but said she had bitten him and denied choking her.

This was suspicious enough to persuade the cops to dig further into Ridgway's background. They found the records of his 1982 arrest for soliciting a police decoy and the 1983 incident near the school ballpark. From his two ex-wives and an ex-girlfriend, they learned about his appetite for outdoor sex—and found he had arranged trysts, camped out or picked blackberries at as many as seven of the body dump sites. …

Investigators worked out the details and found that on all the 27 dates and times that could be pinpointed for victims' disappearances, Ridgway was, in their words, "available as a suspect."

The evidence was all circumstantial, but it was enough for a local judge. In April 1987 the police got a search warrant and went through Ridgway's house looking for anything that would tie him to the murders. Under the warrant, they took hair cuttings and had Ridgway chew on a piece of gauze to take a sample of his saliva. Neither they nor their suspect realized how important that would be 14 years later.

One problem hampering the investigation was that all of the parties involved had their own theories, and each new suspect resulted in a new chase that burned time and diverted resources, as reported in Gumbel (2001):

In 1984, after an internal inquiry that lambasted the investigative efforts undertaken thus far, the authorities shifted into an entirely different gear, setting up a special Green River Task Force, sending officers out undercover to learn more about the world they were investigating, and moving operations from the sheriff's department in downtown Seattle to a district office just a mile from the Strip. The trouble was that, by then, most of the prostitutes had left in terror, and indeed, the killing seemed to have stopped. Bodily remains kept being unearthed on a regular basis, but there was little to be done except go back over and over the voluminous files and hope some pattern or clue would emerge.

Investigators started cracking under the pressure. An FBI profiler called John Douglas was struck down with viral encephalitis and almost died. A county investigator, John Blake, became fixated with a lawyer that he thought was the murderer, and had to be discharged from his job on mental disability. Jim Pompey, a police captain who took over the Task Force in 1986, died in a diving accident after less than a year on the job. The King County sheriff, Vernon Thomas, resigned in 1987, largely because of the failure of the Green River investigation, and shortly afterwards, the budget for the Task Force was slashed, making further progress near-impossible. All through this, suspects were identified and processed, but never to much avail. All sorts of terrifying rapists and kidnappers came out of the woodwork—apparently inspired by the killings and, in one case, by a passage from Ezekiel in the Bible inveighing against prostitutes—but none fit the killer's profile.

A cab driver who first came forward to volunteer information to the police was considered a suspect for years because he seemed to know an awful lot about the dead women. But there was never any hard evidence against the man, Melvyn Foster, and inordinate amounts of time were wasted either tailing him or responding to his ever more indignant complaints about his civil rights.

There were other major errors: the media-circus arrest of a suspect in 1986 who turned out not to be a suspect at all; the failure to follow up on a driving license belonging to one of the murdered women, which was found by a cleaner at Seattle airport (the license was destroyed by airport police after six months, as were the passenger manifests for any relevant flights); and a years-long obsession with a pink glass-like substance found at many of the crime scenes, which turned out to be fragments of garnet stone sprinkled all over the Pacific Northwest by the eruption of Mount St Helens in 1980.

And then there was Ridgway. The police could have got to him as early as 1983, which was when the father and the boyfriend of 17-year-old victim Marie Malvar tracked down the truck that had picked her up and found it in the drive of Ridgway's home. At the time, investigators were not interested. They did catch up with Ridgway in 1987, when a couple of fresh-eyed new investigators saw a convergence of incriminating evidence, all of it circumstantial. He had links to three of the murdered women. He had a history of frequenting prostitutes, including one who accused him of trying to strangle her, and [he] liked to scavenge for junk car parts near the Green River. Employment records showed that he had not been at work at the time of any of the murders, either because he was not on shift or because he had called in sick. And his house was near an intersection with the Strip where four of the murdered women had last been seen.

One of those with theories about the true nature of the Green River Killer was then FBI Profiler John Douglas. He was one of several experts consulted by the task force to help them sort through the suspect pool. More than a few investigators found his profiles of the case to be less than helpful, as Sunde (2002, p. A1) explains:

In the 1980s, King County police turned to an FBI profiler, John Douglas, who provided a report on the possible characteristics of the killer responsible for the deaths of a growing number of women.

Court documents have kept the profile and follow-up work that Douglas did a secret, but some details of a possible suspect have come out: a white man in his 20s or 30s who is divorced and frequents prostitutes.

The problem, at least one key investigator said, is that Douglas' work was general enough to rule in nearly everyone who cruised Pacific Highway looking for a streetwalker.

FIGURE 22.3
Former detective Dave Reichert interviewing Gary Ridgway in his capacity as King County sheriff on August 20, 2003. His interview method involved staring Ridgway down over a period of time while slowly moving his face closer and closer (as discussed in Kamb, 2006).

Gary L. Ridgway ultimately confessed to 48 murders and received a life sentence as part of a plea arrangement, avoiding the death penalty (Figure 22.3). Some of the bizarre details of his deal, and how he earned it, were provided to the media by detectives and discussed on CBS News (2004):

> In the days before Ridgway pleaded guilty, [one of Ridgway's attorneys, Mark] Prothero observed then-secret meetings the lawman held with the killer. Decked out in his full sheriff's regalia, Reichert met with Ridgway, though little substantive emerged. "It appeared to be a prolonged photo-op for Reichert's next political campaign," said Prothero, noting stills taken from police video later showed up in the press. ...

> In 1982, when the bodies of three women were found in or near Washington state's Green River, homicide detective Dave Reichert was called in. Today, he's the county sheriff.

> "I knew I was gonna be talking to pure evil, a monstrous killer. But I had a job to do, and every one of those detectives that walked into that room probably wanted to throttle him," says Reichert. "But they all had a job to do and they did it."

> [T]o get answers on the other cases, police and prosecutors struck a deal with Ridgway. If he told the truth about all the killings, he could avoid the death penalty. ...

> "To me, women are something to have sex with—kill and take the money back," says Ridgway on tape.

> Faced with questioning a killer who couldn't remember his victims, detectives decided to do something unique to get at the truth. They secretly moved Ridgway out of jail and into their headquarters, where he lived in a small office in the center of the room for nearly six months—sleeping on a bare mattress. ...

> Every day, Ridgway would come to a room, take a seat before the camera, and begin to answer questions. ...

> Sometimes, the truth had to be pulled out. But eventually, Ridgway admitted stabbing a small boy as a teenager, and acknowledged having problems with women—beginning with his mother. "I hate women," he said on tape.

Ridgway also admitted to writing an anonymous letter to the press in 1984, in which he confessed to the crimes. The existence of the letter had not been made public. At the time, then FBI profiler Douglas advised King County detectives that the anonymous letter wasn't the real thing—that it should be ignored. King County detectives were perplexed, because the letter contained information about the crimes that had not been released. Douglas suggested that this was because the letter writer had access to the task force files. Regardless, detectives apparently followed Douglas' advice, because they did not pursue it as a lead.

In 2003, when Douglas was confronted with his error, he denied he'd ever written such an opinion—that it wasn't something he would do. Then he was provided with a copy of his written opinion, addressed to the detectives, with his signature (Wilson, 2003, p. B1):

FBI criminal profiler John E. Douglas misidentified an anonymous 1984 letter from Green River killer Gary L. Ridgway in the midst of the nation's worst serial-killing spree.

Douglas wrote that the letter was "a feeble and amateurish attempt" by someone who "has no connection with the Green River Homicides."

He was wrong.

Ridgway, as part of his confession to police, admitted earlier this year that he wrote that letter. Police say that had they known that, it could have helped them catch him earlier.

The Ridgway letter and Douglas' analysis were released yesterday by the Green River Task Force under the state's open-records law.

The only known communiqué from the Green River killer in the midst of the murder spree: Gary Ridgway says he sent this letter to a newspaper Feb. 20, 1984. …

FBI profiler John E. Douglas replied that the letter was "a feeble and amateurish attempt" by someone who "has no connection with the Green River Homicides." Yesterday, Douglas learned he was wrong. …

King County sent the letter for FBI analysis because it contained information that had not been made public.

Yesterday, Douglas at first denied he would have written such an opinion; then, when shown the letter, he conceded it was his signature but said he remembered nothing about it.

"This thing, it's amazing, I have no recollection but I'll stand by it because I'd use some of those terms and that's my signature," he said.

Douglas had been seriously ill with stress-related viral encephalitis from December 1983 to May 1984. He reviewed the Ridgway letter in August 1984. "Maybe I wasn't ready mentally after coming back to work," Douglas said.

Ridgway had killed at least 40 women by the time he sent the anonymous letter, two more between then and the date Douglas analyzed it, and at least six more afterward, according to his confession.

Ridgway, 54, of Auburn, has pleaded guilty to 48 charges of aggravated murder in return for a sentence of life rather than death. …

Ridgway told police he typed and mailed the letter to the *Seattle Post-Intelligencer* [P-I] on Feb. 20, 1984.

The typed letter has no spaces between words and is titled, "whatyouneedtonoaboutthegreenriverman." It was signed "callmefred." The letter was marked "dontthrowaway" and the envelope was marked "very important."

The P-I gave a copy of the letter to Green River detectives.

They noticed it contained some details of the crimes that had not been made public, notably that some victims' fingernails had been cut off to eliminate trace evidence, that the killer had had sex with some victims after they were dead, and that one victim was posed with a wine bottle and fish.

"Some of the information contained in the letter has not been made public, which leads us to believe the person writing it may somehow be involved," Tonya Yzaguirre of the King County Department of Public Safety wrote when sending the letter to the FBI for analysis in July 1984.

Douglas' opinion was sent back a month later by registered mail to Detective Bruce Kalin of the task force. "It is my opinion that the author of the written communiqué has no connection with the Green River Homicides," Douglas wrote. "The communiqué reflects a subject who is average in intelligence and one who is making a feeble and amateurish attempt to gain some personal importance by manipulating the investigation. If this subject has made statements relative to the investigation which was not already released to the press, he would have to have ACCESS to this information (Task Force)."

Yesterday, Douglas wasn't sure why he suspected the letter writer could have had inside information from the task force.

Douglas found it surprising that Ridgway didn't follow up on the letter after the newspaper and police "sloughed it off." He said the fact that police reported no communications from "callmefred" between receiving the letter in February 1984 and his analysis six months later might have made him believe at the time that the letter was a fake. "Usually when they start calling or writing, they keep doing it," Douglas said.

He also said he should have talked with the task force, rather than evaluating the letter in isolation. Records released by King County yesterday show no other communication between Douglas and the task force about that letter. ...

Finally, Douglas said he doubted it would have helped the investigation even if he had said the letter was surely or possibly written by the real killer. "Let's say I say that is him. Now what do we do? It's typewritten. If it was handwritten, we could release information publicly. ... Did I hold up the investigation? There was never another communiqué. He never did anything again after that, other than to continue the ways of his killing."

Apparently, Douglas was unaware of the variety of forensic evidence that can be gathered even from typed letters and corresponding envelopes (aside from being able to link a specific typewriter to the letter at some later date should a suspect be developed)—to include fingerprints, hairs, fibers, and other forms of trace-transfer evidence. Additionally, today's forensic techniques are able to retrieve DNA from the saliva left behind when someone licks a stamp or envelope.

In the end, the Ridgway case is a cautionary tale of investigative folly. Faulty assumptions were made. The task force jumped from suspect to suspect without staying focused. Evidence and witnesses were ignored. Profilers were relied upon as viable sources of information and expertise despite being vague and lacking insight.

Were it not for DNA collection and preservation efforts and the close attention of a few dedicated investigators, the case would likely have remained unsolved to this day. And everyone would assume, as many did until Ridgway's arrest, that serial murderers don't stop until they get caught, go to jail, or die; if the killings stop for a protracted period, there's no need to keep looking. If nothing else, we've learned that this assumption is a faulty one.

SERIAL RAPE

Rape is many things. It is a goal in and of itself. It is an instrument of torture. It is a means of proving masculinity. It is a means of getting sex. Many men rape. They have all done something very wrong. Most of them have not done something particularly extraordinary.

—Katherine Baker (1997, p. 563)

A serial rapist is one who has committed two or more related offenses involving rape or sexual assault behavior. By definition, serial rapists are successful criminals because law enforcement fails to connect their crimes and fails to identify and apprehend them before multiple offenses have been committed. However, as with serial murderers, they are not limited to committing the crime of rape or even sex crimes in general.

In the rush to investigate, it is easy to think of rapists as only rapists and forget that they can be, and likely have been, involved in other crimes. An example of the harm that ignorance on this issue can cause is given in Simon (1997, p. 387):

> In the late 1980s, Tucson, Arizona was terrorized by a serial rapist called "the prime time rapist" because he would break into people's homes during the evening news and rape, rob, and terrorize whole families. This rapist was able to avoid detection for several years until an informer turned him in.
>
> Unfortunately, law enforcement officials focused on looking for someone with a prior record of sexual offenses. The rapist, when apprehended, turned out to have no record for sex offenses, but did possess multiple convictions for other types of serious offenses, including drug offenses, burglaries, and robberies. As this example illustrates, focus on the most serious crime(s) an offender has committed can obscure the fact that he or she commits varied and less serious crimes as well. This, in turn, can hamper law enforcement efforts to apprehend a dangerous offender.

To alleviate or at least mitigate that harm in some way, it is necessary to explore the issue of why rapists rape.

Rapist Motivation

Rape cannot simply occur in a vacuum, spontaneously. It is an extreme form of behavioral expression that the offender visualizes and to some degree thinks out before it happens. Before any sex crime can occur, four preconditions must exist (Hamill, 2001):

1. These offenders must be motivated to commit the offense
2. They must have some strategy for overcoming their internal inhibitions (for giving themselves permission to commit the offense)
3. They must be able to overcome any external constraints and gain access to the victim
4. They must be able to overcome the victim's resistance in order to engage the victim in the sexual act

If a sex crime has occurred, it is evidence that these conditions have been met. It also follows that the rapist's motive must have been strong enough to impel the offender through the subsequent preconditions. All rapists are motivated differently, but their motives may be discussed in general terms, such as offered throughout this text (see Chapter 13).

In her research of rapist behavior and motivations, Katharine K. Baker, J.D., assistant professor of law at the Chicago-Kent College of Law, departs somewhat from the mainstream sound bites and platitudes used to explain criminal behavior. In presenting her own rapist motivational typology, which incorporates the Groth typology, she wisely argues (Baker, 1997, pp. 575–576):

> The answers to the "why" question vary in different situations; rapists do not all rape for the same reasons. We learn essential lessons about what rape is—and why juries respond to it as they do—by delving into the question of why men rape.

This view is echoed in Hamill (2001), who discusses rape behavior and motivation as follows:

We all experience a need to feel sufficiently in control of our lives. Many child molesters who use strategies of enticement or seduction feel more powerful when they are able to persuade children to engage in sexual acts. So-called "power rapists" use violent sexual acts to enhance their feeling of personal control over their victims and, in a broader sense, their lives. Other sexual abusers are motivated primarily by a desire to create a greater degree of emotional intimacy with another. Some child molesters, and even some stalkers, are motivated primarily by this desire for interpersonal closeness. For others, the sexual offending is a strategy for venting anger. Some rapists use sexual assaults as a means of "dumping" their anger and frustration. Certain exhibitionists also share this motivation, venting their anger at strangers by shocking them. Still another motivation is a desire to feel competent. Some sex offenders, both juvenile and adult, do not feel competent in their knowledge or experience of sexuality compared to their peers, so they choose to "lower the bar" and become involved with younger children. Other sex offenders commit their offenses to satisfy their curiosity about sexuality. This is particularly true with adolescents.

Certainly, some perpetrators commit sexual offenses to enjoy sexual gratification. For many of them, crimes like rape or sexual abuse of children are manifestations of the perpetrator's sexual orientation.

The author has a keen interest in the Baker typology. Not so much in the precise classifications but in the underlying rapist–victim relationships that they describe. The implications regarding the formation of rape behavior are fairly disturbing. The Baker typology provides seven rapist motivations, explained in the sections that follow (Baker, 1997).[5]

Sex and Lovemaking

For rapists, rape behavior represents a confused attempt to experiment sexually and find intimacy. This experimentation may become coercive because many boys are taught that power, dominance, and violence may be arousing to women. As Baker (1997, p. 576) argues,

> On the evenings of the rapes in question, these men might well have sought to practice communicative sexuality. They may have been looking for shared sexual pleasure and intimacy. That was what motivated them. That was what they wanted. That was what sex was supposed to represent and help them achieve. But, in reality, they had no idea what they were looking for. The abstract goal may have been lovemaking, but it is exceedingly difficult to understand communicative sexuality, sexual pleasure, and intimacy, particularly when one is young and inexperienced.

Sex and Shoplifting

Because we live in a culture (even a world) where sex is viewed and treated as a commodity that may be purchased or used to sell other products, some offenders come to treat women similarly. When something is so

---

[5] Though not discussed in Baker (1997), which was written from the point of view that women are objectified, marginalized, and treated as property by men, it is the opinion of this author that the Baker typology may be applied to any sex crime, regardless of the victim's sex. Anyone can be objectified, anyone can be sexually marginalized, and anyone can be treated as property. Though, again, the author concedes that women are victimized at a far higher rate than men in such ways.

devalued and objectified, it is easier to see it as a commodity that, as well as being purchased, may also be stolen. As Baker (1997, p. 577) argues,

> Most men are taught that sexual desire is like hunger: when it is there, you satisfy it. Women are candy bars. Of course, food is not free and neither is sex, but precisely because men can and do pay for sex, taking it without consent becomes much less morally reprehensible than other violent crimes. Thus, it is not surprising that one study found that thirty-nine percent of convicted rapists were caught in the course of a robbery. As many of these men conceded, they raped because she was there. They were already breaking the laws of trespass and ownership—why not take one more thing?

Uniting

The *uniting* motive describes certain group- or gang-related rape behavior. It involves rape committed out of the need to prove something to a group or to form a sense of belonging within a group. As Baker (1997, p. 578) argues,

> Men often rape women to demonstrate their strength, virulence, and masculinity to other men. For these men, having an audience is critical; intercourse is instrumental.

Dividing

The *dividing* motive involves the perception that women are the property of other men, and rape is used to establish power over them. As Baker (1997, p. 579) argues,

> This use of rape to insult or denigrate other men has particular impact in racial contexts. Perhaps Eldridge Cleaver described it best: "Rape [is] an insurrectionary act. It delighted me that I was defying and trampling upon the white man's law, upon his system of values, and that I was defiling his women. ... I felt I was getting revenge." As Cleaver himself admits, he started out raping black women for practice, but what motivated him to keep raping white women was a desire to send a message to white men.

Power

The *power* motive describes rape used to assert power over a particular victim. It can describe the motive for many prison rapes and marital rapes. As Baker (1997, p. 580) argues,

> This kind of motivation explains a variety of kinds of rape. For instance, the prison rapist may rape to establish himself above his victim in the prison hierarchy; by dominating his victim, he elevates his own position. He may also establish power in the prison community because, like others who share or display their rapes, he sends the message that, "because I rape, I deserve your respect."

> Unlike many of the rapes that were described in the previous section, however, power rapists also rape to establish control over their particular victims. The identity of the subject/victim is critical. Power rapists want to control their particular victim. They use rape to do so. ...

> A husband rapes in order to assert control over a wife who is somehow defying his command. His wife may not want to have sex, or she may simply have annoyed him. He rapes her to control her, to make her his subject. Often, the husband also assaults his wife in less sexual ways: he punches her, he throws her downstairs, he shoots bullets at her, he chokes her. Sometimes he just rapes her. Unlike the man in prison, the husband has many weapons in his arsenal; his penis is just one of them. But like the man in prison, he uses his penis to establish control over his victim.

Anger

The anger rapist attacks all parts of the victim's body, forces the victim to engage in repeated, nonsexual degrading acts, and uses much more violence than is necessary to force the victim into submission.

Sadism

Making the same mistake as Groth (1979), Baker (1997) argues that sadism is a product of anger becoming eroticized aggression over time—that sadistic behavior develops from anger. (For a discussion of the problem with this interpretation of sadism, see Chapter 18.)

At the conclusion of her discussion of this motivational typology, Baker (1997, p. 581) provides the following warning:

> Seventy percent of rape victims report no physical injury and another twenty-four percent report only minor physical injury. Most rape victims are not victims of angry, sadistic rapists. This does not mean that most rape victims are not raped; it does not mean that rape victims fabricate their stories; and it does not mean that what happens to them is okay. It does belie the common belief that rapists are crazy men whose sadistic hunger for sex or hatred of women compels them to rape.

This is a useful and welcome insight.[6]

CASE EXAMPLES

The following case examples (as well as the other examples of serial rape adduced in this text) are provided to give readers an applied sense of the variety of actual serial rape offenses, as well as the motivational possibilities. Readers are once again reminded that rape and homicide are behaviors, not motives, and express offender needs. Approaching cases from this perspective should provide for a more penetrating understanding of an offender in a given case.

Terrance Bolds: Serial Rape and Burglary

Terrance Bolds was tried and ultimately convicted of burglary, sodomy, and forcible rape charges relating to attacks on four different victims, including a pregnant mother, all of which took place during the summer of 1997.

Regarding the rape of P.M., the record provided in Missouri v. Terrance Bolds (2000) provides the following details:

> [On August 21, 1997, around 6:20 a.m., Bolds] entered P.M.'s house with a revolver. P.M., who was two months pregnant at the time of the incident, lived with her three-year-old son. Defendant instructed P.M. not to scream and directed her to the living room. Defendant forced the victim to undress and perform oral sex on him, while pointing the gun at her. Before leaving, defendant told victim, "You better not call the police or I will come back and kill you and your son." Afterwards, defendant took P.M.'s television, car keys, a diskette with her son's photo on it, Rolodex, ATM card, credit card and a receipt from a doctor's visit.

---

[6] The excerpt does give the impression that the false reporting of rapes is low. For a detailed rendering of this subject, see Chapter 10, "False Reports."

Regarding the rape of J.J. on August 23, 1997, the record provided in Missouri v. Terrance Bolds (2000) provides the following details:

[Bolds] entered J.J.'s apartment through a window in her four-year-old son's bedroom around 4:00 a.m. Defendant forced the victim, under gunpoint, to undress and to put on a compact disc and dance for him. Shortly after that, defendant forced the victim to perform oral sex on him. Defendant raped her vaginally and anally, had her perform oral sex on him again and raped her vaginally and anally a second time. Afterwards, defendant tied J.J. up in the bathtub, bound her wrists together, placed her facedown in the tub, and bound her ankles to her wrists. A while later, defendant put an egg in J.J.'s mouth, gagged her with a pair of her "biker pants," and left. Defendant also took J.J.'s Illinois identification card, a Victoria's Secret bag, an Adidas bag, and a Dooney-Burke bag.

Regarding the rape of W.T. on August 26, 1997, the record provided in Missouri v. Terrance Bolds (2000) provides the following details:

[Bolds] assaulted W.T. Inside the house, defendant took two rings from W.T.'s fingers at gunpoint. Defendant raped her several times, vaginally and anally. He also forced her to perform oral sex on him. Throughout the assault, defendant held a gun to W.T.'s head.

Regarding the rape of R.F. on August 29, 1997, the record provided in Missouri v. Terrance Bolds (2000) provides the following details:

[A]round 5:00 a.m. defendant assaulted R.F. Defendant entered R.F.'s bedroom with a gun in his right hand and wanted her to perform oral sex on him. When the victim did not cooperate, defendant forced his penis into her mouth. After defendant switched the gun from his right hand to the left hand, R.F. attempted to take the pistol from the defendant. A struggle ensued and defendant told her "Bitch, you are going to die now," and repeatedly hit and bit R.F. R.F. pulled off the defendant's ski mask and got the pistol away from him. She tried to shoot defendant with the gun but the gun would not fire. Defendant took the pistol and told R.F. to turn around, that he was going to shoot her. The gun would not fire and he ran out of the house.

During the struggle, R.F. heard her ten-year-old son moving around and yelled at him to call the police because a stranger was in the house. Unfortunately, her son's phone was not working. After defendant ran out of the house, she called the police. While she was trying to call the police, defendant came back and tried to open her bedroom door. When he could not open the door, he fired two shots through the door. Bullet fragments hit R.F.'s thigh. She also had scratches on her face and hands and bite marks in five different places. Her car keys, water pitcher, and CDs were missing and the children's bedroom window was broken.

At trial, Bolds's former girlfriend testified that she left him because (Missouri v. Terrance Bolds, 2000):

[H]e used to hit me before and he did—basically he scared me. He would threaten me. I was pregnant when I left. I was about a month pregnant and his behavior was getting more and more violent whereas, you know, I had to leave because he would, you know, want to have sex all the time. And he also would leave, you know, late at night and then come back in the morning, by the time it was time to go to work. And sometimes he would come in the middle of the night and want to have sex and he'd leave and come back in the morning and he would take my car, you know, and he would have my car and he would leave at night.

This case involves power-assertive and profit-oriented offense behaviors that were meant to satisfy Bolds's need to sexually control and possess his victims through physical and verbal degradation, as well as terror.

The modus operandi (MO) indicates planning via numerous precautionary acts, as well as reflecting a history of burglary offenses. These rapes were not, however, sadistic in nature.

Steven Sera: Serial Rape and Rohypnol

Steven Sera, the 39-year-old owner of the Chandler Lumber Company of Dallas, Texas, was tried for multiple rape and kidnapping charges relating to sexual attacks on two victims in Arkansas. A peculiar feature of this case was use of the drug Rohypnol to render victims unconscious so that Sera could videotape the sexual attacks without the victims' knowledge.

Sera claimed that these relationships were actually consensual and that he was guilty only of bad judgment for taping his sexual encounters with Melanie Hataway, a 32-year-old Colleyville, Texas, woman; Jackie Haygood, a 26-year-old Arkansas woman; and Patty Coleman, 18, his sister-in-law, then a college freshman. He testified that they consented to be videotaped. The victims in turn agreed that while there were preexisting relationships with Sera, some of which were sexual, they did not consent to the sexual attacks that had been videotaped while they were unconscious. They each testified that they must have been drugged and then raped. Similar testimony from two additional victims was allowed during this trial.

This case was brought to light when Sera's wife, Nancy Sera, found the videotape that he had made, showing him committing sexual acts with unconscious naked women, at their home. According to police, the tape showed Sera having sex with women from several different states, including Texas and Arkansas. Nancy Sera reported that she and Steven Sera had been married 8½ years and that she was pregnant with their second child when he was arrested.

According to the record provided in (Arkansas v. Steven Anthony Sera, 2000),

> Nancy testified that until mid-1996, she believed she and Sera had a strong marriage, and she became pregnant with the couple's second child in July, 1996. She testified that Sera was "thrilled" with the news. But, by early 1997 she suspected Sera was having an affair, and confirmed this during the Hataway incident. According to Nancy, in December 1996, a man came to the door, and Sera pretended to be his own brother, Tony, when he spoke to the man. She identified the person at the door as Fred Daugherty. Daugherty later became the private investigator for Nancy's divorce attorney. According to Nancy, she found the videotape sometime in mid-June 1997 after she and Sera had separated. Sera's testimony contradicted her and he contended that Nancy found the tape much earlier. Nancy explained that she had gone to their house (she was living in an apartment at the time) to get the video camera Sera had purchased to record an upcoming family event. Nancy still had a key and thus access to the home. After returning to her apartment, she checked the videotape in the camera and saw the videotaped incidents of Sera with three women including her own younger sister, Patty Coleman. Nancy called her divorce attorney who told her to give the tape to Daugherty who in turn gave it to the police after having copies made. Daugherty had it copied onto some VHS tapes at a video store where he took many of his work projects.

> Nancy also testified that once when she cleaned out Sera's suitcase after a trip, she found a bottle labeled "Rohypnol," and she hid the bottle with several pills in it. When Sera looked for his pills, he became very upset when he could not find them, according to Nancy. Nancy eventually gave this bottle to Daugherty in the course of his investigation.

> When Nancy confronted Sera about the tape and told him that she had taken it to the police, he told her that if she didn't get the tape back, he would go to jail. He then took their daughter Chandler

and left town for several days. Nancy and Daugherty returned to the house some time later, and Daugherty searched the house and took packets of medicine from Sera's shaving kit.

At the trial, Steven Sera testified that there were actually several sexual encounters with Patty Coleman, and that they had mutually agreed to videotape these episodes. He also claimed that he and Patty Coleman had taken still photographs of each other, and further, that Nancy Sera had found them and burned them in the fireplace. He asserted that Nancy, his wife, was aware of his relationship with her sister.

In terms of his character, everything about Sera suggests a pattern of psychopathic behavior, from the manipulation and grooming of his victims, to the web of deceit woven for the benefit of his wife to conceal his numerous affairs with other women. As Wrolstad (1997) observes,

> Dozens of interviews and court documents indicate that he was an alternately charming and arrogant salesman whose success hid a succession of firings; whose vanity about weight and age led him to pursue a second round of liposuction and plastic surgery between his rape arrests; whose schemes were so bold that while allegedly carrying a fourth victim into an inn, he was unknowingly interrupted by a former girlfriend.

An expert from Hoffman-LaRoche, the manufacturer of Rohypnol, testified at trial as to the pharmacological effects of the drug. He testified that Rohypnol is in the class of drugs called benzodiazepines, a class that includes Valium, and that the effects of the drug on the human body can include sleep, total muscle relaxation, and loss of memory. He also described the test he developed to detect the presence of Rohypnol metabolites in urine samples; the results determine if and when someone had ingested the drug. He found those metabolites in Jackie Haygood's urine. He further testified that, after watching the videotape of Sera having sex with several unconscious victims, he believed it was possible that these women were under the influence of Rohypnol; however, he could not rule out the presence of other drugs.

The jury ultimately did not believe Sera's version of events, and he was convicted of multiple rape and kidnapping charges relating to the sexual attacks on the two victims in Arkansas. This conviction withstood Sera's appeal.

EVALUATING SERIAL BEHAVIOR

To help develop competent investigative strategies for the successful identification and apprehension of serial offenders, as well as for the development of competent insight into offender motive and intent, the author recommends that the following behavioral considerations be examined.

Victim/Target Selection

If we can understand how and why a serial offender selects a particular victim (or target), then we may also be able to establish the relational links between the victim and that offender. Additionally, if we can come to understand an offender's overall strategy for the selection of victims, then we have a better chance of predicting the type of victim that the offender may select in the future.

When determining how an offender may have selected a particular victim, the profiler must ask of the behavioral evidence certain basic questions in order to begin eliminating the possibilities:

1. Was the victim opportunistic or targeted?
2. If the victim was targeted, what appears to be the offender's selection criterion?

- Location type (indoor, outdoor, apartment complex, parking lot, woods, supermarket, etc.)
- Occupation (prostitute, homeless, exotic dancer, student, banker, teacher, etc.)
- Vulnerability (intoxicated, tired, distracted, etc.)
- Physical characteristics (height, weight, hair style/color, clothing, etc.)
- Activity (jogging, hiking, driving, shopping, sleeping, Internet, etc.)

3. If the victim appears to have been targeted, what presurveillance behaviors would be required by the offender, given the activity of the victim? What activities do investigators and patrol need to be on the lookout for to spot an offender who may be engaged in presurveillance relating to the series of crimes at hand?

4. If the victim could not have been targeted or presurveyed, then did the offender have to step outside of his or her daily, non-criminal routine to acquire victims, or was the offender likely trolling for potential victims?

5. If the offender was not actively trolling and the victim could not have been preselected or presurveyed, then the offender likely acquired the victim during his or her daily routine. This suggests that a reconstruction of the victim's lifestyle, habits, and routines may give direct insight into the lifestyle, habits, and routines of the offender.

Offender Departure Strategy

How an offender chooses to leave behind living victims after an attack is concluded gives insight into the motive and intent of the offender's offense behavior (and skill level). The departure strategy may also reveal information regarding where the offender intends to go after the offense, the offender's personal schedule, how much time the offender needs to get away, and how concerned the offender is that the victim might recognize him or her at a later date. These are, of course, just some of the elements involved, and they can be used in combination, depending on the offender and the circumstances of the attack. For example, the offender may do the following:

- Leave the victim conscious
- Leave the victim unconscious (nature of the force involved?)
- Leave the victim clothed
- Leave the victim partially clothed or nude (was clothing discarded at the scene, near the scene, or taken from the scene?)
- Exert no restraints on the victim
- Restrain the victim physically (type of controlling force used?)
- Leave the victim able, mobile
- Disable the victim physically, making the victim immobile or in need of medical attention (nature of the force involved?)
- Leave the victim at or near the point of contact
- Leave the victim at a location far away from the point of contact
- Take the victim to a remote location to drop him or her off after an attack
- Take the victim to wherever the victim wishes to go (work, home, friend's house)
- Use a physical threat: "Don't follow me or I'll kill you!" "Don't call the police or I'll find you and cut your throat!"
- Use an implied threat: "Don't follow me or else!" "Don't tell anyone or you'll be sorry!"
- Give commands: "Don't follow me!" "Count to 500 and then leave."
- Offer rationalization: "You shouldn't have been walking out here alone." "I could have done a lot worse to you." "You deserved it."
- Apologize: "I'm sorry." "This isn't me." "I didn't mean to hurt you."

Disposal Site Aspects

How an offender chooses to leave behind deceased victims in the disposal site also gives insight into the motive and intent of the individual's offense behavior (and skill level). Criminal profilers must try to establish the relation of the victim's body to the disposal site and the evidence that is in it. The disposal site aspects are useful for answering the following questions:

1. Whether an offender intended that the victim's body be found
2. Where an offender intended that the victim's body be found
3. When an offender intended that the victim's body be found
4. Whom an offender intended would find the victim's body

Convenience Aspect

A convenience aspect refers to a disposal site that an offender chooses by virtue of the fact that it is available or less difficult to access than another location. The convenience aspect may apply when an offender is constrained by time or by the inability to move a victim's body either physically or without being observed or detected.

Remorse Aspect

A remorse aspect refers to a disposal site where there is evidence that the offender felt some regret over the victim's death. This can be seen in behaviors that attempt to "undo" the homicide, including washing the blood off a victim, dressing the victim in clean clothes, and placing the victim in a natural state position, such as a sleeping posture, sitting in a chair, or in the seat of a vehicle.

Preselected Aspect

A preselected aspect refers to a disposal site that an offender chose before actually committing an offense, by virtue of its being particularly suitable for the activities with which the offender wishes to engage the victim. It may be a small outdoor clearing just out of sight and earshot from a well-trodden path or an indoor location that the offender must transport the victim to.

Precautionary Aspect

A precautionary aspect refers to a disposal site where an offender has gone to some effort to destroy evidence or otherwise hamper the investigative effort. This can be in the form of mutilating the body to prevent identification, disposing of it in water to wash away evidence, disposing of it in a remote or hard-to-reach location, or burying it very deep to forestall or prevent its recovery.

Staged Aspect

A staged aspect refers to a disposal site that an offender has altered to purposefully mislead the investigation. Staging may include the murderer's placing a gun in the hand of a shooting victim or his attempts to make a ligature strangulation appear to be a suicide by hanging.

Arranged Aspect

An arranged aspect refers to a disposal site where an offender has arranged the body and the items within the scene in order to serve ritual or fantasy purposes. For example, victims' bodies may be displayed postmortem in a very public location, victims may be placed in humiliating sexual positions after death, and the position of the body may serve the purposes of a particular offender ritual. An important question in cases where the offender has arranged the body or the scene is: Who is meant to see the arrangement: the offender, law enforcement, or others who would happen upon the scene?

SOLVING CASES

In most texts on the subject of serial murder or rape investigation, little or no attention is given to how cases are solved. Keppel (1989, p. 4) comes the closest when he offers the following general remarks regarding why cases are solved:

> The successful completion of a serial homicide investigation is dependent upon a combination of so-called solvability factors. These are:
>
> 1. The quality of police interviews with eyewitnesses.
> 2. The circumstances which led to the initial stop of the murderer.
> 3. The circumstances which established the probable cause to search and seize the physical evidence from the person and/or the property of the murderer; specifically, the solvability factors in each case.
> 4. The quality of the investigations at the crime scene(s).
> 5. The quality of the scientific analysis of the physical evidence seized from the murderer and/ or his property and its comparison to physical evidence from the victims and the homicide scenes.

This is not actually a list of how cases are solved, but rather a list of elements that the successful apprehension and prosecution of serial offenders depends on. Certainly, the list emphasizes quality and thoroughness and is therefore not unhelpful. But it does not quite give us what we need. What we need is a list of mechanisms by which serial investigations are most often solved—that is to say, a list of the most common ways that suspects are initially identified by law enforcement.

As we have discussed, criminal profilers and criminal profiles do not typically solve cases. In the investigative phase, they inform investigative processes and decisions that lead detectives to suspects. Good suspects are most commonly brought to light in a serial investigation via the following mechanisms:

1. A confession
2. Another offender turning in the serial offender
3. The coming forward of an offender's spouse, family members, friends, co-workers, or neighbors to report evidence of aberrant, suspicious, or criminal activity
4. The identification of an offender by a witness to the crime
5. The identification of an offender by a victim who has eluded or evaded an attack
6. The identification of an offender by a victim who has suffered an attack but was subsequently released by the offender
7. The identification of an offender by a victim who has suffered an attack but subsequently escaped from captivity
8. The routine stopping of an offender for a minor violation (expired vehicle tags, traffic violation, parking violation, and so on)
9. The arrest of an offender for an offense unrelated to violent, predatory activity (burglary, purse snatching, indecent exposure, assault, and so on) and subsequent linkage to physical evidence on file associated with unsolved crimes, such as fingerprints, photo ID, or DNA
10. The linkage of a known offender to a series of offenses by the use of data base information or evidence like gun registrations, driver's licenses, fingerprints, or DNA

11. Good detective work, which includes following up on all tips, investigating all leads to their conclusion, sharing information and collaborating with other law enforcement agencies, and working the physical evidence until it is an exhausted possibility

The full utilization and exploitation of these mechanisms requires an alert, educated, and responsive law enforcement community. The ideo-deductive criminal profiling process of behavioral evidence analysis, applied as investigative philosophy, prepares detectives to be just that.

Using the Media

As suggested in the previous section, the public availability of discriminating information regarding an unsolved serial case can be a useful tool for getting witnesses, family members, and previous victims to come forward with vital information regarding the identity of suspects. This makes the media an investigative lifeline to the community. If we want the community to work with us on these cases, we have to give them enough information to work with.

The criminal profile can be a constructive part of this effort. But as we all know, the media is a double-edged sword. Detectives are charged with the task of giving enough information to the public so they can be an effective extension of the investigation. However, they have the equally important responsibility of holding enough specific details back to:

■ Prevent offenders from understanding the full nature of investigative efforts and significantly altering their MOs, depriving the investigators of the ability to link cases
■ Screen copycats and those who would give false confessions

Detectives should also closely monitor the media coverage of a given serial case and keep track of which case details are made public and when. Subsequently, the dissemination of this information should be tracked with known offender behavior to monitor any changes in the offender MO, no matter how subtle or discrete. If the offender is paying attention to news coverage and either learning or reacting to it, detectives will want to be the first to know.

Task Force Praxis

In theory, using a task force is the best way to investigate serial crime (see Baeza, 1999). Generally, it is meant to work like this: Get representatives from the appropriate jurisdictions and agencies to come together as a team; have regular meetings; create a nexus for information; distribute the workload; keep everyone in the loop; compile, analyze, and distribute every piece of old, new, or related information to everyone concerned; ensure that nobody is left without everything they need; and put somebody in charge to run everything without compromise or impediment from the other agencies. Again, it's a good theory that assumes everyone is working toward the same goal—the identification and apprehension of the suspect. The problem is that the human ego, specifically its compensatory need for public recognition for personal gain in the form of professional celebrity or advancement, can cause task force members and others to impede the task force's progress. And that's just what goes wrong before the first meeting.

Problems

Over the course of the past 12 years, the author has had occasion to work as a member of, or as a consultant to, more than a dozen law-enforcement task forces in the United States and other countries concerned with the investigation of serial murderers, serial rapists, and serial burglars. Some of the involvements have been exceptional and productive—resulting in arrests and other clearances. Some of them have not. However, each experience has been educational, with its own share of successes and failures to learn from. Common problems have included:

Lack of qualified leadership. Sometimes the people put in charge of the task force do not know what criminal investigation actually requires and don't understand the resources needed and the time that can be involved with particular tasks. These people may be identified by their constant referencing of TV and film with respect to brainstorming efforts, as opposed to prior case successes.

Lack of actual leadership. Even when qualified people are put in charge, sometimes they aren't all that interested in leading. These are people who can't be bothered to read memos, investigative reports, or other intelligence being gathered. They can often be identified by their frequent absence from task force meetings—they may send an assistant or phone in, signaling their lack of interest. In extreme cases, they may put an end to task force meetings entirely.

Task force bystander apathy. Important yet mundane tasks may be dropped or de-prioritized by those assigned them because they assume that someone else is going to doing them, if anyone has been assigned at all. The larger the task force, the more likely it is that good intelligence is being lost, missed, or ignored because of the assumption that it is being handled by someone else.

Personnel overload. It is not uncommon that a task force has so many people that nothing is actually getting done. Too much time may be spent on the logistics of getting people together, disseminating intelligence, and obtaining a consensus to take action on priority items. If it regularly takes more than 30 minutes to figure out what everyone is having for lunch—there's a problem.

Sabotage. In many cases, unhealthy interagency and interdepartmental rivalries can cause task force members to work against each other. In extreme cases, some task force members may actually sabotage the efforts of others by failing to share intelligence, hiding or "losing" evidence, or arresting suspects prematurely to get credit for the collar. Why such conduct is tolerated within any task force, at any level, is unfathomable. It is also one of the biggest problems with forming a task force—you give other agencies a chance to harm or seriously impede your investigation for their own gain, whatever that may be.

Loss of vital personnel. Invariably, there are vital personnel who hold or control a particular piece of the task force that is necessary for its function (such as access to particular skills, a particular resource, or a source of intelligence). Loss of personnel to training, vacations, and even retirement is a reality. However, when vital people are reassigned simply to serve the needs of the bureaucracy or internal politics, it is a ridiculous waste.

Interference. Task force members and leaders can receive conflicting directives, instructions, or advice from various supervisors and department heads, to say nothing of political figures. This is really a leadership problem, more than anything else, resulting from an absence of an identifiable chain of command with respect to task force members. The less clear task force members are about who their supervisor is, the more interference is tolerated.

These problems were not constrained by culture or continent.

Solutions

Based on a consideration of these and other problems common to task force management, as described in Baeza (1999) and Buhler (1999), the author proposes the following unconventional considerations for task force formation:

1. Smaller task forces mean more accountability, faster decisions, and higher mobility. Task forces should be as small as possible—two to four investigators, two data analysts, one office, and two hard-line phone numbers. Everybody gets dedicated computers (or laptops), and everybody gets a dedicated cell phone. If other agencies want to form their own effort and coordinate, that's fine. If other agencies want intelligence that has been gathered, that's fine, too.

2. Task forces should not cross agency lines, nor do they need to. Most agencies cooperate just fine with outside agencies without having to be told. Creating a task force will not make an uncooperative agency or unprofessional investigator less of a problem. If information or resources are being withheld, work around it and move on.

3. Every bit of information that comes in should be put into a single database by one of the two analysts, with updates every day to all of the investigators. The data analysts should become human repositories of information related to each of the cases. Anyone lacking these skills or abilities should not be in the analyst position. In this way, investigators in the field can get the intelligence they need with a phone call.

4. Investigators should assume that, if they aren't doing it, it's not getting done—mainly because if they aren't, then it isn't.

5. Investigators should be accountable to one senior investigator who is an active member of the task force and is accountable directly to the top entity in the agency only. There should be no intermediate supervisors.

6. Cooperation with the task force must be mandatory. Anyone in the agency found not to be cooperating with, or withholding information from, the task force should be sanctioned in writing. This is key to getting cooperation from everyone.

7. All new case information that even appears remotely related should be copied to the task force. Individual investigating officers should retain their standing on their cases, but they must coordinate their activities with the task force and update the task force with intelligence directly.

8. Investigators must be assigned to the task force on the basis of their ability and results. Investigators with personal solve rates lower than 80% should not be considered. Investigators with political connections or aspirations should also not be considered.

9. The task force must report its findings each week directly to the commanding entity. This increases direct accountability.

10. There should be no press conferences. Nobody should be talking to the press about who is on the task force or what it is doing. The task force is not formed for public relations purposes; it is formed for accomplishing specific tasks. If there is information to be released to the public, it should be done in writing via a press release from the chief's office.

The task force concept is a good one, but currently task forces tend to be bloated and impotent, serving political and public relations goals as opposed to substantive ones. To be effective at the task of solving crime, they must be smaller, more accountable, and less encumbered by politics, personal agendas, information drought, and bureaucracy. They must also be able to move quickly and effectively in response to good intelligence rather than suffering from information spread so thin across members that nobody knows what is known or has been done, or who is responsible for either.

Ironically, serial crime investigations tend to follow the above proposed construct as fractures occur, alliances form, and good detectives set to the task of solving or working around internal problems. Cleaving as many political features from the task force as possible to ensure that detectives have everything they need to move a case forward must be a priority. Giving investigators the time, resources, permission, and support to run down leads is another. If this doesn't happen naturally, it must happen by design, or it may not happen at all.

CONCLUSION

The tendency has, thus far, been to view serial offenders as belonging to discrete categories. Consequently, their natures may be conceived and presupposed based on a false relationship to an immobile cluster, likely by virtue of their criminal behavior at only a few points in time. This narrow, inductive tendency for classification and prediction is troubling and must cease.

There are consequences for labeling criminal behavior arbitrarily or based only on what has been seen and recognized. Linkages can be missed, profiles can be uninformed, investigations can suffer, victims can suffer unnecessarily, and justice can be delayed if not entirely sabotaged, to say nothing of misinforming our criminological understanding of what serial criminals are, how they are motivated, and what they are capable of.

Just because we identify an offender as a serial murderer, we cannot assume this is all the offender has ever been or will ever be. Adjusting our perceptions is a necessary step toward understanding and investigating serial crime and all that this entails. Currently, nomothetic study has created an oversimplified big picture that plays and sells well to the public, while up close the understanding is necessarily unclear if not entirely inaccurate. Further ideographic study of serial crime by current and future students is needed to alleviate this limitation of our "serial" comprehension.

SUMMARY

Many serial offenders commit crimes of multiple types in the course of a criminal season or career. Unfortunately, because of the way that crime is reported, studied, investigated, and prosecuted, many believe that the opposite is true. This has led to stereotyping, pigeonholing, and serial offenses that have gone unrecognized.

The term serial killer was developed by FBI profilers to assist with the allocation of investigative resources. The use of the term by the media and in popular culture has resulted in mythical serial killer archetypes, characterized by deeply reflective, intelligent, or romantic offenders unfettered by the rules of society. The attention and celebrity are born not out of admiration for the characteristics of real-life serial murderers but out of the need to maintain specific yet varied illusions that many in the general public find comforting and entertaining. These images are actually manufactured by the industry that is in the business of profiting from serial killer fictions.

By definition, serial rapists are successful criminals because law enforcement fails to connect their crimes and fails to identify and apprehend them before multiple offenses have been committed. However, as with serial murderers, they are not limited to committing the crime of rape, or even sex crimes in general. Unlike many forms of homicide, rape is an extreme form of behavioral expression that the offender visualizes and to some degree thinks out before it happens. Each rapist is motivated differently, but the rapist's motives may be discussed in the general terms already provided in this text.

To help develop competent investigative strategies for the successful identification and apprehension of serial offenders, as well as for the development of competent insight into offender motive and intent, the author recommends that in each case the following be examined: how and why a serial offender selects a particular victim, how and why an offender chooses to leave behind living victims after an attack is concluded, and how and why an offender chooses to leave behind deceased victims in the disposal site. It is recommended that the media be used judiciously and only when necessary in serial cases. It is also urged that serial task force efforts be made smaller, with more authority, more resources, and with fewer political and bureaucratic burdens.

Questions

1. True or False: Serial offenders tend to commit the same type of crime over and over again throughout their criminal careers—that is, rapists only commit rape, murderers only commit murder, and so forth.
2. This chapter discusses several myths regarding serial killers. List two.
3. Explain the relationship between the films, true-crime novels, and serial killer archetypes.
4. Regarding rapist's motives, some refer to the fact that the act of rape can be uniting for a group. Give an example.
5. The interval during which offenders psychologically disconnect, separate, or compartmentalize themselves from the behaviors and motives that led to or culminated in homicidal behavior and then reintegrate back into their non-criminal lives and activities may be referred to as _____.

REFERENCES

Abbott, K., Langbein, S., 2005. Cops Balked on Arrest: Brents Warrant Prepared Late Last Year, Sat Unsigned for More than a Month. *Rocky Mountain News* (February 18), A5.

Arkansas v. Steven Anthony Sera, 2000. No. CR 98-1222, May 25, 2000 (2000 WL 675546 (Ark.)).

Baeza, J., 1999. Task Force Management. In: Turvey, B. (Ed.), Criminal Profiling: An Introduction to Behavioral Evidence Analysis. Academic Press, London, England, pp. 415–428.

Baker, K., 1997. Once a Rapist? Motivational Evidence and Relevancy in Rape Law. Harvard Law Review 110 (3), 563–624.

Buhler, M., 1999. The Fugitive Task Force: An Alternative Organizational Model. FBI Law Enforcement Bulletin 68 (4), 1–5.

Cabrera, L., 2001. New Tool Faces Old Mystery: DNA Tests May Help Solve the Case of the Green River Killer. *The Columbian* (August 27), 2.

CBS News, 2004. The Mind of a Serial Killer. 60 Minutes II July 7.

Ebrite, T., 2005. Toward a Balanced Equation: Advocating Consistency in the Sentencing of Serial Killers. Oklahoma Law Review 58, 685–722.

Egger, S., 1984. A Working Definition of Serial Murder and the Reduction of Linkage Blindness. Journal of Police Science and Administration 12, 348–357.

Fox, J.A., Levin, J., 1998. Multiple Homicide: Patterns of Serial and Mass Murder. Crime and Justice 23, 407.

Groth, A.N., 1979. Men Who Rape: The Psychology of the Offender. Plenum Press, New York, NY.

Gumbel, A., 2001. The Mystery of the Green River Killer. *Independent,* UK (December 19).

Hamill, R., 2001. Recidivism of Sex Offenders: What You Need to Know. Criminal Justice 15 (4), 24–34.

Herdy, A., 2005. Brents Details Crimes, Alleges Abuse at Parents' Hands. Denver *Post* (July 7), A4.

Hickey, E., 1991. Serial Murderers and Their Victims. Brooks/Cole, Belmont, CA.

Hinch, R., Hepburn, C., 1998. Researching Serial Murder: Methodological and Definitional Problems. Electronic Journal of Sociology 3, 2.

Homant, R., Kennedy, D., 2005. Serial Murder: A Biopsychosocial Approach. In: Petherick, W. (Ed.), Serial Crime. Elsevier Science, Boston, MA.

Ith, I., Smith, C., Guillen, T., 2001. Ridgeway Awaits Charges. Seattle *Times* (December 2), A1.

Kamb, L., 2006. Reichert Touts Law Record, but Critics Don't See It His Way. *Seattle Post-Intelligencer* (October 6).

Kennedy, J., 2006. Facing Evil. Michigan Law Review (May), 1287–1304.

Keppel, R., 1989. Serial Murder: Future Implications for Police Investigators. Anderson, Cincinnati, OH, pp. 1287–1300.

Langbein, S., 2005. 190 More Years for Brents Assault Victims: Mom Says Family's Kindness Paid Back with "Evil". *Rocky Mountain News* (July 9), A6.

Langbein, S., 2006. Victims of Brents to Split Settlement. *Rocky Mountain News* (January 31), A7.

Lindsay, S., 2005. Chilling Details in Brents Case: Suspected Sexual Predator to Stand Trial on 72 Counts of Rape, Attempted Murder. *Rocky Mountain News* (May 3), A5.

Maryland v. Metheny, 2000. July 24 (755 A.2d 1088).

McCarthy, T., 2002. River of Death. Time (June 3), 59–67.

Missouri v. Terrance Bolds, 2000. No. ED 75483, February 7 (11 S.W.3d 633).

Pankratz, H., McPhee, M., 2005. Suspect's Sex Crimes Began in Early Teens. Denver *Post* (February 17), A1.

Petherick, W., 2005. Serial Crime. Elsevier Science, Boston, MA.

Ressler, R., 1992. Whoever Fights Monsters. St. Martin's Press, New York, NY.

Simon, L., 1997. The Myth of Sex Offender Specialization: An Empirical Analysis, Symposium: The Treatment of Sex Offenders. New England Journal on Criminal and Civil Confinement 23 (2), 387–403.

Sunde, S., 2002. Searching for an "Invisible" Menace in Our Midst. *Seattle Post-Intelligencer* (January 18), A1.

Turvey, B., 2004. Modus Operandi, Motive, and Technology. In: Casey, E. (Ed.), Digital Evidence and Computer Crime: Forensic Science, Computers and the Internet, second edition. Academic Press, Boston, MA.

Wilson, D., 2003. Profiler Can't Recall Why He Said Letter Wasn't from Green River Killer. Seattle *Times* (November 26), B1.

Wrolstad, M., 1997. Wife's Discovery of Sex Tapes Leads to Serial Rape Case. *Dallas Morning News* (November 16), A–29.

CHAPTER 23

Introduction to Terrorism: Understanding and Interviewing Terrorists

Brent E. Turvey, Majeed Khader, Jansen Ang, Eunice Tan, and Jeffery Chin[*]

Profiling is often the means to detention, prosecution, and/or deportation.

—Choudhury, "Terrorists and Muslims" (2006, p. 18)

CONTENTS

[*] These authors comprise the Behavioral Sciences Program, Home Team Academy, Ministry of Home Affairs, Singapore.

KEY TERMS

Al Qaeda
Divine mandates

Moral mandates

Reciprocity

On September 11, 2001, terrorist attacks were effectively coordinated against U.S. civilian and government targets along the East Coast. The terrorists consisted of 19 men affiliated with the Islamic extremist group Al Qaeda.[1] They hijacked four commercial airliners, crashing two into World Trade Center towers and one into the Pentagon. The fourth airliner was initially hijacked, but then passengers and crew attempted to regain control when they learned what the terrorists planned to do—the terrorists intended to fly into the White House. Ultimately, they crashed the airliner in a field near the town of Shanksville in rural Somerset County, Pennsylvania. While many are still debating the total losses resulting from that day's events, it is known that all of the terrorist hijackers died, along with all of the airline passengers, and thousands of victims on the ground were instantly killed.

Since that time, the author has received nonstop requests to assist with terrorist profiling efforts from agencies and governments around the globe. The most common question is: Can we profile terrorists based on race? This is routinely followed up with: What is the profile of a terrorist? The inclusion of this chapter arises out of these requests.

The purpose of this chapter is to discuss the viability of profiling terrorists in the context of the global war on Islamic extremist terror groups, the inherent problems with current nomothetic approaches, and then finally to provide strategies for rapport-based interviewing of individual terrorists.

Interviewing techniques are offered in the second part of this chapter for two reasons. First, the intelligence on most terror networks ranges from unreliable to ridiculous. Law enforcement and the military alike often have no idea who terrorists are, how they think, what they want, or what they are willing to do to get it. Their idea of what a terrorist looks like comes from watching films and television—through media archetypes that are at best dangerously under-informed (Choudhury, 2006).[2] As a consequence, we are often torturing good suspects instead of learning from them and building resentment in the noncriminal Islamic community instead of enlisting their help. We need to be building knowledge through competent interviews, and not imposing archetypes with iron-fisted policies. Second, many of the purported terrorism experts who offer lectures, training, and advice on the subject have had no actual contact with terrorists in their careers and have no working knowledge of terrorists' nature and activities other than what they see on the news. To address these limits in available training and literature, the author has enlisted the assistance of colleagues from the Behavioral Science Unit, Home Team Academy, Singapore. Not only do they have experience assisting with the investigation of terrorist networks, including those affiliated with Al Qaeda, but also they have experience interviewing terrorists.

---

[1] Al Qaeda is Arabic for "The Base." It is an international terrorist organization that was originally formed in 1988 by Osama bin Laden and his associate Mohammed Atef to rally and assist Arabs who fought in Afghanistan against the Soviet invasion. Since its inception, Al Qaeda has formed alliances with many other Islamic fundamentalist organizations with goals similar to its own: to overthrow heretical regimes and to restore rule by fundamentalist Islamic law through force. Al Qaeda is violently anti-Western and views the United States and its foreign policy as a primary corrupting influence on the various Islamic states that it seeks to overthrow and restore.

[2] Also refer to the "Power of the Media" section of the third edition of this book, which discusses the 24 effect.

To the unknowing, Singapore may seem a remote place from which to draw this kind of expertise; however, it is not. Singapore is a hub for trade and commerce between countries and cultures that historically have had tension. It is the middleman and sometimes the banker for the region, if not for many parts of the world. In an applied sense, this means that for everything to run efficiently in Singapore, everyone has to get along. It is one of the few places on the planet where people of different religions and cultures, Muslim and Christian alike, have gathered together for a common purpose (e.g., trade) without killing each other over their beliefs.[3]

By itself, Singapore's necessary cultural peace makes it a perfect target for Islamic extremists, such as those associated with Al Qaeda, bent on unseating "heretical" regimes through violence. This is to say nothing of the fact that it is a perfect indirect target for groups wishing to inflict harm on the United States, as approximately 17,000 Americans are residing in this city-state along with 6,000 multinational companies, several of which are American and are among its biggest employers. As Elegant (2002) explains,

> Singapore's much-vaunted internal security apparatus still hasn't quite recovered from the shock of discovering a well-advanced al-Qaeda plot to detonate seven large truck bombs at embassies and other key sites in the city-state late last year. "They were absolutely horrified at how close the plan was to execution," says a source who has worked closely with the Singapore authorities on terrorism issues. Not that the authorities didn't swing into action with characteristic efficiency once the plot was uncovered. With nearly 40 alleged militants now in prison, Singapore officials insist there is no longer "any credible threat" from Jemaah Islamiah cells inside the island republic. But as terror expert Zachary Abuza points out, ultimately, a successful attack in Singapore remains top of the wish list for JI, even if achieving that takes years. "Singapore has enormous symbolic importance as the capitalist center of the region," says Abuza.
>
> Such concerns were highlighted earlier this year when Prime Minister Goh Chok Tong revealed that Mas Selamat Kastari, the "most dangerous" of the 12 or so members of the Singapore Jemaah Islamiah cell who escaped arrest and fled the country, had been planning an attempt to crash a plane into Singapore's Changi Airport. The airport is now reportedly protected by anti-aircraft missiles, as are the huge refinery facilities on the island's southwest section of Jurong, where multinationals such as Shell and Exxon Mobil maintain large facilities. In mid-October Singapore deployed units of its armored division around the area as further safeguards.

What this means is that the Singapore Home Ministry has accrued no small amount of experience dealing with terrorist organizations, marked by no small measure of success. We know this because of the failure of terrorists to successfully attack a target in Singapore despite repeated threats and because of the plots that the Singapore Home Ministry has uncovered and continues to uncover before they come to fruition. Consequently, the Singapore expertise is the substance of the second part of this chapter.

NOMOTHETIC TERRORIST PROFILES: OVERSIMPLIFIED, UNINFORMED, AND UNADAPTIVE

To borrow a quote from the fictional Dr. Ian Malcom in the film *Jurassic Park* (1993), the exercise of Western scholars developing nomothetic terrorist profiles of Islamic extremists "is the worst idea in the long, sad history of bad ideas."

---

[3] In early 2007, members of the Singapore Police Force's Behavioral Science Unit invited the author to give training at the Home Team Academy in Singapore. The result was an important cultural and educational exchange. One of the most important cultural lessons the author learned was how diverse Singapore is and how well everyone gets along—no matter which countries, ethnicities, or religions are sitting at a given table.

First, nomothetic terrorist profiling models are too often based on oversimplified and uninformed prejudices, not actual insight into criminal behavior itself. In fact, we know this problem all too well, which is why racial profiling was on track to be eradicated in the United States only a decade ago. That is, until the events of September 11, 2001 (Reynolds, 2007, p. 667):

> It is a prevailing belief that most criminal acts, excluding the "intellectual" crimes of CEOs involved in the recent Enron and Martha Stewart fiascos, are typically committed by the poorest, darkest, and newest members of American society.

> By the mid-1990s society treated racial profiling by law enforcement as the great taboo. In 2000 eighty percent of Americans surveyed in a Gallup poll stated that they had not only heard of the act of profiling but believed the practice should be stopped. Between January 1999 and September 2001, thirteen states had moved to pass legislation that banned racial profiling or required police departments to collect data on the act. Yet, in the wake of the September 11 terrorist attacks, the consensus of profiling in the nation changed. All nineteen of the hijackers were Arabic men. In no less than "a month [after] the attack, surveys showed that a majority of Americans favored more intensive security checks for Arab and Middle Eastern people." Clearly, however, the profiling had to do with gender as well as race. Gender was the crux basis of the new terrorist profile because all of the hijackers were men; historically the ... members of such fundamentalist Islamic groups are male.

As a result of 9/11, public attitudes toward racially profiling terrorists softened as the sense of urgency regarding future terrorist attacks increased. This took shape when intense new security measures were deployed at airports, borders, and other potential terrorist targets across the country. These enhancements, in an environment of urgency and fear, did not make the rationale behind racially profiling terrorists any more valid. As Taslitz (2005, p. 1186) explains,

> Perceived urgency is a dangerous thing. Intense time pressure leads to rigid, less adaptive thinking. Rather than carefully comparing alternative courses of action on a wide range of measures, decision makers may too readily discard options not obviously having the presumably most-desired attribute. In other words, they too easily narrow their options and their field of attention, ignoring much information that may help in making higher quality, better-informed choices. Perhaps even worse, they increasingly rely on well-learned habits and stereotyping. Time pressure can also create a sense of threat, compromising the ability to reason clearly. Cognitive function suffers an overall decline in the face of time pressure.

> The increased reliance on often subconscious stereotypes, the sense of threat, and the limited ability to gather and effectively assess accurate information in a time-pressured environment increases the likelihood of at least subconscious racial stereotyping. ...

In fact, the continued public and even law-enforcement appetite for racial profiling indicates that we haven't actually learned anything from our experiences with domestic terrorism. As Davies (2003, p. 78) explains,

> The collection of terrorist acts that have occurred on American soil should make any careful thinker hesitate before concluding that persons of Middle Eastern origins are in fact more likely to be terrorists than others. Several "home-grown" terrorists belie this claim. Timothy McVeigh, a white male from upstate New York, committed an act of terrorism responsible for the loss of 168 innocent lives, and over 500 injuries. Had he had his way, the death toll would have been much higher. It was purely and simply a fortuity not in any way creditable to him that more people were not killed when

he detonated the bomb outside the Murrah Federal Building. When asked if he had any regrets, McVeigh replied that his only regret was that the building had not collapsed completely. Before the events of September 11, McVeigh's malicious and premeditated crime was frequently referred to as "the deadliest act of terrorism ever committed on American soil."

Nevertheless, no one suggested after the bombing of the Alfred P. Murrah Federal Building in Oklahoma City that the effort to bring to justice those responsible for that bombing and the deaths of 168 innocents could properly involve acts of police profiling that would subject to extra scrutiny young, closely-cropped, white males simply because they shared those physical characteristics with McVeigh. And why not? I suspect that it is because, when we are faced with the criminality of a white suspect who may have accomplices, we do not fall prey to the same tortured reasoning to which we seem so easily to fall prey when we are faced with a minority suspect. In such a setting, we seem instinctively to know that the odds of capturing additional culprits by treating all young, white males with suspicion are so astronomically small, and the burdens we place on innocent white males in the process are so astronomically large, that it is a course of investigative conduct that makes no logical sense.

Additional examples provide further reason to doubt the first premise of the syllogism posed above [Middle Easterners are more likely to commit acts of terror than non-Middle Easterners]. Like Tim McVeigh, Ted Kaczynski also fails to fit the currently popular stereotype of the Arab or Muslim terrorist. Kaczynski, another native of upstate New York and a white American, was responsible for a string of bombings occurring over the course of seventeen years which resulted in the deaths of three people and injuries of twenty-three others. Unlike the post-9/11 reaction, however, one would search in vain for calls for increased surveillance of scrubby, white male recluses after Kaczynski's reign of terror. And rightly so.

If racial profiling is not viable, what then of general terrorist typologies? For example, Holmes and Holmes (2001) offer descriptions of at least three types of mass killers that could be used in an attempt to help classify individual terrorists: the disciple mass killer, the idiological mass killer, and the set-and-run mass killer. While these may be valid descriptors of some domestic terrorists, they will necessarily fail with respect to gaining insight and understanding into those grown beyond our borders. The reason is fairly straightforward. We in the United States are generally ignorant of Islamic beliefs, cultures, and customs. We do not comprehend the complexities and variations within the different Islamic communities or even that there are complexities and variations. Consequently, we are literally among the last people on the planet who should be trying to impose any kind of research model, typology, or classification structure on non-U.S. terrorists. As Choudury (2006, p. 8) explains,

Despite the increased coverage of all things Islamic in all its variety, writers, analysts, and policymakers routinely fall back on an image of singularity to which they address their advice and excoriations. It seems that in an effort to create the knowable, all Muslims and the myriad of places they live have been collapsed into a fungible people and a seamless geography. This tendency to create simplicity from complexity is not confined to the media. Indeed, the desire to reduce the heterogeneous Muslims into a knowable subject has also been felt by the State and by Muslims in the West. The way in which an otherwise unruly plurality is ordered is through the creation of meta-identities which Muslims are then expected to perform.

At the current level of ignorance and disarray in the Western profiling literature with respect to non-U.S. terrorism, the best thing we can do is spend the next decade learning about the subject from those with a great deal more knowledge, as is described in the next section.

INTERVIEWING TERRORISTS: SUGGESTIONS FOR INVESTIGATIVE INTERVIEWS

This section covers three main areas: a brief look at terrorism research, the profiling of terrorists, and how to conduct interviews with terrorists. It is not meant to be comprehensive or exhaustive but rather to provide practitioners with suggestions based on our practical experiences of interviewing terrorists.

Readers who may be in interested in a broader perspective of terrorism-related issues should refer instead to the main researchers in this field, including Randy Borum (Borum, 2004), Martha Crenshaw (Crenshaw, 1994), Rohan Gunaratna (Gunaratna, 2003), Fathali M. Moghaddam (Moghaddam and Marsella, 2004), Ministry of Home Affairs (Singapore) (2003), and Jeff Victoroff (Victoroff, 2005). Another point for the reader to note is that many of the examples used in this section relate to Islamic extremists, particularly to those in the Jemaah Islamiyah group, which exists within South East Asia (because the authors are most familiar with this group), but the suggestions made here are general enough to be employed when interviewing extremists from other groups as well.

Terrorism Research: A Brief Background

Dr. Andrew Silke, a leading researcher on the subject of terrorism, has made a poignant comment about the current state of research. He says, "Terrorism research is not in a healthy state. It exists on a diet of fast food research: quick, cheap, ready-to-hand and nutritionally dubious. … It was found that the problems identified in 1988 remains as serious as ever" (Silke, 2001). Indeed, several problems plague the field.

First, there doesn't appear to be a consensus among experts on the definition of terrorism. Others have noted that more than 100 definitions of terrorism have appeared in the professional literature (Borum, 2004). Without a clear definition, would it be possible to develop a rich knowledge base or conduct consistent research? This seems unlikely.

Second, Silke, who reviewed terrorism research published in the field's primary journals during the five-year period from 1995 through 1999, observed that an overwhelming number of articles were mainly "thought pieces" based on open-source documents. Only about 20% of those articles provided substantially new knowledge and understanding.

Third, many terrorism "experts" have never actually spoken to a terrorist or are reluctant to reveal who their sources are or at least vaguely where they are from.[4] To be perfectly fair, it is not always necessary to have experience speaking directly with terrorists when one is attempting to understand and analyze the phenomenon of terrorism. However, it seems a basic prerequisite when one advises others on the behavioral competencies of communicating with them, such as how to interpersonally engage, build rapport, or conduct an interview. The authors have some advantage in this regard, as they have had direct contact interviewing and engaging a variety of terrorists in the course of their work. They have also worked and spoken directly with officers who have interviewed terrorists.

---

[4] Ironically, members of Al Qaeda and most other terrorist groups tend to be highly suspicious of those who boast loudly about what they do, where they have been, and what they have seen of any terrorist networks, as such individuals represent a security risk to the organization.

Profiling Terrorists: An Impossible Task?

The early behavioral research conceptualized terrorism as psychological and behavioral deviance. The psychopathology of terrorism was believed to be driven by unconscious motives and impulses that had their origins in childhood. For example, psychiatrist Frederick Hacker (1976) proposed one of the first known psychological typologies of terrorists, called Crusaders, Criminals, Crazies.

With greater understanding, the general consensus among modern experts is that there is no compelling reason to believe that terrorists are psychologically abnormal, insane, or of a unique psychological profile. For example, the authors' experience indicates that, on the whole, terrorists can appear as "normal" as anyone else, perhaps with the exception of being deeply religious/committed, generally agreeable, and very likable. They were also found to be rational and compliant, with conservative thinking, and possessive of a pleasant demeanor absent of psychopathology.[5]

Consider the cold logic behind the rationale for the employment of suicide bombers, as described in Madsen (2004):

> The boldest form of asymmetric warfare, suicide terrorism represents "value for money." It is cheap, brutally efficient, and difficult to stop, making it an attractive option when compared to more traditional terrorist tactics (e.g., car bombings, assassinations, etc.). Indeed, the decision to deploy suicide terrorists results from a crude cost-benefit analysis. The group will consider the impact in employing suicide terrorism on its profile. Will it incur heavier casualties on its enemy? Is the overall benefit (or cost) greater than a conventional attack? Does the attack mobilize public support for the group's activities? Thus, rather than the act of lone or crazy individuals, we see that suicide terrorism is a corporate effort, from the recruitment and training of the bomber, to the intelligence gathering on the target, and getting the suicide bombers to their final destination. These chilling advantages form the core rationale for terror groups to use the tactic.

As a consequence of their sanity, normalcy, and diversity, it is challenging to determine an accurate physical or ethnic profile of any terrorist type. Dr. Rohan Gunaratna, for example, has documented that the Al Qaeda organization recruits members from 74 different countries and among at least 40 different nationalities. This practice makes it difficult to identify any particular ethnic group or nationality as uniquely associated with the group's cause. This is one example of many that suggest that there is little point in arguing that there may be a distinct physical, ethnic, or personality profile of a terrorist.

This does not mean, however, that an organizational or operational terrorist profile of sorts is not feasible. Many terrorist groups are structured organizations that are operationally inclined, hierarchical, or networked. As a consequence, they tend to hold fast to specific ideological beliefs, causes, and operational objectives. Many terrorist groups are, for example, organized to conduct particular actions, such as reconnaissance, kidnappings, assassinations, or bombings. Related behaviors and thinking styles can be anticipated. This makes certain elements and mechanics of terrorist organizations highly predictable. Hence, the group's ideological, operational, and developmental stages of radicalization can be profiled, if one knows what to look for. For security considerations and because it goes beyond the scope of this work, these are not discussed in detail here.

However, the issue of idiology is interesting enough to warrant elaboration. Idiology helps to provide "the moral and political vision that inspires violence, shapes the way in which they see the world, and defines how they judge the actions of people and institutions" (Drake, 1998). Taylor (1988), for instance, explains

---

[5] These features were not always present or consistent, and they are certainly not distinguishing.

that "the way idiology controls behavior is by providing a set of contingencies that link immediate behavior (e.g., violence) to distant outcomes (e.g., new Islamic state, reward in the afterlife). Idiologies therefore, especially religious ones, may contain mandates that impel its adherents to act."

Skitka and Mullen (2002), for example, define two types of idiological mandates: moral and divine. Moral mandates are the specific positions that people develop out of a moral conviction that something is right or wrong, moral or immoral. Moral mandates, they explain, share the characteristics of strong attitudes—that is, extremity, importance, and certainty—but have an added motivational and action component because they are imbued with moral conviction. Divine mandates, on the other hand, are a unique feature of the extremist driven by religious idiology. They are convictions said to be in accordance with the will of God or some other divine authority. Therefore, with respect to terrorists, interviewers are advised to try to understand the nature and origins of their individual idiological beliefs, since they can bear directly on the issue of motive and facilitate the building of rapport.

Suggested Strategies for Rapport-Based Interviews

The strategies for effecting rapport-based interviews with terrorists follow.

Adopt Good Standards for Investigative Interviewing before Commencing

The first piece of advice for all interviewers is to look up, study up on, and seek out training in investigative interviewing techniques. Several models have been developed worldwide, and they can be adopted for interviewing terrorists. The authors advise interested readers to refer to Becky Milne's *Investigative Interviewing: Psychology and Practice* (Milne and Bull, 1999), Fisher and Geiselman's *Memory-Enhancing Techniques for Investigative Interviewing: The Cognitive Interview* (Fisher and Geiselman, 1992), and the more recently edited *Investigative Interviewing: Rights Research and Regulation* by Tom Williamson (Williamson, 2005). If a doctrinal framework for investigative interviewing has not been set up, it should be established before such interviews begin. Interviewers must have a framework to fall back on and guide them as they encounter problems throughout. Such a framework should, of course, be legally and ethically grounded as well.

Torture Does Not Make for a Good Investigation

Even though it often goes without saying, this cannot be overstated: An interview is not a torture session—and torture does not result in a good interview. First, there is the issue of efficacy. Few experienced professionals believe that torture produces good information, as is detailed anecdotally in Applebaum (2005):

> Meet, for example, retired Air Force Col. John Rothrock, who, as a young captain, headed a combat interrogation team in Vietnam. More than once he was faced with a ticking time-bomb scenario: a captured Vietcong guerrilla who knew of plans to kill Americans. What was done in such cases was "not nice," he says. "But we did not physically abuse them." Rothrock used psychology, the shock of capture and of the unexpected. Once, he let a prisoner see a wounded comrade die. Yet—as he remembers saying to the "desperate and honorable officers" who wanted him to move faster—"if I take a Bunsen burner to the guy's genitals, he's going to tell you just about anything," which would be pointless. Rothrock, who is no squishy liberal, says that he doesn't know "any professional intelligence officers of my generation who would think this is a good idea."
>
> Or listen to Army Col. Stuart Herrington, a military intelligence specialist who conducted interrogations in Vietnam, Panama and Iraq during Desert Storm, and who was sent by the Pentagon in 2003—long before Abu Ghraib—to assess interrogations in Iraq. Aside from its immorality and its

illegality, says Herrington, torture is simply "not a good way to get information." In his experience, nine out of 10 people can be persuaded to talk with no "stress methods" at all, let alone cruel and unusual ones. Asked whether that would be true of religiously motivated fanatics, he says that the "batting average" might be lower: "perhaps six out of ten." And if you beat up the remaining four? "They'll just tell you anything to get you to stop."...

An up-to-date illustration of the colonel's point appeared in recently released FBI documents from the naval base at Guantanamo Bay, Cuba. These show, among other things, that some military intelligence officers wanted to use harsher interrogation methods than the FBI did. As a result, complained one inspector, "every time the FBI established a rapport with a detainee, the military would step in and the detainee would stop being cooperative." So much for the utility of torture.

Given the overwhelmingly negative evidence, the really interesting question is not whether torture works but why so many people in our society want to believe that it works. At the moment, there is a myth in circulation, a fable that goes something like this: Radical terrorists will take advantage of our fussy legality, so we may have to suspend it to beat them. Radical terrorists mock our namby-pamby prisons, so we must make them tougher. Radical terrorists are nasty, so to defeat them we have to be nastier.

There are also unintended consequences of using torture. Using techniques like isolation, sleep deprivation, food deprivation, or other more extreme methods in order to decrease resistance to questioning may be analogous to winning the battle but losing the war. The long history of terrorism has shown that stories of torture from released prisoners, often documented with scars, only fuel the fire for generations of terrorists to come who will inevitably seek to retaliate. This was described in Applebaum as reciprocity—one of the "side effects of torture" (2005):

Worse, you'll have the other side effects of torture. It "endangers our soldiers on the battlefield by encouraging reciprocity." It does "damage to our country's image" and undermines our credibility in Iraq. That, in the long run, outweighs any theoretical benefit. Herrington's confidential Pentagon report, which he won't discuss but which was leaked to The Post a month ago, goes farther. In that document, he warned that members of an elite military and CIA task force were abusing detainees in Iraq, that their activities could be "making gratuitous enemies" and that prisoner abuse "is counterproductive to the Coalition's efforts to win the cooperation of the Iraqi citizenry." Far from rescuing Americans, in other words, the use of "special methods" might help explain why the war is going so badly.

As an example, the photographs documenting prisoner abuse by American soldiers in Abu Ghraib, Iraq, are powerful evidence of prison personnel both untrained and out of control. In the early days of that investigation, the military fought hard to prevent the photographs' public release (Preston, 2005):

Senior Pentagon officials have opposed the release of photographs and videotapes of the abuse of detainees at Abu Ghraib prison in Iraq, arguing that they would incite public opinion in the Muslim world and put the lives of U.S. soldiers and officials at risk, according to documents unsealed in federal court in New York.

General Richard Myers, the chairman of the Joint Chiefs of Staff, said in a statement in support of the Pentagon's case that he believed that "riots, violence and attacks by insurgents will result" if the images are released.

The papers were filed in U.S. District Court in Manhattan in a lawsuit by the American Civil Liberties Union, which is seeking to obtain under the Freedom of Information Act the release of 87 photographs and four videotapes taken at Abu Ghraib. The photographs were among those turned over to army investigators last year by Specialist Joseph Darby, a reservist who was posted at Abu Ghraib.

The documents show both the high level and the determination of the Pentagon officials who are engaged in the effort to block the disclosure of the images, and their alarm at the prospect the photographs might become public.

In this case, the military understood the harm that could come from bad press relations, but the entire event could have been avoided if such methods were prohibited from the start by virtue of adherence to a legal and ethical investigative interviewing framework.

A legal and ethical interviewing framework oriented toward rapport building is the bedrock of good investigative interviewing techniques. A competent framework will explicitly underpin the point that any torture (be it physical or psychological) does not make for a good investigation. Torture erodes trust, leads to unreliable information, results in acts of terrorist reciprocity, and even assists terrorist recruitment efforts.

A Terrorist May Have Different Needs than a Criminal

While terrorist groups may undertake criminal acts, the needs that drive or create a criminal (that is, his or her criminogenic needs) may be different from the needs of an individual terrorist or terrorist group. There can be similarities (e.g., both may join groups to be with friends and family, for protection, or to find a sense of community; both can be impelled by a sense of revenge; both can employ the same types of methods and weapons); however, their idiological needs and individual motivations/rationalizations can be quite dissimilar. For example, while many criminals may act out of a desire for monetary gain or to feed a drug habit, many individual terrorists act out of a sense that they are serving a higher cause or justice. It is fair to say that drug addicts are not committing their crimes because of a personal calling to preserve what they perceive as divine will and that burglars have no written doctrine supporting or justifying their cause. For this reason, while there are instruments designed to establish the criminogenic needs of criminals (such as the LSI-R[6]), they are not necessarily appropriate to assess the needs of terrorists.

Good interviewers should therefore attempt to understand their particular interviewee's psychosocial and personal needs on a case-by-case basis—without trying to lump all of the interviewees into a group using an inappropriate measure. This process can provide for engagement and can help build rapport. For example, an interviewee with a strong social need for friendships may enjoy frequent meetings or casual discussions with his interviewer; one with strong cognitive/cerebral needs may appreciate greater intellectual discussions with his or her interviewer about idiologies or philosophies. It is the interviewer's responsibility to ask questions, pay attention to the answers, and learn which is the case.

---

[6] The Level of Service Inventory—Revised (LSI-R) examines 10 criminogenic domains: criminal history, education/employment, financial, family relationships, accommodations, leisure and recreation, companions, substance use, emotional health, and attitudes/orientations. It is used to identify high-risk offenders and to determine what factors exist that cause one to be at high risk.

Respect Begets Respect

While it is almost a cliché, the point cannot be overstated: Respect begets respect. This is especially true when interviewing religiously inclined terrorists who perceive themselves to be on a higher moral plane than the interviewer and can therefore sometimes appear arrogant or reticent. In such cases, and most others, it is generally ineffective and imprudent to engage in any of the following:

Talking down to an interviewee
Being domineering toward an interviewee
Humiliating an interviewee
Yelling or screaming at an interviewee
Engaging in name-calling or heated arguments with an interviewee

Such tactics might get an interviewee to give information of varying quality in the short term, but they destroy trust in the longer term. As terrorism investigations tend to be long term with respect to investigations into individual actions and ongoing with respect to the investigations of groups, it makes good sense not to kill the proverbial "golden goose." The general adage of good interviewing should thus be adhered to: Respect and sincerity are valuable rapport-building tactics. Don't make it personal by making personal attacks.[7]

One word of caution: Some highly skilled terrorists may be charming, eloquent, charismatic, and yet manipulative. Interviewers should constantly check themselves or check on one another (using a team-based approach) to see if they are being manipulated into over-empathizing with the interviewee.

Interviewer–Interviewee Matching

In instances where the interviewee is a senior or respected figure within the terrorist organization, it may be operationally advantageous to use an investigator who matches in terms of background, age, and seniority. This strategy of matching/mirroring may build rapport and has been shown to work in other settings (e.g., counseling). However, this doesn't mean that someone with a different background would be at a disadvantage. Interviewers can always explain that they do not fully understand the interviewee's background/jargon and can use this as a premise to make clarifications, build rapport, and find out more. In an ideal situation, the interviewing team could comprise a combination of both matched and unmatched interviewers.

Attempt to Understand the Cultural Background of the Interviewee

The interviewer must make every effort to understand the background of the interviewee. This means understanding the things that are culturally important to the interviewee. Also, this will help to avoid any cultural faux pas. For example, the use of dogs or pigs to frighten a Muslim interviewee would be ineffective in building rapport. It should also be noted that in the Middle East, Asia, and other collectivistic cultures (as opposed to cultures that emphasize individualism), there is a high degree of respect for collectivistic ideals like family and community. Family and community wellness may be deemed more important than individual wellness. Hence, a threat to individual liberty may not work well as an interviewing strategy. On the other hand, explaining to the individual being interviewed that cooperating with the authorities means completing the interview earlier, so that he or she can return to his or her family,

---

[7] While these tactics may be satisfying on a visceral level, they are the hallmark of the inexperienced and unskilled.

may be fruitful (this should not be used as a threat, but as a motivation for the interviewee to cooperate). This idea itself is not new; multicultural therapy and counseling have for some time been recognized as important aspects of appreciating the cultural milieu of the client and motivating the client as part of an attempt to build rapport.

Understand Some of the Jargon or Language Used by Your Interviewee

While it is not realistic for the interviewer to understand the language that the terrorist uses, it is useful to have some working knowledge, especially when one is trying to make basic conversation.

Failure to understand common terms and basic concepts can lead to miscommunications as well as unnecessary work. For example, an understanding of the key concepts of jihad, bai'ah, hadith, ummah, halal, haram, and kafir when interviewing Muslim terrorists can be vital. In one case, an interviewer was told that a piece of information he wanted could be found in the Hadith (a compilation of the acts and sayings of the Prophet Mohammad). He mistook it to mean "hard disk." This led to a lot of work searching an associated hard disk, and nothing was found on it.

It can also leave the terrorist with the impression the interviewer is ignorant and may be easily deceived. This is not the impression that an interviewer wants to leave, accurate or not. By demonstrating a basic understanding of key terms and concepts and using them properly, the interviewer can gain credibility with the interviewee and build rapport.

Again, it may not be absolutely necessary to understand or speak the terrorist's language fluently (although this does help in many instances), but some basic understanding of the terms used is important.

Talk to the Individual, but Don't Forget the Group That's Behind Him

Terrorism is a group phenomenon. The group may be a physical one, but in today's virtual world it could be a virtual community. When radicalized by a physical group, the individual is socialized by other group members to attend training, mini operational missions, and religious educational presentations.

A recent trend is that of self-radicalization, which involves individuals who surf the Internet looking for jihadi Web sites or who join newsgroup discussions where like-minded radicals discuss jihad and other related issues. Therefore, it may be necessary to understand the group psychology that is operating. This point is sometimes missed by law-enforcement officers, who are more accustomed to dealing with criminals who operate as individuals (with the exception of those who deal with organized crime groups).

The terrorist is not only about himself. Terrorists also possess a unique identity within the group that is in many instances something deep and meaningful. For example, they may be the group's lead trainer, its expert in bomb making, or its deputy leader for financing. The individual's group role is worth exploring because there may be something emotionally rewarding or reinforcing about the role. This includes social companionship (through social contact in gatherings), the sense of mission and cause, the sense of importance the individual carries within the group, or the person's kinship (by blood or marriage) to other members in the group.

Asking about his or her role in the group may create greater rapport and understanding during the interview. It shows interest and gives interviewees a chance to talk about things that matter to them. And of course, it is also an excellent topic for developing further intelligence about the group, its organization, its activities, and its potential.

Attempt to Understand the Interviewee's Idiological Beliefs

To the average police or prisons officer, idiology is gobbledygook. But there is a need for interviewers to appreciate the idiological beliefs of their interviewees, whatever the nature of the idiology, be it religious, political, ethnic, or sociological. In current terrorism issues, which are religious-political, such idiologies could operate at two levels. The first is to understand the overall political tone, and the second is to appreciate and understand the secondary thinking and messaging behind such broad idiologies that may carry dangerous tones. An example of the first would be how the Jemmah Islamiyah group in South East Asia intends to set up a political conglomeration based on Islamic Shariyah law called the Daulah Islamiyah comprising several countries within South East Asia. This concept and its strong political overtones can be difficult to appreciate, as it is often foreign to the law enforcer who is used to hearing stories from offenders who commit crimes for greed, lust, or other motives. It is hard to appreciate why anyone or any group would be interested in setting up an Islamic Caliphate and the advantages of such an entity! To appreciate the second type of idiological belief, it may be useful to read Eidelson and Eidelson's article on "five dangerous ideas" (Eidelson and Eidelson, 2003) that influence the lives of individuals and groups and contribute to interpersonal and intergroup conflict. The Eidelsons argue that these are beliefs about vulnerability, injustice, distrust, superiority, and helplessness. Some understanding of the interviewee's idiology and grievances can be useful because it enables the interviewer to understand the frustrations of the interviewee. Moreover, if the interviewee feels particularly strong about any particular issue, for example, a perceived sense of injustice about how the person's group is being treated worldwide, this makes for excellent conversation and helps to build rapport further.

Expect Deception and Learn to Be a Better Lie Detector

Finally, interviewers should expect a high degree of deception—which is particularly challenging when terrorists can be charming, agreeable, and friendly (in fact, this was the dominant personality type noted). Many terrorist groups train their cell members to avoid questions when captured and to think about covering their tracks when moving from point A to point B. Therefore, interviewers should try to make themselves competent in the study of deception and the detection of deception. In worldwide studies, however (see Bond and Atoum, 2000), the general consensus appears to be that people all over the world, including law-enforcement officers, are poor at detecting deception and that training may not make much of a difference. However, Professor Aldert Vrij at the University of Portsmouth (United Kingdom) has argued that there may be ways to raise the chances of detecting deception, including combining verbal indicators of deception with nonverbal indicators (Vrij, 2000, 2004). Furthermore, there are growing numbers of new techniques to detect deception, although some are still experimental. They include the use of thermal imaging, brain fingerprinting, and functional magnetic resonance imaging, although the research on these techniques is still preliminary. Remembering that the individual always works in a group, it may also be useful to cross-check all information provided by one person against the information provided by the others or against the physical and forensic evidence obtained to ensure that any deception is quickly detected.

CONCLUSION

The purpose of this chapter has not been to throw in the towel with respect to nomothetic research of terrorist profiles. Rather, it is intended to serve as a wake-up call to Western investigators, examiners, and researchers who think that they are capable of operating with the vaguest understanding of Islamic terrorist organizations despite not speaking or reading Arabic, to say nothing of their overall lack of contact with terrorists and the cultures they come from, and an overall ignorance with respect to related histories. Without this basic context, it seems unlikely that we can perform adequately informed research and casework. A step in the right direction would be to shift from an antagonistic and torture-oriented model of interrogation that builds resentment to a rapport-oriented model of interviewing that gains actual intelligence. In this way, we can combat the stereotypical thinking that has misled our efforts thus far.

SUMMARY

Nomothetic terrorist profiling models are too often based on oversimplified and uninformed prejudices, not actual insight into criminal behavior itself. In fact, we know this problem all too well, which is why racial profiling was on track to be eradicated in the United States only a decade ago. However, racial profiling gained new life with the terrorist attacks organized against the United States on September 11, 2001. Subsequently, public attitudes toward racially profiling terrorists have softened as the sense of urgency regarding future terrorist attacks has increased.

Unfortunately, profilers in the United States are generally ignorant of Islamic beliefs, cultures, and customs. We do not comprehend the complexities and variations within the different Islamic communities, or even that there are complexities and variations. Consequently, we are literally among the last people on the planet who should be trying to impose any kind of research model, typology, or classification structure on non-U.S. terrorists.

Worldwide, actual experts on terrorism are few in number. There doesn't appear to be a consensus among experts on the definition of terrorism. Most research on the subject consists of "thought pieces" based on open-source documents. And many terrorism "experts" have never actually spoken to a terrorist or are reluctant to reveal who their sources are or at least vaguely where they are from.

As a consequence of terrorists' sanity, normalcy, and diversity, it is challenging to determine an accurate physical or ethnic profile of any terrorist type. However, it can be said uniformly that the torture of individual terrorists not only fails to produce good information, but also fuels the fire for generations of terrorists to come who will inevitably seek to retaliate. The best techniques for interviewing terrorists involve rapport-building strategies that include the adoption of ethical interviewing practices, learning about interviewee culture and language, encouraging mutual respect, and expecting deception.

Questions
1. True or False: It is easy to identify terrorists in the United States based on their ethnicity or manner of dress.
2. Give an example of a moral mandate.
3. What is the relationship between Singapore, terrorism, and the United States?
4. List three problems with current terrorism research.
5. Explain why, if torture does not work, it is still considered a viable intelligence-gathering option.

REFERENCES

Applebaum, A., 2005. The Torture Myth. The Washington Post, January 12, p. A21.

Bond, C.F., Jr., Atoum, A.O., 2000. International Deception. Personal and Social Psychology Bulletin 26, 385–395.

Borum, R., 2004. Psychology of Terrorism. University of South Florida, Tampa, FL.

Choudhury, C.A., 2006. Terrorists and Muslims: The Construction, Performance, and Regulation of Muslim Identities in the Post 9/11 United States. Rutgers Journal of Law and Religion 7, 8–48.

Crenshaw, M. (Ed.), 1994. Terrorism in Context. Pennsylvania State University Press, University Park, PA.

Davies, S., 2003. Profiling Terror. Ohio State Journal of Criminal Law 1, 45–101.

Drake, C.J.M., 1998. The Role of Ideology in Terrorists' Target Selection. Terrorism and Political Violence 10 (2), 53–85.

Eidelson, R.J., Eidelson, J.I., 2003. Dangerous Ideas: Five Beliefs That Propel Groups toward Conflict. American Psychology 58, 182–192.

Elegant, S., 2002. SINGAPORE: Strict Measures. Time (November 25).

Fisher, R., Geiselman, R.E., 1992. Memory-Enhancing Techniques for Investigative Interviewing: The Cognitive Interview. Charles C Thomas, Springfield, IL.

Gunaratna, R., 2003. Inside Al Qaeda: Global Network of Terror. Columbia University Press, New York, NY.

Hacker, F., 1976. Crusaders, Criminals, Crazies: Terror and Terrorism in Our Time. W. W. Norton, New York, NY.

Holmes, R., Holmes, S., 2001. Mass Murder in the United States. Prentice Hall, Upper Saddle River, NJ.

Madsen, J., 2004. The Rationale of Suicide Terrorism. Review of International Social Questions (September 8).

Milne, R., Bull, R., 1999. Investigative Interviewing: Psychology and Practice. Wiley, Chichester, England.

Ministry of Home Affairs (Singapore), 2003. The Jemaah Islamiyah Arrests and the Threat of Terrorism. Ministry of Home Affairs, Singapore.

Moghaddam, F.M., Marsella, A.J. (Eds.), 2004. Understanding Terrorism: Psychosocial Roots, Consequences, and Interventions. American Psychological Association, Washington, DC.

Preston, J., 2005. Pentagon Fights Release of Abu Ghraib Images. International Herald Tribune August 13.

Reynolds, A., 2007. So You Think a Woman Can't Carry out a Suicide Bombing? Terrorism, Homeland Security, and Gender Profiling: Legal Discrimination for National Security. William and Mary Journal of Women and the Law 13 (24), 667–699.

Silke, A., 2001. Devil You Know: Continuing Problems with Terrorism Research. Terrorism and Political Violence 13 (4), 1–14.

Skitka, L.J., Mullen, E., 2002. The "Dark Side" of Moral Conviction. Analyses of Social Issues and Public Policy 2, 35–41.

Taslitz, A., 2005. Racial Profiling, Terrorism, and Time. Pennsylvania State Law Review 109, 1181–1204.

Taylor, M., 1988. The Terrorist. Brassey's, London, England.

Victoroff, J., 2005. The Mind of the Terrorist: A Review and Critique of Psychological Approaches. Journal of Conflict Resolution 49, 3–42.

Vrij, A., 2000. Detecting Lies and Deceit: The Psychology of Lying and the Implications for Professional Practice. Wiley, Chichester, England.

Vrij, A., 2004. Invited Article: Why Professionals Fail to Catch Liars and How They Can Improve. Legal and Criminological Psychology 9, 159–181.

Williamson, T., 2005. Investigative Interviewing: Rights, Research and Regulation. Willan, Cullompton, Devon, England.

Threshold Assessment

Homicide of Armida Wiltsey

Body Found: Tuesday, November 14, 1978, at approximately 10:15 p.m. by Roy English, East Bay MUD Ranger.
Investigating Agency: Contra Costa County Sheriff's Department.

Report by:
Jodi Freeman, MCrim
Date: September, 20, 2010
jodi.freeman@rogers.com
Report for:
Brent Turvey
Forensic Solutions LLC
bturvey@corpus-delicti.com

PURPOSE

After reviewing the case materials, a determination was made by the examiner that insufficient investigation and forensic analysis have been performed in this case to warrant the rendering of a criminal profile. The purpose of this report is to provide investigative suggestions by means of a threshold assessment. A *threshold assessment* is an investigative report that reviews the initial physical evidence of crime scene related behavior, victimology, and crime scene characteristics for a particular unsolved crime, or a series of potentially related unsolved crimes, in order to provide immediate investigative direction (Turvey, 2008). A threshold assessment involves the employment of scientific principles and knowledge, including Locard's exchange principle, critical thinking, analytical logic, and evidence dynamics (Turvey, 2008).

> *Locard's exchange principle,* a cornerstone of the forensic sciences, states that when an offender comes in contact with a location or another person, an exchange of evidence occurs (Saferstein, 1998).
> *Critical thinking* may be described as the process of actively and skillfully conceptualizing, applying, analyzing, synthesizing, or evaluating information gathered from, or generated by, observation, experience, reflection, reasoning, or communication, as a guide to belief and action (Turvey, 2008).

Analytical logic involves the ability to study a crime scene and any subsequent documentation and arrive at logical, well-reasoned conclusions. This ideally involves the formation of hypotheses that can be tested against the established facts of the case. The end result of this process is that conclusions may be drawn that follow naturally from the evidence that is present. Such conclusions may be referred to as deductions (Thornton, 1997).

Evidence dynamics refers to any influence that changes, relocates, obscures, or obliterates physical evidence, regardless of intent. Evidence dynamics are at work even before the crime happens and also during the interval that begins as physical evidence is being transferred or created (Chisum and Turvey, 2007).

This threshold assessment is limited to the assumption that the evidence and investigative reports at the time of examination were correct. As the evidence changes, so will the results provided in this report. Should any new information be provided, the findings in this threshold assessment must be reconsidered.

CASE MATERIALS

The examiner rendered this threshold assessment based on a careful examination of case evidence. This evidence included, but was not limited to, the following:

- Contra Costa County police interviews
- Contra Costa County police reports and evidence examination reports
- Contra Costa County witness statements and line-ups
- Contra Costa County crime scene photos
- Contra Costa County crime scene sketches
- Contra Costa County bloodhound tracking report
- Autopsy report and photos of Armida Wiltsey
- Lafayette Reservoir map and brochure
- Media report "Jogger is Strangled, Raped at Reservoir"

BACKGROUND

According to the Contra Costa County police reports, the body of Armida Wiltsey (40, WF) was found laying in the southeast corner of the Lafayette Reservoir, at approximately 10:15 p.m. on Tuesday, November 14, 1978, by Roy English, an East Bay MUD ranger.

The victim was found 40 yards off of the main jogging trail, lying in a brushy area.

Crime scene photos indicate that the victim was found partially clothed, lying on her left side in a curled-up position. The victim was wearing a blue jogging shirt and blue jogging shoes. Her blue jogging pants and white underwear were found lying partially on top of the victim and partially to her side and her jogging shirt was lifted up, exposing her breasts. Crime scene and autopsy photos evidence fecal matter on the victim's buttocks and clothing. Abrasion marks on the victim's face are also evident, along with pressure marks on her neck and wrists. According to Armida Wiltsey's autopsy report, the cause of death was asphyxiation due to neck trauma.

According to police interviews and victimological inquires, Armida Wiltsey was a dedicated mother who spent the majority of her time with her family and involved with her son's school. On the day of the homicide, the victim left her residence at some point before 9:00 a.m. and was reported missing by her neighbor,

Larry Busboom, at approximately 7:00 p.m. after she failed to pick up her son from school. The victim's vehicle was subsequently located across the street from the main entrance of the Lafayette Reservoir, commencing a search of the area. Armida Wiltsey's body was discovered at approximately 10:15 p.m. with the assistance of three dog-handlers.

TIMELINE

The following timeline information was taken from Contra Costa County police interviews and reports.

Tuesday, November 14, 1978

At some point before 9:00 a.m., Armida Wiltsey helped her husband, Boyd Wiltsey, pack for a business trip. That morning, she told her husband that she was concerned about taking their son to school. Armida Wiltsey left her residence and dropped her son off at school before driving to the Lafayette Reservoir to go for a jog.

At approximately 9:00 a.m., Armida Wiltsey's vehicle, a 1975 Datsun, was seen by Gail Overra across the street from the Lafayette Reservoir, where it was eventually discovered. It is estimated from police interviews with witnesses in the area that the victim was "pulled into the bushes" between 9:30 a.m. and 9:45 a.m.

At 12:00 p.m., Armida Wiltsey failed to pick up her son from school, which was routine for her to do. At 7:00 p.m., the victim was reported missing by her neighbor, Larry Busboom. At some point between 7:00 p.m. and 9:50 p.m., police discovered the victim's vehicle across the road from the Lafayette Reservoir. At 9:50 p.m., a search of the reservoir commenced, involving a search by foot, vehicle, helicopter and bloodhounds. At approximately 10:15 p.m., the body of Armida Wiltsey was found by Roy English, an East Bay MUD Ranger.

Wednesday, November 15, 1978

At approximately 12:30 a.m., police met the victim's husband, Boyd Wiltsey, at the airport to inform him that his wife was dead.

VICTIMOLOGY

Victimology is the process of investigating, establishing and evaluating victim traits and history: learning everything there is to know about victims, who they were, where and how they spent their time, and how they lived their life (Petherick and Turvey, 2009). A victimology requires an extensive examination of the victim's lifestyle exposure and situational exposure, as well as knowledge of the underlying sociological theories that contribute to these exposures.

Name: Armida Wiltsey
Race: Caucasian
Ethnicity: Hispanic
Sex: Female
D.O.B: October 29, 1938
Age: 40
Height: 62 inches
Weight: 105 lbs.

Eye Color: Brown
Hair Color: Black
Family legend:
Armida Wiltsey: Victim (40)
Boyd Wiltsey: Victim's husband
Name Unknown: Victim's biological son (10)
Daniel Boyd Wiltsey: Victim's stepson (19)
Michael Wiltsey: Victim's stepson (23)
Residence location: 4169 Cora Lee Lane, Lafayette, Contra Costa, California. USA.
Residence type and description: Armida Wiltsey lived with her husband, Boyd Wiltsey, and their 10-year-old son at their residence located at 4169 Cora Lee Lane in Lafayette, California. The residence type is unknown but police interviews suggest that the Wiltseys lived in an upper-middle class residence. This is evident by the employment of a live-in nanny, Julie Doherty (18, WF), who lived with the family at their residence, providing light housework and babysitting for their 10-year-old son.

The criminal history of the residence and surrounding neighborhood is unknown.

Family history: Armida Wiltsey was married to Boyd Wiltsey. The length of their marriage is unknown. According to the police interview with Boyd Wiltsey, he had no problems with his wife and they had no history of major arguments or disagreements. The last time he saw Armida Wiltsey was on the morning of the homicide, before he left for his business trip. Boyd Wiltsey frequently traveled for business.

Armida Wiltsey and Boyd Wiltsey had a 10-year-old son together. Boyd Wiltsey also had two sons from a pervious marriage, Daniel Boyd Wiltsey and Michael Wiltsey. Michael Wiltsey was living in Oregon at the time of the homicide. It is unknown where Daniel Boyd Wiltsey was residing. According to the police interview with Julie Doherty, Daniel Wiltsey had a drug problem. The extent of his drug problem is unknown.

Social history: Armida Wiltsey was a homemaker. She did not work outside of the home and according to Julie Doherty, her life was devoted to her family and spending time with friends in the area. Her activities included participating in the P.T.A at her son's school and volunteering for the school library.

Armida Wiltsey jogged 3–5 mornings a week at the Lafayette Reservoir. She had been jogging for approximately 3–4 months prior to the homicide and had started her jogging program gradually.

According to police interviews with Julie Doherty, Susan Todd, Gail Overra, Sandy Busboom, and Kim DeStPaer, Armida Wiltsey had no male friends other than her husband and no problems in her marriage to Boyd Wiltsey. However, an anonymous letter received by the Oakland Police Department stated that Guy Icalaolle had an affair with Armida Wiltsey and was responsible for the homicide.

Criminal history: Armida Wiltsey's criminal history is unknown.

Drug and alcohol use: There is no known evidence of drug or alcohol use by the victim. According to Armida Wiltsey's autopsy report, there were no substances in the victim's body at the time of the homicide.

According to Julie Doherty, Daniel Wiltsey had a drug problem. The extent of his drug problem is unknown.

Medical and mental health history: Armida Wiltsey's autopsy report indicates that she was generally in good health and her body was well developed and nourished. According to the victim's neighbor, Larry Busboom, she was seeing a doctor for "female problems." According to the victim's medical records, she had last seen her physician two weeks prior to the homicide for a vaginal infection.

Armida Wiltsey had no known mental health issues.

VICTIM EXPOSURE

Victim lifestyle exposure: *Lifestyle exposure* refers to the frequency of potentially harmful elements that exist in a victim's everyday life as a consequence of biological and environmental factors, as well as past choices (adapted from Petherick and Turvey, 2009).

Armida Wiltsey was a *low-exposure victim* who was rarely exposed to the possibility of suffering harm or loss (adapted from Petherick and Turvey, 2009). This is due to the following circumstances:

1. The victim's daily routine revolved around her family, specifically her son. There is no evidence to suggest that she engaged in activities outside of her family interests, except for her routine jogging.
2. The victim's family and friends knew her daily jogging routine and she was accountable to her husband, son, friends, and live-in babysitter. These individuals acted as capable guardians who would have noticed if she had gone missing (Petherick and Turvey, 2009).
3. The victim's autopsy report reveals that she was healthy, well nourished and not suffering from any underlying medical issues.
4. The victim did not have any issues with anyone around her. There is evidence to suggest that she may have had an affair but the validity of this information has not been established.
5. The victim's stepson, Daniel Boyd Wiltsey, had a drug problem at the time of the homicide. However, it is unknown whether the victim was routinely exposed to this behavior. This factor would increase the lifestyle exposure of the victim.

Victim situational exposure: *Situational exposure* refers to the amount of actual exposure or vulnerability experienced by the victim to harm, resulting from the environment and personal traits, at the time of victimization (Petherick and Turvey, 2009).

Armida Wiltsey was a *low-medium exposure victim* who was vulnerable to some harm or loss immediately prior to victimization (adapted from Petherick and Turvey, 2009). This is due to the following circumstances:

1. The homicide occurred during daylight hours and the reservoir was populated with joggers.
2. The victim did not have auditory interference and was alert to her surroundings.
3. The victim's autopsy report reveals that she tested negative for alcohol and drugs. The victim was not under the influence of substances at the time of the homicide.
4. The reservoir was located in a secluded area with dense shrubbery. This environment increased the victim's situational exposure but did not completely remove the capable guardianship of other joggers in the area (Petherick and Turvey, 2009). This is evident in police interviews that state that other joggers witnessed individuals in the bushes on the day of the homicide.
5. The victim was jogging alone at the time of the homicide. This factor increased the situational exposure of the victim.
6. There were no security features at the park and the entry gate was left open. This factor increased the situational exposure of the victim.

CRIME RECONSTRUCTION

A *crime reconstruction* is the determination of the actions and events surrounding the commission of a crime. A reconstruction may be accomplished by using the statements of witnesses, the confession of a suspect, the statement of a living victim, or by the examination and interpretation of physical evidence (Chisum and Turvey, 2007).

Findings

The available physical evidence supports the following sequence of events that occurred on Tuesday, November 14, 1978. Should any new information be provided, this sequence of events and the subsequent findings must be reconsidered.

1. At some point before 9:00 a.m., Armida Wiltsey left her residence and drove to the Lafayette Reservoir.
2. At some point before the attack on Armida Wiltsey, the evidence suggests that the victim walked by the portable toilets at the Lafayette Reservoir.
3. At some point after 9:00 a.m., the offender acquired the victim and immediately covered her mouth with his hand.
4. At some point after the offender acquired the victim, she engaged in physical resistance.
5. At some point after the victim resisted, the offender manually strangled the victim, causing her to lose consciousness and die. It is unknown whether the victim died immediately after the strangulation. The evidence suggests that this attack occurred in an area between the jogging path and the disposal site.
6. At some point after the victim was unconscious, her hands were bound.
7. At some point after the victim was unconscious, she was anally penetrated. The evidence suggests that the offender removed the victim's pants and underwear, pulled up the victim's shirt, and anally penetrated the victim while she was lying on her left side.
8. At some point after the offender penetrated the victim, the offender wiped off the object used in the penetration.
9. At some point after the attack, the offender removed the ligatures.
10. At some point after the offender removed the ligatures, the evidence suggests that the offender took the ligatures from the crime scene.
11. At some point after the attack, the offender carried the body of the victim to the disposal site and placed her there.

Discussion

1. At some point before 9:00 a.m., Armida Wiltsey left her residence and drove to the Lafayette Reservoir. This is supported by the following facts:
    a) According to the police interview with Boyd Wiltsey, Armida Wiltsey was at home that morning.
    b) According to the police interview with Gail Overra, Armida Wiltsey's vehicle was seen across from the Lafayette Reservoir at approximately 9:00 a.m.
2. At some point before the attack on Armida Wiltsey, the evidence suggests that the victim walked by the portable toilets at the Lafayette Reservoir. This is supported by the following facts:
    a) The bloodhound search for the victim started at the victim's car and proceeded to the portable toilets before locating the victim's body.
    b) Crime scene photos reveal sand on the bottom of the victim's shoes and footprints in the sand near the portable toilets at the reservoir. The footprints match the pattern of the victim's shoes. This suggests that the victim walked in this area, however, the footprints cannot be individuated (Chisum and Turvey, 2007). It is unknown whether the footprints were left on the day of the homicide.
3. At some point after 9:00 a.m., the offender acquired the victim and immediately covered her mouth with his hand. This is supported by the following facts:
    a) According to police interviews, witnesses at the Lafayette Reservoir did not report hearing any screams or unusual noises. This suggests the offender immediately covered the victim's mouth to functionally prevent her from screaming.

b) Autopsy photos reveal injuries to the victim's mouth that are consistent with control-oriented force. They also reveal a contusion on the victim's lower lip in the shape of a finger. This injury indicates that the victim was struggling with the offender upon the initial application of force.

4. At some point after the offender acquired the victim, she engaged in physical resistance. This is supported by the following fact:
   a) Criminalistic reports and autopsy photos reveal debris, including fibers, tissue and traces of blood, under the victim's fingernails. This evidence suggests that that victim scratched the offender.

5. At some point after the victim resisted, the offender manually strangled the victim, causing her to lose consciousness and die. It is unknown whether the victim died immediately after the strangulation. The evidence suggests that this attack occurred in an area between the jogging path and the disposal site. This is supported by the following facts:
   a) The offender manually strangled the victim, causing her to lose consciousness and die.
      i. The victim's autopsy report reveals that the cause of death was asphyxiation due to neck trauma.
      ii. Autopsy photos evidence hand marks on the victim neck.
      iii. Autopsy photos reveal that the victim's blood was not pumping after the strangulation, indicating that she did not regain consciousness.
   b) The evidence suggests that the attack occurred in an area between the path and the disposal site.
      i. The reservoir was populated with joggers on the day of the homicide but the crime was not witnessed. This suggests that the attack did not occur on the jogging path.
      ii. The victim was moved to the disposal site after the attack (See *Crime reconstruction section 11* of report).

6. At some point after the victim was unconscious, her hands were bound. This is supported by the following facts:
   a) Autopsy photos reveal ligature marks on the victim's wrists.
   b) Autopsy photos reveal that the ligature marks do not contain tearing of the skin. This indicates that the victim was unconscious (or deceased) at the time she was bound.

7. At some point after the victim was unconscious, she was anally penetrated. The evidence suggests that the offender removed the victim's pants and underwear, pulled up the victim's shirt and anally penetrated the victim while she was lying on her left side. This is supported by the following facts:
   a) The offender removed the victim's pants and underwear.
      i. Crime scene photos evidence the victim naked from the waist down and partially covered with her jogging pants and underwear.
   b) The victim was anally penetrated.
      i. The victim was found naked from the waist down. This suggests that a sexual act took place.
      ii. Police reports and crime scene photos evidence fecal matter at the crime scene, on both the victim's buttocks and clothing. The presence and location of the fecal matter indicate anal penetration occurred.
      iii. The autopsy report reveals a linear tear of the victim's perineum. This injury is consistent with anal penetration.
   c) The evidence suggests that the victim was lying on her left side at the time she was penetrated.
      i. Autopsy photos evidence scratch marks and abrasions on the victim's left side. There is an absence of similar injuries anywhere else on the victim's body.

8. At some point after the offender penetrated the victim, the offender wiped off the object used in the penetration. This is supported by the following fact:
   a) Crime scene photos evidence fecal matter on the clothing of the victim. This suggests that the offender wiped off the material from the object used to penetrate the victim.

9. At some point after the attack, the offender removed the ligatures. This is supported by the following fact:

   a) Crime scene and autopsy photos evidence the victim without ligatures.

10. At some point after the offender removed the ligatures, the evidence suggests that the offender took the ligatures from the crime scene. However, this cannot be concluded until the twine found at the crime scene is further examined.

11. At some point after the attack, the offender carried the body of the victim to the disposal site and placed her there. This is supported by the following facts:

    a) Crime scene photos evidence the victim in a heavily bushed area that would significantly minimize the ability of the offender to sexually assault her in this location. The victim's autopsy report also reveals injuries that are inconsistent with the assault occurring at the disposal site. The victim would have injuries present on both sides of her body.

    b) The victim's injuries, including multiple scratch-type abrasions, are consistent with the victim being carried through the bushes to the disposal site.

    c) Crime scene photos reveal the victim's pants were caught above her on a branch, suggesting the victim was placed at the disposal site.

    d) Crime scene photos reveal a lack of drag marks or transfer material present on the victim's clothing, hair, and body, eliminating the possibility that she was dragged to the disposal site.

CRIME SCENE CHARACTERISTICS

Location type: The crime scene existed in an outdoor environment. The victim's body was found outside in a brushy area, exposed to the elements of nature. This is evident in crime scene photos, police sketches and police investigative reports.

Location of the scene: The crime scene in this case was in the southeast corner of the Lafayette Reservoir, located at 3949 Mount Diablo Road in Costa County, California. According to police reports, the victim's body was found 40 yards from the jogging path on the hillside, enclosed in brushy vegetation. The path was frequently used by joggers and had multiple access points, including foot trails from the parking lot and jeep trails from residential neighborhoods. The temperature on the evening of the homicide was 40–50 degrees Fahrenheit, as evidenced in the police reports and crime scene photos that reveal frost on the ground. The criminal history of the location is unknown.

Crime scene type: The known crime scene in this case was the *disposal site*[1] of the body. Crime scene and autopsy photos strongly suggest that the victim was moved to this location (see *Crime reconstruction* section of report). The location of the *primary crime scene*[2] is unknown. The primary crime scene cannot be established without a further search for evidence. This search should focus on reviewing the crime scene photos in an attempt to locate transfer evidence or fecal matter in the surrounding area, as well as clothing or other evidence that indicate the victim's presence in a specific location. The investigation should also focus on the victim's clothing in an attempt to locate transfer evidence that may suggest that she was assaulted in another location.

---

[1] *Disposal site* is used to describe a crime scene where a body is found (Turvey, 2008).

[2] *Primary crime scene* is the location where the offender engaged in the majority of his or her attack/assault upon the victim or victims (Turvey, 2008).

Victim selection: *Victim selection* refers to the process by which an offender intentionally chooses or targets a victim (Turvey, 2008). In this case, the evidence and location of the crime suggest that a prior relationship between the victim and offender was not necessary for the commission of the crime (see *Knowledge of victim* section of this report). The victim was an *opportunistic victim,* chosen based on availability and opportunity.

Victim location: *Victim location* refers to the characteristics of the victim's location prior to the *point of contact.* In this case, the victim location shares the same characteristics as the location of the scene (see *Location of the scene* section of report).

Point of contact: *Point of contact* refers to the precise location where the offender first approached or acquired the victim (Turvey, 2008). The point of contact in this case is unknown. Further investigation into the location of the primary crime scene may provide investigators with knowledge of where the victim was first contacted (refer to *Crime scene type* section of report).

Method of approach: *Method of approach* refers to the offender's strategy for getting close to a victim (Turvey, 2008). In this case, it is unknown whether the offender approached the victim with a surprise approach or a con approach. Crime scene photos suggest that the brushy area around the jogging trail may have provided the offender with the opportunity to surprise the victim at a moment of vulnerability. However, the offender may have also gained the victim's trust by use of deception. The method of approach cannot be inferred from the available evidence.

Method of attack: *Method of attack* refers to the offender's mechanism for initially overpowering a victim after making the approach. It is appropriate to describe a method of attack in terms of the weapon and the nature of the force involved (Turvey, 2008). In this case, the offender initially overpowered the victim by applying control-oriented force to her mouth (see *Use of force* section of report). Armida Wiltsey's autopsy photos evidence injuries to her mouth, consistent with force used to prevent the victim from screaming. A contusion is also evident near her lip that indicates she was struggling during this initial application of force.

Use of force: *Use of force* refers to the amount of force used by the offender during an attack (Turvey, 2008). The amount of force used against the victim in this case may be characterized as *lethal-force.*[3] The strangulation of the victim involved physically aggressive behavior that was sufficient to kill the victim. The strangulation may also be referred to as *control-oriented force,*[4] used to restrict the victim's movements by rendering her unconscious. The offender also engaged in control-oriented force by binding the victim's hands together to prevent movement and delay her escape. Control-oriented force was also applied to the victim's mouth to prevent her from screaming, and further used to move the victim from the initial point of contact to the location at which the attack occurred. It is the opinion of the examiner that the control-oriented behavior of the offender was functional.

Methods of control: *Method of control* refers to the means an offender uses to manipulate, regulate, restrain, and subdue victim behavior of any kind throughout the offense (Turvey, 2008). The offender applied multiple levels of control-oriented force to the victim during the commission of the offense (see *Use of force* section of report).

---

[3] *Lethal force* is a term used to describe physically aggressive behavior that is sufficient to kill. It includes the intentional infliction of injuries to vital areas such as the head, heart, or neck. It may involve a weapon, chemical, or bare hands (Turvey, 2008).

[4] *Control-oriented force* is a term used to describe the physically aggressive behavior that is intended to restrict victim movement.

Use of weapons: According to Armida Wiltsey's autopsy report, the victim died of asphyxiation due to neck trauma. The absences of gunshot wounds or other sharp force injuries indicate that no weapons were used in the commission of this crime.

Victim response: *Victim response* refers to the victim's reaction to offender behavior (adapted from Turvey, 2008). The criminalist report suggests that the victim engaged in physical resistance by scratching the offender. Traces of blood and debris found under the victim's fingernails were noted in the report and material under the victim's fingernails is also visible in autopsy photos. The contusion under the victim's mouth also suggests that the victim resisted the offender at the time her mouth was covered.

Verbal behavior: The injuries to the victim's mouth indicate that the offender applied control-oriented force to prevent her from screaming. This suggests that the verbal behavior of the victim was limited. The extent of the verbal behavior of the offender is unknown but police reports state that witnesses did not hear voices or unusual noises in the area.

Sexual acts: A *sexual act* is any offender behavior involving sexual organs, sexual apparatus, or sexualized objects (Turvey, 2008). Crime scene photos reveal that the victim was found naked from the waist down, suggesting that the offender engaged in a sexual act during the commission of the crime. The fecal matter found on the victim's clothing and buttocks indicates that the victim was anally penetrated (see *Crime reconstruction* section of report).

Time: The exact amount of time the offender spent with the victim is unknown.

Multiple offenders: There is no evidence in this case to suggest that multiple offenders were involved in the commission of this crime.

Evidence of planning: The extent of offender *planning* may be determined by assessing whether or not the offender possessed the means for the commission of the crime (Turvey, 2008). In this case, it is the opinion of the examiner that the offense was planned. This is supported by the fact that the offender chose a location which he or she knew would contain potential victims, the offender chose a location in which an offense could be carried out in a hidden area, the offender brought ligatures to the crime scene and the area itself was secluded and required offender knowledge (see *Knowledge of crime scene* section of report).

Opportunistic elements: *Opportunistic elements* refer to any unplanned elements that the offender seized on for inclusion in an offense (Turvey, 2008). The examiner found no evidence of the use of opportunistic elements in the commission of this crime, except the victim (see *Knowledge of victim* section of report).

Precautionary acts: *Precautionary acts* refer to behaviors that an offender commits before, during, or after an offense that are consciously intended to confuse, hamper, or defeat investigative or forensic efforts for the purpose of concealing the offender's identity, connection to the crime, or the crime itself (Turvey, 2008). It is the opinion of the examiner that the offender committed precautionary acts during the commission of the crime. This opinion is supported by the following facts:

1. The body of the victim was moved after she was attacked (see *Crime reconstruction* section of report). This suggests that the offender wanted to delay the investigative effort to find the body and draw investigative efforts away from the primary crime scene.
2. The offender removed the ligatures on the hands of the victim (see *Crime reconstruction* section of report). This suggests that the offender removed evidence that would link him or her to the crime scene.
3. The offender took the object used to penetrate the victim (see *Crime reconstruction* section of report).

4. The offender engaged in control-oriented force to prevent victim resistance. These behaviors intended to conceal the offender's identity by preventing individuals in the area from witnessing the crime. These behaviors included the manual strangulation of the victim to render her unconscious, the force applied to the victim's mouth to prevent her from screaming, and the ligatures used to bind the victim's hands to delay her escape.

Missing items: The only known items taken from the crime scene were the ligatures used to bind the victim's hands and the object that the offender used to penetrate the victim with (unless the offender's penis was used to penetrate the victim). It is the opinion of the examiner that the ligatures, and possible object, were evidentiary items, taken as a precautionary act.

The body: The body of the victim was carried to the disposal site at some point after the attack (see *Crime reconstruction* section of report).

Evidence of staging: *Staging* refers to a crime scene in which the offender has purposely altered evidence so as to mislead authorities or redirect the investigation (Turvey, 2008). It is the opinion of the examiner that there is no evidence to indicate that the offender attempted to stage this crime scene.

MOTIVATION

It is the opinion of the examiner that there are crime scene behaviors that support both a *power-reassurance* and *power-assertive* motivation. The basis for this opinion resides in the consideration of the following:

1. A *power-reassurance* motive is evidenced by crime scene behaviors that are intended to restore the offender's self-confidence or self-worth through the use of low-aggression means (Turvey, 2008).
   a. The lack of victim injuries is consistent with a power-reassurance motive.
   b. The placement of the victim in the disposal site is consistent with a power-reassurance motive.
2. A *power-assertive* motive is evidenced by crime scene behaviors that intend to restore the offender's self-confidence or self-worth through the use of moderate to high aggression means (Turvey, 2008).
   a. The sexual behavior the offender engaged in with the victim reflects a power-assertive motive.
   b. The victim was unconscious and therefore not involved in the sexual act. The offender forced the victim to submit to the offender's sexual behavior. This behavior is consistent with a power-assertive motive.
3. The examiner can eliminate the possibility of an *anger retaliatory*[5] motivation. The crime scene behaviors and victim injuries lack consistency with this motivation. The victim's injures would have evidenced high levels of force and *overkill*[6] and the crime scene behaviors would have evidenced anger.
4. The examiner can eliminate the possibility of a *sadistic motivation.*[7] This can be supported by the fact that there was a lack of torture inflicted on the victim. The autopsy photos reveal a lack of injuries consistent with torture and the victim was unconscious at the time of the sexual attack, eliminating a necessary component of sadism (Turvey, 2008). The crime also lacked a controlled environment. The reservoir was populated with joggers who would have witnessed elements of torture, including verbal resistance of the victim. The amount of time the offender would have to engage in sadistic behavior would be minimal at that location.

---

[5] *Anger retaliatory* motive is evidenced by crime scene behaviors that indicate a great deal of rage, either toward a specific person, group, or institution, or a symbol of either (Turvey, 2008).
[6] *Overkill* is injury beyond that needed to cause death. It involves the repeated infliction of injury subsequent to the application of lethal force (Turvey, 2008).
[7] *Sadistic* crime scene behaviors are those that evidence offender sexual gratification from victim pain and suffering (Turvey, 2008).

5. The examiner can eliminate the possibility of a *profit motivation*.[8] This can be supported by the fact that the offender did not take any items of value from the victim. Police reports reveal the victim was found with her ring, earrings, and car keys.

OFFENDER CHARACTERISTICS

Knowledge of Crime Scene

It is the opinion of the examiner that the offender had knowledge of the crime scene prior to the homicide. Local knowledge of the crime scene was not required, but the evidence suggests that the offender had, at the very minimum, knowledge of the existence of the location. This is supported by the fact that the Lafayette Reservoir is not a location that can be seen from the open road, suggesting that the offender had knowledge of the location and engaged in pre-surveillance. The level of planning associated with this offense suggests that it is unlikely that it was opportunistic or accidental (see *Evidence of planning* section of report).

A series of *contradictory acts* were also evident that increased the offender's likelihood of drawing the attention of the authorities and being identified during or subsequent to the crime (Turvey, 2008). The following contradictory acts were present:

1. The offense took place during daylight hours, increasing the likelihood that the victim or other witnesses in the area would identify the offender.
2. The offender acquired the victim while she was out for a routine jog. The victim was accountable to her capable guardians who would have noticed if she was gone for an extended period of time.

Familiarity with the crime scene increased the confidence level of the offender to the point at which the offender was comfortable enough to increase the level of risk associated with the crime, as evidenced by the offender's contradictory acts.

Knowledge of Victim

It is the opinion of the examiner that a prior relationship between the offender and the victim was not necessary for the commission of this crime. The crime took place in an area that was routinely populated with individuals, increasing the number of accessible victims. There is no further evidence to suggest that pre-surveillance of the victim occurred prior to the homicide.

Knowledge of Methods and Materials

It is the opinion of the examiner that the offender had both knowledge of the methods and materials that were used in the commission of this crime. Knowledge of materials was demonstrated by the fact that the offender brought the ligatures to the crime scene and possessed the physical ability and confidence to use them. However, no special skills or abilities were required to commit this crime (see *Evidence of criminal skill* section of report). Knowledge of methods is demonstrated by the fact that the offender knew how to control the victim and carry out the offense.

---

[8] *Profit-oriented* behaviors include those that service material or personal gain (Turvey, 2008).

Evidence of Criminal Skill

Criminal skill may be thought of as a function of the offender's *planning* and their *precautionary acts* (Turvey, 2008). It is the opinion of the examiner that the offender had a *medium level of criminal skill*. This is demonstrated by the fact that the offender was skilled in the victim takedown, which resulted in little injury to the victim, suggesting that the offender had engaged in this type of behavior previously. The offender also possessed the criminal skill necessary to move the body to a hidden location and remove the ligatures on the victim's wrists.

The examiner cannot conclude the offender *lacked forensic awareness* because there is no evidence to indicate that the twine found at the crime scene was left by the offender. If the twine found at the scene was used in the crime, this may indicate a lack of forensic awareness or interruption. If the twine was not used in the crime, this may indicate forensic awareness because the offender took the ligatures from the crime scene to remove evidence that may have linked the offender to the crime. No other evidence was found that addressed the issue of forensic awareness.

Physical Characteristics

It is the opinion of the examiner that the offender possessed a level of physical strength necessary to carry the victim's body. The evidence indicates that the body of the victim was placed at the disposal site at some point after the attack (see *Crime reconstruction* section of report).

INVESTIGATIVE SUGGESTIONS

The following is a list of suggestions for further investigating and establishing the facts of this case:

1. A thorough examination of the crime scene photos and the photos of the surrounding area should be conducted in an attempt to locate the primary crime scene. Investigators should focus their attention on the photos in an attempt to locate possible fecal matter, transfer evidence, or other evidence that may indicate victim–offender interaction occurred. This should include:
   a. Photos of the location where the victim's earring was discovered.
   b. Photos of the area surrounding the portable toilets. According to the police reports, the bloodhounds traveled from the victim's car to portable toilets in the reservoir before locating the victim's body. This evidence coupled with the footprints in the area suggests that the victim was in this area prior to the attack. This may provide evidence that will assist in the location of the primary crime scene or the point of contact.
   c. The tissues found in the victim's vehicle should be tested in comparison to the tissues found in the reservoir.
2. The clothing of the victim should be examined in an attempt to locate transfer evidence that may suggest the location at which the offender acquired or assaulted the victim.
3. Thorough interviews should be conducted with the family and friends of the victim to establish a more thorough victimology. Victimological inquiries should include the following:
   a. The nature of the victim's relationships with other males.
   b. The nature of Daniel Wiltsey's drug problem.
   c. The reason why the victim was worried about taking her 10-year-old son to school on the day of the homicide.
   d. The criminal and mental history of Armida Wiltsey.

4. DNA tests should be conducted on the victim's fingernails clippings. John Patty examined fingernail clippings from the victim's hands and noted debris, including fibers and tissue. On two of the fingernails from the victim's right hand, he saw a very thin trace of blood.
5. DNA test should be conducted on the hairs found on the victim's clothing.
6. The vaginal and anal swabs of the victim should be tested for epithelial cells to indicate whether the victim was penetrated with a penis.
7. The fecal matter on the victim's clothing should be tested for transfer evidence and DNA.
8. Tests should be conducted on the twine found at the crime scene to determine whether the twine was used in the commission of the crime. This includes testing the twine for the victim's DNA and establishing whether the twine matches the victim's injuries evidenced in the autopsy photos.
9. Crime statistics from the Lafayette Reservoir and other parks in the area should be reviewed.
10. Offenders with a similar *modus operandi*[9] should be reviewed. These crimes include, but are not limited to, kidnapping, sexual assaults, and muggings.

The examiner is available for discussion of these suggestions.

Jodi Freeman, MCrim

REFERENCES

Chisum, J., Turvey, B., 2007. Crime Reconstruction. Elsevier, San Diego, CA.

Petherick, W., Turvey, B., 2009. Forensic Victimology. Elsevier, San Diego, CA.

Saferstein, R., 1998. Criminalistics: An Introduction to Forensic Science, sixth edition. Prentice-Hall, New York, NY.

Thornton, J.I., 1997. The General Assumptions and Rationale of Forensic Identification. In: Faigman, D.L., Kaye, D.H., Saks, M.J., Sanders, J. (Eds.), Modern Scientific Evidence: The Law and Science of Expert Testimony, vol. 2. West, St. Paul, MN.

Turvey, B., 2008. Criminal Profiling: An Introduction to Behavioral Evidence Analysis, third edition. Academic Press, London, England.

---

[9] *Modus operandi* is the offender's method of operation, consisting of their habits, techniques, and peculiarities of behavior (Turvey, 2008).

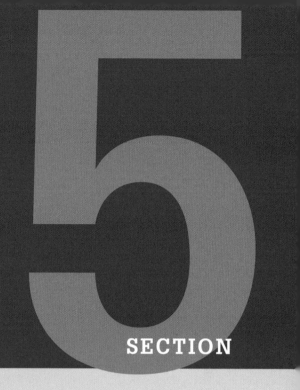

SECTION

5

Professional Issues

CHAPTER 24

Ethics and the Criminal Profiler

Brent E. Turvey

We have to condemn publicly the very idea that some people have the right to repress others. In keeping silent about evil, in burying it so deep within us that no sign of it appears on the surface, we are implanting it, and it will rise up a thousand-fold in the future. To stand up for truth is nothing. For truth you have to sit in jail.

—Alexsandr Solzhenitsyn, *The Gulag Archipelago*

CONTENTS

KEY TERMS

Comfortainment	Forensic fraud	Pseudoexperts
Dissemblers	Murdertainment	Simulators
Ethics	Perjury	

The term *ethics,* as we use it, refers to rules or standards that have been established to govern the conduct of members of a profession. The problem here is that only a handful of criminal profilers have begun to professionalize.[1] Most criminal profilers operate outside of a specific or written code of professional ethics. Consequently, one could make an effective argument for the position that many criminal profilers are still allowed the luxury of giving expert opinions without having to worry about being held responsible for them.

The author is alarmed by the continual examples of reckless, unethical behavior in the criminal profiling community. Many do not seem to be in touch with, or concerned by, the real-world consequences of their conduct. In fact, many seem dangerously preoccupied with recognition and status (and that has come to mean media attention).

Responsibility is the key. Keep in mind that a profiling method may be incompetent and a profiling result may be incorrect. But only the behavior of the criminal profiler can be referred to as unethical (e.g., a profiler who continues to use a method that he or she knows to be inaccurate). If criminal profilers perceive no duty to actually assist an investigation and see themselves only as academics with a higher scientific or academic goal in mind, then this absolves them of any ethical responsibility to a case. That means having no moral obligation to the validity of their opinions.

How dare we.

This chapter discusses the various types of unethical conduct and fraud that occur in the profiling community and offers readers an opportunity to learn from specific case examples. Additionally, a code of ethical conduct is provided as a preventative educational measure.

---

[1] On March 16, 1999, the author and five other professionals from the investigative, behavioral, and forensic disciplines formed the Academy of Behavioral Profiling (ABP). This was the first nonpartisan, independent professional organization dedicated to criminal profiling. As ABP president, Michael McGrath, M.D., stated: "To begin the task of professionalization, individuals of varied but specific backgrounds have joined together to found this concerted, multidisciplinary effort. As practitioners in our own disciplines, we struggle with what has been done in the past, what we are doing now, how we are doing it, and why." The ABP Web site is located at www. profiling.org.

WHEN PROFILING HARMS

Dr. Paul Wilson, a professor and criminologist at Bond University in the Gold Coast, Australia, articulated the issue of ethics as it relates to criminal profiling very well. According to Kocsis et al. (1998, pp. 8–9),

> There should be an onus on experts to point to the limitations of profiling. …
>
> [P]rofiling is no more unethical than any other investigative technique. It is how profiling (or any other technique) is used in any given case, which is important.

Essentially, there are numerous ways that profiling can cause harm, not limited to the following:

1. Delaying the apprehension of an offender by providing false leads
2. Delaying the apprehension of an offender by pointing to false suspects
3. Delaying the apprehension of an offender by excluding viable suspects
4. Harming the personal life of a citizen by an implication of guilt based solely on the characteristics in the profile

The first three represent the fruits of inaccurate methods of profiling. Only the fourth represents a breach of ethics by virtue of misuse. However, an argument for unethical behavior is warranted if a criminal profiler continues to advocate and use methods, without proper warning to the end user, that are known to result in the first three.

There are numerous examples of the unethical uses of criminal profiles. Keep in mind what is meant by unethical use. Also keep in mind that what is unethical is not necessarily criminal. Consider the following cases.

Colin Stagg

In July of 1992, 23-year-old Rachel Nickell, her 2-year-old son, Alex, and their dog went for a walk on Wimbledon Common in London, England. Ms. Nickell was stabbed 49 times, right in front of her son. It was the country's most publicized crime of that year. Law enforcement accepted the help of a psychologist who prepared a profile that reportedly described a man named Colin Stagg with a great deal of accuracy. However, law enforcement lacked any evidence that the man had committed a crime. They decided, with the psychologist's help, to have a female officer engage in suggestive correspondence with him (Kocsis et al., 1998). According to Edwards (1998, p. 149),

> Through an attractive blond undercover policewoman, the psychologist initiated an eight months' liaison with the 31-year-old Stagg in which she shared violent sexual fantasies, confessed to the ritual sexual murder of a baby and a young woman, and egged him on to match her stories; even telling him that she wished he were Nickell's murderer because, "That's the kind of man I want."
>
> Stagg never claimed credit for the killing, but from 700 pages of letters and transcribed telephone conversations and public meetings, the psychologist [Paul Britton] concluded that Stagg's fantasies, modeled upon information fed to him by those familiar with the details of the crime, revealed unique knowledge of the crime scene which could only be known by the murderer. Dragged before a judge in open court at the Old Bailey, defense quickly pointed out that Stagg hadn't even made good guesses—he didn't know the location of the crime and had wrongly asserted that the victim had been raped. …

> Clearing the accused and acknowledging the understandable pressure on the police, the judge was nevertheless forced to conclude that the operation betrayed "not merely an excess of zeal, but a blatant attempt to incriminate a suspect by positive and deceptive conduct of the grossest kind."

This case involved a psychologist who stepped beyond his expertise into the interpretation of crime scene behavior, who ignored inconsistencies in the suspect's stories, and who ultimately set out to prove the police theory regarding the case despite the established facts.

Ultimately, Colin Stagg was not the only victim of this circumstance. On June 12, 1998, BBC News (1998) announced the following:

> A woman detective at the center of a controversial undercover operation into the murder of model Rachel Nickell has taken early retirement.

> The 33-year-old officer—who has been known only by her cover name of Lizzie James—has left the Metropolitan Police on health grounds following her "traumatic" role in the investigation of Miss Nickell's death. …

> Conversations and correspondence between Lizzie and Mr. Stagg formed the basis of the prosecution case when he went on trial at the Old Bailey. …

> Lizzie, who has served 13 years in the Metropolitan Police, including time with Scotland Yard's SO10 covert operations squad, continued to work following the Nickell investigation.

> Fellow officers have claimed she never recovered from the trauma she suffered during her harrowing work on the Nickell inquiry, which was ultimately perceived as a failure.

Richard Jewell

On July 27, 1996, a backpack with a bomb in it was placed next to the AT&T Global Village stage in Centennial Park, in Atlanta, Georgia. Centennial Park was an open facility, crowded with people at the time, housing sponsors' tents for the 1996 summer Olympic Games. The device, a pipe bomb, exploded at 1:20 a.m., killing Alice Hawthorne of Albany, Georgia, and injuring 111 others. A Turkish cameraman also died of a heart attack as a result of the blast.

Richard Jewell, a security guard working in the park, had just alerted police to the suspicious knapsack and was helping to evacuate people from the area moments before it exploded (CNN, 1996).

The portly 34-year-old security guard, with a soft Southern drawl and a passion for police work, was hailed for his bravery and professionalism after he found a bomb underneath a bench in Atlanta's Centennial Olympic Park.

He helped clear people from the area before the bomb went off early on July 27, 1996, quick action that likely saved lives. But despite what he did, Jewell never claimed the mantle of hero for himself. He was, he insisted, just doing his job.

But within days, the story of the Olympic Park bombing seemed to take an unbelievable, melodramatic turn: The Federal Bureau of Investigation (FBI) suspected that Jewell had planted the bomb himself. The tidal wave that overwhelmed Jewell began on the afternoon of July 30 when the *Atlanta Journal-Constitution*, citing unidentified law enforcement sources, published a special edition saying the FBI considered him a suspect (CNN, 1997b).

An FBI agent leaked information to the press that a psychological profile had identified Jewell, a private security guard at the time, as the likely perpetrator. The press published that Richard Jewell was indeed the FBI's prime suspect, saying that he matched an FBI profile that described the bomber as a former policeman who longed for heroism.

In their quest for potential clues, federal agents removed everything from firearms to dryer lint from the apartment in Atlanta that Jewell shared with his mother, Barbara, 60. In its original request for a search warrant, the FBI cited evidence that Jewell "had no girlfriend … lives and breathes police stories," and "was exposed to explosives and bomb instruction and lectures on two separate occasions." In short, the one-time police officer and campus security officer fit what some agents felt was the profile of a law enforcement wannabe who might plant a bomb and then "discover" it to win acclaim (Hewitt, 1996).

This was combined with the reports of other items taken from Jewell's home during the service of search warrants, such as a collection of newspaper clippings describing Jewell as a hero. These elements added fuel to the media fire. When Jewell was brought in for questioning by the FBI, he was lied to. He was told that the questioning was not formal, nor was their interest in him as a genuine suspect. They led him to believe that they were using him as part of a training video for federal agents. It was an appeal to their perception of his need for attention.

However, when this all came to light and the search warrants failed to produce physical evidence of any kind, the FBI ultimately capitulated. Jewell was issued a notification that he was no longer a suspect. According to Collins (1996),

> The letter that finally arrived from US Attorney Kent B. Alexander, the prosecutor investigating the Atlanta bombing, fell far short of an apology, but it did free Jewell from the fear that he would be arrested at any moment. Jewell, the letter stated, was "not considered a target" of the investigation. "Barring any newly discovered evidence," it continued, "this status will not change."
>
> That language does not foreclose a future investigation of Jewell, and some FBI agents still wonder if he was somehow involved. But absolutely no evidence has been found to link him to the bombing. The search of his mother's house yielded nothing. It would be impossible to make a bomb as crude as the one at Centennial Olympic Park without handling the powder, but no trace of explosives was discovered anywhere on Jewell, in his truck or at his home, even by the vaunted devices used by the FBI that can detect one part per trillion. "They knew within days of going through his apartment that he didn't do it, but they continued to accuse him," says G. Watson Bryant Jr., one of Jewell's attorneys. "Their conduct is just despicable."

The special agent who had leaked the information to the press regarding the psychological profile was eventually reprimanded:

> FBI agents in Atlanta rallied in support of a fellow colleague Thursday after he returned to work following a five-day suspension without pay for his role in interviewing Olympic bombing suspect Richard Jewell.
>
> Several dozen people applauded as agent Don Johnson entered Atlanta FBI headquarters.
>
> Asked if [he thought] Johnson was a political scapegoat, agent Harry Grogan said, "Yes, I do." The FBI suspended Johnson last week and censured Atlanta special-agent-in-charge Woody Johnson and Kansas City special-agent-in-charge David Tubbs for their roles in the Jewell investigation.

Jewell was never charged in the 1996 bombing at Olympic Centennial Park, and the FBI eventually cleared him of suspicion (CNN, 1997a).

ETHICAL GUIDELINES FOR THE CRIMINAL PROFILER

To both educate and restrain its members, the Academy of Behavioral Profiling (ABP) was the first professional organization to publish a set of ethical guidelines specifically designed to address the potential misconduct of criminal profilers. It also served the task of professionalizing criminal profiling as a formal discipline. The ABP Ethical Guidelines for Professional Conduct were first published in March of 1999. They were designed to prevent, check, and govern potential abuses of criminal profiles by criminal profilers engaged in research or casework. In 2010, the ABP changed to reflect the growth of the organization and the challenges facing the profession, and renamed itself to The International Association of Forensic Criminologists (IAFC). Additionally, the ethical guidelines were updated. According to the guidelines set forth by the IAFC (see www.profiling.org/abp_conduct.html),

1. Members shall conduct themselves in a professional manner.
2. Members shall not have a felony conviction, nor a conviction of a misdemeanor based on a felony charge. If a member is arrested on a criminal charge, membership will be suspended until the charge is resolved. If guilty, membership will be terminated.
3. Members shall not have a conviction related to perjury or false testimony. If a member is arrested on such a charge, their membership will be suspended until the charge is resolved. If guilty, membership will be terminated.
4. Members shall conduct all examinations and research in a generally accepted scientific manner.
5. Members shall assign appropriate credit for the work and ideas of others.
6. Members shall maintain an attitude of independence and impartiality in order to ensure unbiased analyses and interpretations.[2]
7. Members shall render opinions and conclusions strictly in accordance with the established facts and evidence in the case.
8. Members shall not misrepresent their qualifications.
9. Members shall not misuse their positions as professionals for fraudulent purposes, or as a pretext for gathering information for any individual, group, organization, or government.
10. Members shall not practice outside their area of competence.
11. Members shall recognize an obligation to be knowledgeable regarding the methods and research in their areas of practice, to include the scientific limitations for all professional opinions and testimony. They shall also strive to make those limitations clear to others, and to refrain from leaving false impressions of their findings or certainty. [*Note*: This guideline is of particular importance for members whose expert opinions and testimony may encroach upon the "ultimate issue." In such cases, members are admonished to refrain from couching their findings in terms of guilt or innocence, as these are legal issues for the court to decide. They are further admonished to refrain from assuming guilt or innocence in their analysis, unless these issues have been conceded.]
12. Members shall not use a position off authority to exploit or coerce students or subordinates.
13. Members shall recognize an obligation to maintain the ethical standards of the professional community, and carefully weigh the need to report unethical conduct that they have observed to

---

[2] This author has a great deal of respect for the discussion on the subject of objectivity offered in Thornton (1997, p. 21): Personal bias may be reduced to a very low level but no prudent scientist would claim that it was forever absent. Personal bias is capable of being vanquished in a practical sense, but some circumspection and effort is required to do so. Bias that would cause the forensic scientist to embrace a position concerning the guilt or innocence of an accused is clearly improper. That sort of bias is easily recognized for its evil en se, however. More insidious is the sort of bias in which an analyst will engage to protect findings once they have been developed.

the appropriate authorities when feasible. [*Note*: This guideline is intended to recognize that IAFC members have an obligation to work toward reducing unethical conduct that exists in their sphere of influence. However, not all unethical behavior must be treated in the same fashion. Careful deliberation is required before action should be taken. The IAFC acknowledges that some ethical issues involve subjectivity; that the recognition and acknowledgment of unethical behavior may be treated as a training opportunity; and that reporting unethical behavior can involve consequences that outweigh any benefits of reporting. The IAFC also acknowledges that there are authorities who ignore such reports or who punish those who make such reports, rather than dealing with the offending parties. These and related factors may weigh in the balance with the respect to the decision of IAFC members to report unethical conduct.]

These guidelines do not represent a radical departure from those of other well-established professional and forensic organizations, such as the American Society of Criminologists (ASC), American Board of Criminalists (ABC), and the California Association of Criminalists (CAC). However, until we apply these guidelines to ethical issues that exist in the real world, they can seem too abstract, too obvious, or even irrelevant. Nothing could be further from the truth. Not only are these considerations vital and relevant to the issue of professional character, they have been ignored by many of those in the profiling community. This may be caused by an ignorance of good practice that is common to the less educated in the community, or it may be caused by the draw of fame and recognition—such as may be the case with profilers who establish themselves as perpetual media pundits.

THE MEDIA AND ENTERTAINMENT INDUSTRY: CONFLICTS OF INTEREST

Because of the high amount of emotional and sexual voyeurism inherent in the criminal profiling process, it has an equally high entertainment value. This attracts not only a large number of consumers to profiling-related media but arguably a high number of students to college courses on the subject as well. In any case, criminal profilers are constantly being asked to contribute to, to consult on, or to opine for, media-related projects on real or fictional offenders and offenses.

The relationship between the criminal profiler and the media should be the same as any other—the profiler should be there to educate. Not to alarm. Not to sensationalize. Not to judge. Not to condemn. Not to assume facts or guess about whether or not a missing child is dead or whether a suspect is guilty. The profiler is either a source of competent and informed knowledge based on objective forensic practice or serving no valid professional purpose whatsoever.

Books, Films, and TV

It is commonplace for film and television studios to call on the expertise of those with specialized knowledge to consult on projects that deal with technical subject matter or where an element of realism is crucial to the effectiveness of a project.

One example is author Thomas Harris, who was allowed the incredible, unprecedented privilege of consulting with the FBI's then Behavioral Sciences Unit (BSU) for character and plot development relating to his acclaimed written work of fiction, *Red Dragon*, and the sequel, *The Silence of the Lambs*. In 1986, the De Laurentis Entertainment Group released the feature film *Manhunter*, based on *Red Dragon*, and in 1991, Orion Pictures released the Academy Award–winning film, *The Silence of the Lambs*.

Bringing these works of written fiction to film elevated the members of the FBI's then Behavioral Sciences Unit to superstar status. Arguably, this hurt the image of the BSU more than it helped it.

The precedent set by the success of *The Silence of the Lambs* and other films, as well as the subsequent popularity of the published memoirs of several former FBI profilers, originally opened the door. Criminal profilers have been invited by the entertainment industry to act as creative consultants on numerous film and television projects dealing with the subject in the years since. Many of these programs promote the myth that criminal profiling involves psychic or paranormal ability. Given the bulk of the published literature in the field, it is evident that many criminal profilers seem to agree with this position. The ethical dilemma for the criminal profiler, then, is whether to participate as a creative consultant on a fictional project that endorses the supernatural as an aid to criminal profiling. This ultimately represents a public endorsement of misinformation about the field. As is discussed in the Preface to the Third Edition, there are a fair number of profilers who have no problem with this association, and even seek to promote it—based on personal beliefs as opposed to verifiable evidence.

True Crime

The true-crime market is in the business of dramatizing, vilifying, packaging, and selling the acts of violent, predatory offenders to the public. This has been the case for more than a few generations. As Vollmer (1949, p. 1) states,

> While it is true that glorifying crime is reprehensible and the making of heroes out of psychopathic criminals is abhorrent, there seems to be little that the public can do about it.

As we have already discussed, criminal profilers have made successful publishing forays into the realm of true crime through published memoirs. An ethical concern arises, however, when criminal profilers seek endorsement from those whose business is selling cases rather than solving them. This speaks to the old saying that one person cannot effectively serve two masters. One cannot effectively service the objective investigation of fact while financially attached to the dramatization of that fact for public consumption.

News Agencies

Very often, news agencies will contact criminal profilers and ask them to opine on a case that has captured the attention of the public for whatever reason. The first decision that a profiler should make is whether he or she is qualified to speak about a particular case. The second consideration is whether there is enough publicly available information to form any kind of relevant opinion. The third consideration is whether the public dissemination of the profiler's opinion will be of harm or advantage to the case. It is not the policy of this author to give opinions on a case without a great deal of specific case information, which the media typically do not have. In most cases, the author will only discuss general profiling techniques and how they may be generally applied to a certain type of investigation. However, there are occasions when case material and court filings are available and can be the basis for specific comments.

A very real danger arises when a criminal profiler begins to perceive media attention as a form of professional validation. The profiler's inflated ego can become so used to reading its own name in print that it becomes lonely for itself when not seen in the paper or heard on the news. Profilers may begin to do things specifically to attract media attention, or they may begin to solicit the attention of the media directly. In either case, this type of behavior inevitably undermines one's public and professional credibility.

Case Example: Murdertainment

During the so-called Beltway Sniper shootings in October of 2002, criminal profilers from around the globe participated in wall-to-wall coverage of the investigation that ensued. Many offered specific profiles of the unknown suspect.[3] One such commentator was Dr. Jack Levin of Northeastern University. As McGrath and Turvey (2003, p. 133) explain,

> Professor Jack Levin, director of the Brudnick Center on Violence and Conflict at Northeastern University and author of several works on the subject of criminal profiling, came out with a profile similar to that offered by [former FBI profiler Clint] Van Zandt.
>
> "The truth is he has other responsibilities in his life," criminologist Jack Levin said on Larry King's program on CNN last week. "He may be married. He may be playing with his children, watching football on Sunday, or he may have a part-time job" (Farhi and Weeks, 2002).
>
> When the snipers were captured, this profile proved to be inaccurate. Levin argued that even though inaccurate, his opinions were a public service that was intended to comfort.
>
> "My predictions were not that close. But the average American was hungry for information," he said. "People wanted a story of who this guy was. What we did, by providing it, comforted them" (Gettlemen, 2002).

In this example, the prediction, based on nomothetic profiles that have been circulating for years, was inaccurate. There were two snipers; one was divorced and unemployed; neither was from the area; and both were black. In defense of these inaccurate opinions, it was argued that the purpose of having profilers on TV is to comfort the public in times of crisis—any information, even if false, is helpful. This author disagrees wholeheartedly and would argue that profilers have an ethical duty to refrain from participating in what can only be described as comfortainment, in service of the murdertainment industry that has arisen to satisfy the appetite of the 24-hour news cycle.[4] Ironically, the criminologist in question revisited the sniper case a year later with an op-ed piece in *USA Today*, which asked the question, "So how did we start down this road to our exaggerated view of serial snipers?" (Fox and Levin, 2003).

HIGH STATION: ABUSING POSITIONS OF POWER

Criminal profilers, whether employed by an investigative agency, a university, or in private practice, may find themselves in positions of authority over students or other subordinates. For ethical profilers, this is a chance to mentor a new mind and help influence their educational journey. It is an opportunity to give opportunities and to build much-needed confidence and esteem. It is an occasion to help shape a future colleague. For unethical profilers, these relationships are an opportunity to exploit students and subordinates for personal gain. This can involve everything from uncredited work to trading on sexual favors.

---

[3] It should be noted that three of those who refrained from giving specific profiles for lack of information were the author of this text, Dr. Michael McGrath, and Det. John Baeza (NYPD, retired). Restraint in the face of great pressure to be entertaining and give certain answers is not easy, but it is responsible.

[4] Comfortainment is defined by the author as providing reassuring, if incorrect, opinions and commentary to the public through media programs designed to entertain more than they are designed to provide accurate information. Murdertainment is defined by the author as providing sensational coverage of incidents involving death and violence through media programs designed to entertain more than they are designed to provide accurate information.

Far from being a unique problem to the field of criminal profiling, subordinate abuse by those in positions of power is common. It may come about because those in high station exert an influence—either conscious or unconscious—on those who are below them or because those lower in station seek out the higher up to gain purchase in an already competitive field.

The temptation to engage in exploitative relationships can be substantial. It is up to the individual practitioner to recognize and to assess every subordinate relationship for what it is worth and the subsequent solutions to individual problems when they arise. While inappropriate relationships and solutions are many and varied, the best cure is prevention; avoid any such relationships at all costs and learn from any mistakes that one may make in recognizing they exist.

That such inappropriate relationships exist at all is a real issue worthy of consideration, but as with all things there are various levels of severity within the abuse of power. For instance, the profiler who finds himself or herself in a situation where ethics and integrity are compromised is one thing, but the profiler who knowingly and repeatedly places himself or herself in such positions—even plans for and anticipates them—is another. Different again is the situation whereby the individual actively exploits subordinates, such as may exist for research benefit or where the subordinate produces work product under the name of the supervisor—that is, prostituting the student for personal gain while leading the student to believe there will be something for him or her in the relationship at the end of the day.

In defense of such relationships, it is often argued that the subordinate is not a victim at all, but a mature volunteer in a consensual arrangement. However, the disparity of power prevents such seemingly logical decisions from being made. What's more, any such situation may not become an issue until some part of the relationship goes bad. If and when this happens, the student will always be on the losing end of the transaction.

To be clear on this issue, the critique is not aimed at those few people who establish friendships or deep and meaningful relationships with students or colleagues who may at some time have served under the professional in question. Rather, it is aimed at the professionals who have made a habit of preying upon those who are subordinate to them, whether they are students or colleagues, through the abuse of their position as someone in authority. Many institutions have actually anticipated this problem by ruling against such relationships, certain bodies may terminate the employment of individuals who are habitually absive, and others may ignore it entirely for fear of a wrongful termination suit. Ethical profilers will strive to avoid such off-balance relationships and will further seek to develop their students and subordinates rather than exploit them.

ETHICS IN PUBLISHING

Criminal profilers have a responsibility to ensure that any research they publish is both relevant and honest. This means that the data being studied must be related to the questions posed, as well as the subsequent problems that the research will be applied to. This also means that publications may not assume facts for the purpose of convenience, and they must strive not to misrepresent the existing literature.

Example: Assuming or Inferring Legal Guilt for Research Purposes

A recent publication that raises concerns is an article by Santilla et al. (2003), titled "Inferring the Characteristics of an Arsonist from Crime Scene Actions: A Case Study in Offender Profiling," which was published in a police journal. The purpose of the article was to showcase investigative psychology (IP) as a valid profiling technique using a single case example. An IP profile was rendered during a criminal investigation, and the results were later compared against the primary suspect in the case. As explained in Santilla et al. (2003, pp. 5 and 12),

> The accuracy of these predictions was evaluated against information concerning the suspect in the case. ... The characteristics predicted, based on the findings of Canter and Fritzon (1998), were in good accordance with the actual characteristics of the suspect in the case. Also, it was possible to provide fairly good estimates of the home location of the suspect based on the crime locations. There was a difference between those predicted characteristics that were based strictly on the Canter and Fritzon model and the spatial predictions which were more accurate compared to predictions based on "common sense."

To be clear, the stated purpose of the article was not to merely provide a case example and showcase the IP method. It was to argue the veracity of IP by determining if the results were "in good accordance with the actual characteristics of the suspect." On the surface, and to a primarily law enforcement audience, this may seem an acceptable practice.

However, the only way to measure the accuracy of IP predictions in this case is by a direct comparison with the characteristics of the actual offender. The suspect in the case at hand was not charged, let alone convicted, of any offense. The article presents the suspect and begs the reader to assume guilt, as the authors do, because he is the suspect. The distinction between suspect and offender is not clear in the purpose and mechanics of the article. By comparing the profile to the suspect, the article is either assuming guilt or proposing guilt. Otherwise, again, any comparison of predicted characteristics has no value.

The author wrote one of the co-authors of this case study and requested clarification of these ethical issues. In her response, the co-author asserted that the issue of actual guilt had been raised before publication among the co-authors, but that the purpose of the article was not to address the accuracy of the method so the point was moot. This response stated precisely the opposite of the language in the publication. The co-author then explained that the suspect was essentially as good as guilty from a law-enforcement perspective, and that's what gave the case study value (Fritzon, K., personal communication, July 30, 2007):

> In fact, the outcome was that the state prosecutor (an independent nonpolice body in Finland) decided that the direct physical evidence was not strong enough to proceed. This is quite different from being found not guilty, as you know. There was, in fact, a lot of circumstantial evidence (i.e., he was seen leaving the scene of several of the arsons). ...
>
> I think that the validity and utility of the profile to some extent depends on the perspective. From the police perspective, they found it a helpful and interesting input to their investigation. You may not find it "scientific" although, in fact, it remains an open hypothesis as further evidence may at some point be gathered.
>
> I would finally add that the article was peer reviewed and also commented on by the editor, and no one seemed to have a problem with the issue.

It is true that the IP profile may have been helpful to police in their investigation. However, this is separate from the issue of publishing the profile in comparison with the suspect's characteristics to validate IP methodology. Unless readers can assume guilt, this exercise cannot satisfy the stated purpose of the article. Suspect guilt is a hypothesis in this case. So is suspect innocence. These are legal determinations outside the scope and service of scientific research.

To be abundantly clear, comparing a profile against the characteristics of a suspect is an exercise in futility with respect to testing the veracity of a given method. The only exception would be if that suspect has been found guilty in a court of law. Even then, guilt is a legal classification—those who are actually innocent may be found legally guilty and the opposite is also true. These limitations must be boldly expressed along with the conclusions of any such study in the interests of scientific honesty.

CRIMINAL PROFILING AND FORENSIC FRAUD

Criminal profilers engage in forensic fraud when they provide sworn testimony, opinions, or reports bound for court that contain deceptive or misleading findings, opinions, or conclusions, deliberately offered to secure an unfair or unlawful gain. As Turvey (2003) notes, forensic frauds tend to fall into one of three general categories: simulators, dissemblers, and pseudoexperts.

Simulators

Simulators, the most common form of forensic fraud, are described in Turvey (2003):

> Simulators are those who physically manipulate physical evidence or related forensic testing. This means that they either fabricate evidence or destroy it for a particular gain. The inept simulator seeks to conceal their own lack of skills, abilities or proficiency, much like a plagiarist that hands in a term paper they did not write. They are aware of their own shortcomings or mistakes, and will fabricate or destroy evidence to keep it a secret. The apathetic simulator is lazy, crunched for time, or strapped for resources. In any case, they are not concerned about the consequences of falsifying results, and may even feel entitled to do so. The less they do, the easier it is for them all around. The egotistic simulator invents results specifically for personal and/or financial gain. They have a reputation for results, and they are going to maintain it at all costs. By doing so, they hope to ensure their use on future cases and in some extreme cases maintain their "celebrity" status amongst colleagues. The altruistic simulator fabricates or destroys evidence to assist the circumstances for someone that they feel will otherwise be denied justice, such as a criminal defendant or a colleague. They feel that fabricating or destroying evidence is sometimes morally right, and therefore necessary.

In the criminal profiling community, simulators are not unheard of. Consider the following case example.

Case Example: JonBenet Ramsey

On December 26, 1996, 6-year-old JonBenet Ramsey was found murdered in the basement of her parents' home in Boulder, Colorado, 8 hours after she was reported missing. Suspicion immediately fell on the parents. They hired an attorney, a publicist, and a retired FBI profiler to publicly defend their interests.

In January of 1997, the retired FBI profiler appeared on *Dateline NBC*. He stated, based on his interview of John and Patsy Ramsey (together) and his examination of the facts of the case, that he knew in his heart that they could not have killed their daughter. To bolster his opinions, he stated that officials involved with the case had briefed him on the autopsy report.

Reporters following the story tried to verify the retired FBI profiler's account, but they could not find any officials who would admit to having briefed him about the autopsy report. When that story broke, the retired FBI profiler was forced to change his story. Two days later on *Larry King Live*, he stated that the only briefing he received on the JonBenet Ramsey autopsy report came from the Ramsey family lawyers; his knowledge of her autopsy was third-hand. As Brennan (1997) explains,

Former FBI profiler John Douglas has conceded that the only briefing he received on the JonBenet Ramsey autopsy report came from the Ramsey family's lawyers.

In a one-hour interview Thursday on *Larry King Live*, the criminal profiler hired by John and Patricia Ramsey to help solve their 6-year-old daughter's murder said his knowledge of her unfinished autopsy report is third-hand.

"I was briefed by the attorneys" representing the Ramseys, Douglas said. He said he has not seen the final report.

This contradicts statements on *Dateline NBC* Tuesday night that Douglas had been briefed on the autopsy report. The next day, no officials connected to the murder investigation admitted having done so.

Boulder County coroner John Meyer will ask at a Feb. 12 hearing in Boulder District Court to have the report sealed. It is not expected to be completed until then.

Los Angeles criminal defense attorney Leslie Abramsom, who defended Erik and Lyle Menendez in the murders of their parents, was also a guest on King's show.

"How could the defense attorneys be briefing Mr. Douglas on the autopsy when they don't have a report?" she asked.

When King repeated the question, Douglas answered, "You'd have to bring them on as a guest."...

Douglas defended his analysis concerning the murder of JonBenet, who was discovered in a remote room of her family's basement Dec. 26, about eight hours after her mother discovered a ransom note demanding $118,000 for the girl's safe return. ...

Douglas told King that he was limited in what he could say about the murder because he'd been told by the Ramseys' lawyers he may be called before a grand jury.

In this case, the retired FBI profiler simulated the existence of evidence (an autopsy report) and individuals (unnamed officials and attorneys), whom he claimed to have been briefed by with respect to autopsy findings. He then used these nonexistent briefings as part of the basis for his interpretations about the nature of the crime and his subsequent opinions regarding the Ramseys' innocence—to bolster his credibility with respect to having examined evidence. Unfortunately, his accounts were not consistent, and nobody would corroborate them.

Dissemblers

Dissemblers are those forensic examiners who exaggerate, embellish, lie about, or otherwise misrepresent their actual findings. They are the second most common form of forensic fraud. As Turvey (2003) describes,

Dissemblers exist on a continuum from those who lie outright about the significance of their findings to those who simply present a biased or incomplete view. As discussed in Saks (2001):

A more ambiguous version of this [forensic fraud] is the proffered expert who comes from a field that has valid knowledge and is capable of doing sound work, but in the case at bar the expert has failed to perform according to the expected standards ("with the same intellectual rigor," as some courts and commentators have put it) and that looseness has produced less reliable results (which presumably leads to conclusions that tilt the testimony further in the direction of the proponent's preferred position).

Consider the following case example, which involves confessions of dissembling.

Case Example: Waco

In April of 1993, the siege of the Branch Davidian property (at Mount Carmel) in Waco, Texas, by the FBI and the ATF ended after 51 days with the death of their charismatic leader, David Koresh, and 85 of his followers.[5] The dead included men, women, and children, all of whom died in a fire that started about six hours after FBI agents began spraying in tear gas and ramming the building with tanks (Hancock, 2000).

When an FBI profiler warned the FBI against breaching the compound, he was told to change his opinions or he would be sanctioned. According to the *New York Times* ("FBI Agent at Waco Says Bureau Pressured Him on Koresh Reports," 1995),

> Peter Smerick, the FBI's lead criminal analyst and profiler of Koresh, has broken his silence to charge that bureau officials pressured him into changing his advice on how to resolve the situation without bloodshed.
>
> Smerick, now retired from the bureau and working as a consultant in the Washington area, said he had counseled a cautious, non-confrontational approach to Koresh in four memos written from Waco for senior FBI officials between March 3 and March 8, 1993.
>
> But he was pressured from above, Smerick says, as he was writing a fifth memo March 9. As a result, that memo contained subtle changes in tone and emphasis that amounted to an endorsement of a more aggressive approach against the Davidians.
>
> The following month, the FBI got the go-ahead from Attorney General Janet Reno for its plan to inject tear gas into the compound. Koresh and his followers then set the place on fire, according to a Justice Department review of the siege.

Also, according to Hancock (2000),

> Although no one plainly stated that he would be censored, Mr. Smerick said in 1995, he felt unmistakable pressure to change his advice. He added in the confidential interview that he believed that "the traditionally independent process of FBI criminal analysis ... was compromised at Waco."
>
> Mr. Smerick told interviewers that he quit writing after submitting an "acquiescent" final memo that omitted previous cautions against pushing the sect and incorporated suggestions from his Washington boss for tactical pressure. He said he left Waco "in frustration" on March 17, though he kept in contact with some negotiators.

Smerick admitted to altering his opinions under pressure before Congress, as discussed in Zeliff (1995):

> Opening statement, Congressman William H. Zeliff, Jr., Tuesday, August 1, 1995:
>
> ... How much more plainly do words come than as written by Roger Altman in his striking memo of April 15th to Secretary Bentsen. Mr. Altman is not in the decision-making process, yet he sees the predictable nature of the tragedy—"the risks of a tragedy are there," he says.
>
> Meanwhile, Mr. Smerick at the FBI writes four memos discouraging a shift away from negotiations to a tactical response. He writes until—he feels that he has to change his recommendation because—in his words—he must please those above him, including the director of the FBI.

---

[5] The actual number of victims killed at Waco is a matter of some debate. Reliable news agencies as well as the FBI report the number differently. The FBI claims that David Koresh is to blame for these discrepancies because he gave out false information about the number of people living at Mount Carmel.

Peter Smerick's then supervisor, John Douglas, has corroborated this version of events. According to Worden (1999),

> Among the negotiators embroiled in the conflict, and one who felt pressured to remain silent about information provided to him from negotiators in the field, was John Douglas. A 25-year veteran of the FBI, he was at the time chief of the FBI's investigative support unit that supplied negotiators to the operation. ...
>
> "I felt I had no choice but to keep my mouth shut or I'd be rustling cattle somewhere," he said.
>
> Douglas was part of the behavioral science group, comprised of criminal profilers, analysts and psychologists. The group clashed repeatedly with the hostage rescue team—the more powerful tactical side—which dismissed the behavioral scientists and wanted action-oriented results, Douglas said. ...
>
> During a meeting at the FBI's command center in Washington a week before the ill-fated assault on the compound, Douglas recalls being asked for a status report by Sessions. Among those in the room, according to Douglas, were FBI Deputy Director Floyd Clarke, Assistant Director of Criminal Investigations Larry Potts, Deputy Assistant Director Danny Coulson, and Criminal Investigations Section Chief Michael Kahoe.
>
> Douglas briefed Sessions on the psychological profile his field negotiators had developed about Koresh and his followers.
>
> "I told [Sessions] there was a possibility of [Koresh] being violent ... although I didn't think he had been driven to that point yet," said Douglas. "I told him as long as he was talking to us, there was no danger he would harm anyone."
>
> About 20 minutes into his presentation, Douglas said, Potts, Coulson, and Kahoe left the room and asked a lower-level agent to bring Douglas outside. "I thought it was very strange being summoned out of a meeting with the director," said Douglas. Outside the room, Douglas said, Kahoe turned to him and said: "We don't want you talking to the director. There are certain things we don't want the director to know. We'll be the ones to brief him."
>
> Douglas said the meeting abruptly ended at that point before he had an opportunity to discuss the widening rift between tactical strategists and the negotiators.

According to both FBI agents involved, Attorney General Janet Reno acted on false information provided by one, who agreed to change his last report under pressure from the other (his supervisor), who was in turn under pressure from his bosses at the FBI to favor a breach at Waco.

According to their own accounts, both agents agreed to alter their professional expert opinions as criminal profilers regarding Waco to favor those of their supervisors, for fear of losing their jobs or other sanctions. This was a decision that both understood could cost lives.[6]

If either now ex-FBI agent gets in front of a jury to offer expert testimony, opposing counsel will likely ask the following question: "Have you ever changed your expert opinion for money when you thought people might die as a result?" For both, given their admissions and congressional testimony, the answer to this question can only be Yes.

---

[6] Changing, altering, or tailoring one's professional/expert opinions for financial reasons is, arguably, one of the most unethical things that a professional can do. Add to this the strong possibility that changing or altering one's opinion may cost lives, and it becomes the most egregious of all unethical conduct, in the opinion of this author.

Pseudoexperts

At times, experts may misrepresent the nature or quantity of their qualifications. Their reasons may be to have the court see them as eminently more qualified than they actually are or to be allowed to give evidence in an area in which they are not really qualified. Either way, it is a form of fraud. Pseudoexperts are those who fabricate or misrepresent expert credentials such as college diplomas, expert certifications, professional affiliations, or case-related experience (Turvey, 2003). Such fraud is without question the easiest form to investigate and screen. Unfortunately, it remains common within the forensic community in general, in forms both subtle and gross. Consider the following case examples.

Case Example: Fabrication of Credentials and Experience

In a 1982 case, the defense discovered and a federal appeals court agreed that a now-retired prison therapist and criminal profiler perjured himself in regard to his qualifications during sworn expert testimony in a double homicide shooting case. According to the record in Drake v. Portuondo (2003),

> The prosecution informed defense counsel on the Thursday evening that it intended to call a psychologist named Richard D. Walter to testify about psychological profiling. On the Friday, the prosecution successfully moved to add Walter as a witness, and Walter mounted the stand. Under the announced schedule, defense counsel would have no more than a weekend to get a competing expert, if needed, or for that matter to prepare his cross-examination.

> The prosecution concedes that Walter's testimony was intended to reinforce what it perceived as weaknesses in the evidence supporting its theory of intent. The prosecution also concedes that Walter was referred to them by Dr. Levine, the forensic dentist, and that the prosecution did not independently investigate Walter's qualifications.

> Walter conceded at the outset that he had not examined Drake or reviewed his medical records, and would rely on his review of grand jury testimony, medical evidence and the police record. Walter opined on that basis that Smith and Rosenthal had been the victims of a specific type of "lust-murder" called "picquerism" (a derivative misspelling of the French verb "piquer," which means, among other things, to stick or poke). See Trial Transcript at 794. According to Walter, picquerists achieve sexual gratification by biting, shooting, stabbing, and sodomizing their victims (though not all picquerists do all these things). This supposed syndrome accounted for much of the physical evidence in medical terms that dovetailed with the prosecution's theory of intent.

> It is now apparent that Walter's testimony concerning his qualifications was perjury. He claimed extensive experience in the field of psychological profiling, including: work on 5000 to 7500 cases over several years in the Los Angeles County Medical Examiner's Office; an adjunct professorship at Northern Michigan University; more than four years as a prison psychologist with the Michigan Department of Corrections; and expert testimony given at hundreds of criminal trials in Los Angeles and Michigan.

> On the Monday following Walter's testimony, defense counsel told Justice DiFlorio that the defense had searched over the weekend to retain a rebuttal psychologist, but could not find any expert who had ever heard of "picquerism." The defense requested a two-week continuance to find a psychologist with the expertise required. The prosecution successfully opposed a continuance.

> Years after exhausting his direct appeals, Drake discovered evidence, through his own research in prison, that Walter had lied about his credentials. Although Walter is a prison psychologist with the Michigan Department of Corrections, Drake found suggestive evidence that Walter lied about

his other credentials. As the prosecution now concedes, Walter performed no criminal profiling in the Los Angeles County Medical Examiner's Office. According to Walter's supervisors there, he was employed as a lab assistant responsible for cleaning and maintaining the forensic lab. There seems to be no record that Walter was ever on the payroll of Northern Michigan University, where he claimed to be an adjunct professor. The Los Angeles County District Attorney's office has found no record of Walter testifying as an expert witness in a criminal proceeding between October 1975 through May 1978.

In 1995, Drake moved to vacate his conviction and sentence pursuant to N.Y. C.P.L. 440.10 on the basis of the newly discovered evidence concerning Walter's perjury. ...

For the foregoing reasons, we vacate the district court's judgment denying Drake's petition for habeas relief, and remand to the district court for discovery and a hearing (if the district court in its discretion considers that a hearing is needed) on whether the prosecution knew (or should have known) that its expert, Richard D. Walter, was committing perjury.

Subsequent to this 2003 decision, further court filings addressed the issue. As explained in Drake v. Portuondo (2006),

On September 30, 2004 Respondent filed the Motion for Summary Judgment in which it argued that Walter did not commit perjury at trial and that, even if the Court concludes that he did commit perjury, the prosecutor neither knew nor should have known of the perjury. On June 15, 2005 Drake filed a response to the Motion. The Court received Respondent's reply on June 21, 2005 and oral argument on the Motion was heard on June 24, 2005.

Federal judge John T. Elfvin ultimately concluded, based on the profiler's testimony and its context, that it was reasonable to presume that he had indeed given false testimony with regard to his qualifications. Moreover, Judge Elfvin found that the profiler had made additional false and misleading statements about his credentials while under oath that could not be conclusively referred to as perjury, which is a specific legal charge. This is detailed in Drake v. Portuondo (2006):

Drake asserts that Walter committed perjury at trial by testifying falsely concerning his qualifications as an expert and concerning his prior work experience. Specifically, Drake challenges Walter's statements as to his work history with the Los Angeles County Medical Examiner's Office, his licensure as a psychologist, his prior scholarly publications, his teaching experience and his prior testimony as an expert witness. In its January 31, 2003 decision, the Second Circuit concluded that Walter had testified falsely. The Court stated:

"He claimed extensive experience in the field of psychological profiling, including work on 5000 to 7500 cases over several years in the Los Angeles County Medical Examiner's Office, an adjunct professorship at Northern Michigan University; more than four years as a prison psychologist with the Michigan Department of Corrections; and expert testimony given at hundreds of criminal trials in Los Angeles and Michigan." Drake, 321 F.3d at 342.

Ordinarily, in light of such a statement by the Second Circuit, Walter's perjury would be presumed. However, Respondent urges the Court to review Walter's trial testimony because it asserts that much of Walter's testimony was true and that—even if portions of Walter's testimony were factually incorrect—Walter did not intentionally testify falsely and thus the incorrect testimony does not constitute perjury under the law. Respondent's argument misses the point that a conviction knowingly based on false evidence, even that which does not rise to the level of perjury, is subject to reversal. See *Thomas v. Kuhlman*, 255 F. Supp.2d 99, 108 (E.D.N.Y. 2003) (citing United States v. Boyd, 55 F.3d 239, 243

(7th Cir. 1995)). On the other hand, perjury is defined as "false testimony concerning a material matter with the willful intent to provide false testimony, rather than as a result of confusion, mistake or faulty memory." *United States v. Dunnigan*, 507 U.S. 87, 94 (1993). Because Respondent argues, in part, that Walter's trial testimony was not false, the Court will examine each of the challenged areas of Walter's trial testimony in turn.

1. Licensure

Drake takes issue with Walter's characterization of his occupation at the time of the trial as a "prison psychologist" for the Michigan Department of Corrections. Drake asserts that such statement is false because, under Michigan law, a psychologist must possess a Ph. D. Drake contends that, as Walter had obtained only a Master's Degree, his license was only that of a "limited psychologist."

Walter testified at trial that he held a Master's Degree only and that he was a "prison psychologist." Trans. at 783.3. On cross-examination Walter confirmed that he did not possess a Ph. D. Trans. at 805. At his deposition in this case, Walter defended his use of the title "prison psychologist." Walter stated that, in Michigan, one with a Master's Degree may receive a limited license in psychology. Walter Dep. at 80. Ordinarily, one with a limited license must work under the direction of a fully licensed psychologist. Id. at 80–81. Walter testified, however, that the Michigan Attorney General in a 1979 Opinion stated that there is no requirement for such supervision when the limited psychologist works for a governmental entity or non-profit organization. Ibid. Based on that same Opinion, Walter testified that limited psychologists are permitted to use the title "psychologist" within such settings. Walter Dep. at 80–81.

This Court cannot conclude that Walter misrepresented his qualifications when he testified at trial that he held only a Master's Degree and clearly stated that he did not possess a Ph.D.; nor can the Court conclude that Walter testified falsely when he characterized his then-current occupation as that of "prison psychologist."[7]

2. Publications

Drake next asserts that Walter testified falsely concerning his prior publications. At trial, Walter was asked if he had written any papers. He responded "Yes." Trans. at 784. At his deposition, Walter reiterated—albeit with some confusion as to the relevant dates—that he had written a paper prior to the Drake trial, but that it was presented and published after the trial. He stated:

Q: Okay. Prior to October 19th of 1982, had you published anything in the Journal of the American Academy of Forensic Sciences?
A: No. [Walter Dep. at 34.]
Q: You said you delivered an address concerning the topic [of the paper] but hadn't actually written the paper yet?
A: I had not published the paper. I had written it not published it.
Q: Okay. And you believe that you delivered it at a January meeting, did you say?

---

[7] The Michigan Department of Corrections recently listed an available position for a "psychologist." Linked to that listing is a copy of the Civil Service job description. That description states that an applicant for the position of "psychologist" must possess a Master's Degree in Psychology. See www.michigan.gov/documents/Psychologist_12904_7.pdf. The job description states that "[e]mployees in this job complete or oversee a variety of professional assignments to provide psychological treatment to residents of state facilities and community based programs. Positions in this class are located in mental health facilities, prisons, youth residential facilities, and veterans hospitals."

A: No, February.

Q: February meeting?

A: Yes.

Q: Which would have been when, what year, if the testimony you gave in the trial—

A: In '81.

Q: —was in 1982 October?

A: Oh, it would have been '82 then.

Walter Dep. at 42–43.

The Court concludes that Walter did not testify falsely at trial when he testified only that he had written a paper prior to his testimony. As Walter never testified at trial that said paper was published, any inconsistency in his deposition testimony regarding the dates of the presentation and publication of that paper is irrelevant.[8]

3.   Teaching Experience

Drake also asserts that Walter testified falsely that he was an "adjunct lecturer" at Northern Michigan University. Drake argues that the term "adjunct lecturer" is an academic title that Drake was not entitled to use and that left a false impression with the jury.

At trial, Walter was asked "Do you teach at all?" Trans. at 784. In response, he stated "I'm adjunct lecturer at Northern Michigan University." Ibid.

At his deposition, however, he elaborated on the nature of his relationship with that institution—to wit, he had lectured as a guest of a professor at Northern Michigan University. Walter Dep. at 68–71.

Walter defended his use of the term "adjunct" as factually correct within its ordinary meaning because he meant adjunct with a lowercase a, not a capital A. Walter Dep. at 68, 72. Although he wished he had used the term "guest," Walter disputed that the jury could have been misled by his testimony at trial.

He stated: "Inasmuch as its [sic] part of the English lexicon, I don't apologize for using the word in its proper context. Whether [the jury] choose [sic] to understand it or not is a misfortune of their's, not mine. I prefer to—I would have preferred to have said guest. I used the word adjunct." Walter Dep. at 75.

While this Court is dismayed at the cavalier attitude displayed by Walter, it cannot conclude that Walter's use of the term "adjunct" rendered his testimony false as a matter of definition. The word adjunct is defined as "a person associated with or assisting another in some duty or service." Webster's Third New International Dictionary 27 (1965). In the context in which the question was asked, however, Walter's response was—at best—misleading.[9]

---

[8] Exhibit 3 to Drake's Memorandum in Opposition to this Motion is a copy of an article entitled "Anger Biting" which was published in the September 1985 issue of the *American Journal of Forensic Medicine and Pathology*. The publication contains a notation that the paper was first presented to the Odontology Section of the American Academy of Forensic Sciences in February 1983.

[9] Neither party addressed the significance, if any, of Walter's use of the present tense. Walter stated, "I'm adjunct lecturer."… No evidence was adduced as to whether—at the time of trial—Walter continued to lecture as a guest at that institution. His response, however, left the impression that his affiliation with that institution was ongoing.

4. Experience as an Expert Witness

Drake further argues that Walter's trial testimony was false with respect to his prior experience testifying as an expert witness. The Second Circuit agreed, noting that Walter claimed to have testified in "hundreds of criminal trials in Los Angeles and Michigan." Drake, 321 F.3d at 342. The Court must first note that the Second Circuit's characterization of Walter's trial testimony is incorrect. Walter never claimed to have testified at hundreds of trials. Rather, he claimed to have been qualified in one or two jurisdictions. Walter was never asked how many times he had been so qualified.

Q: Have you ever been qualified to testify as an expert witness in any criminal court?
A: Yes.
Q: And in what states and jurisdictions, if you would please.
A: In California, Los Angeles County and in Pasadena.

Trans. at 785. Notwithstanding the fact that Walter did not claim to have testified hundreds of times, there is no doubt that even his actual—more limited—trial testimony was factually incorrect and thus, false. At his deposition, Walter reiterated his prior experience as an expert witness. He could recall testifying only in two prior cases, one murder case and the "Mazda" case. When questioned about the substance of his prior expert testimony, however, Walter revealed that he testified in the murder case in his capacity of the custodian of the evidence—a chain of custody matter—not as a psychological expert. Walter Dep. at 87–88. Walter defended his characterization of his testimony as "expert" because he believed that such testimony was in fact expert testimony. Ibid. The second matter in which Walter could recall testifying prior to the Drake trial was the "Mazda" case—a civil, not a criminal, case. Thus, his testimony in that case was not relevant to the prosecutor's question at trial which specified qualification as an expert in any criminal court.

Although Drake has demonstrated that Walter's testimony at trial was factually incorrect, and thus false, he has not shown that Walter gave such false testimony intentionally. However, as discussed above, the relevant issue is whether Walter's trial testimony concerning his qualifications was false.

Accordingly, the Court concludes that portions of Walter's testimony concerning his past qualification as an expert witness were false.

5. Los Angeles County Medical Examiner's Office

Finally, the area of most concern is Walter's trial testimony relative to his work experience in the Los Angeles County Medical Examiner's Office. At the beginning of his testimony on direct examination on this topic, Walter testified that he was: "a student professional worker at the time, while I was taking an academic course work in criminal justice. While I was there I consulted with the prosecutors, the police agencies and various investigative agencies. I related to and the pathologists related to moding cause of death and profiling for possible leads."

Trans. at 788–89. Walter testified that, in his position, he had personal involvement in 5,000 to 7,500 cases. Trans. at 789–790. He testified that, in some cases, he would view the decedent's body, confer with pathologists and others, discuss the case with police and investigators and develop a "profile." Trans. At 791. He testified that the purpose of a profile: "was not only to help the pathologists and the investigating agencies figure out what happened, but also then towards leads in resolving the case, whether it was a completed case or understanding the motive behind what occurred. And sometimes that's very complex, so they would take the aid of the profile." Trans. at 791.

What is problematic about Walter's testimony is that, while he may have engaged in such tasks as he described at trial, he was not employed to engage in those tasks. In fact, his employment was for the purpose of working in and maintaining the toxicology laboratory. There is no evidence to suggest that Walter engaged in profiling activities at the behest of the Medical Examiner's Office. To the contrary, there is evidence in the record to suggest that, when the Medical Examiner's Office required profiling, it was conducted by the Medical Examiner himself.[10]

A portion of the statement contains the following questions and answers:

Q: In the course of your employment with the Medical Examiner's Office, did you and/or the [Forensic Science Laboratory] ever prepare psychological profiles, or utilize psychological modeling, or otherwise employ behavioral science to create a composite of a suspect in a criminal case?

A: No, but the Medical Examiner himself did.

Q: If the answer to the above was yes, please explain[.]

A: In certain high profile cases, the medical examiner—Dr. Noguchi [sic]— would have a psychological profile drawn of a yet to be identified murderer. To my knowledge, he never used his own staff.

Statement of Dr. Ronald Taylor, attached to Drake's Objections to the Report and Recommendation.

An affidavit submitted by Dr. Ernest Griesemer, who worked with Walter at the Medical Examiner's Office, indicates that Walter's primary responsibility was to maintain the laboratories at the Medical Examiner's Office. See Drake's Opp'n Mem. at Ex. 6.

In an effort to demonstrate that Walter was more than a mere student assistant, Respondent points to another letter written by Dr. Griesemer to the Ethics Committee of the American Academy of Forensic Sciences in October 1995.

See Resp't's Summ. J. Mot. at Ex. A. Griesemer's letter states in part: "Richard Walter worked in the Forensic Sciences Laboratories of the Department of Coroner, Los Angeles County, Los Angeles, California for two and a half years from 1/76 to 8/78. He was employed as a Student Professional Worker and worked with Forensic Sciences, Toxicology and Histopathology Laboratories and their storage. …

"While he was working here, I noted that Mr. Walter would read through as many of these report and review items as he could and he was continually discussing cases with Coroner's staff members detectives, and insurance investigators. I always had the feeling he was striving to search out the facts and achieve a more complete understanding of underlying circumstances and individual causes of death for specific Coroner's cases.

"Mr. Walter also attended the periodic case reviews and scientific discussions including Psychological Profiles held by the Coroner. He also attended the scientific departmental discussions in meetings of both the Toxicology Section and the Forensic Investigations Section of the Coroner's Department. He sought and was sought after for one-on-one discussions with pathologists working on specific cases and presented materials in some of the meetings. He discussed evidence and case details with Toxicologists and with Forensic Science Investigators in the Department."

---

[10] Attached as an exhibit to Drake's Objections 7 to the Report and Recommendation issued by Magistrate Judge Schroeder is a sworn statement from Dr. Ronald Taylor, who from 1973 to 1981 was the Director of the Forensic Science Laboratory for the Los Angeles County Medical Examiner's Office. The statement is in the form of Taylor's answers to written interrogatories.

Ibid. [11] While the letter sheds some light on Walter's activities during his employment with the Medical Examiner's Office, it confirms that activities such as seeking out pathologists for one-on-one consultation and discussing cases with detectives and other investigators were not the activities for which Walter was compensated. Indeed, Griesemer's statement that he "always had the feeling [Walter] was striving to search out the facts and achieve a more complete understanding of underlying circumstances and individual causes of death…" contrasts markedly with Walter's own sworn testimony that he developed profiles in order to "not only help the pathologists and the investigating agencies figure out what happened, but also then towards leads in resolving the case. …" Trans. at 791.

Griesemer's letter indicates that Walter attended psychological profiles, not that he developed such profiles or that he was expected to develop such profiles in the course of his duties. What is clear is that Walter engaged in the tasks he described at trial only informally and on his own initiative and that he was not employed by the Medical Examiner's Office to do so. Thus, his trial testimony was false.

Furthermore, the Court cannot conclude that Walter was confused or misled by the prosecutor's question at trial. The prosecutor asked simply, "What did you do for the Medical Examiner's Office?" The natural response to such question is a description of the work one is paid to perform. From all indications, if Walter had performed only those tasks he described at Drake's trial, he would not have been performing the job he was apparently hired to do. Despite all evidence—including Walter's own deposition testimony—demonstrating that one of Walter's primary responsibilities was working in and maintaining the laboratories, at the Drake trial Walter did not even mention any work in the laboratories. Thus, the Court cannot conclude that Walter's false testimony in this regard could have been caused by confusion or mistake. Accordingly, for purposes of this motion, the Court will presume that Walter committed perjury with respect to his testimony concerning his work experience in the Medical Examiner's Office.[12]

As of this writing, there have been no formal consequences to this expert for his false testimony.

Case Example: Misrepresentation of Multiple Professional Credentials and Affiliations

In Australia, one researcher's professional misrepresentations have affected the entire community, as he is perhaps the most prolific author of inductive profiling-related material and research to date. A timeline of events is perhaps the best way to demonstrate these misrepresentations.

In 1998, the researcher made an application for employment to Charles Sturt University for the position of "Lecturer Investigations." According to Kocsis v. Charles Sturt University (2001),

> Mr. Kocsis stated in the curriculum vitae for the position of Lecturer Investigations at CSU that the expected date of completion of the degree of Doctor of Philosophy he was undertaking was December 1998. Mr. Kocsis has still not yet completed this degree.

As is evidenced by these court filings, the researcher had not received his Ph.D. in 1998, and had not yet received his Ph.D. by May 30 of 2001.

---

[11] Although the statements in the letter were not made under oath, it is appropriate for the court to consider the contents of the letter because it is accompanied by Griesemer's affidavit affirming that the statements were true when the letter was written in October 1995 and remain true to present.

[12] The testimony clearly was false. However, the court declines to hold that Walter committed perjury.

In April of 1998, the researcher published "Analysis of Spatial Patterns in Serial Rape, Arson, and Burglary: The Utility of Circle Theory of Environmental Range for Psychological Profiling," *Psychiatry, Psychology and Law*, 5(1), April 1998, 195–206, with co-author Harvey J. Irwin. In this peer-reviewed publication, the researcher is described with the following employment information: "Richard N. Kocsis, State Intelligence Group, NSW Police Service." The New South Wales (NSW) Police Service has not ever employed this individual, as this publication would suggest to any reasonable reader.

Also in April of 1998, the researcher published "Organised and Disorganised Criminal Behaviour Syndromes in Arsonists: A Validation Study of a Psychological Profiling Concept," *Psychiatry, Psychology and Law*, 5(1), April 1998, 117–131, with co-authors Harvey J. Irwin and Andrew F. Hayes. In this peer-reviewed publication, the researcher is described with the following employment information: "Richard N. Kocsis, Department of Psychology, University of New England and NSW Police Service." Again, the New South Wales (NSW) Police Service has never employed this person, as this publication would suggest to any reasonable reader.

In November of 1998, the researcher published "The Psychological Profile of Serial Offenders and the Redefinition of the Misnomer of Serial Crime," *Psychiatry, Psychology and Law*, 5(2), November 1998, 197–213, with co-author Harvey J. Irwin. In this peer-reviewed publication, the researcher is described with the following employment information: "Richard N. Kocsis, University of New England and NSW Police Service." Again, the New South Wales (NSW) Police Service has not ever employed this individual, as this publication would suggest to any reasonable reader.

In January of 1999, the researcher was hired as a lecturer at Charles Sturt University. According to Kocsis v. Charles Sturt University (U no. 21249 of 2000), "Mr Kocsis commenced working as a lecturer at CSU on 25 January 1999."

On July 22, 1999, the researcher presented the seminar "An Introduction to Psychological Profiling and an Empirical Assessment of Its Accuracy in Assisting Violent Crime Investigations" at the Australian Institute of Criminology. His employment information is provided as "Richard N. Kocsis, Unit Chief, Criminal Profiling Research Unit, Charles Sturt University." At no time did Charles Sturt University authorize the creation of a "Criminal Profiling Research Unit," let alone appoint the researcher as its "Director."

In March 2000, Kocsis published "Expertise in Psychological Profiling: A Comparative Assessment," *Journal of Interpersonal Violence*, Vol. 15, No. 3, March 2000, 311–331, with co-authors Harvey J. Irwin of University of New England, Australia; Andrew F. Hayes, Dartmouth College; and Ronald Nunn, New South Wales Police Service, Australia. In this peer-reviewed publication, the researcher is described with the following degree and employment information:

> Richard N. Kocsis, Ph.D., is a lecturer in violent crime investigation at the NSW Police Academy, Charles Sturt University. He is also the unit chief of the Criminal Profiling Research (C.P.R.) Unit.

Again, at no time did Charles Sturt University authorize the creation of a "Criminal Profiling Research Unit," let alone appoint the researcher as its "Unit Chief." Moreover, this individual was never hired as a lecturer at the NSW Police Academy. And finally, he had not yet received his Ph.D.

On November 17, 2000, the researcher was fired/annulled by Charles Sturt University, according to Kocsis v. Charles Sturt University (U no. 21249 of 2000) 2001.

In May of 2001, the researcher was officially awarded a Ph.D. in psychology from the University of New England.

This researcher remains registered as a psychologist with the NSW Psychologists Registration Board, as well as a prolific author on the subject of criminal profiling.

Other examples of unethical conduct in criminal profiling are discussed in Chapter 4, "Forensic Psychology, Forensic Psychiatry, and Criminal Profiling: The Mental Health Professional's Contribution to Criminal Profiling."

SOLUTIONS

The problems associated with unethical behavior are not unique to the profiling community, nor are the necessary safeguards beyond reach. There must be clear ethical guidelines, there must be practice standards, and these must be understood and enforced. Ethical forensic examiners of every kind have a duty to employ established practice standards and to seek out membership in professional organizations with stern codes of conduct. They also have a duty to shun affiliations that provide neither. Professional organizations have a corresponding duty to provide competent standards of practice, to enforce their codes of ethics, and to educate or expel members who fail with respect to either. Finally, individual professionals have an equally important duty to call attention to inept or unethical practice as they find it. No such practice occurs in the dark, and those who give even tacit approval are a part of the problem.

A necessary step in this direction is the metacognitive ability to recognize inept practice and conduct in oneself and others. The context will not always make it clear, and examiners are commonly rewarded for incompetence and unprofessionalism when their employers' interests are being served. It is the onus of the individual practitioner to learn and to exemplify the distinguishing philosophy of professional conduct—that one's first responsibility is to one's profession and not one's employer.

In the words of Marcus Aurelius Antoninus, Roman emperor, CE 169–180 (from "The Meditations," 167 CE), "If it is not right do not do it; if it is not true do not say it." This must be an absolute, even when threatened, punished, or rewarded. Otherwise, we are unworthy of the trust that we have been given within the criminal justice system.

SUMMARY

Most criminal profilers operate outside of a specific or written code of professional ethics. Consequently, many criminal profilers give expert advice and opinions without having to worry about being held responsible for them. This is made apparent by the fact that there are numerous high-profile cases where the unethical conduct of profilers has resulted in harm to the personal life of a citizen. This is most commonly accomplished by an implication of guilt based solely on the public inference that innocent citizens fit the characteristics in a profile.

Criminal profilers are regularly sought out to assist or be affiliated with media-related projects on real or fictional offenders and offenses. Ethical dilemmas arise when a creative consultant position on a fictional project promotes the use of the supernatural, the misrepresentation of the certainty of methodology, or the misrepresentation of case facts for dramatic purposes. The profiler's involvement in any project can represent a public endorsement of misinformation about the field. In such instances, the profiler must speak up or resign entirely, as he or she is either a source of competent and informed knowledge based on objective forensic practice or serving no valid professional purpose whatsoever.

Professionals must also not abuse their positions of authority by compromising or exploiting subordinates, publishing misleading material or research, or engaging in misrepresentation or fraud.

The problems associated with unethical behavior are not unique to the profiling community, nor are the necessary safeguards beyond reach. There must be clear ethical guidelines, there must be practice standards, and these must be understood and enforced. Ethical forensic examiners of every kind have a duty to employ established practice standards and to seek out membership in professional organizations with stern codes of conduct. They also have a duty to inform the community regarding unethical conduct, to act as a disincentive to those who actively disregard the mandates of ethical professionalism.

Questions

1. True or False: Lying under oath is not necessarily perjury.
2. Give two examples of fraudulent behavior committed by *pseudoexperts*.
3. Give two examples of fraudulent behavior committed by *dissemblers*.
4. Give two examples of fraudulent behavior committed by *simulators*.
5. Explain why *comfortainment* is unethical.

REFERENCES

BBC News, 1998. Rachel Nickell Detective Quits at 33. June 12, www.news.bbc.co.uk/1/hi/uk/111406.stm.

Brennan, C., 1997. Profiler Admits His Autopsy Briefing Came from Ramsey Lawyers. Rocky Mountain News February 1.

CNN, 1996. Olympic Bomb Chronology, October 26.

CNN, 1997a. FBI Peers Applaud Suspended Agent in Jewell Case, May 29.

CNN, 1997b. Richard Jewell Faces Cloudy Future, July 7.

Collins, J., 1996. The Strange Saga of Richard Jewell. Time November 11.

Drake v. Portuondo, 2003 Docket No. 01–2217, January 31 (321 F.3d 338); argued: September 9, 2002, decided: January 31, 2003.

Drake v. Portuondo, 2006 United States District Court, Western District of New York, 99-CV-0681E(Sr), Memorandum and Order, March 16.

Edwards, C., 1998. Behavior and the Law Reconsidered: Psychological Syndromes and Profiles. Journal of Forensic Science 43 (1), 141–150.

Farhi, P., Weeks, L., 2002. With the Sniper, TV Profilers Missed Their Mark. Washington Post October 25, p. C1.

FBI Agent at Waco Says Bureau Pressured Him on Koresh Reports, 1995. New York Times May 2.

Fox, J., Levin, J., 2003. Media Exaggerate Sniper Threat. USA Today December 8.

Gettlemen, J., 2002. The Hunt for a Sniper: The Profiling: A Frenzy of Speculation Was Wide of the Mark. New York Times October 25.

Hancock, L., 2000. FBI Misled Reno to Get Tear-Gas OK, Ex-Agent Alleged. Dallas Morning News March 6.

Hewitt, B., 1996. Justice Delayed. People November 11.

Kocsis, R., Lincoln, R., Wilson, P., 1998. Validity, Utility and Ethics of Profiling for Serial Violent and Sexual Offenders. Psychiatry, Psychology and Law 6, 1–11.

Kocsis v. Charles Sturt University, 2001. (U no. 21249 of 2000) Australian Industrial Relations Commission, Application for relief re: termination of employment. Sydney, May 30.

McGrath, M., Turvey, B., 2003. Criminal Profilers and the Media: Profiling the Beltway Snipers. In: Petherick, W. (Ed.), Serial Crime. Elsevier Science, Boston, MA.

Saks, M., 2001. Scientific Evidence and the Ethical Obligations of Attorneys. Cleveland State Law Review 49 (3), 421–438.

Santilla, P., Hakkanen, H., Fritzon, K., 2003. Inferring the Characteristics of an Arsonist from Crime Scene Actions: A Case Study in Offender Profiling. International Journal of Police Science and Management 5 (1), 1–15.

Thornton, J.I., 1997. The General Assumptions and Rationale of Forensic Identification. In: Faigman, D., Kaye, D., Saks, M., Sanders, J. (Eds.), Modern Scientific Evidence: The Law and Science of Expert Testimony, vol. 2. West, St. Paul, MN.

Turvey, B., 2003. Forensic Frauds: A Study of 42 Cases. Journal of Behavioral Profiling 4 (1).

Vollmer, A., 1949. The Criminal. Foundation Press, New York, NY.

Worden, A., 1999. Did FBI Staff Feuds Lead to Waco Disaster? APB News September 3.

Zeliff, W., 1995. Testimony to the House of Representatives, Judiciary, Crime Federal Actions at Waco, Texas on August 1, 1995.

CHAPTER 25

Criminal Profiling on Trial
The Admissibility of Criminal Profiling Evidence

Craig M. Cooley, M.S., J.D.*

Profiling is a natural contradiction. Its masters claim to understand the minds of strangers—often irrational killers. It is a soft, inexact science in a field that demands specifics.[1]

[W]hile handwriting is an inexact science, psychological profiling appears to be even more inexact; … psychological profiling remains primarily a law enforcement device for narrowing the field of suspects and is rarely admissible in court.[2]

In my career of sixteen years in police work, I have found that [profiling is] truly a science.[3]

A profile is an investigative tool. It is not science, it is not DNA, it is not latent fingerprints…. It is just one more tool investigators have. But a profile does not tell you who did the crime.[4]

CONTENTS

---

* Much thanks must be given to Professor Shari Diamond of Northwestern University School of Law, as a large portion of this chapter was written for her spring 2004 "Scientific Evidence" seminar. Professor Diamond is the Howard J. Trienens professor of law at Northwestern University School of Law.

[1] Scott Gold and Greg Krikorian, "Profiling Not Always Model of Accuracy Forensics," L.A. Times, July 18, 2002, A.26.
[2] Valente v. Wallace, 332 F.3d 30, 34 (1st Cir. 2003).
[3] Toney v. State, 1996 WL 183411 *2 (Tex. App.) (testimony of Detective Julie Hardin).
[4] "Hunting the Hunter: Profiling the Sniper," CNN.com, Oct. 9, 2002 (quoting former FBI profiler Clint Van Zandt).

KEY TERMS

Daubert v. Merrell Dow Pharmaceuticals, Inc.	Frye v. United States	Motivational analysis
Expert witness	Ipse dixit	UNSUB profiling
	Linkage analysis	

INTRODUCTION

Criminal profiling has captured the American public's imagination. Incorporated into movies such as *Silence of the Lambs*, *Kiss the Girls*, *Hannibal*, and *Red Dragon*, and televisions series such as *Criminal Minds* and *CSI*, criminal profiling has become associated with expert prediction and foresight regarding the criminal mind. Just as forensic scientists interpret and evaluate physical trace evidence to link an offender to a crime scene, criminal profilers rely on behavioral and psychological trace evidence to deduce an offender's likely characteristics or even to link that person to a series of offenses.[5]

At the request of law enforcement agencies stumped by difficult cases, profilers currently enjoy an ever-growing involvement within criminal investigations.[6] Prosecutors have also increasingly relied on criminal profilers.[7] Since the 1980s, prosecutors have turned to these self-professed mind hunters to help explain the imperceptible psychodynamics of crime scenes, as well as the nature of psychopathic or psychotic criminals. The law enforcement profiler serves as a near-perfect expert witness for prosecutors with weak or highly circumstantial cases, offering reconstructions without evidence, psychological testimony without foundation, a sympathetic/pro–law enforcement outlook, and all at little or no extra cost (law enforcement profilers work either on staff in a police agency or for the Federal Bureau of Investigation [FBI], which does not charge local law enforcement for it is profiling-related services).

---

[5] See David Canter, *Criminal Shadows* (5th ed. 1995).
[6] See Laura Parker, "Profiling: Art of the Educated Hunch; TV Experts Draw Picture Quite Close to Suspect," USA Today, Nov. 1, 2002, A.3 ("Profiling the characteristics of a criminal, once dismissed as conjecture, is widely used today to help investigators solve hard-to-crack cases.").
[7] See infra, Appendixes A–C (listing the profiling case law).

That many of these profilers have found their way into the nation's courtrooms should cause great concern. First, because the FBI originally intended to use profiling as an investigative tool, there is very little research substantiating the many far-reaching claims made by profilers. Moreover, the limited research conducted establishes neither the accuracy of profilers nor the validity of their underlying assumptions.[8] Second, as many recent high-profile investigations have established, profiling has much to prove before it can share the forensic spotlight with DNA or even fingerprinting.[9]

With a suspect empirical foundation, curiosity must be directed at how courts have dealt with profiling testimony since the 1980s. Given the U.S. Supreme Court's trilogy regarding expert testimony since the early 1990s, which forces federal judges to act as gatekeepers by identifying and excluding unreliable expert testimony, attention is directed at whether courts are accurately distinguishing between reliable and unreliable expert profiling testimony.[10] While a number of courts have distinguished between scientific validity and investigative reliability as it pertains to profiling, certain courts have not. Courts that have admitted profiling testimony have typically done so only after performing superficial reliability and validity assessments.

Accordingly, the chapter opens with a brief discussion of the various analyses profilers undertake and testify to in court—namely, UNSUB (unknown subject) profiling, motivational analysis, and linkage analysis. The discussion then turns to the different admissibility standards. Next, we chronicle criminal profiling's empirical record. The chapter concludes with a survey of profiling case law.

CRIMINAL PROFILING: FROM CATEGORIZING TO INDIVIDUALIZING OFFENDERS

The American public comprehends profiling's assigned purpose as the prediction of an unknown offender's personality and traits. However, since the early 1990s, profilers developed two additional profiling techniques aimed at detecting an offender's motivation and identity: motivational analysis and linkage analysis.

Traditional or UNSUB Profiling

Historically, law enforcement viewed profiling as an investigative filtering technique aimed at deducing personality characteristics of unknown offenders (i.e., UNSUB profiling).[11] By focusing on the crime scene characteristics, profilers professed they could narrow the relevant offender characteristics, thereby improving law enforcement efficiency by reducing the potential suspect pool.[12] The profiler's primary goal was to

---

[8] As should become evident, this chapter refers largely to FBI-styled profiling methods (a.k.a. criminal investigative analysis). See D. Michael Risinger and Jeffery L. Loop, "Three Card Monte, Monty Hall, Modus Operandi and 'Offender Profiling': Some Lessons of Modern Cognitive Science for the Law of Evidence," 24 Cardozo L. Rev. 193, 243–253 (2002) (discussing the lack of research and the questionable findings of this research). See infra, §V (discussing profiling's empirical evidence).

[9] Profilers provided inaccurate information and profiles in the D.C. sniper case, the May 2002 pipe bombing case, the Derrick Todd Lee serial killer investigation, the Olympic Park bombing case, the UNI-Bomber case, and the Green River killings investigation. See, e.g., Glenn Garvin, "Profile of a Losing Strategy: The Networks Got It Wrong," Sun Herald (Biloxi, MS); Henry K. Lee, "Pitfalls of Profiling Conjuring Up Psyche of Suspects More Gamble Than Science; Profiles Can Help, But They Often Are Proved Wrong," S.F. Chron., May 12, 2002, A.4.

[10] The U.S. Supreme Court's trilogy consists of Daubert v. Merrell Dow Pharmaceuticals, Inc., 509 U.S. 579 (1993); General Electric Co. v. Joiner, 522 U.S. 136 (1997); and Kumho Tire Co., Ltd. v. Carmichael, 526 U.S. 137 (1999). For a discussion concerning the Daubert trilogy, see Michael J. Saks, "The Aftermath of Daubert: An Evolving Jurisprudence of Expert Evidence," 40 Jurimetrics J. 229 (2000). These cases will be discussed infra, §III.

[11] UNSUB = unknown subject.

[12] See Robert J. Homant and Daniel B. Kennedy, "Psychological Aspects of Crime Scene Profiling—Validity Research," 25 Crim. Just. & Behav., 319, 322 (1998).

provide information to help detectives better facilitate and direct their investigations.[13] UNSUB profiling's basic premise is that the manner in which an offender thinks dictates the individual's criminal behavioral patterns.[14]

UNSUB profiling differs in two respects with the traditional forensic sciences. First, whereas forensic scientists deal with physical evidence deposited at crime scenes, profilers focus on the crime scene's psychological evidence. Second, UNSUB profiling is not aimed at individualizing the psychological residue; instead, it is geared toward categorizing the evidence so investigations can operate more effectively.[15]

Forensic scientists initially examine physical substances in order to identify (or categorize) and quantify these substances; for example, Is there alcohol in the blood, and if so how much?[16] Categorizing or identifying a substance, object, or mark, however, is not the ultimate goal for forensic scientists; rather, individualization is the primary goal. Individualizing an object, substance, or mark simply means it is possible to link the object, substance, or mark back to a unique object (e.g., tool, firearm) or person (e.g., DNA, fingerprints, bite marks), to the exclusion of all other objects or persons in the entire world.

Utilizing the FBI's disorganized–organized dichotomy (see Chapter 3), profilers categorize an offender's behavior as either organized or disorganized.[17] According to the FBI, a correlation supposedly exists between the quantity of organization or disorganization at a crime scene and the offender's criminal sophistication level.[18] In its crudest form, a "crime scene that is messy, with a lot of physical evidence, can be labeled 'disorganized,'" whereas a "crime scene that has very little evidence and appears less chaotic, can be labeled 'organized.'"[19] After inferring the crime scene's organizational makeup, profilers inductively predict the unknown offender's likely characteristics.[20]

Modern-Day Profiling: Motivational Analysis and Linkage Analysis

UNSUB profiling can be a valuable investigative tool; it has had little impact, however, in the courtroom because of its prejudicial effect against defendants. Evidence that attempts to link the general characteristics of serial murderers, rapists, or child molesters to a defendant's specific characteristics is of little probative value and extremely prejudicial, as the defendant is essentially being accused by a witness who was not present at the crime or crimes.[21] Consequently, UNSUB profiling has generally been inadmissible.[22]

---

[13] See Richard Ault and James Reese, "A Psychological Assessment of Crime: Profiling," 49 FBI Law Enforcement Bulletin 3, Mar. 1980, 22, 23.

[14] See Robert R. Ressler et al., "Criminal Profiling from Crime Scene Analysis," 4 Behav. Sci. & L., 401, 405 (1986).

[15] See Bob Baker, "Psychological Profile: Probing Killer's Mind," L.A. Times, Aug. 29, 1985, 1 ("The best [profiling can] … do is save detectives valuable time by winnowing out some of the 2,000 tips that have poured in.").

[16] See generally Michael J. Saks, "Implications of the Daubert Test for Forensic Identification Science," 1 Shepard's Expert & Sci. Evid. Q. 427 (1997) (discussing identification and categorization); Craig M. Cooley, "Forensic Individualization Science and the Capital Jury: Are Witherspoon Jurors More Deferential to Suspect Science Than Non-Witherspoon Jurors?" 28 S. Ill. U. L.J. 273, 303–05 (2004) (discussing categorization and individuality).

[17] See Robert R. Hazelwood and John E. Douglas, "The Lust Murderer," 49 FBI Law Enforcement Bulletin 18, Apr. 1980, 18 (first introducing the disorganized–organized analytical framework).

[18] See John E. Douglas et al., *Crime Classification Manual*, 9 (1992).

[19] Brent Turvey, *Criminal Profiling: An Introduction to Behavioral Evidence Analysis*, 219–220 (2nd ed. 2002).

[20] See Anthony J. Pinizzotto, "Forensic Psychology: Criminal Personality Profiling," 12 J. Police Sci. & Admin., 32, 33 (1984). See Chapter 3 of this text (listing offender characteristics for "organized" and "disorganized" offenders).

[21] See Simmons v. State, 797 So.2d 1134, 1150 (Ala. Crim. App. 1999).

[22] See, e.g., United States v. Pierre, 812 F.2d 417 (8th Cir. 1987); State v. Person, 564 A.2d 626 (Conn.App.Ct. 1989), aff'd, 568 A.2d 796 (Conn. 1990); Gilstrap v. State, 450 S.E.2d 436 (Ga. Ct. App. 1994); People v. Edwards, 586 N.E.2d 1326 (Ill. App. Ct. 1992); State v. Armstrong, 587 So. 168 (La. Ct. App. 1991).

As profiling became increasingly identifiable during the 1980s,[23] profilers began to believe their methods should be employed in court as well.[24] Cognizant that UNSUB profiling would certainly be excluded, profilers were forced to reorient their focus so they could use their mind-hunting skills in court. It was with this objective that the profiling community created motivational analysis and linkage analysis. Rather than narrowing the suspect pool, motivational analysis and linkage analysis identifies two characteristics routinely relied on during criminal trials: (1) motive and (2) identity. In short, the profiling community redirected its focus from criminal investigations to criminal and evidence law.

In terms of criminal law, profilers zeroed in on an assailant's motive. Although not an absolute requisite at trial, a prosecutor without a motive is in essence a sea captain without a boat—both are going nowhere fast.[25] Accordingly, during the late 1980s and early 1990s, the profiling community unveiled motivational analysis. In regard to evidence law, profilers became aware of the often hotly debated topic of character evidence. Profilers either realized or were made aware of the fact that similarities between the crime[s] charged and crime[s] previously committed by the defendant may be offered by prosecutors to establish the identity of the offender who committed the charged offense.[26] Profilers, in effect, intertwined the individuality premise with the legal concepts of modus operandi and signature when they developed linkage analysis.

Motivational Analysis

Motivational analysis concerns detecting the offense's likely motive by evaluating the crime scene characteristics and physical evidence.[27] Motivational analysis centers on criminal law's curiosity and desire for motive evidence.[28] While motive may be an "unfortunately ambiguous" word,[29] legal practitioners have come to understand motive as "[s]omething … that leads one to act."[30]

If motive is not an essential element of any charge, then why and how has the profiling community found a comfortable niche in this area of criminal law? The answer rests in the fact that motive evidence can be instrumental in securing convictions where evidence is entirely circumstantial.[31] In the typical prosecution, there is abundant proof the underlying criminal act occurred. For example, in a murder prosecution, the act's occurrence will typically not be debated. Occasionally, however, there is a justifiable dispute about whether an act occurred. For instance, when a suspected murder victim's body is not found, there remains legitimate doubt a murder actually occurred. Alternatively, the condition of a dead body might not reveal a specific manner or cause of death. Further still, certain cases that lack physical evidence or disinterested witnesses

---

[23] See Stephen G. Michaud, "The F.B.I.'s New Psyche Squad," N.Y. Times, Oct. 26, 1986, 40 (noting the FBI's Behavioral Science Unit's increased notoriety).

[24] For instance, many attribute the Wayne Williams prosecution (Atlanta child killer case) as legitimizing criminal profiling. Most of the work performed by John Douglas, the FBI's head profiler at the time, was conducted during Williams's trial. See Ed Foster-Simeon, "Manhunter: The FBI's John Douglas, Tracking Serial Killers," Wash. Times, Aug. 2, 1989, 1.

[25] See John F. Decker, "Illinois Criminal Law: Student Edition," 114 (2nd ed. 2000) ("Though motive is not a necessary ingredient to proving murder (or any other crime), it may be an important circumstance in determining the defendant's guilt where the evidence is entirely circumstantial. Thus, the state will be allowed to show the defendant's motive if it deems such a showing necessary to establish guilt.")

[26] See Fed. R. Evid. 404 (B); Edward J. Imwinkelried et al., "Courtroom Criminal Evidence," § 907, at 319 (3d 1998) (discussing 404(b)).

[27] See State v. Stevens, 78 S.W.3d 817, 830 (Tenn. 2002) (discussing motivational analysis).

[28] Like many amorphously defined legal terms, motive is no different. Legal scholars have been unable to articulate a precise workable definition. See David P. Leonard, "Character and Motive in Evidence Law," 34 Loy. L. A. L. Rev. 439, 445 (2001) (commenting on the diversity of definitions afforded to motive).

[29] John H. Wigmore, *A Students' Textbook of the Law of Evidence*, 76 (1935).

[30] *Black's Law Dictionary*, 1034 (7th ed., Bryan A. Garner ed., 1999).

[31] Decker, supra note 25, at 114.

can make the criminal acts commission a matter of legitimate dispute.[32] Consequently, when parties dispute the criminal act's occurrence, evidence that the person charged with the act was reasonably motivated to commit the offense can be admissible to prove the act in fact occurred.[33]

Establishing motive can be accomplished by introducing evidence that clearly identifies a specific motive. This evidence is then coupled with circumstantial evidence to prove the defendant's guilt. Suppose, however, no clear motive can be deduced; instead, there is only circumstantial evidence indicating a possible motive (e.g., a sexual motive). More important, inferring this sexual motive can only be accomplished by expert testimony given the jury's general ignorance regarding the psychosexual dynamics of certain crimes. It is under these circumstances profilers have been able to exercise their mind-hunter skills in court. In such cases, prosecutors typically recruit an FBI profiler to interpret the scene and testify whether the defendant acted with a specific motive.[34]

Linkage Analysis

Linkage analysis takes advantage of evidence law's incoherent or "miasmic doctrine"[35] concerning "other crimes' evidence." The "other crimes" doctrine, which is entrenched in Federal Rule of Evidence (FRE) 404 and its counterparts, rules 405, 607, 608, 609 (and perhaps 406's "habit" rule),

> grew out of rules of admission and exclusion developed almost exclusively in criminal trials, as courts tried to come to grips with intuitions concerning the relevance, weight, and potential accuracy-harmful effects of evidence concerning the kind of person a defendant might be, especially when this was to be proved by showing specific prior criminal acts of the defendant not in themselves forming any part of the charged crime.[36]

Under FRE 404(a), a person's character, or general propensity to act in a particular way, may not be offered as a basis for the inference that, on a specific occasion, the person acted in conformity with that propensity or trait.[37] This prohibition, however, has exceptions. Under FRE 404(b), prior acts may "be admissible for other purposes, such as proof of motive, opportunity, intent, preparation, plan, knowledge, identity, or absence of mistake or accident."[38]

Under the identity exception, extrinsic evidence may be utilized to prove the defendant's identity as the perpetrator by demonstrating the defendant committed similar crimes with a distinct modus operandi.[39] It is the similarities between the charged and uncharged offenses, not merely the offender's propensity, that

---

[32] See, e.g., John Lentini, "The Scientific Basis of Expert Testimony on Fires, Arsons, and Explosion," in *Science in the Law: Forensic Science Issues*, 376 (David L. Faigman et al., eds., 2002) ("In nearly every fire case, it is circumstantial evidence which allows cause of the fire to be deduced. Likewise, in nearly every arson case, the corpus delicti is proven by circumstantial evidence, and the jury is read the standard circumstantial evidence charge.").

[33] See id. See also Huey L. Golden, "Knowledge, Intent, System, and Motive: A Much Needed Return to the Requirement of Independent Relevance," 55 La. L. Rev. 179, 206 (1994) (by introducing motive evidence, "the prosecution is able to establish the defendant was more likely to have committed the crime than a person without a similar motive").

[34] See infra Appendixes A–C (listing cases). Motivational analysis is primarily utilized to prove that an offense was sexually motivated. See Masters v. People, 58 P.3d 979, 986 (Colo. 2002) ("unlike many other types of homicides, where a motive may be fairly obvious, the motive in a sexual homicide is typically 'intrinsic, internal, [and] very psychological for the individual'" (quoting Dr. Reid Meloy)).

[35] D. Michael Risinger, "John Henry Wigmore, Johnny Lynn Old Chief, and 'Legitimate Moral Force': Keeping the Courtroom Safe for Heartstrings and Gore," 49 Hastings L.J. 403, 428 (1998).

[36] Risinger and Loop, supra note 8, at 204–205.

[37] Fed. R. Evid. 404(a).

[38] Fed. R. Evid 404(b) (emphasis added).

[39] See, e.g., United States v. Feinman, 930 F.2d 495 (6th Cir. 1991); United States v. Khan, 993 F.2d 1368 (9th Cir. 1993).

makes it reasonable to surmise that whoever perpetrated the uncharged offense must have also committed the charged offense.[40] This pattern of similarity is frequently referred to as the offender's signature or print.[41] Nonetheless, if the prosecution wishes to invoke FRE 404(b)'s identify exception, it must establish a very high degree of similarity between the charged and uncharged offenses.[42]

Traditionally, prosecutors and defense attorneys hashed out identity exception arguments in court—without expert assistance. This is reasonable because many lawyers are good at obscuring the generality of their claimed similarities. Moreover, this practice was entirely acceptable "as long as the game was merely a game of lawyer-asserted speculation about base rates, and lawyer rhetoric in the packaging of similarities and differences."[43] Because lawyers were the ones speculating as to the likelihood the defendant committed not only the uncharged but also the charged offense, the legal system felt that the triers of fact could make reasonably accurate judgments regarding the offender's identity after listening to the lawyers' arguments.[44]

The identity game, however, recently changed; there is "a new brand of asserted expertise that claims to be able to identify the right set of variables [indicative] of similarity in such cases, to give at least general testimony on their individual base rates and proper combination, and even to conclude more reliably than the jury that two crimes were committed by the same person."[45] Profilers dubbed this new technique linkage analysis.[46]

UNSUB profiling is an exclusionary tool; its main objective is to narrow the suspect pool. Motivational analysis is also not concerned with individualizing behavior to a particular offender. Nonetheless, since the 1990s, profilers have disregarded their initial declarations that profiling cannot individualize a specific offender.[47]

Profilers have taken major strides toward amalgamating themselves with forensic scientists, as a number of them have claimed that just as an offender's fingerprints or DNA can be individualized, so too can his or her psychological trace evidence.[48]

Linkage analysis consists of evaluating two or more offenses where at least one offense can be associated to a particular individual. When conducting the analysis, profilers concentrate on two types of behaviors: modus operandi (MO) and ritualistic (or signature) behaviors. MO behaviors include only those actions necessary to carry out the offense.[49] Ritualistic or signature behaviors are those that go beyond the actions required to complete the offense; they are said to serve the offender's psychological needs.[50] By evaluating the MO and signature behaviors from the known and unsolved offense[s], profilers claim they can determine whether the individual who committed the known offense also committed the unsolved offense[s].[51]

---

[40] See Imwinkelried et al., supra note 26, at 319 (3rd ed. 1999).

[41] See, e.g., United States v. McQuiston, 998 F.2d 627 (8th Cir. 1993); United States v. Sanchez, 988 F.2d 1384 (5th Cir. 1993).

[42] See, e.g., Commonwealth v. Hawkins, 626 A.2d 550, 552–553 (Pa. 1993) (18 points of similarity not sufficient enough to qualify under identify exception); see also State v. Dunn, 981 P.2d 809, 811, 814 (Or. App. 1999); State v. Fortin, 745 A.2d 509, 517 (N.J. 2000).

[43] Risinger and Loop, supra note 8, at 209.

[44] See id.

[45] Id.

[46] See Stephen G. Michaud and Roy Hazelwood, *The Evil That Men Do*, Ch. 17 (1998) (discussing linkage analysis).

[47] The exception to this is the community of profilers in the Academy of Behavioral Profiling, the independent professional organization cofounded by several of the authors of this textbook. The ethical guidelines of that organization, discussed in the next chapter, preclude the use of criminal profiles or linkage analysis for the purposes of individuation.

[48] The most glaring example comes from former FBI profiler Roy Hazelwood. According to Hazelwood, "An aberrant offender's behavior is as unique as his fingerprints, as his DNA—as a snowflake." Michaud and Hazelwood, supra note 49, at 177.

[49] See Robert D. Keppel, "Signature Murder: A Report of the 1984 Cranbrook, British Columbia Cases," 45 J. Forensic Sci., 500, 501 (2000).

[50] See Turvey, supra note 19, at 279.

[51] State v. Fortin, 745 A.2d 509, 512 (N.J. 2000) (describing in detail the individualizing process).

Thus, like forensic scientists, profilers evaluate similarities and dissimilarities between known and unknown samples. Accordingly, the three premises that underpin individuality's physical evidence context are applicable to psychological trace evidence. First, an offender's behavioral or psychological tendencies exist in a unique, one-of-a-kind form. Second, these tendencies leave equally idiosyncratic traces of themselves in every environment they encounter. And third, the methods of observation, measurement, and inference employed by profilers are sufficient to link these traces back to the one and only individual who produced them.[52] As we reveal later in the chapter, empirical evidence has yet to substantiate these premises.[53]

The move toward individuality profiling, or linkage analysis, was not motivated by investigative considerations because it does little in terms of narrowing the suspect pool. Rather, the creation of linkage analysis was legally motivated; it was developed as a means of acquiring either the admission of other crimes' evidence, which might not otherwise be admitted, or as a means to persuade fact finders that the other crimes' evidence was more consequential than they otherwise might judge, or sometimes both. In short, linkage analysis "was a not a way to identify unknown perpetrators, but a tool to help build a case against defendants already believed to be guilty."[54]

ADMISSIBILITY STANDARDS: FROM GENERAL ACCEPTANCE TO GATEKEEPING JUDGES

Expert witnesses are fundamental to Anglo-American judicial proceedings. Expert witnesses have influenced the legal system since at least the 13th century when judges called on them to aid in their decision making.[55] Courts and legal commentators, nevertheless, have traditionally been weary of expert witnesses.[56] Similarly, the judiciary has struggled to develop admissibility standards for expert testimony,[57] especially scientific testimony.[58] Developing admissibility standards for scientific evidence is difficult because law and science have different philosophies and objectives.[59] Law prefers prompt resolution and finality, whereas science focuses predominantly on precision. Dubious science and slapdash scientists have only complicated the admissibility standard issue.[60]

During the late 19th and early 20th centuries, experts could testify if qualified, and their testimony was beyond the average juror's range of knowledge. Expertise was implied by the expert's success in an occupation or vocation that comprised the subject matter at issue.[61] In 1923, however, in Frye v. United States,[62] the District of Columbia Court of Appeals affirmed the exclusion of a psychologist's finding, based on blood

---

[52] See Craig M. Cooley, "Forensic Science and Capital Punishment Reform: An 'Intellectually Honest' Assessment," 16 Geo. Mason U. Civ. Rts. L.J. (forthcoming 2007) (discussing individuality's three premises).

[53] See Risinger and Loop, supra note 8, at 243 (arguing that "the research data available to profilers, either from their own research or that of others, neither specifically validate the assumptions of the process nor provide the information from which to construct the profiles they produce").

[54] Risinger and Loop, supra note 8, at 254.

[55] See Stephen Landsman, "Of Witches, Madmen, and Product Liability: An Historical Survey of the Use of Expert Testimony," 13 Behav. Sci. & L., 131 (1995).

[56] See John Pitt Taylor, "Treatise on the Law of Evidence," § 50, at 69 (3rd ed. 1858).

[57] See Samuel R. Gross, "Expert Evidence," 1991 Wis. L. Rev., 1113, 1116.

[58] See David L. Faigman et al., "Check Your Crystal Ball at the Courthouse Door, Please: Exploring the Past, Understanding the Present, and Worrying about the Future of Scientific Evidence," 15 Cardozo L. Rev., 1799, 1801 (1994).

[59] See Edward K. Cheng, "Changing Scientific Evidence," 88 Minn. L. Rev., 315, 329–335 (2003) (discussing these differences).

[60] See, e.g., Peter W. Huber, Galileo's Revenge: Junk Science in the Courtroom (1991) (discussing numerous instances over the past century).

[61] See David L. Faigman et al. (eds.), 1 "Modern Scientific Evidence: The Law and Science of Expert Testimony," § 1–2.1, at 4 (2nd ed. 2002).

[62] 293 F. 1013 (D.C. Cir. 1923).

pressure measurements, that a defendant was truthful when he denied committing a murder. In its opinion, the court of appeals required a showing that the expert's novel scientific test for deception be generally accepted in the scientific community.[63] While many courts embraced Frye's general acceptance standard,[64] it had its shortcomings.[65]

In 1975, Congress signed the FRE into law.[66] Rule 702 employed a "helpfulness" standard, which departed from the common law's stricter "beyond the ken" of an ordinary fact-finder standard.[67] Legal scholars characterized this rule as a "relevancy test."[68] As applied, the test often meant once a court qualified a witness, so too was his or her technique automatically qualified.[69] Ironically, neither the advisory committee's commentary nor FRE 702 mentioned Frye. As a result, "in principle, under the Federal Rules no common law of evidence remain[ed]."[70] The failure to clarify whether FRE 702 superseded Frye produced confusion among federal and state courts during the 1970s and 1980s.

The U.S. Supreme Court partially clarified the issue in Daubert v. Merrell Dow Pharmaceuticals, Inc.,[71] when it "held that Frye had been superseded by the [FRE] and that expert testimony could be admitted if the district court deemed it both relevant and reliable."[72] Daubert said trial judges were obligated to act as "gatekeepers" when screening expert testimony to make certain it was "not only relevant, but reliable."[73] Daubert instructed judges not merely to assess whether a technique or theory was generally accepted, but also whether it was amendable to testing and falsification and whether it possessed an identifiable error rate and had undergone peer review.[74] Daubert failed to address whether "technical" and "specialized" knowledge—the two other forms of expert testimony recognized in FRE 702—must also be viewed through this prism.

---

[63] In one of the most oft-cited passages in evidence law, Judge Van Orsdel articulated the "general acceptance" standard:

> Just when a scientific principle or discovery crosses the line between the experimental and demonstrable stages is difficult to define. Somewhere in this twilight zone the evidential force of the principle must be recognized, and while courts will go a long way in admitting expert testimony deduced from a well-recognized scientific principle or discovery, the thing from which the deduction is made must be sufficiently established to have gained general acceptance in the particular field in which it belongs.

Id. at 1013.

[64] See, e.g., United States v. Addison, 498 F.2d 741 (D.C. Cir. 1974); Reed v. State, 391 A.2d 364 (Md. 1978); People v. Kelly, 549 P.2d 1240 (Cal. 1976).

[65] See Paul C. Giannelli, "The Admissibility of Novel Scientific Evidence: Frye v. United States, a Half-Century Later," 80 Colum. L. Rev. 1197, 1208–1228 (1980) (detailing the various difficulties in applying the vague "general acceptance" rule).

[66] See Act of January 2, 1975, Pub. L. No. 93–595, 88 Stat. 1926.

[67] Federal Rule 702 stated the following:

> [I]f scientific, technical, or other specialized knowledge will assist the tried of fact to understand the evidence or to determine a fact in issue, a witness qualified as an expert by knowledge, skill, experience, training, or education, may testify thereto in the form of an opinion or otherwise.

[68] See Paul C. Gianelli, "Daubert: Interpreting the Federal Rules of Evidence," 15 Cardozo L. Rev. 1999 (1994) (discussing the relevancy approach's origin); C. McCormick, Evidence 363–364 (1954).

[69] See Paul C. Giannelli and Edward J. Imwinkelried, *Scientific Evidence*, §1–6, at 30 (3rd ed. 1999).

[70] Edward W. Cleary, "Preliminary Notes on Reading the Rules of Evidence," 57 Neb. L. Rev. 908, 915 (1978).

[71] 509 U.S. 579 (1993).

[72] United States v. Scheffer, 523 U.S. 303, 311 n. 7 (1998). There was nothing remarkably innovative about a trial judge possessing the authority to make an admissibility determination. Federal Rules of Evidence 104(a) and 702 supported this conclusion, and trial judges barred expert testimony long before Daubert. The majority's decision, however, not only identified this power but also stressed that trial judges were obligated to employ this power when confronted with scientific expert testimony.

[73] 509 U.S. at 589.

[74] See id. at 589–593.

The Supreme Court answered this question in Kumho Tire Co. v. Carmichael,[75] holding that Daubert "applies not only to testimony based on 'scientific' knowledge, but also to testimony based on 'technical' and 'other specialized' knowledge."[76] The Supreme Court felt it would be too difficult if trial judges had to apply different rules to areas of knowledge where "there is no clear line that divides … one from the other."[77] Kumho Tire put forth another significant, though less overt, principle; the gatekeeping decision must focus on the "task at hand" and not the standard reliability of a generally and broadly defined area of expertise.[78]

Congress amended FRE 702 in 2000 by codifying Daubert, Kumho Tire, and General Electric Co. v. Joiner.[79] FRE 702 now reads:

> If scientific, technical, or other specialized knowledge will assist the trier of fact to understand the evidence or to determine a fact in issue, a witness qualified as an expert by knowledge, skill, experience, training, or education, may testify thereto in the form of an opinion or otherwise, if (1) the testimony is based upon sufficient facts or data, (2) the testimony is the product of reliable principles and methods, and (3) the witness has applied the principles and methods reliably to the facts of the case.

Like Daubert and its progeny, FRE 702 forces courts to question the empirical underpinnings of all expert testimony and to exclude those opinions that are "connected to existing data only by the ipse dixit of the expert."[80]

CRIMINAL PROFILING'S EMPIRICAL PROOF, RELEVANCE, AND PREDICTABILITY

Profiling's empirical record is barely visible; the little research generated fails to substantiate the premises that support its continued existence.[81] This is not unexpected because

> profilers tend to exhibit exceptionally strong professional rivalry and jealousy, and thus they hesitate to expose any shortcomings in their profiling expertise where there is no personal gain in their doing so.[82]

Its nonexistent empirical record calls into question whether profiling is even relevant and whether profilers can offer accurate predictions. If evidence is neither relevant nor reliable, it should not be admissible. Lastly, if experts cannot moderately outperform ordinary laypersons in regard to the task that the expert claims expertise in, their testimony is of no benefit to the trier of fact; it is irrelevant and inadmissible.[83] As the Illinois Supreme Court acknowledged:

---

[75] 526 U.S. 137 (1999).

[76] Id. at 141.

[77] Id. at 148.

[78] See D. Michael Risinger, "Defining the 'Task at Hand': Non-Science Forensic Science after Kumho Tire Co. v. Carmichael," 57 Wash. and Lee. L. Rev 767 (2000) (discussing and describing this subtle principle in Kumho Tire).

[79] 522 U.S. 136 (1997) (holding that abuse of discretion is the proper standard of review for district court evidentiary rulings).

[80] General Elec. Co. v. Joiner, 522 U.S. 136, 146 (1997). As the district court in United States v. Hines wrote, Daubert and its offspring "plainly invite a reexamination even of 'generally accepted' venerable, technical fields." 55 F.Supp.2d 62, 67 (D. Mass. 1999).

[81] See, e.g., Richard N. Kocsis et al., "Expertise in Psychological Profiling: A Comparative Assessment," 15 J. Interpersonal Violence 311 (2000) ("Although the efforts of psychological profilers may be of practical value, there has been little empirical study of the abilities that mark proficient profilers"); Risinger and Loop, supra note 8 (same); Andreas Mokros and Laurence Alison, "Is Offender Profiling Possible? Testing the Predicted Homology of Crime Scene Actions and Background Characteristics in a Sample of Rapists," 7 Legal & Criminological Psychol. 25 (2002) (same); Laurence Alison et al., "The Personality Paradox in Offender Profiling," Psychol. Pub. Pol'y & L., Mar. 2002, at 115 (same).

[82] Kocsis et al., supra note 82.

[83] See Risinger and Loop, supra note 8, at 243.

Indeed, there appears to be an implicit recognition in some professional circles that the development of supporting databases of systematic and rigorous case studies will be necessary in order to enhance the credibility of profiling as a discipline in the legal profession and enhance the prospects of profiles being admissible as evidence.[84]

Motivational Analysis

Motivational analysis is similar to UNSUB profiling—it rests on the profiler's ability to distinguish between sexual and nonsexual elements of crime scenes. What this implies is that besides the organized–disorganized dichotomy there appears to be a sexual–nonsexual dichotomy. The words "appears to be" are emphasized because this dichotomy is not explicitly spelled out in the profiling literature like the organized–disorganized dichotomy.[85] The dichotomy can only be piecemealed together by reading the sparse case law and profiling memoirs. This endeavor, nonetheless, still fails to paint a clear picture as to what factors are symptomatic of sexual homicide.[86] More important, even if a list of symptoms or crime scene characteristics could be articulated, one could still question whether they were relevant or probative in determining whether a homicide or crime was sexually motivated.

FRE 401 defines "relevant evidence" as evidence that has "any tendency to make the existence of any fact that is of consequence to the determination of the action more probable or less probable than it would be without the evidence."[87] In a homicide case, evidence that the homicide exhibited a particular crime scene characteristic (CSC) is relevant for proving the homicide was sexually motivated if the symptom's presence increases the chance that the homicide was actually motivated by some sexual propensity. One can ascertain whether a CSC increases the likelihood the homicide was actually sexually provoked by considering two proportions: the proportion of sexual homicide cases in which the CSC occurs and the proportion of nonsexual homicide cases in which the CSC occurs. If the proportion of sexual homicide cases exhibiting the CSC is significantly greater than the proportion of nonsexual homicide cases exhibiting the CSC, then the CSC is relevant for proving the homicide was sexually motivated.[88] Scholars refer to this

---

[84] People v. Metz, 842 N.E.2d 618, 657 (Ill. 2005) (citation omitted).

[85] Although the FBI authored *Sexual Homicide: Patterns and Motives*, the book fails to provide a concrete list of crime scene characteristics that distinguishes between sexual and nonsexual homicides. See Robert K. Ressler et al., *Sexual Homicides: Patterns and Motives* (1995).

[86] See, e.g., State v. Lowe, 599 N.E.2d 783, 784 (Ohio App. 1991) (preplanning is an indicator of a sexual homicide); State v. Stevens, 2001 WL 579054 at *13–14 (Tenn. Crim. App.) (punishment, degradation, humiliation, and pornographic material indicative of sexual homicide); Simmons v. State, 797 So. 2d 1134 (Ala. Crim. App. 1999) (ante and postmortem stabbing of sexually significant areas [buttocks, genitals, breasts] and evidence that the offender cleaned the crime scene before he departed from the scene were indicative of sexual homicide). According to Dr. Reid Meloy, a forensic psychologist who specializes in sexual homicide,

> [t]he features that distinguish a sexual homicide are: (1) primary sexual activity usually involving semen or ejaculation; (2) secondary sexual activities with attention paid to the victim as a sex object, including (a) undressing of a female victim and exposure of the breasts or genitals, (b) acts of violence involving mutilation of the body in the areas of the breast or vagina, (c) insertion of objects into the mouth, anus, or vagina, or (d) posing the body or displaying it in an area where it will be discovered easily.

Masters v. People, 58 P.3d 979, 986 (Colo. 2002).

[87] See Fed. R. Evid. 401.

[88] See Richard O. Lempert, "Modeling Relevance," 75 Mich. L. Rev. 1021, 1026 (1977) ("[E]vidence is logically relevant only when the probability of finding that evidence given the truth of some hypothesis at issue in the case differs from the probability of finding the same evidence given the falsity of the hypothesis at issue.").

ratio of proportions as the *relevance ratio* and suggest that this ratio is the apposite standard against which to calculate expert testimony's relevance.[89]

Profilers frequently testify that certain CSCs are "consistent with" sexual homicide. Under the relevance ratio approach, however, CSCs that are "consistent with" sexual homicide are only relevant for proving the homicide was sexually motivated when the CSC occurs more frequently in sexual homicides than nonsexual homicides. As it is generally utilized in the profiling community, the "consistent with" phrase does not necessitate consideration of the frequency with which the CSC occurs among nonsexually motivated homicides. Accordingly, the "consistent with" language simply represents an observation that at least a number of sexual homicides exhibit the CSC. Consequently, when profilers testify that a crime scene's characteristics are "consistent with" a sexually motivated homicide, this testimony notifies the fact finders that the numerator of the relevance ratio is nonzero, but it fails to inform them about the denominator. The numerator, however, must be judged against the denominator for the CSC's relevance to be comprehended by the fact finders.[90] Besides being unclear as to the actual numerator, profilers have conducted no research to determine the denominator or base rate regarding the few factors that they claim are symptomatic sexually motivated offenses.[91] Simply put, when the "consistent with" phrase is employed in this context, it does not and cannot equate to "probative of."[92]

Moreover, any expertise offered to courts must present with some marginal advantage of performance over the commonplace juror before it can be admissible. Taking this into consideration, one must question whether profilers can actually demonstrate a decipherable advantage of performance over ordinary jurors once jurors are made aware of the common CSCs that are allegedly indicative of sexual homicide. These CSCs do not seem to require expert testimony explaining their sexual nature. For instance, the presence of pornography, stabbing sexually significant body regions, ligatures located on a half-naked body, inserting foreign objects into the anus or vagina, and undressing a female victim, need very little, if any, expert interpretation; the evidence speaks for itself. No juror research has yet established that jurors are so ignorant and sexually uninformed they would not be able to acknowledge the sexual nature of these acts. Given the obvious nature of these CSCs, it is not surprising to find that the only two "comparative proficiency studies" conducted thus far lend no support to the claim profilers are significantly better at distinguishing between sexually and nonsexually motivated offenses (or organized and disorganized crime scenes) than laypersons and nonprofiling professionals (e.g., detectives, clinical psychologists, psychics).[93]

UNSUB Profiling

UNSUB profiling is premised on unsophisticated trait theories of personality, in which forecasting personality traits relies on a paradigm that is nomothetic, deterministic, and nonsituationist. UNSUB profiling is nomothetic because it endeavors to construct general predictions about assailants; it is deterministic because

---

[89] See Thomas D. Lyon and Jonathan J. Koehler, "The Relevance Ratio: Evaluating the Probative Value of Expert Testimony in Child Sexual Abuse Cases," 82 Cornell L. Rev. 43, 46–50 (1996) (discussing and advocating for the employment of the "relevance ratio" in assessing the relevance of expert testimony).

[90] See id. at 51. See also Jeffery J. Rachlinski, "Heuristics and Biases in the Courts: Ignorance or Adaptation," 79 Or. L. Rev. 61, 89–90 (2000) (discussing the "consistent with" fallacy with respect to probativeness and relevance).

[91] See supra note 83 (discussing the research or lack thereof).

[92] See Rachlinski, supra note 83, at 90.

[93] See Anthony J. Pinizzotto and Norman J. Finkel, "Criminal Personality Profiling: An Outcome and Process Study," 14 Law & Hum. Behav. 215 (1990) (finding that profilers sustained a 75% to 80% accuracy rate, which was typical of other nonprofiling groups over a wider range of details); Kocsis et al., supra note 83 (finding that profilers were not significantly better than the nonprofiling test groups).

it assumes the perpetrator's actions are influenced in predictable manners; and it is nonsituationist in its conviction that behavior is thought to remain stable across different environmental circumstances. In short, UNSUB profiling is premised on two fundamental assumptions: (1) behavioral uniformity across offenses and (2) steady associations between configurations of offense behaviors and background characteristics.[94] Although empirical data sustain the former, no evidence exists to support the latter.[95]

Even if trait theory research debunks UNSUB profiling's theoretical foundation and its proclaimed validity, one could still expect reliable conclusions rendered by profilers. Consequently, because one of UNSUB profiling's basic classifications is the distinction between organized and disorganized offenders, and the crime scenes that reflect them, one could still expect profilers to come to the same conclusion when evaluating a murder scene and determining whether it is sexually motivated and whether it is organized, disorganized, or mixed.[96] Unfortunately, as Professor Risinger explains, the FBI's "reliability data can give no comfort to those claiming the high accuracy of the FBI profiling practice."[97]

Linkage Analysis

It cannot be overemphasized what profilers claim they can do when conducting a linkage analysis. They claim they can evaluate two or more offenses and determine, by virtue of the common characteristics, whether the same person committed the offenses. Unlike UNSUB profiling and motivational analysis, which are supported by some research, however problematic, there is no research to substantiate the claims made by profilers engaged in linkage analysis. For the most part, the base-rate issues prevalent in motivational analysis are also problematic in linkage analysis. To infer any true significance about a condition or CSC, the individual deducing the significance must first be aware of how common the CSC is across all crime scenes; this sort of research, however, is nonexistent.[98]

Moreover, identifying the so-called significant CSCs in linkage analysis is left to the profiler's whim. This complicates issues of "data-dredging" or "data-trawling."[99] For instance, in a situation rich with information, which possesses countless prospective data variables, various post hoc associations can be recognized and singled out. Moreover, these associations will not necessarily be the inconsequential sort easily written off because of observably high base rates of occurrence (e.g., the offender had two hands, the suspect has two hands, the offender had five fingers, the suspect has five fingers, and so forth). Quite the opposite may occur, as it does not require many variables to obtain numerous moderately low base-rate associations post hoc, as long as the profiler has not restricted himself or herself to any specific variable(s) before the examination. A false impression of significance can be generated in any context because of this phenomenon, particularly in those situations where reevaluations are carelessly performed on the preexisting information. This reexamination is referred to as *data-dredging* or *data-trawling*.

---

[94] Homant and Kennedy, supra note 13, at 328 ("[P]rofiling rests on the assumption that at least certain offenders have consistent behavioral traits. This consistency is thought to persist from crime to crime and also to affect various non-criminal aspects of their personality and lifestyle, thus making them, to some extent, identifiable").

[95] See Alison et al., supra note 83, at 115.

[96] See "Classifying Sexual Homicide Crime Scenes: Interrater Reliability," 54 FBI Law Enforcement Bulletin 8, Aug. 1985, 13, 16.

[97] Risinger and Loop, supra note 8, at 247.

[98] Professor Risinger's groundbreaking article comprehensively details the numerous ploys and statistical illusions linkage analysis profilers take advantage of when testifying to whether certain crime scene variables are significant enough to infer that two (or more) crimes were committed by the same perpetrator. See Risinger and Loop, supra note 8.

[99] See generally Mark Klock, "Finding Random Coincidences While Searching for the Holy Writ of Truth: Specification Searches in Law and Public Policy or Cum Hoc Ergo Propter Hoc?" 2001 Wis. L. Rev. 1007.

Data-dredging problems are not infrequent in law, especially in today's forensically dependent criminal justice system. Before linkage analysis, DNA database searches represented the most intriguing and emerging trawl search problems.[100] The DNA database dilemma is itself minor when contrasted with the dredging complexities created by linkage analysis. DNA analysts know beforehand the variables for which they are probing; they do not have the luxury of being able to select variables based on correspondences. On the other hand, profilers are not restricted by a preexamination list of variables, which dictate when an association or match is significant. An association is significant if they choose it to be significant (even though the base rate of the association may be moderately high across all murder scenes). Furthermore, so malleable or unfettered is their "significance identifying" discretion that profilers can basically claim pertinent similarity in the face of explicit dissimilarity almost without limit. This can go on to the point where the reasonable becomes untenable; the alleged similarities being claimed are so universal that their asserted exclusivity is anything but exclusive (e.g., the offender in the first crime utilized a weapon, this offender used a weapon). In short, by expanding the criteria of correspondence, profilers can create the illusion of similarity even in situations where no similarities exist.[101]

Lastly, no proficiency testing has yet to be conducted to determine whether profilers can accurately link two or more offenses employing linkage analysis. Such testing does not seem unfeasible; there are many solved serial cases that can be used as sample cases. For instance, profilers could receive three mock cases, with two being committed by one offender (offender A) and the third committed by a different offender (offender B). If profilers can link the two offenses committed by offender A, such an outcome could presumably legitimize linkage analysis. Nonetheless, until a study like this or other studies are conducted, the claimed expertise of linkage analysis is basically premised on the ipse dixit of practicing profilers. This, according to the Supreme Court, is insufficient to garner admissibility.[102]

Remarkably, the profiling community, in an arrogant manner, acknowledged the lack of research regarding profiling's reliability and accuracy during the congressional hearings pertaining to the *USS Iowa* explosion. When a government committee questioned FBI profiler Dick Ault about the validity and reliability of the FBI's profiling techniques, he responded:

> I certainly appreciate that wonderful academic approach to a practical problem. It is typical of what we find when we see people who have not had the experience of investigating either crime scenes, victims, criminals and so forth in active, ongoing, investigations.... [I]n the field of psychology and psychiatry, there are existing raging arguments about the validity of the very techniques that exist. They won't be resolved in this world. So, to ask us to provide the validity [and reliability] is an exercise in futility.[103]

Although profiling's various undertakings may represent invaluable investigative resources to detectives, the research does not establish that these undertakings are reliable or accurate enough to warrant admissibility. As a result, profiling should be utilized with great prudence in criminal investigations, and not at all as confirmatory evidence in court, until research demonstrates its predictive validity and establishes the base-rate occurrences regarding certain CSC.[104]

---

[100] See David J. Balding, "Errors and Misunderstanding in the Second NRC Report," 37 Jurimetrics J. 469 (1997); Peter Donnelly and Richard D. Friedman, "DNA Database Searches and the Legal Consumption of Scientific Evidence," 97 Mich. L. Rev. 931 (1999).

[101] See Risinger and Loop, supra note 7 (discussing this problem in depth).

[102] "[N]othing in either Daubert or the Federal Rules of Evidence requires a district court to admit opinion evidence that is connected to existing data only by the ipse dixit of the expert." Kumho Tire Co., Ltd. v. Carmichael, 526 U.S. 137, 157 (1999) (quoting General Electric Co. v. Joiner, 522 U.S. 136, 146 (1997)).

[103] Norman Poythress et al., "APA's Expert Panel in the Congressional Review of the *USS Iowa* Incident," 48 AM. Psychologist, 8, 9 (1993) (quoting Agent Ault's congressional testimony).

[104] See Kocsis et al., supra note 83.

Profiling in the Courts

The "question of admissibility of profiler testimony in criminal cases has been a matter of some controversy."[105] For the most part, courts have dealt inconsistently with profiling testimony. Whereas UNSUB profiling has characteristically been excluded, the same cannot be said for motivational analysis and linkage analysis; "recent decisions by state supreme courts seem to come down on the side of exclusion, at least where the evaluative testimony of the profiler is not supported by evidence of reliable databases and methodologies."[106] On a positive note, where courts have excluded motivational analysis or linkage analysis, their rulings have generally been premised on the fact this form of expert testimony is merely investigatively reliable and not reliable and relevant in the legal (or scientific) sense.[107]

Traditional UNSUB Profiling

Excluding Courts

In State v. Parkinson,[108] the Idaho Appellate Court affirmed a trial court's decision to exclude an FBI profile offered by the defendant to support his claim he did not fit the sex offender profile. The court premised its holding on three factors. First, "the F.B.I. sex offender profile … was developed for use by law enforcement officials and … its application was more of an art than a science."[109] Second, the profiler "did not identify the components of the profile or explain how it was developed, other than noting that its development involved interviews with convicted sex offenders."[110] Lastly, the profiler "did not state whether or how the resulting profile had been tested for accuracy or identify the technique's error rate."[111] In short, the court did not abuse its discretion because the "testimony did not provide information from which it could reasonably be ascertained that the profile technique was trustworthy, that it was based upon valid scientific principles, or that it could properly be applied in the manner advocated by Parkinson."[112]

In Pension v. State,[113] the Georgia Appellate Court held that the trial judge committed reversible error by admitting an FBI serial arsonist profile. A Georgia jury convicted Pension of burglary and two counts of arson. As part of the prosecution's case-in-chief, an investigator from the state fire marshal's office testified as an arson expert. Through this expert, the prosecution introduced evidence of an FBI serial arsonist profile.[114] The trial judge permitted the expert to discuss the profile if he refrained from opining whether Pension fit the profile. The expert testified that serial arsonists exhibit these common characteristics:

> white males between 18–27, loners, educational failures, homosexuals or bisexuals, history of
> criminal activity, medical or mental problems, poor employment records, alcohol and drug abuse,

---

[105] People v. Mertz, 842 N.E.2d 618, 657–658 (Ill. 2005).

[106] Id. at 657 (citing State v. Fortin, 843 A.2d 974, 1000–02 (N.J. 2004); State v. Stevens, 78 S.W.3d 817, 836 (Tenn. 2002)).

[107] The investigative-reliability argument is based on the assumption that because many law enforcement and forensic agencies utilize a particular technique, the technique must be reliable and valid. While seemingly reasonable, the argument is misleading. Although usage may be a factor to consider in determining a technique's validity, standing alone it is insufficient. If this were true, the information provided by psychics would be considered trustworthy because they are repeatedly relied on in major cases in certain jurisdictions. See Martin Reiser et al., "An Evaluation of the Use of Psychics in the Investigation of Major Crimes," 7 J. Police Sci. & Admin., 18 (1979). Consistency and accuracy can only be established through empirical testing conducted by fair-minded practitioners and scientists and only when the results are consistently correct or accurate.

[108] 909 P.2d 647 (Idaho App. 1996).

[109] Id. at 653 (emphasis added).

[110] Id.

[111] Id.

[112] Id.

[113] 474 S.E.2d 104 (Ga. App. 1996).

[114] Id. at 254.

and dysfunctional family backgrounds … are mainly walkers who set fires within two miles of their home and act on the spur of the moment, usually for revenge.[115]

In reversing Pension's convictions, the court noted,

> [U]nless a defendant has placed [his] character in issue or has raised some defense which the [profile] is relevant to rebut, the state may not introduce evidence of the [profile], nor may the state introduce character evidence showing a defendant's personality traits and personal history as its foundation for demonstrating the defendant has the characteristics of a typical [profilist].[116]

Pension never placed his character in issue. More important, the trial judge's directive to prosecutors not to apply the profile to Pension was considered worthless given the prosecutor's extensive examination of Pension's personal history and personality traits and his noticeable efforts to associate this evidence to the profile. The court never considered whether the profile's conclusions and the methodology employed to deduce these conclusions were reliable or accurate.

In State v. Fain,[117] an Idaho jury convicted Fain of capital murder. Similar to the defendant in State v. Parkinson,[118] Fain wished to introduce an FBI "psychological profile" to demonstrate he did not fit the child-killer profile. The trial judge excluded the profile. On appeal, the Idaho Supreme Court affirmed because the profile represented "nothing more than the [FBI's] guess … as to the personality composite of the unidentified subject."[119] The court said a "profile … is not a physical scientific test conducted upon actual evidence using well-established scientific principles."[120]

Motivational Analysis

Admitting Courts

In Simmons v. State,[121] a capital murder prosecution, the Alabama Criminal Court of Appeals affirmed a trial judge's decision to admit motivational analysis testimony from an FBI profiler. In order for prosecutors to seek death, they had to establish at least one aggravating factor enumerated in Alabama's death penalty statute; one aggravator was Simmons committed the homicide during first-degree sexual abuse. Under this factor, prosecutors had to prove Simmons subjected the victim to sexual contact by forcible compulsion with the intent to gratify his sexual desire.[122] To prove the murder was sexually motivated, prosecutors called an FBI profiler. The profiler testified that "the offense was sexually motivated and that the person who committed the offense did so for sexual gratification."[123] The jury ultimately convicted and sentenced

---

[115] Id. Before the trial court admitted the profile evidence, the prosecution had already established the following:

> Pension was age 26, lived alone, had a tenth grade education, was unemployed, did not own a vehicle, and walked to the scene of the Walker County Rescue Building fire which was 500 feet from his home. The jury could observe for itself that Pension is a white male.

Id.

[116] Id. at 255.

[117] 774 P.2d 252 (Idaho 1989).

[118] 909 P.2d 647 (Idaho App. 1996).

[119] Fain, 774 P.2d at 257.

[120] Id.

[121] 797 So.2d 1134 (Ala. Crim. App. 1999).

[122] See Ala. Code § 13A-5-40(a).

[123] Simmons, 797 So.2d 1150.

Simmons to death. On appeal, Simmons argued the trial judge erred in admitting the profiler's testimony because it did not satisfy Frye's general acceptance standard.[124]

The Alabama Criminal Court of Appeals disagreed; it held motivational analysis "does not rest on scientific principles like those contemplated in Frye."[125] Rather, profiling testimony represented "specialized knowledge" and thus fell outside Frye's scope.[126] The court evaluated the testimony under Alabama Rule of Evidence 702.[127] Under Rule 702, an expert could testify if his or her "specialized knowledge" assisted "the trier of fact to understand the evidence or to determine a fact in issue."[128] Citing Daubert and Kumho Tire, the court held that before the profiling testimony could be admitted, the trial judge had to determine whether it was sufficiently reliable.[129]

The court of appeals held that motivational analysis was sufficiently reliable. First, the court cited the profiler's testimony that "research ha[d] been published within the field and subjected to peer review."[130] Second, the profiler "established the general acceptance of [motivational analysis] when he testified that numerous law enforcement agencies relied upon [motivational analysis] when conducting their investigations."[131] Third, the profiler "detailed the theories supporting [motivational analysis], the way the theories are applied by others with the same 'specialized knowledge,' and the way the specialized knowledge was applied in this particular case."[132]

In United States v. Meeks,[133] prosecutors charged Meeks with two counts of first-degree murder. At trial, prosecutors presented an FBI profiler whose testimony was "limited solely to the analysis of the physical aspects of the crime scene."[134] The profiler testified that the person responsible for the murders went to the scene "with sex and killing on his mind."[135] A military jury ultimately convicted and sentenced Meeks to life in prison.

On appeal, Meeks argued the FBI profiler's testimony was "nothing more than … speculation" and should have been excluded.[136] The military court of appeals disagreed and held the trial judge did not abuse its discretion. According to the court of appeals, under Military Rule of Evidence 702, an expert may testify if his or her "scientific, technical, or other specialized knowledge" assists the jury in "understand[ing] the evidence or to determine a fact in issue."[137] The court of appeals emphasized that an expert "need not be 'an outstanding practitioner,' but need only be a person who can help the [jury]."[138]

---

[124] The Alabama Supreme Court adopted the Frye standard for novel scientific evidence in Ex parte Perry, 586 So.2d 242, 247 (Ala. 1991).

[125] Simmons, 797 So.2d 1150.

[126] Id.

[127] Under Ala. R. Evid. Rule 702,

> If scientific, technical, or other specialized knowledge will assist the trier of fact to understand the evidence or to determine a fact in issue, a witness qualified as an expert by knowledge, skill, experience, training, or education, may testify thereto in the form of an opinion or otherwise.

[128] Id. at 1154 (citing Ala. R. Evid. Rule 702).

[129] Id.

[130] Id. 1155.

[131] Id. This is a quintessential investigative reliability argument. As noted supra, see note 106, usage does not equate to reliability or accuracy. If this were the case astrologers could legitimately claim their professional opinions are reliable and valid.

[132] Id.

[133] 35 M. J. 64 (CMA 1992).

[134] Id. at 66.

[135] Id. (emphasis added).

[136] Id. at 67.

[137] Mil. R. Evid. Rule 702.

[138] Meeks, 35 M. J. at 67 (citation omitted).

The court of appeals held that motivational analysis can "hardly be considered speculation." First, it is "generally recognized as a body of specialized knowledge."[139] Second, "such evidence has been admitted in several state courts."[140] Lastly, the "admission of such evidence is consistent with the practice in Federal civilian courts of admitting evidence from qualified police officers concerning the techniques and methods employed in criminal acts."[141] The court of appeals never indicated or considered whether the profiler's testimony was reliable or accurate. Instead, because the testimony was not considered conjecture the court deemed it helpful and thus admissible.

Excluding Courts

In State v. Stevens,[142] a capital murder case, the Tennessee Supreme Court affirmed a trial judge and appellate court's decision to exclude an FBI profiler's testimony that two murders were sexually motivated.[143] The appellate court's decision, which relied on Kumho Tire, held that despite the nonscientific nature of the profiler's testimony, the trial judge did not abuse its discretion by assessing the profiler's testimony under a Daubert-like standard.[144] In affirming the appellate court's decision, the Tennessee Supreme Court held that the profiler's testimony was "not based on scientific theory and methodology, but rather, is based on nonscientific 'specialized knowledge,' that is, the expert's experience."[145] The Tennessee Supreme Court said the profiler's testimony must still satisfy Military Rule of Evidence 702's reliability requirement—something it could not do.

To begin with, the profiler's opinion that the homicides were sexually motivated was "connected to existing data only by the [profiler's] ipse dixit."[146] Citing General Electric Co. v. Joiner,[147] the court held that

> nothing in either Daubert or the Federal Rules of Evidence requires a district court to admit
> opinion evidence which is connected to existing data only by the ipse dixit of the expert. A court
> may conclude that there is simply too great an analytical gap between the data and the opinion
> proffered.[148]

The court added, "Although we do not doubt the usefulness of behavioral analysis to assist law enforcement officials in their criminal investigations, we cannot allow an individual's guilt or innocence to be determined by 'the ipse dixit' of the expert."[149] Likewise, the court thought profiling testimony was too

---

[139] Id. at 68.

[140] Id. To support this claim, the court cites Dailey v. State, 594 So.2d 254, 258 (Fla. 1991) (sexual battery); State v. Asherman, 478 A.2d 227, 235 (Conn. 1984) (bite mark, hair, and blood); People v. Nolan, 504 N.E.2d 205, 207 (Ill. App. 1987) (crime scene analysis); Hill v. State, 647 S.W.2d 306, 309 (Tex. App. 1982) (defensive nature of wound). None of these cases concerns deducing offender motivation or an offender's personality traits.

[141] Id. United States v. Pearce, 912 F.2d 159, 163 (6th Cir. 1990) (method and techniques employed in drug conspiracy), United States v. Torres, 901 F.2d 205, 236–237 (2d Cir. 1990) (drug operation); United States v. Dunn, 846 F.2d at 762–763 (drug operation); United States v. Espinosa, 827 F.2d 604, 611–613 (9th Cir. 1987) (drug operation), cert. denied, 485 U.S. 968, 108 S.Ct. 1243, 99 L.Ed.2d 441 (1988); United States v. Anderson, 813 F.2d 1450, 1458 (9th Cir. 1987) (drug operation).

[142] 78 S.W.3d 817 (Tenn. 2002).

[143] The Tennessee Appellate Court's decision can be found at State v. Steven, 2001WL 579054 (Tenn. Crim. App.) (profiler's testimony not sufficiently reliable).

[144] Id. at 832.

[145] 78 S.W.3d at 832.

[146] Id. at 835. For instance, the profiler testified that profiling is "not a hard science where you can do controlled experiments and come up with ratios in all this," but the increased demand for such services exemplifies its effectiveness." State v. Stevens, 2001 WL 579054 *16 (Tenn. Crim. App.).

[147] 522 U.S. 136 (1997).

[148] Id. at 146.

[149] Id. at 835.

speculative and unreliable.[150] According to the court, "the FBI's study revealing a seventy-five to eighty percent accuracy rate for crime scene analysis lacks sufficient trustworthiness to constitute evidence of this technique's reliability."[151] The court added:

> In this case, there is no testimony regarding how the FBI determined the accuracy rate of this analysis. For example, was accuracy determined by confessions or convictions, or both? Even then, the absence of a confession does not indicate the offender's innocence and thus an inaccuracy in the technique. Clearly, the accuracy rate alone, without any explanation of the methodologies used in the study, is insufficient to serve as the foundation for the admission of this testimony.[152]

In State v. Roquemore,[153] the Ohio Appellate Court said a trial judge committed reversible error when he admitted profiling testimony in a rape and manslaughter prosecution.[154] When questioned if he had an opinion as to whether a rape occurred, the profiler answered yes.[155] The profiler further testified the rape exhibited an "anger retaliatory type of motivational structure."[156] The prosecution claimed the profiler's testimony rebutted the defendant's claim he did not rape the victim.

From the court's perspective, while the testimony was relevant, it was not sufficiently reliable nor did it assist the jury as required by Ohio law.[157] Although the profiler testified his conclusions were probabilistically manufactured,

> he d[id] not keep files on all the cases he reviews (only approximately twenty-five percent of them), nor d[id] he keep statistics about them. He stated that he used statistics from other sources, including the FBI, *but there is no indication as to how he reaches his conclusions.*[158]

The court held that the triers of fact are "perfectly capable of making the analysis and factual determinations" of whether a rape occurred "without opinion testimony."[159]

In State v. Lowe,[160] the Ohio Appellate Court affirmed a trial judge's decision to exclude an FBI profiler's motivational analysis testimony. The profiler intended to testify that "based upon his review of the crime scene materials, he was of the opinion that the motivation for the [victim's death] was sexual."[161] In affirming, the appellate court said while the profiler's testimony "might be used to investigate … it d[id] not have the reliability to be evidence."[162] First, the profiler repeatedly said his "testimony … could [not] be

---

[150] According to the court, the profiler "acknowledged that his analysis involves some degree of speculation, and he further negated the sufficiency of his own analysis when he conceded that each case is "unique" and that criminals are often driven by any number of motives." Id. at 836.

[151] Id.

[152] Id.

[153] 620 N.E.2d 110 (Ohio App. 1993).

[154] Id. at 112.

[155] Id.

[156] Id. at 114.

[157] Ohio R. Evid. 702 reads:

> If scientific, technical, or other specialized knowledge will assist the trier of fact to understand the evidence or to determine a fact in issue, a witness qualified as an expert by knowledge, skill, experience, training, or education, may testify thereto in the form of an opinion or otherwise.

[158] Id. at 114 (emphasis added).

[159] Id.

[160] 599 N.E.2d 783 (Ohio App. 1991).

[161] Id. at 784.

[162] Id. (emphasis added).

stated to a reasonable scientific certainty."[163] Second, the profiler's lack of relevant training and education undermined the reliability of his testimony; the profiler based his opinion "on the behavioral science of clinical psychology, an area in which he ha[d] no formal education, training or license."[164] Third, the profiler did not base his testimony on "scientific analytical processes" but instead his "intuitiveness honed by his considerable experience in the field of homicide investigation."[165] The court concluded:

> While we in no way trivialize the importance of [the profiler's] work in the field of crime detection and criminal apprehension, we do not find that there was sufficient evidence of reliability [to be admitted under the Ohio Rules of Evidence].[166]

Linkage Analysis

Admitting Courts

In Pennell v. State,[167] a capital murder case, the Delaware Supreme Court affirmed a trial judge's decision to permit an FBI profiler to opine whether the same offender committed three murders. On appeal, the defendant argued the profiler's testimony did not satisfy Frye. The Delaware Supreme Court said the defendant's reliance on Frye was "misplaced" because Frye only concerned the "reliability, accuracy and admissibility of certain scientific tests."[168] Linkage analysis, according to the court, did not involve science or scientific tests because the profiler based his opinion "upon his knowledge and experience in the field of crime analysis."[169] Because the profiler premised his opinion on his "knowledge and experience," the court said admissibility must be evaluated under Delaware Rule of Evidence 702.[170] Under Rule 702, the profiler's testimony was admissible because it was "not possessed by the average trier of fact" and it was "helpful ... in understanding behavior unknown to the general public."[171] The court did not consider whether the profiler's testimony was valid and reliable.

In State v. Code,[172] another capital murder case, the Louisiana Supreme Court affirmed a trial judge's decision to permit FBI profiler John Douglas (the same profiler used in Pennell) and a medical examiner to opine that the same offender committed six murders.[173] The medical examiner testified that "all three crime scenes were signature crimes of one person" because "the harm was done in a sequential manner and there were similarities in how the persons were handled and killed."[174] Douglas testified that each crime scene had "several identical ritual aspects, the most important being the distinctive handcuff ligature."[175] Douglas added he "had never seen this type of ligature before, nor had any crime enforcement personnel he consulted."[176] Furthermore, Douglas said the "ligatures were tied" so uniquely that if "you would put

---

[163] Id. at 785.

[164] Id.

[165] Id. In short, this opinion was premised on his ipse dixit.

[166] Id.

[167] Pennell v. State, 602 A.2d 48 (Del. 1991).

[168] Id. at 55 (emphasis added).

[169] Id.

[170] Delaware R. Evid. 702 reads:

> If scientific, technical or other specialized knowledge will assist the trier of fact to understand the evidence or to determine a fact in issue, a witness qualified as an expert by knowledge, skill, experience, training or education may testify thereto in the form of an opinion or otherwise.

[171] Id. at 55.

[172] State v. Code, 627 So.2d 1373 (La. 1993).

[173] The profiler only testified during a Rule 404(b) admissibility hearing and not during trial.

[174] Id. at 1282.

[175] Id.

[176] Id.

all those cases together in one pile, you would look and say, 'This all happened at one case. This is one instance.'"[177] Douglas said the similarities were so widespread and obvious "'it [was] not even a difficult case for us [the FBI] ... to show the signature aspect.' Each law enforcement officer that visited the three crime scenes was convinced the murders were the work of the same person."[178]

On appeal, the Louisiana Supreme Court did not ask whether Douglas' and the medical examiner's testimonies were valid and reliable. Instead, it simply said:

> The state showed by clear and convincing evidence the commission of the other crimes and the defendant's connection to them. The expert testimony established that these were signature crimes. The ritual aspects of the Chaney homicides, the Ford homicide and William Code homicides were so distinctive as to lead to the conclusion they were the work of the same person. The issue of identity was genuinely at issue in this case. The other crimes' probative aspect on the identity issue outweighed their prejudice to the defendant.[179]

Excluding Courts

In State v. Fortin,[180] a capital murder case, the New Jersey Supreme Court overturned a conviction and death sentence because a trial judge improperly admitted linkage analysis testimony from a former FBI profiler, Roy Hazelwood. Hazelwood based his opinion that the same offender committed two different crimes (a murder and an attempted murder/sexual assault), by claiming the following:

> In my 35 years of experience ... I have never observed this combination of behaviors in a single crime of violence.... [Consequently], it is my opinion that the same person was responsible for the murder of Ms. Melissa Padilla and the subsequent attempted murder of Ms. Vicki Gardner.[181]

During his second appeal, Fortin argued Hazelwood never produced a database of cases from which his opinion was generated, as required by the New Jersey Supreme Court's initial decision and remand order.[182] The New Jersey Supreme Court ordered Hazelwood to produce the database to "ensure that [his] crime-scene comparison techniques would be subject to verification, allowing the defense a fair opportunity to test his methods and credibility in the crucible of cross-examination."[183] When the defense requested the database on remand, Hazelwood said

> he neither had a list of the files of those cases that he had investigated during his years in law enforcement, nor access to them, and that "[n]o database, evidence or scientific studies were

---

[177] Id.

[178] Id. at 1283.

[179] Id.

[180] 2004 WL 190051 (N.J.).

[181] State v. Fortin, 724 A.2d 818, 826 (N.J. Super. Ct. App. Div. 1999).

[182] See State v. Fortin, 745 A.2d 509 (N.J. 2000). In State v. Fortin, 724 A.2d 818, 826 (N.J. Super. Ct. App. Div. 1999), the New Jersey Appellate Division held that while the attempted murder/sexual assault case was admissible to prove identity under New Jersey R. Evid. 404(b), Hazelwood was not qualified to give linkage analysis expert testimony. In State v. Fortin, 745 A.2d 509, 509 (N.J. 2000) [Fortin I], the New Jersey Supreme Court affirmed; the Court held that Hazelwood's linkage analysis testimony lacked "sufficient scientific reliability" to prove that the same perpetrator committed the murder and the attempted murder/sexual assault. On the other hand, the Fortin I Court held that based on his experience Hazelwood could testify as an expert in criminal investigative techniques, and, as such, could discuss similarities between the crimes, provided that he did not draw "conclusions about the guilt or innocence of the defendant."
Nevertheless, the Fortin I Court qualified it holding; it said Hazelwood's testimony could prove beneficial to the trier of fact in demonstrating that the evidence established an "unusual pattern," provided that Hazelwood "can from a reliable database offer evidence that a combination of bite marks on the breast, bite marks on the chin, and rectal tearing inflicted during a sexual attack is unique in his experience of investigating sexual assault crimes." The Fortin I Court emphasized that Hazelwood's testimony would only be admissible if "there is such a database of cases" so Hazelwood's "premise can be fairly tested and the use of the testimony invokes none of the concerns that we have expressed about the improper use of expert testimony."

[183] 2004 WL 190051 at *17 (N.J.).

reviewed in forming [his] opinion." He professed to have "relied upon [his] experience, education and training in arriving at [his] opinion."[184]

The New Jersey Supreme Court scoffed at the State's argument that Hazlewood had the burden of assembling the database "by researching his publications and tracking down all or some portion of the relevant 7,000 cases that he investigated over the course of his law enforcement career."[185] The court said it was hard to believe an FBI profiler, who authored "five books and scores of articles," did not have the necessary data to piece together even a minor database of cases. The court noted,

> Hazelwood … holds himself out as an expert in this field and presumably has kept records for the purpose of conducting research, publishing articles and books, and presenting lectures. We believe that if he had the will to do so, he could provide some credible database for submission to the trial court.[186]

Because Hazelwood failed to produce a database, the court said his testimony should have been excluded because Hazelwood's experience, publications, and curriculum vitae were inadequate proxies to assess the accuracy and reliability of his linkage analysis testimony.[187]

Harmless Error Courts

In People v. Mertz,[188] an Illinois capital case, prosecutors called James Wright, a former FBI profiler, to testify as to whether the same offender committed an arson and two murders.[189] Prosecutors also asked Wright to "evaluate the crimes, evaluate defendant, and render his opinion as to whether defendant was responsible."[190] On direct examination, Wright said profiling was not "a science. Rather, it is assessment and analysis based solely on years of training and experience."[191] Although Wright opined the same offender committed all three offenses, he "did not … testify that defendant committed the Warner murder or burned down the apartment building."[192]

On appeal to the Illinois Supreme Court, Mertz claimed Wright's testimony was unreliable, irrelevant, and should not have been admitted. The Illinois Supreme Court agreed with Mertz's claim that profiling was unreliable. For instance, the court said, "there appears to be an implicit recognition in some professional circles that the development of supporting databases of systematic and rigorous case studies will be necessary in order to 'enhance the credibility of profiling as a discipline in the legal profession and enhance the prospects of profiles being admissible as evidence.'"[193] It added that "[s]everal years ago, the FBI itself conceded that there had been few systematic efforts to validate its profile-derived classifications."[194] It also said it "would be helpful to see supporting statistics when profiling testimony is proffered in future cases."[195]

---

[184] Id.

[185] Id.

[186] Id. at *20.

[187] See id. at *18.

[188] 842 N.E.2d 618 (Ill. 2005).

[189] Prosecutors initially asked Wright to compare the crimes and say "whatever [he] could about the individual that committed the three crimes or if they could possibly be connected." Id. at 634; id. at 655 (prosecutors asked Wright "to compare the McNamara murder, the Warner murder, and the arson, and say 'whatever [he] could about the individual that committed the three crimes or if they could possibly be connected'").

[190] Id. at 634; id. at 656 ("Wright was asked to engage in the process known as profile-defendant correspondence (P-DC), in which the profiler, using the criteria set out in the crime profile, adduces evidence as to defendant's guilt or innocence.").

[191] Id. at 633.

[192] Id. at 656 (emphasis in original).

[193] Id. at 657 (citation omitted).

[194] Id. at 657.

[195] Id. at 657–658.

Although the court found Wright's profiling testimony suspect, it said it need not decide whether the absence of "supporting statistics" rendered his testimony inadmissible because any error in admitting his testimony was harmless error. It was harmless because much of Wright's testimony "was, for the most part, cumulative of testimony given by other witnesses, and any inferences drawn by Wright were commonsense ones that the jurors no doubt had already drawn for themselves."[196] The court added, "Wright's testimony was, in our opinion, cumulative and essentially superfluous on the issue of the defendant's commission of the Warner murder and the arson. Other evidence sufficiently linked defendant to those offenses."[197] The court also said, "As far as Wright's 'psychiatric or psychological' pronouncements are concerned, we view them—with no disrespect intended—as observations that anyone off the street would have made when presented with the same evidence."[198] In the end, the court added, "any inferences drawn by Wright were commonsense ones that the jurors would have already drawn for themselves."[199]

CONCLUSION

The number of courts that critically evaluated profiling's reliability and accuracy is, to be frank, unexpected. By contrast, it is unclear why so many courts refused, for so long, to conduct similar critical assessments concerning other forensic identification techniques.[200] The answer may lie in the fact that physical evidence provides a concrete form of identification that can be visually appraised before rendering an opinion. Psychological trace evidence, on the other hand, is an abstract identification method; it is impossible to visually evaluate the merits of this evidence before opining on its accuracy and validity. Legal scholars have labeled the different treatment regarding concrete and abstract forms of expert evidence as the "show-and-tell" effect.[201] According to this theory, if the fact finders can evaluate—for themselves—the central facts from which the examiner's opinions were drawn, courts will generally admit the evidence. This approach is based on the assumption that triers of fact can in some way authenticate the examiner's conclusions if presented with the underlying information.[202] Consequently,

> [I]f the subject matter of the evidence seems intuitively accessible to the jury on some superficial level—for example, if it concerns footprints, bite marks, or voices, instead of statistics, epidemiology, or microscopic particles—and the basic facts upon which the evidence is grounded are presented to the jury in an engaging, "show-and-tell" manner, then courts seem to deem the evidence less dangerous to admit.[203]

---

[196] Id.

[197] Id.

[198] Id.

[199] Id. at 660.

[200] See Margaret A. Berger, "Procedural Paradigms for Applying the Daubert Test," 78 Minn. L. Rev. 1345, 1353 (1994) ("Considerable forensic evidence made its way into the courtroom without empirical validation of the underlying theory and/or its particular application"); Michael J. Saks, "Merlin and Solomon: Lessons from the Law's Formative Encounters with Forensic Identification Science," 49 Hastings L.J. 1069, 1082–1090 (1998) (arguing that courts have generally subjected forensic science evidence to insufficient scrutiny).

[201] See "Developments in the Law—Confront the New Challenges of Scientific Evidence," 108 Harv. L. Rev., 1481, 1502 (1995).

[202] See id.

[203] Id. For excellent illustrations of the "show-and-tell" effect, see State v. Bullard, 322 S.E.2d 370 (N.C. 1984) (footprint analysis admitted); People v. Marx, 126 Cal. Rptr. 350, 356 (Cal. Ct. App. 1975) (admitting bite mark evidence by distinguishing it from polygraph, statistical, and other evidence by pointing out that "[w]hat is significantly different about the evidence in this case is this: the trier of fact … was shown models, photographs, X-rays and dozens of slides of the victim's wounds and defendant's teeth…. Thus the basic data on which the experts based their conclusions were verifiable by the court"); State v. Temple, 273 S.E.2d 273, 280 (N.C. 1981) (admitting bite mark evidence because "[p]hotographs of the wound and models used by the experts in reaching their conclusion were presented at trial as evidence and were verifiable by the court").

While fingerprints,[204] questioned documents,[205] hair identification,[206] and footprint identification[207] have recently undergone increased scrutiny, courts need to continue judiciously evaluating all investigative techniques that try to enter the courtroom masquerading as science or specialized knowledge. If courts conduct comprehensive evaluations, more often than not they will discover the technique or asserted science is supported by little or no empirical data; instead, the opinions are typically only supported by the ipse dixit of the expert.[208] If this is the case, as it is with profiling, the testimony should not be admitted—even if every law enforcement agency on the planet employs the technique.

Tables 25.1 through 25.3 cite major cases in which the court has considered profiling and related issues. It should be noted that the author is aware of many cases where such testimony is admitted without challenge. In other words, these case citations are representative as opposed to complete.

SUMMARY

With a suspect empirical foundation, curiosity must be directed at how courts have dealt with profiling testimony since the 1980s. Given the U.S. Supreme Court's trilogy regarding expert testimony since the early 1990s, which forces federal judges to act as gatekeepers by identifying and excluding unreliable expert

---

Table 25.1 UNSUB Profiling/Criminal Investigative Analysis (CIA)

Excluded

U.S. v. Thomas, D.Md., 2006 (not reported in F.Supp.2d) (CIA not reliable; not trustworthy; profiler used circular reasoning and contradicted himself)

People v. Schmidt, 2002 WL 31270258 (Cal. App.) (harmless error)

People v. Robbie, Cal. App. 1 Dist., 2001 (profiler invaded the province of the jury; case overturned)

People v. Avellanet, 662 N.Y.S.2d 345 (1997) (not generally accepted)

Pension v. State, 474 S.E.2d 104 (Ga. App. 1996) (improper character evidence; no ruling on reliability or trustworthiness)

State v. Parkinson, 909 P.2d 647 (Idaho App. 1996) (not sufficiently trustworthy)

Cases Prior to Daubert

State v. Fain, 774 P.2d 252 (Idaho 1989) (not sufficiently reliable)

Admitting Cases

People v. Tuite, 2006 (not reported in Cal. Rptr. 3d) (organized–disorganized typology; no inquiry into accuracy and reliability)

People v. Duvardo, Cal. App. 1 Dist., 2004 (not reported in Cal. Rptr. 3d) (crime scene analysis and victimology testimony not profiling)

---

[204] United State v. Llera Plaza, 179 F.Supp.2d 492 (E.D. Pa. 2002) (fingerprint identification technique did not satisfy Daubert requirements for admissibility of an expert witness's opinion that a particular latent print was that of a particular person), vacated and with'd United States v. Llera Plaza, 188 F.Supp.2d 549 (E.D. Pa. 2002).

[205] United States v. Starzecpyzel, 880 F. Supp. 1027 (S.D. N.Y. 1995) (holding document examination does not pass Daubert's reliability test).

[206] Williamson v. Reynolds, 904 F. Supp. 1529, 1558 (E.D. Okla. 1995), aff'd on other grounds, 110 F.3d 1508, 1523 (10th Cir. 1997) (during habeas corpus proceeding, a federal district court found hair and fiber identification to be so unreliable (or of such undemonstrated reliability) that it was deemed inadmissible).

[207] State v. Berry, 546 S.E.2d 145 (N.C. App. 2001) (excluding footprint testimony); State v. Jones, 541 S.E.2d 813 (S.C. 2001) (excluding footprint testimony); Hurrelbrink v. State, 46 S.W.3d 350 (Tex. App. 2001) (holding admission of footprint testimony, if erroneous, was harmless).

[208] General Electric Co. v. Joiner, 522 U.S. 136, 146 (1997).

Table 25.2 Motivational Analysis

Admitting Cases

People v. Hurth, 2002 WL 1172930 (Cal. App.) (no inquiry into accuracy and reliability)

Masters v. People, 58 P.3d 979 (Colo. 2002) (no inquiry into accuracy and reliability)

People v. Masters, 33 P.3d 1191 (Colo. App. 2001)

Simmons v. State, 797 So.2d 1134 (Ala. Crim. App. 1999) (no discussion regarding reliability or accuracy of motivational analysis)

Toney v. State, 1996 WL 183411 (Tex. App.)

Cases Prior to Daubert

United States v. Meeks, 35 M. J. 64 (CMA 1992)

Excluded

State v. Garcia, 2002 WL 1874535 (Ohio App.) (invades province of jury)

State v. Stevens, 78 S.W. 817 (Tenn. 2002) (not sufficiently reliable)

State v. Stevens, 2001WL 579054 (Tenn. Crim. App.) (not sufficiently reliable)

Cases Prior to Daubert

State v. Roquemore, 620 N.E.2d 110 (Ohio App. 1993) (not sufficiently reliable)

Lowe v. State, 599 N.E.2d 783 (Ohio App. 1991) (not sufficiently reliable)

State v. Haynes, 1988 WL 99189 (Ohio App.) (not sufficiently reliable)

Table 25.3 Linkage Analysis

Admitted Cases

Kenneth Bogard (Ca. 1995) (no published opinion)

State v. Russell, 882 P.2d 747 (Wash. 1994)

Cases Prior to Daubert

State v. Code, 627 So.2d 1373 (La. 1993) (no consideration as to reliability or accuracy)

Cleophus Prince (Ca. 1993) (no published opinion)

Pennell v. State, 602 A.2d 48 (Del. 1991) (no consideration as to reliability or accuracy)

Excluded

State v. Fortin, 189 N.J. 579, 917 A.2d 746 (N.J. 2007) (VICAP data unreliable/inadmissible)

State v. Fortin, 2004 WL 190051 (N.J.) (reliability not established)

State v. Fortin, 745 A.2d 509 (N.J. 2000) (profiler may testify as a Hines witness)

State v. Dunn, 981 P.2d 809 (Or. App. 1999) (similarities are not sufficiently great)

State v. Fortin, 724 A.2d 818 (N.J. Super. 1999) (insufficiently reliable)

Commonwealth v. Distefano, PICS Case No. 99-0640 (Lackawanna Common Pleas Court, Pa.) April 1999 (insufficiently reliable) (unpublished opinion)

testimony, attention is directed at whether courts are accurately distinguishing between reliable and unreliable expert profiling testimony. While a number of courts have distinguished between scientific validity and investigative reliability as it pertains to profiling, certain courts have not. Courts that have admitted profiling testimony have typically done so only after performing superficial reliability and validity assessments.

Historically, law enforcement viewed profiling as an investigative filtering technique aimed at deducing personality characteristics of unknown offenders (i.e., UNSUB profiling). By focusing on the crime scene characteristics, profilers professed they could narrow the relevant offender characteristics, thereby improving law enforcement efficiency by reducing the potential suspect pool.

Cognizant that UNSUB profiling would certainly be excluded, profilers were forced to reorient their focus so they could use their mind-hunting skills in court. It was with this objective in mind that the profiling community created motivational analysis and linkage analysis. Rather than narrowing the suspect pool, motivational analysis and linkage analysis identify two characteristics routinely relied on during criminal trials: (1) motive and (2) identity.

Motivational analysis concerns detecting the offense's likely motive by evaluating the crime scene characteristics and physical evidence. Evidence introduced to establish motive is generally admissible. However, profilers have routinely crossed the line with such testimony, resulting in unfavorable court rulings.

Linkage analysis takes advantage of evidence law's doctrine concerning other crimes' evidence. Under the identity exception, extrinsic evidence may be utilized to prove the defendant's identity as the perpetrator by demonstrating the defendant committed similar crimes with a distinct modus operandi or behavioral signature. Linkage analysis consists of evaluating the behavior from two or more offenses where at least one offense can be associated with a particular individual. Not unlike motivational analysis, profilers have routinely crossed the line with such testimony, resulting in unfavorable court rulings.

Criminal profiling has a nonexistent empirical record that calls into question whether it is relevant and whether profilers can offer accurate predictions. If evidence is neither relevant nor reliable, it should not be admissible. Ultimately, courts have dealt inconsistently with profiling testimony. Whereas UNSUB profiling has characteristically been excluded, the same cannot be said for motivational analysis and linkage analysis.

ACKNOWLEDGMENTS

Much thanks must be given to Professor Shari Diamond of Northwestern University School of Law, as a large portion of this chapter was written for her spring 2004 "Scientific Evidence" seminar. Professor Diamond is the Howard J. Trienens professor of law at Northwestern University School of Law.

Questions

1. True or False: FBI profilers have empirically established the reliability of their profiling methods.
2. In State v. Fortin, the court _____ the defendant's conviction and death sentence because a trial judge improperly admitted _____ testimony from a former FBI profiler, Roy Hazelwood.
3. Why is profiling testimony generally inadmissible?
4. True or False: The decision in Kumho asserts that the Daubert standard applies to nonscientific testimony, such as that offered by profilers.
5. *Ipse dixit* is Latin for "he himself said it." It refers to assertions that are not _____

Glossary

A priori investigative bias A phenomenon that occurs when investigators, detectives, crime scene personnel, or others somehow involved with an investigation come up with theories uninformed by the facts.

Academy of Behavioral Profiling The first international, independent, multidisciplinary professional organization for students and professionals engaged in criminal profiling or related disciplines.

Accelerant Any fuel (solid, liquid, or gas) that is used to initiate or increase the intensity or speed of the spread of fire.

Action evidence Evidence that shows what happened during the commission of the crime.

Active signature behaviors Behaviors that result from an offender who is in control and intends to leave a specific psychological impression or satisfy a particular emotional need.

Administrative crime scene behaviors Behaviors those that service financial, material, or personal gain.

Administrative force The delivery of a specific, purposeful amount of injury in order to accomplish a particular goal.

Al Qaeda An international terrorist organization that was originally formed in 1988 by Osama bin Laden and his associate Mohammed Atef to rally Arabs who fought in Afghanistan against the Soviet invasion. It is violently anti-Western and seeks to overthrow what it views as heretical regimes and restore rule by fundamentalist Islamic law through force.

Anger retaliatory crime scene behaviors Behaviors indicating a great deal of rage, either toward a specific person, group, institution, or a symbol of either.

Antisocial personality disorder A condition characterized by persistent disregard for, and violation of, the rights of others that begins in childhood or early adolescence and continues into adulthood. Deceit and manipulation are central features of this disorder.

Arranged aspect A disposal site where an offender has arranged the body and the items within the scene in such a manner as to serve ritual or fantasy purposes.

Arson The intentional setting of a fire with the additional intent to damage or defraud.

Asphyxia A condition that is caused by the loss of oxygen to the brain resulting in unconsciousness and death.

Associative evidence Usually a form of trace evidence that can be identification or ownership evidence.

Assumption of integrity The faulty belief that evidence left behind at a scene is protected and vestal until the arrival of police investigators and other responders.

Autoerotic asphyxia The deliberate self-induction of hypoxia with the intent of causing heightened sexual arousal.

Automated modus operandi Refers to software programs that automate certain methods of breaking into computer systems and hiding incriminating evidence, making multiple offenders appear almost indistinguishable.

Availability heuristic The tendency to answer a question of probability by asking whether examples come readily to mind.

Behavioral commonality Behavioral commonality is present when behavioral factors have been compared and they are similar but not unique.

Behavioral consistency theory The belief that the same criminal will behave in relatively the same way across their offense.

Behavioral dissimilarity Behavioral dissimilarity is present when behavioral factors have been compared and they are dissimilar.

Behavioral evidence Any physical, documentary, or testimonial evidence that helps to establish whether, when, or how an action or event has taken place.

Behavioral evidence analysis (BEA) An ideo-deductive method of crime scene analysis and criminal profiling that requires the examination and interpretation of physical evidence, forensic victimology, and crime scene characteristics.

Bestial pornography Pornography that involves the depiction of sex acts between humans and animals.

Bestiality (or zooerasty) Any human sexual act with an animal.

Blitz An offender's method of attack when there is an immediate, brutal application of controlling, sexual, punishing, or lethal physical force aimed at incapacitating or killing the victim, subsequent to the offender's approach.

Blood libel A false accusation of murder made against one or more persons, typically of the Jewish faith.

Bomb An explosive that is detonated by impact, proximity, timing, or other predetermined means.

Broad targeting The intentional infliction of injury or damage in a wide-reaching fashion.

Brutal force Physically aggressive behavior that involves the onset of one or more injuries that inflict tremendous damage, often until death results.

Case linkage The process of determining whether there are discrete connections, or distinctive behavioral factors between two or more previously unrelated cases by means of crime scene analysis.

Chain of custody The record of everyone who has controlled, taken custody of, or had contact with a particular item of evidence from its discovery to the present day.

Child molestation Child molestation is any sexual contact with a child or adolescent below the age of consent.

Collateral victims Victims whom an offender causes to suffer loss, harm, injury, or death (usually by virtue of proximity), in the pursuit of another victim.

Common sense Native good judgment; knowledge accumulated by an individual that is useful for, but specific to, making decisions in the cultures and locations that they live or frequent.

Competency to stand trial A defendant's current ability to understand his or her legal predicament (for example, charges or possible outcomes) and to assist the attorney with his or her defense.

Con approach An approach characterized by an offender who gets close to a victim by use of a deception or subterfuge.

Confirmation bias A form of observer bias, it is the conscious or unconscious tendency to affirm preexisting theories, opinions, or findings.

Comfortainment Providing reassuring, if incorrect, opinions and commentary to the public through the media, intended to entertain or relax the public despite any inaccuracy and ignorance.

Consent The act of giving permission with full awareness of the consequences.

Contact evidence Something that demonstrates whether and how two persons, objects, or locations were at one point associated with each other.

Contributing motivational factors Any circumstances that support or lead to the development of motive.

Control-oriented force Physically aggressive behavior that is intended to restrict victim movements.

Convenience aspect A disposal site that an offender chooses by virtue of the fact that it is available or less difficult than another location.

Cooling-off period (or cooling interval) The interval during which offenders psychologically disconnect, separate, or compartmentalize themselves from the behaviors and motives that led to or culminated in homicidal behavior and then reintegrate back into their noncriminal lives and activities.

Corpus delicti Translated as "the body of the crime" and refers to those essential facts that show a crime has taken place.

Corrective force Physically aggressive behavior that is delivered in response to, or to prevent, undesirable or harmful victim behavior.

Counter-transference Occurs when the patient evokes the feelings of the therapist. With respect to profiling, this can occur when the facts of a case evoke strong feelings in the profiler to the point that he or she is unable to remain objective.

Crime reconstruction The determination of the actions and events surrounding the commission of a crime.

Crime scene An area where a criminal act has taken place.

Crime scene analysis The analytical process of interpreting the specific features of a crime scene and related crime scenes, involving an integrated assessment of the forensic evidence, forensic victimology, and crime scene characteristics.

Crime scene characteristics The features of a scene as evidenced by offender behavior related to decisions about the victim and the offense, in accordance with their contextual meaning.

Crime scene investigation Crime scene investigation includes crime scene examination and documentation, laboratory analysis of physical evidence, scientific interpretation of results, and scientific crime reconstruction.

Crime scene processing Recognizing, documenting, collecting, preserving, and transporting physical evidence at and from a crime scene.

Crime scene type The relationship of the crime scene to the offense behavior.

Criminal investigative analysis (CIA) An investigative process developed by the FBI that identifies the major personality and behavioral characteristics of the offender based on the crimes he or she has committed—in other words, the FBI's term for criminal profiling.

Criminal motive The emotional, psychological, and material needs that impel and are satisfied by behavior.

Criminal pornography Pornography that involves the depiction of actual sex crimes or underage children.

Criminal profiling Inferring the traits of individuals responsible for committing criminal acts.

Criminology The study of crime, criminals, and criminal behavior.

Critical thinking Indiscriminately questioning all evidence and assumptions, no matter what their source.

Cyberpatterns Repeated, discernable sequences of behavior evident in the cybertrails of victims and offenders.

Cybertrails Digital footprints left behind by victims and offenders as they move through the world, electronic and otherwise, often through third-party systems and providers.

Deductive arguments Arguments in which, if the premises are true, then the conclusions must also be true. In a deductive argument, the conclusions flow directly from the premises given.

Defensive force Physically aggressive behavior that is intended to protect the individual administering it from attack, danger, or injury.

Deification Idealizing victims based on who or what they are, without consideration of the facts (e.g., young schoolchildren, missing adolescents, and others who are favored in the press or by public opinion).

Diagnostic evaluation (DE) Rather than being a single profiling method or unified approach, diagnostic evaluation is a generic description of the services offered by medical and mental health professionals relying on clinical experience when giving profiling opinions about offenders, crime scenes, or victims.

Directional evidence Anything that shows where something is going or where it came from.

Disposal site/dumpsite A crime scene where a body is found.

Dissemblers Forensic frauds who exaggerate, embellish, lie about, or otherwise misrepresent their actual findings.

Distance decay The theory that crimes will decrease in frequency the farther away an offender travels from home.

Divine mandates A unique feature of extremism driven by religious ideology: the divine mandates are convictions said to be in accordance with the will of God or some other divine authority.

Domestic child homicide Homicide that occurs when a parent or caretaker kills a child.

Domestic elder homicide Homicide that involves a caretaker (often a family member, private nurse, etc.) who kills an elder in his or her charge.

Domestic homicide Homicide that occurs when one family member, household member, or intimate kills another.

Dynamic modus operandi A modus operandi that an offender consciously changes frequently, and even completely, to avoid detection.

Equivocal forensic analysis A review of the entire body of physical evidence in a given case, questioning all related assumptions and conclusions.

Error rate The frequency of errors, also known as incorrect answers, opinions, conclusions, or interpretations.

Erotica Sexual images that depict mutually pleasurable sexual expression between people who have enough power to there by positive choice.

Ethics Rules or standards that have been established to govern the conduct of members of a profession.

Evidence dynamics Any influence that adds, changes, relocates, obscures, contaminates, or obliterates physical evidence, regardless of intent.

Evidentiary items Items that the offender believes may link him or her to the victim or to the crime.

Exhibitionism Sexual arousal achieved from showing others one's own genitals, or from sex acts (e.g., masturbation, oral sex, vaginal sex, and anal sex) committed in front of an audience, often in public.

Experimental force Behaviors involving force that fulfills nonaggressive, often psychological, and fantasy-oriented needs.

Expert witness An individual who, by virtue of education, training, experience, or skill, possesses knowledge beyond that of the average person.

Explosion The sudden conversion of potential energy (chemical or mechanical) into kinetic energy with the production of heat, gases, and mechanical pressure.

Expressive offenders Offenders who are defined by their heightened emotional state; their motive is personal, being associated with jealousy, anger, power, or sexual desire.

False report (or false allegation) Any untruthful statement, accusation, or complaint to authorities asserting that a crime did or will occur.

False reporter One who makes false allegations or reports.

False reporting The false report, conveyance, or circulation of an alleged or impending criminal offense.

False swearing A false statement, oral or written, made under oath or penalty of perjury.

Falsification Subjecting a theory to repeated attacks in order to disprove it—testing it against the case facts or alternative theories.

Fetish burglary Burglary committed in whole or in part to gather items for sexual purposes.

Fetishism The attribution of erotic or sexual significance to a nonsexual inanimate object or nonsexual body part.

Forensic analysis The examination, testing, and interpretation of any and all available physical evidence.

Forensic assessment A general term that refers to any examination, evaluation, or appraisal of the evidence record and related to the findings in a given case.

Forensic fraud Forensic fraud occurs when experts provide sworn testimony, opinions, or reports bound for court that contain deceptive or misleading findings, opinions, or conclusions, deliberately offered in order to secure an unfair or unlawful gain.

Forensic identification The methods used to classify or individuate items of evidence for court (a.k.a. forensic purposes).

Forensic individualization When an item has some unique feature or property that distinguishes it from all other items.

Forensic psychiatrist A physician who specialized in psychiatry after completing medical school, with board certification in forensic psychiatry, who for court purposes regularly evaluates and diagnoses patients with physical and mental illnesses.

Forensic psychiatry A medical subspecialty that includes research and clinical practice in the many areas in which psychiatry is applied to legal issues.

Forensic psychologist Typically, a person with at least a Ph.D.-level education in psychology, with board certification in forensic psychology, who regularly performs and interprets psychological measures and evaluates and diagnoses patients with mental illnesses for court purposes.

Forensic psychology The application of the science and profession of psychology to questions and issues relating to law and the legal system.

Forensic victimology The scientific study of victims for the purposes of addressing investigative and forensic issues.

Genocide The deliberate and organized killing of large groups of people who are distinguished by their personal, political and religious beliefs, their nationality, and/or their ethnicity.

Geographical profiling A method of estimating the geographic region of an offender's home location, place of work, or other relevant anchor points based on nomothetic data and assumptions.

Goal-directed crime scene behaviors Behaviors intended to fulfill personal gain specific to the offender.

Grooming The process by which a sexual predator gains control over his victim.

Group Any collection of people unified by shared characteristics such as sex, race, color, religion, beliefs, activities, or achievement.

Homology assumption The hypothesis that different criminals who commit similar acts will have similar traits or characteristics.

Honor killing The murder of an individual, almost always a girl or woman, by members of, at the direction of, or on behalf of, the family.

Identification (or Classification) The placement of any item into a specific category of items with similar characteristic. Identification does not require is imply uniqueness.

Idiographic The study of the concrete: examining individuals and their actual qualities.

Idiographic offender profiles Characteristics developed from an examination of a single case, or a series of cases linked by a single offender.

Individuation The assignment of uniqueness to an item; describing it in such a manner as to separate it from all other items.

Indoor crime scenes Crime scenes that exist inside of a structure with walls and some form of ceiling cover from the elements of nature.

Inductive argument When a conclusion is made likely, a matter of some probability, by offering supporting conclusions. It is at best a prediction about what might be true. Often based on statistics, comparisons, or experience.

Inference A particular type of conclusion based on evidence and reasoning.

Inferred evidence Anything that the reconstructionist thinks may have been at the scene when the crime occurred but was not actually found.

Infidelity Any violation or betrayal of the mutually agreed rules and boundaries of an intimate relationship.

Insanity (a.k.a. criminal responsibility) Commonly associated with pleading "not guilty by reason of insanity," this is a legal term referring to the defendant's inability, because of a mental illness or defect, to appreciate the wrongfulness or criminality of his or her behavior during the offense. It is a legal determination as to state of mind and does not imply a specific disorder.

Instrumental offenders Offenders defined by their desire to achieve a specific end, usually financial or materially oriented.

Intended victim The person, group, or institution that was meant to suffer loss, harm, injury, or death.

Intent The end aim or plan that guides behavior.

Intermediate crime scene Any crime scene between the primary crime scene and a disposal site, where there may be transfer evidence.

Interrupted/incomplete offense An offense that does not contain enough MO behaviors to complete the offense.

Intimate homicide A homicide that occurs when a current or former intimate relationship partner kills the other.

Intimate terrorism Relationships in which only one of the partners/spouses is violent and controlling.

Intuition Knowing or believing without the use of reason, or rational, articulate processes.

Investigative analysis Analysis conducted during an ongoing investigation while facts are still being established.

Investigative link A general class connection between one or more cases that serves to inform the allocation of investigative resources.

Investigative psychology (IP) The study of all aspects of psychology relevant to criminal and civil investigations. IP involves the study of offender groups, the patterns within those groups, and the application of that research to individual cases.

Ipse dixit A Latin phrase that means "he himself said it." It refers to something that is asserted but unproved.

Least effort principle More of a theory than a principle, this involves the belief that given two alternatives to a course of action, people will choose the one that requires the least effort—that is, people will adopt the easiest course of action.

Lethal force Physically aggressive behavior that is sufficient to kill.

Lifestyle exposure The *frequency* of potentially harmful elements experienced by the victim and resulting from the victim's usual environment and personal traits, as well as past choices.

Limiting evidence Evidence that defines the nature and boundaries of the crime scene.

Locard's exchange principle When two objects come into contact, there is an exchange of material, even if only at the microscopic level.

Locational/positional evidence Evidence that shows where something happened, or where something was, and its orientation with respect to other objects at the location.

Location type The physical environment where a crime scene exists.

Location of the scene The descriptive qualities of the crime scene.

Logic The science of valid argumentation and reasoning.

Logical fallacies Errors in logic in reasoning that essentially deceived those whom they are intended to convince. They are brought about by the acceptance of faulty premises, bias, ignorance, and intellectual laziness.

Lustmurder Any sexually motivated homicide.

Mandated reporter Any professional who is bound by law to report evidence of crime, abuse, or neglect.

Masochism Sexual arousal from receiving punishment, bondage, discipline, humiliation, or being in servitude.

Mass murder The murder of multiple victims during a single event, at one or more associated locations.

Metacognition One's ability to estimate how well one is performing, when one is likely to be accurate, and when one is likely to be in error.

Metacognitive dissonance Believing oneself capable or recognizing one's own errors in thinking, reasoning, and learning, despite either a lack of evidence or overwhelming evidence to the contrary.

Method of approach The offender's strategy for getting close to a victim.

Method of attack The offender's mechanism for initially overpowering a victim after making the approach.

Methods of control The means used to manipulate, regulate, restrain, and subdue victim behavior during the offense.

Missing items Any items that originally belonged at a crime scene and were not found during crime scene investigation efforts.

Modus operandi (MO) The manner in which a crime has been committed.

Moral mandates The specific positions that people develop out of a moral conviction that something is right or wrong, moral or immoral.

Motivational analysis Detecting an offense's likely motive by evaluating the crime scene characteristics and physical evidence.

Murdertainment Providing sensational coverage of incidents involving death and violence through media programs designed to entertain more than they are designed to provide accurate information.

Mutual violent control Controlling violence in a relationship in which both spouses are violent and controlling.

Narrow targeting The intentional infliction of specific, focused, calculated amounts of damage or injury to a specific target.

Necrophilia A persistent sexual arousal associated with the dead, or sexual activity with the dead.

Nomothetic The study of the abstract: examining groups and universal laws.

Nomothetic offender profiles Offender characteristics developed by studying groups of offenders. Nomothetic profiles do not represent actual offenders that exist in the real world. They represent varying degrees of theory and possibility.

Non sequitur An inference that does not follow from the premises given or that is unrelated to them. It is an argument that is illogical.

Nonviolent pornography Sexual images that have no explicitly violent content but may imply acts of submission or violence.

Observer bias The conscious or unconscious tendency to see or find what one expects to see or find.

Observer effects A form of bias characterized by distortions resulting from the context and mental state of the forensic examiner, to include his or her employer, peer relationships, and subconscious expectations and desires.

Obstruction of justice Obstructing, delaying, or preventing the communication of information relating to a violation of any criminal statute by any person to a criminal investigator by any means (e.g., bribery, intimidation, and false statements).

Offender exposure The general amount of exposure to discovery, identification, or apprehension experienced by the offender.

Offender signature The pattern or cluster of MO behaviors, signature behaviors, and motivation behaviors that occur across an offense.

Offense gone wrong An offense that contains unintentional, unplanned MO behavior, which increases the offender's risk or criminal status.

"Open" relationship A relationship where intimate partners are free to pursue sexual relationships with other partners.

Opportunistic element Any unplanned element that the offender seizes on for inclusion in an offense.

Opportunistic victim The victim is ancillary to the offense.

Organized/disorganized typology The FBI's binary crime scene and offender classification system. It assumes that crime scenes with characteristics the FBI has designated "organized" will be reflective of "organized" offenders; it further assumed that crime scenes with characteristics the FBI has designated as "disorganized" will be reflective of "disorganized" offenders.

Outdoor crime scenes Crime scenes that are exposed to the elements of nature.

Overkill Multiple injuries beyond that necessary to cause death.

Ownership evidence Any evidence that may be connected to, or associated with, a particular person or source.

Passive signature behaviors Behaviors that result from an offender who is not in control and unintentionally leaves a particular psychological impression.

Peer review The process of subjecting an author's work, research, or ideas to the scrutiny of others who are experts in the same field.

Perjury The act of lying or making verifiably false statements on a material matter under oath or affirmation in a court of law or in any sworn statements in writing. A criminal act, it is not sufficient that the statement be false to be considered perjury; it must be regarding a material fact—a fact that is relevant to the situation.

Personal identification Establishing the precise identity of individuals, typically witnesses, victims, and offenders.

Personal items Items taken from the victim or the crime scene that have sentimental value to the offender.

Physical or mental disability Any physical or mental disease or defect that causes a permanent state of being incapable of rationally appraising the nature of one's own conduct.

Physical torture The intentional and repeated infliction of nonlethal injury to a victim.

Point of contact The precise location where the offender first approached or acquired the victim.

Point of origin The specific location at which a fire is ignited, or the specific location where a device is placed and subsequently detonated.

Pornography Sexualized materials used primarily to stimulate sexual arousal.

Power-assertive crime scene behaviors Behaviors intended to restore the offender's self-confidence or self-worth through the use of moderate to high-aggression means.

Power-reassurance crime scene behaviors Behaviors that are intended to restore the offender's self-confidence or self-worth through the use of low-aggression means.

Practice standards Fundamental rules that set the limits of evidentiary interpretation, offering a standard for evaluating acceptable work habits and application of methods.

Precautionary acts Behaviors that an offender commits before, during, or after an offense that are consciously intended to confuse, hamper, or defeat investigative or forensic efforts for the purposes of concealing the offender's identity, connection to the crime, and the crime itself.

Precautionary aspect A disposal site where an offender has gone to some effort to destroy evidence or otherwise hamper the investigative effort.

Precautionary force Physically aggressive offender behavior that results in wound patterns that are intended to hamper or prevent the recognition and collection of physical evidence.

Preferential bestiality (or zoophilia) A clear preference for engaging in sex with animals.

Preselected aspect A disposal site that an offender chooses before actually committing an offense, by virtue of it being particularly suitable for the activities with which the offender wishes to engage the victim.

Primary crime scene The location where the offender engaged in the majority of his or her principal offense behavior.

Principles The fundamental truths and propositions that provide the foundation for any given field of study.

Probative link Evidenced by either a unique offender behavior, or a unique offender signature that is shared across two or more cases, with limited behavioral dissimilarity.

Profit-oriented crime scene behaviors Behaviors that are intended to fulfill material or financial gain.

Projection Ascribing to others one's own thoughts, feelings, or motives. With respect to profiling, this occurs when a profiler ascribes his or her own thoughts, feelings, or motives to the behavior evident in a given case.

Property Structures, vehicles, or other objects. It includes things that have material or evidentiary value, as well as physical symbols and collateral objects.

Pseudoexperts Forensic frauds who fabricate or misrepresent expert credentials such as college diplomas, expert certifications, professional affiliations, or case-related experience.

Pseudo-rational attribution A form of false deduction defined as the practice of falsely suggesting that traits, conditions, phenomena, or casual relationships exist because they can be traced to a divine or authoritative source—usually written—which was actually penned in response to a prejudice belief rather than proving it with evidence and reason.

Pseudo-rational attribution effects Any of the various consequences of pseudo-rational attribution, including false accusations, witch hunts, and miscarriages of justice such as wrongful arrests, convictions, and executions.

Psychopath A social predator (diagnosed with psychopathy) who often charms and manipulated his or her way through life. Psychopaths are completely lacking in conscience and in feelings for others, taking what they what and doing as they please without the slightest sense of guilt or regret.

Psychopathy A personality disorder evidenced by a distinctive cluster of behaviors and inferred personality traits defined by *Hare's Revised Psychopathy Checklist* (PCL-R).

Psychological evidence Any act committed by the perpetrator to satisfy a personal need or motivation.

Punishment-oriented force Brutal and short-lived levels of force that are reflected in extensive, severe wound patterns.

Rape Nonconsensual sexual penetration.

Reciprocity The phenomenon whereby torture or ill treatment of prisoners and "detainees" encourages an equivalent response from the groups that these individuals represent.

Remorse aspect A disposal site where there is evidence that the offender felt some regret over the victim's death.

Remote assessment A portfolio of methods used to evaluate individuals and groups when direct contact methods (interviews, questionnaires, etc.) are not feasible or desirable.

Sadism The intentional infliction of psychological or physical suffering on a conscious victim, able to experience pain or humiliation for the purpose of sexual gratification.

Sadistic **crime scene behaviors** Behaviors that evidence offender sexual gratification from victim pain and suffering.

Sadomasochism Consensual activity involving polarized role-playing, intense sensations, and feelings, actions, and fantasies that focus on playing out or fantasizing dominant and submissive roles as part of the sexual scenario.

Salem Witch Trials A series of court proceedings and trials in the furtherance of prosecuting those alleged to have committed acts of witchcraft in Massachusetts from 1692 to 1693. Expert "scientific" testimony on the profiles of witches allowed as evidence in court for the first time in what would eventually become the United States.

Science An orderly body of knowledge with principles that are clearly enunciated and reality oriented, with conclusions that are susceptive to testing.

Scientific knowledge Any knowledge, enlightenment, or awareness that comes from examining events or problems through the lends of the scientific method.

Scientific method A way to investigative how or why something works, or how something happened, through the development of hypotheses and subsequent attempts at falsification through testing and other accepted means.

Scripting The language used by an offender during an offense, as well as the language he or she commands the victim to use. Scripting is used to direct the victim verbally and behaviorally.

Secondary crime scene The location where some of the victim–offender interaction occurred, but not the majority of it.

Secondary transfer An exchange of evidence between objects or persons that occurs subsequent to an original exchange, unassociated with the circumstances that produced the original exchange.

Sequential evidence Anything that establishes or helps to establish when an event occurred or the order in which two or more events occurred.

Serial arson Two or more related cases involving fire setting.

Serial bombing Two or more related cases involving the use of explosives.

Serial crime Any series of two or more related crimes.

Serial homicide/murder Two or more related cases involving homicide.

Serial rape Two or more related cases involving rape or sexual assault behavior.

Sexting Engaging in sexually explicit cell-phone conversations via text messaging, with equally explicit images and even video added to enhance narration.

Sexual act Any offender behavior involving sexual organs, sexual apparatus, or sexualized objects.

Sexual arousal An emotional and motivational state arising from an interaction between genital response, central arousal, information processing of sexual stimuli, and behavior.

Sexual asphyxia The consensual or forced reduction of oxygen to the brain to enhance physical or psychological pleasure in association with sexual arousal.

Sexual assault Nonconsensual sexual contact.

Sexual coercion The psychological, emotional, and even physical manipulation of one intimate partner by the other to achieve domination and control.

Sex crime Offenses against an individual or community that either directly or indirectly relate to sex.

Sexual deviance Any eroticized activity that differs from accepted or typical sexual norms.

Sexual fantasy The deliberate act of imagining a behavior, event, or series of events that one finds personally arousing.

Sexual force Aggression or coercion that relates directly to the satisfaction of erotic or libidinous desires.

Signature behaviors Acts committed by an offender that are not necessary to commit the crime but that suggest the psychological or emotional needs of that offender.

Simulators Forensic frauds that physically manipulate physical evidence or related forensic testing.

Situational or incident exposure The amount of actual exposure or vulnerability experienced by the victim to harm, resulting from the environment and personal traits at the time of victimization.

Situational couple violence Individual non-controlling violence in a dynamic context in which neither of the spouses is violent and controlling.

Sociopath This term is used to describe the same behavior manifestations and inferred personality traits as are evident in a psychopath; however, sociopaths have a syndrome forged entirely by social forces and early experiences.

Sodomy Any sexual act that does not involve a penis penetrating a vagina.

Symbol Any person who represents something else such as an idea, a belief, a group, or even another person.

Souvenir A reminder or token of remembrance that represents a pleasant experience.

Speculation A conclusion based on theory or conjecture without firm evidence.

Spanish Inquisition The formal authorization of the Catholic Church to assist the government with the identification of converses, mainly Muslims (Moors) and Jews (*marranos*), who had pretended to convert to Christianity but secretly continued the practice of their former religion.

Spoofing When one person or program successfully masquerades as another by falsifying data and gains an illegitimate advantage.

Staged aspect A disposal site that an offender has contrived so as to purposefully mislead the investigation.

Staged crime scene A crime scene in which the physical evidence has been purposefully altered by the offender to mislead authorities or misdirect the investigation.

Staging A crime scene in which the physical evidence has been purposefully altered by the offender to mislead authorities or misdirect the investigation.

Surprise approach Characterized by an offender who gets close to a victim by lying in wait for a moment of vulnerability.

Target The object of an attack from the offender's point of view.

Targeted victim The primary purpose of the offense, resulting directly from the offender's motive for committing the crime.

Temporal evidence Evidence that specifically denotes or expresses the passage of time at a crime scene relative to the commission of the crime.

Tertiary crime scene Any location where physically evidence is present but there is no evidence of victim–offender interaction.

The *Malleus Maleficarum* One of the first published texts that offered explicit instruction on the subject and practice of profiling criminal behavior—essentially a rationale and guide for those involved with the Inquisition to assist in the identification, prosecution, and punishment of witches.

Threshold assessment An investigative document that reviews the initial physical evidence of behavior, forensic victimology, and crime scene characteristics for a particular case, or a series of related cases, in order to provide immediate direction.

Transference The phenomenon that occurs when a patient reacts with a therapist in a manner that mimics other relationships from the patient's past. With respect to profiling, this can occur when the profiler reacts unconsciously to a case based on some facet that strikes the profiler personally.

Trophy A symbol of victory, achievement, or conquest.

Trust approach Characterized by an offender who gets close to a victim by means of a relationship that exists (or past relationship that existed) between the victim and offender.

Underwater crime scenes Crime scenes that are at or beneath the surface of any body of water.

UNSUB profiling Inferring the characteristics of unknown offenders (subjects).

Valuables Items taken from the crime scene that the offender believes may have financial value.

Vehicle crime scenes Crime scenes that are drivable and therefore mobile.

Victim compliance The situation in which a victim acquiesces to an offender demand readily and without hesitation.

Victim exposure The amount of contact or vulnerability to harmful elements experienced by the victim.

Victim location The descriptive qualities of the victim's physical location immediately prior to encountering the offender.

Victim selection The process by which an offender chooses or targets a victim.

Victim resistance Victim behavior that defies an offender.

Victim response The victim's reaction to offender behavior.

Vilification Viewing a certain victim as worthless or disposable by virtue of who or what they are, without consideration of the facts (e.g., the homeless, the poor, minority groups and prostitutes).

Violent pornography Sexual images that portray explicit violence of varying degrees perpetrated against one individual by another.

Violent resistance A type of intimate personal violence that involves a focal spouse that is violent but not controlling, and his or her partner is violent and controlling.

Voyeurism A sexual interest in, or the practice of spying on, people engaged in intimate or private behaviors, such a undressing, sexual acts, urinating, or defecating.

Weapon Any item found in the crime scene (available materials) or brought to the crime scene by the victim or the offender that is used for the purposes of inflicting injury.

X-factor Any unknown or unplanned influence that can affect crime scene behavior during an offense.

Index

In this index the use of *b* indicates text found in a box, *f* indicates a figure, *ge* indicates a glossary term, *np* indicates a note, and *t* indicates a table.